TREASURES OF BRITAIN

TREASURES
OF
BRITAIN

AND
TREASURES OF IRELAND

Published by Drive Publications Limited, for the
Automobile Association,
Fanum House, Basingstoke, Hants

TREASURES OF BRITAIN

was edited by Drive Publications Limited
Berkeley Square House, London W1X 5PD
for the Automobile Association
Fanum House, Basingstoke, Hants, RG21 2EA

Printed in Italy

Printing and binding by:
POLIGRAFICI EDITORIALE, BOLOGNA, ITALY
Maps produced by:
CLYDE SURVEYS LTD, MAIDENHEAD

The end-papers show details from the border of the Bradford Table Cover,
made in England in the 16th century and now exhibited at the Victoria and Albert Museum

TREASURES OF BRITAIN

The publishers express their gratitude for major contributions
by the following people and organisations:

Malcolm Aird
John Astrop
Norman G. Barber
John Beale
John Blomfield
Michael Borrie
Broadway Arts Ltd
John Bulmer
Mike Busselle
Norman Cook
George Coral
Maurice Craig
Catherine Cruft
Anne Cruikshank
Roy Dickens
Frank Dowling
Tony Evans
E. C. Fernie
Graham Finlayson
Desmond Fitz-Gerald
Andrew Fleming, M.A.
Christina Gascoigne
Charles H. Gibbs Smith
H. Gordon Slade, T.D., A.R.I.B.A., F.S.A.SCOT.
Charles Green
Paul Grinke
Desmond Guinness
Douglas B. Hague
Leslie Harris
John Hayes
Valerie Howard
Tony Howarth
B. J. Hurren
Philip James
David N. Johnson
Peter Keen
Ann Kings
Sally Kington
Alfred Lammer
John Marmaras
Andrew Martindale
Donald Maxwell
Eric Meacher
Lieutenant-Commander George Naish
Sydney W. Newbery
John Newman
Richard Ormond
John Physick
Anthony Radcliffe
L. T. C. Rolt, M.A., F.R.S.L., C.I.MECH.E.
Tom Scott

Derek Shrub
Edwin Smith
Francis Stephens, A.R.C.A.
Dr Roy Strong
Michael Taylor
Pennie Tweedie
Peter Warner
Martin Weaver
James Wentworth Day
Michael Wynne
Doreen Yarwood, A.T.D.(LONDON)
Ian Yeomans
D. Zichy
Jesse Zierler

The British Library, Department of
    Manuscripts
The British Museum
The Chester Beatty Library, Dublin
Courtauld Institute
Department of the Environment
Glasgow City Art Gallery and
    Museum
The Irish Georgian Society
The Lord Chamberlain's Office
Museum of London
The National Gallery
The National Gallery of Scotland
The National Portrait Gallery
The National Portrait Gallery of Ireland
The National Trust
The National Trust for Scotland
Office of Public Works, National
    Monument Branch, Dublin
Royal Commission on the Ancient and
    Historical Monuments of Scotland
Royal Commission on the Ancient Monuments
    in Wales
Royal Scottish Museum
School of Fine Arts, University of
    East Anglia
Scottish National Portrait Gallery
Tate Gallery
Trinity College, Dublin
Trinity House
The Trustees of the National
    Maritime Museum
Victoria and Albert Museum
The Wallace Collection

Many other people, organisations, and publications
were consulted during the preparation of this book, including those
whose assistance is acknowledged on the last page

CONTENTS: *A Grand Tour o*

TREASURES IN THEIR TIME

How the past has shaped our inheritance

PAGES 9–48

GAZETTEER OF THE TREASURES OF BRITAIN

The Nation's heritage described and illustrated

PAGES 49–504

PEOPLE AND PLACES: MEN AND WOMEN WHOSE LIVES ARE WOVEN INTO BRITISH HISTORY

FAMOUS PEOPLE

Their works and whereabouts

PAGES 505–535

MAP SECTION

Where to find the Treasures of the British Isles

PAGES 536–576

GAZETTEER OF THE TREASURES OF IRELAND

The wealth of a unique and little-known land

PAGES 577–632

PEOPLE AND PLACES

W. B. Yeats, Ballylee 582

TREASURES
IN THEIR TIME

*The works of builders and artists, from Stonehenge
to 20th-century statues, are keys to the understanding
of the times in which they were made*

Drive into any city in Britain, and you journey backwards in time.
First the suburbs of the last half century, then an inner ring of 19th-
century building, then the Georgian, Tudor and medieval core,
clustering round the soaring spire of a Gothic or Norman cathedral.
Buried under the tarmac of the modern highway there may well be
the rutted stones of a Roman road. In the country the remains are
fewer, but may be still more ancient. A faint bank and ditch in the
middle of a field shows where prehistoric men gathered for market
or defence; a standing stone marks the spot where generations of their
chieftains were buried.

This introductory section of the book relates these objects, large or
small, ancient or modern, stone wall or carved jewel, to the men who
made them and the times in which they were created. Each period
begins with a brief historical sketch, followed by guides to the architecture, sculpture, painting and decorative arts of the period. The
treasures described range from medieval manuscripts, Wren churches
and Georgian landscape gardens to carved Elizabethan tombs and
pinnacled Victorian town halls.

The 20th century, with all its bewildering changes, needs the points
of reference given by such treasures. Their slow artistic evolution, in
which experiments were adopted only after much trial and error,
gives a sense of the continuity of thousands of years of history.

Ice Age to the Romans

The Romans in the 1st century AD *conquered a land which had seen many cultures, from primitive hunters to the princes of the Iron Age*

THE PALAEOLITHIC PERIOD c. 400,000–8000 BC

During the 'Great Ice Age', which is thought to have lasted about a million years, there were many periods of tens of thousands of years when the ice-cap which covered Britain melted away, and the climate became as warm as it is today. In these interglacial periods primitive races of men first came to this land as hunters and food-gatherers. They were merely large families or small clans, scattered widely over the southern half of Britain. During this period, the Palaeolithic (Old Stone) Age, Britain still formed, at least at times, a part of the Continent. Each time the climate worsened and ice-caps began to form in the hills, the animals and their human predators moved south.

For most of the period the only archaeological evidence we have consists of the implements made by chipping flint nodules or flakes to the required shapes (British Museum).

Modern man (*Homo sapiens sapiens*) is known to have existed in Western Europe during the last 35,000 years. During the later cold spells of the Ice Age, his skills enabled him to clothe himself and to hunt in the areas round the edges of the ice.

In Britain there are a few caves (like those in Cheddar Gorge, Somerset) where family groups found conditions suitable for survival. In some of these the debris of food-bones and broken implements later became sealed by a layer of stalagmite, which has preserved many objects that would otherwise have decayed; so implements of bone survive as well as of flint.

THE MESOLITHIC PERIOD c. 8000–4000 BC

A rise in the sea-level, brought about largely by the melting ice-cap, cut Britain off from the Continent about 9000 years ago; Ireland had been isolated rather earlier.

A steady improvement in the climate allowed the population to increase somewhat; but as long as man had to rely on gathering food, as opposed to farming it, his numbers could never grow large.

The improvement of climate was accompanied by a slow spread of forest from the south, leading to changes in animal life. The cold-weather herds of the steppes disappeared, to be replaced by forest animals, and there was also an increase in the species of fish. This led to changes of diet and modifications of the old hunting methods.

STONEHENGE, Wiltshire, the finest Bronze Age sanctuary in Britain. Built in successive stages, c. 2500–1500 BC. Engraved by Jan Kip, a Dutchman who worked in England at the beginning of the 18th century

STONE CIRCLE, near Tormore, Arran. A highly romanticised water-colour by William Andrews Nesfield (1793–1881)

Of the men themselves of this period we know virtually nothing. All we have are some flint and bone implements. Though many of the occupation sites are known, and have in varying degree been excavated, there are no structural remains.

THE NEOLITHIC PERIOD *c.* 4000–2000 BC

Soon after 4000 BC the first parties of farmer-immigrants established themselves in the chalk Down country of southern Britain. From early beginnings in the Near East, the twin activities of grain cultivation and stock rearing had spread slowly westwards. The visible monuments of this cultural advance are of three kinds—flint mines (Grime's Graves, Norfolk), causewayed camps (Windmill Hill, Wiltshire), and long barrows or long cairns (West Kennet, Wiltshire).

A more regular food supply led to a steady increase of population, which was further increased by the arrival of new settlers and improved farming techniques. During this period, Britain was occupied by many tribes of different cultural levels, probably speaking different languages and certainly different dialects.

The need for open land, both for crop-growing and pasturage, meant that trees had to be felled. On the chalk Downs the woodland was comparatively light and dry, and clearing could be done partly by burning and partly by felling. Tree-felling needed axes, and for these igneous rocks were at first used. Some centuries later, seams of fine flint deep in the chalk were mined.

Causewayed camps, marked by bank-and-ditch rings around hill-tops, have been recognised on a number of sites; the ditches have many causeways for crossing, which correspond with openings in the banks. In this way they can be clearly distinguished from the hill-forts of the Iron Age. They may have been meeting-places for formal communal purposes, and perhaps markets.

The most important monuments are undoubtedly the burial sites. These are called megalithic (from the Greek *mega-*, large, and *lith-*, stone), as the burial-chambers and approach-passages are of large stone slabs; in certain areas, where suitable slabs were not available, drystone walling was used.

Broadly the tombs fall into two main groups—passage-graves, with a passage from the entrance to a circular burial chamber; and gallery-graves, with a long rectangular chamber, the whole of which was used for burials. Some of these have transepts or side-chambers, as in the Cotswold-Severn group. When complete, these structures were concealed below long mounds (although a few are roughly circular) and contained by stone walling. The long ones were usually higher at the entrance end; and here there was often a forecourt, where rites were performed when the tomb was opened for a burial, after which the entrance and forecourt were again masked by a carefully built stone blocking.

In parts of southern and eastern England, long mounds of similar age are to be found, entirely lacking the internal stone structures; excavation has revealed that similar turf and timber structures were often present.

LANYON QUOIT, a Cornish dolmen. The remains of a long-barrow burial chamber after the covering of earth and stones has been removed. The chamber was entered through a passage

CARN EUNY, a 'fogou' near Brane, Cornwall. Primarily associated with Iron Age settlements in Cornwall, fogous were formed by cutting a passage in the soil and concealing it with a covering of stones and earth. Lined and paved with stone slabs, fogous were used either for storage purposes or as escape routes from the village when under attack. The example shown is over 60 ft long

HILL-FORT, Figsbury, Wiltshire. Iron Age forts provided a commanding view of the countryside and a protected area for livestock. Their ditches and ramparts were an effective defence against the principal weapon of the day—the sling

ROMAN THEATRE Aerial view of the 2nd-century AD theatre at Verulamium (St Albans). The only known Roman theatre in Britain

THE BRONZE AGE c. 2000–600 BC

The division of prehistoric cultures into Stone Age, Bronze Age and Iron Age is a useful time-scale based on the technological skills employed in making important tools and weapons; no hard and fast line can be drawn. The first newcomer to Britain with a small metal knife-dagger began the Bronze Age; but the essentially Neolithic way of life, for most people, was not in the least changed, and it was only slowly that the new metal objects spread to all parts of the island.

The new immigrant group coming in from the Low Countries have been called the Beaker People, because of the characteristic drinking vessels found in many of their tombs (British Museum). They also brought with them the custom of individual burials, under round barrows, much smaller than the large, collective long barrows.

The round barrow slowly became the normal tomb of the Bronze Age, although after a time cremation replaced burial. The commonest visible monuments of the Bronze Age are the many thousands of these round barrows (mainly in Dorset and Wiltshire). A few still stand at about their original height; but most have been reduced, often by later agricultural activity, and an unknown number have been completely destroyed, ploughed flat in the last 2000 years. These are now beginning to be revealed by air photography.

In chalk country, houses of this period can be found only by excavation, and show as a pattern of post-holes. In the West Country, notably on Dartmoor (for example, in the Chagford area), where huts were built of stone, settlements of this date may still be seen. The boundaries of Bronze Age corn plots are sometimes visible as slightly raised banks, known as lynchets.

THE IRON AGE c. 600 BC–AD 43

This period began with a further strengthening of the farming communities of the Late Bronze Age type in the south-eastern part of the island, and ended in the southern half with the establishment of Roman sovereignty. Military adventurers, traders, refugees and farming migrants all swelled and enriched the cultural variety of British life. The advent of new weapons, such as the sling or the war-chariot, together with the increase in population, led inevitably to tribal warfare. It is this aspect of Iron Age life, represented by fortified villages, hill-forts, and the fortified homesteads of the extreme north, that is most noticeable in our surviving field monuments.

Hill-forts took many forms, Maiden Castle, Dorset, being one of the finest. Some were simply promontories or hill-spurs, cut off by a bank and ditch at the narrowest point; but the most characteristic were those where a whole flattish hill-top was enclosed. At first, a single bank and ditch was thought to be effective, the bank being laced and revetted with timber. Later the weak points were made stronger, and the entrances became more complex—deeply inturned, with gates and guard-rooms. Later still, the number of ramparts was increased, with as many as three or even four banks and ditches, wide enough to give protection against missiles such as sling-stones. Improved protection of the approaches and gates became common. Forts of this type are the most numerous in the chalk country and the west.

An odd variant is the Scottish vitrified fort, where the stone walls show evidence of molten rock. It is now thought that these were originally laced with timber inside and that when they were set on fire, either deliberately or by accident, the heat of the burning timbers caused the stone to take on a glass-like consistency.

The last groups of invaders were Belgic warriors and refugees, who established themselves in the south-east, where they built their strong places in valleys rather than on hills. In the century before the conquest of Britain by Claudius in AD 43, their grip on the surrounding tribal areas was increased. Their traders, bringing in goods of Roman origin, began the process of Romanisation before the military occupation took place.

IRISH GOLD COLLAR The Irish were expert at making gold ornaments. This collar dates from the 7th century BC

The line between the Forth and Clyde estuaries (later that of the Antonine Wall) seems to have been a racial boundary, north of which the language was different from the 'ancient British' of the south. The eastern area, as far north as the Moray Firth, was the land of the Picts in historic times, and here the vitrified forts are the characteristic defended sites. To the north of Pictland there is a concentration of the defended homesteads known as brochs, and minor concentrations in some Hebridean islands.

Many hill-forts seem to have been no more than tribal refuges, used in times of stress; but the more important ones were permanently occupied, apparently by the tribal chiefs and their followers. These were the *oppida* (Latin *oppidum,* a town), the centres of power in which tribal government was conducted. Though not strictly towns, they foreshadowed in elementary fashion the future towns on which regional government was to be based.

THE ROMANS AD 43-410

For nearly four centuries the Romans made southern Britain a part of civilised Europe, and almost everywhere there is evidence of the Roman occupation. Much of our road system has a Roman origin. London and other important towns are built on Roman foundations.

The Roman conquest began in AD 43 (though Julius Caesar had reconnoitred the country a century before), and within a few years the south-east lowlands were subdued. For a time a number of garrisoned forts of timber and earth were sufficient to keep the peace, but by AD 75 permanent legionary fortresses had been established at Caerleon (Gwent), Chester and York; these were rebuilt in stone about 20 years later. By AD 85, the northern Pennines and the Scottish lowlands had also been subdued, and the northern tribes had been defeated at Mons Graupius (in the Grampian Mts). Afterwards the troops were withdrawn to a frontier established from Solway to the mouth of the Tyne.

MITHRAS, THE BULL-SLAYER Late 2nd- or early 3rd-century relief-carving from the site of the Wallbrook Mithraeum, London. Mithras was the god worshipped by the Roman legionaries

Frontier troubles now led to the building of Hadrian's Wall (*c.* AD 122–35) to link the forts. This wall, 73 miles long, with stone ramparts 8–10 ft thick, still survives in places. The borders were still not pacified, however; and in AD 142 another wall, the Antonine, was built from the Forth to the Clyde. At the end of the 2nd century, due to a shortage of manpower, this wall was deserted. The troops were stationed along Hadrian's Wall.

Meanwhile Romanisation progressed in the south. *Coloniae* (settlements of retired soldiers) were established, and the beginnings of local government were set up. The tribal areas were marked out and organised as locally-governed cantons, administered from the cantonal towns. By this time the local notables had become Romanised, and from them magistrates were selected. Other towns and posting-stations grew up on the main roads, and large-scale agriculture developed on the estates of the country houses (*villae*). Local disturbances led to these towns being protected, at first by timber-revetted banks and ditches, and soon after AD 200 by stone walls added to the banks.

In the 3rd century barbarians began to raid the coasts. A chain of forts was built from the Wash to Southampton Water against the marauding Saxon long-boats, and also as bases for the Roman fleet. Similar forts were built in the west against the Irish raiders, and signal-stations were built on the Yorkshire coast to counter the threat of the Picts, who sought to outflank Hadrian's Wall by sea.

Towards the end of the 4th century, ambitious Roman generals gradually denuded Britain of most of her troops for a series of Continental adventures. In 410, when all the available Roman legions were needed in foreign fields, the British became responsible for their own defence. They engaged Germanic mercenaries, who proved to be a fifth column, opening the doors for the Anglo-Saxon invasion and conquest. During these years many linear earthworks were constructed by the Britons, as regional defences.

PREHISTORIC AND ROMAN ART

Although the Palaeolithic cave paintings of southern France and Pyrenean Spain exhibit remarkable artistic sophistication, Britain has little art to show for the corresponding period. The best we have is a simple incised line-drawing of a hooded man, on a bone from a cave at Cresswell, Derbyshire. Another of these caves has produced engravings of animals on scraps of bone.

The changed way of life of the Neolithic farmers did not at first help the development of the visual arts. Pottery was now in general service; but, as women made the pots for their own household use, they were ornamented only with simple rows of dots or with panels of grooved lines. A few crude sculptures have also been found. In a flint mine at Grime's Graves, Norfolk, where the flint-seam was very thin, a tiny shrine for a crudely carved pregnant woman was found, with offerings thought to be a sacrifice to the fertility goddess. Also at Grime's Graves, fragments of the chalky crust of flint were found, bearing engravings of red deer.

IRON FACE-MASK helmet found during excavations at Trimontium, a late 1st-century Roman fort at Newstead, near Melrose

BRONZE STATUETTE of Mercury from a Roman temple site near Colchester, 2nd century AD

The beakers of the period when Neolithic and early Bronze Ages overlapped show a wider range of decorated pottery; but again the designs are purely geometric, although 'rusticated' decoration was also produced by pinching the wet clay between thumb and forefinger. Later, in the true Bronze Age, small vessels of pottery, amber or occasionally gold are found in the tombs of wealthy Wessex chiefs.

Personal ornaments were also decorated, and the discovery of Irish gold led to its use for such ornaments as the crescent-shaped *lunulae*, worn as collars, which bear simple geometric line decorations. These were copied, in parts of Britain, in elaborate groupings of jet beads. Armlets and torques (twisted bands or belts) were also made in gold and bronze.

Simple designs mark of the best of the pottery and other objects of the first days of the Iron Age, but during this period the decorative La Tène art (named after the Iron Age lake-side settlement at La Tène in Switzerland) was introduced. This was based on the palm-leaf, and had evolved abstract curvilinear patterns.

In Britain this design was to progress to a magnificent climax, but was already deteriorating when the Roman conquest interrupted its course. La Tène art was largely restricted to the weapons, harness-fittings and domestic appointments of aristocratic warriors and their women.

Roman art, on the other hand, was naturalistic, though formal patterns such as the guilloche (two-stranded twist) were commonly used for panel-borders and the like. Architecture, in the real sense of the word, now appeared for the first time. Fine public buildings, both religious and secular, were built and embellished with statues and carved reliefs. The walls were painted and the floors were of *tesserae* (tiny cubical mosaic tiles) set in various designs. Many town and country houses had these embellishments. The great pavement at Woodchester, in Gloucestershire, for example, shows Orpheus playing his lute to the beasts of the field.

It was in grand, Romanised villas that fine silver and glass were used. The Mildenhall treasure (British Museum) and the looted Roman silver found at Traprain Law, near Edinburgh (National Museum of Antiquities, Edinburgh), show the quality of the silversmith's work.

Nor was the lesser man neglected. Pottery for the table was embellished with a wealth of design; and statues of the gods, cast in bronze or pipeclay as small statuettes, were cheap and plentiful. The coinage, at its best, showed great skill in portraiture. Knife-handles took the form of crouching lions, and the knobs of box-lids were shaped like cocks or eagles.

Though this work was Classical in inspiration, much of it showed its British origin. The Celtic craftsman, deserting his curvilinear patterns for the new style, carried over some of the old tradition. As a result, we have that masterpiece, the gorgon's head, which once stared from the pediment of the temple of Sulis-Minerva at Bath (Bath Museum). Even when the Romans had gone, a mixture of Romano-Celtic designs survived. Modified to suit the Nordic taste, these took their place in the pattern-books of Anglo-Saxon craftsmen.

MOSAIC ARTISTRY at Low Ham Villa, Somerset. Part of a mosaic pavement in a large 4th-century Roman house. It depicts scenes from the Romance of Dido and Aeneas in Vergil's *Aeneid*. One of the first examples where a complete story was told in a series of chronological scenes

Saxon and Norman

*Between the 6th and 12th centuries
the arts in Britain followed the
rise and fall of kingdoms, culminating
in the great Norman cathedrals*

BAYEUX TAPESTRY 230 ft long
and 20 in. deep, the 11th-century
tapestry tells the story of the
Conquest in 72 scenes, ending
with the defeat of the English at
Hastings. In this scene a
workman is fitting a weather-
vane to the roof of Westminster
Abbey before the funeral of
Edward the Confessor

ROCHESTER CATHEDRAL, Kent.
Over the 12th-century west
doorway the figure of Christ
is surrounded by angels and the
Four Beasts symbolising
the four Evangelists

When St Augustine landed in Thanet, Kent, in AD 597, under orders from Pope Gregory the Great to convert the heathen English to Christianity, he brought to England a new religion and a new way of life.

The worship of Odin and Thor—the religion of the Anglo-Saxon 'barbarians'—was concerned mainly with manliness, generosity, loyalty and physical courage, and did little to promote learning or art. The arrival of the Christians meant the return of learning to Britain.

The Church, benefiting from the pious gifts of its patrons, acquired vast lands and wealth. Its great cathedrals and abbeys dominated the landscape; and, since the life of Saxon England was centred on the village, the countless parish churches became the focal points of village life. Churches monopolised the skill of the builders until the coming of the Normans in the 11th century, and artists found their chief source of inspiration and employment in adorning them.

It was in the north, in the Kingdom of Northumbria which extended from Edinburgh on the Forth to York and the Humber, that the arts flourished, reaching their zenith in the 8th century. Church and state were more stable in Northumbria than in the surrounding restless kingdoms, and in this more or less peaceful climate the Venerable Bede wrote his *Ecclesiastical History* and the Bishop of Lindisfarne compiled the *Lindisfarne Gospelbook* with its magnificent illuminations.

The invasion of the Danes in the 9th century brought cultural disaster. It disrupted the monasteries, where civilisation had its roots, and the arts barely managed to survive. It was not until the reign of Alfred the Great (871–99), scholar, warrior and administrator, who with his successors made England into one united kingdom, that men could settle again to more leisurely and cultivated pursuits.

Long before the Norman Conquest of 1066 there had been a flow of artistic ideas between the Continent and England. This constant traffic had gone on with few interruptions for over 200 years. The Norman Conquest in 1066 brought a political revolution which stabilised the kingdom; but in the arts its effect was not so much a revolution as an acceleration—sometimes violent, as in architecture—of already existing trends. Since the kings of England were also lords of Normandy and later of Anjou, and constantly travelled to and fro, such Continental influences as Romanesque sculpture infiltrated England. The 12th century and the end of the Norman period marked a high point in English arts.

CATHEDRALS, CHURCHES AND FORTRESSES

Anglo-Saxon and Norman architecture is mainly a story of churches, since no secular buildings earlier than the late 11th century survive. Not many Anglo-Saxon churches are left either. Many were built of wood and easily destroyed—there is a solitary example of an early 11th-century wooden church at Greensted, Essex—or else they were demolished by the Normans in the spate of rebuilding that followed the Conquest of 1066. Among the major Anglo-Saxon churches which perished were Canterbury, Winchester and Worcester.

A few small stone Anglo-Saxon churches survive. The most important are at Brixworth, Northamptonshire, Bradford-on-Avon, Wiltshire, Deerhurst, Gloucestershire, Great Paxton, Cambridgeshire, Wing, Buckinghamshire, and Stow, Lincolnshire. There are also splendid Anglo-Saxon church towers at Earl's Barton, Northamptonshire, Barton-upon-Humber, Lincolnshire, Barnack, Cambridgeshire, and Sompting, W. Sussex. Architecturally, they fall into two periods—the 7th–8th and 10th–11th centuries. Virtually nothing survives from the Danish invasion in the 9th century.

The early period shows Celtic and Roman influence, rather than any indigenous Anglo-Saxon style. One of the best examples is at Brixworth, Northamptonshire, where bricks from a Roman ruin were used by Anglo-Saxon builders to make a simple, large-windowed rectangular building with a semicircular recess at one end (a Roman apsidal basilica). Other examples are the crypt at Hexham, Northumberland, where the abbey was built by Wilfrid in the 7th century, using stone from the ruined Roman townships of Hadrian's Wall; and the crypt at Ripon, N. Yorkshire.

Most of the remaining Anglo-Saxon churches belong to the second phase—the 10th and early 11th centuries. Few of the smaller Anglo-Saxon churches survive intact, though more than 200 churches still have pre-Conquest work in them.

The typical Anglo-Saxon church has a simple plan—two rectangles of unequal size linked by an arch, with the smaller rectangle to the east. An additional chamber or *porticus* could be attached to the church; sometimes there was more than one, as at Bradwell, Essex. The buildings tended to be of a much greater height than width, as at Bradford-on-Avon, Wiltshire. The windows were small and round-headed, set high in the walls.

Interiors were often decoratively painted, with little architectural ornament. The external decoration was often elaborate—usually pilaster-work (vertical strips of stone on the outside walls). The exterior might also have round-headed or triangular blank arcading (a series of arches against a blank wall).

The Norman genius found its finest expression in architecture. Although the Conquerors destroyed the great English churches, they raised on their ruins some of the noblest buildings still extant. The Norman influence in building was at work well before the Conquest. Westminster Abbey, built by Edward the Confessor (1042–66), last of the Saxon kings, was Norman in style.

ST MARY'S CHURCH at Dover. A 19th-century engraving depicting one of the few Norman towers still standing with the round-headed arches characteristic of that period. In the background is Dover Castle

DURHAM CATHEDRAL About 500 years ago the western towers were surmounted by spires; they were made with timber and clad with lead sheeting

This style is characterised by magnificent scale, superb proportions and bold construction. The design was simple yet inventive, and produced an effect of austere grandeur—or so it now seems, though we do not see these churches as they originally were. The bare melancholy now so characteristic of their atmosphere was dispelled by painted interiors, stained glass windows, opulent vestments and furnishings, and the elaborate ceremonial for which the churches formed a setting.

Only three large churches—the cathedrals of Durham, Norwich and Peterborough—remain substantially as they were in Norman times, though fine work can still be seen at Winchester, St Albans, Ely, Gloucester and many smaller churches.

Durham Cathedral, one of the finest Romanesque churches in Europe, was begun by Bishop William of St Carilef in 1093 and completed by 1133. It was the first large building in northern Europe to be rib-vaulted in stone. The ribbed vault was the Normans' greatest contribution to medieval architecture. After passing through all the stages of development and decadence, it ended in the extravagance of the roof of Henry VII's chapel in Westminster Abbey, where the functional ribs evolved into an intricate web of stone decoration.

Though this period saw much splendid ecclesiastical building, the great castles that survive are mainly of later date. The first Norman forts were simple earth mounds with ditches and palisades, and it was not until the 12th century that stone castles began to be built in any numbers. Their characteristic feature is the square Norman keep combining fortress and residence. Two examples survive from the 11th century—Colchester, Essex, and the most famous of all English castles, the White Tower in the Tower of London, completed by 1097. Although the White Tower has been altered, its form is essentially as it was—a four-storey building divided by an internal wall into two parts. One half of the building was again subdivided to the plain but beautiful Chapel of St John, which is the oldest complete Norman church in England.

SCULPTURE: RISE AND FALL OF STYLES

Monumental carved crosses, erected to commemorate persons or events long since forgotten, are found mostly in the north of England and the Kingdom of Northumbria. Apart from a few crosses in the Midlands, no comparable sculptures of that period can be found anywhere else in western Europe. The finest examples are at Ruthwell, Dumfries & Galloway, and Bewcastle, Cumbria; they date from the late 7th and early 8th centuries. They are carved with a vine-leaf decoration and figures of Christ and the Saints.

The artistic tradition that produced the crosses declined as the Northumbrian Kingdom declined. The sculpture produced in the south with the rise of the Kingdoms of Mercia and Wessex was different in character. The carved reliefs at Breedon on the Hill, Leicestershire, of 750–850, include a magnificent figure of Christ, with decoration of grotesque beasts and figures intertwined

NORMAN MOULDINGS An unusually varied selection of mouldings on the blind-arcading and pilasters of St Anselm's Tower, Canterbury Cathedral. From John Britton's *Cathedral Antiquities of England* (1814–35)

NORMAN CARVING was usually in low-relief until the axe was superseded by the chisel in the 12th century. The font at St Michael's, Castle Frome, marks the new freedom offered by this change of technique

with vine tendrils. The workmanship is accomplished, and indicates the existence of a flourishing 'Court school' of sculpture in the Kingdom of Mercia.

The same can be said of outstanding works produced in Wessex at a later period. The late 9th-century carved stone at Codford St Peter, Wiltshire, the flying angels at Bradford-on-Avon, Wiltshire, and particularly the great Crucifixion at Romsey, Hampshire (early 10th century), are works of outstanding quality in which can be discerned for the first time a recognisable Englishness— a dignified restraint and lightness of touch.

The Norman churches built immediately after the Conquest had little sculptural ornament. When in the 12th century English craftsmen began to execute extensive architectural sculptures, they got their inspiration from France, where Romanesque sculpture was developing with the brilliance and assurance that was to culminate in the glories of Chartres Cathedral.

The mutilated Madonna at York (early 12th century) is a work of great dignity, and the 12th-century reliefs in Chichester Cathedral, *The Raising of Lazarus* and *Martha and Mary Greeting Christ*, are possibly the finest sculptures produced in medieval England.

No grand sculpture cycles comparable with those of the French cathedrals have survived, but a band of sculptures of biblical scenes on the west front of Lincoln Cathedral serves to indicate the extent of our loss. Smaller-scale architectural sculptures are fairly plentiful. In the crypt and north transept of Canterbury Cathedral, for example, are capitals carved with the strange beasts and monsters dear to the medieval imagination, and all over England there are carved tympana and doorways.

RELIEF CARVING in whalebone. On a 12th-century *Adoration of the Magi*, a lower frieze features fighting animals

VELLUM AND BURNISHED GOLD

Until the 12th century, graphic art in England is represented solely by manuscripts that were 'illuminated'— that is, painted with pigments whose effect could be enriched by burnished gold laid on the vellum—or else illustrated with line drawings. The subject matter of this art was almost exclusively religious, and its aim was to illustrate and enhance the sacred texts of the Church.

Illuminated manuscripts are the most perfectly preserved of all the works of art left to us by the Middle Ages. Huge numbers of manuscripts were destroyed in the Reformation, when a coloured initial was enough to convict a book of idolatry and condemn it to the flames. But the quality of what has survived shows how the English excelled at this exquisite art.

Outstanding among the earlier manuscript treasures is the *Lindisfarne Gospel-book* (British Museum). Lindisfarne was the great monastery on Holy Island off the coast of Northumberland, founded by St Aidan and his Irish monks from Iona in 635. The *Gospel-book* is the most splendid monument of the Anglo-Irish civilisation which developed in Northumbria after St Aidan's mission and was compiled by Eadfrith, Bishop of Lindisfarne from 698–721. The stylised miniatures of the four Evangelists reflect a Classical influence—evidence of a traffic in books and artistic ideas between England and

THE LINDISFARNE GOSPEL-BOOK A full-page miniature of St Mark from the AD 700 illuminated manuscript of Bishop Eadfrith

MUSICAL INSTRUMENT
Reconstruction of an Anglo-
Saxon harp from the Sutton
Hoo Treasure, discovered
in 1939

GOLD BUCKLE with Anglo-
Saxon engraving inlaid with
niello (silver sulphide). Part
of the Sutton Hoo Treasure

southern Europe at the time. The decoration derives from contemporary metalwork like the Sutton Hoo buckle (British Museum), and consists of geometric and interlaced ornament, interwoven with strange ribbon-like animals into a complex, many-coloured network. The freshness and delicacy of the colours and the intricacy of the workmanship are unmatched in any other manuscript except the later *Book of Kells* (Trinity College, Dublin), which was possibly written at Iona itself between 760 and 820.

When the Vikings sacked Lindisfarne in 793, the monastic life of the North was disrupted and the production of manuscripts seems to have ceased until southern England became united under the Wessex supremacy of Alfred the Great over 100 years later. The art that revived in the 10th century, though no less brilliant than its Northumbrian predecessor, was different. It drew its inspiration, motifs and techniques from the schools of illumination that flourished in the Holy Roman Empire established by Charlemagne in AD 800.

By the late 900's English artists had adapted these Carolingian ideas to their own taste and talent, and founded the Winchester style of illumination—one of the greatest achievements in the history of English art. Its characteristic features are a luxuriant and finely drawn acanthus leaf motif, usually worked into elaborate foliate borders, and a delicate style of figure-drawing.

The first mature example of the Winchester style is the *Foundation Charter of King Edgar to the New Minster at Winchester*, dated 966 (British Museum). It contains a miniature of the king, between the Virgin and St Peter, offering the charter to Christ. The finest example came ten years later—the *Benedictional* or *Book of Blessings* written for St Aethelwold, Bishop of Winchester.

The Norman Conquest had little immediate effect on the style of English illumination, but there was some influence on detail. Some decorative features became more common, such as 'historiated' initial letters (decorated with figures of men and animals), and 'inhabited scrolls', showing arabesques of foliage with animals 'inhabiting' the branches.

During the first half of the 12th century a new style, the Romanesque, entered the country. This grew up alongside the surviving Anglo-Saxon style. It derived from Byzantium and the East, and its characteristics were firmness of line, boldness of execution, and a rigid, monumental dignity in the portrayal of the human figure. A rare example surviving from this time is the wall-painting of *St Paul and the Viper*, in St Anselm's Chapel, Canterbury Cathedral.

The most important English contribution to Romanesque painting is the development of the technique of pictorial narrative and of a complete cycle of illustrations to the Bible. These appeared in the enormous ceremonial Bibles which were produced in the 12th century, in particular the Winchester Bible (Winchester Cathedral), the Lambeth Bible from Canterbury (Lambeth Palace), and the Bury Bible (Corpus Christi College, Cambridge).

The Winchester Bible, in four volumes measuring 23 in. by 16 in., has claims to be the finest. It was probably begun in 1160-70 and is the work of at least six master illuminators. Its design (not completed) called for an elaborate initial letter at the beginning of each book of the Bible, and several full pages of illuminated illustrations. These magnificent Bibles are the greatest achievements in European painting in the 12th century. At the end of the Norman period they won for England the pre-eminence in the graphic arts which in sculpture belonged to France.

WHEN BISHOPS WERE METALWORKERS

The metalwork for which England was famous was a monastic craft until the Conquest and was mostly done for the Church. High-ranking churchmen practised these crafts: both St Dunstan, Archbishop of Canterbury, and St Aethelwold, Bishop of Winchester, were skilled metalworkers. Among the best surviving examples of the craft is an elegant silver bowl of *c.* AD 1000 from Halton Moor, Lancashire (British Museum), decorated with low-relief figures in a Byzantine style; and metal objects decorated with interlace and scroll ornament *c.* 875, found in a hoard at Trewhiddle, Cornwall.

Some fine jewellery survives from the pagan Anglo-Saxon period. Brooches in filagree and cloisonné-work, like the lovely Kingston Brooch (Liverpool City Museum) were made in the 6th- and 7th-century Kentish workshops, and the Sutton Hoo Treasure of the early 7th century (British Museum) includes a large and splendid jewelled buckle and other objects. The magnificent Alfred Jewel, dating from *c.* 880, is made of gold and decorated with a figure in cloisonné enamelling (Ashmolean Museum, Oxford). Two other jewels, less fine but still evidence of a vigorous and inventive craft, are the Minster Lovell Jewel of the late 9th century (Ashmolean Museum, Oxford), and the Dowgate Hill Brooch of *c.* 900 (British Museum).

Among the textiles, the exquisite Anglo-Saxon embroidery known as *opus anglicanum* was prized throughout Europe. Only one example from the Anglo-Saxon period is left—the St Cuthbert Vestments in Durham Cathedral, placed in St Cuthbert's tomb in 934 by King Athelstan. The best-known medieval embroidery is the 11th-century Bayeux Tapestry (at Bayeux, Normandy) —a long strip of linen embroidered in coloured wools with lively, detailed scenes from the life of King Harold, the battle of Hastings and the Norman Conquest.

Carving in ivory of religious objects such as crucifixes or reliquaries was an important craft. Bishop Leofric of Exeter (1050-73) gave his church two crosses, shrines and candlesticks all made of ivory, and two gospel-books bound in ivory. Two early ivories can be seen at the Victoria and Albert Museum, London: a crucifix of *c.* 950, and a crozier head of the 12th century carved with scenes from the Nativity and the Deposition of Christ from the Cross.

Glass painting was of some importance in the 12th century, but little remains. Canterbury Cathedral has the jumbled remnants of some late 12th-century glass which represents one of the earliest narrative sequences in Europe; there are other fragments at York and Lincoln.

12th-CENTURY PLAQUE A colourful early-English enamel of St Paul being lowered from the wall of Damascus

THE STORY OF CAIN AND ABEL Page from an early 11th-century manuscript containing poems based on the Old and New Testament

The Gothic Period

Between the mid-12th and the early 16th century the Gothic cathedrals soared to lofty vaults, while castles evolved from simple keeps to complex palaces

VIEW OF LONDON from the *Nuremburg Chronicle*, 1493. One of the first publications to use woodcuts, which were often personal interpretations rather than accurate records

15TH-CENTURY BRASS from Felbrigg Church, Norfolk, to Sir Simon Felbrygge and his wife Margaret

The adjective 'Gothic' began as the name of a tribe, but it has come to refer only to a particular style of art. It has nothing to do with the original Goths, whose historical importance waned after the 7th century.

The Gothic style was a North French export of the second half of the 12th century and the first half of the 13th, and the importation of the style into this country was a piecemeal operation moving at a variety of speeds, while the best place to put the end of English Gothic is somewhere between 1500 and the Reformation.

Norman architecture was imported into England, because the new patrons were without exception Normans, who disliked the Anglo-Saxon style. The monastic orders, particularly the Cistercians, introduced a style which made it easier for English architects to accept the Gothic innovations when they came. Westminster Abbey, London, is the first clear case of the influence of the royal house on the development of English Gothic architecture. Due chiefly to the alterations inspired by Henry III (1216–72), the abbey came to resemble French High Gothic cathedrals such as Reims. From the time of Henry III on, the Crown was responsible for most important buildings. The great phase of English late medieval architecture, the Perpendicular, was almost certainly initiated in the early 14th century from Court circles in London.

In any case, money commanded the best workmen, designers and artists, so that one would expect royalty to commission masterpieces. The 15th century saw the rise of a new class of patrons—rich merchants with a penchant for fine building.

ARCHITECTURE: CATHEDRALS AND CASTLES

The basis of Gothic architecture was the acceptance, in whole or in part, of the new French style, which involved the creation of a structural and spatial unity out of the ribbed vault, the pointed arch, the flying buttress, and slender supports. Sometimes the formulae were accepted wholesale, as in the eastern parts of Canterbury Cathedral; more often they were watered down with Romanesque élements, as at Salisbury Cathedral.

The two great periods of Late English Gothic are loosely called the Decorated (first half of the 14th century) and the Perpendicular (*c.* 1340–1500). The choir of Gloucester Cathedral is one of the earliest and finest manifestations of the Perpendicular style and is also a classic illustration of how little Late Gothic architecture concerned itself with structural function: the revolutionary elements are little more than a veneer of tracery decoration applied to a pre-existing Norman fabric.

The development of English Gothic architecture can be traced in miniature through the changes in the patterns of ribs applied to vaults. In the second half of the 12th century Continental Gothic vaults were of the simple four-part or six-part type: the square or rectangular form of the vault was divided up either into four areas by two intersecting diagonal ribs, or into six areas by a further transverse rib cutting through the point of intersection of the diagonals. During this period the English often did not bother to vault, as at Ripon Cathedral, N. Yorkshire, or Hexham Abbey, Northumberland.

But in the 13th century they accepted and developed with alacrity the embellishment of the basic Continental type, on to which ridge ribs were added, running both right down the length of the nave and across each bay. A further rib, the tierceron, was then made to run from the springing point of the vault to these ridge ribs.

This stage is illustrated in the nave of Lincoln Cathedral (early 13th century), the impression being of an undulating, all-over design more or less disguising the original concept of vaults in separate bays. The nave of Lincoln appears almost chaste beside the forest of ribs used at Exeter. If ever there was to be a case for the old idea that Gothic architecture derived from wooden architecture and resembled a row of giant trees in a forest, this nave would justify it.

The next stage was the introduction of short ribs, called liernes, linking the main ribs, ridge ribs and tiercerons and creating star-like patterns in the centre of the vault, as in the nave of York Cathedral (c. 1300). The liernes, together with the ogee or reverse-curve arch (excellent examples at Bristol and in the Lady Chapel at Ely), can be said to introduce the Decorated style.

Liernes could be used in two ways—either to make a pattern of odd shapes over the whole surface of the vault, as was attempted at Gloucester in the middle of the 14th century; or to increase the suggestion of a fan already created by the bunches of tiercerons. The second method led to the development of the 'fan-vault', the first example of which appears again at Gloucester, in the cloister, towards the middle of the century. Fan-vaulting only found its full expression when used over main areas in the second half of the 15th century, as at King's College Chapel, Cambridge. Henry VII's Chapel in Westminster Abbey completes the cycle.

The growth of the Gothic style in ecclesiastical architecture has no parallel in castle building. However, the mid-12th century marks a fairly distinct break in the development of castles, in that wooden constructions are as unusual after this date as stone ones were before. Most castles before the 15th century were massive, the spaciousness of Gothic being unsuited to fortification.

Thus the castle of the late 12th and 13th centuries is for the most part the same in form as the Norman one. It is dominated by a heavily fortified keep, generally square but sometimes cylindrical, especially later in the period. There are dungeons and store rooms on the

LINCOLN CATHEDRAL, a 19th-century engraving from Britton's *Architectural Antiquities of Great Britain*. Part of the gable between the two main western towers

HENRY VII'S CHAPEL, Westminster Abbey. An early 19th-century engraving showing the magnificent fan-vaulted ceiling (1503–19). The bronze screen in the foreground encloses the tomb of Henry VII and his queen, Elizabeth of York

ground floor, and an entrance and a great hall with smaller contiguous rooms, often including a chapel, on the first floor. The keep is set on one edge of a large area called a bailey, enclosed by a wall and often a moat, where other buildings and quarters were installed, as with the early arrangements of Dover and Windsor.

The 13th century saw the greatest advance in the development of the castle in England. This was chiefly due to a decline in the importance of the keep, and an increase in the defensibility of the enceinte or perimeter wall, which in turn was made possible by the use of towers on the walls and at the gates. Framlingham, in Suffolk, is an early (13th-century) example of a castle with wall towers. The castle as a whole took on a looser, more rambling quality than previously, and became more like the open layout of a palace. The finest examples of this new stage are found in Wales, as at Caerphilly, Harlech and Beaumaris. The use and enlargement of wall and gate towers reaches such a pitch in this group that it is almost possible to see them as a series of keeps multiplied at intervals around the bailey wall.

There is another way in which one can express this 13th-century development. The keep expands, creating a well and then a courtyard in its centre, and finally evolves into a perimeter on which the old corner turrets become enceinte towers. This results in a symmetrical plan, as at Beaumaris. This type of plan, symmetrical or otherwise, remained the standard of good castle building throughout the period—for example, the late 14th-century Kenilworth, Warwickshire—blurring the difference between military and non-military architecture.

SCULPTURE: SHARP TRANSITIONS

The dependence of carving on the minor arts, particularly manuscript illumination, is much less marked in these centuries than in the Anglo-Saxon and Norman periods. This is partly indicated by the fact that there was a much sharper transition in sculpture between Romanesque and Gothic than there was in illumination.

Once again, as with church architecture, it is to the Ile de France (the area around Paris) that one must look for the source of inspiration. The portal of Rochester Cathedral, Kent (c. 1170), makes use of the columnar figures used at St Denis and Chartres around 1140.

The revolution carried through at Notre Dame in Paris in the first decade of the 13th century changed Early Gothic into High Gothic—that is, into the style which was going to dominate Gothic figure sculpture until its end. But High Gothic did not make an impact on England until 70 years later, for example in the Angel Choir at Lincoln. This chunky style of sculpture itself soon turned into something elegant and very decorative —for example in the tombs of Edmund Crouchback and Aymer de Valence in Westminster Abbey. Sometimes it is almost frivolous, like the tomb of Edward II in Gloucester Cathedral (1330's). All medieval sculpture was painted in some way or another, which meant a heyday for the decorator. The popularity of small alabaster plaques is a manifestation of the same trend.

RICHARD THE LIONHEART, a statue from the late 15th-century choir-screen at York Minster. One of fifteen statues depicting the kings of England from William the Conqueror to Henry VI

PAINTING: FROM RIGIDITY TO REALISM

The Early Gothic style, from the late 12th to the late 13th century, began, like sculpture, by using a short figure covered in fairly heavy drapery with many folds, and with a well modelled head. Scrolls and other decorative details were still coiled and organised, betraying little of the slight shift towards naturalism made in the figures. The change is nicely illustrated by the superb illuminations of the *Winchester Bible* (*c.* 1170), in which the artist known as the Master of the Leaping Figures epitomises the extremes of Late Romanesque design, while the style of the Master of the Morgan Leaf is Early Gothic. This style continued in England until the turn of the century, and is also represented by such masterpieces as the British Museum manuscripts of Bede's *Life of St Cuthbert*, and the *Westminster Psalter*. It was at this time and in this medium of illumination that England and many other countries contributed most to a development which was otherwise chiefly French.

In the 13th century this tight, restrained style gave way to something much looser, made up of tall, willowy figures clothed in fine, loose-fitting garments. Good examples of this new style are the *Evesham Psalter* (British Museum), the *Guthlac Roll* (British Museum) and the work of William of Malmesbury. Decorative work of the period still retains a pre-Gothic liveliness.

The century from *c.* 1270–1370 was characterised by two changes. The tightness of detail was loosened up, so that foliage, for example, moved away from pure design towards naturalism; and there was an increase in the sumptuousness of the decoration (for instance, backgrounds of tooled gold, or small painted repeat patterns), and in the figures themselves, which became almost unbelievably elegant and refined.

This change from Early to High Gothic took place in England during the reign of Henry III (1216–72), just as that reign saw the introduction of High Gothic architecture at Westminster. The change is found in the *Oscott Psalter*, the *de Lisle Psalter* (both British Museum), and the Sion Cope (Victoria and Albert Museum).

Towards the middle of the 14th century there is some evidence of the infiltration of Italian motifs and formulae. This last point is symptomatic of something happening throughout Europe at this time. Countries north of the Alps were being introduced to the intricacies, delights and hazards of the Italian artists' representation of space; while Italy was being educated in the northern traditions of everyday realism and aristocratic flamboyance and manners. The result of this inter-penetration was the emergence, around 1400, of an 'international' style, so-called because of the similarity of its products in different parts of Europe. One of the finest English examples is the *Wilton Diptych* (National Gallery, London).

Parallel to the exploration of space in the international style ran a desire to create scenes with groups of figures, and an interest in portraiture, as exemplified by the portrait of Richard II (1390's) in Westminster Abbey. This makes an interesting comparison with younger and older versions of the same monarch in the *Wilton Diptych* and on the king's tomb in the same abbey.

ILLUMINATED LETTER from a 13th-century manuscript. Certain initial letters were enlarged and embellished with decorative details, in brilliant colour-work. Their treatment was often descriptive of the text

GOTHIC ILLUMINATION from the Evesham Psalter, *c.* 1250. On this page a tiny figure of the Benedictine abbot, to whom the book belonged, kneels at the foot of the cross

Tudor and Jacobean

The adventurers and nobles enriched by Henry VIII and Elizabeth began the English country house tradition, and were lavish patrons of the arts

In 1509 Henry VIII was crowned king in succession to his father, Henry VII, the founder of the Tudor line. Eighteen years old, with unusual talents of body and brain, he became the patron both of sportsmen and of the men of the New Learning, the Renaissance, which was stirring the universities to a new and vigorous life. Henry was a champion at tennis and a fearless hunter; and his great suit of tilting armour in the Tower of London recalls his exploits in the lists. He was an accomplished musician, and fostered music and poetry at his Court.

In the early days of his reign, Henry employed Cardinal Wolsey as Chancellor and virtual ruler of England. Wolsey flaunted his pride and power in the face of king and nobles, helping to prepare the anti-Church revolution that eventually dissolved the monasteries and dispersed many of their treasures. Wolsey was enormously rich from Church revenues—some said almost as rich as the king. He kept a household of 1000 persons and marched in state with silver pillars borne before him. Wolsey's munificence left its mark on English architecture. Under his patronage Italian architects, painters and sculptors were brought over to assist with two great palaces, Hampton Court and York House (later Whitehall Palace). He endowed Cardinal College (later demolished) at Ipswich, and Cardinal College, now Christ Church, Oxford. Being too rich and powerful, Wolsey was inevitably deposed (1529). Henry VIII, wealthy from confiscations from the Church, became a hectic trendsetter in building for the last 20 years of his reign. He made vast extensions to his London palaces at Hampton Court, Whitehall and St James's. A fantastic palace at Nonsuch, Surrey, later destroyed, was built in direct emulation of the châteaux of the French king.

After the fall of Wolsey, Henry cut England off from Rome and proclaimed himself supreme head of the Church. From 1536 to 1539 he dissolved the monasteries, wrecking the ancient buildings and appropriating their wealth. He brought the clergy and their monies into subservience to the Crown. This seizing of monastic lands meant the biggest change in land-ownership since 1066. Much of the Church property was distributed among Henry's courtiers. Monasteries fell into ruin, became national cathedrals, or were cleared away to have country houses erected on the sites.

When Henry VIII died in 1547, his young son, delicate in health and only nine years old, became Edward VI (1547–53), and the Crown was immediately beset by factions of grasping nobles. Years of strife and upset

ELIZABETH I on her way to Blackfriars. Each year the Queen journeyed throughout the kingdom. In the hope of winning her favour, wealthier subjects built splendid houses in which to entertain her

followed. Protector Somerset, the king's uncle, pushed ahead with the sacking of the guilds and chantries, mostly for his own private interest. Out of his share of the loot the original Somerset House (now destroyed) rose on the banks of the Thames. The royal finances collapsed. As a result, the Crown did not re-establish its role as arbiter of the arts until James I came to the throne in 1603. Instead, this role passed to newly ennobled government officials.

It was these men, many owning land snatched from the monasteries, who sponsored the arts in the years to come. Often building on stolen land with stones from ruined abbeys, they raised the great mansions of Elizabethan and Jacobean England—among them Burghley House, Cambridgeshire, Hatfield House, Hertfordshire, Hardwick Hall, Derbyshire, and Audley End, Essex. These were the houses of the new rich—arrogant, bold and spectacular.

From Edward VI's reign onwards ran a strong anti-art current. The Protestant reformers ordered all sculpted or painted religious images to be removed, and the churches whitewashed. This meant the mass destruction of medieval art, and all forms of art came to be regarded with suspicion. On Edward's death, the Crown passed to his Catholic sister Mary (1553-8), whose reign ended in disaster. Although she restored ordered government, she also restored the Catholic faith, began the persecution of Protestants, made an unpopular marriage with Philip of Spain, and lost the war with France, and with it Calais, the English bridgehead on the Continent.

But waiting in Hatfield, Hertfordshire, eager to assume the Crown, was the last and most brilliant of Henry VIII's children, Elizabeth. She was to lead the English back to harmony and prosperity; and on to fresh areas of domination. Foreign artists imbued with Renaissance ideas had attended the court of Henry VIII, and in Elizabeth's reign more were to come. Flemish and German craftsmen settled in the eastern counties, where they influenced the style of the new mansions; and the persecution of Protestants by the Duke of Alva in the Low Countries in the 1560's drove skilled craftsmen to England.

The legendary Elizabethan age was one of intellectual brilliance, and of immense commercial prosperity. When Elizabeth died in 1603, Burghley's son, Robert Cecil, saw to it that her cousin James Stuart of Scotland, styled King James VI and I, should succeed smoothly to the throne. The Stuarts brought England into closer touch with the Continent, especially with France and Italy. James I, inept as he was at politics, was a scholar. Through his art-loving wife, Anne of Denmark, he became the pupil of Inigo Jones, the great English architect who was to change the course of architecture and art in England.

The men of Tudor and Jacobean times produced their artistic triumphs almost in spite of themselves. Trouble and upset at home and the anti-art campaign of the Reformers and later of the Puritans cut England adrift from the Continent, where the Renaissance was flourishing in almost every country. The suppression of the visual arts meant that painting was confined to portraits, sculpture to tombs, and building to dwelling-houses.

NONSUCH PALACE, Surrey, was the most ambitious building ever undertaken by Henry VIII. It was demolished c. 1670. Contemporary drawings show that it was planned around two courtyards and was lavishly ornamented by foreign craftsmen

BURGHLEY HOUSE,
Cambridgeshire. One of
the finest houses of the early
Renaissance period in England,
it was formerly the home
of Lord Burghley, Elizabeth I's
minister of state. His design
consultant was the Dutch
architect 'Master Henryk'

BRICK CHIMNEYS came into
general use early in the 16th
century and were one of the
most characteristic features of
the Tudor house. Often
elaborately carved and
decorated, they offered the
bricklayers the chance to
exploit newly acquired skills

ARCHITECTURE: THE AGE OF THE COUNTRY HOUSE

Architecturally, the Tudor period (1485-1603) might be called the age of the country house, because it is at this time that the country house first emerged as an architectural form. Church building had virtually ceased with the Reformation, and energies were centred on new houses.

Tudor architecture, and the Tudor house in particular, still retained overtones of Gothic from the previous century, and some of its characteristics persisted until the middle of the 17th century. Most Tudor houses were still built round a quadrangular court entered from under a gate-house. Fortified gateways, grand courtyards, battlemented parapets, towers and turrets lingered on for ornament rather than defence; and ornamented chimneys signified comfort within. The hall became a symbol of grandeur: money and artistic skill were lavished on its carved fire-places, oak-panelled walls and timber roofs.

Hampton Court, on the outskirts of London, is a famous surviving example. The original part of the palace, built of mellow red brickwork in diaper (diamond) pattern, has battlemented parapets, a turreted gate-house, many courtyards and ornamented chimneys. The great hall of Henry VIII is its main feature. Later in Henry VIII's reign, the new Classicism of the Renaissance came to England from France. Nonsuch Palace, Surrey (now destroyed), was an embodiment of the new style.

From the death of Henry VIII in 1547 until c. 1570 architecture followed a confused path. The troubles of the middle years of the century were not conducive to the long, peaceful task of raising great buildings. Classical detail, which came to England from France, continued to be superimposed on Tudor Gothic. Somerset House (now destroyed) in the Strand, begun in 1547, represented the first attempt to build a complete Classical façade.

The tradition of French Classicism lingered with some vitality in Burghley House, Cambridgeshire, which was built by Lord Burghley in the French manner in the 1560's. But already a new influence can be seen at work there, promoted by Burghley's friend, Sir Thomas Gresham. Gresham imported from Antwerp a Classicism more flamboyant than the French style, overladen with bulbous detail, such as caryatids (female figures used as pillars), cartouches or scroll ornaments, and strapwork.

After these stops and starts, English architecture quite suddenly, c. 1570, ceased to be derivative and set out on a different, startling path. Two great houses epitomise this. Kirby Hall, in Northamptonshire, now a fairly intact ruin, was built for Sir Humphry Stafford by John Thorpe; from its courtyard giant pilasters soar upwards almost to the skyline. Longleat, Wiltshire, was remodelled from 1573 onwards for Sir John Thynne as the first spectacular instance of the lantern house—a glistening acreage of glass and bay windows. These houses of the 1570's achieve their effects by superimposing Classical detail on a basically restrained architectural shell.

About 1580 architecture took another course. It rejected the Classical and turned back in time to the glories of the English Perpendicular style. The effects aimed at by the builders of King's College Chapel, Cambridge, were developed in late Elizabethan and Jacobean houses: height, huge windows and a distinctive, striking skyline.

Architects did not really exist as a professional group before Inigo Jones at the beginning of the 17th century. But if any two men may be singled out as superb exponents and creators of a style, it would be Robert Smythson and his son John. Their work, beginning with Robert's Longleat in the 1570's, includes some of the greatest examples of the neo-medieval castle style: Wollaton Hall, Nottinghamshire (1580-8), for Sir Francis Willoughby; Robert Smythson's Hardwick Hall, Derbyshire (1590-7), for Bess of Hardwick, the Countess of Shrewsbury; and John Smythson's Bolsover Castle, Derbyshire (begun 1612), for Sir Charles Cavendish.

These epitomise what the Elizabethans most desired in their buildings. They are impressive, almost melodramatic in their setting, often sited on hill-tops. They rise to a great height, penetrating the skyline in a riot of carved brick and stone, crenellation, balustrading, chimneys and cupolas. Their startling effect is enhanced by symmetry, and by acres of glass, making them lanterns of light twinkling in the sun across the countryside.

ALABASTER MEMORIAL, Elmley Castle. A 17th-century alabaster memorial to William Savage and his wife, Katherine, holding their baby son. Like most other effigies of the period it probably depicts the family as they were in their prime rather than at the time of death

SCULPTURE: SUMPTUOUS TOMBS

The feverish pace at which the Tudors built was not carried over into their sculpture, which existed only as a complement to building. Sculptors were artificers, employed to overlay and garnish a building, or to carve a tomb with recumbent effigies. They did not sculpt portraits, busts or mythological groups, as in Italy.

Tudor sculpture opened with a brief, spectacular flirtation with Renaissance Italy in the person of Pietro Torrigiano, who worked for the young Henry VIII. The moving effigies on the tombs of Henry VII, his wife Elizabeth of York, and his mother Margaret Beaufort (in Westminster Abbey) represent this fleeting moment. The hands of the aged Lady Margaret, wrinkled and old, laid on each other in prayer, and her tranquil face, are typical of Torrigiano's talents of characterisation.

English sculpture sank back into the rut of the engaging second-rate. Endless tombs were produced, to proclaim for all time the glory of the new gentry. They lie there, with hands clasped, sumptuously dressed and flanked by coats of arms. Near by kneel figures of children ranging downwards in size; and a laudatory epitaph, offset only by skulls, crossbones and bubbles, reminds the spectator that life is transitory. Beautiful examples of this style are the Hoby family tombs at Bisham, Berkshire; the tomb of Robert Cecil, Lord Salisbury, at Hatfield, Hertfordshire; that of Henry, Lord Norris, in Westminster Abbey; and that of Lady Carey at Church Stowe, Northamptonshire.

SIR THOMAS MORE, in the style of Holbein. A political philosopher, humanist and author of the famous *Utopia* (1516), More steadfastly refused to recognise Henry VIII's claim to be head of the church; he was executed at the Tower in 1535

PAINTING: HOLBEIN AND THE MINIATURISTS

Painting in Renaissance England began quite abruptly with the arrival of a foreigner, the German Hans Holbein the Younger, who lived in England from 1527 to 1529 and from 1531 to 1543. He brought with him all the

NICHOLAS HILLIARD miniature (1576) of Robert Dudley, Earl of Leicester. Miniatures were painted on the backs of playing-cards or sheets of vellum, until the superior quality of ivory was discovered in the 18th century

SUIT OF ARMOUR designed for Sir Henry Lee. From *The Jacobe Album* (1489). The book catalogued the various designs built at the Royal Armouries, Greenwich, during the Tudor reigns of Queen Mary and Queen Elizabeth

discoveries of the high Renaissance in Italy: skill in perspective and illusionism, knowledge of Classical antiquity and an acuteness of psychological observation.

Holbein was welcomed by Sir Thomas More, the foremost exponent of the New Learning, and was later patronised by Henry VIII. His style enables us to visualise, by means of his sublime portrait drawings at Windsor Castle, the burly toughs and tight-lipped beauties of Henry VIII's court.

Hans Eworth, an exile from Flanders, was the only painter of any stature to work during the troubled middle years of the century. His portrait called *Mary I* (Fitzwilliam Museum, Cambridge) betrays Holbein's influence.

So, too, does Nicholas Hilliard (1547–1619), Queen Elizabeth I's miniaturist. His is a delicate, flower-coloured world. In an oval the size of a gull's egg, he captures the great Elizabethans: the haughty queen; proud, pouting Leicester; or romantic, curly-headed Raleigh (all in the National Portrait Gallery). Hilliard produced one of the masterpieces of English art, the *Unknown Youth leaning against a Tree* (Victoria and Albert Museum).

By the turn of the century Hilliard was becoming old-fashioned, and the court took up a new romanticism purveyed in miniature by Isaac Oliver (*c.* 1565–1617) and, larger, by his brother-in-law, Marcus Gheeraerts the Younger (*c.* 1561–1636). Gheeraerts's masterpiece is at Woburn Abbey, Bedfordshire. It is a portrait of Elizabeth's last favourite, Essex, pensive in white and silver against a background landscape. Oliver's large miniature of Lucy Harington, Countess of Bedford, enveloped in billowing gauze veils (Fitzwilliam Museum), is a small-scale counterpart to Gheeraerts's Essex.

DECORATIVE ARTS: EMBROIDERY AND ARMOUR

In the Middle Ages, England had been famous for her embroidery, and in the reign of Elizabeth there was a remarkable revival of this art. But now it was no longer applied to vestments as in medieval times, but to curtains, bed hangings, tablecloths, cushions and costume. Hardwick Hall, Derbyshire, houses embroideries which are wonderful in the invention of their design.

Little English jewellery survives from this period, but where it does, as in the Armada Jewel (Victoria and Albert Museum), it is exquisite. This is said to have been presented by Queen Elizabeth to Sir Thomas Heneage on the defeat of the Armada in 1588. Vast quantities of silver plate still exist—nefs (silver boats), tazzas (saucer-shaped cups mounted on a foot) and standing cups (British Museum and Victoria and Albert Museum).

In Elizabeth's reign handsome suits of decorated armour were produced, in which her knights would joust in her honour; these can still be seen in the Tower of London.

In Elizabeth's reign, also, tapestry was woven in England for the first time, under the auspices of the Sheldon family of Weston, Warwickshire. Some can be seen at the Victoria and Albert Museum. Hatfield House, too, has a splendid set of tapestries of the Four Seasons.

The Stuarts

The first half of the Stuart period (1625–1714) was dominated by the art of Van Dyck; the second half by the architecture of Wren

The arts flourished in the early years of Charles I's reign (1625–49), for they were an essential accompaniment to 17th-century absolute monarchy, when the grandeur of princes and aristocracy was measured by the magnificence of their art collections.

When the Crown fell, the arts declined into decadence. The 11 years of the Commonwealth (1649–60), when England was ruled by an oligarchy of republicans, are of little importance in the history of the arts in England. Cromwell's rule as Lord Protector (1653–8) was a virtual dictatorship, with army officers controlling the country. It was not until after Cromwell's death in 1658, and after the short rule of his son Richard, when the Stuarts returned to the throne in 1660 on a wave of popularity, that the arts began to revive.

Charles II made every effort to put the clock back to the gay, carefree days of the 1630's. Theatres reopened, racing started at Newmarket, clothes blossomed out into ruffles and ribbons, and there was ribaldry and excess. Charles's brother, James II, who succeeded to the throne in 1685, had to flee the country in 1688 for promoting the interests of his Catholic supporters. The 'Glorious Revolution' of 1688 set on the throne William of Orange, Stadtholder of the Netherlands, and his wife Mary, James II's daughter, and established Parliamentary monarchy. Under William and Mary, and their successor Queen Anne (1702–14), Britain gained a political and constitutional equilibrium never again upset.

Charles I accumulated an art collection which, if it had survived intact, would have made England the greatest single repository of Renaissance art in the world. Its sale under the Commonwealth was a horrifying artistic tragedy. Now its treasures lie scattered over the great galleries of Europe and America; but enough remains here to evoke some idea of its spectacular opulence. Charles's collection included, for instance, the Mantegna cartoons (Hampton Court), the Leonardo sketchbooks (Windsor Castle), the Raphael cartoons (Victoria and Albert Museum), and the Wilton Diptych (National Gallery).

Charles I was not only an avid collector, but an enthusiastic and discerning patron who wanted England to be in the forefront of artistic taste and achievement. For this reason he welcomed to England Rubens and Van Dyck to put new life into painting, and the sculptors Le Sueur and Fanelli to civilise our lumpish provincial sculpture; and he entrusted the *décor* of the Court, both architectural and theatrical, to the genius of Inigo Jones.

QUEEN HENRIETTA MARIA by Van Dyck. She was the youngest daughter of Henri IV of France, and queen consort of Charles I. An obstinate woman, her zealous Catholicism did little to help her husband throughout a difficult reign

CHARLES II as a boy-commander, by William Dobson (1610–46), who succeeded Van Dyck as Court painter. Dobson was one of the first English artists of this period to achieve distinction

31

THE BANQUETING HOUSE,
Whitehall, is considered to be
Inigo Jones's masterpiece. Built
as the first stage of a larger
palace, which was never
completed because of the Civil
War, it cost £15,000. The
ceiling-panels in the Banqueting
Hall were painted by Rubens

CHURCH OF ST MARY-LE-
STRAND in London, from an
18th-century water-colour. This
building was the first important
commission by James Gibbs, a
pupil of Sir Christopher Wren,
after a protracted tour of study
in Italy as a young man

Outside the Court was another great patron and collector,
the Earl of Arundel. His antique marbles (Ashmolean
Museum, Oxford) give a clue to the quality of his
collection, as does Holbein's portrait of Erasmus, the
remarkable painting now at Longford Castle, Wiltshire.

After the disruption of the Commonwealth, the Court
never quite re-established its position as arbiter of the
arts. Charles II and James II, with their Catholic-biased
Courts, promoted French baroque in emulation of
Louis XIV's palace at Versailles, while Dutch William
III brought a flavour of Holland to Hampton Court, with
bulbs for the garden and Delftware pottery for the house.
Only at the end of the period, in Queen Anne's reign,
was there a revival of artistic patronage on the grand
scale, when vast baroque palaces were built for the Whig
aristocracy by Vanbrugh and Hawksmoor.

The 17th century was a time of disruption and change,
and it failed to produce a single, settled standard of taste.
But art acquired a status: it became not only respectable
but fashionable. Artists, and in particular painters, ceased
to be regarded as tradespeople, as they were in Elizabethan days, and became gentlemen. Knighthoods were
bestowed on Van Dyck, Lely and Kneller.

The educated upper classes took an acute interest in
the arts. The diaries of Samuel Pepys and John Evelyn
are full of references to painting, sculpture and architecture. Artistic theory came second-hand through translations from the French and Italian; but by the close of the
period Shaftesbury's book *Characteristicks* had launched
the notion of a national school of British art. This
resulted in the campaign for an academy, a plan that
reached fruition three generations later when the Royal
Academy was founded in 1768.

ARCHITECTURE: THE AGE OF INIGO JONES AND WREN

The most important single figure in 17th-century
English art was Inigo Jones (1573-1652). He was the
judge and dictator of taste at the Stuart Court of James
I and Charles I for over 20 years. He was a collector and
antiquarian, a connoisseur of painting and antiquities.
He designed the fantastic stage designs for the Court
ballets (now at Chatsworth House, Derbyshire), as well
as being England's foremost architect.

Inigo Jones had worked in Italy and was deeply
influenced by Classical tradition and its revival in
Renaissance building in Italy. In particular, he admired
the work of the 16th-century Venetian architect,
Palladio, and introduced into England the new Italianate
Classical styles, later called Palladian.

Jones began a revolution: the Banqueting House in
Whitehall (1620-35), with its severely Classical façade—
tall windows, pediments, columns all strictly symmetrical—arose in the midst of the shambling, black and white
timbered houses of Stuart London; his Queen's House
in Greenwich (begun 1616), a Venetian villa in the
Palladian manner, was built astride the main Deptford-
Woolwich Road. Inigo Jones's work and influence
affected the whole course of architecture in England.
English country houses of the mid-17th century were

enlivened by architectural features based on Inigo
Jones's work. At the Restoration in 1660, English
architects had at last to come to terms with the prevailing
European style, the baroque—exemplified particularly
by Louis XIV's great palace at Versailles, which inspired
Charles II's own artistic taste. The story of art and
architecture in the second half of the 17th century is the
attempt to adapt the baroque idiom to English taste.

This was crystallised in the career of Sir Christopher
Wren (1632-1723), who rebuilt 51 City churches and
St Paul's Cathedral after the Great Fire of London in
1666. He was enormously ingenious in planning buildings
on cramped sites; and the interiors of some—St Stephen's,
Walbrook, especially—are particularly noble.

Under the later Stuarts, Wren worked on frustrating
palace projects—Whitehall, Greenwich, Kensington and
Hampton Court. Fragments of the last three remain.
Greenwich (begun 1694) is his secular masterpiece.
Grand blocks form narrowing courtyards which, when
viewed from the Thames, lead the eye to Inigo Jones's
Queen's House. St Paul's Cathedral, built between 1675
and 1710, is his ecclesiastical masterpiece. In it Wren
fulfilled his own creed that 'the glory of that which is
good of itself is eternal'.

While Wren was not fundamentally a domestic
architect, his followers, Nicholas Hawksmoor (1661-
1736) and Sir John Vanbrugh (1664-1726), were
particularly interested in great houses. They often worked
as a team and developed a more flamboyant, openly
baroque style than that of Wren.

INIGO JONES (1573-1651) His
brilliant career as an architect at
Court was brought to an end by
the start of the Civil War. He
was imprisoned and forced to
pay a heavy fine for being a
'courtier', and died in poverty
at the age of 79

SCULPTURE: ECHOES FROM ITALY

English sculpture throughout the 17th century remained
a provincial echo of the great stylistic movements that
emanated from Italy. Not that effort was lacking: for
Charles I imported foreign sculptors, as well as a hoard
of antique statues, to inspire a new generation of artists.
But the Frenchman Hubert Le Sueur and the Italian
Fanelli did not approach the stature of a Van Dyck. Le
Sueur's statue in Trafalgar Square of Charles I on
horseback reflects the fairly low level they achieved.

Towards the close of the century Caius Gabriel Cibber
and Grinling Gibbons adopted a modified baroque style.
The only real sculptural glory of the century was achieved
by Gibbons and his followers in their development of
wood carving (choir stalls of St Paul's Cathedral, and
panelling at Hampton Court). Inspired by Dutch still-life
painting, their swags of flowers, fruit, birds and trophies
transformed interior decoration.

OLIVER CROMWELL An 18th-
century bust by Joseph Wilton,
reflecting the reputed sternness
of the Lord Protector. Although
neither cruel nor tyrannical by
nature, Cromwell had a
repressive influence on the arts
from which they only recovered
after the Restoration

PAINTING: A TRIO OF FOREIGNERS

The history of English painting under the Stuarts can be
summed up by three artists, all foreigners: Sir Anthony
Van Dyck (1599-1641), Sir Peter Lely (1618-80) and
Sir Godfrey Kneller (1646-1723). Between them these
three painters cover the 100 years from the accession of
Charles I in 1625 to the close of George I's reign in 1727.

The style that Van Dyck brought to England in 1632

SIR CHRISTOPHER WREN painted
by Sir Godfrey Kneller,
Principal Painter to the Court of
Charles II. Wren was the first
man to be buried in St Paul's;
his tomb bears the inscription:
'Lector, si monumentum requiris,
circumspice.' (Reader, if you seek
a memorial, look about you)

JACOBEAN EMBROIDERY A
detail from a mid-17th-century
stumpwork fabric. Stumpwork,
or 'embossed' work, was an
elaborate form of embroidery
which used cotton, wool or hair
to achieve raised surfaces. Metal
or seed-pearls were used for eyes
and hands, and faces were carved
in wood or wax

was a muted version of that of Rubens, his master, who
had painted for Charles I the ceiling of the Whitehall
Banqueting House, one of the finest examples of baroque
decoration in Europe. But Van Dyck did not import the
rubicund, fleshy, almost coarse writhings produced by
his master's studio. Instead he studied the gentler mood
of English genteel refinement; he turned every vice of
character or appearance into a virtue.

Van Dyck's virtuosity of interpretation and skilful
handling of paint are displayed at Windsor Castle—in
the portrait of Charles I on horseback riding in triumph
through a Classical archway; the triple portrait of this
sad-faced little man; the hollow-cheeked Queen Henrietta Maria full face and in profile; and, best of all, the
royal children grouped in joyous solemnity.

Van Dyck had a successor—William Dobson, the
talented Englishman who painted the Civil War courtiers
at Oxford. His portrait of Charles II as a boy commander
banishing with a gesture of his baton the snake-haired
figure of Rebellion (Scottish National Portrait Gallery)
catches the mood of this last outburst of Caroline culture.

After the Restoration in 1660 portraiture was dominated by Sir Peter Lely, who fused the bourgeois style
of his native Holland with the refinements of Van Dyck.
Lely's studio maintained what can only be described as
factory production. At his best, as in the burly *Admirals
at Greenwich* (National Maritime Museum), or the
Beauties (Hampton Court), he was capable of considerable spiritedness; fundamentally he was a superficial
recorder of external appearances.

To visualise the Restoration court in depth, it is better
to ignore the acreage of Lely and concentrate on the
inches of Samuel Cooper (1609-72). Influenced apparently
by Rembrandt, Cooper rendered the heavy-lidded
ladies and thick-lipped gentlemen with little concern for
surface glitter (Victoria and Albert Museum).

Sir Godfrey Kneller, like Lely, maintained a torrential
studio production and had a horde of imitators. For 40
years, until his death in 1723, he dominated the scene.
The best collection of his portraits is the famous *Kit-Cat
Club* series in the National Portrait Gallery.

DECORATIVE ARTS: TAPESTRY AND EMBROIDERY

The decorative arts were distinguished in the Stuart
period by the excellence of their tapestry and embroidery.
Furniture and silver, beautiful though they could be,
were mere reflections of styles evolved abroad; but
English tapestry was an art on its own. In 1620 James I
founded a royal tapestry factory at Mortlake. Charles I
acquired the Raphael cartoons to inspire these weavers,
and examples of their work are in the great houses of
England (Belvoir Castle, Leicestershire; Woburn Abbey,
Bedfordshire; Chatsworth, Derbyshire).

Surviving embroidery is mostly domestic in character,
executed by the children and ladies of the household.
The engaging pictorial crudity of these little embroidered
pictures and cabinets, worked in coloured silk and metal
thread, is in direct contrast to the elegance proclaimed
by a Van Dyck or a Lely.

The Georgian Age

The reigns of the four Georges, from 1714 to 1830, saw the creation of landscape gardens, the elegance of Georgian houses, and the start of the romantic movement

The glory of the Georgian age lay in the genius and energy of individuals acting freely, in a community ruled by law and Parliament, not despotism—such men as Wolfe, Clive, Cook, Wellington and Nelson among the soldiers and sailors; Swift, Johnson, Fielding and Wordsworth among the writers; Hogarth, Gainsborough and Blake among the artists; and Handel, Wesley and Watt in music, religion and scientific discovery. The aesthetic principles underlying the arts in this age of rising prosperity and great political families are reflected in its most characteristic achievement, the landscape garden (Stowe, Buckinghamshire; Stourhead, Wiltshire). Gardens were intended to appear natural and irregular, reflecting the 18th-century love of freedom; but in practice they were carefully contrived. Modelled on the landscape paintings of the 17th-century French artist, Claude, they evoked memories of Classical antiquity by means of carefully placed temples and busts. They also aroused feelings of sentiment and melancholy by means of specially built Gothic ruins.

The taste for the elaborate asymmetry of the rococo style was embodied by Capability Brown in his serpentine paths and lakes; and the 'picturesque' school of the latter part of the century, in which open vistas and rolling acres gave way to concealment and surprise, was a foretaste of the romantic and exotic movement which characterised the arts at the end of the Georgian era.

The symbol of Georgian wealth and power was the country mansion, set in acres of carefully landscaped parkland. In order to maintain their status, great landowners felt compelled to live, build and furnish ostentatiously. The state rooms in great houses were designed principally for show, and there were open days when visitors were encouraged to view and admire. Many aristocrats, such as Lord Leicester (Holkham Hall, Norfolk) and Lord Chesterfield (Chesterfield House, London), devoted much of their energy to improving their houses; and some, like Lord Burlington (Chiswick House, and the Assembly Rooms at York) and Lord Pembroke (the Palladian Bridge at Wilton House) even became amateur architects.

Taste was based principally upon the arts and civilisation of Italy and of Classical antiquity. It was customary for the nobility to complete their education with two or three years of travel on the Continent. They were taken to archaeological sites, and to artists' studios, where they bought Classical sculptures, paintings by Canaletto and Pannini, and copies of famous pictures by other artists.

TIMES OF DAY—NOON One of a series of four satirical engravings by William Hogarth (1697–1764), illustrating the uninhibited life of the London streets. The church is St Giles-in-the-Fields

HUNTING SCENE Detail from a landscape by George Stubbs (1724–1806). A great landed aristocrat, the 3rd Duke of Richmond, hunts at Goodwood, with his brother, Lord George Lennox, and General Jones

The experience of the Grand Tour led to the foundation in 1734 of the Dilettanti Society, whose membership was confined to those who had been to Italy, and had a general interest in archaeology. The discovery of ancient Herculaneum (near Naples) in 1738, of Baalbek (Lebanon) and Palmyra (Syria) in 1751, and of Pompeii in 1763, and the lavish publications that followed, had an immediate influence on taste and design.

Much of the Classical sculpture bought by 18th-century collectors was fancifully 'restored' by the trade in Rome, but much also was of fine quality. Special sculpture galleries were built in country houses; examples survive intact at Holkham Hall, Norfolk, and at Newby Hall, N. Yorkshire. Most of the sculpture was Roman; Greek sculpture was little known until the sculptures from the Parthenon (the Elgin Marbles) were bought for the nation in 1816.

Some early 18th-century aristocrats, like Lord Burlington and the Duke of Chandos, had Italian painters to decorate their houses: Amigoni, a Venetian, did fine work for the Duke at Moor Park, Hertfordshire. But the taste for painted wall decoration was in decline, and most patrons concentrated on buying old masters in the grand manner—history paintings by Poussin and the Bolognese followers of Raphael, or landscapes by Claude.

Lord Spencer furnished Spencer House, London, with dramatic paintings by Salvator Rosa and Guercino (now at Althorp, Northamptonshire). Other collections in this taste which still exist were formed by Paul Methuen (Corsham Court, Wiltshire) and Sir Nathaniel Curzon (Kedleston Hall, Derbyshire).

With so many rich collectors vying for the best pictures, the art trade in London expanded enormously. Auction rooms were opened: Sotheby's was founded in 1744 and Christie's in 1766. For some enthusiasts like the portrait painters Jonathan Richardson and Sir Thomas Lawrence, collecting drawings became a passion; others collected prints.

An increasing number of middle-class collectors bought pictures and works of art. Charles Jennens, Handel's friend, collected Dutch pictures rather than Italian, in addition to the work of his own countrymen, such as Hogarth; while Jonathan Tyers commissioned Francis Hayman to paint the decorations for Vauxhall Gardens. But this patronage of British painters was uncharacteristic. While British cabinet-makers and silversmiths were widely patronised, in painting only documentary work, portraits, country house views and sporting pictures were commissioned from British artists.

It was not until the end of the century, when the country was fighting Napoleon, that any systematic encouragement of native painting was attempted. The British Institution, which organised exhibitions and awarded prizes, was started in 1805, and collections of British painting and sculpture were formed by Sir J. F. Leicester, Sir George Beaumont, the friend of Constable, and Lord Egremont, the friend of Turner (whose collection may still be seen at Petworth, W. Sussex).

Patronage and taste under the Georges followed a succession of different fashions. French rococo style

ROYAL ACADEMY, 1771 Detail from a work by the mezzotint engraver Richard Earlom (1743–1822), showing prospective buyers of pictures. The bulky figure may be Dr Johnson

DESIGN BY WILLIAM KENT This pen and ink wash drawing is the design for a side table at Houghton Hall, Norfolk. Kent was an outstanding personality of the Palladian school, and under the patronage of Lord Burlington became the fashionable architect of the 1730's and 1740's. The drawing is dated 1731

began to affect all the decorative arts around 1740, and there was a craze for *chinoiserie*, especially influential in architecture, furniture and gardening, during the 1750's. The feeling for Gothic, stimulated by Horace Walpole's house, Strawberry Hill, Twickenham, was more significant for the future, and reflected a growing interest in British antiquities. The Society of Antiquaries was founded in 1717, and research was begun into Roman as well as medieval Britain. Certain of the cathedrals, Canterbury for example, were cleaned of grime.

Towards the end of the Georgian period there was a Greek revival, foreshadowed by Stuart and Revett's book *Antiquities of Athens* (published in 1762). The Duke of Northumberland was one of the earliest to form a collection of Egyptian sculpture. The collecting of early Italian painting by William Roscoe, Lord Ashburnham and William Fox-Strangways was a development (like the encouragement of contemporary British art and the Gothic Revival), which was to influence Victorian taste.

THE RISE OF THE ARCHITECT

Early Georgian architecture was anti-baroque, in revolt against the exuberant style of the end of the 17th century. It took its principles and its forms from three sources: from Classical Rome; from Andrea Palladio, the 16th-century Italian whose treatise on architecture was translated in 1715; and from Inigo Jones, who founded Britain's Renaissance style.

The chief exponents of the early Georgian style were Colin Campbell (*d.* 1734), Lord Burlington (Chiswick House), and William Kent (Holkham Hall, Norfolk, and the Horse Guards, Whitehall). The Palladian style they evolved was noble and finely proportioned but austere and sparing of ornament; and it soon penetrated the whole of English architecture. Manor houses up and down the country, as well as streets in London and elsewhere, were built in the simple, unadorned manner which has come to be accepted as typically Georgian. At this period countless pattern-books appeared laying down the 'correct' methods of designing. For the first time designing became dissociated from practical building, and successful practitioners began to call themselves architects. A new profession had come into being.

The most notable architects of the mid-18th century, Sir Robert Taylor and James Paine, were still working in the Palladian tradition. About 1760, however, two greater men appeared on the scene—Sir William Chambers (Somerset House, London) and Robert Adam (Syon House, Greater London; Kenwood, Hampstead; Newby Hall, N. Yorkshire; Harewood House, W. Yorkshire; Kedleston Hall, Derbyshire). Although Chambers was Palladian in spirit, he used other sources—a natural consequence of the spate of discoveries of ancient cities, such as Baalbek in the Lebanon.

These discoveries also led to a more flexible attitude among some later 18th-century architects. James Wyatt, for example, did not mind whether he was required to build in Classical or Gothic. Indian (Royal Pavilion, Brighton), Egyptian and other styles were adopted.

ST MARTIN-IN-THE-FIELDS Wooden model of the church built 1722-6 by James Gibbs (1682-1754). His design for what has been called 'the finest parish church of the Grecian style in England' has been widely copied —especially in America

MARBLE FIRE-PLACE at Kedleston Hall, Derbyshire, by Robert Adam (1728-92). Adam designed the interiors of his houses down to the smallest detail. The white stucco figures were made by Joseph Rose

Adam also made use of the new range of Classical forms, but his attitude towards his borrowings was different from that of Chambers. He discarded Classical proportions and used his sources in a personal and inventive way, primarily for the interior decoration of his houses. Adam usually designed all the furniture and accessories for a house, so that the unity of conception was complete (Harewood House, W. Yorkshire), and he envisaged an interior as a sequence of carefully contrasted rooms (Syon House, Greater London). Similarly his exteriors were designed to show what he called 'movement'—a constant variety of silhouette and of recession and projection (Kedleston Hall, Derbyshire).

The picturesque and dynamic qualities of Adam's architecture were developed by John Nash (1752–1835). In his masterpiece, Regent Street (now rebuilt) and Regent's Park, he gave a complicated piece of town planning the sweep and movement of a house by Adam, and parts of it, in particular Cumberland Terrace, the magnificence of Vanbrugh's architecture.

The most original architect of the late Georgian period was Sir John Soane (1753–1837) (Soane Museum, Lincoln's Inn Fields, London; and Dulwich College Art Gallery). Simplicity, a return to the first principles of building and the pruning of Classical forms to bare essentials were the main characteristics of his work.

BUST OF ALEXANDER POPE The most brilliant poet and wit of England's Augustan Age wears, appropriately enough, a Roman tunic in this sculpture by Louis François Roubiliac

SCULPTURE: ROMAN NOBILITY, GREEK ELEGANCE

Georgian sculptors had the same dislike of baroque excess as Georgian architects. They were led by a group of Flemish sculptors, all active in England by 1720: Plumier, Delvaux, Scheemakers and, most notably, Michael Rysbrack (Marlborough Monument, Blenheim Palace). Commissions were mainly for monumental tomb sculpture and for portrait busts, the favoured image of the Georgian landowner, and Rysbrack excelled in both.

Louis François Roubiliac (Argyll Monument, Westminster Abbey), who came to England in 1732, created a considerable sensation with the informal design of his statue of Handel for Vauxhall Gardens (1738). In his busts, which were the finest portraiture of the period, he attempted to catch the idiosyncrasies of the sitter.

The sculpture of the second half of the century was influenced by the recent Classical discoveries. The Roman grandeur of Rysbrack gave way to the Grecian elegance of Nollekens, several of whose tombs are in Westminster Abbey, and to the graceful, flowing style of Thomas Banks; while the linear style of Flaxman derived from a study of Greek vase painting. At the turn of the century the principal commissions were for monuments to national heroes, like Nelson, and for outdoor statues.

MONUMENT TO ISAAC NEWTON The great mathematician, sculpted by Michael Rysbrack, broods within his niche in Westminster Abbey

PAINTING: NATURALISM AND THE GRAND MANNER

Most of the best painters working in Britain up to this time had been foreigners; and wealthy patrons continued to buy or commission foreign rather than British pictures. In 1711 Sir Godfrey Kneller, famous as a portrait painter at the end of the 17th century, started an academy in

London for training British artists; and the St Martin's Lane Academy was revived by Hogarth in the 1730's.

But it remained difficult for painters to find a market for their work. Hogarth started the idea of putting paintings on show at the Foundling Hospital, of which he was a governor; and they are still to be seen there (Brunswick Square, London). However, it was not until the Society of Artists was founded in 1760 that artists had a regular means of exhibiting their paintings.

William Hogarth (*The Marriage à la Mode,* National Gallery, and numerous examples at the Tate Gallery) was a revolutionary influence in many other ways. In *The Analysis of Beauty* he put forward his own theory that painting should be based on a serpentine line; and he evolved a completely new style of painting designed to appeal to middle-class people. His portraits were primarily likenesses, and he introduced the informal group portrait known as the conversation piece—the most popular of all 18th-century genres. He also painted several series of pictures, of which *The Harlot's Progress* was the first, to foster thrift, honesty and hard work.

Equally important as an influence on British painting was Sir Joshua Reynolds. He came back to England in 1753 after studying for several years in Italy, and established himself as the only rival to the Scottish artist, Allan Ramsay, then the leading portraitist in London.

Reynolds was as determined as Hogarth to raise the status of the British painter. As first President of the Royal Academy, founded in 1768, he delivered a series of annual discourses to the students, in which he taught that history painting was the most important genre. Though he painted few history pictures himself, since they were difficult to sell, he tried to invest his portraits with the characteristics of the 'great style'. He painted the defender of Gibraltar, Lord Heathfield (National Gallery), against storm-laden clouds, with cannon visible beneath; and based his *Commodore Keppel* (National Maritime Museum, Greenwich) on the *Apollo Belvedere* in the Vatican. He was capable of a more informal style. His *Georgiana, Duchess of Devonshire, and Daughters* (Chatsworth) is an incomparable image of motherly love.

The only contemporary of Reynolds to equal him in greatness was a painter opposite to him in every way, Thomas Gainsborough (1727–88) (*Lady Howe,* Kenwood; numerous examples at the National and Tate Galleries). Where Reynolds always generalised, Gainsborough was best at detail—the silks and satins of a lady's dress, or the glitter of a sword hilt. Gainsborough's real love was for landscape. In an age when villagers were beginning to migrate to factories and mills, he painted nostalgic pastoral landscapes of cows being driven home in the evening, or peasants at a cottage door.

By the later 18th century the public had developed a taste for sentiment. Francis Wheatley's *Cries of London,* showing the picturesque and deserving poor, proved more acceptable than the pungent satire of Hogarth. Among other notable contemporaries of Reynolds was Richard Wilson, a landscapist, whose work shows an unusual sensitivity to light and atmosphere (National Museum of Wales, Cardiff).

SIR JOSHUA REYNOLDS A self-portrait of Reynolds (1723–92) as a young man. The painting shows the vitality and confidence that were his trade-marks

TINTERN ABBEY, water-colour by Turner (1775–1851). Romantic ruined abbeys and castles were a favourite subject of Turner's early period, and he exhibited water-colours at the Royal Academy from the age of 15

Other leading artists were George Stubbs, the greatest of all English sporting artists (National Gallery, Tate Gallery, British Museum); and Joseph Wright of Derby, who specialised in industrial subjects like the *Experiment on a Bird in the Air-pump* (Tate Gallery).

John Constable (fully represented at the Victoria and Albert Museum) devoted his life to painting the English countryside. Like Wordsworth, he had an almost religious feeling for landscape, and used effects of light and weather to convey different moods and emotions.

J. M. W. Turner (fully represented at the Tate Gallery) was more interested in the wild, romantic aspects of landscape, and specialised in mountain scenes and storms at sea. He was fascinated by effects of light and colour.

Among other romantic painters of the turn of the century who developed often extravagant stylisations of form were Fuseli, Ward, Martin and Danby. The poet William Blake painted religious subjects in a personal, visionary style. Romantic portraiture, in which the sitter was dramatised more than in the Reynolds tradition, was represented in London by Sir Thomas Lawrence and in Edinburgh by Sir Henry Raeburn. In complete contrast were the colourful, descriptive or genre scenes of David Wilkie (1785–1841), which delighted George IV.

GOD JUDGING ADAM William Blake (1757–1827) was almost unknown to his contemporaries; his profundity was utterly opposed to the cold, Classical spirit of the age. This painting illustrates the visionary power that pervades all his work

DECORATIVE ARTS: GRANDEUR AND GRACE

Grandeur was the keynote to early Georgian style in the decorative arts. The furniture designed by William Kent for Holkham Hall and Houghton Hall, both in Norfolk, was ornate and richly gilded. Walls were covered with damasks and Genoese velvets. Mahogany was replacing oak; and grand, beautifully carved mahogany furniture, whose ornament derived from architectural features, was made by Vile and Cobb in the middle of the century. Silver and glass, though plain, were solid and well proportioned.

By 1740, French rococo, an exuberant, curvilinear style, was influencing all the decorative arts. Graceful, curling ornament and boldly asymmetrical shapes were characteristic of the silverware of Paul de Lamerie, and the gilded wall brackets and mirrors of Thomas Chippendale. French *bombé* (serpentine) shapes were used for commodes, and colourful twisted ornament decorated the stems of wine glasses. The figurines produced by the Chelsea and Bow porcelain factories marked the quintessence of this gay and often whimsical style.

TWO LOVERS WITH A BIRDCAGE, Bow porcelain, c. 1755. Idealised rustic lovers were a recurring theme in the pottery and painting of the Georgian era

The Gothic and Chinese designs popular in the 1750's were eagerly absorbed by craftsmen, and Chippendale's famous pattern book *The Gentleman and Cabinet-maker's Directory* (published 1754) included designs for chairs and tables in both tastes. Later in the century Classical shapes and patterns, reflecting the Classical revival, were used in glass and silver, most notably in Wedgwood's pottery.

In furniture, influenced by Adam's style of interior decoration, much of the Classical ornament was painted and gilded. Rosewood, satinwood and inlaid and cross-banded furniture became popular. The elegance and straight lines of Hepplewhite and Sheraton furniture matched the simple interiors of Henry Holland.

The Victorian Age

*Material expansion during the 19th
century was paralleled by artistic
upheavals, as 18th-century gaiety
gave way to pious high-mindedness*

The coronation of Queen Victoria in 1838 seemed to
represent the dawn of a new golden age. Her accession
coincided with the beginning of one of the most dramatic periods of national prosperity in the history of the
world. Success in the Napoleonic wars had won for
England a long period of peace, enabling her to concentrate her wealth and energy on promoting industry. The
spirit of the age had changed, too, from the gay exuberance of the 18th century, with its worship of Classical
art and culture, its cynicism and immorality, to a more
austere, high-minded and religious outlook.

Queen Victoria saw the passing of the Age of Elegance.
Her taste for the landscapes of Landseer and for tartan
wallpaper was that of her subjects. Oddly enough,
Prince Albert had an enthusiasm for early Italian paint-
ings, although his collection was surpassed by those of
William Roscoe (Walker Art Gallery, Liverpool) and
Thomas Gambier Parry (Courtauld Institute, London).
Paintings by the well established masters of the 16th and
17th centuries continued to be popular.

Palladian architecture, introduced from Italy by
Inigo Jones in the 17th century, was thought cold and
formal, and portraits by Reynolds and Gainsborough
changed hands in the sale-rooms for a few pounds. But a
more penetrating artistic judgment led to the growing
popularity of Botticelli and the 15th-century masters,
and also of William Blake (1757-1827).

Taste in the Victorian age was a matter of personal
preference and whim: there were no general rules. For
example, Pugin, noted as a church architect, built the
enormous Alton Towers, Staffordshire, in flamboyant
Gothic style, with a cathedral-type tower, in which Lord
Shrewsbury inhabited a single whitewashed cell. John
Bowes and Baron Rothschild both had elaborate
châteaux built (Bowes Museum, Barnard Castle,
Durham, and Waddesdon Manor, Buckinghamshire) to
house their enormous collections of art treasures.

ARCHITECTURE: CLASSICAL VERSUS GOTHIC

In previous centuries architecture had evolved gently
along traditional lines. The sudden and enormous
material expansion of the 19th century and the far-
reaching social effects resulting from the new discoveries
—steam, gas and electricity—broke up the traditional
pattern of life. In architecture, this break-up was symbolised by the so-called 'Battle of the Styles'. Architects
reverted to Classical or Gothic. Classical was a hang-over

THE HOUSES OF PARLIAMENT:
Sir Charles Barry's design, which
won against competition from 96
other architects. The style-setting
Gothic building was not finished
until after his death in 1860,
and his concept was never fully
completed. The giant archway
shown above, for instance, was
never built

CANNON STREET station, an
engraving of 1866. The railway
stations, practical and awe-
inspiring with their great soaring
arches, have been called 'the
cathedrals of the 19th century'

GOTHIC BEDSTEAD, the epitome of the vulgarity and extravagance so often assumed to be typically Victorian. Shown at the Great Exhibition of 1851. It was probably designed especially for the Exhibition and never actually used

HYLAS AND THE WATER NYMPHS, carved by John Gibson (1790-1866), a sculptor much admired by his contemporaries. He interpreted Classical Greek and Roman themes—rather superficially—and revived the Greek practice of colour tinting sculpture

from the 18th century; Gothic was influenced by the current feeling for medievalism, particularly in literature.

The Classical style continued to be used for public buildings during the first half of the 19th century. Robert Smirke's British Museum (1823), H. L. Elmes's St George's Hall, Liverpool (1839), and Joseph Hansom's Town Hall, Birmingham (1846) were all based on Greek or Roman originals. The battle between Classical and Gothic was particularly heated over public commissions. Sir Gilbert Scott was forced to change from a Gothic to a Classical plan for the Foreign Office in the 1860's and sold the discarded Gothic plan to be used for St Pancras Station; but the designs of Barry and Pugin for the new Houses of Parliament (1836) had been a decisive victory for the Gothic Revivalists.

The Gothic Revival coincided with a revival of religious fervour. Augustus Welby Pugin, a passionate Christian, sought to build in the true spirit of the past. His churches, such as the Roman Catholic Cathedral (St Chad's), Birmingham, show his complete understanding of Gothic architecture. He also built country houses like Alton Towers, Staffordshire, and Scarisbrick, Lancashire, for the older Catholic gentry. The succeeding generation of neo-Gothic architects attempted to use Gothic in an original way. William Butterfield's All Saints, Margaret Street, London (1849 onwards), with its use of multi-coloured bricks, is a good example.

The dominant Victorian style was neo-Gothic, but this did not prevent architects from turning to other styles when it suited them. Barry built the Reform Club, Pall Mall (1837) in an Italianate Renaissance style, while Anthony Salvin's Harlaxton Manor, Lincolnshire (1837 onwards) is modelled on the Elizabethan Hatfield House. In contrast, the factories and warehouses, the great railway stations, or the iron and steel Crystal Palace, built for the Great Exhibition of 1851, express the practical side of Victorian architecture.

Norman Shaw developed a functional and distinctly modern type of domestic architecture, often based on Dutch and Queen Anne styles. The Bedford Park estate at Turnham Green, London, built in the early 1880's, is a good example of this.

Shaw's successors, Charles Voysey, W. R. Lethaby and the early Edwin Lutyens, worked with simpler outlines and made use of projecting wings. The end of the Victorian era was marked by the abrupt buildings of Charles Rennie Mackintosh, whose masterpiece is the School of Arts and Crafts in Glasgow (1896 onwards).

SCULPTURE: CHASTITY AND PRETTINESS

Victorian sculpture was generally uninventive. Figure compositions were usually reworkings of outworn Classical themes, suitably draped and chaste to conform with Victorian scruples.

John Gibson, who lived in Rome for most of his life, was perhaps the most dedicated and successful of the classicising sculptors (*The Tinted Venus* and *The Wounded Warrior*, Royal Academy). There were others who followed his example: E. H. Baily, with *Eve at the*

Fountain (Bristol Art Gallery) and Richard Wyatt with his *Glycera* (Royal Collection, Buckingham Palace).

Victorian high-mindedness, coupled with a depressing lack of originality, more often led to works of conventional prettiness. An exception is *Paolo and Francesca* (Birmingham Art Gallery), by Alexander Munro, which was influenced by the Pre-Raphaelites. Alfred Stevens produced a few highly inventive works. His most ambitious sculpture was the unfinished Wellington Monument in St Paul's. The only other sculptor of originality in the second half of the 19th century was Alfred Gilbert (the Queen Alexandra Monument, outside St James's Palace), who successfully employed sinuous art nouveau patterns and contrasting materials.

THE LAST OF ENGLAND, painted in 1855 by Ford Madox Brown. Although not a member of the Pre-Raphaelite Brotherhood, he was clearly under their spell. This painting was inspired by the departure of the sculptor Thomas Woolner for Australia, and Brown used himself, his wife and child as models

PAINTING: CONFUSION OF STYLES

The first years of Victoria's reign saw no definite line of painting. It was hoped that the grandiose frescoes, begun in 1845, which decorate the Houses of Parliament would foster a native school of history painting. But Daniel Maclise's *Death of Nelson* and the *Meeting of Wellington and Blücher* are the only frescoes with any power and originality.

The most characteristic Victorian school was that of the genre painting—homely renderings of everyday subjects, an expression of an essentially narrative approach to art. Following the success of Wilkie's (1785–1841) early paintings, like *Blindman's Bluff* (Royal Collection), the genre school reached its zenith in William Frith's great scenes of contemporary life: *Derby Day* (1856–8, Tate Gallery), *Ramsgate Sands* (1851, Royal Collection) and *The Railway Station* (1862, Royal Holloway College).

The Victorian era produced no landscape artist of the stature of Constable or Turner. But most early Victorian landscapes have some narrative interest, like Edwin Landseer's *The Monarch of the Glen* (Royal Collection), or William Collins's *The Reluctant Departure* (Birmingham City Art Gallery), and the Pre-Raphaelites fostered a minutely realistic school of landscape painting. Their influence remained strong until the end of the century. Pure landscape painting was largely confined to watercolour such as the Welsh mountainscapes of David Cox or the East Anglian meadows of Peter de Wint.

The Pre-Raphaelite Brotherhood, founded in 1848 as a protest against current academic painting, made the most original contribution to English art. The member painters' meticulous and jewelled canvases have an intense realism that gives a hallucinatory quality to their romantic subjects. D. G. Rossetti's *Girlhood of St Mary Virgin* (Tate Gallery), Holman Hunt's *Awakening Conscience* (collection of Sir Colin Anderson), and J. E. Millais's *Lorenzo and Isabella* (Walker Art Gallery, Liverpool) are works of real power and imagination. The other-worldly pictures of Burne-Jones, based on medieval and Classical legends, owe much to their example, and there were many other followers.

Not all Victorian painters fell under the Pre-Raphaelite spell. G. F. Watts (1817–1904) painted epic allegorical subjects in the manner of the old masters, like *Hope* (Tate

THE DAY DREAM, by Dante Gabriel Rossetti (1828–82), founder of the Pre-Raphaelite Brotherhood. The precision of detail builds up a romantic, dream-like world

Gallery) and *The Horsemen of the Apocalypse* (Walker Art Gallery, Liverpool); while running through the second half of the 19th century is a belated Classical revival led by Frederic, Lord Leighton (*Daedalus and Icarus*, Buscot Park, Oxfordshire), Edward Poynter (*Faithful unto Death*, Walker Art Gallery, Liverpool) and Alma-Tadema (*The Parthenon Frieze*, Birmingham City Art Gallery). Their work was superseded in the 1860's to 1880's by the new ideas from France. James McNeill Whistler (examples in Glasgow Art Gallery and Tate Gallery), an American, was the first artist to bring an Impressionist technique to England. He concentrated on tone, colour and atmosphere to the exclusion of narrative.

As a challenge to the conventionalism of the Royal Academy and the literary approach of the Pre-Raphaelites, the New English Art Club was founded in 1886. Outstanding among the original members were Wilson Steer (1860–1942) and Walter Sickert (1860–1942).

'IMITATION' ANTIQUE VASES, on show at the Great Exhibition of 1851, and imitating the fine-textured white marble obtained from Paros since the 6th century BC. They are made from a mass-produced biscuit porcelain, and illustrate the Victorian taste for anything that appeared 'antique'

DECORATIVE ARTS: ALL FOR COMFORT

The Great Exhibition of 1851 has fostered the misconception that Victorian decoration was over-elaborate and grotesque. In fact, most of the pieces exhibited there, like J. W. Willcox's massive carved sideboard, which is now at Charlecote Park, Warwickshire, were specially designed for the occasion, and do not represent current styles. Early Victorian furniture was relatively simple: it was only towards the middle of the century that the plush, the curves and the twiddles began to come in. Architects often designed the most elaborate pieces, such as the great cupboards of Norman Shaw, William Burges and J. P. Seddon (Victoria and Albert Museum).

Firms like Garrard's and Elkington's continued the tradition of the great Regency silversmith's; but they produced few exciting or new designs. Pugin's church plate, executed by Hardman's of Birmingham, was of much greater quality and originality than most comparable domestic wares. Pottery and glass both followed traditional patterns. Fabrics became increasingly heavy.

William Morris founded his famous firm, Morris & Co., in 1862, as a protest against ugliness and confusion of style. His own designs for wallpapers, chintzes and tapestries, often based on naturalistic flower or bird motifs, are superbly decorative. To everything he produced, whether fabrics, furniture or stained glass, he brought clarity and simplicity. He had a thorough understanding of the materials he used, and a coherent and articulate decorative sense.

WILLIAM MORRIS wallpaper design. Morris (1834–96) founded a firm of artists producing wallpaper, tapestries, furniture and stained glass. He believed that a work of art could not be beautiful unless the artist had enjoyed making it

The Arts and Crafts movement, headed by Voysey and Gimson, carried Morris's ideas a stage further. It discarded medieval overtones, and produced designs for objects of all kinds that were austerely linear, using simple contrasting materials. William Godwin's geometric and delicate furniture, Whistler's plain, wash-coloured walls, William de Morgan's simple pottery shapes, decorated with designs and colours from the East—all represent a decisive move towards the 20th century. The art nouveau movement of the 1890's, with its swirling and sensuous shapes, marked the final end of Victorian attitudes.

The Twentieth Century

Like their fellows on the Continent, British architects and artists have struggled to keep up with the constant changes of the last half century

In the 20th century the private patron has given way to patronage by museums and the state—for example, the growing collection of modern art at the Tate Gallery, and the travelling exhibitions organised by the Arts Council. The Tate Gallery especially has played a key part in the appreciation of modern art, both British and foreign. The Tate was founded in 1897 as the national collection of British painting, and in 1915 its scope was widened by Sir Hugh Lane's bequest of foreign paintings. In 1946 the gallery received its first Government grant for buying pictures, and the total annual grant now comes to more than £1,800,000. The Tate is to modern art what the National Gallery is to the art of past centuries.

Dramatic new concepts in science and engineering have been echoed in all the arts to the point where the word 'functional', invented by the architects, can almost be applied to modern art. This continuing contact between art and day-to-day life has led to a reciprocal attitude on the part of industry, which is finding increasing employment for artists. It has also achieved the breaking-down or blurring of the traditional divisions between architecture, painting and sculpture, inasmuch as painting frequently becomes three-dimensional, and sculpture tends to make use of architectural and even mechanical structures. The successful sales of abstract art in the auction-rooms have demonstrated its final acceptance on a wide scale.

LEICESTER UNIVERSITY The Engineering Building by architects Stirling and Gowan (1959–63). The wall in the foreground supports the roof trusses over the laboratory. The ends of the trusses have been developed in a sculptural manner to provide top-lighting over the benches

ARCHITECTURE: FUNCTIONAL STEEL AND CONCRETE

It was almost 30 years before the new image of 20th-century architecture was accepted in Britain. On the Continent and in America, concrete and steel structures were challenging the skies long before they were accepted here. The Victorians had discovered the advantages of prefabrication and the use of glass as a structural element as early as 1851, in Paxton's Crystal Palace; and slowly steel and concrete began to replace bricks and iron for public buildings. But in spite of this, most architects still looked on Georgian housing as ideal.

The one architect from the turn of the century to stand out from his fellows was Charles Rennie Mackintosh, who designed the Glasgow School of Art, begun in 1897; this rock-like building is remarkable for its bold handling of mass.

In the early years the garden city movement developed in London. It originated in Bedford Park, Chiswick, designed by Norman Shaw in the 1880's, and was emu-

UNIVERSITY OF WARWICK The Benefactors' Building by architects Yorke, Rosenburg and Mardall. A characteristic example of modern design where ornament has been sacrificed in favour of elegant proportions, precise detailing and simplicity of form

KING AND QUEEN (1952-3) by
Henry Moore. Probably the
greatest living British sculptor,
Moore simplifies the human
form in order to emphasise
ideas. *King and Queen* illustrates
their dignity and repose, yet
preserves an anonymity that
suggests the present-day decline
of monarchy

STANLEY SPENCER (1891-1959)
A mystic who spent most of
his life in the Berkshire village
of Cookham, the setting for
many of his paintings. *Swan
Upping* was started in 1914 and
finished four years later after
his return from the war

lated less successfully in Welwyn Garden City (Louis de
Soissons and Arthur W. Kenyon, 1918-20), and in
Hampstead Garden Suburb (Lutyens, 1908).

The exciting experiments in functional architecture
taking place in Berlin and Vienna were looked on with
distrust in Britain. The work of Edwin Lutyens, with its
return to a simplified Georgian Classicism, in both public
and domestic building, typifies the conservatism of the
period (Viceroy's House, Delhi, 1920-31; Deanery
Gardens, Sonning, Berkshire).

In the 1930's the influx of architects from Nazi
Germany left an indelible impression on the British
architectural scene. Walter Gropius designed the Village
College at Impington, Cambridgeshire; Erich Mendelsohn, in partnership with Serge Chermayeff, designed
the De la Warr Pavilion at Bexhill-on-Sea, E. Sussex;
and Marcel Breuer planned a garden city (never built)
with F. R. S. Yorke. The new functionalism infiltrated
British design, and Maxwell Fry's Frognal House, built
in 1936, was a perfect example.

The immediate post-war years showed a widening
gulf between the new and old generations of architects.
The young men were committed to the idea of the
Welfare State, put forward by the 1945 Labour Government, and to the revolutionary theories of Le Corbusier
in France, and Mies van der Rohe and Frank Lloyd
Wright in America, the use of reinforced concrete and
fitness for purpose being the key factors. The older
generation looked back to indigenous English themes.

The major projects of the post-war Government were
the new schools and the new towns. Only 50 out of
1000 London schools survived the war; and the low-cost
single-unit housing of new town projects created not just
dormitory suburbs on the old garden suburb plan, but
completely new and distinct townships. Stevenage,
Harlow, Crawley and Basildon are examples.

The 20th century has seen four major cathedrals built
in Britain. Liverpool Cathedral, the earliest, designed by
Sir Giles Gilbert Scott, was begun in 1904 and is still not
completed. Guildford Cathedral (begun 1936, consecrated
1961) was designed by Sir Edward Maufe; and after the
war Sir Basil Spence designed Coventry Cathedral
(consecrated 1962). Most recent is Frederick Gibberd's
Roman Catholic Cathedral at Liverpool, built in record
time and completed in 1967.

New universities, and new colleges at Oxford and
Cambridge, gave great scope to architects: St Catherine's,
Oxford, by Arne Jacobsen; Leicester University Engineering Building, by Stirling and Gowan; Sussex University,
by Sir Basil Spence; and the Sainsbury Centre, East Anglia,
by Norman Foster.

SCULPTURE: LEADERS FROM BRITAIN

This century is the first to see a really significant body of
sculpture in Britain. The work of Sir Jacob Epstein
(1880-1959; Tate Gallery, London; also Birmingham,
Manchester, Hull) was never accepted by the public
during his lifetime. Before moving to massive, often
religious, figure subjects in a rough-hewn expressionist

mould, and a prolific series of portraits, Epstein produced one really remarkable piece of sculpture, *The Rock Drill* (1913–14, Tate Gallery).

Sculpture after the Second World War revolved around one major figure, Henry Moore (*b.* 1898; Tate Gallery), who dominated British sculpture until the late 1950's, by which time he had won an outstanding international reputation. Reclining figures and mother and child groups interested him from the start and have continued to do so both in figurative and non-figurative styles (*Recumbent Figure*, 1938; *Project for Madonna and Child*, 1943; both at the Tate Gallery). Moore's feeling for space is echoed by the work of Barbara Hepworth (*Corinthos*, 1954, Tate Gallery).

Among other sculptors who first began to exhibit in the late 1940's is Reg Butler. He was the prime exponent of the 'rod and wire' school, a linear style which moves away from the masses so skilfully deployed by Henry Moore. His work can best be seen in the *Monument to the Unknown Political Prisoner* (Tate Gallery). Of the later sculptors Anthony Caro and Eduardo Paolozzi stand out (Tate Gallery). Caro's painted metal sculpture and Paolozzi's robot-like, menacing images have a real feeling for the mechanics of the machine age. Contemporary eclecticism is represented by Carl André's brick composition *Equivalent VIII* (Tate Gallery).

LA MITRAILLEUSE (The Machine-gun) by C. R. W. Nevinson (1889–1946). An official war artist during the First World War, his soldiers were depicted as dehumanised components of their fighting machines, expressing 'a life of steel, fever, pride and headlong speed'

PAINTING: FROM ABSTRACT TO POP ART

In the years before the First World War British painting was still trying to free itself from the dominance of the Royal Academy and its offshoot, the New English Art Club, of which two outstanding members were Wilson Steer (1860–1942) and Walter Sickert (1860–1942). The New English had been formed in 1886 as a protest against academic conventions, but was now losing its impetus as an element of protest.

Meanwhile from the Slade School, a part of the University of London under the direction of Henry Tonks, came a tradition of fine draughtsmanship. From it emerged two remarkable individualists—Augustus John (1878–1961; Tate Gallery), a master of figure drawing; and Stanley Spencer (1891–1959; Tate Gallery), a religious mystic. His painting *The Resurrection*, done in the churchyard of his native village of Cookham, Berkshire, is remarkable both in idea and execution.

In 1911 the Camden Town Group was formed at the inspiration of Walter Sickert, and largely echoed his own delight in the London street scene. At the same time a highly vocal body, stimulated by the painter-critic Roger Fry, formed an aggressive splinter group led by the painter and writer D. B. Wyndham Lewis, with his Vorticist movement and his magazine *Blast*.

The First World War gave English artists first-hand experience of the realities of battle. C. R. W. Nevinson (1889–1946; *La Mitrailleuse*, Tate Gallery) saw war in the field with the Red Cross, and much of his work achieved a semi-abstract quality, as did that of Paul Nash (1889–1946; *Totes Meer,* Tate Gallery), who was commissioned as a war artist. Their stark lunar landscapes of the Flanders

POSTER ART E. McKnight Kauffer was an American who settled in Britain shortly after the First World War. A successful practitioner of 'persuasive art', he became famous for his London Underground posters. The use of symbols is typified by his 1924 advertisement for Eno's Fruit Salts

BARBARA HEPWORTH *Madonna and Child*. Much of Barbara Hepworth's sculpture is purely abstract; this *Madonna and Child*, carved in 1954, shows the effects of the abstract discipline—the simplified figures creating a basically oval shape without losing their naturalness. The quality of the stone is preserved as if a pebble or a boulder has been animated by the sculptor's art

ASHBEE PEACOCK PENDANT A piece of art nouveau jewellery in gold, turquoise and enamel, now in the Victoria and Albert Museum. The peacock was a favourite of the art nouveau school and appeared in paintings, fabrics and book decorations

battlefields provided a sympathetic climate for the early stirrings of abstractionism in post-war England.

By the early 1930's a handful of major talents had established themselves—Henry Moore, Barbara Hepworth, Ben Nicholson. Nicholson, son of artist Sir William Nicholson, was the outstanding painter of the group. With his balanced geometrical shapes, sensitive line and harmonious combinations of colour, he had dedicated himself to abstractionism since the 1920's.

In 1936 the Surrealist Exhibition demonstrated the freeing of the artist from all the traditional concepts of art. Deeply influenced by this movement was Graham Sutherland (Tate Gallery), hitherto an etcher, engraver and landscape painter. A former pupil of Sutherland, Francis Bacon (Tate Gallery), developed an intuitive style of painting in the 1940's. His distorted images are often taken, like Picasso's, from familiar masterpieces and photographs. Contemporary with Bacon, but quite opposed in style and concept, John Piper (Tate Gallery) also came to the fore, renouncing abstractionism and reverting to romantic architectural subjects.

The 1950's saw L. S. Lowry (Leicester Art Gallery), pursuing a solitary path in his creation of a personal landscape of the industrial north. A new realistic school was recognised in this period, labelled 'the kitchen sink school'. Led by John Bratby, they were concerned with the humdrum things of everyday life. Figurative art returned in the shape of 'pop art', which sought to reflect the images of popular life. Peter Blake, R. B. Kitaj and David Hockney established themselves as leaders of the English movement, and remained in the forefront in the mid-1980's.

THE DECORATIVE ARTS

The influence of William Morris, who revived the idea of the artist-craftsman, lingered on in the firm of Morris & Co. well into the 20th century and did much to raise the level of design. Craft Guilds (co-operatives of artist-craftsmen), founded by A. H. Mackmurdo and C. R. Ashbee towards the end of the 19th century, continued the unification of the arts of design and paved the way for the reception of art nouveau, a style characterised by a sinuous, whiplash line and stylised floral ornament.

The first new movement embracing the decorative arts was Roger Fry's Omega Workshop of 1913—a return to the idea of painted furniture briefly advocated by the Pre-Raphaelites. But it was a painter's movement, and failed because it was essentially decorative and had little grasp of functional design. Its major benefit was to introduce light colours into the home.

The decorative arts lagged behind the Continent after the First World War, although Sir Ambrose Heal produced well-made English versions of the German Bauhaus furniture designs. After 1933, with the closure of Bauhaus schools, a number of refugee teachers and students gave a new impetus to design. New materials—chrome and glass—began to appear in decoration, as in architecture, and motifs taken from abstract painting made their appearance.

THE TREASURES
OF BRITAIN

A guide to the public and private possessions

which make up the national heritage of

England, Scotland and Wales

In towns, villages and hamlets, and sometimes in the loneliest corners of the countryside, heirlooms from the pageant of Britain's past are liberally scattered. They range from cathedrals and grand houses to works in museum showcases.

In the following gazetteer pages the most notable of them are described. The selection has been based on experts' judgment of their significance, beauty and value. To avoid disappointment visitors are advised to check beforehand that treasures can be seen when they wish. Some property owners and curators require notice of a visit. Many churches are kept locked; often the key is obtainable from somebody near by, but some churches may be viewed by appointment only. Some ruins, though accessible, may be neglected and should be approached with care.

All these gazetteer entries are linked to the maps (pages 537-76) by a simple reference code, and are pinpointed on the map by symbols.

The gazetteer includes picture features on notable people associated with particular places. Where towns and buildings are rich in treasures several pages are devoted to illustrating them.

Abbey Dore *Heref. & Worcs.* 546Ad
The monastery was founded in 1147, and the surviving church belongs mainly to the end of the 12th century. The eastern end was added a little later, *c.* 1200, and this part of the building, with its moulded arches and long lancet windows, is particularly striking. A few fragments remain of the nave. The site of the monastic buildings, which lay to the north of the church, has been excavated, and virtually nothing of these buildings can be seen. Work was still continuing on the church in 1260, and it was consecrated *c.* 1275; it eventually became derelict. In 1634 Viscount Scudamore restored what was left, and added the great oak screen. The nave had gone; what remain now are the transepts, crossing and chancel, and the 17th-century tower added on the south side. There are many fragments of sculpture from the ancient church and the monuments include two cross-legged knights of the 13th century.

Abbotsbury *Dorset* 540Cc
A village of stone and thatch houses at the foot of the Downs near the Fleet—the lagoon between Chesil Bank and the mainland. In the village are ruins of the 12th-century Benedictine Abbey of St Peter; the Church of St Nicholas was once part of the abbey and so was the great 15th-century tithe barn, 276 ft long. The swannery created by the monks continues today and, like the sub-tropical gardens near by, is open to the public.
CHURCH OF ST NICHOLAS There was once a Benedictine abbey here; ruins of some of its buildings are to be seen, and the great tithe barn, *c.* 1400, is of much interest. The church has a west tower and is to the north of the abbey; it was built mainly in the 14th and 15th centuries. The chancel has a plaster ceiling of 1638, and a large reredos of 1751 completely fills the east wall. There are various monuments including an effigy of an abbot of *c.* 1200 and a fine early 17th-century canopied pulpit.
ST CATHERINE'S CHAPEL This 15th-century chapel (key available at No. 1, Back Street) was built on a hilltop, perhaps as a beacon for sailors. The hill is terraced with Bronze Age lynchets (small fields).

Abbotsford House *Borders* 562Dd
Sir Walter Scott bought the original house in 1811 and lived at Abbotsford until his death in 1832. He rebuilt the house and planted most of the trees in the grounds. The house contains Scott's relics and a collection of weapons.

Abbots Langley *Herts.* 547Hc
CHURCH OF ST LAWRENCE The church has 12th-century arcades to the nave, and a 14th-century south chapel, a west tower, an octagonal Perpendicular font and 14th-century wall-painting of SS Thomas of Canterbury and Lawrence. Among the monuments is one to Lord Raymond (*d.* 1732) by Sir Henry Cheere, and seated beside him an allegorical figure holding a portrait medallion. A later monument to the 2nd Lord Raymond (*d.* 1756) is by Peter Scheemakers. The church was damaged by fire in 1969 and has since been restored.

Aberaeron *Dyfed* 544Ff
This attractive Georgian port grew until the 1880's, when the coming of the railway ruined coastal shipping. It has survived almost intact to the present day. There is a harbour and a large square. The houses have good fan-lights and are finished with coloured stucco. Its pleasant style has influenced a number of neighbouring villages.

Aberdeen *Grampian* 567Ge
ART GALLERY Housed in a modern building with an unusual arcade of polished granite pillars and a fountain group in the entrance court, the gallery has an important collection of paintings including Monet's *La Falaise à Fécamp* and Renoir's *La Roche Guyon*. Other works by Boudin, Maris, Forain, Vlaminck, Bonnard and Vuillard can also be seen, along with water-colours by de Segonzac, Kokoschka and others. Scottish painting and sculpture are represented by Ramsay, Nasmyth, Wilkie and Raeburn, and a collection of early English water-colours includes works by Turner and Cozens. Bronzes by Rodin can be seen in the sculpture section with works by Degas, Bourdelle, Henry Moore, Barbara Hepworth, Zadkine and Epstein. There are also contemporary sculptures by Reg. Butler and Eduardo Paolozzi. The James McBey Print Room has a collection of McBey's etchings, drawings and water-colours. The gallery has a large collection of modern prints.
CATHEDRAL OF ST MACHAR A mainly 15th-century granite nave with an impressive west front. The transepts are ruined. The heraldic ceiling of 1520, depicting the unity of Scotland, Europe and Holy Church, is a unique and eloquent treatment of a great medieval theme.
KING'S COLLEGE This group of buildings in the High Street, Old Aberdeen, was built *c.* 1500. The chapel has a fine lantern tower in the form of a crown. The oak rood screen, stairs and choir stalls, some with misericords, are covered with elaborate and delicate carving.
MARISCHAL COLLEGE The present college was started in 1844 when the eastern range of buildings was built to plans by Archibald Simpson. The Perpendicular Gothic façade to Broad Street, built in Kemnay granite to the designs of A. Marshall MacKenzie, was finished in 1906. Together with the Mitchell Tower and the adjoining Greyfriars Church the college forms one of the finest complexes of granite buildings in the country.
MERCAT CROSS This unique cross, designed by John Montgomery of Old Rayne in 1686, was rebuilt in 1821 and moved to its present site in 1841–2. Its central shaft is surmounted by a marble unicorn rising from a hexagonal platform on a circular, arcaded base. The balustrade has a series of portraits of Scottish sovereigns from James I to James VII and the royal and burgh Arms.
MUSIC HALL One of the finest buildings in Union Street, the construction of which led to the development of the 'Granite City' in the 19th century. Designed with a six-columned portico by Archibald Simpson in 1820 as the assembly rooms, the superb neo-Greek card and supper rooms are noteworthy. The Music Hall was added in 1858–9 by James Matthews.
OLD ABERDEEN Episcopal burgh associated with St Machar's Cathedral, incorporated in 1891 to form the present City of Aberdeen. The medieval street lay-out is still visible. High Street, with the town house of 1787 at the head, still retains some 18th-century houses with their gables facing the street. The Chanonry and Don Street, originally containing the manses of the cathedral clergy, now contain simple granite houses, mostly of the 18th and 19th centuries.
PROVOST SKENE'S HOUSE Built *c.* 1545, this striking town house was greatly extended *c.* 1670 after George Skene, merchant and Provost of Aberdeen, purchased the property. The building was remodelled, becoming a four-storey rubble block with flat roof. Some interior work survives from all periods, notably a coved ceiling of 1626 painted in tempera representing religious subjects. It is now a museum, containing relics of local history and local social and domestic life.
ROBERT GORDON'S COLLEGE Founded in 1729 by Robert Gordon, an Aberdeen merchant, as a

GENERAL WADE'S BRIDGE, ABERFELDY

General Wade (1673–1748) and his troops, in their campaign to overcome the rebellious Scottish clans and maintain peace for George I, made some 250 miles of roads and bridges, and these are still the main lines of communication in Scotland. Many of the bridges cost *only £40 to construct, but this one was designed by William Adam and built in 1733 at a cost of £4000. Of the five stone arches, the central one has a span of 60 ft, and the four obelisks crowning the parapets make an unusual feature.*

hospital for the education of destitute boys. The central block of three storeys, attic, cupola and spire was designed by William Adam and finished in 1746; the advanced wings and colonnade by John Smith of Aberdeen were added 1830–3. The statue of the founder by John Cheere was placed in the niche over the main entrance in 1753. The planning of the early building still survives, with an interesting scale-and-platt stair.

UNIVERSITY ANTHROPOLOGICAL MUSEUM The museum has items of archaeological interest from all parts of the world: the Henderson Collection of classical vases; the Grant-Bey Egyptian Collection including scarabs and mummies; Chinese bronzes of the Shang Yin period, Tang Dynasty horses and carved jade of the Ming Dynasty. The museum also houses the Sir William MacGregor general ethnographic exhibit. Local antiquities in the collection include skeletal remains and urns of the Beaker People, who came to Britain from Europe c. 1800 BC.

Aberdour Castle *Fife*   *562Bf*
The castle's oldest part is the 14th-century tower which is rhomboidal in plan. Other parts were added in the 16th and 17th centuries. A fine circular dove-cote is well preserved.

Aberfeldy *Tayside*   *566Bb*
GENERAL WADE'S BRIDGE This picturesque five-arched bridge, designed by William Adam in 1733, carries Wade's military road to the central Highlands. Raised quoins and voussoirs add architectural finesse to arches and buttresses while tall obelisks dominate the central span.

Abergavenny *Gwent*   *545Jd*
ABERGAVENNY AND DISTRICT MUSEUM The museum is accommodated in a 19th-century stone hunting lodge, built in the grounds of a ruined medieval castle. The exhibits are mainly items made or used locally, including harness and saddlery, farm tools and domestic equipment, firearms, dolls, costumes, Welsh harps and local archaeological finds. One room is a replica of a Welsh Border farmhouse kitchen as it might have appeared in 1870.

PRIORY CHURCH The church of the Benedictine priory founded in the 12th century, cruciform and with a central tower. Not much Norman work remains, and the building is mainly 14th century. There are canopied choir stalls, a number of monuments, the earliest of which is a lady of c. 1270, and a large wooden figure of Jesse.

Abernethy *Tayside*   *562Bg*
The capital of the Picts, an early Scottish people who were united with the Scottish Celts under King Kenneth MacAlpin in 843.

CASTLE LAW One of a series of forts usually associated with Picts or an Iron Age people at the beginning of the Roman occupation. The fort was vitrified when its construction of timber and rocks was partially destroyed by fire about AD 100.

ROUND TOWER This 'Irish' round tower is one of only two such structures on the Scottish mainland (the other is at Brechin, Angus); it is 74 ft high and dates from the 12th century.

Aberystwyth *Dyfed*   *544Fg*
ABERYSTWYTH ARTS CENTRE Housed in the Great Hall Gallery, University College of Wales. Permanent collection of ceramics, prints and drawings. Exhibitions during term times include work by contemporary artists and Welsh Arts Council travelling exhibitions.

NATIONAL LIBRARY OF WALES The library houses a large collection of books, manuscripts, documents, pictures and maps, mostly relating to Wales and other countries of Celtic origin. Many of the books and maps were acquired under the Copyright Act. Temporary exhibitions of portraits, landscapes, paintings and photographs from the library's own collections or elsewhere are shown every month.

Abingdon *Oxon.*   *546Fc*
An ancient wool and agricultural town, the county town of Berkshire until 1888, when it ceded that distinction to Reading. Abingdon has some famous almshouses, in Long Alley (built 1446), in Brick Alley (1718) and Twitty's Almshouses (1707).

ABBEY Founded in 675, Abingdon Abbey was once rich and powerful, but most of its ecclesiastical buildings were demolished during the Dissolution in 1538 and there are now few visible remains. These include the main abbey gateway, adjoining the medieval parish church of St Nicholas, and three buildings by the millstream. The oldest of these is the 13th-century Checker (perhaps originally the Exchequer), a square stone building with an unusual and interesting chimney —the gabled roof of the chimney has triple lancets for the smoke to escape. There is also a 15th-century guesthouse, the Long Gallery; and built into the abbey granary is the Unicorn, a theatre constructed in 1953 in the Elizabethan style. In the abbey grounds there are some artificial ruins built in the 19th century.

ABINGDON BRIDGE Over 150 yds long, it is really three bridges: Abingdon Bridge proper, over a backwater of the R. Thames and Burford Bridge, over the mainstream to the south (both built in 1416 by the town's Guild of the Holy Cross). The third bridge, three stone arches known as Hales Bridge, was built in 1458 by William Hales, a London mercer, across the marshy area at the approach to Burford Bridge. The whole bridge was widened in the 19th century and in 1927 much of its fabric was replaced.

BOROUGH MUSEUM (COUNTY HALL) The borough museum and county archives, including ten borough charters, the earliest of which is dated 1556, are housed in the County Hall. There are relics from medieval Abingdon Abbey; pewter plate; costumes, uniforms and arms from the 16th–19th centuries; children's toys and books; coins; pottery, implements and ornaments from local Saxon graves; a collection of fossils and items from past and present local industries.

The museum also has exhibits relating to the local jail and police force, including lanterns, whistles, and uniform buttons.

CHURCH OF ST HELEN The splendid 13th-century steeple rises high above this riverside church that is wider than it is long: there are five aisles inside, dating from rebuilding in the 15th and 16th centuries. The ceiling of the Lady Chapel is panelled and was painted c. 1390 to show the Tree of Jesse. There is interesting woodwork: the pulpit of 1636, the mayor's seat of 1706, and the organ case of 1725. There are monuments from the 15th century onwards; two of the late 18th century are John Hickey's for Elizabeth Hawkins and one by J. Nollekens for Dr John Crossley. The 19th-century stained glass includes some by C. E. Kempe, and the marble font was shown in the Great Exhibition of 1851.

COUNTY HALL The County Hall at Abingdon was built under the supervision of Christopher Kempster, 1678–82. Kempster was one of Sir Christopher Wren's masons at St Paul's Cathedral in London. The two-storied building has cellars and an attic; the main façade is to the market-place. Giant pilasters of the Composite order extend the height of the two main storeys, flanking the windows on the first floor and the arcade openings on the ground floor. The sloping roof is decorated with a deep cornice and balustraded, with a cupola. At the back a square tower contains the staircase. The market hall occupies the ground floor within the open arcade, and the large courtroom is on the floor above.

GUILDHALL Originally outbuildings of Abingdon Abbey, the Hospital and Chapel of St John the Baptist were sold to the Corporation in 1561. The chapel became the courtroom (which now houses two magistrates' benches) and the Hall was adapted to accommodate Abingdon School, re-founded on his 63rd birthday by John Roysse, who required the room to be 63 ft long to accommodate 63 boys. When the school was moved in the 19th century, the Roysse Room was linked to the 18th-century council chambers.

Abington *Northants.*   547Gf
CHURCH OF SS PETER AND PAUL A small church on the outskirts of Northampton, with remains of work dating from c. 1200. There is a wide nave, a 15th-century font with cover, and a good late 17th-century pulpit, richly carved. Many memorial tablets by the local family of Cox, and a monument with a robed, standing man by Samuel Cox, c. 1730.

Accrington *Lancs.*   552Bh
HAWORTH ART GALLERY This mock-Jacobean building, with fine plaster ceilings and wood-panelling, was constructed in 1909 for William Haworth, a cotton manufacturer, and given to the Corporation in 1921 to be used as an art gallery. It contains a collection of about 130 pieces of Tiffany glass, the invention of Louis Comfort Tiffany of New York (1848–1933).

Also on display are notable watercolour land-scapes and Victorian narrative paintings by Peter de Wint, Paul Sandby, David Cox, John Varley, Samuel Prout and others. The oils include work by Lord Leighton and Claude Vernet.

Achamore *Isle of Gigha, Strathclyde*   560Dd
Large gardens, with roses and flowering shrubs.

Ackworth School *W. Yorks.*   558Da
A Georgian building erected in 1750 as an appen-dage to the London Foundling Hospital; it is all

ABINGDON COUNTY HALL
In many towns the town hall served at least two purposes; the lower part was an open colonnade, used for market stalls, while the upper part served as court and assembly rooms.
Abingdon County Hall is one of the finest examples of the style. The designer is not known, though the in-fluence of Sir Christopher Wren is evident. Under the supervision of Christopher Kempster the hall was completed in 1682. The finely proportioned courtroom on the first floor is 57 ft long and 30 ft wide. The plaster ceiling is a modern restoration.

that survives of the hospital. Since 1779 it has been run by the Society of Friends (Quakers) as a boarding school. (By appointment.)

Acle *Norfolk*   554Eb
CHURCH OF ST EDMUND The church has an 11th-century round tower, but the octagonal upper stage and battlements are of a later date. Both north and south porches are two storeys high. The font dates from 1410, with carvings of lions, wild men, the Trinity, and emblems.

Acton *Cheshire*   552Ad
CHURCH OF ST MARY A large 13th- and 14th-century building, the west tower rebuilt after storm damage in 1757. The best of several monuments is a large and canopied knight's effigy,

c. 1400, and another, of *c.* 1660, has two good effigies. There is a Norman font, 17th-century screens and stalls, and a fine 18th-century brass chandelier. In the churchyard there is a 17th-century sun-dial.

Acton *Suffolk* 548Ce
CHURCH OF ALL SAINTS Originally built *c.* 1300, but the tower is early 20th century. There is a very good brass of Sir Robert de Bures, *c.* 1302, shown as a cross-legged knight wearing chain-mail and holding a shield; also a monument of *c.* 1722, which might be by Thomas Green of Camberwell, with a reclining man against an architectural background, with his wife sitting at his feet.

Acton Beauchamp *Heref. & Worcs.* 546Be
CHURCH OF ST GILES The nave and chancel were rebuilt *c.* 1816 in a Classical style; the west tower and the Norman south doorway remain from the original church. An Anglo-Saxon carving of the 9th century is used as a lintel to the tower doorway.

Acton Burnell *Shropshire* 552Ab
CHURCH OF ST MARY This 13th-century church lies close to Bishop Robert Burnell's castle, also 13th century. The north transept is paved with medieval tiles, and the font is contemporary with the church. The monuments include one of the finest military brasses in Salop—of Sir Nicholas Burnell (1382). Alabaster effigies to Sir Richard Lee (1591) and his son Sir Humphrey Lee (1632) have figures carved by Nicholas Stone.

Acton Round 546Bg
CHURCH Isolated and small, with a pretty, timbered south porch, and a door with 13th-century ironwork. Among the monuments is one of *c.* 1703 by William Stanton; another, of *c.* 1760, incorporates Gothic elements, and seems to owe something to Sir Henry Cheere.

Acton Round Hall *Shropshire* 546Bg
A Dower House built *c.* 1713 for Aldenham Park; it contains some period panelling.

Adderbury *Oxon.* 546Fe
CHURCH OF ST MARY THE VIRGIN A large cruciform church in the Decorated and Perpendicular styles, with a west tower and spire. Outside are many corbels and gargoyles. The chancel is spacious, and there are brasses, a rood screen, and some early woodwork.

Adderley 552Ad
CHURCH OF ST PETER A cruciform building of red sandstone, standing on the edge of parkland. It was built in the Gothic Revival style in 1801 (though the tower is older, 1712), and the window tracery is of cast iron, typical of the area at that date. The big carved font is Norman, but the north chapel is mid-17th century, and there is a brass to a 14th-century cleric.

Addinston and Longcroft *Borders* 562De
The Iron Age fort of Addinston crowns a hill close to the A68 road north of Lauder. There are two great ramparts, each with an external ditch, the outer having, in places, a counterscarp bank. The enclosed area measures some 280 ft by 160 ft, and the bases of several circular huts are still visible.

The Longcroft fort is less than a mile to the north-east of Addinston and has much more complex defences, which appear to represent more than one period of construction in the Iron Age. There are two outer ramparts with an intermediate ditch and, well within the enclosed area, two further concentric ramparts without ditches. The innermost enclosed area has many circular hut-bases and minor enclosures, and a rectangular foundation, probably of a much later date.

Addlethorpe *Lincs.* 554Ae
CHURCH OF ST NICHOLAS A 15th-century church which lost its chancel in 1706. Some of the medieval glass still remains, and much of the woodwork is original in the screens, pew ends, and angels in the roof. The church has been extensively restored.

Adisham *Kent* 542Ff
CHURCH OF THE HOLY INNOCENTS A cruciform church of Norman monastic origin, with a low central tower capped by a pyramidal roof. There are lancet windows, and a Norman font. The reredos in the south transept was originally in Canterbury Cathedral. (By appointment.)

Adlington Hall *Cheshire* 552Be
Country mansion of mixed architecture, begun in 1315. The great hall was built 1450–1505, and an Elizabethan black and white wing added in 1581. There is a Georgian south front and Palladian portico of 1757. The great hall, in which is installed a Bernard Smith organ, *c.* 1670, has a carved beamed ceiling and fine murals.

Affleck Castle *Tayside* 566Eb
A turreted keep is the main remnant of this 15th-century fortress of the Auchinlecks.

Affpuddle *Dorset* 540Dc
CHURCH OF ST LAURENCE Situated on the river bank of the Piddle Valley, this is a church of the 13th century, with aisle and tower of the 15th century. It contains some pleasant mid-16th-century wood benches and a pulpit of the same date; the font is Norman.

Alberbury *Shropshire* 551Jb
CHURCH OF ST MICHAEL Close to the castle, St Michael's has a massive tower of *c.* 1200 on the north side. The Loton Chapel was built in 1340. In 1972 it was divided from the nave by a glass screen and refurnished. The Lyster and Leighton monuments date from 1699. A three-pipe manual organ from Rowton Castle has been installed.

Albury Park *Surrey* 542Af
The mansion is entered in the Domesday Book. Rebuilt in 1847 by A. W. Pugin with interior alterations by Sir John Soane. It was converted in 1972 by the Country Houses Association into apartments for retired gentlefolk.

Henry Howard, grandson of the sixth Duke of Norfolk, improved the gardens in the 17th century with the advice of the diarist (and arboriculturalist) John Evelyn. When Henry Drummond acquired the estate in 1819 he added plane trees and tulip trees to oaks and chestnuts now up to 400 years old.

Alcester *Warks.* 546Df
A market town with medieval timber-framed buildings. The Old Malt House was built in 1500. There are several 17th-century buildings; the town hall dates from 1618.

Alconbury *Cambs.* 547Jf
CHURCH OF SS PETER AND PAUL The fine 13th-century chancel has three lancets at the east and arcading on the north and south walls. The west tower has a broach spire, and inside are fragments of medieval glass.

Aldborough *N. Yorks.* 558Dc
CHURCH OF ST ANDREW A long 14th-century church with low 15th-century tower. Inside, there is a brass of *c.* 1360 and fragments of stained glass from the same period. A Roman sculpture, with the figure of Mercury, is probably from the town of Isurium Brigantes that once stood here.

Robert Burns

ROBERT BURNS, THE PLOUGH-BOY POET

The Strathclyde countryside is rich in associations with the life of her most distinguished son, who wrote of himself 'I have not the most distant pretensions to being what the guardians of the escutchions call a Gentleman. I am simply Robert Burns at your service. I was born to the Plough.' At 14, Burns was already his father's chief labourer and, as the family moved from one unproductive farm to another, he found increasing solace in literature and lassies. His early love poems and country verses were published by William Creech in 1787, making him the toast of Edinburgh at 28. He died nine years later, and his last child was born as he was being buried.

BURNS COTTAGE *in Alloway, which the poet's father built with his own hands. In the 'butt' or kitchen, his eldest son was born on January 25, 1759, and here spent the first seven years of his life. It is preserved as a museum and contains many relics of the poet's life.*

PUNCH BOWL *of Inverary marble, with silver mounts, and engraved 'Come to my bowl, come to my arms, my friends, my brothers'; it is now in the British Museum, and a replica is at Burns Cottage. The bowl is said to have been presented as a wedding gift to the poet by his wife's father, James Armour. Burns celebrated his love for his wife, Jean, in a poem whose first verse runs:*

> O my Luve's like a red red rose
> That's newly sprung in June
> O my Luve's like the melodie
> That's sweetly play'd in tune.

POEM *engraved on a window-pane at the Globe Inn, Dumfries. These lines from 'Polly Stewart' were cut with a diamond by the poet.*

AULD LANG SYNE *manuscript which the Trustees of Burns Cottage bought in 1952 for £1500. Written by Burns to the music of an old Scottish air, it is one of the 350 Scots songs Burns either wrote or revived for inclusion in 'The Scots Musical Museum'. Four volumes of Burns's annotated version of this work remain at the cottage; the manuscript of the fifth volume, published after the poet's death, is in the British Museum. Burns travelled all over Scotland collecting song material for the 'Museum', but never sought payment for this great work.*

> We twa hae run about the braes,
> And pou't the gowans fine;
> But we've wander'd mony a weary fitt
> Sin auld lang syne.
> We twa hae paidl't in the burn
> Frae morning sun till dine;
> But seas between us braid hae roar'd
> Sin auld lang syne

At Ellisland, Burns's farm near Dumfries, there is a plaque with these words: 'One autumn day in 1790 Robert Burns paced up and down this grassy path crooning to himself in one of his poetical moods the words which became the immortal tale of "Tam o'Shanter". In the last field along the path the poet saw the wounded hare which inspired "The Address to a Wounded Hare".'

Had we never lov'd sae kindly
Had we never lov'd sae blindly
Never met—or never parted,
We had ne'er been broken-hearted.
A silhouette by John Miers of Clarinda (Mrs Agnes Maclehose) to whom Burns wrote these lines. (Scottish National Portrait Gallery)

FIRST EDITION of 'Poems, chiefly in the Scottish dialect', published by John Wilson of Kilmarnock in 1786. 'Old and young, high and low, grave and gay, learned and ignorant were alike delighted, agitated, transported' by the poems. (Burns Cottage)

WOODEN SNUFF BOX mounted on silver, a gift from his friend, John Richmond, whose lodgings Burns shared when he arrived in Edinburgh in 1786. (Lady Stair's House)

MARBLE APPLE given by Burns to his sister-in-law. (Lady Stair's House)

CORDIAL GLASS belonging to the poet. In later years 'blue devils' arose to plague Burns and he became a seasoned drinker avowing 'Freedom and Whisky gang thegither'. (Lady Stair's House Museum, Edinburgh)

RELICS of the poet at Burns Cottage. Despite his great triumph as a poet in Edinburgh, Burns returned to the simple life of a farmer and excise officer. 'I'll be damned if I ever write for money' he said.

PAINTING by W. B. Johnstone of Burns in Sibbald's Circulating Library with distinguished men of the period. 'The man will be spoiled if he can spoil,' said an observer, 'but keeps his simple manners and is quite sober.' (Lady Stair's House)

HENRY MACKENZIE   DR ADAM FERGUSON   JAMES SIBBALD
HUGH BLAIR   ALEXANDER NASMYTH   JAMES BRUCE   MISS BURNETT   LORD MONBODDO
   ROBERT BURNS   DAVID ALLEN   WALTER SCOTT

Aldbourne *Wilts.*   540Fg
CHURCH OF ST MICHAEL Standing by the village green the church was originally 12th-century Norman. There were later enlargements and additions, including a fine 15th-century west tower. The south door is Norman with a two-storey Perpendicular porch, and the interior roofs are 15th century. There is an interesting carved Jacobean pulpit, an octagonal 17th-century font, brasses of the 15th and 16th centuries, and two fine early 17th-century monuments.

Aldbury *Herts.*   547Hd
CHURCH OF ST JOHN THE BAPTIST The church, dating mainly from the 13th and 14th centuries, stands near the village green. The Pendley Chapel, formed later by a stone screen erected within the church, contains a 15th-century tomb with recumbent effigies. There are two brasses and a 16th-century wooden lectern. An unusual feature is the priest's chamber over the porch.

Aldeburgh *Suffolk*   548Ef
Alde House was the home of Elizabeth Garrett Anderson, one of the first women doctors. The 16th-century Moot Hall dates from the town's most prosperous period; timber-framed with brick, it has an outside staircase leading to an upper floor added in the 17th century. In the council chamber maps and prints are on display.
CHURCH OF SS PETER AND PAUL The church stands on a hill overlooking the town. The west tower is of the 14th century, and most of the building is 16th century. The very long south porch of 1539 has three entrances. Inside is a 14th-century font, a 17th-century pulpit, some brasses and monuments.

Alderford *Norfolk*   554Cc
CHURCH OF ST JOHN THE BAPTIST The church and its west tower are 14th century, and there is no chancel arch. The octagonal seven-sacrament font, typical of East Anglian churches, is carved with a Crucifixion and angels. Some medieval stained glass still remains.

Aldershot *Hants*   541Jf
AIRBORNE FORCES MUSEUM The museum exhibits all types of equipment used by Airborne Forces.
ROYAL ARMY DENTAL CORPS MUSEUM Dental instruments and records showing the development of military dentistry from 1620 to the present. (By appointment.)
ROYAL ARMY MEDICAL CORPS HISTORICAL MUSEUM The museum has displays of uniforms, medals, letters, flags and medical equipment. The collection includes relics of Wellington, Napoleon, Florence Nightingale, Lt.-Col. Martin-Leake and Captain Noel Chavasse who both won the Victoria Cross twice.

Aldwincle *Northants.*   547Hg
CHURCH OF ALL SAINTS This has many fine features, with a brass to William Aldewyncle, 1463.
CHURCH OF ST PETER A church of Norman origin with a window to Thomas Fuller (1608–61).

Aldworth *Berks.*   546Fb
High on the Berkshire Downs, this isolated village is near the eastern end of the Ridge Way, a 40 mile long route along the top of the Downs, part of the prehistoric Icknield Way, which ran from the Wash to Salisbury Plain. In the Church of St Mary are huge stone effigies of the medieval family of de la Beche. In the churchyard is a yew tree said to be 1000 years old.

Alford *Lincs.*   553Je
CHURCH OF ST WILFRID A 14th-century church, extensively restored and enlarged by Sir Gilbert Scott in 1869. The south porch is chambered; there is a 17th-century pulpit, and a large monument with effigies dated to *c.* 1668.

Alfriston *E. Sussex*   542Cd
The village lies by the Cuckmere R., overhung by a shoulder of the South Downs on each side. The main street has several fine half-timbered houses, including the Star Inn with much carving, faces and small figures of priests.
CHURCH OF ST ANDREW A 14th-century cruciform church. Inside is an Easter sepulchre, piscina and triple sedilia. There are some fragments of early glass, but a Jesse window in the south transept is by Kempe & Tower, *c.* 1912.
CLERGY HOUSE This pre-Reformation parish priest's house dates from *c.* 1350. It is half-timbered and thatched, and the living-room has cambered tie-beams and moulded king-posts. It was the first building acquired by the National Trust (1896).

Allington Castle *Kent*   542Df
A 13th-century moated castle by the R. Medway, built in the reign of Edward I and altered in Henry VIII's reign. It was restored earlier this century and contains a collection of furniture. The castle is now a retreat house for the Order of Carmelites (White Friars).

Alloway *Strathclyde*   561Gc
BURNS COTTAGE Birthplace of Robert Burns, now a museum of his relics. (See also pp. 54–55.)

Almondbury *W. Yorks.*   558Ca
CHURCH OF ALL HALLOWS The church is mainly Perpendicular, with some Early English work and a big west tower. Inside there is a fine ceiling with decorated bosses dated 1522, a good font cover and some early stained glass showing saints and donors.

Almondsbury *Avon*   540Cg
CHURCH OF ST MARY THE VIRGIN A large cruciform church, with an Early English chancel and Norman remains. There is a central tower with broach spire, and inside a fine 16th-century tomb with two effigies. The nave was restored in 1834.

Alne *N. Yorks.*   558Dc
CHURCH OF ST MARY Basically Norman, with a carved south doorway of that period. The west tower has 18th-century additions. Inside there is a Norman font, and a 14th-century effigy of a lady.

Alnwick Castle *Northld.*   563Gc
A Border castle, the home of the Percy family since 1309. The site has been occupied since the 12th century; parts of the massive keep and the existing curtain walls enclosing the two baileys date from that time. The main part of the castle dates from the 14th century, but the present building is the result of rebuilding and restoration as successive

---

ALNWICK CASTLE

Throughout the Middle Ages the owners of Alnwick occupied an uneasy political position; nominally subjects of the English king and committed to defending the Border against the Scots, they often allied themselves with the Scottish kings if the occasion suited them. The main part of the castle belongs to the 14th century and the period of the first two Percy lords.

The interior was converted into a magnificent Italian Renaissance palace by the director of the Capitoline Museum in Rome for the 4th Duke (1847–65).
CABINET *The ornate ebony veneer cabinet was made for the apartments of Louis XIV at Versailles. It was sold by Louis XV in 1753, and eventually found its way into the hands of the 3rd Duke.*

REYNOLDS *Georgiana, Countess Spencer and Lady Georgiana Spencer*

Sir Joshua Reynolds was the epitome of the successful artist; he was occasionally a great artist. He moved in the best society, and was the first President of the Royal Academy. Reynolds believed greatness in painting only came from observance of rules based on a study of the old masters. He had an extraordinary versatility in composition—far more than Gains- *borough ever had—and treated his society beauties as material for pictorial organisation rather than as emotive subject-matter. His portraits at Althorp are among his happiest—notably this splendidly composed double portrait painted between 1759 and 1761. Here his characterisation has a sensitivity and intimacy which he never rivalled in his later work. (Althorp)*

owners attempted to make the medieval structure conform to later standards of comfort. There were two main periods of restoration—under the 1st Duke of Northumberland (1750–86) who employed Robert Adam as architect, and under the 4th Duke (1847–65) who had Salvin as architect for the exterior. This last work is now most in evidence; the exterior is dominated by the 19th-century Prudhoe Tower. The keep, armoury, guard-chamber, library and other apartments contain Italian paintings, including works by Titian, Tintoretto and Canaletto, and the family state coach is also on view. There is a museum of British and Roman antiquities. In the Abbot's Tower is the Regimental Museum of the Royal Northumberland Fusiliers.

Alrewas *Staffs.* 552Dc
CHURCH OF ALL SAINTS Some of the original Norman work remains, but there is Gothic enlargement, with good 16th-century roofs. The font is of the 15th century and has some carved grotesque heads, and the pulpit is 17th century. There is a monument of *c.* 1707 by Thomas White.

Alstonfield *Staffs.* 552Cd
CHURCH OF ST PETER A Norman church with later additions; the chancel arch is Norman. There are some good 17th-century box-pews.

Altarnun *Cornwall* 538Ed
CHURCH OF ST NONNA A church with an imposing, tall west tower, in a pretty hill-side village. There is a carved Norman font, 79 16th-century bench ends and the remains of a 16th-century rood screen.

Althorp *Northants.* 547Gf
The home of the Spencer family since 1508, where Queen Anne, the wife of James VI of Scotland, stayed on her way to join her husband in London when he became James I of England in 1603. The mansion, of medieval origin, was altered in 1573, 1660, 1733, and finally by Henry Holland in 1787. Robert Spencer, 2nd Earl of Sunderland (1640–1702) installed paintings by Dutch and Italian masters in the Picture Gallery (115 ft long). A daughter of the 1st Duke of Marlborough and his wife Sarah married one of the Earls of Sunderland, and their descendants succeeded to the Marlborough title; Sarah, Duchess of Marlborough's personal collection, and portraits by Reynolds and Gainsborough, are on display.

Alton *Hants.* 541He
Market town, assumed to have been on the Pilgrims Way. Near the market-place is a house (1590) in which the poet Edmund Spenser lived.

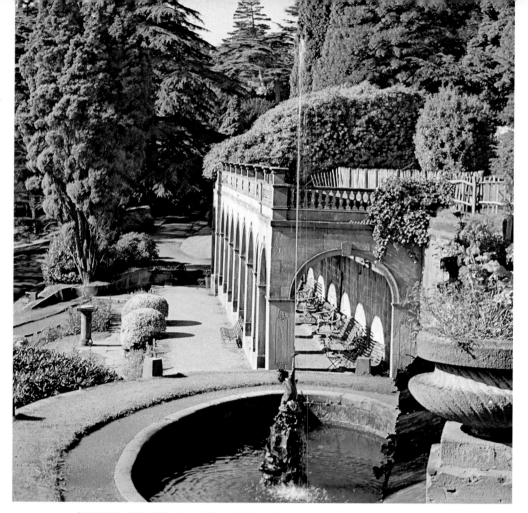

ALTON TOWERS: THE COLONNADE AND ROMAN BATH

Charles Talbot, 15th Earl of Shrewsbury, converted thousands of acres of farmland and wild countryside into a huge, fanciful, ornamental park between 1814 and 1827. At enormous expense he directed scores of craftsmen and labourers who laid out terraces and gardens, and created ponds, lakes, fountains and ornamental buildings. The colonnade and Roman bath erected in Classical style and the Screw Fountain were some of the many elegant or fantastic monuments built by the earl; these ranged from a Chinese temple in Gothic style to a Swiss cottage. The 16th Earl of Shrewsbury was responsible for 'Her Ladyship's Garden', and erected a monument to his predecessor inscribed, 'He made the desert smile.'

ALLEN GALLERY The gallery shows paintings by W. H. Allen (1863–1943). There is a collection of English ceramics from 1550, and some silver including the 12 Titchbourne spoons and the Wickham communion chalice and plates.

CURTIS MUSEUM The collections deal with local history, geology, natural history and crafts of the area. There is also a collection of dolls and other toys.

Alton Towers *Staffs.* 552Cd
A ruined 19th-century neo-Gothic mansion with a splendid park and pleasure gardens. It was formerly the principal seat of the Earls of Shrewsbury, and the hill on which it stands was probably an Iron Age camp. The Alton estates came into the possession of the Talbots (family name of the Earls of Shrewsbury) in the 12th century. The ruins of Alton castle are near by.

Alveley *Shropshire* 546Bg
CHURCH OF ST MARY In a commanding position on a hill, this church was restored by Sir Arthur Blomfield in 1878, but the tower is Norman (with an 18th-century top storey), and there are Norman remains inside, with work from the 13th to the 15th centuries. The embroidered altar frontal is 15th century. There is a brass of 1616, and stained glass by C. E. Kempe of 1882 and 1903.

Amberley *W. Sussex* 542Ad
Few villages have such a consistent architectural style as Amberley, its brick-trimmed, flint and stone cottages not intruded upon by anything more stately or extreme. At one end stand the church and the mighty ruins of the 14th-century castle, once the palace of the Bishops of Chichester. The church dates from the 12th and 13th centuries, with a Norman chancel arch and a square font. The south doorway of *c.* 1300 has carved foliage capitals. There is an interesting brass effigy of a man (*d.* 1424).

Amersham *Bucks.* 547Hc
CHURCH OF ST MARY A large town church dating from about 1140, and heavily restored and furnished in the 19th century. Since 1965 the floors have been repaved and the medieval character restored. St Mary's is one of the richest churches in the county for monuments and brasses. The brasses have been relaid in the north transept. The earliest are brasses to Henry Brudenell and his wife, Eleanor, *c.* 1430. There is an alabaster monument of Henry Curwen (*d.* 1636) by Edward Marshall in the chancel, and notable 18th-century tombs by Andrew Carpenter, Peter Scheemakers and Sir Henry Cheere in the Drake Chapel.

ANTONY HOUSE

The finest Queen Anne house in Cornwall, Antony House was built of granite in 1711–21 for Sir William Carew, whose family had lived at Antony since 1450. In spite of its size and beauty the architect is unknown (though for some time it was thought to be the work of the 18th-century Scottish architect, James Gibbs).

The central block is linked by curved colonnaded screens to the two red brick side wings and the terminal square pavilions with elaborate lead roofs. The main door, behind a grand porte-cochère added in the 19th century, leads into a fine panelled hall, from which an elegant staircase is reached through an arcade.

Amesbury *Wilts.*   540Fe
CHURCH OF SS MARY AND MELOR St Melor was a popular Cornish-Breton saint. The church here, founded in 979, once belonged to the Norman Abbey. In 1177, when the abbey was re-founded by Henry II, the church was altered. Its plan is cruciform, with a central tower. The Purbeck marble font is Norman; there are fragments of 13th-century glass and a 15th-century screen. The remains of a Saxon wheel cross can be seen in a case. The church was restored in 1853 by William Butterfield.

Ampney Crucis *Glos.*   546Dc
CHURCH OF THE HOLY ROOD Cruciform, mainly Early English but with some Norman remains and a 15th-century west tower. In the churchyard is a rare and famous 14th-century cross. Inside the church is a monument of 1584 with effigies of a man, his wife and 12 kneeling children, and a monument of *c.* 1719 by Edward Stanton and Christopher Horsnaile.

Ampney St Mary *Glos.*   546Dc
CHURCH OF ST MARY A Norman church: the nave dates from the 12th century, the chancel from the 13th. Inside are 12th- to 15th-century wall-paintings.

Ampthill *Beds.*   547He
Ampthill is architecturally one of the most attractive towns in Bedfordshire. Professor Sir Albert Richardson, architect and a past President of the Royal Academy, lived in Avenue House, an 18th-century red-brick dwelling in the main street, for many years. A great enthusiast of Georgian architecture, he was responsible for considerable restoration work in the locality; in particular the 14th-century Church of St Andrew with its 15th-century tower and battlements. It has a curious monument to Richard Nicolls, a local inhabitant who became a Royalist, fought the Dutch in America and finally became the first Governor of Long Island. At the Battle of Sole Bay in 1672, Nicolls was shot dead and the cannon-ball respon-

sible for 'his mortality and immortality' can be seen mounted on the monument's pediment. The White Hart Hotel is a Queen Anne house incorporating an earlier Tudor building.

About a mile and a half out of the town is the Oxford Hospital or St John's Almshouses, founded by 'John Cross of Oxford, Gentleman' in 1697 and built in the Wren style.

To the north are the evocative ruins of Houghton Conquest House, the 'House Beautiful' of Bunyan's *The Pilgrim's Progress*. The house is thought to have been designed by Inigo Jones, or one of his pupils, for Sir Philip Sidney's sister, the Countess of Pembroke.

Katherine's Cross was erected in 1773 in memory of Katherine of Aragon, Henry VIII's first wife, who stayed at Ampthill Castle when she was being divorced. The cross was designed by James Essex.

At nearby Marston Moretaine, there is a half-timbered 16th-century manor house with a moat.
AVENUE HOUSE A red-brick house of 1793, later enlarged by Henry Holland. In the grounds is an 18th-century octagonal garden-house designed by Sir William Chambers, architect of the Pagoda at Kew Gardens. (By appointment.)

Ampton *Suffolk*   548Cf
CHURCH OF ST PETER S. S. Teulon restored the church in the mid-19th century. The most interesting feature is the chantry chapel, built after 1479. There are brasses and monuments by John Christmas and Nicholas Stone.

Ancaster *Lincs.*   553Gd
In the main village street, off the Sleaford–Grantham road, is the site of the south gate of the Roman town of Causennae. In the garden on the left, the bastioned south-west angle of the town wall has been excavated. In the large field on the right, there is still visible the earthen bank which backed the wall with, in front of it, the half-filled protective ditch. These defences continue round almost to the north-east angle, but surface traces of the walls have disappeared, though exca-

vation has now revealed their precise line. Causennae was the last posting-station along the main road (Ermine Street) from London to Lincoln.

Anglesey Abbey *Cambs.*   *548Af*
Of the original building of 1135, only the chapter house and canon's parlour remain. In 1926 Lord Fairhaven laid out the magnificent gardens, and filled the house with his art collections.

Anstey *Herts.*   *548Ae*
CHURCH OF ST GEORGE A cruciform church, originally Norman, with a central tower, the arches of which are probably from the mid 12th century. The remainder of the church dates from the 13th to the 15th centuries. The carved font is Norman, and the stalls have carved misericords. A tripartite lych gate, built in the 15th century or earlier, has had one-third converted into a lock-up. The church contains many fascinating examples of medieval graffiti.

Anstruther *Fife*   *562Dg*
The burghs of Easter and Wester Anstruther developed independently on either side of the Dreel Burn. There are 17th- and 18th-century houses in Castle Street and Shore Street, fronting the quay, and in the Esplanade, round the miniature harbour and parish church of Easter Anstruther. Most of the two- and three-storey houses display crow-steps and pantiles, features common to the Scottish tradition in Fife.
MANSE The oldest inhabited manse in Scotland, built in 1590.

Antonine Wall *Strathclyde–Central*
The Roman wall running from sea to sea at the narrowest part of Scotland was built *c.* AD 142 during the reign of Emperor Antoninus Pius. It represented the most north-westerly frontier of the Roman Empire, as well as marking the northern limits of Roman Britain, and is the most important remaining Roman work in Scotland.
It consisted of a turf rampart with a stone foundation. The dimensions of this rampart are uncertain, but it was perhaps 12 ft high, and 14 ft wide at the base, tapering to 6 ft at the flattened top. About 15 ft to the north was a large ditch, some 40 ft wide and 12 ft deep. About 50 yds to the south of the rampart ran a military road 16–18 ft wide. The whole work was 37 miles long, from Bridgeness on the Forth to Old Kilpatrick on the Clyde. It was built not only as a base for military operations into Caledonia but with the political aim of preserving peace by intimidating the enemy barbarians to the north.

From excavations and air surveys, it has been discovered that there were originally six forts spaced out along the wall line with fortlets, or mile-castles between. Later the mile-castles were superseded with extra forts, at 2 mile intervals, amounting to 19 in all. Small turf platforms, perhaps used for signalling, were built against the back of the wall.

The wall was built by detachments of all three legions stationed in Britain, and 'distance slabs'—inscribed stones—exist showing how many lengths of wall each squad completed. Probably 20,000 men were needed to garrison it and other strongpoints in Scotland. From archaeological finds such as children's shoes it is known that families lived with the soldiers at the wall.

The wall was abandoned *c.* AD 170, so it was used by Rome for less than 30 years. It was mentioned by early chroniclers, including Bede, but systematic excavation only began in 1890 and continues today. The ditch is better preserved than the rampart; the military road is almost obliterated.

Many finds are displayed in the Hunterian Museum, Glasgow, and the National Museum of Antiquities, Edinburgh.

Antony House *Cornwall*   *538Fc*
The finest Queen Anne house in Cornwall, built of granite for Sir William Carew in 1711–21 by an unknown architect. The main entrance front is on

ARBORY HILL

The earliest relics of buildings for human habitation in Britain are those of the Iron Age Celtic peoples who came from the Continent from about 550 BC to AD 40; they were gradually pushed northwards and westwards by the invading Romans in the 1st century AD. Their habitations (hill-forts) varied in size from small fortified farmsteads to large defended settlements. The fort on Arbory Hill may well have been still inhabited when the Roman legions were passing along their road in the Clyde Valley below.

ARBROATH ABBEY

William the Lion, King of Scotland, lavished endowments on Arbroath, the abbey he founded in 1178 and dedicated to the memory of his friend Thomas Becket, former Archbishop of Canterbury. King William was buried in 1214 before the high altar—where the Coronation Stone was found in 1951 after it had been taken from Westminster Abbey by Scottish Nationalists.

the south side, and has a large columned *porte-cochère* (entrance porch for carriages) added in the 19th century. On either side of the forecourt are wings of red brick linked by colonnades to the central block and the terminal square pavilions with fanciful lead roofs. The house contains the original panelling, and fine furniture, china, needlework, *objets d'art*, and a collection of Carew family portraits including works by Reynolds. Extensive grounds with fine gardens run down to the R. Lynher.

Apethorpe *Northants.* 547Hg
CHURCH OF ST LEONARD A Perpendicular church, with a monument to Sir Anthony Mildmay, who died in 1617. The south chapel was built in 1621 to house it. Above the recumbent effigies on a sarcophagus is a huge tented canopy, the drapery of which is held by life-size figures of Charity, Justice, Wisdom and Piety.

Appleby *Humberside* 553Gg
CHURCH OF ST BARTHOLOMEW Originally medieval, this church was largely rebuilt in the 19th century. The font is Norman, and there is 19th-century glass by Capronnier and Wailes.

Appleby Magna *Leics.* 552Db
CHURCH OF ST MICHAEL A large, mainly 14th-century church, with many network tracery windows. The plaster vaulting was put in during early 19th-century restoration. The box-pews and west gallery are of the same period. There are fragments of 14th-century stained glass.

Appleton-le-Moors *N. Yorks.* 558Ed
CHRIST CHURCH The architect of this church, with south-east tower and spire, was John Loughborough Pearson, who built it in 1863–5 in Gothic style. The west front has a rose window, and there is stained glass by Clayton & Bell.

Arborfield *Berks.* 547Gb
MUSEUM OF THE CORPS OF ROYAL ELECTRICAL AND MECHANICAL ENGINEERS The souvenirs, mementoes, photographs and documents in the museum illustrate the history of the Corps of REME, which was formed in 1942, and the achievements of its personnel.

Arbor Low *Derbys.* 552Ce
This is a fine example of a Neolithic/Bronze Age henge monument with two entrances in the containing bank. This bank is still more than 6 ft high and the diameter of the enclosure is some 250 ft. The ditch lies between the bank and the central platform and was originally about 6 ft deep. Some 50 stones—or their fragments—now lie prone, but originally probably stood upright to form an outer circle and a central group. A Bronze Age barrow overlaps the line of the bank and appears to have been constructed partly with re-used material. Permission required for access.

Arbory Hill *Strathclyde* 562Ac
This fine Iron Age fort crowns a hill on the east bank of the R. Clyde, immediately above the Roman road running north along the valley. The centre of the fort is a walled area, about 140 ft across, with two entrances. Well outside this wall are two encircling ramparts, each with an external ditch. There are five entrances through these outer defences. There are traces of hut foundations in the central enclosure. (See p. 61.)

Arbroath *Tayside* 566Fb
Now an industrial, fishing and seaside town, it was here in 1320 that Robert the Bruce and the first Scottish Parliament drew up the Declaration of Scottish Independence. The town contains the Signal Tower Museum and 12th-century Kellie Castle. The Bell Rock lighthouse is 13 miles away, built 1807–11 by Robert Stevenson. This is the legendary site of Robert Southey's poem 'The Inchcape Bell'.

Arbroath Abbey *Tayside* 566Fb
Today only ruins remain of this once powerful monastery, founded in 1178 by King William of Scotland. Arbroath was a wealthy abbey, generally ruled by men distinguished for ambition rather than piety. Bernard de Linton, who was elected abbot in 1307, was also Chancellor of the Kingdom under Robert de Bruce, and in 1396 Pope Benedict XIII granted the abbot the privilege of wearing the mitre, ring and other insignia normal to a bishop. At the end of the 15th century the abbacy came to be granted to laymen. The abbey then became merely a source of revenue, the title of 'abbot' surviving until the 17th century, long after the original purpose of the monastery had lapsed. The Round O of Arbroath is a window—still to be seen in the abbey ruin—from which a beacon gave navigational aid to ships at sea. The mortuary chapel, designed for the Allan-Fraser family, was built in 1875–84.

Arbury Hall *Warks.* 546Eg
The novelist George Eliot (Marian Evans, 1819–80) was born on the Arbury estate, where her father was the agent. Set in large grounds with landscaped gardens, the Hall is built on the site of an Augustinian priory, and probably follows much of the plan of the former buildings. In 1580 a house was built of which a few details remain—a mullioned window in the courtyard, for instance. The house came into the hands of the Newdegate family in the 16th century, and in 1674 Sir Richard Newdegate consulted Sir Christopher Wren about stables. A few years later he commissioned the new chapel, which contains a magnificent plaster ceiling laden with flowers, fruit and foliage, the work of Edward Martin in 1678. In 1748–96 the Elizabethan house was transformed into a castellated mansion in Gothic Revival style by Sir Roger Newdegate. Inside are collections of family documents and letters, pictures, fine furniture, porcelain and glass.

Ardifuar *Strathclyde*   560Ef
A fine example of a circular galleried Iron Age
dun. Its diameter is 65 ft and its wall is 10 ft thick,
still standing in places to a height of 10 ft. This
dun has been excavated and, together with some
remains of Iron Age type, a fragment of Roman
pottery points to its occupation in historic times.

Ardoch Roman Camp *Tayside*   562Ag
Visible in the grounds of Ardoch House is a large
Roman fort with multiple ditch-defences—one of
those left by Agricola when recalled to Rome in
AD 84. Abandoned by the end of the century, it
was later rebuilt and occupied as an outpost of the
2nd-century Antonine Wall. Two Roman temporary marching camps have also been excavated
close by.

Ardtornish Castle *Highland*   564Fb
The 14th-century ruins of a castle overhanging the
sea and backed by cliffs; it was the ancient domain
of the Lords of the Isles.

Arkesden *Essex*   548Ae
CHURCH OF ST MARY The church has a 13th-
century nave and chancel, and fine effigies.
WOOD HALL A moated mansion, built in 1652 and
externally much altered.

Arlington *E. Sussex*   542Cd
CHURCH OF ST PANCRAS A little church, with
Saxon and Norman remains, Perpendicular font
and fragments of mural painting.

Arlington Court *Devon*   538Ff
A herd of Shetland ponies, a flock of Jacob sheep,
buzzards and ravens are to be seen in the park.
The Regency house, which was built in 1822,
contains a carriage museum and a collection of
model ships, pewter and snuff-boxes.

Armathwaite *Cumbria*   557Jg
CHAPEL OF CHRIST AND MARY A small chapel
consisting only of chancel and nave, rebuilt in the
17th century after falling into ruin and being used
as a cattle shed. The east window is a late production by Morris & Co., 1914.

Arreton *Isle of Wight*   541Hc
ARRETON MANOR The manor house, which
exhibits toys, dolls, dolls' houses, Jacobean and
Elizabethan furniture and folk items, was built on
the site of an earlier building and completed
c. 1612. Its carved panelling is over 350 years old
and a 14th-century hall screen is still in position.

BLAKE *The Cycle of the Life of Man*

*A water-colour discovered nearly 20 years ago among
rubbish on top of a cupboard in Arlington Court. It
seems that it was bought direct from William Blake
by the first owner of the house, Colonel J. P. Chichester.
Its elaborate composition, its superb condition and its
unusual technique make it exceptional in the whole
range of Blake's art. In addition to the ordinary
technique of water-colour on paper Blake used
tempera on canvas, wood or metal. Towards the end
of his life, however, he acquired a much greater
mastery of his medium and here he used water-colour
on a ground of thin gesso on thick paper. The subject
is complicated and the title conjectural. It seems to*
*represent the cycle of the life of man, spiritual and
material, and according to Sir Geoffrey Keynes 'the
two central figures probably represent Albion or Man
and his female counterpart Vala, who indicates with
her right hand that Man must descend into material
existence, and with her left hand that he can ascend
again to the regions of the spirit. The creator in his
chariot, above, has been stayed in his course by the
act of creation. Below, the cord of generative life in
the River of Death is cut as it reaches the sea, the
circle of symbolic figures, all representing some part of
the mystical process of creation, incarnation, death
and spiritual restoration.' (Arlington Court)*

63

The first manor was owned by royalty from the time of King Alfred to the Norman Conquest. It then passed to the Abbey of St Mary at Quarr. At the Dissolution it became a royal possession again, until Charles I granted it to trustees to pay some debts to the City of London.

CHURCH OF ST GEORGE The appearance is chiefly Norman, but St George's also contains Saxon work: the west front of the original Saxon church is visible on the west wall, and the door now concealed by the heavily buttressed 14th-century tower is of the same period. There are many later additions, and the church was restored in the 19th century. Monuments, also of the 19th century, include two by Sir Richard Westmacott.

NATIONAL WIRELESS MUSEUM This has exhibits from the First World War onwards.

Arundel *W. Sussex* 542Ad
The distant view of the town from the east is spectacular, with a French-looking church silhouetted against the sky, and the massive grey castle backed by beech woods. The town, in fact, like the church, is mostly Victorian. The High Street is dominated by a splendid coaching inn.

CASTLE For 500 years the home of the Dukes of Norfolk, Earl Marshals of England. John Howard, the first Duke of Norfolk of the Howard family, was killed at Bosworth Field in 1485. The castle, in a superb position overlooking the valley of the R. Arun, was begun in the reign of Edward the Confessor. The crenellated keep on top of the motte, barbican and drawbridge all date from Norman times. In 1643 Parliamentary troops besieged the castle; for 17 days it was bombarded by cannon from St Nicholas's church tower, and suffered much damage. It was rebuilt in the 18th century, and the 15th Duke carried out much reconstruction in 1890. The castle contains furniture from the 15th century and its collection

of portraits includes works by Gainsborough, Reynolds and Van Dyck.

CHURCH OF ST NICHOLAS A late 14th-century church, divided into two by a medieval iron screen. The chancel originally formed the collegiate chapel of the Holy Trinity, while the nave and transepts formed the parish church. In 1544 the chancel was sold by Henry VIII to the Duke of Norfolk. It is now the Fitzalan Chapel, containing monuments of the family.

Ascott *Bucks.* 547Gd
A half-timbered hunting lodge built 1870, housing the collection made by Anthony de Rothschild of pictures, French and Chippendale furniture, and ancient Chinese porcelain.

Ashbourne *Derbys.* 552Dd
CHURCH OF ST OSWALD This cruciform church has a central spire more than 200 ft high. Mainly of the 13th and 14th centuries, Saxon and Norman churches preceded it on the site. It contains a 13th-century font and some medieval stained glass. The monuments in the church include the masterpiece of Thomas Banks, the sleeping Penelope Boothby.

Ashburnham *E. Sussex* 542Dd
CHURCH OF ST PETER The west tower is in the Perpendicular style, but the rest of the church was rebuilt in 1665. The pulpit, font, box-pews and west gallery are all 17th century, and so are the iron screens and panelled wagon-roofs. There is a gilt-framed painting (*c.* 1676) of the Commandments and two 17th-century monuments to the Ashburnham family; one by John Bushnell shows a reclining lady with her husband kneeling by her.

Ashby de la Zouch *Leics.* 552Dc
CHURCH OF ST HELEN A 15th-century church, with late 19th-century additions. There is a reredos

ARUNDEL CASTLE

For centuries the fortress of the Fitzalan-Howard family, Dukes of Norfolk, Arundel Castle was begun in the reign of Edward the Confessor on a bluff guarding the gap made by the Arun Valley. It had a stormy history, especially from the time of Henry I. William, 3rd Earl of Arundel and his son Hugh were two of the 25 barons elected to see that Magna Carta was maintained. In 1643, during the Civil War, the castle was besieged by Cromwell's troops. However, the *fortunes of the family changed and since the Restoration the dukedom and office of Earl Marshal of England have been held without break by the Howard family. During the 18th century the castle was rehabilitated and the fine 11th-century stone keep preserved. Considerable restoration was carried out by the 15th Duke during the 19th century, and today the castle, with its circular keep and double bailey, is a smaller version of Windsor Castle.*

CUYP *View on the Maas at Dordrecht*

From his glowing paintings one might think that Cuyp had visited Italy, but he lived all his life in Dordrecht on the Maas and only travelled in his native Holland. The radiant glowing light which we always associate with Cuyp (1620–91) only became an essential part of his painting after the return to his native Utrecht in 1641 of Jan Both, who went to Rome and did landscapes in the style of Claude. There is nothing *Claudian in Cuyp's subject matter which, for a Dutch painter, is unusually varied. He did portraits and still-lifes, but it is his landscapes with cattle and stolid peasants, and his seascapes and river scenes with their 'amber coloured warmth', which made him so popular with English collectors. This picture was once divided into two halves which were reunited by a London art dealer in 1841. (Ascott)*

of 1679, but the main interest lies in the many monuments. Among them is that to the 2nd Earl of Huntingdon (*d.* 1561) with two recumbent alabaster effigies, and that to the 9th Earl, designed by William Kent and carved by Joseph Pickford and J. M. Rysbrack.

Ashdown House *Oxon.*   546Eb
A hunting box built in the late 17th century for Elizabeth of Bohemia by the 1st Earl Craven. The four-storied house, built of chalk blocks, is surmounted by a cupola topped by a golden ball. A notable feature is the great staircase which takes up more than a quarter of the interior. The house is set in fine gardens.

Ashleworth *Glos.*   546Cd
CHURCH OF SS ANDREW AND BARTHOLOMEW Making a group with Court House and a tithe barn, a small church of varying periods. There is a pre-Reformation rood screen, a Jacobean pulpit and priest's stool, and a 15th-century octagonal font. The spire is early 14th century.
TITHE BARN A 16th-century barn, 125 ft long, with stone roof, two projecting porch bays and queen-post roof timbers.

Ashley *Staffs.*   552Bc
CHURCH OF ST JOHN THE BAPTIST The tower dates from the 14th–17th century, but the rest of the church was rebuilt during the 19th century and the interior, by G. F. Bodley, was completed in 1910. There is a fine Elizabethan monument with effigies, and among memorials of the 19th century are works by Sir Francis Chantrey and Matthew Noble.

Ashover *Derbys.*   552De
CHURCH OF ALL SAINTS Mainly of the 14th and 15th centuries, the church has a lead Norman font with figures beneath an arcade, a rood screen of *c.* 1500, brasses and an alabaster monument, *c.* 1518, with effigies, saints, angels and weepers.

Ashridge *Herts.*   547Hd
The children of Henry VIII lived here in a converted 13th-century monastery. In 1808 a new house in Gothic style was begun by James Wyatt for the 7th Earl of Bridgewater, and the 13th-century crypt and Tudor barn are all that remain of the earlier buildings. Wyatt's building has a fine

chapel with an apse, and at the other end a square tower which rises above open arcades. In 1928 the house was endowed as a college of citizenship as a memorial to Andrew Bonar Law, Prime Minister in 1922–3. Since 1959 it has been a management training centre. The grounds were laid out by Humphry Repton.

Ashton *Devon*   539Gd
CHURCH OF ST JOHN THE BAPTIST A large 15th-century church with a west tower. Inside are rood and parclose screens of the same period, with painted figures of prophets, the Annunciation and the Visitation. There is an early 17th-century pulpit, a 15th-century wall-painting of Christ, and some original stained glass.

Ashwell *Herts.*   547Je
A well-preserved village, with timber-framed and brick gable-end houses, representative of some of the finest domestic architecture in England. St John's Guildhouse, with its narrowly spaced timber uprights set close together, is early 16th century. The town house near by, which contains an excellent museum—originally started by two schoolboys—is 16th century. In St Mary's Church, started in the early 14th century, there is the Latin inscription: 'Miserable, wild and distracted, the dregs of the people alone survive to witness . . .', referring to the Black Death which swept through England killing one man in three. On the inside wall of the tower is scratched a unique 14th-century drawing of old St Paul's Cathedral. Other places of interest are Chantry House, Plait Hall, Bear House, Forresters Cottages, and Bluegates Farm at Ashwell End. The manor house at Ashwell Bury is a Victorian dwelling internally reconstructed in the 1920s by Sir Edwin Lutyens, the architect who also reconstructed Lindisfarne Castle and designed the Cenotaph, Whitehall.
ASHWELL VILLAGE MUSEUM The life of an English village from prehistoric times up to the present day is depicted at this folk museum. The exhibits, which include Stone and Bronze Age implements, Roman pottery and tools used by country craftsmen—farmer, shepherd, blacksmith, wheelwright and coachbuilder—are displayed in a timber-framed, early Tudor building which was originally the Ashwell Tithe Office of the Abbot of Westminster. It later became the town house for

market officials, a meeting place of Dissenters, a straw-plaiting school and a tailor's shop. It was restored in 1930 to house the collection of local bygones, and is now scheduled as an ancient monument. Among a wide variety of exhibits are tradesmen's tokens of the 17th and 19th centuries, a unique 16th-century spectacle frame, and a peep show of the Great London Exhibition.

Astbury *Cheshire*   552Be
CHURCH OF ST MARY A large battlemented church, of the 14th and 15th centuries, with a detached tower and spire. Inside there are especially good roofs, and screen, lectern and stalls of *c.* 1500. The earliest of the many monuments in the church and churchyard is a 14th-century knight's effigy; an unconventional 17th-century font cover projects from the wall.

Astley *Warks.*   546Eg
CHURCH OF ST MARY THE VIRGIN This collegiate church of *c.* 1340 was cruciform and had a central tower and spire. After the Reformation, the building fell into disrepair until the tower collapsed *c.* 1600. A few years later the old chancel became the nave of a restored parish church, and a new chancel and west tower were built. The choir stalls, *c.* 1400, have painted figures and misericords. There are brasses and monuments.

Aston Eyre *Shropshire*   546Bg
CHURCH A small Norman church with a superb carving in the tympanum of the south doorway, depicting Christ's entry on an ass into Jerusalem.

Aston Munslow *Shropshire*   546Ag
THE WHITE HOUSE A four-period manor house built on the site of a Saxon township. It is equipped with the furniture and household effects of family occupation through the ages.

Aston Upthorpe *Oxon.*   546Fb
ALL SAINTS CHURCH Recorded as a chapel-of-ease in 1227. The nave may date from the 11th century. There is a Norman window in the north wall, and both the north and south doorways are Norman in shape.

Athelhampton Hall *Dorset*   540Dc
A 15th-century mansion with 16th-century additions, the Hall has a timbered roof, oriel window, heraldic glass, linenfold panels, secret staircases, and a Tudor great chamber. The stables are thatched, and there is a 15th-century dove-cote.

Atherington *Devon*   538Ff
CHURCH OF ST MARY A Perpendicular Gothic church, built about 1200, with a tall west tower which was restored in 1884. The main attractions of the church are its wagon-roofs, the late Tudor windows, the carved bench ends, and the carved screen with enclosed rood loft—'the only one remaining in Devon'. The church also contains 15th-century brass.

Attingham Park *Shropshire*   552Ab
A mansion built in Classical style in 1785 for the 1st Lord Berwick to designs by George Steuart. It stands in front of an older house built *c.* 1700. The south front has a portico which rises through three storeys; it is supported by slender Ionic columns. Two wings project behind the remains of the old house on the north side, masked on the south by curved colonnades. The 2nd Lord Berwick commissioned Humphry Repton to landscape the grounds, and shortly afterwards, in 1807, John Nash was engaged to build a picture gallery. Nash originally thought of supporting the ceiling on novel cast-iron frames, to be made at the neigh-

bouring iron-foundry of Coalbrookdale. However, he changed his mind and used instead the present iron frames with glass lights—an early use of these materials in English architecture. The state rooms contain fine furniture and pictures by Caravaggio, Veronese and Spanish masters.

Attleborough *Norfolk*   554Cb
CHURCH OF ST MARY Formerly cruciform, the church's chancel and apse have disappeared, while the central tower remains. Some Norman work exists and the remainder is mainly Decorated, with a good west window and a two-storey porch. The late 15th-century rood screen has painted decoration. There is a cast-iron lectern of 1816, wall-paintings, and some original stained glass.

Aubourn Hall *Lincs.*   553Ge
A red-brick 16th-century country house with a fine carved staircase and panelled rooms.

Auchagallon *Arran, Strathclyde*   560Ed
The Bronze Age monument here is a little out of the ordinary. The cairn is a rounded mound of stones, but it is surrounded by the stone circle, which consists of 15 standing stones. It stands in the low-lying ground close to the west coast of the island.

Audley End *Essex*   548Ae
The Benedictine Abbey of Walden stood here, but after the Dissolution the site was given by Henry VIII to Lord Audley, who built himself a house in the grounds. The estate descended to Lord Howard of Walden, created Earl of Suffolk by James I; in 1603 the Earl began an enormous Jacobean house, one of the largest in England, with two great courts. About 1721 the 5th Earl employed Sir John Vanbrugh to work on the house, and the outer court was pulled down and the rest of the house much altered. After that the building gradually deteriorated, and in 1747 it was bought by Lady Portsmouth; her nephew, Lord Braybrooke, succeeded to it in 1762 and between then and his death in 1797 carried out renovations. The house contains a fine collection of pictures.

Aughton *Lancs.*   551Jg
CHURCH OF ST MICHAEL A Norman church with later medieval work. The 14th-century tower is square at the base, then octagonal, and is surmounted by an octagonal spire. Inside is a 15th-century font, brass plates of 1661 and 1686, and an altar tomb to a 19th-century rector by J. S. Westmacott.

Auldearn *Highland*   566Cg
BOATH DOOCOT Built in the late 17th century to house the pigeons which provided the local laird's table with fresh food during the winter months. This circular stone cote, rough cast of lime and small gravel, containing 546 nest holes, occupies a prominent position on a mound that was originally the site of Auldearn Castle. Here James Graham, Marquess of Montrose, defeated the Covenanters, the Presbyterian opponents of Charles I, in 1645.

Ault Hucknall *Derbys.*   552Ee
CHURCH OF ST JOHN THE BAPTIST The Norman origins of this church, with its central tower, are easily seen, and some even suggest there may be Saxon remains. The church contains the tomb of Thomas Hobbes, the scholar and philosopher who was tutor to Charles II. There are also funeral hatchments of two of the Dukes of Devonshire. The churchyard has some interesting tombs.

Avebury *Wilts.*   540Fg
Part of Avebury village lies today in the centre of the great henge monument built about 2000 BC. Its

THE HALL AT AUDLEY END

The splendid Jacobean house Lord Howard of Walden, 1st Earl of Suffolk, built when he inherited the estate at Audley End in 1603, eventually became one of the largest in England. It was about twice its present size, with two courts built around the ruins of a Benedictine monastery. After the Restoration Charles II acquired the house, but it was returned to the Howards in 1701, when the 5th Earl called in the architect Sir John *Vanbrugh. On his advice the outer court was demolished and much of the interior altered. But the graceful exterior of the earlier house, with its roof surrounded by a balustrade and topped by turrets, remains—and so does the great hall, entered through two ornate early 17th-century porches, and containing a flat ceiling embellished with wood and plaster panels, and a screen with a riot of carved decoration.*

enclosing bank, 20 ft high with a diameter of 1400 ft, was built with chalk from the inner ditch which was interrupted by four causeways forming entrances. The steep-sided ditch was originally 30 ft deep, with a flat base. A few feet from the inner edge lay the main stone circles. At the centre of the northern inner circle two of the stones of a 'cove' can still be seen (see p. 68), and in the southern circle is part of a setting of smaller stones.

From two of the entrances wide avenues of sarsen stones extended for over a mile. Of the western, which led to Beckhampton, only two stones remain, but much of the West Kennet Avenue to the south has been restored. It leads to The Sanctuary, a circular site on Overton Hill.

ALEXANDER KEILLER MUSEUM The museum, which is reached through the churchyard, is named after its founder, who opened it in 1938 to house the material from his excavations at Windmill Hill and Avebury. In addition, it now displays material from other monuments of the uniquely important prehistoric complex, which includes West Kennet Long Barrow, Silbury Hill, West Kennet Avenue and the Sanctuary.

AVEBURY MANOR An Elizabethan manor house, with period panelling, plasterwork and collections of porcelain and antique furniture.

Aveley *Essex*   *548Ab*
CHURCH OF ST MICHAEL Dating from the 12th to 14th centuries, the church has a 12th-century Purbeck marble font and an early 17th-century pulpit. The brasses include one of Flemish type to Ralph de Knevynton (*d.* 1370).

Avington *Hants.*   *541He*
CHURCH OF ST MARY A brick church built *c.* 1770, with a west tower. The 18th-century interior is unspoilt and contains pulpit, box-pews, family pew, and a west gallery which has an early 19th-century barrel-organ. The 18th- and 19th-century monuments include one to Margaret, Countess of Carnarvon (*d.* 1768), who ordered the church to be built, but died before it was begun.

Avington Park *Hants.*   *541He*
A red-brick mansion in the style of Wren, dating from the 16th and 17th centuries.

Axbridge *Som.*   *540Cf*
CHURCH OF ST JOHN BAPTIST A cruciform Perpendicular church, with a good central tower. There is a fine plaster nave ceiling of 1636, and monuments from the late 15th century.

Aylesbury *Bucks.*   *547Gd*
The town has Parliamentarian associations, especially with John Hampden (1594–1643) who in 1635 refused to pay the Ship Money Tax imposed by Charles I. In the main square is a statue to Hampden, who lived at Great Hampden near by. The 18th-century Prebendal House was the home of John Wilkes (1729–97), satirist and M.P. for Aylesbury from 1757 to 1764. The King's Head Inn dates from the 15th century and has fine medieval windows, gateway and courtyard.

BUCKINGHAMSHIRE COUNTY MUSEUM The museum is housed partly in an early 18th-century building erected for the grammar school, and partly in a private house rebuilt in the early 18th century but retaining its 15th-century roof. The collections relate to Buckinghamshire history, archaeology and natural history, and include finds from the Romano-British villa at Hambleden. A Buckinghamshire Rural Life Gallery was opened in 1975. There is a small display of period costume, and paintings on view which include a set of nine oils of the grounds of Hartwell House (1738 and 1749) by B. Nebot.

CHURCH OF ST MARY A cruciform church of the 13th–15th centuries, unfortunately over-restored by Sir Gilbert Scott in the 1860's. The spirelet on the central tower is a successful copy of a 17th-century original. The beautiful late 12th-century font is circular, and carved with stiff-leaved foliage. There is much Victorian stained glass. The pews have been removed.

Aylesford *Kent*   *542Df*
A restored 13th-century friary, with late 14th-century cloisters, containing unusual items of sculpture and ceramics.

Aylsham *Norfolk*   *554Dc*
There are many good 17th- and 18th-century houses in and about the town. Market Place has several, including the Black Boys Inn, probably Queen Anne. On Blickling Road are the Knoll, *c.* 1700, and Aylsham Old Hall, dated 1689, an excellent example of its time, with hipped-roof and pedimented doorway. On the Norwich road are Old Bank House, *c.* 1710, and the Manor House, 16th and 17th centuries. Abbots Hall, a farmhouse, is an early 17th-century brick house. St Michael's church has a monument to Humphry Repton, the great 18th-century gardener.

Aynhoe Park *Northants.*   *546Fe*
A 17th-century country mansion, built on the foundations of a Norman castle. It was remodelled by Sir John Soane in the 18th century.

Ayot St Lawrence *Herts.*   *547Jd*
SHAW'S CORNER A late Victorian country residence, the home of the playwright, George Bernard Shaw, from 1906 to 1950. It is preserved as he left it. His ashes were scattered in the garden.

Ayr *Strathclyde*   *561Gc*
The seaport centre of the Robert Burns country. The Auld Brig (Old Bridge) dates from the 13th century, and was renovated in 1910. The Tower of St John is the sole remnant of a 12th-century church, enclosed within Cromwell's Citadel in 1652; part of the Citadel wall is still to be seen. In the Wallace Tower (built 1832) is a statue of Sir William Wallace, the Scottish patriot, carved by James Thom, a local sculptor. Loudoun Hall has been restored and is a good example of early 16th-century burgh domestic architecture. The Tam o' Shanter Inn in the High Street is now a Burns Museum. For many years a public house, it was the starting place of Tam o' Shanter's famous ride to Kirkoswald about 10 miles from Ayr, as described in Burns's poem.

TOWN HALL Thomas Hamilton of Edinburgh, given the commission in 1828 to build a new town steeple and assembly rooms in the town of Ayr, designed this neo-Classical building of Cullaloe stone from Fife. The 126-ft spire, formed by superimposed squares and octagons surmounted by an obelisk, still dominates the town.

AVEBURY

The largest stone circle in the British Isles, this circle of sarsen stones or megaliths was constructed of undressed natural blocks of sandstone from the nearby Downs. It is surrounded by a ditch and bank enclosing 28 acres. The stones of this, and the two inside circles of 320 and 340 ft across, stand 5 to 20 ft above the ground, but many have been pillaged for use as building material. The monument, originally approached by two avenues of megaliths, was constructed by Late Neolithic people about 2000 BC or earlier.

B

Babington *Som.*   *540Df*
CHURCH OF ST MARGARET Grouped with Babington House, the church was built in 1750. It has an apse, and a west tower with a cupola.

Babraham *Cambs.*   *548Ae*
CHURCH OF ST PETER The oldest part of the church, the tower, was built about 1200. The new east window was designed by John Piper. A 17th-century sculpture by John Bushnell is of two figures with carved drapery.

Bachwen *Gwynedd*   *550Ed*
Here, close to the sea, stands a typical megalithic burial chamber, with uprights and capstone, from which the circular mound has long since disappeared. The unusual feature here is the wealth of cup-marks which cover the upper surface of the capping. This type of carving, first introduced to Britain at the end of the Neolithic period by the megalith-builders, is fairly well distributed in northern and western Britain, but it is not very commonly found in this position in a grave.

Backwell *Avon*   *540Cg*
CHURCH OF ST ANDREW Dating from the 15th century, on an earlier foundation, St Andrew's has a west tower over 100 ft high. Inside, are a Norman font, a 16th-century screen and a brass.

Bacton *Heref. & Worcs.*   *546Ae*
CHURCH OF ST FAITH This church was first built in the 13th century; the west tower was added in the late 16th century. Some of the stalls are ornamented with poppy-head carving. The most important monument is to Blanche Parry, a local girl who was Queen Elizabeth's maid of honour. She is shown kneeling before the Queen; the inscription to hers ends: 'Allwaye wythe maeden queene a maede did ende my liffe'.

Bacton *Suffolk*   *548Df*
CHURCH OF ST MARY A Decorated and Perpendicular church with a west tower. There is decorative stone and flint work in the clerestory, and a double hammerbeam roof in the nave. Inside is a contemporary font with angels; also benches, screen, and medieval doom-wall painting.

Bacup *Lancs.*   *552Bg*
BACUP NATURAL HISTORY SOCIETY'S MUSEUM Collections devoted to local natural history, geology, archaeology and household bygones are exhibited in a former inn of the late 18th century.

Badbury Rings *Dorset*   *540Ed*
This is a conspicuous Iron Age hill-fort by the Wimborne–Blandford road. A steep hill-top has been strengthened with two massive inner ramparts and a third, much slighter, enclosing them, perhaps built at a later date. There were two entrances and rather complicated defence works. In Roman times there was probably a large settlement as two major Roman roads meet here. One is the main road from Old Sarum to Dorchester, Ackling Dyke, and the other is the road from Bath to Poole. To the north-west of the site are four Bronze Age bowl barrows.

Baddiley *Cheshire*   *552Ad*
CHURCH OF ST MICHAEL A small church, consisting only of nave and chancel; the nave was rebuilt in 1811 but the chancel retains its original

timber construction. The east wall of the nave over the screen is painted with heraldry, the Commandments, Creed and Lord's Prayer, 1663. There are box-pews, west gallery and pulpit of the 18th century, and a large monument of *c.* 1726.

Badgeworth *Glos.*   *546Cd*
CHURCH OF THE HOLY TRINITY An early 14th-century Decorated church, noteworthy for the profusion of 'ball-flower' carving ornamenting the windows and north doorway.

Badingham *Suffolk*   *548Ef*
CHURCH OF ST JOHN THE BAPTIST Originally Norman, with later additions, the church has a pretty hammerbeam roof, and a good example of an East Anglican seven-sacrament font.

Bag Enderby *Lincs.*   *553Je*
CHURCH OF ST MARGARET The chancel, nave and windows of this sandstone church date from the 14th century. The font, of the same period, has carvings of a *Pietà*. The tower and porch are of the 15th century, as is the east window. Some medieval stained glass remains.

Bainton *Humberside*   *558Fb*
CHURCH OF ST ANDREW A fine church, mainly of the 14th century, with a west tower; on the outside are many carved animals and faces. Inside is a Norman font, the brass of a priest, and the effigy of a 14th-century cross-legged knight.

Bakewell *Derbys.*   *552De*
Little but the Holme Bridge, a medieval pack-horse bridge rebuilt in 1664, survives of Bakewell's industrial past of lead mining and cotton milling; but the Bath House of 1697 is a reminder of another tradition, when a dozen or so warm springs made the town a spa.
CHURCH OF ALL SAINTS An embattled cruciform church, of Saxon origin, with an octagonal central tower and spire. Some original pieces remain, including Saxon tombstones in the church porch and an 8th-century cross in the churchyard. The church contains an early 14th-century font, screen, and many monuments with effigies and weepers. The most remarkable is that to Sir Godfrey Foljambe (*d.* 1377) with two upright half-figures on a wall.
OLD HOUSE MUSEUM The Old House was built *c.* 1534 of random limestone, and contains timbered roofs and ceilings, with wattle-and-daub screens and large fireplaces. There is a fine *garde-robe* and a Tudor cupboard belonging to the house. The museum re-creates local life in the Peak District in the past, with costumes, farming equipment and miners', blacksmiths', and wheelwrights' tools. There are also a 19th-century kitchen with equipment, a collection of lace, and another of Victorian dolls and toys, including a Noah's Ark and clockwork trains.

Baldersby *N. Yorks.*   *558Cd*
CHURCH OF ST JAMES A large Victorian church by William Butterfield, designed 1856–8 in the 13th-century style, with a tall steeple and spire. The impressive interior has a tiled floor in the chancel and typical fittings and stained glass of the period.

Baldock *Herts.*   *547Je*
CHURCH OF ST MARY A spacious church, with two-storey south porch and an early 14th-century west tower, embattled, with an octagonal lantern

and small spire. Inside are a 13th-century octagonal font, 15th-century screens, brasses and a monument, of c. 1846, by E. H. Baily.

Ballygowan *Strathclyde* 560Eg
A decorated rock-face with a group of Bronze Age cup-and-ring decorations together with several horseshoe-shaped examples.

Balmerino Abbey *Fife* 562Ch
Ruins of an abbey built by Alexander II (1198–1249) at the wish of his mother Queen Ermengarde (widow of William the Lion), who is buried beneath the high altar.

Balmoral Castle *Grampian* 566Dd
A private residence of the Queen, used by the Royal Family as a holiday estate. Prince Albert, Queen Victoria's Prince Consort, bought it in 1848 and in the following years had it rebuilt in white granite as a castellated mansion in Scottish baronial style. Only the gardens, first laid out by Prince Albert in the 1850's, and planted with rare conifers and other trees, are open to the public, who may also see Queen Victoria's garden cottage and Queen Mary's sunken garden.

Balnuaran of Clava *Highland* 566Bf
A ring cairn, an almost circular structure contained in a broad ring of stony rubble, held on the outside by a stone kerb and internally by upright stone slabs. The average thickness of this ring is about 20 ft. The internal area measures 21 ft by 18 ft. Outside the ring are nine standing stones spaced along the circumference of a circle some 100 ft across. These vary greatly in size; the tallest is about 7½ ft high. On either side of the Neolithic ring cairn is a passage-grave.

Balsham *Cambs.* 548Be
CHURCH OF THE HOLY TRINITY The church is mainly 14th century with additions; there is a west tower with nine buttresses, now made safe with reinforcing. Inside are a good rood screen, two brasses to former rectors, 1401 and 1462, and 14th-century stalls with carving and misericords.

Bamburgh *Northld.* 563Gd
CASTLE There is evidence that buildings existed on the site in Roman times. A wooden Saxon 'city' stood here when Bamburgh was the capital of the Kingdom of Northumbria. This was sacked by the Danes, and was replaced by a Norman castle of which the keep remains. The castle was restored in 1894–1903 and has an exhibition of armour.
CHURCH OF ST AIDAN The church is mainly of the 13th century with later additions, and a west tower. The long, aisle-less chancel has a crypt beneath. There is a monument by Chantrey of 1839; Grace Darling is buried in the churchyard.

Bampton *Oxon.* 546Ec
Bampton is a large village that once had a market, and the 19th-century Italianate town hall survives in the market-place. It has a surprising number of good 'gentry' houses, mostly visible from road or churchyard. The castle, west of the village, preserves fragments of the 13th-century castle of Aymer de Valance, but is now a private house. Behind the church the deanery is a rambling house, externally of the early 17th century. Bampton Manor has an 18th-century Classical façade to the garden, and an early 19th-century Gothic-style porch to the drive. Weald Manor to the south-west, is of c. 1700 and is finished with a quality of detail worthy of a much grander house.
CHURCH OF ST MARY THE VIRGIN An impressive cruciform church with central tower and spire, it has Norman and later Gothic work. Inside are brasses, and a monument with an early 17th-century recumbent effigy.

Banbury *Oxon.* 546Ee
An ancient wool town, whose castle was twice besieged by Parliamentary forces during the Civil War. The castle was demolished in 1648 and no trace remains. The Banbury Cross of nursery rhyme fame was destroyed in 1600 by the Puritans as being Popish: the present hexagonal neo-Gothic cross dates from 1859.
MUSEUM An exhibition covers the local history of the Cherwell Valley from the Stone Age.

Banff *Grampian* 566Fg
One of the most attractive towns in the north of Scotland, exhibiting a wealth of good architecture. The 16th-century market cross, the tolbooth of 1764–7 by one of the Adam brothers, churches in the Classical form, tall gabled houses and simple artisan dwellings ornament The Shore, Waterpath, High Street and Boyndie Street. Here and there a Classical doorpiece and stone quoins add a note of sophistication. Banff Castle of 1750 and Duff House, magnificent baroque by William Adam, 1740–5, are from more affluent days.
DUFF HOUSE A great ornate mansion built for the Earl of Fife in 1735 by William Adam in Classical style, based on the style of the Villa Borghese.

Bangor *Gwynedd* 550Ee
CATHEDRAL A small cathedral of Celtic foundation. A later Norman church here was enlarged during the 16th and 17th centuries, restored by Sir Gilbert Scott in 1868–84 and by Alan Caroe in 1966–71. There is a 15th-century font, a stone with 14th-century low relief, medieval tiles and 'the Mostyn Christ' (1518).

Bannockburn *Central* 561Jf
BORESTONE A monument, erected in 1964, overlooking the traditional site of the defeat of the English army in 1314 by King Robert the Bruce. A rotunda encloses the Borestone site where the Scots standard stood. There is also an equestrian statue of the king.

Banwell *Avon* 540Cf
CHURCH OF ST ANDREW A Perpendicular church with an imposing west tower. There is a Norman font, a 16th-century rood screen, 15th- and 19th-century stained glass, and interesting brasses.

Barden Tower *N. Yorks.* 558Bc
Ruins in Wharfedale, all that remains of a house rebuilt in the 15th century as one of six lodges built for keepers' accommodation and the protection of deer in the Forest of Barden. The lodge was restored in the 17th century and repaired in 1774 but since then it has fallen into disrepair.

Bardwell *Suffolk* 548Cf
CHURCH OF SS PETER AND PAUL Much 15th- and 16th-century building; the south porch has flushwork decoration and Arms, of c. 1430. The hammerbeam roof has some of its original colour left, though most of the angels have gone. There is 15th-century stained glass, and a 17th-century monument with kneeling figures and children.

Barfreston *Kent* 542Ff
CHURCH OF ST NICHOLAS The small Norman village church at Barfreston is externally ornamented with an unusual amount of carving. The decoration was done c. 1180, and is in style similar to other local carving at Rochester and Canterbury. The east end of the church has a row of arcades surmounted by a wheel-window carved with animals, foliage and figures. The arcading is continued round the sides and is topped by a corbel table carved with grotesque figures. There is a less decorated doorway on the south side of the chancel and another on the north side of the nave. The

BARFRESTON CHURCH

No explanation has been found for the profusion of rich Romanesque carving on Barfreston Church. (The village church at nearby Patrixbourne is similarly ornamented, but Barfreston is outstanding.) The carving has the same style as other local carving at Rochester and Canterbury, and was probably done by masons with similar training. The manor belonged to *the de Port family during the 12th century, but no account has survived to explain the building of such an elaborate little church. The interior is less ornamented, but a curious feature is the carved, raised band which runs horizontally beneath the windows of the nave. The nave and the decoration were partly restored in 1840, and some of the present carving dates from then.*

most impressive carving decorates the south door, which was clearly intended as the main entrance. Carved in the centre of the tympanum is Christ in Glory. The meaning of the remainder of the carving is obscure; many of the roundels on the arches appear to be humorous, particularly those of animals playing musical instruments.

Barham *Cambs.* 547Jf
CHURCH OF ST GILES A Norman church, with nave arcade and chancel arch, and a 13th-century chancel. There is a 13th-century font.

Barham *Kent* 542Ff
Seen from the valley road, the village is a cluster of mellow, red-tiled roofs among the trees. Up the hill, along turning and twisting streets, is Barham Court, a handsome Queen Anne building, with early 20th-century additions by Sir Edwin Lutyens.

Barking *Greater London* 548Ab
EASTBURY HOUSE A red-brick, H-shaped manor house of 1572, now in a modern housing estate.
VALENCE HOUSE MUSEUM A 17th-century manor house, still partly moated, with a collection devoted exclusively to local history. The collection includes 17th- and 18th-century portraits relating to the Fanshawe family.

Barlaston *Staffs.* 552Bd
WEDGWOOD MUSEUM TRUST In 1906, many documents and wares were discovered at the Etruria factory, which had been built for Josiah Wedgwood in 1769. This discovery led to the foundation of the museum, which displays only Wedgwood wares and associated documents. Exhibits include three copies of Wedgwood's first edition Portland Vases, as well as two of the six 'First Day Vases' thrown by Wedgwood himself on the opening day of the Etruria factory. Also on show are pieces from the Queen's Ware service made for Catherine of Russia. The museum

complex includes a demonstration area, in which visitors can see the arts of pottery practised in a manner almost unchanged since the days of the first Josiah Wedgwood.

Barmekin of Echt *Grampian* 566Fe
Three ramparts form the outer defences of this hill-fort, and the five entrances are flanked by walls running well into the enclosure. Inside the enclosure, two more stone walls encircle the innermost area, some 370 ft in diameter. It seems clear that this complex resulted from one or two phases of defence-building in the Iron Age.

Barmston *Humberside* 559Gc
CHURCH OF ALL SAINTS The church is mainly of 15th-century work, with a west tower. There is a Norman font with cable-and-diamond decoration, and a 15th-century alabaster effigy.

Barnack *Cambs.* 547Hh
CHURCH OF ST JOHN THE BAPTIST A Saxon church probably dating from the early 11th century. The west tower has 13th-century additions, including the spire and pinnacles, while the remainder of the church is of the 12th to the 16th centuries. Among the contents are a seated figure of Christ in Majesty (early 11th century), an early English font with leaves (13th century) and monuments dating from the 14th century.

Barnard Castle *Durham* 558Be
The town grew up beside the medieval castle on top of a bluff by a crossing point of the R. Tees. The castle was founded by Guy, Lord of Bailleul, and rebuilt in 1112–32 by his nephew, Bernard Baliol, from whom it takes its name. It is now in ruins, but remains of the 14th-century great hall and earlier cylindrical, three-storied keep survive. The castle was besieged in 1569 during the Rising of the Northern Earls, and allowed to decay after its capture by Cromwell. The medieval stone bridge across the river is still in use and on the

EL GRECO: THE TEARS OF ST PETER *Of all the old masters El Greco seems the most 'modern'. Both in spirit and style his work conforms in its air of unreality and individuality with the art of our own time. Born in Crete in 1541 he clearly reflects his Byzantine heritage but in about 1560 he went to Venice and came under the spell of Titian. Then in 1570 he went to Rome where the gesturings and foreshortenings in the late murals of Michelangelo, only six years dead, had prepared the way for* mannerism. *In 1577 he settled in Spain for the rest of his life, and in a wealth of portraits and religious works he developed a more and more personal style. A marked elongation of limbs, flame-like forms, pietistic gazes with eyes rolled heavenwards—as in 'The Tears of St Peter'—and a range of predominantly acid colours are the ingredients of his unique visionary intensity. His abstract conflicting planes create a shallow space similar to that in the cubist work of another Spanish-born painter, Picasso.*

main street of the town are ancient houses and several inns—one of which has links with Dickens's *Nicholas Nickleby*.

BOWES MUSEUM The building, of French design, was begun in 1869 specifically as a museum, and houses an extensive collection of Spanish paintings, including works by El Greco and Goya. French works by Boucher and Courbet amongst others, and Italian paintings including some by Sassetta and Tiepolo. A series of period settings displays English and French furniture of the 17th and 19th centuries and also collections of pottery and porcelain; 16th–18th-century tapestries can also be seen, with smaller collections of sculpture,

miniatures, jewellery, watches and snuff-boxes. There are rooms showing period costume, textiles, musical instruments and local history and dolls, dolls' houses and other toys.

Barnsley *S. Yorks.* 552Dg

MONK BRETTON PRIORY Extensive remains of a large 12th-century Cluniac abbey, with a gatehouse dating from the 15th century and, near by, a late 13th-century guesthouse.

WORSBOROUGH MILL MUSEUM A working industrial site museum, which includes a 17th-century water mill, and a 19th-century mill—both mills powered by a rare 1911 hot bulb oil engine.

FRENCH GOLD SNUFF-BOX *Despite the wars and revolutions of the 18th and 19th centuries, French goldsmiths maintained their high standards of work, and this snuff-box is a fine example. Dated on the lid 'May 27, 1853' it was made of several different coloured golds by the Parisian firm of Martial Barnard. The surface is decorated with silver and with opaque and translucent enamels. An inscription around the sides supports legal government as opposed to revolution.*

SILVER SWAN *This swan is an elaborate musical toy, $27\frac{1}{2}$ in. high, with an articulated neck. When set in motion, it bends down to pick up a fish which it appears to swallow while a tune is played. Said to have been made by James Cox for his 'museum' of mechanical novelties in late 18th-century London, it was restored by a London silversmith in the 1860's. The pointed leaves round the 'pool' probably date from then, but the swan itself seems little changed from the 18th century.*

Barnstaple *Devon* 538Ff
Barnstaple has been a small inland seaport since Norman times. The parish church, consecrated in 1318, has a twisted wood spire, covered with lead in 1636. The Long Bridge has crossed the R. Taw since 1273. Queen Anne's Walk (1560–89) was once a meeting place for ship owners and merchants whose bargains were settled on the Tome Stone. The Three Tuns Tavern (1450) has panelling and fire-places that may be medieval; it was restored in 1947. Horwood and Penrose Almshouses date from the 17th-century. The latter has a granite colonnade façade.

DODDERIDGE ROOM, GUILDHALL Once part of the town house of a rich merchant, it has a collection of plate and ancient seals, and a symbolic Silver Oar showing that the mayor is Water Bailiff holding Admiralty warrant for the post.
ST ANNE'S CHAPEL MUSEUM The upper part of this building probably dates from 1456, but the crypt is much older—it was originally part of a charnel-house. From 1685 the building was used as a place of worship by Huguenots, Protestants who had fled from France to escape religious persecution. The building was a grammar school from the end of the 17th century until 1910; John Gay, who wrote *The Beggar's Opera* in 1728, was a pupil there and items associated with him are in the museum. All the collections are of local interest and include prints, drawings, pottery, seals and fire-arms.
YOULSTON PARK An 18th-century house—four miles north-east of Barnstaple—set in a beautiful woodland garden with a lake. The house has fine plaster ceilings and a Chinese Room.

Barra Castle *Grampian* 567Gf
A partly 17th-century stone mansion with a wing built in the mid-Georgian period.

Barrington Court *Som.* 540Cd
A fine Elizabethan stone mansion, of pure Gothic design, probably built by William Clifton between 1559–64. The stable wing was added in 1680.

Barrowden *Leics.* 553Gb
CHURCH OF ST PETER Mainly 13th century, the church has a 14th-century west tower with spire; 15th-century enlargements include the clerestory and east window. Inside is a late 16th-century monument.

Barr's Hill *Dumfs. & Gall.* 562Aa
HILL-FORT This hill forms part of the narrow ridge separating the lower reaches of Annandale and Nithsdale and gives a wide view of the approaches on both sides. The outer defences are two ramparts with an intermediate ditch. Within this, enclosing the central area, is a massive bank with an external ditch. Outside, on the north-west, there are traces of additional defences. There is a single entrance on the east side. The fort was built in the Iron Age.

Barsalloch Point *Dumfs. & Gall.* 556Cf
The tip of a headland is cut off by two Iron Age ramparts with a broad deep ditch between them.

Barsham *Suffolk* 548Eg
CHURCH OF THE HOLY TRINITY Norman, with later enlargement, Holy Trinity has a round west tower, and a highly decorated east wall with stone and flint flushwork trellis which incorporates the window as part of the scheme. Two fonts, one Norman, the other Perpendicular; Jacobean woodwork includes the pulpit. The 19th-century east window is by C. E. Kempe. There is a brass, and a 16th-century monument.

Barton Turf *Norfolk* 554Dc
CHURCH OF ST MICHAEL AND ALL ANGELS With a battlemented west tower, this 14th- and 15th-century church has 15th-century screens with painted figures. A brass dates from *c.* 1445, and there are monuments from the late 18th century.

Barton-upon-Humber *Humberside* 553Gg
CHURCH OF ST MARY A magnificent Norman church with Decorated and Perpendicular additions, and a 15th-century brass to a vintner, Simon Seman of Hull.
CHURCH OF ST PETER In what was once a major port of Humberside, this church, founded during St Chad's mission to Lindsey in 669, still retains its Saxon tower and west end. The nave and

chancel date from the 14th century. The tracery of the east window is noteworthy. The Department of the Environment now has care of the church.

Basing *Hants.*   *541Hf*
A village of brick cottages, with a splendid brick barn at Grange Farm, lying in the marshy valley of the R. Loddon. The Norman earthworks of Basing Castle stand above it, but the great Tudor house inside them was destroyed in the Civil War. BASING HOUSE RUINS A Saxon fortress, the Old Castle of Basing is referred to in Domesday Book. The Norman New Castle was built on the same site. In 1530 a magnificent Tudor fortified mansion, Basing House, was built on the same spot. Queen Elizabeth I stayed here twice; her second visit lasted 13 days and proved so expensive that her host had to demolish part of his house to pay for it. During the Civil War the house was besieged for three years by Cromwell's troops, and was captured and razed in 1645. Excavations that have been carried out on the site have revealed many items, including Iron Age pottery, Roman coins, 13th- and 18th-century tiles and glassware, 16th- and 17th-century pottery, and relics of the Civil War, all of which are housed in the Hampshire County Museum and the Basingstoke Museum. The Old Bothy, built over the original powder magazine, contains Tudor and Elizabethan sculpture, pottery and fire-backs.
CHURCH OF ST MARY A large Perpendicular church near the ruins of Basing House which was destroyed during the Civil War, when the architect, Inigo Jones, was taken prisoner, 1645. The church was also damaged at the same time, but later repaired, and restored again in 1874. There are several monuments of the 15th and 16th centuries, and one by John Flaxman (1755–1826).

Basingstoke *Hants.*   *541Hf*
WILLIS MUSEUM A collection of clocks and watches and exhibits illustrating local history and archaeology.

Basingwerk *Clwyd*   *551He*
ABBEY Basingwerk Abbey, a Cistercian house, was founded during the 12th century; it is now in ruins.

Baswich *Staffs.*   *552Bc*
CHURCH OF THE HOLY TRINITY This little church was rebuilt during the 18th century, though the medieval tower was kept. There is a three-decker pulpit and, in the north transept of the chancel, a double-decker family pew.

Batcombe *Som.*   *540De*
CHURCH OF ST MARY A 14th–15th-century church with a west tower of 1540. Inside there is a Perpendicular font, and several mural tablets from the 16th and 17th centuries.

Bateman's *E. Sussex*   *542De*
Rudyard Kipling's home is preserved as it was when he lived there from 1902 until 1936; he described its surroundings in *Puck of Pook's Hill.* The house was built in 1634.

Bath *Avon*   *540Df*
The Roman camp established here *c.* AD 44 later became a prosperous spa, Aquae Sulis, based on local warm springs; remains of some of those buildings can still be seen. After 410 the town declined and suffered greatly from Anglo-Saxon raids. Later it became an ecclesiastical centre and wool-manufacturing town. Between 1088 and 1122 the monastic church was rebuilt by John de Villula of Tours, but the present abbey dates

mainly from 1499–1616. During the 18th century Bath revived as a spa and the many fine Georgian buildings date from this period. The city was badly bombed during the Second World War and has been rebuilt; it is still an important spa and cultural centre. (See also pp. 76–77.)
ABBEY Bath Abbey, founded in 1499, is built in a restrained Perpendicular style and the design is remarkably uniform throughout. The present abbey church, although much smaller than the previous Romanesque building, was obviously intended to be ostentatious. Bishop King, the founder, was a royal servant, and the king's masons whom he employed promised to build him the finest vault in England. Whether the vault was in fact designed by them is uncertain, since it contains heraldic carvings which were probably executed after King's death in 1504, and the vault cuts across the frame of the east window, suggesting that its present curve was not the one originally planned. This striking and elaborate vault, which transforms the whole building, took a long time to complete, and the nave vault was not added until the 19th century. The church is crammed with monuments, and carved decoration on the west front shows angels climbing up and down ladders on each of the turrets flanking the window.
HOLBURNE OF MENSTRIE MUSEUM Built in Palladian style in 1796–7 as part of Sydney Gardens (a place of entertainment similar to Vauxhall Gardens in London) the inside of the house was adapted as a museum in 1913–15. It now houses porcelain, ceramics, silver, glass, fine furniture and

EMBROIDERED DOUBLET
OF A 17th-CENTURY LADY

This fine embroidery was worked on a doublet worn by a lady of about 1680. The doublet was a close-fitting garment worn above the waist. In this case it was made of natural-coloured cotton, embroidered with flowers and birds on a background of fine lattice work. The garment also has a fringe of buff-coloured cotton. It is on display at the Museum of Costume in Bath Assembly Rooms, one of the world's largest exhibitions of costumes.

pictures including some by Gainsborough, Reynolds, Stubbs, Barker of Bath and Guardi.

MUSEUM OF COSTUME In Bath Assembly Rooms, built between 1769 and 1771, there is one of the world's largest exhibitions of costume. The period covered is from the 17th century to the present day. All aspects of fashion are covered, from the latest styles to fashionable Victorian costumes displayed against settings of Bath.

ROMAN BATHS The Romans early learnt the medicinal quality of the Bath waters and here they established Aquae Sulis, the leading spa and fashionable town of Roman Britain, even as it later became that of 18th-century England. The great bath-buildings with an attached temple stood in the town centre and much of this complex is today incorporated in the modern Pump Room buildings, where there is also a museum of finds from the site.

VICTORIA ART GALLERY AND MUSEUM No permanent displays, but continuous exhibitions are drawn from the gallery's collections of paintings (17th–20th century), the Kimball collection of etchings by British and American artists (20th century), local topographical prints and drawings, British water-colours, English ceramics and glass, British Delftware, Bohemian glass, miniatures, watches, Bath Mint coins and trade tokens. Collections not on view can often be seen by appointment.

Batley *W. Yorks.*   558Ca
ART GALLERY The permanent collection includes works by Francis Bacon, Max Ernst, Graham

Sutherland and Vivian Pitchforth, and alternates with local and travelling loan exhibitions.

BAGSHAW MUSEUM (WILTON PARK) The archaeology, local history, industry and natural history of the Batley area are the themes of the displays here. There are also collections of Near Eastern antiquities and of Chinese ceramics.

Battle *E. Sussex*   542Dd
A small town clustered by the abbey's mighty gate-house; there is a triangular market-place, and the best house, the Deanery, built in 1669, is beside the church.

CHURCH OF ST MARY A Norman building, enlarged during the 12th century, and with later additions. It has a west tower; the font is Norman and has a 15th-century cover. There are brasses, and a 16th-century monument.

Battle Abbey *E. Sussex*   542Dd
Before the Battle of Hastings William of Normandy vowed he would build an abbey should the victory be his; he did so, and the remains of the Benedictine house stand on the slopes of Senlac Hill, where Normans and English fought.

Battlesbury Hill *Wilts.*   540Ef
This is one of the finest hill-forts in a county with many fine forts. It has an internal area of nearly 24 acres and most of it has a defence system of three ramparts, though the south-east segment has two only. Excavation has shown that there was permanent occupation late in the Iron Age. Outside the north-west entrance were the burials of men, women and children slain by violence, though whether by Roman soldiers or enemies from another British tribe, could not be determined.

Baulking *Oxon.*   546Ec
CHURCH OF ST NICHOLAS This small rustic church, mainly of the 13th century, has a narrow chancel arch with small side openings. The pulpit is 17th century, and a tie-beam on the roof is dated 1708.

Beaudesert *Warks.*   546Df
CHURCH OF ST NICHOLAS This Norman church, with later additions, has a Perpendicular west tower, and a Norman chancel arch. The vaulting of the chancel was added by Thomas Garner in 1865. The 19th-century stained glass is by Holland, and Morris & Co., *c.* 1865.

Beaulieu *Hants.*   541Gd
The pretty village street leads to the bank of the Beaulieu R., where it first opens out as an estuary. Across the river is Palace House, originally the gate-house of the abbey and converted into a mansion shortly after the Dissolution.

ABBEY A Cistercian abbey was founded here in 1204. The 13th-century buildings are now mainly ruined, but the old refectory is now the parish church. Its most important feature is the pulpit reached by way of an open 13th-century arcade in the thickness of the wall; although the present pulpit is new, it rests on the original base decorated with foliage.

NATIONAL MOTOR MUSEUM Incorporating the comprehensive collection of the Montagu Motor Museum, founded by Lord Montagu in 1952 in memory of his father, the 2nd Baron Montagu of Beaulieu, the museum illustrates the history of motor transport with veteran, vintage and modern cycles, motor-cycles and cars. Among the many exhibits are the 1895 Knight—the earliest petrol-driven car of an all-British design; the 1896 Pennington—a three-wheeler with enormous cylinders and a top speed of about 45 mph, the land speed record of its time; the 1898 Cannstatt-Daimler—a tall motor brougham with a centre-pivot

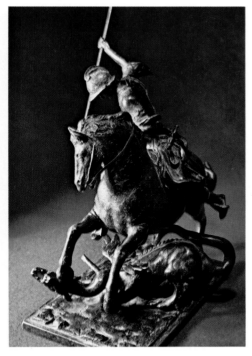

FRANCESCO FANELLI
St George and the Dragon

Fanelli was the most accomplished sculptor working at the Court of Charles I. He probably trained in one of the great bronze workshops in Florence and came to England soon after 1610, bringing with him the art of bronze statuette making, for which he was chiefly patronised during his stay until the outbreak of the Civil War in 1642, when he settled in France. With two exceptions all his known bronzes are of equestrian subjects. (Holburne of Menstrie Museum, Bath)

BATH *Splendour from the waters*

First Iron Age peoples, later the Romans, and later still fashionable society of the 18th and 19th centuries were attracted to Bath, to take the waters. By the time of Agricola (AD 78–84) the town was a thriving spa. In 1705 Beau Nash, leader of London society, went to live there and was soon 'king of Bath'. Once again the town became a major spa and holiday centre, and the finest artists and craftsmen of the time transformed it into a showpiece of Georgian prosperity.

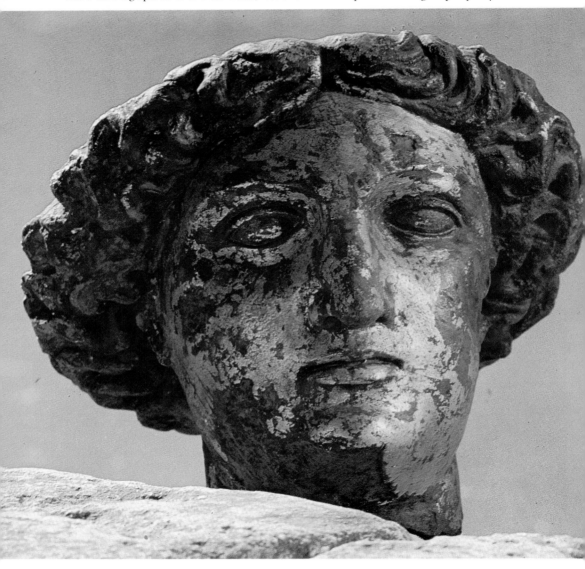

HEAD OF MINERVA *This roughly life-size head is of bronze, hollow-cast and gilded. It had been hacked from the body in ancient times and was found in the 18th century lying in a corner of the Roman bath. The treatment of the back of the head shows that it must originally have worn Minerva's helmet, a separate casting. Here, doubtless, it was the representation of Sulis-Minerva. It was certainly a classical piece and was probably made in a Mediterranean workshop.*

HEAD OF MEDUSA *This frowning, moustached face, radiating locks of hair entwined with snakes, once dominated the temple of Sulis-Minerva at Bath. It was the central figure of a sculpted pediment, and encircled by two oak wreaths. On either side was a Winged Victory on a globe. To the Celts and Romans the head and Victories suggested the healing and evil-averting powers of Sulis-Minerva.*

FAN-VAULTING AT BATH ABBEY in Prior Bird's Chantry is one of the most majestic features of a building which belongs to neither of the city's principal hey-days. Founded in 1499, it occupies the site of the Saxon abbey in which Edgar was crowned King of England in 973. Transformed into a vast minster by the Normans, the building was destroyed by fire in 1137. The present abbey was restored and altered several times between 1603 and the 1960's, when Second World War bomb · damage was finally repaired. The famous west front carvings represent the founder-bishop's dream of angels ascending and descending from Heaven. Inside, 614 memorial tablets make an elaborate mural cenotaph to the many people who have contributed to the grandeur of Bath.

ROYAL CRESCENT, a great sweep of 30 houses with 114 Ionic columns supporting a Palladian cornice, was the work of John Wood the Younger. Other streets followed, and other architects were at work: Thomas Baldwin, who built the guildhall and the Pump Room; Robert Adam, who spanned the R. Avon with the Pulteney Bridge, lining it with shops so that from the road there is no impression of being on a bridge. Meanwhile Ralph Allen, a postal clerk who founded a fortune on his ingenious system for speeding the mail out of Bath, commissioned Sham Castle, a mock Gothic façade which improved the view from his house on North Parade. No. 1, Royal Crescent is now restored and refurnished, and open to the public.

THE EMPEROR HADRIAN looks down at the Great Bath, 80 ft by 40 ft and 5 ft deep, where Romans bathed in hot mineral-spring water. Once roofed, the bath is still supplied with water through the lead conduit fitted by a Roman plumber. There are also remains of another rectangular bath and a circular bath with stepped sides. Relics of mosaic pavements and the temple of Sulis-Minerva have been uncovered in the town.

Bath was destroyed by the Saxons after the Romans' withdrawal from Britain, and many of the city's glories lay buried for more than 1000 years.

CUP AND SALVER When these magnificent pieces, made of silver heavily plated with gold, were given to the city of Bath in 1739 by Frederick, Prince of Wales, to commemorate his visit of the year before, they were described as being 'of an entire new taste, and much admired'. By then they were already six years old, but fashion travelled slowly in the 18th century. The novelty lay in their asymmetrical, or rococo, style, which was replacing the symmetrical forms established ever since the Middle Ages. The new style had developed in France, and was brought to this country by immigrant French goldsmiths like Louis Pantin. Both pieces are superbly engraved with the Arms of the Prince of Wales and the city of Bath, and the finial of the cup is in the form of the Prince of Wales's feathers. The gift may have been made at the suggestion of Beau Nash, a personal friend of the Prince of Wales, and the leader of Bath society.

'MEDIEVAL' DRESSING TABLE

This dressing table, together with a matching bed, was designed by the Victorian architect William Burges for his house in Kensington, London, in 1867. It is made of mahogany and painted red. The style reflects the medieval period, an obsession which Burges shared with some of his contemporaries. The dressing table and bed are in the Cecil Higgins Art Gallery in Bedford, part of a remarkable and unusual collection of 19th- and 20th-century decorative art.

A TURNER MAN-O'-WAR

The painter J. M. W. Turner completed this water-colour between breakfast and lunch for his friend and patron Walter Fawkes. Fawkes had asked for a drawing that would give him an idea of the proportions of a man-o'-war, and Turner produced the water-colour entirely from memory. It was painted during a visit to Fawkes's house, Farnley Hall in N. Yorkshire, in 1818, and Turner was observed throughout by Francis Fawkes, the 15-year-old son of the host. Francis watched him

axle like a horse-drawn carriage, a rear engine and a 4-speed belt drive; and the 1909 Rolls Royce "Silver Ghost". In the motor-cycle section are the 1930 Ascot-Pullin and the 1921 Ner-A-Car—both attempts to produce 'cars on 2 wheels'. Among the bicycles are the 1865 English Bone Shaker, the 1876 Coventry Lever and the 1900 Dursley Pedersen with a unique frame of triangulated tubes and the saddle suspended like a hammock. There is also a national transport library with books, photographs and catalogues.

Beauly Priory *Highland*   *566Ag*
In this 'beau lieu' (beautiful place) stand the ruins of a 13th-century foundation, built by French monks for Sir John Bisset of Lovat in 1230; a façade was added *c.* 1530.

Beaumaris *Anglesey, Gwynedd*   *550Ee*
CASTLE The building of Beaumaris Castle was started at the end of the 13th century by Edward I. The castle is situated in open, level country, and since the architect had no natural obstacles to contend with, the result is a castle of extreme symmetry, unequalled as a piece of military planning and engineering. It was intended that the castle should contain no less than five separate suites of lodgings, each with its own hall, chamber and associated rooms, and it has been estimated that the castle alone cost as much as the town and castle of Conwy together. Work on the castle was never completed, and the curiously truncated

towers are not, as elsewhere, the result of the activities of the Parliamentarians or of stone robbers, but of lack of interest and money in the 14th century. Building continued until the early years of Edward III's reign, *c.* 1330, and then stopped.
CHURCH A 14th-century building with several monuments, including alabaster effigies of a knight and lady. There are also stalls with misericords.
COURT HOUSE This delightful building was erected in 1614 and was thoughtfully altered early in the 19th century. Many of the fittings and the roof are original and there is an 18th-century canopied pew for the mayor and bailiffs.
NO. 32 CASTLE STREET This well restored and maintained building contains the remains of a house of *c.* 1400. The fine woodwork of the medieval roof can be seen from an upper floor inserted during the 17th century.

Beaupre *S. Glam.*   *545Hb*
The carved Renaissance porch in the inner court of this Elizabethan mansion is certainly the finest in Wales, and in quality equals some of the Northamptonshire examples. The house embodies medieval fabric, built by the Basset family when they first settled in the area, but it took its present form in the second half of the 16th century. The ruins have been consolidated, and it is possible to trace most of the original arrangements. The battlemented courtyard wall and the outer gatehouse were more for prestige than for defence.

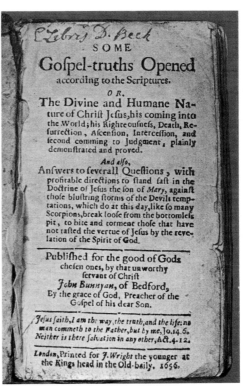

JOHN BUNYAN'S
Some Gospel Truths Opened

Only three copies are known to exist of 'Some Gospel Truths Opened', John Bunyan's first book. An attack on Quaker teaching, it was first published in 1656; four years later he was arrested and imprisoned for Nonconformity. Enforced leisure for 12 years enabled him to produce a spate of books, and during a second term of imprisonment he wrote 'Pilgrim's Progress'. (Bedfordshire County Library.)

pouring wet paint on to the paper until it was saturated, 'working like a madman, and tearing up the sea with an eagle claw of a thumbnail'. The painting, measuring 11¾ in. × 15⅝ in., demonstrates Turner's intimate knowledge of ships and the sea. The artist painted many works at Farnley Hall, but this was the only one to be observed. It is one of several Turners at the Cecil Higgins Art Gallery, Bedford, whose water-colours date from the 17th century.

Beccles *Suffolk*   548Eg
An ancient town on the R. Waveney, with picturesque river reaches. Four fires in the 16th and 17th centuries destroyed much of the old town. It has attractive streets of red-brick Georgian houses. Noteworthy are the old town hall, 1726; St Peter's House, with 18th-century front and 'Strawberry Hill' style Gothic decorations, on the site of a chapel to St Peter; Ravensmere House of 1694; and Leman House on Ballygate Street, a school founded in 1631. On the road to Bungay is Roos or Rose Hall of 1583, a good gabled brick Tudor manor with pedimented windows.

Bedale *N. Yorks.*   558Cd
BEDALE HALL An 18th-century Georgian mansion with a ballroom and museum of domestic arts.

Beddington *Greater London*   542Bf
CHURCH OF ST MARY THE VIRGIN A basically 14th- and 15th-century church, with 19th-century enlargement and restoration. It has a Norman font, brasses, a 16th-century pulpit, carved misericords, and a 17th-century alabaster effigy of a man in armour lying on his tomb.

Bedford *Beds.*   547He
First fortified by the Saxons in 915, Bedford was sacked by the Danes in 1010 and granted a charter by Henry II in 1166. It is notable for its connections with John Bunyan—he was born in the nearby village of Elstow in 1628 and imprisoned for religious dissent in 1660. Bunyan

Meeting House is a memorial to him and contains Bunyan relics; its bronze doors depict in bas-relief ten scenes from *The Pilgrim's Progress*. Near St Peter's Church is a statue of Bunyan by Sir Joseph Boehm. The Muniment Room in the town hall has council minutes dating from 1647, the 'Elizabethan Black Book of Bedford' and records of the Court of Pleas. A statue of John Howard (1726–90), the prison reformer, by Gilbert, who sculpted Eros in Piccadilly, is in Bedford.

CECIL HIGGINS ART GALLERY Several extensive collections are on view. The collection of water-colours and drawings from the 17th century to the present includes works by Cozens, Rowlandson, Turner, Sickert and Ben Nicholson. There are also collections of prints from Dürer to the present, and of sculpture including bronzes by Epstein and Henry Moore. The collection of English and continental porcelain of the 18th and 19th centuries includes examples from the Chelsea, Bow, Worcester, Meissen and Nymphenburg works, and the English and continental glass section includes two pieces by George Ravenscroft.

The gallery also displays 18th-, 19th- and 20th-century furniture.

COUNTY HALL LIBRARY Books about the life and works of John Bunyan are displayed here.

MUSEUM The collections here are devoted to Bedford and its county, and comprise archaeological finds from Iron Age and Roman sites, Saxon urns and brooches, local traders' tokens, agricultural

WOODCARVING AT BELTON HOUSE

This type of naturalistic woodcarving reached its height of perfection in England during the 1680's when many Dutch craftsmen emigrated here. One of the most notable carvers was Grinling Gibbons and although there is no evidence to show that he worked at Belton, the style here is very similar to other examples of his work. The carving is of pear and limewood and is almost certainly Dutch or English: the surface is waxed, and French and Italian works of the time were usually gilded or silvered.

and domestic bygones and exhibits relating to the lace-making and straw-plaiting industries.

Bedingfield *Suffolk*   548Df
FLEMINGS HALL A fine moated wood-frame building of *c.* 1380, altered by the addition of stepped gables, a porch and polygonal chimneys, all in pink brick, *c.* 1580. (By appointment.)

Beeston *Norfolk*   554Bc
CHURCH OF ST MARY The church is mainly Decorated, with Perpendicular clerestory added in 1410. The hammerbeam roof, the painted rood screen and two parclose screens are particularly fine. The churchyard has a memorial to Jem Mace, world champion bare-fisted boxer born in Beeston.

Belas Knap *Glos.*   546Dd
This example of the latest stage of development of the chambered Neolithic long barrow has been carefully restored. The horned forecourt at the north end has a dummy entrance and the four chambers are widely spaced round the sides and south end. The rubble of the mound is held in place by walling.

Belton *Grantham, Lincs.*   553Gd
BELTON HOUSE The home of the Brownlow family for 300 years. The present house, in Wren style, was erected in 1685–8. It is built on an H-plan and has a hipped-roof with dormer windows and, above, an elegant cupola. Between projecting wings a broad flight of steps leads up to the main doorway, above which is a pediment with the Brownlow coat of arms. About 1776 James Wyatt altered the house, and in 1811 his nephew, Sir Jeffry Wyatville, built the orangery. In the house is a fine collection of portraits connected with the Brownlow family.

Among the many fine rooms there is the Chinese Bedroom. It has door mouldings and wall panels decorated to simulate bamboo, hand-painted wallpaper, and a bedcover with Chinese embroidered silk.

Other rooms contain notable displays of Chinese, Japanese and French porcelain; English and French furniture from the 17th century to the Regency period; and Dutch and English tapestries of the late 17th and early 18th centuries.

Next to the Dining Room with its immense wildlife paintings by the 17th-century Flemish artist Melchior d'Hondecoeter is a room specially prepared to display the family collection of silver and silver gilt, acquired by Sir John Cust, an 18th-century Speaker of the House of Commons who married into the Brownlow family.

In the entrance to the former brewhouse, designed by Wyatville and now a shop, is an exhibition of carriages on loan from Lady Brownlow.
CHURCH OF SS PETER AND PAUL There were additions and changes to the original Norman church until the 18th century, and in 1816 Sir Jeffry Wyatville designed a chapel. Notable are the many monuments to the Brownlow family, by William and Edward Stanton, John Bacon, Baron Marochetti and many others.

Belvoir Castle *Leics.*   552Fc
Formerly a fortress, Belvoir was rebuilt during the 17th century by the 8th Earl of Rutland. In 1779 the 4th Duke asked Capability Brown to improve the grounds and restore the house. Brown drew up the plans, but because of the duke's death this work was not carried out. In *c.* 1800 the 5th Duke asked James Wyatt to convert the house into a medieval castle. Wyatt reconstructed the private apartments, rebuilding the south-east range and raising

the Staunton Tower in height. He then added a new range to the south-west with a large round tower, and slightly to the south of this he built two octagonal pinnacled turrets on either side of the lancet windows which light the chapel. The northern part of the castle was reconstructed following a fire in 1816, by the Duchess of Rutland and the Rev. Sir John Thoroton, assisted by Benjamin and Matthew Wyatt. The castle is now roughly rectangular around a large courtyard. In the grounds is a mausoleum built in Norman style in 1826–8 by Thoroton. The castle is noted for its Gobelins tapestries, *objets d'art* and picture collections which contain works by Holbein, Gainsborough and Poussin.

Bembridge *Isle of Wight*   *541Hc*
RUSKIN GALLERIES The largest Ruskin collection in the world, part on display here, part at Brantwood, in Cumbria, Ruskin's former home. The collection consists of drawings and paintings by Ruskin and some by his friends and associates, and a large number of his letters, manuscripts and books. Volumes from Ruskin's own library are also on view. (By appointment.)

Bembridge Windmill   *541Hc*
Isle of Wight
The only remaining windmill on the island. The stone tower with wooden machinery was erected *c.* 1700, and was last used in 1913.

Beningbrough Hall *N. Yorks.*   *558Dc*
A large house of stone and brick, built in 1716 for John Bourchier, possibly by Thomas Archer. It contains woodwork and carving of a high standard—an oak staircase, friezes and panels.

Benington *Herts.*   *547Jd*
In AD 850 Berthulf, King of Mercia, held a council of war here when he heard that the Danish fleet was in the Thames.

The Lordship, a Georgian mansion (not open), adjoins the keep of a ruined Norman castle. The large neo-Norman gate-house 'folly' near by is said to have been designed by a landscape gardener.

Benmore *Strathclyde*   *561Gf*
YOUNGER BOTANIC GARDEN A landscaped woodland garden.

Benthall Hall *Shropshire*   *552Ab*
A 16th-century stone house with mullioned windows and moulded chimneys. Interior alterations were carried out in the 17th century. Notable features are a carved oak staircase, decorated plaster ceilings and 16th-century oak panelling.

Beoley *Heref. & Worcs.*   *546Df*
CHURCH OF ST LEONARD The church is noteworthy for its fine collection of 16th-century monuments to members of the Sheldon family, who began tapestry weaving in England. Outstanding among these are those to William and Ralph Sheldon and their wives, which display much heraldic ornament.

Bere Regis *Dorset*   *540Ec*
CHURCH OF ST JOHN THE BAPTIST An 11th-century church added to in later styles; the Perpendicular tower has the stone-and-flint diaperwork typical of the area. Inside, the fine roof with painting and

THE ELIZABETH SALOON AT BELVOIR CASTLE

The family of the Dukes of Rutland has lived at Belvoir since Henry VIII's reign, and the 5th Duke commissioned James Wyatt to convert the house overlooking the Vale of Belvoir into a romantic Gothic-style castle in about 1800. The Prince Regent visited the castle in 1813 and the Regent's Gallery in the south-west range was named in his honour. It is 130 ft long and a wide bow in the centre forms part of the round tower; along the walls is a series of busts by the sculptor Joseph Nollekens. A disastrous fire in 1816 *destroyed the northern portion of the castle, and the Duchess of Rutland and one of the duke's relatives, the Rev. Sir John Thoroton, employed two of Wyatt's sons, Benjamin and Matthew, to help them rebuild. Thoroton designed the east tower containing the magnificent Elizabeth Saloon, with ceilings painted by Matthew Wyatt and a life-size statue of the duchess by him. The room was decorated by Benjamin Wyatt in French rococo style, soon to become popular in London and repeated in other houses.*

figures dates to the 15th century; the arcades and mid-16th-century seating are also worth noting. There are interesting marble monuments, and a Norman font, with arcading and other decoration.

Berkeley *Glos.*   *546Bc*
CHURCH OF ST MARY THE VIRGIN A fine, mainly Gothic building, but with Norman font and south doorway. There is a magnificent stone screen, and the Berkeley chapel on the south side. There are interesting monuments and wall paintings, including a Doom and a Norman consecration cross.

Berkeley Castle *Glos.*   *546Bc*
Edward II was brutally murdered here in 1327; the murder room is as it was at the time of his death. The perfectly preserved stronghold overlooking the Severn has been the home of the Berkeleys since it was begun in 1153. The massive Norman keep, dungeon, and curtain wall date from that time, and the great hall and kitchen were added in 1340. The state apartments contain paintings, tapestries and fine furniture and silver. The grounds include a terraced garden with an Elizabethan bowling alley.

Berkhamsted *Herts.*   *547Hc*
Only earthworks remain of the 11th-century Norman castle to which came Thomas Becket, Chaucer and the Court of Henry VIII. Berkhamsted is the birthplace of William Cowper (1731–1800), the poet and hymn-writer, whose father was the rector of Great Berkhamsted.

BERKELEY CASTLE

DOORWAY *The door decorated with alternate rows of saints and cherubs was brought to Berkeley Castle from the Continent this century for the doorway of the new clock-tower. Above it are the family Arms supported by two knights. Ten crosses on the shield show that an early member of the family once took part in a Crusade.*
MADONNA AND CHILD *A 15th-century French woodcarving. In his right hand the Infant Christ holds a globe, signifying the world.*

CHURCH OF ST PETER This large cruciform church, originally Norman with later additions, was restored in 1871 by William Butterfield. Fragments of 14th-century stained glass remain. One window is by C. E. Kempe, 1880. There are many brasses and monuments, and a 16th-century 'whistling' weathercock in the vestry.

Berkswell *W. Midlands*   *546Eg*
CHURCH OF ST JOHN THE BAPTIST The best Norman church in Warwickshire, probably built in the late 12th century. It has an impressive vaulted crypt under the chancel, with an unexplained octagonal extension westwards beneath the nave. The 16th-century south porch is half-timbered and two-storied. There is a fine Norman chancel and much remaining work of that period in the nave. The monuments include one by John Bacon of 1795.

Berrington Hall *Heref. & Worcs.*   *546Af*
A country mansion built in 1778–81 by Henry Holland, with fine plasterwork and painted ceilings. The park was landscaped by Capability Brown in 1780.

Berry Pomeroy Castle *Devon*   *539Gc*
Ralph de Pomeroy, who came to England with William the Conqueror, built this Norman castle on top of a wooded cliff. Later a descendant, the Duke of Somerset (1506–52), brother of Henry VIII's wife Jane Seymour, built a great Tudor mansion within the medieval walls while he was Protector Somerset—Regent for Edward VI. The Seymours occupied the castle until late in the 17th century when it was abandoned following extensive damage during the Civil War. Ruins of the mansion, medieval walls and great three-storied gate-house with hexagonal towers remain.

Berry Ring *Staffs.*   *552Bc*
This is an oval area defended by a single Iron Age bank and ditch.

Berwick *E. Sussex*   *542Cd*
CHURCH OF ST MICHAEL AND ALL ANGELS There was a Saxon church here and the font built into the wall probably dates from that time. The present building is 12th century and was restored in 1858. On the walls of the church are murals painted in 1942 by the Bloomsbury Group artists Duncan Grant, Vanessa Bell—sister of Virginia Woolf—and her son Quentin.

Berwick-upon-Tweed *Northld.*   *562Fe*
During the succession of Border Wars between the Scots and the English, Berwick, founded *c.* AD 870, changed hands 13 times. Since 1482 it has been politically in England. The town is surrounded by the 'Elizabethan Wall', some 10 ft thick, completed as a fortification in 1565, and designed specially for gunpowder warfare. Its gates are Scotsgate, Cowport, Ness Gate and Shore Gate. Only fragments of Berwick Castle remain—Bell Tower and Lords Mount.

Three bridges cross the Tweed: Berwick Bridge, in pink sandstone, was opened in 1634; Royal Border Bridge, a viaduct of 28 arches by Robert Stephenson, is a mile and a quarter long and 120 ft above water level and was opened by Queen Victoria in 1850; and Royal Tweed Bridge, opened in 1928, spans the river on four arches.
CHURCH OF THE HOLY TRINITY One of the only two churches built during the Commonwealth under Cromwell. The church, completed in 1652, was built by a London mason, John Young of Blackfriars, and has many Venetian windows.
MUSEUM AND ART GALLERY The art gallery has a collection of pictures given by Sir William Burrell

One of the masterpieces of medieval European art, the tomb with its richly decorated canopy is by tradition that of Lady Eleanor Percy, but was more probably made for her daughter-in-law, Lady Idonea, who died in 1365. As well as the magnificent carving of angels, fruit, leaves and symbolic beasts on the canopy, the minster contains superlative wood and stone carving throughout, especially on corbels, roof bosses, on the nave arcade, in the choir and on and around the great west door, whose panels of the Evangelists and their symbols were designed by Nicholas Hawksmoor. The misericords, carved from Sherwood Forest oak, are some of the best in England; among them can be seen a man shoeing a goose, a pig playing a harp, and men catching a bear in a wicker-work cage. In contrast with these fanciful and expertly worked decorations is the plain 1000-year-old Fridstol or sanctuary chair, a reminder of the minster's ancient Rights of Sanctuary, where fugitives might seek the Peace of St John and at least temporarily gain respite from their pursuers.

including Daubigny's *Cap Gris Nez* and Degas, pastel *Russian Dancer*. The Berwick Room has items of local interest including a 16th-century tempera wall-painting removed from the Old Bridge Tavern, since demolished. The museum contains small collections of bronze, brass, ceramics and glass, mostly from Sir William Burrell's collection, more of which can be seen at the Camphill Museum, Glasgow.

Besford *Heref. & Worcs.* 546Ce
CHURCH OF ST PETER The timber and plaster nave is 14th century; the choir was rebuilt in the late 19th century with timbers replaced in their original positions. The rood screen is 15th century; monuments include one in the form of a painted wood triptych, and one by William Stanton.

Besselsleigh *Oxon.* 546Ec
CHURCH OF ST LAWRENCE This is a small Norman church, with later rebuilding. At the west end there is a two-bell cote; the church was restored in 1632, and has a 17th-century font and canopied pulpit. It is the only church in the county to retain all its box-pews and original seating and ritual arrangements.

Betchworth *Surrey* 542Bf
Hardly more than a hamlet, though the buildings grouped near the church—tiled barns, cottages, a pub and a big, plain Georgian house—are typical of old Surrey.

Betley *Staffs.* 552Bd
CHURCH OF ST MARGARET A 13th-century church in which a surprising amount of timber was used—not only for the roofs, but for nave piers and arches, and the clerestory.

Bettws Newydd *Gwent* 546Ac
CHURCH This church retains an elegant Perpendicular rood screen with its original gallery decorated with open-work tracery.

Beverley *Humberside* 559Gb
Once a walled town, there is now only one 15th-century gate surviving from five originals. There are several fine Georgian houses. The guildhall (1832) has excellent plasterwork in the courtroom. The market cross dates from the 18th century.
ART GALLERY AND MUSEUM The gallery includes paintings by F. W. Elwell of Beverley. There is a small collection of folk material.
CHURCH OF ST MARY The second of Beverley's notable churches, St Mary's is overshadowed by the minster. Cruciform, from the 14th and 15th centuries, with some earlier work, it has a pinnacled central tower. Inside are medieval stalls with misericords and an early 16th-century font. There is a monument by John Bacon the Younger.
MINSTER (CHURCH OF ST JOHN THE EVANGELIST) St John of Beverley (640–721) founded the original Saxon church at Beverley and was buried there. Having been a student at Canterbury under the great Abbot Hadrian, *c.* 687 he was promoted to the bishopric of Hexham and *c.* 703 he ordained the Venerable Bede. In 705 he became Bishop of York. However, he was a lover of solitude and eventually he resigned his diocese, and in 717 retired to Beverley where he died in 721. He was canonised in 1037. His church at Beverley became a college of secular canons in the 10th century, but was badly damaged by fire in 1188. Rebuilding did not begin until the 13th century, and culminated in the early 15th century with the construction of the west façade, with twin towers, one of the finest architectural gems of its period in England.

Beverstone *Glos.* 546Cc
CHURCH OF ST MARY A small Norman church, rebuilt in the 14th century. The three-bay south arcade of the nave is from *c.* 1200 and the south doorway is Norman. There is a fine nave roof and a restored 15th-century rood screen.

Bewdley *Heref. & Worcs.* 546Bf
A museum in the 18th-century butchers' shambles shows crafts extinct in the area, such as charcoal-burning, rope-making and tanning.

Bexhill *E. Sussex* 542Dd
DE LA WARR PAVILION A long, low, white, concrete block with a balconied bow craning toward the sea; a major example of the international style of its date, 1933–6. Designed by Erich Mendelsohn, whose finest work had been done in Germany.
MUSEUM Permanent displays of local natural history, geology and archaeology, with frequent loan exhibitions on a variety of subjects.

Bexley *Greater London* 542Cg
HALL PLACE A stone Tudor house, built by Sir John Champneis, 1537–40, with a 17th-century red-brick extension, set in attractive grounds. It once belonged to Sir Francis Dashwood, the notorious rake. Now used for exhibitions.

Bibury *Glos.* 546Dc
ARLINGTON MILL A 17th-century flour mill, now a museum of machinery, agricultural implements, Victorian costumes and Arts and Crafts furniture.
ARLINGTON ROW A row of early 17th-century stone cottages on the R. Colne. Arlington Row was once a wool factory and the wool was hung out to dry on Rack Island opposite. (Not open.)
BIBURY PARISH CHURCH This great Saxon church was altered by Norman and Gothic builders, and restored by Sir Gilbert Scott in the 19th century. Inside, the casts of Saxon gravestones are especially interesting. The churchyard contains the carved chest tombs and headstones of the 17th and 18th century, the rococo motifs now coloured by lichen.

Bicester *Oxon.* 546Fd
CHURCH OF ST EDBURG The church is basically 12th century, but with considerable later enlargement; the west tower is 15th century. There is a medieval parclose screen, a 13th-century font and an early 18th-century monument with the effigy of a man. Other monuments include ones by Joseph Wilton and Sir Richard Westmacott.

Bicton Gardens *Devon* 539Hd
These Italian gardens were originally laid out in 1735. The pinetum has rare trees, which can be viewed from an 18 in. gauge railway.

Biddenden *Kent* 542Ee
A beautiful Kent Weald village, with ancient weavers' cottages and a medieval Cloth Hall, famous for the 'Biddenden Maids'—Siamese twins (1100–34) who are commemorated by a distribution of food to the poor on Easter Day.

Bideford *Devon.* 538Ff
In the days of sail Bideford was a seaport, and in 1700 was importing tobacco from America on a major scale. Charles Kingsley used the town as the setting for *Westward Ho!* The old town has many medieval streets: in Gunstone, stone cannon-balls were made, and Buttgarden was the site of archery butts. The 24-arch bridge spanning the R. Torridge links the main town with East-the-Water: the original wooden bridge (1280) was replaced by a stone one in the 15th century.

Bigby *Humberside* 553Gg
CHURCH OF ALL SAINTS An Early English church, with late 13th-century west tower. There is a sculpture of the Virgin, made *c.* 1300, brasses, and 16th- and 17th-century monuments. One, of 1581, has 22 mourning children.

Biggar *Strathclyde* 562Bd
GLADSTONE COURT MUSEUM In this small folk museum, everyday items dating back a century and a half are displayed in an indoor street of shops re-created from buildings that existed in the district.

Bignor *W. Sussex* 542Ad
A large Roman courtyard villa, comparable with those at North Leigh and Chedworth. The main buildings completely enclose the courtyard and there are also some detached buildings outside. The establishment as we now see it is the end-process of a long period of remodelling and addition.

It has been calculated that the estate of this villa was upwards of 2000 acres of arable land, together with areas of forest, downland-grazing and marsh.

Its end appears to have been marked by desertion and slow decay of roof and walls. There is no hint of a final catastrophe of fire or slaughter. A museum presents models of a villa of Roman times, with objects found during excavations.

Billinge *Merseyside* 552Af
CHURCH OF ST AIDAN Built in 1717 in a mixture of Gothic and Classical styles, with nave arcades of

MOSAIC FLOOR AT BIGNOR ROMAN VILLA

This great villa built around a courtyard contains many fine mosaic floors, some of which have portraits in medallions set in surrounds of elaborate formal patterns. This floor, however, is in a very different style, for here a variety of small figure-groups occur. These show stages in a contest of gladiators and, on the right, the 'retiarius', with net and trident, has been felled by his opponent swordsman. Amusingly enough, however, these are not true gladiators, but Cupids dressed for the parts. The floor is late 4th century.

Doric columns, panelled walls and a west gallery. The embattled parapet is ornamented with urns.

Billingham *Cleveland* 558Df
CHURCH OF ST CUTHBERT An interesting Saxon west tower, and a nave which was altered during the 12th century. The chancel is modern, dating from 1939. There is a 17th-century font cover.

Bilston *Staffs.* 552Cb
CHURCH OF ST LEONARD The church was built in the Classical style by Francis Goodwin in *c.* 1825. The interior is galleried and has contemporary monuments.

Binham Priory *Norfolk* 554Cd
The layout of the abbey building at Binham is reasonably clear, but the main fragment to survive intact is the west end of the monastic church, which is now used as a parish church. With the exception of the west end, the exact date of the church is not known. It was built mainly during the 12th century, but evidence suggests that it remained unfinished for a considerable time. According to documentary evidence the impressive west front was built between 1226 and 1244, and the decoration, with its arcading, small columns and dog-tooth ornament, confirms that this part of the church was built *c.* 1230. The large window with its geometric tracery is unusual in an English church built before 1241, but irregularities in the masonry suggest that this window was added at a late date. Inside the building, the join between the 12th- and 13th-century work is clearly visible in the arcading on either side of the west end. There is a Perpendicular seven-sacrament font, and the stalls have misericords. Ruins of the old priory surround the church.

Binley *W. Midlands* 546Eg
CHURCH OF ST BARTHOLOMEW Built *c.* 1773 by Lord Craven, and said to have been designed by Robert Adam, the church has a western octagonal cupola, Tuscan columns, and a shallow apsed chancel, with plaster decoration.

Binns, The *Lothian* 562Bf
A country mansion dating from 1612–30, the home of the Dalyells, including General Tam Dalyell who, in 1681, raised the Royal Scots Greys Regiment. The façade has two matching towers and a castellated parapet.

Birchington *Kent* 543Gg
POWELL-COTTON MUSEUM A large collection of zoological specimens, including six dioramas showing African and Indian animals in their natural habitats, is displayed in a furnished Regency house. There are also displays devoted to native arts, crafts and domestic objects from Africa, Asia and the Pacific area; together with one of Britain's most important collections of Chinese Imperial porcelain.

In addition, the museum contains a major collection of cannon and firearms.

Birkenhead *Merseyside* 551Jf
PRIORY OF ST JAMES Only the ruins remain of this Benedictine priory, said to have been founded in 1150. The presence of a ferry across the Mersey in the 13th century meant that travellers often stayed at the priory when weather conditions were bad. To ease the financial burden imposed on the monastery, in 1318 Edward II granted the prior the right to build extra accommodation for travellers and charge them for food and lodging. In 1330, Edward III granted the monastery the additional rights of charging ferry tolls.
WILLIAMSON ART GALLERY AND MUSEUM A large

HOUDON *Bust of Anne Robert Jacques Turgot*
One of the great masterpieces of a period when the art of the portrait bust reached a peak of development, this terracotta bust was created in 1778 in one of the most fertile periods of Houdon's life (1741–1828). Turgot is treated naturalistically and the material is handled in a vivid way. Turgot was Minister of Finance under Louis XVI; he tried to initiate sweeping reforms, but failed and was disgraced.
(Birmingham City Museum and Art Gallery)

group of English water-colours including works by Turner, Cotman, de Wint, Cozens, Gainsborough, Wimperis and Burne-Jones are displayed with oil paintings by Wilson Steer and Liverpool artists. The ceramics section includes Liverpool porcelain. In a separate gallery exhibits, including ship models, illustrate Birkenhead's main industry—shipbuilding.

Birkin *N. Yorks.* 558Da
CHURCH OF ST MARY An almost wholly Norman building, with west tower and apse. Fragments of 14th-century glass remain and a monument, also 14th century, of a man holding a heart. The font is dated 1663, and there is an 18th-century pulpit.

Birmingham *W. Midlands* 546Dg
ASTON HALL A fine Jacobean house built in 1618–35 by Sir Thomas Holte, an ardent Royalist, who in 1642 entertained Charles I at Aston when the king was on his way from Shrewsbury to relieve Banbury Castle. Later the house was taken by Parliamentarians and Sir Thomas was heavily fined and imprisoned. The Holtes lived at Aston Hall until 1794; from 1818 to 1848 it was leased by James Watt, son of the famous engineer. The house contains a grand balustraded staircase, fine long gallery and many magnificent plaster friezes and ceilings. Its rooms are arranged with fine furniture and pictures dating from the Jacobean to Victorian periods.

The house also contains examples of needlework by Mary Holte, and local metalwork, pottery, textiles and furniture.
BARBER INSTITUTE The gallery houses the collection of European paintings belonging to the trustees of the Barber Institute of Fine Arts. They date from the early Renaissance to the early 20th

GAINSBOROUGH *The Harvest Waggon*

Thomas Gainsborough was a painter of landscapes by choice and of portraits by necessity; in one of his letters he talks of being 'sick of portraits'. In stature the equal of Wilson for the development of British landscape art of the 18th century, he owed far less to outside influences. True, he took his cue from French and Dutch sources in his earlier work, but he was an inspired and instinctive painter who created his own version of nature. In 1759 Gainsborough moved from

his native Suffolk to Bath, then at the height of its popularity as a fashionable spa, and there he laid aside the clear, dewy freshness of his East Anglian landscapes (which often included a portrait) for a more idealised style which in 'The Harvest Waggon' owes much to Rubens. In colour a range of virtually monochrome tints is brought to life by the introduction of a single note of strong colour in the red shawl.
(The Barber Institute, University of Birmingham)

century and include works by Rubens, Gainsborough and Degas. There are also medieval ivories, Renaissance bronzes and some furniture.

BLAKESLEY HALL (YARDLEY) A timber-framed yeoman's house built in the late 16th century. The hall, kitchen, long gallery and a bedroom, containing its original wall-paintings, are exhibited as period rooms. The rest of the house contains collections devoted to local history, with particular emphasis on traditional rural crafts of the region.

CANNON HILL NATURE CENTRE The centre is at the south-west entrance to Cannon Hill Park, opposite Pebble Mill Road. It has been designed primarily for children, emphasising the appreciation of nature and the importance of conservation. Living plants and animals, and displays, can be seen in the 6-acre grounds.

CATHEDRAL The baroque Church of St Philip, which became a cathedral in 1905, was begun in 1711. Thomas Archer, designer of the Church of St John in Smith Square, London, was the architect. Archer, unlike any of his predecessors since Inigo Jones, had been to Rome, and the style of the building reflects this. Most of the church was finished by 1719, but the west tower was not completed until 1725. It is a rectangular building with a projection at the east end, added *c.* 1883.

CATHEDRAL OF ST CHAD In 1839 Augustus Pugin began the first Roman Catholic cathedral in England since the Reformation. Pugin, a passionate admirer of medieval architecture, became a Roman Catholic convert in 1834, and his ecclesiastical work culminated with the building of St Chad's. The cathedral was dedicated in 1841.

CITY MUSEUM AND ART GALLERY Outstanding collections of European and English paintings and

Pre-Raphaelite drawings. Also sculptures by Rodin and Henry Moore; costume from the 17th century onwards is displayed. English ceramics are well represented, and there is a good collection of silver from the 17th–19th centuries. There are also archaeological and natural history collections.

GEOLOGY DEPARTMENTAL MUSEUM (UNIVERSITY) Minerals, including precious stones, rocks and fossils from all over the world, are displayed in the museum. Diagrams illustrate the geology of the British Isles. (By appointment.)

MUSEUM OF SCIENCE AND INDUSTRY A variety of heavy engineering exhibits—mill engines, gas engines, steam turbines, electrical generators and various machine tools including a wall planing machine used at Boulton and Watt's Soho Foundry in Birmingham in the 19th century—are housed in the engineering hall. The transport section is devoted to cars, motor-cycles and bicycles, and includes the Napier Railton car in which John Cobb reached 394 mph in 1947—a land speed record which remained unbroken until 1964. Also on show are the Liddell Collection of musical boxes; collections of early organs and gramophones; the City Collection of small arms; scientific equipment; and the Charles Thomas Collection of European and Oriental writing implements.

WEOLEY CASTLE Recent excavation has revealed the foundations of a fortified manor house built in 1264 on the site of an earlier building. Various finds from the excavations are housed in a small museum on the site.

Birstall *W. Yorks.* 558Ca

OAKWELL HALL A moated Elizabethan house, the 'Fieldhead' of Charlotte Brontë's novel *Shirley.* In the Civil War it was searched by Parliamentarians after their crushing defeat at nearby Adwalton Moor on June 30, 1643.

Bisham *Berks.* 547Gb
CHURCH OF ALL SAINTS Standing beside the Thames, with a 12th-century tower and all the rest 19th-century restoration, All Saints is notable for the Hoby tombs in the south chapel: two brothers, Sir Philip (*d.* 1558) and Sir Thomas (*d.* 1566) lie side by side, semi-reclining, in alabaster. Sir Edward's widow (*d.* 1605) is commemorated by an alabaster obelisk with four swans at its base. Sir Thomas's widow (*d.* 1609) kneels, children behind her, under a canopy and wearing a gold coronet.

Bishop Auckland *Durham* 558Cf
CHURCH OF ST ANDREW The church has a Saxon cross which has been rebuilt incorporating fragments of the original. It is carved with Christ and other figures, *c.* 800. The late 13th-century church building has a west tower and a two-storey south porch. Inside sits a cross-legged knight, carved from oak *c.* 1340. There is also a brass of a 13th-century monk which attracts considerable interest among brass rubbers.

Bishops Cannings *Wilts.* 540Ef
CHURCH OF ST MARY THE VIRGIN An impressive Early English church, cruciform with a central tower topped by a 15th-century spire. A few Norman traces remain. A rare item is a meditation seat, on which are painted a large hand and Latin inscriptions about sin and death. There is 19th-century stained glass by Wailes in the east window.

Bishop's Cleeve *Glos.* 546Cd
CHURCH OF ST MICHAEL AND ALL ANGELS A magnificent cruciform Norman church, the central tower of which was rebuilt in 1700. The west

BLACKSTONE EDGE ROMAN ROAD

When they were not fighting, the Roman legions acted as pioneers—building forts, bridges and roads. They covered Britain with a network of straight roads; some stretches are in their original condition today while many more form the basis of roads still in use. This stretch runs north-east from Littleborough in Lancashire, over the moors of Blackstone Edge, and is probably the best preserved section of Roman road in Britain. It goes straight up a steep hill but has resisted centuries of erosion by rain, wind, snow and frost. The surface stones are solidly set on a foundation of sand and rubble, with ditches on both sides. The Romans planned and built with such skill that after they left Britain their roads continued as the chief means of communication for centuries.

front is especially impressive, with turrets and a magnificent Norman doorway; and the two-storey south porch is also striking. The Decorated chancel has a good window. There are some interesting monuments with effigies, including a particularly fine one of 1639.

Bishopstone *Heref. & Worcs.* 546Ae
CHURCH OF ST ANDREW An interesting church, building, of which only a blocked south window remains; there are late 13th-century transepts, and a 14th-century timbered south porch. The pulpit is 17th century and there is some 16th- and 17th-century foreign glass, but the east window dates from 1843. One monument is from 1614.

Bishopstone *E. Sussex* 542Cd
CHURCH OF ST ANDREW An interesting church, originally Saxon with Norman additions and later medieval work. It was restored in the mid-19th century. The west tower is Norman. There is a fine 12th-century coffin-lid with three carved loops of rope enclosing a cross, two birds drinking and the symbols of the Lamb and Cross. In the gable above the south door there is a sundial, inscribed 'Eadric', which is believed to be Saxon.

Bishopstone *Wilts.* 540Fe
CHURCH OF ST JOHN THE BAPTIST Standing amid beeches is this large cruciform church with a Perpendicular central tower. The interior is in both Decorated and Perpendicular Gothic styles, with rib-vaulting in the south transept and chancel, carved sedilia and piscinae, and interesting carving. Some traces of Norman work remain. There are several interesting monuments: outside, by the south transept, a small stone cloister of two vaulted bays shelters a decorated tomb chest, perhaps that of the founder of the church. In the north transept is another richly decorated tomb recess, with stone coffin-lids, and in the south transept a mid-19th-century Gothic monument to a former rector by A. W. Pugin. The church is near the R. Ebble, just south of the main road to Salisbury.

Bishop's Stortford *Herts.* 548Ad
CHURCH OF ST MICHAEL A large 15th-century church with a west tower, heightened in 1812. The pulpit dates from 1658; the 15th-century stalls have carved misericords. There are original roofs. The 15th-century rood screen is richly carved, and the 12th-century font is of Purbeck marble. RHODES MEMORIAL MUSEUM Cecil Rhodes (1853–1902) was born here and the house is now a museum devoted to him.

Bishops Waltham *Hants.* 541Hd
The tight-knit little town, mostly with Georgian brick houses, acts as a foil to the enormous grey ruins of the palace of the Bishops of Winchester. It is Norman, remodelled to a large extent in the later Middle Ages.

Blackburn *Lancs.* 557Ja
MUSEUM AND ART GALLERY More than 1200 Japanese prints are contained in the art gallery, together with a collection of English watercolours, paintings and ceramics. The museum features English, Greek and Roman coins, medieval manuscripts and early printed books, primitive weapons, domestic items and costumes from African tribes, and a small archaeological collection containing Egyptian material.

Blackbury Castle *Devon* 540Bc
This Iron Age single bank-and-ditch fort has an oval interior of 4 acres. The entrance on the south side has a large protective structure. Excavation has shown that the bank was of simple construction without stone or timber revetment, except for a

little wattling near the entrance. Both inner and outer openings in the entrance defences had timber gates with a gravelled path between them. The ditch was originally some 8 ft deep, with a wide, V-shaped profile.

Blackhammer *Rousay, Orkney*   *569Hg*
A Neolithic 'stalled cairn'. The chamber is 42½ ft long by 6 ft wide and is divided by standing slabs into 14 stalls, into one of which the passage leads. The chamber walls, of stone, are very thick. The upper part of the cairn and the roof of the chamber have been removed.

Blackpool *Lancs.*   *557Hb*
GRUNDY ART GALLERY Paintings and drawings by 19th- and 20th-century British artists are exhibited.

Blackstone Edge *Gtr. Man.–W. Yorks.*   *552Cg*
This is perhaps the most remarkable piece of paved Roman road in the country. It formed a part of the road from the fort at Manchester (Mancunium) to that at Ilkley (Olicana) and, as it climbs on to the crest of the Pennines, the paved way, some 16 ft wide, is held in position in the underlying peaty deposits by deeply-set kerbs. The oddest feature is the central paved channel in the roadway. The most likely explanation is that it had a turfy filling which gave a good foothold to horses.

Blair Castle *Tayside*   *566Bc*
The ancient home of the Dukes of Atholl, Blair Castle dates from the 13th century, although its appearance has changed considerably over the years. In 1269 the Crusader Earl of Atholl complained that during his absence John Comyn had started to build a castle at Blair. The foundations of the present Cumming's Tower probably date from this time, although the tower itself has been

rebuilt several times. In 1530 the 3rd Earl built the Hall and the vaulted rooms beneath it.

In 1652 the castle was captured by Cromwell's troops and held for eight years until the Restoration. More violence was in store for the castle in the 18th century—although Queen Anne had made the 2nd Marquess Duke in 1703, by 1745 the only member of the family to support the Hanoverians was the 2nd Duke, Lord James Murray. The Jacobites, led by Bonnie Prince Charlie and the Duke's attainted elder brother, marched on the castle and occupied it, and in the following year the Duke's younger brother laid siege to the castle—the last castle in the British Isles to be besieged.

Because of the extensive damage caused by the Jacobite attack, the 2nd Duke decided to remodel the castle completely in the Classical manner—between 1747–58 the battlemented turrets and stepped gables were removed and sash windows put in. But in 1868, when the Gothic style had once more become fashionable, the 7th Duke employed David Bryce to restore the castle to its former appearance.

The interior of the castle still retains its Classical scheme of decoration. The rooms contain some fine furniture—including Chippendale and Sheraton cabinets displaying a collection of Sèvres porcelain—paintings, among them works by Lely, Hoppner and Zoffany, and many items of embroidery, lace and jewellery. Collections of weapons and armour reflect the history of the castle and the military campaigns of successive Dukes.

Blaise Hamlet *Avon*   *540Cg*
An eccentric disposition of ten cottages of differing design, built in 1809 by John Nash for John

THE TAPESTRY ROOM AT BLAIR CASTLE

The tapestries in this room were bought when much of Charles I's furniture was sold and the bed, belonging to the 1st Duke of Atholl, was moved here in 1709. From 90 to 100 yds of silk costing from 16 to 21 shillings a yard were needed to cover such a bed—and the crimson silk used here would have cost more because the dye was expensive. The bed was probably made around 1690, when tall beds surmounted by vases of ostrich feathers were the height of fashion, in keeping with the baroque taste.

BLENHEIM PALACE

BLENHEIM PALACE *One of the largest mansions in England, the masterpiece of Sir John Vanbrugh, and the gift of the nation to a victorious soldier. Queen Anne rewarded John Churchill, 1st Duke of Marlborough, for his decisive defeat of Louis XIV (1704) with Blenheim Palace; but although a huge sum of money was allocated by Parliament for its erection, the Marlboroughs had to find tens of thousands of pounds to pay for the completion. The headstrong duchess Sarah lost the queen's favour and quarrelled with Vanbrugh, who left before Blenheim was completed. The greatest artists and craftsmen of the day worked on the interior decoration: the magnificent ceiling and wall-paintings in the great hall, which leads to the saloon and the state apartments, are by Sir James Thornhill and Louis Laguerre; the high relief carvings are by Grinling Gibbons, and Michael Rysbrack sculpted the duke's monument in the chapel. The gardens extend over several acres and were laid out by Henry Wise and Capability Brown, who also created the large lake. In 1874 Sir Winston Churchill was born at Blenheim.*

BRUSSELS TAPESTRY *The Brussels weaving industry still produced many tapestries in the 18th century although it had declined considerably by then. Jos de Vos, a weaver in Brussels from 1703 onwards, wove a set of tapestries depicting the 'Victories of the Duke of Marlborough'. The figure of the duke is taken from a panel showing him receiving the surrender of Marshal Tallard after the Battle of Blenheim.*

Harford, to house pensioners of the Blaise estate.
BLAISE CASTLE HOUSE A fine house built in the late 18th century and now used as a museum of social history. A dairy designed by John Nash and an 18th-century corn mill stand in the grounds.

Blakeney *Norfolk*   554Cd
A small picturesque port, well known to yachtsmen, wildfowlers and naturalists, built mainly of flint. The guildhall has a brick vaulted undercroft with stone pillars, probably 15th century. At the west end of the quay is the Red House, a pleasant Georgian building, low, with a three-bay pediment. A little to the north of the church, a house called the Friary incorporates parts of a Carmelite friary of *c.* 1296. To the east of this there is a windmill of brick and flint.
CHURCH OF ST NICHOLAS Outside the town and overlooking the sea, the church has two towers, the Perpendicular west tower and a small tower at the north-east angle of the chancel which is still used as a beacon for Blakeney Harbour. There is a Perpendicular nave, an Early English vaulted chancel with a room above it, and an octagonal font with carved figures.

Blanchland *Northld.*   558Bg
CHURCH OF ST MARY THE VIRGIN The abbey was founded in 1165 for the Premonstratensians, and what remains of their church is the north transept

and chancel. There is a tower at the north end of the transept.

Blandford Forum *Dorset*   540Ed
A fine Georgian market town on the R. Stour. There are few antiquities, for the town has a history of destruction by fire. The most disastrous was probably that of 1731 which destroyed most of the town; only 40 or 50 houses, including the almshouses and the Old House, escaped out of a total of more than 500. This was the making of two local men, John and William Bastard, brothers who played a major part in rebuilding the town.
CHURCH OF SS PETER AND PAUL One of the finest Georgian provincial churches, finished in 1748 to John Bastard's design. It is faced with ashlar and has a fine square tower crowned with a cupola. Inside are Ionic nave columns, a font, box-pews, a western gallery and canopied mayor's seat of the period. In the early 19th century obtrusive galleries were added in the nave but these were removed in 1970. In 1895 a chancel was built. The sanctuary apse was raised on rollers and moved away from the nave to new foundations; the chancel was then built between the sanctuary and nave. The 1794 organ, moved when the chancel was built, has now been restored to its original position in the West Gallery.
TOWN HALL A fine Georgian building designed by

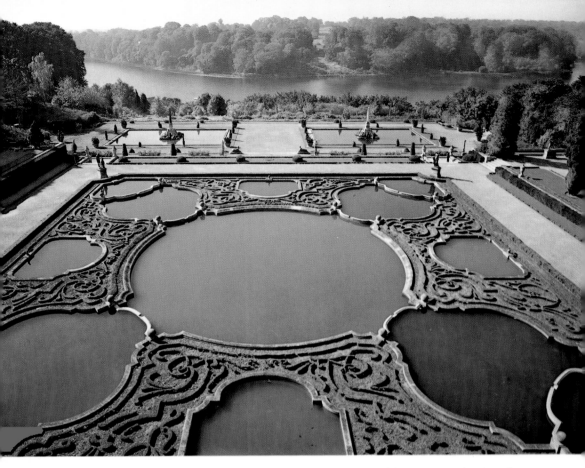

BLENHEIM PALACE GARDENS *The ornamental garden below one of the terraces at Blenheim Palace is the work (1925–32) of the French garden designer Achille Duchêne, trained in the formal tradition of André Le Nôtre. The 9th Duke of Marlborough commissioned Duchêne to create the formal garden with its parterres, ponds and fountains—re-creating the original concept of the garden by Henry Wise, which was destroyed by Capability Brown in his quest for the 'natural garden'.*

Under Brown's direction the grounds were transformed into a charming landscape of trees, woods and grass. Brown also produced one of Blenheim's finest features, by skilfully damming the R. Glyme and converting the marshy ground into the present fine lake beyond Duchêne's garden.

---

the Bastard brothers. Inside is a memorial to Alfred Stevens, born in Blandford in 1818. He was an architect, painter, sculptor and designer, but is best remembered for his magnificent monument to the Duke of Wellington in St Paul's Cathedral, commissioned in 1862.

Blantyre *Strathclyde* 561Je
The Shuttle Row, the former tenement building where the missionary and explorer David Livingstone (1813–73) was born, has been preserved as a memorial to him with a museum containing his relics.

Bledington *Glos.* 546Ed
CHURCH OF ST LEONARD There is Norman and later work in this church, and Perpendicular windows, some with brilliant contemporary glass. The nave gable still retains its 12th-century bell-cote, and the south arcade is Transitional Norman.

Bledlow *Bucks.* 547Gc
CHURCH OF THE HOLY TRINITY A church of Norman foundation on a steep slope in the Chilterns. The interior has nave arcades of *c.* 1200 with carved capitals, and a circular Norman font carved with stiff-leaved foliage. Remains of medieval wall-painting include Adam and Eve, and St Christopher; the south door is of the 13th–14th centuries. In the south aisle are a reredos and

large candlestick with dummy flame, both 18th century. There is one brass of interest, to the vicar William Hern (d. 1525).

Blenheim Palace *Oxon.* 546Ed
The nation's gift to the 1st Duke of Marlborough, Blenheim was designed by Sir John Vanbrugh and built in the years 1705–22. The mansion is in baroque style, with two storeys, and is arranged round three sides of an immense courtyard. The large central building has four turrets and a portico supported by Corinthian columns. Doric columns connect the main building to pavilions on either side. In the state apartments are fine collections of portraits, china, tapestries and furniture. On the ground floor is the small bedroom, with personal relics, where Sir Winston Churchill was born on November 30, 1874.

Henry Wise, gardener to Queen Anne, was the man responsible for the garden designs at Blenheim Palace early in the 18th century. The style was the elaborate formal manner of Le Nôtre, examples of which can be seen in France at Vaux-le-Vicomte and Versailles. The ornamental garden close to the palace consisted of parterres. These were elaborately designed scroll-like patterns with dwarf hedges of clipped box, outlining patterns filled in with brightly-coloured gravels and closely mown turf. Parts of the patterns were planted with

91

flowers, and the whole was punctuated with pyramids and cones of yew. Statuary and fountains were interspersed throughout the design. The kitchen garden was simpler; it was surrounded by thick walls against which fruit trees were trained. Shortly after Wise had finished the ornamental garden, the vogue in garden design changed completely. Formality in the French style was despised, and the natural park-like landscape became fashionable. Except for the kitchen garden, which still exists, Wise's gardens were obliterated by Capability Brown. The grounds, almost up to the palace, were transformed into an idealised scene of trees, woods and grass. One of Blenheim's most singular features was achieved by the same designer. By damming up the little R. Glyme, Brown turned the marshy ground through which it trickled into the present fine lake, spanned by Vanbrugh's triumphant causeway.

Bletchingley *Surrey*   *542Bf*
The village street, curving and falling towards the east, is one of the most pleasant in Surrey. The best houses, however, are a mile away to the north-west, at Pendell, all of red brick: the Court is Jacobean, the House is dated 1636, and is a remarkably restrained design for that date, and the Manor is 15th century with a Georgian façade.
CHURCH OF ST MARY THE VIRGIN Built by the De Clare family *c.* 1090 on a Saxon site, the church retains Norman arches in the tower and sanctuary. Arcades were added in the 13th and 15th centuries, and the church was restored in the 19th century. Inside there are a number of brasses and monuments, in particular one by Richard Crutcher, *c.* 1707, with standing figures in contemporary dress. The pulpit is 17th century.

Blewbury *Oxon.*   *546Fb*
CHURCH OF ST MICHAEL Originally a 12th-century building on the cruciform plan, there were later changes, including the Perpendicular west tower. There is a good parclose screen to the south chapel, and a door to the rood loft; also a 15th-century Perpendicular font and 19th-century glass in the east window. The brasses are of interest, and date from 1496.

Blickling Hall *Norfolk*   *554Cc*
A fine red-brick Jacobean house built for Sir Henry Hobart by Robert Lyminge in 1616–24. Lyminge's building comprised a large central block with long wings on either side terminated by corner turrets with lead caps like those at Osterley Park, Greater London. During the second half of the 18th century the open ends of the court, left by the two wings, were filled in by Thomas Ivory and his family of Norwich. The state rooms contain collections of fine furniture, pictures and tapestries. The grounds include an extensive formal garden, a crescent-shaped lake, and an orangery and temple built by the Ivorys.

Blisland *Cornwall*   *538Dc*
CHURCH OF SS PROTUS AND HYACINTH A church near the village green, with transepts and a north tower. The nave is Norman; the side chapels are early 15th century. Inside is a Norman font, and there are wagon-roofs. The 19th-century stained glass and painted rood screen are by F. C. Eden.

Blists Hill *Shropshire*   *552Ab*
The Blists Hill Open Air Museum is an industrial museum in a woodland setting. It includes the Hay Inclined Plane which moved boats from the Shropshire Canal to the Severn river 200 ft below. A Victorian industrial village of the 1890s is being re-created. It illustrates life at a time when Blists

Hill was a thriving coal mining, iron smelting and brick and tile-making community. The three blast furnaces and the brick and tile works have been restored. Around them is a network of plateways on which freight wagons ran. Lighter industries – candlemaking, shoemaking, joinery, paper-making – are still carried on. Among the reconstructed shops – some brought here from other industrial towns, but all with original equipment – are the establishments of a plumber, a blacksmith and a locksmith, a chemist's shop-*cum*-dentist's surgery, a butcher's shop and slaughterhouse, and a sweet-shop.

BLICKLING HALL

Sir Henry Hobart built Blickling Hall between 1616 and 1628. Although contemporary with Inigo Jones's Palladian Queen's House at Greenwich and Banqueting House in Whitehall, Blickling is very different. Its architect was Robert Lyminge, who had earlier worked at Hatfield House for the Cecils. Lyminge produced a turreted red-brick house in Jacobean style. This was altered in the late 18th century by Thomas Ivory and his family, architects from Norwich. Inside is a fine staircase of the 17th century, altered by the Ivorys, with much carved decorative detail and figures as at Hatfield. Several rooms have ornate chimney-pieces and plaster ceilings, but of those belonging to the original house the most impressive room is the gallery, nearly 130 ft long, lined with windows along one side, and with a decorated plaster ceiling.

Blithfield *Staffs.*   *552Cc*
CHURCH OF ST LEONARD The church adjoins the picturesque Blithfield Hall, and dates from the 13th century, with Victorian restoration work by Pugin. There is some interesting medieval glass, and many monuments.

Bloxham *Oxon.*   *546Ee*
CHURCH OF OUR LADY From the pinnacled 14th-century tower of this magnificent large church rises an octagonally based spire. There is some Norman work, and a monument of 1725 by Andrew Carpenter. The church's restoration in 1866 was carried out by George Edmund Street, who also restored Christ Church Cathedral in

Dublin, and designed the London Law Courts. The east window is by William Morris and Edward Burne-Jones.

Blundeston *Suffolk*   *548Fg*
CHURCH OF ST MARY THE VIRGIN A Norman round west tower, and a 14th-century nave; the chancel was rebuilt in the 19th century. The south and north doorways are basically Norman. Inside are the remains of rood screens and benches.

Blyborough *Lincs.*   *553Gf*
CHURCH OF ST ALKMUND An Early English church, with a 13th-century chancel arch and part of a 15th-century Flemish rood. Later work includes the 18th-century tower. There is a reclining effigy of a priest (*d.* 1434).

Blythburgh *Suffolk*   *548Ef*
CHURCH OF THE HOLY TRINITY An interesting church with tall west tower, dating mainly from the later 15th century. There is a contemporary font, carved stalls, and benches with the Seven Deadly Sins instead of poppy-heads.

Boarstall Tower *Bucks.*   *546Fd*
The stone gate-house of a former fortified house, built in the 14th century and altered in the 16th and 17th centuries. It is almost surrounded by a moat. (Interior not open to the public.)

Bodiam Castle *E. Sussex*   *542De*
Architecturally one of the most satisfying castles, and built during the 14th century. It has a quadrangular plan with the main entrance in the centre of the north side. Although the regular form of the castle follows the development which had already taken place in the 13th century at Harlech and Beaumaris, Bodiam is built on a smaller scale and is intended to combine a high degree of comfort with defence. Before this time there was a tendency for living accommodation to grow up haphazardly inside a castle, but at Bodiam the residential quarters, including the hall and chapel which are still traceable, were carefully planned and built at the same time as the castle itself. The original iron-plated oak portcullis remains.

Bodmin *Cornwall*   *538Dc*
County town of Cornwall. Its features include the Turret Clock which marks the site of the ancient Butter Market; the 144 ft obelisk to Lt.-Gen. Sir Walter Raleigh Gilbert (1785–1853), whose ancestors were the Elizabethan sailors, Raleigh and Gilbert; the assize hall and shire house. In the church of St Petroc is St Petroc's Casket (*c.* 1170), of Byzantine origin, and the town's four silver gilt maces may be seen on application to the town clerk.
CHURCH OF ST PETROC Mainly 15th century; probably the largest parish church in the county. The church tower has Norman masonry at the base. The font is Norman. There is a good monument, with recumbent effigy, to Prior Vyvyan (*d.* 1533). In the south wall is the ivory reliquary of St Petroc.

Bodnant Garden *Gwynedd*   *550Fe*
Bodnant, high above the R. Conwy, looks out over a valley towards Snowdonia. The magnificent gardens of Bodnant, residence of Lord Aberconway, consist of the upper terrace gardens, and the Dell with a pinetum and a wild garden. The upper garden in front of the house has five formal terrace gardens and lawns with fine specimen trees. The high walls and stairways of the terraces, completed in 1914, are planted with huge banks of hydrangeas, camellias and other ornamental trees and shrubs. Among the terraces are two formal lily pools, with numerous fine hybrid

lilies, and the rose terraces whose beds are edged with saxifraga and dwarf campanulas. There are numerous and rare varieties of rhododendrons, and large plantings of azaleas and magnolias. The pinetum contains huge specimens of giant fir,

BODIAM CASTLE

The neighbouring towns of Rye and Winchelsea had been attacked and burnt by the French when Richard II granted his supporter Sir Edward Dalyngrydge a licence to build the castle in 1385. But it was never attacked or besieged and, as a result, survives practically unchanged. Bodiam is an interesting monument to the period when considerations of comfort were beginning to weigh equally with those of defence in castle planning, much of the carefully planned living accommodation being still traceable within the walls.

Douglas fir and redwood trees planted over the past 100 years. There is a large rock garden and another rock garden devoted to dwarf alpine rhododendrons. Paths that wind through the wild garden lead to flowering shrub borders and an avenue of pleached laburnums. (See p. 94.)

Bodrhyddan Hall *Clwyd.*   *551Ge*
This has been connected with the Conwy family since the 1280's when Edward I built the nearby Rhuddlan Castle. The name was probably once 'Bodrhuddlan' meaning 'House of Rhuddlan'. The first house was a wooden one, which was replaced in the 15th century by a grey stone version. Most of the south front is of the 17th century, and the big dining-room is 18th century. The west front driveway and major rebuilding were done in 1874. The symbol of the Saracen's Head, dating back to the Crusades, appears on the former entrance gates. There is a collection of arms and armour in the Hall itself. In 1284 the charter of Rhuddlan was signed by Edward I giving it the status of a borough and the protection of a garrison town. There are portraits by de Troy of the Duc d'Anjou and the Duc de Berry, 1696; Reynolds's portrait of Dr Shipley; and Hogarth's of Mrs Shipley. The St Mary's Well building is attributed to Inigo Jones and was possibly used to celebrate clandestine marriages. The Hall managed to be loyal to both Cromwell and the king during the 17th century, and there are several gifts from both Charles I and Charles II. The porcelain collection is mainly 18th-century Chinese with some later pieces. There is also an ornamental garden.

Bodsey House *Cambs.*   *547Jg*
A moated house, once a hermitage attached to Ramsey Abbey which was dissolved in 1539. The house was later much altered. It has a 17th-century chimney-stack, and a coved and panelled ceiling in one of its rooms. (By appointment.)

Bodwrdda *Gwynedd*   *550Dc*
This fine-looking house, dated 1621, is notable for
being the earliest large brick house in a county
where the traditional building material is stone. In
fact only the wings are of brick; the main block is
of stone incorporating medieval fabric. Three
small medieval windows light the rear wall.
(Exterior viewing only.)

Bokerly Dyke *Dorset*   *540Ed*
This fine late Roman and Dark Age linear earthwork is crossed close to its centre by the modern
Salisbury–Blandford road and runs for some miles
each way. Recent excavations suggest that the first
part was constructed during troubles in the 4th
century. In AD 367, when Pictish raiders threatened
the south country, the check-point opening was
sealed and the more westerly arm of the northern
half was added. Finally, the north-eastern wing of
this northern part was added early in the 5th
century, probably because of a threat by Saxon
raiders from the north-east. The bank still stands to
a good height, particularly to the south of the main
road, and is fronted by a now partly silted ditch.

Bolam *Northld.*   *562Fa*
CHURCH OF ST ANDREW A Norman church with a
tall Saxon tower at the west. There is a mutilated
stone effigy of a cross-legged knight.

Boldre *Hants.*   *541Gc*
CHURCH OF ST JOHN THE BAPTIST Originally
Norman, the church stands in an unusually
isolated position on the edge of the New Forest.
Later additions include the late 14th-century
tower, which has a late 17th-century top stage.
The chancel was rebuilt in the 19th century. A
monument of the mid-17th century shows a man's
head and shoulders. The architect R. Norman
Shaw built Boldre Grange, and shortly afterwards
designed the pulpit of 1876.

Bolsover Castle *Derbys.*   *552Ee*
A castle has stood here since the reign of William
the Conqueror, but nothing of the Norman
building remains. The present castle was begun
during the reign of James I by Sir Charles Cavendish; the keep, with corner turrets, pinnacles and
battlements, dates from *c.* 1615. In *c.* 1660, Sir
Charles's son, the 1st Duke of Newcastle, added a
fine range of terrace buildings in Classical style.

Bolton *Greater Manchester*   *552Ag*
Bolton, once known as Bolton-le-Moors, was
formerly a wool manufacturing town, but by the
18th century it was one of the leading cotton
centres. Here the cotton industry was revolutionised when Richard Arkwright invented his
Water Frame in 1768, and Samuel Crompton
perfected his Spinning Mule in 1779. The black-
and-white house where Crompton worked near
the town, Hall-i'-th'-Wood, is now preserved as
a museum.
MUSEUM AND ART GALLERY The museum's
natural history collection specialises in British
birds, and a local history collection includes
material relating to cotton spinning. There is also a
collection of Egyptology. The art gallery displays
17th-century Italian paintings and 18th- and 19th-
century English water-colours.
TEXTILE MACHINERY MUSEUM A collection of
historic textile machinery, including Hargreaves'
Spinning Jenny, Arkwright's Water Frame and
Crompton's Mule, three inventions which
revolutionised the Lancashire cotton industry in
the late 1700's.

Bolton *Cumbria*   *557Jf*
CHURCH OF ALL SAINTS Two jousting knights are
carved in crude relief over the north doorway of
this Norman church, and both north and south
doorways have carved Norman capitals. The west
turret (with two bells) was built in 1693, and the
chancel screen of open tracery is mid-19th century.

THE DELL AT BODNANT

*An exotic portion of the Andes, Himalayas and China
beside a small stream below the hills of Snowdonia.
A great mass of trees, camellias, magnolias, azaleas
have been planted beside paths along the sides of the
valley. Perhaps the most magnificent of all are the
rhododendrons of the 'Grande' series, brought from
Asia. Primitive plants unchanged for nearly 50 million
years, they flourish outside Asia only in the wetter,
sheltered areas of south-west Scotland and Ireland,
north-west England and Wales, and California.*

Bolton Abbey *N. Yorks.* 558Bb
Charming ruins in a delightful setting of water-falls, woods and meadows; the remains give evidence of the mid-12th century, when the priory was founded by Augustinian canons. The nave, repaired and lengthened, is now the parish church.

Bonawe *Strathclyde* 565Ha
LORN FURNACE A complete early industrial lay-out, with stone blast-furnace, sheds for storage of iron ore and charcoal, and housing for workers and manager. Built in 1753 for iron smelting with local birch charcoal.

Bo'ness (Borrowstounness) *Central* 562Af
A stone slab at the eastern outskirts of the town marks the eastern end of the Roman Antonine Wall.
KINNEIL HOUSE In a cottage on this estate lived James Watt (1736–1819), and there in 1764 he developed the condensing steam engine. The house contains 16th- and 17th-century wall and ceiling paintings. In the Parable Room are six cartoons depicting the story of the Good Samaritan.

Boothby Pagnell *Lincs.* 553Gc
MANOR HOUSE A small Norman manor house, built 1178 in the grounds of Boothby Hall; it had a moat for defence and substantial construction—in places the walls are as much as 4 ft thick—disguised by ashlar stone dressings. Inside is a vaulted ground floor with hall and solar. (By appointment.)

Boroughbridge *N. Yorks.* 558Dc
ALDBOROUGH ROMAN SITE MUSEUM Pottery, coins, inscriptions and bronze, iron, bone and glass objects found in or near the Roman town of Isurium Brigantum are displayed.
DEVIL'S ARROWS These are three great standing stones of millstone grit in a straight line, spaced 200 ft and 370 ft apart. They stand between 18 and 22 ft high and were brought from a quarry at Knares-borough. Their irregular surfaces are due to wea-thering. They were erected during the Bronze Age.

Borthwick Castle *Lothian* 562Ce
On June 6, 1567, three weeks after their marriage, Mary, Queen of Scots and her third husband, Bothwell, came to stay here. But a few days later they were forced to flee; Bothwell left for Dunbar and a day later Mary made her escape disguised as a page. The massive castle, with machicolated towers, dates from 1430 and has a great hall containing a huge fire-place and fine vaulting.

Borwick Hall *Lancs.* 557Jc
An Elizabethan manor house, set in fine gardens and unaltered in form since it was built around portions of an earlier house in 1595.

Bosbury *Heref. & Worcs.* 546Be
CHURCH OF THE HOLY TRINITY A large, late Norman church (c. 1200) in red sandstone, with a font of the same date. The detached tower is 13th century and the Morton Chapel was added in the 16th century. Among the monuments are two Elizabethan ones in the chancel, one of 1573 by John Guldo of Hereford, another of 1578 with recumbent effigies.

Boscobel House *Shropshire* 552Bb
Charles II fled here after the Battle of Worcester in 1651. Because of Parliamentary troops it was too dangerous for him to remain in the house by day, so he hid in an oak tree. The present Royal Oak on the spot is said to have been raised from an acorn of the original tree. The house, built early in the 17th century as a hunting lodge, was altered at a later period.

Bosham *W. Sussex* 541Jd
CHURCH OF THE HOLY TRINITY In a fishing village on Chichester Harbour, the church is of Saxon origin. It features on the Bayeux Tapestry, as it was from Bosham that Harold sailed to Normandy. There is a magnificent tall Saxon chancel arch, and a pre-Conquest tower with later spire. Some 13th-century additions include the five-lancet east window. The font is octagonal, and there are some fragments of medieval stained glass. In the chancel is a recessed 13th-century tomb with the recum-bent figure of a young girl.

Bossall *N. Yorks.* 558Ec
CHURCH OF ST BOTOLPH Late Norman cruciform church, with a central tower. The crossing arches inside are also late Norman, but there are other additions up to the Perpendicular period. The font, with 18th-century cover, may be Norman. There is a brass of 1454, and a 17th-century monument.

Boston *Lincs.* 553Jd
Shodfriars Hall in South Street is a 19th-century copy of a 16th-century timber-framed house with double overhang and two gables. From the custom house (1725) there is a picturesque view of warehouses and old houses running down to the tidal R. Witham. The stone shell of Black-friars in Spain Lane, a Dominican friary built in the 13th century, has been restored and is now a small theatre and arts centre. On the Skirbeck Road stand the ruins of the Hussey Tower, with a stair-turret and some ribbed-vaulting on the ground floor.
The Pilgrim Fathers sailed from here in the *Mayflower* in 1620 and Boston, Massachusetts, was given the name by emigrants from the town.
CHURCH OF ST BOTOLPH In what was formerly a notable port, St Botolph's is one of the largest parish churches in England, with one of the most famous towers, Boston Stump. The Stump (it has an octagonal lantern) is 272 ft high, a landmark for travellers and sailors. The church was begun c. 1310 and building continued through the Dec-orated and Perpendicular periods. The style is sumptuous and unified. The stalls have good misericords, and among the brasses and monu-ments is a large slab to a Hanseatic merchant who died in 1340. There is a 17th-century pulpit, an 18th-century wrought-iron communion rail, Victorian stained glass, and a font by Pugin.
FYDELL HOUSE The best house in Boston, built 1726, with six bays and giant pilasters, a grand entablature and balustraded parapet, and a tall doorway with Doric columns. Internally, there is an elegant staircase, much rococo decoration, some first-rate plasterwork and, in a ground-floor room, an unusually decorative chimney-piece.
GUILDHALL Built 1450, a symbol of medieval Boston's former prosperity; it has a splendid five-light window, much Georgian brickwork and a good example of 15th-century linenfold in the old council chamber. Several Pilgrim Fathers were imprisoned there.

Bothal *Northld.* 563Gb
CHURCH OF ST ANDREW A 13th- and 14th-century church. Many fragments of medieval stained glass remain, and there are alabaster effigies of the 16th century.

Bottesford *Leics.* 552Fd
CHURCH OF ST MARY A large church with a handsome west tower and spire; the building dates from the 13th century, with many later alterations. The font is 16th century and the pulpit 17th century. There are many impressive and impor-tant monuments from as early as the 13th century.

The best known are those to the eight Earls of Rutland in the chancel, by Richard Parker, Gerard Johnson, Nicholas Johnson, and to the 7th and 8th Earls by Grinling Gibbons (c. 1684).

Bottesford *Humberside*   *553Gg*
CHURCH OF ST PETER'S CHAINS The dedication itself is one of the most interesting features of this church; others include the many lancet windows and the small bronze 15th-century Sanctus Bell, which was discovered in a wall during the 19th-century restoration. The church is cruciform.

Bottisham *Cambs.*   *548Af*
CHURCH OF THE HOLY TRINITY Impressive church of the 13th and 14th centuries, with a west tower and porch. Inside, a clerestory, stone rood screen, and wood parclose screens. There are several interesting monuments, including two seated figures of c. 1740, and one with an urn and *putti*—cherub-like children—by John Bacon.

Boughton Monchelsea Place *Kent*   *542Df*
A castellated Elizabethan manor house, set in a deer park; it dates from 1570. Though altered in Regency times, it still has a Tudor kitchen and tithe barn. The house contains tapestries dating from 1680 and manor records going back to 1570.

Bourne *Lincs.*   *553Hc*
Home town of Hereward the Wake, last of the Saxon nobles to resist William the Conqueror. His Saxon manor house stood on the site of Bourne Castle, now marked by mounds and part of a moat. The town has a number of good Georgian houses, including the Maltings and the Manor House. The Tudor cottages in South Street, dated 1636, are single-storey structures in brick with stone gable-ends and wooden mullioned windows. Near by is the Free School, of 1768, with six-light windows. The Roman Car Dyke, the earliest canal to attempt to drain the Fens, flows to the east of the town. At Cawthorpe, a mile and a half away, there are two good Georgian houses: Cawthorpe House and Cawthorpe Hall.
CHURCH OF SS PETER AND PAUL Originally the church of the former Augustinian priory, the present building contains only the nave of the abbey church. The nave arcades are 12th century; the rest largely Early English.
RED HALL A mansion of c. 1620, with three-gabled bays, a two-storey porch with Tuscan columns, mullioned windows and the original staircase.

Bournemouth *Dorset*   *540Fc*
RUSSELL-COTES MUSEUM AND ART GALLERY Collections of 16th- and 17th-century furniture, paintings and ceramics; Victoriana, armour, model ships, butterflies and moths, and local archaeology are displayed, and items from New Zealand, Africa and the Pacific.
Items associated with Napoleon and with Sir Henry Irving (1838–1905), the first actor to be knighted, are on view. The gallery contains collections of oil paintings, water-colours and drawings, mainly from the Victorian period; works by local artists; the Russell-Cotes Oriental Collection representing China, Japan, Burma, Thailand, Tibet and India; South American pottery.

Bourton-on-the-Hill *Glos.*   *546De*
CHURCH OF ST LAWRENCE Of Norman origin with a west tower, St Lawrence's has Norman cylindrical pillars on the south side of the nave and a Perpendicular font.

Bowhill *Borders*   *562Cc*
Ancient seat of the Scotts of Buccleuch, the present house is mainly early 19th century with a collection of paintings by Reynolds, Guardi, Canaletto and Claude Lorraine, and French furniture and *objets d'art*. There are relics of the Duke of Monmouth and Sir Walter Scott.

Bow Hill *W. Sussex*   *541Jd*
On this site are Bronze Age barrows, Neolithic flint mines and lynchets revealing the pattern of prehistoric cultivation.

Bowden Hill and Cockleroy *Lothian*   *562Af*
These two Iron Age forts crown two hills. Each was defended by a single strongly-built stone wall, which enclosed the summit, and each was so disposed that the steeper scarp-slopes aided the defence scheme. It is thought that they were built during the same period. The Bowden Hill fortwall has been robbed in places.

Bowness *Cumbria*   *557Hd*
CHURCH OF ST MARTIN The present church was built in the 15th century, and later restored, but the main interest here is in the medieval stained glass in the east window, which came from one of the neighbouring abbeys such as Furness or Cartmel. There is a carved mural monument (without a figure) by John Flaxman, the neo-Classical sculptor (1755–1826), who prided himself on making monumental sculpture in England more Christian.

Boxford *Suffolk*   *548Ce*
CHURCH OF ST MARY The church has a 14th-century wooden north porch, which is vaulted, and a Perpendicular south porch, with decoration. The west tower has a small spire. Inside is a 17th-century font cover with doors, an 18th-century pulpit and some medieval mural paintings.

Boxgrove *W. Sussex*   *541Jd*
CHURCH OF SS MARY AND BLAISE Norman remains of Boxgrove Priory, founded c. 1108. The important Early English chancel is of the second quarter of the 13th century. The clerestory has Purbeck marble shafts and rich arcades. Of the monuments the most important is the de la Warr Chantry of c. 1532, with a mixture of Gothic and early Renaissance motifs.

Boxley *Kent*   *542Df*
A small village, overshadowed by a green sweep of the North Downs; it consists of a handful of cottages, with some grander houses, each in a luxuriant garden. White weather-boarding and red brick are the characteristic materials here, with a medieval stone house, and a 12th-century tithe barn.

Boxted *Suffolk*   *548Ce*
CHURCH OF THE HOLY TRINITY A flint and stone church, with a hammerbeam roof in the chancel. There is a large pew on the north side for the Poley family and their household. A monument, c. 1587, has wooden effigies, and another, of the 17th–18th centuries with standing figures of husband and wife, might be by John Bushnell.

Boynton *Humberside*   *559Gc*
CHURCH OF ST ANDREW The present church dates from 1768, when it was rebuilt by John Carr of York, who retained the 15th-century tower. In the Strickland Chapel are a number of 17th-century and later monuments.

Boynton Hall *Humberside*   *559Gc*
A Tudor manor house, now divided into flats, built by William Strickland in 1550, with Georgian alterations by Lord Burlington and John Carr.

Bradfield *Berks.*   *546Fb*
A village with a boys' public school. The school is built around an 18th-century manor house, and

has an open-air Greek theatre. The Church of St Andrew, in Transitional style, was largely rebuilt by Sir Gilbert Scott in 1847.

Bradfield St George *Suffolk* 548Cf
YEOMAN'S ACRE A yeoman's dwelling of pre-Tudor origin. (By appointment.)

Bradford *W. Yorks.* 558Cb
BOLLING HALL The manor of Bolling is mentioned in Domesday Book. It was owned by the Bolling family and their descendants from *c.* 1165 until the end of the Civil War when, having supported the Royalist cause, they were forced to dispose of their property. The earliest part of the present house is the south-east defensive tower which dates from the 15th century. Additions were made in the following centuries, and in 1779–80 the north wing was remodelled by John Carr of York in a style reflecting the Adam brothers. The Hall contains fine stained glass and plasterwork, displays of costume, and items connected with folk life and local history, and its furniture illustrates the development of English furniture from the 16th to the 19th centuries.
CARTWRIGHT HALL The Hall contains the city art gallery, with paintings by British and foreign artists including Vasari, Guido Reni, Paul Brill, Gainsborough, Reynolds, Raeburn, Romney, Sickert, Wilson Steer, Corot, John Nash, McEvoy, Stanley Spencer, Ford Madox Brown, Ceri Richards and a comprehensive collection of modern prints. There are changing temporary exhibitions of art, sculpture and ceramics.
CATHEDRAL Formerly the large parish church of St Peter, the cathedral is mainly 15th century; the tower is dated 1508. The font and sculpture date from the same period. The notable monuments include one by John Flaxman to Abraham Balme, and others by John Bacon the Younger, J. F. Moore and Peter Scheemakers. Restored in 1899, the church was enlarged 1954–65, when the chancel and sanctuary were rebuilt and a Lady Chapel and Chapter House were added.
MOORSIDE HOUSE A 19th-century mill-owner's home, refurnished throughout in the style of Bradford's Victorian middle-class.

Bradford Abbas *Dorset* 540Cd
CHURCH OF ST MARY THE VIRGIN Mainly of the 15th century, with a good pinnacled west tower. There are 11 canopied niches in the west face, two of which contain sculptured figures. There is a good nave roof. Inside is a 15th-century stone rood screen, and a font with figures at each corner, medieval bench ends and a 17th-century pulpit.

Bradford-on-Avon *Wilts.* 540Df
A charming small town, in style similar to Bath. It rose to fleeting importance after Dutch spinners arrived to manufacture fine cloth in 1659. Its 12th-century parish church contains the first English Bible to be used in a church—a 1572 reprint of the Bishop's Bible of 1568. The diminutive 8th-century Saxon church is one of the earliest and smallest stone churches in England. The tithe barn, once a granary for Shaftesbury Abbey, dates from the 14th century. It is 167 ft long by 30 ft wide, and is made up of 14 great bays with gabled porches. The Hall, commonly known as Kingston House after the two Dukes of Kingston who owned it in the 18th century, is a 17th-century mansion (not open). The Town Bridge is part medieval and part 17th century; it has a small chapel (in being before 1740), surmounted by a weather-vane in the form of a copper gilt fish, known as the Bradford Gudgeon.
CHURCH OF ST LAURENCE The tiny church of St Laurence—the nave height is 25 ft 5 in., 3 in. more than the length—is one of the few Anglo-Saxon churches to survive intact. It is thought that the church was built by St Aldhelm, a famous scholar and monk, who lived in the late 7th century. The plan and much of the fabric of St Laurence's probably dates from this period, but the external decoration is of a later date. At the end of the 10th century the decorative arcading on the outside was formed by cutting into the stonework of the existing church. At the same time the roof was heightened, and later still the sculptured angels high up in the interior were added. The main loss has been of the south porch, but in essence the church is a near-perfect survival from pre-Conquest times, and—in its oldest part—from the 7th and 8th centuries.
CHURCH OF THE HOLY TRINITY Near the river with visible Norman remains such as the chancel windows, the church has early 14th-century additions, but the west tower with its short spire is of a later date, and there is other Perpendicular work. The squint from the north aisle to the chancel is exceptionally long. There is a medieval wall-painting of the Virgin, and two painted panels of Church Fathers from a former screen. Monuments and brasses include two of the 18th century, by John Nost (*c.* 1701) and Michael Rysbrack (*c.* 1737); 17th- and 18th-century painted glass can be seen in one of the nave windows.
ORPIN'S HOUSE Built in 1780 this was the home of Edward Orpin, parish clerk, whose portrait by Gainsborough is in the Tate Gallery. Considerably restored in 1965, when a stone-arched fire-place with seats and recesses, and a niche with a shell head, both dating from *c.* 1580, were uncovered.

CHURCH OF ST LAURENCE
BRADFORD-ON-AVON

One of the few Anglo-Saxon churches to remain intact, St Laurence's is a superb survival from pre-Conquest England. Its early history is not known, but William of Malmesbury, a historian writing in the early 12th century, described a small church at Bradford-on-Avon, said to have been built by St Aldhelm, a 7th-century scholar and monk. It is now thought that he was referring to St Laurence's. After the 12th century the building was not used as a church —by the mid-19th century it was part cottage and part school—but it is now a church once more The decorative arcading on the outside was probably carved at the end of the 10th century, when the roof was heightened. A little later two sculpted angels were added inside the church—these probably flanked a crucifix, now vanished, and they resemble angels that decorated 10th- and 11th-century English manuscripts.

Brading Villa *Isle of Wight*   *541Hc*
This Roman villa was once a fine country house standing on the sheltered southern side of Brading Down, near the east end of the island. Its known buildings stand on three sides of a courtyard, doubtless a farmyard. On the slopes of the Down, north of the house, there is a complex of 'Celtic' fields, probably a part of the villa's estate. As in many Roman villas, the main central rooms must have been lighted by clerestory windows set high in the walls over the penthouse roofs of the front veranda and rear range.

Bradley *Staffs.*   *552Bc*
CHURCH OF ALL SAINTS An interesting church of Norman origin, with 13th-century nave arcades. There is a Norman font, some fragments of medieval stained glass, and monuments with alabaster effigies.

Bradwell Lodge *Essex*   *548Cc*
An early 16th-century house with an Adam wing added in 1785. In the 18th century the belvedere was used as a studio by Thomas Gainsborough.

Bradwell-on-Sea *Essex*   *548Cc*
CHURCH OF ST PETER'S-ON-THE-WALL Built by St Cedd, Bishop of the East Saxons, in AD 654, this is one of the oldest churches in England. Constructed of Roman materials astride the wall of the Roman fort of Othona, it faces the North Sea. The chancel and porch have disappeared, but the nave with original doorway and west window remain.

Braemar *Grampian*   *566Dd*
CASTLE Built by the Earl of Mar in 1628, it was attacked and burnt in 1689 by John Farquharson of Inverey. Near here, in 1715, the Standard was raised in support of the Old Pretender, son of James II. The castle was bought in 1732 by the Farquharsons of Invercauld. It was garrisoned by English troops after the defeat of Bonnie Prince Charlie at Culloden (1746), and restored in 1748. Now a private residence, it retains its central tower with spiral stair, iron yett, star-shaped curtain wall and underground prison.

Brailes *Warks.*   *546Ee*
CHURCH OF ST GEORGE The church, with a west tower, dates from the 13th century. In the Decorated chancel are some 14th-century sedilia with stone arms to the seats. The church was restored in the late 19th century.

Bramall Hall *Greater Manchester*   *552Bf*
The former ancestral home of the Davenport family, the Hall was built mainly in the 16th century with a 'magpie' black and white exterior and many gables. There are portraits dating from 1575, tapestries and murals.

Bramber *W. Sussex*   *542Bd*
CASTLE The gaunt remains of a Norman castle on the R. Adur, owned by the Dukes of Norfolk from the 14th to the 20th centuries. It was destroyed in the Civil War.
HOUSE OF PIPES A collection of 25,000 pipes and smoking artefacts spanning 1500 years.
ST MARY'S A 15th-century timber-framed house, with rare 17th-century painted panelling, period furniture and a butterfly museum.

Bramfield *Suffolk*   *548Ef*
CHURCH OF ST ANDREW The Norman round tower is isolated from a newer Decorated church. There is a screen of *c*. 1500, and one of Nicholas Stone's best-known monuments, of *c*. 1634, which shows Mrs Coke holding a baby.

Bramham Park *W. Yorks.*   *558Db*
A country mansion, built in 1698 by Robert

Benson, 1st Lord Bingley (1676–1731), politician and Lord Chamberlain to Queen Anne, whose portrait by Kneller hangs in the hall. The house was damaged by fire in 1828 and restored in 1906. The gardens are in the style of Le Nôtre.

Bramley *Hants.*   *541Hf*
CHURCH OF ST JAMES A Norman church with later additions and restorations. It has an early 17th-century brick west tower. Inside are 13th-century wall-paintings, one showing the murder of Thomas Becket, and an 18th-century pulpit and west gallery. The Brocas Chapel on the south side contains a marble monument of *c*. 1777 which has been attributed to several sculptors, including Thomas Banks and Thomas Carter.

Brampton *Cambs.*   *547Jf*
PEPYS'S HOUSE The picturesque, twin-gabled farmhouse or small manor house where Samuel Pepys's uncle lived, and where Pepys, not born here but in London, frequently stayed. In his diary he records how he thanked God he had 'such a pretty spot to retire to'.

Brancepeth *Durham*   *558Cf*
CHURCH OF ST BRANDON Originally 12th-century, the church is in the grounds of the castle: it has a west tower. The chancel was rebuilt in the 15th century. Much of the furnishings were given by John Cosin, rector *c*. 1626.

Brandsby *N. Yorks.*   *558Dc*
CHURCH OF ALL SAINTS Small church designed by Thomas Atkinson, 1767–70, in Classical style with a central cupola.

Brant Broughton *Lincs.*   *553Gd*
CHURCH OF ST HELEN The Decorated west tower and tall spire have crockets all the way up; the arcades are 14th century, and there is a Perpendicular clerestory. The church was restored and the chancel rebuilt in 1876 by Bodley, who also installed some wood carving and wrought iron.

Brantwood *Cumbria*   *557Hd*
The home from 1872 to 1900 of the Victorian artist and writer John Ruskin (1819–1900), the house contains a large number of his paintings and many of his personal possessions. (See pp. 378–9.)

Bratton *Wilts.*   *540Ef*
A village containing many 16th- and 17th-century houses, and a Baptist chapel of 1667.

Bratton Castle *Wilts.*   *540Ef*
A fine Iron Age hill-fort on the north-west edge of the Salisbury Plain chalk massif. The internal area is about 24 acres, with two banks and ditches for most of its defences, though one bank is omitted on the east side. A Neolithic long barrow with quarry ditch lies within the enclosure.
There is a white horse carved into the chalk of the hill-side to the west of the fort. This, sometimes called the Westbury White Horse, is more horse-like than the one at Uffington. But we know that this was recarved in 1778 and it has been reported that the outline of the original horse has been seen from the air, when conditions were suitable, and that this resembled the Uffington Horse in outline. If this is accepted, the earlier horse here may also be attributed to the Iron Age.

Braunton *Devon*   *538Ff*
CHURCH OF ST BRANNOCK Originally Norman, much of the rest of the building is 13th-century and has later additions. The Norman south tower has a later broach spire. The nave is wide, with a wagon-roof of *c*. 1500; there are many carved bench ends, some as late as 1593.

Breamore *Hants.*   *540Fd*
BREAMORE HOUSE Built in 1583, this gabled manor house has been the home of the Hulse family for over 200 years; Sir Edward Hulse (1682–1759) was physician to George II. The interior, which was ravaged by fire in 1856, has been restored; its contents include fine furniture, paintings and tapestries.
CHURCH OF ST MARY This important Saxon cruciform church, also displaying Norman and later work, is on the edge of a park close to a red-brick Elizabethan manor house. Over the archway to the south transept is an Anglo-Saxon inscription meaning 'Here the Covenant becomes manifest to thee'. Over the south doorway is a carved stone rood, protected by a later porch, but badly mutilated at the Reformation.

Brechin *Tayside*   *566Fc*
ROUND TOWER Brechin 'Irish' round tower is one of only two such structures on the Scottish mainland—the other is at Abernethy in Tayside. The Brechin tower, attached to the cathedral, probably dates from the 10th century; it is certainly 200 years older than the oldest part of the cathedral, the spire of which dates from 1360. The tower is about 86 ft high and is capped by a conical roof added in the 14th century.

Brecon *Powys*   *545Hd*
This town was founded by the Normans at the end of the 11th century. Near the centre, in the grounds of the Castle Hotel, a solid tower and part of a wall are all that remain of Brecon Castle, built within 25 years of the Norman Conquest. Many well-known people have lived in the town including John Aubrey, the 17th-century antiquary, Charles Kemble, the 18th-century actor, and his sister, later famed on the London stage as Sarah Siddons.
BRECKNOCK MUSEUM Contains collections of archaeological and geological exhibits, agricultural implements, and domestic and dairy appliances, pottery and an assembly of love-spoons.
CATHEDRAL The church of the former priory here, raised to cathedral status in 1923. The cruciform building has a 13th-century central tower and a chancel with a five-lancet east window. There is a monument by John Flaxman. The building was restored by Sir Gilbert Scott during the third quarter of the 19th century.
SOUTH WALES BORDERERS REGIMENTAL MUSEUM The Regiment was founded in 1689, and its activities since that date are recorded in the items on show. The weapons in the armoury include an example of almost every weapon used since 1800.

Brecon Gaer *Powys*   *545Hd*
A mile and a half to the north-west of Brecon, the hill Pen-y-Crug is crowned by a strongly defended hill-fort, of native type, overlooking the junction-point of several radiating valleys. It was probably the strategic importance of this site which led to the Roman commander, in the early days of the conquest, to site a fort a mile higher up the western valley. The first ramparts and buildings were of earth and timber, but some remodelling in stone took place in the 2nd century. Excavation has shown that the civil disturbances which occurred towards the end of the 2nd century led to much damage here. But the fort was restored and occupied, at least intermittently, until towards the end of the occupation of Britain.

Bredon *Heref. & Worcs.*   *546Ce*
CHURCH OF ST GILES Dating in large part from the 12th century, this fine church has a central tower with a tall spire. Inside there is much of interest, including medieval tiles, tombs, early glass, and a heart burial with a slab showing a pair of hands holding a heart. There is a large 17th-century monument with reclining and kneeling figures,

THE ROYAL PAVILION, BRIGHTON

George IV, as Prince of Wales, first visited the village of Brighthelmstone in 1783 when it was becoming a fashionable resort for the new pastime of sea-bathing. In 1786 he leased a small house in the Steine, a valley running down to the sea; his wife, the former Mrs Fitzherbert, lived in a nearby villa. Soon Prince George commissioned the architect Henry Holland to enlarge his house into a pleasant Classical building with a domed central rotunda. In 1811 George III's mind failed, Prince George became Regent—and the great reconstruction of his Brighton house began. First,

enormous sums of money were spent on the kitchen, entrance hall, long gallery and state apartments. John Nash, the Regent's Surveyor-general, transformed the exterior by adding to Holland's house the onion-shaped dome, tent-like pavilion roofs, and pinnacles and minarets in the style of a mogul's palace. The lavish interior was much influenced by Chinese decoration. The banqueting room has painted walls, a ceiling resembling a huge palm-tree and a bedragonned chandelier. The music room was severely damaged by fire in 1975.

cherubs, columns and heraldry, an impressive product of the period.

Bredon Hill *Heref. & Worcs.* 546Ce
Bredon is a great outlier of the Cotswolds, commanding the Vales of Severn and Avon. A spur on the north side of the hill is defended by two ramparts of an Iron Age hill-fort, each with an external ditch. The inner defences came first, and had a simple staggered entrance. Later, the outer bank and ditch were added. This rampart was faced with stone on the outside, and the two entrances through it were inturned to give long narrow passages to the space between the two banks. At the same time a long 'corridor entrance' was made in the inner bank to replace the first, simpler way into the fort.

The place was sacked, and its defenders slain. Thereafter it lay deserted for an indeterminate period before the Roman conquest. The central openings in the outer bank are apparently comparatively modern.

Bredwardine *Heref. & Worcs.* 545Je
CHURCH OF ST ANDREW A large Norman church, with carved north and south doors and a plain Norman font. The chancel is early 14th-century, and the north-west tower was added in 1790. There are two effigies of knights.

Breedon on the Hill *Leics.* 552Ec
CHURCH OF SS MARY AND HARDULPH The church is built on the site of a Saxon monastery, commanding a view over the Trent Valley. It is mainly Norman, with later work; the nave was destroyed. High up in the south aisle, and between the arcades, are magnificent carved fragments with figures and geometric ornaments, dating from *c.* 800, from the monastery. There are late 16th-century tombs with effigies, made by Royleys of Burton upon Trent.

Breiddin, The *Powys* 551Jb
This massively defended 65-acre hill-fort overlooks the upper waters of the R. Severn. It was occupied in the Late Bronze Age (*c.* 750 BC) and in the Iron Age. An earth rampart, faced with timber, was succeeded by a stone-faced rampart, and circular wooden huts succeeded the earlier small square type. The site was refortified in the 4th century AD.

Brenchley *Kent* 542De
A picturesque village with splendid Tudor half-timbered houses. An avenue of ancient yews leads to the church.

Brent Eleigh *Suffolk* 548Ce
CHURCH OF ST MARY A Decorated church with a later west tower, and a 14th-century south door. Inside are a 17th-century pulpit and font cover and 18th-century box-pews. The reredos is painted, with a 13th-century rood screen; wall-paintings discovered on either side in 1961 have become a focal point for visitors.

Brentford *Greater London* 542Ag
NATIONAL PIANO MUSEUM The collection includes a Steinway-Duo-Art reproducing grand piano belonging to Princess Beatrice, youngest daughter of Queen Victoria, a self-playing violin with piano accompaniment, orchestrions, nickelodeons, music boxes, cylinder gramophones, barrel and player pianos, hand organs, and all sorts of old, odd and interesting keyboard instruments.

Brentor *Devon* 538Fd
CHURCH OF ST MICHAEL DE RUPE This is a primitive mainly 13th-century little church, perched on top of an extinct volcanic cone, a wonderful site 1100 ft above the sea.

Brewood *Staffs.* 552Bb
CHURCH OF SS MARY THE VIRGIN AND CHAD A fine church with a spire, dating from the 13th century with later additions. There are several 16th- and 17th-century monuments with effigies.

Bridestones *Staffs.* 552Be
Most of the mound has disappeared, so that the chamber of the Neolithic long barrow, though somewhat damaged, is visible. There are traces of the semicircular forecourt at the east end and nearly 20 ft of the long gallery is still intact. Originally, the barrow must have been large; it is believed to have exceeded 300 ft in length, which would have made it one of the largest long barrows in England.

Bridge of Dun *Tayside* 566Fb
BRIDGE OVER THE R. SOUTH ESK Three wide arches, ornamented with such Gothic motifs as double crosses and quatrefoil columns, span the river; squat obelisks guard the approaches. By Alexander Stevens, it was completed in 1787.

Bridgnorth *Shropshire* 546Bg
A town on two levels, one part being called the High Town standing 200 ft above the R. Severn, the Low Town being linked by a bridge across the river. Its oldest dwelling is Bishop Percy's House, built 1580, birthplace in 1729 of Thomas Percy who became Bishop of Dromore (Ireland). The town hall (1652) is a half-timbered building, once a barn in Much Wenlock, standing on an open-arched *piazza* of stonework. The castle, of which only the keep remains, was built between 1098 and 1101 and damaged by the Parliamentarians in 1647 after the Civil War.
CHURCH OF ST LEONARD With traces of Norman work in its south tower, this large church was almost entirely rebuilt in the 1860's in Gothic Revival style. The nave roof, of hammerbeam construction, is mid-17th century.
CHURCH OF ST MARY MAGDALENE Begun in 1792 to the design of Thomas Telford the engineer, this church is neo-Classical inside and out. The exterior has large Tuscan columns, a pediment and smooth rustication (the stones smoothly finished, but the joints between them greatly emphasised). The tower is square at first, then octagonal and finally domed. Telford designed the liturgical east end (actually the south end) to be straight but Sir Arthur Blomfield added the apse in 1876. Another Salop church by Telford is at Madeley.

Bridgwater *Som.* 540Be
An inland seaport and market town, birthplace of Robert Blake (1598–1657), admiral and general-at-sea under Oliver Cromwell; Blake's house is now a museum. The rebel Duke of Monmouth was proclaimed king at Bridgwater in 1685. The medieval steeple of St Mary's Church is a notable landmark, 175 ft high. The town possesses many Georgian houses, especially in Castle Street.
ADMIRAL BLAKE MUSEUM The reputed birthplace of Admiral Robert Blake (1599–1657) and containing relics of his life, including his sea-chest and compass. Also on display are relics of the Battle of Sedgemoor (1685) and of the Duke of Monmouth. Collections of local shipping, industry, archaeology and history, topographical prints, drawings and photographs, and examples of domestic and agricultural bygones.

Bridlington *Humberside* 559Gc
ART GALLERY AND MUSEUM, SEWERBY PARK Amy Johnson's Pilot's Log Book, covering the years 1928–38, is the main exhibit in the Amy Johnson Room at Sewerby Hall and Park. The

POSSET POT

Posset was a hot drink of ale, honey and herbs. Refined people spooned their posset out of a silver pot; others sipped it from the spout of an earthenware one, such as this example, made at Bristol in the late 17th century. It is painted with Chinese figures in enamel colours. (Brighton Museum and Art Gallery)

HOVE AMBER CUP

Found buried in the long-barrow grave of a Wessex Culture chief at Hove in 1857, this cup is nearly 3 in. high. An oak coffin was uncovered and inside with bones were the cup, a stone axe-head and a bronze dagger. The cup was turned on a lathe from a single block of amber. (Brighton Museum and Art Gallery)

famous flier opened the Hall as a museum in 1936 and today, her trophies, awards and mementoes are collected here. Sewerby Hall was built *c.* 1720, with later additions dating from 1808–50. It houses a collection of pictures by local artists and an archaeological display of Bronze Age axe-heads and flint implements. Botanical gardens in the park are open to the public.

BAYLE MUSEUM The museum is in the 14th-century stone and brick gate-house of the Augustinian Priory of Bridlington. Structural alterations were made in the 17th century, but some original building remains, including a spiral stair, fire-places and a groined vault. In its time the manor court-house, a school and a prison, the Bayle is still used for meetings by the Lords Feoffees of the Manor, in whose trust the Bayle has been since 1631. The collections consist of local relics, including weapons, domestic and trade untensils (pipe-makers' equipment and farm implements), jewellery, a collection of Valentines, dolls' furniture, model boats and local paintings, prints and maps.

CHURCH OF ST MARY The church is the nave of what must have been an impressive priory church, founded in the early 12th century, but after the Dissolution the east end, transepts and central tower disappeared. The two western towers were completed by Sir Gilbert Scott in the second half of the 19th century.

Bridport *Dorset* 540 Cc
MUSEUM AND ART GALLERY Seven hundred and fifty years of local trade are commemorated in a display of apparatus used in making ropes, nets and lines displayed at the Bridport Museum. Other exhibits include British birds and their eggs, Roman relics from the 1st-century camp near by and items of local history—domestic and agricultural bygones.

The collections are contained in a building dating from the early 16th century, which is reputed to have been the house of a chantry priest of St Leonard.

Brighouse *W. Yorks.* 558 Ca
SMITH ART GALLERY A collection of oil paintings and water-colours, mainly by 19th-century artists.

Brighton *E. Sussex* 542 Bd
MUSEUM AND ART GALLERY The collections include Old Master paintings, water-colours, furniture and ceramics; the Willett Collection of English pottery and porcelain; the Edward James Collection of surrealist paintings; fine and applied art of the Art Nouveau and Art Deco periods; important collections of ethnography and archaeology; and musical instruments.

PARISH CHURCH OF ST PETER A Gothic building by Sir Charles Barry, later the architect of the Houses of Parliament; it was built *c.* 1825, and has the tower at the south end. The chancel by Somers Clark was added in 1896–1902.

PRESTON MANOR An early manor house rebuilt in 1738, and substantially altered in 1905, by Charles Stanley Peach, giving it its present appearance of an opulent country house. It was left to the town of Brighton in 1932 by the late owner, Sir Charles Thomas-Stanford and his wife, on the understanding that it should be preserved as an English country home. It has since been administered as a country-house museum.

The Macquoid and Thomas-Stanford bequests of fine furniture, ceramics, leatherwork, pictures and silver is also on view. The collection of silver includes examples from England, Portugal and Scandinavia, and a collection of Russian silver niello snuff boxes (a form of inlay using a black alloy of silver to emphasise the engraved design). There is a collection of 17th- and 18th-century Chinese Fukien-ware figures. The furniture is mainly Georgian, with some 16th- and 17th-century pieces, and one room contains leather hangings brought from Cordoba by Katherine of Aragon. There are also some 18th- and 19th-century landscapes.

ROYAL PAVILION In 1786 George, Prince of Wales, leased a small house here, and soon afterwards Henry Holland reconstructed it as a Classical building, with a central rotunda and dome. After he became Regent in 1811, Prince George had the house rebuilt; John Nash, his Surveyor-General, transformed Holland's house into something like an Indian mogul's palace by the addition of the great onion-shaped dome, tent-like roofs to the pavilions, numerous pinnacles and small minarets, while the interior was taken to a peak of exoticism, mostly in the 'Chinese taste'. William IV and later Queen Victoria stayed at the Pavilion—though she disliked it as new building in Brighton was robbing it of privacy. The pavilion was closed in 1845 and the furniture removed. The building was bought by the town of Brighton in 1850. Since the Second World War it has been restored to its former brilliance, and furnished with much of the original furniture, returned on loan by the Queen. (See p. 99.)

Brightwell Baldwin *Oxon.*   *546Fc*
CHURCH OF ST BARTHOLOMEW An attractive church, in the Decorated and Perpendicular styles. The stained glass is medieval, the pulpit Jacobean. Inside are brasses and monuments, and a barrel organ made in 1843.

Brinkburn *Northld.*   *562Fb*
PRIORY CHURCH OF SS PETER AND PAUL Founded by Augustinian canons *c.* 1135, in an enchanting position by the R. Coquet. It was in ruins until the 19th century, when restoration took place.

Brinsop *Heref. & Worcs.*   *546Ae*
CHURCH OF ST GEORGE An early 14th-century church, with some interesting Norman carving, including a scene of St George and the Dragon. From the 14th century some wall-paintings of the Annunciation and the Crucifixion, and stained glass also showing St George. The ornate reredos was done by Sir Ninian Comper in 1920–8.

Bristol *Avon*   *540Cg*
CATHEDRAL The Abbey Church of St Augustine, founded in 1140, was given cathedral status by Henry VIII in 1542. From the original Norman building survive the great gatehouse, the entrance to the Abbot's lodging, the walls of the south transept and the east walk of the cloister, and the Chapter House.

The choir of the church, rebuilt in 1298–1330, is unique in England. In most medieval churches the central aisle rises above those at the side, but this is a hall-church in which the aisles are as high as the central space and the external flying buttresses are replaced by stone bridges carrying transverse tunnel vaults across the aisles. The central space itself has the earliest lierne vault in England. Another unusual piece of vaulting, an early 14th-century skeleton vault, appears in the sacristy.

The rebuilding of the Norman nave, begun in 1485, was abandoned when the abbey was dissolved by Henry VIII. The present nave was built to match the choir by G. E. Street in 1868–88. Among the furnishings of the church are stalls with misericords (*c.* 1500).
CHURCH OF ALL SAINTS The earliest parts of the church are Norman and 15th century. The north tower, topped by a cupola, is of the early 18th century, and the chancel was rebuilt in the mid-19th century. The most outstanding monument is by the Belgian sculptor Rysbrack to Edward Colston (*d.* 1721), designed by the architect James Gibbs. Now a diocesan study centre.
CHURCH OF ST MARK (THE LORD MAYOR'S CHAPEL) The chapel originally belonged to Gaunt's Hospital, but at the Dissolution became the property of the city corporation (it is the only church in England owned by a corporation) and from 1721 their official place of worship. There have been many alterations to the original 13th-century building: a tower in the Perpendicular style of 1487 and the 16th-century fan-vaulted Poyntz Chapel, floored with Spanish tiles.

Amongst a wealth of stained glass is some from the eccentric millionaire William Beckford's Gothic extravagance, Fonthill Abbey. A profusion of monuments, ranging from cross-legged knights of the 13th century to the 19th-century work by Sir Francis Chantrey, make this one of the most important churches for monumental sculpture.
CHURCH OF ST MARY REDCLIFFE A magnificent church, one of the largest in England, dating from the 13th century; the outer north porch (*c.* 1280) is lavishly decorated. In the 15th century the tall spire was struck by lightning, and was not rebuilt for 400 years. The church contains many monuments and brasses, and among the fittings are candlesticks, a sword-rest, lectern and wrought-iron screens.
CITY ART GALLERY Built in 1899 and presented to the city by Sir W. H. Wills, of the tobacco family. It contains old and modern paintings, sculpture, water-colours, ceramics, glass and textiles. Among the collections are 19th-century French paintings, works of the Bristol School of the 1820's, Bristol glass and porcelain and the Schiller collection of Oriental ceramics.
CITY MUSEUM Housed in the same building as the art gallery, the museum contains major collections of archaeology, geology, natural history and technology from Bristol and the West of England, and antiquities and ethnography from many parts of the world.
CLIFTON SUSPENSION BRIDGE Built by Isambard Kingdom Brunel, 245 ft above the Avon Gorge; it incorporates chains from the old Hungerford suspension bridge in London.
MARITIME CENTRE Isambard Kingdom Brunel's restored steamer *Great Britain* lies in Bristol docks near a reconstructed dredger, also designed by Brunel, and a display of ship models and paintings accumulated by the shipbuilder Charles Hill.
WESTBURY COLLEGE John Wycliffe (1320–84), who instituted the first translation of the whole Bible into English, was a prebend of the College of Priests; the 15th-century gate-house is all that remains.

Britford *Wilts.*   *540Fe*
CHURCH OF ST PETER A cruciform church of Saxon origin which contains some important 8th- and 9th-century carvings. There are monuments *c.* 1300, a late 17th-century pulpit and pews, and an 18th-century mausoleum. The church was restored *c.* 1875 by G. E. Street.

Brixworth *Northants.*   *547Gf*
CHURCH OF ALL SAINTS The church dates from the 7th century and incorporates many Roman bricks. It was monastic until 870 and the belfry and spire were added to the Saxon tower in the 14th century. There is a 10th-century stair turret and an effigy of a cross-legged knight of *c.* 1300.

Broad Clyst *Devon*   *539Hd*
CHURCH OF ST JOHN THE BAPTIST A large church, mainly 14th- and 15th-century, with a tall pinnacled west tower, the base of which is Norman. The interior has wagon-roofs, and there are several monuments, ranging from a mid-14th-century knight to reclining or recumbent effigies of 1613 and 1622.

Broadstairs *Kent*   *543Gg*
BLEAK HOUSE Here Charles Dickens wrote *David Copperfield*. The house inspired the title of another work, which he planned while living here on the edge of the cliffs. In Dickens' time, the house was a small Regency building: the west wing and castellations were added in 1901.

EDWARD BAILY *Eve at the Fountain*

One of the most successful and prolific sculptors of the first half of the 19th century, Edward Baily is little known today, although his Nelson in Trafalgar Square, London, is one of the most famous statues in Britain. By general consent in his own day 'Eve at the Fountain' was considered his masterpiece. Carved in 1822, it was bought some years later by a general subscription of the citizens of his native Bristol. Strangely enough the model was originally designed as the handle of a silver soup tureen for the Licensed Victuallers Company; the original sketch-model is also at the Bristol gallery.
(City Art Gallery, Bristol)

'OLIVER CROMWELL' PRIVATEER GLASS

A series of Privateer glasses was made in Bristol to celebrate the commissioning of armed merchant vessels in the Seven Years' War (1756–63). The distinction between privateers and pirates was somewhat academic to their victims. This glass is engraved: 'Success to the Oliver Cromwell Privateer', and 'Paul Flyn, Commander'. Standing 6 in. high, it has an enamel twist stem and a conical bowl; most glasses in the series have bucket-shaped bowls.
(City Art Gallery, Bristol)

CLIFTON SUSPENSION BRIDGE, BRISTOL

This bridge was one of the most daring of its kind when designed by Brunel in 1830. The foundation stone of the massive west abutment was laid by Lady Elton in June 1831, but owing to shortage of funds this part alone was completed in Brunel's lifetime. After his death in 1859, the bridge was completed by the engineers Sir John Hawkshaw and W. H. Barlow as a memorial to their late colleague. The suspension chains used were bought cheaply from Brunel's Hungerford Bridge which was then being demolished to make way for the present Charing Cross railway bridge in London. This entailed some alterations to Brunel's original design. The bridge was completed, and opened on December 8, 1864. It has a single suspended span of 702 ft carrying the roadway 245 ft above the R. Avon.

Isambard Kingdom Brunel was born at Portsmouth in 1806. When he was only 19 years old he was resident engineer in charge of the Thames tunnel, and at 24 was elected a fellow of the Royal Society. Three years later he became engineer of the Great Western Railway. To extend its services he turned to shipbuilding and constructed the Great Western, a wooden paddleship which crossed to New York under steampower in 1838; she was followed in 1843 by the Great Britain, the first screw-propelled iron steamship designed for regular Atlantic crossings, and later by the Great Eastern.

Broadwater *W. Sussex* *542Ad*
THE PARISH CHURCH In what was formerly a
village, now part of Worthing, the church is cruciform with a central tower. The Norman building
was added to, and there was much restoration in
the mid-19th century. There are some misericords,
a brass to a former rector (*d.* 1432) and monuments to two Lords de la Warr, of 1524 and 1554.

Broadway *Heref. & Worcs.* *546De*
One of the most famous villages in Britain, with
all the best features of Cotswold stone building.

Broch of Mousa *Mousa, Shetland* *568Ee*
This is certainly the best known and, in many
ways, the finest of the Iron Age brochs. It still
stands some 43½ ft high and has a 50 ft external
diameter at the base. It contains stairs and
galleries, and is particularly notable for the
thickness of its wall.

Brockhall *Northants.* *546Ff*
An Elizabethan manor house, with a wing altered
in the 18th century in the style of Robert Adam.

Brockham *Surrey* *542Bf*
A triangular green, with the church, built of white
firestone, at one end, and a grand sweep of chalky
downland above the houses at the other.

Brockhampton-by-Ross *Heref. & Worcs.* *546Bd*
CHURCH OF ALL SAINTS A stone and concrete
church by W. R. Lethaby, of 1901–2, All Saints
has a central tower. The extremely steep arches of
the nave spring low from the walls, without
brackets. The tapestry was designed by Sir Edwin
Burne-Jones and made by Morris & Co., and
there is some 20th-century stained glass by
Christopher Whall. The altar has a fine alabaster
statue of the Madonna.

Brodick Castle *Isle of Arran, Strathclyde* *560Fd*
Set amid fine formal and woodland gardens below
bleak Goatfell, this castle, dating partly from *c.*
1500, was the former home of the Dukes of Hamilton; the west end and tower were added in the
19th century. The castle contains much fine furniture and collections of porcelain, silver and paintings, including sporting pictures.

Bromham *Wilts.* *540Ef*
CHURCH OF ST NICHOLAS Once Norman, most of
the building is of a later date with an Early English
central tower with Perpendicular spire. The chancel is a Victorian reproduction of the Early English
structure, and the south aisle is 18th-century
Gothic. The church is notable for the very ornate
south chapel with large Perpendicular windows;
it was founded in 1492, and has brasses and
monuments to the Tocotes-Beauchamp and
Baynton families of the 15th and 16th centuries. In
the east window is stained glass by William Morris
after Burne-Jones, *c.* 1870. The poet Thomas
Moore is buried in the churchyard.

Bromsgrove *Heref. & Worcs.* *546Cf*
CHURCH OF ST JOHN THE BAPTIST There is a mid-
14th-century tower with an octagonal crocketed
spire, but St John's is chiefly noteworthy for its
monuments. These include the 15th- and 16th-
century tombs with alabaster effigies to members
of the Talbot and Stafford families. On the Talbot
tomb evidence was found in 1856 establishing the
claim of Lord Talbot of Ingestre to the Earldom of
Shrewsbury; Sir Humphrey Stafford was killed in
the rebellion against government corruption led
by Jack Cade in 1450.

Bromyard *Heref. & Worcs.* *546Ag*
CHURCH OF ST PETER This Norman cruciform
church has a low central tower, flanking aisles, and
a Norman doorway on the south side with a figure
of St Peter in flat relief. There is an interesting tub-
shaped Norman font with decorations.

Bronllys Castle *Powys* *545Je*
All that remains of this castle is the tower, which is
of early Norman date. The tower is 80 ft high and
has two passages inside the wall. The castle was
small with a single keep of the knight's stronghold
type. It was used as a base by William Rufus and
passed to the Bohuns. Later, in the reign of Henry
VII, it was acquired by the Staffords.

Brooke *Leics.* *553Gb*
CHURCH OF ST PETER The church dates from
Norman times, but much was rebuilt during the
16th century, from which time most of the furnishings survive. There is a fine Renaissance tomb
commemorating Charles Noel (1619), which still
has traces of the original colouring. The font is
Norman.

Broomend of Crichie *Grampian* *566Fe*
This is a circular enclosure with external bank and
contained ditch. Its overall diameter is about 110 ft.
The two standing stones near the ditch are contemporary with the Bronze Age monument, but that
at the centre is a later addition; Pictish symbols
are carved on this central stone.

Brougham *Cumbria* *557Jf*
CHURCH OF ST NINIAN There was once a Saxon
church on this site, and then a Norman one which
Lady Anne Clifford of Brougham Castle rebuilt in
1660. Today the church is as she left it, still with its
contemporary furnishing. Near by are St Wilfrid's
Chapel, of about the same date, with an interesting screen and stalls, and the castle.

Broughton *Humberside* *553Gg*
CHURCH OF ST MARY A Norman church, the
building has later work and a Saxon west tower
with a circular staircase addition. Inside there are
interesting monuments of several periods including two fine 14th-century brasses, and two
alabaster effigies of the late 14th century. Another
effigy of *c.* 1670 commemorates Sir Edmund
Anderson, Lord Chief Justice of the Common
Pleas.

Broughton *Oxon.* *546Ee*
CHURCH OF ST MARY THE VIRGIN This spacious
church, near the castle, has a 14th-century tower
and spire and stone chancel screen. Inside there are
many monuments.

Broughton *Staffs.* *552Bc*
CHURCH OF ST PETER An early 17th-century
Gothic church with earlier, medieval stained glass,
depicting figures of saints and heraldic shields.
Inside are contemporary box-pews, and many
tablets, the best being cartouches to William
Bagot, 1687, and Spencer Broughton, 1702.

Broughton Castle *Oxon.* *546Ee*
A moated manor house, with origins dating back
to *c.* 1300, the castle was added to and decorated in
Elizabethan times and has interesting Civil War
connections. It was owned by William of Wykeham (1324–1404) and passed by marriage to the
2nd Lord Saye and Sele in 1451; the Lords Saye
and Sele have lived there ever since. The façade,
fire-places, ceiling and panelling were introduced
in 1554–99.
    Features of the house include a collection of
china and Chinese wallpapers.

Broxbourne *Herts.*   *548Ac*
CHURCH OF ST AUGUSTINE A large 15th-century
church close to the R. Lea. The builder of the
south chapel in 1476 may have worked also at St
Margaret's, Westminster. The nave and chancel
are not divided by a chancel arch. The Norman
font is octagonal, and there are many interesting
monuments and brasses.

Bryn Celli Ddu *Gwynedd*   *550Ee*
This fine cairn covers a passage-grave dating
back to the 3rd millennium BC. It is of a type
that is more common in Ireland. The original
mound, some 160 ft in diameter, was held within
a circle of substantial uprights and, on the north-
east side, a long entrance passage led to a 10 ft long
chamber near the centre. Only one of the original
capstones now remains, but in the chamber there
still stands a carefully rounded upright stone set
there, not as part of the supports, but for some
quasi-religious purpose.

Bryn Yr Hen Bobl *Anglesey, Gwynedd*   *550Ee*
A burial chamber contained in a Bronze Age
kidney-shaped mound. It is unusual in having a
320 ft long narrow terrace leading off to the south
of the mound.

Buckden *Cambs.*   *547Jf*
The Lion Hotel and the George Hotel are notable
old coaching inns. The timber-framed manor
house was built in the late 16th century.
BUCKDEN PALACE A residence of the Bishops of
Lincoln from the early Middle Ages until 1838.
The walls, great tower, and inner gate-house date
from the 15th century, when building was begun
by Bishop Rotherham and finished by Bishop
Russell whose arms are over the gateway.
The ancient gateway with its bold machicolations
overhanging the third storey is probably *c.* 1470,
the same period as the chapel. Katherine of
Aragon, first wife of Henry VIII, lived here from
1534 to 1535 before she was removed to Kimbolton Castle where she died.
The palace now belongs to the Claretian
Missionaries.
CHURCH OF ST MARY The church is near the
former bishop's palace, and is mainly Perpendicular with a tower and spire, and a two-storey
south porch. There is a 17th-century pulpit, and
some fragments of medieval glass and a monument
by E. H. Baily may be seen.

Buckfast Abbey *Devon*   *539Gc*
In 1907, Benedictine monks started to rebuild the
ruins of a 10th-century abbey which had been
dissolved in 1539. The revived abbey was finished
in 1938. It is built of local limestone, in Transitional
Norman-English style, with a tower 158 ft high.

Buckingham *Bucks.*   *547Ge*
Market town with a Georgian-fronted town hall
in the square and, close by, the old gaol, styled as
a small castle and built in 1748. There is a 16th-
century manor house, while the 16th-century
Royal Latin School has a Norman gateway.
CHANTRY CHAPEL Chantry chapels were built
with money left by the pious rich to provide places
where masses might be sung for them and prayers
said. Here the original Norman doorway may still
be seen, having survived the chapel's rebuilding in
1475 and its restoration in 1875.

Buckland *Glos.*   *546De*
CHURCH OF ST MICHAEL Mainly Perpendicular in
appearance (but with traces of earlier work, as in
the late 13th-century nave arcades), it has almost
completely escaped restoration. Outstanding
features inside are the 17th-century oak panelling,

pews and west gallery, and the 15th-century glass
in the east window, depicting three of the seven
sacraments; the tiles in the south aisle and the
finely embroidered pall kept in the north aisle are
also both of the 15th century.

Buckland *Surrey*   *542Bf*
The main road runs between the pretty church and
the prim oblong green, with a black barn on one
side and the village school on another.

Buckland Abbey *Devon*   *538Fc*
In 1581, Sir Francis Drake (1540–96) acquired this
13th-century Cistercian monastery from the
Grenville family, who had made many alterations
in 1576. The monastery nave became the great
hall. The abbey is now a museum with relics of
Drake and Sir Richard Grenville.

Buckland Rectory *Glos.*   *546De*
A house dating from the 12th century; the great
hall has a timber-frame roof and stained-glass
windows of the 15th century.

Bucklers Hard *Hants.*   *541Gc*
This hard (a sloping foreshore) is on the tidal
waters of Beaulieu R. A shipyard flourished here
during the 18th and early 19th centuries.
The wide, late 18th-century street, which is all
there is of the village, runs down to the Beaulieu
R. It was the start of a port which the Duke of
Montagu meant to develop.
MARITIME MUSEUM The museum contains maps,
documents and models relating to shipbuilding on
the Beaulieu R., as well as relics of Nelson and
records of Sir Francis Chichester's ocean voyages.
Many original shipbuilding drawings by Henry
Adams, who built Nelson's favourite ship, the
Agamemnon—which he commanded in 1793—can
be seen. A model of Bucklers Hard in 1803 shows
in detail social life in the village at that time, while
the Information Centre gives the background to
the development of the village and of the river.
There are also paintings and prints of ships built
at Beaulieu and the officers who commanded
them.

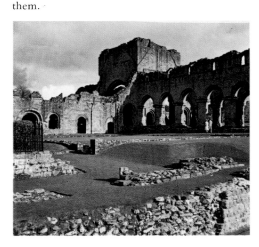

BUILDWAS ABBEY

*The extensive ruins of Buildwas Abbey include the
church and the eastern range of the cloister. The
ruins of the 12th-century church consist of the nave
arcades, the west wall and the choir chapels with their
vaults intact. North of the church lie the chapter
house and two adjacent rooms, all complete with
vaults. The ruins show no signs of enlargements or
alterations from the foundation of the abbey in the
12th century until the Dissolution in 1536, a fact
which suggests that the house was never powerful or
wealthy.*

BURGHLEY HOUSE

One of England's greatest Elizabethan houses, Burghley was begun about 1552 by Sir William Cecil, one of the queen's ministers. Of the earlier part of the building, the grandest room is the great hall, with a double hammerbeam roof incorporating both Gothic and Renaissance elements, especially in the large fireplace with its fluted and bulging supports. Dominating the second stage of the house is the fantastic feature in the courtyard; this is surmounted by a clock on top *of which is a huge obelisk held up by two enormous rampant lions, with obelisks behind them. A feature of the interior is the Roman Staircase, based perhaps on one in the Louvre in Paris. Little of the original decoration remains, but there is carved woodwork by Grinling Gibbons, and much wall-painting by Verrio and others, from the subjects of which some of the rooms take their names—the Hell Room and Heaven Room. The building was completed in 1587.*

Buildwas Abbey *Shropshire* 552Ab
Originally a Savignac house, Buildwas Abbey was absorbed into the Cistercian order with other Savignac foundations in 1147. It was founded from Furness Abbey by Roger de Clinton, Bishop of Coventry and Lichfield. A small railway line now runs close to the south of the ruins, but the seclusion of the setting remains intact. The church, built during the second half of the 12th century, is the best preserved part, giving an idea of the simplicity of early Cistercian architecture. (See p. 105.)

Bunbury *Cheshire* 552Ad
CHURCH OF ST BONIFACE A large, formerly collegiate church of the 14th and 15th centuries, with a west tower. It was damaged during the Second World War but successfully restored. Among the monuments is the 14th-century alabaster tomb, a monument to Sir George Beeston, who fought against the Armada, and a memorial to Sir R. Egerton, Standard-bearer to Henry VIII. The screens and doors are of the 16th century.

Bungay *Suffolk* 548Eg
A small town in the Waveney Valley. A few old houses survived a fire in 1688 but the town is mainly 18th century in character. It has interesting remains of the castle, built by the Bigods in the 12th century and already ruinous in the late 14th century. In the market-place, the Butter Cross of 1689 replaced an older one destroyed by the fire. In St Mary's Street, a 16th-century house has carved woodwork by the windows. There are many pleasant Georgian houses in the town.
CHURCH OF THE HOLY TRINITY With a Norman round tower, the church is Norman with later additions up to 1926, when the chancel was rebuilt. There is 16th- and 17th-century woodwork, and a monument of *c.* 1774 by Thomas Scheemakers.

Buntingford *Herts.* 548Ad
Situated on the R. Rib, with parts of the Roman Ermine Street forming its High Street, is Buntingford: a small and architecturally charming little town. Its famous town clock is over 500 years old, but of greater interest are the 17th-century almshouses founded in 1684 by Bishop Seth Ward, the mathematician and astronomer friend of Sir Christopher Wren. The two-storied brick houses with mullioned windows, a pedimented centre and projecting wings forming a three-sided courtyard look like a mansion from the street.

Bures *Suffolk* 548Ce
CHURCH OF ST MARY Of the 13th to 16th centuries, St Mary's has a Perpendicular font with carved angels and heraldry. There are 14th–16th-century monuments, including an early cross-legged knight of wood.

Burford *Oxon.* 546Ed
CHURCH OF ST JOHN THE BAPTIST Recumbent figures and carved projections decorate many of the numerous monuments adorning this church; the complexity of the church is the result of later additions to the original Norman building. The three-storied south porch is in the Perpendicular style, and the central tower carries a spire.
TOLSEY MUSEUM The history of England, from the Norman Conquest to the Industrial Revolution, can be seen here, as reflected in the records of a small town and its neighbouring countryside. The collection is housed in the Tolsey, or toll house, a 16th-century Cotswold building; it contains maces, seals and documents of Burford Corporation, and local industries, past and present, are represented—stone tiling, rope making, bell founding etc. A 16th-century treasure chest and doll's house with furniture can also be seen.

Burford House Gardens *Shropshire*   546Bf
Gardens beside the R. Teme, noted for their flowering shrubs and an 18th-century summerhouse.

Burgh Castle   548Fh
This is one of the intermediate Roman forts of the Saxon Shore system. The east wall, most of the north and south walls and several of the external bastions, are still standing. Excavation has shown that it was originally planned to have internal turrets in its rounded angles, but these were demolished and the external bastions substituted, before the walls were finished.

The gap in the south wall was made in Norman times, when a motte and bailey castle was built here. The area of the motte at the south can still be seen and its surrounding ditch, now largely re-filled, passed through the wall at this point and is also visible as the external hollow at the south end.

There was also a mid-Saxon monastery within the walls, but no traces of this are now visible.

Burghley House *Cambs.*   547Hh
A superb example of Elizabethan domestic architecture, and the home of the Cecil and Exeter families for over 400 years. The house was begun in *c.* 1552 by William Cecil, who had just been knighted. He inherited the manor which had been bought by his father about 30 years previously. Cecil completed the Renaissance building in two stages, because after 1563 he was building another great house, at Theobalds in Hertfordshire. Flemish masons were probably employed on the mansion, which was completed *c.* 1587 after Cecil became Lord Burghley and Elizabeth I's Lord High Treasurer. Built around a central courtyard, Burghley is a square house with rounded corner towers topped by turrets. The main gate-house on one side comprises four more towers with turrets. Inside the state apartments are painted ceilings, silver fire-places, fine furniture, tapestries and over 700 works of art. There is also a rose garden.

Buriton *Hants.*   541Jd
Edward Gibbon, the 18th-century historian, lived in the Georgian manor house. The village, round a duckpond, stands below one of the high-points of the South Downs.

Burleigh Castle *Tayside*   562Bg
The ruins of a Balfour stronghold, described in Scott's *Old Mortality.* The lower part of the 15th-century keep remains, and traces of the curtain wall and moat are visible. Later remnants include the tower-house, built in 1582, and southern gate-house.

Burley on the Hill *Leics.*   553Gb
CHURCH OF THE HOLY CROSS Although originally Norman, the building was restored by John Loughborough Pearson, *c.* 1870. There is an impressive white marble mourning figure, kneeling, by Sir Francis Chantrey, *c.* 1820, on the monument to Lady Charlotte Finch.

Burnham *Bucks.*   547Hb
This village boasts a fine 13th-century church with a tower surmounted by an oak-shingled spire, but it is perhaps best known for Burnham Beeches, 600 acres of huge pollarded beech trees. This is all that remains of the forest that covered the Chilterns in prehistoric times.

Burnham Norton *Norfolk*   554Bd
CHURCH OF ST MARGARET The church, of the 13th to 15th centuries, has a round tower which may be of Saxon origin. The rood screen is dated 1458, and there is a fine pulpit with painted panels of the donor and the Latin Fathers of the Church (there is

another at St James, Castle Acre). The font is Norman.

Burnley *Lancs.*   558Ab
TOWNELEY HALL The fortified home of the Towneley family from the 13th century until 1902. The present house dates from the 14th century and was altered in the 16th, 17th and 19th centuries. It now contains an Elizabethan long gallery, a 16th-century chapel, an early 18th-century entrance hall and two Regency rooms. Much of the house has been retained as it was, furnished with Tudor and Jacobean furniture and hung with water-colours and oil paintings. There are two modern art galleries and changing museum displays. Each summer there is a series of temporary exhibitions. A museum of local crafts and industries is housed in the former brewhouse in the grounds.

Burnswark *Dumfs. & Gall.*   562Ba
HILL-FORT AND ROMAN SIEGE WORKS The hill on which this Iron Age fort stands is 920 ft high, on the east side of Annandale, with fine views up the dale and down to the Solway Firth and the Cumbrian coast. There are multiple defences which indicate more than one period of construction, the fort being finally an area of some 17 acres.

Two opposite flanks of the hill each have the traces of a Roman siege camp and, in the corner of that on the south-east side, there are the remains of an earlier small Roman fort. This dates from *c.* AD 140 and the later siege camps, it is thought, represent the punitive expedition after the revolt of AD 155. Burnswark has also been identified as the most probable site of the later battle of Brunanburgh (AD 937), where King Athelstan, Alfred's grandson, defeated Olaf Curan and his Norsemen, who were in alliance with Constantine, King of the Scots.

Burntisland *Fife*   562Bf
PARISH CHURCH A square 16th-century church; the gallery on all four sides has painted panels of ships, nautical instruments and other devices. In the centre of the church is an unusual early 17th-century pew with three sides.

Burrough Hill *Leics.*   552Fb
This four-sided Iron Age hill-fort has an internal area of some 12 acres and crowns the steep slopes of a hill-spur. There is still a substantial bank inside a ditch with small counterscarp bank. Near the south-east angle is the main entrance of the developed inturned type. The fort stands in a position of some importance, overlooking the valley which connects Leicester with Stamford.

Burry Holms *W. Glam.*   544Ec
Recent excavations on the island of Burry Holms have been filled in and none of the pre-Norman buildings can be seen, though the outline of some, including the 12th-century church and the later medieval hall and school-room, can be traced. The square chancel with its small stone altar are 14th-century additions; foundations of the original apse were discovered beneath. Above the low, sheltered medieval site a deep ditch and bank mark the defences of an Iron Age promontory fort. The island is accessible for about three hours each side of low water.

Burton *W. Sussex*   542Ad
CHURCH Small church of Norman origin in Burton Park. Restored in 1636, it escaped 19th-century alteration. There is a Perpendicular screen and several 16th-century monuments with brasses. The Arms of Charles I, dated 1636, are painted on a wall.

16th-CENTURY TUDOR CHEST

During the 16th century furniture makers in England copied the practice of marble, metal and timber inlaying developed in Italy during the previous century. Even so, in most English 16th-century interiors, furniture was limited to a few items—chests of drawers and wardrobes were rarely found and the use of the large box was still general. The design of this inlaid wood chest follows the usual pattern of the period, the panels showing the romantic architectural features of Tudor buildings. (Burton Agnes Hall)

Burton Agnes *Humberside* 559Gc
CHURCH OF ST MARTIN A church dating from the Normans, in a setting near the Hall, with a 15th-century west tower. The chancel was rebuilt in the mid-19th century. There is a Norman font and a fine alabaster monument with effigies of the 15th century.

Burton Agnes Hall *Humberside* 559Gc
Mansion, built in 1598–1610 in conventional Elizabethan style except for the bow windows, which were unknown elsewhere at this period. The entrance porch is three-tiered and elaborately decorated. The interior has a carved staircase, Oriental china, and paintings by Renoir, Manet, Corot and Utrillo.

Burton Constable *Humberside* 559Gb
An Elizabethan mansion, built in 1570, with castellated towers and oriel windows. Robert Adam, Wyatt, Carr and Lightoler carried out alterations to the interior. The grounds were laid out by Capability Brown.

Burton upon Trent *Staffs.* 552Dc
MUSEUM AND ART GALLERY The museum is mainly devoted to local history and traces the history of Burton and district from prehistoric times until the present. There is also a gallery of British birds.

Burwash *E. Sussex* 542De
Here is a long street, made handsome with pollarded trees on one side. Rampyndene, dated 1699, is the outstanding house, with a huge roof and chimney-stacks, and rich carving.

Burwell *Cambs.* 548Bf
A large village a mile long on the ancient shore of the once-flooded wilderness of the Old Fen. It has several interesting houses, including the manor house, with notable stone thatched barns, and Maltings Corner, a longstone building with some interesting windows, once part of the ancient Priory of St John. Ramsey Manor is a good 18th-century house, while the Hall, once much larger, contains a recently discovered Perpendicular window. Parsonage Farm, partly pre-Reformation, and Tunbridge, from the 18th century, are both good buildings. The site of the castle, at the siege of which Geoffrey de Mandeville, 'the Devil in human form', was slain, is marked by a moat 9 ft deep. There are two tower-mills.
CHURCH OF ST MARY A glorious Perpendicular church, with a west tower of Norman origin. There is a wheel-window above the chancel arch, and much panelling.

Bury *Greater Manchester* 552Bg
ART GALLERY AND MUSEUM The Wrigley Collection contains paintings by British 19th-century artists including Turner, Constable, Landseer, Webster, de Wint, John Crome and Birket-Foster. The gallery also has paintings and sculpture by Lowry, Steer and Epstein. The small museum is devoted mainly to local history, and displays include Bronze Age items from a recent excavation.
LANCASHIRE FUSILIERS MUSEUM The collection includes Napoleonic relics from when the Regiment guarded him as a prisoner on St Helena, mementoes of Wolfe of Quebec, and a large collection of medals, uniforms and regimental relics.

Bury St Edmunds *Suffolk* 548Cf
The burial place of a martyred Saxon king and the birthplace of Magna Carta; both these events are commemorated in the town's motto, *Sacrarium Regis, Cunabula Legis* (Shrine of a King, Cradle of the Law). Originally a Saxon homestead, known as Beodericsworth, the town was chosen in 636 as a suitable place for a monastery. In 870, King Edmund was brutally killed by the Danes during their raids on eastern England. His mutilated body was buried at Hoxne (4 miles south-east of Diss) where it lay for 33 years. Miracles were attributed to the king; he was canonised, and his body removed to Beodericsworth Monastery. The name of the town was changed to St Edmunds Bury. The Danish-born king, Knut (Canute), who conquered all England in 1016, granted the monastery abbey status in 1032. Edward the Confessor held Edmund's shrine in such reverence that he created the Franchise of the Liberty of St Edmundsbury, approximately modern West Suffolk. At the time of the Norman Conquest the abbot, Baldwin, was a Frenchman, and was able to save Bury St Edmunds from Norman destruction. He planned the town on Roman lines, and built

five gates, each with its own chapel and a hostel for pilgrims visiting the shrine. A period of culture followed the appointment of Abbot Anselm in 1121 and the illuminated manuscripts produced by his monks are now in the British Museum, the Metropolitan Museum, New York, the Vatican, at Oxford and at Cambridge where Corpus Christi College has the Bury Bible. One manuscript, written *c.* 1150–60, is in the form of a diary and gives a picture of life in a medieval monastery.

In 1214, ostensibly meeting to honour St Edmund's Day, King John's barons held a secret conference, and swore on the high altar of the abbey church to force the king to sign Magna Carta—thus the town's claim to be 'Cradle of the Law'.

In 1327, a quarrel between the abbot and the townsfolk reached a violent climax; the monks made an armed attack on the townspeople at their parish church and, in retaliation, the abbey was almost destroyed. The abbey was gutted by fire in 1465, but after rebuilding (completed in 1538), it became one of the architectural glories of England.

The town plan is based on the medieval formula of a square for God and a square for man. The former—just outside the abbey—is now known as Angel Hill; the latter is the market-place, still the commercial heart of the town. Abbot Baldwin's early gates disappeared in the 18th century, but their names are preserved in Northgate, Risbygate, Eastgate, Westgate and Southgate Streets. Athenaeum Lane (formerly Punch Lane), Skinner Lane and Pump Lane date from medieval times. The 12th-century Norman tower was built as a gate to the abbey. The Athenaeum, late 18th-century assembly rooms with 1804 façade and extensions, has a ballroom said to have been decorated by the Adam brothers.

ABBEY The entire precinct of the Abbey of St Edmundsbury survives intact, although the buildings themselves are much mutilated. There were formerly three parish churches on the perimeter of the precinct but only two of these medieval buildings have survived. One of them, St James's, has been the cathedral since 1914, the other, St Mary's, has a particularly impressive interior. Of the abbey buildings, the most complete remains are the two gate-houses, one Norman and the other built during the 14th century. All that survives of the immense abbey church is the west front, entirely robbed of its facing stone, a few columns at the east end which have been similarly robbed, and the crypt of the Norman apse which has now been laid open.

ANGEL CORNER A fine Queen Anne house containing the Gershom-Parkington Collection of clocks by such makers as Quare, Tompion, Vulliamy and others. Watches and other time-recording devices are displayed—for example, a ring-dial (a form of sun-dial) in which the sun's rays are cast, through a conical hole, on to the inner side of a brass ring marked off with hour lines. Clock and watchmaking flourished here in the 18th and 19th centuries.

CHURCH OF ST MARY A great 15th-century church, with a tower at the west end on the north side. There is a fine nave roof with carved angels, and the tomb of Mary Tudor (1496–1533), daughter of Henry VII, who became Queen of France.

CUPOLA HOUSE A 17th-century coffee house, with cupola, belvedere and a projecting second-floor balcony over the street.

GUILDHALL Built in the 15th century; the doorway has dog-tooth ornament. The two flanking wings were built in 1807. (By appointment.)

HENGRAVE HALL Originally built in 1525–38 by Sir Thomas Kyston, of stone and brick, the Hall is now a conference centre. A wing was demolished in 1757, and the moat filled in. The twin turrets to the gate-house are similar to others at Westminster Abbey and King's College, Cambridge. The oratory has a 16th-century window with 21 lights of biblical scenes. There is a minstrels' gallery in the restored banqueting hall. (By appointment.)

MOYSES HALL MUSEUM A 13th-century Monk's Chronicle, written in the abbey at Bury St Edmunds, is preserved in the museum, together with items dating from prehistoric, Roman, Saxon and medieval times. Of these, the most interesting is a late Bronze Age founder's hoard, which was found at Isleham, Cambridgeshire, in 1959. Weighing 185 lb, the hoard comprises palstaves, axes, hammers, spearheads, knives, swords, and what appear to be vehicle fittings. It is the largest fully recorded and complete founder's hoard in Britain, and of major archaeological importance because of the presence of decorated mounts (probably used on leather belts or harness), many of which have no parallel in the British Bronze Age, but bear similarity to decorated mounts found in Hungary, the upper Rhine and western France. Moyses Hall is a Norman building, dating from the 12th century, and is possibly the oldest domestic building in East Anglia.

SUFFOLK REGIMENT MUSEUM Items of historical interest connected with the Regiment.

BURY ST EDMUNDS
NORMAN TOWER

The Norman gateway tower is now the belfry of the nearby cathedral church of St James, the only cathedral in Suffolk. It was formerly the ceremonial gateway for the abbey, once one of the richest monasteries in England, whose abbots exercised considerable power over, and sometimes clashed with, the townspeople. One such clash is commemorated in the abbey gateway, not far from the Norman tower; this was built by the townspeople in 1347, as a punishment for having destroyed the original gateway during a riot in 1327.

UNITARIAN CHAPEL One of the finest Nonconformist chapels in Britain, built in 1711. It has a double-decker pulpit.

Buscot *Oxon.*   546Ec

BUSCOT PARK An estate of 3853 acres running down to the Thames and including the Cotswold stone village of Buscot. The mansion was built in 1780 in the Adam style; amongst the contents are Burne-Jones's *Briar-Rose* paintings and pictures by Rembrandt, Murillo and Reynolds. The park and lake are 18th century; the water gardens were laid out by Harold Peto.

Butley Priory *Suffolk*   548Ee

GATE-HOUSE The second greatest medieval gate-house in Suffolk, the first in Europe with a heraldic display in stone. The 14th-century gatehouse was once part of the Augustinian priory founded by Ranulf de Glanville in 1171, who travelled with Richard the Lionheart on the Third Crusade. Above this huge gateway are cut in stone the Arms of England and France, the three crowns of East Anglia, the Passion, and the Holy Roman Empire, with Leon and Castile. Below them is the blazonry of many great East Anglian families. The central block of ashlar and blue-grey flints is flanked by huge buttresses. Lancet windows,

pierced and foliated, give grace and light. The gate-house is surrounded by one of the oldest forests in England: the pre-Druidic Staverton Forest. Behind it, in the farmyard, somewhere beneath the ruins of the priory, is said to lie the silver coffin of Michael de la Pole, Earl of Suffolk, killed at Agincourt.

Butser Hill *Hants.*   541Hd

Butser has an irregularly rounded top joined on the south-west by a narrow ridge to a rather lower hill. The multiple defences of the Iron Age hill-fort, consisting of three widely separated bank-and-ditch structures, cross this ridge at various points to protect the wide top of Butser Hill. There are also minor defence-works at different places on the hill-top itself. To the south-east of the hilltop, the slopes reveal the lynchets of an area of 'Celtic' fields. They were probably cultivated in both Iron Age and Roman times.

Buxton *Derbys.*   552Ce

An important Roman station built around the natural hot spring known as St Ann's Well on the route from Manchester to Lincoln. The Old Hall by the well was built *c.* 1600 by the Earl of Shrewsbury and was enlarged by the 3rd Duke of Devonshire in 1670. The 5th Duke of Devonshire

THE SALOON AT BUSCOT PARK

Standing in grounds running down to the Thames, *Buscot Park was built in Adam style in 1775–80 by Edward Loveden Townsend. It was carefully restored to its original form by Lord Faringdon in the 1930's. In the house is the 'Briar-Rose' series of art-nouveau paintings by Sir Edward Burne-Jones*

(1833–98). *The magnificent saloon contains the group depicting the story of Sleeping Beauty. Burne-Jones originally intended taking holy orders, but under the influence of Dante Gabriel Rossetti he became a member of the Pre-Raphaelite brotherhood of painters and devoted himself to art.*

built the elegant crescent opposite the well in 1780–4, and the assembly room (now the clinic). Many other buildings followed as the repute of the medicinal waters converted the original village to a thriving spa in the 19th century. On the southern outskirts of the town is Solomon's Temple, a folly tower, erected in 1896 to honour Solomon Mycock, a farmer who had permitted the excavation of a prehistoric barrow on his land in 1894. MUSEUM Items illustrating local history and geology are on view. There are also collections of ornaments of Ashford Marble (a local stone) and Blue John (a blue mineral found locally), paintings, prints, pottery and glass.

Byland Abbey *N. Yorks.*   558Dd
The remains of this large and prosperous monastery include the west front of the church—the longest Cistercian church in England—and the lay-out of the entire monastic site. Byland Abbey was the final home of a community of monks who had lived temporarily at various other places since its foundation in 1134. The architecture suggests that lay-brothers set to work preparing the site before the arrival of the monks in 1177. The west wall has a large rose window. There is medieval tiling in green and yellow geometrical patterns. In a museum near the ruins are preserved the nave capital, decorated with foliage carving.

C

Caburn, Mount *E. Sussex*   542Cd
First occupied in Iron Age times without defences; these were later added and consisted of the low inner bank with its external ditch. The much larger outer bank, together with its ditch, was erected at the time of the Roman conquest. This bank was revetted with timber both inside and out, and crossbeams through the bank connected the two. The entrance was also remodelled at this time.

Cadbury Castle *Som.*   540De
This is the traditional site of the fabled Camelot, seat of King Arthur's court. Attempts have been made by excavation to learn its secrets, attempts tinged for many with the romantic hope that the Camelot tradition may be confirmed and that a historical man, perhaps a war chief of the sub-Roman Britons, may have been the original of the king of the story-cycle.

The fort crowns an isolated hill and is defended by four, and in places five, ramparts with ditches between them. The innermost bank was revetted with drystone walling, and the internal area is some 18 acres.

Excavations from 1966 to 1970 have shown both Neolithic and Late Bronze Age domestic occupation of the hill-top. The hill-fort defences were erected in the Iron Age and were remodelled at least four times. To this period belong numerous timbered houses and military equipment suggesting a workshop for its manufacture. There is a 'shrine' belonging to the last days before the Roman Conquest, when the defences were destroyed by a Roman military party in temporary residence.

An additional defence of timber and dry stonework was added at the time of the historical Arthur (*c.* AD 500), making this the most formidable fortification of his day. A timber gate-tower and a large feasting hall with auxiliary buildings were also discovered. In late Saxon times, King Ethelred the Unready established a royal mint here, for which further defences were constructed. The mint was destroyed by King Canute.

The excavations have been filled in to preserve the remains. Access to the defences is limited.

Cademuir Hill *Borders*   562Bd
HILL-FORTS A long spur runs south-west from the central massif of Cademuir, and the larger of these two forts is set upon its south-west end. It has a single stone wall enclosing an 8 acre area and there are traces of the foundations of many Iron Age houses. It is thought to have been deserted soon after the Roman occupation of the Lowlands. The smaller fort lies half a mile to the north-east on the same spur of hill. Its central area is enclosed in a substantial drystone wall and outside this on the east side is an area studded with upright boulders set into the ground, designed to prevent the rush of a body of men.

Cadney *Humberside*   553Gf
CHURCH OF ALL SAINTS There is Early English work here; the body of the church is early 13th century, and the south arcade is late Norman. There is a Perpendicular east window and screen. The font is Norman, and there is a 12th-century stone coffin-lid.

Cadzow Castle *Strathclyde*   561Je
The ruins of a castle visited by Mary, Queen of Scots in 1568. A herd of White Cattle roam the park beside the R. Avon.

Caerlaverock Castle *Dumfs. & Gall.*   562Ba
The castle is triangular in plan and surrounded by a moat. Over the gateway between two round towers is carved the crest of the Maxwells, Earls of Nithsdale, who owned the castle for over 400 years. It was built during the reigns of the Scottish Kings Alexander II and III, destroyed during Border Wars in 1312 and 1356, and rebuilt; it was finally left to ruin after destruction by the Covenanters, Presbyterian opponents of Charles I, in 1640. Robert Paterson, 'Old Mortality' of Sir Walter Scott's novel of that name, was buried in the churchyard of Caerlaverock Church, about a mile away.

Caerleon *Gwent*   545Jc
CHURCH OF ST CADOC A Norman church largely rebuilt at the end of the 15th century, and again during the 19th century. The west tower is at the end of the south aisle. The organ case was designed by A. E. Caroë. There is a series of 19th-century glass commemorative windows.

The church stands at the centre of Isca, the 50 acre permanent fortress of the 2nd Augustan Legion. Founded by the Romans *c* AD 75 on the banks of the tidal R. Usk, Isca was a busy seaport; its first clay and timber defences and buildings were rebuilt in stone *c* AD 100. Parts of this fortress wall and some internal buildings may still be seen. More spectacular, however, are the bath-house, and the amphitheatre outside the south-west wall, now fully excavated and preserved. The amphitheatre was the legion's drill-ground. Also outside lay the *vicus,* the civilian suburb which grew up as military needs permitted. The fortress was occupied until the end

CAERNARFON CASTLE

The first castle at Caernarfon was built during the Norman settlement of Wales, but it was reconquered by the Welsh in 1115 and all traces of any buildings dating from that period have now vanished. The castle was entirely replaced by another begun in 1283–4, during Edward I's conquest of Wales, and completed about 1330. According to ancient Welsh tradition Caernarfon was the birthplace of the Emperor Constantine, and in 1283 it is reported that 'Magnus Maximus', allegedly the father of Constantine, was dug up at Caernarfon and reburied in the church there. In 1284 the future Edward II was created Prince of Wales there and in 1911 the future Edward VIII was also invested with the Principality.

of the 3rd century, when it was partly replaced by the fort at Cardiff, though it was not finally deserted until the latter part of the 4th century. Finds from the site are displayed in the museum.

Caernarfon *Gwynedd*   550Ee
ROMAN FORT Here, on the hill-slopes outside Edward I's castle and the modern town, stand the remains of the Roman Segontium. It had a long history. Placed to overlook the outer end of the Menai Strait and its coastlands, it was first founded in the early days of the Roman occupation. A period of unrest in the second half of the 2nd century AD led to its being rebuilt in stone. Further reconstruction took place at the beginning of the 3rd century and, after the Irish raids of AD 367, yet another reconstruction took place. Its garrison seems finally to have been withdrawn by Maximus in AD 383 to aid in his continental adventure.
SEGONTIUM MUSEUM The museum stands next to the remains of Segontium Roman fort, which was excavated by Sir Mortimer Wheeler in 1921–3, and houses the objects found in the fort.

Caernarfon Castle *Gwynedd*   550Ee
Caernarfon Castle was begun in 1283–4 as part of Edward I's plan for the control of Wales and attained its present form in *c.* 1330. The Eagle Tower was one of the largest single towers ever to be built in the Middle Ages. The walls of Caernarfon Castle are built of different coloured masonry and the angle-towers are polygonal. These walls in fact bear a striking resemblance to the walls of Constantinople, and in adopting this design Edward I may have been seeking to link the castle with the traditional belief that the Emperor Constantine was born at Caernarfon. Surveys in the 16th century suggest that the castle was neglected and in a ruined state at that period. In the

17th century Caernarfon narrowly escaped demolition after the Civil War, and it was only in the 19th century that the castle was repaired.

In 1284 Edward II was born here and presented to the Welsh people by his father, Edward I, as Prince of Wales—'one who could speak neither English nor Welsh'. The investiture of HRH Prince Charles as Prince of Wales took place here in 1969.

Caerphilly Castle *Mid Glam.*   545Jb
Due to the immense reconstructions carried out by the former owner, the 4th Marquess of Bute, and since 1949 by the Department of the Environment, Caerphilly Castle, reflected in its great lakes, is a splendid example of early military architecture. Remarkably advanced in plan, the building was begun in 1268. It bristles with ingenious details of internal defence; but its masterpiece is the brilliantly conceived water defence, designed to keep out of range the deadly military catapults, which, at short distance, could batter down the most robust walls.

Caerwent *Gwent*   546Ac
The Roman city of Venta Silurum, some 9 miles east of Caerleon, was the cantonal town of the Silures. Originally defended by double earthen banks and ditches, a 30 ft high stone wall was added late in the Roman period as a defence against the raids of Irish pirates. Like Caerleon most of the site of Caerwent is free from modern buildings. Venta was the only walled civilian town in Wales.

Cairnholy *Dumfs. & Gall.*   556Dg
These are two chambered Neolithic cairns standing about 150 yds apart near the east side of Wigtown Bay. The larger of the two is about 170 ft long and about 50 ft wide. Its great hollow forecourt is outlined by tall standing stone slabs

and inside the entrance there is a double chamber, now somewhat ruined. Most of the covering mound has now disappeared.

The northern cairn is smaller, being only some 70 ft long by 40 ft wide. This also has a double burial chamber.

Cairnpapple *Lothian*   *562Ae*
Cairnpapple Hill is crowned by a complex of henge, cairns and burials. The first structure was a group of three enormous boulders and an arc of large stones in conjunction with a late Neolithic cemetery. This was superseded by a henge monument with two opposed entrances. Inside the ditch of this henge, stones were set in a great oval Then came a cairn, 50 ft in diameter, on the site of the henge. This had a stone kerb. Later, the cairn was enlarged; it now had a diameter of 100 ft and received cremations in urns of Middle Bronze Age type. Finally, later burials were intruded, probably in the Iron Age.

Caisteal Grugaig *Highland*   *565Gf*
The remains of this Iron Age broch are in good condition, and still stand some 13 ft high. A good entrance, wall-chambers, a stair-lobby with part of the staircase and part of a gallery are all evident.

Caister Castle *Norfolk*   *554Eb*
An impressive ruin of a castle built for Sir John Fastolf in 1432–5. The moated remains include the 98 ft high round tower with stair turret, a gate-house and stretches of wall. It was the home of the Paston family from 1459 to 1599 (except for five years) and some of the 'Paston Letters', which give a vivid account of 15th-century domestic life, were written here. In the grounds is a motor museum.

Caister-on-Sea *Norfolk*   *554Eb*
Here, on the higher land overlooking the former open estuary and harbour, stood a Roman walled town. Much of it has been excavated, but the part preserved for inspection contains part of the south gate with an adjacent length of wall-base, and part of a great building just inside the gate, possibly a hostelry for seamen and travellers from the ships. South from this gate, a road led down to the quay and harbour, some 400 yds away. The latter is now the drained marsh-pasture on the south side of West Road, opposite Grange Farm, and the site of the quay is marked here by the new roadway running along the side of this pasture to the new estate. The first occupation began early in the 2nd century and the town survived until the end of the Roman occupation of Britain. Later, a Saxon settlement grew up in its ruins but, at the time of the Danish settlement in AD 880, this was deserted and a new village was formed to become the centre of modern Caister.

Caistor *Lincs.*   *553Hf*
CHURCH OF SS PETER AND PAUL Among the interesting monuments in this church is one in the vestry to Sir Edward Maddison, who died in 1553 at the age of 100. The west tower is Saxon and the nave arcades are 13th century. There are some 13th- and 14th-century stone effigies and a 15th-century brass on the chancel floor. The 19th-century stained glass includes some by C. E. Kempe.

Caistor St Edmund *Norfolk*   *554Db*
Venta Icenorum, the cantonal town of the Iceni, stood on a valley site not far from the confluence of the Yare and Wensum. At first a minor open town, it was walled soon after AD 200, a central area only of some 35 acres being enclosed. On the north side, the outer face of the wall is visible in places, though rather overgrown, but in general the wall today stands no higher than the earthen rampart inside it. The interior, much of which has been excavated, is now under pasture.

Cakemuir *Lothian*   *562Ce*
Of 15th-century origin, the house was considerably altered in the 17th century. Of note is a spiral staircase between stone walls 6 ft thick. Two sentry-boxes stand on the parapet around the original tower. (By appointment.)

Calder Abbey *Cumbria*   *557Ge*
The remains of a 12-century Cistercian abbey beside a river. The ruins include those of the church and the 13th-century chapter house.

Callaly Castle *Northld.*   *562Fc*
A 17th-century mansion, with Georgian and Victorian additions. Some parts of a 13th-century castle remain.

Callanish *Lewis, Western Isles*   *568Bc*
STONE CIRCLE AND CAIRN The standing stones form the most imposing feature of the group. A pillar over 15 ft high stands centrally in a circle 37 ft in diameter, formed by 13 tall slabs. North from this circle runs a double avenue of stones for a distance of 270 ft. Ten stones on one side and nine on the other still survive, though originally there may have been 20 on each side. Other shorter stone-lines radiate from the circle, 50 ft on the east and 40 ft on the west.

The remnants of the chambered cairn lie in the eastern part of the circle. There is also another low mound, perhaps another cairn, lying immediately to the north-east of the first. The complex is of Bronze Age date.

Camber Castle *E. Sussex*   *542Ed*
The ruins of one of Henry VIII's coastal defence castles, built in 1539 as a protection against French raids. Originally it was near the sea, but because of silting up of the coast is now over a mile inland. It had fallen into decay by 1626.

Camborne *Cornwall*   *538Bb*
PUBLIC LIBRARY AND MUSEUM The building was given to the town in 1894 by John Passmore Edwards, a philanthropist who founded 70 public institutions. The museum, in one room of the library, houses mainly archaeological, historical, mineral and mining items of local interest. In the archaeological section there are Neolithic and flint implements found on ancient camp sites.

Cambridge *Cambs.*   *548Af*
Much of the charm of Cambridge is in the small streets and passages such as St Edward's Passage off King's Parade. In Botolph Lane off Trumpington Street there is a group of attractive small houses. Little St Mary's Lane, also off Trumpington Street, is a fascinating byway which has been skilfully restored. It overlooks an old churchyard. The Little Rose Inn, in Trumpington Street, c. 1600, was probably the last Cambridge inn to have extensive stables. No. 2 Chesterton Road is Wentworth House, an elegant dwelling of the late 18th century; Nos. 4–10 are attractive one-storey cottages. Near the corner of Beche Road and Priory Road there are the small but notable 13th-century remains of the Cellarers Chequer House of the original Barnwell Priory, founded 1092 and now vanished, apart from its Chapel of St Andrew the Less.

Good houses on the outskirts of Cambridge include Chesterton Hall close to the highway, a smallish Jacobean mansion, with three big gabled

CLARE COLLEGE GATES AND BRIDGE

Thomas Grumbold was Christopher Wren's mason for Trinity College Library. When he sketched out his first design for a Classical bridge across the Cam in 1638 he was paid three shillings for his work. Clare College at the time was about to undergo rebuilding and Grumbold's bridge was probably intended to make the transportation of building materials easier. The wrought-iron gateway was made by a local smith named Warren in 1713–15, following a sudden taste for ornamental ironwork stimulated by Mary II and the superb work of the French smith Jean Tijou.

Warren also made two other gates for Clare College, replacing ones of timber. The bridge and gates give Clare College access to the Backs, one of Cambridge's chief pleasures. These sweeping lawns beside the Cam, set with willow trees, and affording fine views of the riverside colleges, stretch from St John's College, past Trinity, Trinity Hall and Clare Colleges to King's College and Queens' College. They were largely the work of Richard Bentley, Master of Trinity College from 1699 to 1734, who made them from what was then rough marshland.

dormers; Fen Ditton Hall behind the famous Ditton Meadow, a charming red-brick house *c.* 1720, with three different types of Dutch gable; Newnham Grange, late 18th century; and the Malting House (1909).

ABBEY HOUSE Built in 1678, it is part timber-framed and part brick, with splendid chimney-stacks; it was noted for its alleged population of ghosts, for example the Ghost of Squire Butler who died in 1765; the White Lady; the Ghostly Squirrel; an Astral Hare; a Disembodied Head; a Clanking Chain; and a poltergeist. In recent years the ghosts were solemnly exorcised by a parson with bell, book and candle. The house has fine panelled rooms, but is not open to viewing.

CHURCH OF THE HOLY SEPULCHRE Known as 'The Round Church', this is one of England's four surviving Norman round churches, with a vaulted ambulatory. The oak roofs in the choir and the north aisle were carved in the 14th and 15th centuries.

EAGLE INN Off Bene't Street, the last remaining coaching inn in the city, with a cobbled courtyard and first-floor gallery.

FITZWILLIAM MUSEUM A great Corinthian portico in Trumpington Street is a feature of the entrance to the world-famous museum founded by the 7th Viscount Fitzwilliam of Merrion, who in 1816 bequeathed to the university the sum of

£100,000 plus his library and collection of 144 paintings and 130 medieval illuminated manuscripts and other *objets d'art*. The building was begun in 1837 and opened to the public in 1848; its interior has a wealth of marblework, statuary, mosaics, friezes, and rococo enrichments in the mid-Victorian taste. The museum's collections comprise West Asiatic, Egyptian, Greek and Roman antiquities, European ceramics and other applied arts, Islamic art, Far Eastern art, manuscripts, paintings, drawings and miniatures, and prints. There is also a library, which includes a collection of music and literary autographs. (See also pp. 120–1.)

HOBSON'S CONDUIT Built between 1610 and 1614 to carry water to Cambridge from Nine Wells near Great Shelford, it commemorates Thomas Hobson who died in 1631. He was the famous Cambridge carrier who coined the phrase 'Hobson's Choice', since anyone who wished to hire a horse from his livery stable had to take the first one on the list—and no other. The monument, transferred from Market Hill to the corner of Lensfield Road in 1855, is octagonal with strapwork ornamentation on top and a cupola.

JESUS COLLEGE This college was founded in 1496 by Bishop Alcock of Ely in the buildings of the former Benedictine nunnery of St Radegund. Alcock suppressed the nunnery and took over the buildings as a working unit—which shows how similar the respective corporate existences of college and convent were. The chapel remained the chapel, but was reduced in size, the prioress's lodging became the Master's lodging, the refectory became the dining-hall, although Alcock enlarged and improved the building. He also added an extra storey to the living quarters. In addition, he made improvements in the outer court, particularly to the attractive main gate.

KING'S COLLEGE CHAPEL The chapel was the only completed medieval part of this college founded in 1441. The first stone was laid in 1446 and the chapel, in Perpendicular style, was completed in 1515. Subsequent buildings of the college belong mainly to the 19th century, apart from the Gibbs Building, a fine addition in Classical style, begun in 1723. The whole assembly of buildings stands on a magnificent site overlooking the banks of the R. Cam.

KING'S PARADE Houses and shops of differing styles, heights and periods without a dull frontage among them; they face the delicate stone tracery of King's College screen, and the Classical lines of the Senate House. No. 17 has a timber-framed and overhanging upper storey. No. 14 is an 18th-century brick house.

LITTLE TRINITY GUEST HOUSE The most handsome private house in Cambridge. Five-bay, c. 1800, with dark brick and a doorcase including Ionic pilasters, it stands back from Jesus Lane behind iron gates and gate piers. No. 32 Jesus Lane is another excellent 18th-century brick house. The Pitt Club, also in Jesus Lane, is an assembly room building with an elegant Ionic portico and a medallion of Pitt above the doorway.

MARKET-PLACE The cobbled Market-Place, dominated by the modern Guildhall, is the very heart of Cambridge. Bookstalls sell second-hand textbooks, as their predecessors did in the Middle Ages, while undergraduates of various persuasions harangue the jostling market-day crowd. The Guildhall contains the city treasures, including the Great Mace (1710) and four other gilt maces dating from 1723.

NORTHAMPTON STREET AND MAGDALENE STREET Here are the best medieval houses and cottages in the city—a long range of two- and three-storied plastered and timbered houses, many with oversailing upper floors. This group, with the old houses opposite Magdalene College, are reminders of what medieval Cambridge looked like.

PEMBROKE COLLEGE CHAPEL The first of Cambridge's ecclesiastical buildings in a purely Classical style. Bishop Wren of Ely gave £5000 to Pembroke College in 1663 for a new chapel and this was completed by 1665 to designs by his nephew, Sir Christopher Wren, who probably based his design on drawings of a Roman temple published in a book by the Italian architect Sebastiano Serlio. Serlio's books ran to many editions and were an important source for architectural forms during the early English Renaissance. The street front of the chapel is pedimented, and has four Corinthian pilasters dividing the three bays; above is a small hexagonal wooden cupola. In 1880 George Gilbert Scott enlarged the chapel when he moved the east wall eastwards and rebuilt it.

PETERHOUSE COLLEGE This is the oldest college in Cambridge. It was founded in 1284 and still retains some of its original masonry.

ST JOHN'S COLLEGE Founded in 1511 by Lady Margaret Beaufort—great-granddaughter of John of Gaunt and grandmother of Henry VIII—St John's has three magnificent red-brick courts with a fine gate-tower, a 17th-century library, and a

TRINITY COLLEGE LIBRARY

Sir Christopher Wren designed Trinity College Library in 1676; it marks a transitional point in his work. Wren first proposed a domed free-standing building, but in the end had to design a building to close off the two arms of Nevile's Court, which resulted in this elegant Classical building, some 150 ft long, facing the court on one side and the R. Cam on the other. The library, raised to first-floor level, is a vast hall; bookshelves line the walls beneath the windows and also stand at right angles to form a series of small bays. There is much work by the 17th-century master of woodcarving, Grinling Gibbons. In addition there are busts by Louis Roubiliac, Michael Rysbrack, Peter Scheemakers and John Bacon the Elder.

chapel designed by Sir Gilbert Scott. The picturesque 'Bridge of Sighs' crosses the R. Cam.

SCHOOL OF PYTHAGORAS Never a school, and probably never a part of the university; it is, however, the oldest secular building in the city, built of clunch-rubble before AD 1100. It has an undercroft and a hall on the upper floor, a 13th-century solar and 14th-century buttresses. Merton Hall, a 17th-century gabled house now belonging to St John's College, is next to the school.

SCOTT POLAR RESEARCH INSTITUTE Established in 1920 as a memorial to Capt. R. F. Scott, RN, and the four companions who died with him on the return journey from the South Pole in 1912, the Institute is part of the Department of Geography of the University of Cambridge, and exists to promote and conduct research in the Arctic and Antarctic. Its museum features relics of Arctic and Antarctic expeditions, among them some 400 watercolours and pencil sketches made by Edward Wilson during Scott's Antarctic expeditions on the *Discovery* (1901–4) and *Terra Nova* (1910–13), and others by E. L. Moss and J. E. Davis during 19th-century expeditions. There are also Eskimo soapstone carvings and stone-cuts and other exhibits of current scientific activities in both regions.

SENATE HOUSE James Gibbs, the Scottish architect of St Martin-in-the-Fields in London, designed the

Senate House in 1722. It is the only part built of a complex of university administrative buildings designed by him. The building is two storeys high, and nine window bays long. The upper windows are round-headed, but those of the lower level have alternating straight and curved pediments. Between the bays are giant Corinthian columns or pilasters, with the three central bays beneath a pediment. Christopher Cass, a master-mason who died in 1734, was employed to carve much of the decoration. A first-class craftsman, he had also been associated with Gibbs in the building of St Martin-in-the-Fields and with other architects at St Paul's Cathedral.

TRINITY COLLEGE Two early colleges supplied the main elements: King's Hall, founded by Edward II in 1317 and enlarged by his son in 1337, and Michaelhouse, founded in 1324 by Hervey de Stanton, Chief Justice and Chancellor of the Exchequer. The buildings occupied adjacent sites, and with further endowments amalgamated in 1546 into a single college. It is on this that some authorities ascribe the founding of the college to Henry. Some of the remains of King's Hall, with a main entrance that was built between 1490 and 1535, are still visible. But even older than King's Hall is King Edward's Tower, which was built in 1428–32. This is the earliest of all the great Cambridge gate-houses, but it is no longer on its original site. It was taken down in 1599 and rebuilt on a site north of its earlier position. Thomas Nevile, who was Master of the college from 1593 to 1615 and later became Dean of Canterbury, made further additions to the heterogeneous collection of buildings of different dates and converted them into one great quadrangle.

TRINITY COLLEGE LIBRARY The library was begun in 1676 to designs by Sir Christopher Wren. It made a fourth side to Nevile's Court, previously an open yard facing the R. Cam. A relatively plain Classical building, the library is raised to first-floor level above a ground floor open to the court through a round-arched arcade. On the parapet stand four figures representing Divinity, Mathematics, Law and Physics, for which the 17th-century sculptor Caius Gabriel Cibber was paid £80 in 1681. The river front is plainer than the court side, as there is no open arcade; instead there are windows and three great doorways, one in the centre and one at each end. The door openings are very low because the height of the first floor of the library was dictated by the level of the existing buildings in Nevile's Court. (See p. 115.)

UNIVERSITY BOTANIC GARDEN Founded in 1761, the garden covers more than 40 acres, and has an entrance in Bateman Street and a frontage along Trumpington Road.

UNIVERSITY LIBRARY The origins of the library are probably 13th century: the earliest catalogue, begun c. 1424, lists 122 books. Until 1934, when the new building designed by Sir Giles Scott was opened, the University Library was housed in buildings known as Old Schools, and the collection had reached a total of 1¼ million volumes. It now has 72 miles of shelving that hold more than 3¾ million books, more than 20,000 manuscripts, 800,000 maps and 380,000 items of printed music.

Among the present collections are: The Royal (Bishop Moore's) Library, presented by George I in 1715; the Bradshaw collection of Irish books (1868–70); the Wade collection of Chinese books (1886); the Taylor-Schechter collection of Hebriaca from the Cairo Genizah (1898); the Acton Historical Library (60,000 volumes), presented by Viscount Morley in 1902; and a collection of incunabula (books printed before 1501). Its treasures include the Codex Bezae manuscript of the Gospels, the only perfect copy of Caxton's *Golden Legend*, and the Gutenberg Bible (c. 1450).

The library is entitled (under the Copyright Act) to claim a copy of every work published in the British Isles: it does not necessarily exercise this right, but its resources are continually being enlarged by gifts and purchases of foreign volumes.

The red-brick library is the biggest building in Cambridge: the main reading room is 200 ft long on its west side; the front, or east side, is over 400 ft long. At the main entrance are great metal honeycomb-pattern doors beneath a tower that dominates the landscape. The library is open each afternoon, Monday to Friday.

UNIVERSITY MUSEUM OF ARCHAEOLOGY AND ANTHROPOLOGY Collections of archaeological items from Europe, Asia, Africa and America, and ethnographical material from America, Africa, Oceania and S.E. Asia.

UNIVERSITY MUSEUM OF CLASSICAL ARCHAEOLOGY A large representative collection of casts of Greek and Roman sculpture is on view.

WESTMINSTER COLLEGE The best-looking college building not belonging to the university; built of red brick in the Tudor style in 1899, it has short wings, a good staircase, a turret with a lantern and a dining-hall with a wagon-roof.

WHIPPLE MUSEUM OF THE HISTORY OF SCIENCE Housed in the original Cambridge Free School (1618–24), the museum contains a collection of early scientific instruments, calculating devices and surveying instruments, and books on the history of science.

GATEWAY TO ST JOHN'S COLLEGE

Lady Margaret Beaufort, Countess of Richmond and Derby, and mother of Henry VII, was one of the great benefactresses of Cambridge. She lived from 1443 to 1509, and in 1505 founded Christ's College. At the suggestion of her confessor and advisor, Bishop John Fisher, she founded a college in honour of St John the Evangelist, but did not live to see it; Fisher continued her work and the college opened in 1511 on the site of a former hospital. The gate-house is a three-storey brick and stone building, the ground floor richly fan-vaulted. It was probably built by the master-mason William Swayne, who also worked at Christ's College and King's College Chapel. The heraldic decoration commemorates Lady Margaret and Henry VII. In the centre the Beaufort Arms are supported by two yales—fabulous beasts with antelopes' bodies, goat-like heads and the ability to swivel their horns about. Above the coat of arms is the Beaufort crest—an eagle's head and wings rising from a coronet, while to the left and right are the Tudor and Beaufort badges—rose and portcullis. All around are strewn daisies and borage, Lady Margaret's flowers. In the niche above is a figure of St John, put there in 1662 to replace the original statue removed during the Civil War.

Beyond the gate lies First Court, the original building of St John's College. The doorway at the far side of the court leads to two further courts, the first of them one of the finest in Cambridge. Beyond these is the famous Bridge of Sighs over the Cam, named after the Venetian bridge. It leads to New Court cloisters, the Backs, and St John's excellent new buildings. To the right of First Court is the 19th-century college chapel by Gilbert Scott. It contains some of the stalls from the original chapel, and a monument of about 1522 to Hugh Ashton, Archdeacon of York, who is represented by effigies, one in life, the other in death.

CAMBRIDGE *Treasures of the Colleges*

The Cambridge colleges have gained their treasures from many sources: from kings and queens, bishops and travellers, craftsmen from the far side of Europe and from the town itself. The quality and variety would be amazing anywhere except in such a great centre of culture as this.

THE TRINITY APOCALYPSE *This is probably the finest of the medieval manuscripts inspired by the visions of the Apocalypse of St John. It was made about 1250. In the upper half St John stands on the left of the Third Beast, or false prophet, which is then shown sitting on a mound faced by the Second Beast and worshippers. Below, three men kill three martyrs and two men worship the Second Beast. (Trinity College)*

PEDESTAL DISH FROM COCLÉ, PANAMA *The Coclé region of Panama has some of the most unusual pottery in a continent notable for its remarkable pottery styles. This dish is decorated with crocodile heads and characteristic pointed hooks. Most Coclé pottery has been found in graves dating from the 14th century to the Spanish conquest, around the 16th century. (University Museum of Archaeology and Anthropology)*

KING'S COLLEGE CHAPEL *This chapel, in royal tradition (King's College was founded by Henry VI in 1441), has probably the finest and purest set of fanvaults in England. They are based on the 14th-century cloisters of Gloucester Cathedral. The angel stands on top of the organ case. It was designed in 1859 by Gilbert Scott and is based on an engraving of the chapel made in 1690 which shows the original angels later removed during alteration.*

BERTEL THORVALDSEN: LORD BYRON *The great Danish neo-Classical sculptor Bertel Thorvaldsen (1770–1844) is usually associated with a particularly severe brand of neo-Grecian nude—the museum devoted to his work in Copenhagen makes a chilly impression. But here, suiting the spirit of his statue to its subject, he produced a highly romantic work—one of his masterpieces: Byron sits among the ruins of Athens, composing part of 'Childe Harold'. (Trinity College Library)*

RUBENS: THE ADORATION OF THE MAGI *El Greco's work shows the ingredients of the Mannerist style—asymmetry, deliberate elongation of the human figure and a preference for rather acid and hard colours. In the succeeding baroque period the soaring figures, the exaggerated gestures, the facial contortions were subordinated to a dramatic whole in which the splendour of rich resonant colour played a major part. It was an international, largely Catholic style and although its origins were in Italy and the Counter-Reformation it flourished in Flanders, Southern Germany, Central Europe and Spain. Rubens (1577–1640), whose vigour and robustness are unequalled, was the greatest figure in northern baroque; his version of the style was admirably suited to vast canvases glorifying Church and State. This is one of his great altar-pieces painted originally for a convent in Louvain and paid for in 1634. By this time the movement of Rubens's forms had become less energetic and apart from the splash of red which he so often introduces, as here in the robe of the king prostrating himself, the colour range too is quieter.*
(King's College Chapel)

THE BETRAYAL OF CHRIST BY JUDAS *A detail from a stained glass window in the Chapel of King's College, the only medieval English church, apart from Fairford, Glos., to retain all its original glass. This panel is one of a series portraying scenes from the lives of the Virgin and Christ; most of the panels were designed, painted and glazed by Dirick Vellert of Antwerp and Galyon Hone, a Netherlander, two of the many foreign craftsmen working in England during the reign of Henry VIII. In many great churches splendid windows frequently told the whole history of man from the Creation to the Fall. Those at King's College are the last great example of the medieval glaziers' art in England.*

ST BEDE'S COMMENTARY ON THE APOCALYPSE *The main characteristic of Romanesque art—the portrayal of the human figure in rigid poses expressing abstract qualities—is well illustrated in this drawing from a manuscript written between 1150 and 1155. It shows St John as a bishop with a monk, the writer of the manuscript, at his feet. The Anglo-Saxon technique of coloured outline drawing is adapted to the Romanesque demands with marvellous economy and skill—a striking example of how line was emphasised in English art throughout the stylistic changes of the 10th, 11th and 12th centuries. (St John's College)*

QUEENS' COLLEGE DIAL *The dial in the Old Court at Queens' College is one of the finest examples of sun-dial art in the country, and one of the few moon-dials in existence. It was repainted in the mid-18th century, although records show a dial here in 1642. The small ball on the style is a unique feature of the dial and makes possible many of the calculations. The shadow cast on to the golden Roman numerals is apparent solar time. The table of figures below the dial is an aid to telling the time by moonlight, providing the moon is strong enough to cast a readable shadow. The altitude of the sun can also be observed, the date, the time of sunrise and sunset and the sign of the zodiac in which the sun lies.*

FITZWILLIAM MUSEUM, CAMBRIDGE

The Fitzwilliam is one of Europe's major museums. Its collections cover Egyptian, Greek and Roman antiquities, coins and medals, medieval manuscripts, painting and drawing of all periods, prints, and the applied arts. Outstanding are the collection of coins and medals, the collection of paintings, and the collections devoted to the applied arts, especially ceramics, glass and armour.

LIMOGES ENAMEL TRIPTYCH *This enamel triptych was made in 1538 in Limoges by Pierre Reymond, who lived from about 1513 to 1584 and was a leading master of the art of enamelling in the Renaissance.* *Reymond and his contemporaries used coloured enamels applied to a design incised on metal, usually copper. The centre panel here is based on a composition by Raphael. The sides show St Peter and Daniel.*

GREEN JADE BUFFALO *This Chinese piece, 15¾ in. long, is unusually large for a carving in jade, which is generally found in smaller pieces. Until the Revolution of 1911 it formed part of the Imperial collection in Peking, where it was attributed to the Han period, but it is now thought to have been carved during the Ming dynasty.*

FIGURE OF OCEANUS *Modelled between 1762 and 1765 by Konrad Linck for the Frankenthal factory in Germany, this figure of Oceanus is an example of the popular 18th-century trend for using gods as the subjects for table centre-pieces. The figures were designed to be seen from all angles and so every detail is carefully finished. Sea-green crêpe paper would have been placed on the table to imitate waves, and figures (originally confectionery but by the 18th century porcelain) representing Neptune, Oceanus and mermaids would be placed on imitation rocks and shells.*

18TH-CENTURY GLASS GOBLET *The Royal Arms of England are painted on this lead-glass goblet, the Prince of Wales' feathers and motto 'Ich Dien' ('I serve') being on the reverse. Painted by William Beilby around 1762, the goblet has a bucket-shaped bowl and an enamel-twist stem. The bowl, stem and foot of the goblet were all formed separately and joined together in the final stage of manufacture.*

16TH-CENTURY ITALIAN PARADE HELMET *Bought for a few shillings from a theatrical costumier in 1937, this helmet was probably originally made for a Renaissance prince. Its style is Classical, based on Roman armour, showing that it was designed for show rather than for combat. The visor is in the form of a lion's mask. The skull was beaten out of a single piece of steel, and is embossed in relief with trophies of arms and musical instruments, foliage, and two nude females representing Fame and Victory. Little now remains of the original gold and silver which covered the surface decoration, and both the cheekpieces have also been lost. Despite these defects it displays the art of the Renaissance metalworker to perfection, and there is little doubt that it is the work of Filippo and Francesco Negroli of Milan, the greatest masters in this field.*

DOMENICO VENEZIANO: THE ANNUNCIATION *One of the five predella panels of the St Lucy altarpiece, painted for a church in Florence by Domenico. He was one of the major painters in 15th-century Florence but few of his works have survived. He contributed a feeling for atmospheric colour and the semblance of real light to the development of perspective and the study of anatomy which were the main preoccupations of Florentine painters, obsessed as they were with a love of abstract ideas and formal relations.*

CANTERBURY ROMAN GLASS

Glass-blowing was invented in Roman times, probably in the last century BC. The two-handled flagon is from the 3rd century and was dredged from a lake at Bishopsbourne in 1846. To the right is a 1st-century jug found in a Roman grave at Faversham; it comes from the Rhineland, a great centre of glass-making. The two glass bracelets, found in the 19th century in a field at Milton Regis, may possibly be Anglo-Saxon. (Canterbury Royal Museum)

Cambuskenneth *Central*   *562Af*
ABBEY Picturesque ruins, beside the R. Forth, of the Augustinian abbey founded in the mid-12th century by King David I. A magnificent 13th–14th-century bell-tower is still intact.

Cameley *Avon*   *540Cf*
CHURCH OF ST JAMES A small, isolated church dating from the 12th century, with interesting fittings—pulpit, pews, reredos and communion rail.

Campsall *S. Yorks.*   *552Eg*
CHURCH OF ST MARY MAGDALENE A large cruciform building, of Norman origin with later additions. There is a tall rood screen and a family monument by Flaxman, 1803. The stone altar in the Lady Chapel is by Pugin.

Camster *Highland*   *569Ld*
GREY CAIRNS OF CAMSTER The first of the two Neolithic cairns is the 200 ft Camster long cairn. The horns at the eastern end enclosed a ritual area, in which fires were lit in front of a low platform below the great revetment wall; the area was then deliberately filled with stones. The long cairn covers two little round cairns with chambers.

Two hundred yards to the south-east is a round cairn, a mound of loose stones some 55 ft in diameter. It has a 20 ft long passage leading to a triple chamber, partly roofed by stone slabs and partly by corbelling. Some 140 yds to the south-west is a third round cairn, 27 ft in diameter.

Cannock Wood *Staffs.*   *552Cb*
CASTLE RING This is an important Iron Age fort standing on an isolated elevation to overlook the surrounding country. To the north and west there are two protective banks, each with an external ditch, but on the opposite side, where there is no steep slope, there are no less than five banks with

four ditches. The entrance is on the east side, with the inner bank inturned to provide an entrance passage.

Cannon Hall *S. Yorks.*   *552Dg*
A 17th-century mansion which was rebuilt in the 18th century by Carr of York. It contains furniture and paintings, and stands in a fine park.

Canon Pyon *Heref. & Worcs.*   *546Ae*
CHURCH OF ST LAWRENCE A 13th- and 14th-century church with a south tower. There is an octagonal Perpendicular font, some misericords, and stalls with poppy-head carving. Also a monument (1753) by Louis Roubiliac, the foremost sculptor of his period in this country.

Canterbury *Kent*   *542Ff*
During the Second World War bombs destroyed one-third of the old city of Canterbury, and in so doing revealed ancient foundations which enabled archaeologists to trace the story of its occupation from the Iron Age through Roman and medieval times. A settlement of *c.* 300 BC had become a centre of the Belgae tribe when the Romans invaded, and was the Saxon town of Cantwarbyrig when St Augustine arrived on a mission from Rome in AD 597; in 602 Canterbury became the metropolitan city of the English Church. The Normans built a castle, now in ruins, between 1070 and 1094, and in 1067 the cathedral, sacked by the Danes in 1011, was completely rebuilt. In 1170 Thomas Becket was murdered in the cathedral and, from that date until Henry VIII destroyed the martyr's shrine, Canterbury was the destination of pilgrims from all over Europe. In the late 16th century many Flemish and Huguenot immigrants settled there.

The town is dominated by the long grey pile of the cathedral with its three great towers. The roughly oval plan of the medieval town is easy to make out still, and large stretches of the town walls survive, especially on the east and south sides. The most spectacular building after the cathedral is the West Gate, built in Edward III's time. Since the bombing in the Second World War, the east half of the town has been much rebuilt, but the close medieval texture remains in the streets on both sides of St Peter's Street, especially in the lanes leading to the great Christ Church Gate and the cathedral precincts, with their lofty overhanging houses. The King's School, to the north of Mint Yard in the precincts, has a splendid Norman staircase entrance.

CATHEDRAL Canterbury Cathedral was founded in 597, but of the early buildings nothing survives from before the Conquest. The internal appearance of the present cathedral is dominated by the work of two men—William of Sens, who designed the choir and apse after the fire of 1174, and Henry Yevele, who designed the nave in 1374. The exterior is dominated by the central Bell Harry Tower designed by John Wastell in the late 15th century. In the Trinity Chapel, on the south side, is the magnificent tomb of Edward the Black Prince, Edward III's son, who died in 1376; on the north side lie the bodies of Henry IV, who died in 1413, and his queen, Joan of Navarre, in a splendid canopied tomb with elaborate alabaster effigies. Much of the monastic building has survived. The 12th-century monastery had an unusually fine system of sanitation and plumbing; a fresh water supply was piped in from outside and distributed to all the main buildings. The so-called Water Tower still exists although its upper part, which was rebuilt at the beginning of the 15th century, is now used as a vestry.

CANTERBURY CATHEDRAL

CANTERBURY CATHEDRAL *Despite its great antiquity and illustrious origins, the life of Canterbury during the Middle Ages centred on the shrine of St Thomas Becket. The place of his martyrdom is marked by a plaque on the wall, and the shrine was behind the high altar. Most Archbishops of Canterbury were statesmen. Some, like Becket and Archbishop Sudbury, who became Chancellor and was murdered during the Peasants' Revolt in 1381, came to grief. Henry Chichele, on the other hand, was a great early 15th-century figure and the founder of All Souls College, Oxford, while Archbishop Bourchier, consecrated in 1454, survived to crown in succession Edward IV, Richard III and Henry VII.*

CRYPT *The Norman crypt at Canterbury is the largest in England; its main feature is the Chapel of our Lady, whose fine stone screens were a gift from the Black Prince, who had intended the chapel to be his last resting place. The Black Prince's Chantry is an early Norman chapel used by the Huguenots; it takes its name from alterations made for the Black Prince.*

St Gabriel's Chapel has frescoes dating from the early 1100's and pillar capitals carved with figures and animals; some of the original paintwork remains. Opposite the north transept are two Romanesque chapels, St Mary Magdalene and St Nicholas, and in the great east crypt is another superb Chapel of our Lady, the ceiling decorated with crowned 'M's.

THE BLACK PRINCE'S ACHIEVEMENTS *The armour of noblemen was carried at their funerals and then placed on their tombs as Achievements—emblems of distinction. This is part of the armour of Edward, Prince of Wales—the Black Prince; it was borne at his funeral in Canterbury Cathedral in 1376. The helm has a moulded leather crest in the form of a lion standing on a cap; the loose garment, a surcoat, is embroidered with the prince's coat of arms in gold and silver thread, which also appear in moulded leather on the wooden shield. The gauntlets are of gilded latten— a kind of brass—and the remains of a red leather sword-scabbard are decorated with gilt studs. The buckle is attached to remnants of a linen belt which originally supported either a sword or a shield; and there is a piece of guard chain for the helmet. It is unlikely that the armour was ever used in warfare, although it may have been worn in tournaments.*

NATIONAL MUSEUM OF WALES, CARDIFF

Prosperity came late to Cardiff. With its bustling streets and docks it seems a child of the Industrial Revolution but its roots stretch back to Roman and Norman times. To preserve this heritage the museum was founded in 1907 'to teach the world about Wales and the Welsh people about their own fatherland', but Welsh achievements are shown against a wider cultural background.

SILVER-GILT TOILET SERVICE *The tray with the Arms of Williams-Wynn, an influential Welsh family, and the ornate box, both belong to a silver-gilt toilet service made in 1768 by Thomas Heming,* the principal goldsmith to George II and George III. *Heming's work reflects the gradual change in design from the elaborate rococo to a more severe Classical style that took place in the late 18th century.*

THE DOLGELLAU CHALICE AND PATEN—*so named because they were discovered by chance in 1890 buried by a road near Dolgellau, Gwynedd—are among the earliest examples of church plate in Britain.* *The style of the chalice, the shallow bowl, the lobed knot halfway up the stem and the cusped lobes at the foot, indicate that they were made about 1250. The paten's centre shows Christ enthroned.*

DYNEVOR PLATE *In the second decade of the 19th century, Swansea had one of the best porcelain factories in Britain. This plate, part of the Dynevor service, is of a delicately fragile whiteness. Its hand-painted flower decorations are attributed to a Welsh artist named Evans. The museum porcelain section contains not only Welsh treasures but also English and continental porcelain, and shows Welsh contributions to the main stream of European culture.*

THE LLANDAFF DIPTYCH *This ivory carving, originally the right-hand part of a French 14th-century diptych, showing Christ with the Virgin and St John, was discovered accidentally in 1836 when the Old Well House at Llandaff was demolished.*

BRONZE TRITON *One of the most unusual treasures of the museum is a bronze triton attributed to Severo da Ravenna, one of the Italian bronze sculptors practising their art in Padua in the late 15th and early 16th centuries. Padua was then leading the world in this art form, and the small bronzes produced by its masters were an inspiration to artists in other lands. Although a Paduan writing at the time listed all the sculptors working in the town and hailed Severo as the greatest master of them all, little is in fact known about him. Only one bronze, a sea-monster which he signed (now in New York), can with certainty be attributed to him. But as more bronzes in the Severo manner come to light, it should soon be possible to distinguish his work from that of his contemporaries.*

ROMAN PAVEMENT The remains of a Roman town house, including two mosaic floors and hypocaust, are preserved *in situ* in this underground museum.
ROYAL MUSEUM AND ART GALLERY (BEANEY INSTITUTE) Many items on exhibition in the museum were excavated in and around the city. There are Belgic, Roman and Anglo-Saxon coins, Roman swords, a hoard of Roman silver spoons, Roman and Saxon glass and jewellery. (See p. 122.) One part of the art gallery is devoted to works by T. S. Cooper R.A. (1803–1902), who was born in Canterbury.

The building also houses the BUFFS REGI-MENTAL MUSEUM with its uniforms and trophies illustrating the history of the Royal East Kent Regiment, 3rd Foot.
ST AUGUSTINE'S ABBEY Canterbury had two great monasteries. The church of one became the cathedral, but its powerful rival is now a ruin of very great interest with Saxon and Norman work, while just to the east is the very early church dedicated to St Pancras. Two of the abbey's gates remain incorporated in mid-19th-century buildings that were once a theological college and are now part of the King's School.
WEST GATE MUSEUM Collections of arms and armour, both British and foreign, are housed in the West Gate, the only surviving city gate in Canterbury. It was built on the site of a former gate by Archbishop Sudbury and finished in 1380. From 1543 to 1829 it was used as the city gaol.

Capel Garmon *Gwynedd* 550Fd
A roughly wedge-shaped Neolithic cairn some 140 ft long with a forecourt at the east end. This however leads to a dummy portal. The true entrance to the triple chamber is on the south side, from which leads a passage to the central oval chamber, on either side of which is another, roughly circular. The passage and chamber walls are of large stone slabs, with the gaps filled with drystone walling. Only one of the chamber capstones remains, but parts of the passage were also roofed with large covering stones, other parts being corbelled. The stones of the cairn were held by a drystone walling revetment, and the whole structure had a final covering of earth.

Capel Newydd *Gwynedd* 550Dc
Licensed on October 6, 1769, Capel Newydd is the oldest surviving Nonconformist chapel in North Wales. It was carefully restored in 1956–8 when it was on the verge of collapse. The church members' poverty and self-conscious attempt to make their place of worship unlike a church give the building a barn-like appearance. The present two doors were originally windows, and the original earth floor has been retained.

Capesthorne *Cheshire* 552Be
A country mansion built in 1722 on the site of an earlier house and altered by Blore and Salvin. It contains fine paintings, furniture, silver, Greek vases, and documents dating from Domesday times. A small Georgian chapel adjoins the house.

Cardiff *S. Glam.* 545Jb
Cardiff has grown, in little more than 150 years, from a sizeable village to become capital of the Principality of Wales, a major seaport, and a university city. Its prosperity dates mainly from the docks, introduced by the Marquess of Bute in the early 19th century.
CARDIFF CASTLE Robert, Duke of Normandy, was confined here for 28 years following his defeat by his younger brother, Henry I of England, at the Battle of Tenchebrai (Normandy) in 1106 (Normandy remained annexed to the English Crown until the reign of King John). A motte with

wooden buildings was raised in *c.* 1093 on the site of a Roman fortification; the present stone keep was erected to replace the wooden buildings in the late 12th century and additions were made in the 15th century and each century following. In 1861 the 3rd Marquess of Bute and William Burges designed additions in the Gothic, Arab and Classical Greek idioms. The Arab Room represents a harem with trellised windows, and throughout the decoration is a riot of inventiveness and allegory, often in exotic materials—lapis lazuli, for example.

NATIONAL MUSEUM OF WALES See pp. 124–5.

ROMAN FORT Adjoining the fine open spaces which surround Cardiff's civic centre, there stands this Roman fort. Built about the end of the 3rd century, it is of the same pattern as the later forts of the Saxon Shore, with rectangular corners and projecting bastions. It was placed here to protect the harbour and coast against the raids of Irish pirates. Its special spectacular interest lies in the fact that a former Lord Bute, its owner, had its curtain wall completely reconditioned, even to the castellation along the wall-top, so that, standing in a modern main street, the exact semblance of a late Roman fort may be viewed.

WELCH REGIMENT REGIMENTAL MUSEUM Military items connected with the Welch Regiment are on display.

Cardoness Castle *Dumfs. & Gall.* *556Eg*
The ruined home of the McCullochs; a 15th-century tower-house on a rocky hill by the Water of Fleet.

Carew Castle *Dyfed* *544Dc*
The noble ruins of a 13th-century castle on an inlet of Milford Haven. The castle was enlarged during the 15th century when the great hall was built, and the fortress became a fine Tudor residence. It was destroyed during the Civil War. Near the entrance to the castle is a carved Celtic cross, 14 ft high.

Carew Cheriton *Dyfed* *544Dc*
CHURCH A fine, mainly 14th-century church, which is cruciform with a 15th-century tower. There are monuments of the 14th and 17th centuries with effigies. There is also a 19th-century memorial by John Evan Thomas, who exhibited at the Great Exhibition of 1851.

Carisbrooke *Isle of Wight* *541Gc*
CHURCH OF ST MARY A Norman building, formerly the monastic church of the Benedictine priory which was suppressed in 1415. The 15th-century tower is outstanding. The chancel was demolished in the 16th century, but there is a Norman nave and arches, and the south aisle is Early English work. The font and pulpit are 17th century.

Carisbrooke Castle *Isle of Wight* *541Gc*
Roundheads kept Charles I a prisoner here from 1647 until shortly before his execution on January 30, 1649; his children Prince Henry and Princess Elizabeth were brought here in August, 1650. Less than a month later the 15-year-old Princess Elizabeth died. Prince Henry was released in 1653. On the site of a Roman fortress the Norman keep was built by William Fitz-Osborn, Earl of Hereford, in the reign of William I. The gate-house was built *c.* 1470. The outworks were added *c.* 1588 when the Spanish Armada threatened England, and a well, 161 ft deep, dates from that time.

Carlisle *Cumbria* *557Hg*
Near the Scottish–English border, Carlisle occupied an important position for 1700 years, but has few remaining monuments to its turbulent history. A Roman town on Hadrian's Wall, it was abandoned during the Danish invasions and revived by the Normans.

BORDER REGIMENT AND KING'S OWN ROYAL BORDER REGIMENT MUSEUM, Carlisle Castle. Uniforms and trophies illustrate the history of military units of Cumbria.

CASTLE Built by William Rufus *c.* 1092 and enlarged in the next century. It was a bastion during all the Border Wars, a palace and stronghold: in 1568 Mary, Queen of Scots, came as a guest and stayed as a prisoner. In the Civil War the castle was besieged and captured by Parliamentary forces; in the rising of 1745 it surrendered to Bonnie Prince Charlie. Early in the 19th century large parts were destroyed, including the banqueting hall where Edward I (the 'Hammer of the Scots') held his Parliament and the apartments where Mary, Queen of Scots, was held prisoner. The most important remains are the 14th-century main gate, Queen Mary's Tower and the impressive central keep.

CATHEDRAL Built between 1092 and 1419. First the church of an Augustinian priory, it became the cathedral when the Diocese of Carlisle was founded in 1133. Part of the Norman work was pulled down in the Civil War, but this small cathedral comprises all periods of architecture. The truncated nave is the Border Regiment chapel. There is a beautiful Early English choir dominated by the cathedral's two chief glories, the unique painted barrel-vault ceiling and the huge east window with some 14th-century stained glass—perhaps the finest Decorated window in the country and reputedly designed by the master mason of York Minster. The choir stalls are carved with misericords and tabernacled canopies. There are monuments by Thomas Banks, John Adams-Acton, Hamo Thornycroft and H. H. Armstead. Sir Walter Scott was married in the cathedral.

MARKET-PLACE The centre of Carlisle; here are the 18th-century town hall and 14th-century guildhall.

MUSEUM AND ART GALLERY Displays of Roman archaeology, decorative arts and local history housed in a Jacobean mansion, Tullie House.

Carl Wark *S. Yorks.* *552De*
A small enclosure, roughly rectangular, with steep natural scarps on three sides. On the west and south sides there is a stone-faced earth and turf rampart, the stonework in places still nearly 10 ft high. On the south-west is an inturned entrance. Evidence produced by recent excavations would tend to make this an Iron Age hill-fort.

Carnasserie Castle *Strathclyde* *560Eg*
The remains of a fortified house built in the late 16th century by John Carswell, the first Bishop of the Isles after the Reformation. A parapet wall with gun loops and ports connects round corner-towers, and many rooms survive.

Carneddau Hengwm *Gwynedd* *550Fc*
Here stand two Neolithic long cairns. Neither is in very good condition, but enough of their essential structure is visible to work out the chambers and the blocked portal at the east end of the south cairn. Close by are the two henge circles known by the same name. Of these two the northern circle, some 120 ft in diameter, was never more than a circular ditch with an earthen bank, for excavation has shown that there were never any upright stones set in the circle. The southern circle, however, still has a few stones in their sockets and the excavation exposed the holes in which the missing stones had stood.

CASTELL COCH

A Victorian fairy-tale castle resulted when in 1875 the 3rd Marquess of Bute commissioned William Burges to rebuild his ruined medieval castle on a hill. Burges found only foundations and fragmentary walls and during the next 20 years he created this medieval fantasy of three round towers capped by conical roofs and connected by a curving curtain wall which forms a courtyard. The whole building is a fascinating exercise in late 19th-century romanticism. In the decoration of the hall and the main rooms in the keep, Burges allowed full reign to his imagination of things medieval. The walls and ceilings are covered with painted birds, stars, monkeys, butterflies, scenes from Aesop's Fables and heraldic devices. The chimney-pieces have carved and painted animals, and in the drawing-room are three large carved figures of the Fates. Burges also designed the furniture, and in the bedrooms, known as the 'Lord's' and the 'Lady's', there are painted beds.

Carreg-Cennen Castle *Dyfed* 545Gd
Legend says that one of King Arthur's knights, Sir Urien, had a fortress here on the great rock above the R. Cennen. The present castle was built by a Welsh prince and saw much fighting in the wars between the Principalities. In 1277 it was taken by the English, and John of Gaunt and Henry Bolingbroke were subsequent owners. The defences were damaged in 1462 and now only the ragged ruins remain.

Carrock Fell *Cumbria* 557Hf
In addition to the natural defence provided by the steep scarp-slopes, there is a 5 acre enclosure within a stone wall. This hill-fort is tentatively attributed to the Iron Age, though its inmates may well have not advanced beyond a Bronze Age culture.

Near its east end, the wall encloses a cairn of somewhat earlier date, and there are many more of these in the area to the north of the fell. They may well cover earlier Bronze Age burials.

Carshalton *Greater London* 542Bf
Although in the midst of suburbia, Carshalton has a number of Regency cottages around the church and pond, and the splendid Carshalton House, built *c.* 1714, with gardens by Charles Bridgeman and a water house looming above the road, designed perhaps by Vanbrugh.

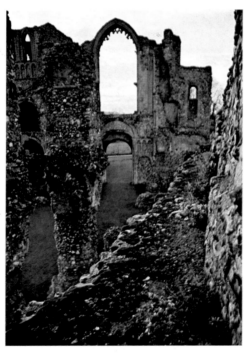

CASTLE ACRE PRIORY

Castle Acre is probably the most impressive surviving ruin of an English Cluniac house. The order of Cluny, a reformed type of Benedictinism originally established in Burgundy, was introduced into England by William de Warenne when he founded Lewes Priory in 1077. His son William founded Castle Acre about 1090. The Cluniacs were often criticised for their wealth and ostentation, and the excessively decorated west front at Castle Acre and also the decoration inside the church at the west end probably aroused much criticism. During the Middle Ages there were usually about 25 to 35 monks in residence, but by the Dissolution the number had dwindled to 11, including the prior. A series of scandals suggests that by the 14th century discipline at Castle Acre was slack.

Cartmel *Cumbria* 557Hd
PRIORY CHURCH OF ST MARY AND ST MICHAEL A great medieval parish church that is cruciform and basically of late Norman work, with Perpendicular windows and a diagonally-set upper stage of the central tower added in the 15th century. After the Dissolution the building decayed, and by 1618 was roofless, at which time its restoration began. From this date are the magnificent Renaissance screens and stall-canopies, erected by George Preston of Holker when he was in charge of the restorations. Among many fine monuments is the 14th-century Harrington memorial, with recumbent effigies.

Cartmel Fell *Cumbria* 557Hd
CHURCH OF ST ANTHONY A small, early 16th-century church; the attractive interior has two large family pews, a three-decker pulpit and some good medieval glass.

Castell Coch *S. Glam.* 545Jb
A 13th-century castle existed here, but for centuries it was a ruin. In 1872 the 3rd Marquess of Bute asked William Burges to rebuild it. Burges found only foundations and fragmentary walls, and during the next 20 years he created this medieval fantasy of three round towers capped by steep conical roofs and connected by a curving curtain wall forming a courtyard. The castle is approached only by a wooden drawbridge over a dry moat, and at the entrance is a portcullis. (See p. 127.)

Castell-Y-Bere *Gwynedd* 550Fb
Beautifully sited and remote ruins of a 13th-century castle with two D-shaped towers—a characteristic feature of Welsh castles. The quality of the carved stonework is high, and it seems likely that Castell-Y-Bere was intended to be a centre of considerable importance to the Welsh princes.

After the English conquest Edward I founded a borough here, but it was abandoned during the 14th century.

Castle Acre *Norfolk* 554Bc
The village, lying at the crossing point of the Peddars Way and the R. Nar, has a combination of military and monastic ruins unlike anything else in East Anglia. The Peddars Way is a Roman road that linked Suffolk with the Wash, and Castle Acre is the only large village on its line across Norfolk. To the east of the village is the castle, to the west the priory.

CASTLE A motte and bailey fortress, going back to the 11th century, it fell into decay in the 14th century, and was pillaged by local builders. Only the 13th-century gateway with two round towers stands, spanning the village street; there are traces of the keep and ditch. The site covers about 15 acres.

CHURCH OF ST JAMES Near to the castle and the priory, the church was built mainly between the 13th and 15th centuries. There is a west tower, and a Perpendicular pulpit with painted panels of the Latin Fathers of the Church (as at Burnham Norton in Norfolk). The rood screen has paintings of *c.* 1400 and the font has a tall Perpendicular cover with some original colour left. The stalls have misericords.

PRIORY Impressive remains of a Cluniac priory, founded by William de Warenne, 2nd Earl of Surrey, *c.* 1090. The 12th-century arcaded west front of the priory church is built of hewn stone and flint. The sacristy, prior's lodging and chapel with its wooden ceiling of *c.* 1500 and 14th-century murals, and the 16th-century gate-house, also survive.

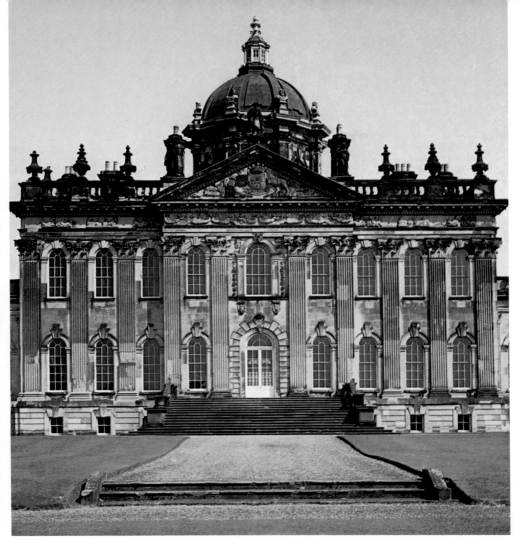

CASTLE HOWARD

One of the largest and most spectacular houses in the country, Castle Howard was designed in about 1700 for the 3rd Earl of Carlisle by Sir John Vanbrugh, assisted by Nicholas Hawksmoor, one of Sir Christopher Wren's assistants. Vanbrugh's scheme was for a great central domed block, flanked by two smaller side wings, but he died in 1726, long before the work of building was finished, and Sir Thomas Robinson continued the scheme, building one of the side wings. There was a disastrous fire in 1940 which destroyed the central dome, but this has been restored. Beneath the dome is the great hall, 52 ft square, reaching to the full height of the dome; it has arches on huge Composite pilasters, statues in niches, and is flanked by staircases. The charming Temple of the Four Winds in the grounds was designed by Vanbrugh and completed by Hawksmoor, who also erected the circular colonnaded mausoleum on a nearby hill.

Castle Ashby Northants.   547Gf
The Compton family (who became Marquesses of Northampton) have lived in this Elizabethan mansion since it was begun in 1574. It was finished in 1635 and the south wing is attributed to Inigo Jones. The parapet surmounting the house is formed by letters cut in stone. The house contains fine moulded ceilings, panelling, staircases and chimney-pieces dating from 1600–35; fine furniture and Brussels tapestries of 1660–1700; and a collection of Dutch, Italian and English pictures. The grounds were landscaped by Capability Brown.

Castle Bromwich Hall W. Midlands   546Dg
An early Jacobean mansion, bought in 1657 by Sir John Bridgeman, who added the Restoration-style porch.

Castlecary Central   561Jf
CASTLE CARY Remains of a rectangular 15th-century tower house. (By appointment.)
ROMAN FORT The remains of a stronghold, one of the line of forts along the Antonine Wall.

Castle Combe Wilts.   540Eg
A Cotswold village, elected the prettiest in England in 1962, set in a river valley. There is a 15th-century market cross, stone houses and cottages. The church is mostly Perpendicular; it was restored in 1851 but the original tower still stands.

Castle Ditch Cheshire   552Ae
Iron Age earthworks enclose the whole 11-acre summit of Eddisbury Hill. The defences have been remodelled more than once. The first was a timber stockade, which was soon replaced by a bank and ditch with counterscarp bank, though these did not include the whole hill-top. The entrance was on the east side, flanked by guard-houses. The bank and ditch were then extended to include the whole area, with a second entrance. Finally, another bank and ditch were added to the complex, outside the earlier ones, and the entrances were remodelled and revetted with stone. In historic times, Aethelfled, Lady of the Mercians, refurbished the defences and made it one of her burhs, or strong-points, against the Danes of the Danelaw.

Castle Dore *Cornwall*   *538Dc*
This small Iron Age hill-fort has a roughly circular internal area, protected by two banks and ditches, the outer bank being extended on the east side to make it oval in plan. In the first phase, the banks were contained between turf walls, but later the inner one was revetted with stone. Probably at this time the elaborate entrance was constructed, a passage between inturned banks with a bridge over the wooden gate. After the Roman Conquest it fell into disuse but later a Dark-Age occupation gives some support to the legend that this was the castle of King Mark of Cornwall, the husband of Tristan's Iseult.

Castle Fraser *Grampian*   *566Fe*
One of the most spectacular of the Castles of Mar, begun *c.* 1575 and completed in 1636.

Castle Haven *Dumfs. & Gall.*   *556Eg*
This is an Iron Age galleried dun with a D-shaped plan, and is enclosed in a larger structure of a similar plan. The inner structure encloses a space some 60 ft by 35 ft and has wall-galleries.

Castle Hedingham *Essex*   *548Be*
A small town once dominated by a mighty castle built by the powerful de Veres, Earls of Oxford, in *c.* 1130. The Norman keep of Hedingham Castle still stands, and is one of the best preserved examples of its type in England. It is four storeys high, with square turrets, and walls averaging 11 ft thick. Inside are arches with zigzag decoration, a hall on the second floor, and some original plastering. A late 15th-century bridge crosses the moat.
CHURCH OF ST NICHOLAS A Norman church with a later clerestory. The tower bears the date 1616. The nave has a double hammerbeam roof. The north and two south doorways are originals of the 12th century and the contents include carved misericords and a 14th-century rood screen.

Castle Howard *N. Yorks.*   *558Ec*
An obelisk in the grounds is inscribed 'Charles the

III, Earl of Carlisle, of the family of the Howards erected a castle where the old castle of Henderskelfe stood, and called it Castle-Howard'. The mansion, which was commissioned by the young Earl of Carlisle, is by Sir John Vanbrugh, who was aided by Nicholas Hawksmoor, an assistant to Sir Christopher Wren.

The house was begun in 1700. The south façade comprises a central block, surmounted by a dome, between two wings. Corinthian fluted pilasters accentuate the height of the central block. The mansion contains a notable long gallery, chapel, hall, and much fine furniture, pictures and statuary; the paintings include works by Reynolds, Gainsborough and Holbein.

The stables, built in 1781 by John Carr, house an exhibition of 18th- to 20th-century costumes in period settings. The grounds include a circular mausoleum designed by Hawksmoor, a Temple of the Four Winds designed by Vanbrugh and completed by Hawksmoor, and a massive gatehouse, crowned with a pyramid. (See p. 129.)

Castlerigg Stone Circle *Cumbria*   *557Hf*
This stone circle is ovoid in plan, with some 38 stones still standing. Its greatest diameter is more than 100 ft. It also has an inner enclosure at its east end.

Castle Rising *Norfolk*   *554Ac*
A small, pretty village that was an important port, until the sea receded in the 15th century and the River Babingley silted up.
CASTLE Built by William de Albini, mid-12th century. It was acquired by Thomas Howard, Duke of Norfolk, in 1544, and still belongs to the Howards. The main moat is nearly 60 ft deep, crossed by a brick bridge, and there is a gate-house. The impressive hall-keep of two floors is divided into several rooms with arches and vaulting. They are reached by principal and lesser staircases.

Castle Rising is surrounded by an immense earth rampart about 64 ft high, and the outer ditch which surrounds the wall goes down a further

CASTLE RISING

Castle Rising stands on some of the most spectacular earthworks in England. The site has not yet been fully excavated, and although the smaller enclosures to the east and west may date back to the Roman occupation, the origin of the main earthworks is uncertain. In the 12th century the property was owned by the Albini family, and the castle itself was built about 1150 by William de Albini, Earl of Sussex, who married the widow of Henry I. The castle was apparently never subjected to any major siege, and only enjoyed one

brief period of fame when, about 1330, it became the chief residence of Queen Isabella, wife of the murdered Edward II and mother of Edward III. Nominally in disgrace for her liaison with the executed Roger Mortimer and her part in the fall of Edward II, she appears to have lived comfortably at the castle, and was visited there by both Edward III and his son, the Black Prince. In the 15th century the castle decayed, and in 1544 it passed to Thomas Howard, Duke of Norfolk.

CASTLERIGG STONE CIRCLE

Surrounded by a rim of mountains two miles east of Keswick is this great prehistoric stone circle known as Castlerigg or Keswick Carles. It is one of a great many such circles in Britain which date from the Neolithic and post-Neolithic periods. While many megalithic circles were burial monuments, those as large as this one were probably built as places for religious or ceremonial meetings, the most famous being Stonehenge in Wiltshire. Castlerigg has 38 stones standing or lying to make an oval that is 100 ft to 110 ft in diameter, and a further ten stones beside the circle at the south-east arranged to form a rectangle.

60 ft below it. The main enclosure is roughly circular and the distance round the circumference is about 1000 yds. This rampart cuts across extensive earthworks on a smaller scale which extend east and west.

TRINITY HOSPITAL A group of 17th-century almshouses founded by Henry Howard, Earl of Northampton in the reign of James I. The brick-and-tile building consists of nine dwellings arranged round a centre court, with a chapel, hall and treasury tower. On Sundays the elderly women who live there wear scarlet cloaks embroidered with the Howard badge. The traditional tall, black, conical hats are reserved for special occasions, such as the Founder's birthday.

Castle Tioram *Highland*   564Fc
The ruins of a 13th-century fortress of the MacDonalds of Clanranald, destroyed in 1715.

Castleton *Derbys.*   552Cf
A village set charmingly among the hills of the Peak District, near numerous caves and disused lead mines. The Church of St Edmund dates from Norman times and has fine plasterwork and box-pews of the 17th century. The ruined Norman keep of Peveril Castle stands above the village and was the setting of Sir Walter Scott's novel, *Peveril of the Peak.*

Castletown *Isle of Man*   556Cc
NAUTICAL MUSEUM The museum is housed in a three-storied boat-house, almost 200 years old. Among the exhibits is a schooner-rigged yacht, the *Peggy,* which was built in 1791 and is probably the oldest craft of her kind. There are also models of deep sea vessels and local fishing boats, and a reconstruction of a sailmaker's workshop.

Castor *Cambs.*   547Hg
A village on the north bank of the R. Nene that was once part of a Roman settlement.
CHURCH OF ST KYNEBURGHA The only church in the country dedicated to the eldest daughter of the pagan King Penda of Mercia whose children all became Christians. Kyneburgha founded a house at Castor of which she became the Abbess. The dedication in 1124 is recorded by an inscription in stone over a door of the Norman church which contains wall-paintings dating from the 14th century.

Caterthun, Brown and White *Tayside*   566Ec
Brown Caterthun stands alone with its six lines of defence. The outermost, a rampart with external

ditch, encloses an area 1000 ft by 900 ft. This has eight entrances, as has the second line of defence, a ditchless rampart. Then come two more ramparts with an intervening ditch and, close inside these, a greater rampart with a boulder facing. Finally, the innermost line of defence is a stone wall with a single entrance. Its detailed history is not known, but this wealth of defence clearly indicates a history of remodelling and amplifying the defences.

White Caterthun, a mile to the south-west of its neighbour, is a hill-top oval, surrounded by two enormous stone walls, now rather ruinous. Outside these are lesser ramparts with quarry ditches. Again the sequence of construction is unknown, though probably more than one period is represented. Both forts are of Iron Age date.

Cauldside *Dumfs. & Gall.*   556Dg
Here, at the head of the Cauldside Burn, stand the remains of two cairns, two stone circles and a large stone block carved with cup-marks and spirals, all of the Bronze Age. The larger cairn is 63 ft across, stands 10 ft high and there is an exposed chamber visible in the top. The second, of which only the foundations remain, lies 150 yds to the north. Each cairn had a stone circle immediately to its south. The first, some 70 ft across, still has ten of its stones standing, but the more northerly one has almost disappeared. The cup-marked stone stands nearly a quarter of a mile north-west of the larger cairn.

Cavendish *Suffolk*   548Ce
A pretty village in the Stour Valley, with thatched almshouses fronting on to the green. Nether-hall Farm is a 16th-century timber-framed Tudor house; also from the 16th century are Manor Cottages and the Old Rectory (now the Sue Ryder Home for survivors of concentration camps). A mile from the village is the Regency Cavendish Hall.
CHURCH OF ST MARY The church has a west tower and a clerestory. There is a 15th-century brass eagle lectern, and a 16th-century wooden one.

Caverswall Castle *Staffs.*   552Cd
The turreted castle, of medieval origin with Jacobean alterations, stands in a dried-up moat. (Not normally open.)

Cawdor Castle *Highland*   566Bg
Picturesque medieval building, with central tower dating from 1372, moat, drawbridge and iron yett (protective gateway grille).

CHATSWORTH

One of the great mansions of England, Chatsworth dates from 1687 when the 1st Duke of Devonshire employed William Talman, who had also worked at Hampton Court, to rebuild his Elizabethan house in Classical style. When the duke died in 1707 his house was finished.

THE GREAT CHAMBER *The largest room of the state suite and one of the few rooms left unaltered during the 6th Duke of Devonshire's enlargements to the house. Designed in 1690–1700, it has the only ceiling of the suite that was painted by Verrio. The carving of the chimney-piece, although often attributed to Grinling Gibbons, is in fact by Samuel Watson and complements the ceiling. The carved and gilded tables were designed by William Kent, and some were originally part of the Burlington House collection.*

Cawston *Norfolk* 554Cc
CHURCH OF ST AGNES An impressive church with 15th-century additions. The west tower is plain and the nave roof is hammerbeam with widespread winged angels. In the south transept is a piscina with a wild man and a dragon.

Caythorpe *Lincs.* 553Gd
CHURCH OF ST VINCENT The church dates from the 13th century, with a central tower and tall spire, and has a fine early 14th-century nave arcade. There are fragments of a wall-painting over the tower arch.

Cedar House *Surrey* 542Af
An H-shaped building of the 15th century, altered in the 17th and 18th centuries. The great hall has a fine timbered roof. (By appointment.)

Cerne Abbas *Dorset* 540Dd
This charming little village was once the seat of an important Benedictine Abbey, built in 987; scattered remains of a gate-house and a guest house can still be seen near the present Abbey House.

CHURCH OF ST MARY The church is of mainly 15th- and 16th-century work, with a west tower. There are fragments of 14th- and 15th-century stained glass, and some 14th-century wall-paintings. The pulpit dates from 1640, and the stone rood screen from the 15th century, as do the remains of a cross in the churchyard.

Cerne Abbas Giant *Dorset* 540Dd
Carved in outline on a hill-side east of the Dorchester–Sherborne road, close to the village of Cerne Abbas, is the huge figure of the Giant—a naked man bearing a club; it is some 180 ft high. References to 'Helith', apparently its early name, and its relationship to spring-time fertility rites, lead to the belief that it is a representation of the Roman Hercules, identified with some local deity. Similar figures of Hercules are known from Roman times and the Giant is generally considered to be of Romano-British origin.

Cerrig-y-Gof *Dyfed* 544De
A burial chamber of unique design among the

THE GRAND CASCADE *The three great periods of garden design—17th-century formal, 18th-century landscaped, and mid-Victorian—are illustrated at Chatsworth. The garden was first altered in 1688 by George London in the formal style of the Frenchman, André Le Nôtre, and parts that still remain include the canal and fountains, and the temple of the Grand Cascade designed by Thomas Archer in 1696. Capability Brown gave a more park-like aspect to the grounds in the 18th century. They were altered again in 1826 by Sir Joseph Paxton, who in 1843 constructed the second highest fountain in Europe—throwing a jet of water 296 ft high—and also built the giant conservatories. Although none now remain, one was the prototype of the Crystal Palace. The larger flower-beds planted with modern herbaceous plants and roses show 20th-century tastes for less elaborate vistas.*

THE CHAPEL *One of the few rooms of the great house hardly altered since 1694. The altar-piece was designed by Caius Gabriel Cibber although only the two large figures on either side were carved by him. The rest of the altar-piece was carved of the same alabaster by Samuel Watson. The walls and ceiling were painted by Laguerre and Ricard, and the painting above the altar, 'Doubting Thomas', is by Verrio. On the walls are carvings in limewood on cedar by Watson and a group of London carvers. The close collaboration between Laguerre and Cibber is shown in the paintings on either side of the altar-piece—they are an extension of the carved design and not connected with the other wall-paintings.*

many fine monuments, mainly of Bronze Age date, dotted along the coast west of Cardigan. In the outer edge of a circular mound are set five megalithic chambers, rectangular in plan, which face outwards, a real departure from the characteristic chamber of uprights supporting a capstone.

Chaddesley Corbett *Heref. & Worcs.* 546Cf
CHURCH OF ST CASSIAN This is an interesting church with a Norman nave, and later work of the 14th century. There is an early Norman font carved with interlaced work and dragon-like creatures. There are several monuments, including some of the early 14th century. The tower and spire were rebuilt at the end of the 18th century.

Chalbury *Dorset* 540Ed
CHURCH Not a large building, the church is of 13th-century origin, and has plastered walls and timbered bell-cote. The east window is 14th century; the interior has some good 18th-century wood fittings (such as gallery, box-pews, pulpit and a pillared division between nave and chancel).

Chaldon *Surrey* 542Bf
CHURCH OF SS PETER AND PAUL This little church has a south tower with a shingled spire, and dates from Norman times. It is famous for its great wall-painting, possibly of the early 12th century, showing the Ladder of Salvation. Little naked men and women climb the ladder to Heaven, or go down it to Hell where wait fearsome demons with great fires into which people are hurled.

Chalfont St Giles *Bucks.* 542Ah
MILTON'S COTTAGE The half-timbered house where John Milton the poet lived during the plague in 1665. He finished his epic 'Paradise Lost' here, and began writing 'Paradise Regained'.

Chalgrave *Beds.* 547Hd
CHURCH OF ALL SAINTS An interesting church in the fields. It has 13th-century and later work, including carved corbels and wall-paintings with saints. There are tombs with effigies, and bench ends. The tower fell during a gale at the end of the 19th century.

Chanctonbury Ring *W. Sussex*   *542Ad*
A ring of beech trees planted in 1760 around the area enclosed by an Iron Age hill-fort—a small enclosure, surrounded by a single bank and ditch, with a supplementary defence to the west of the enclosure. The remains of a Roman temple, together with other contemporary buildings, stand at the centre of the site.

Chard *Som.*   *540Bd*
This town was first granted a charter in 1234, and became a royal borough in 1285. It contains several interesting buildings, including a 15th-century church with gargoyles, an Elizabethan Court House and a Guildhall.

Charing *Kent*   *542Ef*
Typical of Kent, Charing seems a tiny town rather than a village. There are no specially grand houses, just a medley of mellow walls and roofs and, by the church, the ivy-covered ruins of a palace of the Archbishops of Canterbury. The barn to the east of these was built in the 14th century as the archbishops' great hall.

Charlecote *Warks.*   *546Ef*
CHURCH OF ST LEONARD A mid-19th-century building in Gothic style, by John Gibson. The stained glass is by O'Connor, Kempe and Willement. The north chapel has 17th-century monuments, with effigies in alabaster, and black and white marble.

Charlecote Park *Warks.*   *546Ef*
An Elizabethan mansion built of stone in 1558. It was altered and reconstructed in the 19th century but the gate-house was left untouched. The grounds were laid out by Capability Brown.

Charleston Manor *E. Sussex*   *542Cd*
Domesday Book recorded that William the Conqueror's Cup-bearer owned this manor of 'Cerlestone'. A Tudor wing was added to the original Norman house, and a Georgian front was built in 1710–30. (Gardens only open to public.)

Charlton *Greater London*   *542Cg*
CHURCH OF ST LUKE Originally a medieval church; rebuilt *c.* 1630, with later additions. Among its many monuments is one by Nicholas Stone, and there is a bust by Sir Francis Chantrey of Spencer Perceval, Prime Minister 1809–12.

Charlton Marshall *Dorset*   *540Ed*
CHURCH OF ST MARY THE VIRGIN The 15th-century tower remains, but St Mary's was rebuilt in a Classical style at the beginning of the 18th century. The pleasant contemporary fittings include a good canopied pulpit and mural monuments.

CHANCTONBURY RING

The beeches that lift Chanctonbury above other hills were planted in 1760 by Charles Goring of Wiston, which lies beneath the slope of the South Downs.

Charlton-on-Otmoor *Oxon.*   *546Fd*
CHURCH OF ST MARY THE VIRGIN A 13th- and 14th-century church, with an impressive Perpendicular screen; the vaulting of the loft remains, though the gallery has gone.

Charminster *Dorset*   *540Dc*
CHURCH OF ST MARY An aisled 12th-century church with original Norman arcades and chancel arch. It has a 16th-century tower, and late Gothic additions include an attractive 19th-century chancel. There are marble monuments and fragments of mural paintings.

Charney Bassett *Oxon.*   *546Ec*
CHURCH OF ST PETER This tiny church, originally 12th century, stands near the local manor house. There is a Norman south doorway with a tympanum showing a man with two griffins. Rebuilding took place in the 15th century and there is an unusual rectangular 17th-century bell-cote.

Charterhouse *Surrey*   *542Af*
The school moved here from London in 1872. The buildings, by P. C. Hardwick, make the most complete Victorian group in the area; the skyline is a barrage of steeples, and the lofty chapel was built in the 1920's by Sir Giles Gilbert Scott.
CHARTERHOUSE SCHOOL MUSEUM The school's collection of local antiquities, classical pottery, ancient Peruvian pottery, natural history and relics of the school are housed in a museum next to the library.

Chartwell *Kent*   *542Cf*
The former country home of Sir Winston Churchill (1874–1965), now kept as a memorial to him with many souvenirs of his eventful life. The grounds include a fine rose garden.

Chastleton House *Oxon.*   *546Ed*
Robert Catesby, a conspirator in the Gunpowder Plot, once owned the site of this fine Jacobean manor house which, like many great houses of the area, also has associations with the Civil War. The house was built in 1603 by Walter Jones; it is unaltered, and an inventory made in 1633 reveals that much of the original furniture survives. The rooms also contain fine ceilings, panelling, porcelain and tapestries. The gardens, laid out *c.* 1700, are famous for their ornamental hedges clipped into fantastic shapes.

Chatham *Kent*   *542Df*
A settlement existed here in Anglo-Saxon times, but Chatham was not important until the 16th century when Henry VIII established a dockyard, which later became a naval depot. Nelson's *Victory,* launched in 1795, was one of the ships built here.
MUSEUM OF THE CORPS OF ROYAL ENGINEERS The development of military engineering is shown in this museum, which covers the history of the Corps.

Chatsworth *Derbys.*   *552De*
William Talman built this Classical mansion for the 1st Duke of Devonshire in 1687–1707. After he succeeded to the title in 1755 the 4th Duke employed James Paine to build the stables and convert the old kitchen into an entrance hall. During this period landscaping of the park began and the duke had most of the buildings visible from the house destroyed. The 6th Duke made further alterations in 1820–30; his architect was Sir Jeffry Wyatville, who built the orangery and an extension on the north-east side of the house, which includes the ballroom and picture and sculpture galleries. The 6th Duke also completed the destruction of Edensor village and rebuilt it out of sight. The house contains fine furniture, pictures, sculpture, books and manuscripts.

The extensive gardens at Chatsworth illustrate four periods of garden design. In 1688 George London, leading garden designer of his day, created a formal garden in the valley of the Derwent, laid out with canals, fountains and an orangery. Parts of this early garden remain and include a canal, with a fountain of Neptune with sea nymphs before the south front of the house. A slightly later addition is the great cascade, designed by Thomas Archer and unequalled in Britain. During the 18th century much of London's garden was destroyed when Capability Brown created a woodland park on the banks of the Derwent. Early in the 19th century Joseph Paxton transformed the then neglected gardens into a showplace, building huge but since-destroyed conservatories which were said to be his prototypes for the Crystal Palace. He planted rare conifers, made the large rockery and designed the Emperor fountain which can throw a water jet 296 ft high. The new greenhouse has three sections at different temperatures. The hottest has a lily pool kept at 85°F.

Chawton *Hants.* *541He*
JANE AUSTEN'S HOME Jane Austen lived in this house from 1809 to 1817, and here she wrote *Emma* and *Persuasion*. The house is now a museum containing her personal effects and other relics.

Chearsley *Bucks.* *547Gd*
CHURCH OF ST NICHOLAS An unspoilt village church with a 13th-century nave and chancel and a west tower. There is a Norman font, a brass of 1462, box-pews and an 18th-century west gallery. The church is worth seeing, as it seems to have escaped 19th-century restoration.

Checkendon *Oxon.* *547Gb*
CHURCH OF SS PETER AND PAUL The wall-paintings in this Norman church show how Christ and the Apostles were imagined in the 12th century. The church has an apsed chancel higher than the nave, and a 16th-century west tower.

Checkley *Staffs.* *552Cd*
CHURCH OF ST MARY AND ALL SAINTS An impressive church dating from the Norman period, with later enlargements. There is some medieval stained glass with heraldry and figures, as well as alabaster effigies, screen, stalls and a Norman font. There are the remains of Saxon crosses in the churchyard.

Cheddar *Som.* *540Cf*
GOUGH'S CAVE This cave was occupied during the last phase of the Ice Age, and excavation revealed large quantities of flint and bone implements and ornaments, as well as much food debris. A burial of this period was also found and this is preserved in the museum on the site. The uppermost layers of the cave floor contained evidence of occupation in Iron Age and Romano-British times.

Chedworth *Glos.* *546Dd*
CHURCH OF ST ANDREW Not far from the famous Roman villa of Chedworth, the church conceals its Norman origins on the outside by a fine range of Perpendicular windows. Inside, the north nave arcade and the font with its interlacing arcades are both Norman; the pulpit, of carved stone, is 15th century; and the nave roof is late Gothic.

Chedworth Villa *Glos.* *546Dd*
This is one of the best preserved Roman villas in the country. Many of the original walls stand several feet high and these have been extended and roofed so that the buildings may be entered. On the north side is the wing where, in later Roman days, Cotswold wool was processed. The many finds from the site are displayed in a small museum.

PIERCE *Monument to Lady Warburton*

Edward Pierce was the most sophisticated English exponent of the baroque style; much of his work was done for Sir Christopher Wren. Several monuments reflect his style, but none is certainly by Pierce, except for this one, for which his drawing exists in the Victoria and Albert Museum. The monument was probably begun in or soon after 1693, when Lady Warburton died, and finished after Pierce's death by the Flemish sculptor John Nost. The dramatic motif of a skeleton holding up a shroud was probably inspired by French tombs. (Church of St John the Baptist, Chester)

Chelmsford *Essex* *548Bc*
CATHEDRAL Made the cathedral in 1914, the Cathedral Church of St Mary has a 15th-century west tower, with spirelet of 1749, and a south porch containing a 17th-century library in an upper room. There is much 19th-century work, and 16th–18th-century monuments.

Chelsworth *Suffolk* *548Ce*
One of the prettiest villages in Suffolk, on the R. Brett. A two-arched bridge crosses the river, and there are attractive timber-framed thatched houses; the Grange is dated 1694 and the rectory was built in the late 18th century.

Cheltenham Spa *Glos.* *546Cd*
A town with Anglo-Saxon origins, Cheltenham became a fashionable watering-place after the discovery there of saline springs in 1716. There are good Georgian buildings, including the Pittville Pump Room and Montpellier Rotunda. ART GALLERY AND MUSEUM Dutch paintings, oils, water-colours and prints may be seen; the museum contains Chinese porcelain, English pottery and porcelain, and 17th- and 18th-century furniture.

Chenies *Bucks.* *547Hc*
CHURCH OF ST MICHAEL Rebuilt in the 15th century and again in the 19th, St Michael's has some interesting fittings—Norman font, 15th- and 16th-century brasses—but is famous for the Russell family tombs in the Bedford Chapel, built 1556. Monuments range from one of the 15th century to a member of the Cheyne family

[signature: Winston S. Churchill]

SIR WINSTON CHURCHILL
THE ARCHITECT OF VICTORY

'YOU HAVE BEEN SO FAITHFUL AND SO LOVING TO US, YOU HAVE FOUGHT SO STOUTLY FOR US, YOU HAVE BEEN SO HEARTY IN COUNSELLING OF US THAT WE SHALL NEVER FORGET YOUR FAVOUR TOWARDS US'. This tribute to Churchill appears in an illuminated book given him by Members of the House of Commons on his 80th birthday. The book is on view at Chartwell in Kent, his home for 37 years and now open to the public. Churchill was more than 50 years in Parliament and his fighting orations delivered as Prime Minister during the Second World War rank among treasures of the 20th century. His second enduring interest was writing and he won the Nobel Prize for Literature for his four volume work *Marlborough, His Life and Times*. First editions of this and his other works are on view at his home at Chartwell.

PORTRAIT BY WALTER SICKERT *painted in 1927 when Churchill was Chancellor of the Exchequer. At this time he wrote 'The World Crisis', a personal account of the First World War. (National Portrait Gallery)*

SCHOOLBOY LETTER *written by Churchill from Harrow School to his mother. Churchill made little headway scholastically and said 'Examinations were a great trial to me. The subjects which were dearest to the examiners were invariably those I fancied least.' But failure did not quell his spirit and it is recorded that companions would chase him round the bathing pool until he was out of breath, in a desperate attempt to stop him talking. (Library of Harrow School)*

DETAIL FROM 'DISTANT VIEW OF VENICE' *painted by Churchill and presented to Harrow School in 1966 by Lady Churchill. His interest in painting began with annexation of his children's water-colour boxes, and developed into a passion. 'If it weren't for painting I couldn't live, I couldn't bear the strain of things', he said.*

GARTER ROBES *belonging to Sir Winston Churchill and Garter Star worn by his ancestor the 1st Duke of Marlborough. Churchill was created Knight of the Garter when he was Prime Minister in 1953. He retired from Office two years later at the age of 80. (Chartwell)*

MODEL OF MULBERRY HARBOUR *inset into the library wall at Chartwell. 'He has at least a hundred ideas a day,' said President Roosevelt, 'of which four are good.' This idea is an artificial harbour which was towed across the Channel after D-Day and named Port Arromanches.*

WALL AT CHARTWELL *demonstrating Churchill's skill as a bricklayer. When invited to join the Union, Churchill sent a cheque for 5s. for registration as an 'adult apprentice'.*

DESK *with box for cigars (he smoked 3000 a year) and busts of Napoleon and Nelson with family photographs. (Chartwell)*

BOER WAR POSTER *for Churchill's capture, dead or alive, describing the escaped War Correspondent as '25 years old, about 5 ft 8 in. tall, indifferent build, walks with a forward stoop, pale appearance, red brownish hair, talks through his nose and cannot pronounce the letter 's' properly'. (Chartwell)*

FIRST WORLD WAR TANK *Derided in 1914, tanks and Churchill's vision led to the army's first decisive victory in 1917. (Bovington Museum, Dorset)*

CHURCHILL'S GRAVE *in the quiet churchyard at Bladon. It is within view of Blenheim Palace, where the room he was born in may be seen.*

to one to the 9th Duke of Bedford (*d.* 1891). Though not open to the public except by permission (obtainable from the Bedford Estate Offices, London), the chapel is visible through glass screens.

Chepstow *Gwent*   546Ac

CASTLE The Norman fortress, on a cliff above the R. Wye, was a centre of fighting during the Civil War, in 1645; in 1648 it was confiscated by Parliament and used as a prison until 1660. It was built by William Fitz-Osborn in 1067 as a defence for the Roman road leading to South Wales, and was rebuilt and extended by the Clare family in the 13th century. Now a ruin, it has four courtyards dominated by a keep (40 ft high) and surrounded by thick curtain walls, strengthened by towers. The entrance gate-house has two drum towers with a portcullis chamber between.

CHURCH OF ST MARY Formerly a large Norman church with a central tower, but this fell in 1700. The present west tower dates from 1706. There are Norman nave arcades, and the monuments include one to the Earl of Worcester (*d.* 1549), with canopy and reclining figures, and two of the 18th century by James and Thomas Paty, of Bristol. The 17th-century organ came from Gloucester Cathedral.

Cherry Willingham *Lincs.*   553Ge

CHURCH OF SS PETER AND PAUL A small mid-18th-century building with an octagonal lantern at the west end. It has a little apse, and a flat ceiling. In the chancel is a good contemporary reredos.

Chester *Cheshire*   551Je

No city in Britain is richer in archaeological and architectural treasures than Chester, which has preserved to this day the walls built in Roman and Saxon times. It was originally the fortress site of the 20th Legion, the town being known then (*c.* AD 70) as Deva, and it became a major trading port. The Romans withdrew *c.* AD 400, and the prosperous city fell prey to marauding Danes and Saxons to such an extent that it was virtually derelict by 900. The Norman conquerors reached Chester *c.* 1070, and its fortunes revived so that by the 13th century it had again become a ship trading centre, a port serving Scotland, Ireland, France and Spain. The last Norman earl died in 1237, and the earldom passed to the Crown: the eldest son of the reigning monarch now enjoys the title of Earl of Chester. In the 14th century began the Mystery Plays and pageants for which the city became famous. Henry VII granted a charter in 1506 and in 1541 Chester was made a bishopric.

By the 15th century the Dee began to silt up, and gradually the seaborne trade died. Impoverished by this natural action, further disasters came with fighting in the Civil War. But throughout this chequered history, Chester's walls remained virtually intact. They extend in a 2-mile circuit, and give a vivid reminder of what a medieval fortified town was like. In the Middle Ages several towers and gates to the walls were made: the most important of these was at Eastgate, now astride a main thoroughfare and crowned with an anachronistic clock that commemorates Queen Victoria's diamond jubilee (1897). King Charles's Tower, on the site of the north-east corner of the Roman fortress, retains a medieval appearance after restoration in 1613 and in 1658. From it Charles I is said to have watched the defeat of his forces at Rowton Heath in 1645. The tower now houses an exhibition devoted to the Civil War. The massive Water Tower at the north-west angle of the walls was originally New Tower, built in 1322 by John de Helpston, a mason, for £100. Newgate is modern—it was opened in 1938—but just east of it

is the site of a Roman amphitheatre, believed to be the largest in Britain with dimensions of 314 ft by 286 ft, and with an arena measuring 190 ft by 162 ft. The most distinctive medieval feature of the city is The Rows. These are double-level walkways with a continuous line of balconies, and with shops at street and first-floor levels. The Rows are unique and were certainly in being in the 14th century. Throughout the city are splendid Tudor and Elizabethan buildings, the richest example being Bishop Lloyd's House. This divine was Bishop of Chester 1604–15; his brother David was mayor 1593–4. Stanley Palace in Watergate Street is a magnificent half-timbered house built in 1591.

ABBEY SQUARE Opposite the Victorian town hall (1869), and entered through a massive gateway built 1377, Abbey Square was originally the outer court of the Abbey of St Werburgh, and the Chester Mystery Plays were enacted at the gateway.

CASTLE Originally a timber structure of *c.* 1069, the castle was given stone walls and towers by Henry III. It retained its medieval appearance until 1789 when the battlements and defensive walls were removed to be replaced by a severe group of buildings erected 1789–1813. The 14th-century chapel of St Mary de Castle remains.

CATHEDRAL A church was built on the site in the 10th century as a shrine for the relics of St Werburgh, a Mercian princess who died *c.* 707. In 1092 Hugh Lupus, the 2nd Norman Earl of Chester, made the church into an abbey of Benedictine monks, with the help of St Anselm. The abbey was dissolved in 1540 and in 1541 became the cathedral of the newly formed diocese of Chester. In the choir are superbly carved stalls of the late 14th century. In the south-west corner of the nave is the consistory court of the diocese with furnishings dating from 1636. The church was largely rebuilt in the 14th and 15th centuries and underwent a great deal of restoration by Sir Gilbert Scott in 1870. Some of the monastic buildings are remarkably well preserved, and include the cloisters, chapter house and refectory. A grotesque figure known as the Chester Imp is in the north clerestory of the nave.

CHESHIRE MILITARY MUSEUM The museum, located in Chester Castle, contains items associated with the Cheshire Regiment, the Cheshire Yeomanry, the 3rd Carabiniers, and 5th Royal Inniskilling Dragoon Guards, and material captured by General Sir Charles Napier in India.

CHURCH OF ST JOHN THE BAPTIST This large and impressive Norman building would have been a cathedral, had the See not moved to Coventry. The nave has fine Norman pillars and arcades; the east end is in ruins. In the south aisle a monument, *c.* 1693, shows a shrouded skeleton. (See p. 135.)

GROSVENOR MUSEUM The museum's archaeological exhibits are mainly from the Roman legionary fortress of Deva and include important inscribed stones. There is also a display of local natural history.

Chesterfield *Derbys.*   552De

CHURCH OF ST MARY AND ALL SAINTS The twisted spire is 228 ft high; it is made of lead-covered wood, which has warped through the ages, and caused the curious twist.

Chester-le-Street *Durham*   558Cg

CHURCH OF SS MARY AND CUTHBERT The west tower has an octagonal upper stage, and a spire, and is of *c.* 1400. There is a series of 14 effigies of ancestors of Lord Lumley, who brought them here, or had them carved, *c.* 1590.

Chesterton *Cambs.*   *547Hg*
CHURCH OF ST MICHAEL Much of the church is of
the 14th century, to which has been added an 18th-
century chancel. There is a good 17th-century
monument with kneeling figures at a prayer-desk,
and a host of praying children.

Chetwode *Bucks.*   *546Fd*
CHURCH OF SS MARY AND NICHOLAS The body of
the church was once the chancel of an Augustinian
priory church of *c.* 1250. There is a fine east end
with lancet windows, and the 13th- and 14th-
century stained glass in the chancel is matched by
early Victorian glass in the east window. The
piscina and sedilia have dog-tooth carving.

Chewton Mendip *Som.*   *540Cf*
CHURCH OF ST MARY MAGDALENE An originally
Norman church, of which there are still remains
among the later additions. These include the
imposing 16th-century tower. Inside are fragments of medieval glass, and recumbent 14th-
century effigies on a monument.

Chicheley *Bucks.*   *547Ge*
CHURCH OF ST LAWRENCE The nave and north
aisle are 14th century, the central tower 15th
century, but the chancel was rebuilt *c.* 1708 and is
all in good Classical style. The rood under the

CHICHESTER CATHEDRAL
The Raising of Lazarus
*The Norman cathedral at Chichester was founded on
its present site in 1085. Before that the bishop's
church had been at Selsey, and it was refounded on the
site of a Saxon church at Chichester, a city dating from
Roman times, in accordance with William I's policy
that cathedrals should be moved to the centres of
population. In 1829, two 12th-century panels of
Purbeck stone with scenes from the legend of Lazarus
were found built into the eastern piers of the crossing
of the cathedral. Now re-erected in the south aisle of the
choir, they are perhaps the greatest works of Romanesque monumental sculpture in England. The two
panels are not the work of the same artist—one is more
sophisticated; the other, from which this detail is taken,
is more expressive—but they are both from the same
workshop, and must be the only two surviving sections
from a series. No other sculptures from this workshop
are known, and the panels, because they date from
1125 to 1150, are exceptional for their strong
emotional content. The deeply drilled eyes would
originally have been inlaid with metal.*

tower arch is by Sir Ninian Comper, 1904. There
are two interesting monuments, the earlier of 1576
with a bizarre representation of a naked corpse,
and caryatids on either side. The other, 1635, has
two kneeling figures under a canopy.

Chichester *W. Sussex*   *541Jd*
A Roman, medieval and Georgian city, Chichester is the administrative centre for West Sussex.
The plan of the Roman town is still evident in the
two long, straight streets that cross at right angles
in the city centre. At the crossing stands the market
cross, one of the most elaborate structures of its
kind in England, erected by the bishop in 1501 to
give shelter to country people selling their produce. The cathedral stands informally against West
Street, not set like most cathedrals within a close.
In the bishop's palace, the chapel and walls of the
great kitchen are 13th century, and the gateway is
14th century. Half the palace is now used by the
bishop and half by the Prebendal School. But
Chichester is the stateliest town in Sussex because
of its Georgian town houses. The finest of them
are at the far end of West Street, and especially
between East Street and South Street. Best of all
is Pallant (or Dodo) House of *c.* 1712, with dodos
on the gate piers (see page 140). The Council
House was built in 1731; James Wyatt added the
east wing in 1783, and set in the outer wall by the
entrance is a Roman inscription dedicating a
temple to Neptune and Minerva.
CATHEDRAL The present cathedral at Chichester
was founded *c.* 1080, and is still substantially the
same building as that begun under Bishop Ralph
de Luffa, who became bishop in 1091. Considerable additions and alterations were made to the
church after a fire in 1187, and changes after that
date included the addition of the central spire to the
earlier tower and the building of a separate bell-
tower in the 15th century. The bell-tower still
stands to the west of the cathedral, but the central
tower collapsed in 1861 and was replaced in 1861–6
by the existing replica. Luffa's building, particularly the nave and choir, bears a striking resemblance to William the Conqueror's foundation of
St Stephen's at Caen, although the stone itself came
from the Isle of Wight and was not imported from
Caen, as was the usual practice at that time. To the
east is the retrochoir, part of the late 12th- and early
13th-century building; the use of shafts and
columns of Purbeck stone in this building was
inspired by the new east end of Canterbury Cathedral which was rebuilt, after a fire, in 1184.
CORPS OF ROYAL MILITARY POLICE MUSEUM The
first Provost Marshal of the British Army was
appointed in 1511. This museum portrays the
history and exploits of Provost Marshals since
then, and of the Corps of Royal Military Police,
and contains uniforms and equipment, medals,
flags and documents.
DISTRICT MUSEUM In an 18th-century corn store,
converted into a museum in 1964, collections
devoted to local history and archaeology are on
view; they include Romano-British pottery and
coins, medieval pottery, and a set of stocks on
wheels which used to be pulled around the city
cross in the 18th and early 19th centuries while
onlookers threw refuse and abuse at the offender
locked in them. There is also 17th-century
furniture from the Grange, a demolished house in
the city.
GUILDHALL MUSEUM The building was originally
built in the 13th century as a chapel for Grey Friars
and was later used as a guildhall. It contains a
collection of Romano-British relics, including
pottery from the Roman cemetery at Chichester.
PALLANT HOUSE GALLERY A fine Queen Anne

building is the setting for the Walter Hussey Collection of paintings, drawings, prints and sculpture, ranging from Rembrandt and Tiepolo etchings to figures by Barbara Hepworth and Henry Moore. Also on display are Bow porcelain and 18th-century English glass.

Chiddingfold *Surrey* 542Ae
A handsome, spacious village. The church faces a pond, a triangular green and a row of Georgian and tile-hung cottages. To the east is the red-brick manor house, 1762, standing in a dell.

Chiddingstone *Kent* 542Ce
The whole village belongs to the National Trust, and has a fine group of Tudor half-timbered houses. To the west there is a view across a lake to Chiddingstone Castle.
CHURCH OF ST MARY THE VIRGIN The first mention of a church on this site is dated 1072, but the present building dates from the 14th century. It was restored and enlarged in 1624–9. It has a Perpendicular west tower, and faces a row of timbered houses. There is some original stone carving, and a Jacobean font, cover and pulpit.

Chiddingstone Castle *Kent* 542Ce
An 18th-century restoration of a much earlier manor house, in Gothic style. It contains Royal Stuart and Jacobite pictures, manuscripts and relics; an Ancient Egypt collection; Japanese lacquer, and weapons; and Buddha figures. In the grounds are caves and a lake.

Chilcomb *Hants.* 541Ge
CHURCH OF ST ANDREW A lonely downland church with much Norman work—windows, doorways and chancel arch. The font is in the 18th-century Gothic style, and there is tilework.

Chilham *Kent* 542Ff
Village squares are rare in South-east England. Chilham is especially delightful, on the top of a hill reached via narrow lanes leading into the square.

Chilham Castle *Kent* 542Ff
A Jacobean castle built to the designs of Inigo Jones on the site of an earlier castle and completed in 1616. There is a Norman keep, and gardens designed by Capability Brown.

Chillingham *Northld.* 562Fc
CHURCH OF ST PETER Originally Norman, there is a crypt below the chancel. Inside is a magnificently decorated monument, *c.* 1443, to Sir Ralph Gray, with 14 small figures of saints in niches.

Chillington Hall *Staffs.* 552Bb
Seat of the Giffard family since the 12th century. The house was rebuilt in Georgian style, south front by Francis Smith in 1724, and main front, hall and state rooms by Sir John Soane in 1785. Park and lake are by Capability Brown.

Chilworth *Hants.* 541Gd
CHURCH OF ST DENYS Built in a Gothic style in 1812, with transepts; there are lancet windows all down the nave, beneath a plaster vault with roof-bosses. The pews are contemporary with the church, but the font is Norman.

Chippenham *Cambs.* 548Bf
A splendid example of a squire's model village with attractive cottages and larger houses, many dating from *c.* 1800. Chippenham Park Mansion, rebuilt in 1886, replaced the earlier 17th-century mansion of the Earl of Orford.

Chippenham *Wilts.* 540Eg
A stone-built town of the Cotswolds, on the R. Avon, with many fine houses. The timbered Yelde Hall, which now houses a museum, dates from the 15th century.

WROUGHT-IRON GATES
AT CHIRK CASTLE

There was a story that these gates were the work of a local smith and his daughter, but in fact they were made by two brothers—Robert and John Davies, Welsh smiths who did most of their work between 1702 and 1755, and who were strongly influenced by the French smith, Jean Tijou. The gates were made for Sir Robert Myddleton in 1719–21, and were probably the brothers' first commission. The work is ambitious; the gates are enclosed by two large square piers of wrought iron, each crowned with a lead wolf representing the Myddleton coat of arms.

Chipping Campden *Glos.* 546De
CHURCH OF ST JAMES An imposing church, mainly of the 15th century, with a fine west tower; the chancel is of the 14th century. There are brasses, a 15th-century brass lectern, and several 16th-century monuments with effigies, one of them by Joshua Marshall.
MARKET HALL A fine arcaded Jacobean building with pointed gables.

Chipping Norton *Oxon.* 546Ed
CHURCH OF ST MARY THE VIRGIN This is one of the largest churches in Oxfordshire. The south porch is hexagonal and two storeys high. The nave is clerestoried, and there is a west tower. Many brasses, and 16th-century monuments with recumbent effigies.

Chipstead *Surrey* 542Bf
CHURCH OF ST MARGARET A large early 12th-century cruciform church with a central tower and late 19th-century additions by R. Norman Shaw. The screen is 15th century, the pulpit 17th, and fragments of medieval glass remain.

Chirk Castle *Clwyd* 551Hd
Sir Thomas Seymour, who married Henry VIII's widow, Catherine Parr, and Robert Dudley, Elizabeth I's favourite, were granted this Border castle, which was in the gift of the Crown for 280 years from its completion in 1310 during the reign of Edward II. The castle, with round towers and battlements, has been lived in continuously ever since Sir Thomas Myddleton acquired it in 1595 and it now belongs to the National Trust. Charles I stayed here in 1645. The interior has tapestries and portraits and decorations and furnishings of the 17th–19th centuries. There are traces of Offa's Dyke in the grounds.

Chislehampton *Oxon.* 546Fc
CHURCH OF ST KATHERINE Urns decorate the roof-line of this pretty, bell-coted little building of 1763. The pews, pulpit, font and other fittings are contemporary with the church.

Chittlehampton *Devon*   *539Gf*
CHURCH OF ST URITH (OR HIERITHA) The saint to whom the church is dedicated was local, murdered by pagans. The church is largely late Perpendicular with a 115 ft high west tower, a stone pulpit, original wood ceilings, and monuments with recumbent or reclining figures of the 17th century. A brass in the floor dates from the late 15th century.

Cholmondeley *Cheshire*   *552Ad*
CHURCH OF ST NICHOLAS The chapel of Cholmondeley Castle, originally 13th century, but rebuilt in the early 18th century. The chancel roof is probably late 15th century, and there is a good screen of 1655 with stalls, pulpit and other furnishings of about the same date. A large family pew extends across the west end of the church. (By appointment.)

Cholsey *Oxon.*   *546Fb*
CHURCH OF ST MARY A large flint and stone church. It is basically Norman, with interesting architectural details; the interior was extended in the 13th century, and the Early English chancel has two 19th-century windows by C. E. Kempe.

Chorley *Lancs.*   *552Ag*
ASTLEY HALL A large mansion, built in 1666. The great hall is glazed on three sides and contains a small art gallery. The Long Gallery incorporates a massive, original, shuffleboard table. The drawing-room ceiling is so festooned with plasterwork that it resembles a suspended grotto. The house contains a collection of fine furniture, pottery, tapestries and pictures.

Christchurch *Dorset*   *540Fc*
CASTLE The 12th-century keep, now ruined, stands on a well-preserved motte, or artificial mound; its walls are nearly 10 ft thick.
CONSTABLE'S HOUSE The ruins of a Norman house built in the late 12th century for the resident steward of the castle.
PRIORY Originally built *c.* 1100 by Ralph Flambard, Bishop of Durham, but added to and completed in 1485–1509. The priory was dissolved by Henry VIII, but the priory church is still as it was originally built (though part of it has been restored); the surrounding Norman fortifications were demolished in the Civil War. Carvings in the choir are probably 200 years older than those in Westminster Abbey. There is a fine mid-14th-century reredos with a sculptured Tree of Jesse, several misericords and many monuments, including John Flaxman's famous group to Viscountess Fitzharris of *c.* 1815, and H. Weekes's monument of 1854 to the poet Shelley.
RED HOUSE MUSEUM AND ART GALLERY The main part of the Red House dates from *c.* 1760, when it was built as a workhouse; the art gallery is housed in the former stables and coach house, built in 1887. The museum concentrates mainly on displays of the geology, natural history, archaeology and history of the region. The archaeological section includes material from the Bronze Age (the Deverel Rimbury phase), from a late Palaeolithic 'Reindeer Hunters' camp site at Hengistbury, and from the port and settlement which existed there from the Early Iron Age to Roman times.
An example of local industry is seen in the making of minute Fusee chains—used in the compensating mechanisim of Verge watch movements and widely exported—confined almost solely to this district throughout the 19th century. Smuggling relics and 19th-century local domestic and dairy equipment can also be seen, including an original open hearth fire-place and equipment. Other Victorian items include lighting, smoking, letter-writing and needlework materials. Children's toys and games are on display, and dolls are shown in a Victorian setting which includes a selection from the extensive Druitt Collection of 18th- and 19th-century fashion plates. A collection of costumes covers the period between 1865 and 1915; and there are plans for extending it to the 1960s. The natural history section concentrates on the richness of the surrounding district, and there is an aquarium and herb garden.

Christ's Hospital *W. Sussex*   *542Ae*
Often called the Blue Coat School because of the traditional long, dark blue coat with girdle still worn by the boy scholars, this school moved here from London in 1902. It was founded by Edward VI in 1552 in the buildings of the Grey Friars monastery in Newgate Street, in the City of London. A painting, 87 ft by 16 ft, by Antonio Verrio (*c.* 1639–1707) commemorating the foundation of the Royal Mathematical School of Christ's Hospital by Charles II in 1673, hangs in the school dining-hall.

Church Crookham *Hants.*   *541Jf*
The Gurkha Museum, opened by Field Marshal Lord Harding in 1974, records the outstanding contribution made by the Gurkhas to the British Crown since 1815. From a photographic display recounting the early days, the evolution of the Gurkha Brigade can be followed up to the present day. Apart from uniforms, kukris and Gurkha regalia, there is a section on Nepal, a fine collection of badges relating to all Gurkha Regiments, and a display of medals. One end of the museum is devoted to the British and Gurkha recipients of the Victoria Cross. Three Victoria Crosses and a George Cross are on display.

Church Eaton *Staffs.*   *552Bc*
CHURCH OF ST EDITHA A Norman church, with a spire added to the tower in the 15th century. The east window is Gothic, almost filling the wall. Most of the glass in the church dates from the 19th century, some showing scenes from the life of Christ.

Church Hanborough *Oxon.*   *546Ed*
CHURCH OF SS PETER AND PAUL Between the lintel and arch of the north door to this fine church sits St Peter, holding the key to the Kingdom of Heaven. This carving on the tympanum, and the whole doorway, is Norman workmanship. The church itself contains later additions to the original Norman fabric—the Perpendicular west tower, for example, with its tall spire—and inside is a 14th-century carved font. Amongst its furnishings are screens, brasses and a carved pulpit.

Church Stowe *Northants.*   *546Ff*
CHURCH OF ST MICHAEL The church is interesting externally because of the Saxon west tower and a Norman doorway; there is much later work, internally renewed. The outstanding monuments include a cross-legged knight of the 13th century, Nicholas Stone's monument to Lady Carey, with a lovely marble effigy of *c.* 1620, and the strange monument to Dr Turner (*d.* 1714), President of Corpus Christi College at Oxford. By Thomas Stayner, it has two life-size figures, one standing on a celestial globe and the other on a terrestrial globe. There is a good tablet of *c.* 1757 in architectural style by John Middleton.

Chysauster *Cornwall*   *538Ab*
A remarkable Iron Age village, with four pairs of houses each fronting a village street. Each house is oval in plan, but the rooms are roughly circular, set

CLANDON PARK

Clandon was built on land acquired in 1641 by the Onslow family, three of whom became Speakers of the House of Commons. In about 1731 the 2nd Lord Onslow commissioned the Venetian architect Giacomo Leoni to build him a new house. Leoni's house is in Classical style. The hall is a single cube, 40 ft by 40 ft by 40 ft. In it are two chimney-pieces, each with a relief carved by Michael Rysbrack, one of the foremost sculptors of the early 18th century. One relief shows the goddess Diana, and the other is a representation of a sacrifice to Bacchus. The house contains some fine plasterwork, probably by Artari and Bagutti.

in thick walls and all opening to a central courtyard. Now open to the sky, the rooms were apparently roofed with corbelled stone or with thatch, though the courtyards were open. When excavated, querns, pottery and other domestic debris, together with hearths, were found lying on the paved floors. Each house also had a stone-fenced back garden.

Cilgerran Castle *Dyfed*   544De
The ruin of a castle standing on a promontory between the Teifi and Plysgog rivers, which was painted by Richard Wilson in the 18th century, and later by Peter de Wint and Turner. The Normans first established a castle here during the 12th century, but the remaining towers and walls date from the 13th century.

Cirencester *Glos.*   546Dc
During the Roman occupation, Cirencester, then called Corinium Dobunnorum, served as the administrative centre for a large part of the West Country. The Roman city was the second largest in Britain when its defences, enclosing 240 acres, were set up in the 2nd century. When the Romans left, their town was destroyed piecemeal by Saxon raids, and now only fragments remain. After the Norman invasion, William Fitz-Osborn built a castle, which had disappeared by the end of the Middle Ages, and in 1539 the formerly rich abbey was dissolved. In the 19th century the once thriving wool trade gave place to a considerable market for corn and cheese. In Cirencester Park the 1st Earl Bathurst rebuilt the original Elizabethan house in 1718, and laid out the great park in 1704–35. The house is not open to view, but the public may walk or ride in the park.
CHURCH OF ST JOHN THE BAPTIST It was originally Norman, but as a result of considerable additions during the 14th and 15th centuries by rich local wool merchants, it is now regarded as one of the most beautiful Perpendicular churches in England. There is a three-storey south porch completely covered in Perpendicular tracery, and a west tower. Impressive inside is the high clerestoried nave and the window over the chancel arch; and there is elaborate ornamental stonework over the nave and aisle. Also worth noting is the 15th-century pulpit (one of the few pre-Reformation pulpits in the county), the fan-vaulting in St

Katharine's Chapel, and the monuments in the Lady Chapel, one to Lord Bathurst (c. 1776) by Joseph Nollekens.
CORINIUM MUSEUM The museum gets its title from the Roman name for Cirencester, and its exhibits are concerned with that period of British history. Provincial Roman sculpture, architectural detail, mosaic work and domestic items are on display.

Cissbury Ring *W. Sussex*   542Ad
A group of disused Neolithic flint-mines was in the area enclosed by an Iron Age hill-fort in the 3rd century BC. This ceased to be used before Roman times, but was refurbished and occupied for a time early in the Dark Ages.

Clackmannan *Central*   562Af
CLACKMANNAN TOWER On a hill to the west of the town, the tower is 79 ft high, of 14th-century origin with 17th-century additions, and was reputedly built by Robert the Bruce.

Clandon Park *Surrey*   542Af
A Classical mansion built by Giacomo Leoni for the 2nd Lord Onslow c. 1731–5. It is rectangular in plan, and the roof is hidden behind a balustrade. On the west front is the main entrance, beneath a pediment (and now with a disfiguring porch added during the 19th century). The original gardens were formal, following the fashion of the time, but during the 1770's Capability Brown designed a more fashionable informal arrangement. The house contains fine furniture, pictures and porcelain.

Clapham *Beds.*   547He
CHURCH OF ST THOMAS OF CANTERBURY Noteworthy for its tall Saxon tower, which was incorporated in the Norman church. Inside is a large, 17th-century monument with little *putti*—cherub-like children—one holding a skull.

Clare *Suffolk*   548Be
A small, ancient town with fragments of a 13th-century shell-keep, part of Gilbert de Clare's castle. The town has houses from all periods, including the Ancient House, c. 1473, once the priest's house; the Grove, five-gabled, c. 1500, with oriel bracket of huntsmen and hounds; Chapel Cottage or Wentford Chapel, late 12th century; the Bell Hotel, well restored; the Swan

Inn; Cliftons, with splendid 17th-century chimneys; Nethergate House and Stour House, with oversailing upper storey. There are also the remains of an Iron Age camp.

CHURCH OF SS PETER AND PAUL A large church, mainly of the 14th to 15th centuries, but with an earlier west tower. There is a Perpendicular font and 17th-century woodwork.

Claremont *Surrey*   *542Af*

The former house on this site was built by Sir John Vanbrugh for the 1st Duke of Newcastle. It was bought by Clive of India in 1768 and he replaced it with the present Palladian mansion, started in 1770 and built to designs by Capability Brown. The house, on high ground, comprises two floors above a basement. It is rectangular in plan, and the hall is approached by a flight of steps beneath a portico of Corinthian columns, which rises to the full height of the house on the southern side. Henry Holland, assisted by John Soane, was largely responsible for the interior decoration. During the present century some interior decoration has been altered, but much of the work of Brown, Holland and Soane remains. Claremont is now a girls' school.

Claverley *Shropshire*   *546Bg*

CHURCH OF ALL SAINTS Founded by Roger de Montgomery, William the Conqueror's cousin (*d.* 1094). The fine north arcade and the carved font are Norman, but most of the rest of the church was rebuilt between the 13th and 15th centuries. Most important is a large wall-painting in the nave, of *c.* 1200, showing battling knights on horseback: they are reminiscent of those in the Bayeux Tapestry.

The chancel roof is post-Reformation (1601) and there are two monuments, of 1448 and 1558, the latter with children as the mourners.

Claverton Manor: *540Df*
The American Museum in Britain *Avon*

This mansion contains furnished rooms in the style of 17th- to 19th-century American homesteads, brought complete from across the Atlantic. Also on show are examples of American Indian art, Spanish Colonial rooms from New Mexico and a folk art collection. In the grounds are a reproduction of part of George Washington's flower garden from Mount Vernon, a Conestoga (covered) wagon, a herb garden and herb shop. A maritime section covers aspects of immigration into America, sea battles, the whaling trade and the China traders. The house, in 120 acres of park, was built in 1820 in Greek Revival style and was opened as a museum in 1961.

Claybrooke *Leics.*   *552Ea*

CHURCH OF ST PETER This basically 14th-century church contains a contemporary chancel, and a Perpendicular nave. The windows have flowing tracery and fragments of medieval stained glass.

Claydon House *Bucks.*   *547Gd*

The Verney family came into possession of land here in 1463, and the family still lives at Claydon. The 16th-century manor house was enlarged by the 2nd Earl of Verney in the middle of the 18th century. Parts of the house were demolished in the mid-19th century, when a new south front was built. Florence Nightingale was a sister of Parthenhope, Lady Verney, and often stayed at Claydon; her bedroom is on view.

CLAVERTON MANOR

In 1897, at the age of 23, Winston Churchill made his first political speech at Claverton Manor, a country house outside Bath. Today, Claverton houses the first American museum to be established outside the United States, with reconstructions of American rooms from the 17th to 19th centuries. The museum was opened in *1961 with a wide range of exhibits, including this country store and post office, to illustrate the history and development of culture in America. Some rooms of the museum at Claverton have wooden panelling and flooring that was originally fitted in American homes.*

Cleeve Abbey *Som.* 540Ae
Founded in 1198, it forms a small but interesting complex of buildings whose main fabric belongs to the 13th century. The church itself has been almost destroyed, but the convent buildings survive in a remarkably complete state. In the late 15th century the refectory was reconstructed, and this medieval hall, with its superb timber roof, is one of the finest surviving in this part of England. Incorporated into the lower floor of the rebuilt refectory are two small sets of rooms, each with its own lavatory or garderobe, which indicate that by the Dissolution in 1537 the monks' dormitory had been split up into cubicles.

Cleeve Cloud *Glos.* 546Cd
This Iron Age promontory fort on a Cotswold spur high above the Vale of Severn is small, hardly more than 2 acres in extent. To the west it is adequately protected by the steep slopes of the hill, but on the east it is cut off from the main hill-top by two banks each with an external ditch.

Clevedon Court *Avon* 540Cg
Thackeray wrote much of *Vanity Fair* while staying here, and he used the house as a background to his novel *Henry Esmond*. The once-fortified manor house, with additions made in every century since the 12th, has been the home of the Elton family since 1709; it contains the Elton Ware pottery collection and a display of Nailsea glass. The 14th-century chapel is noted for its beautiful window tracery.

Cley next the Sea *Norfolk* 554Cd
A picturesque town that was a busy port in the 14th century. It is rich in small, attractive flint houses, some with Dutch gables, and is dominated by a windmill. The old custom house is red brick with Georgian windows. The Maison de Quai has a brick and cobble wall, and a 15th-century doorway.

Cliffe *Kent* 548Bb
CHURCH OF ST HELEN This was a church of considerable importance during the Middle Ages. The present structure dates from the 13th century, but the aisles were widened, the chancel rebuilt and the two-storey porch added in the 14th century. Some of the wall-paintings in the transepts are part of the original decoration.

Clifton Campville *Staffs.* 552Db
CHURCH OF ST ANDREW A magnificent, mainly 13th- and 14th-century church, with a tall tower and spire. It has screens, stalls, misericords, remains of wall-paintings, and monuments, including one by J. M. Rysbrack and one by William Behnes.

Clifton Reynes *Bucks.* 547Ge
CHURCH OF ST MARY THE VIRGIN Though originally Norman, with a Norman west tower remaining, there were many additions to St Mary's in the 13th to 15th centuries, including the battlemented exterior. Particularly interesting are the 14th-century font with carved figures of the Trinity, the Virgin and saints, and the monuments, with stone and oaken effigies to the Reynes family. One 14th-century tomb chest has little mourners standing round. The tomb of Alexander Small (*d.* 1752) has a terracotta bust by Peter Scheemakers.

Clipsham *Leics.* 553Gc
CHURCH OF ST MARY On the edge of a small, well wooded park, St Mary's is large and mainly 14th century, with some 12th-century work. The sturdy west tower has a broach spire of unusual design. Of the original Norman work in the interior, the font and capitals of the north arcade

remain. The window tracery is part of the 14th-century reconstruction.

Cliveden *Bucks.* 547Hb
Famous political centre and country home of Lord Astor in the 1930's. This is the third house to be constructed on the site, the great red-brick terrace dating from 1666. The present mansion was built in 1851 by Sir Charles Barry, the architect of the House of Commons; it overlooks the Thames, and in the grounds, designed by Capability Brown, are temples dating from *c.* 1735 by Leoni, and magnificent formal gardens.

Clodock *Heref. & Worcs.* 545Jd
CHURCH OF ST CLODOCK On the edge of the Black Mountains, this church has a Norman nave and chancel arch, a late 17th-century three-decker pulpit and pews, and a west gallery of *c.* 1715.

Clun *Shropshire* 551Ja
CHURCH OF ST GEORGE A large church with a massive Norman west tower that has an unusual double pyramid roof. There is more Norman work in the church, but this and work of later centuries was restored by G. E. Street in 1877. The Jacobean pulpit has a horizontal sounding board and the altar a handsome wood canopy. Outside is a copy of the original 17th-century lychgate.

Clyffe Pypard *Wilts.* 546Db
CHURCH OF ST PETER In a beautiful position on a wooded ridge stands St Peter's, dating mainly from the 15th century (the west tower, nave and aisles with rood and parclose screens are all of that period), but restored by William Butterfield in 1874 when the chancel was rebuilt. There is a Victorian carved font. Among the many monuments is an unusual one by John Deval Junior to a carpenter, dated 1786. The carpenter stands, in white marble, with his tools.

Clynnog-Fawr *Gwynedd* 550Ed
CHURCH OF ST BEUNO This is one of the most impressive churches in North Wales, probably founded by St Beuno (a 7th-century abbot) whose shrine was here. It is a late Perpendicular cruciform building with west tower, joined by a 17th-century passage to St Beuno's Chapel. There is a 16th-century screen and a simple pulpit of *c.* 1700.

Coalbrookdale *Shropshire* 552Ab
MUSEUM OF IRON This is housed in the Coalbrookdale Company's great warehouse and traces the history of ironmaking through the vital roles of the Darby family and the Coalbrookdale Company. Near by are the remains of the original furnace used by Abraham Darby I to smelt iron from coke. (See also Ironbridge and Blists Hill.)

Coalport *Shropshire* 552Ad
Built as a new town towards the end of the 18th century, Coalport was a shipping junction of the Shropshire Canal and the R. Severn. But its major industry was china making, and it remained so until 1926. Today, the buildings of the china works house a museum and exhibit a unique display of Coalport china.

Coate *Wilts.* 546Db
RICHARD JEFFERIES MUSEUM Manuscripts, first editions and personal items of the writer Richard Jefferies (1848–87), are displayed in his birthplace, Coate Farmhouse, together with similar mementoes of another local writer, Alfred Williams.

Coates-by-Stow *Lincs.* 553Gf
CHURCH OF ST EDITH A small charming church without aisles. It has a Norman south doorway, font, and a Perpendicular rood screen which still

has its gallery, a great rarity in England. There is a monument of the Commonwealth period to Brian Cook, some fragments of medieval glass, and 15th-century pulpit and bench ends.

Cobham *Kent* 542Dg

COBHAM HALL The Hall was built in three distinct phases. During the late 16th century it assumed its basic form—a central block with two wings at right angles, each with an octagonal turret. In the mid-18th century the central block was rebuilt, probably by Inigo Jones and John Webb. Further alterations were made at the end of the 18th century by James Wyatt, who also built the mausoleum in the grounds which was never used. At this time Humphry Repton and his son John laid out the grounds and fine gardens. The mansion is now a girls' public school.

Cochwillan *Gwynedd* 550Ee

This is probably the best late medieval house in Wales, being built *c.* 1450 by William ap Gruffydd, who later fought at Bosworth and was made High Sheriff for the county for life by Henry VII. Careful restoration of the building after its long use as a barn has made it possible to appreciate the excellent quality of the original woodwork, especially the hammer-beams and frieze. The hall contains the original great fireplace and is partitioned from the living accommodation by a massive oak screen at each end. (By appointment.)

Cockermouth *Cumbria* 557Gf

The ruined castle dates from 1134 and has a good example of an oubliette dungeon—one with entrance only from above by a trap door.

WORDSWORTH HOUSE The house where William Wordsworth and his sister Dorothy were born is preserved and contains relics of them.

Cockleroy See Bowden Hill and Cockleroy.

Cogges *Oxon.* 546Ec

CHURCH OF ST MARY The north-west tower is square at the base and octagonal above. Remains of the Norman church include the south doorway and the font. One of the monuments shows a 14th-century lady in a wimple; there are windows with interesting late Decorated tracery, and some medieval glass fragments.

Coity Castle *Mid Glam.* 545Hb

The ruins of a medieval castle. The 12th-century square keep is surrounded by curtain walls. Later additions include the 13th-century round tower adjoining the great hall, and the 14th-century eastern gate-house. The castle was abandoned and left to decay in the late 16th century.

Colchester *Essex* 548Cd

There was probably a settlement at Colchester in the 5th century BC, and in the 1st century AD, Cunobelin (Shakespeare's Cymbeline) was king at Camulodunum. Roman invaders occupied Colchester in AD 43 and five years later established a major colony there. In AD 60 the Britons under Queen Boadicea's command revolted against Roman rule, massacred the Roman occupants, and destroyed the temple. In the Dark Ages the Danes frequently raided the town. By *c.* 1085 the Normans had built a castle on and around a former Roman temple. The town's charter was granted by Richard I in 1189. St John's Abbey, of which only the gate-house remains, and St Botolph's Priory, ruined during the Civil War, date from *c.* 1100. The castle keep is now a museum. The Hollytrees Museum, in a Georgian house (1716–18), is the centre for the Essex Archaeological Society.

TOMBSTONE OF A CENTURION

One of the finest gravestones from Roman Britain, and possibly the earliest. It commemorates Marcus Favonius Facilis, a centurion of the 20th Legion. Made of Bath stone, the memorial is 6 ft high and was probably carved by a sculptor from the Mediterranean region; it dates from before AD 60, from the military occupation preceding the colonial town of Colchester, for Facilis is not described as a veteran. Traces of plaster on the stone suggest it was once coloured. (Colchester and Essex Museum)

BOURNE MILL A fishing lodge built in 1591 from material of St John's Abbey, with elaborately stepped and curved Dutch gables. It was later converted into a mill.

CHURCH OF THE HOLY TRINITY A church with a Saxon west tower, and triangular-headed west doorway; its builders made much use of Roman materials. Now a natural history museum.

COLCHESTER AND ESSEX MUSEUM The museum is divided into four parts. Most of the collections are housed in the castle keep, a Norman building of *c.* 1085, constructed on the vaults of the Roman Temple of Claudius, built in AD 50. Here exhibits illustrate local history from the earliest Stone Age to the 17th century; the Roman section includes fine jewellery, coins, pottery, bronzes and statues, glassware, implements and models of Roman Colchester. Domestic antiquities and costume are housed at Hollytrees, a Georgian house near by; exhibits there illustrate local history from the 18th century. Items of local crafts, shipping and transport are displayed in the former Church of the Holy Trinity. The natural history museum is in the former All Saints' Church.

WATTS MORTUARY CHAPEL, COMPTON

An exotic circular chapel, in style part Byzantine, with Tuscan and Norman touches, built in 1896 by a team of amateurs under Mary Watts, wife of the 19th-century artist, George Frederic Watts. After the couple had settled in Compton, Mrs Watts, who had studied art before her marriage, started classes in clay-modelling for local people. Encouraged by the success of the classes, she decided to build the chapel with the help of her pupils, who even made their own

bricks. It is 24 ft across with four transepts representing the Circle of Eternity with the Cross of Faith running through it. The outside is plain, but the interior is startling—every inch of walls and vaulting is covered in rich art nouveau decoration, all designed by Mrs Watts with symbolic meaning. Here winged messengers stand under the Tree of Life. The plasterwork is incised in some places and built up in others to give the effect of light and shade.

MINORIES A Georgian house, rebuilt in 1776 and now an art gallery; it contains Georgian furniture, pictures, portraits and drawings by Constable, and 20th-century paintings, prints and sculpture.

Coldridge *Devon* 539Ge
CHURCH OF ST MATTHEW Originally a Norman building, of which some details remain, most of the church now dates from the 15th century. The font is Norman. Other features include rood and parclose screens, bench ends of the early 16th century, and a stained-glass figure.

Coldstream *Borders* 562Ed
BRIDGE OVER THE TWEED This severe but beautifully proportioned seven-arched bridge crosses the river between England and Scotland. Designed by John Smeaton and built 1763–6, it still has the Marriage House, famous as the venue of runaway weddings before 1856, on the Scottish side of the R. Tweed.

MARKET PLACE A tablet recalls that General Monk raised the Coldstream Guards here in 1659.

Coleford *Glos.* 546Bd
A town of special interest to metallurgists and industrial archaeologists: 5125 cu. ft of wood from the Forest of Dean were used to produce one ton of iron bar. The local trade declined during the first half of the 18th century, when further deforestation on this scale was forbidden. A local 'free-miner' named Robert Forester Mushet (1811–91) discovered the value of speigeleisen for restoring the quality of 'burnt iron'. Applying this discovery to the Bessemer process, he produced cast steel.

Coleridge Cottage *Som.* 540Be
Samuel Taylor Coleridge, poet and philosopher, lived here from 1797 to 1800, when he wrote 'The Ancient Mariner' and the dream poem 'Kubla Khan'.

Coleshill *Oxon.* 546Ec
A great estate (3620 acres) adjoining Buscot Park, including the village of Coleshill with its fine Cotswold stone cottages and farmhouses, Bradbury Hill on which is an Iron Age fort, and Great Coxwell village with its fine tithe barn.

Colne *Lancs.* 558Ab
BRITISH IN INDIA MUSEUM The exhibits, which include paintings and photographs, coins, medals and uniforms, illustrate the impact of the British presence in India during the century and a half before the transfer of power in 1947. There is a diorama showing the last stand of the 44th Regiment at Gandamak, a model of the Simla railway, and the dress of an Afghan princess who was presented to Queen Victoria.
CHURCH OF ST BARTHOLOMEW Though mostly late Perpendicular, St Bartholomew's was begun in the 12th century. The 16th-century roof was exposed during restoration in 1856–7. There are noteworthy mid-18th-century monuments to the Emmott family by Sir Robert Taylor.

Combe Bank *Kent* 542Cf
An 18th-century mansion, with Adam-style rooms, now a girls' school. It contains decoration by the 19th-century artist, Walter Crane. (By appointment.)

Combe Gibbet *Berks.* 546Ea
This Neolithic long barrow is apparently one of those without internal megalithic chambers. The quarry-ditches along the sides are still partly visible and the 50 ft wide broader end still stands more than 6 ft high. It lies on Inkpen Beacon, near the village of Combe, and gets its odd name from the fact that, some 300 years ago, a gibbet was erected on the mound on which to hang the murderers of two small children.

Compton *Surrey* 541Jf
CHURCH OF ST NICHOLAS A Norman church with several fascinating and unique features, including a west tower which is probably Saxon; a two-storey chancel, the lower part vaulted, above is a Norman wood screen; a Norman nave roof; and a scratched carving on a chancel pillar of a soldier straight from the Bayeux Tapestry.
WATTS GALLERY Featuring the pictures and sculptures of George Frederic Watts (1817–1904), the gallery was founded by Mrs Watts in memory of her husband.

Compton Acres *Dorset* 540Fc
Eight gardens in English and foreign styles, with statuary in bronze and marble and many rare plants.

Compton Beauchamp *Oxon.* 546Eb
CHURCH OF ST SWITHIN A small cruciform church of chalk near Compton House, dating probably from the 13th century, with a pyramid roof to the tower. The font is late Gothic, and there is 14th-century stained glass in the east windows. The 20th-century reredos, rood, communion rail and some other details are by Martin Travers. There are good monuments of 1737 and 1771.

Compton Castle *Devon* 539Hc
The house of Sir Humphrey Gilbert (1539–83), founder of Newfoundland, the first British colony in North America, and half-brother of Sir Walter Raleigh. The fortified manor house was built in 1320, added to in the 15th and 16th centuries and restored in modern times.

Compton Martin *Avon* 540Cf
CHURCH OF ST MICHAEL A Norman church, with a Perpendicular west tower. There is a Norman font and a twisted pillar of the same period.

Condover *Shropshire* 551Jb
CHURCH OF SS ANDREW AND MARY The original Norman north transept remains, but much of the rest of the building is later 17th century, including the west tower. There are many monuments, including one of *c.* 1746 by Louis Roubiliac of Roger Owen of Condover Hall and his daughter.

Condover Hall *Shropshire* 551Jb
A gabled and mullioned Elizabethan house, E-shape in plan, built of pink stone and noted for its examples of the mason's craft. It is now a school for the blind. (By appointment.)

Congleton *Cheshire* 552Be
CHURCH OF ST PETER The present building of 1742, in Classical style, replaced an old church which had become dilapidated. The lower part of the 14th-century tower remains. Inside there are galleries with box-pews, various 18th-century monuments, coats of arms and a 17th-century pulpit placed centrally before the altar.

Congresbury *Avon* 540Cf
REFECTORY Built in Perpendicular style in the late 15th century, it has fine moulded beams and roof timbers. In 1824–7 a Regency wing was added. (By appointment.)

Conington *Cambs.* 547Jf
CHURCH OF ST MARY A church of many dates; nave 18th century, chancel late 19th century, and the tower of the 14th century. There is a signed monument by Grinling Gibbons, the great wood-carver of the late 17th century; and earlier work attributed to Joshua Marshall, *c.* 1658.

Conisbrough Castle *S. Yorks.* 552Ef
The present buildings at Conisbrough were probably built by Hamelin Plantagenet, Henry II's half-brother, to whom the estate passed in 1163. The outer bailey is now represented by an earthwork; the inner bailey was surrounded by a stone wall which has mostly survived; on the west and east sides of the wall are projecting turrets (an early instance of the use of round turrets). Dominating the whole site is the 90 ft tall circular keep—interesting because in England before *c.* 1165 keeps had always been rectangular in shape. The walls of the keep are supported by six heavy buttresses which in effect form small turrets. The planning within the keep is ingenious. The hall is on the first floor, and above it are the solar and chapel. The chapel itself is an unusual shape—an elongated hexagon squeezed into the thickness of the wall and one of the flanking buttresses.

Coniston *Cumbria* 557Hd
JOHN RUSKIN MUSEUM Dedicated to John Ruskin who lived at his house, Brantwood, 1¼ miles away, during the last part of his life (1872–1900). The museum contains, among other things, a large part of his mineral collection, engravings of his work, a few original drawings, many of his books, his hand-bells, paintbox and sketchbooks. A corner of the museum is dedicated as a memorial to Donald Campbell, who died on Lake Coniston trying to break the world water speed record.

Conwy *Gwynedd* 550Fe
ABERCONWY A medieval house dating from the 14th century and now housing an exhibition.
CASTLE Conwy Castle, built mainly between 1283 and 1287, is one of the outstanding achievements of medieval military architecture in Europe. The castle, with its eight drum towers and 21 semicircular towers, was built in a curve to follow the lie of the restricted land available. The outer ward, which occupies more than two-thirds of the main castle area, contains the

CONWY CASTLE

The time-worn dark grey stone of Conwy Castle looms over the lighter stone of Robert Stephenson's tubular railway bridge over the River Conwy, built in a matching castellated style in 1848—nearly six centuries later.

Conwy was one of the castles built by King Edward I late in the 13th century to consolidate the English hold over Wales. Eight massive drum towers and 21 smaller towers punctuate walls 15 ft thick and half a mile around.

remains of the great hall, while the inner ward contains the royal apartments. Although the timber fittings of the castle have long since perished, the stonework is virtually complete. The town walls were built at the same time as the castle, and neither has been altered in any important detail.

PLAS MAWR It took from 1572 to 1596 to complete this fine Elizabethan town house, the last addition being the handsome gate-house on the main road. This is one of the few houses of its kind without significant additions and alterations, and almost all the original plasterwork survives. All the ceilings are flat and enriched. There are some fine examples of Tudor screenwork and two interesting wooden spiral staircases, but most notable is the rich treatment of the elevations with their elaborate crow-stepped gables.

SUSPENSION BRIDGE In 1826 work was completed on the suspension road bridge over the R. Conwy. Thomas Telford, architect of the Menai road bridge, here repeated his successful suspension bridge on a smaller scale. Close to the bridge is the medieval Conwy Castle, and Telford designed the two castellated tower supports to harmonise with the castle. The original suspension bridge has now been replaced by a new and wider road bridge, but Telford's magnificent achievement has been preserved.

TUBULAR BRIDGE Adjacent to the road bridge is Robert Stephenson's railway bridge. It is a tubular iron construction, built in 1848 and, unlike Stephenson's Britannia tubular bridge over the Menai Strait (1850), is in a single span.

Copford *Essex* 548Cd

CHURCH A remote Norman church, one of the most impressive in Essex, whose nave, chancel and apse are original. A south aisle was added later. The remains of 12th-century paintings which once covered all the walls—Christ in Glory, signs of the zodiac, and so on—were restored in the 19th century.

Corbridge *Northld.* 558Bg

The important Roman site, Corstopitum, stands near the modern town where the R. Tyne is crossed by the Roman road to the north (now the A68). Established in the 1st century (probably AD 78–84) as a fort to protect the crossing, it was abandoned *c.* AD 125 when Hadrian's Wall was built, 3 miles to the north. In the 2nd century, the occupation for a time of the Antonine Wall in Scotland left Hadrian's Wall with a skeleton garrison only, so the fort was re-constituted and re-occupied from *c.* AD 140 until the northern wall was abandoned and the troops returned to Hadrian's line.

About the beginning of the 3rd century, important rebuilding took place and the site became a supply town for the Wall's garrison. It was then occupied by a considerable civilian population until the Wall was finally abandoned near the end of the 4th century.

CORBRIDGE GRANARY

To allow air to circulate around the garrison's corn supplies, so keeping them fresh, the flagstones forming the floor of the East Granary at the Roman fort of Corstopitum were laid over a series of parallel channels. The grain fed troops protecting a strategic crossing of the River Tyne.

Important excavations have been carried out during this century. Much of the site has been preserved and laid out for inspection.

There are visible remains of two granaries, a fountain, and a massive, uncompleted storehouse. Elsewhere are the foundations of the headquarters building and its strongroom, where the garrison's pay was kept before distribution. The Stanegate, a Roman road running parallel to Hadrian's Wall and linking the forts to the south of it, passes through the fort.

The small museum attached to the site has a remarkable collection of military and civilian material, including tools and other equipment, and a fine series of sculptured and inscribed stones, such as the famous 'Corbridge lion'. This consists of a fountain-head depicting a lion devouring a stag.

Corfe Castle *Dorset*   540Ec
Though now no more than a majestic ruin, Corfe dominates the countryside as it has for a thousand years. Its long history is one of blood and treason; the 18-year-old Edward, son of King Edgar, was murdered here in 978 by his step-mother, and the Duke of Brittany and other French captives were starved to death in the dungeons on the orders of King John. The castle was captured during the Civil War through the treachery of its own garrison. Afterwards, Oliver Cromwell's engineers blew it up to stop it being used again as a fortress. Stone from the ruins was incorporated in the buildings of the old village of Corfe Castle.

Corhampton *Hants.*   541Hd
CHURCH A Saxon church with long-and-short work. The east wall, however, was rebuilt of brick in the 19th century. The chancel arch is Saxon and there is a Saxon sun-dial. The circular font is Norman, and there are wall-paintings dating from the 13th century.

Cornworthy *Devon.*   539Gc
CHURCH OF ST PETER This 14th-century church has a circular Norman font and an 18th-century pulpit with a sounding board. The box-pews and panelling probably date from c. 1800. The church was restored in the early 19th century.

Corrimony *Highland*   565Jf
CHAMBERED CAIRN A Neolithic passage-grave in a roughly circular mound, some 60 ft in diameter, standing about 8 ft high. There is a stone kerb round its edge. The 23 ft long passage leads to a circular chamber some 12 ft across; the roof was corbelled and then covered by a great capstone with cup-marks. The mound is surrounded by a circle of 11 spaced standing stones.

Corsham *Wilts.*   540Eg
CHURCH OF ST BARTHOLOMEW A large church extensively altered by G. E. Street who demolished the central tower and built the present one. The original church was Saxon, to which aisles and an extra bay were added in the 12th century. The aisles were rebuilt in the 14th, and the east end of the church completely re-modelled in the 15th century. The chapel on the north of the chancel contains the tomb of Thomas Tropenell who built Great Chalfield Manor House. There are also memorials to the Methuen family.
CORSHAM COURT An Elizabethan mansion of 1582, with Georgian additions. The Methuen collection of old masters hangs in the gallery, which has a fine ceiling and carpet, and is lined with damask of 1769. The furniture includes chairs by Chippendale and mirrors of Adam design. The park was laid out by Capability Brown.

Cotehele House *Cornwall*   538Fc
A medieval manor house, dating from 1485–1627. It was constructed of grey granite around two courts on the site of an earlier house and is one of the least-altered houses of its period in the country. It was for centuries the home of the Earls of Mount Edgcumbe and was given to the Treasury by the family in 1947 in lieu of payment of death duties. The contents includes furniture, tapestries, armour and needlework, mainly of the 17th and early 18th centuries. It stands in more than a thousand acres of ground with gardens and pools at different levels.

FRA FILIPPO LIPPI
The Annunciation

In the period of Florentine painting following Masaccio and Donatello, there were two tendencies—one towards a logical and scientific outlook, and another towards a more sensuous reaction to the visible world, which is reflected in Fra Angelico's devotion to the beauty of holiness and his exquisite radiant colours, and in the similar work of Fra Filippo Lippi, who was only a few years younger. Lippi was also a painter-friar, but his life was far different. His seduction of the nun, Lucrezia Buti, and the birth of their son the painter Filippino Lippi indicate a more worldly make-up—and a feeling for human rather than spiritual beauty distinguishes Filippo's later work. His painting became gradually more decorative and even humorous. His luscious colour becomes scumbled, anticipating the tonal painting of Leonardo. This late 'Annunciation' was painted in 1463. (Corsham Court)

149

Cottesbrooke *Northants.*   *547Gf*
CHURCH OF ALL SAINTS A church of *c.* 1300—originally cruciform, but it has been restored; there is a west tower. Inside is a rare 18th-century movable, wood pedestal font with cover. Fortunately left by the 19th-century restorer are the three-decker pulpit, box-pews and the two-storey pew of the Langham family. Among monuments from the early 17th century are some by Thomas Cartwright, and J. F. Moore.

Cottingham *Humberside*   *559Gb*
CHURCH OF ST MARY THE VIRGIN The church is cruciform with a central tower, and dates from the 13th to 15th centuries. There is a 14th-century brass of a priest.

Coughton Court *Warks.*   *546Df*
In 1605, wives of several conspirators engaged in the Gunpowder Plot waited for news of the enterprise in a room of the great central gate-house of this house, the home of the Throckmorton family from 1409 to 1946. The battlemented gate-house dates from 1509 and there are two half-timbered Elizabethan wings and Georgian Gothic additions. The house contains Jacobite relics.

Coventry *W. Midlands*   *546Eg*
CATHEDRAL The old cathedral, which was the parish church of St Michael until 1918, was built in the 14th and 15th centuries; it was a magnificent example of Gothic church building, with a unique pentagon-shaped east end. The square west tower, built from 1373 to 1394, changes to an octagonal lantern supported by flying buttresses, and is crowned by a spire completed in 1433; this rises to 299 ft and is exceeded in height only by the spires of Salisbury and Norwich Cathedrals. The outside walls and tower are all that remain after the bombing of November 14, 1940. An extensive restoration programme to preserve the tower and the spire was brought to completion in May 1978. The new cathedral, built on the north side of the old and joined to it by a porch, was designed by Sir Basil Spence and completed in 1962. The great west screen of clear glass by John Hutton enables the old cathedral to be seen from inside the new. The exterior is relatively simple, and the main features are the two free-standing circular chapels, of Unity and of Christ the Servant, the saw-edge elevations of the nave walls and windows, the slender spire which was lowered by helicopter on to the roof, and the large bronze group of St Michael and the Devil by Epstein. (See pp. 152–3.)
CHURCH OF THE HOLY TRINITY A medieval parish church, with one of the famous three spires of Coventry. The oldest part of the present building, the north porch, was built early in the 13th century. A stone seat along the length of the south wall of the church was provided for the sick and elderly: the congregation then stood to worship, and 'the weakest goes to the wall'.

Cowbridge *S. Glam.*   *545Hb*
This small town was originally defended by a circuit of medieval walls, of which only the 13th-century south gate survives. The church is worth a visit, and the main street contains a number of ancient houses.

Cow Castle *Strathclyde*   *562Bd*
This complex contains two settlements, not contemporary with each other. The earlier, larger one, which was constructed in the Iron Age, occupies the south-west end of a ridge raised above what was once a watery marsh. It had a single rampart and, in places, an external ditch. The smaller, later settlement was built either in the Iron Age or the Dark Age, on top of the remains of the earlier one. There are traces of hut-bases visible both of the earlier and later periods. The ridge also shows some evidence of other banks and ditches.

Cowdray Park *W. Sussex*   *541Jd*
The Cowdray ruins are all that is left of a mansion built *c.* 1530 by the Earl of Southampton, but largely destroyed by fire in 1793. The remains include the east side of a large quadrangular court, and some parts of the west side where the three-storey gate-house, with turrets, stands nearly intact. The hall porch is almost square, with octagonal buttresses: the entrance arch bears a mutilated carving of the Arms of Henry VIII, who visited Cowdray in 1538.

Cowes *Isle of Wight*   *541Gc*
The most famous of all yachting centres, Cowes, East and West, is divided by the Medina estuary. West Cowes has the character of a seaside town, but in the 19th century two castellated mansions were built across the estuary; one, John Nash's own castle, has been pulled down, but the other, Norris, makes a splendid sight from the Solent. More famous is Osborne, designed by Thomas Cubitt and the Prince Consort as Queen Victoria's country home.

Coxwold *N. Yorks.*   *558Dd*
CHURCH OF ST MICHAEL A 15th-century church with a distinctive octagonal west tower. The 18th-century chancel is by Thomas Atkinson. Among the furnishings is an unusual 18th-century communion rail and pulpit, and monuments to the Bellasis family include one by Nicholas Stone, *c.* 1632, with kneeling effigies.

Craigellachie *Grampian*   *566Df*
SPEY BRIDGE A cast-iron bridge with a single 160 ft span, designed by Thomas Telford in 1815 and built to carry the road south from Elgin. It is now used only as a footbridge: road transport uses a modern addition.

Craigie Castle *Strathclyde*   *561Hd*
The overgrown remains of the 13th-century castle—once the seat of the Lindsays—still shows evidence of fine stonework, including a Gothic arched ceiling and a barrel-vaulted cellar.

Craigievar Castle *Grampian*   *566Fe*
An example of the Scottish tower-house style, with conical caps to its French château-like turrets. Completed in 1626 by William Forbes, a prosperous merchant turned landowner, the castle was repaired 200 years later, but survives fundamentally unaltered. The hall, which is in medieval style, has a musicians' gallery, carved oak panelling, and fine Renaissance plasterwork including a Scottish Royal arms – evidence that the laird had the right of 'pit and gallows' – of imprisonment and execution. Plaster and panelling – some in 17th-century Memel pine, reflecting Forbes' Baltic trading interests – are features of most of the other rooms. Visible in a number of places is an inscription reading 'Doe not vaiken sleiping dogs'—the motto of Craigievar.

Craigmillar Castle *Lothian*   *562Ce*
The central tower of Craigmillar Castle is massive but simple, in plan rather like a squat letter L. On the first floor is the great hall, and adjoining it another smaller room, presumably a living-room or solar. In 1427 the tower was enclosed by a roughly rectangular curtain wall with heavily machicolated parapets which still survives. A gun-port in one of the towers commanding the approaches to the castle is an early instance in

CRAIGIEVAR CASTLE

A tall, dramatic castle, Craigievar is a magnificent Scottish 'tower-house'; it has remained unchanged since it was built between 1610 and 1626 for William Forbes, and his descendants occupied it until 1963. Built on an L-shaped plan, the castle rises straight through seven stories. Its turrets are corbelled, and capped with plain conical roofs like candle-snuffers.

Inside there is a fine plaster ceiling in the groined vault of the great hall. This was executed by craftsmen from London and has pendants and portrait medallions, foliage and heraldic devices in relief. Also in the hall are a huge fire-place, a fine wooden screen, a musicians' gallery and, over the grand staircase, the inscription, 'Doe not vaiken sleiping dogs'.

Scotland of provision for artillery in the defence of a castle. It is not clear whether further domestic accommodation was attached to the curtain wall at this time but such accommodation was certainly added in the 16th century when a range, including a kitchen, was built inside the east wall. Finally, in 1661 more commodious living quarters were added along the west wall.

Craignethan Castle *Strathclyde* 562*Ad*
The ruins of a 16th-century fortress, the 'Tillie-tudlem Castle' of Scott's novel *Old Mortality*.

Craigston Castle *Grampian* 566*Fg*
A castle built in 1604–7 by John Urquhart in Renaissance style and still occupied by his family. (By appointment.)

Crail *Fife* 562*Dg*
The oldest of the five royal burghs of the East Neuk of Fife. In Marketgate, Rumford and Shoregate are groups of traditional 17th- and 18th-century houses with crow-stepped gables and red pantiled roofs. The 16th-century tolbooth, reconstructed in 1776 and added to in 1814, dominates the south side of the Marketgate. The stone-spired parish church is surrounded by a fine churchyard with mural monuments.

Cranborne *Dorset* 540*Ed*
CHURCH OF SS MARY AND BARTHOLOMEW Little remains of the Norman origins, except the fine north doorway; the church is now mostly of the 13th and 15th centuries, with 19th-century restoration in the chancel. There are a 15th-century pulpit, several 17th-century monuments with figures, 13th-century wall-paintings over the south arcade, and a font of 1240.

Cranbrook *Kent* 542*De*
Cranbrook was a centre of the Wealden cloth-making industry which flourished in the 15th century. The church was built then, but the building which appears at every turn of this intricate little town is the windmill, built in 1816, and set on a high base to help it catch the wind.

Cranford *Greater London* 547*Hb*
CHURCH OF ST DUNSTAN An aisle-less church with a west tower; the nave was rebuilt in 1716 after a fire. St Dunstan's was restored in 1895. There are several monuments, the most noteworthy being that to Sir Roger Aston (*d.* 1612) and his wife, by William Cure, with kneeling figures and a large arched canopy on Corinthian columns.

Crantock *Cornwall* 538*Cc*
CHURCH OF ST CARANTOC An interesting Norman church which once had a central tower; the tower is now at the west. The chancel is 14th century; there is a Norman font. The church was restored by E. Sedding at the turn of this century.

Crarae Lodge *Strathclyde* 560*Fg*
A woodland garden of rare trees and flowering shrubs by Loch Fyne.

Crathes Castle *Grampian* 566*Fd*
A house built in 1553–96 in Scottish baronial style, with turrets and battlements; a Queen Anne wing, destroyed by fire in 1966, has been rebuilt in the same style. An iron-studded entrance door gives access to a spiral staircase leading up to the main floor, above ground level. The great hall has a carved Elizabethan fire-place. The house is noted for its painted ceilings, especially those in the Chamber of the Nine Nobles (dated 1602). The Green Lady's Room is reputed to be haunted; it has a painted ceiling, and along the crossbeams biblical texts are inscribed.

The garden, dating from the early 18th century, contains some of Britain's finest plant collections. The lime avenues were planted in 1702, as were the dense yew hedges which are now used to divide the garden into units. Each enclosure has a distinctive horticultural personality. The Pool Garden is planted in a colour scheme of purple foliage and red and yellow flowers. The yew borders shelter plants which show off well against the sombre green: yellow-flowered witch hazel and *Eucryphia*, which has blooms of white flowers carrying golden tassels.

151

COVENTRY CATHEDRAL

Throughout the night of November 14, 1940, Coventry endured the longest single air raid ever suffered by a British city. During the attack fire bombs destroyed all but the outer walls and tower of the Gothic cathedral. These now form a prelude to the magnificent new cathedral. Work to Sir

Basil Spence's competition-winning design began in June 1954, and the cathedral was consecrated in 1962. The interior, a basilica 270 ft by 80 ft, gives the impression of great space, and this is enhanced by the slender concrete columns supporting a canopy ceiling beneath the concrete roof.

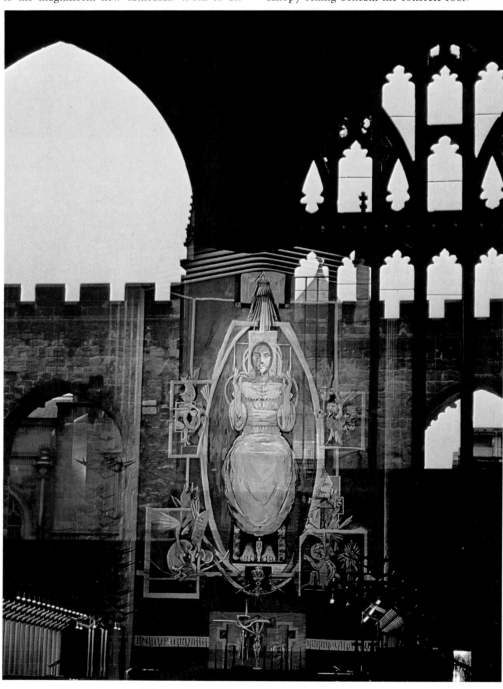

THE NAVE AND HIGH ALTAR *The tapestry of Christ in Glory above the high altar is seen here through the west screen, in whose glass are reflected the ruins of the old cathedral. The tapestry, the largest in the world, takes the place of the traditional east window. It was designed by Graham Sutherland, woven in France, and took 30,000 hours to make. The design is based on* the vision of St John the Divine from the Book of Revelation. The enthroned Christ, Man between his feet, is surrounded by four symbolic creatures—man, eagle, ox and lion; they are worshipping Christ. Above the lion, St Michael casts down the Devil. At the bottom right of the picture, seen as a golden glow, is the Chapel of Christ in Gethsemane.

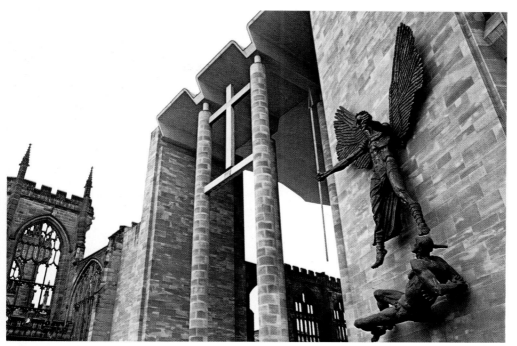

PORCH *The ruins of the 14th-century church are linked to the new cathedral by a porch. To the right of it is Sir Jacob Epstein's bronze sculpture of St Michael, the cathedral's patron saint, defeating the Devil in chains. This was Epstein's last religious sculpture before his death. The cathedral is built of Hollington stone from a quarry in Staffordshire.*

THE CHAPEL OF CHRIST IN GETHSEMANE *The golden mosaic by Steven Sykes shows the angel who appeared to Christ during his agony in the garden of Gethsemane, and strengthened him before his betrayal and crucifixion. The chapel is for private prayer.*

BAPTISTRY WINDOW *The largest window in the new cathedral, containing 200 panels, designed by John Piper and made by Patrick Reyntiens. It has alternating panels of stone and of stained glass in a chequer-board pattern. The magnificent range of stained glass windows in the new cathedral culminates in this huge one, which suggests the power of the Holy Spirit at work in the world, reaching up to heaven and down to earth.*

Crediton *Devon*   *539Ge*
CHURCH OF THE HOLY CROSS A cruciform church of cathedral proportions whose history began with St Boniface, Apostle of Germany, born in Crediton in 680. There is a Norman font and the tower over the crossing is part of the original 12th-century structure. The Chapter House has relics of Cromwell, and there are notable tombs.

Creech *Dorset*   *540Ec*
GRANGE ARCH A folly, built in 1740 of Portland stone, by Denis Bond of Creech Grange; it is also known as Bond's Folly.

Cressing *Essex*   *548Cd*
CRESSING TEMPLE The manor here was given to the Knights Templar in 1135, and was their earliest English possession. The two magnificent barns, the Barley Barn and the Wheat Barn, were built by the Templars, probably during the first half of the 13th century. There is a stable with granary dated 1623, a moat, and a walled garden of the late 16th century. (By appointment.)

Creswell Crags *Derbys. and Notts.*   *552Ee*
In the sides of a cleft in the limestone are several caves which excavation showed were inhabited in Upper Palaeolithic times. Many flint and bone implements were found, as well as fragments with engraved decoration. This early occupation was probably concentrated close to the mouth of each cave. They continued to be occupied into the early Mesolithic period and, after millennia of desertion, use was again made of them in Roman and even early English times. The best caves have now been excavated. They are closed to the public, being unsafe.

Crich *Derbys.*   *552Dd*
THE TRAMWAY MUSEUM As a form of transport, trams have almost disappeared. At Crich, however, they can be seen in operation, and visitors can take rides. The tramway was built by volunteer members of the Tramway Museum Society and carries a selection of tramcars.

Crichton Castle *Lothian*   *562Ce*
A solid rectangular tower-house, probably built in the late 14th century with a hall on the first floor, was the basis of Crichton Castle. Early in the 15th century the tower's defences were immensely strengthened by the addition of a gate-house tower which had its own hall (on the first floor). The living accommodation in the original tower was probably abandoned at that time, since no communication was provided between the first tower and the gate-house. Further domestic rooms were provided late in the 15th century when an extension was built along the west side of the courtyard. Finally, in the 16th century, a considerable amount of rebuilding along the north side provided a further range of domestic quarters behind an Italianate Renaissance façade.

Criccieth *Gwynedd*   *550Ed*
A resort on Tremadog Bay. Earl Lloyd George, Prime Minister at the end of the First World War, lived at Brynawelon, a house on the hill-side above the town. He was brought up and is buried at the nearby village of Llanystumdwy, where there is a small museum devoted to him. His tomb was designed by Sir Clough Williams-Ellis, the architect of Portmeirion. Criccieth includes the remains of a small castle that was rebuilt by Edward I, and at nearby Rhoslan there is a megalithic tomb.

Cricklade *Wilts.*   *546Dc*
CHURCH OF ST SAMPSON Dominating this church is the four-pinnacled tower at the crossing of the nave, chancel and transepts. It was built during the

CRICHTON CASTLE

Strategically positioned on the banks of Tyne Water about ten miles from Edinburgh, the castle was first a simple rectangular tower-house, probably built in the late 14th century by a John de Crichton. This tower was gradually enlarged, and now reflects the changes in military and domestic design, and architectural fashion, which took place during its development. In the late 15th century Crichton came into the possession of the Earls of Bothwell, one of whom was for a short period the husband of Mary, Queen of Scots. After Bothwell's downfall the castle was forfeited to the Crown, and was later conferred by James VI on Francis Stewart, Earl of Bothwell, who entertained the king there in 1586. Francis Stewart, who himself forfeited the castle in 1593, has been described as 'an eminently cultured ruffian'. He travelled widely in Spain and Italy, and was responsible for the Italianate façade added in the 16th century.

16th century and has a lierne-vault with much heraldry and bosses. The body of the church is of Saxon origin, with Norman additions and alterations. St Sampson was a Welsh-Breton saint. Cricklade has another Norman church, St Mary's.
SAXON BURH A large rectangular enclosure surrounded by a defensive bank and ditch. Test excavations have indicated, though perhaps not finally proved, that this was a defensive *burh* established in the reign of King Alfred.

During his campaigns against the Danish armies, Alfred had seen that the ease with which they had overrun the country was largely due to the absence of defensive points which could be garrisoned when necessary. And so, after peace was established, a series of these *burhs*, south of the Thames from Kent to Devon, was set up and finally completed by his son Edward the Elder.

Croft *Heref. & Worcs.*   *546Af*
CHURCH OF ST MICHAEL AND ALL ANGELS Standing by Croft Castle, this church has an interesting monument to Sir Richard Croft (d. 1509) and his wife, with effigies, a canopy and four figures of saints. There are some medieval tiles, and box-pews and a west gallery of the early 18th century. The nave and chancel are of *c.* 1300.

Croft *Lincs.* 554Ae
CHURCH OF ALL SAINTS An interesting church, which contains some good 15th-century screens and benches. The pulpit is dated 1615, and there is an impressive eagle lectern in brass, which is late pre-Reformation. Among several fine monuments are two 17th-century pieces with kneeling figures, and an early brass of a mail-clad knight in the south chapel.

Croft *N. Yorks.* 558Ce
CHURCH OF ST PETER A low church with west tower, originally Norman but now mainly later work. There are some engaging carvings on sedilia and elsewhere, and a fragment of a Saxon cross remains. The massive 17th-century family pew is reached by stairs; there are monuments from the 15th century, including one to Lewis Carroll.

Croft Castle *Heref. & Worcs.* 546Af
A Welsh Border castle owned by the Croft family from Domesday until 1957, except for the years 1750–1923. The ancient walls and four round corner-towers of pink stone, dating from the 14th or 15th century, survive, in spite of modifications made to the castle in the 16th and 17th centuries and in the mid-18th century, when the Georgian-Gothic staircase and ceilings were installed.
CROFT AMBREY An Iron Age hill-fort with multiple banks and ditches. An early rampart, *c.* 550 BC, was built just inside the present defences, which were erected around 400 BC. The site was occupied continuously until the Roman Conquest, as shown by the frequent replacement of post-holes for the huts and gates (east, west and south-west). The population of about 500–1000 lived in small square huts arranged in streets, and obtained their pottery from manufacturers in the Malvern Hills area.

Cromarty *Highland* 566Bg
A unique survival of the 18th century, this burgh contains good houses, a Classical court-house of the 1770's and a parish church of the 17th century. Two 18th-century buildings represent the past industry of the burgh: a brewery of red freestone and an attractive group of buildings comprising a rope-works. A simple lighthouse and attached dwellings were built near the harbour in 1846.
HUGH MILLER'S COTTAGE The birthplace of Hugh Miller (1802–56), geologist, stone-mason, accountant and author; now a museum devoted to him.

Cromford Bridge *Derbys.* 552Dd
A 15th-century bridge across the R. Derwent, with rounded arches on one side and pointed arches on the other. On the south side are ruins of a 'temple' which is inscribed as *Piscatoribus Sacrum* (sacred to fishermen). A stone tablet in the bridge commemorates a feat of 1697 when a man on horseback jumped unharmed into the river some 30 ft below.

Cromford Old Mill *Derbys.* 552Dd
Here, in 1771, Richard Arkwright first used water power to drive a cotton mill.

Crondall *Hants.* 541Jf
CHURCH OF ALL SAINTS A church with Norman origins, of which several portions remain. There was once a central tower, but this was pulled down in the mid-17th century, when the present tower was built. The chancel and clerestory are Early English. The church was restored in the second half of the 19th century. There are brasses, and other monuments.

Croome d'Abitot *Heref. & Worcs.* 546Ce
CHURCH OF ST MARY MAGDALENE An early Gothic Revival church, built for the Earl of

CROOME D'ABITOT CHURCH

Overlooking Croome Court is a small early Gothic Revival church, built for the Earl of Coventry c. 1761; its architect was Capability Brown. Inside are Gothic plaster ceilings, a pulpit with delicately carved canopy, and beautiful Classical font carved with foliage and winged cherub-heads. The monuments are outstanding; they are to the Coventry family and are mostly a century older than the present building. A fine reclining 17th-century lady holds her baby, and on the north side of the chancel is a large work of 1690 by Grinling Gibbons commemorating Lord Coventry. He lies gesticulating on a sarcophagus between two standing allegorical ladies. For many years he wore a coronet placed on his head during a restoration. It was too small for the noble head and looked absurd. The coronet is now back on the cushion where Gibbons intended it to be.

Coventry, *c.* 1761, near his country home, Croome Court. The church has a pinnacled west tower attached on the east side only; on the other three sides are large arches at ground level. Inside, the monuments are superb, but there is one significant omission. In 1700 William Stanton carved a monument to the 1st Earl, but because it displayed a false genealogy for his widow—a servant whom the Earl had married in his old age—the 2nd Earl refused to have it in the church. The deposed monument is now in the village church of Elmley Castle, about 4 miles south-west of Evesham.

Crosby Garrett *Cumbria* 558Ae
SETTLEMENT GROUP Here are three villages set roughly in line, the overall distance being about 1000 yds. The largest of the three is the south-west village; this has near-rectangular huts and paddocks, and a larger rectangular hut. The middle village, 700 yds from the first, is similar but smaller, and the third compares closely with the second. All three villages are set in a complex of small square fields of characteristic 'Celtic' type, with boundary banks and pathways.
The settlement probably began in the Iron Age, but occupation may have continued into the Roman period.

Crosby Ravensworth *Cumbria* 557*Je*
SETTLEMENT GROUP An excellent group of upland settlements within a fairly small area. They probably originated in Iron Age times, but it is known that Ewe Close continued to be occupied in the Romano-British period. Burwens has an enclosing stone wall and comprises almost an acre of ground with many circular and irregularly shaped huts. Cow Green lies some distance to the west, and consists of two groups of huts of rather different type. Ewe Close is still farther to the west and is larger than Cow Green, covering about 1¼ acres. There are two main groups of circular huts and a subsidiary to the south. Ewe Locks lies some 700 yds south of Ewe Close and again has two main hut-groups, one with an enclosing wall. Howarcles lies to the north-east of Burwens, and is grouped on both sides of a roadway. Its huts are both oval and sub-rectangular in plan.

Croscombe *Som.* 540*Ce*
CHURCH OF ST MARY A 15th- and 16th-century church, one of the most interesting in Somerset; it has a west tower and spire. There are some Tudor pews, a pulpit dated 1616 and many Jacobean fittings including a rood screen, pews and parclose screens.

Crosscanonby *Cumbria* 557*Gf*
CHURCH OF ST JOHN THE EVANGELIST Originally a Norman church, with later additions. There are some interesting Saxon and early Norman carvings, and woodwork of the early 18th century.

Crosthwaite *Cumbria* 557*Gf*
CHURCH OF ST KENTIGERN Mainly late Perpendicular of the early 16th century, with a west tower. There are several monuments and one brass, including one by J. G. Lough to Robert Southey.

Crowhurst *Surrey* 542*Bf*
CHURCH OF ST GEORGE This 11th-century church contains the tomb brasses of Sir John Gaynesford (1450) and his son (1460), showing the enormous development in the armour of the period.

Crowland *Lincs.* 553*Hb*
ABBEY Founded in 716 by King Ethelbald, in memory of St Guthlac, who had built a cell on the Fen island. The abbey was burnt by the Danes, rebuilt *c.* 930, burnt again in 1091, rebuilt in 1114, shaken by an earthquake in 1117, partly burnt in 1146, completed in 1190 and remodelled *c.* 1281. The relics of St Guthlac were taken there in 1195. His cell, at the west end of the south aisle, was excavated in 1908, but filled in again. The abbey is now the parish church; the west front is sculptured, and inside there is a 15th-century oak screen. Hereward the Wake is said to be buried here.
TRIANGULAR BRIDGE Probably unique in Europe, the bridge consists of three 14th-century stone arches meeting at an angle of 120 degrees. They originally spanned three streams of the R. Welland, but now stand over dry land. The carved figure on the bridge was put in position in 1720, and probably came from the abbey.

Croxden *Staffs.* 552*Cd*
ABBEY The abbey was founded in the 12th century, though most of the ruins are of a later date. The west front is impressive, with lancet windows.

Cubert *Cornwall* 538*Cc*
In this village, the manor house of Ellenglaze and Chenoweth Farm are mentioned in Domesday Book. To the west, at Trevornick Farm, is the restored 14th-century holy well of St Cubert.

Cuckfield *W. Sussex* 542*Be*
The village street winds up a gentle hillside, between houses of all the typical South-east England materials, brick, weather-boarding, tile-hanging and, a Sussex speciality, honey-coloured sandstone.
CHURCH OF THE HOLY TRINITY This is a church of the 13th and 14th centuries, the west tower having a broach spire. The roofs, however, are 15th century. G. F. Bodley and others restored the building in the second half of the 19th century and there is much stained glass of this time, including two good windows by C. E. Kempe. Of the many monuments one is attributed to Epiphanius Evesham (17th century) and there are later ones by Thomas Adye, John Flaxman, Sir Richard Westmacott and John Bacon Junior.

Cuddesdon *Oxon.* 546*Fc*
CHURCH OF ALL SAINTS A fine cruciform church with central tower. Much remains of the original Norman building, such as the Transitional tower arches and the font. The medieval west door has its original iron hinges and binding.

Culbone *Somerset* 539*Gg*
CHURCH OF ST CULBONE The smallest (35 ft x 12 ft) complete medieval church in regular use in England. The windows, one hewn from a single sandstone block, are Saxon, while the walls and porch date from the 12th and 13th centuries. Coleridge wrote his fragmentary poem 'Kubla Khan' in the farmhouse that stands above the church.

Cullercoats *Tyne & Wear* 558*Ch*
CHURCH OF ST GEORGE Dating from 1884, St George's is by John Loughborough Pearson, architect of Truro Cathedral in Cornwall. There is a tall tower and spire on the south side.

Cullerlie *Grampian* 566*Fe*
STONE CIRCLE Eight undressed boulders set equally spaced round the circumference of a circle 32 ft across. Excavation has shown that within the circle were seven cremation-burials, one at the centre, the remainder in the space around. The circle and burials date from the Bronze Age.

Culloden *Highland* 566*Bf*
On this bleak moor in April 1746 the Jacobite cause was finally lost—Bonnie Prince Charlie and his followers were routed by 'Butcher' Cumberland (the Duke of Cumberland). The Memorial Cairn, 20 ft high, was erected in 1881 by Duncan Forbes where the bloodiest fighting took place. The graves of the Clans and the Field of the English are marked by stones.

Cullompton *Devon* 540*Ad*
CHURCH OF ST ANDREW An impressive Perpendicular church. The west tower of 1545 has gargoyles and pinnacles. Light interior with clerestory and an unusual second aisle, fan-vaulted, built *c.* 1525 by wool merchant John Lane. There is no division between the nave and chancel and the fine wagon-roof runs the whole length of the church, while a painted rood screen stretches across its entire width. The rood beam and parclose screens remain, and there is a stained glass window of 1904 by Morris & Co.

Culross *Fife* 562*Af*
BISHOP LEIGHTON'S HOUSE The Causeways radiating from the market cross contain 17th-century houses with red pantiled roofs. In Mid Causeway is the house said to have been inhabited by Bishop Leighton of Dunblane. (Not open to public.)
PALACE Built (1597–1611) by Sir George Bruce, whose salt-panning and coal-mining businesses brought prosperity to Culross and largely created the lower town below the abbey. Grouped round a

CULZEAN CASTLE

A great sham Gothic castle overlooking the Firth of Clyde. Robert Adam began the present huge mansion for the 10th Earl of Cassillis in the 1770's and the work continued until 1792. Adam incorporated the original building—a stronghold of the Kennedy family for centuries—into the south side of his mansion. Next he built the north wing with its massive round tower on the seaward side, which houses the saloon. This left a rectangular house with a central courtyard, and into this Adam built one of his masterly staircases.

ENGLISH SIDEBOARD

Although the sideboard as a single item of furniture existed before the late 18th century, it is at that time that an interesting development occurs. Earlier, rectangular side-tables ornamented with Greek and Roman motifs stood between pedestal cupboards used as storage units and plate warmers, and these were surmounted by urn-shaped water containers. This piece of early 19th-century furniture brings together all three components introduced into Britain by Robert Adam. (Culzean Castle)

courtyard with traditional crow-stepped gables and pantiled roofs, it is one of the finest domestic buildings in Scotland. The interiors contain outstanding 17th-century tempera painting. An attractive terraced garden lies to the north.
STUDY, THE Built *c.* 1600, this fine L-shaped house with projecting stair-tower wing is at the end of the descent from the abbey down the Tanhouse Brae, itself lined with examples of some of the best vernacular burgh architecture in Scotland. One room illustrates three centuries of domestic life in Culross.
TOWN HOUSE The Sandhaven, the old meeting place of the burgh of Culross, is dominated by the town house, originally built in 1626. In 1783 a new front with double forestairs and clock tower with bell-shaped roof was added. A ceiling of 1626, painted in tempera, is to be found in the town council meeting room.

Culzean Castle *Strathclyde* 561Gc
In this Gothic-style mansion there is a memorial room to General Dwight D. Eisenhower, Supreme Commander of the Allied invasion of Europe in 1944 (later President of the U.S.A.). The house, set in magnificent gardens, was designed by Robert Adam and built between 1777 and 1792; it contains an unusual oval staircase, round drawing-room and much fine plasterwork.

Cuween *Mainland, Orkney* 569Hf
CHAMBERED CAIRN This Neolithic cairn had been damaged in the past, but is now repaired for inspection. Its mound is 55 ft in diameter and stands $8\frac{1}{2}$ ft high. An 18 ft long passage leads to the central chamber, a rectangle about 10 ft long by 5 ft wide. The present roof, at $7\frac{1}{2}$ ft above the floor, is a repair, and lies a little lower than the original. Other small cells open off the main chamber.

D

Daglingworth *Glos.* 546Cc
CHURCH OF THE HOLY ROOD The church displays many interesting features of the Saxon church from which it grew. The west tower was added in the 15th century and the chancel was rebuilt in the 19th century. During the 19th century some of the original Saxon carvings were found in the chancel arch; three of these are now set on the walls of the nave: a Crucifixion, Christ in Majesty and St Peter.

Dale Abbey *Derbys.* 552Ed
CHURCH OF ALL SAINTS A small (26 ft x 25 ft) 12th-century church with a farmhouse under the same roof. In the 15th century it became the infirmary chapel of Dale Abbey, now a ruin. The church has several items of 17th-century furniture, including a pulpit with a reading pew and a 'cupboard' altar—a table with a cupboard under it for storing sacred vessels.

Dalmeny *Lothian* 562Bf
CHURCH A good example of the Romanesque style in Scotland, dating from the second half of

the 12th century. There is an apse, and the chancel, apse arches and south doorway are impressively carved.

Dalton Holme *Humberside* 558Fb
CHURCH OF ST MARY The church is a large mid-19th-century Gothic Revival building, with a lofty central tower and spire; the architect was John Loughborough Pearson. Inside is a late 17th-century monument with an effigy supported on a slab by four Virtues.

Dalton-in-Furness *Cumbria* 557Gc
A 14th-century tower remains in the main street of the village.

Danby Rigg *N. Yorks.* 558Ee
ARCHAEOLOGICAL REMAINS These varied remains are grouped on a steep-sided spur of a hill. Scattered over the northern end are several hundred small stony mounds. They are probably clearance heaps associated with the cultivation of the area in prehistoric times, but some of the larger ones may also have been used as burial mounds in

the Bronze Age. South of the mounds a stony bank crosses the spur, and some 700 yds beyond it there are three more banks with two ditches. Within the area enclosed by the banks are two earth and stone circles, one of which has a standing stone at its edge. They are Bronze Age cremation cemeteries.

To the east of the main site there is a complex of embanked fields, which appear to have belonged to the prehistoric inhabitants.

Danny *W. Sussex* 542Bd
A late Elizabethan E-shaped house in red brick, home of the Campion family for centuries. It was built *c.* 1595 by George Goring. In 1728 the south front was refaced in Queen Anne style and part of the interior, including the great hall, was altered. It contains Campion portraits.

Darlington *Durham* 558Ce
CHURCH OF ST CUTHBERT An important cruciform town church of the 13th century, with central tower and spire. There is a stone screen across the tower arch in the nave. Inside are stalls, misericords, font cover and 19th-century stained glass by Clayton & Bell and others.

Darrington *W. Yorks.* 558Da
CHURCH OF ST LUKE AND ALL SAINTS A Norman church, with additions of the 13th and 14th centuries. There is an unusual arcaded gallery between the vaulted north chapel and aisle. Furnishings include carved bench ends and stalls with misericords, and there are 14th-century effigies of a cross-legged knight and a lady.

Dartford *Kent* 542Cg
BOROUGH MUSEUM Devoted to the history and natural history of Dartford and district, including the Darent Valley. Archaeological finds include prehistoric stone implements, and items, including jewellery, from the Roman and Saxon periods. Medieval relics are also on view. The natural history collection includes fossils, as well as plants and animals.

Dartmouth *Devon* 539Hb
The great international fleet of English, French, German and Flemish ships bound for the Second Crusade assembled at Dartmouth in 1147. In 1341, Edward III granted the first charter. To guard against Breton raids, two castles (which still guard the mouth of the R. Dart) were built between 1488 and 1502, and nine ships from Dartmouth joined Drake against the Spanish Armada. Thomas Newcomen (1663–1729) of Dartmouth produced the first practical industrial steam-engine: one of the originals is preserved in Royal Avenue Gardens. In 1905 the Royal Naval College was opened, to train officers for the Royal Navy.
BUTTERWALK A row of four shops, above which timbered houses, supported by 11 granite columns, project over the pavements. They were built in 1635–40, damaged by a bomb in 1943, and restored in 1954.
TOWN MUSEUM The museum is housed in a merchant's house, one of several 17th-century colonnaded houses on the Butterwalk which were visited by Charles II in 1671. The nautical collection includes fine ship models, relics of famous sailors, old maps and marine pictures. One of Newcomen's atmospheric steam-engines may also be seen in Royal Avenue Gardens.

Deal Castle *Kent* 543Gf
Built *c.* 1540 by Henry VIII as part of a military defence system against possible invasion by the French. In all, 20 forts were probably built by Henry VIII, all of them unlike most medieval castles: in plan they resemble the rose badge of the Tudors. Deal Castle consists of a circular court or keep from which six semicircular bastions radiate, all equipped with guns, with an outer curtain wall of six more semicircular bastions. Altogether there were 145 openings for guns, with an all-round view.

Dean *Beds.* 547Hf
CHURCH OF ALL SAINTS The church, with a spire, has portions of the 13th-century building, but was

DEAL CASTLE

With the close of the Middle Ages fortified castle building came to an end, but the castle at Deal is one of many forts built along the south coast by Henry VIII in about 1540. The king's break with the Church of Rome prompted the Pope to advocate a crusade against England, and Henry VIII built about 20 artillery forts as a precaution against a French invasion. Several of these castles were along the Thames, at Tilbury and Gravesend, for instance, while in Kent there were castles at Deal, Walmer and Sandown and Sandgate. That at Sandown is in ruins and Walmer Castle is the official residence of the Lord Warden of the Cinque Ports. Deal Castle is the most spectacular example of Henry's low, squat forts—with thick walls, rounded parapets, tiers of embrasures for guns and sparse living quarters for the garrison.

largely rebuilt in the 15th century. The roofs are fine specimens of this period, and there are good screens at the west end of both chapels and also across the chancel arch. The font is 14th century, and there is a pre-Reformation pulpit.

Deane *Greater Manchester* 552Ag
CHURCH OF ST MARY A spacious Perpendicular church with a Decorated west tower. Like many other churches of the same period, St Mary's has no chancel arch division; the continuous roof of nave and chancel is panelled, and is a 19th-century copy of the original built in 1510.

Debden *Essex* 548Ae
CHURCH OF ST MARY THE VIRGIN AND ALL SAINTS Originally 13th century, but it was partly rebuilt in 1793 by R. Chiswell from the designs of John Carter. There are 18th- and 19th-century monuments and a Coade stone font of 1789.

Dedham *Essex* 548De
A lovely town in the Stour Valley, one of Constable's favourite subjects. On its two principal streets are some interesting houses: the Sun Hotel, a half-timbered early 16th-century building with stable yard; the Marlborough Head Inn of *c.* 1500; the old grammar school, dated 1732; and Shermans, also Georgian. South of the village is Southfields, timbered and gabled, once the offices, warehouse and living quarters of a prosperous weaver; it was built around a courtyard *c.* 1500.
CASTLE HOUSE The former home of Sir Alfred Munnings, containing many of the paintings and unfinished works of this 20th-century artist who specialised in painting horses.

Deene *Northants.* 547Hg
CHURCH OF ST PETER The west tower dates from the 13th century, but most of the remainder is a restoration of *c.* 1868 by Sir M. Digby Wyatt, with some later decoration by G. F. Bodley. The contents include monuments to the Brudenell family, a bust of Anne, Duchess of Richmond (*d.* 1722) by G. B. Guelfi and, in medieval tradition, a monument by Sir J. E. Boehm to the 7th Earl of Cardigan (*d.* 1868).

Deene Park *Northants.* 547Hg
The turreted and towered Tudor home of the Brudenell family since 1514, preserved in its original state. The 7th Earl of Cardigan (James Thomas Brudenell (1797–1868), who led the Charge of the Light Brigade at Balaclava, 1854, lived here. The park, with fine gardens and a lake, is noted for rare trees and shrubs.

Deeping St James *Lincs.* 553Hb
CHURCH OF ST JAMES Once the church of a priory founded in 1139, this is a large church which offers a representation of all the architectural styles from Norman to 18th century. The transepts of the original cruciform building have since gone; there is an impressive Norman arcade in the nave, and the late Norman font is adorned with a design of intersecting arches. The west tower and spire are work of the 18th century. There are monumental effigies of the 14th century.

Deerhurst *Glos.* 546Cd
CHURCH OF ST MARY This is an extremely interesting Saxon church, probably of 7th-century origins, with an apsidal east end; it once belonged to the former priory. It retains much of the original tower, though the top is medieval. Inside the nave are the famous triangular-headed windows opening from the tower's east wall. The magnificent Saxon font with its carved decoration is in a remarkable state of preservation.

Near by is Odda's chapel, again Saxon and dated 1056. This, until the 19th century, was part of the farmhouse which has been built on to it.

Delapre Abbey *Northants.* 547Gf
A former Cluniac nunnery which now houses the Northamptonshire Records Office.

Delgatie Castle *Grampian* 566Fg
The 13th-century home of the Clan Hay, the castle was altered in the 16th century and contains fine painted ceilings dating from 1570, and collections of paintings and armour. (By appointment.)

Denbigh *Clwyd* 551Ge
One of the few Welsh towns set on a hill, and the site of a native settlement before the castle and town walls were commenced in 1282, after the English conquest. The castle gate-house is a more complete example of the three-towered arrangement designed for the King's Gate at Caernarfon Castle. On Castle Green are the remains of an incomplete 16th-century church intended to replace the ancient and tiny cathedral of St Asaph,

ST CATHERINE WINDOW

This panel showing St Catherine holding her wheel is in the west window of the south aisle in the priory church. St Catherine is depicted in the characteristic 'S' pose of the 14th century. The architectural canopy above her is typical of such panels of the period; these were often set half-way up the windows, and surrounded by small diamond panes, some plain and some painted with foliage and flowers. (Church of St Mary, Deerhurst)

6 miles away. The many other buildings of historic interest in Denbigh include the 16th-century County Hall and the Golden Lion Inn, which has a timber-framed archway of the 15th century.

Dennington *Suffolk*   548Ef
CHURCH OF ST MARY A Perpendicular church, with an earlier chancel, and a west tower. The furnishings include lavish 15th-century parclose screens, 17th-century pulpit and box-pews. The 15th-century bench ends have interesting carving. There is medieval stained glass, and 15th- and 17th-century monuments.

DERBY PORCELAIN ICEPAIL WITH LINER AND COVER

This Derby porcelain icepail was painted with overglaze enamels by William Pegg in 1800. The neo-classical shape and clear colours are typical of Derby porcelain of the period. (Derby Museums)

Derby *Derbys.*   552Dc
A trading centre in medieval times, with a charter (1154) from Henry II and another (1554) from Mary Tudor, Derby was crippled by outbreaks of the plague in 1349, 1592, 1637 and 1645. In 1693 there were only 694 houses in the borough. A change took place in two stages of the Industrial Revolution: first from 1715 to 1850 the silk and hosiery trade flourished and the manufacture of Derby porcelain and chinaware became a major industry; secondly, with the coming of the railway, the town became an engineering centre.

The Old Silk Mill gates, by Robert Bakewell, are a masterpiece of wrought-iron work (1728); County Hall in St Mary's Gate was built in 1660.
CATHEDRAL The early 16th-century western tower was part of a medieval church on the site, the rest of which was demolished in the early 18th century, and replaced by a building designed by James Gibbs. Gibbs had studied in Rome, first for the priesthood, and then as a pupil of the late-baroque architect, Carlo Fontana. His church is dwarfed by the massive earlier tower, but like St Martin-in-the-Fields, London, which he also designed, it shows Fontana's influence. The building was completed by 1725; the builder was Francis Smith of Warwick, a member of a family which has great importance in Midland architecture.

Wrought-iron work is by a local smith, Robert Bakewell; pulpit and choir stalls of the late 19th century by Temple Moore; the altar by Sir Ninian Comper. Monuments include that to Bess of Hardwick (Elizabeth, Countess of Shrewsbury, *d.* 1607), and others by Roubiliac, Rysbrack, Nollekens, Chantrey and Westmacott. The church was raised to the status of a cathedral in 1927.

MUSEUMS AND ART GALLERY A room in the museum commemorates the visit to Derby of Bonnie Prince Charlie during the 1745 rebellion. Other collections cover the archaeology, natural history and history of Derby city and county. In the industrial section is a working model of the Midland Railway, and a collection of Derby porcelain. There are also paintings and drawings by Joseph Wright of Derby (1734–97).
OLD SILK MILL INDUSTRIAL MUSEUM A new museum giving an introduction to Derbyshire industries. There is a historic collection of Rolls-Royce aero engines.

Devil's Bridge *Dyfed*   545Gg
Three bridges span the R. Mynach here, where it enters a deep gorge in a series of waterfalls; they are built on top of each other, and the oldest, the bottom bridge, was built in the 11th century by monks from Strata Florida Abbey.

Devil's Dyke *Cambs.*   548Bf
This remarkable bank and ditch runs straight across country for a distance of some $7\frac{1}{2}$ miles. It faces south-west and straddles the main road, the A11, which here overlies the Icknield Way, a prehistoric trackway which has served East Anglia for more than 2000 years. The Dyke's north-west end rests on the Fen-edge and its south east end would originally have reached the virgin forest which at that time lay around the R. Stour basin. Some 6 miles to the south-west, the smaller Fleam Dyke served a similar purpose; it is almost certain that these defences were erected early in the 7th century when East Anglia began to be threatened by its neighbour, the midland kingdom of Mercia.

Devizes *Wilts.*   540Ef
A small market town, with timbered buildings dating from the early 16th century, and some fine 18th-century houses. There are two 12th-century churches, both enlarged in the 15th century. The castle, built in the 19th century, is on the site of a former Norman strongpoint.

Above the town is Roundway Down, where in 1643 Roundhead and Royalist troops met in battle. Near the battle site is an Iron Age camp.
MUSEUM (WILTSHIRE ARCHAEOLOGICAL AND NATURAL HISTORY SOCIETY) Collections of Neolithic, Bronze, Iron Age and Roman finds from Wiltshire. The most important is the Stourhead Collection of Bronze Age urns, beakers and grave

ROMAN COCKEREL

A small bronze ornament found on the site of a Roman temple at Nettleton in Wiltshire, not far from Foss Way. The comb and feathers of the bird are represented by boldly marked ornamental hatching, and on its back is a candle holder. (Devizes Museum)

BUSH BARROW CONTENTS

The Bush Barrow, one of the Normanton Down group close to Stonehenge, was excavated in 1808. The grave, that of a 'tall and stout' man, as the skeleton was described, was so richly furnished and the barrow itself was so prominent, that it has been regarded as belonging to one of the greatest chiefs of the Wessex Culture. Some of the finds—the large lozenge-shaped gold plate which lay over the breast, the two daggers, *and a ceremonial mace, as well as a gold hook of a belt, which were close to the right arm, and the flanged bronze axe found near the right shoulder—are shown here. When first found, the smaller of the daggers had a wooden pommel patterned with thousands of minute gold pins. This fell to pieces, as did what may have been a wooden shield or helmet with bronze fittings. (Devizes Museum)*

goods and ornaments excavated from barrows on Salisbury Plain in the early 19th century.

Dilwyn *Heref. & Worcs.* 546Af
CHURCH OF ST MARY A large, light church—only the chancel has stained glass—whose Norman west tower (*c.* 1200) is surmounted by a small 18th-century spire. The present church dates from the 13th century, with a clerestory and tall rood screen. There is some 14th-century stained glass and tiles, and the tomb of a knight made 1300–10.

Dinedor Hill *Heref. & Worcs.* 546Ae
An Iron Age hill-fort, reputedly occupied by the Roman general Ostorius Scapula, in his operation against the British chief Caractacus.

Din Lligwy *Gwynedd* 550Ef
This is one of the best preserved and finest examples of its type, a 'native' British village which was occupied throughout Roman times and for some time after. A strongly built wall encloses the settlement-area; within it stand a number of stone-built houses, rectangular or circular in plan. These were not squalid huts but commodious dwellings, built at various periods. The quality of the buildings suggests that Din Lligwy must have been an important settlement, the seat of a person of rank in the native hierarchy. To the south of the village is a Stone Age grave of *c.* 2500 BC, in which about 30 men, women and children were buried, probably over a long period. A capstone weighing 25 tons covers the grave.

Dinmore Manor *Heref. & Worcs.* 546Ae
A manor house dating from the 14th century. Only the garden, chapel and music room are open to the public. The medieval chapel was once part of a Commandery (headquarters) of the Knights Hospitaller of St John of Jerusalem.

Dirleton Castle *Lothian* 562Df
Edward I besieged and took this castle, but in 1311 it was retaken by the Scots. It fell to Cromwell's troops in 1650 and was not rebuilt. Three 13th-century drum towers and part of the walls remain; there is also a 16th-century dove-cote.

Disley *Cheshire* 552Cf
CHURCH OF ST MARY THE VIRGIN A 15th-century hill-top church partially rebuilt in 1824–35. The nave has a timbered roof of exceptional beauty, with bosses and angels. There is German stained glass in the east window, mainly of the 16th century, and a monument to Thomas Legh, of nearby Lyme Park, by the 19th-century Cheshire-born sculptor Alfred Gatley.

Ditchley Park *Oxon.* 546Ed
The family of General Robert E. Lee, who fought for the South in the American Civil War, owned this 18th-century mansion for three and a half centuries, and it is now an Anglo-American conference centre. The house was designed by James Gibbs, who entrusted the building work to Francis Smith of Warwick. It is the supreme example of the work of Gibbs, and has magnificent interiors by William Kent and Henry Flitcroft. During the Second World War it was a week-end headquarters of Sir Winston Churchill.

Ditherington *Shropshire* 552Ac
In 1796 a flax mill was erected here. The oldest known surviving iron-framed building, it is now used as a maltings, and is an early ancestor of the modern skyscraper.

Doddington Hall *Lincs.* 553Ge
A gabled gate-house guards the entrance to this Elizabethan manor house crowned with belvederes and cupolas. It was built in 1593–1600 and

contains Stuart and Georgian furniture, tapestries and a collection of china.

Doddington Moor *Northld.* 562Fd
DOD LAW The western enclosure of these hill-forts is roughly D-shaped, with a double earth and stone bank, and an internal area of about half an acre. On one side is a small annex enclosed within a single bank. In the main enclosure are the remains of stone huts ranging up to 18 ft in diameter. The eastern enclosure is larger, more nearly square and is enclosed within a bank and ditch. The enclosures are late prehistoric, probably of Iron Age date. In the area are many rocks with characteristic Bronze Age cup-and-ring markings.

Dodington Hall *Som.* 540Be
Tudor mansion containing a great hall with minstrels' gallery. (By appointment.)

Dodington House *Avon* 540Dg
The Regency-style house was built in 1796–1813 on the site of a 16th-century house; it was designed by James Wyatt for Christopher Codrington. The house is almost square, and on the west side is a portico with huge Corinthian columns, so spaced that a carriage could drive through them to the main entrance. The grounds containing fine gardens and many great trees were laid out by Capability Brown in 1764. Two lakes were created: one is higher than the other, and flows into the lower lake via a Gothic cascade.

DODINGTON HOUSE

The Codrington family has lived at Dodington since 1578; an ancestor, John Codrington, was Standard-bearer to Henry V at Agincourt and Harfleur in 1415. In 1796 Christopher Codrington employed James Wyatt to build him a great house in Regency style, and it was completed in 1813. In that year Codrington was indirectly responsible for Wyatt's death: on September 14, he and Codrington were travelling back to London when their coach overturned near Marlborough and Wyatt was killed. The house is almost square. Inside, the spacious entrance hall has scagliola columns, and a marble floor, patterned in black, red and white; the ceiling has sunken panels and is terracotta in colour, enriched with gold. The stair hall rises the full height of the building and is lit by four semicircular windows beneath a dome. The stair-case is magnificent; it divides into two flights, to left and right, from the first landing. Mid-18th-century wrought-iron work brought from Fonthill (Wiltshire) which Wyatt was rebuilding was incorporated in the stair railings.

Dollar *Central* 562Ag
DOLLAR ACADEMY William Playfair of Edinburgh produced a building of great dignity when in 1818–20 he built this school, endowed by John McNabb, for poor children of the parish of Dollar. The principal façade, dominated by a fine six-columned portico with Tuscan columns, faces west over a magnificent park under the Ochil Hills. The nearby Academy Place contains simple ashlar houses designed by Playfair for the staff.

Dolwyddelan Castle *Gwynedd* 550Fd
This was a popular subject for early 19th-century painters. There is a tradition that it was the birth-place of Llywelyn the Great, and the earliest part of the keep may date from the 12th century. It was held for a short time by the English and then abandoned, until occupied by Maredudd ab Ieuan in the late 15th century. Finally it was restored in the mid-19th century.

Doncaster *S. Yorks.* 552Ef
MANSION HOUSE This is one of only three mansion houses in England originally provided as mayoral residences (the others being in London and York). It was built in 1745–8 by James Paine, and has a splendid ballroom with ornamental ceiling. (Interior by appointment only.)

Dorchester *Dorset* 540Dc
The history of Dorset's county town goes back to the Stone, Bronze and Iron Ages. It was the Roman stronghold of Durnovaria in AD 70–400. To the west was Poundbury Camp, and to the south Maumbury Rings, a Stone Age stone circle. The Romans adapted this site as an amphitheatre, which even in the Middle Ages was used for bull-, bear- and badger-baiting. Dorchester was a Saxon centre in AD 660, and a Saxon mint town under Athelstan (925–39); it was taken by the Normans, and used by King John as a hunting centre. The plague struck Dorchester, and a great fire in 1613 destroyed 300 houses. Puritan emigrants led by John White left the town in the early 17th century to establish a church at Dorchester, Massachusetts. In 1685, the notorious Judge George Jeffreys was sent to hold an Assize to punish the Duke of Monmouth rebels after the Battle of Sedgemoor: 300 were tried at the 'Bloody Assize' and 292 sentenced to death; 80 were executed—the rest were whipped or transported. Thomas Hardy was born near by at Bockhampton in 1840 and the area provides a setting for many of his Wessex novels.
DORSET COUNTY MUSEUM All the collections concern Dorset, and the county's geology, natural history, archaeology and local history are covered. A collection of finds from the Iron Age fort at Maiden Castle is included. The Thomas Hardy Memorial Collection includes manuscripts of his novels and poems, letters, drawings, notebooks and other personal items; much of it is housed in a reconstruction of his study at his house in Max Gate (Dorchester). The museum also contains relics of the Dorset poet William Barnes, and pictures of Dorset by Dorset artists.
DORSET MILITARY MUSEUM The history of the Dorset Regiment, the Dorset Militia, the Volunteers and Queen's Own Dorset Yeomanry from 1660 is illustrated by pictures, uniforms, medals, weapons and battlefield relics. A desk from Hitler's Berlin Chancellory and relics of Clive of India are on view.
OLD SHIRE HALL Here six men, the Tolpuddle Martyrs, were sentenced to seven years transportation for forming in their village of Tolpuddle,

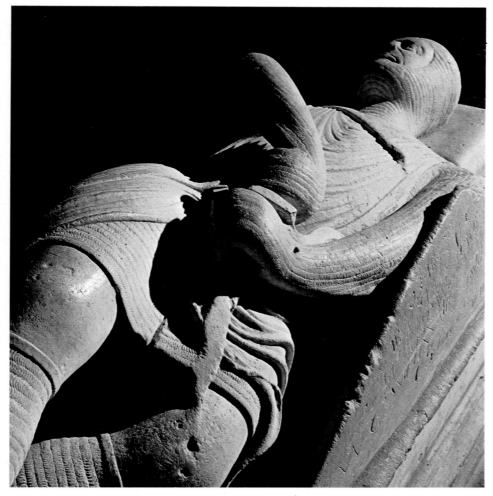

EFFIGY OF A KNIGHT

The dynamism of this powerful figure is unique in English sculpture of its time. Cross-legged effigies are common, but here the whole body of the knight is con- *torted by violent action. The figure was probably carved about 1300, and the sculptor may have come from the Abingdon workshops near by. (Dorchester Abbey)*

7 miles north-east of Dorchester, 'The Friendly Society of Agricultural Labourers'; this 'crime', which took place in 1834, is considered to be the start of the Trade Union movement in England. The farmworkers asked for a wage rise from 9s. to 10s. per week, and promptly had their wages reduced to 8s., and, on their complaining, to 7s., to teach them a lesson. The martyrs were given a free pardon two years later.

Dorchester *Oxon.*   *546Fc*
ABBEY CHURCH OF SS PETER AND PAUL The church of Dorchester has an unimpressive exterior, and inside is a strange mixture of Norman and Gothic architecture. The church dates back to the 7th century and became an abbey from about 1072. The most interesting features of the abbey church are found in the choir, three windows dating from the early 14th century. The window in the north aisle represents the Tree of Jesse; the stone tracery consists of carved figures of the descendants of the Patriarch; stone and glass are combined in an unorthodox style. The east window is stabilised by a buttress down the centre. The south window has a funeral procession carved on its lower part. Beneath this window is a stone sedilia with rear wall pierced by windows containing 13th-century glass.

Dorfold Hall *Cheshire*   *552Ad*
A Jacobean country house, *c.* 1616, with period plaster ceilings and panelling.

Dorney *Bucks.*   *547Hb*
CHURCH OF ST JAMES A church grouped pleasantly with its house, Dorney Court. Originally Norman, the church has an added Tudor west tower and a porch of 1661, both brick. Inside, the woodwork includes a 16th-century family pew and a west gallery and pulpit of the mid-1600's. Traces of medieval painting show two Annunciation figures. In a chapel is an alabaster monument to Sir William Garrard (*d.* 1607) and his wife, kneeling, with their 15 children, some holding skulls. There is a 12th-century carved font.

Dorset Cursus *Dorset*   *540Ed*
This enormous cursus (Neolithic ceremonial monument), the longest in the country, stretches for some 6 miles across country roughly parallel to and rather more than half a mile south of the Salisbury–Blandford road. Outlined by a bank and ditch, its south-west end is marked on Thickthorn Down by two long barrows, as is the north-east end close to the Bokerley Dyke. Two other long barrows were included in its course. Near the centre it is crossed by the bank of a Roman road.

Thomas Hardy.

THOMAS HARDY, THE WESSEX GENIUS

Hardy was only a few months old when his mother found him sleeping in the garden with a snake coiled asleep on his chest. This early affinity with nature was fostered by the isolated situation of his birthplace, which now belongs to the National Trust. Hardy trained as an architect in Dorchester, and one of his notebooks is on display at the County Museum. Also on show are many of Hardy's manuscripts and his reconstructed study. At 22 he travelled to London and in 1863 won the essay prize offered by the Royal Institute of Architects. Writing poetry in his spare time, he now began to write prose. His first novel *Desperate Remedies* cost him £75 to have published, but £60 was returned to him on the sales. Two years later he found success with his fourth novel *Far From The Madding Crowd*. In 1910 Hardy received the Order of Merit and the Freedom of Dorchester. The most astonishing period of his life began at 70 when he launched into a career of lyric poetry, until his death at 87. His poetry was surprisingly original in theme and matter, and *The Dynasts* is the fullest expression of his genius. The portrait of Hardy is by R. G. Eves.

HARDY'S TWO WIVES *On the left Emma Lavinia Gifford, to whom he was married for 38 years, and Florence Dugdale whom he married in 1914, when he was 73 and she 35. Hardy was attracted by the concept of the well-beloved migrating from woman to woman. Both portraits at the Dorset County Museum, Dorchester.*

HARDY'S BIRTHPLACE *in the hamlet of Bockhampton, near Dorchester. The boy inherited his love of the countryside from his father, a builder, who liked to lie on a bank in warm weather 'with grasshoppers leaping over him'.*

THE AUTHOR'S PENS *which have on their handles the names of the works he wrote with them. These items can be seen at the Dorset County Museum where Hardy's study has been reconstructed as it was in his home.*

THE WESSEX COUNTRYSIDE

As described by Hardy in his prose and poetry, it is not limited entirely to the county of Dorset but covers the Wessex kingdom of Saxon times, including Berkshire, Wiltshire, Somerset, Hampshire, Dorset and Devon. The author is unique in the way he harnesses nature's atmosphere to heighten the drama of his fiction. For instance, the love of Tess of the d'Urbervilles grew and matured in the lush valley of the Frome, whereas her betrayal took place among the sombre yews of Cranborne Chase. But it is the areas around Dorchester (which has grown to be synonymous with Casterbridge) that Hardy utilises most frequently for his atmospheric settings and some are here illustrated: EGDON HEATH, or 'haggard Egdon' as Hardy called the wild country stretching eastward from the doorstep of his birthplace. This untameable heathland, with its ancient barrows, rush-filled pools and gaping pits, forms a potent background to violent happenings in 'Tess of the d'Urbervilles', 'The Dynasts' and 'The Fiddler of the Reels'. GREY'S BRIDGE, which crosses the Frome outside Dorchester, is where the distracted Mayor of Casterbridge saw his own effigy floating down the river and DURDLE DOOR, near to Lulworth Cove, is where Sergeant Troy commits fake suicide in 'Far From The Madding Crowd'.

MEMORIAL WINDOW to Hardy in the church at Stinsford. Hardy was not a religious man and said 'I have been looking for God 50 years and I think if he had existed I should have discovered him.'

HARDY'S DESK, spectacles and blotting paper in Dorset County Museum. He wrote all his work in longhand.

HEART TOMB OF HARDY, whose dying wish was to be buried in his parish churchyard. His fame as an author and poet however, earned him a place in the Poets' Corner of Westminster Abbey. After his death his family compromised by burying his heart at Stinsford and the ashes of the rest of his body at Westminster.

Dorstone *Heref. & Worcs.* 545Je
ARTHUR'S STONE There are indications that this Neolithic long barrow may have suffered some disturbance to its original form. The entrance at the south end opens to a passage leading into a large oval chamber; this is walled by nine upright slabs which support an enormous capstone. Other scattered stones may at one time have formed a part of the barrow.

Doune Castle *Central* 561Jg
Before his murder at Donibristle in 1592, this was the home of the 'Bonnie Earl of Moray' of the ballad. Here Bonnie Prince Charlie (Prince Charles Edward) kept important prisoners after the Battle of Falkirk in 1745. Restored in 1883, the castle was built by the Duke of Albany, Regent of Scotland for James I, in the late 14th century. It stands on a hill between the R. Teith and Ardoch Burn, and is surrounded by a moat.
MOTOR MUSEUM The museum houses Lord Moray's collection of veteran, vintage and post-vintage cars, including a 1905 Rolls-Royce.

Dover *Kent* 543Ge
Episodes of invasion and defence make Dover's history. On a clear day the coast of France, 21 miles away, can be seen from its White Cliffs. In 55 BC Julius Caesar landed near Dover with 6000 men of the 7th and 10th Legions, carried by 80 oar- and sail-driven boats. In the 650 years following the Roman occupation, invading Angles, Jutes and Saxons landed at or near Dover, and at the time of the Norman invasion, William the Conqueror's half-brother, Bishop Odo of Bayeux, landed with the prefabricated parts for a castle stronghold, to be erected on the heights above Dover. In 1588 two galleons of the Spanish Armada, the *San Bernard* and the *Pereira*, were wrecked on the nearby Goodwin Sands.

Dover Castle inevitably became the most important building in the town. In the Civil War, Cromwell's supporters seized it, and it was considerably fortified against invasion during the Napoleonic Wars. On the Western Heights are cavernous brick shelters built to house a large part of the British army, in case Napoleon invaded England. In the First World War the town was the centre for the Dover Patrol, whose job was to safeguard the Straits, and in the Second World War Dover endured much bomb damage and shelling by long-range guns sited in France.

There are many memorials in Dover to heroism and achievement. The dead of both World Wars are commemorated by the Dover War Memorial, and at St Margaret's Bay, 5 miles along the cliffs to the east, is a granite obelisk commemorating the Dover Patrol.
CASTLE The main fortifications of Dover Castle belong to the late 12th and 13th centuries. The keep was built in the 1180's in the middle of an inner bailey, and the fortifications of the surrounding outer bailey were begun soon after, although these were not completed until the reigns of John and Henry III. The castle is of particular interest because it is one of the earliest in England in which the fortifications were arranged concentrically. Much of the architectural effect of its circuits of enclosing walls was destroyed during the Napoleonic period when the tops of many towers were cut off and the remaining stumps strengthened to provide gun emplacements.
CHURCH OF ST MARY-IN-CASTRO The church of St Mary was built in the late 10th and early 11th centuries, and the Roman lighthouse became a free-standing bell-tower to this church, which incorporated a considerable amount of Roman material. St Mary's was much restored in the 19th century from a state of ruin, and the interior at least must rank as a 19th-century building.
DOVER MUSEUM Part of the museum is housed in Maison Dieu, built as a hall for pilgrims in 1203. Its magnificent stained-glass windows depict events in Dover's long history, and there are displays of portraits and armour. Other items on show include archaeological finds from prehistoric and Roman times.
ROMAN LIGHTHOUSE The Roman *pharos* near the castle keep is the earliest lighthouse in Britain, and probably dates from the 1st century AD. The top floor of this octagonal structure has been removed; it must have been carried on a stone vault, as the original light would have been in the form of an open brazier. In medieval times it was used as a church tower. It is comparable to the larger square Roman tower at La Coruña in north-west Spain, which is almost certainly the oldest lighthouse in the world still working.
ROMAN PAINTED HOUSE More than 400 square feet of brilliantly coloured wall-paintings adorn the inside of the house, which in the 2nd century AD may have been the home of a Roman port official or naval commander. The paintings consist mainly of large rectangular panels, each of which contains a motif such as a tree.

Dowdeswell *Glos.* 546Cd
CHURCH OF ST MICHAEL A cruciform church, with central tower and broach spire, St Michael's was considerably rebuilt during the 16th and 17th centuries. Inside there are several later monuments, including one of *c.* 1731 by Christopher Horsnaile the Elder.

Down Ampney *Glos.* 546Dc
CHURCH OF ALL SAINTS A cruciform church with an Early English tower and spire, it was restored in 1897. The interior, however, retains the 13th-century arcades and a number of medieval effigies of knights and ladies, and the south chapel has a Gothic screen. In the north chapel is a tomb to Sir Anthony Hungerford.

Downe *Greater London* 548Aa
DOWN HOUSE The home for 40 years of Charles Darwin (1809–82), the Victorian naturalist, where he wrote *The Origin of Species*. The house, built mainly in the 18th century, contains relics of Darwin.

Downholme *N. Yorks.* 558Bd
CHURCH OF ST MICHAEL The Norman south door and arcades remain but St Michael's has Early English and later additions. The Norman font was converted to the Perpendicular style in the 19th century.

Doyden Castle *Cornwall* 538Dd
Perched on Doyden Point, the castle is a cliff-edge folly, built *c.* 1830.

Drem *Lothian* 562Df
CHESTERS, THE The interesting feature of this fort lies in its position. Instead of being sited on a hill from which it could command the surrounding country, it is low-lying and is immediately overlooked by a steep scarp from which it could easily have been assaulted with missiles of any description. Its internal area is well defended by multiple ramparts and ditches, which appear to represent more than one period of construction. There are indications of circular stone-hut foundations inside the enclosure. Some of these appear to be later than the defences, which they overlie, but all belong to the Iron Age.

DOVER CASTLE

DOVER CASTLE *was constructed mainly in the late 12th and 13th centuries on a magnificent site which shows evidence of occupation or fortification from prehistoric times. The castle commands an important harbour opening on the shortest sea route to the Continent and was for centuries vital to the defence of the kingdom.*

A 13th-century chronicler described it as the 'Key of England'. The medieval kings spent vast sums of money fortifying the site, and these fortifications have been continuously brought up to date. Within the walls is the Roman lighthouse, the earliest in Britain, probably built in the 1st century AD.

QUEEN ELIZABETH'S POCKET PISTOL *Despite its popular name, this brass gun is really a type of cannon, being 24 ft long with a 4¾ in. calibre. It was made in Utrecht in 1544—before Elizabeth came to the throne—and the whole surface is decorated in relief with bands of fruit, flowers, grotesques, and figures symbolising Liberty, Victory and Fame. The Tudor*

coat of arms has beneath it a verse in Dutch, translated as: 'Break, tear every wall and rampart Am I called, Across mountain and valley pierces my ball By me striken.' In 1613–22 the gun was known to be capable of firing a 10 lb ball a distance of 2000 yards: a local rhyme declares: 'Use me well and keep me clean I'll send a ball to Calais Green.'

Dreva *Borders*   562Bd
This Iron Age hill-fort commands the valley connecting the Upper Tweed with the Clyde Valley. The top of the prominent crag is encircled by two stone walls. On the south-west is a slope studded with boulders, set in the earth to break the rush of a close body of men. To the north-east of the fort are the traces of a later settlement; a similar one is on the north-west slopes of the hill.

Druim An Duin *Strathclyde*   560Ef
A small galleried Iron Age dun, some 30 ft by 50 ft. In places its wall is 16 ft thick and stands about 9 ft high. There are two entrances, one of which has a guard-chamber inside the wall. The dun is on a ridge overlooking Loch Sween.

Drum Castle *Grampian*   567Gd
In 1323, Robert the Bruce gave the 12th-century keep of this castle to William de Irvine, whose descendants have owned it ever since. A residential wing was added *c.* 1619. The castle, set in extensive gardens, contains fine collections of furniture, antique porcelain and paintings.

Druminnor Castle *Grampian*   566Ef
A 15th-century castle, the former home of the Lords Forbes.

Drumlanrig Castle *Dumfs. & Gall.*   562Ab
Home of the Duke of Buccleuch and Queensberry. A magnificent castle with 15 lead-capped turrets built on a former Douglas stronghold, 1679–91. Many art treasures.

Drummond Castle Gardens *Tayside*   562Ag
Gardens originally laid out in 1630 by John Drummond, 2nd Earl of Perth.

Drumtroddan *Dumfs. & Gall.*   556Dg
Altogether in this group there are three rock-faces, each one carved with cups, cup-and-ring markings, radial grooves and other channels. They belong to the early Bronze Age.

Dryburgh Abbey *Borders*   562Dd
Sir Walter Scott and Field Marshal Earl Haig, British Commander-in-Chief in France in 1915, were interred in the abbey. Founded by King David I of Scotland in 1150, and added to in the

12th to 15th centuries, it was several times damaged by the English during Border Wars; in the 16th century it was left to decay. A memorial to James II of Scotland survives in the grounds.

Dryslwyn Castle *Dyfed*   *544Fd*
A ruin on a high point overlooking the valley of the Towy, once the fortress of a Welsh prince.

Dudley *W. Midlands*   *552Ba*
BLACK COUNTRY MUSEUM A 19th-century village is being reconstructed.
CENTRAL MUSEUM A fine collection of geological specimens features local limestone and coal fossils. There is a permanent art collection, and temporary exhibitions are held in the art gallery.
CHURCH OF ST THOMAS THE APOSTLE This is a dominating church in Regency Gothic, designed by W. Brooks, 1817–19, with a good spire and plasterwork of the same style in the interior vaulting and panelling. Above the marble altar is a carving of St Thomas, by Samuel Joseph. Most of the 19th-century glass has now gone, although that in the east window, depicting the Ascension, remains, and is by Joseph Backler, 1821. There are monuments by Peter and William Hollins.

Dudley Castle *W. Midlands*   *552Ba*
A ruined 13th-century castle, with 16th-century additions, standing in extensive grounds containing a zoo. Near by is a ruined priory.

Dufftown *Grampian*   *566Df*
BALVENIE CASTLE The ruins of a castle owned in turn by the Comyns, Douglas and Atholl families; the Atholl motto is carved on the 15th–16th-century front. A notable feature is the yett (a massive iron grille) guarding the entrance to the tower.

Duloe Circle *Cornwall*   *538Ec*
Eight standing stones in a small circle some 39 ft in diameter. It is unique in Cornwall as a megalithic structure, because its builders used quartz instead of Cornish granite. It appears to have been used in the Middle Bronze Age.

Dumfries *Dumfs. & Gall.*   *562Aa*
Dumfries was given a royal charter by William the Lion in 1186, and another by Robert III in 1395. It is known especially for its links with Robert Burns and Sir James Barrie. Burns moved into Dumfries from a farm at nearby Ellisland to a house in Bank Street (1791) and then to Mill Street where he died (1796). Burns and his family are buried in a mausoleum (built 1819) in St Michael's churchyard, and the Burns Statue in the High Street was erected in 1882. A collection of the poet's relics are on display in the Burns House. Sir James Barrie was a pupil at the Academy.
DEVORGILLA BRIDGE A six-arched stone bridge with massive piers spanning the R. Nith. Steps lead up from the eastern bank to a narrow carriageway still used by pedestrians. Traditionally called Devorgilla Bridge after the foundress of Sweetheart Abbey, its origins nevertheless are 15th century.
MID STEEPLE In the middle of the High Street this three-storey tolbooth with a square squat tower rising from the north end was designed by John Moffat of Liverpool, and built by Tobias Bachup of Alloa. It was finished in 1708; on its façade is the standard measurement of a Scots ell (37 in., 8 in. less than the English ell). It was the town hall and municipal building until 1867.
OBSERVATORY (DUMFRIES MUSEUM) The oldest part of the building is the windmill, built *c.* 1760, which was converted into an astronomical and weather observatory in 1835. A camera obscura was added in 1836, and a hall in 1862. The exhibits

cover the natural history and human history of the area from Gretna Green to the Mull of Galloway. Archaeological finds include an Iron Age plough from Elshielshiels Moss and a Romano-Celtic head from Birrens Roman fort.
OLD BRIDGE HOUSE MUSEUM A 17th-century house containing rooms with fine furniture from several periods and a Victorian childhood room.

Dunadd Hill-fort *Strathclyde*   *560Ef*
Built upon a rocky hill, the defences of this fort consist of stone walls at different points and levels on the various rocky outcrops, the central area measuring no more than 100 ft by 45 ft. Close to the entrance of this, a rock-face has been carved with various Pictish symbols. The fort may first have been built in the Iron Age, but the symbols are currently attributed to the Dark Ages, probably late 7th–8th century AD. There is a historical reference in an Irish chronicle to Dunadd, for we are told that, in AD 683, a force of Picts and Scots besieged a party of Britons here. This has led to the suggestion that the attacking force succeeded and that the symbols were carved to mark the victory.

Dunaverty Castle *Strathclyde*   *560Ec*
Ruins of a castle of the Lords of the Isles, where in 1647 a garrison of 300 men was besieged by Covenanters, Presbyterian supporters of the English Parliament. The defenders were forced to submit because of thirst and were slain by the Covenanters.

Dunbar *Lothian*   *562Df*
TOWN HOUSE An early 17th-century town house situated on the east side of the High Street. A three-storied main block with a slated irregular hexagonal tower terminates in a slender spirelet. Inside are the usual arrangements of council chamber and prison cells.

Dun Bharpa *Barra, Western Isles*   *564Be*
A circular Neolithic cairn of the passage-grave type. The mound is about 85 ft in diameter and is surrounded by upright stone slabs of heights varying up to 7 ft. The entrance is on the east side and the passage leads to a chamber near the centre. This itself cannot be seen, but its great capstone, 10 ft by 5 ft 8 in. by 1 ft thick, is visible at the top of the mound, which is some 17 ft high.

Dunblane *Central*   *561Jg*
CATHEDRAL The cathedral was founded in the middle of the 12th century and largely completed by the 1250s. Towards the end of the 16th century, the nave roof collapsed, and for 300 years remained open to the elements. It was eventually restored in the late 1800's. Margaret Drummond, wife of James IV of Scotland, and her two sisters are buried in the choir.

Dun Carloway *Lewis, Western Isles*   *568Bd*
This fine Iron Age broch stands on a rocky ridge overlooking the 'black-houses' of the later village. Though robbed, it is still in fair condition and parts of its 11 ft thick wall still stand 30 ft high. The internal enclosure is 25 ft in diameter. The structure displays all the best features of the broch walls. From a wall-chamber at ground level, a staircase ascends to the galleries, the construction of which is clearly displayed.

Dundee *Tayside*   *566Ea*
MCMANUS GALLERY The gallery contains a collection of Dutch, Italian and French paintings executed from the 16th to the 18th centuries, and British works of art from the 18th to the 20th centuries, especially Scottish paintings of the Victorian age. In the museum is an archaeological collection, a collection of Scottish silver and other

rooms devoted to Egyptology, decorative arts, ethnology, geology and natural history.

CUSTOM HOUSE Designed by James Leslie and John Taylor in 1842–3 with a sympathetic addition by C. & L. Ower in 1884. An elegant three-storey building with four Greek Ionic columns at the upper floor level surmounted by a pediment.

HIGH SCHOOL A portico dominates the façade of this handsome building, built in 1834. The designer, George Angus, based the portico on the style of the Parthenon in Athens.

Dundrennan Abbey *Dumfs. & Gall.* *556Eg*
The ruined Cistercian abbey, founded in 1142, where Mary, Queen of Scots spent her last night in Scotland.

Dunfermline *Fife* *562Bf*
ABBEY The beautiful Norman church of the Benedictine abbey is only a fragment of the original, but fortunately most of the nave survives intact. The east end and central tower are modern.

Dun Fiadhairt *Skye, Highland* *564Dg*
The wall of this Iron Age broch is about 12 ft thick and encloses an area some 31 ft in diameter. There is a guard-room in the wall-thickness on each side of the entrance.

DUNKELD CATHEDRAL

The early history of Dunkeld Cathedral, on the banks of the Tay, is obscure. The See was revived in 1107, but the existing church dates only from the 13th century when the boundaries of the diocese were redefined and a body of secular canons installed in the cathedral. During the 13th century the Bishops of Dunkeld were frequently involved in affairs of State. Bishop Richard of Inverkeithing was appointed one of Alexander III's guardians, and in 1264 was auditor of accounts in the Exchequer, while Bishop Mathew de Crambeth, elected in 1288, was sent to negotiate with the King of France in 1295. The See survived until its suppression in 1571, although the cathedral had already been 'purged of superstition' in 1560. The choir was ultimately used as a kirk. The cathedral's isolated position dates from the sacking of the town of Dunkeld in 1689 during a battle between government troops and Jacobite supporters. The town was burnt to the ground, and the new town grew up farther to the east.

Dungarry and Suie Hill *Dumfs. & Gall.* *556Eg*
Two small Iron Age forts standing nearly 2 miles apart at opposite ends of a hilly ridge.

Dungarry, at the northern end, is enclosed by two stone walls. The outer wall is about 6 ft thick, but the inner has twice this thickness. There is an entrance on the east side with additional external defences, and an annex to the north of the entrance. The fort on Suie Hill, at the southern end of the ridge, is similar to this.

Dungeness *Kent* *542Fd*
LIGHTHOUSE A light was first displayed on this dangerous coast early in the 17th century. In 1792 James Wyatt designed a handsome tower; this was severely damaged by lightning in 1822 but survived until 1904 when a tower 140 ft high was erected. The keepers' houses built around Wyatt's tower can still be seen, the demolished tower being an open area. Finally, the construction of the atomic power station made it necessary to re-site the lighthouse, and in 1961 the present slender reinforced concrete tower was built. The previous lighthouse is still there, and is open to the public.

Dun Grugaig *Highland* *565Ge*
The Iron Age dun stands on a cliff-top above the precipitous side of a gorge; its wall does not completely encircle the inner area, but curves from cliff-edge to cliff-edge. This wall is 14 ft thick, with internal chambers and an entrance passage with sockets for the bar which held the door. The wall, though ruinous, still stands some 8 ft high.

Dun Hallin *Skye, Highland* *564Dg*
The outer enclosure is surrounded by a 6 ft thick wall and within it stands the Iron Age broch, a fortified tower-dwelling still some 12 ft high, with a wall about 11 ft thick. There are two wall-chambers and a stair-lobby.

Dunkeld *Tayside* *566Cb*
A seven-arched bridge of 1809, built by Thomas Telford, heralds the approach to late Georgian shops and houses, the only part to be built of a new town planned by the Duke of Atholl in the same year.

CATHEDRAL The plan of Dunkeld is unusual in not being cruciform; the aisle-less choir and long aisled nave make the cathedral look more like an enormous parish church. The earliest parts of the existing church date from the 13th century. The rebuilding of the nave, now a roofless ruin, was begun by Bishop Robert de Cardeny in 1406 and continued by Bishop Thomas Lauder. The design of the nave is also unusual; the arcade is supported on heavy drum columns reminiscent of an earlier period, and the tribune gallery between the arcade and the clerestory, dating from the early 15th century, is an extremely archaic feature for that time. The choir in its present form is largely the result of restorations in 1815 and 1908. No traces of the canons' houses or bishop's palace survive.

DUNKELD LITTLE HOUSES Forty houses in Cathedral Street and High Street, built mainly after 1689 when the town was damaged during the siege of 1200 Cameronians in the town by 5000 Highlanders. The houses were restored in the years 1950–65.

Dun Lagaidh *Highland* *568Fb*
A fort on the lower ground bordering the southwest shore of Loch Broom. It has a 12 ft thick wall which shows traces of vitrified material. There are additional defences outside the east gate. The broch was later built within the eastern part of the fort, but detailed description is difficult because of the surrounding debris. Both are of the Iron Age.

DUNSTABLE

THE FAYREY PALL *Every religious fraternity, City livery company and noble family in the later Middle Ages possessed its own funeral pall (coffin covering). The Fayrey family gave this pall to the Fraternity of St John the Baptist, which was founded in 1442 in Dunstable. The sides show St John preaching, with barren tree trunks and rocks representing the wilderness. Henry Fayrey, a wealthy merchant of Dunstable who died in 1516, is leading the fraternity to the Baptist from one side, and from the other, Henry's wife Agnes presents a row of ladies. The centre portion (bottom right) is of Florentine brocade on cloth-of-gold. St John is depicted in his rough coat of camel's hair, and the Arms*

shown are those of the Fayrey family and the ancient Arms of the Mercers' Company (a demi-figure of Our Lady, crowned). The silk is Italian, the style Flemish, but the workmanship undoubtedly English. (Victoria and Albert Museum)

DUNSTABLE SWAN BADGE *This gold-and-enamel badge was made in the 15th century and may have been worn by a king or noble who claimed descent from the legendary Knight of the Swan, a figure of medieval romance who appears in a boat drawn by a white swan, then vanishes for ever in the same boat. Found in Dunstable in 1965, the badge is now in the British Museum.*

Dunnottar Castle *Grampian*   567Gd

In 1652 this castle was the only one in Royalist hands and here the crown and sceptre of Scotland were taken for safe-keeping. After eight months of siege the castle fell to Cromwell's troops and was plundered, but the regalia were smuggled to safety. Records show that in 1685 167 Covenanters were held in the dungeon. The castle was dismantled after the Jacobite rebellion of 1715; the ruins, with tower and chapel dating from the 14th century, and gateway of *c.* 1590, stand on top of a rocky cliff, 160 ft above the sea.

Dunollie Castle *Strathclyde*   565Ga

The remains of an 11th-century MacDoughall keep crown an 80 ft rock surrounded by the sea on three sides and overlooking Loch Linnhe.

Dunrobin Castle *Highland*   569Jb

The castle, overlooking the Moray Firth, has parts dating back to 1401, plus additions made in the 18th and 19th centuries. A wing, destroyed by fire in 1915, has been restored. Rooms on view house Louis XV furniture, Mortlake tapestries and paintings by Canaletto, Romney, Ramsay and Reynolds. Collections of uniforms and court dress, and of wild animals shot by the 5th Duke of Sutherland, are also on view. The 19th-century gardens are laid out in the style of Versailles.

Dunsinane *Tayside*   566Da

The internal area of this conspicuous Iron Age fort is enclosed by a strong rampart, which may have been timber-laced. Additional ramparts add to its strength. Inside the fort was a small earth-house (souterrain). This is reputedly the site of Macbeth's castle.

Dun Skeig *Strathclyde*   560Ee

This oval fort crests a steep hill overlooking West Loch Tarbert, and has a heavily vitrified wall. A roughly circular dun with a thick wall and a single entrance lies outside the fort. Both are of the Iron Age.

Dunstable *Beds.*   547Hd

CHURCH OF ST PETER The magnificent Norman nave of 1150 survives from the priory church; the east end has disappeared since the Dissolution. The west front includes both Norman and Early English work, and the north-west door has rich ornamentation of the 13th century. There is a 15th-century chancel screen, one of the monuments is by Thomas Green of Camberwell.

Dunstaffnage Castle *Strathclyde*   565Ga

The castle was built in the 13th century on the site of a former home of the Scottish kings, who by then had moved their capital to Scone. Dunstaffnage was captured from the MacDougalls by Robert Bruce. He appointed MacArthur—a distant relative of the Campbells—as the constable, and 'Captain of Dunstaffnage' eventually became a hereditary Campbell title. Flora Macdonald was imprisoned here after leading Bonnie Prince Charlie to safety following the Battle of Culloden. Ruins of three round towers and the walls of a 15th-century stronghold remain.

Dunstanburgh Castle *Northld.*   563Gc

The remains of an extensive castle standing on high cliffs above the North Sea. The castle was begun in 1313 by the Earl of Lancaster, and enlarged by John of Gaunt in the 14th century. It was surrounded by defensive walls, even on the seaward side, and covered 11 acres. It was taken by the Yorkists in the Wars of the Roses and afterwards dismantled.

Dunster Castle *Som.*   539Hg

This crenellated hill-top castle dominates the little

market town. Dating from 1070 and modified in the 17th and 19th centuries, it has been the home of the Luttrell family since 1376. It contains a bedroom once occupied by Charles II, a fine carved staircase installed in 1681, and a banqueting hall with hanging leather panels embossed to show the story of Antony and Cleopatra.

Dun Suledale *Skye, Highland* 564Eg
Similar to the broch Dun Hallin, for again the outer wall is some 6 ft thick. The broch wall is 12½ ft thick and the internal area about 42 ft in diameter. The western entrance has a guard-chamber. Also in the wall-thickness are other cells and a gallery. It dates from the Iron Age.

Dun Telve & Dun Troddan *Highland* 565Ge
These two Iron Age brochs stand close together in the glen below Dun Grugaig. They are regarded as the best preserved of their type on the mainland of Scotland. Dun Telve has an inner area 32 ft across, surrounded by a wall 13½ ft thick at its base. In places it stands more than 33 ft high. It contains the usual galleries and chambers. Dun Troddan, a little higher up the glen, is slightly smaller. Its internal space is 28 ft in diameter, surrounded by a wall 13½ ft thick, which still stands 25 ft high in parts.

Duntisbourne Rous *Glos.* 546Cc
CHURCH OF ST MICHAEL A small church of Saxon origin, with Norman additions. The 15th-century west tower has a saddle-back roof. Under the chancel is a Norman crypt. Inside the church are a fine Norman font and medieval misericords.

Dun Torcuill *North Uist, Western Isles* 564Bh
The wall of this Iron Age dun is rather variable in thickness, ranging from 7½ ft to 12⅓ ft. It encloses

a space some 38 ft in diameter. In the wall are cells and galleries. In places it still stands some 10 ft high.

Dun Troddan See Dun Telve & Dun Troddan.

Duntrune Castle *Strathclyde* 560Ef
A modernised 17th-century fortress on the shores of Loch Crinan. (By appointment.)

Dunvegan *Isle of Skye, Highland* 564Dg
The home of the chiefs of the Clan MacLeod since 1200, the castle has a 15th-century dungeon, a 16th-century tower, and was restored in the 19th century. Among its treasures are relics of Bonnie Prince Charlie, manuscripts of Sir Walter Scott and Dr Johnson, the Rory More drinking-horn and the 'Fairy Flag of Dunvegan'. The flag, which is surrounded by legends, probably came from Syria or Rhodes and may have been brought back to Scotland by a MacLeod taking part in the Crusades.

Dunwich *Suffolk* 548Ff
Once a considerable port, with monastic houses, hospitals and many churches, Dunwich now lies at the bottom of the still-encroaching sea. All that remain are the 19th-century Church of St James, and by it the apsed chapel of the Norman leper hospital. There are some ruins of the Franciscan friary, a few houses and crumbling cliffs.

Durham *Durham* 558Cf
Ancient and modern buildings jostle for space on a natural fortification site, for here the R. Wear makes a hairpin bend, almost encircling a great sandstone outcrop. In 1072 William the Conqueror built the castle on the narrow neck of land commanding the approach to the city. This was founded in 995 when a Saxon church was built on the river-girt rock. The Norman cathedral and monastery were begun on the same site in the 11th century. Around the cathedral and castle are many fine 17th- and 18th-century houses. There is little industry in the city, which now straddles the river; the university was founded in 1832, and the city is the administrative centre of County Durham. It has always been a route focus—it lies on the Great North Road—and seven bridges span the Wear: the Elvet and Framwellgate bridges are preserved as ancient monuments; Prebends' Bridge (footbridge) dates from 1778, and Baths Bridge (footbridge) leads to a former House of Correction. The Kingsgate footbridge and the Milburngate road bridge were built in the 1960's, and New Elvet Bridge opened in 1975. On the western outskirts of the city a cross marks the left flank of the English forces who defeated the Scots in the Battle of Neville's Cross, 1346.
BISHOP COSIN'S HALL AND ALMSHOUSES Built *c.* 1666 on Palace Green near the cathedral.
CATHEDRAL AND CASTLE Durham Cathedral, one of the most outstanding examples of Romanesque architecture in Europe, stands on a great rock surrounded on three sides by the R. Wear. The complex of buildings at the summit is dominated by the cathedral and castle. The cathedral was begun by Bishop William of St Calais in 1093, and the Norman work was finished by 1133. This part of the church, which has survived almost intact apart from the east end, shows the first use of ribbed vaulting on an extensive scale in a church. The main additions after 1133 were the Chapel of the Nine Altars at the east end in the middle of the 13th century, Bishop du Puiset's Galilee Chapel at the west end in the late 12th century, and the central tower in the last half of the 15th century. The interior of the cathedral, which is richly ornamented, contains many interesting tombs and

LEATHER HANGINGS

One of six magnificent leather panels in fine condition, richly coloured and relieved in places with impressed designs made by iron tools. The panels tell the story of the Roman, Mark Antony and the Egyptian queen, Cleopatra. Originally made in the Low Countries in the 17th century, the panels must have been intended for a particular house, as they vary greatly in size. (Dunster Castle) furnishings, including a magnificent screen behind the high altar (1372–80) and the north door's famous 12th-century knocker. (See pp. 174–5.)

Durham Castle lies to the north of the cathedral and the earliest of its existing buildings date from *c.* 1070. Of the magnificent buildings erected by Hugh du Puiset, who became bishop in 1153, only the main entrance to his hall survives. This entrance is the most extravagant piece of Norman work to survive in the county and, in the nearby Constable's Gallery, is another piece of striking decorative arcading. Much of the rest of the castle was renewed at a later date. The great hall was probably built in Bishop Bek's time (1284–1311), while the keep is the work of Bishop Hatfield (1345–81). All these buildings were restored in the 19th century and later adapted for use by the university.

DURHAM UNIVERSITY ORIENTAL MUSEUM The only museum in Britain devoted wholly to Oriental art. The many treasures on view include the Hardinge Collection of Chinese carved jade, Tibetan paintings and sculpture, the MacDonald Collection of Chinese pottery and porcelain, Chinese paintings and textiles, and the Northumberland Collection of Egyptian antiquities. The museum also houses temporary exhibitions of ancient and modern Eastern art. (See p. 176.)

GRAMMAR SCHOOL Founded in 1541 by Henry VIII; the present building dates from 1661.

UNIVERSITY OF DURHAM A collegiate university founded in 1832. Part of it is housed in the castle.

Durisdeer *Dumfs. & Gall.* 562Ab
CHURCH A 17th-century church with the mausoleum of the Dukes of Queensberry on the north side. A monument to a duke who died in 1711, by

John Nost, has columns, flying cherubs, and the duke reclining beside his dead wife. Nost's original design is in the Bodleian Library, Oxford.

Durrington Walls *Wilts.* 540Fe
This great circular structure is almost bisected by the Amesbury–Marlborough road. The bank, now largely eroded, enclosed a ditch some 80 ft wide and 20 ft deep. There were two entrances. New road construction led to an emergency excavation being made on part of the site in 1967. This showed that, within the circle, there were once many round buildings constructed on a pattern similar to those at the Woodhenge monument which stands close by to the south-west. It is fairly clear that this complex at Durrington was an important religious centre before this was transferred to Stonehenge at the very end of the Neolithic period.

Dwarfie Stane *Hoy, Orkney* 569Hf
A great block of sandstone, 28 ft long by 14 ft wide by 8 ft deep. Into it a passage has been cut, 7½ ft long by 2 ft 4 in. high and 2 ft 10 in. wide. On either side there is a cell cut into the rock. Each is about 5 ft wide by 3 ft deep and 2½ ft high. The square block which now lies outside the entrance was originally used to stop it. No other such rock-cut tomb is known in Britain, though a comparable one is at Glendalough in Ireland. It is of the Neolithic period.

Dyce *Grampian* 567Ge
CHURCH OF ST FERGUS The churchyard contains two Pictish stones, one with mysterious incised symbols and the other carved in relief. Two miles west is a remarkable circle of standing stones, some of which are more than 11 ft high. The circle is over 60 ft in diameter.

DUN TELVE BROCH

One of the best preserved brochs on the mainland of Scotland, situated in the picturesque glen above Glenelg. These drystone circular structures were built as defensive dwelling-places some time between 100 BC and AD 100, usually beside cultivable land, and are peculiar to Iron Age Scotland. At Dun Telve the hollow central tower, enclosing an area 32 ft across at its base, had a wall 13½ ft thick at the bottom and which tapered inwards. As buildings of strength these

towers with their single entrance were perhaps the greatest in prehistoric Europe. Inside the thickness of the walls was a series of galleries and living chambers reached by stairs; the chambers or cells had no windows on the outside of the tower. Parts of the outer wall with its one defended entrance still survive around the tower-like inner structure, and the enclosed space would probably have included a number of defended small out-buildings.

DURHAM CATHEDRAL

Durham is no stranger to power. For centuries its mighty Norman cathedral and castle, sited on a rock 70 ft above the R. Wear, have dominated one of Britain's arteries, the Great North Road; the coal and industry of the surrounding area still give it immense economic strength. William the Conqueror, when he first visited it in 1072, immediately saw its importance, and he and his successors made certain of the loyalty to the Crown of its prince-bishops.

DURHAM CATHEDRAL AND CASTLE *The first church on the site of Durham Cathedral was built in the 10th century AD by the guardians of the remains of St Cuthbert who, according to legend, were guided to the spot by a maiden searching for her lost cow. The Norman cathedral was not planned until 100 years later. By then William the Conqueror had ordered the construction of the castle and had, in order to stabilise the North, conferred special powers on the Bishops of Durham who as a result became important political figures. The castle is now part of Durham University.*

ANGLO-SAXON STOLE *Durham Cathedral is the home of one of the oldest surviving embroidered stoles in Western Europe. Originally made for Bishop Frithestan of Winchester who died in 931, and later presented by King Athelstan to the shrine of St Cuthbert, it is now displayed, with other relics, in the Treasury. The prophets Daniel and Jonah, who are still recognisable, are embroidered in a style strongly influenced by Byzantine art.*

THE CARILEF BIBLE *One of the most splendid works in Durham Cathedral's library is an illuminated Bible in two volumes bequeathed by William of St Carilef or St Calais, Bishop of Durham from 1081 to 1096, who not only founded the Norman cathedral we know today but also its library. As in all illuminated manuscripts, the initial letters are most elaborately decorated and in this instance none more than the letter B. In the upper part of the B the stylised foliage customary in illuminated manuscripts merges with a grotesque creature, also made of foliage and in the lower part King David sits playing his harp.*

THE CONYERS FALCHION *A falchion, a broad, curved, convex-edged sword in use in the Middle Ages, and one of the treasures preserved at Durham, had to be presented by the head of the Conyers family who held their lands from the Bishops of Durham, to every new prince-bishop as he first entered his diocese. Failure to do so was tantamount to refusing to render military service to their feudal overlord and entailed forfeiture of their lands.*

THE SANCTUARY DOOR KNOCKER *at Durham Cathedral recalls the days and nights in medieval times when debtors and other fugitives from the law could seek protection from arrest in places of worship like Durham Cathedral. The Rights of Sanctuary which went back to Old Testament times were eventually, because of blatant abuse, abolished in 1540.*

DURHAM CATHEDRAL, *proudly dominating its surroundings, is one of the finest examples of the Romanesque style of architecture. Though the style varied in different countries, the round arch and ever more ambitious experiments in vaulting were common features everywhere. The ribbed vaulting in the north and south aisles of the choir of Durham Cathedral is the earliest of its kind in Europe.*

IRON HORSE *The Chinese preferred such small-headed horses of South Russia to their own large-headed ones,* *and fine iron casting became one of their skills during the 10th century AD when this statue was made.*

EGYPTIAN BOXWOOD FIGURINE *A servant-girl of 1580 –1314 BC; such statues were put in tombs in the belief that the persons portrayed became real in the next world.*

18TH-CENTURY TIBETAN TANKA *showing a compassionate being, reborn to help end suffering; he is with a goddess, surrounded by Buddhas, saints and deities.*

Dyrham *Avon* 540Dg
CHURCH OF ST PETER Mainly in Perpendicular style, but a late Norman arcade survives in the nave. A tower stands over the west end. Inside the church is a fine Norman font and a brass of 1416 depicting the armoured figure of Sir Maurice Russell and his wife. There is also a large monument to Sir George Wynter, with recumbent effigies, mourning children and gloriously flamboyant heraldry.

Dyrham Park *Avon* 540Dg
A country mansion in a deer park, the house was built between 1692 and 1704 for William Blathwayt, Secretary of State at War to William III. The east front and the orangery were designed by William Talman. The interior expresses the Dutch-influenced taste of William's reign, with gilt leather hangings, delftware, paintings by minor Dutch masters and furniture which has associations with the 17th-century diarists Pepys and Evelyn.

E

Eaglesham *Strathclyde* 561Hd
An interesting 18th-century village lay-out. The plan conceived by Alexander, 10th Earl of Eglinton, in 1769 takes the form of an elongated triangle. One- and two-storey traditional harled houses frame the large grassy area in the centre, some being distinguished by Classical details such as fan-lights and pilastered doorways.

Eardisley *Heref. & Worcs.* 545Je
CHURCH OF ST MARY MAGDALENE Originally a Norman building, with later additions, most interesting for its cup-shaped font of *c.* 1150, whose carvings show men fighting with spear and sword, the Harrowing of Hell, a large lion, and other figures and ornaments.

Earls Barton *Northants.* 547Gf
CHURCH OF ALL SAINTS The tower of this church was probably built in the late 10th century, and must at some time have been incorporated into the defences of the nearby Norman castle. The decoration of the tower includes a row of arches and two rows of chevron decoration set between narrow pilaster strips. The origin of this type of decoration is obscure, but it may derive from timber construction or it may have been an imitation of building techniques on the Continent. The original west entrance survives at the base, a massive and clumsy piece of Saxon architecture. It is popularly believed that the doors which open out of the first floor were used for access when the church was used for defensive purposes, but this is unlikely since there were three external doorways—in the west, south and east faces. The upper storey contains openings separated by characteristic Saxon baluster-shaped pillars. The Normans added a small nave and chancel to the Saxon tower, and the church was further enlarged in the 14th and 15th centuries. The tower battlements were added in the 15th century.

Earl Stonham *Suffolk* 548Df
CHURCH OF ST MARY A cruciform church of various dates, with a west tower. There is a magnificent hammerbeam nave roof with angels, and another in the chancel; carved octagonal font, a 17th-century pulpit with hour-glasses, and interesting bench ends.

Earn's Heugh *Borders* 562Ee
These hill-forts and settlements stand on the cliff-edge, not far from St Abb's Head; owing to marine erosion, they have suffered some loss. They were probably originally roughly circular enclosures. The eastern site is defended by a single bank and external ditch with an entrance on the west. The other, clearly later, as its defences partly cover those of the first, has a double rampart with an intermediate ditch. The settlement, itself defended by a single rampart without a ditch, is sited within the earlier fort, and contains the foundations of several circular huts. The evidence suggests that the original forts were of the Iron Age and that, some time later, a settlement of the later Roman period was sited within the earlier defences.

Easby *N. Yorks.* 558Ce
CHURCH OF ST AGATHA Stands near the ruins of a 12th-century abbey, and is basically of the same period, with 13th-century additions. Sir Gilbert Scott made restorations in 1869. The medieval wall-paintings are of biblical scenes.

Easington *Durham* 558Dg
CHURCH OF ST MARY THE VIRGIN Originally Norman with later enlargements, the church has a west tower. There are pews with poppy-heads, and two 13th-century monuments with effigies, one of a lady, the other of a cross-legged knight.

Eassie *Tayside* 566Eb
A fine Pictish symbol stone stands in the ruins of Eassie church. It is carved on one side with a cross and figures; the other has an 'elephant' symbol, disc and Z-rod symbols, together with men and animals.

Eastbourne *E. Sussex* 542Cc
THE REDOUBT A fortification built against Napoleon now houses a military museum illustrating the theme of 'Sussex at war' up to the Hitler threat of 1940. A separate collection is devoted to the story of the Royal Sussex Regiment from 1704.
TOWER 73: THE WISH TOWER A restored Martello tower. It is one of 74 such towers built along the Kent and Sussex coasts between 1804 and 1808 as defences against possible French invasion during the Napoleonic Wars. Tower 73 now contains a museum which includes displays describing the history of Martello towers and their garrisons, together with exhibits of 18th- and early-19th-century weapons and uniforms. The name 'Wish Tower' is probably derived from the wash or marsh on which the Martello was originally built.
TOWNER ART GALLERY The house was built *c.* 1776 and was later used as a manor house. The collections include the works of British 18th-, 19th- and 20th-century painters; contemporary original prints by artists such as John Piper, Ceri Richards, Picasso, Michael Rothenstein; sculptures by Elizabeth Frink; works by Sussex artists, and a set of Georgian caricatures by George and Henry Cruickshank. Frequent temporary exhibitions are held here.

East Dereham *Norfolk* 554Cb
CHURCH OF ST NICHOLAS The church is cruciform, with a lantern tower over the crossing and a

detached bell-tower. Work dates from all periods from Norman to Perpendicular. The seven-sacrament font cost £12 in 1468. St Nicholas's contains a brass lectern, *c.* 1500, 19th-century stained glass and a monument by John Flaxman to the poet Cowper, 1802.

East Grinstead *W. Sussex*　　　　*542Be*
In the main street is a group of fine houses: Cromwell House, 16th century and timber-framed as was standard at that time, and an 18th-century red-brick building, Dorset House, dated 1705. Opposite these is Sackville College, a generous piece of philanthropy by the Earl of Dorset. The buildings, of local sandstone, are dated 1619, and lie around a quadrangle.

East Guldeford *E. Sussex*　　　　*542Ed*
CHURCH OF ST MARY Standing on the fringe of the Romney Marsh, below Rye, this brick church, with no tower, has the appearance of a barn. Built at the turn of the 15th century, it has immense triangular buttresses at the west end. Inside the church there are early 19th-century box-pews and a pulpit.

East Hagbourne *Oxon.*　　　　*546Fc*
CHURCH OF ST ANDREW The church is of the 12th–15th centuries; the south aisle can be dated from brass plates commemorating the founder and his wife (*d.* 1403 and 1414). Some good 14th-century glass shows the Nativity and the Presentation, and the large painted Arms are of Charles II.

East Ham *Greater London*　　　　*548Ab*
CHURCH OF ST MARY MAGDALENE A Norman church, with an early 16th-century west tower, fragments of 13th-century wall-painting and some good 17th-century monuments, including one to Edward, Earl of Westmorland.

East Harling *Norfolk*　　　　*554Ca*
CHURCH OF SS PETER AND PAUL The west tower has a small spire surrounded by flying buttresses, with pinnacles. Other features include a clerestory, a hammerbeam roof to the nave, an octagonal font with decorated panels, remains of screens and some original stained glass in the east window. Some 15th- and 16th-century monuments with effigies are dedicated to the Harling and Lovell families.

East Lambrook Manor *Som.*　　　　*540Cd*
A 15th-century house with 16th-century additions. The gardens are informal and contain some rare plants.

Eastleach Martin *Glos.*　　　　*546Dc*
CHURCH OF SS MICHAEL AND MARTIN A Norman church with a low west tower and fine Norman doorways. There is later Early English work, a 14th-century font and medieval carved benches.

Eastleach Turville *Glos.*　　　　*546Dc*
CHURCH OF ST ANDREW A small church with a saddleback tower and a fine Norman south doorway, richly ornamented with dog tooth, chevron and hobnail carving. The door is surmounted by a carving of Christ in glory, with cherubim and seraphim in adoration.

East Linton *Lothian*　　　　*562Df*
PHANTASSIE John Rennie, the bridge engineer, was born here in 1761. On the estate is a 16th-century rubble-built beehive dove-cote, now harled and colour washed. Thick walls taper to a slated roof and attractive stone hood sloped to the north. Pigeon entries situated below the eaves on the south side are also found in a wooden dormer. Fixed ladders inside enabled the 544 stone nests to be reached.

PRESTON MILL A picturesque rubble-built pantiled corn mill of the 18th century, containing a circular drying kiln with conical roof, a cast-iron wheel made by the Carron Iron Co. in 1760, and machinery in working order; the mill-pond also remains.

East Looe *Cornwall*　　　　*538Eb*
LOOE MUSEUM Housed in the former Magistrates' Court in the 15th-century Guildhall, the museum illustrates the life and culture of Cornwall. One collection deals with pilchard-fishing (including model boats); others include weights and measures, regalia of mayors and town criers, porcelain, and old photographs.

East Markham *Notts.*　　　　*552Fe*
CHURCH OF ST JOHN THE BAPTIST A large church of the 15th century. There are some fragments of early glass, and a late 19th-century window by Sir Ninian Comper. There are also monuments, and a brass to a lady, *c.* 1419.

East Meon *Hants.*　　　　*541Hd*
A picturesque downland village on the R. Meon. There is a fine red-brick William-and-Mary house and a medieval courthouse.
CHURCH OF ALL SAINTS A Norman cruciform church, with a central tower with lead spire, and much Norman work inside. The magnificent black Tournai marble font dates from the mid-12th century, and is carved with the Creation, Temptation, the Expulsion from Eden, birds and animals. A similar font is in Winchester Cathedral. Most of the stained glass is by Sir Ninian Comper who also restored the church.

Eastnor *Heref. & Worcs.*　　　　*546Be*
CHURCH OF ST JOHN THE BAPTIST A 14th-century tower and some 12th-century work remain, but the rest of the building is by Sir Gilbert Scott, who used the 'Middle Gothic' style in 1852. The east window is by C. E. Kempe. There is a monument of 1778 by Thomas Scheemakers, from a design by James 'Athenian' Stuart, the painter and architect whose accurate accounts of the monuments in Athens helped to introduce the Greek style of architecture to London, and an effigy, *c.* 1883, by Sir J. E. Boehm, who designed the Wellington Statue at Hyde Park Corner.

Eastnor Castle *Heref. & Worcs.*　　　　*546Be*
A neo-Gothic castle, built in 1814; it contains collections of armour, tapestries and paintings, and stands in spacious grounds.

Easton Maudit *Northants.*　　　　*547Gf*
CHURCH OF SS PETER AND PAUL Mainly of the Decorated period, the church has a tower with a spire, pinnacles and flying buttresses. Two large monuments with effigies, and children kneeling at the bottom of them, date from the early 17th century.

East Riddlesden Hall, *W. Yorks.*　　　　*558Bb*
A manor house, built in 1640, with a Gothic rose window and battlements to one wing. It contains oak furniture, pewter and pictures. A fine medieval tithe barn stands in the grounds.

Eastrington *Humberside*　　　　*558Ea*
CHURCH OF ST MICHAEL A magnificent church, originally Saxon, but largely Norman. There is a monument of *c.* 1456 to a judge, who wears armour, robes, and has a pigtail.

East Wellow *Hants.*　　　　*541Gd*
CHURCH OF ST MARGARET OF ANTIOCH There has been a church here since 931. The present church

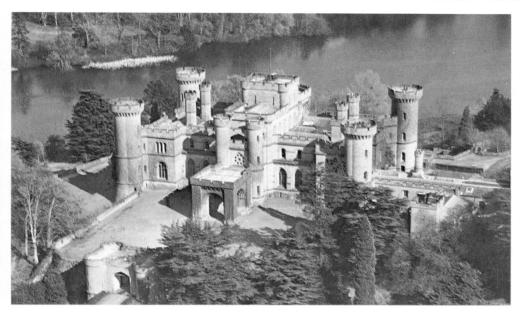

EASTNOR CASTLE

An impressive collection of towers, which could be a Norman castle. But Eastnor is a neo-Gothic castle dating only from the beginning of the 19th century. It was built for the 1st Earl Somers by Sir Robert Smirke in 1810–15 in the fashion of the period. The interior *contains the great hall by Sir Gilbert Scott, 56 ft high and 60 ft long, the ballroom in flamboyant Gothic style by A. W. Pugin, and the long library by George Fox. The British Museum is the finest work by Sir Robert Smirke to survive.*

dates from 1215; there are 13th-century wall-paintings of St Christopher, a knight, and the murder of Thomas à Becket. Florence Nightingale is buried in the churchyard. There is a copy of Magna Carta in the porch.

Eaton Bishop *Heref. & Worcs.*   *546Ae*
CHURCH OF ST MICHAEL AND ALL ANGELS A spacious church, enlarged in the 13th century. The Norman west tower remains, with a later broach spire. There is a clerestory of lancet windows, and a window above the chancel arch. Stained glass of the early 14th century has figures of the Virgin, saints, and a representation of the Crucifixion.

Eaton Bray *Beds.*   *547Hd*
CHURCH OF ST MARY THE VIRGIN Externally, the 15th-century reconstruction and a simple modern west tower belie the original 13th-century interior, with carved foliage capitals on the nave arcade. The font is also of the 13th century: a large bowl with four columns at the corners, rich with foliage carving. The 13th-century ironwork of the south door is by Thomas of Leighton, who also made the grille round Queen Eleanor's tomb in Westminster Abbey.

Ebrington *Glos.*   *546De*
CHURCH OF ST EADBURGHA A mainly Perpendicular church, but Norman work remains in the north and south doorways. Of interest inside are a Saxon stone coffin, wall monuments, benches, a canopied 17th-century pulpit and medieval glass.

Ecclefechan *Dumfs. & Gall.*   *562Ba*
CARLYLE'S HOUSE The birthplace of Thomas Carlyle (1795–1881), essayist and historian; it contains Carlyle relics and some of his manuscripts.

Eccles *Greater Manchester*   *552Bf*
MONKS HALL MUSEUM Housed in a Tudor building with 17th-century additions, the museum opened in 1961 and has items of local interest. The Nasmyth Room contains early machine tools, in-

cluding a steam hammer made at the local Bridgewater foundry by the engineer James Nasmyth. There is a permanent display of toys, and regular exhibitions of arts, crafts and bygones.

Ecclesfield *S. Yorks.*   *552Df*
CHURCH OF ST MARY A spacious church, mainly Perpendicular, with crossing tower and battlemented exterior. Inside are carved stalls and benches, medieval and 19th-century glass, an effigy of *c.* 1640, and a font of 1662.

Eccleshall *Staffs.*   *552Bc*
CHURCH OF THE HOLY TRINITY A magnificent church with a tower nearly 100 ft high. The nave is transitional Norman and the chancel Early English. There are tombs of four bishops—three Tudor and one Victorian.

Eccleston *Lancs.*   *552Ag*
CHURCH OF ST MARY A 14th-century church with later additions, including the late Perpendicular south aisle. It was restored in the 18th and 19th centuries. There is an altar tomb with a 15th-century brass of a priest, and there are 18th-century wall monuments.

Eckington *Derbys.*   *552Ee*
CHURCH OF SS PETER AND PAUL The church, with its massive tower and spire, has 13th- to 15th-century work. The south aisle was rebuilt in Georgian style in the 18th century, and the chancel is 19th-century Gothic.

Edensor *Derbys.*   *552De*
The village was re-sited and designed by Joseph Paxton for the Duke of Devonshire in 1839. It incorporates an extraordinary array of styles, including a Swiss chalet and Tudor chimneys.

Edgcote House *Northants.*   *546Fe*
Mid-18th-century Palladian mansion with rococo interior, good fire-places and plasterwork.

EDINBURGH CASTLE

Castle Rock was probably the site of an Iron Age fort, but may have been refortified around the early 7th century. In the 11th century the castle was used as a residence by Malcolm III and his pious English queen, Margaret, who was eventually canonised. The Scottish kings continued to use the castle during the following century, and by the late 13th century the state records and royal treasures were kept there.

In 1566, after the brutal murder of her secretary David Riccio at Holyroodhouse, Mary, Queen of Scots moved to the castle to give birth in safety to her son, later James VI of Scotland and I of England. After the kingdoms of England and Scotland were united under James in 1603, the castle was only occasionally visited by the reigning monarch and was used mainly as a fortress.

Edgehill *Warks.*　　　　　　　　　　546Ee
Scene of the Battle of Edgehill (October 23, 1642), marked by an octagonal stone tower (now the Castle Inn) erected in 1749 on the position of Charles I's royal standard at the start of the fight.

Edinburgh *Lothian*　　　　　　　　562Be
CANONGATE TOLBOOTH Built 1591, it is now a city museum, with the J. Telfer Dunbar Collection of Highland Dress.
CASTLE Edinburgh's principal building, dominating the city. It is perched on a basalt rock, that juts up 443 ft above sea-level and has been a fortress site since the 7th century. No 11th-century castle buildings survive, but St. Margaret's Chapel, built by Malcolm III's wife, remains from the 11th century. In 1314 all the other early buildings were destroyed to make the castle useless to the invading English. King David's Tower—a large L-shaped keep at the south-east corner of Castle Rock—was built in 1367, and a fragment of this tower, which was later greatly reduced in height and incorporated into Half Moon Battery (1574), still survives. Many alterations have been made, especially in the 17th century, to the King's Lodging and the great hall, which were built in the 15th and early 16th centuries. The palace buildings inside the castle precincts form three sides of a square, the fourth being the impressive Scottish National War Memorial. The United Services Museum is at the west end of Palace Yard. On the south side is the great hall, former Parliament meeting place and banqueting hall: it contains a collection of weapons and armour. On the east side are the royal apartments.
　The Scottish regalia—crown, sceptre, sword of state—is kept in the castle, in the stone-vaulted Crown Room. The crown (dated 1540) is of Scottish gold, set with 94 pearls, 10 diamonds, 33 gems.
CATHEDRAL The High Kirk of Edinburgh (St Giles) is large, mainly 14th and 15th century, and has a central tower crowned by a lantern supported on flying buttresses. There are monuments with effigies, and the ornate Chapel of the Order of the Thistle, added in the 20th century, with knights' stalls and banners.
CHAMBERS STREET The University of Edinburgh,

founded in 1582, has a number of buildings here; here also is the Heriot-Watt University, founded in 1854. The Old College building of Edinburgh University is in South Bridge, and was erected between 1789 and 1834.
GENERAL REGISTER HOUSE Built mainly between 1774 and 1789 to Robert Adam designs, and completed 1822–7 by Robert Reid. Its documents go back to the 13th century.
GLADSTONE'S LAND A 1620 house, with outside stairway, crow-stepped gables, painted ceilings and period furniture.
HOLYROOD ABBEY The abbey was founded in 1128 by King David I, in thanksgiving, it is said, for his escape from an enraged stag after the sudden appearance of the Cross between himself and the animal. Very little can now be seen of the original buildings. Parts of the nave are 12th century, but the surviving arcade belongs to the first half of the 13th century. As frequently happened, the nave was kept as a parish church; its present ruined state dates from the collapse of its vault in 1768.
HUNTLY HOUSE Built 1570, it is a museum of local history, with collections of Edinburgh silver and glass, and Scottish pottery.
　There are also items relating to Field-Marshal, Earl Haig.
JAMES' COURT David Hume, the philosopher and historian (1711–76) lived here, and here James Boswell entertained Dr Samuel Johnson.
JOHN KNOX'S HOUSE Built 1490, and occupied by the famous preacher 1561–72. Many religious items are in this museum, which has a splendid Oak Room with a painted ceiling, of *c.* 1600.
KIRK OF GREYFRIARS Here the National Covenant was signed in 1638.
LADY STAIR'S HOUSE Built in 1622, now a literary museum with manuscripts of Scottish writers.
MAGDALEN CHAPEL Once a mortuary, it has exceptional pre-Reformation stained glass. The steeple dates from 1618.
MERCAT CROSS Originally of the 14th century, but the present structure was opened by W. E. Gladstone; it is the appointed place for reading royal proclamations by the Lord Lyon King of Arms, and was once an execution site.
MUSEUM OF CHILDHOOD A collection of about

10,000 items illustrating childhood throughout the ages—toys, dolls, games, books and costumes.
NATIONAL GALLERY OF SCOTLAND Amongst the artists represented in this collection of European painting, sculpture and drawing are Gainsborough, Constable, Turner, Rembrandt, Watteau, Goya and Velasquez; the collection of Scottish painting is unrivalled. (See pp. 186–7.)
NATIONAL LIBRARY OF SCOTLAND Founded in 1682 as the Library of the Faculty of Advocates, this is one of the four largest libraries in Britain, containing over 4,500,000 books and a large collection of manuscripts.
NATIONAL MUSEUM OF ANTIQUITIES OF SCOTLAND The collections deal with Scottish history from the Stone Age to modern times. As well as Bronze Age ornaments, Roman silver, Viking and Highland weapons, there are personal relics, including some of Mary, Queen of Scots, and Prince Charles Edward. In the same building is the Scottish National Portrait Gallery. (See p. 183.)
OLD TOLBOOTH Built in 1466, it no longer remains but is commemorated near St Giles' Cathedral by a heart-shaped pattern of cobble-stones laid in 1817. This old tolbooth provided the opening scene in Scott's novel Heart of Midlothian.
PALACE OF HOLYROODHOUSE James IV of Scotland began this palace adjacent to Holyrood Abbey in 1501, with the building of the north-west tower. During his son's reign additions were made, but much was destroyed by fire in 1650 while Cromwell's troops occupied the building. The damage was made good, but when Charles II was restored to the thrones of England and Scotland, he undertook a major reconstruction of the palace. Sir William Bruce was the architect and in 1671–9 the south-west tower was built to match that of James IV, and the apartments behind the west façade were added. George V and Queen Mary had the throne room and state rooms renovated and redecorated; they were refurnished with period furniture and hung with tapestries and portraits of Scottish kings and queens.
PARLIAMENT HOUSE The Scottish Parliament met here 1639–1707. It is now the Supreme Court, Court of Session and High Court. In Parliament Hall the south window depicts the inauguration of the Court of Session by James V in 1532. In Parliament Square is Edinburgh's oldest statue, of Charles II, completed in 1685.
PRINCES STREET The principal thoroughfare; completed in 1805, it marks the beginning of the new town. One side is open to the castle and Princes Street Gardens, where the Scott Monument is.
REGIMENTAL MUSEUM OF THE ROYAL SCOTS The British army's oldest and most senior infantry regiment displays its collection of campaign medals and decorations, uniforms, equipment, silver, prints and portraits in Edinburgh Castle.
ROYAL COLLEGE OF SURGEONS OF EDINBURGH The building was erected in 1832 to designs by Playfair. Collections in the museum have the history of surgery and pathology as their theme, and can be viewed by appointment.
ROYAL SCOTTISH ACADEMY The Scottish counterpart of the Royal Academy of Arts in London. It was founded by a group of artists in 1826, received a royal charter in 1838 and has held annual summer exhibitions of works by living artists ever since. During the Edinburgh Festival special exhibitions of works by masters from all over the world take place. (By appointment.)
ROYAL SCOTTISH MUSEUM In the natural history section is material collected by early explorers. The geology section has fossil and mineral collections, and in the department devoted to technology are

THE GUTENBERG BIBLE
Until the 15th century the need to copy books by hand was a barrier to the rapid spread of knowledge; but with the invention of individually cast metal types by Johann Gutenberg of Mainz, Europe entered the modern age. The Gutenberg or Mazarine Bible, produced about 1456, was the first substantial work to be printed from such types. (National Library of Scotland)

scale models which can be operated by visitors, exhibits devoted to shipping, navigation and mining, and much historical material. There is a fine collection of prehistoric Japanese pottery, and African, Egyptian and ancient American works. (See pp. 184–5.)
SCOTTISH NATIONAL GALLERY OF MODERN ART Inverleith House, in Belford Road, contains the 20th-century collection of the National Galleries of Scotland. There are paintings, sculptures, drawings and prints, including works by Picasso, Matisse and Giacometti.
SCOTTISH NATIONAL PORTRAIT GALLERY A collection of over 2000 portraits of the main figures in Scottish history since the mid-16th century. Best represented are Mary, Queen of Scots, Sir Walter Scott and Robert Burns. The paintings include works by Lely, Reynolds and Gainsborough.
SCOTTISH UNITED SERVICES MUSEUM The only museum in the United Kingdom dealing with all three services at all periods of their history. The displays of uniforms, head-dresses, arms and equipment, medals, portraits, engravings and prints, housed in the museum, illustrate the history of the armed forces in Scotland. There is also an extensive library on military affairs.
SCOTT MONUMENT A memorial to Sir Walter Scott, it was completed in 1844 to the design of George Meikle Kemp. This neo-Gothic edifice has a statue of Scott under a canopy of arches and tiers, with niches in which are 64 statuettes of characters from Scott's novels. The monument is 200 ft high.
WHITE HART INN Frequented by Burns and Wordsworth. In Tanners Close in the nearby West Port lived Burke and Hare, the murderers hanged in 1829, who sold the bodies of their victims for surgery.

ROYAL EDINBURGH

Edinburgh has long been the capital of Scotland. By the reign of Malcolm Canmore (1057–93) the castle included the royal palace where the Celtic and Stuart kings often resided. About 1500 James IV began the Palace of Holyroodhouse, beside the abbey founded by David I. Linking castle and palace is the Royal Mile, a series of narrow streets —the centre of Edinburgh life until the elegant New Town was built in the 18th century. The Scottish Regalia is kept in the castle.

PALACE OF HOLYROODHOUSE *These magnificent 20th-century wrought-iron gates lead to the official residence in Scotland of the reigning monarch.*

SCOTTISH REGALIA *The crown, of Scottish gold, was remodelled for James V in 1540. The sword of state, from Italy, was given by Pope Julius II to James IV.*

NATIONAL MUSEUM OF ANTIQUITIES

Situated in the same building as the Scottish National Portrait Gallery, the National Museum of Antiquities contains the most comprehensive collection in existence of the history and everyday life of Scotland from the Stone Age. Launched in 1781 by the Society of Antiquaries of Scotland, the collection at first set out to attract antiquities from all over the world but in time it became progressively more specialised, concentrating on exhibits to illustrate the story of Scotland and her people.

PAIR OF SCOTTISH BELT-PISTOLS *King Louis XIII (1601–43) may be regarded as the first gun-collector, in the modern sense of the term. At the age of 12 he owned 50 guns, and by the time he died many hundreds, both ancient and modern. The collection was catalogued, and pieces from it can still be identified. Among them is this pair of pistols; they may have been presented to* *Louis by his Scots Guard. Apart from the silver tubes under the barrels for the missing ramrods, and the iron working parts, they are made entirely of brass, engraved with scrolling foliage and originally gilt. The barrels are engraved with the date 1611, the French royal Arms, the inscription* LOUIS XIII ROY DE FRAC, *and a maker's mark ascribed to James Low of Dundee.*

THE TORRS 'CHAMFREIN' *Though the parts of this piece are certainly ancient and genuine relics of the Iron Age, its shape is a puzzle and it must have been wrongly reconstructed when found in 1829. Recent study shows it to be a pony-cap with earholes, not a mask or chamfrein with eyeholes. When it was reconstructed the horns were attached to the main section front to back.*

ST NINIAN'S ISLE TREASURE: HEMISPHERICAL BOWL *In 1958 a hoard of treasure was discovered below the nave of a ruined medieval church on St Ninian's Island in the Shetlands. As well as a hanging bowl, in many ways similar to those found in earlier Anglo-Saxon graves, brooches, shallow bowls, cone-shaped objects, chapes, a sword pommel, and a spoon and pricker were among the 28 silver and silver-gilt objects discovered. They were buried late in the 8th century, probably in order to avoid the Viking raids on the islands. It is thought that most of the pieces were made in Scotland.*

ROYAL SCOTTISH MUSEUM

Situated in Chambers Street, immediately to the west of the Old College of the University of Edinburgh, the Royal Scottish Museum, founded in mid-19th century, combines collections of exhibits which reflect human endeavour not only in Scotland, but in other countries. Though rich in Scottish examples from many fields, it is representative of all the world. It is the largest comprehensive museum of science and art (excluding painting) in the British Isles.

AN EMPEROR'S SUGAR BASIN *The richness and magnificence of the French Empire style is well illustrated by this silver-gilt basin which forms part of an elaborate tea service made for Napoleon I in 1810. The service was brought to Scotland in 1830 by the 10th Duke of Hamilton, a fervent admirer of Napoleon, and is now divided between the Royal Scottish Museum and the Louvre.*

MEISSEN LION *In the 1730's Meissen porcelain was already of a high quality—as shown by this model of a lion. Taken from a model by Kirchner about 1732, it was probably made for the Japanese Palace in Dresden of the Elector Frederick I of Saxony (1694–1733).*

SWORD OF BATTLE ABBEY *Like most medieval swords, the Battle Abbey sword is a straight, two-edged weapon with a simple cross guard and a shaped knob—the pommel—at the top to counter-balance the blade. Made between 1417 and 1434 the steel pommel and cross are overlaid with silver which was originally gilt, and engraved with Gothic foliage. The pommel is engraved with the Arms of Battle Abbey in E. Sussex, and with the letters 't.m.', the initials of Thomas de Lodelowe, Abbot of Battle. The abbey's arms include a sword to symbolise the right of administration of justice granted by William the Conqueror.*

EMBROIDERED BOX *This box, made about 1670, with its fine silk thread laid in graded colours with animals and floral motifs worked in satin-stitch, is typical of the needlework boxes in which young English ladies kept their small personal belongings; it is lined with silk. The ladies did their own embroidery and, having first practised the craft on samplers and, perhaps, on embroidered pictures, they worked the strips and panels for their boxes. These were then assembled by a cabinet-maker who added handles, and fitted secret drawers for jewellery, and mirrors. The edges of the boxes were often trimmed with silver braid.*

MOSQUE LAMP *An enamelled mosque lamp dating from about 1340, containing an oil vessel; such lamps were suspended by chains from the ceilings of Egyptian mosques. Most were inscribed with names and titles of the Mameluke Sultans of Egypt or their officers and until about 1400 were made in Syria. The museum also contains a small but important collection of antiquities from Ancient Egypt.*

BLACKWORK PANEL *This panel dates from the 16th century, when blackwork was used mainly as a decoration on undergarments, sleeves and cuffs, and head-dresses of both men and women. Such examples of its use appear in portraits by Holbein. The formal pattern is made up of running stitches worked entirely by the thread of the linen. The flowing black outline is then filled in with various stitches.*

GREAT HELM OF SIR RICHARD PEMBRIDGE *This great helm made about 1360 for Sir Richard Pembridge, who fought beside the Black Prince in France, is constructed from three riveted plates with rounded and oblique surfaces to deflect and resist sword and lance thrusts. It is made of steel so hard that a modern pen-knife cannot scratch its surface, and was worn over a smaller helmet during battle.*

NATIONAL GALLERY OF SCOTLAND

The National Gallery of Scotland was designed in the Grecian style and opened to the public in 1859. It contains one of the most exquisite collections of paintings in the world. It boasts some of the most important and intriguing groups of works by masters such as Raphael, Titian, Rembrandt, Gainsborough, Poussin, Degas and Cézanne as well as a section devoted to Scottish artists.

WATTEAU: FÊTES VÉNITIENNES *The 18th century in France produced two great masters of painting, Watteau and Chardin. Their worlds were poles apart. Chardin's scenes come from the nursery and kitchen: Watteau created a make-believe world of gallants and their ladies dancing, play-acting or love-making in enchanted gardens. There is in his art, as well as precise drawing, keen observation and ravishing colour, a magical elusive mood.*

DEGAS: DIEGO MARTELLI *The portrait of Martelli, a Florentine art critic, seen in his study, carpet-slippered, in his shirt-sleeves and amid a confusion of papers, gave Degas the chance to display his psychological penetration of the sitter's character and surroundings and for his superb draughtsmanship and gift for colour. Although Degas helped to organise the first Impressionist exhibition in 1874, and consistently exhibited with Impressionists, he was not really one of them. He hated the word 'Impressionist' and tried to prevent its adoption by the group. But he approved of their sense of immediacy and their choice of subjects from everyday life.*

TITIAN: THE THREE AGES OF MAN *The cornerstone of Venetian art was colour and the artist's gift, which is particularly noticeable in Titian's paintings, to make his work come alive by his superb handling of oil paint. 'The Three Ages of Man' belongs to Titian's early period. Its composition is simple and uncomplicated:* immature childhood is represented by the three putti, old age by the man with the skulls in the background and the earthly paradise of requited love by the boy and the girl. The radiant sensuousness of the glowing flesh tints reveals the maturing Titian's master touch.

GAINSBOROUGH: THE HONOURABLE MRS
GRAHAM *Gainsborough did not belong, as did Sir
Joshua Reynolds, his contemporary and fellow society
portrait painter, to the world of his fashionable sitters.
His friends were musicians, actors and painters. But
he had to paint society ladies for a living. Mrs Graham* *was one, and the artist reacted emotionally to her
beauty. His brushwork in the scintillating carmine
skirt is impassioned and looks forward to Renoir.
French too, is the Watteau-like setting of the figure
in a landscape, a feature of his late portraits done in
London after he had left Bath.*

Joseph Lister

JOSEPH LISTER, THE MAN WHO MADE SURGERY SAFE

Joseph Lister came from a gentle but industrious background, and his father's lively scientific interests led him to delight in experiments—at first into the causes of inflammation, which often led to gangrene. 'Having got a frog from Duddingston Loch I proceeded last night to the investigation, and a most glorious night I had of it', wrote Lister from his house at 11 Rutland Street, Edinburgh. The Infirmary where he worked is now the geological department of Edinburgh University. Lister acted on the results of his experiments when he moved to Glasgow as Professor in 1860, insisting on cleanliness and the dressing of wounds with carbolic acid gauzes; as a result, his wards remained entirely free of hospital diseases, when others were frequently closed because of gangrène. Relics of this period in his life may be seen at Glasgow University. In 1877 he moved to London and a memorial bust in Portland Place, near his house in 12 Park Crescent, recalls the man who brought about an incalculable saving of lives and suffering.

PRESCRIPTION BOOK *written up by Lister when Professor at the Glasgow Royal Infirmary. The death-rate in unhealthy wards was drastically reduced by his Antiseptic System. (Wellcome Institute, London)*

LORD LISTER *with his staff in the Victoria Male Casualty Ward, King's College Hospital, in 1891. When he first came to London his ideas were cautiously received, but his revolutionary methods were successful.*

CARBOLIC ACID *was the liquid chosen by Lister as an antiseptic in surgery, after reading that it had been used to purify sewage in Carlisle. This liquid, used on gauze to cover wounds after an operation, prevented putrefaction and gangrene.* (Glasgow University Museum)

LADY LISTER *at the time of her marriage in 1856. She was the daughter of Lister's chief in Edinburgh, Professor Syme, and was of great practical help to her husband. Nearly all his early notebooks of experiments are in her handwriting.*

SURGICAL INSTRUMENTS *used by Lister, a great practical surgeon. The first man to dare to open the abdominal cavity, he occupied the Chair of Clinical Surgery at King's College, London, for 15 years.* (Glasgow University and Wellcome Institute)

CARBOLIC SPRAY *introduced by Lister to purify the air, this one operated by steam.*

SPENCER-WELLS, *a well-known surgeon of the 1880's, performing an operation under antiseptic conditions using Lister's spray.* (Wellcome Institute)

LISTER'S MEDICINE CHEST AND MICROSCOPE *The companions of 'his faultless patience, his unyielding will, beautiful gentleness and splendid skill'.* (Royal College of Surgeons, Edinburgh and London)

QUEEN VICTORIA'S DEDICATION *on the flysheet of her book on Balmoral, presented to Lister after his success in lancing an abcess in her armpit.* (Private collection)

189

EDZELL CASTLE

The intricate and formal garden (left) is thought to be the oldest Renaissance garden in the British Isles, laid out in 1604 by Lord Edzell. Three sides of the garden are enclosed by the original sandstone walls; the fourth by the castle. Mary, Queen of Scots often stayed in Stirling Tower (right) on visits to Edzell.

Edington *Wilts.* 540Ef
CHURCH OF SS MARY, KATHARINE AND ALL SAINTS A 14th-century monastic church, cruciform in plan with fairly low embattled central tower, and battlements all round. The monastery was founded by William of Edington in 1358, and the church consecrated three years later. Font cover, pulpit and altar rails are early 17th century. There are monuments from the 15th century onwards, including a fine one of *c.* 1630 with recumbent effigies, children and angels, and another of *c.* 1817 by Sir Francis Chantry. The nave has a 17th-century panelled plaster ceiling.

Edin's Hall *Borders* 562Ee
A complex and unusual group of monuments. The fort, which is the earliest feature, does not crest the hill, Cockburn Law, but is on its sloping north-east side. It is defended by two banks with external ditches and has an entrance at the west end.

The broch is large and circular, some 55 ft in diameter, with 17 ft thick walls, within which are groups of chambers and guard-rooms.

The settlement is sited in the western half of the fort and extends in part over the original defences, which here it has virtually levelled. It consists of many stone foundations of circular huts and the walling of minor enclosures.

The time covered by the three settlements extends from the later Iron Age to the end of the Romano-British period. (By appointment.)

Edlesborough *Bucks.* 547Hd
CHURCH OF ST MARY Standing isolated on a mound, this large church is 13th century in its oldest part, was added to in the two following centuries and restored in Victorian times. It has fine Gothic woodwork: a delicate Perpendicular pulpit with tester, fine rood screen and carved misericords on the stalls. The Victorian contributions include stained glass by Warde & Hughes, and Kempe, and painting in the nave. There are also good brasses dating from 1395 to 1540.

Edmondthorpe *Leics.* 553Gc
CHURCH OF ST MICHAEL A Decorated church with a 13th-century west tower that was finished in the 15th century, when the clerestory was added to the building. Inside are several monuments of the 17th and 18th centuries.

Edzell Castle *Tayside* 566Fc
Ruins of a 16th-century castle. The walled Renaissance garden was laid out in 1604; its walls have carvings of the 'Cardinal Virtues', the 'Liberal Arts' and the 'Planetary Deities'.

Eggardon *Dorset* 540Cc
This fine Iron Age hill-fort has three banks with intermediate ditches and additional defences at the east and north-west entrances. The visible hollows in the 20 acre internal area are grain storage-pits. Also within the defences are two Bronze Age round barrows.

Egilsay (Isle of) *Orkney* 569Hg
The ruined 'Irish' round tower is incorporated in the church where St Magnus was murdered, *c.* 1115. Both tower and church date from the early 12th century. The tower, now roofless and 48 ft high, was probably at least 60 ft high when first built.

Egleton *Leics.* 553Gb
CHURCH OF ST EDMUND The chief interest of this mainly Norman church is the richly carved south doorway and west tower.

Egmanton *Notts.* 552Fe
CHURCH OF ST MARY One of the best churches in which to see the work of Sir Ninian Comper, who reconstructed the rood screen and designed the pulpit and organ case for the Duke of Newcastle, *c.* 1898. There is Norman architecture in the nave, but the glass in the east window is also by Comper.

Eildon Hills North *Borders* 562Dd
HILL-FORT AND SIGNAL-STATION This great Iron Age fort shows evidence of three structural periods. It began with the building of a rampart to enclose the top of the hill, a structure which is now almost obliterated. It was followed by a new work which included the first area and additional ground on the north and north-east slopes of the hill. Finally, two strong ramparts were thrown round the hill to enclose a 40-acre area. This was the chief settlement of the Selgovae tribe. It appears to have been evacuated in AD 79 when the Romans occupied this area and built their fort at Newstead close to the foot of the hill. A small signal-station, used by the Roman garrison, was erected close to the top of the hill, and the shallow circular ditch,

broken by a causeway, which lies just to the west of the hill-top, is the last trace of it.

Eilean Donan Castle *Highland*   *565Gf*
Built in 1220 by Alexander II of Scotland, on an islet where Lochs Duich, Alsh and Long meet, to ward off Danish raiders; it later passed to the Clan Mackenzie (Earls of Seaforth). In 1719 it was held by Spanish Jacobite troops and bombarded by the *Worcester*, an English warship. It remained a ruin for 200 years before being rebuilt.

Elford *Staffs.*   *552Db*
CHURCH OF ST PETER There is a 16th-century tower, but the rest is mostly a restoration by Anthony Salvin, *c.* 1848, and G. E. Street, *c.* 1870. The church is full of interesting monuments, many with effigies; outstanding is the mid-15th-century figure of a boy holding a tennis ball, pointing to his head to indicate where the ball had struck and killed him. There is also good ironwork on the door to be seen, and interesting carved work in the corbels and capitals.

Elgin *Grampian*   *566Dg*
ANDERSON'S INSTITUTION Founded in 1831 by Lt.-Gen. Anderson as the Elgin Institute for Support of Old Age and Education of Youth. Designed by Archibald Simpson of Aberdeen in the Greek Revival style with recessed two-column Ionic portico surmounted by a tall dome dominating the north front. A six-column Doric portico adds interest to the west elevation.
CATHEDRAL Elgin Cathedral, now in ruins, belongs mainly to the 13th century, although the Diocese of Moray had been founded in 1107. The oldest existing fragments of the building, the choir and transepts, are usually dated after 1224, although their style suggests an earlier period. The presbytery has a great eastern façade composed of rows of lancet windows similar to buildings in England of *c.* 1240–50, although it is usually dated after a great fire of 1270. On the north side is an octagonal chapter house, built in the 13th century but re-roofed and repaired after a further great fire in 1390. The See was dissolved in 1560 and the cathedral no longer required. The lead was stripped from the roof in 1567 and gradual ruination followed. A monument to the Duchess of Gordon survives; the original design by Peter Scheemakers is in the Victoria and Albert Museum.
GRAY'S HOSPITAL Occupying a superb position at the west end of the High Street, this hospital, endowed by Dr Alexander Gray in 1815, was designed by James Gillespie Graham of Edinburgh. A central cupola with octagonal base surmounts a three-storied building with impressive four-column portico.
NO. 7 HIGH STREET Dated 1694, this three-storey house with dormers, crow-stepped gables and stone slated roof was from 1702 to 1722 the home of William Duff of Dipple and Braco, Bankers. The ground floor has an arcade or *piazza* to the street, once a feature of the Elgin street scene.

Elie *Fife*   *562Dg*
A spacious burgh with attractive kirk of 1726 on the north side of the High Street. Houses in the Scottish native tradition front South Street, some with carved doorpieces and pediments. The Castle, a fine L-plan house of the 17th century in South Street, is the most notable building in the burgh.

Elkstone *Glos.*   *546Cd*
CHURCH OF ST JOHN THE EVANGELIST A Norman church, the Perpendicular west tower with musician gargoyles. Over the south doorway is a sculpture showing Christ in Glory and the four evangelists surrounded by rows of grotesque carvings. There is a dove-cote over the chancel. Inside is a fine Perpendicular font.

Elmley Castle *Heref. & Worcs.*   *546Ce*
CHURCH OF ST MARY At the end of a pretty street, beneath Bredon Hill. Here one can see the change in English sculpture during the 17th century. An early work of the century in alabaster, still in the medieval tradition, with recumbent effigies, heraldry, weepers and so on, faces a large marble creation by William Stanton. This has columns, pediment, reclining figure, and standing angels with gilded wings, and is of 1700. There is a 400-year-old sundial in the churchyard.

Elmore Court *Glos.*   *546Bd*
A country mansion with Elizabethan, Stuart and Georgian features. It contains collections of period furniture and tapestries, and a selection of historical manuscripts; it has a 16th-century staircase and fine chimney-pieces. (By appointment.)

Elmswell *Suffolk*   *548Cf*
CHURCH OF ST JOHN The west tower has flint-work decoration. The chancel was restored in the late 19th century. There is a carved font, and a monument to Sir Robert Gardener, Chief Justice of Ireland, ascribed to Maximilian Colt (1619).

ELGIN CATHEDRAL

The Diocese of Moray was founded in 1107 when the Scottish Church was reorganised under Alexander I, but the cathedral at Elgin was not established until 1224. The See was dissolved in 1560 and the buildings gradually disintegrated after 1567 when the lead was stripped from the roof. The stones of the cathedral were used for local building until preservation measures were taken in the 19th century. Many of the Bishops of Moray were employed in the royal service. Bishop Richard (1187–1207) was chaplain to William the Lion, who was one of Elgin's great benefactors. David Murray (1299–1325) was an ardent opponent of Edward I; in 1304 he preached, as though for a crusade, that those who supported Robert the Bruce would acquire as much merit 'as if they had set out from the Holy Land against the Pagans and Saracens'.

ELY CATHEDRAL

ELY CATHEDRAL *Originally the monastery and town of Ely were situated on an island in the midst of an immense expanse of marshy Fenland; even today, Ely Cathedral rises clear of the surrounding countryside—the now-drained Fen. The original religious community was founded in 673 by St Etheldreda. The present* *building dates from 1083. There are two heavily carved but very mutilated chantry chapels at the east end of the church. One was built by Bishop Alcock who died in 1501; and the other, by Bishop West who died in 1534, is particularly interesting for its early use of Renaissance motifs.*

Elsdon *Northld.* 562Fb
CHURCH OF ST CUTHBERT A mainly 14th-century church. Inside is a Roman tombstone, brought from a Roman fort at High Rochester.

Elsing *Norfolk* 554Cc
CHURCH OF ST MARY The church was built by Sir Hugh Hastings, *c.* 1330, with a battlemented west tower. The nave has no aisles, but is nearly 40 ft wide. The octagonal font has a good canopied cover, with some original colouring. Figures in stained glass date from the 14th century. A magnificent brass to the founder, who died in 1347, shows small representations of some of his relatives, including Edward III, on either side of the armoured figure.

Elstow *Beds.* 547He
Famous principally for its associations with John Bunyan, who was born there in 1628. His cottage home has, however, since been demolished. The Moot Hall, now a museum, is a splendid red-bricked half-timbered 16th-century building that was once a meeting-place for Bunyan's followers. The ground floor was originally used for shops and stalls.

William the Conqueror's niece founded a nunnery at Elstow which celebrated a three-day fair every year. This involved considerable merrymaking among trenchermen and became notorious throughout the country; Bunyan used it in *The Pilgrim's Progress* as the model for his 'Vanity Fair', which Thackeray used as the title of a novel nearly 200 years later.

CHURCH OF SS MARY AND HELEN The present church occupies the nave of a Norman monastic church built *c.* 1100 and extended westwards in the 13th century. The eastern part of the church was demolished after the Dissolution, but the Norman nave arcades and north door remain. Extensive restoration work was carried out in the late 19th century. The church has a detached tower to the north-west and contains a 16th-century monument with effigies and a brass of a 16th-century Abbess. John Bunyan was baptised here.

To the south of the church are the remains of Elstow Place, a 17th-century house incorporating part of the 14th-century refectory and cloister. Its 18th-century porch is attributed to Inigo Jones.

Elton Hall *Cambs.* 547Hg
The 15th-century gate-house and vaulted crypt are all that remain of a house destroyed during the Commonwealth period. The present Jacobean house was built by Sir Thomas Proby in 1662–89, and his descendants still live there; it has 18th-century alterations and additions. There is a fine library containing early English Bibles and prayer books, including Henry VIII's prayer book with his signature and that of Mary Tudor. There is also a collection of pictures including works by Constable, Reynolds and Frans Hals.

SOUTH TRANSEPT *The magnificent painted roof.*

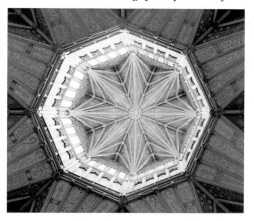

LANTERN *Inside the unique octagonal lantern tower, built to replace the Norman crossing tower that collapsed in 1322.*

NAVE *The majestic Norman nave, 208 ft long; its ceiling was painted by le Strange and Gambier-Parry in the 19th century.*

Ely *Cambs.* 548*Ag*

Ely, the Cathedral City of the Fens where Hereward the Wake, 'The Last of the English', held out against William the Conqueror, has some good domestic buildings. They include the half-timbered St Mary's Vicarage, also known as Cromwell House, where Oliver Cromwell lived for 11 years from 1636; and a charming jumble of small cottages on Waterside, the most picturesque street in the town. The prior's house, now part of the King's School, has 14th- and 15th-century work with some large windows. The Treasury, or Audit Chamber, was added in the 14th century. Near by is Prior Crauden's Chapel, a classic example of the Decorated style, built *c*. 1325.

BISHOP ALCOCK'S PALACE Built in the late 15th century, of which the east tower and parts of the west tower remain.

BISHOP'S HOUSE Built into the former great hall of the monastery, which has a 13th-century vaulted undercroft with 13th-century buttresses outside. It was partly rebuilt in the 18th century.

CATHEDRAL The present cathedral was begun in 1083. The choir was rebuilt in the 13th century to provide a more adequate setting for St Ethel-dreda's shrine, and in the 14th century a very elaborate Lady Chapel was added to the north transept. In 1322 the Norman crossing tower collapsed, and was replaced by a larger, octagonal tower surmounted by a timber vault carrying an octagonal lantern. This crossing tower is unique in medieval English architecture and is the cathedral's most characteristic feature. The 11th- and 12th-century decoration of the south-west transept is the cathedral's finest carving. Two doorways of *c*. 1130 survive—originally they opened into the cloister of which little remains—and the quality of the carving and its excellent state of preservation place them among the most important survivals of Norman architecture.

CHANTRY The Chantry lies on the north side of Palace Green, with a high brick front wall incorporating an 18th-century wrought-iron gate. The front dates from Charles II's reign; the rear from about 40 years later. Interior features are a rococo ceiling (18th century), made of papier-mâché, and an Ionic chimney-piece of stripped pine.

ELY PORTA The great south gate-house, which was begun in 1397, is unusually broad with square rooms on either side of the gateway and square angled turrets. The long 14th-century barn is now the dining-hall of the King's School. Powchers Hall has an early 16th-century third storey; Walsingham House, built for Alan of Walsingham in 1335, has a late 12th-century Norman doorway, and the Black Hostelry opposite, once a hostel for visiting Benedictine monks, is partly mid-13th century. The rest of the cathedral precinct includes the almonry with a vaulted 12th-century undercroft and the sacristy which was once Alan of Walsingham's offices.

KING'S SCHOOL School house has a splendid late Norman doorway in the part known as the Storehouse. There are flat 12th-century buttresses on the street front.

Empingham *Leics.* 553Gb
CHURCH OF ST PETER A church of grand proportions, it has a west tower with crocketed spire, west front of notable 14th-century work, and a mainly Early English interior, with the arcades and south transept retaining traces of mural paintings. There are fragments of early stained glass.

Enfield *Greater London* 547Jc
CHURCH OF ST ANDREW Parish church dating from the 13th century; St Andrew's was later enlarged with a 14th-century nave, choir and (probably) west tower. Good monuments include a 15th-century brass with canopy and a standing monument to a Lord Mayor of London (*d.* 1646).
FORTY HALL Built in 1629-32 for Sir Nicholas Raynton, Lord Mayor of London, the Hall has a courtyard archway attributed to Inigo Jones The interior contains 17th-century strapwork ceilings, a carved screen, and moulded medallions of 1787. On permanent display are 17th- and 18th-century paintings, water-colours, pottery and furniture, and there are some furnishings on loan from the Victoria and Albert Museum. There are frequent temporary exhibitions.

Enstone *Oxon.* 546Ed
HOAR STONE This much-denuded Neolithic long barrow has lost virtually all its mound, so that the roughly rectangular megalithic chamber at the east end stands exposed. Three of its sides are still

extant, and fallen stones close by doubtless comprise the capstone and additional parts of the chamber and its entrance structure.

Epworth *Humberside* 552Fg
OLD RECTORY John Wesley (1703-91), the founder of Methodism, and his younger brother Charles, the hymn writer, were born here while their father was Rector of Epworth. Early in 1709 the rectory was burnt down by a mob of people opposed to their father's political views; the house was rebuilt later that year.

Erddig *Clwyd* 551Jd
Built in the late 1600s with additions in the succeeding century, the house retains a lot of its original furniture. A feature is the series of paintings of household servants commissioned by their employers – coachboy, blacksmith, gardener, gamekeeper and others. The outbuildings – laundry, bakehouse, sawmill, smithy – also have their original equipment, which is in working order. The garden has been restored to its 18th-century design, to include kinds of fruit trees grown in it at the time, such as Orange Apricock and Spanish Musk Pare.

Erith *Greater London* 548Ab
ERITH LIBRARY There is an archaeology exhibition and museum study centre.

Erwarton Hall *Suffolk* 548De
Much of the present Hall dates from 1858, when it was rebuilt incorporating features of Sir Philip Parker's house of 1570. The red-brick gatehouse, however, with its rounded arch, buttresses and pinnacles, belongs to a still earlier house of 1549. There is a fine Jacobean staircase, overmantel and

ETON COLLEGE

Eton College is the largest of the ancient English public schools. It was founded by Henry VI in 1440 as a collegiate church with a school and almshouse attached. Henry had ambitious plans, but was deposed in 1461. Under his successor, Edward IV, the college narrowly escaped annexation to St George's Chapel, Windsor Castle, but was firmly established by the reign of Henry VIII. The left-hand picture shows School

Yard looking east, with College Hall, one of the Founder's few surviving buildings, in the right background. In the centre is his statue. College Chapel is no more than the choir of the cathedral-sized church as conceived, and the right-hand picture is of one of its wall-paintings of miracles and legends of Our Lady. Dating from 1479-88, they are the finest of their kind surviving in England, and show strong Flemish influence.

pargeted ceiling. Anne Boleyn often visited the ~~ouse~~, and it is said that her heart was secretly ~~b ried~~ in the nearby church. A heart-shaped casket d ~~c overed~~ in 1836 helps to confirm the story. (By a ~~p intment~~.)

~~E comb~~ *Durham* 558Cf
~~CH URCH OF ST JOHN THE EVANGELIST~~ One of the ~~m st~~ striking features of Escomb church is the ~~qu lity~~ of the masonry—squared ashlar, varying ~~sl htly~~ in size, laid in regular courses—which is ~~Ro man~~ in origin. This Saxon church, which is ~~one~~ of the most important survivals of early ~~Ch ristian~~ architecture in Britain, consists of a nave ~~and~~ small chancel separated by an arch with ~~car efully~~ fitted Saxon long-and-short work on the ~~side~~ supports. Some of the original windows, small ~~wit h large~~ embrasures inside, can still be seen.

~~E crick~~ *N. Yorks.* 558Eb
~~CH URCH OF ST HELEN~~ A mid-Victorian Gothic ~~re vival~~ church by F. C. Penrose, who held the ~~app ointment~~ of Surveyor to St Paul's Cathedral. ~~Th ere~~ are monuments sculpted by Matthew Cotes ~~W yatt~~ and by Prince Victor of Hohenlohe-~~La ngenburg~~, as well as one of a medieval knight.

~~Es her~~ *Surrey* 542Af
~~CH URCH OF ST GEORGE~~ A delightful 16th-century ~~ch urch~~, with additions of the 18th and 19th ~~ce nturies~~, such as the brick transept and upper west ~~ga llery~~. A marble monument commemorates ~~Pr incess~~ Charlotte of Wales (George IV's daugh-~~te r~~), who died at nearby Claremont in 1817.

~~E ssendine~~ *Leics.* 553Gb
~~CHURCH OF ST MARY~~ A small church, largely ~~N orman~~, consisting of nave and chancel. Once the ~~ch apel~~ of the adjoining castle, which has disap-~~p eared~~, it has been restored and rebuilt. The south ~~d oorway~~ has a fine carving of Christ.

Etchingham *E. Sussex* 542De
CHURCH OF SS MARY AND NICHOLAS A former collegiate church, a good example of the Decorated style, built by Sir William de Echyngham, who died in 1389 and is buried here. The church has a tall central tower, and inside the stalls have interesting misericords. Original tiles and fragments of stained glass remain, but the east window is of 1857, by J. Clayton. There are brasses of the 15th century to the Echyngham family.

Eton College *Berks.* 547Hb
Eton was founded in 1440 by Henry VI as a collegiate church, with a grammar school and almshouse attached. Only College Hall and Kitchen, in use by 1450, survive as designed. College Chapel is the choir of the Founder's church as originally conceived, and also served Eton parish until 1852. The Founder intended it to be second only to Canterbury as a place of pilgrimage and devotion to Our Lady, to whom he dedicated his college. But the Wars of the Roses cut short Henry's plans. In School Yard (the outer quadrangle), Long Chamber (originally the scholars' dormitory), Lower School and the north range were probably completed in the late 15th century. The lower storeys of the North and East Cloisters beyond are also 15th century. The west range of the Cloisters with the great gate-house, Lupton's Tower, was added in the early 16th century, and Upper School was built *c.* 1690.

Ettington Park *Warks.* 546Ee
CHURCH OF ST NICHOLAS In the ruined church is a good example of the work of the London sculptor John Francis Moore. It is the monument to Earl Ferrers, *c.* 1775, and admirably illustrates Moore's love of coloured marbles. (By appointment.)

TOMB OF ALICE DE LA POLE

In 1437 William de la Pole, Duke of Suffolk, and his wife, Alice, founded an almshouse near the Perpendicular church at Ewelme. In the church is Alice's tomb, with a splendid alabaster effigy. Alice, who died in 1475, was the daughter of Thomas Chaucer, lord of Ewelme Manor, and granddaughter of Geoffrey Chaucer the poet. (Church of St Mary the Virgin, Ewelme)

Euston *Suffolk* 548Cg
CHURCH OF ST GENEVIEVE The church was rebuilt in 1676, on the foundations of an earlier building, by an unknown architect. There is a high-quality carved wood pulpit and reredos, attributed by some to Grinling Gibbons.

Evesham *Heref. & Worcs.* 546De
ABBEY Benedictine abbey of pre-Conquest foundation, though little now remains above ground-level of the 11th-century and later buildings. The most prominent remaining part is the early 16th-century bell-tower.
ALMONRY MUSEUM A 14th-century half-timbered building with Roman, Saxon and medieval items.

Ewelme *Oxon.* 546Fc
CHURCH OF ST MARY THE VIRGIN The well-preserved Perpendicular church was built (apart from the 14th-century tower) to a single design, with the attached almshouse cloister and school, by Alice de la Pole, Duchess of Suffolk (*d.* 1475), and her husband. She was the granddaughter of Geoffrey Chaucer, the poet. The Chapel of St John contains her magnificent alabaster tomb, with her two effigies on top and below, the first as in life, the second as a corpse. Next to it is that of her father, Thomas Chaucer, Lord of the Manor of Ewelme, Constable of Wallingford Castle, and Speaker of the House of Commons, who fought at Agincourt, and of her mother; it is decorated with fine brasses and enamelled coats of arms. The timber ceiling of the chapel with its carved angels, the rood screen and the elaborate 15th-century font cover and counter-weight are all notable features of the church.
GRAMMAR SCHOOL AND ALMSHOUSE The original buildings of the pre-Reformation almshouse survive. The almshouse is built around a small courtyard at the west end of the church. It was founded in 1437 by William, Duke of Suffolk, and his wife Alice for two chaplains and 13 poor men. Originally one chaplain was to be Master of the almshouse, the other a Grammar Master of the school alongside it. There is now no Grammar Master, and in 1605 the mastership of the almshouse was combined with the Regius Professorship of Medicine at the University of Oxford. The almshouse still functions and the school survives near by.

Ewenny Priory *Mid Glam.* 545Hb

A monastery with serious military defences. The priory was established in 1141 as a cell of the Benedictine abbey at Gloucester. The walls are mostly 13th century, but there is evidence that they replaced earlier defences. The nave of the mid-12th-century church is still used for services, but the transept and chancel have been cleared for use as a museum. The crude vault of the chancel, which was heightened at an early date and lengthened, is the best Norman work in the county. There are a number of medieval sepulchral slabs with Norman French inscriptions cut in Lombardic characters. Part of the convent building which stood to the south is incorporated in a mansion, whose private grounds extend to the south walls of the church.

Ewerby *Lincs.* 553Hd

CHURCH OF ST ANDREW A fine example of Decorated Gothic architecture, the church has a west tower and an impressive broach spire. The font, which is contemporary with the church, incorporates Norman work. There are some good screens and a late 14th-century effigy in the north aisle.

Ewloe Castle *Clwyd* 551He

This small castle with a D-shaped tower is a well-preserved example of a Welsh castle built before Edward I's conquest at the end of the 13th century.

Exeter *Devon* 539Hd

The Roman town founded in AD 50–55 as the fortress of the Second Augustan Legion became in about AD 80 the centre of government and the capital of the West Saxon kingdom. The Danes sacked the city in 1003. After the Norman invasion, Exeter was a centre of West Country resistance, but William secured its submission in 1068. A Parliament was held at Exeter in 1286. The impostor Perkin Warbeck led 6000 rebels against the city in 1497, but was forced to withdraw. The Devon sea captains—Drake, Frobisher, Hawkins, Gilbert, Raleigh, Carey—are claimed to have frequented Mol's Coffee House in the Close.

Many Exeter men joined in the Duke of Monmouth's rebellion against James II: Chief Justice Jeffreys held one of his 'Bloody Assizes' in the city, and 14 rebels were ordered to be hanged.

Near the town centre is a small port, to which sea-going ships of up to 300 tons have access by means of a 5½-mile canal. The canal became necessary after Isabel, Countess of Devon, built a weir across the R. Exe in Henry III's reign. The original lock canal, the oldest in the country, was cut in 1564–6.

CATHEDRAL Exeter Cathedral, situated in the centre of the city, was established as a cathedral church in 1050. The two large transept towers are the main remnants of the Norman church; the position of the towers is unusual for the period, and the plan may have come from the Continent. The outer nave walls appear to be Norman as well, but the present cathedral is, in fact, the result of a rebuilding which was begun *c.* 1270. Almost the entire church was remodelled from east to west, the façade being finished *c.* 1360. In spite of the length of time involved, the cathedral has a remarkable unity of style; the main differences occur in the treatment of details, such as the carving of foliage and the design of window tracery.

DEVONSHIRE REGIMENT MUSEUM The Devonshire Regiment was raised in 1685 as The Duke of Beaufort's Musketeers, to help fight the Duke of Monmouth, a natural son of Charles II, who landed at Lyme Regis to claim the English Crown; he was defeated at Sedgemoor (Somerset) and

EXETER CATHEDRAL
FIGURES ON THE WEST FAÇADE

The largest surviving array of 14th-century sculpture in England graces the west façade of Exeter Cathedral. The cathedral interior, remodelled in the 13th century, is ornate, with multiplication of mouldings on the arches and piers. The vaulting has more ribs than any other 13th-century church in England, and great cones of descending ribs resemble palm branches. The bishop's throne has some of the most impressive woodcarving of 14th-century Europe. Bishop Stapledon was Edward II's Treasurer; associated with an unpopular ruling clique, he was murdered by a London mob in 1326.

THE EXETER BOOK OF
OLD ENGLISH VERSE

This book, the longest single source of Anglo-Saxon poetry, was written between 950 and 1000 and given by Bishop Leofric of Exeter to the cathedral library. This poem, 'The Wanderer', is an exile's lament: 'Oft a solitary mortal wishes for grace, his Maker's mercy. Though sick at heart he must long traverse the watery ways, with his hands must stir the rime-cold sea, and tread the paths of exile.'
(Exeter Cathedral Library)

later beheaded on Tower Hill. The Regiment amalgamated with the Dorset Regiment in 1958. Its history is told in the museum's collection of uniforms, medals, weapons and documents.

GUILDHALL Claimed to be the oldest municipal building in England; it is referred to in a document of 1160. The main hall and roof were rebuilt in 1466, and the mayor's parlour—with a portico overhanging the pavement—in 1592–4.

MARITIME MUSEUM Housed in a group of old warehouses on the quayside, the museum's collection of craft includes an Arab pearling dhow, a reed boat from Lake Titicaca and a 320-ton Danish steam tug. The vessels are taken out to sea as much as possible, helping to preserve traditional sailing techniques.

ROUGEMONT HOUSE MUSEUM Temporarily closed, the museum re-opens in 1987 with displays of costume and lace.

ROYAL ALBERT MEMORIAL MUSEUM AND ART GALLERY The main museum has permanent displays of oil paintings, water-colours, sculpture, glass, china, clocks and watches, local archaeology, anthropology and natural history. There are also collections relating to the Royal Devon Yeomanry, and of Exeter silver.

Exmouth *Devon* 539Hd
A LA RONDE A house of circular plan, with a shell gallery, built in the style of the Church of San Vitale, Ravenna, in 1798.

Exton *Leics.* 553Gb
CHURCH OF SS PETER AND PAUL Extensively rebuilt in the mid-19th century after lightning damage, the church contains an impressive series of monuments from the 14th to 18th centuries; there are fine 16th-century tombs with effigies, and work by Grinling Gibbons, Joseph Nollekens, and some attributed to Nicholas Johnson.

Eyam *Derbys.* 552De
In 1665 some cloth was sent from London to the village tailor, and thus the great plague (then raging in London) was brought here. The villagers voluntarily isolated themselves to stop the plague spreading farther, and within a year some 259 of the 350 villagers were dead. Each year on the last Sunday in August the Eyam Plague Commemoration Service is held, with a procession to Cucklet Dell, where the villagers worshipped during the plague.

Eye *Suffolk* 548Df
Once surrounded by water, and named after the old Saxon word for island, this agricultural town received its first charter from King John in 1205. Its Norman castle reverted to the Crown five times, and was finally demolished by Cromwell's army in 1655. Stones from the castle were used to make a castellated folly on the original site in the 19th century. Only the old guest house and fishponds remain of the Benedictine monastery founded in 1066. The guildhall is early 16th century and there are some good 18th-century houses.

CHURCH OF SS PETER AND PAUL The 15th-century west tower is one of the best in the county; there is flint and stone panelled decoration from ground to battlements. The 15th-century rood screen, with painted figures, was restored in 1925, together with the rood and loft, by Sir Ninian Comper.

Eye Manor *Heref. & Worcs.* 546Af
A 17th-century Renaissance manor house, built by Ferdinando Gorges, a slave-trader of Barbados. Its fine plaster ceilings resemble those of Holyroodhouse. It contains exhibitions of period costumes and costume dolls, needlework and books.

Eynesbury *Cambs.* 547Jf
CHURCH OF ST MARY THE VIRGIN Originally Norman, the church was altered in the 13th century and later; the tower on the south dates from the later 17th century. There are many 16th-century benches with carved poppy-heads, and an 18th-century pulpit. (By appointment.)

F

Faenol Fawr *Clwyd* 551Ge
This Elizabethan house has the date 1597 on a fireplace, and also has a fine stair. It was built by John Lloyd, who was registrar of the Diocese of St Asaph, and has attractive elevations with crow-stepped gables and dormers. Now a restaurant.

Fairford *Glos.* 546Dc
CHURCH OF ST MARY THE VIRGIN A late 15th-century church with a good central tower, reflecting the prosperity of local wool merchants. The church has 28 windows with magnificent contemporary stained glass illustrating biblical stories; there are also screens, monuments, misericords, and fine roofs. (See p. 198.)

Falkirk *Central* 562Af
ROUGH CASTLE The site of a large Roman fort, one of a line of strongholds built by Agricola in AD 80; the forts stretched across the narrow neck of Scotland from Bowling on the Clyde to Bo'ness on the Forth, and 60 years later were linked by the Antonine Wall.

STEEPLE An elegant steeple surmounted by a tapering octagonal spire. It was designed by David Hamilton of Glasgow and built 1813–14 on the foundations of a steeple of 1697, demolished in 1803. It is square in plan and built in four stages.

Falkland *Fife* 562Cg
Lying in the Fife hills this burgh, with its palace completed in 1542 by James V as the centrepiece, possesses many buildings of interest. Key House of 1713, thatched Nicoll Moncreif's house dated 1610, and Cameron House are the best of the houses of some pretension in the High Street. The Classical town house of 1801 with octagonal belfry is another notable building.

Some 18th-century weavers' houses, many built using the solid rock as a foundation, border the narrow streets leading from the Bruce Fountain of 1856.

FALKLAND PALACE A 16th-century hunting palace of the Stuart Kings until the death in 1625 of James VI of Scotland (James I of England). The palace was frequently used by Mary, Queen of Scots. The gardens have been restored to the plan of a 17th-century engraving.

Falkland Memorial *Berks.* 546Fa
A 19th-century monument to Lucius Cary, 2nd Viscount Falkland (1610–43) who fell at the first Battle of Newbury.

Falmer *E. Sussex* 542Bd
The new University of Sussex is one of the most dramatic groups of modern buildings. It was

begun in 1961, and Sir Basil Spence was the architect. The dominant motif, which recurs again and again in different sizes and proportions, is of red brick and exposed concrete lintels.

Falmouth *Cornwall*   *538Cb*
The great natural harbour of Falmouth only began to be developed as a maritime port in 1688 when it was selected as a station for the Mail Packet Service. By 1827 this service had 39 vessels conveying mail to America, the West Indies, South America and the Mediterranean; but when steam replaced sail the service was transferred to Southampton and Falmouth declined.

Fareham *Hants.*   *541Hd*
The old High Street has the longest and most varied stretch of Georgian architecture in Hampshire, a relic of the days when it was fashionable for naval officers from Portsmouth to retire here. The locally made bricks glow with colour. The Kintyre Hotel, one of the best houses, is dated 1756.

Faringdon *Oxon.*   *546Ec*
CHURCH OF ALL SAINTS A large, cruciform church, with low central tower that lost its spire in the Civil War. All Saints dates from the 12th to 19th centuries, with the 13th predominating. The north door is Norman, *c.* 1170, the font is Perpendicular, and the 13th-century south door has decorative ironwork with dragon heads. Monuments include those to the Unton (16th century) and Pye (17th and 18th century) families.

Farleigh Castle *Avon*   *540Df*
The ruins of a castle built *c.* 1383 by Sir Thomas Hungerford. The inner bailey containing the domestic buildings is surrounded by a curtain wall with round towers. There are monuments to the Hungerford family in the chapel, which was originally a parish church.

Farnborough Hall *Warks.*   *546Ee*
A country mansion, mainly rebuilt in the 18th century, with fine plasterwork designed to harmonise with Italian paintings and sculptures. The grounds contain a terrace walk and two temples.

Farnham *Surrey*   *541Jf*
There are two fine streets in the town. West Street has two sumptuous Georgian houses, Willmer House of 1718, and Sandford House of 1757. Castle Street, a picture of domestic variety, leads to the castle.
CASTLE The Norman keep was begun in 1138 by Henry de Blois, grandson of William the Conqueror, brother of King Stephen and Bishop of Winchester 1129–71. The foundations of the massive centre tower can still be seen on top of the existing (artificial) mound. In 1155 Henry II ordered everything de Blois had built to be destroyed, and the present shell was built soon afterwards, in the late 12th century.

For 800 years, the castle served as a palace for the Bishops of Winchester, and later Guildford. Of the palace buildings, the Great Hall, built about 1170 and extensively modified in 1677, a Norman refectory and chapel, a massive red-brick tower built in 1470 and an Elizabethan guest-house remain. Seventeenth-century additions include a fine staircase and Bishop Morley's Chapel.
FARNHAM MUSEUM (Willmer House) This early Georgian house has a façade of cut and moulded brick dated 1718, and contains fine carving and panelling. Its collections include archaeological finds, 17th- and 18th-century furniture and clocks, folk material, and items associated with local artists, architects and inventors. There is also a collection of 19th-century English and French glass paper-weights.

STAINED GLASS OF A DEVIL'S HEAD
The parish church at Fairford is the only one which has kept its complete set of medieval stained glass windows. These were painted between 1495 and 1505 when the present church was built. This devil's head is a detail of the western windows depicting the Day of Judgment. In the north clerestory window other devils stand above the Persecutors of the Church. The series of 28 windows also shows events from the Gospels, saints and martyrs from Church history, and prophets of the Old Testament. The strong Flemish influence suggests that some of Henry VII's men were employed here. The king himself was the owner of the manor and many of his glaziers were of Flemish origin. (Church of St Mary the Virgin, Fairford)

Farningham *Kent*   *542Cf*
Once an important stop for coaches on the Dover Road, hence the handsome 18th-century houses, and the splendid red-brick Lion Inn.

Farnworth *Cheshire*   *552Af*
CHURCH OF ST LUKE Originally 12th-century, but now mainly Decorated and Perpendicular Gothic, with 19th-century restoration. There are many monuments, some to the Bold family by Pietro Tenerani, Sir Francis Chantrey and the firm of Franceys of Liverpool, who employed as an apprentice John Gibson, one of the most successful 19th-century English sculptors.

Faversham *Kent*   *542Ef*
A quiet old town. It was once a flourishing port, and the best street, Abbey Street, has wharves behind it. Recently well restored, Abbey Street perfectly expresses modest Georgian prosperity.
ARDEN'S HOUSE A 15th-century house, sometimes called the Old Abbey because of its 12th-century abbey remains. It commemorates the name of Thomas Arden, who was murdered here in 1550 by his wife and her lover. The story inspired the 16th-century melodrama, 'Arden of Feversham'.

Fawsley *Northants.*   *546Ff*
CHURCH OF ST MARY Mainly Decorated, the church has 13th-century details in the arcade. There is a west tower. Main interest lies in the many monuments to the Knightley family, which include brasses. A magnificent painted alabaster

altar-tomb of 1534 has recumbent effigies. Two large urns on pedestals of *c.* 1681 and *c.* 1715 might possibly be the work of William Stanton and his son Edward, and there is also a mid-19th-century work by John Gibson.

Fedw Deg *Gwynedd*   *550Fd*
Part of this 16th-century house has been destroyed, but the surviving section has been restored. Typical of this slate area is the arched door-head, cut out of a single slab; also of interest is the primitive 'pre-glazing' wooden mullioned window. The parish of Penmachno in which the house stands is rich in 16th- and 17th-century houses.

Felbrigg *Norfolk*   *554Dd*
CHURCH OF ST MARGARET The church, which has Decorated and Perpendicular work, is remarkable for its brasses, from 14th to 17th century. They include the brass to Simon de Fellbrigg (*d.* 1416), Standard-bearer to Richard II. Other monuments are to William Windham (*d.* 1686), for which Grinling Gibbons was paid, and William Windham (*d.* 1813) by Joseph Nollekens. Other features of the church are a 14th-century octagonal font, box-pews and a wall oven in the vestry.

Felmersham *Beds.*   *547Hf*
There are many stone-built houses of great charm here, a great buttressed tithe barn opposite the 13th-century Church of St Mary the Virgin, and the picturesque Six Ringers Inn.
CHURCH OF ST MARY THE VIRGIN An impressive 13th-century church, and a fine example of Early English work, especially the west façade. There is a central tower; during the 15th century the nave walls were raised to give a flat-pitched roof and clerestory. A delicate screen of the same period contrasts with the massive piers of the crossing.

Fenny Bentley *Derbys.*   *552Dd*
CHURCH OF ST EDMUND A Gothic church with a restored west tower. There is a good early 16th-century rood screen still with its vaulting. From slightly later in the same century come the two macabre tomb-effigies.

Fenstanton *Cambs.*   *547Jf*
The home of Capability Brown, the famous landscape gardener. Brown, his wife and their eldest son are buried in the church.

Festiniog Railway *Gwynedd*   *550Fd*
This 13 mile long narrow-gauge railway was built to connect the slate quarries of Blaenau Ffestiniog with Porthmadog. It opened in 1836 as a horse-drawn tramway; in 1863 steam engines were introduced. This was in many ways a pioneering railway: in 1865 it became the first narrow-gauge railway in Britain to carry passengers, in 1869 it adopted the Fairlie patent articulated locomotive, and in 1873 bogie coaches were introduced. Today, the little railway, whose gauge is only 1 ft 11⅝ in., attracts holidaymakers and engineering enthusiasts from all over the world.

Fettercairn *Grampian*   *566Fc*
In the main square is the shaft of the old Kincardine Tower Cross (1670) which is notched to show the length of the Scottish ell (37 inches).

Ffynnon Gybi (St Gybi's Well) *Gwynedd 550Ed*
Set in a valley immediately north of the church, the two well chambers with attached cottage and a small privy, although simple in style, form the most elaborate establishment of its kind in the county. To the north of the larger well is a smaller one of the kind adjacent to many old churches in the area. Although archaic in appearance the larger building is most likely to be the work of a

Merioneth squire, who *c.* 1750, 'caused proper conveniences for Bathing, and other improvements to be made'.

Filkins *Oxon.*   *546Dc*
SWINFORD MUSEUM Village life over a period of more than 150 years is reflected in the display of items made and used in the farms, workshops and cottages of Filkins and the surrounding district. The museum is housed in a small Cotswold stone cottage and village lock-up. (By appointment.)

Finavon *Tayside*   *566Eb*
VITRIFIED FORT A long, narrow Iron Age fort which excavation showed had a wall about 20 ft thick, still standing some 16 ft above its original ground surface. This wall had been timber-laced and it is thought that the burning of these timbers resulted in heavy vitrification of the stone.

Finchale Priory *Durham*   *558Cg*
Finchale Priory was founded *c.* 1237 on the banks of the R. Wear and laid out on the normal monastic plan. This plan proved unsuitable for the revised establishment of the 14th century, when Finchale became the holiday house for the monks of Durham Cathedral Priory, and the church was drastically reduced in size; the refectory seems to have been abandoned in the 15th century, when part of it was turned into chambers for the monks. The life of this community centred on the prior's lodgings, a well-developed domestic residence, with its own hall, chamber, chapel and kitchen.

Finchingfield *Essex*   *548Be*
An unspoilt village, with a charming street of varied houses climbing the hill from the green and duckpond to the church. There is a guildhall of *c.* 1500; a late 18th-century hexagonal thatched cottage, the Round House; and a windmill. One mile north is Spains Hall, a red-brick house of *c.* 1570 with a two-storey porch and seven gables.

Finlarig Castle *Central*   *566Aa*
The ruined stronghold of the Earls of Breadalbane at the head of Loch Tay, built in *c.* 1609. Near the entrance tower is the beheading pit where executions were carried out by means of a crude guillotine—called The Maiden or sometimes The Widow. The castle is described in Scott's *Fair Maid of Perth*.

Firle Place *E. Sussex*   *542Cd*
The home of the Gage family since the 15th century. General Thomas Gage was Commander-in-Chief of the British army at the beginning of the American War of Independence (1775–83) and the house contains items he brought from America. The original Tudor house was reconstructed in Georgian style *c.* 1730 and contains French and English furniture, Sèvres porcelain and old masters from the Cowper Collection.

Fishbourne *W. Sussex*   *541Jd*
On a site which had been used for military and civil occupation at the time of the Conquest, a great Roman palace was built in the decade AD 71–80. This outstanding building covered an area of some 250,000 sq. ft and has been attributed to Cogidubnus, king of the Regni, who was recognised by the Romans as their 'sub-ruler' and made a Roman citizen. A wing of the building and much of the Roman garden have been conserved and are available for inspection. (See p. 200.)

Fishlake *S. Yorks.*   *552Fg*
CHURCH OF ST CUTHBERT Originally a Norman church, with alterations up to the 15th century. There is a fine Norman south door with lavish carving. Inside are a medieval carved font, screens and a monument of *c.* 1505.

Five Knolls *Beds.* 547Hd
This is an unusual barrow group with a triple bell barrow and two normal bowl barrows. In addition, there are what may be two of the rare pond barrows. Excavation of the mounds showed them to belong to the Early Bronze Age, with surviving Neolithic traces. Mutilated human remains found in one mound have been dated late Roman or early Saxon and probably resulted from a skirmish.

Flamborough *Humberside* 559Gc
CHURCH OF ST OSWALD Dating from the 14th century, it has a Norman chancel arch and font. There is a 15th–16th-century screen with one of the two surviving Yorkshire rood lofts, which still has some of its original colouring; there are parclose screens as well, and some monuments.

Flamstead *Herts.* 547Hd
CHURCH OF ST LEONARD The church tower is Norman, the main structure 12th century. There is a fine Early English arcade with interesting capitals. The 12th- to 15th-century wall paintings were recently restored—Christ in Glory, Three Living and Three Dead Kings, and Passion Cycle. Monuments by William Stanton and John Flaxman.

Flatford Mill *Suffolk* 548De
One of the 18th-century water-mills owned by the father of John Constable (1776–1837). Near by, beautifully situated beside the mill stream, is Willy Lott's Cottage, an early 17th-century house, which figures in his painting *The Hay Wain*. (Interiors not open.)

Fleet *Dorset* 540Dc
CHURCH OF THE HOLY TRINITY An attractive Gothic church with a west tower, built in 1827–9 to replace a church that was badly damaged by the sea during a gale in 1824. The apsidal chancel has a good vaulted plaster roof, and contains a large marble monument with mourning figures, *c*. 1818.

Fleet *Lincs.* 553Jc
CHURCH OF ST MARY MAGDALENE A 14th-century Fenland church, with tower and spire detached from the main building. Apart from the chancel, rebuilt in 1862, the remainder of the church is in the Decorated style, except for Early English arcades and the Perpendicular west window.

Flint Castle *Clwyd* 551He
The ruined Flint Castle has a great round tower or donjon outside the circuit of the walls. It is the only example of this plan used by Edward I, who in all his other castles used the more 'modern' form of great, independently defended gate-houses.

Flitton *Beds.* 547He
CHURCH OF ST JOHN THE BAPTIST The church is mainly 15th century, and is noted for its many monuments to Earls and Dukes of Kent; the later ones are in a family mausoleum. Among sculptors whose work is represented are Thomas Banks and Matthew Noble. There is also a number of brasses.

Floors Castle *Borders* 562Ed
A large 18th-century mansion, designed in 1721 by William Adam and enlarged by William Playfair, with an abundance of capped turrets surmounting a façade that shows Tudor influence.

MOSAIC FLOOR AT FISHBOURNE ROMAN PALACE

There were several phases of construction at this great Roman house, and late in the 2nd century this fine floor was laid. On the panel, roughly 18 ft by 18 ft and surrounded by a chequered border, the central medallion shows a winged boy astride a dolphin, and the semicircles show sea-horses and sea-panthers.

Fochabers *Grampian* 566Eg
The 4th Duke of Gordon replaced the old burgh of Fochabers, *c.* 1780, by a new planned village at a respectful distance outside the castle walls. Laid out by Thomas Mylne, his surveyor, the traditional two-storey houses and church with portico and steeple were designed by John Baxter in 1798. The village was planned on the rectilinear principle with main street and parallel back streets and large open space in the centre. Milne's Institute, designed by Thomas MacKenzie of Elgin in 1843, is a notable later building.

Folkestone *Kent* 542Fe
Until the railways acquired the port in 1842 for the sum of £18,000, the town had little significance except as a smuggling centre, which flourished *c.* 1800. It is now a holiday resort and cross-Channel port. Just to the north is an ancient fortification called Caesar's Camp. On the Leas, a shrub and floral coastal walk, is a statue of William Harvey, the great anatomist who discovered the circulation of blood, born in Folkestone in 1578.

Folkingham *Lincs.* 553Hc
CHURCH OF ST ANDREW An interesting church, with an outstanding Perpendicular tower, it retains evidence of its Norman origins. Inside are 14th-century arcades, early 15th-century windows, a good screen, and an Early English chancel.

Forde Abbey *Dorset* 540Bd
A Cistercian monastery, founded in 1141, notable for its collection of tapestries and 25-acre gardens.

Fordham *Norfolk* 554Ab
SNORE HALL A little-known house built of brick *c.* 1480–90. It has buttresses with pinnacles, an embattled porch, and on the west side a gable and a panelled shaft running up the middle. On the south side are Elizabethan (or Jacobean) windows and a big chimney-stack of the same period. (Not open to the public.)

Fordwich *Kent* 542Ff
Once a town, now a tiny village, Fordwich has kept its half-timbered town hall, on the quay-side by the R. Stour.

Foremark *Derbys.* 552Dc
CHURCH OF ST SAVIOUR Built in 1662, it has a Gothic exterior with an embattled west tower. The interior is Renaissance with a 17th-century screen, a three-decker pulpit, box-pews and iron communion rails, probably by Robert Bakewell.

Forfar *Tayside* 566Eb
FORFAR MUSEUM AND ART GALLERY Devoted to the history of Forfar, its geology and natural history. It has paintings by J. W. Herald and a bridle used during the burning of witches.

Forrabury Common *Cornwall* 538Dd
A unique survival of the Celtic (pre-Saxon) system of land tenure—stitchmeal. There are 42 'stitches' or small fields grouped at the edge of the common, each containing some good and some poor soil.

Forse *Highland* 569Ld
SETTLEMENT COMPLEX The remains of this homestead are complex, and their sequence obscure. The first structure was probably the circular enclosure, some 45 ft across, with a 4 ft thick wall. This may have been sited within an outer enclosure measuring about 40 yds by 35 yds, formed by an earthen bank. The complex is of Iron Age type.

Fort Augustus *Highland* 565Je
Built in 1715–30 to help quell the Jacobite rebellion, the fort is named after William Augustus,

Duke of Cumberland—'Butcher' Cumberland of Culloden. The site was given to the Benedictine order in the 19th century and the abbey, with cloisters and tower designed by Pugin, was built.

Fort George *Highland* 566Bg
Constructed after the Jacobite rising in 1745 under the direction of Colonel William Skinner, with William Adam and later John Adam as master mason. The barrack blocks and chapel are encircled by irregular polygonal walls and six bastions.
REGIMENTAL MUSEUM OF THE SEAFORTH HIGHLANDERS, THE QUEEN'S OWN CAMERON HIGHLANDERS AND QUEEN'S OWN HIGHLANDERS The history of these regiments is reflected in the uniforms, medals, weapons, silver, prints and pictures displayed in a building erected over 200 years ago to designs by Robert Adam.

Forth Railway Bridge 562Bf
The first plans for a bridge over the Forth, to link Edinburgh with the north of Scotland, were drawn up by Sir Thomas Bouch. However, following the disastrous destruction of his bridge over the Tay in 1879, these were dropped. Sir John Fowler and Sir Benjamin Baker drew up new plans, and in 1882 work began on the present enormous cantilever construction, with 1700 ft main spans—a world record for many years. The bridge, about 5300 ft long altogether, and 360 ft above high water, was opened in March 1890.

Forton *Staffs.* 552Bc
CHURCH OF ALL SAINTS An interesting combination of Georgian and medieval work, All Saints was begun in Norman times, enlarged during the Gothic period, and altered in the 18th century. An 18th-century south wall and nave link the squat medieval tower with the Decorated east end.

Fort William *Highland* 565Hc
The base for climbers scaling Ben Nevis, the highest mountain in the British Isles (4406 ft).
THE FORT The stronghold was built in 1655 to restrain the Highlanders; it was rebuilt by General Wade in 1715, but dismantled in 1855.

Fossdyke *Lincs.* 553Ge
Still a navigable canal with a tow-path which can be walked from end to end, this waterway links the R. Witham at Lincoln with the R. Trent at Torksey. It formed part of a system of water-transport designed by the Romans, probably to convey the corn of East Anglia to the garrison at York and thence north by road. Much of the first part of that system, the Car Dyke, which ran from the R. Cam near Cambridge to the central river-system of the Fens and then from the Nene to the Witham, is now filled in or incorporated in the Fenland dyke-drainage system. But the Fossdyke was reconditioned in post-Roman times and still provides a route by water from Lincoln to the Trent and so down to the Humber and up the Yorkshire Ouse.

Foston Old Rectory *N. Yorks.* 558Ec
Designed and built of pink brick in 1813–14 by Sydney Smith, Rector of Foston and an essayist noted for his wit. (By appointment.)

Fotheringhay *Northants.* 547Hg
CHURCH OF ST MARY AND ALL SAINTS Part of a college founded in 1411, the church was partially demolished after the Dissolution when the chancel was pulled down. All that remains is the nave and aisles. The west tower becomes a pinnacled octagonal lantern at its upper stage. There are flying buttresses from the high clerestory and a Perpendicular pulpit with a vaulted tester. The contract for the nave survives and is dated 1434.

MarieR

MARY, QUEEN OF SCOTS, SCOTLAND'S TRAGIC QUEEN

Mary Stuart, 'the fairest and most cruel queen on earth' became Queen of Scotland at eight days old. She married the Dauphin of France at 15, sending a miniature of herself to her cousin Elizabeth, which remains in the Royal Library, Windsor. In 1558 Mary became heir apparent to the English throne and in 1559 Queen of France as well. Her troubles began when her young husband died and the 18-year-old Papist queen returned to Protestant Scotland. Her personal apartments at Holyroodhouse can be visited and a brass plate marks the spot where her favourite secretary was murdered at the instigation of her jealous second husband, Lord Darnley. At the Castle of Loch Leven Mary was held after the mad episode of her abduction and marriage to the Earl of Bothwell and the disaster of the Battle of Carberry Hill. At 26 Mary fled to England, where she was imprisoned for 19 years. Her embroideries can be seen at Holyrood and Hardwick Hall.

LE DEUIL BLANC *(white mourning) portrait of Mary showing her when she was 17 and Queen of France. This is a copy of the famous painting by Clouet, who sketched her at the French court. It gives some idea of her striking colouring, but a poor impression of her vivacity and charm. (Scottish National Portrait Gallery)*

GOLD DUCAT *of extreme rarity struck for the wedding of Mary and the Dauphin of France, with the arched crown of Scotland suspended between them. They became king and queen when Henri II died after being accidentally struck in the eye at a tournament. (British Museum)*

CHILD PORTRAIT *of Mary's son who was crowned James VI of Scotland at the abdication of his mother, when he was 14 months old. In 1603, he was also crowned James I of England. (Scottish National Portrait Gallery)*

HENRY, LORD DARNLEY *and MARY STUART. Mary's headlong infatuation and marriage to her 19-year-old cousin culminated in his murder 18 months later at Kirk o' Field. (Engraving at the British Museum)*

SILVER CASKET *said to be identical with the one discovered under the bed of one of Bothwell's servants after Darnley's murder. It contained love letters from Mary to Bothwell and other documents incriminating the queen in the murder of her husband. It is now thought that these were forgeries.*
(Lennoxlove, Lothian)

THE PENICUIK JEWELS AND FAN *that belonged to Queen Mary. She divided her personal treasures between her attendants just before her execution, but it is thought that these pieces had previously been given to one of her maids of honour. The locket has a tiny miniature of the queen on the front. On the back is a miniature of her son as a boy of about ten. (National Museum of Antiquities of Scotland)*

GOLDEN ROSARY, CRUCIFIX AND PRAYERBOOK *carried by Mary, Queen of Scots to her execution. On the steps of the scaffold she spoke to the assembly 'with joyous countenance' saying 'I have been brought before a company who will witness that I die a Catholic.' (Arundel Castle, W. Sussex)*

SCOTTISH PENNY, *about 1554, with the earliest likeness of the queen as a 12-year-old child. Aged six she went to be educated with the French royal children, having been engaged to the Dauphin. Her mother remained in Scotland as Regent. (British Museum)*

MARY'S SIGNET RING, *the shoulders ornamented with leaves and flowers and engraved with the emblem of Mary. In the hoop at the back are the marks of Mary and Francis, her first husband. (British Museum)*

DEATH MASK *of Mary. When the executioner held up the head crying 'God Save the Queen', her wig came off, showing her hair to be 'as grey as if she had been three score years and ten, polled very short'. The head was placed in the castle window for an hour so that the crowd could see it. (Lennoxlove, Lothian)*

EXECUTION SCENE *of Mary at Fotheringhay in 1587. The hall was draped in black, lit by flaring torches and a large fire. The queen, dressed in red satin, died with regal dignity. (Scottish National Portrait Gallery)*

HIGHLAND HARP *or clarsach said to have been given by Queen Mary to Beatrix Gardyne. This Highland harp was probably made about AD 1450. (National Museum of Antiquities of Scotland)*

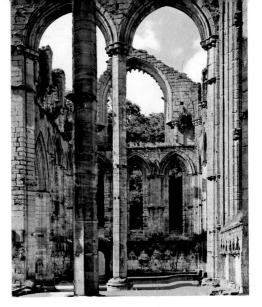

FOUNTAINS ABBEY

Fountains Abbey was founded in 1132 on a site which was later described as 'fit more for the dens of wild beasts than for the uses of man'. At first the monks suffered considerable privations and hardship, but the abbey ultimately became the richest Cistercian house in England, although its inmates were not especially distinguished either for holiness or scholarship. The ruins of the abbey form one of the most complete sets of Cistercian buildings to survive the Dissolution of the monasteries.

Foulden *Borders*   562Fe
TITHE BARN One of the few remaining tithe barns in Scotland, situated in the north-east corner of the churchyard belonging to the parish church of 1786; it has two floors with crow-stepped gables and outside stone stairs leading to the first floor. (Interior closed to the public.)

Fountains Abbey *N. Yorks.*   558Cc
The buildings of Fountains Abbey, founded in 1132, were reconstructed between 1148 and 1179 after enemies of the abbot had broken in and destroyed the abbey by fire. The only major additions after 1179 were the north tower, built by Abbot Huby (1479–94), and the Chapel of the Nine Altars at the east end of the church, built between 1203 and 1247. The whole ground plan has survived, and the positions of the refectory and the lay brothers' quarters (peculiar to Cistercian monasteries) can be clearly seen. The abbey also possesses the most imposing surviving medieval provisions for waterworks and drainage, most of the 12th-century tunnelling constructed to conduct the R. Skell along the chosen course being still visible. The abbey is now approached through the beautiful grounds of Studley Royal.

Fountains Abbey Garden See Studley Royal.

Fountains Hall *N. Yorks.*   558Cc
Built *c.* 1611 by Sir Stephen Proctor, the Hall is constructed with stones from Fountains Abbey, which was sold to Proctor in 1597 by Sir Richard Gresham (connected with the merchant bank in London) to whom it had passed at the Dissolution.

Fowlis Easter *Tayside*   566Da
CHURCH A mid-15th-century church, which retains some of the painted panels of its former rood screen. There is also an ambry (tabernacle) with a sculpture of the Annunciation.

Fowlis Wester *Tayside*   566Ca
A fine Pictish symbol stone, 10 ft high, stands railed within the village. Its carvings are elaborate

examples of Pictish work, but today it is weathered.

Foxdenton Hall *Greater Manchester*   552Bf
A Stuart mansion, reconstructed in 1700 and restored in 1965.

Fox's Hospital *Wilts.*   540Fe
A group of 12 red-brick, Flemish bond almshouses, designed by Wren and modernised in the 20th century. They were built in 1681–2 through the bounty of Sir Stephen Fox, Paymaster to the Armed Forces of Charles II.

Framlingham *Suffolk*   548Ef
An old market town with some pleasant domestic architecture on Castle Street and Market Hill; also the late 17th-century Ancient House with pargeting, and two sets of almshouses of 1654 and 1703.
CASTLE When built by Roger Bigod, the 2nd Earl of Norfolk, *c.* 1190, it was the most modern type of defence then known. The keep and bailey plan was being abandoned in favour of a uniform curtain wall with projecting towers, and Framlingham is an early English example of this style, built before square towers had been replaced by round ones. The rebellious medieval owners of Framlingham frequently forfeited the castle to the Crown. It was attacked and taken by King John's forces in 1215 but underwent no other siege. In 1553 when it was held by the Crown, it was the home of Mary Tudor, and became a rallying point for her supporters at the beginning of her reign, when her succession to the throne was in doubt. In the 17th century Pembroke College, Cambridge, received the castle as a bequest, and was instructed to build a Poor House, which still exists on the site of the Bigod great hall (fragments of which are embedded in the present building).
CHURCH OF ST MICHAEL Rebuilt from mid-15th century, it has a west tower and a magnificent nave roof. It is famous for its 16th-century monuments to the Duke of Richmond (1536), and to members of the family of the Dukes of Norfolk, with carved recumbent effigies. From the mid-18th century is a minor work by Louis Roubiliac.

Frampton *Dorset*   540Dc
CHURCH OF ST MARY Later additions to the original 15th-century church include the 17th-century west tower, the 18th-century north aisle, and the south porch, added in 1820. Monuments include 17th-century recumbent effigies, and a large wall monument of *c.* 1750 with a bust and flying cherub, probably by Sir Henry Cheere.

Frampton Court *Glos.*   546Bc
Built in 1731 by Vanbrugh or a pupil, it has fine panelling and 18th-century furniture. An ornamental canal leads to an orangery of 'Strawberry Hill' style Gothic design. (By appointment.)

Frampton-on-Severn *Glos.*   546Bc
CHURCH OF ST MARY This church, with its pinnacled west tower, is mainly Decorated and Perpendicular Gothic. The lead font is Norman. Monuments with effigies of a knight and lady date from the 14th century; the pulpit is dated 1622.

Freiston *Lincs.*   553Jd
CHURCH OF ST JAMES The remains of the church of the former 12th-century priory; the present building shows Norman work. Inside are good screens, and a Perpendicular font with cover.

Fressingfield *Suffolk*   548Eg
CHURCH OF SS PETER AND PAUL A Decorated and Perpendicular church, with west tower, clerestory and vaulted two-storey south porch. Inside are good benches with carving.

FRAMLINGHAM CASTLE

By the middle of the 12th century Framlingham was one of a group of castles in the eastern counties held by the powerful Bigod family, Earls of Norfolk. Framlingham was destroyed in 1174, but Roger, the 2nd Earl, built a new and stronger castle about 1190. The layout of the rooms is now almost completely lost, although the house was still inhabited in the 16th century when it had passed to the Howard family. The destruction seems to have occurred in the 17th century when the castle was bequeathed to Pembroke College, Cambridge, which was instructed to pull it down 'saving the stone building'.

FURNESS ABBEY

Originally a Savignac house, this abbey was taken over by the Cistercian order in 1147, and became the second richest Cistercian house in England after Fountains Abbey, acquiring extensive property in northern England and the Isle of Man. The piscina and sedilia in the presbytery are among the finest to survive from the 12th and 13th centuries. The 'bays' to the right are the sedilia, and the piscina at the left formerly had a basin with towel recesses on each side.

Freston Tower *Suffolk*   548De
A slim, dramatic, six-storied tower-house with a spiral staircase linking each floor, it was built of red diapered brickwork *c.* 1550. In its early days it was occupied by the Latimers, the early English Church reformers. In the decade following 1767, it was used for the reception of patients undergoing the new treatment of inoculation against smallpox. (Not open to the public.)

Fritton *near Great Yarmouth, Norfolk*   548Fh
CHURCH OF ST EDMUND The church has a thatched roof and is built on Saxon foundations (the chancel floor is AD 750); 12th-century paintings have been uncovered in the apse.

Frome *Som.*   540Df
A town of Saxon origin, and the scene of brutal executions following the Duke of Monmouth's rebellion in 1685. A waterway runs along the centre of Cheap Street, emerging from paving stones at one end and disappearing at the other.

Froyle *Hants.*   541Je
CHURCH OF THE ASSUMPTION The brick nave, dating from the early 19th century, is by James Harding, but the chancel is part of the original church and dates from the late 13th century, while the west tower is of *c.* 1720. Fragments of medieval heraldic stained glass remain, and the windows of 1874–97 are by C. E. Kempe.

Furness Abbey *Cumbria*   557Gc
Furness Abbey was founded in 1123, but the present buildings belong almost entirely to the period after it became a Cistercian house in 1147. A great deal of the abbey survives, including the east end of the church and the transepts up to roof level, and the east side of the cloister with the adjoining 13th-century chapter house. The surviving parts of other monastic buildings make it possible to appreciate the size of the abbey. The dormitory was over 200 ft long, the infirmary 126 ft, and the refectory nearly 150 ft (at Fountains Abbey the refectory is about 100 ft long and the dormitory about 110 ft). The abbey's great size created problems, and the refectory in particular seems to have been made smaller, possibly *c.* 1500.

G

Gaddesby *Leics.* 552Fb
CHURCH OF ST LUKE An impressive medieval church, primarily late 14th-century work. The south side is lavishly decorated with stone carvings of the same period, and most of the original wood remains in the 14th-century oak pews. There is a life-size statue of Colonel Cheney on horseback at Waterloo, by J. Gott, in the chancel.

Gainford *Durham* 558Ce
With its Georgian houses surrounding a wide and handsome green, Gainford is regarded as one of the prettiest villages in the county.

Gainsborough *Lincs.* 552Ff
A market town identified with 'St Ogg's' in George Eliot's *Mill on the Floss*. The 15th-century Old Hall in the town centre is traditionally the scene of the assassination of Sweyne, King Canute's father.
OLD HALL The original medieval Hall was wrecked during the Wars of the Roses; the present house, partly of brick and partly in half-timbering, was built *c.* 1500. In the late 16th century it was the meeting place of the early Dissenters, later known as the Pilgrim Fathers. John Wesley, the founder of Methodism, preached at the Hall several times. It is now a museum which has a Richard III exhibition, and collections of furniture and paintings.

Garn Boduan *Gwynedd* 550Dd
A mile from the sea, south of Nevin, stands an isolated hill, on the crown of which is this Iron Age hill-fort. The defences, though originally of some strength, are no longer in good condition, but relics of its occupation still survive in the form of many round stone-built huts, still quite well preserved. The crest of the hill, which is on private property, is marked by rubble remains.

Garway *Heref. & Worcs.* 546Ad
CHURCH OF ST MICHAEL AND ALL ANGELS This was one of the round churches of the Knights Templar, an order of the knighthood founded *c.* 1118 to guard pilgrims on their way to Jerusalem; it dates from the late 12th century. Part of the original round nave is visible, but the present nave is 13th century. The Norman chancel arch remains. The early 13th-century west tower was once detached from the church. The stalls, benches, communion rails and panelling are all of the 16th and 17th centuries. South of the church is a dove-cote dated 1326.

Garynahine *Lewis, Western Isles* 568Bc
STONE CIRCLE The stones comprise a central slab surrounded by a ring of boulders. Outside these is a second ring composed of upright stone slabs, the tallest rising to a height of 9 ft. Five of these uprights remain, the sixth having disappeared. The circle dates from the Neolithic period or the Bronze Age.

Gatehouse of Fleet *Dumfs. & Gall.* 556Eg
A pleasant burgh of two-storey traditional stone houses with symmetrical three-window elevations distinguished here and there by pedimented door-ways and window surrounds painted in a darker colour. High Street and Fleet Street run from east to west. A wide street to the south leads to the gates of Cally House, which was designed by Robert Mylne in 1759–63.

Gatton *Surrey* 542Bf
Gatton was a 'rotten borough', and the houses were all swallowed up in a gentleman's landscaped park. The so-called town hall is a tiny Classical temple with an urn in front. It was built in 1765, and two Members of Parliament were solemnly elected there, although there was hardly anyone to vote for them.

Gawsworth *Cheshire* 552Be
CHURCH OF ST JAMES Gawsworth is a picturesque village, and St James's is a fine 15th-century building with a tall pinnacled west tower, decorated with heraldic shields. There are good roofs in the nave and chancel, and several 17th-century monuments to the Fitton family, who lived at the Hall near by.

Gawsworth Hall *Cheshire* 552Be
A 16th-century Elizabethan half-timbered manor house, the former home of Mary Fitton (*c.* 1600), who is considered by some to have been Shakespeare's 'Dark Lady' of his Sonnets. Right from its origin, the hall has been held by only five families, one of which, 'The Fighting Fittons', held the tenure from 1316 to 1662. The house has a fine collection of paintings, including examples of works by Rubens, Constable and Correggio. In the grounds there is a collection of coaches and carriages, and the park encloses a medieval jousting ground.

Gawthorpe Hall *Lancs.* 558Ab
The home of the Shuttleworth family since 1330. The present mansion was built around an earlier house in the late 16th century and houses a collection of textiles and early European furniture. Closed until 1987.

Gayhurst *Bucks.* 547Ge
CHURCH OF ST PETER A complete rebuilding in 1728 of an older church by an unknown architect. It stands next to Gayhurst House, a 16th–17th-century house. The square west tower is crowned with a cupola. It is rusticated below, and there are Ionic pilasters around the exterior. The pleasant interior has been almost untouched in the intervening centuries, having giant pilasters, and decorated plaster ceiling, while panelling, box-pews, two-decker pulpit and reredos are all woodwork of the time. The showpiece is the monument to Sir Nathan Wright and his son (*c.* 1728) with two standing figures in contemporary dress and wigs, the architectural background with looped curtains, all in marble.

Geddington *Northants.* 547Gg
Geddington has the best preserved of the 'Eleanor' crosses, set up by Edward I in memory of his wife, Eleanor of Castile, and marking the places where her coffin rested on its journey to London from Harby in Nottinghamshire after her death in 1290. Only three of the original 12 crosses remain.

Gedney *Lincs.* 553Jc
CHURCH OF ST MARY MAGDALENE The Early English tower has an unfinished Perpendicular spire. There are remains of 14th- and 15th-century glass in the north aisle. Monuments include a 13th-century brass of a lady, a 17th-century alabaster coloured effigy, and part of a 13th-century figure of a knight.

GLAMIS CASTLE

During the 1715 Jacobite rebellion, James Francis Edward Stuart, the Old Pretender, was entertained in this magnificent 'tower-house' castle; since 1372 it had been the home of the Lyon family, later Earls of Strathmore and Kinghorne, and forbears of Queen Elizabeth the Queen Mother. It was also visited by Mary, Queen of Scots, and was occupied by Cromwell's troops. The original tower dates from the 15th century, *but in 1650 the 3rd Earl began enlargements in French-château style—the wings and rounded turrets, castellations and corbels were added, eclipsing the nucleus of the castle. Inside, delicately worked plaster ceilings, also showing Renaissance influences, were installed. About this time, several castles, including Craigievar and Caerlaverock, also 'flowered' in this way, and the style became known as Scottish baronial.*

Gibside *Tyne & Wear* 558Cg
CHAPEL In the grounds of Gibside House, an interesting building now a ruin, the chapel, now used as a church, was designed by James Paine in 1760; it was originally intended as a family mausoleum.

Giggleswick *N. Yorks.* 558 Ac
CHURCH OF ST ALKEDA This Perpendicular church, dedicated to an obscure Anglo-Saxon saint, contains some fine 17th-century furnishings including a pulpit, reading desk, communion rail and poor box. There is a battered effigy of Sir Richard Tempest, who donated a chantry to the church. The story goes that when he was buried here in 1488, the head of his favourite horse was interred with him.

Gilling Castle *N. Yorks.* 558Ed
An Elizabethan house with a front added in the early 18th century. The Elizabethan great chamber still retains its original ribbed plaster ceilings, and the frieze, oak panelling and stained glass were rescued from a London warehouse, to which they had been sent by the American millionaire, William Randolph Hearst, and re-installed. The grounds include fine terraced gardens.

Glamis *Tayside* 566Eb
GLAMIS CASTLE This imposing castle has been the home of the Lyon family since the 14th century. The head of the family, forbears of Queen Elizabeth the Queen Mother, was made Earl of Strathmore and Kinghorne in 1606; Princess Margaret was born here. The castle was remodelled in French-château style by the 3rd Earl in 1650–96, but the tower dates from the 15th century.
KIRK WYND (ANGUS FOLK MUSEUM) Agricultural and domestic equipment, cottage furniture, hand looms and workmen's tools, all collected in Angus, are displayed in a row of five cottages, built between 200 and 300 years ago.

Glandford *Norfolk* 554Cd
MUSEUM OF SHELLS A collection of shells from all over the world. The museum also includes jewels, pottery and relics of Pompeii.

Glasgow *Strathclyde* 561He
St Mungo the missionary founded this city on the R. Clyde in the 6th century; he is its patron saint and the 12th-century cathedral is dedicated to him. In 1451 Bishop William Turnbull founded the university. During the Border Wars Glasgow was a rallying point for Scottish armies engaged in feuds and battles with England, in particular with the city of Carlisle. It remained a small port, and market and university city, until the 18th century. Then the dredging of the Clyde improved navigation and the city's trade, shipbuilding and manufacturing increased rapidly. The city grew, quickly expanding beyond the limits of the old town centred round the cathedral; today it is Scotland's largest city.
ART GALLERY AND MUSEUM (KELVINGROVE) Opened in 1902, this red sandstone building houses displays representing the Italian, Dutch, Flemish and French schools and British and Scottish art, especially Scottish Colourists. There are exhibits of ceramics, jewellery and silver, and examples from the zoology, botany and geology collections of the Natural History Department.
BOTANIC GARDENS Kibble Palace, a wrought-iron conservatory, was transferred to the gardens in 1873. It contains a collection of rare tree ferns.
BURRELL COLLECTION Housed in a purpose-built gallery in Pollok Park is the lifetime's collection of Sir William Burrell, a rich shipowner. More than 8,000 items (a quarter to a third of them on show at any one time) cover the world of art from French Impressionist paintings and Assyrian reliefs to Chinese bronzes, medieval European tapestries, and Roman glass.

Glasgow is fortunate in having the finest municipal collections in Britain. They are housed in the Kelvingrove Art Gallery and Museum and in the city's branch museums (see p. 210).

FRENCH TAPESTRY OF THE 15TH CENTURY *The popular medieval millefleurs motif—a field of flowers forming the background to unlikely scenes and strange events—greatly influenced designers of a later age, such as William Morris. This tapestry, probably made in the late 15th century, mixes legend and fact: Charity, on an elephant, strikes down Envy dressed as a knight. (Burrell Collection)*

KIFWEBE MASK *A fine dance mask of the Baluba people of south-eastern Zaire. Such masks are worn by members of the secret Kifwebe society in dance ceremonies performed on the death of a chief and the installation of his successor. (Kelvingrove)*

15TH-CENTURY MILANESE ARMOUR *The earliest complete suit of armour which can be seen in Britain, made about 1440 for a member of the Matsch family of Churburg in South Tyrol. It is also one of the earliest and finest surviving examples of Italian Gothic-style armour. It was designed for a mounted knight—the holes to the right of the breastplate were used for attaching a lance-rest. Carefully tailored to its owner's figure like a well-made suit, it gives the effect of 'sculpture in steel'. (Kelvingrove)*

GIORGIONE: THE ADULTERESS BROUGHT BEFORE CHRIST *Giorgione died in 1510 at the early age of 33 and there are perhaps no more than a dozen pictures in the world which can be assigned to him without question; but he brought to Venetian painting a rare poetic quality. Some of this he inherited from his teacher Giovanni Bellini and he passed it on to his* fellow pupil Titian to such an extent that it is difficult to decide which artist did some paintings. The 'Adulteress' is one of these, but the balance of opinion is in favour of Giorgione, if only because it has that particular gift of his—a sort of melancholy grace. Being a Venetian, Giorgione creates his ideal world out of colour rather than form. (Kelvingrove)

THE WARWICK VASE *The fragments of this vase were found in a lake near Hadrian's villa in Tivoli near Rome in 1771. Sir William Hamilton, husband of Lord Nelson's Emma, had the vase restored in Rome, and it was later acquired by the Earl of Warwick, who* had it taken to Warwick Castle in 1788. It remained there until 1979, when it was bought by the City of Glasgow for the Burrell Collection. It is of white marble, is 5 ft 6 in. high, and dates from the 2nd century AD. (Museum of Transport)

HUNTERIAN MUSEUM

Chardin (1699–1779) gives each subject its own special quality. Forsaking the brilliance of high society, he records the dignity of simple people and humble occupations with a superb mastery of form, an exquisite eye for colour and an exceptional feeling for paint. His technique captures marvellously the different textures of the wooden tub, the coarse linen apron and the maid's rough, red hands.

This 19th-century oil bowl from British Columbia was fashioned from the horns of a Big Horn sheep and is decorated with a carving of a man and a shark.

Gorgets, or chest shields, were worn for protection from wooden spears in the battles that took place frequently in the Society Islands in the 18th century. This one, probably made for a chief, is from Tahiti and has a wickerwork base ornamented with feathers, dogs' hair, sharks' teeth and mother-of-pearl.

CALEDONIA ROAD CHURCH The shell of a fine Grecian-style church built in 1857 by Alexander 'Greek' Thompson, with a tall, thin unadorned tower and a fine Ionic portico.

CATHEDRAL Dedicated to St Mungo, the well preserved cathedral was built between the 12th and 15th centuries. It is cruciform in plan, with a low central tower and spire. Beneath the east end is a crypt. Most of the fittings are 19th century.

HUNTERIAN MUSEUM AND ART GALLERY, UNIVERSITY OF GLASGOW The museum, as well as holding one of the four major collections of British coins, has relics of prehistoric and Roman Scotland and archaeological finds from the Mediterranean area including Egypt, Jericho and Jerusalem. The ethnographical material includes some from the South Sea Islands brought back by Captain Cook, and in the geological collection of minerals, rocks and gemstones is a set of casts of fossil footprints. A model of James Watt's Newcomen engine is displayed. The art collections include works by Rembrandt, Rubens, Chardin, Stubbs, Whistler and C. R. Mackintosh, Scottish paintings of the late 19th and early 20th centuries, and a large selection of prints.

HUTCHESON'S HOSPITAL Built in 1802–5 and designed by David Hamilton in the neo-Classical style with a traditional Scottish 'town house' steeple. Statues of the founders George and Thomas Hutcheson made in 1649 by James Colquhoun are those from the original hospital building.

MERCHANT'S STEEPLE Built into the Fish Market of 1872, this relic is all that remains of the guildhall and hospital built by the Merchants of Glasgow in 1659. Gothic and Renaissance details add charm to the 164-ft steeple, which was completed in 1665. Originally it stood as part of the garden frontage entered from the Bridgegate.

MUSEUM OF TRANSPORT Exhibits show the development of transport with horse-drawn vehicles, bicycles, locomotives, cars, an outstanding collection of ship models, and a model railway.

PEOPLE'S PALACE A museum of Glasgow history in the oldest park in the city with an adjoining Winter Gardens housing exotic plants.

POLLOCK HOUSE Contains a fine collection of Spanish paintings and European decorative art.

PROVAND'S LORDSHIP The oldest house in Glasgow, built in 1471 as part of the Hospital of St Nicholas. It is now a museum.

ROYAL BANK OF SCOTLAND AND ROYAL EXCHANGE SQUARE A fine unit, comprising a central block of two storeys with Greek Ionic portico and pediment. Archways set in coupled Ionic columns link the bank with the symmetrical flanking buildings, whose first and second floors are fronted by the Ionic order. Archibald Elliot of London designed the bank in 1827. David Hamilton and James Smith designed Nos. 1–29 and 2–40 in the square.

ST VINCENT STREET CHURCH Alexander 'Greek' Thompson built this delightful Grecian church in 1859. Its elaborate tower is a hill-top landmark, and the church itself rises sheer from a great podium. Originally built for the United Presbyterians, it is now used by St Vincent Street Free Church of Scotland. Outside are magnificent Ionic porticos. The interior of the church is spacious, with galleries and two tiers of strange columns in Pompeian red, blue, white and gold.

SCHOOL OF ART In 1895 a competition was held to choose designs for a new, larger School of Art. The competition was won by a Glasgow firm with designs by Charles Rennie Mackintosh. Building began in 1897 and the first portion was finished

INTERIOR AT GLASGOW SCHOOL OF ART

Charles Rennie Mackintosh (1868–1928) was a Scottish art nouveau architect who designed the interiors, furniture and fabrics for many of his buildings. The Glasgow School of Art, built 1897– *1909, shows his preference for black-and-white colour schemes. He is remembered for his high-backed chairs —some were made about 5 ft tall; but in their surroundings Mackintosh designs do not look incongruous.*

within two years; there was then a pause of some years and the remainder was not completed until 1909. The school is practically designed with large windows. Some of it is decorated in the flowing art nouveau style which had recently become fashionable, but much of it is simply designed and forms a link between Victorian architectural style and the modern trends of the 20th century.

STIRLING'S LIBRARY David Hamilton, one of the principal architects of the new town of Glasgow, designed the Royal Exchange in 1829, incorporating the earlier Cunningham Mansion of 1778. A massive portico of the Corinthian order surmounted by a tower dwarfs the equestrian statue of Wellington by Marochetti which stands in front.

TOLBOOTH STEEPLE Erected in 1626. Originally a handsome tolbooth of five storeys fronting the north side of the Trongate, with the surviving seven-storey steeple at the east end. An open cross with balustrade crowns the steeple, and the lintels are embellished with carved strapwork containing emblems of St Mungo and royalty.

UNIVERSITY OF GLASGOW The second oldest university in Scotland, founded in 1451. The original buildings were in the High Street, but in 1870 the university moved to Victorian Gothic buildings in Kelvingrove Park, designed by Sir Gilbert Scott, who also designed the Albert Memorial, London.

UNIVERSITY OF STRATHCLYDE Founded in 1964 and formerly the Royal College of Science and Technology.

Glastonbury *Som.* 540Ce

ABBEY The most substantial remains at Glastonbury, apart from two great columns where nave and chancel meet, are of the Lady Chapel (at the west end). The ruins of the chapel, which stands on the site of the 7th–8th-century church, date from 1187 when rebuilding began after a fire had destroyed the earlier buildings. The chapel is remarkable for its sculptured doorways and elaborate late Norman architectural decoration; the sculpture appears to date from the late 13th century. Near by, the abbot's kitchen, dating from the late 14th century, is the chief monastic building still visible. It is one of the most complete medieval kitchens to survive in Europe. The monastic gatehouse has a small museum and a model of the abbey as it is believed to have existed up to 1539.

LAKE VILLAGE MUSEUM Glastonbury was once— from the 2nd century BC to the Roman conquest— an important trading site, built near navigable water on artificial islands or platforms of brushwood or timber; archaeological finds from the Iron Age Celtic lake village are now housed in a 15th-century building known as the Tribunal, which used to be the courtroom of the Abbot of Glastonbury.

Glencoe *Highland* 565Hc

A tall stone cross marks the scene of the massacre of February 1692 when a party of Campbells led by their Captain killed 40 Jacobites of the Macdonald clan. To this day the glen is known as the Glen of Weeping.

Glencorse *Lothian* 562Be

CASTLE LAW FORT AND EARTH-HOUSE This interesting fort has been excavated, and the sequence of its various defences determined. Its first enclosure was a simple timber palisade, soon succeeded by a timber-laced rampart which did not quite coincide with the line of the first stockade. Later, two ramparts, each with an external ditch, were constructed outside the first, so that finally there was a trivallate hill-fort shortly before the early Roman expeditions reached southern Scotland. The earth-house (souterrain) is a small underground apartment entered from the inner of the two later ditches; it may be of the 3rd century AD.

Glendurgan Garden *Cornwall* 538Ca

The garden at Glendurgan lies in a small wooded valley which drops down to the fishing village of Durgan. At the head of the garden stands the house. On the front lawn tropical succulents such as giant agaves flower in Cornwall's temperate climate. A path down one side of the valley is planted with exotic flowering shrubs, and branches off to a group of giant camellias. There is a water garden surrounded by primulas and bluebells. The path to the house on the other side of the valley runs beside an extremely rare Bunya-bunya tree from Australia and an unusual maze.

Glenesk *Tayside* 566Ec

FOLK MUSEUM In a converted shooting lodge, it is part of the Glenesk Trust, sponsored by Lord and Lady Dalhousie. It contains folk material, period costumes and a music library.

GLOUCESTER CATHEDRAL

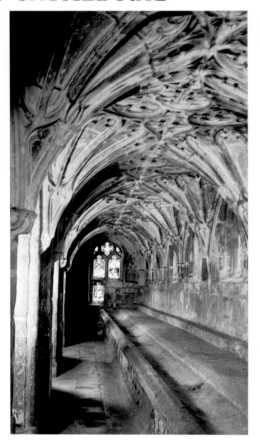

TOMB OF EDWARD II *In 1327 Edward II was murdered. The body of a murdered king is a difficult thing to find a home for, but it was finally taken for burial by the Abbot of Gloucester. Within a few years the new king, Edward III, began to make a cult of his father's memory, and this magnificent tomb was his first move in establishing it. With its elaborate stone canopy, it dates from soon after 1330, and was the work of London Court sculptors. The alabaster head is not a portrait but an idealised symbol of saintly majesty. The rather effeminate style of this period is appropriate to the subject.*

TOMB OF ROBERT, DUKE OF NORMANDY, *the eldest son of William the Conqueror, is carved in oak painted to represent life, and dates from the end of the 12th century; but the chest under it is 15th-century. The figure was broken during the Civil War but was later restored. Robert was his father's natural successor but he twice revolted against William, so that when the Conqueror died he named his second son Rufus heir to the throne of England. The dissatisfied Robert eventually died a prisoner in Cardiff Castle in 1134.*

THE MONKS' LAVATORIUM *The Abbey of St Peter at Gloucester was founded before the Conquest but, like many English abbeys, was reformed soon after the arrival of the Normans. The first Norman abbot, Serlo, began the existing church in 1089, and the main work was complete by the consecration of 1100. In appearance, Romanesque Gloucester is similar to the neighbouring abbey church of Tewkesbury. The origin of the design of these buildings, which both have cylindrical columns in the nave, can be found in Burgundy and Italy rather than in Normandy. The superb choir stalls are 14th century, and the organ case, the oldest in any English cathedral, dates from 1663. The 'choir organ' (a small case beneath the big one on the eastern side of the organ) may date from the time of Henry VIII, and if so is by far the oldest organ case in England. The fine ring of twelve bells in the tower, with England's heaviest medieval bell by an unknown founder, was restored in 1979.*

Glenfinnan Monument *Highland*   565Gd
A tall, narrow tower, on which the statue of a Highlander stands, was erected in 1815 on the site where Prince Charles Edward (Bonnie Prince Charlie) raised his standard for the Jacobite rebellion on August 19, 1745.

Glenkiln *Dumfs. & Gall.*   562Aa
William J. Keswick has turned his 3000-acre moorland and woodland estate, between Dunscore and Shawhead, into an open-air gallery of works by Henry Moore, Jacob Epstein, Auguste Rodin and other sculptors.

Glenluce Abbey *Dumfs. & Gall.*   556Cg
The abbey, founded in 1190, is now a ruin, but the vaulted chapter house remains intact.

Glenquicken *Dumfs. & Gall.*   556Dg
STONE CIRCLE This Bronze Age circle, with a 50 ft diameter, comprises 28 boulders set with their narrow edges outwards (radially). In the centre of the circle is a larger rectangular stone which stands almost 6 ft high.

Another similar circle of nine stones in the circumference and a central stone $5\frac{1}{2}$ ft high, lies $1\frac{1}{4}$ miles to the south-east.

Gloddaeth Hall *Gwynedd*   550Fe
Gloddaeth Hall was greatly extended in the 19th century, but most of the older parts are concentrated around the entrance front. Although dating from the 16th century, the Hall with its open roof is medieval in inspiration; of particular interest is

the coved ceiling at the end where the high table would have been set. Behind this are two rooms, both lined with Elizabethan wainscoting, the upper room or solar having a roof similar to that over the hall. The wing to the north-east has a fine late 17th-century staircase. By appointment.

Gloucester *Glos.* 546Cd
BISHOP HOOPER'S LODGING Housed in a group of 15th- and 16th-century timber-framed buildings, the museum illustrates the crafts and agriculture of the region, such as the different fishing methods used on the R. Severn.
CATHEDRAL Building was begun in 1089 and the Norman part finished *c.* 1160. The east end was remodelled by London masons after Edward II was buried there in 1327, and although much of the Romanesque work survives, the internal face was covered with a skin of masonry in the new Perpendicular style. To the east, the Norman apse was removed and replaced by one of the largest Perpendicular windows in England. This window retains its superb 14th-century glass. The cloisters were also rebuilt in the 14th century. They contain the earliest surviving fan-vaulting and, down the south walk, the carrels (miniature studies used by the monks for reading and working). Historic plate is exhibited in a Treasury provided in 1977 by the Goldsmiths' Company.
CHURCH OF ST MARY-DE-CRYPT A cruciform church, of Norman origin, with a central tower. It contains brasses, and several 17th- and 18th-century monuments, including one (the design for which is in the Victoria and Albert Museum) by Peter Scheemakers, who carved Shakespeare's bust in Westminster Abbey.
CITY MUSEUM AND ART GALLERY The archaeology and natural history of the area are featured, one of the most important archaeological items being the late Iron Age bronze Birdlip mirror from *c.* AD 25. English furniture, pottery, silver, glass and costume can be seen, and temporary art exhibitions are held throughout the year.
ROBERT OPIE COLLECTION At Gloucester Docks is a museum devoted to more than a century of British packaging and advertising, from the colourful tins, boxes, bottles and posters that helped to sell the goods of Victorian grocers, confectioners, chemists and tobacconists to the early TV commercials of the 1950s.

Glyn Cywarch *Gwynedd* 550Fc
The earliest part of this attractive Welsh country house is an example of the curious custom seen in this part of Wales, of an extension (dated 1616 in this case), taking the form of a separate house joined at one point to the original. This is thought to be connected with the practice of gavelkind, the equal division of property among heirs, as opposed to the English custom of primogeniture, by which property is inherited by the eldest son. (Exterior only.)

Glynde *E. Sussex* 542Cd
CHURCH OF ST MARY THE VIRGIN A Classical church, built in 1765, probably to the designs of Sir Thomas Robinson. The interior, with its 18th-century furnishings—pulpit, box-pews, gallery— is somewhat spoilt by the big 19th-century screen. There is some 16th- and 17th-century Netherlandish stained glass, as well as some late 19th-century stained glass by C. E. Kempe.

Glynde Place *E. Sussex* 542Cd
Richard Trevor (1701–71), Bishop of Durham, lived in this 16th-century quadrangular mansion built of flint and brick; in 1752 he rebuilt much of the house and added the stable block. The house contains a long gallery with 17th-century panelling, a collection of bronzes by Bertos, fine needlework, and paintings by Rubens, Kneller, Hoppner, Lely, Weenix and Zoffany.

Glyn Pits *Gwent* 545Jc
At Glyn Pits are preserved the only two early steam-engines in Wales. The smaller building houses the pumping engine and is dated 1845; opposite is the winding engine, which lifted cages in the two shafts, now filled in. (Exterior only.)

Gnosall *Staffs.* 552Bc
CHURCH OF ST LAWRENCE The impressive cruciform building was begun by the Normans, whose tower arches still remain. There is work of all periods to the 15th century. The east window has some good Decorated tracery and 20th-century glass. There is also an effigy of a knight.

Godalming *Surrey* 542Ae
The polygonal white market hall, built in 1814, with arcades and a cupola, is the focal point of the long street. There is also a fine coaching inn, the King's Arms, built in 1753.
BOROUGH MUSEUM The museum is housed in the old town hall or Hundred House, built in 1814 to replace an earlier building on a site which was a centre of local government for over 1000 years. The exhibits are arranged to show the story of the town and the Godalming Hundred (a medieval county division) from prehistoric times.

GLYNDE PLACE

Bishop Trevor, a favourite prelate of George II, made extensive alterations to this Elizabethan manor house and in the course of them made the east front, which faces the park, the entrance to the house. Among its treasures is Rubens' original sketch for the ceiling of the Banqueting House in Whitehall.

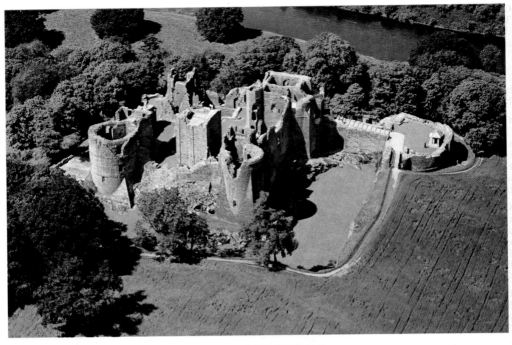

GOODRICH CASTLE

Goodrich Castle is set on an outcrop of red sandstone overlooking the R. Wye, and throughout the 12th and 13th centuries its importance lay in the fact that it was a Welsh Border castle. It came into the possession of the Crown in the 12th century and was granted to William Marshall, Earl of Pembroke, who had made his fortune by winning prize money in tournaments. In 1247, after the death of his son, the property passed to William de Valence, a half-brother of Henry III, whose enamelled tomb can still be seen in Westminster Abbey. The castle has not been inhabited since the 16th century.

CHURCH OF SS PETER AND PAUL A cruciform church with a central tower and spire; it stands on a Saxon site, and contains work of all periods—from Norman times to the 19th century.

Godinton Park *Kent*   *542Ee*
A Jacobean gabled mansion containing carved panelling, particularly in the hall and on the staircase, fine furniture, paintings and china. The grounds, originally laid out in the 18th century, were extended and improved in the 19th century by Sir Reginald Blomfield. They contain formal gardens with fine topiary work.

Godmanchester *Cambs.*   *547Jf*
Twin town of Huntingdon, with several 16th- and 17th-century half-timbered houses, some thatched. CHURCH OF ST MARY THE VIRGIN A 13th- and 14th-century church, with a 15th-century clerestory. The 17th-century tower has a spire. Inside are noteworthy 15th-century choir stalls, with carving, and a series of misericords.

Godolphin House *Cornwall*   *538Ba*
The country mansion home of the Earls of Godolphin. It is partly of Tudor date, with Elizabethan and Stuart additions; the colonnaded façade was added in 1635.

Godshill *Isle of Wight*   *541Hc*
CHURCH OF ALL SAINTS Conspicuous on its hilltop site, a church of the 14th and 15th centuries. In the south transept is a 15th-century wall-painting of Christ crucified on a lily cross. Among interesting monuments, from the 16th to 19th centuries, the best is to Sir John Leigh and his wife.

Goodmanham *Humberside*   *558Fb*
CHURCH OF ALL HALLOWS Norman church, with Gothic additions, which is believed to be on the site of a pagan temple destroyed during the 7th century after its priest was converted to Christianity. There is a Norman chancel arch and doorways, and a Perpendicular font.

Goodrich Castle *Heref. & Worcs.*   *546Bd*
Goodrich, or 'Godric's', Castle is first mentioned in a document of c. 1095, but the existing buildings are all later. On the south side of the main enclosure stands a square Norman keep built c. 1160–70. Any 12th-century outworks there may once have been have now vanished, and the keep is surrounded by late 13th-century walls; these were designed to bring the defences up to date, and in fact made the keep militarily almost unnecessary. During the conquest of Wales by Edward I, William de Valance, half-brother to Henry III, made extensive additions to Goodrich, which had passed to him in 1247. He gave the castle an almost square inner ward, an outer ward covering two sides, a barbican covering the main gate and, inside, a suite of living rooms including a great hall, upper chamber, chapel and kitchen.

Goodwood House *W. Sussex*   *541Jd*
Seat of the Dukes of Richmond, Lennox Aubigny and Gordon, the Jacobean house was rebuilt in Sussex flintwork in 1780–1800 by Charles Lennox, the 3rd Duke (1735–1806), with James Wyatt as architect. It contains paintings by Canaletto, Van Dyck, Romney and Lely, sporting pictures by Stubbs and Wootton, furniture of the Louis XV period, and a collection of Sèvres porcelain.

Gop Cairn *Clwyd*   *551He*
Crowning Gop Hill, the largest prehistoric cairn in Wales. Over 60 ft high, it was partly excavated in 1866 when it was found to be built entirely of drystone.

Gorhambury *Herts.* 547Hc

The home of the Earl of Verulam, kinsman of the great Elizabethan essayist and scholar, Francis Bacon. The house was designed by Sir Robert Taylor and completed in 1784; it contains portraits and books formerly belonging to the Bacon family. The older 16th-century manor house, home of Francis Bacon, is now a ruin in Gorhambury Park.

Gorsey Bigbury *Som.* 540Cf

This Neolithic 'henge' is marked by a circular bank some 200 ft in diameter, with an internal ditch cut into the underlying rock. One of the few henges to have been fully excavated, it was revealed that, soon after it was constructed, it was occupied for a time by some Beaker People, perhaps as a camping site.

Gosfield *Essex* 548Bd

GOSFIELD HALL A Tudor courtyard house, much altered in the 18th century, and added to and restored in the 19th century by the Courtauld family. It has a Tudor panelled long gallery, ballroom and hidden room. Now owned by Country Houses Association.

Gowthorpe Manor *Norfolk* 554Db

Sir William Boleyn, grandfather of Anne Boleyn, acquired this Tudor manor between 1494 and 1505. It passed to Thomas Aldrych, twice Mayor of Norwich, in 1525. The west wing dates from *c.* 1530. The great chamber was shortened by 26 ft in 1669, and the oak framing by the spiral stair and the fire-place in the south room are additions, *c.* 1550. In 1669, Thomas Berney cased the oak-framed west wing with brick; and his son Thomas (1674–1720), introduced the 18th-century fire-places in the drawing-room and a bedroom, and also built a walled garden with new entrance gates. The Steward family bought the property in 1810; it was used as a farmhouse until 1908, when John Henry Steward moved the main front door from the west to the east of the house, at the same time building a new kitchen wing. (By appointment.)

Goxhill Priory *Humberside* 553Hg

Often regarded as a mystery building, since there is doubt about its religious origins. The records of the Wentworth family show that Marjorie, the last heiress of the le Despensers, whose family seat was at Goxhill, married Roger Wentworth of Nettlehead (*d.* 1452), and that Goxhill was a Wentworth possession until Sir Richard Wentworth's death in 1528. This 14th-century house, therefore, seems likely to have been a Despenser manor house, and not a priory. The main doorway carries shields and spandrels and there is a spiral staircase in the south-west corner, a three-light Perpendicular window on the west side and three wide blank arches on the north and south. (By appointment.)

Grantham *Lincs.* 553Gc

Originally a staging point between London and Lincoln, the town was sacked in 1461 during the Wars of the Roses. In 1483 at the 14th-century Angel Inn, Richard III signed the death warrant of the Duke of Buckingham. The Early English church has a spire 272 ft high. Notable buildings are the elegant George Hotel of 1780, Vine House in Vine Street (1764), and Grantham House, dating from 1380 but with Elizabethan additions of *c.* 1570. The Beehive Inn in Castlegate has as its sign a beehive that is actually used by bees. In front of the guildhall is a statue to Sir Isaac Newton, who was born in 1642 at Woolsthorpe Manor by Colsterworth, about 6 miles south of Grantham.

ANGEL AND ROYAL HOTEL The inn dates from the 14th century. At the front of the decorated two-

18th-CENTURY FRENCH WRITING CABINET OR SECRETAIRE

Made by one of the leading 18th-century Parisian cabinet makers, Bernard van Risenburg, this cabinet may have been at the Palace of Versailles, as it is similar to other pieces made by Risenburg for Louis XV and Madame de Pompadour. It shows Risenburg's taste for the exotic in the Oriental lacquer. Louis wanted smaller rooms as well as the grand salons of Versailles and so smaller furniture was required. Risenburg achieved this diminution in size without offending the French taste for grandeur.
(Goodwood House)

COMPOTIÈRE AND COVER

Made in 1756, the year when the French porcelain factory moved from Vincennes to Sèvres, this compotière (dessert-dish) and cover were probably decorated by Armand Aine. He used the popular 'bleu céleste' or 'heavenly blue' glaze, and the panel is painted with birds in overglaze enamels. The collection of Sèvres porcelain at Goodwood was accumulated by the 3rd Duke of Richmond when Ambassador to Louis XV. (Goodwood House)

storey structure two bay windows flank a central archway. The medieval windows were at some later date replaced by sash windows. Originally the property of the Knights Templar, the inn later belonged to the Hospitallers.

CHURCH OF ST WULFRAM A magnificent church, with work of all periods. The tower and spire are fine work of the 14th century, and the main body of the church is of the same period; the north aisle, however, is earlier. Beneath the south chapel is a vaulted 14th-century crypt. There is late Decorated work in the north porch, and the chantry chapel in the north aisle is late Perpendicular. The font, which is Perpendicular, is richly carved with figures and biblical scenes.

GRANTHAM HOUSE Princess Margaret, daughter of Henry VII, stayed here in 1503 on her way north to marry James IV of Scotland. The original house, including the hall used by the princess, is late 14th century; it was enlarged in the 16th century and extensively altered in the 18th century.

LIBRARY AND MUSEUM Sir Isaac Newton was educated at Grantham Grammar School, and items associated with him are included in the collections which reflect the social and industrial history of the town from the Bronze Age onwards. Relics of the Beaker People, who came to Britain *c.* 1800 BC, and Romano-Britons are included.

Grasmere *Cumbria*   *557He*
DOVE COTTAGE Home for 8½ years of the poet William Wordsworth. His house and personal belongings are preserved; there is also a Wordsworth Museum. The poet is buried in St Oswald's churchyard.

Gravesend *Kent*   *542Dg*
CHURCH OF ST GEORGE A fine Georgian church of red brick with stone facings, built *c.* 1731 on the site of a medieval church destroyed by fire. Its architect was Charles Sloane. An aisle was added in 1897. Princess Pocahontas, the first Red Indian to become a Christian, visited England with her English husband, John Rolfe, but died at Gravesend on the return journey to Virginia in 1616. She was buried in the chancel and is commemorated by a life-size statue.

Grays *Essex*   *548Bb*
THURROCK LOCAL HISTORY MUSEUM The main collections are of local archaeological finds from Palaeolithic times, the Early and Late Bronze Age —including a Celtic founder's hoard—and Romano-British ceramics, glass, bronzes and ornaments, with a hoard of Roman silver coins of the 1st and 2nd centuries AD. There are also pre-Christian Saxon ceramics, domestic items, ornaments and weaving equipment, and local social history is represented by items relating to the railways, fire-fighting and other services. Local engravings and water-colours are also exhibited.

Great Amwell *Herts.*   *548Ad*
CHURCH OF ST JOHN THE BAPTIST A pre-Norman church, with an apse and a 15th-century west tower. It also has a brass, a 17th-century pulpit and several large 18th-century monuments in the churchyard.

Great Badminton *Avon*   *546Cb*
CHURCH OF ST MICHAEL AND ALL ANGELS Standing in the park of the Dukes of Beaufort, for whom it was rebuilt in 1783, the church is in the Classical style of the period. Inside, there are notable contemporary fittings, including box-pews and canopied pulpit, and a great number of marble monuments to the Beaufort family, including two by J. M. Rysbrack, of the mid-18th-century. (By appointment.)

Great Bardfield *Essex*   *548Bd*
CHURCH OF ST MARY THE VIRGIN A 14th-century church, with a Norman west tower and chancel. Some fragments of late 14th-century stained glass remain and there is a stone rood screen of the same date.

Great Barrington *Glos.*   *546Dd*
CHURCH OF ST MARY THE VIRGIN Of Norman origin, with work of the Early English and Perpendicular periods, the church has a pinnacled west

tower; inside, the nave roof is a fine example of 15th-century work, and the chancel arch is Norman.

The monument to two children who died of smallpox in 1711 and 1720 may be by Christopher Cass, who carved the coat of arms over the portico of St Martin-in-the-Fields, London. The designs for this and for the large mourning figure by Joseph Nollekens are both in the Victoria and Albert Museum.

Great Bookham *Surrey*   *542Af*
CHURCH OF ST NICOLAS Originally a Norman building; most notable of the later additions are the chancel, built by John Rutherwyke, Abbot of Chertsey in 1341, and the south aisle, widened in the 15th century. There is a timber tower, with shingled spire, on a stone base. Restorations took place in the second half of the 19th century. There are brasses and monuments of all periods.

Great Brington *Northants.*   *546Ff*
CHURCH OF ST MARY A large church with a west tower, mainly of the Decorated and Perpendicular periods. The north chapel, dating from the early 16th century, was built by Sir John Spencer as a chapel for his family. The series of Spencer monuments includes work by Jasper Hollemans, Nicholas Stone, Joseph Nollekens and John Flaxman.

MONUMENT TO
SIR EDWARD SPENCER

Carved in marble by John Stone—probably the third son of the famous mason Nicholas Stone (1586–1647) —the monument shows Sir Edward's effigy emerging from an urn. (Church of St Mary, Great Brington)

Great Bromley *Essex*   *548Dd*
CHURCH OF ST GEORGE A mainly 15th-century church, it has a fine west tower, a south porch with flushwork panelling, a clerestory to the nave and a double hammerbeam roof. There is a 15th-century brass to a priest.

Great Budworth *Cheshire*   *552Ae*
CHURCH OF ST MARY AND ALL SAINTS The church and its imposing west tower both date from the 14th and 15th centuries. Inside there are some original roofs, medieval stalls and chest, and a 15th-century font. The monuments include one to Sir Peter Leycester, Cheshire historian (*d.* 1678) and the alabaster figure of Sir John Warburton (*d.* 1575).

Great Casterton *Leics.* 553Gb
CHURCH OF SS PETER AND PAUL A large 13th-century church, with a west tower added in the 15th century. The font is Norman; there are traces of 13th-century mural painting and a carved effigy of a priest.

Great Chalfield *Wilts.* 540Ef
CHURCH OF ALL SAINTS Small, with a square bell-turret, the church stands with the manor house built by Thomas Tropnell. He also added a chapel to the church in 1480, where wall-paintings of the life of St Katharine and a heraldic stone screen still remain. The church contains a 17th-century three-decker pulpit.

Great Chalfield Manor *Wilts.* 540Ef
A moated house built *c.* 1480 of yellow-grey Corsham stone on the site of a fortified manor. It is a good example of domestic Gothic architecture, with a fine great hall that can be viewed from the solar room through squints in the form of hollow masks. The exterior is remarkable for the detail of its arches and buttresses, and for the intricate stone figures carved on the gable ends.

Great Coggeshall *Essex* 548Cd
PAYCOCKE'S Great Coggeshall has several interesting houses, such as the gabled Wool Pack Inn, late 15th century, but this is its most noted building, a complete, richly ornamented merchant's house of *c.* 1500. It has a remarkable façade with oriel windows, a slightly overhanging second storey, and a carved frieze with the builder's initials, T.P. Inside the house there are rooms with carved and moulded beams, and the original fire-places.

Great Coxwell *Oxon.* 546Ec
GREAT BARN The monks of Beaulieu built this enormous tithe barn of stone in the 13th century. Its size indicates the productiveness of the local tithe, or levy, on crops. The roof is of unusual timber construction with stone tiles. The barn, considered by many the finest in England, is 152 ft long, 44 ft wide and 48 ft high.

Great Cressingham Manor *Norfolk* 554Bb
The remains of a once great house built of brick in 1545. It has been partly rebuilt, but the original south front exists showing an ornate string course of terracotta forming a frieze of arches and leaves, and above it terracotta panelling decorated with such emblems as a hawk on a fist and a wreath with a monogram.

Great Dixter *E. Sussex* 542De
A half-timbered manor house, built *c.* 1450 and recently restored. It has oriel windows and a great hall showing hammer-beams alternating with tie-beams. The gardens were laid out by Sir Edwin Lutyens, who carried out restoration of the house in 1910.

Great Dunmow *Essex* 548Bd
A former small market town that is now best known for its Trial of the Dunmow Flitch, one of England's oldest traditional ceremonies. There are several good buildings in the town. The town hall was built in the 16th century, but enlarged subsequently, and the brick and timber Clock House of *c.* 1600, with a square clock turret, is a good example of its time. Bigods, a late 16th-century house, has an attractive Elizabethan summer-house. In the Doctor's Pond, Lionel Lukin tested one of the first lifeboats, 1785.

Great Gaddesden *Herts.* 547Hd
CHURCH OF ST JOHN THE BAPTIST A 12th-century church with later, mainly 15th-century, additions;

the north-east chapel dates from 1730. The monuments, mainly of the 18th century, include one of *c.* 1782 by John Flaxman.

Great Gidding *Cambs.* 547Hg
BAPTIST CHAPEL Built in 1790, the chapel contains nearly all its original furnishings.

Great Glemham *Suffolk* 548Ef
CHURCH OF ALL SAINTS A west tower with flush-work decoration, and a good roof with bosses. Inside is a seven-sacrament font, and fragments of medieval stained glass. All Saints was restored in the 19th century.

Great Malvern *Heref. & Worcs.* 546Be
PRIORY CHURCH OF SS MARY AND MICHAEL A beautiful, mainly 15th-century building, containing tiles, some good choir stalls and magnificent 15th-century glass. Earlier work, of the 12th and 13th centuries, can also be seen, and there are Norman nave arcades. A kiln discovered locally in the 19th century gives weight to the suggestion that all the tiles were made *in situ*.

Great Milton *Oxon.* 546Fc
CHURCH OF ST MARY THE VIRGIN A fine church with work of the Early English to Perpendicular periods, but also with traces of Norman work. The large west tower has a stair-turret capped by a spirelet, and the south porch is two-storied. The choir roof is Perpendicular; fragments of medieval glass and an imposing tomb of *c.* 1618 remain.

Great Packington *Warks.* 546Dg
CHURCH OF ST JAMES This late 18th-century church is the work of Joseph Bonomi (1739–1808). With a plain brick exterior, it has four small towers, one at each corner. The stone-faced, vaulted interior has Greek Doric columns. The altar-piece is a painting by J. F. Rigaud, set into a frame of marble columns and pediment. The 18th-century organ was designed by Handel. (By appointment.)

Great Salkeld *Cumbria* 557Jf
CHURCH OF ST CUTHBERT An austere battle-mented tower was added to the Norman nave of St Cuthbert's during the 14th century, obviously as a defensive measure against raids from the neighbouring Scots. There is a good Norman south doorway, and a 14th-century effigy of a priest.

Great Sampford *Essex* 548Be
CHURCH OF ST MICHAEL Most of the church dates from the 14th century when it was rebuilt by the Knights Hospitaller, though the south chapel remains from an earlier building. It has a 14th-century font, and when the nave was redecorated in 1979 some 14th–15th-century murals depicting the seven deadly sins were uncovered.

Great Staughton *Cambs.* 547Jf
The village cross, erected in 1637, has a complicated sun-dial on three of its four faces.

Great Warley *Essex* 548Bc
CHURCH OF ST MARY THE VIRGIN An outstanding example of an art nouveau church, built in 1904; there is a screen in the form of trees with angels standing among the foliage. The architect was Harrison Townsend, the designer of the White-chapel Art Gallery, London, and most of the interior fittings are by Sir William Reynolds Stevens.

Great Witcombe Villa *Glos.* 546Cd
A fine Cotswold Roman villa which nestles in a sheltered combe of the scarp and looks out over the Vale of Gloucester. When first excavated, some of the walling still stood to a height of about 6 ft. The

GREAT WITLEY CHURCH

This elegant parish church of St Michael and All Saints stands beside gaunt Witley Court, a roofless ruin of a once palatial house. The church is a surprising excursion into baroque style in such a remote place. It dates from the 18th century, when the decision was made to rebuild the medieval church. Much of it has its origins near London. In the suburban wilderness of Edgware once stood Canons, the palatial house built for the 1st Duke of Chandos, who had amassed a colossal fortune as Paymaster-General to Marlborough. After the duke's death, his heir was forced to sell the property and later the mansion was demolished. Lord Foley of Witley Court bought from the chapel the painted-glass windows, made about 1719 by Joshua Price from designs by Francesco Sleter, a Venetian, and the magnificent plaster and painted ceiling panels, the work of Antonio Belucci, and installed them in the church at Great Witley. The organ case may also once have been at Canons. In the south transept is a towering monument to the 1st Lord Foley by Michael Rysbrack, the foremost sculptor in England during the first half of the 18th century.

remains contain tessellated pavements and there is a bath wing. The fabric of the remains has been renovated.

Great Witley *Heref. & Worcs.*   *546Bf*
CHURCH OF ST MICHAEL AND ALL ANGELS There was a medieval church here beside Witley Court, once the home of Lord Foley, but early in the 18th century the decision was made to rebuild it. In 1735 the present baroque church, the same size as the old building, was consecrated. It is a hall-like building with transepts at the east end, and a tower over the western end where the entrance is. But it is the interior, with its magnificent painted glass, and painted, plaster and papier-mâché ceilings, which makes the church important.

Great Wymondley *Herts.*   *547Jd*
An attractive village linked with the 16th-century kings of England, who granted the lord of the manor the right to be Cup-bearer at coronations. DELAMERE HOUSE Built *c.* 1600, named after one of these lords, it is a three-storied brick building occupying the site of a dwelling where Henry VIII was once entertained by Cardinal Wolsey.

Great Yarmouth *Norfolk*   *554Eb*
A great herring port, a 19th-century resort and now a popular holiday centre, Yarmouth is a long town stretching north–south on a gridiron plan. Already settled at the time of the Conquest, it was granted a charter by King John in 1208.

ELIZABETHAN HOUSE MUSEUM An Elizabethan-style house with a Georgian front. There are fine 16th-century panelled rooms with exhibits illustrating domestic life, mainly that of the 17th and 19th centuries. Lowestoft china and glass decorated by William Absolon is shown.
MARITIME MUSEUM FOR EAST ANGLIA Covers herring fishing, lifesaving and shipbuilding.
MARKET-PLACE A large open space merging into Church Plain, with the Fishermen's Hospital or almshouse of 1702. A fine one-storey building around a courtyard, it is picturesquely gabled with a cupola, a pediment with relief and a statue of Charity in the yard. Near here stood the Benedictine priory of St Nicholas, *c.* 1100, of which the refectory remains. Close by is the vicarage of 1718, which has an elegant doorway with shell-hood, and then the great parish church of St Nicholas. King Street is a shopping street with some good buildings, including the Elizabethan White Lion Inn, the early Georgian house (No. 51), and other 17th- and 18th-century houses.
QUAYSIDE On the R. Yare; over a mile long, one of the finest quays in England. Hall Quay has the Victorian town hall of 1882, the Duke's Head Hotel dated 1609 and the Elizabethan Star Hotel. South Quay has a sequence of notable houses: Nos. 1 and 2 are of 1700; No. 4 was built in 1596 and has a panelled Elizabethan room with an excellent plaster ceiling. Nos. 5, 20 and 74–75 are all early

18th century; No. 20 is now the customs house, the most ambitious house on the quay, with big porch and Doric columns. The Old Merchant's House (museum) is of 17th-century brick with later west front. Off South Quay are the remains of the Franciscan (Greyfriars) friary of the 13th century, and near these the old tolhouse of 1362, badly bombed but restored, with Early English doorways. The narrow streets here called the Rows were also badly bombed.

TOLHOUSE A 14th-century civic building restored in 1961 after bomb damage in the Second World War. There is a series of dungeons and the house contains displays depicting local history.

Greenock *Strathclyde* 561Gf
MCLEAN MUSEUM AND ART GALLERY James Watt, who perfected the steam engine, was born in the port of Greenock; the museum contains his tools and other items associated with him. There are sections devoted to geology, natural history and shipping, with model ships and engines. Collections of British pewter and of arms from Japan and West Africa are also on view.

Greensted-juxta-Ongar *Essex* 548Ac
CHURCH OF ST ANDREW One of the best-known churches in England because of its pre-Conquest log nave. The chancel is of Norman flint, repaired with brick in the early 16th century.

Greenwich *Greater London* 542Cg
BOROUGH MUSEUM Collections of local history and natural history. Also the Dawson Collection of butterflies. (By request only.)
CHURCH OF ST ALFEGE Designed by Wren's assistant, Nicholas Hawksmoor, this Portland stone church of c. 1715 has a tower by John James. The fine woodwork of the interior, damaged by fire in the Second World War, was restored in 1953. The gardens were redesigned in 1975.
QUEEN'S HOUSE At the beginning of the 17th century Greenwich Palace was a conglomeration of Tudor buildings on the south bank of the Thames, with the Woolwich–Deptford road running alongside just to the south. In 1616 Inigo Jones was commissioned to build a house for Queen Anne, wife of James I; it was to be Palladian, on either side of and bridging the Woolwich road. Two years later work stopped: it was not resumed until 1630—for Henrietta Maria, wife of Charles I. It was completed c. 1635. The house is of brick with Portland stone dressings; as the road went through at ground level, the H-shape of the plan appeared only at first-floor level. A little later John Webb,

Jones's assistant, built two other bridges over the road at each end of the house, which now give it the appearance of a rectangular building. It now forms part of the National Maritime Museum.
NATIONAL MARITIME MUSEUM The exhibits, arranged chronologically, range from Tudor times to the present day, and include a large collection of portraits and seascapes, including some by Turner, Hogarth and Reynolds. There are also navigational instruments and charts, model ships and relics of Nelson, including the uniform worn by him at Trafalgar. In the Barge House, the barges of Mary II (1689) and Frederick, Prince of Wales (1732) can be seen. The Old Royal Observatory is part of the museum and contains displays illustrating the history of astronomy and time-keeping. (See pp. 220–221.)
ROYAL NAVAL COLLEGE A rambling Tudor building, Greenwich Palace (known also as Placentia) stood on this site. It was demolished in 1662 and all that remains today is the vaulted crypt beneath the present Queen Anne's Block. In the same year the foundations of King Charles's Block, designed by John Webb, Inigo Jones's assistant, were laid; this building near the Thames was finished in 1669. At the end of the 17th century Mary II planned to build a hospital for disabled men of the Royal Navy. After the death of William III, Sir Christopher Wren was appointed architect for the new hospital, although at that time he was fully employed with St Paul's Cathedral, Hampton Court and churches in the City of London. Wren incorporated the existing King Charles's Block and Inigo Jones's Queen's House in a single grand design. By 1714 Queen Anne's Block near the river, and Queen Mary's and King William's blocks nearest to the Queen's House, were complete. Although the whole conception was Wren's, he was assisted by Nicholas Hawksmoor and his successor as surveyor to the hospital, Sir John Vanbrugh. In 1873 the hospital was given over to the Royal Naval College. (See p. 221.)

Greystoke *Cumbria* 557Hf
CHURCH OF ST ANDREW A large church, mostly of the 15th century, with a west tower. Inside are misericords, brasses and alabaster effigies. The east window consists mostly of 15th-century glass.

Grime's Graves *Norfolk* 554Ba
Of the hundreds of filled mine-shafts in this immediate area, 16 have been excavated and two are kept open for inspection, though covers have been

GREENSTED-JUXTA-ONGAR

The Church of St Andrew at Greensted in Essex dates from AD 845 and is said to be the oldest wooden church in the world. Some of the timber in the north and south walls is from split tree trunks that were used in construction of an earlier church on the site nearly 200 years before the present one was built.

GREENWICH

placed over them as a protection from the weather. Layers of flint occur naturally in chalk, the quality varying considerably. Here and there in the sides of this ancient valley, the best flint, the floorstone as it is known, outcrops. Neolithic man, knowing its approximate depth, dropped these shafts to reach it, sometimes as deep as 40 ft. From the central shaft, he ran out galleries in all directions. The waste material from a new shaft was then thrown into the adjacent exhausted mine.

Nearby Brandon is the last centre of the flint-knapping industry, and from here flints are exported all over the world.

Grimsby *Humberside*   553Hg
The coming of the railway in 1848 transformed this medieval fishing port into a great trading centre. Today, Grimsby's 2800 fishermen supply a market handled by 300 merchants and one fresh filleting factory deals with up to 200,000 lb of whole fish a day.

CHURCH OF ST JAMES Among the finest of Grimsby's churches is the parish church of St James, built in the 13th century. Not all the stone-work is original—the tower was rebuilt in 1365, and the chancel restored in 1881.

WELHOLME GALLERIES More than 200 ship models include some made by French prisoners of war in the 18th and 19th centuries, and a large group of fishing vessels. The Doughty Collection of china and a small group of paintings, mainly of local interest, are also exhibited.

Grimspound *Devon*   539Gd
In the *Hound of the Baskervilles*, Sir Arthur Conan Doyle gave Sherlock Holmes the remnants of a hut

ROYAL NAVAL COLLEGE *By the time Charles II was restored to the throne in 1660, the old Tudor buildings of Greenwich Palace, where Henry VIII and Elizabeth I were born, had been so neglected that it was decided to demolish them. In 1662–9 they were replaced by King Charles's Block which was designed by John Webb, Inigo Jones's assistant. At the end of the 17th century Mary II proposed the foundation of a hospital for disabled men of the Royal Navy, and Sir Christopher Wren was appointed architect. Not far from the site was Inigo Jones's Queen's House, and this Wren decided to make his central feature. He designed two magnificent colonnades leading towards the house and away from the existing palace, and above each colonnade he placed an elegant dome. The colonnades form the sides of Wren's Queen Mary's and King William's Blocks. Since 1873 the hospital has been the home of the Royal Naval College.*

FREEDOM BOX *Enamelled boxes like this were made in Great Britain and Ireland during the 18th century to contain the written grant of the freedom of a town or city. This box is not only a superb example of its kind but also has great historical interest. It is of two-colour gold, decorated with a scene in painted enamel showing the Battle of the Nile. The sides are set with four plaques which bear coats of arms, the initials of Captain Edward Berry, trophies, and the British lion and Egyptian crocodile on either side of a pyramid. The box contained the freedom presented to Captain Berry, captain of the admiral's ship under the command of Nelson at the Battle of the Nile on August 1, 1798, by the City of London to thank him and his fellow sailors for 'their gallant services . . . manifesting to the world an additional instance of the superior Discipline and irresistible Bravery of the British Seamen'.*
(National Maritime Museum)

in a prehistoric settlement in which to bivouac; his model was this Bronze Age village. Surrounding a roughly circular 4 acre area is a stone wall some 9 ft thick, and in it are the remains of 24 circular huts of about 15 ft diameter. A raised stone bed-place was a luxury that several enjoyed. The inhabitants made sure of a water supply by enclosing part of a stream with the wall.

Grinton *N. Yorks.* 558Bd
CHURCH OF ST ANDREW St Andrew's was built by the Normans, but is now mainly in the Perpendicular style. There is a carved Norman font, and fragments of medieval stained glass; also screens and an early 18th-century pulpit.

Groombridge *Kent* 542Ce
The brick church, built in 1625, is surrounded by tile-hung cottages on a sloping green.

THE PLACE A Restoration country house built *c.* 1660 with interior panelling from the Elizabethan manor which once stood on the site. The old moat was retained for decorative purposes to harmonise with the stone-walled garden which was constructed during the 17th century. Garden open occasionally.

Grosmont Castle *Gwent* 546Ad
This 13th-century castle, now a ruin, figured largely in the history of the Welsh uprisings. It was besieged in 1405 by Owain Glendwr, but he was defeated and captured by the future Henry V. The castle was dismantled by Edward IV.

Guildford *Surrey* 542Af
The High Street is one of the finest streets in southern England. Abbot's Hospital, the great almshouses begun in 1619, and the town hall, of

1683, with a cupola and great clock, are particularly impressive. The ruined keep of the Norman castle lies to the south, nearer the valley bottom. CATHEDRAL The Second World War held up the building of the cathedral. Sir Edward Maufe's design was accepted in 1932 but the building was not consecrated until 1961. The style of the building is simplified Gothic, the exterior being of red brick with Clipsham stone dressings. Among those whose work decorates the building was Eric Gill, whose *St John the Baptist* stands outside the south transept; he also designed the sculpture around the circular east window. Other sculpture is by Vernon Hill, and by Alan Collins, who carved the font. There is stained glass by Moira Forsyth and Rosemary Rutherford, and glass engraved by John Hutton, who engraved the glass screen at Coventry Cathedral. The sanctuary carpet was designed by Sir Edward Maufe.
CHURCH OF THE HOLY TRINITY A large church rebuilt in the mid-18th century, after the tower collapsed. The east end, however, dates from the late 19th century. Michael Rysbrack may have been the sculptor of a man in Roman dress on the monument to Speaker Onslow (*d.* 1768). There are important monuments in the south chapel.
MUSEUM The museum is housed in a 17th-century brick building adjoining the medieval Castle Arch. Lewis Carroll (Charles Dodgson), author of *Alice in Wonderland*, often visited his family in Guildford, and died there in 1898; his letters and other relics are preserved in the museum. Other exhibits show items from the 6th-century Saxon cemetery at Guildown, finds from the Guildford friary, examples of Wealden ironwork, needlework and needlework implements.
WOMEN'S ROYAL ARMY CORPS MUSEUM On display are women's uniforms of the First World War, of the ATS of the Second World War, and of the WRAC. Also shown are photographs, decorations and medals.

Guisborough *Cleveland*   *558Ee*
CHURCH OF ST NICHOLAS This late 15th-century church, restored *c.* 1905, stands near the ruins of a 12th-century priory. There are fragments of the original glass, and a good early 16th-century monument brought from the priory at the Dissolution, with carved figures of knights and saints.
PRIORY An Augustinian priory was founded here in 1119 by Robert de Brus, a member of the French family—ancestors of Robert the Bruce of Scotland—who had come to England with William the Conqueror and settled at Skelton.
All that now remains of the priory, which was once the third richest in Yorkshire, are the 12th-century gatehouse and dovecot, and the late 13th-century east end, the window adorned with elaborately carved vine tracery.

Gunby Hall *Lincs.*   *553Je*
Tennyson's 'haunt of ancient peace' was built of red brick and stone dressings by Sir William Massingberd in 1700. It is a fine example of William-and-Mary architecture, and reflects the influence of Wren. Inside are panelled rooms containing fine furniture.

Gunton *Norfolk*   *554Dc*
CHURCH OF ST ANDREW The church, designed by Robert Adam in 1769, has a portico of Tuscan columns. The organ is in the west gallery, which is supported by Corinthian columns.

Gunwalloe *Cornwall*   *538Ba*
CHURCH OF ST WINWALOE An isolated church on a sandy beach. The detached tower is built into a rock. St Winwaloe's is mainly of the 14th and 15th centuries. Inside are rood screen fragments with painted panels, and a Norman font.

Gurness *Mainland, Orkney*   *569Hg*
The archaeological remains are a complex of several occupations, but the site is very close to the sea and parts of the outworks have been eroded.
First came the broch, which stood within a walled area. Much of this outer wall has now disappeared. Outside this was a ditch and other ramparts and ditches farther out were probably contemporary.
Later, after the broch had ceased to be occupied, the outer space between it and the ditch was filled with many other small buildings and occupation seems to have persisted until Viking times.

Guthrie Castle *Tayside*   *566Fb*
A 15th-century castle on the site of an earlier fortress. The square tower dates from 1468 and additions were made in the 19th century. It contains 15th-century wall-paintings. (Exterior viewing only.)

Gwydir Castle *Gwynedd*   *550Fe*
This romantic building, wrongly called a castle, was for many years the principal seat of the influential Wynn family. Its founder, Maredudd ab Ieuan, moved into the area in the late 15th century, and after living at Dolwyddelan Castle came to Gwydir and built the tall block opposite the entrance *c.* 1500. Many additions were made during the next 100 years; medieval stonework from the dissolved abbey at Maenan was used during that period, and also re-used and copied in the 19th century. The building was burnt out in this century, and restored to its present appearance.

Gwydir Uchaf Chapel *Gwynedd*   *550Fe*
The small private chapel of Gwydir Uchaf, built by Sir Richard Wynn in 1673, has a painted ceiling representing the Holy Trinity.

H

Hackness *N. Yorks.*   *558Fd*
CHURCH OF ST PETER The church was begun in the 11th century and added to later; the chancel arch, however, may be Saxon, and fragments of a Saxon cross may be seen. The 15th-century chancel has stalls with misericords. There is a Perpendicular font cover and there are 19th-century monuments by Sir Francis Chantrey and Matthew Noble, who was born at Hackness.

Haddenham *Bucks.*   *547Gc*
Some of the houses in the village are made of wichert—chalk marl compressed with straw.
CHURCH OF ST MARY A 13th-century church with a good west tower with arcades. Inside is an early 19th-century plaster ceiling, which masks the 14th-century timber roof. There is a Norman font, and medieval glass in the north chapel. Two brasses show 15th-century priests.

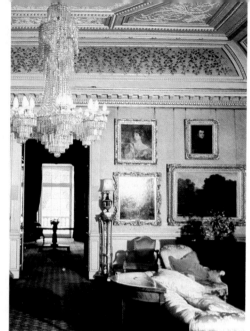

HADDO HOUSE

Like Hopetoun House near Edinburgh, Haddo House is basically the work of the Scottish architect William Adam, whose sons John and Robert were to become famous architects during the second half of the 18th century. The house, begun for the 2nd Earl of Aberdeen in the 1730's, was a simple but elegant building with a central block and a curving flight of steps up to the first-floor entrance; on either side two wings were connected to the main house by colonnades, which in 1780 were turned into corridors, and a second storey added. In the 1880's the house was further enlarged by Lady Aberdeen: a new entrance hall was created and a library and chapel added. All the new decoration was carefully chosen in keeping with Adam's work. The drawing-room is a magnificent example of Adam revival taste.

Haddenham *Cambs.*   *548Af*
Haddenham, the highest village in the Fen country, 120 ft above sea level, has an air of spacious dignity, enhanced by three or four good houses including the red-brick Porch House of 1657 with a central porch, and Vine House and The Limes, both of the 18th century. The Church of Holy Trinity was built in the 13th and 14th centuries, and heavily restored from 1876.

Haddington *Lothian*   *562De*
CHURCH OF ST MARY A large cruciform church, with a central tower, of the 14th and 15th centuries. It was restored in 1972–4.

Haddo House *Grampian*   *567Gf*
For over 500 years the home of the Gordons of Haddo, who became Earls of Aberdeen; the 4th Earl was Prime Minister from 1852 to 1855. The present mansion was designed by William Adam in 1731 but altered in 1780 and again in the 1880's. It contains fine furniture, portraits of the Gordons, and a chapel designed by G. E. Street, and is the centre for the Haddo House Choral Society.

Haddon Hall *Derbys.*   *552De*
Surrounded by a 12-ft wall built during the crusades, Haddon Hall was restored this century and is now the Derbyshire seat of the Duke of Rutland. The Hall is devoid of ornamental frills, and the oldest parts date back to the 12th century. Among the special features is the long gallery (110 ft), panelled in oak and walnut, with a decorative ceiling that has an acoustic function. Haddon Hall passed to the Earls of Rutland in the 16th century when Dorothy Vernon eloped with Sir John Manners, but by the 18th and 19th centuries the Rutland family were using Belvoir Castle as their main country residence, and Haddon Hall was abandoned. Detailed restoration, using the same stone as when the hall was originally built, was begun in the early 20th century and completed by the 1930's. On the south side, terraced gardens descend to the R. Wye.

Hadleigh *Suffolk*   *548De*
A market town which was once a centre of the East Anglian cloth trade, it has a remarkable grouping of buildings by the church. The 15th-century guildhall is timber-framed with two overhanging storeys. There are several attractive medieval and Georgian houses throughout the town.
CHURCH OF ST MARY A spacious 14th- and 15th-century church with tower and spire. Inside is a 14th-century font, with modern cover, screens and bench ends, and a fine early 18th-century organ-case. There are brasses, and monuments by Charles Regnart, c. 1793, and Eric Gill, c. 1935.
DEANERY The house has an early Tudor brick gateway. The Deanery Tower of 1495 is the surviving gate-house of an archdeacon's palace. It is of brick, with panelled and embattled turrets. The interior has a Georgian panelled room, an octagonal oratory with brick vaulted ceiling, and remains of a secret hiding place (By appointment.)

Hadrian's Wall *Cumbria–Northld.*   *557Jg*
As a barrier against infiltration by barbarians from Scotland and as a base against attack by them, a great wall was built by order of the Roman Emperor Hadrian in the years AD 122–30. It ran for 73 miles, from Wallsend-on-Tyne in the east to Bowness on the Solway Firth in the west, taking advantage of every natural point of strength and, at its highest, following ground 1230 ft above sea level. It is the chief monument of the Roman occupation in Britain, and the most remarkable of all Roman frontier works.
Built of stone and 20 ft high in its eastern part, and of turf and 12 ft high in its western sector, it had 17 large forts about 5 miles apart, and a line of smaller forts each a Roman mile apart. Between each pair of these 'milecastles' were built two

signal towers 20 ft square. On the northern side of the wall ran a continuous protective ditch, averaging 27 ft in width and 9 ft in depth. On the southern side was the *vallum*, a flat-bottomed ditch about 20 ft wide and 10 ft deep, with earthworks on either side; it ran straight from point to point like a Roman road and therefore often deviated from the course of the wall. This ditch seems to have served as the civil boundary. A road, now known as the Military Way, was built later between wall and *vallum* and was about 20 ft wide.

The wall was garrisoned by infantry and cavalry, usually auxiliaries from all parts of the Empire under Roman officers. Detachments from the three Roman legions always stationed in Britain were sent to the wall only for special duties, for example when it was under attack. Garrisons were lodged in the forts and the milecastles. The wall was abandoned in AD 197 and a century later, but each time was rebuilt and regarrisoned. It was finally abandoned in AD 383.

The first important survey was made by William Camden, scholar and historian, who first published his *Britannia* in 1586. Archaeological research has continued from his day to the present. The wall suffered much destruction after the Jacobite rebellion of 1745, the stones being used to build a new road from Newcastle to Carlisle; and even in the Second World War 300 yds of it were quarried for military use. There are museums at Housesteads and at Chesters Fort, and the museums in Carlisle and Newcastle also have excellent collections from the wall. Among these are votive stones and altars dedicated to many different deities—Jupiter, Fortune, Germanic gods, the Mother Goddesses, and the soldiers' god, Mithras. On the wall at Carrawburgh (Brocolitia fort) a Mithraic temple has been excavated.

Hadstock *Essex*   548Ae
CHURCH OF ST BOTOLPH This was probably the church built by Canute in 1020 to commemorate his victory over Edmund Ironside at nearby Ashdon. Much of the original structure remains, including a Saxon oak door, which may well be the oldest in the country. Beneath the iron straps were found fragments of human skin, assumed to be that of a Danish invader. There are 14th-century additions, but the screen across the south transept and the west tower are both 15th-century work. The chancel, of much later date, was built by William Butterfield in 1884.

Hailes *Glos.*   546Dd
ABBEY The Cistercian abbey was founded in 1246 by Richard, Earl of Cornwall, the younger brother of Henry III, in gratitude for an escape from shipwreck in the Scilly Isles. In the Middle Ages, its holy relics included what was said to be some of Christ's blood, an object of reverence for pilgrims which is mentioned by Chaucer in *The Canterbury Tales*. The abbey fell into ruins after the Dissolution of the Monasteries in 1539 and the only substantial building that remains above ground is the shell of the cloister. However, archaeological excavation has revealed the footings of other walls.
CHURCH The Norman parish church of Hailes was built *c.* 1130, before the nearby abbey, which later owned it. It is not known to whom the church was dedicated. Inside, there is medieval stained glass and a series of well-preserved wall paintings of *c.* 1300, including representations of St Catherine and St Margaret. Many of the tiles were brought to the church from the abbey. The oak canopied pulpit dates from the 17th century, as does much of the panelling and the choir stalls. The pews are from before the Reformation.

Hailes Castle *Lothian*   562Df
At one time Hailes Castle belonged to the Hepburns, one of whom, James, 4th Earl of Bothwell, abducted and married Mary, Queen of Scots in 1567. The ruined castle comprises 13th-century masonry with 14th- and 15th-century additions; the dungeons and water-gate still survive.

Halifax *W. Yorks.*   558Ba
BANKFIELD MUSEUM Housed in the former home of the local mill owner and philanthropist Edward Akroyd, who built a model workers' estate here in the 19th century, the museum contains a comprehensive collection of costumes and fabric, specialising in peasant work from the countries of the Balkans and Burma. There are also displays of items connected with the Duke of Wellington's Regiment and collections of stamps, coins and local natural history.
CHURCH OF ST JOHN A large building, mainly of the 15th century, but with some 12th-century fragments. The west tower is Perpendicular. Inside are medieval stalls and font cover.
SHIBDEN HALL A 15th-century timber-framed house, with a collection of early furniture. The outbuildings and grounds form an open-air folk museum.

HADRIAN'S WALL

The greatest monument of the Roman occupation of Britain. The wall, shown near Housesteads in Northumberland, was first built in AD 122–30 by order of the Emperor Hadrian, to act as a defence against the Celts from Scotland. Built of stone in the east and turf in the west, it stretched 73 miles, from Wallsend-on-Tyne in the east to Bowness on the Solway Firth, and ran from one natural vantage point to the next. It was garrisoned by troops from all over the Roman empire, but was finally abandoned in AD 383.

HAM HOUSE

HENRY BONE: MINIATURE OF LADY DYSART *This enamel miniature by Henry Bone (1755–1834), Painter in Enamel to the Prince of Wales, copies a portrait of Lady Dysart as Shakespeare's heroine Miranda painted by Sir Joshua Reynolds in 1775. Bone, one of the last and best practitioners of enamel-painting in miniature, specialised in miniatures of portraits by great contemporary artists. He achieved the fine detail and delicate modelling first seen on enamel miniatures in about 1630.*

THE GREAT STAIRCASE *Thomas Carter, the joiner responsible for the boldly carved staircase at Ham House, charged £7 for the 24 yds of wainscot beside it and £6 for the arch that separates it from the hall in 1637–38. The wood was painted and grained to look like walnut.*

TOWN HALL In the summer of 1859 Queen Victoria opened the great town hall at Leeds. In the same year Sir Charles Barry, architect of the Houses of Parliament, began to draw up plans for a civic palace in Halifax. The foundation stone was laid in 1861, but before the building was finished Barry had died and the work was completed by his son. During the town hall's construction the Prince Consort had also died and Queen Victoria refused to open the building herself in 1863, delegating the task to the Prince of Wales, later Edward VII.

The 180 ft high tower, strangely Gothic in appearance in spite of its classical components, is decorated with large sculptured groups representing Europe, America and Africa by John Thomas. He, too, died before finishing the work, and the final group, of Asia, was completed under the supervision of the painter Daniel Maclise.

Hallaton *Leics.* 552Fb
CHURCH OF ST MICHAEL There are Norman fragments, including a tympanum in the porch depicting St Michael and the Dragon, but the body of the church is 13th century, including the west tower with broach spire. The aisles are a 14th-century addition; at the east end of the north wall there is an elaborately decorated turret, surmounted by a little spire. Some good 13th-century ornamentation remains in the chancel. There is a small crypt under the north aisle, and some good 19th-century stained glass.

Hall-i'-Th'-Wood *Greater Manchester* 552Bg
A black-and-white timbered manor house, built in 1483. A stone wing was added in 1591, and a further wing in 1648. The spinning-mule, an improved version of Hargreaves' spinning-jenny

for fine cottons, was developed here by Samuel Crompton (1753–1827), in 1779. The house is now a folk museum.

Halsall *Lancs.* 551Jg
CHURCH OF ST CUTHBERT A 14th-century church, one of the best in Lancashire. The 15th-century octagonal tower rises from a square base, and has a spire. There is a good chancel, with a fine medieval doorway and the original oak door with traceried top. A 14th-century tomb recess contains a later effigy, and a table-tomb of *c.* 1523 also has effigies.

Halstead *Essex* 548Cd
BLUE BRIDGE HOUSE Between 1700 and 1712, John 'Carcase' Morley, a local butcher who became the friend of men of letters, including the poet Alexander Pope, added a Queen Anne façade to the original Tudor house. Blue Bridge stands in a walled garden and has fine wrought-iron gates. Over the porch are the arms of the Butchers' Company, carved out of stone. Inside the house there is a collection of English, French and Italian furniture of the 17th and 18th centuries.
CHURCH OF ST ANDREW Mainly of the 14th to 15th centuries, but restored in the 19th century, the church has a reredos of 1893 by Sir Arthur Blomfield and several monuments to the Bourchier family, including a brass and effigies.

Haltwhistle *Northld.* 558Ag
CHURCH OF THE HOLY CROSS A church was founded here by William the Lion in 1178, but the present building is 13th century. There are fine stone grave covers, a 14th-century effigy and a hexagonal font dating from the 17th century. In the south wall of the chancel is a three-stalled sedilia. The east window is by William Morris.

HAMPTON COURT

TIJOU SCREEN *Decorative ironwork flourished in England in 1685 to 1740 as never before, and the acknowledged master of the art was the Frenchman Jean Tijou, who came to England in 1688 with William III and stayed until 1712. At Hampton Court Tijou made wrought-iron gates, balustrades, and a magnificent screen for the Fountain Garden (now in the Privy Garden). Above is a detail of one of the 12 decorative panels which are connected by plainer palisades. These panels are typical of Tijou's work; he liked elaborate flowery effects, and used much repoussé work such as the mask at the top here.*

HAMPTON COURT *Cardinal Wolsey started to build the largest house in England in 1514. The magnificent result and the cardinal's ostentation, however, irritated the king and Wolsey, in an unsuccessful attempt to stave off his displeasure, thought it prudent to 'present' the house to him. Between 1531 and 1536 Henry VIII added the great hall, with its magnificent hammerbeam roof, and various other buildings. He lavishly embellished the chapel with a fine fan-vaulted wooden ceiling, which looks like stone. After that no significant additions were made until William III, who ascended the throne in 1689, and who disliked living in London, employed Sir Christopher Wren to enlarge the palace. The cloistered Fountain Court dates from this period, and the Cartoon Gallery was built to house a set of great tapestry designs by Raphael. Wren also decorated the chapel, designing the paintings and the oak reredos carved by Grinling Gibbons.*

After William's death from a riding accident in 1702 there were no more major changes to the building. The state apartments in Wren's building (shown here) contain painted decoration by Laguerre, Verrio and Sir James Thornhill, and works by leading sculptors of the late 17th century, such as John Nost, Grinling Gibbons and Caius Gabriel Cibber. The French smith Jean Tijou was responsible for a great deal of the ornamental ironwork. In the gardens, mainly designed for William and Mary by Henry Wise and George London, are the maze and the vinery with the Great Vine planted in 1769. The Banqueting House overlooking the river, with walls and ceiling decorated by Verrio with classical subjects was built for William III about 1700.

Hambledon *Hants.*   541Hd
The cradle of cricket, the village lies in a valley-bottom, half-way along which a charming short street opens up, with the church at the top. Cricket as we know it was first played a mile or so away, on Broadhalfpenny Down, in the late 18th century.

Hambledon Hill *Dorset*   540Ed
The prominent earthworks are the defences of a major Iron Age hill-fort, remodelled two or three times. Within the ramparts may be seen a fine Neolithic long barrow, and small scooped terraces for Iron Age huts. To the south is a Neolithic enclosure once edged by causewayed ditches. The

recent discovery of skulls in these ditches hints at ritual activities at the site of periodic regional assemblies.

Ham House *Greater London*   542Ag
HAM HOUSE The original Ham House was built in 1610 as a modest country residence by Sir Thomas Vavasour. In the middle of the century it was bequeathed to Elizabeth, Countess of Dysart, by her father. After her marriage to the Duke of Lauderdale, Minister at the Court of Charles II, the house was enlarged and redecorated in 1673–5 in the flamboyant baroque style of the period. Much of the original furniture and interior ornament has

been retained. Paintings include works by Kneller and after Van Dyck in the great hall, works by the Dutch, Venetian, Roman and Flemish schools elsewhere in the house, and a fine collection of miniatures including a Nicholas Hilliard, Isaac Oliver's portrait of an unknown man against a background of flames, and a Samuel Cooper. In the room over the chapel is an interesting collection of textiles, including a complete 'wedding set' all of tissue of blue silk and silver thread, of early 18th-century French work.

The rest of the textile collection consists of furnishing fabrics, carpets, and a large collection of tapestries of English, French and Flemish manufacture. Particularly notable among these are the 17th-century Flemish tapestries in the Yellow Sitting Room, after paintings by Poussin in the Louvre depicting incidents in the life of Pyrrhus, King of Epirus in the 3rd century BC.

There is also a rich display of furniture mainly of the 17th century, particularly Dutch and English work. A plasterer named Joseph Kinsman seems to have been extensively employed in the 1630's to provide ornate decoration on ceilings and walls; and outstanding work of the same period is the handsome staircase with carved and pierced panels depicting trophies of arms. (See p. 225.) The garden has been restored to its 17th-century layout.

Hampton Court *Greater London* 542Ag
Thomas Wolsey, Archbishop of York and subsequently Cardinal and Lord Chancellor of England, began this enormous palace in the early 16th century. He fell from power in 1529, having already in 1526 offered Hampton Court to Henry VIII in an attempt to regain favour. Its size and splendour made it suitable as a royal palace and with additions and alterations it remained a royal residence up to the death of George II in 1760; five of Henry VIII's wives lived there. The palace is roughly symmetrical, and there is some Italianate detail, showing the influence of Renaissance ideas from the Continent. But in general, the building is still a large rambling medieval palace built around a series of courtyards. Much of Wolsey's building survives in the Tudor portions of the complex, although the great hall was built for Henry VIII. The astronomical clock in Clock Court was made for Henry in 1540—the dial remains, but the mechanism was renewed in 1879. Adjoining the palace is the closed tennis court built by Henry in 1529, and to the north-west lie the Tiltyard Gardens, laid out on the site of the Tudor tiltyard where, in Henry's time, tournaments were held.

Most of the external façades date from the accession of William III, when Sir Christopher Wren was commissioned to improve and extend the palace. Originally his plans involved the destruction of all the existing buildings except the Great Hall, but his eventual scheme, begun in 1689, left the Base Court and the Clock Court standing, while the third courtyard, round which the State Rooms were grouped, was demolished to make way for the series of rooms and galleries which now surround Fountain Court.

The palace contains a magnificent collection of tapestries, furniture and clocks and the paintings include works by Titian, Tintoretto, Veronese, Correggio, Andrea del Sarto, Holbein and Lely.

Hanbury *Staffs.* 552Cc
CHURCH OF ST WERBERGH A 13th-century church, restored during the 19th century. It contains several good and interesting monuments of the 16th and 17th centuries.

Hanbury Hall *Heref. & Worcs.* 546Cf
A red-brick H-plan house with a cupola, built at the beginning of the 18th century for Thomas Vernon, whose grandfather had bought the estate in 1631. The date 1701 is carved over the entrance.

The house itself is in the style of Wren, although the architect is unknown. The interior decoration was commissioned in 1710 from Sir James Thornhill, at a time when he was embarking on his masterpiece, the ceiling of Greenwich Hospital.

The entrance hall is relatively simple, the full impact being reserved for the staircase. Here the walls are painted with scenes from the life of Achilles, while a group of gods and goddesses look down from the ceiling. There are also panels of trophies, and realistically painted fluted Corinthian pilasters, cornices and moulding.

Other rooms in the house, notably the Long Room, contain some fine plasterwork.

Harberton *Devon* 539Gc
CHURCH OF ST ANDREW A battlemented church of the 13th and 14th centuries with a long barrel roof which has some 80 carved bosses. There is a fine 15th-century vaulted screen and gilded parclose screens. The vaulted screen was restored in 1871 and the panels are believed to depict young ladies of the congregation. The 15th-century stone pulpit has 17th-century carved figures. The font is Norman.

Hardingstone *Northants.* 547Gf
On high ground stands a fine stone cross, one of twelve erected by Edward I in 1291–4 to mark sites where the body of Queen Eleanor rested on its way from Harby (Nottinghamshire) to Westminster Abbey. The cross was restored in 1840 and 1884.
CHURCH OF ST EDMUND The church has a 13th-century tower and a 14th-century nave arcade. There are two 17th-century monuments to the Harvey family, one with kneeling figures in two tiers, and a large wall monument with portrait medallions by J. M. Rysbrack, *c.* 1760.

Hardwick Hall *Derbys.* 552Ee
This magnificent Elizabethan house was begun in 1591 by Elizabeth, Countess of Shrewsbury (Bess of Hardwick). Work progressed incredibly quickly for that time, considering the size of the house. Within three years the structure had been completed and by 1597 the house was decorated and furnished ready for occupation. It has four great towers, one at each corner, and huge windows which increase in size the higher they are. Parapets incorporating the initials E. S. (Elizabeth Shrewsbury) stand against the sky and proclaim the builder. It is thought that Robert Smythson was the architect. The house contains fine furniture, needlework, tapestries and portraits, and is set amid extensive gardens with yew hedges and borders. (See p. 228.)

Hardwick Heath *Suffolk* 548Cf
Noted for its cedar trees, said to be the finest in Britain.

Hardy Monument *Dorset* 540Dc
A tall column on a hill near Portesham commemorates Vice-Admiral Sir Thomas Masterman Hardy (1769–1839), who was Flag Captain in the *Victory* at the Battle of Trafalgar, and with Lord Nelson when he died; the column was erected in 1846.

Hardy's Cottage *Dorset* 540Dc
A thatched cottage where the novelist Thomas Hardy (1840–1928) was born.

'Bess of Hardwick', a much married lady and one of the most powerful personalities of Elizabeth I's reign, built herself this magnificent house. Bess, who was born in 1520, was first married at the age of 12, and as each of her husbands died she became richer and richer. Her fourth and last husband was George, Earl of Shrewsbury, for many years the custodian of the imprisoned Mary, Queen of Scots. The Countess of Shrewsbury eventually tired of this arrangement and left her husband; he died in 1590, leaving her yet more money. Assisted by Robert Smythson, she at once started on the building of Hardwick and by 1597 it was ready for her to move into. Inside the house are large ornate chimney-pieces and a rambling staircase. In the High Great Chamber is a splendid elaborate plaster frieze showing such scenes as Diana and Venus with the infant Cupid, based on 16th-century engravings.

Harefield *Greater London*   547Hc
CHURCH OF ST MARY There is a low embattled tower at west end of the north aisle here, and an impressive array of monuments, the most sumptuous being to the Countess of Derby (d. 1636). Others are by Grinling Gibbons, William Stanton and John Bacon Junior. There is also some splendid woodwork.

Haresfield Beacon *Glos.*   546Cc
South of Gloucester, a great spur of the Cotswolds projects far into the Vale of Gloucester; its outer part bears a fine Iron Age hill-fort of double construction. The outer end of the spur, the Beacon, has a single bank-and-ditch defence. The enclosed area was later greatly increased by a further series of defences on the east.

From here may be had perhaps the best view across the Vales of Gloucester and Berkeley to the Forest of Dean and, when visibility permits, to the Black Mountains and Brecon Beacons.

Harewood *W. Yorks.*   558Cb
CHURCH OF ALL SAINTS A Perpendicular church, altered in the 19th century by Sir Gilbert Scott. There is an impressive series of 15th-century alabaster effigies lying on tomb chests, on which are angels, heraldry and figures of weepers. There is an oak communion-rail in memory of George V.

Harewood House *W. Yorks.*   558Cb
The home of HRH The Princess Royal, Countess of Harewood, until her death in 1965, this fine country mansion was built in 1759–71 by John Carr of York for Edwin Lascelles, who became the 1st Earl of Harewood; Robert Adam decorated the interior. In 1843 Sir Charles Barry carried out alterations which changed the Classical balance of the house. The library and entrance hall have Adam ceilings, and the ceiling in the music room is set with ten medallions above a similarly patterned carpet. Much of the furniture was designed by Adam and made by Chippendale especially for Harewood House, which also contains paintings by old masters, Sèvres porcelain and fine silver. The park and gardens were laid out by Capability Brown, but the formal terrace gardens were added later.

Harlech Castle *Gwynedd*   550Ec
One of Edward I's Welsh castles, built of local grey sandstone in 1283–90 on a rocky spur near the sea. It was fruitlessly defended so many times that it is sometimes called the Castle of Lost Causes. It was taken by Owain Glyndwr in 1404 and occupied by him until 1409. During the Wars of the Roses it was besieged by Yorkists for eight years until 1468, and this long struggle inspired the song 'Men of Harlech'. By Elizabethan times all but the gatehouse was in ruins, but even so Harlech was the last Royalist stronghold in Wales during the Civil War. The castle is rectangular in plan with two concentric sets of walls. On the east side the massive four-towered gate-house—the focal point of the castle where the living-quarters were—leads into the inner courtyard which has a round tower at each corner. (See p. 230.)

Harlington *Beds.* 547Hd
HARLINGTON MANOR A many-gabled 17th-century house in the village of Harlington, it contains the panelled room in which John Bunyan was brought before Francis Wingate, Justice of the Peace, and committed to Bedford gaol for Nonconformist preaching. The author of *The Pilgrim's Progress* served two prison terms for his beliefs.

Harlington *Greater London* 547Hb
CHURCH OF SS PETER AND PAUL A small Norman church, with a fine south doorway and 15th-century south porch. There is a 12th-century nave, 14th-century chancel, and a tower added in the next century. A recessed monument of *c.* 1545 was also used as an Easter sepulchre. Brasses include one of a 15th-century priest with half-effigy; the tomb chests of the mid-19th century are by R. C. Lucas. A wall monument of *c.* 1695 incorporates winged cherub-heads and three portrait busts.

Harpley *Norfolk* 554Bc
CHURCH OF ST LAWRENCE Most of the church dates from between 1294 and 1332, the period when John de Gurney was rector. There is a finely carved door, and the west window, depicting angels and saints, is in the style of the Medieval Norwich School. Harpley Long Barrow, 150 ft long by 90 ft wide, is on the heath near by.

Harpswell *Lincs.* 553Gf
CHURCH OF ST CHAD The Saxon tower of this church has an inscription which records that the clock that once stood there was given to commemorate the Battle of Culloden. There is a Norman font, and a 14th-century south aisle. In 1891 the effigy of a priest was found in the floor, and there are also two other effigies, of the 14th and 17th centuries. On the north wall of the chancel is the Whichcot brass, depicting a knight and his lady.

Harrogate *N. Yorks.* 558Cb
A spa town, famous for its sulphur and iron springs, which was a fashionable watering-place of the 18th and 19th centuries. The Royal Baths are now a holiday and trade fair centre. The Royal Pump Room over the main spring, erected by Lord Rosslyn in 1842, is a museum.

HAREWOOD HOUSE

THE GREEN DRAWING ROOM *Home of the late Princess Royal, Countess of Harewood and daughter of George V, the magnificent Harewood House was begun in 1759 by Edwin Lascelles, 1st Earl of Harewood, who employed John Carr of York as architect. Robert Adam*

assisted Carr and was responsible for the Classical interior decoration of the house; he also designed much of the furniture. The entrance hall has a splendid plaster ceiling and decoration by Joseph Rose, and the long gallery has painted panels by Angelica Kauffmann.

CARVED PELMET *An illustration of baroque illusionism, this pelmet is carved in wood to imitate the gathered cloth of the curtains. Probably designed by Robert Adam, it was made with great skill by Thomas Chippendale's workshop, and shows the high standards they achieved. Illusionism was never generally popular in England, but a few patrons of the arts who had been on the Grand Tour of Europe favoured it. A series of these pelmets adorns the windows of the gallery at Harewood, and show fine craftsmanship, wealth and imagination.*

HARLOW CAR GARDENS The Northern Horticultural Society's gardens—55 acres of ornamental gardens and woodland.

Harrow *Greater London* 547Hb
CHURCH OF ST MARY The spire at the west end of St Mary's is a prominent landmark. The church is of Norman origin and there are 11th-century remains in tower. There were 13th- to 15th-century additions, and restorations in the 19th century. There is some 19th-century glass, and an east window by Sir Ninian Comper. Among the monuments is that by Flaxman (1815) to John Lyon, Founder of Harrow School, with figures of boys said to be the sons of Spencer Perceval, the murdered Prime Minister.

Harrow Hill *W. Sussex* 542Ad
Here is a representative group of Neolithic flint-mines, one of which, when excavated, proved to be 22 ft deep, with six radiating galleries at its base. Close by, and partly overlying some of the mine-shafts, is a small enclosure with a single bank and ditch. The bank was strengthened by the use of timber and the western entrance had a substantial timber gateway. There was apparently no regular occupation, so this was doubtless a stronghold intended for use in emergency.

Hartford *Cambs.* 547Jf
This picturesque village has a number of charming cottages, the 17th-century manor house on the main road and the 18th-century Hartford House. In August 1964, during the construction of Longstaff Way, workmen dug up 1108 English and foreign silver coins of the 15th and 16th centuries, ultimately declared Treasure Trove. The vicarage is said to have been part of the marriage settlement of Oliver Cromwell's wife.

Hartington *Derbys.* 552Ce
A small town near Beresford Dale, with old cottages in the market-place. King John granted the market charter in 1203 and the foundations of the church of St Giles date from the same period. Hartington Hall was rebuilt in the 17th century.
FISHING TEMPLE A fishing lodge of 1674 in Beresford Dale, used by Charles Cotton and Izaak Walton, who wrote *The Compleat Angler* in 1653.

Hartlebury *Heref. & Worcs.* 546Cf
CHURCH OF ST JAMES While parts of the medieval chancel still remain, and the west tower is of 16th-century construction, the body of the church was restored in the 19th century in Gothic Revival style, with slender nave columns and a plaster vault.

Hartlebury Castle *Heref. & Worcs.* 546Cf
The residence of the Bishops of Worcester for more than 1000 years. The present mansion was erected in 1675 on the site of a moated medieval castle, and carefully restored in 1964. The state rooms include a great hall with portrait gallery and an 18th-century rococo saloon. The castle also contains the library of Richard Hurd (1720–1808), a noted divine. The Hereford and Worcester County Museum is housed in the north wing.

Hartlepool *Cleveland* 558Df
CHURCH OF ST HILDA An impressive 12th-century church, with a battlemented west tower. The chancel was restored by W. D. Caroë in 1927. There is a brass dated 1593. The font is from 1728 and there is 19th-century glass.

Harvington Hall *Heref. & Worcs.* 546Cf
A moated Tudor manor house, associated with religious persecution of Catholics and featuring priests' hiding places, and painted walls.

Harwich *Essex* 548Ed
LIGHTHOUSE During the 17th century the great increase in coal shipments from Newcastle to London caused demands for many coastal lights, and in 1665 two were built at Harwich. These were crude structures, the upper light being a coal fire displayed in an open room above the town gate; the lower, which was a primitive candle-lit wooden tower on the shore, figures in a painting by Constable. These functioned until 1818, when they were replaced by octagonal brick towers, interesting examples of early cavity-wall construction. Owing to movement of the channel both had to be replaced in 1862 by the Dovercourt Lights, which in their turn became redundant.
REDOUBT In 1808–11, when Napoleon's armies were poised to invade England, the redoubt—a granite fort with moat and earthworks—was hastily built to defend the port.

HARLECH CASTLE

One of Edward I's great military projects in his conquest and settlement of Wales, Harlech Castle was begun in 1283 and virtually complete by 1290—an extraordinarily rapid achievement made possible by an enormous expenditure of money for an army of workmen. It has been estimated that, in modern terms, Harlech Castle cost nearly £5,000,000. The labour force at its greatest was about 950 men, and the weekly average during the summers of 1286 and 1287
was about 850. Like the other castles of this period, Harlech is not merely a fine example of military design but a considerable achievement in administration: workmen were brought from all over England. This was not voluntary service—the King of England then had the right to impress labour for his service. But the cost was prodigious—in modern terms the bill for Beaumaris, Conwy, Caernarfon and Harlech together was over £30,000,000.

MONUMENT TO ROBERT CECIL, 1st EARL OF SALISBURY

The effigy of Sir Robert Cecil, holding the white staff of Lord Treasurer, lies on a slab of black marble supported by four kneeling Virtues; underneath is a skeleton. The monument was carved by Maximilian Colt (or Poultrain) a Huguenot who carved Elizabeth I's tomb at Westminster. He also carved river barges for the Royal Family and, besides money, received an annual suit of broadcloth and fur for life. Cecil's tomb was ordered before his death to ensure a good likeness, a common practice in 16th-century England—'thereby to prevent the negligence of heirs and to mind him of his mortality'. Colt made a model of the tomb for Cecil in 1609, although he did not die until 1612. (Church of St Etheldreda, Hatfield)

Haslemere *Surrey* 541Je
There are several generously scaled Georgian houses in the wide main street, which slopes downhill and up to the back of the town hall. Behind the town are the woods of Blackdown.
EDUCATIONAL MUSEUM Started in 1888 by a surgeon, Sir Jonathan Hutchinson, who saw the function of a museum to be not merely the display of random collections of rare or extraordinary objects, but a means of explaining the story of the earth and its life. The exhibits here are mainly concerned, therefore, with geology, zoology and human history. In the geology gallery the display of rocks and fossils is supplemented by an analysis of local geological history through relief-models, maps and diagrams, and by show-cases dealing with such themes as the story of fossils, the story of coal, and precious stones. There is a display of minerals which, when lit by an ultra-violet lamp, fluoresce in spectacular colours. In the history gallery there are illustrations of life in each period, a collection of prehistoric tools, and panels indicating the phases through which people in Britain were passing relative to other civilisations. The zoology gallery covers vertebrates, invertebrates and insects. Particularly notable are the collection of British mammals, an exhibit on bird biology and the collection of British birds.
JESSES This house contains a fine collection of early European musical instruments, on view to the public by appointment.

Haslingfield *Cambs.* 548Ae
CHURCH OF ALL SAINTS A church of the 14th century, but with earlier work. The west tower has embattled pinnacle turrets. There are remains of a three-storey pulpit and a Jacobean font cover. Fragments of stained glass, and a standing figure of a man in contemporary dress, *c.* 1675, possibly by William Stanton of Holborn.

Hastings *E. Sussex* 542Dd
The old town of Hastings was one of the Cinque Ports. The Battle of Hastings, when Harold was defeated by William the Conqueror in 1066, actually took place at Battle, known to the invaders as Senlac, about 6 miles to the north-west.

To record the history of the Norman invasion, Matilda, the wife of the Conqueror, ordered the weaving of the 213 ft long Bayeux Tapestry. To mark the 900th anniversary of the Norman invasion, the Royal School of Needlework embroidered a similar strip of tapestry, the Hastings Embroidery, 243 ft long, recording in detail 81 of the great events of British history since 1066.
PELHAM CRESCENT With the church of St Mary-in-the-Castle at the centre of the arc, the crescent was built in 1824–8 by a little-known architect, Joseph Kay. The architecture is more distinguished than any of the contemporary terraces at Brighton.

Hatchlands *Surrey* 542Af
Admiral Boscawen, who defeated the French fleet at Louisberg (1758), built the exterior of the mansion *c.* 1756. In 1759 Robert Adam carried out the fine interior decoration—his earliest known work in England.

Hatfield *Herts.* 547Jc
Fore Street has a charming row of small Georgian dwellings that were stepped up the hill to exploit the slope. At the bottom, on the corner of Park Street, is the timber-framed and gabled Eight Bells Inn, *c.* 1630. Dick Turpin is said to have leapt from one of the upper windows on to his horse Black Bess, and galloped away as the Bow Street runners entered the place. Several other houses of interest, with oversailing upper floors, are in Park Street, and a good group of half-timbered late 16th-century houses can be found in Church Street.
CHURCH OF ST ETHELDREDA The nave was rebuilt by David Brandon in 1872, with the east end, chancel and transepts from an older building. The north chapel was built in 1618 as a family chapel for the Cecils. Monuments include the work of Maximilian Colt, Nicholas Stone, Rysbrack and others, the latest being by Goscombe John of the early 20th century. Of the 19th-century stained glass, one window is by Morris & Co. from a design by Burne-Jones.

Hatfield Broad Oak *Essex* 548Ad
CHURCH OF ST MARY THE VIRGIN Formerly a priory founded by Aubrey de Vere in 1135, the

church consists only of the nave. There is much 15th-century work, including the west tower and south porch. In 1708, a library was built to the east of the south chapel. The contents include a 15th-century screen, an 18th-century reredos by John Woodward, and several monuments, of which one is by J. F. Moore, another by John Flaxman.

Hatfield House *Herts.*   547*Jc*
The original palace here was completed in 1497 for Bishop Morton of Ely. After the Dissolution it became a royal residence, but James I exchanged it for the home of Robert Cecil, 1st Earl of Salisbury. The remains of the palace, including the banqueting hall, still stand in the west gardens. In 1607 Salisbury asked Robert Lyminge to design a new house. This Jacobean building kept to the usual E-plan of Elizabethan houses and was completed in 1611. In size it is impressive—it is nearly 300 ft long and 150 ft wide. The wings are wide and have square turrets at each corner. Still the home of the Cecil family, it contains fine portraits, including the Rainbow portrait of Elizabeth I by Isaac Oliver, and manuscripts and relics of her. There are fine gardens and an extensive park.

Haughley Park *Suffolk*   548*Cf*
Although not built until 1620, this small red-brick mansion is typical of an Elizabethan house with its E formation, crow-stepped gables and star-topped chimneys. The house is set in over 250 acres of parkland, and the interior, recently restored, contains fine furniture and pictures.

Haughmond *Shropshire*   552*Ac*
ABBEY One of the most impressive of all abbey ruins, Haughmond was founded by the Augustinians at the beginning of the 12th century. Most of the church has gone, but there are remains of the various monastic buildings dating from the Normans.

Haughton-le-Skerne *Durham*   558*Ce*
CHURCH OF ST ANDREW A Norman church, including the chancel arch, but the transepts are from the 19th century; there is a west tower. Inside are 17th-century furnishings—box-pews, font cover and pulpit. There are some Saxon carved fragments and a 16th-century brass depicting a woman with twin babies.

Hawkshead *Cumbria*   557*Hd*
In Ann Tyson's cottage the poet William Wordsworth (1770–1850) lodged when a scholar at the 16th-century grammar school; the cottage has an outside staircase. The medieval gate-house of Hawkshead Hall survives almost intact.

Haworth *W. Yorks.*   558*Bb*
BRONTË PARSONAGE MUSEUM The home of the Brontë sisters from 1821 until 1849, where Anne, Charlotte and Emily Jane wrote their novels. Manuscripts and personal effects of the sisters are exhibited in the bleak Georgian house, which is preserved as it was in their day.

Hawstead *Suffolk*   548*Cf*
CHURCH OF ALL SAINTS Norman and later; the west tower is Perpendicular, with flushwork decoration. The nave has hammerbeams and angels, but was restored in the mid-19th century. There are attractive furnishings—benches, 16th-century pulpit, lectern—a large number of brasses, and monuments by Nicholas Stone, the two John Bacons and others from the 13th century onwards. The screen is 15th-century.

Hawthornden *Lothian*   562*Ce*
A mansion rebuilt in 1638 by the poet William Drummond (1585–1649), who is buried in the

THE HALL AT HATFIELD HOUSE

At the Dissolution Henry VIII seized the palace of Hatfield which belonged to the Bishops of Ely. His daughter, Mary Tudor, lived there and during her reign her half-sister, the Princess Elizabeth, was kept virtually a prisoner at Hatfield. There in 1558, while in the park, Elizabeth heard of her accession to the throne. James I coveted Theobalds, the nearby home of Robert Cecil, 1st Earl of Salisbury, and he exchanged houses with Salisbury. From 1607 Salisbury set about building a great new Jacobean house at Hatfield. Inside is the two-storey hall with a carved screen at one end; at the other end a door leads to the magnificent carved wooden staircase, much decorated and with standing figures of boys and heraldic lions. The long gallery runs the entire length of the south front, 180 ft long. In King James's Drawing-room is a large chimney-piece, by Maximilian Colt, with a painted plaster statue of James I. The chapel retains its original stained glass. The relics on display include letters exchanged between Mary, Queen of Scots and Elizabeth, the warrant for Mary's execution, the cradle of Charles I and armour worn by men of the Spanish Armada. In the Marble Hall is a 17th-century tapestry of the Four Seasons.

churchyard of the nearby Norman church in Lasswade. In the grounds is a tree commemorating a visit by Ben Jonson in 1618. (By appointment.)

Hawton *Notts.*   552*Fd*
CHURCH OF ALL SAINTS The interest here is nearly all centred in the magnificent chancel built by Sir Robert de Compton before 1330; he is buried in it near the richly ornamented Easter sepulchre, opposite which is an equally richly decorated sedilia.

Heaselands *W. Sussex*   542*Be*
The gardens contain a wide variety of flowering shrubs—notably rhododendrons and azaleas—water gardens and aviaries.

Heaton Hall *Greater Manchester*   552*Bg*
Built by James Wyatt in 1772, the Hall was formerly a residence of the Earls of Wilton. It contains one of the few surviving Etruscan rooms, with painted walls and ceiling by Biagio Rebecca. Other contents include an organ built by Samuel Green (1790) and furniture and paintings of the 18th century.

HATFIELD HOUSE: DETAIL FROM A TAPESTRY OF 'SPRING'

This tapestry is one of a set of four depicting 'The Seasons', a favourite subject for a tapestry room. The engravings of a Flemish artist, Marten de Vos (1531–1603), provided the main theme of the gods surrounded by seasonal activities. The detail here shows hunts in progress through fields and woods, with much incidental detail around the central subjects. Made in 1611 the tapestry also shows the signs of the zodiac for each season, and emblems with their Latin tags fill the borders.

Heckington *Lincs.*   *553Hd*
CHURCH OF ST ANDREW One of the best Decorated churches in Britain, with a tall tower and spire. Inside there is a very fine Easter sepulchre with carved figures, including a mermaid and a man playing bagpipes. The loss of the chancel screen detracts from the medieval proportions, but the tracery work in the east window is a masterpiece.

Hedon *Humberside*   *559Ga*
CHURCH OF ST AUGUSTINE A cruciform church which is mainly of the 13th century at the east end, and has a 14th-century nave. The central tower is 14th century. G. E. Street restored St Augustine's during the third quarter of the 19th century. There is fine tracery in the windows, lancet arcading, and a 14th-century font with carved angels.

Hellen's *Heref. & Worcs.*   *546Be*
A brick Jacobean manor house, with parts dating from 1292, once visited by the Black Prince. The dovecot dates from 1641.

Helmingham *Suffolk*   *548Df*
The Tudor Hall stands within a deer park; it is moated, with functioning drawbridges, and has crenellation added by Nash in the 18th century. It was built in 1490 by the Tollemache family to whom there are many monuments in the church. (Hall gardens only open.)

Helpston *Cambs.*   *547Hh*
A memorial to John Clare (1793–1864), known as the Peasant Poet, stands at the cross-roads in this village in which he was born. The son of a Northamptonshire labourer and without education, his poems about the countryside and those written during his confinement in Northampton asylum are among the finest in the language.

Helston *Cornwall*   *538Ba*
CHURCH OF ST MICHAEL Built during the second half of the 18th century. The west tower has obelisk pinnacles.
MUSEUM Situated in the old Butter Market, folk collections illustrating all aspects of local life in the Lizard Peninsula are displayed. In 1901 Marconi successfully transmitted the first wireless message across the Atlantic from Poldhu Point, just south of Helston, and a small section of the museum is devoted to the early days of wireless. Another display illustrates the work of Henry Trengrouse (1772–1854) a Helston cabinet-maker who invented the rocket line for saving life at sea.

Hembury *Devon*   *540Ad*
When excavated, this fine hill-fort was seen to cover an earlier Neolithic causewayed camp. The hill-fort itself had been remodelled. At first it had a single bank and ditch with two entrances. The bank was held by a timber revetment with an external palisade, and the entrances had timber gates

QUEEN ELIZABETH *painted by Nicholas Hilliard. (National Portrait Gallery)*

ELIZABETH I, THE GREAT GLORIANA

'In my opinion', said the Mantuan envoy, 'she exceeds the bounds of gravity and decorum.' The subject of his displeasure was a young queen, 'as tall as a door', as she described herself, with tawny hair and clothed in cloth-of-gold, who was 'very cheerful and smiling and giving everyone a thousand greetings' on her progress through the streets of London to her coronation. In a few weeks Elizabeth had captured the devotion of the City and established herself as her own Prime Minister, a position she was to maintain, in peace and war, through nearly 45 years. In her reign Shakespeare wrote *Hamlet*, Drake circumnavigated the globe, and England rose from a second-class nation to the dominant power of the 16th-century world. Her tomb is at Westminster Abbey.

MEDAL *commemorating the defeat of the Spanish Armada. (British Museum)*

ESSEX RING *reputedly given by the queen to Essex to return if he were ever in danger. (Westminster Abbey Museum)*

MINIATURE BY NICHOLAS HILLIARD, *and its original case, of Elizabeth, with her hair flowing loose in token of her maidenhood. 'I will never marry', she is reported to have said as a child of eight, when Catherine Howard, the step-mother whom she loved, was beheaded. (Victoria and Albert Museum)*

ARMADA JEWEL. *(Victoria and Albert Museum)*

THE OLD PALACE AT HATFIELD, *Elizabeth's residence before she became queen. At 15 she wrote to her brother 'The face, I grant I may well blush to offer, but the mind I will never be afraid to present.'*

ELIZABETH'S VIRGINALS. *One day she was alone, and playing these virginals, when she was surprised by the envoy of Mary, Queen of Scots, and she jealously asked him if she played better than her cousin Mary, if she danced better, and which of them was fairer. The envoy told her that she was 'the whiter' but that her cousin was very lovesome. (Victoria and Albert Museum)*

WHITE HORSE *which the queen rode to review her troops before the Armada. (Hatfield House)*

BUCKSKIN RIDING BOOTS AND EMBROIDERED GLOVES *belonging to the queen, a superb horsewoman. She was very proud of her long, slim hands and had the habit of constantly drawing her gloves on and off when she was thinking.*
(Ashmolean Museum, Oxford)

THE ARMADA PORTRAIT *painted soon after the defeat in 1588 of Philip II's Spanish fleet, which is shown in the two background panels. The queen, with her hand resting assertively on the globe of the world, is the personification of the splendour, stability and supreme power of England. (Woburn Abbey)*

with bridges over. Later, additional banks and ditches were constructed to deepen the defences and, finally, more banks and ditches were put in, crossing the interior of the fort and blocking the west gate. The entrances are fine examples of the inturned type. This most westerly of the cause-wayed camps appears to link its builders with the tribes of the Salisbury Plain area. The fort dates from the Iron Age.

Hemel Hempstead *Herts.* 547Hc
CHURCH OF ST MARY A large, mainly Norman, cruciform church with a central tower and tall spire. The chancel, decorated by G. F. Bodley in the 1880's, has a mid-12th-century ribbed vault. The church contains a 14th-century brass and some 19th-century stained glass.

Hemingbrough *N. Yorks.* 558Ea
CHURCH OF ST MARY A splendid cruciform church, of the 12th to 15th centuries, with a squat central tower and lofty spire. There is good medieval woodwork in the roofs, screens, bench ends and misericords. The pulpit dates from 1717.

Hendon *Greater London* 547Jc
CHURCH OF ST MARY The original church dates from the mid-13th century, but was greatly enlarged in 1914-15. There are interesting fur-nishings and a fine square Norman font carved with intersected arcading on all sides. Monuments include a bold heraldic slab cf 1677 and one of *c.* 1703 with a reclining bewigged figure.
HENDON HALL The home of David Garrick, the celebrated actor-manager, in 1756.

Henley-on-Thames *Oxon.* 547Gb
A small town set in beautiful wooded country in the Thames Valley. The bridge dates from the 18th century and there are many fine Georgian houses with gardens running to the river.

Hereford *Heref. & Worcs.* 546Ae
CATHEDRAL A cruciform cathedral dating from the 11th century, but with much alteration. There was, besides the central tower, one at the west end as well; this fell in 1786, knocking down part of the Norman nave. James Wyatt restored the west end, and this again was rebuilt at the beginning of the 20th century. The central tower dates from the 14th century, and is studded with ball-flower dec-oration. Inside are many brasses and monuments, and some fine 14th-century stalls with misericords.
CHURCHILL GARDENS MUSEUM The collections of costume, accessories, dolls, furniture and paintings date from 1750.
CITY MUSEUM AND ART GALLERY Historical exhibits include a Bronze Age burial, finds from Iron Age hill-forts and discoveries made at the Roman town of Magna (Kenchester). There are also natural history and geological displays, collec-tions of agricultural and domestic bygones, Chinese ceramics, English china and glass and water-colours by local artists, including David Cox and Joshua Cristall.

Herefordshire Beacon *Heref. & Worcs.* 546Be
This Iron Age hill-fort is marked by its com-manding position and complex earthworks. In the centre are the first defences, a single ditch with bank and counterscarp bank. Later, the internal area was extended to some 32 acres by a great ditch with bank and counterscarp. This incorpor-ated the earlier bank on the west, but stretched away outside it on the east. In Norman times, a castle was built at the centre of the original works and its earthworks add to the fascinating display of 2000 years of military engineering.

Hergest Croft *Heref. & Worcs.* 545J
Only the garden and park, noted for their flowering shrubs and woodland, are open to the public.

Hermitage Castle *Borders* 562Dl
A Border castle owned by the Earl of Bothwell the lover of Mary, Queen of Scots, who rode 40 miles there and back from Jedburgh to visit him Four great square towers are linked by curtain walls which date from the 14th century.

Herstmonceux Castle *E. Sussex* 542D
The home of the Royal Observatory since 1948 Herstmonceux was built by Sir Roger Fiennes Lord Treasurer under Henry VI, in 1440. With it large windows, and relatively thin walls, it wa never intended for defence and is really a mano house. From 1777, when it was dismantled, unti the restorations of 1933, the castle was a ruin (Interior not open.)

Hertford *Herts.* 547J
CASTLE Built *c.* 1100, the oldest building in Hert ford, which until the reign of Elizabeth I wa closely connected with royalty. When Edwar III's mother Queen Isabella died, he recruited guard of 14 poor persons at twopence a day, fo three months, to watch over her body. The Kin of Scotland, David Bruce, was imprisoned there as was King John of France, after the battle a Poitiers. Here also Henry Bolingbroke, Duke o Lancaster, drew up the charges against Richard I which subsequently dethroned him in 1399. Jame I's son, Prince Charles, sold the castle to William Cecil, Earl of Salisbury, whose family have owne it ever since. The present building includes th Mount, some of the 12th-century curtain wall, postern gate and an octagonal tower. The lat 15th-century gate-house was considerably altere *c.* 1800. Castle Street has timber-framed cottage and in Water Lane Nos. 4-16 are thought to b former outbuildings of the castle.
FORE STREET Many of the buildings have splendi pargetting or ornamental stucco work including variety of floral decoration. Shire Hall is a simpl and unpretentious building designed by Rober Adam's brother James, in 1768-9. Nos. 3-13 hav excellent 17th-century pargetting.
LOMBARD HOUSE On Bull Plain, the 17th-centur home of Henry Chauncy, the Hertfordshir historian and judge, who presided over one of th last witchcraft trials in England. The gables an beams of the house have a Georgian façade ove them. The house now contains the Hertford Clu
MUSEUM A half-timbered town cottage of th mid-17th century houses objects of local origin archaeological finds, geological specimens, paint ings, photographs and prints of Hertfordshire, an the collections of the Hertfordshire Regiment.
ST ANDREW'S STREET No. 43, the Old Verger' House, is a half-timbered structure with oversail ing upper storeys dating from the 15th century

Hessett *Suffolk* 548C
CHURCH OF ST ETHELBERT A 14th-century churc with a 15th-century west tower, nave and porc with flushwork decoration. There is a 15th century font, a screen and benches, and a monu ment by John Stone of *c.* 1653. Mural painting depict the Seven Deadly Sins, St Barbara, S Christopher and Christ of the Trades. The 14th century Vestry was once an anchorite's cell an still has its own altar and squint.

Hetty Pegler's Tump *Glos.* 546E
This Neolithic transeptal chambered long barrow was excavated in the 19th century, and has bee

HEREFORD CATHEDRAL

RICHARD OF HALDINGHAM'S MAPPA MUNDI
*This map of the world (mappa mundi) is one of the
largest (65 in. by 53 in.) and most elaborate medieval
maps in Europe. Richard, who died about 1313, was
Treasurer of Lincoln Cathedral and Prebendary of
Hereford, and the prominence given to Lincoln on the
map, together with the sketchy impression of Hereford,
suggest he painted it in Lincoln about 1275. The map,
worked on vellum, embodies all the Middle Ages'
fundamental beliefs about the shape and nature of the
world, which is drawn centred on Jerusalem; east is
at the top.*

CHAINED LIBRARY *The largest library of its kind in
the world, with nearly 1500 books, handwritten and
printed. Each has a chain attached to the front edge of
one cover and to a rod on the bookcase; they can be read,
but not removed. The oak bookcases were made in 1611.
Seventy books were printed before 1500, two by
Caxton.*

THE ENTRANCE HALL AT HEVENINGHAM HALL

Sir Robert Taylor designed this, the loveliest Palladian house in England, for Sir Gerald Vanneck in 1779. Taylor had started his career as a sculptor and had been an assistant to Sir Henry Cheere; he did not turn to architecture until the mid-18th century. He carved the sculpture in the pediment of the Mansion House in London—a commission he won as the result of a competition in which there was stiff opposition from his former master, Cheere, and Louis Roubiliac. The interior decoration at Heveningham was entrusted to James Wyatt. The superb hall has screens of columns at either end, and in the saloon the ceilings and walls were painted by Biago Rebecca.

consolidated and kept open so that its structure and some of the interior chambers may be seen. A deep forecourt leads to an entrance, inside which is a gallery with two chambers on either side (two of which are now sealed) and a fifth at the inner end.

Half a mile south lies Uley Bury, a fine Iron Age hill-fort.

Heveningham Hall *Suffolk*   548Ef
Sir Gerald Vanneck inherited this estate with its small 18th-century house in 1777, and had a great new house built. He employed as architect Sir Robert Taylor, who left to the University of Oxford £180,000 with which the Taylorian Institute was founded. Taylor's Palladian house is a pillared centre block rising from an arcaded basement, with a pedimented wing on either side. James Wyatt decorated the interior of the house and also built the orangery. The grounds, containing a lake, were laid out by Capability Brown *c*. 1780. The entrance hall, Etruscan Room and library have their original furniture and contents. The estate still belongs to the Vanneck family.

Hever *Kent*   542Cf
CHURCH OF ST PETER A good example of 14th-century work, with west tower and spire, and barrel roof. There is a 15th-century brass to a lady in the chancel, but more important is one on an altar-tomb in the north chapel to Sir Thomas Boleyn (*d*. 1538), the father of Anne Boleyn. He wears full Garter robes, and lies with his head resting on his helmet.

Hever Castle *Kent*   542Cf
The girlhood home of Anne Boleyn (1507–36) second queen of Henry VIII and mother of Queen Elizabeth I. The late 13th-century moated castle was altered in the 15th century. The grounds contain a formal garden in Italian style.

Hexham *Northld.*   558Bg
A town famous in Saxon times when, under the name of Hagulstald, it became a bishopric in AD 678. However, it was largely destroyed by the Danes in 810. From those times the priory church dates, though much reconstruction took place in the 13th century; its treasures include a wooden pulpit, a pre-Conquest stool which gave sanctuary to anyone seated upon it, a crypt and fine choir screen. In 1464 the Yorkist army of Edward IV routed the Lancastrian forces of Henry VI at the battle of Hexham. The bridge across Haglut Burn dates from the 13th century. The Moot Hall, *c*. 1400, and the Manor Office, *c*. 1330–2, were the court-house and prison of the Manor of Hexham. In the Market Place is the Shambles, an unusual columned market building built in 1766.

Hexham Abbey *Northld.*   558Bg
Hexham Cathedral, founded *c*. 675–80, survived until 821. The town was sacked in 876 and there are no records of the church until the Archbishop of York refounded it as a house of Augustinian canons in 1113. The church is the main building to survive from the refoundation, but the external view from the east is dominated by the 19th-century façade, built *c*. 1858. Behind this stands a church begun *c*. 1180, which is an excellent example of Early English style, with its long lancet windows and clustered column shafts. The nave was destroyed in 1296 but rebuilt in 1908. One outstanding feature is the massive staircase in the south transept, which led up to the canons' dormitory, and was used by them to descend directly into the church to sing the night offices. Inside is a Roman tombstone and a chair called Wilfrid's Throne, dating from the 7th century and said to be the bishop's seat from the Saxon church. Also known as the *frith stool* (peace chair), it afforded the right of sanctuary to a fugitive. Beneath the buildings is Wilfrid's crypt of the same date, which utilises Roman stones in its construction. The rood screen, stalls with misericords and two chantry chapels, one with curious stone sculptured figures, are 15th century.

Heysham *Lancs.*   557Hc
CHURCH OF ST PETER Parts of the church date from the 10th century, although the present building is largely 14th century, with 15th- and 17th-century additions. The hog-backed stone, a curved grave stone carved with figures of men and animals, probably dates from the 10th century. In the churchyard is the carved shaft of a 9th-century cross. There are several stone grave covers and an 11th- or 12th- to 13th-century stone coffin.

To the west of the present church is the ruin of St Patrick's Chapel, a Celtic church believed to date from the 5th century and probably founded by Irish missionaries. West of this again is a row of six coffins carved out of the solid rock.

HEVER CASTLE

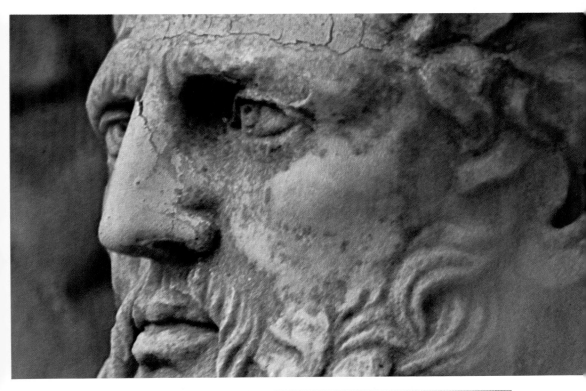

ITALIAN GARDEN *William Waldorf Astor, who had been American Minister to Italy, acquired Hever in 1903. He restored the building to its Tudor glory, and created the Italian Garden as a setting for Classical sculptures he had collected in Italy; it has a pergola and grottoes—one is shown here.*

DISGRACED QUEEN *Bored with his mistress Mary Boleyn, Henry VIII persistently courted Mary's younger sister Anne (pictured here by an unknown artist), and finally married her in January 1533. Little more than three years later she was dead, beheaded allegedly for adultery, but in fact for failing to provide Henry with a son. The prayer book she carried with her to the scaffold on Tower Green is shown below the painting. It is a Book of Hours, bearing an exhortation to readers in Anne's own handwriting to remember her in their prayers.*

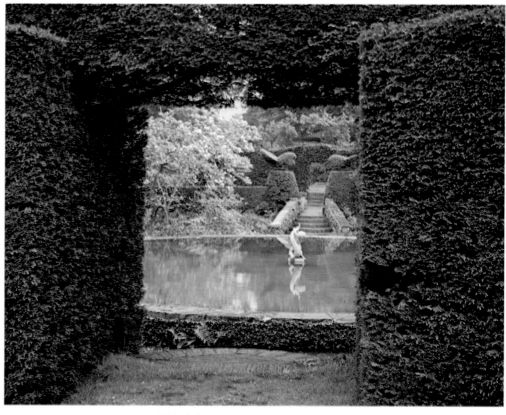

HIDCOTE MANOR GARDENS

Lawrence Johnston, an American, bought this estate in 1907 and created a series of delightful gardens, both formal and informal. The site was inhospitable: the soil was limestone, limiting the choice of plants, and there was little shelter from the wind in the wide valley with its small stream running down the Cotswold escarpment to the vale of Shakespeare's River Avon. Johnston planted protective hedges and these were often unorthodox—red-leaved beech was mixed with the usual kind, and golden-leaved with green yew. They form a series of compartments with plants

from all over the world, and each garden has a particular quality—one is full of red-foliaged and flowered plants and shrubs.

The stream part of the garden is quite different. A path rambles downhill along it, roughly parallel to the formal axis. It is overhung by fine trees, while beside the banks are choice shrubs and alongside the water primulas and other moisture-loving plants grow in profusion. By the house a large kitchen garden has its paths lined with old-fashioned roses and many kinds of clematis.

Heytesbury *Wilts.*   *540Ee*
CHURCH OF SS PETER AND PAUL A large cruciform church with a central tower, collegiate in the 12th century. Its origins are Norman, but there is much 13th-century work and additions up to the 15th century. There is a fine stone screen to the north transept with fan-vaulting on both sides. It was restored by William Butterfield in 1866–7.
HOSPITAL OF ST JOHN An almshouse founded in the 15th century by the Hungerford family. The present Georgian building dates from 1767, when it was rebuilt after a fire.

Hidcote Manor Gardens *Glos.*   *546De*
These gardens in the Cotswolds have been called the most beautiful gardens of the 20th century. In 1907 an American officer, Lawrence Johnston, began to transform what was virtually a wilderness into a series of superb gardens. A cedar of Lebanon, a clump of fine beech trees, barren fields and a stream trickling through a small valley were the raw materials. First, the limestone windswept Cotswold scarp was converted into broad terraces. Along these unusual hedges were planted to form a series of compartments linked by a central vista. Each compartment has a special quality, such as the garden of plants all with red foliage and flowers.

The gardens contain many rare and exotic plants and lime-hating rhododendrons, camellias and magnolias are grown in beds of sawdust. From the last terrace an alleyway of pleached hornbeam leads through a gate into a holly-grove.

High Banks *Dumfs. & Gall.*   *556Eg*
There is a rock-face exposed about a mile south-east of High Bank Farmhouse. This 100 ft surface bears groups of Bronze Age cup-and-ring markings, remarkable for the unusual grouping-patterns they display.

High Bridestones and Flat Howe   *558Fe*
N. Yorks.
The Bridestones are the remains of two circles of standing stones, each originally nearly 40 ft across. A few stones only remain upright; more have fallen, and the rest have disappeared. There are also single standing stones outside the circles.

Flat Howe is a round barrow about a quarter of a mile to the east of the circles. Its mound has a visible kerb of stones. All are of the Bronze Age.

Highdown Hill *W. Sussex*   *542Ad*
The site of a Bronze Age settlement, overlaid by an Iron Age hill-fort. Remains of a Roman bath-

house and a Saxon cemetery have been excavated. Finds from the site are in Worthing Museum.

High Melton *S. Yorks.* *552Ef*
CHURCH OF ST JAMES The nave is Norman, but St James's is mainly a Perpendicular church; the west tower is of that period. There is a parclose screen and some medieval stained glass, and a 20th-century rood screen and reredos by Sir Ninian Comper.

High Wycombe *Bucks.* *547Gc*
CHAIR AND LOCAL HISTORY MUSEUM Since the 18th century High Wycombe has been a major centre of the chair-making and furniture trades; up to the First World War, it was almost the town's sole source of employment. The museum displays an extensive collection of the domestic chairs (mainly Windsors) and chair-making equipment that are part of this local craft. A small collection of local bygones is also among the items on show.

Hillesden *Bucks.* *547Gd*
CHURCH OF ALL SAINTS A lonely and most interesting church, all late Gothic though the west tower was built somewhat earlier than the rest. The walls are impressively battlemented, and there is a two-storey north vestry with a delicate canopy to the tower. Below the chancel roof is a row of carved stone angels holding music scrolls. The rood and parclose screens have linenfold panelling, and the 16th-century stained glass shows stories of St Nicholas. There are several monuments, one of marble to Sir A. Denton and wife (*d.* 1733) by Sir Henry Cheere. Sir Gilbert Scott made a thorough restoration in the 19th century.

Hillingdon *Greater London* *547Hb*
CHURCH OF ST JOHN THE BAPTIST Mainly 14th century, although the chancel arch dates from 1260 and the west tower was built in 1629. The church was restored by Sir Gilbert Scott in 1848. There are notable brasses and monuments: that of 1657 is to Sir Edward Carr, and that of 1743 to Henry Paget, Earl of Uxbridge. In the churchyard is the tomb of John Rich (1682–1761) founder of Covent Garden theatre. (By appointment.)

Hill Top *Cumbria* *557Hd*
Beatrix Potter lived here and wrote the *Peter Rabbit* books. The 17th-century house contains her pictures, china and furniture.

Hilton *Dorset* *540Dd*
CHURCH OF ALL SAINTS A 15th-century church, with superb arch over the main aisle. After the Dissolution, several windows from the cloister of Milton Abbey were fitted in the north aisle; it is thought that the fan-vault of the porch may also have come from there. In the tower are 12 tall panels with painted figures of the Apostles, also from Milton, of the early 16th century; there is a 17th-century pulpit and a Norman font.

Hindley *Greater Manchester* *552Ag*
CHURCH OF ALL SAINTS In 1766 the earlier church here was rebuilt in the Classical style. All Saints is brick with traceried windows; the galleried interior contains panelling and woodcarving.

Hingham *Norfolk* *554Cb*
A small, unspoilt town between Norwich and Watton. Samuel Lincoln, weaver and ancestor of Abraham Lincoln, was baptised here in 1622 in the splendid medieval church. Shortly before Lincoln left England the Puritan rector, Robert Peck, fled to America, to the newly founded town of Hingham, Massachusetts. A bronze bust of Abraham Lincoln is in the church.

MARKET PLACE Has a number of elegant houses: Beaconsfield House, early Georgian; the Admiral's House with embattled wings; Quorn House with a Tuscan porch and pediment. The Mansion House in Pond Street has imposing Flemish gables and chequer brickwork.

Hintlesham Hall *Suffolk* *548De*
A mid-Tudor mansion with additions in Queen Anne style made in 1842; now a restaurant.

Hinton Blewett *Avon* *540Cf*
CHURCH OF ST MARGARET OF SCOTLAND Mainly 14th century, with a later north aisle of *c.* 1530. Inside is a Norman font and a canopied pulpit dated 1638 which originally had three tiers.

Hinwick House *Beds.* *547Hf*
The Orlebar family have lived here since 1230. The present Queen Anne mansion was built in 1710; adjacent buildings date from 1430. The house contains paintings by Van Dyck, Lely, Kneller and Pieter Breughel, Mortlake tapestries and 17th- and 18th-century furniture.

Hirwaun Iron Works *Mid Glam.* *545Hc*
The works closed down in the mid-19th century, and the furnaces fell into decay, but sufficient remains above the surface to see that the builders worked in a grand manner. Particularly interesting is the use of wrought-iron reinforcement bars, in the furnaces and in the slender tram-road embankment; some of the stone sleepers of the tram-road are still *in situ*.

Hitchin *Herts.* *547Jd*
CHURCH OF ST MARY A large embattled church, mostly dating from the 14th and 15th centuries. The west tower is earlier. The stone font dates from the 15th century. Of the monuments, one of *c.* 1697 appears to be typical of the style of William Stanton of Holborn.

ST NICHOLAS WINDOW

There are eight panels in this 16th-century window illustrating stories from the Miracles of St Nicholas, and here is a detail of a scene from the 'Boy and the Gold Cup'. A rich nobleman promised that if he had a son, he would present a gold cup to the altar of St Nicholas. A son was born and the cup was made, but only a duplicate was offered to the Saint. During the voyage to the church the boy fell into the sea with the cup. Part of the medieval ship and sailors are depicted here. The glass in the Church of All Saints, Hillesden, is rich in colour, and the drawing style shows a strong Flemish influence.

HOLKHAM HALL

Thomas Coke succeeded to the Holkham estates when he was ten years old. In 1712, at the age of 15, he set out on the Grand Tour and spent six years travelling, returning to England in 1718. During his time abroad, his most impressionable years, Coke met the remarkable William Kent, then an art student, but destined to become a brilliant painter, architect, interior decorator and designer of sculpture and furniture. The two were travelling companions for a year, and later Coke, by then Earl of Leicester, employed Kent to design his new house at Holkham, built in 1734–62. The interior is sumptuous and ornate. The main hall is 50 ft high— the full height of the building—and occupies most of the central block; it has a superb coffered plaster ceiling. Much of the furnishings and decoration of the state rooms, including the saloon (above) and state bedroom (right), was designed by William Kent.

Hoarwithy *Heref. & Worcs.*   *546Ad*
CHURCH OF ST CATHERINE An Italianate Roman-esque church of the late 19th century by J. P. Seddon, with a bell-tower and a cloister walk on the south side. Inside is a Byzantine east end with gold mosaic work by Italian and local craftsmen.

Hod Hill *Dorset*   *540Ed*
Across the valley from Hambledon Hill lies this second great Iron Age hill-fort, with an internal area of 50 acres. Again there are multiple defences with well protected entrances. Remodelled three times, this hill-fort was one of the settlements reduced by Vespasian and his 2nd Legion in the early days of the Roman conquest. Shortly after-wards, the Romans erected a small fort in one corner and this was occupied for a time by both legionaries and some auxiliary cavalrymen.

Hodnet *Shropshire*   *552Ac*
CHURCH OF ST LUKE An unusual church, for the present wide south aisle was originally the nave, and the present nave the former north aisle. The semi-circular Norman arches above the doorway and windows in the south aisle are particularly interesting. Nineteenth-century restoration in-cluded the addition of the Heber Chapel in 1870. Interesting 18th- and 19th-century tombs include

one by John Carline, one to Bishop Heber (*d.* 1826) by Sir Francis Chantrey, and one of *c.* 1752 attributed to Sir Henry Cheere.

Hodnet Hall Gardens *Shropshire*   *552Ac*
Hodnet Hall, a large red-brick mansion designed in the 19th century by Salvin in the Tudor style, stands on the bank of a small valley. An adjacent hall houses a collection of big game trophies. The surrounding Victorian garden was of no great merit, but the countryside abounded with streams and pools. In 1921 Brigadier Heber-Percy created the first water garden in the valley and added a lake in 1923, but work was then halted until 1953. A chain of many pools covering 60 acres now fills the valley; massed primulas, irises, giant gunneras and other moisture-loving plants grow beside the water. The water gardens are linked to the house on the bank by formal terraces covered with lawns and massed rhododendrons and azaleas. Daffodils and early flowering shrubs provide brilliant spring colours.

Hoghton Tower *Lancs.*   *557Ja*
Relics of James I's visit to this house in 1617 are preserved here. The house, rebuilt in 1565 and re-stored during the late 19th century, contains 17th-century panelling and pictures of local interest.

Holbeach Lincs. 553Jc

CHURCH OF ALL SAINTS A church of particular
interest to architects, since it shows features of the
transition between the Decorated and Perpendicular styles. Its austere beauty is enhanced by
the total lack of structural alteration since the
building was completed in 1380. There are,
however, one or two mysterious oddities. The
north porch is flanked by two 30 ft turrets which
may have been taken from Moulton Castle. There
is also a fine 14th-century tomb containing the
remains of Sir Humphrey Littlebury, who is
depicted praying with his head resting upon his
helmet, above which appears another figure.

Holker Hall Cumbria 557Hd

Former residence of the Dukes of Devonshire, the
Hall was built in the 17th century and restored in
1873 after a fire. The interior has woodcarvings
by local craftsmen, period furniture and paintings.
In the grounds are rare shrubs and a deer reserve.

Holkham Camp Norfolk 554Bd

This is a camp or fort lying on an island of solid
ground in a surrounding drained salt marsh. It is
defended by one or two banks and a single ditch,
except where the natural slope and the water
which formerly surrounded it gave adequate pro-

tection. It has never been excavated and its date is
very uncertain, but it is generally thought to
belong to the latter part of the Iron Age.

Holkham Hall Norfolk 554Bd

A Palladian mansion, built in 1734–62, which symbolises planned progress as seen in the 18th
century. It was built near Wells by Thomas
Coke to show how an area of dunes and salt
marshes could be reclaimed and utilised, and how
the style of an Italian palace could be harmoniously
introduced into an English setting. Coke's plans
were crystallised after discussions with Lord
Burlington and William Kent; the result was a
mansion of H-plan, with four wings to a central
section: the overall front is 340 ft, with a great
central portico. The interior became as lavish as
the exterior is arid: a marble pillared and galleried
entrance hall leads to a saloon of dark red velvet
and gold with the Rubens painting of *The Return
from Egypt* as its dominant theme. All the main
rooms have a full measure of 18th-century magnificence—ceilings, paintings, tapestries and statuary. The interior was planned to give long vistas
of connecting rooms. Holkham Hall was part of
the inheritance of Thomas Coke's more famous
great-nephew 'Coke of Norfolk'.

Hollingbury *E. Sussex*   *542Bd*
Very early in the Iron Age, a simple defensive fort
was built here, traces of which remain. But more
than a century later, the present main structure was
built in substitution. Its rampart was revetted with
substantial timbering and there was also timbering
enclosed within the ramp. The west gate has an
inturned entrance, but that on the east side was of
much simpler construction.

Like the fort on Harrow Hill, this was apparently used only in times of emergency.

Holm Cultram Abbey *Cumbria*   *557Gg*
This was a Cistercian foundation of the mid-12th
century, and the nave survives as the parish church
of St Mary. This has a good Norman west
doorway, and a 16th-century west porch. The east
window appears to be a 17th-century form of
Perpendicular.

Holme Lacy *Heref. & Worcs.*   *546Ae*
CHURCH OF ST CUTHBERT An interesting church
with 14th-century arcade dividing the nave and
south aisle, which are almost of the same width.
The late 17th-century font is carved, and the stalls
have misericords. There are many monuments to
members of the Scudamore family from the 16th
century, that of 1571 with alabaster effigies, and
there are two (1859 and 1871) by Matthew Noble.

Holme Pierrepont *Notts.*   *552Fd*
CHURCH OF ST EDMUND A Gothic church of the
later 17th century, with a west tower. There is a
15th-century font, and many monuments, from *c.*
1300 up to early 19th-century work by John
Flaxman.

Holt *Wilts.*   *540Ef*
This pleasant village, composed largely of 17th-
and 18th-century houses surrounding a green, was
a well-known spa in the early 1700's. The well still
exists, incorporated in a factory.
THE COURTS Local weavers brought disputes to
this house for adjudication until the end of the 18th
century. Its decorated façade dates from 1700.

Holt *Heref. & Worcs.*   *546Cf*
CHURCH OF ST MARTIN This mainly Norman
church, with the 14th-century castle near by,
stands remote from all other buildings. It has rich
12th-century decoration on the doorway and
chancel arch; there are some fragments of
medieval glass of fine quality, a number of monuments and some good 19th-century mosaics.

Holtye *E. Sussex*   *542Ce*
It has been shown by excavation that the Roman
roads crossing and linking sites in the Weald were
often paved with slag from the iron-smelting
works in the area. Many of the minor roads,
indeed, appear to be have constructed largely to
serve these sites. At Holtye a section of such a road
has been excavated and left open for inspection. Its
surface of slag has consolidated with the passage of
time and it still shows the ruts and wear of the
traffic which passed along it.

Holyhead *Anglesey, Gwynedd*   *550Df*
CAER GYBI Holyhead was an important harbour as
early as Roman times. Here, in the latter part of the
Roman occupation, when the Irish were raiding
and settling on the Welsh coast, a tiny fort was
built. Its pattern resembles those later forts of the
Saxon Shore in South-east England, and two of
its projecting bastions still stand. It was this Irish
threat which led the British authorities, at the
beginning of the 5th century, to move the leaders
of the Votadini, and many of their tribesmen, from
the Lothians of Scotland to settle in North Wales as
a bulwark against invaders.

CHURCH OF ST CYBI A cruciform church, with a
west tower. Much of the building is the 15th- and
16th-century enlargement of the earlier church
whose chancel dates from the 13th century. The
church is set within the curtain wall of the Roman
fort of Caer Gybi.

Holy Island *Northld.*   *563Gd*
LINDISFARNE CASTLE A small castle on a high rock
above the sea. It was built in 1549 as a protection
against Scottish raids; stones from the nearby
ruined abbey founded in 635 were used in its
construction. From the Civil War until 1900 the
castle was in ruins; it was made habitable again by
Sir Edwin Lutyens, who designed the Cenotaph in
Whitehall, London.
LINDISFARNE PRIORY St Aidan founded a monastery here in 635, but this was destroyed by the
Vikings in 793 and sacked again in the 9th century
by the Danes. It was not until the 11th century
that the present building was begun for the Benedictines of Durham. Now only ruins remain, but
they are impressive and evocative.

Holywell *Clwyd*   *551He*
ST WINIFRED'S CHAPEL This well chapel and well
chamber, built in the late 15th century, is one of the
most perfect buildings of its kind in Britain. The
well forms the basement of the chapel and consists
of a large stone basin with steps for pilgrims to
descend into the water. The spring is said to mark
the spot where St Winifred's head was cut off by an
importunate lover. According to the legend it was
miraculously replaced, and she recovered to
become Abbess of Gwytherin.

Honeychurch *Devon*   *539Ge*
CHURCH OF ST MARY A remote Norman church,
with chancel arch and wagon-roofs in the nave.
The Norman circular font has cable and zigzag
carved decoration and a Jacobean cover. The west
tower and bench ends are of the 15th century.

Honington Camp *Lincs.*   *553Gd*
Hill-forts are almost unknown in Lincolnshire, but
this small Iron Age fort must have been placed here
for much the same reason that the early Roman
defences at Ancaster, which preceded the civilian
town of Causennae, were established. Both lay on
the southern slopes of Ancaster Gap, an ancient
channel eroded through the upland of Lincoln
Edge. Honington stands on the hill-slopes at its
south-west end and commands the Witham Valley
at its junction with the Gap. Its internal area of
about an acre is guarded by no less than three banks
with two intermediate ditches.

Honiton *Devon*   *540Ad*
Once famous as a wool town, Honiton suffered
disastrous fires in 1672, 1747, 1754 and 1765: its
houses are mainly Georgian and Victorian. It is
noted for its pottery and its lace which is similar to
Brussels lace, and which was worn by Queen
Charlotte, Queen Adelaide and Queen Victoria.
HONITON AND ALLHALLOWS PUBLIC MUSEUM
The museum is housed in what was probably the
chancel of the oldest church in Honiton and the
chapel of Allhallows School, whose tower and
nave were demolished in the 1820's to build the
present church of St Paul. The original shape of the
building and some of the original windows can still
be seen. The museum's collection centres on a
display of the lace for which Honiton is famous.
There are old and new examples of the lace, and a
collection of different types of Continental lace.
Other exhibits include a collection of bones of
prehistoric animals, all about 100,000 years old,
and a display of military and other relics of the
two World Wars.

HOPETOUN HOUSE

An enormous house on the south bank of the Firth of Forth, not far from the Forth Bridges. In 1721 William Adam, father of the two famous architects and decorators, John and Robert, began enlarging the existing house, built by Sir William Bruce for the 1st Earl of Hopetoun. Work went on for 30 years and when their father died in 1748, the Adam brothers *carried on, finished the house and decorated the new building with its two flanking wings joined to the main block by colonnaded quadrants. The interior is magnificent with woodcarving and plasterwork. The chimney-piece in the Red Drawing Room is the work of Michael Rysbrack, one of the most successful sculptors of the first half of the 18th century.*

Hopes, The *Lothian*   *562De*
One of the many large hill-forts scattered on the northern edge of the Lammermuir Hills. Built at one end of a ridge, its many ramparts appear to indicate at least two phases of construction. The inner area is protected by three ramparts without intervening ditches. Outside these are various lengths of rampart with external ditches, which do not encircle the whole area but curve from one steep scarp to another.
The fort is Iron Age.

Hopetoun House *Lothian*   *562Bf*
The house was begun in 1699 by Sir William Bruce, enlarged by his pupil William Adam and completed by Adam's sons Robert and John. It has a central building and two flanking wings surmounted by towers and cupolas, and is richly furnished. In the damask-hung Yellow Drawing Room are paintings by Rubens, Rembrandt and Titian. The Red Room is hung with silk. The house has most of its original furniture, including work by James Cullen.
The house is set in 100 acres of parkland, in which are herds of red and fallow deer, and the rare black four-horned St Kilda sheep.

Hopton Castle *Shropshire*   *546Ag*
Though this square Norman castle, incorporating some 14th-century additions, now lies in ruins, its setting in a hollow among wooded hills is strikingly beautiful. In 1644 it was the scene of a famous siege when 33 Roundheads, commanded by Colonel Samuel More, held the castle for three weeks against 500 Royalist troops.

Horncastle *Lincs.*   *553He*
A small market town on the site of the Roman station at Banovallum, with traces of Roman walls and other relics remaining. The parish church, St Mary's, is notable for the excellent brasses of the Dymoke family—Hereditary Champions of England. There are some good Georgian houses, principally Rollestone House, No. 2 West Street, the naturalist Sir Joseph Banks's old house, and No. 28 East Street. The Fighting Cocks Inn in West Street still has a cockpit in the yard. Bull-baiting was practised in the Bull Ring until 1835. Horncastle was once famous for its annual horse-fairs, which were said to be the largest of their kind in the world.

Horningsham *Wilts.*   *540De*
In the village is the Old Meeting House, built in 1566, with a thatched roof. It is the oldest Nonconformist chapel in England, erected by Scottish workmen engaged on the mansion of Longleat.

Horsey *Norfolk*   *554Ec*
WINDMILL The 200-year-old windmill was rebuilt at the beginning of this century by the millwright Dan England.

Horton Court *Avon*   *546Bb*
A Cotswold manor house, altered in the 19th century but with a 12th-century Norman great hall and early Renaissance features. In the garden is an unusual late-Perpendicular ambulatory, or covered walk.

Horwood *Devon*   *538Ff*
CHURCH OF ST MICHAEL A small, remote church standing in the hills above Bideford Bay. It has a low west tower with pinnacles. There is only one aisle, situated on the north side of the church. The Norman font is square, and the piscina is distinguished by its curling horn-shaped drain. There is some 15th-century stained glass, 16th-century bench ends and a pulpit of 1635. A mid-15th-century alabaster monument shows a woman in horned headdress, with children.

Hough-on-the-Hill *Lincs.*   *553Gd*
CHURCH OF ALL SAINTS The west tower is Saxon, with an exterior circular stair turret. Inside, the pillars of the aisle arcades are Early English, and the arches on the north side of the chancel leading into a chantry chapel are 13th century.

Houghton and Wyton *Cambs.*   *547Jf*
Houghton and Wyton, 2 miles from St Ives, have many picturesque cottages and riverside views. Houghton Water-mill is believed to be the oldest on the Great Ouse. The 'Gothic' village pump on the green, an elaborate cast-iron affair, is unique. Magdalene College Farm in Wyton was built in 1600, and an adjoining farmhouse is dated 1648.

Houghton-le-Spring *Tyne & Wear*   *558Cg*
CHURCH OF ST MICHAEL AND ALL ANGELS A large cruciform church, with a central tower; originally Norman, now mainly of the 13th to 15th centuries. There is tracery in the east and west windows, and stone effigies of 13th-century cross-legged knights.

Houghton Regis *Beds.*   547Hd
CHURCH OF ALL SAINTS A large 14th- and 15th-
century building, with a west tower. It possesses
brasses, a monument of a knight in armour, a
Norman font, and a 15th-century screen.

Hougue Bie *Jersey*   540Ea
A prehistoric burial ground containing a tomb
dating from the New Stone Age (*c.* 3000 BC). Great
stones dragged from the nearby beach were
arranged to form a central chamber reached by a
passage with three side chambers. The whole was
then covered by earth and rubble. When opened in
1924 the tomb was found to have been plundered.
The hill is crowned by the 12th-century Chapel of
Notre Dame de la Clarté (Our Lady of the Dawn),
probably built to banish pagan associations still
clinging to the mound. The Jerusalem Chapel was
added *c.* 1520 by Dean Mabon on his return from a
pilgrimage to Jerusalem; in the crypt is a replica of
Christ's tomb in the Church of the Holy Sepulchre
in Jerusalem.
AGRICULTURAL MUSEUM A small museum with a
collection of old farming implements. An old
manual fire engine is also displayed.
GERMAN OCCUPATION MUSEUM An extensive
German underground installation contains a large
collection of Nazi relics and samples of food,
clothing and personal effects used by the civilian
population during the Second World War.

Howden *Humberside*   558Ea
THE MINSTER CHURCH OF ST PETER A magnificent
cruciform church, formerly collegiate, with a very
tall central tower; the building dates mainly from
the 14th century. The chancel has been in ruins
since the end of the 17th century, and just to the
south are the ruins of a charming octagonal
chapter house. There are a number of medieval
and later monuments.

Howell *Lincs.*   553Hd
CHURCH OF ST OSWALD There is much Norman
work here, with additions in the Transitional and
Decorated styles. Some fragments of medieval
stained glass remain, and the font and bell-gable
are 14th century.

Huddersfield *W. Yorks.*   558Ba
CHURCH OF ST JOHN A Gothic Revival church
with a tall spire, designed in 1852–3 by William
Butterfield, in the style of *c.* 1300.
CHURCH OF ST THOMAS THE APOSTLE Built in
1858–9 by Sir Gilbert Scott, this Victorian church
has a tower and a broach spire at the south-west.

Hughenden Manor *Bucks.*   547Gc
The home from 1847 to 1881 of Benjamin Disraeli,
Earl of Beaconsfield, whose portrait by Sir Francis
Grant is on show. Disraeli (1804–81) has a monu-
ment in Westminster Abbey but is buried at
Hughenden.

Huntingdon *Cambs.*   547Jf
Linked by a bridge across the R. Ouse, the twin
towns of Huntingdon and Godmanchester lie at
the intersection of three Roman roads. Huntingdon suffered from Danish raids, endured the Normans, but was nearly wiped out by the plague in
1348. From 1205 to 1686 it was granted 18 charters
of privileges. Its bridge was built in 1332.
    Oliver Cromwell and Samuel Pepys were pupils
at the grammar school, converted from the
Hospital of St John the Baptist in 1565. The
building is now a museum of Cromwelliana.
HINCHINGBROOKE HOUSE The early 13th-century
Benedictine nunnery here was handed over to the
Cromwell family at the time of the Dissolution,
and around it Sir Richard Cromwell, the great-

grandfather of the Protector, built a Tudor country
house. His son, Sir Henry Cromwell, entertained
Queen Elizabeth here in 1564 and Sir Henry's son
received King James here before selling the house
to Sir Sidney Montagu in 1627. Extensive alterations were made to the house in 1660, when
Edward Montagu was created 1st Earl of Sandwich, and it was restored after a fire in 1830. It
is now a school.

Huntly Castle *Grampian*   566Ef
This castle was once the home of the Gordon
family, the Marquesses of Huntly, after whom the
'Gay Gordons' dance was named. Now derelict, it
dates from *c.* 1600 when it replaced the medieval
Palace of Strathbogie.

Hurlers, The *Cornwall*   538Ec
This is a group of three Bronze Age stone circles set
in a straight line. They range from 105 ft to 135 ft
in diameter. Perhaps half of the original number
of uprights has been lost. These uprights appear to
have been carefully shaped and are of equal height.
The central circle also had a single stone at its
centre. The north-east circle appears originally to
have had the unusual refinement of a paved floor.

Hursley *Hants.*   541Ge
CHURCH OF ALL SAINTS The church (all but the
tower) was rebuilt by John Keble, *c.* 1848. Keble,
the poet, essayist and designer in whose memory
Keble College, Oxford, was founded in 1869, is
buried in the churchyard. In the chancel is buried
Richard Cromwell, son of Oliver who, unlike his
father, preferred being lord of the manor at

HUGHENDEN MANOR

*Benjamin Disraeli, Queen Victoria's favourite Prime
Minister, bought the house in 1847 and completely
remodelled the Georgian structure to conform with his
ideal of a Victorian gentleman's country seat. The
house contains manuscripts of Disraeli's novels, his
study, left as it was at the time of his death, and an
inscribed copy of Queen Victoria's* Journal of Our
Life in the Highlands. *The hall and staircase (above),
Disraeli's 'Gallery of Friendship', house portraits of
intimate political friends, among them the Earl of
Derby, the Marquess of Salisbury and Horace Walpole.*

Hursley to being Lord Protector of the Realm. MERDON CASTLE Remains of the castle, built *c.* 1138 by Bishop Henry de Blois, are in Hursley Park.

Hurstbourne Tarrant *Hants.* 541Gf
A picturesque valley village, with many thatched cottages, and a prim white Regency house by the church.

Hurworth *Durham* 558Ce
This largely Georgian village was the birthplace and home of William Emerson, the 18th-century mathematician and eccentric, whose tomb is in the churchyard. He was born in what is now the Emerson Arms pub in the village.

Hylton Castle *Tyne & Wear* 558Cg
An imposing 14th-century keep built by William de Hylton to defend the ford over the Wear against the Scots. It is allegedly haunted by the Cauld Lad—the poor, shivering ghost of a stable-boy, thrown down the courtyard well in 1609.

Hythe *Kent* 542Fe
This small, attractive seaside resort is one of the ancient Cinque Ports. The Royal Military Canal, built in 1805 as part of the coastal defences against Napoleon, runs through the town.
CHURCH OF ST LEONARD In a commanding position on the side of a steep hill, this large church is celebrated for its soaring 13th-century chancel, rising 13 steps above the nave. There are Norman remains in the nave and transepts. Below is a crypt containing thousands of human bones, part of an ancient processional way beneath the altar. The 13th-century tower fell in 1739 and was replaced in 1750 when the south aisle was rebuilt. The altarpiece in the south choir aisle is by Henry Armstead the sculptor (1828–1905).

I J

Ickleton *Cambs.* 548Ae
CHURCH OF ST MARY MAGDALENE An interesting church, with Romanesque nave incorporating several Roman columns, and medieval wall paintings. Formerly cruciform (the north transept has gone), there is a crossing tower with a spire, and a vaulted south porch.

Ickwell Green *Beds.* 547Je
A beautiful village with a permanent maypole on the green. The May Day ceremonies continue a tradition probably 400 years old. The village also has many picturesque cottages. Nearby Old Warden has a number of cottages with thatched roofs and Elizabethan chimneys.

Ickworth *Suffolk* 548Cf
A 700 ft long building devised and begun by the eccentric Frederick Augustus Hervey, 4th Earl of Bristol and Bishop of Derry. From an oval rotunda housing a central hall the main rooms are reached via two curved corridors. The rotunda is 100 ft high with a shallow dome; round the outside is a frieze of reliefs by Casimiro and Donato Carabelli from Milan, after John Flaxman's designs based on Homer. The house, designed in 1794 but not completed until 1830, contains Regency furniture, magnificent silver, paintings and *objets d'art*. The park was landscaped by Capability Brown. (See p. 248.)

Idsworth *Hants.* 541Jd
CHURCH OF ST HUBERT This small chapel stands in a field, and has a nave and chancel with an 18th-century bell-turret at the east end. Though basically of the 11th century, the chapel, after years of neglect, was restored *c.* 1912 by H. Goodhart-Rendel. Some of the fittings are of the 18th

ICKWORTH

An eccentric bishop with a taste for travel had the idea of building this unusual house to display his fine collection of paintings and sculpture—but he lost most of the collection before the house was completed. The bishop was Frederick Hervey, 4th Earl of Bristol and Bishop of Derry, who decided in 1792 to build a house with an oval ground plan on land which his family had owned since the 15th century. Five years later, with the building still in its early stages, the bishop *was unlucky enough to be in Rome when Napoleon occupied the city. He was imprisoned, and his collection confiscated. Back in England he saw work on the house progress under the architect Francis Sandys, but the bishop died in 1803 with the building only half completed. After a halt of several years, the 1st Marquess of Bristol completed the house and furnished the main rooms. Antonio Canova, the great Italian sculptor, carved the chimney-piece in the library.*

century—box-pews, and a pulpit with sounding board. The 14th-century wall-paintings may represent the legend of St Hubert, or perhaps the life of St John the Baptist. In the chancel are the painted figures of SS Peter and Paul.

Iffley *Oxon.*   *546Fc*
CHURCH OF ST MARY One of England's most famous Norman churches, dating from the late 12th century. It has a nave, tower and chancel; the later sanctuary is Early English. There is a spectacular west front with doorway, a circular window and three arched windows, all with zigzag decoration. The south doorway and the tower arches inside are also richly decorated, and there is a Norman font.

Ightham *Kent*   *542Cf*
CHURCH OF ST PETER A historically interesting church in a picturesque village; the main fabric of St Peter's is 15th century, but some Norman work remains. There are fine box-pews. Two interesting monuments are the 14th-century effigy of Sir Thomas Cawne, who lived at Ightham Mote, and one by Edward Marshall, one-time assistant to Nicholas Stone, to Dorothy Selby (*d.* 1641).

To the south-west of the village are ancient habitations, the Iron Age hill-fort and Stone Age rock dwellings on Oldbury Hill.

Ightham Mote *Kent*   *542Cf*
The manor house stands at the foot of a hill surrounded by the moat that gives it its name. The manor is a late-medieval building, that was extensively remodelled in the early 16th century, and altered throughout the next 600 years by successive owners.

The Great Hall (1340) has original oak rafters and the Tudor Chapel (1520) its original painted ceiling—a decoration scheme from this period of great rarity. The east end of the Chapel has some fine linen-fold panelling.

The manor has a Jacobean staircase—built to replace stone stairs—by Sir William Selby, who inherited the Mote from his uncle, the first Sir William Selby, in 1611. The staircase's newel post is carved to represent a Saracen's head, the crest of the Selby family.

Hanging on a wall nearby, is a portrait of Sir William's wife Dorothy, who died in 1641 at the age of 69.

Ilam *Staffs.*   *552Cd*
In the churchyard there are two Saxon crosses; in the church itself is a carved font showing St Bertram, and a tomb designed by Sir Francis Chantrey. St Bertram's 13th-century shrine is in a side chapel of the church.

Ilford *Greater London*   *548Ab*
CHURCH OF ST MARY Originally Norman, St Mary's has later additions. There are fine roofs, a rood screen fragment with painted figures, and a brass, *c.* 1483.

SILVER ICE-PAIL

One of a pair, this ice-pail was made about 1715 by the Huguenot silversmith Philip Rollos. Driven out of France by Louis XIV's persecution, Rollos settled in London, and was patronised by William III. But like many of his exiled compatriots, he still followed French developments in taste. The ice-pail is decorated in régence manner, a later elaboration of the baroque style of Louis XIV's reign. (Ickworth)

Ilfracombe *Devon* 538Fg
LIGHTHOUSE The tiny medieval chapel of St Nicholas crowns Lantern Hill. The first reference to the display of a light is in 1522, but one may have been shown when the building was erected in the 14th century. The light was originally shown from a projecting window on the north side; after the Reformation the chapel became a house, and a lantern was devised on the west gable. This was replaced by the present one in 1819; it still carries a light. Although there are several records of medieval chapels showing coastal lights, this is one of the few to survive.

Ilkley *W. Yorks.* 558Bb
MANOR HOUSE MUSEUM AND ART GALLERY In AD 79, the Romans built a fort on the site now occupied by the 16th-century manor house and the parish church. The original manor house was founded by Anglo-Saxon invaders, using stones from the Roman fort. The house escaped pillage by Norman and Scots invaders, and early in Elizabeth I's reign it was rebuilt and enlarged. It has been restored, and its contents illustrate the history of Ilkley from prehistoric times. Exhibitions of sculptures, paintings and pottery are held.

Ilkley Moor *W. Yorks.* 558Bb
On Rombald's Moor are many scattered rocks carved with the characteristic Bronze Age cup-and-ring ornamentation. Many of the best have been brought down and now stand in the gardens facing St Margaret's Church. The Swastika Stone, which may belong to the Iron Age, still lies out on the moor.

On the moor are also several stone circles, three of which, the Twelve Apostles Circle, the Grubstone Circle and the Horncliffe Circle are of some importance. The others lie to the east of the Grubstones.

Inchcolm *Fife* 562Bf
ABBEY The ruins of the abbey are on an island in the Firth of Forth, and are extensive and well preserved, due no doubt to their isolation. The buildings date from the 12th century onwards.

Ingatestone *Essex* 548Bc
The village has a 16th-century inn, The Bell, and a number of pleasant Georgian brick houses. There are some good mock-Tudor houses built in the 19th century by George Sherrin.
CHURCH OF SS EDMUND AND MARY With a 15th-century diapered brick west tower, the church was originally Norman, but has later additions. Several monuments with effigies are dedicated to 16th- and 17th-century members of the Petre family.

Ingestre *Staffs.* 552Cc
CHURCH OF ST MARY THE VIRGIN The design of this Classical church is attributed to Sir Christopher Wren, c. 1676. The magnificent interior has four-cluster columns in the nave, plaster roofs, and monuments by Sir Francis Chantrey, Richard Westmacott the Younger, and others.

There is a splendid tripartite screen with pilasters, surmounted by the Royal Arms, and a canopied pulpit nearby. Both are thought to be the work of Grinling Gibbons.

The centre window in the north wall (by Burne-Jones) and the opposite window in the south wall, were both made in the William Morris workshops.

Ingestre Hall *Staffs.* 552Cc
Of early 17th-century origin, the Hall was twice reconstructed in the 19th century to the original Jacobean style. The church is probably the work of Sir Christopher Wren.

IGHTHAM MOTE

The east façade—the lower part of Kentish ragstone and the upper storeys half-timbered. The gable end of the Old Chapel (1340) can just be seen. The bridge leads to the kitchen courtyard.

Inglesham *Wilts.* 546Dc
CHURCH OF ST JOHN THE BAPTIST This is a small church near the Thames, without a tower but with a bell-cote. It is interesting because, although repaired in 1888–9, it was saved by William Morris from the prevalent over-restoration or falsification. Mainly of the 13th century, it has a 17th-century pulpit and 17th-century box-pews.

Ingoldmells *Lincs.* 554Ae
CHURCH OF SS PETER AND PAUL This is a large and impressive church with a 15th-century porch. The chancel was demolished in the early 18th century. An interesting brass of the 16th century depicts a man named William Palmer with his 'stylt' or crutch at his side.
The church has a fine Perpendicular font.

Inveraray Castle *Strathclyde* 560Fg
The home of the Dukes of Argyll and headquarters of the Clan Campbell since the 15th century. The present castle, greatly admired by Sir Walter Scott, was built in the 18th century by Roger Morris and Robert Mylne in French château-style, with corner towers and conical turrets. The castle, set in extensive grounds, contains old masters, tapestries, fine furniture and plate, and early Scottish armaments. Dr Johnson and Boswell stayed here in 1773.

Inveresk Lodge *Lothian* 562Ce
A garden created by the National Trust for Scotland with the object of demonstrating plants suited to the smaller garden and the interesting varieties now available. There is a rose border and a selection of climbing roses.

Inverewe Gardens *Highland* 568Ea
In 1862 Osgood Mackenzie built a house on a rocky peninsula in Loch Ewe, and three years later he began to create these Highland gardens, now

INVEREWE GARDENS

Osgood Mackenzie began these superb gardens in 1865, on barren, rocky moorland beside Loch Ewe.

Now a wide variety of trees and plants from the world over flourish in the almost sub-tropical climate.

famous for rare and sub-tropical plants. A large shelterbelt of pines was planted to break the Atlantic gales, and tons of pebbles were replaced by fertile soil. In these sheltered gardens, warmed by the Gulf Stream, thrive tender rhododendron species, Himalayan and Chinese magnolias, daisy bushes and, from New Zealand, *Hoherias* with fragrant, pure white flowers. There are giant eucalyptus and tree-ferns, and the extremely rare giant forget-me-nots and many other plants from Australia and South America.

Inverness *Highland* 566Af
A beautifully situated town on the R. Ness, with mountains to the east and west, the Moray Firth to the north and the Caledonian Canal and Loch Ness to the south-west. St Andrew's Cathedral was built in the 19th century; its font is a copy of the famous angel font in Copenhagen. There are many 18th-century town houses, and the museum houses a collection of Jacobite relics.
ABERTARFF HOUSE A 16th-century house, now restored. It is the headquarters of the Highland Association.

Inverurie *Grampian* 566Fe
MUSEUM The museum has a display of local archaeology, including a Neolithic bowl, a 'cushion' mace-head and a large collection of arrowheads, polished stone axes, flint knives, etc. The geology section has a collection of Scottish minerals and fossils, and local bygones can be seen, including snuff boxes, communion tokens and mortsafe tackle. (A mortsafe was a heavy stone lowered on to the coffin as a temporary measure to protect it from grave robbers. When the grave itself was filled in, the mortsafe was raised.)

Iona *Strathclyde* 564Da
The island of Iona has been associated with the spread of Christianity in northern and central Britain since the 7th century. St Columba, the missionary from Ireland, landed on this island in AD 563 and built a monastery, but it was constantly ravaged by raiding Norsemen. One of its most famous monks was St Aidan, who later founded a bishopric at Lindisfarne. In *c*. 1203 an abbey and nunnery were founded by Benedictines and these were restored early in this century. St Columba's cell, with the stone slab on which he slept, has been excavated. Eight Norwegian kings and many Scottish kings, including Macbeth, were buried

in the graveyard. Three of the 360 tall crosses that once stood here remain: St John's Cross (9th century), St Martin's Cross (10th century) and Maclean's Cross (15th century).

Ipswich *Suffolk* 548De
An ancient port on the Orwell estuary, pillaged by the Danes in 991 and again in 1000. A borough before the Norman Conquest, its first charter was given by King John in 1200. It reached its zenith as a wool port in the 16th century, declined in the 17th and 18th centuries, but revived after harbour improvements in the 1840's. Much of the town was built or rebuilt in the 19th century, but 12 medieval churches and several 16th-century buildings survive. Cardinal Wolsey was born here

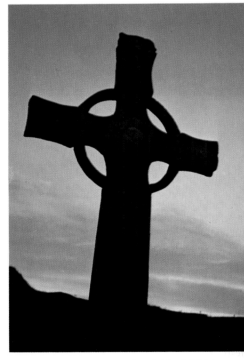

CELTIC HIGH CROSS, IONA

One of three stone crosses left standing on Iona after the Reformation; its circle symbolises Eternity.

IRONBRIDGE

Abraham Darby built this, the first iron bridge, in 1777–9. The delicate, airy, cast-iron structure over *the R. Severn is nearly 200 ft long, with the largest semicircular span being 100 ft, and is 45 ft high.*

c. 1475, and Thomas Gainsborough, the painter, was a resident. The Great White Horse Inn was the scene of some of Mr Pickwick's misfortunes. Today the town is a thriving port, handling coal, grain and malt, and an industrial centre; it is also the county town of Suffolk.

ANCIENT HOUSE Charles II hid in the chapel of this house, built in 1567 and owned by the Sparrowe family from 1603.

CHRISTCHURCH MANSION Tudor country house begun in 1548 on the site of the 12th-century Augustinian Priory. The domestic nature of the house has been retained, and there are collections of furniture. Suffolk portraits, and paintings by local artists (Gainsborough, Constable, Churchyard, Steer, Munnings), are displayed in the attached art gallery.

CHURCH OF ST MARY-LE-TOWER The civic church, rebuilt in the late 19th century with a tower, 176 ft high. It contains fine carvings.

MUSEUM Most of the material exhibited here relates to Suffolk, and includes Stone Age flint implements; weapons and jewellery from the pagan Saxon cemetery at Hadleigh Road, Ipswich; and replicas of the Mildenhall and Sutton Hoo Treasures (now in the British Museum). There is also an ethnographical section and collections of tropical and British birds.

OLD CUSTOM HOUSE A handsome house in miniature Palladian style, built on the quay in the 1840's.

WOLSEY'S GATEWAY The sole remains of a College of Secular Canons founded by Cardinal Wolsey in 1528.

Irnham *Lincs.* 553Gc
CHURCH OF ST ANDREW A large church dating from Norman times, it has a wooded setting and represents architectural styles of the 13th–15th centuries. Of the two brasses, the earlier one (1390) to Sir Andrew Luttrell is particularly interesting.

Iron Acton *Avon* 546Bb
CHURCH OF ST JAMES THE LESS A handsome church, mainly of the 14th and 15th centuries; it has a pinnacled west tower and, in the churchyard, a rare 15th-century memorial cross. Interesting features inside include a canopied 17th-century pulpit, 19th-century mosaic floors, and attractive modern reredos and side chapel screen. Some of the stained glass and a series of effigies of the Poyntz family date from the Middle Ages.

Ironbridge *Shropshire* 552Ab
The bridge over the R. Severn, from which the town takes its name, was the first iron bridge constructed in England. This was the beginning of industrial architecture's use of iron, which culminated in the great spans of the 19th-century railway stations such as Paddington, and the glory of the Crystal Palace housing the Great Exhibition in Hyde Park in 1851. The bridge was built between 1779 and 1781 with iron from the Coalbrookdale foundry. The furnace, once used to make iron, is now in the grounds of the Museum of Ironfounding at Coalbrookdale. Today the river banks, which were gradually moving together and threatening to crush the bridge, have been held apart by a concrete slab. (See also Coalbrookdale and Blists Hill.)

Isel *Cumbria* 557Gf
CHURCH OF ST MICHAEL A 12th-century Norman church, containing some fragments of 10th-century carved crosses.

Isleham *Cambs.* 548Bf
CHURCH OF ST ANDREW A spacious, cruciform, 14th- and 15th-century building. The hammer-beam roof, of 1495, is embellished with angels. Inside are stalls with misericords of *c.* 1350, a font, brasses, and effigies of knights. There are two big monuments of *c.* 1590 and 1616 and an eagle lectern dating from the 15th century.

Isle of May *Firth of Forth* 562Dg
LIGHTHOUSE Although reduced in height, this strange structure gives an excellent idea of the appearance of an old coal-fired beacon. A carved panel over the door is dated 1636, and there is a carved fire-place bearing the Arms of the owner. The survival of the building was due to Sir Walter Scott, who in 1814 persuaded the engineer Robert Stevenson, who was engaged on the present 'Gothic' tower, to 'ruin it *à la pittoresque*'.

Iver *Bucks.* 547Hb
IVER GROVE A house, built by Sir John Vanbrugh, the dramatist turned architect, in 1722–4 in the Baroque style. The only original fitting to survive is the staircase. (By appointment.)

Iwerne Minster *Dorset* 540Ed
CHURCH OF ST MARY Details may still be seen of the original Norman church; later additions include the 19th-century south chapel designed by J. L. Pearson.

Ixworth Abbey *Suffolk*   *548Cf*
A house incorporating the 12th- and 13th-century cloister ranges of the Augustinian priory that was founded here in 1170. There are 17th- and 18th-century additions, and fine woodwork.

Jarlshof *Shetland*   *568Ed*
A complex of buildings comprising a Bronze Age settlement, an Iron Age broch and wheelhouses, and Viking houses of 1000 years later. Sir Walter Scott chose the site as the setting for his novel *The Pirate* and it was he who coined the name 'Jarlshof'.

Jarrow *Tyne & Wear*   *558Ch*
CHURCH OF ST PAUL The present sanctuary is the Saxon church of the monastery of the Venerable Bede (*d.* 735). A unique stone records the date of the dedication as April 23, 683, and there is Saxon glass reset in an original window. The tower and ruins are of an 11th-century monastery.

Jedburgh Abbey *Borders*   *562Dc*
In 1118, before he became king, David I of Scotland founded an Augustinian priory here, beside Jed Water. The Abbey, of local red sandstone, was built after he came to the throne in 1147. The church dates mainly from the period 1150–1220, when first the Romanesque choir and transepts, followed by the Transitional nave, were built. In addition, *c.* 1200 the choir was extended eastwards. In the choir and transepts the triforium is contained within the giant main arcade which springs from ground level. The nave, on the other hand, is arranged after the more usual manner in clearly distinct rows of arcading, one on top of the other. Jedburgh also has a magnificent west door.

Jervaulx Abbey *N. Yorks.*   *558Cd*
The abbey was of the Cistercian order, who moved here during the second half of the 12th century; now in ruins.

Jullieberrie's Grave *Kent*   *542Ff*
An unchambered Neolithic long barrow, far from others of the type, with a now-filled quarry-ditch. One end of the barrow has been mutilated, but what is left is still nearly 150 ft long and some 7 ft high. Romano-British burials have been found in the filling of the quarry-ditch at its south end.

JEDBURGH ABBEY

Many times in its history this retreat of Augustinian monks has been wrecked and burnt by invading armies —the price it has had to pay for being so close to the Scottish border with England. It was ransacked in 1297 by Edward I's army under Sir Richard Hastings, burnt in 1523 and again only 11 years later. Little has survived this devastation apart from the church begun in 1150, three years after David I came to the throne of Scotland. Parts of the building were still being used in Victorian times as a place of worship for the surrounding parish. When a new church was founded in 1875 the remains of the abbey were conscientiously restored.

K

Kedington *Suffolk*   *548Be*
CHURCH OF SS PETER AND PAUL Dating from the 11th century and later. The Barnardiston family pew is constructed from a 15th-century screen. There are Perpendicular benches, 18th-century box-pews, and a three-decker 17th-century pulpit and screen. Also interesting is a Saxon carved Crucifix, and several monuments to the Barnardiston family with effigies, 16th to 18th centuries.

Kedleston Hall *Derbys.*   *552Dd*
The home of the Curzon family for over 850 years. The present mansion was originally designed *c.* 1757 by Matthew Brettingham for Sir Nathaniel Curzon. But Curzon then turned to the most prominent architect of the mid-18th century, James Paine, to remodel his house in a more fashionable Classical manner. Paine had built the north front by 1761. It has a noble portico of six Corinthian columns above a ground storey, on either side of which is a double staircase. There

are no windows between the columns, but niches for statues instead. In 1760 Curzon called in Robert Adam to continue work on the new house and for a while he and Paine worked amicably together. Behind Paine's north front, Adam built the Great Hall, 70 ft long and 40 ft high, with Corinthian columns supporting the coved ceiling. The south front is Adam's, based on the triumphal arch of Constantine in Rome. Behind it the domed Rotunda, even higher than the Great Hall which it adjoins, has painted decoration by William Hamilton and Biagio Rebecca. The Dining Room, Music Room, Library and Drawing Room are also Adam's work. The house, set in extensive gardens, contains fine furniture and a collection of old master paintings.

In the grounds is the 12th-century church containing the Marquess Curzon of Kedleston Memorial Chapel, and also a museum containing the silver-ivories, weapons and works of art collected by the Marquess when he was Viceroy of India in 1898–1905.

Kegworth *Leics.* 552Ec
CHURCH OF ST ANDREW A mainly early 14th-century church, with west tower and chapel at the east end of the aisles adding to the impressive external view. The interior has fragments of medieval stained glass.

Kelham *Notts.* 552Fd
CHURCH OF ST WILFRID A good example of 18th-century sculpture is the monument to Lord Lexington (*d.* 1723) who reclines with his wife, in marble, back to back on a free-standing tomb.

Kelmscott *Oxon.* 546Ec
CHURCH OF ST GEORGE A cruciform church whose south doorway and font remain of the original Norman work. Inside there are carved corbel heads, medieval glass, and wall-paintings. William Morris lived near by at Kelmscott Manor, and is buried in the churchyard.

Kelmscott Manor *Oxon.* 546Ec
William Morris, poet, craftsman and socialist, made this gabled Cotswold Tudor house, in the Thames-side village of Kelmscott, his home from 1871 until his death in 1896. The house dates from the late 16th century. (By appointment.)

Kelso *Borders* 562Ed
ABBEY The abbey, in Norman and Gothic styles and probably the largest of the Border abbeys, was founded by Benedictine monks from Tiron (in Picardy, France) in 1128; it was destroyed during the Border Wars of 1523–45.

Kempsford *Glos.* 546Dc
CHURCH OF ST MARY THE VIRGIN Originally Norman, St Mary's has a fine central tower built by John of Gaunt, with large Perpendicular north and south windows in the lower stage, and weather-vanes on all the crocketed pinnacles. The vaulting within has carved and painted heraldic shields as bosses. Victorian stained glass contributes to the effect of darkness: some of it is by Kempe. The chancel was enlarged by G. E. Street in 1858. On the walls of the nave are framed Puritan texts.

Kendal *Cumbria* 557Jd
A fine town in the Lake District. Kendal was made a barony by William the Conqueror. In 1331, under the protection of Edward III, Flemish weavers set up a woollen industry which gave the town its motto: *Pannus mihi panis* (Wool is my bread). In the Norman castle, now a ruin, was born Katherine Parr, last queen of Henry VIII. The castle dairy, rebuilt in 1564 and open by appointment, is a fine example of Tudor domestic architecture. In the town hall are seven paintings by Romney, and Katherine Parr's book of devotions, exquisitely penned and bound in solid silver.
ABBOT HALL ART GALLERY The house, built in 1759 by John Carr of York, retains its original decor on the ground floor, which exhibits period furniture. The upstairs rooms contain a growing collection of modern paintings and sculpture.
KENDAL MUSEUM Collections devoted to the natural history, archaeology and local history of the area are on view.

Kenilworth Castle *Warks.* 546Ef
Elizabeth I was entertained here by her favourite, Robert Dudley, Earl of Leicester, for 18 days in July 1575 at a cost of £1000 per day. The enormous ruins of Kenilworth Castle suggest its importance as a fortress during the Middle Ages. It

KEDLESTON HALL

18TH-CENTURY MIRROR *Using an exotic design of palms, this mirror was probably designed by John Linnell, a cabinet-maker employed by Robert Adam. Within the frame of carved and gilded wood, several sizes of glass were used; this allowed the framework to be fragile in appearance, yet not overwhelmed by an unrelieved area of mirror—in any case, at that time it was expensive to produce single sheets of glass in such a large size. Mirrors of this type were usually placed above side-tables, opposite or between windows, so as to give the illusion of a larger room.*

18TH-CENTURY SOFA *Made of carved, gilded wood, this sofa is primarily a work of art, but it is also functional. The extravagant design is reminiscent of the 17th-century sculptor Bernini and contrasts with the Classical interior of Kedleston designed by Robert Adam. The sofa, however, is probably not by Adam but by John Linnell, a cabinet-maker employed by him. Unlike Adam, Linnell tended to emphasise the sculptural rather than the architectural form in his work; he is comparatively little known as, unlike Chippendale, he did not publish his designs.*

KENILWORTH CASTLE

This fortress has stood for over 800 years, a stronghold for the kings and lords of England capable of withstanding attack from mighty armies. It was founded about 1122 by Geoffrey de Clinton, royal Treasurer to Henry I, but within 50 years it had become too important to be left in private hands, and was taken over by Henry II. It stayed the property of the kings of England until 1244 when it passed to Simon de Montfort, Earl of Leicester, later a leading rebel against Henry III. In 1266 Henry's army surrounded Kenilworth, but its fortifications withstood the siege until famine forced the defenders to surrender. The fortress was later turned into a medieval palace by the addition of living quarters, and flourished in the late 16th century as the home of Robert Dudley, Earl of Leicester, a favourite of Elizabeth I, who was frequently entertained there at great expense. The castle has been unoccupied for 300 years.

was founded by Geoffrey de Clinton *c*. 1122, and within the next few decades the immense keep was built. In the 14th century John of Gaunt turned the fortress into a palace by adding large domestic quarters. Much of John of Gaunt's banqueting hall survives, together with other domestic offices. During the reign of Elizabeth I the Earl of Leicester added more living quarters and the great northern gate-house. The keep was partially destroyed in the Civil War, and the castle was never re-occupied after the Restoration.

Kentchurch Court *Heref. & Worcs.*   *546Ad*
A fortified manor house on the Welsh border, with a 14th-century great gateway and tower. Owain Glendwr, the Welsh hero who fought against the English, spent the last years of his life here. The interior has Grinling Gibbons carvings. (By appointment.)

Kentisbeare *Devon*   *540Ad*
CHURCH OF ST MARY The west tower of this 14th- and 15th-century Perpendicular church is chequer-patterned in red and grey stone. There are wagon-roofs, that of the chancel plastered in 1757, a good rood screen, and a pulpit and desk of *c*. 1737.
OLD PRIEST'S HOUSE A medieval house with a minstrels' gallery and oak screens.

Kenton *Devon*   *539Hd*
CHURCH OF ALL SAINTS An impressive 14th-century red sandstone church, built mainly between 1360 and 1370. The west tower is about 120 ft high, and the two-storied south porch is embattled. The massive screen has painted panels, with some restoration. There is a 15th-century carved pulpit, and a monument of 1628 with seated figure of a woman. The 19th-century stained glass in the east window is by Clayton & Bell.

Kent's Cavern *Devon*   *539Hc*
A Palaeolithic cave-dwelling first investigated in the early 19th century, when evidence of human occupation from the Middle Palaeolithic Age onwards could not be accepted because it clashed with the prevailing views on the date of the Creation (biblical calculation suggesting that Adam had lived only about 4000 BC). The finds are in the Torquay Museum and the Natural History Museum, London.

Kerry *Powys*   *545Jg*
CHURCH OF ST MICHAEL AND ALL ANGELS
Dedicated in 1176, the church was largely restored in the 14th century; traces of the original structure remain, however, in the north arcade and the tower. The church contains a 14th-century warden's chest, a chained Welsh Bible and a Tudor font sculpted with Instruments of the Passion.

Kersey *Suffolk*   *548Ce*
A picturesque village with the R. Brett running through it. Kersey cloth probably originated here, and the timber-framed houses date from the village's days of greatness in the wool trade. Priory Farm has remains of a 13th-century Augustinian priory.
CHURCH OF ST MARY Situated on high ground, St Mary's has a 15th-century west tower, but the church was restored in the mid-19th century. There is a Perpendicular font with carved angels, and painted panels to the rood screen; also a mural painting of St George and the Dragon.

Kettles, The *Northld.*   *562Fc*
An Iron Age promontory hill-fort with some-what complex defences, ranging from one to three stone ramparts in different parts of the peri-meter. The total internal area is some $4\frac{1}{2}$ acres.

KEW GARDENS

Kew Gardens' connection with royalty goes back to George II. The king owned Richmond Lodge Estate, which ran along the R. Thames from Richmond Green through Old Deer Park to Queen Elizabeth's lawn. His son Frederick, Prince of Wales, leased the adjoining Kew House estate in 1730. The botanic garden was started in 1759 by George III's mother Augusta, Dowager Princess of Wales, helped by Lord Bute (a keen amateur botanist) and the head gardener William

Aiton. The original site of the garden was 9 acres. Sir Joseph Banks later became unofficial director of the garden and used his influence as President of the Royal Society to send plant collectors to many parts of the world. The botanic garden was taken over by the nation in 1840 to become a centre for botany, agriculture and horticulture. The gardens have been gradually enlarged to their present 286 acres by the addition of adjoining portions of the royal estate.

Ketton *Leics.*   *553Gb*
CHURCH OF ST MARY A large church, mainly early 13th century, with late 12th-century work on the west front, and some 14th-century work. The building is dominated by the impressive central tower and spire. The chancel was rebuilt in the 19th century, there is some fine work by Comper and the panelled roof has been repainted in medieval colours and design.

Kew *Greater London*   *547Jb*
The 18th century is dominant at Kew, in the church on the spacious green and in the terraces of houses round it. Kew Gardens, however, contain, at the north end, the Dutch House, dated 1631, and the world-famous botanical gardens, 286 acres in extent, partly landscaped by Capability Brown for George III and opened to the public in 1841. The Palm House, forerunner of the Crystal Palace, was erected in 1844.
CHURCH OF ST ANNE Originally an early 18th-century church, St Anne's has late 18th- and 19th-century enlargements by J. J. Kirby and Robert Browne. There is a mausoleum *c.* 1850 to the Duke and Duchess of Cambridge.
PAGODA, ROYAL BOTANIC GARDENS The royal park at Kew became a national property in 1840. The garden had partly been laid out, under the auspices of George III and his mother, to designs by Capability Brown. The Orangery and most of the small Classical temples and pavilions are the early work of Sir William Chambers. He also designed the Chinese Pagoda (1761), which took only six months to complete and shows the influence of his travels in the Orient.
PALM HOUSE, ROYAL BOTANIC GARDENS This great glass house was built in 1844–8 to designs by

Decimus Burton, who also built the Athenaeum Club in Waterloo Place at the corner of Pall Mall. The Palm House is plain and functional. The iron-work for it was constructed by Richard Turner at his Hammersmith Works in Dublin. The building is 362 ft long, and at the centre 100 ft wide and 66 ft high, and required 45,000 sq. ft of glass. The boiler house was built nearly 500 ft away in order not to impair the graceful lines of the building. A tunnel was constructed to the boiler house, where the chimney was disguised as an architectural feature, and also contained the water tanks.
ROYAL BOTANIC GARDENS MUSEUMS OF ECONOMIC BOTANY The General Museum contains displays of plants useful to man, and their products, together with displays of botanical art and ethnographical material. The Wood Museum, with a display of timbers, mainly of the Commonwealth, is housed in Cambridge Cottage, which was used by the Royal Family in the reign of Queen Victoria.

Kidwelly Castle *Dyfed*   *544Ec*
A fortress built from about 1275–1325; it has a 14th-century gate-house. The outer curtain wall follows the line of the earlier Norman earthworks and the courtyard is enclosed by four round towers. The castle is now in ruins.

Kilbarchan *Strathclyde*   *561He*
WEAVER'S COTTAGE A handloom weaver's house, built in the 18th century; restored as a museum. A loom over 200 years old is still in operation.

Kilchurn Castle *Strathclyde*   *565Ha*
A ruined castle, built in 1440, and altered and extended in the 16th and 17th centuries by Sir John Campbell (1635–1716), 1st Earl of Breadalbane and Holland.

Kildoon *Strathclyde* 561Gb
VITRIFIED FORT This Iron Age fort crowns a rocky ridge overlooking the valley of the R. Girvan. Here a more modern monument has been erected and this has destroyed a part of the fort's defences. The size is about 150 ft by 100 ft, and its rampart is vitrified. In addition, there are two ramparts with external ditches on the west side which gave additional protection along the approach-route.

Kildrummy Castle *Grampian* 566Ee
Imposing ruins of a fortress of the Earls of Mar in the Don Valley, so old that it had to be rebuilt in 1303; it was reduced to a pathetic pile after the Jacobite rebellion of 1715. The hall, chapel and 14th-century gate-house remain.

Kilkhampton *Cornwall* 538Ee
CHURCH OF ST JAMES A large church, with a west tower, and a Norman south doorway. Inside are carved bench ends and wagon-roofs; the organ is reputed to be from Westminster Abbey and dates from 1698.

Killerton Gardens *Devon* 539He
Hill-side gardens noted for rare trees and shrubs.

Kilmartin *Strathclyde* 560Eg
Though the present village was built in the mid-19th century, there is considerable evidence of a much earlier settlement. The churchyard, for instance, contains three fine crosses and a number of medieval sculpted stones. Important prehistoric remains near by include four large stone burial chambers, one of which is carved with representations of bronze axes and the 'cup-marks' of Bronze Age date.

Kilmuir *Isle of Skye, Highland* 564Eh
An Ionic cross stands in the churchyard to mark the grave of Flora Macdonald (1721–90), the Jacobite heroine who aided the escape of Bonnie Prince Charlie after the Battle of Culloden.

Kilpeck *Heref. & Worcs.* 546Ad
CHURCH OF SS MARY AND DAVID A small Norman church, one of the finest in Britain. Built *c.* 1145, it is now well preserved and noted for its carving. This is extremely interesting, as none of it can be traced back directly to Normandy—the motifs of the carving on the chancel arch have been traced to the transept façade of St James's at Santiago de Compostela in northern Spain. Outside is a series of carved corbels running round the church. But the main decorative feature is the south door. Perhaps nowhere in Europe is it possible to find such a strange mixture of ideas and motifs—fruit, flowers, warriors, serpents and dragons intertwine in a mass of detail. A corner of the nave is Saxon, several windows date from late medieval times and the bell-cote was restored in the 19th century, but apart from these the church is purely Norman in style. A. W. Pugin designed the stained glass of the apse window in 1849.

Kilpheder *South Uist, Western Isles* 564Be
This Iron Age round-house, or wheel-house, has an outer wall enclosing a circular area 29 ft in diameter. Within its circle stand 11 drystone pillars free of the wall, with a central space 18 ft across.

Kilphedir *Highland* 569Kc
BROCH The outer enclosure is protected by a bank and external ditch and a second ditch to the north-east. The broch wall is 15 ft thick and encloses a space some 32 ft in diameter. There is a wall-chamber. It belongs to the Iron Age.

Kimbolton *Cambs.* 547Hf
CHURCH OF ST ANDREW A 13th-century church, with a west tower and spire of a century later.

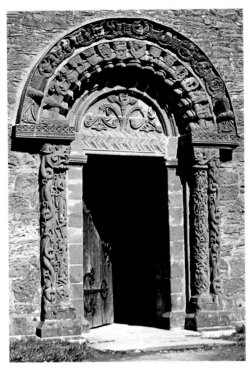

CHURCH OF SS MARY AND DAVID, KILPECK : SOUTH DOOR

Nowhere in Europe is there such a strange mixture of ideas and motifs as in the decoration around the south door of this little church ; another decorative feature is the chancel arch. Oliver de Merlimont founded nearby Shobdon church about 1140, and Kilpeck probably followed in the next ten years. Oliver had made a pilgrimage to St James's at Santiago de Compostela in Spain and the figures that decorate the Kilpeck chancel arch are similar to those on the transept façade of St James's. Almost nothing in the decoration of the church can be traced back directly to Normandy—a reminder that 12th-century architecture and carving in England was not always Norman in origin. Other examples of decoration by what is now known as the Herefordshire School of carving may be found at Brinsop and Stretton Sugwas near by.

Inside are painted medieval screens, some fragments of glass, carved roof bosses, and 17th-century monuments with figures.

Kimbolton Castle *Cambs.* 547Hf
The original medieval mansion here was remodelled in the reign of William and Mary. In 1707 part of the building collapsed and the owner, the 1st Duke of Manchester, commissioned Sir John Vanbrugh to rebuild the castle. Vanbrugh's building is quadrangular around an inner courtyard, and has a Classical battlemented exterior. The south front was completed *c.* 1708 and the rest by 1714. In *c.* 1766 Robert Adam added the outer gate-house and the gateway on the west side. The castle is now a school.

King Arthur's Cave *Heref. & Worcs.* 546Ad
Site of the discovery in 1870 of flints fashioned by Early Man, and remains of hippopotamus, elephant, and other animals long extinct in Britain.

King Arthur's Round Table 557Jf
and Mayburgh *Cumbria*
The Round Table is an embanked circle, some 300 ft across, with an internal ditch. There were once

two entrances, though that on the north side has disappeared. Here there were once two standing stones and another stone structure stood near the centre of the circle.

Mayburgh lies a few hundred yards to the west. It is a circular enclosure slightly larger than the Table and has a single entrance on the east. The bank here is higher than usual. Near the centre is a single standing stone, of which there were once four, with others at the entrance. Both circles belong to the late Neolithic period.

Kings Langley *Herts.*   *547Hc*
CHURCH OF ALL SAINTS Most of the church is of the 15th century, but the piscina in the chancel dates from the 13th century. There is a 17th-century pulpit and several 19th-century stained glass windows by Clayton & Bell and Ward & Hughes. Monuments include one to Edmund of Langley, with heraldry (14th century) and an altar-tomb to Sir Ralph Verney, *c.* 1500, with effigies.

King's Lynn *Norfolk*   *554Ac*
An ancient port on the R. Ouse, near the Wash; it is still a busy harbour for agricultural produce, and a beautiful small town. Before the bishop's manor became royal property it was called Bishop's Lynn, and was linked to the Continent through trade, principally in wool, and by pilgrims on their way to the shrine at Walsingham. It was once a walled town, but now only a small part of the wall and the south gate remain. Many monastic orders were settled there, and are remembered in the names of streets and buildings: Greyfriars, Whitefriars, Blackfriars and Augustine Friars. There are notable merchants' houses and municipal buildings.

BRIDGE STREET This street contains the Greenland Fishery House, built 1605 as a merchant's house, with a cruck-based roof, 17th-century wall-paintings and an overhanging upper floor. At the end of Bridge Street is the stone and brick 14th-century gateway to the former Whitefriars' house, one of King's Lynn's many vanished monastic buildings.

CHAPEL OF ST NICHOLAS Very large, it was founded in 1146, but built in the 15th century. The tower at the south-west is earlier, but has a spire of 1869. St Nicholas's has many interesting fittings and monuments. (By appointment.)

CHURCH OF ST MARGARET One of the few parish churches with two western towers (mid-12th century). Part of the interior of the building is 18th-century Gothic by Matthew Brettingham, *c.* 1745. The outstanding possessions are two brasses of *c.* 1349 and *c.* 1364, which are the largest in England, and minutely detailed.

CLIFTON HOUSE The façade is Georgian, and there is a portal decorated with barley-sugar columns; a 15th-century undercroft remains. A tall Elizabethan tower gives good views of the town.

CUSTOM HOUSE Designed by the local architect Henry Bell in 1683; a small and charming building on the quay reminiscent of Dutch styles. There is a statue of Charles II in a niche, and the building is surmounted by a lantern tower.

GUILDHALL OF THE HOLY TRINITY Built in chequer-board pattern of flint and stone, it dates from 1421; there were additions in the 18th century and in 1895 municipal offices were added to make it the modern town hall. The Treasury here contains city regalia, including King John's Cup, gilded and embossed with enamelled panels showing hawking and hunting scenes of the mid-14th century; King John's Sword; the notable

Mayoral Chains dating from 1512; the Nuremberg Cup of *c.* 1600, an elaborate piece by a German Court goldsmith; and various 17th- and 18th-century treasures. Another guildhall is that of St George, a fine medieval building.

HAMPTON COURT A 14th-century former warehouse on the river, converted to dwellings in the 17th century and one of the best of the town's merchant buildings. The others include the Hanseatic Warehouse (1428), a depot for the German commercial league known as the Hansa; Greenland Fishery House (1605), a merchant's dwelling that became an inn and then a museum; and Clifton House, a medieval dwelling modernised in 1708, from whose Elizabethan tower there is a good view of the town.

KING STREET The best street for pleasing Georgian and 19th-century houses; also includes St George's Guildhall, the largest and oldest example in England of a medieval Merchant Guild's house. Built in the early 15th century, it was restored and adapted as a theatre in 1951.

LYNN MUSEUM Displays relate to geology, archaeology, local history and natural history of north-west Norfolk.

MUSEUM OF SOCIAL HISTORY Exhibits include costumes, toys, ceramics, glass, local prints and paintings.

KING JOHN'S CUP

This cup is the earliest surviving piece of English medieval secular plate. It is decorated in translucent enamel, which is fragile and tends to flake. The cup was restored four times between 1692 and 1782 but the enamels on the bowl, showing men and women hunting, are mostly original. Tradition says the cup was among the treasure lost by King John in the Wash, but its style shows it to date from a century later. Translucent enamelling came into fashion late in the 13th century; the design was engraved on silver and showed clearly through the enamel. A play of light and dark was obtained by varying the depth of the engraving. (Town Hall, King's Lynn)

QUEEN STREET AND SATURDAY MARKET Four contiguous buildings of different dates and styles: the guildhall (1421) of chequer-board flint and stone with low ground-floor windows and a tall seven-light upper window beneath a gable; next to it the fanciful Elizabethan extension in the same flint chequer. Behind these are the assembly rooms of 1766, plain but containing a magnificent rococo mirror.

RED MOUNT CHAPEL Built in 1485, it stands in a park area known as The Walks. The chapel has three storeys inside an octagonal shell, the top storey being a cruciform chapel with beautiful fan-vaulted roof. This Chapel of Our Lady of the Mount was a stopping place for the many pilgrims to Walsingham.

ST MARGARET'S LANE Has an interesting timber-framed warehouse, with an overhang, known as the Hanseatic Warehouse.

SOUTH GATE The only surviving town gate, embattled, dating from 1520. Remains of the town wall can be seen in Kettlewell Lane, Wyatt Street, The Walks and St Ann's Street.

THORESBY COLLEGE Founded in 1500 for priests of the Trinity Guild; it now mostly consists of 17th-century work, but an original archway and door survive.

TUESDAY MARKET-PLACE A fine open space dominated by the Duke's Head Hotel (1683–9), probably by the same Henry Bell who designed the Custom House.

King's Norton *Leics.* 552Fb

CHURCH OF ST JOHN THE BAPTIST An impressive Gothic Revival church rebuilt entirely between 1760 and 1775 by J. Wing the Younger of Leicester. The interior is dominated by the central pulpit, and the fittings are all 18th century. The spire was destroyed by lightning in 1850.

HALS *Portrait of a Lady*

In 1624, Frans Hals painted one of the most popular portraits—the 'Laughing Cavalier'—in which his brushwork can be compared with the touch of the Impressionists, although it had none of their atmospheric quality. The paint is laid on thickly; his sitters have extrovert expressions and the swagger of their poses is enhanced by a low viewpoint. From the 1640's onwards Hals developed a more restrained style, but what he lost in panache he gained in intimacy. To this demure young woman the painter has brought an unusually profound sympathy of observation. The paint surface is now thin, and the treatment of the costume is summary but this serves only to emphasise the exquisite modelling of the face.
(Ferens Art Gallery, Kingston upon Hull)

Kingston *Dorset* 540Ec

CHURCH OF ST JAMES Built of local materials in 1880 by G. E. Street. It is one of his finest churches and shows French influence. The imposing central tower is a notable feature; the chancel is vaulted. The fittings are also Street's work, and include some impressive ironwork.

Kingston Lacy *Dorset* 540Ed

This late-17th-century house was built by Sir Ralph Bankes, son of Charles I's chief justice, and altered more than a century later by Charles Barry. It contains carvings, tapestries and furnishings, mainly from Italy and Spain, and a splendid collection of paintings by Rubens, Titian, Velázquez, Tintoretto, Breughel, Van Dyck and others. There is a fine landscape garden.

Kingston upon Hull *Humberside* 559Ga

Originally a 12th-century trading settlement known as Wyke upon Hull. It changed its name when it was acquired from the Abbots of Meaux (France) by Edward I in 1293, and it received its first royal charter in 1299. By 1331 it had prospered sufficiently for a mayor to be appointed; he was William de la Pole, whose statue now stands at Victoria Pier. The town was enclosed and fortified in 1321, with a moat and walls of brick.

Among the ancient buildings are Holy Trinity Church (Early English), St Mary's Lowgate (*c.* 1400), and the Old Grammar School founded in 1583. Among the pupils who attained fame in later years were Andrew Marvell, the 17th-century poet and politician, and William Wilberforce.

CHARTER HOUSE HOSPITAL Founded in 1384 by Sir Michael de la Pole (later Earl of Suffolk) the original building was demolished during the Civil War and the present one dates from 1780.

CHURCH OF THE HOLY TRINITY One of the largest parish churches in England; it is cruciform with a grand central tower, and is mainly 14th and 15th century, with some early brickwork and huge windows. Inside are medieval roofs, screens and benches, and a carved font.

FERENS ART GALLERY Opened in 1928, the gallery has an important collection of old masters including works by Frans Hals, Guardi, Canaletto, Maffei and Philippe de Champaigne. Sculpture by Henry Moore, Barbara Hepworth and Paolozzi can be seen with a wide selection of modern paintings by Victor Pasmore, David Hockney, Allen Jones and Alan Davie, among others.

HULL TRINITY HOUSE Founded as a religious body in 1369, the organisation responsible for pilotage in the Humber. In 1787 the brethren established a Navigation School, and the characteristic uniform of the Trinity House boys, patterned on that of the R.N. midshipman of the period, is a familiar sight in and around Hull. The headquarters building dates from 1753, and is richly furnished.

MAISTER HOUSE A mansion rebuilt in 1744 with a Palladian hall and staircase, and ironwork by Robert Bakewell.

TOWN DOCKS MUSEUM A maritime museum in the former dock offices. Displays on whales and whaling, ships, and the fishing industry.

TRANSPORT AND ARCHAEOLOGY MUSEUM The transport section contains a collection of coaches, motor cars, bicycles and other road vehicles. There are also fine Roman mosaic pavements from Rudston and Brantingham.

WILBERFORCE HOUSE A 17th-century merchant's house where William Wilberforce (1759–1833) was born. It contains a museum of material from his anti-slavery and philanthropic activities, and a collection of dolls and toys.

Kingston upon Thames *Greater London* *542Ag*
CORONATION STONE Seven Saxon kings were
crowned at this ancient market town during the
10th century, and the traditional coronation stone
(King's Stone) now stands in front of the guildhall.

King's Weston *Avon* *540Cg*
At Sea Mills, 2 miles away on the Avon estuary,
was Abone, a small port at the end of the road from
Silchester (Calleva Atrebatum). From here travellers could ferry across to Caerwent (Venta
Silurum) and Caerleon (Isca). Considerable
excavation of this Roman villa has been made and
the remains are on display. The skeleton of a man,
killed by the sword, was found in the ruins of a
hypocaust.

Kingussie *Highland* *566Bd*
HIGHLAND FOLK MUSEUM A major collection of
items relating to the social and cultural history of
the Scottish Highlands. The six acres of exhibition
space include an open-air museum with an 18th-
century shooting lodge, a 'black' house and a clack
mill from the Isle of Lewis. Other displays
include Highland craftsmanship in wood and
precious metals, straw, heather and thorn; and a
farming museum with a stable, dairy, barn, and
displays of carts, ploughs and harrows.

Kinlet *Shropshire* *546Bg*
CHURCH OF ST JOHN THE BAPTIST Standing in the
grounds of Kinlet Hall (1729, now a school), but
isolated from other buildings, this Norman church
has many later additions including the Early
English west tower with Perpendicular top. Also
Perpendicular is the timber-framed clerestory
(restored by Oldrid Scott, 1892). There is stained
glass of 1814 in the east window. Among many
interesting monuments (the oldest date from the
1400's) there is one of 1584 to Sir George Blount
and his wife.

Kinneff *Grampian* *567Gc*
CHURCH The Honours of Scotland (the crown
jewels) were temporarily concealed for safety in
1652 in a church on this site. They had been
daringly smuggled from Dunnottar Castle by the
minister's wife just before the castle fell to
besieging Roundheads.

Kinross *Tayside* *562Bg*
KINROSS HOUSE Built in 1685–92, and one of the
best period works by Sir William Bruce. The
house is set in beautiful gardens on the shores of
Loch Leven. Gardens open in summer.

Kintraw *Strathclyde* *560Eg*
CAIRNS AND STANDING STONES These monuments stand at the roadside close to the head of
Loch Craignish. There are four cairns, three of
which are quite small. The fourth, 8 ft high and
nearly 50 ft across, has been excavated. When
built, it was heaped round a central post fixed in
the ground. The burial chamber was double and
close to the cairn's edge. The mound is contained
by a stone kerb. Close by stands the upright stone,
some 13 ft high. All belong to the Bronze Age.

Kirby Hall *Northants.* *547Hg*
A house begun in 1570 by an unknown architect.
In 1575 it came into the hands of Sir Christopher
Hatton who added to the building. Kirby is of
architectural significance, though now a ruin,
because it incorporates motifs occurring in French
architecture; this appears to be the only instance of
their use in England and they were probably based
on books of engravings. Later, in the first half of
the 17th century, more building was undertaken, it
is said, by Inigo Jones; this is not confirmed

KIRBY HALL

*Kirby Hall was begun in 1570 for Sir Humphrey
Stafford. The architect is unknown, but the mason
was Thomas Thorpe; and his seven-year-old son
John, who later became an architect, laid the first
stone—as he himself recorded in one of his later
drawings. When Stafford died in 1575 the estate was
bought by Sir Christopher Hatton, who continued the
building work. Further additions were made in the
17th century and then the architect may have been
Inigo Jones. The house, now a ruin, combines
elements of early Renaissance architecture of Elizabeth
I's time with elements of Inigo Jones's period.*

although it is known that one of the leading sculptors of the period, Nicholas Stone, was employed
here. The Hall remained in the possession of the
Hatton and Finch-Hatton families but had become
ruinous by the 19th century.

Kirkby Lonsdale *Cumbria* *557Jd*
CHURCH OF ST MARY THE VIRGIN Ruskin praised
the view from the churchyard here, and Turner
painted it; it is one of the finest in the county,
embracing Howgill and Casterton Fells, and the
R. Lune.
Much remains of the original Norman church,
and the interior is impressive, with massive pillars
in the north arcade alternating with piers of
clustered shafts. There is a 17th-century six-sided
pulpit, and many 18th-century mural tablets.

Kirkby Malham *N. Yorks.* *558Ac*
CHURCH OF ST MICHAEL A Perpendicular church
with a west tower. There is a Norman font, and
17th- and 18th-century pews.

Kirkcaldy *Fife* *562Cf*
The picturesque ruins of Ravenscraig Castle,
built *c.* 1440 and inhabited until the Restoration,
overhang the sea near by. Adam Smith (1723–90),
the political economist, was born here; the house
in the High Street where he wrote *The Wealth
of Nations* may still be seen. In 1816 the historian
Thomas Carlyle was a master at the burgh school.
MUSEUM AND ART GALLERY The museum was
founded as a First World War memorial by John

KIT'S COTY HOUSE

On the side of the Downs above Aylesford stand these relics of the most spectacular of the barrows in Kent that date from the Neolithic period. Such earth burial mounds were oval in plan, and contained chambers made from drystone walling and megaliths—or great stones. The Neolithic peoples were the first farmers in Britain and came from the Continent to the chalk uplands of south-eastern England about 3700 BC. They interred their dead in these chambered barrows in groups, possibly in families, often with their pots and stone implements. The earth mound at Kit's Coty House has now disappeared, leaving the remains of the burial chamber, with the great capstone which formed the roof, and the stone supports.

EARLY 17th-CENTURY CHAIR

Upholstered chairs with X-shaped legs enjoyed a period of popularity during the early 17th century. Their design recalls the folding chairs of ancient Rome, but they were made with broader seats and backs for greater comfort, and were covered in rich fabric. The entire framework of this chair is covered in patterned silk, and the fringe, made of strands of silk, is attached to the frame by nails with decorated heads. The cushion, covered with silk and stuffed, is another concession to rising standards of comfort after the austerity of the carved wooden chairs which were the fashion in Elizabethan times. (Knole)

Nairn, a local linoleum manufacturer. The collection is devoted to the history, industries, and natural history of Fife and includes many pieces of Wemyss ware, a distinctive, finely crazed pottery, originally made *c.* 1883 at Robert Heron's Fife Pottery in Gallatown by Karel Nekola, a Bohemian immigrant. Other items include duelling pistols used in Fife in the 19th century; the inkstand used by Kirkcaldy-born Adam Smith when writing *The Wealth of Nations*; and paintings by William McTaggart.
SAILOR'S WALK A harbour-side group of 17th-century houses. (Not open to visitors.)

Kirkham Priory *N. Yorks.*　　　　　　*558Ec*
An Augustinian priory was founded here *c.* 1125 by a judge, Walter l'Espec, after his son's death in a riding accident. It was substantially enlarged in the 13th and 14th centuries. It is now in ruins, but the 13th-century gatehouse retains some fine carving.

Kirkleatham *Cleveland*　　　　　　　*558Df*
CHURCH OF ST CUTHBERT An earlier church was rebuilt in 1763 to make St Cuthbert's; the mausoleum was designed by James Gibbs in 1740. There are delightful 18th-century fittings and many monuments, some by Peter Scheemakers and Sir Henry Cheere.

Kirknewton *Northld.*　　　　　　　*562Ed*
CHURCH OF ST GREGORY Mainly a 19th-century rebuilding which contains two important examples of primitive building: a transept and chancel which appear to be vault only—the walls are so low that they are hardly apparent. There is also a crude stone-carving depicting the Adoration of the Magi, which probably dates from the 12th century.

Kirkoswald *Cumbria*　　　　　　　*557Jf*
CHURCH OF ST OSWALD A church of various dates, with a 16th-century chancel built by Lord Dacre when he founded a college here. There is a detached tower some distance away, which was built in 1897, and several coffin-lids.

Kirkoswald *Strathclyde*　　　　　　*561Gb*
SOUTER JOHNNIE'S COTTAGE The home of John Davidson (Souter Johnnie), the village cobbler of Burns's 'Tam O'Shanter'. The cottage contains Burns relics.

Kirkstall *W. Yorks.*　　　　　　　*558Cb*
ABBEY One of Yorkshire's ruined Cistercian abbeys, Kirkstall was founded in the 12th century; much of its building survives surprisingly well, even the seemingly precarious wall of one side of the church's central tower.
ABBEY HOUSE MUSEUM See Leeds.

Kirkstead *Lincs.*　　　　　　　　*553He*
CHURCH OF ST LEONARD Once the 13th-century south chapel of the former Cistercian abbey of Kirkstead, founded during the 12th century, and now surrounded by the ruins of various abbey buildings. There is an early effigy of a knight in armour, *c.* 1250.

Kirkwall *Mainland, Orkney*　　　　*569Hf*
The capital of Mainland and the Orkneys. The Cathedral of St Magnus dates mainly from the 12th century: its nave is notable, and there are many memorials of different periods.

Kirkwhelpington *Northld.*　　　　　*562Fa*
CHURCH OF ST BARTHOLOMEW A 12th- and 13th-century church, originally cruciform, with a west tower. The church was considerably damaged during the border raids of the 14th century. The

roof was burnt off three times and the transepts and side aisles were never restored. The chancel was altered in the 18th century and has elegant plasterwork and sash windows. There is a large monument dating from the same period.

Kirriemuir *Tayside*   566Eb
MUSEUM Sir James Barrie (1860–1937), author and playwright, described Kirriemuir as the town of Thrums in *The Little Minister* and *Window in Thrums*. Barrie was born at No 9, Brechin Road, which is now a museum of his achievements. The outside wash-house was his first 'theatre' and may have been the model for his 'Wendy House'.

Kirtling *Cambs.*   548Bf
CHURCH OF ALL SAINTS Originally Norman, All Saints has a good south doorway, with a carving of Christ in Majesty. The rest of the fabric is of various dates, up to c. 1500. There are many monuments to the North family, including two big and ornate ones of the 16th century.

Kirtling Tower *Cambs.*   548Bf
The best and finest tower gate-house in the county. It dates from 1530 and is of red brick, with blue diapers, two tall polygonal outer turrets, slender turrets behind and a superb semicircular oriel window squashed in between.

Kirton in Lindsey *Humberside*   553Gf
CHURCH OF ST ANDREW The huge Early English west tower has pilaster buttresses; the south doorway is contemporary with it. There are remains of Norman work, including the priest's door in the chancel, which has a tympanum of strapwork. Restoration was carried out in the mid-19th century.

Kisimul Castle *Isle of Barra, Western Isles 564Ad*
A castle on a sea-girt rock, begun in 1030; it has been the stronghold of the chiefs of the Clan Macneil since then, except for the years 1838–1937, and has been greatly restored. (By appointment.)

Kit's Coty House *Kent*   542Df
These are the remains of the most spectacular of the small group of Kentish Neolithic chambered barrows. The covering mound has now disappeared. Of the megalithic structure, there survive the uprights on which the great capstone still rests, probably what is left of a burial chamber, though it has sometimes been interpreted as a false entrance.

Knap Hill *Wilts.*   540Ff
This Neolithic assembly-place crowns a hill bordering the north side of the Vale of Pewsey. The external ditch has causeway crossings corresponding with openings in the inside bank, which encloses a 4 acre area. Half a mile to the west, on the opposite hill, stands a prominent long barrow. Adjoining the causewayed camp on its eastern side, a smaller earthwork may be traced. This is of a later date, having been erected as the outer protection of an Iron Age farmstead.

Knaresborough *N. Yorks.*   558Cc
CHURCH OF ST JOHN The church was once cruciform, but the transepts were absorbed in 15th-century rebuilding. The central tower has a small spire. Inside is a Perpendicular font with a later cover, and monuments to the Slingsby family.

Knebworth *Herts.*   547Jd
CHURCH OF ST MARY AND THOMAS OF CANTERBURY Norman, with later enlargements, the church stands in the grounds of Knebworth House. The monuments include two (1700–10) by Edward Stanton, and one with the standing figure of Lytton Lytton (d. 1710) which has been attributed to Thomas Green of Camberwell, an outstanding statuary of the early 18th century.

Knebworth House *Herts.*   547Jd
The Victorian statesman and romantic novelist, Sir Edward Bulwer-Lytton (1st Lord Lytton) who wrote *The Last Days of Pompeii*, succeeded to this

THE VENETIAN AMBASSADOR'S ROOM AT KNOLE

Nicolo Molino, a Venetian ambassador at the court of James I, once occupied this room, and it is named after him; his portrait, painted by Mytens about 1640, hangs by the bed. The furniture and bed, decorated with cupids and the letters JR, may have belonged to *James II. Thomas Roberts, cabinet-maker to Charles II and James II, made the chairs and stools. The tapestries, depicting landscapes with mythical figures, are Flemish, and were woven by Francis Spierinck in the late 16th or early 17th century.*

property in 1843. He lived here until his death in 1873, and was visited by Disraeli, Charles Dickens and other literary friends. The house was begun in 1492 by Sir Robert Lytton; it was partly demolished in 1812, but the Tudor great hall survives. The exterior was redecorated in Gothic style by the 1st Lord Lytton in 1843. The house, set in fine gardens, contains 17th- and 18th-century furniture, portraits, and relics and manuscripts of Bulwer-Lytton.

Knockderry Castle *Strathclyde*   561Gf
On the east side of Loch Long, this castle was built *c.* 1850 on the site of the original Knockderry Castle which features as Knock Dunder in Scott's novel *Heart of Midlothian*. It is now a hotel.

Knole *Kent*   542Cf
One of the largest private houses in England, Knole was built by Thomas Bourchier when Archbishop of Canterbury (1456) and used as a retreat by bishops until Archbishop Cranmer released it to Henry VIII, from whom it passed to Queen Elizabeth I. Elizabeth granted it to her courtier, the politician and poet Thomas Sackville, 1st Earl of Dorset, who extended the property in 1603–8.

The house contains pictures, tapestries, rugs and silver up to the 17th century. The Brown Gallery has portraits and 17th- and 18th-century English furniture. The fire-place in the great chamber resembles a high altar, and the ornamental great staircase, introduced by Sackville, set a fashion previously unknown in private houses. The great hall dates from *c.* 1460.(See also pp. 260–1.)

Knowe of Lairo *Rousay, Orkney*   569Hg
A long four-horned Neolithic cairn, somewhat mutilated but still showing its essential structure. It is about 180 ft long, 16 ft high above the chamber, which is tripartite, and with an entrance passage 18 ft long.

Knowe of Yarso *Rousay, Orkney*   569Hg
A small Neolithic 'stalled cairn' containing four compartments.

Knowlton Circles *Dorset*   540Ed
Here are three Neolithic henge-circles in a row. The largest, some 800 ft in diameter, is roughly bisected by the Cranborne–Wimborne road, and the other two lie to the north. A ruined Norman church with later additions stands in the middle of the central circle. To the east of this circle is an enormous Bronze Age round barrow, and smaller barrows are grouped close by.

Knutsford *Cheshire*   552Be
CHURCH OF ST JOHN THE BAPTIST A brick Classical church, it was built in 1744. The west tower has urns at each corner of the parapet, as does the body of the church; the windows have stone dressings. It replaced earlier chapels of ease, and parochial registers date back to 1581.

Kymin, The *Gwent*   546Ad
In 1804 Lord Nelson dined in the many-windowed Round Tower. It stands on the Kymin Hill overlooking the Wye and Monnow Valleys and was built in 1794 by a dining club which, in 1802, erected a 'naval temple' near by in honour of the Royal Navy.

L

Lacock *Wilts.*   540Eg
One of the most beautiful villages in England, with houses dating from the 15th to 19th centuries.
CHURCH OF ST CYRIAC Built mainly in the 14th and 15th centuries, the church is cruciform with a west tower and spire. The north-east chapel was built *c.* 1430, has a notable lierne-vault with pendants, and an outstanding monument to Sir William Sharington, who converted Lacock Abbey into his dwelling. His tomb is a decorative example of mid-16th-century work.
LACKHAM COLLEGE OF AGRICULTURE: AGRICULTURAL MUSEUM Tools and implements, farm machinery and granaries are exhibited.
LACOCK ABBEY Here in 1839–41, William Henry Fox Talbot perfected his calotype technique which laid the foundations of modern photography. About 1540 Sir William Sharington, one-time Treasurer of the Mint at Bristol, acquired the abbey overlooking the Avon and adapted it as a Tudor mansion, adding an octagonal tower and twisted chimneys and retaining the 13th- and 15th-century cloisters, chapter house and nuns' parlour. The house was altered in neo-Gothic style in 1754 and further alterations were made in 1828.

Ladle Hill *Hants.*   541Gf
The special interest of this Iron Age hill-fort lies in the fact that its defences were never completed and that what was done shows well the method of construction. A shallow marking-ditch enclosing some 7 acres was first dug, and used in part a length of a Bronze Age ditch. Gangs thereupon began work by scraping off the topsoil and dumping this

in heaps inside the line of the future rampart. They then widened and deepened the marking-ditch by cutting into the chalk and piling the rubble spoil inside the ditch-line to form the core of the bank. Apparently the threat which had led to the beginning of the work soon passed. The site was thereupon deserted.

Several disc, bell and saucer barrows of Early Bronze Age date may also be seen on the hill-top.

Laindon *Essex*   548Bc
CHURCH OF ST NICHOLAS A small church, mainly of the 14th and 15th centuries, with carved wood decoration in the south porch. Attached to the west end is a two-storied priest's house of the 17th century. The font is 13th century. (By appointment.)

Lambert's Castle Hill *Dorset*   540Bc
Site of an Iron Age fort, and a round barrow. From the hill are superb views to Chesil Bank in the east and Dartmoor in the west.

Lambourn *Berks.*   546Eb
SEVEN BARROWS This famous barrow group is one of the finest in England. 'Seven' is a misnomer, for there are 26 in the whole group, which today is split by a minor road. Those to the north of this road lie in two straight rows with a few outliers. South of the road, the grouping is irregular and more scattered. These Bronze Age barrows are of various types, including bowl, disc, bell and saucer, as well as an earlier Neolithic long barrow. Some have almost disappeared, but others still stand to heights of 10 ft.

THE GUILDHALL AT LAVENHAM

In the Market Square stands this fine early Tudor timber-framed building. It was the former Hall of the Guild of Corpus Christi and was erected shortly after the guild's foundation in 1528. A full-length figure of the founder of the guild, the 15th Earl of Oxford, is carved on an elaborate corner-post. The early guilds were formed for the benefit of trade, yet they had strong religious connections, and in their halls traditional miracle plays and pageants were performed. Lavenham, a thriving centre of the wool trade in the 16th century, had three guildhalls; that of the Guild of Corpus Christi was the first to be built.

Lampeter *Dyfed* 544Fe
ST DAVID'S COLLEGE Founded in 1822, it was built to the pattern of an Oxford college in 1827, in neo-Gothic, by architect Charles Cockerell. At the north gate of the old building is a Norman motte: the college site was known as Castle Field.

Lamphey *Dyfed* 544Dc
BISHOP'S PALACE This small palace was a rural retreat of the medieval Bishops of St David's. As at St David's, most of the building took place between the 13th and 15th centuries; here, too, is a great hall built by Bishop Gower, using the same kind of arcaded roof parapet as appears at St David's and Swansea Castle. After the Reformation, Lamphey was for a time a private house and some of the alterations can still be seen; but it was soon abandoned and used as a stone quarry.

Lamport Hall *Northants.* 547Gf
The Hall was built in two stages: the central block by John Webb *c.* 1655, the wings by Francis Smith in 1730–8. The music hall contains 18th-century plasterwork.

Lancaster *Lancs.* 557Hc
An old town and port on the R. Lune. Its medieval castle stands on the site of a Roman military station; John of Gaunt, Duke of Lancaster and father of Henry IV, stayed there in 1385 and again in 1393. The town gave lodging to Bonnie Prince Charlie and his army on their ill-fated march south during the Jacobite rebellion of 1745. Lancaster is the county town of Lancashire and contains many fine old buildings. The Friends' Meeting House dates from 1690. The Custom House was built in the 18th century; at its front stand graceful Ionic columns, each carved from a single block of stone. Skerton Bridge was constructed *c.* 1787.
CASTLE In 1102 the Normans built a great square stone keep to replace the Saxon wooden tower on

Castle Hill, the site of Roman fortifications. King John built a curtain wall with round towers and a massive gateway around the keep, enclosing a roughly circular area, 380 ft by 350 ft. Under Edward III's son, John of Gaunt, the gateway towers were added and banqueting halls and fine apartments were built. The castle was a Parliamentary stronghold in the Civil War. George Fox, founder of the Friends (Quakers), was imprisoned there in 1663–5. Besides being a prison the fortress has also been a judge's lodging, and a Crown Court was opened there in 1796. The Shire Hall within the castle contains over 600 heraldic shields. The keep, 78 ft high with walls 10 ft thick, is surmounted by a beacon tower known as John of Gaunt's Chair; from it the approach of the Spanish Armada was signalled.
LANCASTER CITY MUSEUM The museum is in Lancaster Old Town Hall, built in 1781, and contains archaeological and historical exhibits, including important Roman inscribed and sculptured stones, prehistoric and medieval antiquities and model ships. It also houses the museum of the King's Own Royal (Lancaster) Regiment. Works by local artists, topographical paintings, portraits, drawings and prints make up the museum's art collection, with English and oriental pottery and porcelain and examples of Gillow furniture.
PRIORY CHURCH OF ST MARY The church dates from Saxon times, but all that remains of the Saxon church is a doorway at the western end. Most of the present Perpendicular church was built in the 14th and 15th centuries; the belfry was added in 1759. Inside are elaborate oak choir stalls, carved *c.* 1340, and a Jacobean pulpit; there is also a monument by Louis Roubiliac.

Lanchester *Durham* 558Cg
CHURCH OF ALL SAINTS A Norman and Early English church, with a good Norman chancel

arch. Later additions include the Perpendicular clerestory and windows in the south aisle. There is a Roman altar in the porch. The church also has some 13th-century stained glass.

Landwade *Cambs.*   548Bf
The comparatively new Hall incorporates part of the original mansion built in 1445. The treasures of this remote and quiet hamlet, which consist of Hall, church and a few cottages, are the superb tombs, in the church, of the Cotton family who first settled in Landwade in the 15th century.

Laneast *Cornwall*   538Ed
CHURCH OF ST SIDWELL Originally Norman, and with a west tower, the cruciform church has later additions. Inside is a Norman font, carved bench ends, rood screen, and fragments of stained glass. There is a Celtic cross nearby.

Lanercost Priory *Cumbria*   557Jg
Founded in 1169 for Augustinian canons by Robert de Vaux, the priory is built largely of stones from the Roman wall and incorporates an altar to Jupiter. The nave and north aisle were restored in 1740 for use as the parish church. Inside is part of an inscribed cross, erected in 1214. There are several interesting monuments and some stained glass by Burne-Jones.
  Spanning the river close to the priory is a Tudor bridge.

Langham *Leics.*   553Gb
CHURCH OF SS PETER AND PAUL An imposing church, mainly of the 14th century, when a Decorated spire was added to the 13th-century west tower. Inside there is a Perpendicular clerestory, and some early 20th-century stained glass by Sir Ninian Comper.

Langley Marish *Berks.*   547Hb
CHURCH OF ST MARY There are vestiges of Norman work, but the varied architecture has much of the 17th century, including the brick tower, the Kedermister Chapel (south transept), and a surprising library to the west. These were added by the Kederminster family in the 1600's. In the chapel there is a painted wooden screen and, leading into the chapel, a later Coade (artificial) stone screen of 1792; panelling in the library is painted with landscapes of Windsor and Eton. There are monuments to the Kedermister family dated 1599, and one to David Harvey (*d.* 1788).

Langport *Som.*   540Ce
A small market town whose architectural curiosity is the Hanging Chapel—a chapel over an arch.

Langwell *Highland*   569Lc
HOMESTEAD Buildings of this type are not uncommon in the northern part of Scotland, but very little is known of them or their purpose. They are believed to date from the Iron Age.
  The main structure is a 6 ft thick wall enclosing a circular area some 27 ft across. There is an entrance from the outside and another into an adjoining rectangular structure enclosed by a similar wall and measuring about 48 ft by 14 ft. This rectangular building is halved by a cross-partition wall. Also inside it are three stone pillars which supported roofing slabs also resting on the walls.

Lanhydrock House *Cornwall*   538Dc
Overlooking the R. Fowey, the house was begun by Lord Robartes in the 17th century. The gatehouse and north wing are original, but the remainder was built mainly in the 19th century, following a fire. The picture gallery (116 ft long) has a plaster ceiling with scenes from the Old Testament. In the grounds (424 acres) are formal gardens (1857) with a number of bronze urns from the Château de Bagatelle, which were designed by Louis XIV's goldsmith, Louis Ballin. The formal gardens include a typical Cornish sycamore avenue-approach to the house.

Lanteglos-by-Fowey *Cornwall*   538Db
CHURCH OF ST WYLLOW A somewhat isolated, mainly 14th–15th-century church. The west tower has openings into nave and both aisles. There are fragments of early stained glass.

Lanyon Quoit *Cornwall*   538Ab
A huge granite slab, 17 ft by 9 ft, and 18 in. thick, rests on three upright stones—all that remains of a re-erected Neolithic chamber tomb.

Lapworth *Warks.*   546Df
CHURCH OF ST MARY THE VIRGIN The battlemented tower with a steeple is detached from the main body of the church, which has Norman remains. The nave is tall, with a clerestory of Perpendicular square-headed windows. There is a two-storey south porch. Inside, the features include an early 14th-century octagonal font, and a carved monument, *c.* 1928, by the sculptor, wood-engraver and type-designer Eric Gill.

Largs *Strathclyde*   561Ge
SKELMORLIE AISLE A building erected in 1636 as a mausoleum for Sir Robert Montgomerie, in Italian baroque style with elaborate paintings and carvings.

Lasborough Manor *Glos.*   546Cc
A Cotswold manor house, built in 1609, with a garden noted for herbaceous borders and shrubs. (By appointment.)

Laugharne *Dyfed*   544Ed
The attractive township is strategically set at the mouth of the R. Taf, where its medieval castle could be serviced from the sea; evidence of its later use by coastal shipping can be seen in the ruined wharf buildings. There is an interesting courthouse, where a corporation still meets under its portreeve. Laugharne was the home of the poet Dylan Thomas (1914–53) and the possible inspiration for his play *Under Milk Wood*.

Launcells *Cornwall*   538Ee
CHURCH OF ST SWITHIN Set in an attractive position in a valley, with a delightful unrestored interior, St Swithin's has carved bench ends, a wagon-roof, and some 15th-century tiles. There is a monument *c.* 1644, with effigy.

Launceston *Cornwall*   538Ed
CHURCH OF ST MARY MAGDALENE This church was built in 1511–24 by Sir Henry Trecarrel. It has a 14th-century south-west tower, and is noted for extravagant carving all over the granite exterior. There are many early fittings and monuments.

Lavenham *Suffolk*   548Ce
Lavenham has superb timber-framed houses dating from the prosperous 15th century when wool was practically as valuable as gold itself (today the Lord Chancellor still sits on the Woolsack). Its exquisite houses include: the Old Wool Hall, *c.* 1500, the Tudor shops, the superb De Vere House, Nos. 11, 12, 13 and 15 Church Street, the old grammar school, Mulet House, Shilling Old Grange, the Swan Hotel, the Guildhall, *c.* 1529, Woolstaplers, and the Little Hall. Of particular interest is some of the finely executed pargetting work on house façades.
CHURCH OF SS PETER AND PAUL A very well-known church, it is mainly from the 15th century, with a tall west tower, and has a nave, clerestory,

chancel and chapels with very large windows. There is a 14th-century rood screen, and good screens to the chapels. Also interesting are the stalls and carved misericords, and there are some 15th- to 17th-century monuments with effigies. Some of the glass is medieval, some mid-19th century.
GUILDHALL A timber-framed building of 1529, originally the Hall of the Guild of Corpus Christi.

Laxton *Notts.* 552Fe
CHURCH OF ST MICHAEL A large, late 12th-century church, with clerestory, tall chancel and west tower. The north aisle screen is of 1532. There are many monuments from the 13th century.

Layer Marney *Essex* 548Cd
CHURCH OF ST MARY THE VIRGIN Standing near a Tudor gate-house, the church was rebuilt in brick by the 1st Lord Marney at the beginning of the 16th century. It has a west tower and a 15th-century mural of St Christopher. There are monuments which show the mingling of Perpendicular and Renaissance motifs.

Layer Marney Tower *Essex* 548Cd
This mansion, which was never completed on its original scale, consists of an enormous gate-house with smaller ranges of buildings clinging to it. As an example of a phase in the development of English domestic architecture it is both impressive and interesting. The house dates from the early 16th century, and the main part of it was intended to face south. Only the eight-storied gate-house, with its adjacent small buildings, was finished. This was clearly intended as the showpiece of the mansion. The gate-house had emerged, centuries earlier, as a dominant feature of castle structure, and the trend was continued in domestic building. At Layer Marney this architectural feature was developed almost to excess: it is the largest of all gate-houses of its kind. The decorations in terracotta on the battlements and windows are typical early Renaissance motifs of Italian character. It was built between 1510 and 1525. Henry, 1st Lord Marney and John, 2nd Lord Marney, whose tombs are in St Mary's Church, died in 1523 and 1525.

Leamington Spa See Royal Leamington Spa.

Learable Hill *Highland* 569Kc
Several stone-rows stand on the hill-slope down to the R. Helmsdale. Many cairns are also scattered over the area and a standing stone with a cross carved on its face dominates the hill-top. All are believed to date from the Bronze Age.

Leatherhead *Surrey* 542Af
Among many interesting buildings is the Running Horse Inn, mentioned by the poet John Skelton (1460–1529) in his 'The Tunnyng of Elynour Rummyng'. The council offices house two 18th-century cannons. Anthony Hope, author of *The Prisoner of Zenda,* is buried in the churchyard.

Lechlade *Glos.* 546Dc
CHURCH OF ST LAWRENCE Perpendicular church of the 15th century, with west tower and spire. Inside there is a curious roof boss depicting wrestlers, similar to one in Lincoln Cathedral. The font is embellished with carved panelling, and there is a monument (*c.* 1769) by Nicholas Read.

Ledbury *Heref. & Worcs.* 546Be
CHURCH OF ST MICHAEL AND ALL ANGELS A church of Norman origin, but now mostly of the late 13th and early 14th centuries. There is a detached 13th-century tower, with a spire built 1727–34. There is early stained glass, and windows by C. E. Kempe of 1895–1904. Monuments and brasses, mainly from the 15th to 19th centuries,

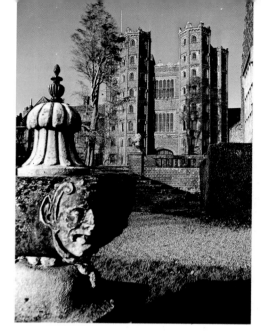

LAYER MARNEY TOWER

A folly-like building, this enormous gate-house—the largest of its kind—is the only completed part of a magnificent early 16th-century mansion. The original intention was to build the main part of the house to the north, but this never materialised. Since Edward I's time it had become the fashion to make the gate-house instead of the keep the aggressive and dominating component of a castle; the trend also became a feature of domestic building, and at Layer Marney the idea was developed to excess. The terracotta decoration on the battlements and windows is one of the earliest uses in England of Italian Renaissance motifs.

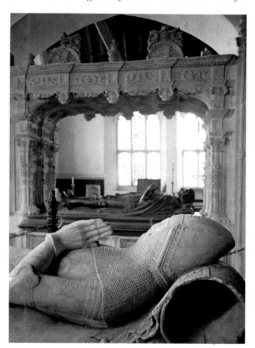

MARNEY TOMBS

The effigy of Sir William Marney in full armour is a typical example of English alabaster work of the 15th century, but the black marble figure of Henry, 1st Lord Marney under its elaborate terracotta canopy is a complete departure from English tradition—the work of Italian artists employed at Layer Marney Tower. (Church of St Mary, Layer Marney)

18th-CENTURY SHIP'S CANNON

This bronze cannon, one of a pair, was made in 1747, probably by José Solano in the royal cannon-foundry at Seville. The guns were almost certainly made for the Spanish navy and captured in 1762 by the British fleet in Havana; they are 41 in. long and have a calibre of $3\frac{1}{4}$ in. (Council Offices, Leatherhead)

---

include work by Charles Regnart (1800), John Flaxman (1803) and J. G. Lough (1857), but the finest of all is perhaps a praying priest of the late 13th century.

Ledsham *W. Yorks.*   *558Da*
CHURCH OF ALL SAINTS An essentially Saxon church, with a Saxon nave and chancel arch and a doorway in the tower. There is Norman and Gothic work and, inside, a Norman font and some medieval glass. There are 17th-century monuments with effigies, and one of *c.* 1739 by Peter Scheemakers.

Leeds *W. Yorks.*   *558Cb*
Many natural routes lead to and from Leeds; in the Middle Ages it was a market centre, and in 1626 Charles I created it a municipal borough to protect and regulate the wool trade. By the 19th century it was an obvious focal point for the Industrial Revolution's developing road, rail and canal system, and was raised to the status of a city in 1893. In 1933 George V opened the new civic hall.
ABBEY HOUSE MUSEUM The building was originally the great gate-house of Kirkstall Abbey, founded in 1152 by Cistercian monks from Fountains Abbey.
At the Dissolution of the monasteries John Ripley, the last abbot, converted the gate-house into a private dwelling and continued to live there; it was occupied for 800 years. Now a folk museum, it contains—as well as items of costume, dolls and toys, musical instruments and domestic bygones—three 'streets', with houses, cottages and shops, removed from the Leeds area and rebuilt in the museum.
CHURCH OF ST PETER A large 19th-century church which replaced the medieval one, but which contains effigies of knights and monuments by Andrew Carpenter, John Flaxman and Baron Marochetti. There is also a Saxon cross.
CITY MUSEUM The collections are mainly of geology, natural history and archaeology, the main emphasis being on Yorkshire, but with displays from all over the world.
Also in the museum is a model coal pit, which shows in minute detail all the workings of a full-scale mine.
TOWN HALL As a result of a competition held in 1853 and judged by Sir Charles Barry, Cuthbert

Brodrick's design for a new town hall was chosen.
His building, with a many-columned exterior, has a columned clock tower over 200 ft high. Work began in 1855, and the new town hall was opened by Queen Victoria in 1859. The building was decorated with sculpture by Matthew Noble and John Thomas. To commemorate the opening, Noble carved an 8 ft high statue of Queen Victoria as part of the decoration.

Leeds Castle *Kent*   *542Df*
There has been a stronghold at Leeds for more than 1,000 years and for 300 of them, from 1272, it belonged to the rulers of England. Edward I presented the castle to his queen, Eleanor of Aquitaine, establishing a tradition of queenly ownership that continued until the 15th century, when Catherine of Valois received Leeds from Henry V, victor of Agincourt. Henry VIII loved the castle and spent lavishly in adapting it to meet his extravagant tastes. Just before his death in 1547, he decided to make a gift of Leeds to Sir Anthony St Leger, Lord Deputy of Ireland. The banqueting hall bearing Henry's name is 75 ft long and richly furnished with tapestries and a wall-carpet. There is also a gallery of Impressionist paintings.

Leek *Staffs.*   *552Cd*
ART GALLERY The gallery exhibits work of the Leek Embroidery Society, and houses temporary exhibitions of paintings.

Leez (or Leighs) Priory *Essex*   *548Bd*
A 13th-century priory here was rebuilt by Lord Rich in 1536. The greater part of the house was razed in 1753, leaving only outer and inner gate-houses and parts of the outer quadrangle, all in richly ornamented red brick. Foundations of the priory church have been excavated.

Legis Tor *Devon*   *538Fc*
This Bronze Age settlement covers more than 4 acres. There are four walled enclosures with accompanying huts. The enclosure-walls were of stone-revetted earth, and the huts had low stone walls with timber and thatched roofs.

Leicester *Leics.*   *552Eb*
The history of the city goes back 2000 years to the Celts, whose settlement on the banks of the R. Soar grew into the Roman town of Ratae.
BELGRAVE HALL An house and gardens, which has 18th- and 19th-century furniture, and a collection of agricultural implements.
CATHEDRAL Formerly a parish church, raised to cathedral status in 1927. Originally Norman, there was much rebuilding until the 19th century, when Brandon, Street and Bodley did work there. There is a monument of 1656, which is signed by Joshua Marshall.
CHURCH OF ST MARGARET The south doorway and south arcade of the nave are 13th century; the rest of the building is of the 14th and 15th centuries and there is a large west tower. It was restored twice in the 19th century, once by Sir Gilbert Scott and then by G. E. Street. The stained glass, of *c.* 1840, is by T. Willement.
GUILDHALL This fine timbered building, begun in 1340, incorporates an ancient public library, first recorded in 1587. Among its collections is the *Codex Leicestrensis*, a 15th-century Greek manuscript of the New Testament.
JEWRY WALL In Roman times Ratae Coritanorum stood here, the cantonal town of the Coritani. Most of it is buried below modern Leicester, but the substantial fragment known as the Jewry Wall can be seen. It was the ornate façade of a great public baths-building and its covered exercise hall, which stood close to the centre of the town.

'THE LOVELIEST CASTLE IN THE WHOLE WORLD'

Seen from across the broad waters of its surrounding lake, fed by the River Len, Leeds is 'the loveliest castle in the whole world', according to Lord Conway, the great 19th-century castle expert. Its site, on two rocky islands, was chosen in the 9th century by Ledian, or Leed, chief minister to King Ethelbert IV of Kent. Ledian put up a wooden stronghold, linked to the shore by a drawbridge. The stone castle was started in 1119 by Robert de Crèvecoeur, a member of a Norman family related to William the Conqueror, and enlarged by a succession of owners, including Henry VIII, who transformed it into a sumptuous residence while retaining all its defensive features. Henry added the Maiden's Tower to house the Maids of Honour to his court, and Ann Boleyn may have stayed there before moving to the main castle as Henry's second queen. Leeds was extensively restored in 1822 and again from 1926. In its grounds there is a wild wood garden, and a duckery.

JEWRY WALL MUSEUM Remains of Roman public baths, pavements and wall-paintings. Displays of archaeology of Leicestershire, from earliest times to the Battle of Bosworth (1485).

LEICESTERSHIRE MUSEUM AND ART GALLERY It contains English paintings, modern art, ceramics and sculpture.

NEWARKE HOUSES MUSEUM Presents a social history of the city and county from 1500 to the present day. The museum of the Royal Leicestershire Regiment is housed in the Magazine close by.

Leighton Bromswold *Cambs.*　　547Hf
CHURCH OF ST MARY THE VIRGIN A medieval cruciform church, with nave and tower rebuilt in the early 17th century; the west tower has obelisk-pinnacles. On either side of the nave are twin pulpits. The church contains 16th-century monumental effigies.

Leighton Buzzard *Beds.*　　547Hd
CHURCH OF ALL SAINTS A large and impressive church, dating from the 13th century, it has a central tower and lofty spire completing its cruciform composition. Inside there is much to see, including a 13th-century font, 15th-century misericords and a wooden eagle lectern. The magnificent timber roofs have the flat pitch typical of 15th-century construction; the collegiate chancel dates from the same period and its screens and seating are still intact. The fine ironwork decoration on the west door is by Thomas of Leighton, who was also responsible for the grille on the tomb of Eleanor of Castile, the wife of Edward I, in Westminster Abbey. An interesting feature of the interior is the *graffiti* on piers and walls, all medieval. Many of the windows have good 19th-century glass by C. E. Kempe.

Leighton Hall *Lancs.*　　557Jc
In *c.* 1800 a neo-Gothic façade was superimposed on this Classical house, set in fine gardens. It contains examples of early Gillow furniture and for a time belonged to the Gillow family.

Leiston *Suffolk*　　548Ef
ABBEY Leiston is an industrial town; a mile away is Leiston Abbey, founded 1182 and transferred to its present site and rebuilt 200 years later. The remains are extensive but fragmentary; there is an early 16th-century gate-house with turrets.

Leith *Lothian*　　562Cf
LAMB'S HOUSE A merchant's house of *c.* 1600; it originally combined a residence and warehouse and was renovated in the 18th century.

Leith Hall *Grampian*　　566Ef
The country home of the Leith family since 1650, the Hall has numerous conical towers capped in the fashion of French châteaux. It contains many family and Jacobite relics and in the grounds is a fine rock garden.

Sam: Johnson

DR SAMUEL JOHNSON,
THE GREAT LEXICOGRAPHER

'Cut out the cant' is perhaps the central theme of the man who has gone down in history as the embodiment of a typical Englishman. Johnson was the son of a Lichfield bookseller; his birthplace is now a museum, and the Dame's School and Grammar School where he was educated can still be seen in Lichfield. At 28, Johnson rode to London to make his fortune. 'No man but a blockhead ever wrote except for money', he said, but in the following 18 years of hack-writing he barely made enough to live on. His articles in *The Rambler* made his name, and the publication of his dictionary confirmed his reputation as the most formidable figure in literary London.

SAMUEL JOHNSON *by Sir Joshua Reynolds (1756),* close friend who painted him several times. Johnson stoo 6 ft among his contemporaries, whose average height wa 5 ft 5 in., and such was his humanity that he would hoi sick beggars on to his back and carry them home to foo and comfort. (National Portrait Gallery)

PORTABLE DESK *belonging to D Samuel Johnson. He said of his craft ' man may write at any time if he set h mind doggedly to it'. (Johnson Birth place, Lichfield)*

DICTIONARY OF THE ENGLIS LANGUAGE *published in 1755 afte eight years work. The entry unde 'Lexicographer' reads 'a writer dictionaries—a harmless drudge'.* (First edition at the British Library)

THE GARRET *where Johnson compile the dictionary can be seen at 17 Goug Square, London. When the messenge who carried the last sheet of th dictionary to the publisher returne Johnson asked him 'Well, what d he say?' 'Sir', answered the messenge 'he said—"Thank God I have don with him."' 'I am glad,' answered th doctor, with a smile, 'that he thank God for anything.'*

A TAVERN SCENE by Samuel Percy, made out of wax. It shows Dr Johnson holding court among members of 'The Club', which met once a week at the Old Cock Tavern. This Literary Club was founded in 1773 by Joshua Reynolds—no mean conversationalist himself—'in order to give Dr Johnson unlimited opportunities for talking'. The figures are traditionally identified, from left to right: a servant holding a mop in mock homage, Dr Johnson, Reynolds with his ear trumpet, an unidentified man, Thomas Gainsborough the painter, General Paoli, the Corsican leader who was lionised in London at this time and Charles James Fox the statesman. Johnson had many close friends, and in 1763 rescued the author and dramatist Oliver Goldsmith from a debtors' prison. (London Museum)

JOHNSON'S CHAIR, used during last illness. 'Sir, you cannot ceive with what acceleration I ance toward death', he said to a end; he died on December 13, 1784. hnson Birthplace, Lichfield)

WEDDING RING belonging to Mrs Johnson. 'Marriage has many pains but celibacy has no pleasures', wrote the doctor. He was a 26-year-old hack writer when he married a well-to-do widow almost twice his age, with three children. Johnson was not inclined to discuss his 'beloved Tetty' with his young friends, but the marriage was one of strong affection. Mrs Johnson died in 1752, two years after Johnson had become recognised as a writer with his twice-weekly essays in 'The Rambler'; her husband took this ring from her finger and wore it thereafter himself. His grief was profound; but work, good company and talk helped to keep melancholia at bay. (Johnson Birthplace, Lichfield)

DR JOHNSON'S TEAPOT He was a 'hardened and shameless tea drinker . . . who with tea amuses the evening . . . and with tea welcomes the morning'. Like talk, it was a passion with him. (Johnson Birthplace, Lichfield)

OLDE CHESHIRE CHEESE, a 300-ar-old inn, with sawdusted floor, in ine Office Court, close to Johnson's use in Gough Square. The doctor ieved 'a tavern chair is the seat of man felicity', and is said to have quented this inn. The seat he is pposed to have favoured is marked th a brass plate. On one wall hangs aricature of Johnson and Boswell by sley, an American artist of the early th century, which was discovered ently in the cellars. James Boswell t Johnson in 1763, and though the st sentence the great man spoke to n was a snub, the persistent Scot an to make notes of Johnson's versation almost at once, with a w to writing his life. This 'Life of nuel Johnson', which occupied the xt 20 years of his life, was published 1791, seven years after Johnson's th, and to it both he and Boswell e their immortality.

THE WEST FAÇADE OF
LICHFIELD CATHEDRAL

*Lichfield is the only English cathedral to preserve
three stone spires—though the central one was
destroyed during the Civil War and was rebuilt.
Lichfield also has the distinction of having once been
the seat of an archbishopric. The See was established
by the missionary, St Chad, in 669, as the main
centre of Christianity in the Kingdom of Mercia.
In the 8th century, during the reign of Offa, Mercia
became the dominant English kingdom and Offa
obtained papal permission to have his bishop elevated
to the dignity of archbishop in 785. However, Offa
died in 796 and his successors quickly lost Mercia's
pre-eminence, and in 803 Lichfield was down-graded
again to the status of bishopric. The existing cathedral
dates only from the 13th century. From 1200 to 1240
the choir, transepts and chapter house were built, and
the nave followed about 1250. The west façade, built
about 1300, has the appearance of a magnificent
screen filled with sculpture, and dominates the small
doorways at its base.*

Lennoxlove *Lothian* 562De
Formerly Lethington Tower, the home of the
Maitlands; William Maitland (1528–73) was secretary and counsellor to Mary, Queen of Scots—the
lime avenue in the grounds is called 'Politician's
Walk' after him. The mansion has a pre-15th-
century tower, and the entrance door dates from
1626. Mary's death mask is on view.

Leominster *Heref. & Worcs.* 546Af
CHURCH OF SS PETER AND PAUL The priory was
built in the 12th century, but most of the buildings
disappeared after the Dissolution of the monasteries. The nave survives on the north side, with a
Norman arcade and triforium, a west doorway,
and the north aisle. The south aisle was completed

in 1300. There is a pre-Reformation chalice and a
ducking-stool on display.

Leonardslee Gardens *W. Sussex* 542Be
Spring-flowering gardens famous for camellias,
magnolias and the Loderi rhododendron.

Leonard Stanley *Glos.* 546Cc
CHURCH OF ST SWITHIN The cruciform church,
largely 12th-century Norman, was originally part
of the Augustinian priory. The massive central
tower has a fine stair turret. Perpendicular windows have been inserted on the north of the nave,
and all have clear glass. There are some good
Norman doorways and tower arches. The original
cloisters have disappeared.

Lerwick *Shetland* 568Ee
SHETLAND MUSEUM The history of Shetland and
man's life there is the theme of the museum.
Archaeology, folk life, shipping and seafaring, and
textiles and art are among the themes of the
collections.

Leuchars *Fife* 562Ch
CHURCH OF ST ATHERNASE A modern church built
on to a magnificent chancel and apse dating from
the 12th century—one of the best examples of
Norman work in Scotland. Above the apse is a
17th-century bell-turret.

Levens Hall *Cumbria* 557Jd
An Elizabethan mansion added to a 13th-century
pele tower. It contains fine pictures and Charles II
furniture. A unique collection of steam engines is
in steam when the house is open. The famous
topiary garden was laid out in 1692 and is little
altered.

Leverington *Cambs.* 553Jb
LEVERINGTON HALL One of the better houses in
the county, part Elizabethan and part built 1660–
75. There are two chimney-breasts, mullioned
windows, straight gables of the 18th century and a
good staircase. The parish has several other 17th-
and 18th-century houses, including Hallcroft and
Lancewood. Beechwood, half a mile south of the
church, has a dove-cote of 1600 or earlier. Park
House and the rectory, half a mile north-west of
the church, are good 18th-century houses. (By
appointment.)

Lewes *E. Sussex* 542Ca
The county town of the area and one of the most
worth-while towns in the county to walk around.
The High Street contains most of the best work.
Georgian houses predominate: many have mathematical tiles, which give the impression of their
having brick fronts. North of the street is the
Castle, its early 12th-century keep on a high
mound and protected by a massive 14th-century
outer gatehouse or barbican.
ANNE OF CLEVES HOUSE A half-timbered house
built *c.* 1500 and given to Anne of Cleves by
Henry VIII after their divorce in 1540, it is now a
folk museum. As well as furniture, costumes and
household equipment it contains a collection of
ironwork.
BARBICAN HOUSE Elizabethan house, with later
adaptations, now a museum of Sussex archaeology
of the prehistoric, Roman, Saxon and medieval
periods. It also contains a collection of Sussex
paintings and prints.

Lewknor *Oxon.* 547Gc
CHURCH OF ST MARGARET A small church, with a
late medieval west tower. There is a good
Norman font with sculptured roundels, and some
17th- and 18th-century monuments, one by Sir
J. E. Boehm of *c.* 1882.

Lichfield *Staffs.* *552Cb*

Lichfield has been given six royal charters, the earliest granted by Richard II in 1387. The charter of Mary I in 1553 made the city a county in its own right, separate and distinct from Staffordshire, electing its own sheriff. Its outstanding feature is the cathedral, built in the years 1195–1325: it is the only English cathedral to retain its group of three spires, which are known as the Ladies of the Vale. In the close, the canons' houses are splendid examples of Tudor domestic architecture.

Ancient buildings include the friary and friary gardens, with links with the Grey Friars of 1229, and Dame Oliver's School where Dr Johnson was a schoolmaster. The Vicar's Close has buildings of the 14th and 15th centuries. Milley's Hospital, founded in 1423 and endowed and rebuilt in 1504 by Dr Thomas Milley, has a fine gateway. Lichfield, for long a centre of pilgrimage to St Chad, was the birthplace of Dr Samuel Johnson (1709–84), the great lexicographer, whose childhood house in the Market Square is now a museum. Other famous men of Lichfield were Joseph Addison (1672–1719), essayist, poet and statesman, and David Garrick (1717–79), the actor who was Dr Johnson's first pupil.

CATHEDRAL England's only medieval three-spired cathedral, originally of Saxon foundation, and dedicated to St Chad, appointed Bishop of Mercia in 669. Chad lived at Lichfield, which became a place of pilgrimage, and the cathedral was built with money donated by the pilgrims. The present church suffered badly at the hands of Cromwell's troops: they shot down the central tower, and pillaged lead and other metals. After the Restoration of the Monarchy in 1660, the long task of rebuilding began. In the 18th and 19th centuries restorers were more keen to replace than to preserve. On the west front there are more than 100 carved statues. The cathedral contains what is probably the most famous of Sir Francis Chantrey's monuments, *The Sleeping Children*, which he completed in 1817. Other monuments are by E. H. Baily, Edward Stanton, Richard Westmacott the Elder and Sir Jacob Epstein.

STAFFORDSHIRE REGIMENTAL MUSEUM This amalgamation of the former North and South Staffordshire Regimental Museums consists of uniforms, weapons, battle trophies, medals, documents and pictures. Relics of Field Marshals Wolseley and Colin Campbell can be seen, along with relics of the American War of Independence. The museum is at Whittington Barracks.

Lilleshall *Shropshire* *552Bc*

CHURCH OF ST MICHAEL AND ALL ANGELS The 13th-century church contains the extravagant Leveson Monument dating from 1764. There is also an excellent Saxon font.

Lilleshall Abbey *Shropshire* *552Bc*

Impressive ruins of a house founded for Arroasian canons *c.* 1148. The main survival is the church, which is entered through a large round-headed door of the late 12th century. Remains of the façade exist, with some Early English arcading. The church was aisle-less, a feature commonly found in Augustinian churches. The canons' choir lay to the east, under the crossing. Much of the transept is destroyed, but the two chapels off the south transept still exist. Probably the best surviving piece of architecture is the south door from the church to the cloister—a fine example of late 12th-century Norman decoration. Still traceable to the east are the chapter house and slype (the dormitory would have been above these).

Limpsfield *Surrey* *542Cf*

DETILLENS An early 18th-century frontage with bays conceals a 15th-century hall house typical of those built by the yeomen of the Weald. It has a fine king-post roof in the upper room, and contains collections of furniture, porcelain and china, military items and medals.

Lincoln *Lincs.* *553Ge*

The ancient British town of Lindon was renamed Lindum by the Roman occupation forces, and, on development, was raised to colony status, giving Lindum Colonia as the root for the present name. In AD 48 a Roman military garrison was set up to command the meeting of two great highways, Ermine Street and Fosse Way.

CARDINAL'S HAT Situated at the corner of Grantham Street and High Street, a splendid example of a late 15th-century house. Named after Cardinal Wolsey, it was restored in 1953. Near the lower end of the Strait is a row of good timbered houses.

CASTLE Built on a Roman site by William the Conqueror in 1068; the surrounding ditches and banks enclosed nearly 14 acres of land. Entry was through the surviving eastern gateway, a structure which has a Norman tunnel-vault internally but a 15th-century façade. The castle's remains include a Norman gateway, part of a barbican and an early 19th-century inner gateway. The gaol, *c.* 1780, is now the Lincolnshire Archives Office and has the largest collection of local records in England. The castle walls carry three interesting towers: to the south-east the Observatory Tower (built by a prison governor in the 19th century for observing the stars as well as possible escapees); the Lucy Tower, a Norman shell-keep standing on a separate mound, *c.* 1200; and Cobb Hall, the small north-east tower, *c.* 1400.

CATHEDRAL The original Norman cathedral was begun in 1072, and parts of this building remain at

WEST FRONT FRIEZE,
LINCOLN CATHEDRAL

The west front of Lincoln Cathedral, one of the earliest Norman cathedrals in England, was built by Bishop Remigius between 1072 and 1092. It was enlarged in the following century, and a sculptured frieze showing scenes from the Old and New Testaments was added at the same time. This detail from the frieze, which runs above the niches, is from the panel showing Noah building the ark.

LINCOLN CATHEDRAL

Lincoln became the centre of a bishopric in 1072, when the See was transferred from Dorchester (Oxfordshire). A cathedral was begun at once, but much of the present church dates from after an earthquake in 1185. It has been little altered since its completion about 1280. Lincoln has had one of the most varied successions of bishops of any English See. Among them were Alexander the Magnificent (1123–48), the illegitimate son of the influential royal servant, Bishop Roger of Salisbury, who was probably responsible for the Romanesque parts of the west front; St Hugh of Avalon (1186–

1200), an ascetic Carthusian, brought unwillingly from his monastery; and Robert Grosseteste (1235–53), a strong supporter of Oxford University in its early years, when it fell within the Diocese of Lincoln. Inside the cathedral, St Hugh's choir and the nave are impressive examples of early Gothic architecture, with fine columns of Purbeck stone; over the choir is a complicated system of arches—the 'crazy vaults of Lincoln'. To the east, the Angel Choir is one of the most heavily decorated of its period. The whole interior is dominated by the immense traceried window in the east end.

the west end of the present church, where three elaborate Norman portals are surmounted by a magnificent sculptured frieze which dates from *c.* 1145. The main cathedral is in Gothic style; the rebuilding of the choir was begun in 1192, and rebuilding of the western part of the church followed. The Angel Choir—so-called from its interior decoration—was added in 1254–80. Thereafter only small additions were made to the cathedral. On the south side is a sculptured porch. The decagonal chapter house, on the north side, is the earliest Gothic polygonal chapter house in England. Great Tom of Lincoln—a sonorous 5 ton bell—hangs in the central tower. (See also p. 271.) The Medieval and Wren Libraries contain a fine collection of manuscripts and early books.

CATHEDRAL TREASURY Sponsored by the Worshipful Company of Goldsmiths and Silversmiths, the Treasury was opened in 1960 in the renovated 'Medicine Chapel' of the cathedral. It shows a changing collection of gold and silver plate from the diocese as well as a few permanent exhibits. The latter include medieval chalices and patens taken from the graves of the Bishops Grosseteste, Sutton and Gravesend. The Treasury also contains the cathedral's original of Magna Carta and the foundation charter of William the Conqueror.

CITY AND COUNTY MUSEUM The museum, which displays collections of armour, local archaeological finds with emphasis on Roman Lincoln, and natural history, is in an early 13th-century building, originally a church for the Greyfriars.

HIGH BRIDGE Built on one side of the bridge spanning the R. Witham are 16th-century timber-framed houses and shops; the bridge is one of the

few surviving examples of its kind in England.

HOUSE OF AARON THE JEW Situated at the corner of Steep Hill and Christ's Hospital Terrace, this 12th-century house is said to be the oldest inhabited dwelling in England; it takes its name from the original owner, a rich merchant. Lower down the hill is the better known Jew's House, of the same date, and one of the best known houses of its period in England.

JAMES STREET Contains two notable houses: Deloraine Court, whose Georgian façade hides a Norman undercroft and a well-panelled room dated 1602; and No. 7, the Burghersh Chantry, founded in 1345 for five priests, but now mainly mid-18th century.

JEW'S HOUSE In 12th-century England Jews could often afford to build themselves modest town houses of stone, for in the English economy then, Jews were essential as money-lenders and financiers because Christians were forbidden to lend money at interest. One of the greatest of the Jewish businessmen was Aaron the Jew of Lincoln. His operations were known to have extended over 25 counties from Kent to Cumberland. His clients included the King of Scotland and the Archbishop of Canterbury. It is not certain whether Aaron lived at the Jew's House, since a further 12th-century building traditionally attached to his name survives. Both houses are interesting reminders of the presence of Jews in 12th-century England. These stone houses were symbols of power and wealth, and they were also places of strength. The Jews were only too useful, but in return they were hated and up to their expulsion under Edward I in 1290, periodic anti-Jewish riots occurred.

NOLLEKENS *Venus and Cupid*

Joseph Nollekens (1737–1823) carved this marble statue of Venus chiding Cupid for one of his chief patrons, Lord Yarborough. Nollekens, one of England's greatest portrait sculptors, worked for ten years in Rome, and it is for his severely Classical busts, like that of Dr Johnson in Westminster Abbey, that he is chiefly remembered. Much less well known are his statues of goddesses, but he probably considered them to embody his best work. Nollekens was probably the shrewdest businessman of English art, and amassed a fortune of £200,000. (Usher Gallery, Lincoln)

ROMAN TOWN GATE Roman Lincoln (Lindum) began as a legionary fortress in the middle of the 1st century AD. By AD 75 the soldiers had gone and, *c.* AD 90, it was made a *colonia*, a settlement of time-served soldiers who formed a self-governing local community of importance. This *colonia* covered the site of the earlier fortress on the hill-top to the north of the Witham. Fragments of its stone wall are still visible. But the most important fragment, unique in Britain, is the Newport Arch which straddles the main road to the North out of the town. The south face of this arch is the original Roman stone, though behind it there is much medieval reconstruction and the original north (outer) face has disappeared. The area of the *colonia* was later extended down the slope to the south. This too was walled, and the new south gate stood only a little way above the still-visible medieval gateway, the Stonebow. The city museum contains many remains from the Roman occupation.
STONEBOW AND GUILDHALL The Stonebow is a 16th-century gateway with the guildhall above it: it stands on the site of a 13th-century gate and an earlier Roman one. The guildhall, partly panelled and with a magnificent open-timbered roof, contains portraits and carries on the roof the Mote Bell. The oldest bell of its type in the country, dated 1371, it is still rung to summon Council members to meetings. The civic insignia and royal charters include a 14th-century fighting sword, believed to have been presented to the city by Richard II in 1387.
USHER GALLERY The Usher Collection of watches, miniatures and porcelain, and the Peter de Wint Collection of oils, water-colours and drawings are the principal exhibits in the gallery. There are also portraits and various relics of the poet laureate Alfred, Lord Tennyson (1809–92).

Lindisfarne Castle See Holy Island.

Lindisfarne Priory See Holy Island.

Lindores Abbey *Fife*   *562Ch*
The ruins of a Benedictine abbey founded in 1178.

Lingfield *Surrey*   *542Be*
CHURCH OF SS PETER AND PAUL 15th-century, but with some earlier work in the south-west of the building. The fittings are contemporary: font, screens, stalls with misericords, and lectern with a chained Bible. Among many brasses and monuments with effigies there is a good series devoted to the Cobham family.

Linlithgow *Lothian*   *562Af*
CHURCH OF ST MICHAEL A fine medieval parish church with a west tower, transepts and a three-sided apse. There are several sculptured slabs, two of which depict the Mocking of Christ and the Agony in the Garden.
PALACE The ruined palace where Mary, Queen of Scots was born on December 8, 1542. A royal manor has existed on this site since early in the 12th century. During the campaigns of Edward I in the early 14th century the area was fortified by a ditch and palisade. Edward used Linlithgow as a base of operations, particularly during the siege of Stirling Castle. However, it was retaken by the Scots *c.* 1313, and the fortifications were demolished. James I of Scotland began the present building in 1424 and the work continued into the 16th century, particularly under James V. By the late 16th century parts of the palace had become derelict and in 1607 the north side collapsed; it was repaired in 1618–33.

Little Bytham *Lincs.*   *553Gc*
CHURCH OF ST MEDARD The church incorporates Saxon work from the original building (in the south-east corner of the nave), and there is Norman work too. In the south chancel doorway is an interestingly carved tympanum, with a sunken circular medallion in its centre, which is said to have once contained the skull and arm-bone of St Medard, the patron saint of the church.

Little Casterton *Leics.*   *553Gb*
CHURCH OF ALL SAINTS A small church with a west bell-cote. It dates from the 12th century, and has carvings of that date. Some 14th-century wall-painting remains, and there is a good medieval brass in the chancel of a man and his wife.

Little Chesterford *Essex*   *548Ae*
MANOR HOUSE A rare surviving manor house of the early 13th century, with thick stone walls and arched doorways inside. An aisled timber-framed hall was added later.

Little Coggeshall *Essex*   *548Cd*
The remains of a Cistercian abbey of *c.* 1140, interesting for the early use of brickwork. The church has disappeared, and after the Reformation a house was built into the monastic ruins, dated 1581. The Abbey Gate Chapel of St Nicholas survives as a rectangular building of *c.* 1225.

Littlecote *Wilts.*   *541Gg*
MANOR HOUSE A gabled Tudor mansion built between 1490 and 1520, Littlecote House has a splendid great hall. There are plans to devote other rooms to a Civil War museum, featuring Littlecote's fine collection of Cromwellian arms and armour. The house contains period panelling and plasterwork, tapestries and furniture.

An early 19th-century watch made by James Rigby of London. The gold and blue enamel case has a double border of half pearls set with brilliant cut diamonds.

A French repeater watch of the early 19th century. The engine-turned case has an enamelled dial with a pierced design showing Venus receiving an apple from Cupid.

The chased and pierced gold outer case of this quarter repeater is set with diamonds, rubies and moss agate plaques; a mid-18th-century watch made by Ferron of London.

The enamelled outer case of this watch depicts Venus rising from the sea. Vienna-made in the 1800's in 17th-century style, it has a gilt and champlevé enamel dial.

This watch dates from the late 18th century; it was produced by Gregson of Paris. The outer case has an enamelled design showing Narcissus at the pool.

The gold outer case of this watch, made by Baillon of Paris in the mid-18th century, has an enamelled miniature, 'Abraham offering Isaac', on its back.

ROMAN VILLA In the early 18th century, William George, steward of the Littlecote estate, found, in the manor house deer park, the remains of a Roman villa, including a large mosaic floor. George died shortly afterwards and the location was subsequently lost. Archaeologists have been excavating the site since 1978.

Little Dunmow *Essex*   *548Bd*
CHURCH OF ST MARY The remnants of an early 12th-century Augustinian priory church, which was once cruciform with a central tower; all that remains is the 13th-century south chapel, or Lady Chapel. The arcade along the north wall would have been the south arcade of the chancel of the former church. Monuments include one by Thomas Adye, 1753.

Little Gidding *Cambs.*   *547Hg*
Outside the door of the small church in the village is the table-tomb of Nicholas Ferrar, whose family

manor house (now destroyed) stood near by. Nicholas Ferrar (1592–1637) was a friend of religious poets John Donne and George Herbert. He founded a religious community known as the Arminian Nunnery, which was used by T. S. Eliot as an example of achieved spiritual life in the last of his 'Four Quartets' entitled 'Little Gidding'.

Little Malvern *Heref. & Worcs.*   *546Be*
CHURCH OF ST GILES There was a 12th-century Benedictine monastery here, and the adjoining court incorporates part of its domestic buildings, but all that remains of the church is the central tower and east end, dating from the 15th century. The 15th-century stained glass in the east window depicts Edward IV and his family. Much of the 15th-century floor tiling remains, and there are also misericords.

Little Maplestead *Essex*   *548Ce*
CHURCH OF ST JOHN THE BAPTIST One of the five round churches of England, built *c.* 1340 by the

A French musical watch of the early 19th century. The gold case is set with pearl borders and on the back is an enamelled picture above moving figures in a ballroom.

This early 19th-century Swiss watch is in the form of a mandolin. The gold case is embellished with pearls and enamel.

An early 19th-century French repeater striking on wire gongs. The gold case has mechanical figures in vari-coloured gold on the face and an engine-turned back.

A quarter repeater made by Justin Vulliamy in London during the mid-18th century. An enamelled miniature of 'Hope nursing Love', after Reynolds, decorates the case.

W. Ilbery of London made this early 19th-century watch for the Chinese market. Its gold case has an enamelled miniature of girls and a youth butterfly hunting.

This watch, hall-marked London, 1824/5, was made by Viner and Co. The chased vari-coloured gold case is set with 54 emeralds and the watch has a cylinder movement.

Knights Hospitaller. The chancel projecting towards the east has an apse, and dates from the same period.

Little Moreton Hall *Cheshire* 552Bd
Built between 1450 and 1580, Little Moreton is one of the most picturesque half-timbered houses in the county. With leaning walls, ornate gables and windows, it looks like a vast, unstable dolls' house. There is a wealth of carved timber, indoors and out, and the long gallery retains its original panelling. Contemporary oak furniture and pewter are on view.

Little Sodbury Manor *Avon* 546Bb
A 15th-century mansion built for Sir John Walsh; its outstanding feature is the great hall. The north-west wing was destroyed by fire in 1702.

Little Stanmore *Greater London* 547Jc
CHURCH OF ST LAWRENCE (WHITCHURCH) There is a 14th-century west tower, but the rest of the church dates from the early 18th century when it was rebuilt by the Duke of Chandos, whose great house by Talman was near by. There are paintings by Louis Laguerre, Antonio Verrio and Antonio Bellucci, and monuments in the Chandos Mausoleum, the largest being that of the duke by Grinling Gibbons. The furnishings include contemporary pews, a west gallery, and an organ on which Handel occasionally played.

Littleton *Surrey* 542Ag
CHURCH OF ST MARY MAGDALENE The church is of the 12th century, with additions right through to the 18th century. The west tower is brick. There are good furnishings from the 15th to the 18th century.

Little Walsingham *Norfolk* 554Bc
The site of the famous shrine of Our Lady of Walsingham, one of the chief centres of pilgrimage in England from early medieval times until the Reformation. The shrine was founded in 1061 by

THE ANGLICAN CATHEDRAL, LIVERPOOL

EXTERIOR *The largest Anglican cathedral in the world is 671 ft long and has a central tower 331 ft high. It was completed in 1978, after nearly 75 years' work. Standing on high ground overlooking the Mersey, the massive, towering cathedral is the overpowering achievement of one man: Sir Giles Gilbert Scott, grandson of Sir George Gilbert Scott, architect of the Albert Memorial. Scott was 22 when, in 1901, he won a competition to design it. Building began in 1904, but two World Wars and rising costs delayed progress, and by the time Scott died, in 1960, his original design had been modified several times.*

THE HIGH ALTAR *The interior of Scott's cathedral lacks the rich ornamentation of Victorian Gothic architecture; he has re-interpreted Gothic forms to create an atmosphere of vastness, grandeur and silence, rather than of gloom. The massive piers seem to lose themselves in the darkness as they soar uninterrupted towards the lofty vaults. The windows,* set in thick walls, admit only glimmerings of light. Liverpool will probably be the last cathedral in Britain to be built entirely of stone; it may also, perhaps, turn out to be the finest ecclesiastical building of the 20th century—economic difficulties and the decline of the mason's craft have put a stop to cathedral-building on such a gigantic scale.

Richeldis de Faverches, a young widow and Lady of the Manor, as the result of a vision in which she was transported to Nazareth. In the vision she was commanded by the Virgin to build a replica of Christ's birthplace. She did so at Walsingham and, as the story spread, pilgrims came from all over Europe to pay homage in the little village. There are 14th- and 15th-century remains of the Augustinian priory that looked after the shrine, whose exact site is that of the raised area of lawn just north of the church. Modern pilgrims attend the Slipper Chapel, where their forbears left their shoes before walking the last mile barefoot: there is also an Anglican shrine, built 1931–7.

The village has many interesting houses in the Common Place (which has a Pump House of c. 1550 topped by a brazier), High Street and Market Place. In part of the priory ruins is Abbey House, late 18th century. On the Fakenham road are the ruins of the Franciscan (Greyfriars) friary of 1347.

Little Wymondley *Herts.*   547Jd
WYMONDLEY HALL An early 17th-century timber-framed house with a fine group of Elizabethan chimneys.
WYMONDLEY PRIORY A medieval barn 100 ft long and 40 ft wide, with the remains of 13th-century arches in the farmhouse alongside.

Liverpool *Lancs.*   551Jf
The city holds a charter granted by King John in 1207. It had a Norman castle (on the site of the present Queen Victoria memorial) the ruins of which were removed in 1725. At the time of the first Stuarts the population was only 1000, but by the early 18th century the town had a thriving trade mainly connected with the West Indies, and was also concerned with the slave trade. The coming of the railways altered Liverpool entirely, and it was from this port that the first ocean steamship line operated across the Atlantic in 1840.

Sudley Gallery, an early 19th-century merchant's house, supplements the treasures of the Walker Art Gallery. The Picton, Hornby and Brown libraries together have more than 200,000 volumes. Liverpool University originated with University College (1881), which was raised by royal charter in 1903 to full university status. The city has two cathedrals, Anglican and Roman Catholic.
ANGLICAN CATHEDRAL The red sandstone Anglican cathedral of Liverpool was begun in 1904 by Sir Giles Gilbert Scott, the Lady Chapel was consecrated in 1910 and Scott himself laid the last stone of the 331 ft central tower—the cathedral's dominant feature—in 1925. However, it was not until 1978 that the vast building was completed. The west end of the cathedral was the last section to be finished. Among its features are a bridge spanning the nave and a great window containing 1,600 sq ft of glass. The style of the cathedral is Gothic, but Scott's design, modified during construction, is essentially original.
BLUECOAT CHAMBERS An example of Queen Anne architecture, built in 1717, the building was acquired in 1927 as a centre for painters, sculptors, musicians and the arts generally under the supervision of the Bluecoat Society of Arts. (By appointment.)
COUNTY MUSEUM The original building, designed by John Weightman and built in 1860, was destroyed by fire in 1941, leaving the façade intact. The museum has now been rebuilt. The newest gallery has sections devoted to Ancient Egypt, Greece, Etruria, Cyprus and Rome, and the Dark Ages. There are also displays on Africa (mainly Yoruba, Ebo and Benin), New Guinea and

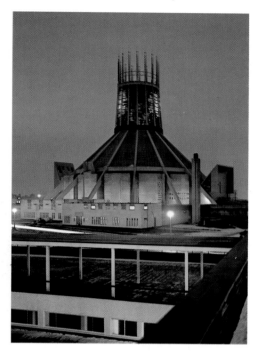

THE ROMAN CATHOLIC
CATHEDRAL, LIVERPOOL

This cathedral of Christ the King, constructed to a strikingly modern design, was consecrated in May 1967. A vast circular building set on a hill, it was achieved at the third attempt. Edwin Welby Pugin designed a cathedral in 1853, but only the Lady Chapel was built. In 1928 Sir Edwin Lutyens conceived an enormous Classical domed building on the present site; work started but was interrupted at the outbreak of the Second World War when the crypt was nearly completed. After the war, Lutyens' design was abandoned because of the astronomical cost involved. In 1959 Archbishop Heenan offered the design for a new cathedral to open competition and Sir Frederick Gibberd's design was chosen from 300 entries. The building rises from a large base, part of which forms a vast piazza over Lutyens' crypt. The altar is in the centre of the cathedral and the congregation is able to participate in services to a greater extent than in a conventional cathedral.

primitive art. Other collections include historical musical instruments, porcelain, enamels, ivories, arms and armour, coins, clocks and watches, English silver, pottery, costumes and textiles. There are also galleries devoted to natural history, a planetarium and an aquarium.
HORNBY LIBRARY This library of about 8000 books includes medieval manuscripts, early printed books, and natural-history works with hand-coloured illustrations and fine bindings. There are good collections of the work of Bewick, Cruikshank and modern private presses. Among the prints are Dürer woodcuts, Rembrandt etchings and engraved portraits by Nanteuil. There are also signatures of Elizabeth I, Nelson and Napoleon.
ROMAN CATHOLIC CATHEDRAL The circular cathedral was consecrated in 1967; its dominant feature is the central lantern tower with slender, spiky pinnacles, some 290 ft high, above an aluminium roof. This lantern, with stained glass by John Piper and Patrick Reyntiens (who also worked on Coventry Cathedral) illuminates the interior of the cathedral with a pool of light over

TREASURES OF LIVERPOOL

ERCOLE: PIETÀ *Ercole de Roberti, who lived about 1450–96, belonged to the northern Italian school of Ferrara; but he softened the harshness of the Ferrarese style—the petrified landscapes, grimacing faces, contorted figures. However, the style has still left its mark here, in for example the hard, jagged outline of the Virgin's robe. The Pietà—Christ's body lying across the Virgin's knees—is a theme which originated in Germany in the 13th century. Ercole's painting, which was in the Church of San Giovanni in Monte at Bologna, is similar in arrangement to the marble Pietà at St Peter's, which was the masterpiece of Michelangelo's early period. It is tempting to assume that Michelangelo saw this painting during his stay in Bologna in 1494–5. (Walker Art Gallery)*

LE HONGRE: CUPID *This intimate, informal bronze figure is one of the rare examples of French baroque sculpture in Britain. It is by Étienne le Hongre (1628–90), one of the small army of artists employed on the decoration of Versailles for Louis XIV. Le Hongre lived and had his workshop in the Palace of the Louvre in Paris. (Walker Art Gallery)*

ST JOHN THE BAPTIST *A striking Byzantine ivory, showing the Court style of Constantinople at its most refined. The Baptist holds a scroll which says, in Greek: 'Behold the Lamb of God, who taketh away the sins of the world.' The figure and scroll date from the late 10th century, but the background is modern—the original one was lost. (County Museum)*

KINGSTON BROOCH *This great gold brooch, 3·3 in. across, is the finest example of the work of the 'Kentish School' of Anglo-Saxon jewellers. It belongs to the first half of the 7th century, and the technique is known as 'cloisonné'—the jewels, flat pieces of red garnet, blue glass and shell, are set in small prepared cells, the cloisons. (County Museum)*

BRACKET CLOCK MADE BY DANIEL QUARE *Bracket clocks (more accurately called table clocks) were designed to be carried from room to room because of their scarcity and value. They were fitted with a handle and their backs are as decorative as their fronts. This clock, made in 1685, has a case of ebony lined with red silk, gilded brass mounts and a pierced basket top. (County Museum)*

MARTINI: CHRIST DISCOVERED IN THE TEMPLE *The 14th-century Sienese school reached its zenith in the work of Simone Martini (1284–1344). His figures have a new suppleness and grace. This picture, dated 1342, was painted after he had reached Avignon, then the seat of the Papacy. His work there had an important influence on the development of the sophisticated 'International Gothic' style. (Walker Art Gallery)*

PLAS NEWYDD, LLANGOLLEN

Famous as the home of the 'Ladies of Llangollen', two Irishwomen who left their native land in 1778 with their maid, Mary Carryl, and settled in Wales. They lived in the house for some 50 years, and their powers of conversation, coupled with a reputation for eccentricity, drew scores of interesting visitors. The playwright Sheridan, the statesmen Burke, Castlereagh and Canning, emigrés from the French Revolution, the Duke of Wellington, Sir Walter Scott and William Wordsworth were all drawn to this beautiful but out-of-the-way spot by the fascination of the 'Ladies'. The ruined castle on the hill is Dinas Bran.

the central altar. Radiating from the walls are chapels of various shapes, with stained glass windows and austere ornament. At the west is a wedge-shaped belfry-cum-porch, 90 ft high, forming the principal entrance. (See p. 277.)

ST GEORGE'S HALL Liverpool possesses one of the great Victorian Classical buildings—St George's Hall, masterpiece of the young architect, Harvey Lonsdale Elmes. He began work on it in 1842, but died at the age of 34 in 1847, long before the project was finished. The great vault was the work of Sir Robert Rawlinson, to Elmes's designs, and C. R. Cockerell completed the exterior and the interior decoration. St George's Hall, inaugurated in 1854, stands in the centre of the city. The Hall is of Classical Greek design; the façade has a great portico of Corinthian columns, and is further decorated with partly free-standing square piers of the same order. There is another, smaller portico of columns at the south end of the Hall, while the north end is semicircular.

SPEKE HALL A timber-framed manor house in the ornate South Lancashire and Cheshire style. It was built around a courtyard from 1490 to 1612 by the Norris family, who owned it until 1736. Internally it is like a maze, with secret chambers and hideaways. The great parlour has an early 17th-century stucco ceiling, and the great hall has a wainscot of 1560–4. The contents include furniture of the 17th, 18th and 19th centuries, tapestries, domestic utensils, and William Morris wallpaper.

SUDLEY ART GALLERY The house, built *c.* 1823 and extended in 1883 for George Holt, contains his collection of Victorian paintings, with works by Turner, Holman Hunt, Millais and Landseer. Fine 18th-century portraits include Gainsborough's *Viscountess Folkestone*, and French 19th-century works include a Corot. There are marbles by Gibson, Spence and Wyatt.

TOWN HALL The present building was completed in 1754 to the design of John Wood of Bath. The original building was largely destroyed by fire in 1795; immediate rebuilding on the original idea was begun, a council chamber being added in 1811. On a newly devised dome, Felix Rossi's statue of Minerva was mounted in 1802.

WALKER ART GALLERY Named after Sir Andrew Barclay Walker, who donated the money for its construction. It has a notable collection of European and British paintings, including work by the Pre-Raphaelites; there are 20th-century paintings and sculptures. (See pp. 278–9.)

Llananno *Powys*   545Hf
CHURCH A little church with an extravagant Perpendicular rood screen with much carved foliage decoration; the gallery has a row of canopied niches containing carved figures.

Llandaff *S. Glam.*   545Jb
CATHEDRAL The first church here was probably built in the 6th century, but the present building was founded during the early 12th century. There are some remains of this early work, but most of the present cathedral is Early English and Decorated Gothic. After the Reformation the building lost its roofs, and the south-west tower collapsed. In the 19th century the building was restored, and a new tower and spire built, but even then the cathedral's troubles were not over, for it was bombed during the Second World War. This damage has now been repaired. A new feature of the interior is the great concrete arch in the nave supporting the organ, and a figure of Christ by Sir Jacob Epstein.

Llandegai *Gwynedd*   550Ee
A model village built by Lord Penrhyn during the first half of the 19th century. *Cottages ornés* and two school-rooms are grouped round the entrance to the medieval parish church.

Llandegley *Powys*   545Jf
THE PALES There are few old Quaker Meeting Houses in Wales, and this tiny building, dating from 1716, is one of the most attractive. A simple rectangular building is divided by a screen into a school-room and meeting-room. Most of the seating is original, and the roof is thatched.

Llandrindod Wells *Powys*   545Hf
A small town of red and yellow brick buildings, one of four small spas in central Wales which flourished in late Victorian and Edwardian days. Caebach chapel (1715) is an early dissenters' meeting-house. The town has a small museum.

Llandwrog *Gwynedd* 550Ed
CHURCH OF ST TWROG A mid-19th-century church, but among its 18th-century monuments is one of *c.* 1749 with a good bust—almost certainly the work of Sir Henry Cheere.

Llanegryn *Gwynedd* 550Eb
CHURCH The pride of the church is its rood screen with the original wide gallery on top, decorated with a wealth of delicate carving, *c.* 1520. There is also a Norman font.

Llanengan *Gwynedd* 550Dc
CHURCH This beautiful and large church stands on the route to Bardsey Island for pilgrims from the south. Doubtless it became wealthy as a consequence, and in the later medieval period, from which most of the building dates, it became a place of pilgrimage itself. Many of the churches in Lleyn have double aisles (one, Llangwnadl, has three): this has in addition a fine tower dated 1534, and a porch. Internally the original roofs survive, as does one of the rood screens and lofts; the second screen has lost its loft. Buried outside the east wall is a Roman Catholic priest, Fr Hughes, who attempted to re-establish a monastery on St Tudwal's East Island some 2 miles off Abersoch. This island has been partly excavated, but all that can be seen is the plan of a medieval hall similar to that found on Burry Holms, W. Glamorgan, and an 18th-century building which was erected across the west end of the medieval church.

Llanfihangel Crucorney *Gwent* 545Jd
LLANFIHANGEL COURT A gabled Elizabethan manor house, the front of which was rebuilt in 1559. The interior was remodelled in 1660 and is rich in period furniture.

Llangollen *Clwyd* 551Hd
An old town on the R. Dee in the beautiful Vale of Llangollen, described by George Borrow in *Wild Wales*. The river is spanned by a fine 14th-century stone bridge built by a Bishop of St Asaph. Every summer since 1947 the International Eisteddfod has been held in the town. The roof of St Gollen's church is carved with angels, flowers and animals, and is reputed to have been brought from nearby Valle Crucis Abbey—a 13th-century Cistercian foundation now in ruins. On a hill overlooking the town are the remains of Castell Dinas Bran.
PLAS NEWYDD An 18th-century black and white house, once the home of the 'Ladies of Llangollen'.
CANAL MUSEUM Exhibits and displays trace the development of Britain's canal system, and horse-drawn canal boats depart for Pentrefelin basin.

Llanmelin *Gwent* 546Ac
Llanmelin stands on a spur of hill close to and overlooking Caerwent. Defended by stone-faced multiple banks, with additional earthworks at one point, it was occupied for some two centuries. It was probably the chief settlement of the Silures tribe and, after the firm establishment of Roman government in South Wales, the new cantonal town was placed in the open country below, as was done in many tribal areas.

Llanrhydd *Clwyd* 551Hd
CHURCH OF ST MEUGAN A simple church about a mile from Ruthin. There is a 15th-century roof and screen, and a 17th-century altar. Monuments include one of the 16th century, with kneeling figures, and there is 19th-century stained glass.

Llanrwst *Gwynedd* 551Fe
CHURCH The church was rebuilt during the late 15th century and enlarged towards the end of the 17th century. Like some other Welsh churches it possesses a good rood screen with its original

gallery. The Gwydir chapel contains monuments to the Wynne family.
TU HWNT I'R BONT A 15th-century stone building, once a court-house.

Llanrwst Bridge *Gwynedd* 550Fe
Until 1826, when Telford's suspension bridge at Conwy was opened, this was the major bridge over the R. Conwy. It consists of a central segmental arch 60 ft high, flanked by slightly lower ones. It was built in 1636, and the western arch, which has a poorer foundation than the eastern arch, has been rebuilt at least once.

Llanthony Priory *Gwent* 545Jd
The ruins of a priory founded *c.* 1108 for Augustinian canons in the Honddu Valley in the Black Mountains. The present buildings are early 13th century, and much of the church remains.

Llantwit Major *S. Glam.* 545Hb
The centre of this small town contains a number of attractive stone houses dating from medieval times to the 18th century. The parish church, a complicated building, stands on or near the site of an important Celtic monastery, and in it are preserved some good pre-Conquest memorials.

Lochinch Castle *Dumfs. & Gall.* 556Bg
A 19th-century building in Scottish baronial style set in landscaped gardens on a peninsular flanked by the White and the Black Lochs. Near by are the ruins of Castle Kennedy, the Kennedy Clan's stronghold, which was erected in the reign of James IV (1473–1513). Gardens only open.

Loch Leven Castle *Tayside* 562Bg
Rugged ruins of a 15th-century fortress set on an island in Loch Leven. William Douglas helped Mary, Queen of Scots escape from it in 1568 after a year of imprisonment.

Lochnaw Castle *Dumfs. & Gall.* 556Bg
This is the ancient home (1426) of the Agnew family, who were hereditary sheriffs of Galloway for 300 years. It is a picturesque building, in an area famous for its rhododendrons. (By appointment.)

Lockington *Humberside* 558Fb
CHURCH OF ST MARY THE VIRGIN Originally Norman, with later additions, the church has a 17th-century pulpit and an 18th-century screen. There is a Norman doorway. Inside is much display of heraldry, some old glass and a 17th-century monument.

Lockleys *Herts.* 547Jd
A red-brick Georgian mansion (*c.* 1720) now used as a school.

Loddon *Norfolk* 554Db
CHURCH OF THE HOLY TRINITY A 15th-century church, with large clerestory, west tower and a two-storey south porch with stair-turret. The pulpit is Jacobean. Of the monuments and brasses, the most notable is the reclining Lady Williamson (d. 1684) in marble.

Logan *Dumfs. & Gall.* 556Bf
Logan House, built in 1701, lies halfway down the Rhinns of Galloway, and the influence of the Gulf Stream and the sheltered position on Luce Bay create a temperate, near frost-free climate. The gardens contain a collection of sub-tropical trees and shrubs, rare in the British Isles. The walled garden is now managed by the Royal Botanic Garden in Edinburgh. Round the Lily Pond there are clusters of giant New Zealand palm trees and eucalyptus (blue gum) from Australasia. Elsewhere tall, magnificent specimens of hybrid rhododendrons thrive with Chinese hydrangeas and Australian tree-ferns.

LONDON

Proud pageant of the nation's wealth

At the heart of the sprawling London conurbation are two cities which had distinct beginnings and have always had different roles, characters and styles. The City of London is the crowded centre of Britain's trade and finance; Westminster is the home of the Court, government and high society.

Underlining them both is the Thames, England's major outlet to the sea, and the reason why the capital is where it is.

A little lump of a hill (later Cornhill), after miles of marshland along the river banks, gave the invading Romans in AD 43 a first defensible stronghold at the lowest point where the river was narrow enough to be bridged; there has been a London Bridge near by ever since. Roman London grew with astounding speed, though it was sacked in its infancy, in AD 60, by Queen Boadicea. Less than 100 years later it was a walled city, with its own forum and the largest known basilica outside Rome, on the site of the modern Leadenhall Market. None of the original wall survives above ground level, but excavations have revealed some important Roman remains, including the Temple of Mithras, unearthed on a Walbrook building site in 1954.

After the Roman evacuation, London was settled by the Saxons, sacked by the Danes and rebuilt by Alfred—only to be sacked again by the Danes. Little of Saxon London remains above ground, though traces of a recently discovered Saxon church can be seen in the crypt of St Bride's, Fleet Street.

To find the medieval City of London is almost an archaeological pursuit. Most of it was destroyed in the Great Fire in 1666, giving a young inventor and astronomer, Christopher Wren, the chance to show his genius as an architect. As the builder of St Paul's Cathedral, the Monument to the Fire, and 51 City churches, Wren inspired a new generation of architects and craftsmen.

The City today is a complex of modern sky-scrapers and imposing Victorian and Edwardian masonry—the handsome cladding of affluent commerce; but the ground plan of medieval London still shows through, with some of the streets little wider than alleys. North of the Fire area a few churches of the Middle Ages and the Tudor period can be found more or less intact, such as Great St Helen's. But some churches which had survived the Fire were gutted in the later tragedy of the Blitz.

The Tower of London was the most notable building to survive the Fire. Built by the Normans—and built to last—as fortress, prison and palace all in one, the Tower is now the oldest major monument in London.

Most of the City's great public buildings have tended to re-shape themselves through the centuries. The Royal Exchange, for example, built in 1565, was burnt down twice, and finally rebuilt in 1844 to present a portico of gigantic columns as the proud face of the Victorian empire.

Most of the Halls of the City Livery Companies, originally guilds of master craftsmen, have been rebuilt several times since the Middle Ages; but they still house a wealth of antique furnishings, pictures and plate. Particular streets came to be associated with particular crafts and trades. The Grocers were to be found in Soper's Lane (now Queen Street), the Merchant Taylors in Birchin Lane, the Drapers in Candlewick. The Fishmongers were at Billingsgate, and the Fishmongers Company still controls Billingsgate market, with officers known as 'fish meters' checking on the freshness of the wares.

The Goldsmiths had the authority of a royal proclamation for their presence in Cheapside and Lombard Street. This was a form of medieval 'window dressing': Cheapside was the highway into London for foreigners coming from the docks, and the idea was to impress them with the taste and wealth of the capital.

In cracks in the present commercial masonry more convivial needs are met by the lively City chop-houses and taverns. Such are Simpson's, down Ball Court, and the George and Vulture (Mr Pickwick's pub, but Chaucer knew it too, when it was only the George).

The border between the City and Westminster is marked by a strip of gardens, courts, lawns and passages running north from the Thames for about three-quarters of a mile. This is legal London, the Inns of Court where the lawyers work—and some still live.

To the west is Westminster, with an antiquity almost as venerable as that of the City. There was a small Roman settlement there, but its national importance began with Edward the Confessor, who started rebuilding Westminster Abbey c. 1050. For nearly 1000 years, and almost without a break, Westminster has remained the site of the Court and the seat of government. William III moved his court to Kensington, but the Georges moved back to Westminster—to St James's Palace. And Queen Victoria finally settled at Buckingham Palace.

By the mid-18th century the Prime Minister was established in what is now Downing Street; and in time, the apparatus of government, the Civil Service, absorbed virtually the whole of Whitehall. The present buildings housing the great departments of State, such as the Home Office and the Foreign Office, mostly date from the confident mid-Victorian era.

About half of London is built on land held under lease—a system begun by the 4th Earl of Southampton in 1660, when he laid out Bloomsbury Square as a speculative development.

Speculative building had started 29 years earlier, when the Earl of Bedford was granted a licence to build on Covent Garden, once the garden of Westminster Abbey's convent. The earl commissioned Inigo Jones as his architect; London acquired its first square, and the Russells an investment that remained in the family until 1914.

After the Restoration (1660), the high servants of the Crown moved into the area around St James's. The Earl of St Albans developed St James's Square, the first of the great squares of the West End. Grosvenor Square was started in 1725, on land which had been the country estate of Sir Thomas Grosvenor. Lord Edward Harley and Lady Henrietta Cavendish developed Cavendish Square with the help of John Prince, the self-styled 'Prince of Builders'. Among other West End squares of this period were Hanover, Soho and Bedford. In the 19th century, a further expansion created the stuccoed opulence of Belgravia.

What Wren had been to the City, John Nash (1752–1835) was to the West End. In an age of patrons he had the greatest patron of all—the Prince Regent (later George IV), who gave Nash the chance to set about town-planning on an ambitious scale. Between 1810 and 1830 he planned Regent's Park (from a rough heathland belonging to the Duke of Portland), Waterloo Place, Carlton House Terrace and Regent Street.

Nash's buildings in Regent Street have vanished almost entirely, but the theatrical scale of his conception can be assessed from surviving terraces at Carlton House and round Regent's Park. With Wren, he is perhaps the greatest of those artists and craftsmen who, finding that London has always offered them the best patronage and livelihood, have responded generously to make it the unique and fascinating city it is.

LONDON GAZETTEER

The sites described here are all in the main
metropolitan area, and are listed alphabetically
with their addresses. At the end of the section are picture spreads
on the major museums and art galleries.

ALBERT MEMORIAL (KENSINGTON GARDENS, W8) The vast monument to the Prince Consort of Queen Victoria was designed by George Gilbert Scott, who was later knighted for this achievement. Scott said that when designing the memorial he had in mind early Christian ciboria and 'metal-work shrines of the Middle Ages', notably the one at Aachen. Nearly ten years were spent erecting the 175 ft high memorial. The shrine is a metal construction, lavishly ornamented with mosaics, gilt, precious metals and enamels, and embellished with extravagant sculptures by the foremost artists of the Victorian period. The monument was completed in 1876.

APOTHECARIES' HALL (BLACKFRIARS LANE, EC4) The Society of Apothecaries, one of the City livery companies, was founded in 1617 under charter from James I and had the monopoly of buying and selling drugs within the City of London. Their hall was built in 1670 and renovated in 1786. Through the entrance arch, with its red and gold coat of arms, is a charming courtyard, quiet in

contrast to the noise of Blackfriars traffic outside. Inside the brick building the great hall and the courtroom have fine old panelling and interesting pictures, including a portrait of John Hunter, the surgeon, by Sir Joshua Reynolds. (Interior open by arrangement.)

APSLEY HOUSE See Hyde Park Corner and Wellington Museum.

BANQUETING HOUSE (WHITEHALL, SW1) Cardinal Wolsey's house by the Thames was appropriated by Henry VIII after the cardinal's fall from power. It was enlarged by Henry and remained a royal residence until the late 17th century when William III preferred life away from London at Kensington Palace or Hampton Court. After a fire in 1619, Inigo Jones built the present Banqueting House on the site. The building is in severe Classical style, with a flat roof surrounded by a balustrade. George I converted it into a royal chapel, and in 1894 the building became the Royal United Services Museum. It has been restored, and has reverted to its original purpose.

ALBERT MEMORIAL

In 1861 the Prince Consort died and it was proposed that a national monument should be erected: the design was to be left to the Queen, who set up a committee. The winning design, by George Gilbert Scott, includes a bronze figure of the Prince, by J. H. Foley, holding a catalogue from the Great Exhibition.

BANQUETING HOUSE

The Double-cube Room in the Banqueting House is 110 ft long, 55 ft wide and 55 ft high. The magnificent ceiling was painted by Peter Paul Rubens for Charles I in 1634. Rubens received £3000 for the work and was knighted six years later. The ceiling panels represent the 'Apotheosis of James I', in the centre, the 'Union of England and Scotland' and 'Benefits of the Government of James I' (north and south panels).

BEDFORD PARK (W4) London's first garden suburb, which influenced all similar developments in the country. It was begun in the late 19th century by Jonathan Carr, a merchant, who disliked the current outward spread of London in rows of streets and houses. Carr chose Edward Godwin, the architect who designed Northampton Town Hall, and Norman Shaw, designer of London's former police headquarters at New Scotland Yard, as his architects. They laid out the site to take advantage of the existing trees, with houses, a church, an inn and an art school.

BETHNAL GREEN MUSEUM (CAMBRIDGE HEATH ROAD, E2) The cast-iron and glass structure was part of temporary buildings erected in 1856 for the South Kensington Museum. It was moved to Bethnal Green in 1867, encased in brick and opened in 1872. The exhibits include a collection of dolls, dolls' houses, toys, model theatres and children's costumes, and some important works by Rodin.

BRITISH LIBRARY (GREAT RUSSELL STREET, WC1) This was created in 1973 from the library departments of the British Museum and other national libraries. The reference division contains some 10 million printed books, about 75,000 Western and 30,000 Oriental manuscripts, 100,000 charters and rolls, 18,000 seals, 3000 Greek and Latin papyri and a fine collection of Egyptian papyri. There are also extensive collections of maps, music and postage stamps. Among the manuscripts are two copies of Magna Carta and a preliminary version of *Alice in Wonderland* with Lewis Carroll's own illustrations, the logs of HMS *Victory*, and an eye-witness account of the execution of Mary, Queen of Scots, sent to the ministers of Elizabeth I. (See pp. 313–17.) The printed books include Shakespeare's First Folios and many other rare editions. The British Library's galleries are—at present—in the British Museum.

BRITISH MUSEUM (GREAT RUSSELL STREET, WC1) One of the world's greatest treasure-stores founded in 1753 on the collections of Sir Hans Sloane. The money to house them, and those of Robert and Edward Harley and Sir Robert Cotton, the Elizabethan scholar, was raised by public lottery. Today the museum possesses a vast array of antiquities, including the Elgin marbles from the Parthenon, the Rosetta stone that provided the key to Egyptian hieroglyphics, ancient artefacts in stone, bronze and gold, and collections illustrating the course of Western Asiatic civilisations. (See pp. 313–17.)

BRITISH MUSEUM (NATURAL HISTORY) (CROMWELL ROAD, SW7) Opened in 1880 in a building designed by Alfred Waterhouse, the museum contains five principle collections embracing the history of plants, minerals and the animal kingdom. These range from the Whale Gallery's 91 ft model of a blue whale to the Botanical Gallery's section on insect-eating plants. A series of new permanent exhibitions has been opened, among them the spectacular 'Dinosaurs and their living relatives'.

BROOMFIELD HOUSE MUSEUM (BROOMFIELD PARK, N13) A late 17th-century building, which has since been altered, containing a mural painting and ceiling by Gerard Lanscroon (early 18th century). Collections of local and natural history are on show, and there are monthly exhibitions of art and ceramics.

BUCKINGHAM PALACE The Queen's London residence, where James I's mulberry orchard once grew. It was built by the Duke of Buckingham and Chandos, and bought by George III in 1761; in

1826–30 John Nash made alterations for George IV, and further alterations were made for Queen Victoria and George V, who employed Sir Aston Webb to reface the east front in 1913. The state apartments are never open to the public. See also Queen's Gallery and Royal Mews.

CARLYLE'S HOUSE (CHEYNE ROW, SW3) This house, built in 1708, is a fine example of an 18th-century town house. It is much as it was when Thomas Carlyle and his wife Jane lived there from 1834 to 1865 and were visited by Dickens, Thackeray, Browning, Tennyson and other eminent Victorians. Many of the Carlyles' letters, personal possessions and furniture are preserved, including an early piano played by Chopin and the desk at which Carlyle wrote all his books.

CENOTAPH, THE (WHITEHALL, SW1) The National Memorial to the dead of both wars was designed by Sir Edwin Lutyens, and unveiled in 1920. Its name in Greek means 'the empty tomb'.

CHARLES II STATUE (CHELSEA HOSPITAL, SW3) In the main court a bronze statue by Grinling Gibbons honours the founder of the hospital. On May 29 (Oak Apple Day and also Charles II's birthday) the statue is decorated with oak leaves in memory of the day after the Battle of Worcester (1651) when Charles escaped capture by hiding in an oak tree at Boscobel House.

CHARTERHOUSE, THE (CHARTERHOUSE SQUARE, EC1) Founded as a Carthusian monastery in 1371, the buildings became a private dwelling after the Dissolution of the monasteries in 1537. Thomas Sutton bought them in 1611 and endowed them as a charitable foundation; part of the foundation became a school and part a 'hospital' for gentleman pensioners. The school moved to Godalming, Surrey, in 1872, but about 40 'brethren'—single men over 60 who were formerly officers or professional men—remain at Charterhouse. The buildings, mainly of 16th-century origin, were badly bombed in 1941. In 1947–9 excavations were possible around them and the original monastic plan, much overlain since the Dissolution, was discovered. The buildings themselves, which formed the 16th-century manor house, have been carefully restored. They include an Elizabethan great hall c. 1571 and a great chamber built later. In the chapel is the tomb of Thomas Sutton. Washhouse Court is the best preserved of the earlier monastic buildings. (Interior by appointment.)

CHISWICK HOUSE (BURLINGTON LANE, W4) Chiswick House was built in 1725 for the Earl of Burlington to his own designs. Lord Burlington became the patron of the Palladian school of architecture, whose most prominent members were the architects Colin Campbell and William Kent.

The partnership of Lord Burlington and William Kent produced the Palladian villa, Chiswick House, in 1725–9. Of two storeys, the upper is the principal floor, and is approached through a great portico, supported by columns and with a pediment above the entablature. Near the portico are decaying statues of Palladio and Inigo Jones, carved by Rysbrack. In 1788 two wings, now demolished, were added by James Wyatt.

The villa contains interior decorations by William Kent, and paintings by Kneller, Ferdinand Elle, Guido Reni, Anthonie Schooyans, Danielo da Volterra, Dobson, Kent and Sebastiano Ricci; adjoining it is the Summer Parlour, built some time before the villa by Colin Campbell, the Earl of Burlington's first guide and tutor. In the 18th century the house was a popular meeting place for poets, artists, aristocrats and statesmen.

CHRIST CHURCH (COMMERCIAL STREET, E1) Built between 1714 and 1729, this is one of Nicholas Hawksmoor's East London churches, and has a huge tower with spire. Among the monuments is a statue of a former Lord Mayor of London by John Flaxman. (Interior by appointment.)

CHURCH OF ALL HALLOWS BARKING BY THE TOWER (BYWARD STREET, EC3) Of Saxon origin, this church survived the Great Fire of London in 1666, but was bombed during the Second World War, allowing some of the early church to be uncovered. It was rebuilt by Lord Mottistone and Paul Paget and re-dedicated in 1957. The font cover is by Grinling Gibbons, and in the crypt are remains of a Roman floor.

CHURCH OF ALL SAINTS (MARGARET STREET, W1) The site on which William Butterfield in 1849 began to build the Victorian Gothic Church of All Saints was so narrow and cramped that the only way in which Butterfield could express his love of massed shapes was by building towards the sky. The church was highly original—and controversial—for its day, and a century later it still appears startling. Butterfield used red bricks, which were then unfashionable; both the exterior and interior brickwork is decorated with geometrical patterns and horizontal bands of black brick and stone. The narrow 230 ft tower ends in an octagonal steeple. The church, completed in 1859, was an early example of Butterfield's highly individual style, which reached its perfection with his polychrome design for Keble College Chapel, Oxford.

The effect of space and size in the interior is amazing, and so is the riot of colour, gilding, mosaics and painting. The church is on a strictly Tractarian plan—one altar visible from all parts of the church, no screen, light from the west end, and the chancel extremely sumptuous.

CHURCH OF ALL SAINTS (OLD CHURCH STREET, SW3) Chelsea 'Old Church' was severely damaged during the Second World War, although the chapel restored by Sir Thomas More in 1528 survived almost intact. The church has since been rebuilt. Monuments from the 16th century onwards include one designed by Pietro Bernini (1672).

CHURCH OF ALL SOULS (LANGHAM PLACE, W1) Designed by George IV's favourite architect, John Nash, as a feature of the new Regent Street, the church was completed by the end of 1824. Nash's circular Ionic portico is surmounted by the tower with a slender spire. The interior was restored in 1951, and a major reconstruction took place in 1975–6.

CHURCH OF ST ANNE (COMMERCIAL ROAD, E14) Designed by Wren's assistant Nicholas Hawksmoor, the building was started in 1712 and consecrated in 1730. The tower is famous as a landmark from the Thames; the church was restored in the 19th century.

CHURCH OF ST AUGUSTINE (KILBURN PARK ROAD, NW6) This is a large, brick, cruciform church, with a spire over 250 ft high, designed by J. L. Pearson in 1870. There are windows by Clayton & Bell, and contemporary paintings and ironwork.

CHURCH OF ST BARTHOLOMEW THE GREAT (SMITHFIELD, EC1) The impressive remains of a Norman priory church, founded by Rahere in 1123, the same year he founded St Bartholomew's Hospital. Only the choir and Lady Chapel remain, as the long nave, originally of ten bays, was demolished after the Dissolution. The church was

CHISWICK HOUSE

Lord Burlington designed this villa for himself after his first Grand Tour in 1714–15. In Italy he became greatly impressed by the work of the 16th-century architect Andrea Palladio, who had influenced Inigo Jones so much a century earlier. Chiswick House was inspired by Palladio's Villa Capra (The Rotunda) near Vicenza. The interior decoration was by William Kent, and the most important room is the central domed hall, round which all the other rooms are built. The magnificent gallery (above), completed in 1729, runs the length of the house; it was designed as a setting for part of Burlington's art collection.

restored during the late 19th century by Sir Aston Webb. The most important monument is that of *c.* 1500 on the north side to the founder Rahere, with a recumbent effigy.

CHURCH OF ST BENET (PAUL'S WHARF, EC4) First mentioned in the early 12th century, and by Shakespeare in *Twelfth Night*, this church was rebuilt by Wren after the Great Fire, in 1677–85. It has an almost Dutch exterior of red and blue brickwork, and a hipped-roof. The interior has galleries to the north and west between Corinthian columns. Henry Fielding was married here in 1748. The architect Inigo Jones is buried in St Benet's, which is the church of the College of Arms.

CHURCH OF ST BOTOLPH (ALDERSGATE, EC1) A medieval church that was rebuilt in two stages, in 1754 and 1787–91 by Nathaniel Wright. The exterior is of modest red brick with a small west

tower. The well preserved interior is late 18th century, with two coffered apses and three dark wooden galleries with Corinthian columns. In the west gallery is an organ-case of 1778; the east window of 1788 shows the Agony in the Garden. There are some monuments from the old church, and a simple monument with portrait medallion, by Louis Roubiliac, to Elizabeth Smith (*d.* 1750).

CHURCH OF ST BOTOLPH (ALDGATE, EC3) Built 1741–4 by George Dance the Elder, the interior was restored in 1889 by J. F. Bentley, who reconstructed the galleries and introduced an unusual ceiling. Further restoration took place after a fire in 1965. The pulpit dates from 1621, and the organ was built for a private house in Houndsditch. Among 16th- and 17th-century monuments are two to victims of Henry VIII, who were beheaded in 1537 and 1538.

CHURCH OF ST BRIDE (FLEET STREET, EC4) The present church, by Godfrey Allen, is the eighth on the site and is a faithful restoration of that built by Christopher Wren 1670–1703 and burnt out during an air raid in 1940. It has some superb woodwork and carving. In the crypts can be seen the line of a 1st-century Roman ditch, the remains of a 2nd-century Roman pavement and those of five previous churches.

CHURCH OF ST CLEMENT DANES (STRAND, WC2) The church was rebuilt after the Fire of London by Wren, only to be destroyed again during the air raids of 1941. But the walls and James Gibbs's elegant tower survived, and the church has now been restored as that of the Royal Air Force.

CHURCH OF ST ETHELBURGA-THE-VIRGIN (BISHOPSGATE, EC2) It is believed that this is the only Anglican church in the country to have this dedication. It is the third oldest in the City, is built of ragstone and brick, and is a survivor of the Great Fire that destroyed so many of the original City churches. Since 1954 it has been one of the 14 guild churches of the City—such churches are found only in this 'Square Mile'. The interior is mainly 15th century, and there is an outstanding Hans Feibusch mural on the east wall.

CHURCH OF ST HELEN'S (BISHOPSGATE, EC3) A large and interesting church, the remains of a Benedictine nunnery founded c. 1210. The nuns' church was built on to an existing parish church, and hence there are two naves. The exterior has embattled gabling and a 17th-century bell-turret.

CHURCH OF
ST MARTIN-IN-THE-FIELDS

There has probably been a church here since before the 13th century when fields stretched between the City and Westminster. A 16th-century church had become unsafe by 1720, and James Gibbs was asked to build the present one—his masterpiece—with his name and the completion date (1726) carved on the pediment.

There are many architectural features of the 13th to 15th centuries, and some later furnishings, including a Jacobean pulpit and marble font of 1632. St Helen's is rich in monuments and brasses. There are the tombs of Sir John Crosby of Crosby Hall (d. 1476), Sir Thomas Gresham (d. 1579), Sir John Spencer and his wife (c. 1609) and one to Sir Julius Caesar Adelmare (d. 1636).

CHURCH OF ST JAMES (CLERKENWELL GREEN, EC1) Designed by James Carr c. 1790, St James's replaced an earlier building. It still has galleries in spite of restoration in the late 19th century. The monuments date from the 16th century.

CHURCH OF ST JOHN (CAMBRIDGE HEATH ROAD, E2) Built c. 1825 to Sir John Soane's design; the church is of brick with an unconventional stone bell-cote. In 1878 St John's was remodelled by G. F. Bodley.

CHURCH OF ST KATHARINE CREE (LEADENHALL STREET, EC3) On the site of a vanished Augustinian priory (Christchurch, whence Creechurch), the body of this church was built in 1628–31, a rare period for church building in England. It was consecrated by Archbishop Laud. The tower is older, 1504. The interior is a mixture of Classical and Gothic styles, containing Corinthian columns, plaster vaulted ceiling and a large east window incorporating a Catherine wheel in the tracery. The organ of 1686 is by Father Schmidt.

CHURCH OF ST LEONARD (SHOREDITCH HIGH STREET, E1) An unpretentious, somewhat ponderous church by George Dance, Senior. Completed in 1740, it is in red brick and Portland stone. The gilt clock case in the gallery, and a monument by Francis Bird to Elizabeth Benson (d. 1710), on which two skeletons tear apart the tree of life, are among the features inside. (By appointment.)

CHURCH OF ST LEONARD (STREATHAM HIGH ROAD, SW16) Due to be rebuilt in 1976 following a fire in 1975, St Leonard's still has its 15th-century tower and font. There are brasses and monuments from that period, including a brass of a rector in full vestments who died in 1513 and a monument of the Master of the Revels for Elizabeth I.

CHURCH OF ST LUKE (SYDNEY STREET, SW3) Designed by John Savage in 1819 and consecrated five years later, St Luke's was one of the first neo-Gothic churches. It has an impressive tower and porch, and a roof of fine stone vaulting. Charles Kingsley, the novelist, held a lectureship at the church, and Charles Dickens was married here to Catherine Hogarth in 1836.

CHURCH OF ST MARK (NOEL PARK, N22) Designed by Rowland Plumbe and consecrated in 1889. The east wall is decorated with fine mosaics resembling those in St Mark's, Venice.

CHURCH OF ST MARTIN-IN-THE-FIELDS (TRAFALGAR SQUARE, WC2) The present church, built 1722–6, is the most prominent work by the Scottish architect, James Gibbs. A disciple of Wren, Gibbs evolved his own architectural style, and his designs for St Martin-in-the-Fields influenced ecclesiastical architecture beyond Britain, especially in the U.S.A. Many churches in different American states are erected in accordance with Gibbs' arrangement of St Martin's. The rectangular church is approached by a broad flight of steps and has a great Corinthian portico. The large carved armorial achievement of George I in the pediment is the work of Christopher Cass. The steeple, which rises above the portico, is in Ionic pilaster form; above the clock Corinthian columns are capped by the actual spire. Gibbs, architect of the Radcliffe Camera, Oxford, also designed monuments. His use of a figure leaning on a large urn set a long-lasting fashion in sculpture.

CHURCH OF ST MARY (BATTERSEA CHURCH ROAD, SW11) Rebuilt c. 1775 by Joseph Dixon in brick, the church contains 17th-century glass and, among its numerous monuments, one by Louis Roubiliac, c. 1751. It stands on the bank of the Thames opposite Lots Road power station. The crypt holds the remains of Benedict Arnold.

CHURCH OF ST MARY ABCHURCH (ABCHURCH LANE, EC4) A rebuilding by Sir Christopher Wren of a church that was first mentioned in the 12th century. The plain brick exterior has stone dressing and the tower in the north-west bears a pretty lead spire. The domed interior was restored by Lord Mottistone after bomb-damage in the Second World War. The carved wooden altar-piece of 1686 is by Grinling Gibbons, and the marble font of the same date is by Christopher Kempster, one of Wren's masons at St Paul's Cathedral.

CHURCH OF ST MARY ALDERMARY (WATLING STREET, EC2) First mentioned in the 11th century, St Mary Aldermary's was rebuilt by Wren after the Fire of London, the money being given on condition that the new building was a copy of the old. Certainly this is in Perpendicular Gothic style, with plaster fan-vaults in aisles and nave. The tower has large polygonal buttresses ending in tall pinnacles. Interesting furnishings include the pulpit, and the font and sword-rest, all of 1682.

CHURCH OF ST MARY-AT-HILL (LOVAT LANE, EC3) Rebuilt by Wren soon after the Great Fire, in 1670–6, it replaced a church first mentioned in 177. The exterior is plain and has a projecting clock. The interior is domed and vaulted, the central dome supported by Corinthian columns that form a cross shape. There is much good woodwork, and box-pews. There are elaborate wrought-iron sword-rests, and a sculptured relief of the Resurrection, c. 1600, which comes from the old church. The clock is the only one of its kind in the City—the workings are in the tower but the face is in the next street.

CHURCH OF ST MARYLEBONE (MARYLEBONE ROAD, NW1) The original medieval church was rebuilt in the first half of the 18th century, but soon proved too small. The present church was designed by Thomas Hardwick and consecrated in 1817. An expensive Corinthian church built in Portland stone, its portico and steeple terminate Nash's stucco York Gate leading out of Regent's Park. The galleried interior was elaborately decorated in Victorian times. The poets Robert Browning and Elizabeth Barrett were married here in 1846. The church is close to the Barrett home in Wimpole Street.

CHURCH OF ST MARY-LE-BOW (CHEAPSIDE, EC4) The legend of 'Bow Bells' originated from a curfew bell that hung here in the 11th century. The church was severely damaged in 1941, and the original bells had to be recast and rehung. The church was reconsecrated in 1964 after restoration.

CHURCH OF ST MARY-LE-STRAND (STRAND, WC2) James Gibbs (1683–1774), a follower of Sir Christopher Wren, studied architecture in Italy, and his Italian training shows clearly in St Mary-le-Strand, built 1714–17. The church stands on an island site, like its near neighbour, St Clement Danes. The nave and chancel have rich, vaulted ceilings.

CHURCH OF ST MARY MAGDALEN (BERMONDSEY STREET, SE1) There was a medieval foundation here of which only the tower remains. The church was rebuilt in 1680 after the style of Wren, and the west front was remodelled in 1830 by George Porter in stucco Gothic. There is a font of 1808.

CHURCH OF ST MARY WOOLNOTH (KING WILLIAM STREET, EC3) A church built by Wren's assistant, Nicholas Hawksmoor, in 1716–26. The unusual tower divides at the top into two small turrets. The façade is heavily rusticated. The interior was restored by William Butterfield in 1875 and the galleries were then removed, but much of Hawksmoor's woodwork remains. Corinthian columns in groups of three are arranged in each corner, and above are semicircular clerestory windows and a moulded plaster ceiling. There is an organ by Father Schmidt.

St Mary Woolnoth is a guild church and, as such, ministers to City workers; it is closed at the week-end. It is also the church of the Worshipful Company of Goldsmiths.

CHURCH OF ST PANCRAS (EUSTON ROAD, NW1) A fine example of Greek Revival architecture, designed by William Inwood and his son Henry William, and built in 1819–22. At the west end is an impressive Ionic portico with three huge doors. Above, following the example of St Martin-in-the-Fields built 100 years before, projects the steepled tower; this comprises a tower with a smaller edition of the same tower on top, and incorporates elements freely taken from the Temple of the Winds in Athens. The rest of the church is based on the Erechtheum in Athens. At the east end, on either side of the Ionic apse, are two small vestries which incorporate versions of the caryatids of the Erechtheum temple on the Acropolis. In Athens H. W. Inwood made plaster casts of the original figures and these were turned into terracotta copies by J. C. F. Rossi and his son Henry. These were then built up around the true supports, cast-iron columns. The flat-ceilinged interior contains galleries supported by columns.

CHURCH OF ST PAUL (RECTORY GROVE, SW4) Rebuilt in the 19th century and recently restored. The important monuments from the early church include two to the Atkins family (one, c. 1689), and another to William Hewer, friend of Samuel Pepys, in whose house Pepys died in 1703.

CHURCH OF ST PETER (LIVERPOOL GROVE, SE17) Designed by Sir John Soane, c. 1823. His steeple rises above four large Ionic columns. The interior retains its galleries.

CHURCH OF ST STEPHEN WALBROOK (WALBROOK, EC4) Rebuilt by Wren in 1672–7, the church has a plain exterior with a tower and steeple finished in 1717. The interior, however, is elaborate, with a large dome, the first built in England, supported at ground level by 12 Corinthian columns, three in each corner. Contemporary furnishings include the organ, pulpit and reredos, and there is a fine painting, *The Burial of St Stephen*, by Benjamin West.

CLEOPATRA'S NEEDLE (VICTORIA EMBANKMENT, SW1) A 68½ ft high obelisk of granite given to the nation in 1819 by Mohammed Ali of Egypt. It did not reach England until 1877, when it was erected on the Embankment. The monument has no connection with Cleopatra, Queen of Egypt (69–30 BC), but was carved in honour of Thothmes III, King of Egypt 1490–1436 BC. It originally stood with a companion obelisk (now in New York) outside the temple at Heliopolis.

289

HANDEL'S KEYBOARD AND COPY OF THE 'MESSIAH'

Written at great speed between August 22 and September 14, 1741, Handel's 'Messiah' was first performed in Dublin in 1742. The organ keyboard (right) was used by him for performances of the oratorio before large audiences throughout the country. In Handel's lifetime all performances of the work were for charity, many for the Foundling Hospital, now the Thomas Coram Foundation. The manuscript copy, one of several still in existence, is open at the passage: 'And the Angel said unto them, "Fear not, for behold I bring you good tidings of great joy".' Blind for the last eight years of his life, Handel died in 1759 at the age of 74. He was buried in Westminster Abbey. (Thomas Coram Foundation for Children)

COLLEGE OF ARMS (QUEEN VICTORIA STREET, EC4) A plain brick building which replaced one burnt down in the Great Fire of London of 1666, it was built *c.* 1671 to be the headquarters of the Officers of Arms, first incorporated by Richard III in 1484. The Kings of Arms have exclusive powers to grant armorial bearings, and the site and building, libraries and collections are the property of the corporation of the Kings, Heralds and Pursuivants of Arms. The large wrought-iron gates were presented to the college in 1956.

COMMONWEALTH INSTITUTE (KENSINGTON HIGH STREET, W8) The institute exists to promote mutual understanding between the peoples of the Commonwealth. The modern building, opened in 1962, acts as a cultural, educational and social centre. Displays illustrate each member country's development and way of life; there is a theatre for documentary films and live shows; and the art gallery exhibits paintings and other works by Commonwealth artists.

CORAM FOUNDATION FOR CHILDREN (BRUNSWICK SQUARE, WC1) This charity, founded in 1739 by Thomas Coram, the mariner, empire-builder, philanthropist and pioneer in child welfare, with the aim of helping unwanted children, was known until 1954 as the Foundling Hospital. It has always enjoyed the support of artists, and William Hogarth, a founder member, was more than anyone else responsible for fostering this link. He gave to the foundation a full-length portrait of Thomas Coram, which hangs on the first landing. His example was followed by many other artists, prominent amongst whom were Allan Ramsay, Thomas Gainsborough and Sir Joshua Reynolds. Another Hogarth painting was won in a lottery with a ticket presented by the artist himself. In the picture gallery hangs *The Massacre of the Innocents*, a portion of one of twelve cartoons for a tapestry depicting scenes from the life of Christ.

The original organ in the chapel was presented by Handel. The keyboard of this organ and a fair copy of the manuscript of the *Messiah* are on display. Both the oak staircase and the courtroom to which it leads on the second floor are from the original hospital. The Foundation's present-day activities are long-term foster care, a pre-school Children's Centre and an Adoption Project, specialising in placing children with special needs.

COURTAULD INSTITUTE GALLERIES (WOBURN SQUARE, WC1) A collaboration between Viscount Lee of Fareham and Samuel Courtauld, an art collector and a textile manufacturer, led to the foundation of the Courtauld Institute of Art in 1932. Their aim was to create a department for the teaching of art history and to provide an art gallery for London University, and to this end they both bequeathed their art collections to the university. Other bequests make up the main part of this collection, namely the Roger Fry Collection, the Sir Robert Witt Collection of old master drawings and the Gambier-Parry Collection of Italian Renaissance paintings and *objets d'art*.

The Samuel Courtauld collection is the most representative selection of Impressionist and post-Impressionist paintings in the country and centres around a collection of paintings by Cézanne that includes his *Lac d'Annecy, Mont Ste-Victoire* and *Card Players*. Manet's *Déjeuner sur l'Herbe* and Renoir's *La Loge* are notable in a collection which includes works by Degas, Pissarro, Monet, Seurat, Bonnard, Modigliani and Utrillo.

The Lee Collection of old masters is shown in rooms decorated with furniture and other works of art in the collection. The most outstanding painting is probably Rubens's *Descent from the Cross*, which was the model for the large altarpiece in Antwerp Cathedral, but works by Lely, Veronese, Bellini, Botticelli, Gainsborough, Goya, Van Dyck and Tintoretto may also be seen.

The bequest of the Gambier-Parry Collection has added a fine selection of 14th- and 15th-century Italian paintings along with splendid collections of majolica and Venetian glass, medieval ivories and Limoges enamels. Examples of early 16th-century Turkish 'Rhodian' pottery and inlaid Islamic metalwork are also displayed.

The 20th century is represented by the Fry Collection, which illustrates the most advanced

English taste in the years preceding the First World War. It includes works by Renoir, Sickert, Bonnard, Marchand, Rouault and Roger Fry, and examples of African sculpture. (See pp. 320–1.)

CROSBY HALL (CHEYNE WALK, SW3) A remarkable medieval hall, of great interest to scholars, is incorporated in this building on Chelsea Embankment. The original Crosby Hall was part of a 'large and sumptuous building' known as Crosby Place, built in Bishopsgate in 1466 by Sir John Crosby, alderman of the City of London and a rich merchant. He owned it from 1466 until his death in 1475. Richard, Duke of Gloucester, lived there in 1483, and in this connection, Crosby Place is mentioned three times in Shakespeare's *Richard III*. Sir Thomas More bought it in 1523 and then sold his 41-year lease to a rich merchant, Antonio Bonvisi, for £200. The house was burnt down in the 17th century, but the great hall survived. In 1910, as a result of an appeal to preserve it, the hall was transferred to Chelsea and rebuilt exactly as the original on part of the site of Sir Thomas More's Chelsea garden. The hall is still used as a dining-hall; of particular interest is the lofty oriel window occupying the whole of one bay, with the Crosby crest in the vaulting, and the magnificent oak roof.

CUMING MUSEUM (WALWORTH ROAD, SE17) The exhibits concentrate on the archaeology and the history of the Southwark area and on London superstitions. They include fragments of a Roman boat found under Guy's Hospital, shaped stones from the palace of the Black Prince at Kennington and from the great abbey at Bermondsey, the pump of the Marshalsea debtors' prison in which Dickens' parents were imprisoned and the Dog and Pot shop sign he noted as a boy.

CUSTOM HOUSE (LOWER THAMES STREET, EC3) The headquarters of the Collector of Customs for the Port of London, this early 19th-century building has a fine neo-Classical façade to be seen from the river. In the Long Room (199 ft long), ships' masters and agents come to register the arrival and departure of ships. (By appointment.)

DICKENS HOUSE (DOUGHTY STREET, WC1) In this house, the only survivor of his London residences, novelist Charles Dickens, in 1837–9, completed *Pickwick Papers* and wrote *Oliver Twist* and *Nicholas Nickleby*. It houses a museum and library containing manuscripts, letters and personal relics of Dickens including the Suzannet collection. It is also the headquarters of the Dickens Fellowship.

DULWICH PICTURE GALLERY (COLLEGE ROAD, SE21) The first public art gallery to be opened in London (in 1814), it was designed by Sir John Soane. There are fine collections of Dutch paintings, and of portraits by 17th- and 18th-century British artists. There are also important works by members of the French, Flemish, Italian and Spanish schools.

FENTON HOUSE (HAMPSTEAD GROVE, NW3) This small, attractive mansion was built towards the end of the 17th century when, following the discovery of mineral springs, Hampstead was being developed as a fashionable spa. The names of the first owner and architect are unknown, and it was not until 1793 that the house was acquired by Mr Fenton, a Baltic merchant. Today it contains fine furniture and porcelain bequeathed by Lady Binning, and a collection of keyboard instruments including a harpsichord used by Handel.

GEFFRYE MUSEUM (KINGSLAND ROAD, E2) Originally built *c.* 1715 as almshouses, the museum

PORCELAIN GOATHERD AND MILKMAID

Porcelain was originally imported from China, but was so expensive and difficult to obtain that some European potteries were encouraged to copy it. Started in 1709 at Meissen, Germany, porcelain production eventually reached England during the 1740's. In 1749 the famous 'soft-paste' pottery at Bristol was founded by William Miller and Benjamin Lund. By this time the Meissen potteries were producing small porcelain figures, enamelled with colour, as replacements for the sugar and wax table-decorations used by the rich at their banquets. At first the figures were modelled to be seen from all sides, but the growing practice of using them as ornaments on mantelpieces and side cabinets resulted in the figures being set against a leafy bower or background feature. This pair of Bristol porcelain figures, the Goatherd (left) and the Milkmaid, date from 1775. Enamelled in several colours, they incorporate a background or bocage. (Fenton House)*

GEMS IN THE GEOLOGICAL MUSEUM

The Geological Museum contains one of the largest and finest collections of gems and ornamental stones in the world. The picture shows:

1 green demantoid garnet
2 oval aquamarine
3 emerald cabochon
4 lilac-coloured kunzite
5 rich red spinel
6 drop-shaped brown topaz
7 yellow sapphire
8 purple amethyst
9 olive-green zircon
10 brown zircon
11 carved tourmaline pendant
12 brilliant colourless danburite

contains furniture and woodwork from the Elizabethan period to 1939 arranged in a series of room settings.

GEOLOGICAL MUSEUM (EXHIBITION ROAD, SW7) Contains a magnificent and famous collection of gemstones, the best in Europe. British fossils and rocks, and minerals from all parts of the world, form part of the museum's permanent exhibitions. A major exhibition, the 'Story of the Earth', outlines the 5000-million-year history of our planet, including an animated volcanic eruption and a simulated earthquake.

GEORGE INN (BOROUGH HIGH STREET, SE1) The only surviving galleried inn in London, built in 1677. It was a famous coaching terminus in the 18th and 19th centuries, and is mentioned in Dickens's *Little Dorrit*. Still functions as an inn.

GOLDSMITH'S HALL (FOSTER LANE, EC3) Contains a fine collection of antique plate, much of it with interesting historical associations. There is also the largest collection of modern silver and jewellery in the country. (By appointment.)

GRAY'S INN (HIGH HOLBORN, WC1) Dates from 1272, but most of the buildings are modern restorations. The Elizabethan essayist and philosopher Sir Francis Bacon lived and worked here for 50 years. It has been said that the first performance of Shakespeare's *Comedy of Errors* was performed in the Hall. (Interior by appointment.)

GUILDHALL (EC2) The City of London's Hall where the Court of Common Council, which administers the City, meets, and where the Lord Mayor and the Court of Common Council entertain famous visitors to London. The original building dates from 1411, but only the walls of the great hall, the porch and the crypt survive today, for the Guildhall suffered damage both in the Great Fire and in the Blitz when the council chamber and the 19th-century roof of the great hall were destroyed. The building has been restored; the interior was completed to designs by Sir Giles Scott in 1952. The Corporation Art Gallery, within the Guildhall, has paintings of great state occasions over the past 100 years. The Guildhall Library, also badly bombed in 1940, contains such treasures as the First, Second and Fourth Folios of Shakespeare's plays, a map of London of 1593 and a deed of sale for a house, signed by Shakespeare.

GUILDHALL ART GALLERY (EC2) The collection started in 1670 with the commissioning of portraits of the judges who dealt with property claims after the Great Fire. The gallery opened in 1886. It exhibits selections from the permanent collection that includes E. W. Cooke drawings of London Bridge, W. Alister Macdonald water-colours of London and the Charles Gassiot Bequest of English 19th-century paintings.

GUY'S HOSPITAL (ST THOMAS STREET, SE1) Founded in 1721 by Thomas Guy (1644–1724), a bookseller who made a considerable fortune by the importation and printing of Bibles. Late in life Guy greatly increased his wealth by investment in the South Sea Company, and this enabled him to build and endow his great hospital. The first patients were admitted in 1726. The view of the original building with its two later wings and its remodelled façade has changed little since 1780. Scheemakers' statue of Thomas Guy in the centre of the forecourt dates from 1733. The medical school was established in 1769 and the poet John Keats was a student there from 1814 to 1816.

HAYWARD GALLERY (BELVEDERE ROAD, SE1) The first major gallery to be built in London since the war, the Hayward Gallery is under the direction of the Arts Council of Great Britain and has temporary exhibitions of British and foreign art.

HOGARTH'S HOUSE (HOGARTH LANE, W4) William Hogarth's 'little country box by the Thames' which he occupied from 1749–64. Though badly damaged in a 1940 air raid, the house has now been perfectly restored and contains many examples of the artist's work, including his savage satires on the London life of his day—'The Harlot's Progress', 'Marriage à la Mode' and 'The Election'.

HORNIMAN MUSEUM (LONDON ROAD, SE23) Built in 1901 to designs by C. H. Townsend, the museum has extensive ethnographical collections. There is a fine collection of musical instruments, natural history specimens from every continent, British fossils, an aquarium and a library.

HOUSES OF PARLIAMENT OR PALACE OF WESTMINSTER (SW1) In deference to nearby Westminster Abbey, a Gothic design by Sir Charles Barry was chosen when the Palace of Westminster was rebuilt following a fire in 1834. Work on the new building began in 1840. The palace comprises a central hall and corridor with the two Chambers (Houses of Lords and Commons) to the north and south, with identical projecting pavilions at either end of the river façade. There are strong vertical features in the massive Victoria Tower, the clock tower and the spire over the central hall. This Classical plan is masked by Gothic detailing, nearly all produced by Augustus Pugin. The clock tower, housing Big Ben, the bell named after the first Commissioner of Works, Sir Benjamin Hall, was completed in 1858 and the Victoria Tower two years later. The stone chosen

GUILDHALL

This medieval hall is the centre of administration for the City. Here kings and distinguished visitors have for centuries been received—in 1419 the mayor, Richard (Dick) Whittington received Henry V, the victor of Agincourt. Today ceremonies granting the honorary Freedom of the City, and the election of the Lord Mayor, still take place here. The annual Lord Mayor's Banquet is a reminder of the great medieval feasts. Around the walls are monuments to the two Pitts, Wellington and Sir Winston Churchill, and two mythical giants, Gog and Magog—the last survivors of Albion—stand guard on either side of the gallery at the west end.

QUEEN ELIZABETH'S CORONATION CUP

This gilt and crystal cup, dated 1554, was presented to the Worshipful Company of Goldsmiths by its most famous Prime Warden, Sir Martin Bowes. Almost certainly it was used at Queen Elizabeth I's Coronation banquet, at which the Lord Mayor of London would have fulfilled his traditional role as butler to the newly crowned monarch. For this service his customary fee was the standing cup from which the Sovereign had drunk, and no doubt this was paid at the accession of Elizabeth I. But how the cup came into the possession of Sir Martin is a mystery, for though he had been Lord Mayor in 1545, he was not so in the Coronation year, 1558. Sir Martin's story resembled that of Dick Whittington; apprenticed as a goldsmith at 14, he rose to become the Master of the King's Moneys, M.P., Sheriff and 13 times Prime Warden of his Company. (Goldsmith's Hall)

for the building did not stand up to London's atmosphere and has been gradually replaced by a more durable type. In 1941, during the Second World War, the main chamber of the House of Commons was gutted by incendiary bombs: a new Chamber was opened in 1950.

HYDE PARK The Manor of Hyde was given by William the Conqueror to Geoffrey de Mandeville, who owned it when the Domesday Book was made in 1086. On his death he gave the manor to the Abbey of Westminster which held it until Henry VIII appropriated it c. 1536 and used it as a royal deer park. It was first opened to the public by Charles I in 1635, when it was used for horse-racing and quickly became a rendezvous for society people; it was also a popular place for duels. The mile-long track of Rotten Row was used for riding and was a favourite parade of the fashionable in their horse-carriages.

The Serpentine, an artificial lake formed from the R. Westbourne, was constructed at the order of Queen Caroline in 1730. A fine bridge built in 1826 by George Rennie and known as Rennie's Bridge crosses the lake between Hyde Park and Kensington Gardens.

In 1850 Joseph Paxton began building the Crystal Palace in the park for the Great Exhibition of 1851. The building remained there for a year and was subsequently removed to Sydenham. Twenty years later the Albert Memorial was put up slightly west of the site.

In the Victorian age the park became a centre for popular orators; for years meetings were forbidden, until a serious riot led to a special place, now known as Speakers' Corner, being designated for assemblies in 1872. The park covers 360 acres.

HYDE PARK CORNER (SWI) Until the beginning of the 19th century London ended here and the country began; Apsley House was known as 'No. 1 London' and many of the distances to England's towns were measured from the Corner. Near Apsley House is the screen at the entrance into Hyde Park, and the Constitution Hill Arch. Apsley House was built by Robert Adam for Lord Apsley during the 1770's, and was later acquired by the 1st Duke of Wellington, the victor of Waterloo, who employed Benjamin Wyatt to enlarge the building c. 1828. At this time the Waterloo Gallery was built. Behind the house is the statue of Achilles, erected by women's subscription to commemorate Wellington's victories. Apsley House was given to the nation by the 7th Duke of Wellington after the Second World War; now the Wellington Museum. (See p. 296.)

The screen and arch were designed by Decimus Burton c. 1825, and when the arch was erected it was much nearer the screen than it is today. The sculptured frieze on the screen is the work of John Henning and his sons John and Samuel, and is based on the Elgin Marbles, now in the British Museum. In 1846 a huge equestrian statue of Wellington was hauled to the top of the arch. It was ridiculed for years and when the arch was moved further down Constitution Hill in the 1880's, the statue was moved to Aldershot, where it still towers over the trees. The arch now supports a bronze group, known as *Victory* or *Peace* but more usually as *The Quadriga*, by Adrian Jones.

The arch, also called the Wellington Arch, is now on the central traffic island, with the statue of Wellington by Sir Edgar Boehm; the Royal Artillery war memorial in the form of a huge stone gun, by C. Jagger; *David*, and the war memorial of the Machine Gun Corps by Francis Derwent Wood.

ARTHUR WELLESLEY, DUKE OF WELLINGTON, HERO OF WATERLOO

Arthur Wellesley joined the army at 19, and as a colonel in India defeated the notorious Tippoo Sahib, whose sword can be seen at Apsley House, now a museum, where Wellington lived for 35 years. In July 1808 he sailed from Cork with 9000 men, to pit himself against the legions of Napoleon. 'They may well overwhelm me,' he said 'but they will not out-manoeuvre me.' Six weeks after landing on Portuguese soil he had won two decisive victories, and in the end he chased the French across the Pyrenees. The two great soldiers faced one another on the field of Waterloo on June 18, 1815. The duke rose early that morning, wrote three letters before 3 a.m. and was in the saddle of his horse Copenhagen by 8 a.m. It was dusk when the 'Saviour of Europe' rode back through a battlefield littered with 45,000 dead and dying soldiers.

PORTRAIT BY GOYA *at the National Gallery; this famous portrait was painted in Madrid in August 1812, after Wellington's victory at Salamanca. For the battle he was awarded the Golden Fleece, which can be seen amoung the collection of his decorations.*

WELLINGTON SHIELD *shows the duke mounted, and surrounded by a group of officers, with the figure of Victory flying above and carrying a laurel wreath. The ten compartments of the shield show scenes of the duke's campaigns. After the Battle of Waterloo, honours were showered on the 46-year-old duke and in the years which followed he acted as administrator, diplomat, and even Prime Minister during 1828–30. The shield was given to him by the merchants and bankers of the City of London and designed by Thomas Stothard. (Apsley House)*

DRESSING CASE *illustrating the duke's Spartan habits. He often slept in his clothes and ate when convenient. 'I conceived a horror for the two words "cold meat" and "daybreak"', said one of his officers. (Apsley House)*

PENCILLED ORDERS *sent by the duke to unit commanders at Waterloo. The writing could be erased and the skin used again. During the battle he spent 13 hours in the saddle. (Apsley House)*

THE AGONY IN THE GARDEN *by Correggio; believed to have been the duke's favourite painting, it was one of the masterpieces captured from Joseph Bonaparte's baggage train at Vitoria. (Apsley House)*

WELLINGTON'S FUNERAL CARRIAGE *in the crypt of St Paul's. One and a half million mourners lined the streets at his funeral.*

PORTUGUESE SERVICE *Items from the famous service of silver plate presented by the Regent of Portugal to the duke in gratitude for delivering his country from the French. The service is one of the major examples of silversmithing of the neo-Classical period. It took 142 craftsmen three years to make, and was delivered in 1816. Only the centre-piece is shown above. (Apsley House)*

A WELLINGTON BOOT *A caricature of the duke as Commander-in-Chief of the Army. He wore such boots, and the style has since been named after him. On each point of the spur is an initial of one of the duke's many orders. (Apsley House)*

THE GOLD BATON *presented to Wellington by the Prince Regent in return for Marshal Jourdan's baton, captured on the field of the Battle of Vitoria, and* THE ORDER OF THE ELEPHANT, *Denmark's supreme order, given to the duke for his great victory at Waterloo. (Apsley House)*

VELASQUEZ *The Water-seller of Seville*

*Velasquez, one of the greatest portraitists of all time, began his career as a painter of religious subjects and scenes of peasant life. His needle-sharp eye for the appearance of things, his ability to subject his appetite for detail to the overall wholeness of the picture, his sheer technical skill in defining the unique texture of glass, fabric, metal or wood, and his restraint as a colourist all combine to make these early works masterpieces of realism. In the 'Water-seller', painted about 1619 when Velasquez was only 20, the high-*lights and strong shadows bespeak a debt to Caravaggio, whose style had a strong influence outside Italy in the early 17th century. The old water-seller was a Corsican and a well-known character in Seville where Velasquez was born, and the youth was a studio boy who served as a model several times. Four years later Velasquez showed the picture to King Philip in Madrid, and he kept it and the artist—who became Court painter for the rest of his life.*
(Wellington Museum, Apsley House)

IMPERIAL INSTITUTE TOWER (PRINCE CONSORT ROAD, SW7) The Imperial Institute in South Kensington was built behind the Royal Albert Hall to mark the celebration of Queen Victoria's Jubilee. In 1887 the queen had reigned for 50 years, and the architect T. E. Collcutt began the construction of the great Imperial Institute. Later the Institute became the Commonwealth Institute (see p. 290) and moved to its new building in Holland Park. In recent years the original buildings have been demolished and replaced by a modern glass complex. Towering over the new buildings of the Imperial College of Science and Technology is the elegant central tower of the Imperial Institute. The 280 ft high copper-domed tower is built of white stone and houses a peal of bells; it is all that now remains of the Imperial Institute.

IMPERIAL WAR MUSEUM (LAMBETH ROAD, SE1) The building, originally the home of Bedlam (Bethlehem Hospital for the Insane), dates from c. 1815. The museum illustrates the two World Wars and other military operations involving Britain and the Commonwealth since 1914. There is a wide range of weapons and equipment, and films are shown at weekends. Exhibits include a Mark V tank, a Battle of Britain Spitfire, Lawrence of Arabia's rifle, and the original German surrender document signed by Field-Marshal Montgomery.

The museum has a major collection of paintings by official war artists, with works by Paul Nash, Stanley Spencer, Graham Sutherland and Henry Moore. There is also a collection of sculpture, with works by Jacob Epstein.

Associated with the museum is HMS Belfast, a cruiser which featured in the Second World War and is now a floating naval museum, permanently moored in the Pool of London.

INNS OF CHANCERY These Inns, of lesser importance than the Inns of Court, have largely disappeared. Staple Inn, Holborn, a fine survival of an Elizabethan house, is no longer connected with the legal profession. The other former Inns of Chancery were Clement's Inn, Clifford's Inn, Barnard's Inn, Lyon's Inn, Furnival's Inn, Thavies' Inn, Strand Inn and New Inn; none survives except in some cases as names of modern buildings and streets.

INNS OF COURT Lincoln's Inn, the Inner Temple, the Middle Temple, and Gray's Inn are the four great Inns of Court which largely govern the practice of barristers in England and Wales. The Inner and Middle Temples adjoin each other between Fleet Street and the Embankment, an area that was once the seat of the Knights Templar.

IVEAGH BEQUEST See Kenwood.

JEWEL TOWER (OLD PALACE YARD, SW1) A surviving fragment of the medieval Old Palace of Westminster, built 1365-6 as a moated treasure house for Edward III. It now houses a museum of relics of the Old Palace.

JOHNSON'S HOUSE (GOUGH SQUARE, EC4) A house of the late 17th century where Dr Samuel Johnson, the critic and lexicographer, lived (1748-59) and where he compiled his *Dictionary*. The house contains many of his relics. Also on show are a first edition of the *Dictionary*, Johnson's portrait by Barry, one of Boswell by Reynolds, and a fine collection of 18th-century prints.

KEATS HOUSE (KEATS GROVE, HAMPSTEAD, NW3) Keats, with his friend Charles Armitage Brown, lived in half of the house at Wentworth Place, John Street, as it was then called, from December 1818 to September 1820. In the other half lived the Brawne family. It was then that Keats fell in love with the eldest girl, Fanny Brawne, and it was there that he wrote some of his best work—the 'Ode to a Nightingale', 'Ode on a Grecian Urn', and 'Hyperion'. A unique collection of Keats relics are to be seen in the house, among them are Keats letters, Fanny Brawne's portrait and her engagement ring, books belonging to Keats and annotated by him, and early editions of his poems. In the garden a plum tree has replaced the one under which it is thought Keats wrote the 'Ode to a Nightingale'.

KENSINGTON GARDENS Adjoining Hyde Park, they were originally part of the 26 acre garden of Kensington Palace, laid out by William III in the formal manner of the time. They were extended by Queen Anne and later by Queen Caroline, and now cover 274 acres. In the early 19th century they were open to the public from spring to autumn and it was at this period that Shelley was seen sailing paper boats on the Round Pond.

Features of the garden are the modern sunken garden with its lily pond and pleached lime walks, and Queen Anne's Orangery designed by Wren, 1704-5, an elegant brick building. Also in Kensington Gardens is the popular statue of Peter Pan designed by Sir George Frampton in 1912 in honour of J. M. Barrie's play of that name.

KENSINGTON PALACE (W8) The country home of the Earl of Nottingham was in 1689 acquired by William III, who commissioned Sir Christopher Wren to carry out numerous alterations and additions. The palace was further enlarged during the reign of Queen Anne, for whom Wren designed the orangery. The brick building is roofed with green slates, and Grinling Gibbons decorated the interior with carved panels, fluted columns and flower-bedecked archways. William Kent fashioned the interior of the palace for George I, and walls and ceilings are painted in profusion. Kent also laid out the gardens. It was in the Palace, at 5 a.m. on June 20, 1837, that the 17-year-old Victoria learnt she had become Queen.

KENWOOD (IVEAGH BEQUEST, HAMPSTEAD, NW3) Kenwood is in a large park of beeches, oaks and chestnuts. The original 17th-century house was owned at various times by the Duke of Argyll and the Earl of Bute before coming into possession of the 18th-century Lord Chief Justice, the Earl of Mansfield. Robert Adam then remodelled the present mansion in neo-Classical style. The principal façade, facing south, has two projecting wings, one of which contains Adam's splendid library. The portico on the north front has a decorated pediment supported by four fluted Ionic columns. In 1922 the 6th Earl of Mansfield sold the contents of the house by auction, and the furniture was dispersed. The mansion itself was in danger of being demolished, but in 1925 Lord Iveagh bought the property. On his death in 1927 the estate was left to trustees for the nation, and Kenwood was opened to the public the following year. It contains a collection of paintings by Rembrandt, Vermeer, Van Dyck, Aelbert Cuyp, as well as English masters—Gainsborough, Reynolds, Romney, Lawrence and Turner. A notable recent acquisition is a Stubbs portrait of a prancing horse which was painted for the Marquis of Rockingham in 1762 and is now on loan from the Trustees of the late Lord Fitzwilliam's Estate. (See p. 298.)

LAMBETH PALACE (LAMBETH PALACE ROAD, SE1) The official home of the Archbishops of Canter-

REMBRANDT *Portrait of the Artist*

Rembrandt Harmenszoon van Ryn was born in Leyden in the Netherlands and lived from 1606 until 1669. His autobiography is unique in its sincerity and humanity. It was not written but painted, drawn and etched in over 100 self-portraits. Every change in his features and his fortunes is dispassionately reflected. Sometimes he is in armour or a fur-trimmed robe or some other richly embroidered garment from his store of studio properties, or again in a beggar's rags. In his last period—that is, from about 1650—his self-portraits reach a monumentality, a poignancy and a maturity which remind us of the last of other great creative artists—the last quartets of Beethoven or the final religious works of Titian. In the portrait at Kenwood, usually dated 1663, we see Rembrandt old before his time—he was only 57. He shows himself not dressed up but as a painter in a composition of majestic simplicity and almost Classical geometry. The baroque flourish has gone and the pyramidal figure is set off by a background relieved only by two large arcs which may symbolise globes in his earlier portraits. The expression is not tortured. He was now bankrupt but had been saved from ruin by his son Titus and second wife, who made him their employee. He could paint his last masterpieces in peace for his own satisfaction. His brushwork, becoming steadily freer, took on a vitality of its own and the surfaces of his pictures seem to vibrate. The paintings show his increasing detachment from the throes of the world. (Kenwood)

298

bury, built when the Thames was the great highway of London, and it was convenient to have a large riverside residence with its own water-gate. The red-brick exterior dates from the late 15th century, the main gate being the work of Archbishop Morton *c*. 1495. The chapel, much restored, dates probably from *c*. 1230; it was rebuilt after war damage, and has modern stained glass by Powell and Edwards. Under the chapel the crypt, the earliest part of the palace (*c*. 1200), has Purbeck marble pillars. The main medieval buildings are of the 15th and 16th centuries. Apart from a considerable amount of rehabilitation in the 19th century, the main post-medieval building is the hall, erected *c*. 1660–3 to replace one destroyed under Cromwell's Commonwealth. It is 93 ft long and has a hammerbeam roof. Lambeth Conferences of Anglican bishops have been held in the hall, which is now part of the magnificent library of illuminated manuscripts and early printed books.

LANCASTER HOUSE (STABLE YARD, SW1) Lancaster House is one of the finest surviving examples of early Victorian architecture. Benjamin Wyatt, who enlarged Apsley House, the Duke of Wellington's town residence, started to build Lancaster House for the Duke of York in 1825: and when the mansion passed into the possession of the Dukes of Sutherland in 1827 alterations were made to the staircase hall by Sir Charles Barry.

LEIGHTON HOUSE (HOLLAND PARK ROAD, W14) The house was built in 1866 by Lord Leighton, one-time President of the Royal Academy, with help from architect George Aitchison, and was his home until his death in 1896. The house, with a collection of the artist's drawings and paintings, was transferred to Kensington Borough Council in 1926. It is one of the earliest examples of a purpose-built studio house. The Arab Hall, with its fine Middle East tiles of the 15th, 16th and 17th centuries, has stained glass windows from Damascus, wooden screens from Cairo, a mosaic frieze by Walter Crane and fine marble columns. Examples of William de Morgan's tiles and pottery are also on view. Loans from the Tate Gallery and the Victoria and Albert Museum are included in a permanent exhibition of paintings, sculpture and furniture.

LINCOLN'S INN (WC2) Has been on its present site near Chancery Lane since at least 1422. Its name may come from the Earl of Lincoln, legal adviser to Edward I. The Old Hall, dating from 1492, the Victorian New Hall and the library (founded in 1474 and the biggest law library in England) are open on application. The quadrangle and gardens are open to the public at midday. Among many famous men connected with Lincoln's Inn are Sir Thomas More, John Donne, William Penn, Disraeli and Gladstone.

LINCOLN'S INN FIELDS (WC2) A large open space with trees, lawns, tennis courts and band concerts in summer. The Royal College of Surgeons stands on its south side, Sir John Soane's Museum to the north, and there are many handsome houses around the square.

LONDON TRANSPORT MUSEUM (COVENT GARDEN, WC2) A superb display of nostalgia on wheels that contains such venerable exhibits as No. 23, the Metropolitan Railway locomotive that served Londoners from 1866 to 1948, and a 'B' type bus of the breed that carried troops to the Front in 1914. Trams, trolleybuses and a collection of posters evoke the London of yesteryear, while the Metropolitan's milk van of 1896 illustrates the Underground's versatility. (See p. 453.)

THE RAMILLIES STAIRCASE
AT MARLBOROUGH HOUSE

A magnificent staircase, with wrought-iron balustrade and black marble steps, decorated with scenes from the Battle of Ramillies (1706), one of the Duke of Marlborough's most notable victories over the French. Louis Laguerre, a Frenchman who settled in England in 1684, completed pictures depicting most of the duke's battles about 1711, for the house designed by Wren.

LORD'S CRICKET GROUND (ST JOHN'S WOOD, NW8) Named after Thomas Lord (1755–1832), a groundsman to the White Conduit Club, in 1780, Lord's has been the headquarters of the Marylebone Cricket Club—the governing body of cricket—since 1814. Lord's Cricket Memorial Gallery includes the urn for the original Ashes.

MALL GALLERIES (THE MALL, SW1) The exhibition galleries of the Federation of British Artists, an organisation to which more than 20 art societies and groups are affiliated.

MANSION HOUSE (EC4) The official residence of the Lord Mayor of London was designed in the Palladian style by George Dance the Elder, and built 1739–53, but has been altered since. A suite of state rooms in 18th-century style, including the 88 ft long Egyptian Hall, can be visited on written application.

MARBLE ARCH (W1) Originally the main gateway to Buckingham Palace, which John Nash designed when he repaired and enlarged the palace in 1825–36. It was moved to its present position in 1851, and in 1908 was closed to traffic and has been purely ornamental since then. A small tablet on the traffic island at the junction of Edgware Road and Bayswater Road marks the site of Tyburn Tree, London's former place of execution. The gallows and public galleries stood here from 1196 until 1783; thereafter executions took place at Newgate.

MARLBOROUGH HOUSE (SW1) Marlborough House was the home of Queen Mary until her death in 1953. It was built by Sir Christopher Wren for the victorious Duke of Marlborough,

THE CUMBERLAND TANKARD

This 7 pint silver tankard was made in 1746 for the Duke of Cumberland, to commemorate his victory over Bonnie Prince Charlie in April of that year. A sketch of the Battle of Culloden is engraved on the upper part of the tankard; it depicts the Duke sitting on his horse while the fight rages behind him. To the left, the Young Pretender flees the field, while at the bottom some of the defeated Jacobite troops plead for mercy. (National Army Museum)

owner of Blenheim Palace (Oxfordshire), *c.* 1705. The red-brick house had certain additions made to it during the 19th century, when it was the home of Edward VII when he was Prince of Wales. Inside are superb wall-paintings by the French painter Louis Laguerre, depicting famous battles of the duke—Blenheim, Ramillies and Malplaquet.

MAYFLOWER INN (ROTHERHITHE STREET, SE16) This Thames-side inn juts out into the river and is named for the famous ship which in 1620 carried the Pilgrim Fathers to America. The Master, Christopher Jones, is buried in the nearby churchyard of St Mary's.

MIDDLE TEMPLE HALL (THE TEMPLE, EC4) Elizabethan, but most of the buildings date from after the reign of Elizabeth I or the Great Fire. Extensive damage was done in the Second World War, but has been repaired. The Temple has been the home of many famous men, among them Thackeray, Dr Johnson and Charles Lamb; Shakespeare placed the incident that began the Wars of the Roses in its gardens (*Henry VI, Part I*). By appointment.

MONUMENT (FISH STREET HILL, EC4) Wren's fluted Doric column, surmounted by a golden globe rising from flames, commemorates the Great Fire of London in 1666, which started in nearby Pudding Lane. Built in 1671–7, it is 202 ft high; a spiral staircase of 311 steps leads to the balcony. On the base are three panels recording in Latin the story of the fire and the subsequent rebuilding of London. The fourth side (to the west) has a sculptured bas-relief by Caius Gabriel Cibber showing Charles II giving protection to the devastated City.

MUSEUM OF LEATHERCRAFT (WITHIN THE GUILDHALL MUSEUM, 52 BASINGHALL STREET, EC2) Exhibits in the museum show some of the wares made by the principal London guilds who were users of leather—the Leathersellers, Cordwainers, Glovers, Saddlers, Sheathers, Girdlers, Forcers and Bottellers. The displays include ancient pouches and purses, a 17th-century fireman's helmet, a leather lantern, footwear from Roman times to the present day, knife and dagger sheaths, a replica of an Iron Age leather shield, heraldic regalia, a fine 18th-century coffer, a saddle with pinion and medieval ornamented boxes for valuables. There is also the famous Edmondson collection of leather bottles, bombards (jugs) and drinking vessels, some examples of gilt-leather wall hangings, and a variety of modern leather goods made by the trades that grew out of the ancient guilds.

MUSEUM OF LONDON (LONDON WALL, EC2) The old Guildhall and London (Kensington Palace) Museums provided the nucleus of the Museum of London, whose collections reflect the history and life of the city from earliest times to the present day. Displays include relics of Roman London, paintings, drawings and prints, theatrical exhibits, material relating to the suffragette movement and collections of Royal memorabilia spanning two centuries. (Opening 1977.) (See pp. 322–3.)

MUSEUM OF THE CHARTERED INSURANCE INSTITUTE (ALDERMANBURY, EC2) The museum has a large collection of British and foreign fire marks and a small collection of objects associated with the history of insurance.

NATIONAL ARMY MUSEUM (ROYAL HOSPITAL ROAD, SW3) Founded in 1960, the museum was housed for ten years in temporary accommodation at the Royal Military Academy, Sandhurst. It was transferred to a new building near the Royal Hospital, Chelsea, in 1970 and was opened to the public the following year. The main permanent display is devoted to the history of the British army since 1485 and illustrates its development and its role in British and world affairs. Also depicted are the history of the Indian Army up to 1947 and that of colonial forces up to the date of independence. The picture gallery houses important military paintings, and an adjacent gallery has a full range of uniforms.

NATIONAL GALLERY (TRAFALGAR SQUARE, WC2) The building was designed by William Wilkins and was built between 1834 and 1837. The collection covers European paintings up to *c.* 1900 and is particularly rich in works of the Italian, Netherlandish and Dutch Schools. The paintings are a comprehensive national collection and, apart from those in the loan collection, are on permanent display at Trafalgar Square. (See pp. 324–9.)

NATIONAL PORTRAIT GALLERY (ST MARTIN'S PLACE, WC2) A unique collection of more than 8000 portraits re-creates a visual history of Britain from the 16th century to the present day in terms of her famous men and women and a panorama of changing tastes and fashions, conventions and culture. Monarchs and their consorts are represented with their friends and enemies, politicians, civil servants, ecclesiastics, explorers, scholars, writers, soldiers, sailors, musicians, architects and artists. The portraits are not confined to formal full-length oils but range from state portraits to watercolours, caricatures and daubs of friends and relatives. The advent of photography has revolutionised the whole concept of the recorded image and plays an important part among the 20th-century portraits in particular. As well as the permanent exhibition, the gallery stages special exhibitions from time to time.

NATIONAL POSTAL MUSEUM (KING EDWARD STREET, EC1) Documents and stamps comprising one of the world's greatest philatelic collections are on show in this museum specially designed for the purpose. The Phillips Collection documents the conception, planning and issue of this British invention, the world's first postage stamp. In 45 volumes it illustrates the history of 19th-century stamps in Great Britain and traces design development and manufacture in British stamp production during the 19th century.

Also in the museum is the Post Office's own collection of stamps and documents, including the registration sheets (final proofs) from the 1840 Penny Black to the most recent issues, and a unique collection of artists' drawings, colour trials and proofs of all British 20th-century stamps. There is also a collection of some quarter of a million stamps from all parts of the world.

NATURAL HISTORY MUSEUM See British Museum.

NELSON'S COLUMN See Trafalgar Square.

PASSMORE EDWARDS MUSEUM (ROMFORD ROAD, E15) Completed in 1899–1900, the building incorporates every possible architectural style current at that time. The collection of the Essex Field Club formed the nucleus of the museum's exhibits which have been augmented by items from west Essex and the eastern Greater London area, which the museum covers. A gallery opened in 1970 is devoted to the geology, archaeology and local history of the area and includes a wide range of items from a dinosaur's footprints to pieces of Bow porcelain that were made near the museum. The Natural History Gallery has live animals and an aquarium.

PERCIVAL DAVID FOUNDATION OF CHINESE ART (GORDON SQUARE, WC1) The collection is devoted to Chinese ceramics of the 10th–18th centuries (Sung, Yüan, Ming and Ch'ing dynasties). Most of the pieces were made for or collected by the emperors and the nobility.

PHARMACEUTICAL SOCIETY'S MUSEUM (BLOOMSBURY SQUARE, WC1) Displays include crude drugs used in the 17th and 18th centuries, early printed works relating to pharmacy, English drug jars, leech jars, medicine chests, dispensing and other apparatus formerly used in the preparation of medicine. (By appointment.)

PUBLIC RECORD OFFICE (CHANCERY LANE, WC2) The home of the nation's state papers, records and documents dating from the time of the Norman Conquest. The museum's collection includes the Domesday Book (1086), two 13th-century enrolments of Magna Carta, papers connected with the Gunpowder Plot of 1605, Shakespeare's will and the Master's log of the *Victory* at the Battle of Trafalgar. The building, a neo-Gothic palace erected in 1851–71, was designed by Sir James Pennethorne; the Chancery Lane wing by Sir John Taylor was erected 1892–5.

QUEEN ELIZABETH'S HUNTING LODGE (RANGERS ROAD, E4) A 16th-century Tudor building used as a base for hunting expeditions into Epping Forest and as an observation post. It was an open framework exposed to the weather, and the upper floors were cambered to allow for drainage. It has a massive arch-braced roof, an Elizabethan staircase with a rare square hollow newel, and a 17th–18th-century chimney stack some 9 ft wide. Displays include animal, bird and plant life and other items of local interest.

QUEEN'S CHAPEL (ST JAMES'S, SW1) An exquisite small chapel opposite St James's Palace, built by Inigo Jones between 1623 and 1627 for the wife of Charles I, Henrietta Maria, though it had been intended for the Spanish princess whom it was hoped Charles would marry. It is in Classical style and was Jones's first ecclesiastical building. Inside there is a fine coffered ceiling and a west gallery (with a fire-place), originally a royal pew.

QUEEN'S GALLERY (BUCKINGHAM PALACE, SW1) Housed in the former chapel of Buckingham Palace, the gallery mounts a series of exhibitions showing selections of paintings and other works of art from the Royal Collection.

REGENT'S PARK Probably the most beautiful and certainly the most elegant of all London's royal parks. It was designed by John Nash in 1811 for the Prince Regent, after whom it was named. The park was the culmination of Nash's plan for Regent Street, which begins at Carlton House Terrace in the Mall, where the Regent lived, and sweeps in a broad curve to Portland Place, whose wide straight road, flanked on either side by elegant houses, terminates in Regent Crescent and the great green open space (410 acres) of the park.

The park is surrounded by a carriageway, the Outer Circle, connected by two roads with the Inner Circle, originally a sawdust and sand track for horse-riding, but now a tarmac road. This encloses the beautiful garden now known as Queen Mary's Garden, which was taken over from the Royal Botanic Society in 1932 and replanted. A small lake includes an island rock garden devoted to alpines and miniature perennials.

On the north side of Queen Mary's Garden is the open-air theatre, where Shakespeare's plays are performed in the summer. In the Zoological Gardens in the north-east of the park are the huge artificial rocks of the apes' Mappin terraces, the aviary designed by Lord Snowdon and the concrete elephant-house by Sir Hugh Casson.

ROOSEVELT MEMORIAL (GROSVENOR SQUARE, W1) A statue of the American President, Franklin Delano Roosevelt (1882–1945) by Sir William Reid Dick, was erected in 1948, near the site of the American Embassy (designed by Eero Saarinen and opened in 1960).

ROYAL ACADEMY (BURLINGTON HOUSE, PICCADILLY, W1) Founded in 1768 by George III; the Academy's first president was Sir Joshua Reynolds. The Summer Exhibition is of works by living artists, but loan exhibitions are held during the rest of the year. (See p. 302.)

ROYAL ALBERT HALL (KENSINGTON GORE, SW7) The Hall, completed in 1871, was erected in memory of Prince Albert to designs by General H. Scott. It is in the form of a huge oval arena, surrounded by tier upon tier of boxes and galleries, and roofed by a shallow metal and glass dome. Encircling the exterior below the dome is a terra-cotta frieze which illustrates man's progress through the arts and sciences through the centuries.

ROYAL COLLEGE OF MUSIC: MUSEUM OF INSTRUMENTS (PRINCE CONSORT ROAD, SW7) Displays include Handel's spinet, Haydn's clavichord and a large number of early stringed and wind instruments. There is an extensive library of printed music and original manuscripts. (By appointment.)

ROYAL COLLEGE OF SURGEONS—HUNTERIAN MUSEUM (LINCOLN'S INN FIELDS, WC2) Founded by John Hunter (1728–93), surgeon and anatomist, to illustrate his experiments on anatomy, physiology and pathology. (By appointment.)

MICHELANGELO *The Virgin and Child with the young St John the Baptist*

By common consent Michelangelo is regarded as the greatest sculptor who ever lived, and this beautiful marble roundel is the only major work of his in Britain. Probably carved about 1503 for Taddeo Taddei, it was bought in Rome in 1823 by Sir George Beaumont, who presented it to the Royal Academy.

Its unfinished state is not unusual, for Michelangelo failed to carry many of his greatest works to completion, but Michelangelo's statue of the Virgin and Child in Bruges, carved about the same time, gives an indication of the kind of surface it would have had if he had completed it. (Royal Academy)

ROYAL COURTS OF JUSTICE (STRAND, WC2)
Following the successful result of the collaboration between Augustus Pugin and Sir Charles Barry over the new Gothic Palace of Westminster, the style of George Edmund Street's Royal Courts of Justice, built in 1868–82, was again Gothic. However, this time an adaptation of the more austere 13th-century style was used. The centre-piece is the stone-vaulted great hall, about 80 ft high, whose roof is surmounted by a tall, narrow spire, best seen from the distance, rising above the roof-line; in the gable is a fine rose window. The Strand stone-faced façade has a tower with a hipped-roof and a clock projecting over the roadway, open screens of pointed arches, and small turrets with pointed caps clinging to the walls. The back of the building in Carey Street also has a tall tower, but here the emphasis is on exposed brick with bands of stone as decoration.

ROYAL EXCHANGE (ROYAL EXCHANGE, EC3) The Royal Exchange was destroyed by fire twice and was rebuilt for the third time in 1844 by Sir William Tite, whose building still stands. It was first instituted and built in Elizabeth I's reign by Sir Thomas Gresham, the richest London merchant and financier of his time, and son of a lord mayor. The Exchange was built in Flemish style round a quadrangle where the merchants transacted their business, and was surrounded by two colonnades, called Pawns, containing more than 100 small shops. Statues of English monarchs stood in niches looking down on to the quadrangle. The first meeting of merchants in the Exchange was probably held in 1569. When Gresham died in 1579 he entrusted the Exchange to the City Corporation and to the Mercers, his livery company. It was destroyed in the Great Fire, rebuilt by Edward Jarman and again burnt down in 1838.

The foundation stone of the third building was laid by the Prince Consort in 1842. A broad flight of steps leads up to the sheltered portico, with its eight Corinthian pillars; a sculpture in the tympanum by Sir Richard Westmacott represents Commerce, in the form of British and foreign merchants and City worthies. Like its predecessors the Renaissance-style building surrounded an open quadrangle, which was roofed over in 1882. In front of the Exchange is a statue of the Duke of Wellington by Sir Francis Chantrey (1844) and a war memorial to Londoners who served in the two World Wars. On the walls of the quadrangle are paintings depicting famous scenes in British History. For the last 40 years no exchange business has been done there.

ROYAL FUSILIERS MUSEUM (EC3) The museum, in the Tower of London, has uniforms including those worn by George V as Colonel-in-Chief, regimental silver and china, four dioramas of famous battles, and campaign medals, among them seven Victoria Crosses including the prototype approved by Queen Victoria.

ROYAL GEOGRAPHICAL SOCIETY (KENSINGTON GORE, SW7) A private society founded in 1830, dedicated to the diffusion of geographical knowledge and to aiding exploration and discovery. The Society's house includes a library, and map room (open to the public) containing over 600,000 maps.

ROYAL HOSPITAL (CHELSEA, SW3) The Royal Hospital, founded by Charles II in 1682, houses over 400 veteran and invalid soldiers, known as Chelsea Pensioners. The building was designed by Christopher Wren and took ten years to build. It is of brick with stone cornices, cornerstones and door dressings. Although Robert Adam and Sir John Soane made alterations and additions, the main building remains virtually unchanged. The pensioners' uniform today—a scarlet frockcoat in summer and blue greatcoat in winter—dates from the time of Marlborough in the early 18th century. Chelsea Flower Show is held every year in the hospital grounds.

ROYAL MEWS (BUCKINGHAM PALACE, SW1) The Gold State Coach, with its panels painted by the Florentine artist Cipriani, is the most spectacular exhibit at the Royal Mews. It was made in 1762, and has been used for every coronation since that of George IV in 1820. Many other state coaches and carriages are on display, including the Irish State Coach and the Scottish State Coach made for the Queen in 1969. The Speaker's State Coach is also kept in the Royal Mews: this was formerly a royal coach, designed for William III in 1698 by Daniel Marot, a fugitive French Huguenot in Holland, and was handed over to the Speaker of the House of Commons by Queen Anne. Private driving carriages and royal sleighs are on display. The Windsor Grey and Cleveland Bay carriage horses are kept in the stables which, together with the coach houses, were designed by John Nash and completed in 1825.

ROYAL OPERA HOUSE (COVENT GARDEN, WC2) The chief theatre for grand opera and ballet in London, originally opened in 1732 and twice destroyed by fire. The present building was designed by E. M. Barry in 1858.

ST BARTHOLOMEW'S HOSPITAL (WEST SMITHFIELD, EC1) London's oldest hospital, founded in 1123 by Rahere at the same time as the priory and church of St Bartholomew the Great; both were erected in thanks for Rahere's recovery from malaria while on a pilgrimage to Rome. The hospital is on the original site and the gatehouse, built in 1702, still makes a fine entrance. Above the

THE IRISH STATE COACH

A Lord Mayor of Dublin, M. Hutton, built this coach in 1852. It was bought by Queen Victoria when she visited Dublin, and she used the coach on the only two occasions on which she opened Parliament during her widowhood, in 1887 and 1897. Later sovereigns have driven to the opening of Parliament in the coach and it is used by the Queen on other State Drives. The wooden body was originally painted maroon but successive varnishings have given it a black appearance. The coach is drawn by four or six horses. (Royal Mews)

THE GOLD STATE COACH

Made of gilded oak, this coach, completed in 1762, was used at the coronation of George IV, and has been for every coronation since. Four Tritons support the coach body. Eight palm trees form its framework and nine painted panels depict allegorical scenes. On the roof are three cherubs representing the genii of England, Scotland and Ireland. The coach weighs 4 tons, and the harness is of red morocco. (Royal Mews)

gatehouse arch there is a statue of Henry VIII who suppressed the priory in 1539 and granted the hospital to the City of London in 1546. Through the archway is the hospital church of St Bartholomew the Less where Inigo Jones was christened in 1573. It was rebuilt by Dance in 1787 and by Hardwick in 1823. The hospital was rebuilt between 1730 and 1769 according to the plans of James Gibbs, who also designed the Great Hall and incorporated a stained glass window showing Henry VIII handing the grant of the hospital to City officials in 1546. On the staircase are two murals by Hogarth, and in the great hall are portraits of physicians and surgeons by Kneller, Thomas Lawrence, Millais and others.

ST JAMES'S PALACE (PALL MALL, SW1) Charles I spent his last night here before walking through St James's Park to his execution in Whitehall in January, 1649. Built by Henry VIII in 1530-6 on the site of a leper hospital dedicated to St James the Less, the palace was the Sovereign's principal residence for only 140 years, but foreign ambassadors

ST PAUL'S CATHEDRAL

WEST FRONT *The old St Paul's, one of England's largest and finest Gothic buildings, was destroyed in September 1666 during the Great Fire. Sir Christopher Wren prepared a first design for a new cathedral in 1670. A second design in the form of a Greek cross, usually called the Great Model design, was submitted in 1673, but was also rejected by the Church Commissioners. Wren's third design, on which the present cathedral is based, was a compromise between Wren's insistence on a Classical cathedral with a dome and the clergy's preference for a cruciform plan. This design received the Royal Warrant in 1673, and the foundation stone was laid in 1675. In 1708 the last stone in the lantern above the dome was laid by Wren's son, and by 1711 the cathedral was complete.*

THE CHOIR *The new high altar, with its imposing domed canopy by S. E. Dykes Bower and Godfrey Allen (suggested by existing drawings by Wren for St Paul's), was consecrated in 1958. It took the place of the high altar and reredos of 1888 which were severely damaged by bombing in 1940. Seen between the columns of the canopy is the Jesus Chapel, now restored as a memorial to the Americans based in Britain who died in the Second World War. Grinling Gibbons carved the choir stalls.*

MONUMENT TO JOHN DONNE *Donne, the great English poet and Dean of St Paul's, died in 1631, and this monument to him by Nicholas Stone (1587–1647) was carved in the same year. Towards the end of his life Donne was obsessed by death, and Stone's carving was made from a painting which Donne posed for in a shroud shortly before he died. The monument, although discoloured, was the only complete figure to be salvaged after the Great Fire and was re-erected in Wren's new cathedral. Stone, one of the most successful sculptors of his day, was the son of a Devon quarryman.*

are still accredited to the 'Court of St James's'. The gatehouse, some of the courtyard turrets, the Chapel Royal and certain state apartments remain from the original building, much of which was destroyed by fire in 1809. Charles I took his last Communion in the Chapel Royal, and Queen Victoria was married there. A number of apartments are occupied by those working in the royal households. The State Apartments are not open to the public.

ST JOHN'S WOOD CHURCH (WELLINGTON ROAD, NW8) On the crest of a hill, this building, with its Ionic Portland stone portico and turret above, is seen to good advantage. It was begun in 1813 after designs by Thomas Hardwick, who had in the same year started building the parish church of St Mary. The interior, which is all white, has monuments of the 19th century by Sir Francis Chantrey, W. Behnes, E. Physick, S. Nixon and others.

ST PANCRAS STATION (EUSTON ROAD, NW1) One of the three great 19th-century railway stations in North London; the other two were Euston and King's Cross. Along the main road spreads Sir Giles Gilbert Scott's Gothic Revival hotel, designed in 1865–71, with spires and pinnacles. Behind is W. H. Barlow's splendid station-shed, roofed by a magnificent iron span of 243 ft—a world record at the time of its construction.

ST PAUL'S CATHEDRAL (EC4) A great Gothic cathedral stood on this site. Its spire was nearly 500 ft high, but this was destroyed by fire in 1561. The building was generally neglected at that time and by 1600 there was concern for its safety. Inigo Jones patched up certain parts, but the cathedral was neglected again during the Commonwealth. After the Restoration in 1660, Christopher Wren put forward proposals for renovating the cathedral, the most important of these being his intention to demolish the central tower and build a dome instead. However, the building was virtually destroyed in September 1666 during the Great Fire of London. The present magnificent domed building was erected to Wren's designs in 1673–1711. During recent years the exterior has been cleaned of two and a half centuries' accumulation of soot, revealing the carved decoration by Francis Bird, Caius Gabriel Cibber, Edward Pierce and Grinling Gibbons.

ST THOMAS HOSPITAL (LAMBETH PALACE ROAD, SE1) Founded near London Bridge as part of the priory of St Mary Overie early in the 12th century. It was separated from the priory following a great fire in 1212 and was rebuilt in Long Southwark (now Borough High Street) where it remained until 1862. It was closed by Henry VIII in 1540 and re-opened by Edward VI in 1552. Extensions to the railway at Charing Cross compelled a change of site, and in 1871 the hospital was re-opened on its present site by Queen Victoria. It suffered heavily from bombing in the Second World War and is being rebuilt on the same site facing the Houses of Parliament. An operating theatre used in the middle of the last century has been preserved as a museum, and this is open to the public in St Thomas Street.

SCIENCE MUSEUM (SOUTH KENSINGTON, SW7) Opened in 1857 in company with its sister museum, the Victoria and Albert, when their respective collections formed the South Kensington Museum. By 1909 the two became separate entities, and the east block of the Science Museum, designed by Sir Richard Allison, was built 1914–18. The collections cover all aspects of science including industrial and technological develop-

GEORGE STEPHENSON'S 'ROCKET'

In 1829 the owners of the unfinished Liverpool and Manchester Railway offered a prize of £500 for the most improved locomotive. Three engines—the 'Rocket', the 'Sans Pareil' and the 'Novelty'—competed in the trials held at Rainhill in October 1828. The 'Sans Pareil' and the 'Novelty' failed to finish the course, but the 'Rocket', drawing three times its own weight (4¼ tons), completed the 35 mile course at an average speed of 14 mph, and became the forerunner of the steam-driven passenger train. (Science Museum)

ments. Many working models, as well as actual locomotives, planes, machinery of both historical and contemporary interest, combine to give an all-embracing panorama of science through the ages.

SOANE MUSEUM (13 LINCOLN'S INN FIELDS, WC2) Founded by Sir John Soane, RA, in the house he originally built for himself in 1812, it contains collections for 'the promotion of the study of Architecture and the Allied Arts'. It includes Hogarth's famous paintings of *The Rake's Progress*. Soane's house next door, built in 1792, has recently been added to the museum.

SOMERSET HOUSE (STRAND, WC2) Old Somerset House was begun in 1547. Its architecture probably derived from the work of contemporary architects such as Philibert de l'Orme; later additions were made by Inigo Jones and John Webb, but the building was completely demolished in the 18th century and replaced by the present palace, designed by Sir William Chambers. This frames a courtyard about 350 ft by 310 ft, and originally reached to the river. The river front, now nearly 800 ft long, was raised on a high base because of the slope of the land towards the Thames, and there were entrances from the river. These have now lost their significance, and are not usually recognised for what they were since the construction of the Victoria Embankment and the roadway over the underground railway. The sculptured decoration of the exterior of the building is by Agostino Carlini, Nathaniel Smith, Joseph Ceracchi, John Bacon, Joseph Nollekens and others. To the west side is the 1856 extension made by Sir James Pennethorne, while to the east is King's College (London University) designed by Sir Robert Smirke and built in 1829–35.

SOUTH LONDON ART GALLERY (PECKHAM ROAD, SE5) The gallery was started as a private venture in 1868 by William Rossiter in a shop in the Camberwell Road. Supported by leading figures in the art world, notably Lord Leighton, G. F. Watts and the actor Henry Irving, Rossiter obtained the present site and the gallery was built in 1891.

The gallery's main collection is of some 300 paintings from the Victorian and earlier eras, including works by Hogarth, Millais, Leighton, G. F. Watts and John Opie, and with drawings by Ruskin. There is a small but growing collection of modern British paintings including works by Sickert, Piper and Christopher Wood, and an artistic record of the London Borough of Southwark shown by paintings dating from the 18th century to the present day. There is also an important reference collection of 20th-century original prints. (By appointment.)

SOUTHWARK CATHEDRAL (LONDON BRIDGE, SE1) Originally the priory church of St Marie Overie. After the Dissolution of the Monasteries, it became a parish church, and in 1905 it was made the Cathedral of Southwark Diocese. The Norman church was begun in 1106 and was destroyed by fire about 100 years later. The present Gothic building was started early in the 13th century. The choir and the retro-choir are extremely beautiful Early English work: the influence of contemporary French Gothic is seen in the handling of the vaulting shafts and ribs. The whole is complemented by an elaborate early 16th-century altar screen, which is comparable with that at Winchester and at St Albans. The crossing under the central tower and both transepts are all fine examples of medieval architecture. The nave was demolished in 1838, and the present one was built in 1890-7 in strict harmony with the 13th-century choir.

STAPLE INN (HOLBORN, WC1) A medieval inn, dating from the 14th century when it got its name from its use as a hostelry where wool was weighed and excise duty collected. A wool-pack

is still to be seen on the wrought-iron gate of the garden. Its quaint half-timbered façade with overhanging gables, said to be the oldest in London, was added in 1586 by the Benchers of Gray's Inn, who bought the building in 1529, and is the only surviving example of Elizabethan domestic architecture in London. Extensive reconstruction was carried out in 1937. The Inn was built round two irregular courtyards in 1545–89 but rebuilt to a large extent in the 18th century. Dickens describes it in *The Mystery of Edwin Drood* as 'one of those nooks turning into which out of the clashing street imparts to the relieved pedestrian the sensation of having put cotton in his ears and velvet soles on his boots'. Nathaniel Hawthorne had the same impression: 'In all the hundreds of years since London was built it has not been able to sweep its roaring tide over that little island of quiet.' It was there that Dr Johnson in 1759 wrote *Rasselas*, in the evenings of one week, to defray his mother's funeral expenses.

TATE GALLERY (MILLBANK, SW1) Sir Henry Tate, the sugar refiner, commissioned the gallery to which he donated his own collection of paintings. The building, in Classical style, was designed by S. R. J. Smith and was opened in 1897. Works by Turner and Blake figure predominantly in a vast collection, only a small percentage of which is displayed at any given moment. The British paintings cover all important artists for the past 450 years and there is also much sculpture; the foreign collections include a representative selection of work by French Impressionists and Post-Impressionists. (See pp. 330–2.)

TEMPLE BAR (EC4) From 1301 a bar (gateway) stood at the boundary of the Cities of London and Westminster. In 1672 a fine gateway designed by Wren was erected. This was removed in 1878 and

SOMERSET HOUSE

Designed in 1726 by Sir William Chambers—one of the founder members of the Royal Academy—Somerset House in the Strand had a Thames-side frontage 800 ft long. Built expressly to house government offices, the Royal Academy and other learned societies, it was the first office building of its kind in England. The rooms on the Strand front contain painted ceiling panels by Giovanni Battista Cipriani, left behind when the Academy moved to the National Gallery in 1837. Started in 1776, the building took ten years to complete. It stands on the site of the former Somerset House built about 1547 for Protector Somerset, Regent for Edward VI.

now stands at Theobald's Park in Hertfordshire; a pedestal surmounted by a dragon marks its former site at the junction of the Strand and Fleet Street. There is a misconception that when the Sovereign drives into the City the carriage must stop at the boundary for the Lord Mayor to give his formal assent to the Sovereign to enter the area, which is under the supreme control of the Lord Mayor. In practice, the carriage drives just across the City boundary, which is marked by a cord stretched across the road on such occasions, and the City Sword is proffered to signify the Lord Mayor's surrender of his authority while the Sovereign is in the City.

TEMPLE CHURCH (EC4) This church, which dates from the 12th century, is the finest monument in England to the Knights Templar. The earliest part of the church is the circular nave, erected c. 1160–85. The circular shape is common to most churches associated with the Templars. The Knights were the self-appointed guardians of the Church of the Holy Sepulchre in Jerusalem, and their round English churches were reminders of this duty and privilege. The design combines Gothic and Romanesque architectural characteristics. Purbeck marble, which centuries later became a favourite decorative material with English masons, was used for the main columns. To the east of this Romanesque church a chancel was added in the 13th century in the form of a three-aisled hall.

THOMAS CORAM FOUNDATION See Coram Foundation for Children.

TOWER BRIDGE (E1) London's best-known bridge. Its centre span is formed by two bascules which are raised two or three times a week to allow ships to pass to and from the Pool of London. Furthest downstream of the Thames bridges, it was opened in 1894.

TOWER OF LONDON (TOWER HILL, EC3) The Tower of London has been a fortress, palace and prison, and it is one of the most important works of medieval architecture to survive in England. It was intended as a royal fortress from which to control the City of London, and represents a system of medieval defences frequently brought up to date. At the core of the whole system stands the White Tower, a massive Norman keep built under William I and William II, and probably finished by 1097. This was built just within the Roman city walls, and it is likely that these were utilised in the original fortress. In the 13th century, following developments in military thought and planning, the White Tower was encircled by two lines of walls and received substantially the form in which it is today. The palace buildings have now all disappeared but evidence for the use of the Tower as a prison is plentiful. Many of the towers have inscriptions carved by former inmates and the records provide a list of illustrious names, including those of Sir Thomas More, Archbishop Laud, Lady Jane Grey and Anne Boleyn, Henry VIII's second wife. (See pp. 308–9.)

TOWER OF LONDON (ARMOURIES) Great Britain's national collection of armour and arms, based on the arsenal of Henry VIII (1509–47), is housed in the 11th-century White Tower of the Tower of London, and in the 17th-century building known as the New Armouries. The collection has been added to over the years and now illustrates the evolution of weapons and defensive armour in Europe from the Middle Ages to 1914. The Armouries, the oldest national armoury still in its original home, can claim to be the oldest museum in Britain.

TOWER OF LONDON (CHAPEL ROYAL OF ST PETER AD VINCULA) The chapel is first mentioned in the reign of Henry III, but it was rebuilt by Henry VIII after a fire in 1520. The chapel was a place of worship for prisoners, and many of those executed are buried here. It was restored in 1876, and again in 1971.

TRAFALGAR SQUARE (SW1) London's most famous square was designed by John Nash early in the 19th century, and was named for the great naval victory of 1805. Its chief monument is Railton's column with Nelson's statue by Bailey, the base of which is guarded by Landseer's four bronze lions. On its north side stands the National Gallery.

VICTORIA AND ALBERT MUSEUM (CROMWELL ROAD, SW7) The vast Victoria and Albert Museum was built as a result of the Great International Exhibition in 1851. Contrary to popular expectations the exhibition, staged by Prince Albert, was a great success, and made so large a profit that a commission was set up to administer the money. The commission bought land south of Hyde Park, commemorated by Exhibition Road in South Kensington, and gradually a cultural and educational centre came into being. The Victoria and Albert Museum was the first establishment of this centre, which grew haphazardly. The first director was Sir Henry Cole: Francis Fowke and H. Scott, army engineers, were among the architects associated with the series of buildings grouped round a central garden. Lord Leighton, Godfrey Sykes and Reuben Townroe did much of the interior decorations. Sir Edward Poynter, Philip Webb and William Morris decorated the old restaurant, which has been preserved as one of the period rooms. By the end of the 19th century the rapidly growing collections had taken up all available space, and in 1899 Queen Victoria laid the foundation stone for the main galleries facing Cromwell Road. Sir Aston Webb, who designed the Victoria Memorial (in front of Buckingham Palace) and the Admiralty Arch, was the architect of the new building. It is dominated by the richly ornamented doorway below a crown-shaped tower. The façade is decorated in the Renaissance style with sculptures and figures set in niches. (See pp. 333–8.)

WALLACE COLLECTION (MANCHESTER SQUARE, W1) The collection is housed in a building begun in 1776 by the 4th Duke of Manchester, which later became the Spanish Embassy and passed to the Hertford family in 1797. On the death of the 4th Marquess in 1870, it passed to his natural son Sir Richard Wallace, who altered it considerably to house his father's art collection and also added many new works—Renaissance and medieval paintings and European arms and armour. The collection was bequeathed to the nation in 1897 by Sir Richard's widow Lady Wallace.

The collection includes paintings by such masters of the Flemish and Dutch schools as Rembrandt, Rubens, Van Dyck and Frans Hals. French schools are well represented with works by Watteau, Boucher, Fragonard, Lancret, Pater and Nattier. Spain and Italy are represented by Velasquez, Murillo and Titian among others, and the British school includes works by Reynolds, Gainsborough, Romney, Hoppner and Lawrence.

Most of the furniture is 18th-century French, much of it from the royal palaces of France, and includes works by some of the greatest French craftsmen—A. C. Boulle, Riesener, Oeben, Weisweiler and Carlin. There is a large collection of Sèvres porcelain, and of Italian majolica, mostly

TOWER OF LONDON

Tradition points to Julius Caesar as the founder of the Tower of London, but its fame begins with the Normans. The White Tower, the massive keep at its heart, was built under William I and William II as a fortress from which to control London. The two outer walls were added in the 13th century. The Tower is famous for its Yeomen Warders, or Beefeaters, resplendent in their Tudor uniforms; its magnificent collection of medieval armour; and as the home of the Crown Jewels. It is even more famous—or infamous—in its role as prison and place of execution and secret murder. Oliver Cromwell ordered the demolition of part of the palace buildings, but there is ample evidence of the use of the Tower as a prison—including the numerous inscriptions scratched by former inmates. The story of the murder of the Princes in the Tower is perhaps of questionable authenticity, but there is poignancy enough in the list of those known to have spent their last days there. State prisoners were commonly admitted through the Traitors' Gate in St Thomas's Tower, and executions took place both on Tower Hill and inside the Tower. Among the illustrious prisoners in the Tower were Sir Thomas More, Sir Walter Raleigh, Archbishop Laud, Lady Jane Grey, Anne Boleyn, Henry VIII's second wife, and Elizabeth I before she became queen.

ST EDWARD'S CROWN *Edward the Confessor, who died in 1066 and was the only English king to be canonised, is said to have placed regalia in Westminster Abbey for the use of his successors. But most of what still survived of these early Crown Jewels by the time of Charles I, was destroyed by order of Parliament after his execution in 1649. The frame of St Edward's Crown is possibly one of the few pieces which escaped destruction; but it more probably derives from the old Imperial Crown of Henry VII, which in turn incorporated earlier materials. The crown is of gold, and it was re-worked and set with diamonds and other precious and semi-precious stones after the Restoration of the Monarchy in 1660. With the minever-trimmed purple velvet Cap of Estate inside, it is traditionally used to crown English sovereigns. (Jewel House)*

STATE SALT *This silver-gilt salt was presented to Charles II by the City of Exeter in thanks for the Restoration. It was used during the coronation banquets of all the monarchs from Charles II to George IV, and has been re-gilded and repaired several times. The condiment was placed in boxes along one side and in receptacles on the tops of the towers. The salt may have been bought second-hand and embellished for presentation to the king. The decoration of lizards and frogs on the base, and the gems and enamelling, suggest that it was made on the Continent in the latter part of the 17th century. The feet and other details appear to date from 1660. (Jewel House)*

ST JOHN'S CHAPEL *The older of the Tower's two Chapels Royal, built about 1080 under William I and improved by William Rufus. Henry III had it painted in high colours. Knights of the Bath spent all-night vigils in the chapel before being dubbed. Later, the chapel became neglected, and under Charles II it was dismantled and used as a storehouse for records. Prince Albert, the Prince Consort, restored it to its former glory, and it is still used as a chapel.*

HENRY VIII'S GUN *The king had this gun—one of the earliest recorded breech loaders—made in 1537. It is almost certainly the gun referred to in accounts of the setting up of targets at Greenwich Palace and Windsor Castle 'for the Kynge to shotte at with his handgoune'. The royal monogram is incorporated in relief ornament on the barrel. (Armouries)*

SPORTING GUN *It is almost certain that this gun was commissioned by Louis XIV to present to Charles Lennox, 1st Duke of Richmond and Lennox, an illegitimate son of Charles II. It was made by Bertrand Piraube, gunmaker to Louis, probably in the early 1680's and is unusual in having a silver barrel. It is unlikely that it was intended for use. (Armouries)*

HENRY VIII'S ARMOUR *(left) In 1515 Henry set up the Almain Armoury at Greenwich Palace. Staffed by Almains (Germans and Flemings)—expert armourers —it made armour for the upper classes only, maintaining a high standard of work. This set of foot-tournament armour was made for the King in 1540. Of bright steel, it has etched and gilded borders probably designed by Hans Holbein the Younger. (Armouries)*

ARMOUR OF ROBERT DUDLEY, EARL OF LEICESTER *This armour (above, right) of Elizabeth I's favourite was made at the Almain Armoury at Greenwich about 1585. A tilt-armour fitted with reinforcing pieces, it has finely etched scrollwork with the initials RD. (Armouries)* from the 16th century. Bronze and gold work of the Renaissance and the 18th century are well represented. There is also an Oriental armoury and a European armoury with many decorated pieces of the 16th and 17th centuries. (See p. 339.)

WELLCOME INSTITUTE FOR THE HISTORY OF MEDICINE (EUSTON ROAD, NW1) The Wellcome Trust, by which this institute and its library are maintained, was established by the American founder of a great pharmaceutical firm—Burroughs Wellcome and Co.—to advance medical research throughout the world. The library contains more than 750,000 items, excluding issues of periodicals. They include manuscripts and printed books from the 11th to the 20th century, and the original letters, notebooks and documents of medical and scientific pioneers. Among these are letters from Florence Nightingale, and the laboratory notebook of Marie Curie, who first isolated radium. There are nearly half a million learned monographs, 50,000 pamphlets, 100,000 prints, drawings and paintings, 2,000 photographs, and 20 films. Special collections include Oriental texts (about 11,000 manuscripts in 43 languages, in addition to printed books), and 14,000 printed books and 150 manuscripts from North, Central and South America dating from between the 16th and 19th centuries. There is extensive material from the collections of, among other bodies, the Royal Society of Medicine, the Medical Society of London, the Royal Society of Health, and the Society for the Study of Addiction.

WELLINGTON MUSEUM (APSLEY HOUSE, HYDE PARK CORNER, W1) Originally built by Robert Adam for Baron Apsley during the 1770's and acquired by the 1st Duke of Wellington in 1817 as his London home. He employed Benjamin Wyatt to enlarge the building in 1828. In 1947 Apsley House was given to the nation by the 7th Duke of Wellington to be preserved as a museum. (See pp. 294–6.)

WESLEY'S CHAPEL AND HOUSE (CITY ROAD, EC1) John Wesley, 1703–91, the founder of Methodism, opened this 'mother-church of world Methodism' in 1778. The chapel, which was recently restored, has the pulpit from which he preached.

Next to the chapel is the 18th-century house, which he lived in for the last 12 years of his life, and in which he died. His tomb is in the graveyard behind the chapel.

The house is now a museum—with Wesley's study and bedroom, and the room which he used for private prayer—containing much of his original furniture.

WESTMINSTER ABBEY (SW1) Built between the 13th and 16th centuries, this church with its great rose windows, its outstanding height, and its flying buttresses, is closer to French Gothic architecture than any other English church. The design of the building seems to have been particularly inspired by the cathedrals of Rheims and Amiens, and the palace chapel of the Kings of France in Paris, Sainte Chapelle. Henry III did not complete the abbey, and the nave was finished only after 1375. However, the Master of the King's Works at that time, Henry Yevele, followed the design of the 13th-century building so closely that the abbey, apart from the Hawksmoor towers, has the appearance of a building designed and built at one period. The 13th-century sculpture on Westminster Abbey is of an extremely high quality. The best-known pieces are probably the figures of angels high up in the interior of the transepts, although much more survives on the lowest

WESTMINSTER ABBEY

Since the 11th century Westminster Abbey has been the usual place for the coronation of English monarchs, and most of the medieval English kings from the time of Henry III were buried there. The present abbey was begun by Henry III (1216–72) on the site of the 11th-century building erected by the royal saint, Edward the Confessor, whose body lies in the great 13th-century shrine at the east end of the church. Henry III never finished the building, and it was not completed until the 16th century; but the French Gothic style was faithfully adhered to, so that most of the abbey gives the impression of a building designed and built as a whole. The latest major addition was Henry VII's Chapel, begun in 1503; it is the chapel of the Order of the Bath and the banners of the knights of the order hang there. The west front gives the appearance of having been constructed during one period, but it represents 600 years of alterations and restorations. In the 18th century, both Christopher Wren and Nicholas Hawksmoor worked on its two main towers.

CORONATION CHAIR *Since the reign of Edward II, all but two English sovereigns have been crowned on the Coronation Chair in Westminster Abbey. It was made of English oak to hold the Stone of Scone, the coronation seat of Scotland's kings, which was seized by Edward I in 1295 to demonstrate Scotland's subservience.*

HENRY VII'S CHAPEL *Raised above the general level of the abbey and approached by a broad flight of steps, the chapel (above) contains the magnificent tomb of Henry VII and his wife, Elizabeth of York. Enclosed by a Gothic screen, the white and black touchstone tomb is the work of the famous Florentine sculptor Torrigiani (1472-1528). Commissioned by Henry VIII in 1512, Torrigiani was paid £1500 and took six years to complete the work. The chapel vault with its intricate and lace-like fan-vaulting is one of the finest of its kind.*

ELEANOR OF CASTILE *This effigy of Edward I's wife, cast in bronze and gilt by William Torel, a London goldsmith, in 1291, is the earliest of its kind in England. It lies on a tomb of Purbeck marble in the Chapel of Edward the Confessor.*

arcading round the walls in the Chapel of St Faith and elsewhere. Henry VII's Chapel, built 1503–c. 1512, is the Chapel of the Order of the Bath. Also used as a royal burial place, it is among the most brilliant and ostentatious works to survive from the Middle Ages; it has an extremely elaborate fan-vault and an unequalled amount of surviving figure sculpture. The latest additions to the abbey are the west towers designed by Nicholas Hawksmoor, which were built from 1735–45.

WESTMINSTER CATHEDRAL (ASHLEY PLACE, SW1) A Roman Catholic cathedral in Byzantine style, built in 1895–1910. John Francis Bentley, the architect, did not live to see the building finished. The dominant feature of the exterior is the tall thin campanile (bell-tower), which rises without ornamentation except for bands of stonework contrasting with the brick, to a graceful octagonal lantern. The tower was for years a prominent feature of the London skyline, but it is now dwarfed by neighbouring office blocks.

WESTMINSTER HALL (HOUSES OF PARLIAMENT, SW1) The scene of many famous trials, including those of Sir Thomas More (1535) and Charles I (1649), the Hall was the chief law court of England from 1224 until 1882. Since then monarchs and famous men have lain in state there before burial. The Hall, part of the medieval Old Palace of Westminster, was built by William Rufus in 1097. It was rebuilt in its present form for Richard II in 1394–1402 by Henry Yevele; the fine hammer-beam roof was the work of Hugh Herland.

WESTMINSTER CATHEDRAL

A great Byzantine-style cathedral, the achievement of Cardinal Vaughan. Built in 1895–1910, it is a large church, impressive in scale inside, the nave and sanctuary comprising four square, domed bays. Originally there was no decoration and the large areas of brickwork were austere. But now marble and mosaic are being added to the walls and vaults, as in this Chapel of the Blessed Sacrament. Some of the earlier mosaics were by R. Anning Bell.

THE 'WOODPECKER' TAPESTRY

In 1881, William Morris (1834–96) the poet, designer, art critic and political thinker, bought Merton Abbey, once a silk factory. There he set up looms for carpets and tapestries, and workshops for other crafts. He revived the 17th-century Gobelins method of high-warp tapestry weaving, and also studied medieval and later tapestries. The 'Woodpecker' tapestry, woven in 1885, was his second full-size tapestry; his friend Philip Webb drew the birds. The design was inspired by the 16th- and 17th-century 'verdures' from Enghien (near Brussels) which usually consisted of a field filled with scrolling leaves similar to acanthus, sometimes with flowers but more usually with birds and insects. Later Morris tapestries included human figures drawn by Sir Edward Burne-Jones.
(William Morris Gallery and Brangwyn Gift)

WHITTINGTON MEMORIAL (HIGHGATE HILL, N19) London's most famous mayor, Sir Richard Whittington, is commemorated by a stone, surmounted by his famous cat, at the foot of Highgate Hill. Here, legend says, the runaway boy heard the sound of Bow Bells three times calling him back to be mayor. At his death in 1423, he was buried in the City church of St Michael Paternoster Royal, bombed during the Blitz.

WILLIAM MORRIS GALLERY AND BRANGWYN GIFT (LLOYD PARK, FOREST ROAD, E17) A collection of work by William Morris and the Morris firm, and by his contemporaries and forerunners of art nouveau is exhibited in Morris's boyhood home. The house is Georgian, has been altered very little, and has much of its original panelling.

BRITISH MUSEUM and THE BRITISH LIBRARY

The nucleus of the British Museum, established by an Act of Parliament in 1753, was the collection of scientific books and manuscripts bequeathed to the nation by Sir Hans Sloane, the fashionable 18th-century physician. As other valuable collections were rapidly acquired, either as gifts, bequests, purchases or copyright deposits, the museum's original premises had to be substantially enlarged. The present building, designed by Sir Robert Smirke and built between 1823 and 1847, has since become the home of priceless man-made objects from all over the world. The British

Library was formed in 1973 from the library departments of the British Museum and other national collections. It is no longer part of the British Museum, and will eventually move out of the Museum building. The reference division has about 10 million printed books and tens of thousands of manuscripts, including the Chinese *Diamond Sutra* of AD 868, the world's first dated printed work, some illuminated manuscripts such as the Lindisfarne Gospels, some early music manuscripts, and two of the four extant copies of Magna Carta.

MILDENHALL TREASURE: THE GREAT DISH *In 1942 a group of silver vessels was found buried near Mildenhall on the borders of the Fens; the hoard was probably hidden for safety and never recovered. This great dish is perhaps its finest piece. Inside the beaded rim, the figure-frieze depicts the triumph of Bacchus over Hercules. The figures include Bacchus (the god of wine), Hercules, Silenus (a foster-father of Bacchus), Pan, satyrs and priestesses of Bacchus.*

Inside this is a zone of sea-nymphs riding on sea-monsters and, in the central medallion, there is a bearded mask, probably of Oceanus, a sea-god. The dish, probably dating from the 4th century, is approximately 2 ft in diameter and weighs more than 18 lb. It was probably made in a workshop in the Mediterranean area, perhaps in Rome, and was buried during the troubled years that saw the end of Roman rule in Britain.

ROYAL GOLD CUP *Made about 1380 for the Duc de Berri, this solid gold cup is decorated with translucent enamels depicting scenes from the life of St Agnes. It had a chequered career in the royal houses of France and England and was acquired by the museum towards the end of the last century from a Spanish convent near Burgos.*

PAINTED WOODEN COFFIN *of Pen-sen-Heru, a Libyan who died in Egypt during the 22nd Dynasty, about 900 BC. The central band of the coffin shows a brightly-painted judgment scene in three sections, culminating in the dead man adoring the god Osiris.*

GOLD COIN OF CHARLES I *The troubled reign of Charles I is reflected in his coinage, which is more varied than that of any other English monarch. This pattern for a gold five-unite piece, was struck at the Tower Mint in 1631–2. As the king's quarrel with Parliament grew worse, local mints were set up throughout the country to supply him with money to continue the struggle. During the Civil War coins were issued in towns and castles under siege.*

GREEK SILVER COIN *One of the masterpieces of Greek colonial coinage, this tetradrachm of 460 BC comes from Naxos, a vine-growing district near Mount Etna, and the oldest Greek colony in Sicily. Appropriately, it carries a portrait of Dionysus, god of fertility and the vine; his great black beard overlaps the frame of the coin. The Greeks made their coins by hand, re-heating the metal after it had been cast while molten, and impressing the design with a bronze or iron stamp.*

GOLD CORONATION MEDAL *Henry Basse, chief engraver to the Mint in 1544–9, made this medal to mark the coronation of Henry VIII's son, the boy-king Edward VI, in 1547. Known only from castings, in both gold and silver, it is England's first official coronation medal. The art of casting portrait medals was introduced in Italy by Renaissance artists, and developed in France, Germany and the Netherlands; but it had little vogue in England until the 17th century.*

SCOTT'S LAST MESSAGE *The last entry, dated March 29, 1912, in Captain Robert Falcon Scott's diary of his ill-fated expedition to the South Pole. It was written in his tent in the Antarctic wastes, and by the time he came to the postscript, 'For God's sake look after our people', his companions, Dr Wilson and Lt. Bowers, were dead beside him. (British Library)*

THE ROSETTA STONE *From the inscriptions on this slab of black basalt, found in the Nile delta in 1799 by one of Napoleon's officers, the French scholar Champollion deciphered Egyptian hieroglyphs, or picture-writing, and formulated the system of decipherment used today. The inscriptions are in two languages but in three scripts: the hieroglyphs in the top section were the form used for monumental purposes; the demotic script in the centre was used almost exclusively for secular purposes; and the Greek in the lower portion was the official language of Egypt at that time. The text on the stone is a copy of a decree passed by the council of Egyptian priests in the ninth year of the reign of Ptolemy V (205–180 BC).*

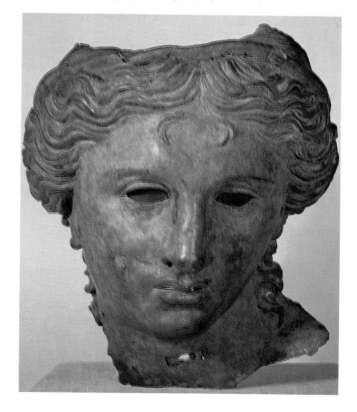

HEAD OF A GODDESS *This bronze head, 15 in. high, is from a statue larger than life, found at Sadak, once a great city of Armenia Minor. The statue, of which the left hand holding drapery has also survived, may represent the Persian goddess of love, Anahita. The eyes of the bronze were originally inlaid; this Greek work is about 2000 years old.*

IRON AGE SHIELD *One of several Iron Age shields found in Britain, this was recovered from the Thames at Battersea. Its gleaming golden-bronze surface is decorated with patterns hammered into relief from the reverse side and embellished with a series of small, quartered, red glass studs. The pattern on the shield reveals an unusual symmetry of design, rarely seen in British work of this period.*

THE HORSE OF SELENE *from the east pediment of the Parthenon, the great temple of the goddess Athene. This marble horse was one of the four (two are in Athens; one is lost) that drew the chariot of Selene across the night sky until dawn, when her chariot sank into the ocean while the chariot of her brother Helios, the sun-god, emerged from the ocean to bring a new day. The Selene and Helios groups stood on opposite sides of the Parthenon's east pediment, in striking contrast—Selene's horses weary after their journey, Helios's fresh and ready to begin. These and a number of other architectural fragments from the Parthenon were brought to England in 1802–11 by Lord Elgin, Ambassador to Turkey. He had seen the neglect many of the sculptures were suffering following the partial destruction of the Parthenon by a Venetian shell during the Turko-Venetian war of 1687. The British Government paid Elgin £35,000—half the cost of bringing the sculptures to England.*

FROISSART'S CHRONICLE *A page from a 15th-century copy of the chronicle, written and illuminated in France, covering the events of the last ten years of Richard II's reign. It starts with the state entry of Charles VI's bride, Isabella of Bavaria, into Paris in 1389 and finishes with Richard's deposition in 1399. The jousts depicted took place at St Inglevert in 1390 for a period of 30 days. Froissart was born in Valenciennes, France, about 1337 and came to London in 1361, where he gained favour with Queen Philippa, Edward III's wife. He stayed five years as the official chronicler at the English Court during the Hundred Years War—already a quarter of a century old. Froissart fell from favour on the death of the Queen and ultimately returned to France where he died in 1404. The Harley Froissart, from which this miniature comes (Harley MS 4379, folio 23b), contains only a small portion of his work. (British Library)*

SEAL OF KING JOHN *The original seal of wax attached to the document submitted by the barons to King John at Runnymede in 1215. The document was later developed into Magna Carta, the great charter of English liberties. Four copies of Magna Carta survive: two are at the British Library, one at Lincoln and one at Salisbury. The obverse of the seal (above) shows John seated in his coronation robes and with regalia. (British Library)*

316

THE SNETTISHAM TREASURE *Related hoards of Iron Age metalwork and coins were found at Snettisham, Norfolk, during 1948–73. Three separate hoards were first found in 1948 when a field was being deep-ploughed for the first time. This beautiful gold torc, or collar, was found at Ken Hill, near Snettisham, in November 1950, with a gold bracelet and a damaged gold 'buffer-ended' torc. It was declared treasure trove and was acquired by the British Museum through the National Art Collections Fund. The torc illustrated consists of eight strands, each of eight twisted wires, soldered into decorated terminals, and is the only complete torc with these elaborate ring terminals to have been found in Britain. Its date was determined by a gold coin c. 50 BC, that was found inside one of the torc terminals.*

BRITISH MUSEUM
MUSEUM OF MANKIND

The Museum of Mankind has one of the world's finest collections of art and material culture from the tribal and pre-industrial societies of Africa, Australia and the Pacific Islands, North and South America, and from parts of Europe and Asia. These collections include material from ancient as well as recent contemporary cultures.

The museum moved from the ethnography galleries in Bloomsbury to more spacious apartments in Burlington Gardens—just behind the Royal Academy—in 1970. A selection of the department's most important pieces can be seen in the permanent exhibition 'Treasures from the Ethnographic Collection'. Other, regularly changing exhibitions, illustrating a variety of non-Western societies and cultures, are 'The Aborigines of Australia', 'The Solomon Islanders' and 'Hawaii'. The library and reserve collections are open to researchers.

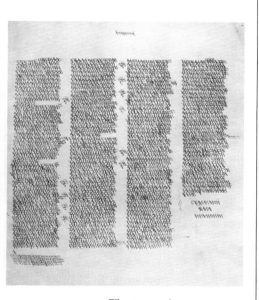

CODEX SINAITICUS *The great 4th-century manuscript of the Bible, in Greek capitals, was bought from the Soviet Government in 1933 for £100,000. The name Sinaiticus is derived from St Catherine's Monastery on Mount Sinai, the former home of the manuscript where, in 1844, a German scholar found a basket filled with old parchment, about to be burnt as rubbish. In this basket were 129 leaves of the Codex. He was allowed to take away 43 leaves, now in the Leipzig University. The remainder were bought by the Imperial Government for 9000 roubles and later sold to Britain. The photograph shows the end of St John's Gospel from chapter 21. (British Library)*

BRONZE HEAD *Head of a queen mother found at Benin, centre of one of West Africa's medieval empires. This head, which dates from the early 16th century, is among the finest pieces of cast-bronze from Benin. It is now at the Museum of Mankind in Burlington Gardens, London, which contains the ethnographic collections of the British Museum.*

317

BRITISH MUSEUM (NATURAL HISTORY)

The lofty halls of the Natural History Museum provide nearly four acres of gallery space where exhibits relating to the products of nature and of early man are on display. Properly, the museum should be called the British Museum (Natural History), for it is an offshoot; the natural history departments were moved from Bloomsbury in 1881, when the parent British Museum was bursting at the seams for lack of space—a condition which has become almost routine. The vast natural history collections are based on the original collection of Sir Hans Sloane (1660–1753), a physician who built his fortune on a rich marriage a fashionable practice and an early appreciation of the value of quinine. The specimens on display are, in fact, only a small selection from the museum's riches. Unseen to the general public are the laboratories, workshops and libraries where the museum's scientific and technical staff are engaged in research. As part of the museum's educational work, schoolchildren are encouraged to study and draw exhibits.

THE FIRST BRITON? *In 1935–6 two fragments of a human skull (right) were found during excavations in a gravel pit at Swanscombe in Kent. Then, in 1955, not many yards away from the site of the original finds, a third fragment was unearthed; the three pieces fitted together perfectly. Close by were a number of flint axes, skilfully chipped to a fine cutting edge. Both the skull, thought to be that of a young woman in her twenties, and the associated implements, are about 250,000 years old— by far the most ancient of any human remains ever discovered in Britain. No one knows how the young woman lived or died, but almost certainly she belonged to a group of nomadic hunters who crossed the land bridge that then existed between England and the Continent. The axes were general-purpose tools, killing implements that were also used to flay and butcher the carcases of the hunters' prey. Pieces of charcoal found near the axes suggest that Swanscombe men knew the use of fire.*

HIBISCUS DRAWING *(left) by Sydney Parkinson. Originally a draper by trade but with a passion for drawing, Parkinson was enlisted by Sir Joseph Banks as an assistant. Together they accompanied Captain Cook, on the Endeavour, on a voyage to the South Seas in 1768. Parkinson, as natural history draughtsman, was paid a salary of £80 a year. He made numerous drawings, but completed only a few, for he contracted a fever and died at sea, aged 26, on the homeward voyage. Other artists were engaged by Banks to make finished drawings from his sketches. The voyage of the Endeavour established the practice for explorers to carry artists with them to record the plants, birds and animals of the new lands.*

CHELIDONIUM DRAWING *(right) by George Dionysius Ehret. Born in 1708 in Heidelburg, the son of humble parents, Ehret spent much of his youth as a gardener's apprentice, practising drawing in his spare time. After a period of study and travel on the Continent when he made hundreds of drawings, he finally settled in England in 1736. Here he met Dr Mead, the Royal Physician, who bought 200 of his paintings and introduced him to Sir Hans Sloane and the Duchess of Portland. By the middle of the 18th century Ehret dominated botanical drawing and was contributing to Linnaeus's 'Genera Plantarum'. In 1750 he was elected to the Botanic Gardens at Oxford as a draughtsman and was finally made a Fellow of the Royal Society in 1757—the only foreigner then so honoured.*

glaucium.

CHELIDONIUM *pedunculis unifloris,*
foliis amplexicaulibus sinuatis, caule glabro. Linn.

COURTAULD INSTITUTE GALLERIES

In 1932 Samuel Courtauld and Viscount Lee of Fareham founded the Courtauld Institute of Art for London University. They both gave their magnificent art collections to the Institute, and these formed the nucleus of the present collections, enlarged by further bequests to the university.

GAUGUIN: NEVERMORE *Gauguin reacted against Impressionism, introducing into his paintings simple outlines of form and large areas of flat, strong colour. His desire for intensity and simplicity, and passion for the exotic, drove him to seek the simple life—in 1895 he left his Danish wife and Western civilisation, and went to live in the South Sea Islands. This, one of his finest paintings, was done in 1897 and depicts a native girl called Paa'ura who, at the age of 14½, went to live with him.*

VAN GOGH: PEACH TREES IN BLOSSOM *In February 1888 Van Gogh suddenly left Paris for Arles and the warmth of a southern climate. Almost immediately the orchards of Provence became a foaming cascade of blossom and the next eight months were the happiest of his short life. In April he painted 15 orchards in blossom. This one he painted in the plain of Crau in the following spring. He used colour with brilliance and originality but with such conviction and sincerity that it works—the force of expression is reflected in his personal technique of dots, stripes and whorls rained on to the canvas with dramatic vehemence.*

320

MANET: A BAR AT THE FOLIES-BERGÈRE *In the 1860's Manet fought a lone battle against the artificiality and sentimentality of official art in Paris. He disregarded the mellow shading of the studio in favour of the harsher contrasts of light and shade in full light, and the use of full colour. He was an inspiration to the Impressionists—but himself desired more naturalism than is possible in the diffuseness of full Impressionism. Manet scandalised the public in his early days and it was just as much his defiance of the accepted way of painting as his subject matter which infuriated them. This painting, his last major work, was exhibited in 1882, and although it may lack the sparkle of his earlier works it is a compact design with the reflections of the barmaid and her customer.*

CÉZANNE: MONT STE-VICTOIRE *Cézanne (1839–1906) was one of the leaders of the inevitable reaction against the sketchy methods and lack of structural form of the Impressionists. He worked out of the studio to achieve his identification of colour with form, and made calculated distortions of form for structural strength. Mont Ste-Victoire, which he could see from his studio near Aix-en-Provence, became a kind of holy mountain which he portrayed many times. In this distant view the components of the intervening landscape form an overall geometric pattern.*

ITALIAN DRUG JAR *One of a set of jars that would have been displayed colourfully on a pharmacist's shelf. The inscription denotes that it contained the drug Zucaro Buglossato. Made in 1510–15 at Deruta in Central Italy, this jar of traditional shape is made of earthenware covered with an opaque-white tin glaze and is painted in colours—a technique called majolica. Originally the name majolica was probably given by Italians to similar Spanish ware imported into Italy by ships sailing from Majorca.*

MUSEUM OF LONDON

The museum, which opened in December 1976, merges the two museums specialising in London's history—the City's Guildhall Museum, dating from the early 19th century, and the London Museum (recently at Kensington Palace) founded in 1912. In its new building in the Barbican, London's two great historical collections show the complex story of how 1 sq. mile of Roman Londinium developed into the 610 sq. mile conurbation of Greater London. The galleries, arranged chronologically, display 2000 years of London life. Tools (the earliest dates from 250,000 BC) and products of urban crafts, household and personal effects, toys and costumes, vividly portray the ordinary Londoner through the ages, while Coronation robes and the Lord Mayor's Coach reflect the pomp and ceremony of the capital.

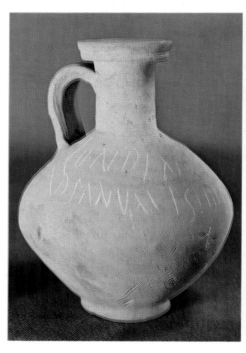

ROMAN JUG *This 10 in. high earthenware jug (right) was found in Southwark. It is inscribed with the words 'Londini Ad Fanum Isidis' (In London, by the Temple of Isis), and was possibly a temple offering or a tavern jug. It dates from the late 1st century AD, and is the earliest example of an inscription using the Roman name for London.*

FIRE ENGINE *The inhabitants of London presented this fire engine (above) to Frederick Hodges, a Lambeth distiller, in 1862 in appreciation of his efforts to fight local fires. Fire protection did not become a public responsibility until 1866 when the Metropolitan Fire Brigade (now the London Fire Brigade) was founded.*

THE CHEAPSIDE HOARD *This hoard of jewellery (right), probably part of a city merchant's stock-in-trade, hidden in Cheapside early in the 17th century, provides a unique record of the taste in jewellery of the middle classes at that period. One of the most exquisite objects is a scent bottle or pomander (bottom right, on a chain) set with a sapphire, opals and diamonds.*

NATIONAL GALLERY

Since its foundation, in 1824, the National Gallery has grown to be one of the greatest museums of art in the world. It is remarkable for the balance of its collections: all of the important national schools and almost all of the major old masters are represented. The rich collection of Dutch masters includes 19 Rembrandts. The gallery, founded when the Government voted £60,000 to purchase and exhibit 38 paintings from the Angerstein Collection, moved to its present site, then newly built, in 1838. It now has more than 2000 paintings. As a matter of policy, drawings, watercolours and pieces of sculpture are not acquired; but an exception was made in the case of the Leonardo cartoon presented through the National Art Collections Fund in 1962.

GOYA: DOÑA ISABEL COBOS DE PORCEL *The art of Goya (1746–1828) is one of astonishing versatility —his drawings, etchings, frescoes, and cartoons for tapestry, as well as about 500 oil paintings, include portrayals of daily life in Madrid, religious works, portraits, a savage indictment of the brutality of war, and finally horrific visions from the unconscious. The great period for his portraits was 1800 to 1808; acuteness of observation is matched by the beauty of his often restrained colour, and his handling of paint often foreshadows Impressionism. This picture was probably exhibited by Goya in Madrid in 1805.*

BELLINI: THE AGONY IN THE GARDEN *With Bellini the Venetian painter's instinctive feeling for colour takes the form of an emotional reaction to light, as in this work of about 1464. In his brother-in-law Mantegna's earlier painting of the subject (also in the National Gallery) the figures merge into a flinty world of geological strata as if they themselves were rocks. Here the apostles are sleeping men in human attitudes —not fallen columns—and Christ towers against a sky flushed with magic dawn light.*

LEONARDO: CARTOON *Leonardo da Vinci (1452–1519) drew this, a full-scale composition of the Virgin and Child with St Anne and infant St John the Baptist, possibly before he left Milan, between and 1499. It is universally admired as one of his most beautiful works. Leonardo's follower, Luini, did a painting from it, but there is none in it by Leonardo himself. An unfinished painting, now in the Louvre, shows how he wanted to get away from the markedly vertical composition of the cartoon, and from the arrangement of having two heads on the same level. The Paris painting does not include St John the Baptist.*

THE WILTON DIPTYCH *Largely because of Henry VIII and Cromwell, few medieval paintings survive in England. This famous diptych, probably by an English artist working in the International Gothic style, represents Richard II and his patron saints who are presenting him to the Virgin and Child.*

SEURAT: UNE BAIGNADE, ASNIÈRES *Seurat (1859–91) did not so much reject Impressionism as reduce it to order. His figures are precisely contoured and are arranged to obtain a perfect integration of space and forms. He analysed the exact proportions of colour and separated them into dots (points) of uniform size which are then blended optically by the spectator. This, his masterpiece, was the first of five major works on a large scale: his 'pointillism' is not fully developed and his system has not yet become an end in itself.*

PIERO DELLA FRANCESCA: THE BAPTISM OF CHRIST *Today Piero is widely regarded as the greatest painter of the mid-15th century, although previously held in low esteem. He was born in the small Umbrian town of San Sepolcro about 1415, but was known to have worked in Florence in 1439. By 1442 he was back in his native town, where he worked for the rest of his life, making visits to Rome and the northern courts of Ferrara and Rimini. His work holds a fine balance between reality and abstraction. The pursuit of geometry and the development of perspective were his particular interest, and he used pale, cool, flat colours to give the effect of a fusion of light and colour. In this picture, probably dating from the 1440's, Christ's body seems almost to be carved out of light and has a radiance and impassivity—keynotes of Piero's art.*

327

DUCCIO: VIRGIN AND CHILD *Duccio (c. 1255–1319) has been called the last artist of the old world. He lived in Siena, where painting was conservative and decorative; in Florence at about the same time, art was vigorous and experimental, with a strong feeling for solidity and form. Duccio's painting was a late* flowering of the Byzantine style, with its emphasis on flat pattern, against a sumptuous gold background. Another quality of Duccio's art, as of all Sienese painting, is the elegance of the draughtsmanship, exemplified in the central panel of this triptych by the graceful weaving line of the Virgin's headscarf.

CARAVAGGIO: THE SUPPER AT EMMAUS *The Italian Caravaggio was one of the great rebels of art. His tempestuous life, punctuated by brawls, came to an untimely end when he was only 37. His painting shocked his contemporaries with its realism and its dramatic lighting. He chose the common people as his* models, and is said to have once fished a corpse out of the Tiber to serve as a model for the Madonna. In this work, done about 1600, Christ is shown without any aura of holiness, and the disciples are rough peasant types. Caravaggio had a Flemish passion for incidental details—note the wormholes in the fruit.

VAN EYCK: THE MARRIAGE OF ARNOLFINI *The Flemish artist Jan van Eyck, who died in 1441, perfected a new technique of painting in oils and varnish which allowed the building up of detail after acutely observed detail in brilliant colours, emphasising the beauty of surface and texture in fabric, fur, glass and metal. This famous double portrait, showing the symbolic marriage of the Bruges merchant Arnolfini and his* bride Giovanna Cenami, is full of elaborate symbolism —the single lighted candle symbolises Christ, the fruit stands for innocence, the dog for faithfulness, and the pattens Arnolfini has taken off show that he stands on holy ground. In the mirror between the espoused couple are two figures in a doorway, one of which must be van Eyck himself, for he has written on the wall, 'Jan van Eyck was here: 1434'.

TATE GALLERY

Of all London's great art collections, the Tate Gallery is, to modern tastes, the most rewarding. It makes no attempt to cover the whole range of art, but comprises two distinct collections—British painting and modern foreign paintings, drawings and sculpture. The gallery, opened in 1897, was built by the sugar refiner, Sir Henry Tate, who also gave to it works from his own collection of British paintings. The Tate sets out to cover all that is significant in British painting from the 16th century to the present day; it houses a number of superb Constables, some of the most powerful work of the visionary William Blake, as well as important Pre-Raphaelite and 20th-century works. But pride of place in the British section must go to its unparalleled collection of Turners—the Tate owns more than 280 of his oil paintings. The modern foreign collection began with the bequest of 39 paintings, mostly French, by Sir Hugh Lane in 1916. It now ranges from the French Impressionist painters to recent examples of 'conceptual art'. The sculpture collection includes works by Rodin, Epstein, Barbara Hepworth, Butler, Giacometti and Henry Moore. The sculpture hall was the gift of the late Lord Duveen in 1937.

HOGARTH: THE GRAHAM CHILDREN *Hogarth (1697–1764) is often remembered only as a painter of social and political satire and as a vigorous campaigner against social ills. But he was also a superb portraitist with a very individual power of observation and exquisite sensibility in the technical handling of paint. This picture is a 'conversation piece'—an informal group portrait—a feature of English painting of 1730–1830. The four children of Daniel Graham, apothecary to Chelsea Hospital, are shown with their cat. The composition is admirably designed and the cherries held by the elder girl form an inspired accent of colour.*

MODIGLIANI: STONE HEAD *Amedeo Modigliani one of the most fascinating sculptors of this ce although his sculpture is much less well known his paintings. An Italian by birth, he went to in 1906 and joined a group of avant-garde which included Picasso. He took up sculpture in but in 1915 devoted himself again to painting his early death in 1920. This powerful stylised probably dates from 1911 or 1912, and was one series of several stone heads which were orig conceived to form a sculptural ensemble. Those survive are now widely scattered.*

PICASSO: THREE DANCERS *In 1925 Picasso's career saw a turning point, marked by the 'Three Dancers'. The classical spirit of his sculptural nudes and serene still-lifes of the early 1920's is exchanged for a mood of torment. His distortion of the human body is now emotional rather than intellectual, and the abandon of the three figures heralds a phase of expressionist violence. Images can have more than one meaning— the circle on the chest of the left dancer can be read as a breast or as an eye.*

KANDINSKY: COSSACKS *A water-colour of 1910 by the Russian artist Kandinsky. In Munich in 1910–14, he was cautiously moving towards a whole-hearted abstraction and painted his 'Improvisations' and 'Compositions'. The former were direct expressions of the subconscious mind; for the latter he did a series of preparatory studies, of which this is one. The forms are still based on reality—a castle, mounted Cossacks, birds. But these vestiges of representation are not the message of the picture—it produces an emotional effect merely by lines, shapes and colours. 'Cossacks' is one of Kandinsky's early works—an amalgam of representational and abstract art.*

331

© by S.P.A.D.E.M. Paris

MATISSE: THE SNAIL *In 1950, at the age of 80, Matisse gave up oil painting (easel painting) because of his ill health. For the last four years of his life he worked on a grand scale with cut-outs of sumptuous hand-coloured paper. These works have no perspective, but the flat, sharply defined areas of pure colour are arranged to create forms that exist in space. The work shown above is named from the disposition of the paper cut-outs.*

MONDRIAN: COMPOSITION WITH RED, YELLOW AND BLUE *Mondrian (1872–1944) is now seen as one of the most influential and individual exponents of abstract art. But the style by which he is best known, shown in this work of about 1940, was reached only after ruthless self-discipline. This ascetic style, with its horizontal-vertical grid and primary colours on a brilliant white background is based on a limited number of elements in maximum contrast.*

BRAQUE: GUITAR AND JUG *Picasso and Braque were the joint inventors of Cubism—the use of arranged geometrical forms to represent what is seen. With Picasso the ideas, often expressed with lightning speed, are more important than the painting; but in Braque (1882–1963) painting is the reality—the technique is* deliberate and shows a craftsman's feeling for his material. After 1918, his liaison with Picasso over, he developed his own post-Cubist style. But in this work —one of a series of rich, sensuous still-lifes of the 1920's —the Cubist idiom is retained in division of the jug into halves to suggest volume without tonal shading.

VICTORIA AND ALBERT MUSEUM

Prince Albert, the Prince Consort, planned a great complex of museums and colleges at South Kensington. With money derived from the Great Exhibition of 1851, the South Kensington Museum, a collective museum of science and art, was erected. Opened in 1857, it incorporated the collections of the Museum of Ornamental Art opened at Marlborough House in 1852. The art departments grew rapidly to include fine and applied arts of all kinds, represented chiefly by post-Classical European art and that of the Near and Far East. Eventually, because of lack of space, the science exhibits were moved to the new Science Museum near by. In 1899 Queen Victoria laid the foundation stone of the present building, designed by Sir Aston Webb. She stipulated that the title be changed to 'Victoria and Albert Museum' and in 1909 Edward VII opened the new building; it now contains one of the world's outstanding collections of fine and applied arts.

THE SION GOSPELS COVER *A German manuscript cover, revealing an unusually high degree of craftsmanship in the use of repoussé—ornamental metalwork that has been hammered into relief from the reverse side. The book dates from about 1000 and has a beech-wood cover veneered with gold, its surface richly decorated with precious stones and cloisonné enamels. The centre panel depicting the seated figure of Christ is very likely 12th-century work and it is probable that some of the larger stones are also later additions. Much speculation surrounds the manuscript's origins and some authorities link it with the Gospels of Charlemagne, a book which belonged to the abbey of St Maurice d'Agaune, in Valais, Switzerland. It is more popularly supposed to have been made for the ancient church of Notre Dame de Valère, also in Valais. A contemporary inscription verifies that the manuscript was there during the 17th century and later transferred to the care of the Cathedral of Sion. In 1851 a dealer at Geneva bought the book from the cathedral authorities and later sold it to the Marquis de Ganay. It was eventually acquired by the Spitzer collection towards the end of the century and has been carefully restored. It is 10 in. high.*

THE SYON COPE *A cope, or large semicircular cloak, is the main vestment worn at numerous ecclesiastical ceremonies. The origins of the Syon cope are unknown, but the wealth of heraldic Arms surrounding it suggest that the cope was made in about 1300–20. It certainly once belonged to the nuns of the convent of Syon in Middlesex, whose community, founded in 1414–15, was exiled in Elizabeth I's reign and only returned to England about 1810. Embroidered on the cope in silver and silver-gilt thread and coloured silks are figures of the apostles and saints, including St Michael (above), six-winged seraphim, and two priests who may have been the donors. It is a good example of the medieval English embroidery known as 'Opus Anglicanum', renowned throughout Europe during the 13th and 14th centuries; the type of stitch used is peculiar to medieval embroidery, and was used particularly for metal threads which were pulled in little loops through to the back of the base material and caught with linen thread.*

THE ELTENBERG RELIQUARY One of the finest surviving examples of Romanesque coppersmiths' work, this reliquary was made in Cologne, probably during the last quarter of the 12th century. By the time of the French Revolution it belonged to the Benedictine nunnery of Eltenberg in Holland. The nunnery was pillaged during the Revolutionary Wars, but the reliquary was saved by one of the nuns who hid it and other treasures in a chimney. The total effect of the reliquary is one of disciplined richness and magnificence; the principal decorative motif is a stylised floral scroll, but geometrical and scale patterns are also used.

MEDICI PORCELAIN BOTTLE The first European soft-paste porcelain was made in Florence under the patronage of the ruling Medici family in about 1570–80. The factory was set up to discover the porcelain formula after Marco Polo had brought back pieces of blue and white porcelain from China. Wares such as this bottle, made about 1580, were produced in soft-paste porcelain decorated under the glaze in mauvish-blue. This bottle is unmarked, but the pieces usually bore a mark incorporating the dome of Florence Cathedral and 'F' in underglaze blue.

RAPHAEL: THE MIRACULOUS
DRAUGHT OF FISHES *It is a miracle
that Raphael's seven tapestry cartoons survive. They are painted in
distemper on paper, for they had to
be sent away to Brussels where the
original tapestries were made. There
they were cut into strips as patterns
for the weavers. Not until the late
17th century, in England, were they
pasted together on canvas. Raphael
was at the height of his powers when
Pope Leo X commissioned a set of
ten cartoons, and seven of the finished
tapestries were hung in the Sistine
Chapel on Christmas Day, 1519.
The cartoons are one of the noblest
monuments of that peak of western
Renaissance art which lasted 30
years, from Leonardo's painting of
the 'Last Supper' until the sack of
Rome in 1527.*

THE BURGHLEY NEF *Nefs—vessels shaped like ships
—were a favourite subject for medieval and Renaissance
goldsmiths. In France they were often used to mark the
highest place at table, like the English great salts, and
the Burghley Nef has a salt container fitted in the poop.
It was made by the Parisian goldsmith, Pierre le
Flamand, known to have been working about 1462.*

THE STUDLEY BOWL *A beautifully proportioned and
decorated bowl and cover made of silver-gilt in England
in the latter half of the 14th century. Made to hold
porridge or similar food this piece of domestic silversmiths' work was once owned by the church at Studley
Royal, near Ripon, N. Yorkshire. Fine chased and
engraved ornament covers both bowl and lid. On each
part a black-letter alphabet is shown preceded by a
cross and followed by various literary symbols and
contractions of the type used in contemporary Latin
manuscripts. Each alphabet is incorporated in a leafy
wreath. On the cover knob is the letter 'a'. Together
the pieces stand 5⅝ in. high and the whole testifies to
the high level of technical and artistic perfection attained
by English silversmiths in the Middle Ages.*

HILLIARD: AN UNKNOWN YOUTH LEA
AGAINST A TREE AMONG ROSES *Hilliard
greatest English artist of the Elizabethan age. N
paintings by him are known, but he is the best
the contemporary miniaturists after Holbein.
obtained a position at court in 1572 and was L
(painter) to the Queen, whom he painted. He
duced the three-quarter view and the full-l
miniature. This miniature, 5½ by 2¾ in., is the
known and is a landmark in English painting.
subject is thought to be the Earl of Essex.*

SILVER-MOUNTED GUN *This intricately decorated air-gun is said to have belonged to George II. It was made about 1735 by the German gunsmith Johann Gottfried Kolbe. The carved walnut stock is inlaid with silver and the steel stock is chiselled in relief with foliage and the figure of Jupiter brandishing a thunderbolt.*

PRESENTATION SWORD *This sword was presented by the East India Company to Lt.-Col. James Hartley for gallantry during the Mahratta War in 1779. It was made by James Morisset, and the hilt is solid gold.*

17TH-CENTURY GERMAN RAPIER *The rapier, with its hilt to protect the swordsman's hand, was developed in the 16th century. In its more elaborate forms it became a piece of masculine jewellery. This sword-hilt was made about 1610 by one of the German brothers Emmanuel and Daniel Sadeler of Munich. Their work is identical, and is often characterised by minute designs in chiselled relief.*

WALLACE COLLECTION

The Wallace Collection is said to be the most valuable single gift ever made by an individual to any nation. It was built up mainly in Paris by the 3rd and 4th Marquesses of Hertford and by Sir Richard Wallace (1818–90), son of the 4th Marquess. In 1871, after the siege of Paris by the Prussians, Sir Richard came to live in England, bringing most of the collection over with him. It was bequeathed to the British nation by Sir Richard's widow, Lady Wallace, who died in 1897.

RUBENS: RAINBOW LANDSCAPE *In the landscapes Rubens painted at Steen—the Belgian château he bought in 1635—the rocks, torrents and serpentine movement of earlier landscapes give way to a lowland countryside, bathed in light of an unprecedented intensity. His superb draughtsmanship is seen in the painting's detail.*

From A. K. Snowman's '18th Century Gold Boxes of Europe' (Faber)

PRINCE HENRY'S SWORD *Medieval cross-hilted swords were briefly revived during the early 17th century when James I re-introduced the ancient ceremony of making Knights of the Bath. This sword was made about 1610 for Henry, Prince of Wales, who died in 1612.*

ENAMELLED GOLD BOXES *Part of a collection of 89 boxes largely built up by Richard Seymour-Conway, the 4th Marquess of Hertford, and added to by his son Sir Richard Wallace. The 'Fantaisie' box in the form of a coach seat (top right) is a great rarity, for work of this kind was never made in great quantity, and little of it has survived. It was made in 1756–7 by the Parisian goldsmith Aymé-Antoine Chollet. Below it is a shell-shaped box with white peacock-feather decoration, made in 1743–4 by Jean Ducrollay of Paris.*

Long Ashton *Avon* 540Cg

CHURCH OF ALL SAINTS A church of the 14th and
15th centuries with a west tower. The most interesting monument is that to Lord Chief Justice
Choke, who died in 1486. This has recumbent
effigies, heraldry, many angels and a canopy.

Longbridge Deverill *Wilts.* 540Ee

CHURCH OF SS PETER AND PAUL Of Norman
origin, the building has work of various periods.
There is a west tower, and inside on the north side
of the nave are Norman arches. At the end of the
south aisle is some classical-style panelling, and
a 17th-century font. Among the interesting
monuments there is a medallion portrait by Sir
Francis Chantrey, and a memorial font by Alfred
Gilbert of *c.* 1887.

Long Crendon *Bucks.* 547Gc

COURT-HOUSE A partly half-timbered, 14th-
century court-house or staple hall, which was
probably once used as a wool store.

Longdon-upon-Tern *Shropshire* 552Ac

Here in 1796 Thomas Telford built the world's
first cast-iron aqueduct. It still stands, though the
canal that it carried is no longer in use.

Longleat House *Wilts.* 540De

A great early Renaissance house, begun for Sir
John Thynne in 1568. Thynne had bought the land
and original priory buildings at Longleat in 1541.
He at once set about building a new house, but
much was destroyed by fire in 1567. A year later,
the architect Robert Smythson arrived on the
scene and work on the present house began, but
was not finished when Thynne died in 1580.
Longleat, one of the great exploits of Elizabethan
architecture, is symmetrical, except for the great
hall, found to one side, as in most medieval houses;
at Wollaton (Nottinghamshire), Smythson's later
house, the hall is at the very centre of the house,
where in earlier buildings there had usually been an
open courtyard. Longleat has a flat, not gabled,

LONGLEAT HOUSE

STATE DRAWING-ROOM *One of
the great Elizabethan houses, Longleat was designed by Robert Smythson for Sir John Thynne, Elizabeth
I's Lord High Treasurer. In 1789 a
descendant of Thynne was created
Marquess of Bath. In 1860, the 4th
Marquess, returned from a Grand
Tour, employed J. D. Crace to
Italianise the state rooms, Italian
craftsmen being imported.*

SILVER CENTREPIECE *The death of
Sir Bevill Grenville, an ancestor of
the Marquess of Bath, is depicted in a
massive 19th-century silver table
piece in the state dining room at
Longleat. Grenville, a Royalist,
was killed in 1643 in the last
charge during the battle of Lansdown
Hill, near Bath.*

roof, with domed pavilions, and is characterised by the large number of windows in each of the four three-storey façades. Sir Jeffry Wyatville made alterations to the house in 1807–11. The magnificent state rooms contain fine furniture and paintings, and include a superb library. The mansion and colourful gardens are in the middle of a park, landscaped by Capability Brown.

Long Meg and Her Daughters *Cumbria*   *557Jf*
This Bronze Age stone circle is oval in plan and measures 120 yds by 100 yds. Of a former total of 59 stones, 27 are still standing. Long Meg herself is a single standing stone, some 12 ft high, on the south-west side; note the ear-rings.

Long Melford *Suffolk*   *548Ce*
Long Melford is the stateliest small town in Suffolk, with an unrivalled main street, long and wide. It has a magnificent church, a beautiful green, three 'great' houses and other worthwhile buildings.

On the green are: the church; Melford Hall, a large Elizabethan mansion of *c.* 1550, with turrets, gate-house and summer-house; and Holy Trinity Hospital, almshouses founded in 1573 (restored 1847). North of the church is Kentwell Hall, *c.* 1564, moated and with a great avenue of limes planted in 1678.
CHURCH OF THE HOLY TRINITY A huge 15th-century church, with magnificent windows, and a three-gabled Lady Chapel. The west tower is a replacement by G. F. Bodley, *c.* 1900, of one of the 18th century. A feature of the interior is the large amount of 15th-century stained glass. There are many brasses and monuments, including that by William Cure to Sir William Cordell (*d.* 1580). There is a carved alabaster panel of the Adoration of the Magi, and, outside, memorial inscriptions run in bands on the walls.

Longnor *Shropshire*   *551Jb*
CHURCH OF ST MARY THE VIRGIN A small and unaltered example of an Early English church, *c.* 1300, standing near Longnor Hall. The nave and chancel are in one, and there is iron Gothic tracery in the east window. There are 18th-century box-pews, reader's desk and pulpit, and galleries.

Longstanton *Cambs.*   *548Af*
ALL SAINTS' CHURCH An interesting, mainly 14th-century church containing monuments to the Hatton family, one of whom was patron to Francis Drake. The Hatton crest, a golden hind, appears both in glass and stone, and it was after this emblem that Drake renamed his famous ship.

Long Sutton *Lincs.*   *553Jc*
CHURCH OF ST MARY This church has an excellent Early English tower with lead spire slightly set apart from the main building. The work on the interior includes some Norman fragments, and there is a handsome 15th-century south porch. Worth noticing is the medieval brass eagle lectern.

Longthorpe Tower *Cambs.*   *547Jg*
An interesting 13th-century fortified manor house. The two lower storeys have stone-vaulting. Some fascinating wall-paintings from the 14th century were discovered on the first floor *c.* 1945 and show, among other scenes, the Seven Ages of Man, the Labours of the Months, the Three Quick and the Three Dead.

Long Wittenham *Oxon.*   *546Fc*
CHURCH OF ST MARY Not far from the Iron Age hill-top fort known as Wittenham Clumps (Sinodun Hill), St Mary's still has the original Norman chancel arch and 13th- and 14th-century additions.

OUR LADY OF PITY

The north-door window of this church was re-assembled in the 20th century, using the magnificent 15th-century stained glass that escaped destruction during the 16th and 17th centuries when much of the church's glass was destroyed. The window depicts the Virgin seated on a decorated throne, holding in her arms the body of Christ crowned with thorns; a detail is shown above. (Church of the Holy Trinity, Long Melford)

There is much 17th-century woodwork—font cover, pulpit and a screen which, together with the stalls, came from Exeter College, Oxford. In the Crusader Chapel is a piscina which is also a monument, with a small figure of a knight.

Looe *Cornwall*   *538Eb*
Seaport town, divided into East Looe and West Looe by the Looe River. It has many houses of medieval origin, and the 16th-century Old Guildhall has the original magistrates' bench and pillory. (See East Looe.)

Loose *Kent*   *542Df*
WOOL HOUSE A half-timbered farmhouse of the 16th century. (By appointment.)

Loseley House *Surrey*   *542Af*
Sir Thomas More's kinsman, Sir William More, built this Elizabethan mansion, set in a large park, in 1561–9; his descendants still live in the house, which incorporates stone from Waverley Abbey near Farnham. Inside are fine ceilings, panelling from Henry VIII's Nonesuch Palace, a unique chimney-piece carved from local chalk, fine furniture and tapestries.

Lostwithiel *Cornwall*   *538Dc*
CHURCH OF ST BARTHOLOMEW A church with an octagonal spire and a 14th-century font, magnificently carved. During the Civil War it was used by Parliamentary troops as a stable and prison. There are also several mural monuments.

341

CARVED MISERICORD

The comparatively austere interiors of medieval churches gradually changed during the 15th and 16th centuries, with a profusion of carved and painted furnishings. The clergy were no longer required to stand erect throughout the long services, and misericords —projections on the undersides of the hinged seats of the choir stalls—began to appear. These served as supports for standing clergy when the seats were turned up, and were often finely carved. Because they were less exposed to view than other church carvings, a far greater freedom of interpretation was permitted. (Church of St Laurence, Ludlow)

Lound *Suffolk*   548Fh
CHURCH OF ST JOHN THE BAPTIST A pretty church with a round Norman tower, and a Perpendicular font with carved lions and angels. The rood and organ case, and the font cover, are early 20th-century works by Sir Ninian Comper.

Louth *Lincs.*   553Jf
There are a few remains of a Cistercian abbey, *c.* 1139, in Louth Park, an intricate pattern of streets and a number of good 17th- and 18th-century houses. Cromwell House was built *c.* 1600, and the Mansion House in the late 18th century.

Thorpe Hall, at the exit from the town, has the remains of its west front, 1584. Most of the rest is 18th-century red-brick and hipped-roof construction, with Elizabethan terraces leading down to the river.
CHURCH OF ST JAMES A magnificent church, and one of the last great medieval Gothic masterpieces, it has one of the most famous spires in England; dating from the early 16th century, it rises to a height of 294 ft, with pinnacles and flying buttresses. Rebuilt by the local inhabitants in the 15th century, and restored by James Fowler during the 19th, the church contains fine wood-carving.

Lower Beeding *W. Sussex*   542Be
SOUTH LODGE Has an attractive garden of flowering shrubs and trees.

Lower Brockhampton House   546Bf
Heref. & Worcs.
A small moated manor house in half-timber which dates from the 14th century, with a detached gatehouse of later date and the ruins of a 12th-century chapel.

Lower Largo *Fife*   562Cg
ROBINSON CRUSOE STATUE Defoe's Robinson Crusoe was in real life Alexander Selkirk (1676–1721), who was put ashore on Juan Fernandez island by his shipmates in 1704, and rescued in 1709. A statue to his memory is on the site of the cottage where he was brought up.

Lower Peover *Cheshire*   552Be
CHURCH OF ST OSWALD A 13th-century timbered church with a massive sandstone tower. Inside, dark oak of the wooden columns, arches and exposed roof timbers is well set off against the whitewashed walls. The fittings, mainly 17th century, are distinguished, particularly the gated-pews, screens, pulpit and cover on a font.

Lowick *Northants.*   547Hg
CHURCH OF ST PETER An impressive church, with fine early 14th-century glass. The west tower is of the late 15th century and has an octagonal upper storey with pinnacles and buttresses. The 15th-century monuments include the canopied effigies of Sir Ralph Greene and his wife, and brasses of Henry and Margaret Greene.

Lowther Castle *Cumbria*   557Jf
The castle, a partial ruin, stands in a 3000 acre park with a mausoleum containing Lowther family tombs. An early member of the Lowther family, Sir Richard, was responsible for guarding Mary, Queen of Scots, during her imprisonment in Carlisle Castle: an alabaster memorial to him is in the church.

Luddesdown Court *Kent*   542Df
A flint-built manor house said to be the oldest continuously inhabited house in the country. Its great hall has an 11th-century fire-place and there is a red-brick chimney dated 1471. There are Tudor additions, and the house features a columbarium —dove loft. (By appointment.)

Ludham *Norfolk*   554Dc
CHURCH OF ST CATHERINE The 14th- and 15th-century church contains a decorated sedilia and a hammerbeam roof to the nave. The octagonal font is carved with figures and lions, the screen has painted figures of saints. A mural of the Crucifixion is painted on the chancel arch.

Ludlow *Shropshire*   546Af
The building of Ludlow started in the 12th century around the Norman castle, and much of the original town remains. Old buildings include fine Tudor, Queen Anne and Regency houses, and the largest parish church in England.
CASTLE Begun by Roger de Lacy in 1085 as a key fortress on the stormy Welsh border, Ludlow Castle was transformed into an elaborate palace in the 13th and 14th centuries.

In 1326 the castle's owner, Roger Mortimer, became virtual ruler of England when he helped his mistress, Queen Isabella, to murder her husband, Edward II, and put her son on the throne.

In 1501, Prince Arthur, Henry VIII's elder brother, came here with his bride, Catharine of Aragon. He died five months later and his heart was buried in the church.

The castle is now in ruins, but the unusual circular Norman chapel of St Mary Magdalene and the Gothic splendour of the late 13th-century state rooms can still be seen.
CHURCH OF ST LAURENCE Earliest remaining work dates from 1199, but the misericords on the choir stalls and the stained glass date from the 14th century. The church was restored by Sir Gilbert Scott and Sir Arthur Blomfield in the 19th century.

FEATHERS HOTEL An elaborate 15th-century half-timbered inn, with embossed ceilings, carved panelling and wall paintings.

MUSEUM Twenty thousand fossils from Salop and adjoining counties are the main feature of the museum's geological collection. Exhibits cover local history from prehistoric to Victorian times, with special reference to Ludlow Castle.

Lullingstone Castle *Kent* 542Cf
Lullingstone is mentioned in the Domesday survey. The castle was founded in early Tudor times, but was largely rebuilt in Queen Anne's reign. The Henry VII period gate-house still remains. The castle contains family relics and a collection of portraits from Tudor times to the 18th century. The Queen Anne drawing-room, with its Elizabethan ceiling, is a notable feature.

Lullingstone Villa *Kent* 542Cf
Modern techniques of excavation have revealed much of this remarkable Roman villa. Apart from its quality as a country house it has what must be accepted as a private Christian chapel, together with many other finds which confirm this interpretation; there are also fine decorative features.

Lundin Links *Fife* 562Cg
At one time a Bronze Age circle of stones stood here. Today, three only remain, but their size is impressive. The shortest is 13 ft high and has 5 ft wide sides. The others stand 17 ft and 18 ft high.

Luton *Beds.* 547Hd
CHURCH OF ST MARY In spite of the industrial surroundings, this fine cruciform town church of the 13th to 15th centuries stands out as a magnificent building. There is a 13th-century font enclosed in a pinnacled and gabled canopy, and a fine, octagonal 14th-century baptistry. There are also brasses and monuments.

MUSEUM AND ART GALLERY Originally a Victorian private residence, the Luton museum displays collections of considerable range. The local history collections include among the archaeological exhibits some important Saxon jewellery found in the Luton area. Also represented are the decorative arts of costume, domestic textiles, furniture and wood carvings.

Luton Hoo *Beds.* 547Hd
'Hoo' is an Anglo-Saxon word meaning 'the spur of a hill'. This great mansion of the Wernher family has Adam associations, but little more than the façade remained after a fire in 1843. It is the contents which now matter, and these are incomparable. The tapestries include those woven at Beauvais (1711–22) depicting the Story of the King of China, the main feature of the dining-room. The collection of English porcelain and china has examples of Chelsea, Worcester, Staffordshire, Derby, Bristol, Liverpool, Swansea and Rockingham. The former chapel is now the main gallery. The racing interests of the Wernhers are indicated in the Brown Jack Room, named after their famous racehorse. There is also a collection of jewelled pieces by Fabergé, and the Russian Room contains robes worn at the Court of the Tsars, and personal mementoes of the Imperial family. Works of art include paintings by Rembrandt and Titian, and the unique *St Michael* by Bartolemé Bermejo (*c.* 1470). One section of Luton Hoo is occupied, but the Wernher Collection is open to the public. (See pp. 344–5.)

Lutterworth *Leics.* 546Fg
The church has a memorial to John Wycliffe who, while living in the village in the 14th century, made the first English translation of the Bible.

Lydbury North *Shropshire* 551Ja
CHURCH OF ST MICHAEL AND ALL ANGELS The handsome 15th-century nave roof was revealed by J. T. Micklethwaite's restoration in 1901. The cruciform plan is Norman; the west tower is 13th century. There is a timbered south porch and early 17th-century box-pews and pulpit. Above the

MOSAIC FLOOR AT LULLINGSTONE ROMAN VILLA

During reconstruction of the villa in the 4th century, this fine mosaic was laid. The foreground illustrates the Greek myth of the abduction of Europa by Zeus in the form of a bull. The Latin couplet above refers to Virgil's 'Aeneid', and indicates the high level of literary education of the villa's upper-class owners.

LUTON HOO

CIGARETTE BOX *Nicholas II and Alexandra, the last Emperor and Empress of Russia, are depicted on a presentation cigarette box (c. 1913) from the workshops of Peter Carl Fabergé. The box is in gold decorated with translucent green enamel and the Emperor and Empress are portrayed within a double-headed Eagle, symbol of imperial Russia, picked out in diamonds. Fabergé, whose family came originally from France, earned a worldwide reputation as a master craftsman with the exquisite jewellery and objets d'art he created for the royal family and aristocracy of Russia.*

CHELSEA PORCELAIN FIGURES *These unusual figures in Turkish costume were made about 1748 at the Chelsea factory which made fine porcelain from 1745 to 1769. The right-hand figure bears the rare voilet-anchor mark.*

JACOPO SANSOVINO: ST JOHN THE BAPTIST *The art collections of the late Sir Julius Wernher at Luton Hoo include one of the finest groups of Italian Renaissance bronzes in private hands in Britain, and this is one of the rarest and most beautiful pieces. Jacopo Sansovino (1486–1570) was one of the most influential Italian Renaissance sculptors. By birth a Florentine, he worked in Rome, but after the sack of the city in 1527 moved to Venice, where he founded a new school of sculpture. Some of his finest work was done on a small scale in bronze.*

rood screen are the Commandments and Creed in painted lettering, dated 1615.

Lyddington *Leics.* 547Gg
CHURCH OF ST ANDREW The tower and chancel are 14th century, the nave and aisles *c.* 1500. Medieval remains include glass and wall-paintings.

Lyddington Bede House *Leics.* 547Gg
Thomas Cecil, son of Elizabeth I's Lord High Treasurer, Lord Burghley, converted the medieval palace of the Bishops of Lincoln into a bede house (almshouse). The former banqueting hall in the upper floor contains a fine ceiling and wooden panelling. The building has been restored.

Lydiard Mansion *Wilts.* 546Db
Formerly the country seat of the St John family, whose splendid tombs are in the nearby church. Of medieval origin, the mansion was considerably altered when Georgian façades were added in 1743–9.

Lydiard Tregoze *Wilts.* 546Db
CHURCH OF ST MARY The style is mainly Perpendicular with alterations made *c.* 1633. The furnishings include a pulpit of the early 17th century and a St John family pew of this date. There is a richly worked wrought-iron communion rail of *c.* 1700 and several medieval murals, but the main interest here centres on the many St John monuments,

RELIQUARY OF ST SEBASTIAN *One of the most impressive examples of German late 15th-century Gothic art in Britain, this reliquary was made to contain a saintly relic acquired by Abbot Georg Kastner for his Cistercian monastery of Kaisheim, near Donauworth in Swabia. Possibly designed by Hans Holbein the Elder about 1497, the reliquary is of silver and partly gilded, and came from the great goldsmithing centre of Augsburg, also in southern Germany. The elaborate base creates an effective contrast to the simplicity of the figure of St Sebastian bound to the leafless tree trunk. The relic is decorated in relief with figures of Our Lady of Pity, with saints, monks and sinners beneath her protective cloak. The relic is set at the back, protected by crystal in an opening ornamented with gems.*

TRAY BY FABERGÉ *Nephrite, or Russian jade, was used a great deal by the royal goldsmith Peter Carl Fabergé (1846–1920) in his workshops at St Petersburg, Russia. This tray, made about 1900, is typical of his work, the dark nephrite contrasting with the gold handles with their enamel and diamond decoration.*

GERMAN PENDANT *An elaborate example of South German goldsmiths' work, this pendant was made about 1600 of enamelled gold, set with rubies, emeralds, diamonds and three pearl drops. It is really a piece of miniature sculpture, the gems being subsidiary elements in the design. A falconer stands against an openwork scrolled background, with a falcon on his wrist and two hounds at his feet—the modelling and enamelling of this miniscule group was the goldsmith's triumph.*

from the 17th century onwards, showing members of the family kneeling, lying or standing. One monument has panels painted with a heraldic genealogical tree, another has a gilded figure standing under a canopy, and yet another is by Michael Rysbrack.

Lyme Park *Cheshire* 552Cf

This estate was in the hands of the Legh family from 1397 until 1947. The present Elizabethan house was much altered by Giacomo Leoni c. 1720, when the exterior was extensively rebuilt, but the long gallery has remained unchanged since 1541. The state rooms contain fine panelling, wood carving and tapestries, and four Chippendale chairs said to be covered with material from the cloak worn by Charles I at his execution in 1649. The house is surrounded by a deer park and moorland.

Lyme Regis *Dorset* 540Bc

CHURCH OF ST MICHAEL The original Norman church had a tower between nave and chancel, but the present church was built to the east of the tower c. 1500; the old nave is now the west porch. Inside are a 17th-century oak lectern, many wall monuments, and a fine pulpit dated 1613.

PHILPOT MUSEUM The collections are devoted to local geology and history, and include old prints, documents, coins, and a fire engine of 1710.

TOMB OF CHRISTOPHER ROPER

The 2nd Lord Teynham lies with his feet resting on a lion and a red cloak over his armour. Beside him kneels his wife in widow's weeds. On the front of this tomb in the Roper Chapel are 17th-century carvings of Roper's two sons and five daughters by Epiphanius Evesham. (Church of SS Peter and Paul, Lynsted)

Lymington *Hants.* 541Gc
A centre of yachting. The town is most happily related to the broad estuary. From the cobbled Quay Hill, the way leads into the High Street, broad and straight, rising over a brow to the church at the far end.
CHURCH OF ST THOMAS THE APOSTLE The church has a south-east tower of 1670, crowned by a cupola. There is some 13th-century work in the chancel and north chapel. The interior of the nave is mainly 18th century with interesting galleries on twin Tuscan columns. Features include an 18th-century font, a mid-19th-century stained glass window, and monuments by J. M. Rysbrack. One monument to a naval captain is by John Bacon.

Lympne Castle *Kent* 542Fe
A rugged medieval castle with terraced gardens looking out over Romney Marsh and across the Channel to France. The tower dates from the 12th century, the rest was rebuilt *c.* 1360, and the whole castle was restored in 1905.
STUTFALL A Roman fort of the Saxon Shore, it guarded Lympne—in Roman times accessible by sea. The structure of Stutfall marks it as one of the last shore forts to have been built. The curtain wall has subsided on the slippery subsoil to give the present odd distribution of wall fragments. The fort can be viewed from the castle gardens, 300 ft above.

Lynsted *Kent* 542Ef
This village has many timbered Tudor cottages and an Elizabethan manor house.
CHURCH OF SS PETER AND PAUL Mainly Perpendicular, with a wooden belfry and spire. There are several monuments, one by Epiphanius Evesham, newly restored, and interesting brasses.

Lytes Cary *Som.* 540Ce
This manor house was the home of the Lyte family for 500 years. Sir Henry Lyte, botanist, translated the *Niewe Herball* (a new history of plants) which was published in 1578 and was the most notable horticultural work of the time. The chapel was built in 1343; the great hall was added in 1450, and the quadrangle buildings in 1535.

Lyveden New Bield *Northants.* 547Hg
Sir Thomas Tresham began this Renaissance house in *c.* 1600; its plan is cross-shaped to symbolise the Passion. However, Sir Thomas was a Papist and his family were involved in the Gunpowder Plot, so the house was never finished; only its shell remains. Lyveden Old Building is an Elizabethan farmhouse.

M

Macclesfield *Cheshire* 552Be
CHURCH OF ST MICHAEL A church which has had much rebuilding, but is of great interest for its tombs with effigies, from the 15th century onwards. The monument to the Legh family depicts Pope Gregory the Great.
WEST PARK MUSEUM Built and presented to the town of Macclesfield by the Brocklehurst family in 1898, the museum contains a collection of Egyptian antiquities, Victorian paintings with works by Landseer and others, a scold's bridle, a stuffed giant panda shot by Captain Brocklehurst on the borders of China and Tibet, and local and topographical items.

Machrie Moor *Arran, Strathclyde* 560Fd
The remains of seven Bronze Age stone circles are grouped within the space of 1 mile. Nearby, there are traces of Stone Age hut circles and tombs.

Madeley *Shropshire* 552Ab
CHURCH OF ST MICHAEL Designed by Thomas Telford, the engineer (his other Salop church is St Mary Magdalene at Bridgnorth). The exterior is octagonal with a square west tower, but inside it is rectangular as the vestries cut off angles. The original design had no chancel, but one was added in 1910. In the churchyard there are 19th-century tombs in the unconventional material of cast iron. (By appointment.)

Madingley *Cambs.* 548Af
CHURCH OF ST MARY MAGDALENE There is a west tower, with rebuilt spire, all mainly of the 13th and 14th centuries. The late 17th-century communion rails are from Cambridge. There are 15th- and 16th-century stained glass fragments, and monuments to members of the Cotton family, one perhaps by Edward Stanton, *c.* 1707. From a century later there is a large monument of a flag and anchor to an admiral by John Flaxman.
MADINGLEY HALL An Elizabethan mansion where the future Edward VII lodged when he was an undergraduate. His father, Prince Albert, fell ill there and died a few days later at Windsor. Today it belongs to Cambridge University. The nearby post-mill (in which the whole body of the mill revolves on the base), removed from Ellington, Cambridgeshire, to Madingley in 1936, is worth seeing. There is a small, thatched, late-medieval manor house in the village.

Madley *Heref. & Worcs.* 546Ae
CHURCH OF THE NATIVITY OF ST MARY THE
VIRGIN Some parts of the original Norman
building can still be seen in this 13th- and 14th-
century church. The contents include six roundels
of early 13th-century stained glass and fragments
of a 14th-century Jesse window.

Maes Howe *Mainland, Orkney* 569Hf
This is the finest Neolithic chambered cairn in
north-western Europe and is still in fairly good
condition. It is a great domed mound of clay and
stones, 115 ft across and 24 ft high, encircled by a
wide, shallow ditch. The chamber, 15 ft square, is
lined with massive stone walling, and is entered by
a 36 ft long passage, again walled beyond the inner
doorway by great slabs, which also form its roof.
The roof of the chamber is corbelled, and corner
pillars aid in supporting the weight. The cairn has
been entered many times in the past. Several times
parties of Vikings have left runic inscriptions, the
language being Old Norse. One of these, surely
the first, records that they found a treasure,
doubtless of gold.

Maesmawr Hall *Powys* 551Ga
Powys is famed as the Welsh county richest in
timber-framed houses. Maesmawr, a hotel, is a
good example. Although timber-framed houses
may date from medieval times, the majority are
17th century, and a number, of which this house
may be an example, are of the early 18th century.
(By appointment.)

Maesyronen Chapel *Powys* 545Je
A Dissenters' chapel dating from 1696. Apart from
the lowering of the pulpit, the internal arrangements, including the communion table, are little
altered and preserve the atmosphere of humility
and domestic warmth lacking in more pretentious
larger chapels. The adjacent chapel house is earlier,
and the party wall contains fragments of an even
earlier cruck-truss, which would once have held a
primitive arch in position, part of a building once
occupying the site of the chapel.

Maiden Bower *Beds.* 547Hd
Iron Age hill-fort built on the site of a Neolithic
causewayed camp. The hill-fort has a single bank
and ditch enclosing about 11 acres. When first dug,
this ditch was some 10 ft deep. Excavation of the
entrance on the south side has shown the post-holes
of a gate with a sentry-walk over it. From the air,
hut-circles have been seen within the fort.

Maiden Castle *Cheshire* 551Jd
This is an Iron Age promontory fort, protected on
the south-east, where it joins the main hill-top, by
a double bank with a shallow ditch between. At
one end is the entrance, where the inner bank is
well inturned to make a tapering passage to the
gate. This inner bank is of stone laced with timber,
and the sandy outer bank has a stone revetment
which replaced an earlier one of timber. The other
sides of the fort are protected by steeply scarped
hill slopes.

Maiden Castle *Dorset* 540Dc
This is perhaps the best known hill-fort in
England. Extensively excavated by Sir Mortimer
Wheeler, the long and varied history of the site is
well established. Concealed below the rampart of
the first Iron Age defences were those of a Neolithic causewayed camp of about 10 acres.
Towards the end of the Neolithic period, an enormous long barrow with quarry-ditches was built
on the hill-top and its line kinks where it crosses the
defences of the earlier camp. The first Iron Age
hill-fort, of 15 acres, occupied the eastern part of

TOMB OF LORD RIVERS

*This monument to Thomas, Earl Rivers of Rock
Savage, was erected in 1696 in his parish church.
The tomb is baroque in style, and above the figure of
the earl is a massive canopy supported by marble
Corinthian columns from which hang curtains in
marble. Between them a long inscription sets out the
titles of Earl Rivers and his two wives. The church,
founded in the 13th century, was rebuilt in 1739 and
1898–1901. (Church of St Michael, Macclesfield)*

THE PROPHET EZEKIEL

*This is one of the figures in stained glass depicted on
three panels in the east window of this church, which
were taken from a richly coloured 14th-century Jesse
window. The prophet's hair and beard are worked in
gold stain against the red background and green vine
leaves of the Jesse tree. (Church of the Nativity of St
Mary the Virgin, Madley)*

MAIDEN CASTLE

THE RAMPARTS *This Iron Age hill-fort was built on the site of a much earlier causewayed camp; Neolithic defences have been uncovered below the Iron Age* *ramparts, and there is a late Neolithic long barrow on the hill-top. The fort was captured and reduced by Vespasian's 2nd Roman Legion.*

IRON AGE OBJECTS *Both pots are of the second main Iron Age culture in Britain. Both have 'bead-rims' and the smaller one also has two countersunk handles. The pierced holes in the pot were intended to take a cord for suspension. Between the pots is a sample of slingstones found in the fort. The curved iron blades are probably primitive sickles. On the book are weaving combs of the first main Iron Age, and some clay slingstones. (Dorset County Museum, Dorchester)*

NEOLITHIC FINDS *These objects were all found at Maiden Castle. The smaller pot probably dates from the same period as the causewayed camp, while the larger one is contemporary with the great long barrow. The darker axe-head to the left is one of a small number made of epidiorite, or greenstone, a rock found in western Cornwall. The other axe-head, of chipped flint has not been polished. On the book are several worked flints. (Dorset County Museum, Dorchester)*

the hill. This comparatively insignificant fort was enlarged and remodelled again and again until, in the days of the last generation before the Roman conquest, the defences received their final refurbishing. The fort was one of the settlements reduced by Vespasian's 2nd Legion and, outside the east gate, the hastily buried skeletons of the inhabitants killed in the fight were found. Doubtless the chief *oppidum* (settlement) of the local tribe, the Durotriges, it was then superseded by Dorchester (Durnovaria), the Roman cantonal town, in the valley below. In the second half of the 4th century, a Romano-Celtic temple and priest's house, the foundations of which can still be seen, were built in the eastern part of the fort. It was near the gates of this hill-fort that great reserves of slingstones were found, proving that, in later Iron Age times, the sling was an important weapon.

Maidenhead *Berks.*   547GI
This town on the Thames was an important coaching stage between London and Bath. The 128-fi arches of Brunel's railway bridge, built in 1837–8 just downstream from the road bridge, are believed to be the longest brick spans ever constructed.
HENRY REITLINGER BEQUEST In a typical Edwardian Thames-side house, the museum contains a wide selection of Chinese, Persian, Peruvian and European ceramics, as well as African and European sculpture, glass, paintings and drawings.

SCULPTURE AT MALMESBURY ABBEY

Some of the finest carving to have survived from the 12th century. The figures of apostles surmounted by an angel are under vaulting on the east and west walls of the porch of the abbey church.

Maiden Stone *Grampian* 566Fe
An exceptionally fine and well preserved example of a Pictish symbol stone, still standing close by a minor road near Chapel of Garioch. It is of red granite, carved in relief with a varied series of men, fish and monsters.

Maidstone *Kent* 542Df
A former 'station' for Roman soldiers on the R. Medway, the town was of considerable importance in the Middle Ages. It possesses an archbishop's palace and several other fine buildings of those times. It has always been a market and route centre, giving rise to industrial and commercial activity; it is the administrative centre (county town) of Kent.
ARCHBISHOP'S OR OLD PALACE The palace belonged to the Archbishops of Canterbury until Henry VIII's day. It contains a fine panelled banqueting hall. The palace stables house a magnificent collection of carriages.
CHILLINGTON MANOR A former manor house, containing art, natural history and archaeological collections, and relics of William Hazlitt, the essayist, born in Maidstone in 1778.
CHURCH OF ALL SAINTS A fine, former collegiate church, built by Archbishop Courtenay in 1395 on the banks of the R. Medway beside the archbishop's palace, and mainly of the 14th and 15th centuries. There are several monuments, one by Joseph Nollekens, *c*. 1795; also misericords and brasses. The 19th-century restoration is by J. L. Pearson.
OLD COLLEGE The Master's House has links with a 14th-century ecclesiastical college, dissolved in 1547. It has been renovated and preserves a 16th-century staircase and archways. It is now a centre of the Kent Music School. (Visitors by appointment.)

Maldon *Essex* 548Cc
BLUE BOAR HOTEL The plain front conceals 15th-century stabling and 17th-century panelling. The 15th-century Swan Hotel is also notable.

CHURCH OF ALL SAINTS The church was originally of the 13th century, but later additions include a unique triangular tower with a spire. The brick Gothic nave dates from 1728. The 14th-century south aisle is lavishly decorated, and there is a crypt. Monuments date from the 17th century.
MOOT HALL Sometimes called D'Arcy's Tower after its builder; a plain brick building of *c*. 1435, like a defensive tower with a higher stair turret. In the 19th century windows were added, and a porch with columns. (By appointment.)
PLUME LIBRARY Founded in 1704 by Dr Plume, Archdeacon of Rochester, on the site of the ruined St Peter's Church. The embattled church tower is the library entrance.
ST GILES LEPER HOSPITAL The remains of a 12th-century chapel.
VICARAGE Built in the 15th century, timbered and gabled.

Malmesbury *Wilts.* 546Cb
Part of the 12th-century Benedictine abbey remains, its church being notable for a porch with splendid medieval carvings of the Apostles. The late medieval market cross survives.
ABBEY CHURCH The present church, dating from the mid-12th century, is a fragment of the original abbey church, which had transepts, a tall central spire and a western tower. All that is left is the nave with aisles. The nave was saved after the Reformation, and became the parish church. The south porch contains some of the best Romanesque sculpture in England. There is a 15th-century tomb with a reclining effigy, said to be that of King Athelstan. The Norman interior has 14th-century lierne vaulting.

Malpas *Cheshire* 551Jd
CHURCH OF ST OSWALD A spacious church, mainly of the 14th and 15th centuries, with large Perpendicular windows and a west tower. There are good timber roofs and screen work, stalls with misericords and a 13th-century chest with decorative iron binding.

BEN NICHOLSON *Au Chat Botté*

This painting is of a shop window in the French town of Dieppe, with the name of the shop, Au Chat Botté, printed in bold letters across the glass. The French name (it means 'Puss in Boots') fascinated Nicholson and brought back memories of childhood fairy-tales. His picture of the shop was the culmination of a set of still-life studies produced between 1929 and 1932. Like his other works in different styles, it shows a coolness and a lyricism which is completely English, and a quality which he describes himself as 'musical and architectural'. Here the 'music' lies in the way he combines colour and form, and the 'architecture' in his use of space. The picture shows three planes: the window, reflections in the glass, and objects on the table inside. Nicholson later turned to abstract reliefs in the 1930's, and semi-abstract still-lifes in the 1950's. But this progress to non-figurative works has not altered his basic style—the 'music' and 'architecture'. (City Art Gallery, Manchester)

Mam Tor *Derbys.* 552C
This Iron Age hill-fort has an internal area of 1 acres; it is the largest in the Peak District, anc comparable in size with many in south-western England. It has a ditch with internal bank and outer counterscarp bank and an entrance to the south-west. Here there is a fine inturned entrance passage some 100 ft long. There are also traces of a similar but smaller entrance at the north end of the enclo-sure. Recent excavation has shown that the hill-top was in domestic occupation in the Late Bronze Age, but there is no evidence that the defences had been erected by that time. Two earlier Bronze Age round barrows lie within the enclosure.

Manchester *Greater Manchester* 552Bf
This great industrial city has for long been the centre of the cotton industry. Construction of the Ship Canal in 1894 converted it into the third largest port in England.
CATHEDRAL The 15th-century collegiate church of St Mary, St Denys and St George was given cathedral status in 1847. It is a magnificent example of Perpendicular Gothic church building, with a suitable tower added in 1868, but its glory is its woodwork—the stalls with their intricate canopies and misericords, and the wooden pulpitum and parclose screens. Among the monuments is work by John Bacon the Younger, E. H. Baily and William Theed the Younger.
CHETHAM'S LIBRARY Founded in 1653, the library contains printed books and manuscripts, including a fine collection of works of the 16th–18th centuries.
CITY ART GALLERY This Classical building, designed by Sir Charles Barry, architect of the Houses of Parliament, was originally opened to

EPSTEIN *Bronze bust of C. P. Scott*

Scott was perhaps the most famous of English editors. He was only 25 when he took charge of the 'Manchester Guardian' in 1872, and he transformed it from a local paper into one of the most influential in the world. He founded its liberal and progressive tradition, and under him it boldly championed many unpopular causes. Its opinions were quoted far outside its native city. This bust was presented to the city of Manchester in 1926

on his 80th birthday by a group of subscribers which included leading statesmen of the day, English and foreign. The choice of artist was fitting, since Jacob Epstein was himself, like Scott, a courageous innovator who was involved in controversy throughout most of his career. The bust captures with striking fidelity the pugnacious spirit of its subject. C. P. Scott died in 1932. (City Art Gallery, Manchester) the public in 1829 as the headquarters of the Royal Manchester Institution. In 1882, it was given to the corporation, together with a number of pictures and other possessions which had been acquired over the years, for use as an art gallery. Its fine collection of paintings specialises in the development of the English School from the 16th century, and includes a large collection of the Pre-Raphaelites. There are also Italian, Flemish, Dutch and French paintings, as well as glass, sculpture, porcelain and silverware.

COURTS OF JUSTICE Rebuilt in 1957, they replace the bombed-out buildings of 1864.

FLETCHER MOSS (DIDSBURY) A former late-Georgian and early-Victorian parsonage which now houses the Manchester City Art Galleries Collection of material relating to local history, including photographs of old Manchester and paintings of local subjects.

FREE TRADE HALL Rebuilt after bombing, it takes in much of the original stonework of 1843 and 1856, and dates from 1951 in its present form. Its large hall is 123 ft long, 78 ft wide, 60 ft high, with maximum accommodation for 2500 people. It is the home of the Hallé Orchestra.

GALLERY OF ENGLISH COSTUME, PLATT HALL (RUSHOLME) Built in the early 1760's, Platt Hall is now a branch of the Manchester City Art Galleries and houses an important collection of English costumes from the 17th century to the present day. The grounds are a public park.

GALLERY OF MODERN ART British and European paintings, prints, drawings, sculpture and decorative arts since 1900 are the theme of this collection, which includes works by Sickert, Gauguin, Matisse, Giacometti, Spencer, Lowry, Pissarro, Modigliani, and Nash.

JOHN RYLANDS UNIVERSITY LIBRARY The present library was created in 1972 by merging the John Rylands Library with that of Manchester University. It is partly housed in a neo-Gothic building designed by Basil Champneys. Its collection of early printed books and manuscripts is known throughout the world and includes one of the three known copies of the Gutenberg Bible, early printed books from Italy and a set of books printed by William Caxton. The illuminated manuscripts include Persian and Arabic as well as European examples. Items from the collection are on display.

LIVERPOOL ROAD STATION Built in 1830, this is the oldest passenger railway station in the world. The original building, which is scheduled as an ancient monument, is intact.

UNIVERSITY OF MANCHESTER Originally Owens College; its buildings, begun in 1870, are a free interpretation of 'French Gothic' and are noted as Victorian collegiate architecture.

PORTICO LIBRARY Opened in 1806, the library was designed in Classical style by Thomas Harrison, who also designed Chester and Lancaster Castles. Peter Mark Roget, compiler of Roget's Thesaurus of English Words, was its first secretary, and John Dalton (1766–1844), the physicist, was once a member. The library's collections include rare historical works.

TOWN HALL This magnificent Gothic Revival building was erected in 1868–77 to designs by Alfred Waterhouse (1830–1905), who was later architect of Eaton Hall in Cheshire. His design was chosen from 123 submitted in a competition held in 1867 by the Manchester authorities. The Town Hall's interesting features include the Lord Mayor's staterooms, and the magnificent Large Hall containing the Ford Madox Brown murals depicting Manchester's history from Roman times to the mid-19th century.

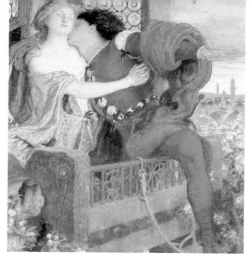

MADOX BROWN *Romeo and Juliet*

Ford Madox Brown (1821–93) was a follower of the German Nazarene school of painting, which sought to bring back into art a pre-Renaissance purity of style and composition. Although he was not a member of the English Pre-Raphaelite Brotherhood, he was closely identified with it, and for a year taught one of its leaders, Dante Gabriel Rossetti. Madox Brown's work is characterised by accurate draughtsmanship and the use of repeated areas of colour. As well as historical and literary subjects, such as his depiction of Romeo and Juliet, he also developed social and moral themes. (Whitworth Art Gallery, University of Manchester)

EMBROIDERED BOX

Well-bred young ladies of the 17th century embroidered boxes like this, in fine silk thread, and used them as containers for personal belongings. (Whitworth Art Gallery, University of Manchester)

WHITWORTH ART GALLERY, UNIVERSITY OF MANCHESTER Watercolours, Old Master drawings, prints and textiles form the main collections of this gallery. The water-colours and drawings are by British artists of the 18th–early 20th centuries (with large groups by Turner and the Pre-Raphaelites), and continental artists such as Cézanne, Gauguin, Van Gogh, Klee and Picasso. There is also a collection of works by contemporary British artists. Prints include a large Japanese group and Italian and German

15th-CENTURY STAINED GLASS

King David, playing the harp, and King Solomon, who holds the tabernacle, are shown on this 15th-century east window, with their names behind them. The three lights of the window contain remains of the original Jesse tree, which has been partly restored. The use of white as a colour is unusual for stained glass of this period. (Church of St Margaret, Margaretting)

Renaissance engravings and woodcuts. The textiles collection ranges from ancient Egypt to contemporary fabrics and includes examples of European, Middle Eastern and Oriental workmanship, costume and tapestries.
WYTHENSHAWE HALL (NORTHENDEN) A half-timbered manor house, set in parkland, and the home of the Tatton family for over 500 years. It contains 17th-century paintings and furnishings, and exhibits drawn from the City Art Gallery's Oriental collections.

Manorbier Castle *Dyfed* 544Dc
One of the few Norman castles containing comfortable, spacious living quarters. The moated fortress was begun in the 12th century. Little remains of the outer ward, but the inner court remains intact. The vast gate-house, hall and chapel form the nucleus of the castle and, with the domestic buildings (not open to the public), have windows looking on to the inner court. The castle was never attacked. Because of its seclusion it has often been used by smugglers in the past.

Mansfield *Notts.* 552Ee
MUSEUM AND ART GALLERY The collection contains 150 water-colours of old Mansfield painted by A. S. Buxton—one-time principal of the Mansfield School of Art—and specimens of British birds and mammals. Two other galleries display loan collections of art, photography, sculpture, embroidery and other exhibitions.

Mapledurham House *Oxon.* 547Gb
Grounds running down to the Thames beside wooded hills are the background to the Elizabethan mansion used by John Galsworthy as one of the settings for *The Forsyte Saga* and by Kenneth Grahame for *The Wind in the Willows*. Here, too, Alexander Pope visited Martha and Theresa Blount, whom he immortalised in his verses.

March *Cambs* 548Ag
CHURCH OF ST WENDREDA A magnificent Perpendicular church, with a west tower and tall spire. St Wendreda's has a double-hammerbeam roof in the nave, with angels everywhere, wings outstretched. There are early 16th-century brasses.

Marford *Clwyd* 551Jd
An unusual and attractive village of which the most conspicuous feature is the fenestration; all the windows are curiously shaped, either as ogee eyelets, or in 'church-warden Gothic' style. A mile to the north is the multi-gabled Elizabethan house, Trevalyn Hall, opposite a fine timber-framed water-mill.

Margam *West Glam.* 545Gb
ABBEY The abbey was founded for the Cistercians in 1147 by Robert, Earl of Gloucester. The nave of the Norman building now serves as the parish church, and contains some fine 16th-century alabaster tombs and a modern triptych and window by Frank Roper. The museum in the churchyard has a good collection of Celtic crosses and other carved stones, including the Cumbrian Cross depicted on a 1969 postage stamp issued to mark the investiture of the Prince of Wales.

Margaretting *Essex* 548Bc
CHURCH OF ST MARGARET In addition to its famous 15th-century Jesse window, the church has good timbering in its north porch and tower and an octagonal font, all of which date from the 15th century.

Markenfield Hall *N. Yorks.* 558Cc
A medieval moated manor of 14th-century origin, with 15th- and 16th-century additions

Market Harborough *Leics.* 552Fa
CHURCH OF ST DIONYSIUS A 13th–15th-century church, with notable window tracery, and a truly impressive west tower and broach spire. The interior is galleried.

Marlborough *Wilts.* 540Fg
This elegant market town, famous for the boys' public school that stands at the end of the High Street, has many interesting old buildings and historical associations. During the Civil War, for example, the town was stormed and captured by the Royalists; scars of the battle may still be seen on the north face of St Mary's Church tower. Due to fires that devastated the town centre on various occasions over the centuries, the oldest houses are to be found mainly in the side streets. However, the partly arcaded High Street, with its coaching inn and hung tile houses, still retains much of its Georgian charm.

Marlow *Bucks.* 547Gb
MARLOW PLACE A red-brick, baroque house built in 1720 for John Wallop, later Earl of Portsmouth. (By appointment.)

Marnhull *Dorset* 540Dd
CHURCH OF ST GREGORY A good cruciform church with a west tower; it has 12th-century origins, but was refashioned in the 14th century and enlarged in the 19th. The tower is mainly 15th century, and the bowl of the font is made from the old village preaching cross.

Marquess of Anglesey's Column 550Ee
Anglesey, Gwynedd
Erected in 1816 by the inhabitants of Anglesey and Caernarfon to commemorate the Marquess's military achievements in Spain and at the Battle of Waterloo, the column stands on the south-east coast of Anglesey, in view of Plas Newydd Mansion—the late 18th-century mansion in which the Marquess lived. It is crowned by a 12 ft bronze statue of the Marquess, wearing his uniform as Colonel of the 7th Hussars, executed by the then fashionable sculptor Matthew Noble. The overall height of the column is 112 ft.

Marston Morteyne *Beds.* 547He
CHURCH OF ST MARY THE VIRGIN A pretty church, begun *c.* 1340, but practically rebuilt in 1445. It has

JOHN NOST *Perseus*

John Nost left Belgium to settle in England in 1678, and became a successful sculptor, specialising in lead statues for gardens. Some of his works were direct copies, but others, like this one in the baroque style of his native Flanders, were original. It is one of a group completed in 1699–1705. (Melbourne Hall)

THE PERGOLA AT
MELBOURNE HALL

A beautiful example of English wrought-iron work, designed and made about 1706 by a local man, Robert Bakewell of Derby. Viewed from below, the graceful work shows the light touch and flair for design of this relatively obscure craftsman. Little is known of his life, but not long after making this arbour he was 'miserable poor'. However, other fine examples of his work exist at Okeover Hall in Staffs., All Saints Cathedral in Derby, and at the Radcliffe Camera in Oxford where he worked in 1744. The pergola stands at the far end of a pond in the Melbourne gardens, designed by the royal gardener under William III, Anne and George I— William Wise. At Melbourne, Wise designed in the manner of the French gardener André Le Nôtre, who laid out the gardens at Versailles.

a massive west tower set slightly apart from the main building. Inside can be seen carved bosses and angels on the roofs, interesting screen paintings, brasses, and a monument with recumbent effigy. In 1969, a massive (16 ft by 11 ft) Doom Painting was uncovered on the wall above the chancel arch. It seems to have been painted at the beginning of the 16th century and depicts the Day of Judgment, with the dead rising from their graves to be dispatched either to Heaven or Hell by a seated figure of Christ. Such paintings served as constant moral reminders to illiterate congregations.

Martley *Heref. & Worcs.* 546Bf
CHURCH OF ST PETER A fine church dating from Norman times, with later additions. Interesting medieval mural paintings include one of St Martin, heraldry and animals. There is a mid-15th-century alabaster effigy of a recumbent knight.

Martock *Somerset* 540Cd
TREASURER'S HOUSE A 14th-century house that was once the residence of the treasurers of Wells Cathedral. The solar, or great chamber, is of even earlier date—probably 13th century.

Marwick Head *Mainland, Orkney* 569Hg
KITCHENER MEMORIAL On June 5, 1916, while outward bound from Scapa Flow to Russia, Field Marshal Earl Kitchener of Khartoum, Secretary of State for War, was drowned when the *Hampshire* struck a mine. The memorial stands at the point nearest to the place where the cruiser went down.

Masham *N. Yorks.* 558Cd
CHURCH OF ST MARY The west tower is Norman in its lower stages, but most of the church, including the spire, dates from the 14th and 15th centuries. The shaft of an important Saxon cross is in the churchyard, and there are several monuments from the early 17th century together with a number of later date.

Mathry *Dyfed* 544Cd
LONGHOUSE A Bronze Age burial chamber. It is walled by no fewer than seven upright slabs which support a great capstone. The covering mound has long disappeared, and its outline cannot now be traced.

Mawley Hall *Shropshire* 546Bf
An 18th-century mansion, possibly designed by Francis Smith of Warwick, with period plaster-work and panelling. (By appointment.)

Maxstoke *Warks.* 546Dg
CHURCH OF ST MICHAEL The church was probably built c. 1336, when a priory was founded here, and has no internal division between nave and chancel. The interior was remodelled during the 18th century.

Mayfield *E. Sussex* 542Ce
At the top of the village there are the remains of a palace of the Archbishops of Canterbury, with a grand 14th-century hall, and in the street several substantial houses, stone or half-timbered. The Middle House Hotel, one of the most spectacular pieces of decorative half-timbering in the Home Counties, is dated 1575. The imposing convent and school is on the site of the 10th-century palace of St Dunstan, Archbishop of Canterbury.

Meare *Somerset* 540Ce
ABBOT'S FISH HOUSE The 14th-century stone building was used for salting and storing fish for the summer palace of the Abbots of Glastonbury.

Medmenham Abbey *Bucks.* 547Gb
The ruins of a 12th-century Cistercian abbey, made notorious by Sir Francis Dashwood as a

meeting place for his Hell Fire Club in 1745—a congregation of young bloods whose motto was 'Do what you will' and whose orgies and rituals mocked all religion. (Not open.)

Meigle Museum *Tayside*   566Db
Here, in a small museum, is a fine collection of 25 Early Christian and Pictish symbol stones. These show a great range of different types.

Meini Gwyr *Dyfed*   544Dd
The Prescelly range of mountains runs parallel to the coast and on the fringes of its southern slopes, which border Pembrokeshire's central valley, stand many isolated monuments. Among them this Bronze Age circle is unique in its design, for its stones are not set directly in the natural surface but are set in a raised ring that was made to receive them.

Melbourne *Derbys.*   552Dc
CHURCH OF ST MICHAEL WITH ST MARY An impressive, cruciform, Norman church, with two west towers, as well as one at the crossing. The interior is well preserved, with a triforium placed in front of the clerestory windows.

Melbourne Hall *Derbys.*   552Dc
A country mansion built on a site used by the Bishops of Carlisle since 1280, but developed by Sir John Coke (1563–1644) and transformed and further developed by his great-grandson, Sir Thomas Coke, between 1710 and 1744. Sir Thomas was Vice-Chamberlain to Queen Anne and George I, whose portraits hang in the drawing-room. The home of Lord Melbourne, the 19th-century statesman, the Hall is now owned by the Marquess of Lothian. The gardens are laid out with long avenues, tunnels of yew, fountains, statuary, a shell grotto and a unique wrought-iron

bird-cage pergola of 1725, by Robert Bakewell, a blacksmith. (See p. 353.)

Melbury Bubb *Dorset*   540Cd
The Anglo-Saxon font in the church is curiously carved with upside-down wrestling animals.

Melford Hall *Suffolk*   548Ce
Elizabeth I visited Sir William Cordell, her Master of the Rolls, in this fine mansion he had built between 1554 and 1578, in the year it was finished. Its two towers stand sentinel to the two wings that flank the main entrance court. The mansion houses the Hyde Parker Collection of Chinese porcelain, fine furniture and old masters.

Mellerstain House *Borders*   562Dd
A castellated country home belonging to Lord Binning, descendant of the Scottish poetess and heroine, Lady Grisel Baillie (1665–1746), who lived here. William Adam built the wings of the house in 1725 and his son, Robert, the central block *c.* 1773. Inside the house are decorated plaster ceilings, old masters and much fine furniture; the library has a frieze of Classical figures over the book-shelves. The extensive grounds include a garden in the Italian style.

Mellor *Greater Manchester*   552Cf
CHURCH OF ST THOMAS An early 19th-century Gothic church that retains from an older building a Saxon font, crudely carved with figures, and a beautiful 14th-century wooden pulpit.

Mells *Som.*   540Df
CHURCH OF ST ANDREW The 15th-century church has a Mendip tower with pinnacles. Inside are fragments of medieval stained glass and a monument by Sir Alfred Munnings.

THE LIBRARY AT MELLERSTAIN HOUSE

William Adam began this battlemented house in 1725, but built only the side wings. After a pause of some years his son Robert completed the house in the 1770's, and was responsible for the interior, a masterpiece of delicate Classical decoration and colour—pale blues, greens and white, with plaster decoration in low relief, of which he was so able a practitioner. Robert's *genius as a designer is evident in the library with its fine Classical friezes, and its ceiling in the style of Zucchi, with a painting of Minerva in the central medallion. The right-hand bust in the far corner is of Lady Grisel Baillie, wife of Mellerstain's first owner; it was carved by Louis Roubiliac in 1746 when Lady Grisel was 81.*

MELROSE ABBEY

This abbey was founded by Cistercian monks on a site in the valley of the Tweed in 1136. The location was ideal for sheep farming, which produced a large part of the abbey's income, and nearby Berwick provided a convenient market for the monks to sell their wool. The house was close to the main road from England to Edinburgh, and so received visits from many eminent *people whose donations made it one of the wealthiest abbeys in Scotland. But the situation soon became a source of danger in any dispute between the kings of England and Scotland. Melrose was sacked by Edward II in 1322 and by Richard II in 1385. The church had to be rebuilt (it continued in use until 1810), but the abbey never recovered from a final sacking in 1547.*

Melrose Abbey *Borders* 562Dd
A Cistercian house founded by David I in 1136 for monks brought from Rievaulx in Yorkshire. Built of local red sandstone, it eventually became one of the richest abbeys in Scotland, but it was near the border where constant warring between England and Scotland occurred. In 1385 the troops of Richard II sacked the abbey seriously enough to warrant rebuilding of the church. This is now the main survival, largely because it was used as a parish church until 1810. It has many features of northern English architecture. For instance, the façades of the south and east arms compare with the west and east façades of York Minster (14th century). It was a splendid church, and its reconstruction lasted into the 16th century. The abbey was extensive—excavations have revealed most of the lay-out. But in 1547 Melrose was again sacked by the English, under the Duke of Somerset, and never recovered. A small museum in the Commendator's House, part of the abbey buildings, houses pottery and floor tiles found during excavations of the abbey site and adjoining grounds.

Melton Mowbray *Leics.* 552Fc
An ancient agricultural centre famous for its hunting, pork pies and Stilton cheese. It has a 17th-century Bedehouse near the church and several elegant 18th-century houses.
CHURCH OF ST MARY A large cruciform building, mainly 13th and 14th century, with a central tower about 100 ft high; the lower stage of this is 13th century, the upper *c.* 1500. There is an outstanding clerestory, rare double-aisled transepts, two 18th-century candelabra and an effigy of a cross-legged Crusader.

Melverley *Shropshire* 551Jc
CHURCH OF ST PETER Built in 1404 to replace the Saxon church burned down by Owain Glendwr in 1401, it is the only remaining church of that period in the country with its original exterior and interior. It is half timbered and the divisions between the massive oak uprights are filled with soft concrete. There is a chained Bible, an Elizabethan altar and a Saxon font.

Menai Suspension Bridge and 550Ee
Britannia Tubular Bridge *Gwynedd*
Thomas Telford was a well-known bridge engineer when he was asked, in the early 19th century, to design a bridge across the Menai Strait. This became his most famous and important work. The Menai road bridge was originally of cast iron, supported by 16 wrought-iron chains passing over tall masonry towers on either bank and anchored below ground. The original deck was replaced by a concrete one in 1938–40, and the chains are now made of steel. The bridge, nearly half a mile long with a central span of 579 ft, opened to traffic in 1826. The Britannia railway bridge was built farther up the strait by Robert Stephenson in the years 1846–50. Stephenson's problems were as great as those which had faced Telford, for a suspension bridge would be unable to carry heavy rail traffic. The bridge was eventually constructed of two great iron tubes supported by five red sandstone piers—one on each bank and three in the strait. The tubes have been removed and replaced by steel arches, but the original supports remain.

Mendlesham *Suffolk* 548Df
CHURCH OF ST MARY Of 13th-century origins, with later additions; the west tower and two porches have much flushwork decoration in flint and stone. There is a good font cover and pulpit of 1630. The north porch contains an unusual feature —a parish armoury (by appointment), with pieces of armour from the 15th to 17th centuries.

Menstrie Castle *Central* 562Ag
The birthplace of Sir William Alexander (1567–1640), poet and statesman, later 'Lieutenant for the Plantations of New Scotland', otherwise known as Nova Scotia, commissioned by James VI

(James I of England) in 1621. The foundation of the colony of Nova Scotia was assisted by the creation of Scotian baronetcies; and the coats of arms of 107 baronets are displayed at the castle.

Mere *Wilts.*   540De
CHURCH OF ST MICHAEL This is a large church of various dates, mostly Decorated though with later Perpendicular work, for example the tower, *c.* 1450. The octagonal font is Perpendicular, and the fine rood and chapel screens are of the same period. The stalls have misericords; there are brasses of 1398 and 1426, and medieval stained glass.

Merevale *Warks.*   546Eg
CHURCH OF ST MARY Originally built as the 'capella ante portas' (chapel at the gates) of the Cistercian Abbey, which was founded in the mid-12th century and is now but fragmentary ruins near by. The church itself dates from the 13th century, but what can be seen now is mainly of the 14th and 15th centuries. Glass of this period includes a 14th-century Tree of Jesse window. There is a medieval organ loft from the abbey church, and a 13th-century effigy.

Mersham *Kent*   542Ee
CHURCH OF ST JOHN THE BAPTIST A Norman church, later enlarged, with a west tower which has a pyramidal roof. The great west window is unique for its tracery and contains some original glass *c.* 1400. Among monuments is one to Sir Wyndham Knatchbull, *c.* 1765, by William Tyler.

Merthyr Mawr *Mid Glam.*   545Gb
Most Welsh roofs are of slate, but in the Vale of Glamorgan there are one or two villages where thatch is used. Merthyr Mawr, a small village near the mouth of the Ogmore, is one of the best preserved. It also has a medieval bridge, a ruined oratory containing pre-Conquest memorials, and within a short distance are the castles of Ogmore, with its splendid stepping-stones, and Candleston, standing on the edge of extensive sand dunes which have covered an area rich in prehistoric sites.

Merthyr Tydfil *Mid Glam.*   545Hc
MUSEUM AND ART GALLERY (CYFARTHFA CASTLE) The neo-Gothic castle, built in 1825 by the Crawshay family of ironmasters, has exhibits relating to the history and natural history of the district.

Methwold *Norfolk*   554Bb
CHURCH OF ST GEORGE The spire of this 14th-century church is famed as a landmark of the Fens, and as an architectural near-impossibility. It consists of a 60 ft tower surmounted by a 30 ft corona, topped by a 30 ft spire, all brick-built from the inside. There are interesting relics (seen by appointment) including the first murrain document in England—a 1747 form of compensation for foot-and-mouth disease.

Michelham Priory *E. Sussex*   542Cd
The Augustinian priory, founded in 1229, is encompassed by a 14th-century moat covering some eight acres. A gate-house was built in the 1300's and the property was adapted as a Tudor farmhouse in the late 16th century. It contains a collection of fine furniture, tapestries, Sussex ironwork, ancient stained glass, musical instruments, a dolls' house, a forge and wheelwright's shop, and farm equipment.

Mid Calder *Lothian*   562Be
CALDER HOUSE It was in this 15th-century house in 1556 that John Knox administered one of the first Protestant communions in the manner of the Reformed Scottish Church.

16th-CENTURY STAINED GLASS
WINDOW

This church was extended in the early 16th century by Sir Richard Assheton, lord of the manor, as a thanks offering for victory at the Battle of Flodden (1513) where he and his archers had distinguished themselves. The war memorial window, set up by Sir Richard in 1524, much altered, now stands in the south chancel. The line of 16 English archers kneeling in prayer is still recognisable, each dressed in blue with a long-bow on his shoulder. Above each bow is the archer's name. Sir Richard and his wife Anne are also included, and their chaplain, Henry Taylyer.
(Church of St Leonard, Middleton)

Middlesbrough *Cleveland*   558De
CAPTAIN COOK BIRTHPLACE MUSEUM The museum (at Marton) was built to commemorate the 250th anniversary of the birth of the explorer James Cook (1728–1779), and contains displays illustrating his voyages of discovery.
DORMAN MUSEUM Collections devoted to the natural history, geology and archaeology of north-eastern Yorkshire are on display.

Middleton *Greater Manchester*   552Bg
CHURCH OF ST LEONARD Rebuilt in the 15th century and extended in the 16th. The old tower has a gabled wooden belfry cap, added in 1709. There is a window inserted by Sir Richard Assheton in 1520, recalling his command of local archers at Flodden Field.

Middleton Hall *Cumbria*   557Jd
A late 14th-century manor house to which extensions and a security wall enclosing a courtyard were added in the 15th century. A Roman milestone marking the 53rd mile from Carlisle was found near the hall in 1836: it now stands in a field close to where it was discovered. Near by is an ancient cross called The Standing Stone of Whilprigg.

Mid Howe *Rousay, Orkney*   569Hg
Here is the largest known 'stalled cairn'. The chamber is lined with drystone walling and the outer face with slabs that are set slantwise in courses. It is of the late Neolithic period.

Midhurst *W. Sussex* *541Jd*
In Tudor times Midhurst shared with Rye the privilege of making town tokens for use by private traders: the Midhurst Farthing had a weaver's shuttle as its device. A local quilt-maker founded the grammar school in 1672. Among its pupils were the statesman Richard Cobden, the novelist H. G. Wells and Sir Charles Lyle, the geologist.

Midmar Castle *Grampian* *566Fe*
A fine early 17th-century Scottish baronial building with many turrets, said to have been built by Sir William Wallace. (By appointment.)

Midsummer Hill *Heref. & Worcs.* *546Be*
A large Iron Age hill-fort lying towards the south end of the Malvern range. It is a 'contour' fort, its defences following the natural contours of the hill, and comprises a bank and ditch with counterscarp bank. The bank was faced with drystone walling, and some of the material came from internal quarry ditches. South of the fort on the adjoining hill are a Neolithic long barrow and several round barrows of the Bronze Age.

Mildenhall *Suffolk* *548Bf*
CHURCH OF SS MARY AND ANDREW A major church of Suffolk—very long and with a tall west tower. There is some 13th-century work in the chancel, but the remainder is mainly Perpendicular. The east window, *c.* 1300, has extraordinary and unique tracery design, and the magnificent roofs have angels and other carved decoration. The font is of Purbeck marble, and there is a monument, with effigies, of *c.* 1620.

Milford Haven *Dyfed* *544Cc*
A natural harbour, for centuries a middle-water fishing port, and now a major harbour for oil tankers too large to be accommodated elsewhere. Milford Haven was the departure point from which in 1172 the forces of Henry II set out to conquer Ireland, and Henry Tudor landed here on his way to Bosworth Field in 1485, where he defeated Richard III and was proclaimed king as Henry VII. Much of Milford Haven now lies within a national park.

Millport *Isle of Cumbrae, Strathclyde* *561Ge*
ROBERTSON MUSEUM AND THE AQUARIUM The museum is devoted to natural history, and the aquarium exhibits marine life found in the Clyde sea area.

Millom *Cumbria* *557Gd*
CHURCH OF THE HOLY TRINITY A Norman and later church, near the castle. Inside are box-pews, and monuments to the Huddleston family, one of *c.* 1494 with alabaster effigies. The remains of a wooden figure in the chancel are thought to be those of an effigy of Sir Richard Hudleston who fought at Agincourt and was known locally as 'Terrible Dick'.

Milton Abbas *Dorset* *540Dd*
In the second half of the 18th century Lord Milton swept away the little market town of Milton Abbas and constructed the present delightful 'model' village nearly a mile away. Identical double thatched cottages with gardens, church, almshouse and inn curve upwards on the slope of the road to Blandford.

Milton Abbey *Dorset* *540Dd*
Milton Abbey was dissolved by Henry VIII, and the estate sold. Eventually Lord Milton bought it in 1752, and employed John Vardy, the former assistant of William Kent, to undertake rebuilding of the former monastic buildings. However, during the early 1770's Milton commissioned Sir William Chambers, one of the most outstanding architects of the 18th century, to build him a new Gothic house. After Milton and Chambers quarrelled in 1774, James Wyatt continued the work of building. He was responsible for most of the Classical interior decoration, with fine ceilings. Of the original abbey, which was destroyed by fire in the 13th century, the abbot's hall survives and is incorporated in the 18th-century mansion, now used as a school.

Close by is the abbey church, which was rebuilt in the 15th century. But the western side was never finished: it is thought that a plague in Dorset at the time of rebuilding prevented completion. The

MILTON ABBEY

Two buildings in the Gothic style stand side by side at Milton Abbey. But three centuries separate them. The abbey church (centre) was erected in the 15th century, secularised after Henry VIII's dissolution, and bought in 1752 by Lord Milton. The church contains a marble monument, c. 1775, with reclining effigies to Lord and Lady Milton, carved by Agostino Carlini. Work on the house (right) started 20 years later. Sir William Chambers, designer of Somerset House in London, first directed construction, then James Wyatt took over. One of the chimney-pieces is the work of Joseph Wilton; others are by Wyatt.

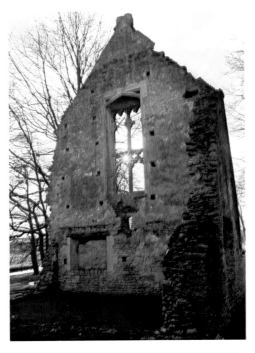

MINSTER LOVELL HALL

The unluckiest owner of this house must surely have been Francis, 9th Baron Lovell, who started life a rich and powerful aristocrat and is said to have died in hiding in one of its vaults. Francis gambled his future on supporting the Yorkists in the Wars of the Roses—unlike his predecessor John, who was a Lancastrian. At first this change of sides brought rewards, and Francis was made a viscount by Richard III in 1483. Two years later, Richard and his supporters were defeated at the Battle of Bosworth. Francis never gained the favour of the new king, Henry VII, and after an unsuccessful rebellion in 1487 he is said to have gone into hiding in a vault at Minster Lovell Hall. Two centuries later, in 1708, workmen making alterations to the house found 'the entire skeleton of a man, as having been at a table which was before him with a book, paper, pen . . . all much mouldered and decay'. Minster Lovell Hall probably belonged to the Lovell family as early as the 12th century, but it was rebuilt in the 15th century.

church contains much good vaulting under the tower and a carved altar screen.

Milton Manor *Oxon.*   *546Fc*
A small 17th-century manor house with Georgian wings. The chapel and library are in the neo-Gothic style. Among items on view is the telescope of John Benbow (1653–1702), Vice-Admiral of the Blue, 1701, and a Viking sword.

Minstead *Hants.*   *541Gd*
CHURCH OF ALL SAINTS The church was originally a 13th-century building, of which the chancel and north-porch arches remain. During alteration in the late 18th century, the west tower was built and fittings added—including the three-decker pulpit, two west galleries and two squire's pews, one with a fireplace in it. The font is pre-Norman. Sir Arthur Conan Doyle, creator of Sherlock Holmes, is buried in the churchyard.

Minster, Isle of Sheppey *Kent*   *542Eg*
ABBEY CHURCH OF SS MARY AND SEXBURGHA One of the oldest monastic foundations in England,

dating from about 674. The building contains much Saxon stonework and a Saxon window survives. There are two famous brasses; that of Lady Joan de Northwode (*d.* 1335) being one of the oldest known of an English lady. There is also a monument to Sir Robert de Shurland (1307) and his horse.

Minster, Isle of Thanet *Kent*   *543Gf*
CHURCH OF ST MARY A beautiful cruciform church, with a west tower capped by a slender spire. The nave is Norman; there are misericords and several monuments. Tradition has it that the church is built on the site of a nunnery founded by Ermenburga *c.* 670.
MINSTER ABBEY Arguably the oldest lived-in dwelling-place in the country, the original monastic foundation was built in 670 by the great-granddaughter of King Ethelbert of Kent. In 1027 it was rebuilt by the monks of Canterbury, and part of this building is still occupied by nuns of the Benedictine order. During excavations in 1929, the apse of the original church was discovered and found to contain part of the tomb of St Mildred, the Saxon saint who died as Abbess of Minster in 725. (Closed on Sundays.)

Minster Lovell *Oxon.*   *546Ed*
CHURCH OF ST KENELM A cruciform church with a central tower, nearly all of the 15th century. The tower is narrower than the rest of the building, and the tower piers in the nave are set in, considerably narrowing the east end. There is some medieval stained glass, a Perpendicular font and good woodwork. An effigy of a knight, *c.* 1430, probably depicts a member of the Lovell family.

Minster Lovell Hall *Oxon.*   *546Ed*
The ruins of Minster Lovell Hall stand in an attractive position on the banks of the R. Windrush. The ruins of the Hall never formed part of any religious establishment, although the owners of the property established a small religious foundation near by, which was subject to Ivry Abbey in Normandy and was therefore termed an 'alien priory'. The site of this priory is now lost. The remains are those of a 15th-century manor house. The chief fragments are of the hall and its porch, and part of the north and west sides of the court. The present ruined state of the Hall is the result of demolition *c.* 1750.

Moat Hall *Suffolk*   *548Ef*
A 15th-century moated manor house that has been restored. (Interior by appointment.)

Moat House *Leics.*   *552Db*
Nothing remains of the 14th-century manor house (home of Sir Edmund de Appleby, who fought at the Battle of Crécy) except part of the moat, an old stone well, and a cobbled courtyard now beneath the present garden. The stone gate-house was rebuilt in the 15th century and a timber-frame building added to it to make a yeoman-type dwelling. In the grounds is a 16th-century dove-cote, originally of stone but restored in red brick.

Mobberley *Cheshire*   *552Be*
CHURCH OF ST WILFRID AND ST MARY THE VIRGIN The origins are 13th century, but most of the work was done in the following two centuries. There is a good rood screen of *c.* 1500, a fine medieval nave roof and some old stained glass. The remains of a wall painting show St Christopher.

Moccas *Heref. & Worcs.*   *546Ae*
CHURCH OF ST MICHAEL AND ALL ANGELS A Norman church of nave, chancel and apse, with

windows of c. 1300. Some stained glass dates from the 14th century, and there is a cross-legged knight on a monument of the same period.

Moignes Court *Dorset*   *540Dc*
One fragment dates from 1280, and contains windows and a doorway of the Early English period. (By appointment.)

Mold *Clwyd*   *551He*
CHURCH OF ST MARY A spacious Perpendicular church, with a west tower rebuilt in 1773. Inside, there is sculptured decoration on capitals and panelling below the clerestory windows. Many memorials by Sir Henry Cheere, Benjamin and Solomon Gibson (brothers of the more famous John) and Michael Rysbrack.

Monk Fryston *N. Yorks.*   *558Da*
CHURCH OF ST WILFRID The west tower is Saxon, but the rest of the church is mainly Early English and Decorated Gothic. There is a square Early English font, and some medieval stained glass.

Monkwearmouth *Tyne & Wear*   *558Dg*
The monastery of Monkwearmouth was established in 674 and that at Jarrow, 6 miles to the north-west, in 684. Both were founded by Benedict Biscop, who had travelled widely in Europe; his churches are outstanding examples of the northern revival of building in stone. By the 8th century the two monasteries were so famous that together they housed nearly 600 monks. At one period the church at Monkwearmouth became buried under piles of ballast, but extensive restoration was carried out in 1866. The most interesting part is at the west end, where the tower incorporates a lower porch dating from Biscop's time. The entrance, which is flanked by heavy stone balustrades, is tunnel-vaulted and is the earliest medieval vault in England. Above the entrance on the outside are the battered remains of a large standing figure carved in relief. This figure also dates from Biscop's time and is one of the earliest surviving pieces of large-scale architectural sculpture in Britain.

Monmouth *Gwent*   *546Ad*
After many changes of ownership—from 1086 when William FitzBaderun acquired the town from the Breton Abbey of St Florent de Saumer, until 1387 when Henry V was born in the castle— Monmouth fell into decay in the Wars of the Roses. It became a Lancastrian holding until it was sold to the Earl of Worcester in 1630, and its fortunes revived. Part of Monmouth was at one time known as 'Cappers Town' because it was the centre of a flourishing industry that produced 'Monmouth' knitted caps. The Shire Hall, in Agincourt Square, is a fine Georgian building erected in 1724 on the site of Old Market House. In the middle of its façade is a statue of Henry V. In the centre of the Monnow bridge is a gateway which was constructed in the 13th century as a toll house and defence tower with portcullis. Great Castle House was built by the 1st Duke of Beaufort in 1673, and c. 1875 it became headquarters of the Royal Monmouthshire Royal Engineers; it has superb plaster ceilings. (By appointment.)
CHURCH OF ST MARY Originally a Norman church with Gothic enlargements, it was pulled down during the 18th century and rebuilt in a Classical style by Smith of Warwick. The 14th-century west tower was retained but given a tall slender spire. In c. 1880 G. E. Street Gothicised and enlarged the building. Monuments of the 18th and 19th centuries include work by James Paty the Younger of Bristol, and Sir Richard Westmacott.

There are some 15th-century wall tiles and some 19th-century glass by C. E. Kempe in the church.
MONMOUTH MUSEUM Among items relating to Lord Nelson, Lady Hamilton and their contemporaries are collections of silver, china and glass, a model of the Battle of Trafalgar, ships, swords and naval equipment; also a collection of Nelson's letters, and items relating to local history.

Montacute House *Som.*   *540Cd*
An Elizabethan house built in 1588–1601. It has fine windows and is surrounded by balustraded parapets. On the west side is a fine porch which dates from the early 16th century; this came from Clifton Maybank, a house a few miles away, when it was demolished in 1786. Carved statues of the Nine Worthies (Joshua, David, Judas Maccabeus, Hector, Alexander, Julius Caesar, Arthur, Charlemagne, Godfrey of Bouillon) stand in niches on the east front, originally the main entrance side of the house, and in the east forecourt are two domed pavilions. The house contains fine heraldic glass, plasterwork and panelling, portraits of the English School, and furniture. It was in the possession of the same family from 1601 to 1931. (See p. 360.)

Montgomery *Powys*   *551Hb*
CASTLE The castle stands on a spur overlooking the R. Severn, and was built by Henry III c. 1223 about a mile from the site of an earlier Norman motte and bailey. It has been a ruin since the defences were slighted by Parliamentary troops in 1649, following the Civil War.

Montrose *Tayside*   *566Fb*
This is an ancient royal burgh with several treasures and curiosities. In the steeple of the Old Church is the Big Peter bell, cast in Rotterdam in 1676, which tolls the curfew at 10 p.m. each night. Also in the church is a chandelier shaped as a hearse, which was presented by a Swedish admiral in 1627.

Four of the books in the old Montrose library were printed before 1501. The old library was replaced in 1790, and a third or 'new' library now incorporates the contents of the previous buildings. James Graham, Marquess of Montrose and Scotland's most famous soldier after Robert the Bruce, was born at Old Montrose in 1612.

Moor Park *Herts.*   *547Hc*
A mansion built in 1620 by the 3rd Earl of Bedford, and later owned by the Duke of Monmouth, executed for treason in 1685. In 1720, the house was restored by Leoni, who encased the old Jacobean brick in stone. It contains fine paintings by Amiconi and Thornhill.

Moretonhampstead Almshouses   *539Gd*
Devon
A row of thatched houses built of granite over an open colonnade facing the street; erected in 1637.

Morley *Derbys.*   *552Ed*
CHURCH OF ST MATTHEW Of the Norman original, only some parts of the nave arcade remain; the remainder of the church is 14th and 15th century. Some of the stained glass dates from the 15th century. Many of the medieval monuments and brasses are dedicated to the Sacheverell family.

Morpeth *Northld.*   *563Gb*
CHURCH OF ST MARY Mainly 14th century. There is a stained glass Tree of Jesse of the same date in the east window, and fragments of old glass in other windows.

Morville *Shropshire*   *546Bg*
CHURCH OF ST GREGORY Making an attractive group with Morville Hall, this Norman church has a chancel arch as early as 1118, and most of the

MONTACUTE HOUSE

MONTACUTE HOUSE *One of the most beautiful country houses of the reign of Elizabeth I, Montacute was built in 1588–1601 for Sir Edward Phelips, who later became Speaker of the House of Commons during the reign of James I. It is possible that its designer was William Arnold. The northern part of the ground floor comprises the great hall, one storey high, with a stone screen at one end; at the other end is a plaster panel* representing *a husband who, after being hit by his wife in retaliation, is further punished by the parish by being carried round tied to a pole—a procedure known as the 'Ride to Skimmington'. On the second floor of the house is a 172 ft long gallery extending the whole length of the building. There is much heraldic stained glass, especially in the windows of the library, formerly the great chamber.*

18TH-CENTURY ENGLISH CHAIR *In England during the reigns of Queen Anne and George I there was a division of opinion about furniture materials and designs. Some preferred an ornate classicism to a restrained baroque style. Natural walnut veneer, as in this chair, was preferred to marquetried wood, and the straight rectangular-shaped back contrasts with contemporary French baroque curves. The legs are en cabriole—a French term meaning 'to caper'.*

KNIGHT IN TAPESTRY *This very fine Gothic tapestry of a knight, fully armed and mounted, hangs in the dining-room. It was probably woven in Tournai c. 1480; the 'mille fleurs' background to the figure, similar to that of the famous Dame à la Licorne tapestries in Paris, reflects the Gothic love of floral decoration. The knight himself is unidentified, but he may be one of the Nine London Worthies—prominent citizens and warriors of the period.*

interior is 12th century. An interesting Norman tub font is carved with large faces; there is 12th-century ironwork on the south door. A chancel window has early 14th-century stained glass.

Morville Hall *Shropshire* 546Bg
An Elizabethan house, altered and added to in the 18th century. (By appointment.)

Morwenstow *Cornwall* 538Ee
CHURCH OF ST JOHN Standing high above the sea, this is an impressive church with west tower and much still remaining of the original Norman building: the north arcade, the south doorway, and the font. There is also work of the 13th, 15th and 16th centuries, and some fine wagon-roofs. During the last century, the poet Robert Hawker was vicar here.

Moseley Old Hall *Staffs.* 552Bb
An Elizabethan house where the Whitgreave family sheltered Charles II after the Battle of Worcester in 1651; the bed he used and his secret hiding place can be seen. The house contains fine furniture, and documents, portraits and other relics of the Whitgreaves.

Mottisfont Abbey *Hants.* 541Ge
At the Dissolution of the monasteries this 12th-century Augustinian priory came into the hands of Lord Sandys, Chancellor to Henry VIII, and he converted it into a fine house for himself; the wall of the church nave forms the north front of the house. It was altered and redecorated during the 18th century. There are Gothic-style *trompe l'oeil* paintings by Rex Whistler in the drawing room.

Moulton *Lincs.* 553Jc
CHURCH OF ALL SAINTS An impressive church, with a late Perpendicular tower and spire. There is fine work in the foliage capitals of the pillars in the nave, and an 18th-century font, recently restored, is embellished with figures of Adam and Eve.

Mount Grace Priory *N. Yorks.* 558De
The ruins of a Carthusian priory, founded in 1397 for 20 monks who, according to their strict rule, lived in separate cells. The priory was dissolved under Henry VIII, but part was made into a house in 1654.

Mow Cop *Cheshire–Staffs.* 552Bd
A sham castle crowns this hill on the Cheshire-Staffordshire border. It was built to enhance the landscape by Randle Wilbraham *c.* 1750, and comprises a ruined round tower and ragged curtain wall broken by archways. On the summit of the hill Hugh Bourne, a Staffordshire carpenter, began to hold open-air camp meetings in 1807 similar to the revivalist camp meetings then sweeping America, and out of these meetings Primitive Methodism was born.

Muchalls Castle *Grampian* 567Gd
Built in 1619 by the Burnetts of Leys, this fortified mansion is notable for its 17th-century elaborate plaster ceilings and fire-places.

Much Cowarne *Heref. & Worcs.* 546Be
CHURCH OF ST MARY A 13th- and 14th-century church consisting of nave and south aisle only—the arcade of the demolished north aisle can be seen from the outside. Among the monuments is a cross-legged knight of the late 13th century.

Muchelney Abbey *Som.* 540Ce
As its Anglo-Saxon name signifies, the abbey once stood on a 'big island'; after Glastonbury, it is the oldest monastic foundation in the county, and exercised considerable influence from the 10th

century until the 16th, when it was dissolved by Henry VIII's commissioners. The medieval Abbot's Lodging is still intact and contains fine wall paintings. It has one of the best-preserved pre-Reformation fire-places in the country. The reredorter, or privy attached to the monks' dormitory, can also be seen. Adjoining the abbey is the parish church. Its waggon roof is decorated with 17th-century paintings of angels in clouds.

Much Hadham *Herts.* 548Ad
An attractive village with a number of delightful small 16th- and 17th-century cottages alongside larger 18th-century dwellings. The Lordship in the main street is a large nine-bay house of *c.* 1740 with a number of later additions. The gabled dwellings opposite are 17th century and next to them is the Earl of Euston's chequered brickwork house, North Leys. Other good examples from this period are Woodham House with its fine doorway; the Old House with exposed timbers; Green Shutters near by and Gaytons, a large three-gabled brick house. Much Hadham Hall, a five-bay house of 1735 with a hipped-roof, is the dominant house of the village street. To the south lies the Hall's handsome stable range and arched carriageway. Moor Place, 1775, is a two-storied five-bay brick house with blank arcading on the ground floor. Inside there is a splendid three-flight staircase.

Other houses of interest around Much Hadham are Yewtree House, dated 1697, at Hadham Cross; the moated Grudds Farm and the sympathetically modernised Bucklers Farm at Perry Green. The rectory is a brick and plastered-timber Jacobean house.
CHURCH OF ST ANDREW Although originally of the 12th century, the church dates mainly from the 13th–15th centuries; there is an embattled west tower with spire. The contents include two late 14th-century sedilia, some stained glass of the 15th and 19th centuries, and brasses.

Much Marcle *Heref. & Worcs.* 546Be
CHURCH OF ST BARTHOLOMEW The nave was built in the 13th century, and has a clerestory of lancet windows. The tower is central, and the long chancel was lengthened late in the 13th century. The array of monuments, with effigies, includes one of the beautiful Lady Grandison, who died in 1347, and a rare, painted wooden effigy of a 14th-century gentleman, believed to be Walter de Helyon.

Much Wenlock *Shropshire* 552Ab
Medieval town associated with the poet A. E. Housman. Its showpieces include Raynald's Mansion (1682) with fine galleries, the manor house (1577) and the timbered guildhall with panelled rooms and movable stocks.
HOLY TRINITY CHURCH Founded in Saxon times as part of the abbey, but largely rebuilt *c.* 1150. St Milburga, granddaughter of King Penda of Mercia, worshipped and was buried here. So, too, was Dr W. Penny Brookes, 19th-century pioneer of physical education and the modern Olympic games.
WENLOCK PRIORY All the turbulence of early English history is recalled by these ruins. The original priory, which was founded in the 7th century by St Milburga, daughter of a Mercian king, was sacked by the Danes *c.* 896. A later college for priests, founded by Lady Godiva, was demolished at the time of the Norman Conquest; it was rebuilt by a Norman knight, Roger de Montgomery, in 1080 but was destroyed again by Henry VIII's soldiers. The buildings, including the ruined church, date mainly from the 11th century

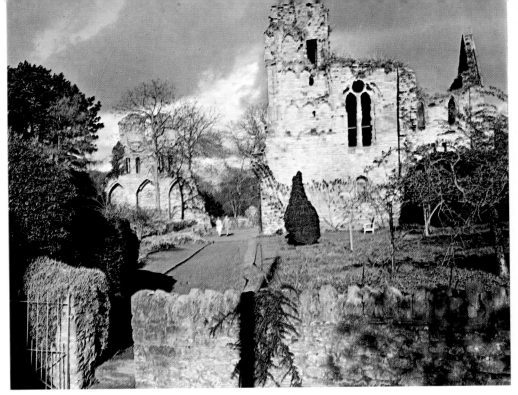

WENLOCK PRIORY

The nunnery founded by St Milburga at Much Wenlock about 680 was destroyed by the Danes 200 years later, and refounded for monks about 1050. In 1080 the Norman Earl of Shropshire, Roger de Montgomery, established a third foundation, which survived until the Dissolution of the monasteries. The Cluniac priory was subject to the French monastery of La Charité-sur-Loire, and paid an annual tax to the mother house. There were many such 'alien priories'

in England—until the wars with France at the end of the 13th century, when the king began to penalise them for this allegiance. During the next century the property of the alien houses was continually being seized by the king, who also taxed them harshly. Eventually, in 1395, Wenlock Priory severed all links with La Charité and, in return for a large cash payment, was released from paying the king's special taxes.

and are in Early English style with Norman arcades. The ruins of a 15th-century prior's lodging also survive.

Mullion *Cornwall* 538Ba
CHURCH OF ST MELAN In the village on the coast above Mullion Cove. Inside are many carved 16th-century bench ends and decorative work by the 20th-century stained glass artist F. C. Eden.

Muncaster Castle *Cumbria* 557Gd
The castle has been the home of the Pennington family since the 13th century. During the Wars of the Roses it provided a sanctuary for the fugitive Henry VI who, in gratitude, presented the

Penningtons with an engraved glass bowl. So long as the bowl—known as the Luck of Muncaster—remains intact, a Pennington will hold the castle. Understandably, only a replica is on view, but there are fine paintings, tapestries and furniture. The views from the terrace are splendid, and the rhododendron gardens world-famous.

Mutford *Suffolk* 548Fg
CHURCH OF ST ANDREW St Andrew's has a circular Norman west tower, and there are other Norman features. The carved font dates from *c.* 1380; there are benches, and an interesting wall-painting of St Christopher.

N

Nanteos *Dyfed* 544Fg
A fine Georgian mansion, with rococo plaster-work, built between 1739 and 1757 by the Powell family. The name, by which an earlier house, now destroyed, had become known at the end of the 17th century, means Valley of the Nightingale. It contains fine period furniture and paintings, and a good first-floor salon in the style of Isaac Ware.

Nantwich *Cheshire* 552Ad
An ancient town, originally prosperous in Roman times because of its brine springs. A great fire devastated the town in 1583, but it was rebuilt in a rich Elizabethan style. The almshouses, which are

decorated with carved figures, are notable and were built in 1638 by Sir Edmund Wright. On the outskirts of the town is Dorfold Hall (1616).
CHURCHE'S MANSION A merchant's house, built in 1577, it is half-timbered and contains some fine oak panelling.
CHURCH OF ST MARY One of Cheshire's finest churches, cruciform, and with a central octagonal tower. The styles are Decorated and Perpendicular, and St Mary's was restored in the 19th century. The vaulted chancel contains magnificent late 14th-century choir stalls with canopies and delightful misericords. There is also a 15th-century stone pulpit.

Narborough *Norfolk* 554Bb
CHURCH OF ALL SAINTS The church has Norman origins with later additions. There are some pieces of 15th-century stained glass. There are monuments dating from *c.* 1300, to members of the Spelman family, many with effigies. That to Clement Spelman (*d.* 1672), which has been mistakenly attributed to Caius Gabriel Cibber, shows him standing dressed in the costume of the period. The story is that, being a proud man, he insisted on being interred standing up so that no one would be able to walk on him. In 1865 the monument was opened, and it was found that the coffin was indeed upright.

Naseby *Northants.* 552Fa
BATTLE AND FARM MUSEUM This contains relics and model layouts of the nearby battlefield where, on June 14, 1645, the Royalist forces under Charles I were decisively beaten by Cromwell's New Model Army. The battlefield has changed little since that day and is marked by two obelisks, the earlier of which, erected in 1823, is incorrectly placed. Farm tools and vintage tractors are also on display in the museum.

Navenby *Lincs.* 553Gd
CHURCH OF ST PETER This fine church has a Decorated east window that is an exceptionally good example of its kind. The Easter Sepulchre, which stands on the north side of the chancel, is decorated with delicately carved figures, including those of three Roman soldiers. The western-most of the pillars on the north side has an ancient seat at the bottom.

Nayland *Suffolk* 548Ce
Nayland has many good 15th- and 16th-century houses, including the handsome White House and Queen's Head Inn.
ALSTON COURT In Church Street, a splendid half-timbered courtyard house, built *c.* 1450 and added to in 1524, incorporates part of an Edward IV house. (Not open.)

Neath Abbey *W. Glam.* 545Gc
The ruins of a Cistercian abbey founded in 1130. It was much enlarged during the 13th century. A fragment of the main gateway to the abbey precinct remains.
Close by are the sites of a Roman camp and a Norman castle.

Needham Market *Suffolk* 548Df
A graceful town that reflects the centuries-long agricultural prosperity of East Anglia. The Georgian houses in the High Street are of especial interest; so, too, is the Bull Hotel, with its carved corner post, the Friends' Meeting House and graveyard, and the 17th-century grammar school.
CHURCH OF ST JOHN THE BAPTIST One of the most superb hammerbeam roofs in England, such a daring piece of design and carpentry that it makes one wonder how it stays up.

Neidpath Castle *Borders* 562Bd
The ruins of the former fortress of the Border Hays beside the R. Tweed, where James VI stayed in 1587. The castle was besieged by Cromwell's troops in 1650 but never surrendered. The original 14th-century tower-house was added to in the 17th century. In 1563, Mary, Queen of Scots stayed in a bedroom on the second floor.

Nether Alderley Mill *Cheshire* 552Be
A 15th-century, water-driven corn-mill that was in use until 1939, when the mill was closed. It was restored in 1976 and is once again in working order. Inside, there is Elizabethan woodwork.

HALL CHAIR AT NEWBY HALL

An 18th-century English entrance hall was really a luxurious waiting-room, far more a focal point of the house than the staircase. Hall chairs would be grouped around fires, and were often equipped with small leather cushions for the comfort of visitors. This mahogany chair shows how Robert Adam thought an entrance hall should be furnished—with simplicity in the style and a hint of luxury in the material.

Nether Winchendon House *Bucks.* 547Gd
A medieval and Tudor mansion, with 18th-century additions. It was the home of Sir Francis Bernard, Governor of New Jersey (1758) and Massachusetts Bay (1760–8).

Netley *Hants.* 541Gd
ABBEY The abbey was founded during the first half of the 13th century by monks who came from the Cistercian abbey not far away across the water at Beaulieu. Like so many abbeys it is now a ruin.

Nettlestead *Suffolk* 548De
CHACE, THE A 19th-century brick house; the gateway is nearly 18 ft high, has a rounded arch, fluted columns and is decorated with the Wentworth Arms.
HIGH HALL An Elizabethan wool merchant's house. It is of red brick with pillared porch and mullioned windows with pediments over. (Exterior viewing only.)

New Alresford *Hants.* 541He
The new town was laid out by the Bishop of Winchester in 1200. He also made the wide, straight Broad Street, now quiet and tree-lined, and dammed the R. Arle to make a reservoir, originally six times its present size.

Newark-on-Trent *Notts.* 552Fd
CHURCH OF ST MARY MAGDALENE One of the most impressive churches in the county, with a tall west spire about 250 ft high. The earliest part is the crypt, while the chancel with its tremendous east window is late 15th century. There are fragments of early glass, many monuments, rood screen and choir stalls, *c.* 1500. A wall-painting depicts the *Dance of Death.*

HIGH LEVEL BRIDGE, NEWCASTLE UPON TYNE

Robert Stephenson designed this bridge, an engineering marvel of its day, to carry road and rail traffic on separate decks over the R. Tyne. It was completed in 1849, and is the finest example of an early cast-iron bridge still in use. The lower bridge in the foreground is a swing bridge built in 1876.

MUSEUM AND ART GALLERY Housed in the former Magnus Grammar School, the museum exhibits archaeological items and relics of local history which include the cheekpiece of a Roman cavalry helmet, Anglo-Saxon cremation urns, relics of the Civil War, and two interesting 17th-century coin hoards.

Newburgh Priory *N. Yorks*   558Dc
A Renaissance mansion, that was the home of Sir George Orby Wombwell—the last surviving officer to have been at the ill-fated Charge of the Light Brigade in 1854. He died in 1913, aged 81. Newburgh Priory was originally an Augustinian priory, founded during the middle of the 12th century, and dissolved in 1529, when it was passed to Anthony Bellasis, Henry VIII's chaplain. Ruins of the priory can be seen in the house.

MUMMY FROM THEBES

This mask is from the mummy of a young woman named Bakt-Hor-Nekht, who was probably embalmed during the 21st or 22nd Dynasty of Egypt (1085–730 BC) when mummies were as life-like as possible, right down to rouge on the cheeks. It was bought in Qurna, Thebes, in 1820. (Hancock Museum, Newcastle upon Tyne)

Newbury *Berks.*   546Fb
At the foot of the Berkshire Downs, the town site has prehistoric links. Its prosperity dates from medieval times when 'Jack of Newbury' (John Winchcombe) extended the local cloth trade by establishing the first true factory in England—having 200 looms and employing over 1000 men, women and children.

Newbury was a battle area in 1643 and 1644; Donnington Castle was ruined in the Civil War. The Jacobean Old Cloth Hall is now a museum of local interests.

DISTRICT MUSEUM Housed in the former Cloth Hall, built in 1627 and restored in 1829, 1897 and 1902, the museum has collections of local archaeology from Palaeolithic to Roman times, and of geology and natural history including a display of moths and butterflies. There are also items dealing with the Civil War period in Newbury, and objects relating to the cloth industry, the Weavers' Company and the Newbury Coat.

Newby Hall *N. Yorks.*   558Cc
A country mansion, built in 1705, with alterations and additions by Robert Adam made in 1770–6. The furnishings include Gobelins tapestries and a collection of Classical statuary. It is surrounded by fine gardens. (See p. 363.)

Newcastle upon Tyne *Tyne & Wear*   558Cg
This important engineering city was once known as Pons Aelii, on the Roman Wall, a fragment of which is visible on the south side of Denton bank. The name Newcastle is derived from the Norman castle built in 1080 by Robert, eldest son of William the Conqueror, and replaced by the existing castle between 1172 and 1177. The Black Gate, which was the gatehouse to the castle, dates from 1247.

During the early 19th century, many fine streets and squares in the city centre were constructed by builder Richard Grainger to the designs of John Dobson, the well-known architect. Outstanding examples of their work are Grey Street, Eldon Square and Grainger Street.

CATHEDRAL The Cathedral Church of St Nicholas, a large and grand parish church, was given cathedral status in 1882; it has a famous tower whose lantern soars on flying buttresses. The building dates mainly from the 14th and 15th centuries.

The interior contains an ornate pinnacled font cover of c. 1500, and a brass lectern of the same date. There are many monuments to be seen, including ones by such sculptors as John Flaxman, E. H. Baily and W. Theed. The Thornton brass is

one of the oldest Flemish brasses in the country.
CENTRAL LIBRARY Here is a notable collection of wood engravings by Thomas Bewick (1753–1828).

DEPARTMENT OF MINING ENGINEERING, THE UNIVERSITY Miners' lamps and miscellaneous mining relics are on display, along with water-colours by T. H. Hair of coal-mines in Northumberland and Durham from 1830 to 1840.

GREEK MUSEUM, THE UNIVERSITY A large collection of ancient Greek and Etruscan antiquities and works of art.

HANCOCK MUSEUM The nucleus of the collections originally belonged to Marmaduke Tunstall of Wycliffe, who died in 1790 leaving a large collection of stuffed animals and birds and a large number of ethnological specimens. These are mainly from the South Sea Islands and Africa, and many are thought to have been brought back by Captain Cook from his Pacific voyages. There is also a small collection of Egyptian mummy-cases. Recent improvements include an entire bird room housing the collection of the 19th-century zoologist John Hancock.

HATTON GALLERY, THE UNIVERSITY A collection of mainly European paintings of the 14th to 18th centuries and a small collection of modern English paintings and drawings. There is also the only remaining sculptured wall by Kurt Schwitters: it was removed from a barn in the Lake District.

HIGH LEVEL BRIDGE Built by Robert Stephenson in 1849, this 146 ft high bridge of cast-iron girders on masonry piers carries road and rail traffic on separate levels over the R. Tyne.

JOHN G. JOICEY MUSEUM This is in Holy Jesus Hospital, a late 17th-century almshouse recently restored, and is adjacent to the medieval Austin Friars tower. Local historical exhibits, furniture and armour are on view.

LAING ART GALLERY AND MUSEUM Oil paintings of the British School from the 17th century onwards, and water-colours illustrating the development of this art in England, are shown. There are displays of silver, ceramics, glass, and historic costume.

MUSEUM OF ANTIQUARIES OF THE UNIVERSITY AND SOCIETY OF ANTIQUITIES Founded in 1813, this houses one of the oldest collections of antiquities in Britain. There are Bronze Age relics, Romano-British jewellery, facsimiles of Roman armour and weapons, inscribed and sculptured stones from Hadrian's Wall. There is also a model of the Wall and a full-scale reconstruction of a temple of Mithras.

MUSEUM OF SCIENCE AND ENGINEERING Exhibits are concerned mainly with the achievements of the north-east in the fields of mining, shipbuilding and engineering. Outstanding are Sir Charles Parsons's original SY *Turbinia* of 1894, the builder's 18 ft model of the *Mauretania* and George Stephenson's locomotive for Killingworth Colliery, built *c.* 1830.

PLUMMER TOWER Part of the medieval fortifications of the city, the tower was altered in the 18th century and given a Classical façade.

New Lanark *Strathclyde* 562Ad
South of Lanark, in the gorge of the R. Clyde, are the textile mills of New Lanark. Here, in 1800, social reformer Robert Owen established his model town. It is being restored and an exhibition illustrates the work in progress. (See p. 366.)

Newland *Glos.* 546Ac
CHURCH OF ALL SAINTS This huge church in the Forest of Dean was mainly built during the 13th and 14th centuries; it also has later additions, and

THE GREYHOUND
BEWICK *The Greyhound*
The revival of wood engraving was largely due to Thomas Bewick, who was born at Cherryburn, near Newcastle. He is best known for his engravings for the History of British Birds (1797–1804). The engraving shown above was made for the History of Quadrupeds (1790). (Central Library, Newcastle)

19th-century restoration. The west tower is impressively pinnacled; inside, there are brasses, including a unique miner's brass, and recumbent effigies of medieval knights and ladies.

Newland *Heref. & Worcs.* 546Ce
CHURCH OF ST LEONARD The mid-19th-century Gothic church replaced the original medieval one which was demolished. The interior is lavishly decorated, notably by splendidly Victorian paintings of biblical scenes on the walls.

Newlyn *Cornwall* 538Aa
NEWLYN ART GALLERY Temporary exhibitions of works by modern artists are held in the gallery.
Works by artists of the Newlyn School are also held.

Newmarket *Suffolk* 548Bf
The centre of racing and racehorse breeding; the Rutland Arms Hotel, with red-brick front, and courtyard with stables behind, and the Jockey Club, Georgian and rebuilt by Sir Albert Richardson in 1933, are worth noting. Newmarket Heath to the west (with the Devil's Dyke earthworks), and the race-course, form a pleasant setting for the town.

Newport *Essex* 548Ae
Once an ancient market town, Newport is now an attractive village chiefly of a single street. On the main street, Monk's Barn is a 15th-century half-timbered house with brickwork and an oriel window with carving of the Virgin and angels below it. On the green are Crown House with pargeting and a shell-hooded doorway of 1692, and Martin's Farmhouse and barn of the 15th century.

CHURCH OF ST MARY THE VIRGIN Formerly collegiate, the church dates from the 13th to the 15th centuries. The west tower was restored in 1858. The church contains a 13th-century font, a late 13th-century painted chest—which is now used as a portable altar—some 14th-century stained glass, a pre-Reformation lectern, and several brasses.

Newport *Isle of Wight* 541Gc
The most urbane town in the island, with a central square, and a town hall or guildhall by John Nash. The most important building is Carisbrooke Castle, on the outskirts to the south-west. It has a Norman keep, Norman curtain walls and, at the lowest level, Elizabethan bastions.
The castle now contains a museum of the island's history.

NEW LANARK

A unique factory and model-village settlement founded by the social reformer Robert Owen after he became a partner in the New Lanark mills in 1800. Welfare schemes for his 2000 workers included reducing the working day to 10½ hours and the opening of a shop where they could exchange cash tokens (one is shown above) for low-priced goods of sound quality. For his workers' children, Owen set up some of the first infant schools in Britain—and abolished corporal punishment.

Newport *Gwent*   *545Jb*
CATHEDRAL The Cathedral of St Woolos is one of the few remaining old buildings in Newport. A church probably stood on this site in the latter part of the 5th century. The cathedral contains some magnificent Norman work with Gothic additions, especially the 15th-century aisles. There was mid-19th-century restoration, and the new reredos and rose window are by John Piper.
MUSEUM AND ART GALLERY Archaeological remains from the Romano-British town of Caerwent are the main attraction, and the museum also has a collection of Pontypool and Usk japan-ware. The art gallery specialises in early English watercolours, British 20th-century works and paintings by Welsh artists, including Augustus John, Sir Frank Brangwyn and Ceri Richards.

New Shoreham *W. Sussex*   *542Bd*
CHURCH OF ST MARY DE HAURA An impressive Norman church, with tower and transepts; the nave disappeared in the 17th century. There is an Early English vault to the chancel, a clerestory and flying buttresses. The interior has a lot of rich ornamental carving, with dog-tooth and foliage, and there is a Norman font with decoration.

Newstead Abbey *Notts.*   *552Ed*
The family of Lord Byron, the poet, lived here from 1540 until 1817, when he was forced to sell the property to pay his debts. The original priory was founded *c.* 1170; it was converted into a house known as Newstead Abbey by Lord Byron's ancestor, Sir John Byron, in the 1540's, but part of the old priory survives. In the 19th century the house was restored in Gothic style to designs by John Shaw. It contains Byron relics, and the furniture collection includes some fine 18th- and 19th-century pieces, together with a rare collection of the poet's letters, first editions and manuscripts. There is a collection of pictures. The grounds are noted for rare trees and shrubs.

Newtimber Place *W. Sussex*   *542Bd*
A 17th-century house, with water-filled moat, at the foot of the South Downs. The hall has late 18th-century Etruscan-style wall-paintings.

Newton Abbot *Devon*   *539Gc*
BRADLEY MANOR A small 15th-century house of roughcast stone, with a great hall, buttery, solarium, and a chapel in Perpendicular style.

Newton Kyme *N. Yorks.*   *558Db*
CHURCH OF ST ANDREW Some Norman work remains, but St Andrew's is largely 13th century, with a small 15th-century west tower. Access to the church is only across the meadow in front of the hall.

Niddry Castle *Lothian*   *562Bf*
The ruins of a 15th-century castle to which Mary, Queen of Scots fled with Lord Seton in 1568 after her escape from Loch Leven Castle.

Norbury *Staffs.*   *552Bc*
CHURCH OF ST PETER A 14th-century church, with an 18th-century brick tower. St Peter's contains four stone sedilia in the chancel, and the tomb and brass of the founder's widow, Hawys Botiller.

Normanby Hall *Humberside*   *553Gg*
A 19th-century mansion, designed by Sir Robert Smirke, the architect of the British Museum. Many of the rooms are furnished throughout in the Regency style, with life-size figures in period costume. There is a 19th-century nursery and an Edwardian bathroom.

Norman's Law *Fife*   *562Ch*
HILL-FORT This hill, nearly 1000 ft high, stands close to the southern shore of the Firth of Tay over which, away to the Sidlaw Hills in the north, it gives a wide view. The defences of the Iron Age fort at the top are complex and represent various phases of construction, though the exact sequence is uncertain. The summit itself is enclosed by a stone wall; well outside this, and including a part of the lower slopes, is a second wall.
   Later, a smaller oval area was enclosed in a 12 ft thick wall of post-Roman origin.

Normanton *W. Yorks.*   *558Da*
CHURCH OF ALL SAINTS This church has a Perpendicular exterior, but much earlier work inside, including the north arcade of *c.* 1300. Fragments of stained glass—the finest in any of Yorkshire's parish churches—include a *Pietà* that is probably 15th-century Flemish; there are monuments of the 16th and 18th centuries.

Normanton Down *Wilts.*   *540Fc*
This is one of the most remarkable barrow groups in Britain. Many of them have been excavated in

the past and the contents, mainly of the Early Bronze Age, show them to have been the graves of people of importance of the 'Wessex culture'; one of them, the Bush Barrow, may well have been that of a paramount chief of his day. It seems certain that these barrows were placed here to be close to Stonehenge, which is surrounded for miles by a concentration of fine barrows. A few of those in this group have suffered some ploughing, but most stand to a considerable height. Apart from a single earlier long barrow, there are 26 round barrows of bowl, bell, disc and saucer types. Finds from the site are in Devizes Museum.

Northampton *Northants.* 547Gf
The town has little to show of its long and eventful history in Norman, Tudor and Elizabethan times, as a great fire gutted the whole of the central portion (600 houses) in 1675. The Eleanor Cross on the London Road is one of the few survivors of the crosses marking Queen Eleanor's funeral procession from Harby (Nottingham) to Westminster (1290).
ABINGTON PARK MUSEUM A reconstruction of an 18th-century street, Northamptonshire lace, exhibits of children's toys, agricultural and domestic bygones, and horse-drawn fire engines are exhibited in a manor house that was medieval in origin but much altered in the 17th and 18th centuries. It also houses the weapons, medals, uniforms and silver of the Northamptonshire Regiment, 1741–1960.
CENTRAL MUSEUM AND ART GALLERY Shoemaking, the local industry, is the focus of a comprehensive collection that includes Queen Victoria's wedding shoes, and ballet shoes of Nijinsky, Ulanova and Fonteyn. Among the other varied collections is the Irchester hoard of 42,000 3rd-century coins, archaeological finds from the Iron Age to medieval times, medieval pottery, paintings and furniture.
CHURCH OF ALL SAINTS A big church in the centre of the town, rebuilt soon after the fire which destroyed Northampton in 1675. A 14th-century tower has a cupola of 1704 and there is an impressive west portico with Ionic columns. The elegant interior has a crossing dome on Ionic columns and retains the medieval crypt below the chancel. The font and pulpit are of *c.* 1680.
CHURCH OF ST MATTHEW A Gothic Revival church that contains a painting of the Crucifixion by Graham Sutherland and a carving of the Madonna and Child by Henry Moore.
CHURCH OF ST PETER A small, interesting Norman church whose west tower was rebuilt in the 17th century; the east end was also rebuilt, *c.* 1850. There are Norman doorways, and the interior has much ornate carving on arches and capitals.
CHURCH OF THE HOLY SEPULCHRE One of England's rare Norman round churches, built *c.* 1110 and shaped like its prototype in Jerusalem. A long 13th-century chancel and massive tower with spire; the apse was added by Sir Gilbert Scott in 1860. The interior is dimly lit, and the circular nave has piers. There is much 19th-century glass and a good 17th-century brass.
TOWN HALL This large town hall was designed by Edward William Godwin in 1861–4 in the Romanesque and Gothic tradition at a time when the Gothic style was becoming unfashionable for secular buildings. The two-storey hall building is in Venetian Gothic style with a clock tower and a gable flanked by two turrets. There is much statuary on the façade, representing sovereigns and patron saints of the United Kingdom. A newer wing by Matthew Holding was added in 1889–92, and is also much decorated with statuary. The

windows are richly ornamented; on the lower floor sculptured groups depict scenes connected with the history of the county, such as the trial of Thomas à Becket at Northampton Castle in 1164, Henry II granting the town its charter in 1189, and the destruction by fire of most of Northampton in 1675. (By appointment.)

North Barningham *Norfolk* 554Cd
CHURCH OF ST PETER The church is mainly of the Decorated period, and has good but damaged piscina and sedilia, and a Perpendicular west tower. Tiles and a stone circular window are laid out in the nave floor. Various monuments are dedicated to the Palgrave family, notably Sir Austin (*d.* 1639) with two busts, and to his sister, Mrs Pope (*d.* 1621), showing her kneeling beneath a canopy with angels.

North Berwick *Lothian* 562Df
BURGH MUSEUM Built in 1876 as a public school, the museum has a natural history collection displaying birds, fish, butterflies and some animals. Medieval relics from the former 12th-century Cistercian priory can be seen, along with Scottish pottery, costumes and bygones. There are also exhibits directly associated with the former Royal Burgh of North Berwick.

Northborough *Cambs.* 547Jh
MANOR HOUSE The gate-house opens on to the main street. Built *c.* 1330, with a porch added in 1500. The house stands as a good example of a small fortified stone-built dwelling, now carefully restored to its original medieval state. Gabled, with a buttress on the south side, it has a Gothic chimney, a crow-stepped angle, and three highly ornamented carved stone doorways to kitchen, buttery and pantry.

North Cerney *Glos.* 546Dc
CHURCH OF ALL SAINTS Partly Norman, this cruciform church has a saddle-back west tower; three windows have 15th-century glass, and the stone pulpit is of the same period. Incised on the outside south wall of the transept and on the south-west tower buttress are the grotesque figures of a mantichora, a man-eater with the head of a man and the body of a lion.

North Creake *Norfolk* 554Bd
CHURCH OF ST MARY The church, built *c.* 1300, has an elaborate Easter Sepulchre, sedilia, and piscina. The Perpendicular additions are the clerestory, nave windows, hammerbeam roofs and the tower. Above the chancel arch there is a faded 'Doom' painting, and internally, above the north door, the Royal Arms of Charles I. On the sanctuary floor there is the Calthorpe Brass, depicting the 15th-century donor holding a model of the church he restored. It may be the work of a Flemish craftsman.

North Elmham *Norfolk* 554Cc
The ruins of an early 11th-century Saxon cathedral blend with the ruins of a manor house of 1386, lying in a moated enclosure; the Saxon remains can be distinguished by the large blocks of dark brown stone. Elmham was the See of the Bishop of the 'North Folk' from *c.* 600 or even earlier. The See was moved to Thetford in 1071 and not long after was finally settled in Norwich.
CHURCH OF ST MARY The original church was built in 1093 as an act of penance for simony— purchase of ecclesiastical benefices. One of the original Norman windows can be seen on the south side. Features include a rood screen with many painted saints, and 14th-century stained glass.

North End *Essex* 548Bd
BLACK CHAPEL This little building is unusual for

17th-CENTURY CUSHION

This 'Turkey-work' cushion, decorated with the arms of the city, is from a set given to Norwich Cathedral in 1651 by Thomas Baret, then mayor. Weavers adapted techniques copied from Turkish carpets, using European designs. (Strangers' Hall, Norwich)

THE READE SALT

Alderman Peter Reade commissioned this salt, made by a Norwich goldsmith in 1568, 'to serve the mayor and his successors for ever'. The shape, decoration and domed cover surmounted by a warrior, show strong Renaissance influence. (City Hall, Norwich)

three reasons: few timber-framed church buildings survive; there are few old chapels left in Essex; and the priest's house is built into the church. Nave, chancel and the priest's dwelling are of the late 15th century, and there are some modern additions. The attractive interior has benches and a screen of *c.* 1500, early 18th-century communion rails and 18th-century box-pews.

North Foreland *Kent*   *543Gg*
LIGHTHOUSE When built in the 17th century, the tower was about half its present height and carried an open coal fire. In the 18th century attempts were made to enclose the fire in a glass lantern, but

the result was so unsatisfactory that it had to be removed. At the end of the century the tower was raised to its present height (188 ft above sea level) and oil lamps fitted; later, some of the earliest experiments in electric lighting were made here.

North Grimston *N. Yorks.*   *558Fc*
CHURCH OF ST NICHOLAS Though not large, the church has a good Norman chancel arch, and quite a large font of the same period, with rough carvings of the Last Supper, Descent from the Cross and St Nicholas.

Northleach *Glos.*   *546Dd*
CHURCH OF SS PETER AND PAUL A large and impressive building of the 15th century for the most part, the church has many of the characteristics of similar products of prosperous wool centres in the Cotswolds. It has a lofty west tower and a fine south porch with a vaulted ceiling and a room above it. The clerestory over the chancel arch was built by John Fortey in the 15th century; his brass is in the floor of the nave. The stone pulpit is Perpendicular; the font has carvings of faces.

North Lees Hall *Derbys.*   *552Df*
Originally built *c.* 1410, almost a ruin by the 20th century, the Hall was restored in 1959. The tower walls with parapet are 3 ft thick, and original: the plasterwork is partly modern restoration to the period of 1594. The Hall was the home of the Eyre family and is said to have been the basis of Thornfield Hall in Charlotte Brontë's novel, *Jane Eyre*. The spiral staircase is a notable feature. (By appointment.)

North Leigh Villa *Oxon.*   *546Ed*
This is a fine Roman courtyard villa, excavated and preserved for inspection. It is of special interest in that it was shown to have been twice remodelled after its first building, the earliest house on the site being a villa-residence of somewhat simpler type. It is large, the overall area being almost 300 ft in each direction. Its fine mosaics, like the best of those in Gloucestershire, appear to have been laid by men of the Cirencester workshop.

North Luffenham *Leics.*   *553Gb*
CHURCH OF ST JOHN THE BAPTIST A church of the 13th and 14th centuries, but there is a continuous list of rectors going back to 1206. The window tracery is 14th century, the arcades 13th century. Remains of wall-paintings can be seen, and there is some medieval glass in the chancel.

North Marden *W. Sussex*   *541Jd*
CHURCH OF ST MARY A tiny Norman church by a farm; it consists of nave and apse only, and there are perhaps only four such churches in England. The south doorway was carved in the 12th century, and the apse has a 13th-century piscina.

North Newbald *Humberside*   *558Fb*
CHURCH OF ST NICHOLAS A Norman cruciform church with a central tower, but no aisles. There are Norman doorways and windows; one of the doors has a carving of Christ in Majesty. Inside is a 12th-century font, with a 17th-century cover.

North Runcton *Norfolk*   *554Ac*
CHURCH OF ALL SAINTS One of the finest 18th-century churches in Norfolk. It was built 1703–13, and is attributed to Henry Bell, designer of King's Lynn custom house. The west tower has a lantern. The nave has a slight projection north and south, while the chapel, which projects on the south side of the chancel, is a late 19th-century addition. In the nave four Ionic columns support a dome, and there are other Ionic columns and pilasters. The panelling and reredos, designed by Henry Bell in

1684, come from St Margaret's, King's Lynn. The paintings in the reredos are Florentine.

North Stoneham *Hants.*   *541Gd*
CHURCH OF ST NICHOLAS Rebuilt in the late 15th century, the church was restored in 1826 and again at the end of the 19th century. Several monuments include one of *c.* 1613 with reclining effigies, and another, *c.* 1787, by J. F. Moore to Admiral Lord Hawke, with a marble relief of a naval engagement. Fragments of heraldic glass date from 1826. (By appointment.)

Northwold *Norfolk*   *554Bb*
A village of several attractive houses grouped around the church and, farther to the west, Manor Farm, with a gable-end dated 1635.

Norton *Cleveland*   *558Df*
CHURCH OF ST MARY In an attractive village, the church is cruciform, and a rewarding Saxon remnant, as the tower arches and windows survive. There is stained glass by C. E. Kempe, of 1896, and an early 15th-century effigy of a knight.

Norwich *Norfolk*   *554Db*
Norwich began as a Saxon settlement over 1000 years ago. It is the capital city of Norfolk and the market centre for a large part of East Anglia.

Norwich has a cathedral, 32 pre-Reformation churches, a Norman castle, a 15th-century guildhall and Georgian assembly rooms. As a medieval town it was built on an irregular pattern and there is no central square or main street, but cathedral, market place and castle act as its centres.
BRIDEWELL MUSEUM The oldest part of this building, for 350 years one of the city prisons, dates back to the early 14th century. Displays illustrate the trades and industries of Norwich. The two most important industries—textiles, and boots and shoes—are illustrated from the tools to the finished products. Also represented are the food and drink industries, iron-founding and engineering, printing and a variety of other trades. Other notable objects on view are a steam engine, a fine collection of locally made clocks, and a complete Victorian bar.
CASTLE MUSEUM The castle, with a splendid Norman keep dominating the city, was opened as a civic museum in 1894. Galleries are devoted to the work of the Norwich School of landscape painters, notably John Sell Cotman and John Crome; but there is also work by 17th-century Dutch and Flemish artists, and by a wide range of

PAINTED RETABLE

The medieval retable, or altar-piece, in St Luke's Chapel (two panels are shown), was given to the cathedral by Bishop Despenser in 1380. Later converted into a table, it escaped destruction by the Puritans. Rediscovered in 1847, it was returned to the chapel in 1957. The centre panel shows the Crucifixion with the Virgin supported by St John; to the right is the Resurrection. (Norwich Cathedral)

British painters down the ages, from Thomas Gainsborough to Edward Seago and Alfred Munnings. There is locally made silver from the time when Norwich had its own assay office, set up in 1565 when the city's churches were ordered to melt down their Roman Catholic chalices and re-make them into Protestant communion cups. British ceramics and glass are represented, notably by a display of 18th-century Lowestoft porcelain.

Archaeologists' finds spanning a quarter of a million years of local history show life as it was lived by the rich and powerful, such as the owners of a Bronze Age shield and gold jewellery and a Roman cavalry parade helmet; and by the ordinary citizen in Saxon, Viking and medieval Norfolk. There are also firearms and other weapons.
CATHEDRAL The cathedral was begun in 1094 when Bishop Herbert de Losinga abandoned Thetford and made the more populous Norwich the centre of the diocese; it was complete by 1145. Subsequent changes included the replacement of the Norman roof by stone vaults (15th and 16th centuries) and the remodelling of the upper part of

ELM HILL, NORWICH

Elm Hill is the most complete and best preserved of several streets in Norwich which still have a late   *medieval appearance, even though some of the buildings in them date from the 17th century.*

the choir and presbytery (14th century). The present magnificent spire was added in the 15th century. The cathedral is surrounded by a close—the precinct of the medieval monastery, for the cathedral was served by monks. The close is entered by three gateways: two are land-gates, and the third a water-gate, on the river by Pull's Ferry, through which the stone for the construction of the cathedral was brought by boat from Caen, in Normandy. Within the close the cloisters lie to the south of the cathedral, and are unusual in having a first floor running right around the cloister court. There is elaborate vaulting in the cloisters, and the prior's door to the cathedral is of fine Decorated design (c. 1320). Beside the cloisters there is an exhibition for visitors and pilgrims.

CHURCH OF ST GEORGE, COLEGATE Of 15th and 16th centuries with a west tower, and a two-storey south porch. It has 18th-century furnishings which include the reredos, pulpit and west gallery on which is the organ of 1802. There are many monuments, including work by Thomas Green of Camberwell, Thomas Rawlins of Norwich and John Bacon the Younger.

CHURCH OF ST PETER MANCROFT The most impressive of Norwich's many interesting churches. It was begun in 1430, and consecrated in 1455. There is a richly decorated west tower, and a little lead spire with flying buttresses dating from 1895. The interior, with a long clerestory, is a hall without a chancel arch. The roof to the nave has hammerbeams concealed by false vaulting. Other features include a canopied font cover with carved supporting posts. Most famous of all the church's monuments, and a Mecca for physicians, is that of Thomas Browne, author of *Religio Medici*.

CITY HALL Built in 1932–8 to the design of C. H. James and S. R. Pierce, this is one of the foremost public buildings erected between the wars. It has a 202 ft high tower. (See p. 368.)

EARLHAM HALL West of Norwich, Earlham Hall is now the Centre of East Anglian Studies.

ELM HILL Elm Hill, which winds down from the church of St Peter Hungate (now a museum) to the R. Wensum, contains the huge nave of the former Dominican church (now St Andrew's Hall) and a series of attractively coloured timber-framed houses. The street is cobbled, and broadens in the middle into a small square or court. (See p. 369.)

GREAT HOSPITAL Founded in 1249 by Bishop Walter de Suffield to provide shelter and food for the poor, the Great Hospital escaped the Dissolution by Henry VIII and survived as a hospital for the aged. The chancel and nave of St Helen's Church were incorporated with the original building and they are still used as part of the present old people's home. The grounds and cloister are open to the public.

MADDERMARKET Near the market-place is the Maddermarket, where red madder dye was sold, with the Maddermarket theatre built as a replica of an Elizabethan theatre. Assembly House, Norwich's best example of Georgian architecture, was re-opened in 1950 as a social and educational centre.

MARKET-PLACE The Norman market-place is surrounded by several notable buildings. On one side is the modern city hall (1938) with central library; on another side the small flint guildhall, built 1413 (with a council chamber dating from 1534), visited by Elizabeth I in 1578.

OLD MEETING Norwich has two noted Nonconformist churches, the Old Meeting (one of the earliest in England, 1693) and the Octagon Chapel with a neo-Classic interior.

PRIORY Some of the priory buildings are now part of the grammar school (founded by Edward VI) where Nelson was a pupil. Nurse Edith Cavell, executed in 1915 for her part in helping Allied fugitives to escape, is buried near the cathedral.

ROYAL NORFOLK REGIMENT MUSEUM Relics of the Regiment—uniforms, weapons and medals including a Victoria Cross—are displayed here.

ST PETER HUNGATE CHURCH MUSEUM Church art is housed in this former parish church originating in the 15th century. A considerable amount of Norwich painted glass of the 15th and 16th centuries remains in the windows. The majority of the exhibits are English, mainly East Anglian, but there is also interesting continental material. The collection of manuscripts includes both English and European material of the 13th–16th centuries, many illuminated, and contains a number of service books and theological works. Outstanding among these is the Wycliffe Bible, c. 1388.

STRANGERS' HALL The house, which has 14th-century origins, was given to the city of Norwich, together with the owner's collection of furniture and historic domestic equipment, in 1922. Rooms

NOTTINGHAM CASTLE MUSEUM

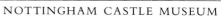

VIRGIN AND CHILD *This alabaster statuette was excavated, with two others, at Flawford, near Nottingham, in the late 18th century. It had been buried to escape the wholesale destruction of church sculpture at the Reformation. Alabaster carvings, more often in the form of panels in high relief than of statuettes, were produced in large quantities in the Midlands (Nottingham was one of the main centres) from about 1350 until the Reformation put an end to this industry—for an industry it undoubtedly was. A flourishing export trade in alabasters was built up, and examples have been discovered in France, Spain, Portugal, Italy and even as far afield as Russia. This is an early example, dating from before 1370. In later years, as production increased, the quality of the workmanship declined considerably.*

THE BLES BOWL *The crown surmounting the lid of the Bles Bowl may mean that it was made for a royal occasion—perhaps to commemorate the accession of James II in 1685. The addition of lead oxide was the great English contribution to glass chemistry, and this bowl is a good example of English lead crystal.*

are furnished in the style of different periods, from early Tudor to late Victorian. There are late 15th-century Flemish tapestries in the great hall and parlour, and mid-17th-century 'stumpwork' embroidery in the large bedroom; the Walnut Room contains marquetry furniture (1690–1720), and the Georgian dining-room a late 18th-century chandelier. There are also examples of the harp-lute and a late 18th-century tambourine in the Regency music room; a good collection of cooking equipment of the early 19th century in two kitchens; and 19th-century dolls' houses with contemporary dolls and furnishings in the toy room. In the coach house are the Lord Mayor's coach and a Panhard Levassor car of 1899.

TOMBLAND Close by the cathedral is Tombland, now a Georgian square. Beyond that, across the R. Wensum, is Magdalen Street; this was the centre of the old weaving industry in Norwich, and has been repaired and restored by the Civic Trust. On this street is Gurney's Court, where the Quaker reformer Elizabeth Fry was born.

Nostell Priory *W. Yorks.* 558Da

A country mansion, developed on a former priory site acquired by an Elizabethan merchant, and one of the first ventures in architecture by James Paine. Work was begun in 1733 to the order of Sir Roland Winn. On his death in 1765 his son called in Robert Adam, who made both external and internal additions and alterations. The house contains fine pictures, paintings and Chippendale furniture. In the park is a lake and a motor-cycle museum.

Notgrove *Glos.* 546Dd

A Neolithic transeptal-chambered long barrow, with two chambers on either side of the gallery and a fifth at the inner end. The gallery leads in from a forecourt. Beyond these chambers excavation revealed a further circular chamber of drystone walling (now concealed), an unusual feature in barrows of this type. The rubble of the mound was held in position by a double wall.

Nottingham *Notts.* 552Ed

The county city of Nottinghamshire, with a turbulent history until modern times. The city was once a Danish Borough called 'Snottingham', but acquired its present spelling because of the Normans' difficulty in pronouncing the sound 'sn'.

The Norman castle was occupied during the Civil War by Parliamentarian forces under Colonel Hutchinson, and demolished in 1651. In 1674 a mansion was built on the site for the Dukes of Newcastle. It was severely damaged by fire during the riots over the Reform Bill in 1831, and remained empty for over 40 years. It was restored and adapted as a museum in 1878. (See pp. 370–1.)

In the 18th century, Richard Arkwright, James

NYMANS GARDEN

The gardens, which cover about 30 acres, are famous for their rare collection of trees and plants. Designed *by Lt.-Col. L. C. R. Messel in the first years of this century, they comprise a series of separate gardens.*

Hargreaves and John Heathcoat opened the way to a vast increase in production, but also caused serious Luddite-type riots. These lasted for years, and their cause had hardly been settled when the proposed political reforms were strenuously blocked by the Duke of Newcastle. This led to violence at the Goose Fair of 1831, when the Duke's mansion was reduced to a smoking ruin as the Chartists brought havoc to the city.

From the time of the 1832 Reform Bill, Nottingham again became prosperous. In 1897 it became a city, and by the turn of the century one-third of the knitting frames in Britain were here, and Nottingham lace had achieved world-wide fame.

The medieval Goose Fair, once a prolonged week of merry-making, has now been reduced to three days in the first week of October, with amusements rather than trade as the main motif.

The University of Nottingham was established by royal charter in 1948 after 67 years as University College.

Robin Hood, as fact or fiction, is commemorated by one of four murals in the shopping arcade beneath the Council House dome, frescoes in the cupola of the Council House, and by a statue on Castle Road, below the castle walls.
CHURCH OF ST MARY An imposing Perpendicular church, mainly of the 15th century, with a large central tower. There are many 19th-century windows by Ward & Hughes, Clayton & Bell, and others; also several monuments.
CITY MUSEUM AND ART GALLERY (NOTTINGHAM CASTLE MUSEUM) The painters Bonington and Sandby are the subjects of special collections. There is also a ceramics section, with Nottingham 18th-century stoneware and Wedgwood.

CASTLE GATE COSTUME MUSEUM This is near the castle and contains a large collection of handmade and machine-made lace, and Lord Middleton's collection of Elizabethan and Jacobean embroideries. There are also furnished period rooms of the 18th, 19th and 20th centuries.

In addition the museum has some fine examples of 17th-century Nottinghamshire tapestries.

Nuneaton *Warks.* 546Eg
MUSEUM AND ART GALLERY Personal possessions of George Eliot, who lived in the district, are in the museum. There are relics of the local pottery industry from the 11th century onwards and ethnographic displays, of which the Baffin Land collection is particularly important. The gallery has engravings by Hogarth and Turner, fine water-colours and changing exhibitions.

Nun Monkton *N. Yorks.* 558Dc
CHURCH OF ST MARY The church is formed from the nave of the 12th-century Benedictine nunnery that stood on this site. It was much restored in 1873 and the east window contains stained glass by William Morris and Burne-Jones.

Nunney Castle *Som.* 540Df
The ruins of a rectangular moated castle begun in 1373 by Sir John de la Mare, whose family tombs are a feature of the nearby 13th-century church.

Nunnington Hall *N. Yorks.* 558Ed
A manor house dating mainly from the 17th century, with panelled hall and staircase. The west wing dates from 1580.

Nymans Garden *W. Sussex* 542Be
About 30 acres of rare conifers, shrubs and plants.

O

Oakham *Leics.* 553Gb
CASTLE In the Norman great hall of this fortified manor house is a remarkable collection of horseshoes left by royalty and peers of the kingdom. The church in Oakham has a Bible contemporary with the Magna Carta, and there are punishment stocks in the market-place.

Titus Oates (1649–1705) of the infamous Popish Plot was born here.
CHURCH OF ALL SAINTS An attractive country town surrounds this fine church, which has an impressive 14th-century west tower with spire of ashlar limestone. Inside there are a number of interesting sculptured capitals and arcades. Additions in the 15th century include the clerestory and Perpendicular windows.
RUTLAND COUNTY MUSEUM This is a former indoor riding school that was built c. 1795 and has a timber roof spanning nearly 60 ft. Displays include Anglo-Saxon jewellery and local tools.

Oaksey *Wilts.* 546Cc
CHURCH OF ALL SAINTS A church of 13th-century origin, with 14th- and 15th-century additions and perhaps some Norman work. There is a Perpendicular clerestory but no north aisle. The screen and choir stall panels are 15th century. Large medieval wall-paintings of Christ of the Trades and of St Christopher were uncovered in 1933. There is some painted glass dating from the 14th century.

Ockham *Surrey* 542Af
CHURCH OF ALL SAINTS A medieval church, with a fine east window and a 15th-century tower. A brick mausoleum contains a carved monument to Lord Chancellor King (d. 1734) by Rysbrack.

Oddington *Glos.* 546Dd
CHURCH OF ST NICHOLAS This is a fine church with its tower at the east end of the south aisle. Once Norman, it is now mainly Gothic in appearance. A large wall-painting of the Last Judgment covers the north wall. The altar, communion rail and pulpit are 17th century.

Odell *Beds.* 547Hf
A lovely village with good limestone houses and cottages, and a country-style house built near the site of a vanished 11th-century castle.
CHURCH OF ALL SAINTS There is a massive pinnacled west tower to this 15th-century church, and the whole building is a good and complete example of the period. The interior has tall arcades and a medieval rood screen. Among the remaining stained glass is a particularly fine group of angels in the east window of the south aisle. There is a monument, c. 1807, by John Bacon the Younger.

Odiham *Hants.* 541Jf
One of Hampshire's impressive broad streets. Here the houses are mostly colour-washed, and unusually low and set back behind sweeps of mown

MONUMENT TO SIR SAMUEL ONGLEY

The classical Roman costume in which Peter Scheemakers (1691–1770) and Laurent Delvaux (1695–1778) chose to dress this monument to Sir Samuel Ongley was typical of the taste of a time when both George I and George II were often represented as Caesar. Scheemakers, whose original design for the monument is now in the Victoria and Albert Museum, London, was born in Antwerp. He worked in Rome and then came to London. Among his other works are the monuments to Dryden and Shakespeare in Westminster Abbey. Delvaux, from Ghent, also enjoyed popularity as a sculptor. (Church of St Leonard, Old Warden)

grass. Near the east end is Marycourt, an impressive Georgian house, and at the west end a Queen Anne mansion with Elizabethan work at the back.
CASTLE A picturesque ruin of Norman origin where Simon de Montfort imprisoned his captive, Prince Edward. David Bruce, King of the Scots, was imprisoned here and released in 1357 on payment of a ransom of 100,000 marks.
CHURCH OF ALL SAINTS This 13th- and 14th-century church, restored in the late 19th century, stands near some 17th-century almshouses. There is a round chalk font, and an early 17th-century pulpit and west gallery. Two of the stained-glass east windows are by Patrick Reyntiens.

Offa's Dyke   *546Ac*
The north end of this great earthwork lies near Prestatyn at the seaward end of the Dee estuary, and passes through 120 miles of glorious country, taking advantage of every natural bastion, to end at

the mouth of the R. Wye opposite Chepstow. It is not absolutely continuous, and some of the gaps certainly represent areas where, when it was built, forest cover made the earthwork unnecessary.

All the evidence points to its having been constructed to the orders of Offa, the great Mercian king who reigned in the second half of the 8th century. It defined, for all men to see, the boundary between his kingdom and Welsh land.

Wat's Dyke, a similar but shorter earthwork, runs from Basingwerk on the Dee estuary to the Morda Brook, south of Oswestry. It lies, therefore, to the east of Offa's Dyke and is roughly parallel. Its date is not known, but it is generally thought to have been a somewhat earlier frontier-line in a difficult area, to be superseded later by the more ambitious work of Offa.

Ogmore Castle *Mid Glam.*   *545Gb*
First built by William de Londres in 1116 to guard the Ewenny river, the castle later became a prison. The ruins are said to be haunted by a ghost that guards long-buried treasure, and the river by misers who died without disclosing their wealth.

Okehampton *Devon*   *538Fd*
This small market town on the northern fringe of Dartmoor was originally a stage point, for those crossing central Devon to and from Exeter. To protect travellers, Baldwin de Brionne built Okehampton Castle (now in ruins but open to the public) shortly after the Norman Conquest. The town suffered badly in the plague of 1625. William Pitt, Earl of Chatham, was M.P. for Okehampton.

Today, the town is a main centre for Dartmoor, 365 square miles of wild countryside with Yes Tor (2029 ft) and High Willhays (2038 ft) as high points.

Old Bewick *Northld.*   *562Fc*
An Iron Age hill-fort, protected on its south side by very steep scarp-slopes. On the opposite side, great curving ramparts enclose two areas which are further defended by a single bank and ditch lying farther to the north. These ramparts have been shown to have a clay core, to which the stonework is a facing. The western section contains circular houses, and the eastern was probably used to protect the flocks. Close to the fort on the south-east are several rocks with cup-and-ring decoration.

Old Clee *Humberside*   *553Jg*
CHURCH OF THE HOLY TRINITY AND ST MARY A cruciform church with a Saxon west tower. The Norman work includes both arcades, and the font. There is a tablet on one of the pillars referring to the rededication in 1192 of the Church by St Hugh, Bishop of Lincoln.

Old Fletton *Cambs.*   *547Jg*
CHURCH OF ST MARGARET A Norman church, which incorporates Saxon carvings in two buttresses of the chancel. There is a 16th-century font.

Oldham *Greater Manchester*   *552Bg*
ART GALLERY Early English water-colours, British paintings of the 19th century, and contemporary British art constitute the main part of this collection, which includes a bust of Sir Winston Churchill by Jacob Epstein (1946).

Old Malton *N. Yorks.*   *558Ec*
CHURCH OF ST MARY The remains of a large church of the Gilbertine priory, founded *c.* 1150. Now only the nave, part of the façade with a carved doorway, south-west tower and remains of two of the central tower piers can be seen.

Old Oswestry *Salop* 551Jc
This fine hill-fort was remodelled four times. A rectangle was enclosed by two banks with external ditches and an entrance at each end, the inner banks being here inturned. When rebuilt, a third bank was added to most of its circumference, followed by modifications of and additions to the defences of the west entrance. The last stage was marked by the addition of yet more banks and some re-modelling of the eastern entrance. The fort was occupied throughout the second half of the Iron Age and there was also some evidence of re-occupation during the Dark Ages.

Old Sarum *Wilts.* 540Fe
Here on a hill are the multiple earthworks of the forerunner of modern Salisbury. But only the outermost bank is of Iron Age date; later, because it stood at the crossing of important roads, it became the Roman Sorviodunum. Centuries later, the Norman invaders quickly realised its strength, and the inner earthworks are of Norman origin. Here a small town grew up and an early cathedral was built. Not until the 12th century, when the great cathedral of Salisbury began to grow up in the valley below, did the men of Sarum colonise the new site by the river.

Old Shoreham *W. Sussex* 542Bd
CHURCH OF ST NICOLAS A basically Norman church with fragments of Saxon work, standing on the east bank of the R. Adur, not far from New Shoreham. The plan is cruciform, with a squat central tower. The carved tie-beam in the chancel and the chancel screen are *c.* 1300. There was much restoration in the 19th century.

Old Soar Manor *Kent* 542Df
A rare survival of the solar wing of an early medieval knight's house. With a chapel, it is partly of the 13th century.

Old Warden *Beds.* 547Je
CHURCH OF ST LEONARD A 12th-century church which contains good woodwork, much of it continental of the 16th and 17th centuries. There are several monuments, including a standing 18th-century figure in Roman costume by Peter Scheemakers and Laurent Delvaux. Scheemakers's design for the monument is in the Victoria and Albert Museum.

Old Warden Aerodrome *Beds.* 547Je
SHUTTLEWORTH COLLECTION A collection of historic aeroplanes, cars, bicycles and carriages. The aviation exhibits range from a genuine Bleriot of 1909, several First World War and inter-war types, both civil and military, to the Hurricane and Spitfire. Also on display are aero-engines, propellers, instruments and other related equipment. Most of the aeroplanes are in flying condition and they are demonstrated on special open days.

Ombersley *Heref. & Worcs.* 546Cf
A delightful village with many timbered houses, including the King's Arms. Ombersley Court, a William-and-Mary house, has been refronted.

Onibury *Salop* 551Ja
CHURCH OF ST MICHAEL Like so many Salop churches, St Michael's is of Norman origin, but there is later work as well. The short west tower is battlemented; inside, the chancel arch is Norman, but the west gallery dates from Detmar Blow's restoration in 1902.

Orchardleigh House *Som.* 540Df
A 19th-century mansion, replacing a former manor house, standing in a great park with a lake. A 13th-century church on an island at the head of

ORFORD CASTLE

Orford Castle was built by Henry II between 1165 and 1173 as part of a successful attempt to re-establish royal power in East Anglia. Of the original building only the keep survives. Its internal appointments were planned on a grand scale and include two superimposed halls with adjoining offices and a chapel. The castle was sufficiently important to be kept in reasonable repair throughout the 13th century, but by the beginning of the 14th century its military role had ceased to be great and in 1336 Edward III granted it in perpetuity to Robert of Ufford who, a year later, became Earl of Suffolk.

the lake contains some fine 15th- and 16th-century stained glass. Sir Henry Newbolt, the poet, is buried in the churchyard. (Park only open.)

Orford *Suffolk* 548Ee
CHURCH OF ST BARTHOLOMEW A ruined 12th-century chancel adjoins this 14th-century church, rich in monumental brasses. Benjamin Britten's operas are sometimes performed here.

Orford Castle *Suffolk* 548Ee
Of Orford Castle, the keep alone survives. The castle itself was of great military importance. It was built by Henry II between 1165 and 1173 as part of a successful attempt to re-establish royal power in East Anglia. The plan was entirely up to date: the bailey was surrounded by a curtain wall from which projected flanking turrets, and the keep was no longer of the rectangular plan but circular inside and polygonal outside. It, too, was defended by projecting turrets.

Ormesby Hall *Cleveland* 558De
A house built in the mid-18th century, with fine period plasterwork.

Ormside *Cumbria* 557Je
CHURCH OF ST JAMES The Norman church is situated on a conical knoll on the west side of the R. Eden, overlooking Roman Fell, and its strong western tower was probably intended for defence against marauding Scots. The chancel roof is 400 years old, and the Ormside Cup, a Saxon work in gold and enamel now in the Yorkshire Museum, was excavated from the churchyard in 1823.

OSTERLEY PARK HOUSE

The house at Osterley was originally built during the reign of Elizabeth I for Sir Thomas Gresham, the merchant who founded the Royal Exchange in the City of London. It eventually passed to the Childs, a great banking family, and in 1761 Robert Adam began a reconstruction of the house that was to take nearly 20 years. The rooms of the house retain their original decoration and furniture by Adam. The hall has a fine marble floor and the elegant library is decorated with painted panels by Antonio Zucchi. The gallery is about 130 ft long and contains Beauvais tapestries. In the tapestry room are Gobelins tapestries specially woven for it in 1775. Another room is decorated in Etruscan style, with tall columns and statuary. In the state bedchamber is a great domed bed designed by Adam about 1776.

Ormskirk *Lancs.*　　　　　　　　　　551Jg
CHURCH OF SS PETER AND PAUL The massive tower of this Perpendicular church was added in 1540 to house bells from Burscough Priory after its dissolution. The monuments include 15th-century alabaster effigies to the 1st Earl of Derby and his two wives, also brought from Burscough.

Orton Longueville *Cambs.*　　　　　547Jg
CHURCH OF THE HOLY TRINITY A 13th- and 14th-century church, with a late 17th-century aisle. There are some fragments of medieval glass in a 16th-century wall-painting of St Christopher, a 15th-century font, a 13th-century knight's effigy, and a seated woman sculpted by Sir Francis Chantrey.

Orton Waterville *Cambs.*　　　　　547Jg
The name of this village is a corruption of the feudal family name of de Waltreville. Its 13th-century church has an Elizabethan carved pulpit. The stone-built Manor Farm was built in 1571, and retains its original mullioned windows.

Osborne House *Isle of Wight*　　　　541Hc
Queen Victoria's favourite home, designed in the Palladian style by the Prince Consort and Thomas Cubitt; Victoria died here in 1901, and the state apartments, which are open to the public (the rest of the house is a convalescent home for officers and civil servants), contain many items of Victoriana.

Osbournby *Lincs.*　　　　　　　　　553Hd
CHURCH OF SS PETER AND PAUL The church is mainly Decorated, and has a Norman font. It contains much 15th-century woodwork, including a set of carved bench ends and poppy-heads.

Ossian's Hall *Tayside*　　　　　　　566Cb
A folly in the Hermitage, a wooded gorge of the R. Braan on the estate of the Dukes of Atholl near Dunkeld. A summer retreat was erected by the 3rd Duke in 1758.

Osterley Park House *Greater London*　547Jb
The first occupant of a house at Osterley was perhaps the richest English merchant of his age, Sir Thomas Gresham, the founder of the Royal Exchange and of Gresham's College. The building as it stands today, however, is mainly the creation of Robert Adam, between the years 1761 and 1780. Retaining the original square plan of the Elizabethan house, Adam placed the principal apartments on the first floor, or *piano nobile,* and raised the ground inside the court to that level, providing a wide flight of steps as an approach and throwing an Ionic portico across the open side of the square. The result is an unusual but superb expression of the classical Italian principles of the time. The interior is one of the finest and most complete by Adam; rejecting the heavy and imposing style favoured by his contemporaries, he used delicate decorations of low reliefs, friezes, pilasters, painted ornament and the so-called 'grotesque' style in stucco. Much of the original furniture remains in the rooms for which Adam designed it, some of it representing the best neo-Classical work. Paintings include a pair of large portraits by Hoppner, of Frederick Augustus, Duke of York, second son of George III, and his wife, Frederica Charlotta. Among the many fine tapestries in the house is a series from Arlington Court in Devon, woven in Beauvais between 1780

and 1793, depicting the four continents, a favourite theme of tapestry weavers since the end of the 17th century; and a set of Gobelins tapestries representing the loves of the gods after designs by Boucher.

Oswestry *Salop*   *551Jc*
To the west of this ancient town are the remains of Offa's Dyke which, running from the R. Wye to the R. Dee, was made *c.* AD 800 by Offa, King of Mercia, as a defence or political boundary. The town's charter was granted by Richard II; by the Act of Union with Wales (1535), Oswestry became English. In 1559 a local plague killed one-third of the inhabitants and in 1642 much of the town was destroyed in the Civil War. The town walls and gates were demolished in 1782. In 1860, the Cambrian Railway completely altered the town, leaving it with little of architectural note. It is, however, of interest to canal and railway historians: about 4 miles north, at Chirk, is a stone railway viaduct and an aqueduct with cast-iron trough 850 ft long and 100 ft high.

Otham *Kent*   *542Df*
STONEACRE A typical small Kentish half-timbered manor-house of the late 15th century. It was restored in 1923 and contains a great hall. (Open to the public by appointment.)

Otley *Suffolk*   *548Df*
OTLEY HALL A partly moated 16th-century timber and brick house, with a fine diapered chimney-shaft. The house has fine linen-fold panelling, a good hall screen, heavily beamed ceilings in the hall and Jacobean wall decorations. In the same parish, Otley High House is a fine contemporary timber-framed building. (By appointment.)

Otterden Place *Kent*   *542Ef*
Originally built during the reign of Henry VIII, the house has 18th-century Georgian additions. (Not open to the public.)

Ousdale *Highland*   *569Kc*
BROCH Standing on a burn-side close to the sea; on one side, the steep slope to the stream gives ample protection, and on the other there is an 8 ft thick wall. Within this enclosure stands the Iron Age broch itself, with a 14 ft thick wall. There was a double door and a guard-chamber in the thickness of the wall. Its condition is still good.

Over Denton *Cumbria*   *557Jh*
CHURCH A small Norman church, with Saxon details, which seems to have been built with Roman stones from Hadrian's Wall. Privately owned, it can be viewed by appointment.

Overstone *Northants.*   *547Gf*
CHURCH OF ST NICHOLAS A Gothic building of *c.* 1803, restored a century later. It has a west tower, some 16th-century stained glass in the east window and two early 18th-century monuments by John Hunt.

Overton Hill *Wilts.*   *540Fg*
THE SANCTUARY This henge monument is the termination of 'The Avenue' leading from Avebury. In its latest form it consisted of two circles of sarsens, 130 ft and 45 ft in diameter. This structure dated from the very beginning of the Bronze Age. But it apparently had replaced a previous timber structure of Neolithic times, evidenced by six concentric circles of post-holes. An attempted reconstruction has shown that this was probably of more than one period, and that new holes were dug from time to time to hold replacing timbers as the old ones rotted.

After they had completed their examination of the site, the excavators erected concrete blocks in

OXBURGH HALL

Though Oxburgh Hall dates from 1482, its great hall was demolished in the 18th century and few medieval fittings survive in the rest of the building. There is, however, an original fire-place in the so-called King's Chamber of the main gate-house. Henry VII is traditionally held to have stayed in the chamber when he visited Oxburgh in 1497. The parish church near the hall has two 16th-century terracotta monuments.

the former stone sockets and concrete pillars in the post-holes, so that the whole pattern is now visible for inspection.

Ovingham *Northld.*   *558Bg*
CHURCH OF ST MARY THE VIRGIN A mainly 13th-century church which has a plain tall Saxon west tower. The interior has painted royal Arms. Fragments of Saxon crosses were found here just after the Second World War. Thomas Bewick, the famous wood-engraver, was buried here.

Owl House, The *Kent*   *542De*
A 16th-century half-timbered cottage, formerly used by wool smugglers: only the extensive gardens, noted for roses, are open to the public.

Owlpen Manor *Glos.*   *546Cc*
A Cotswold stone house of 15th-century origin, with barn, mill and court-house. Inside is a fine set of 17th-century painted-cloth wall hangings.

Oxburgh Hall *Norfolk*   *554Bb*
This property came into the possession of the Bedingfield family during the second half of the 15th century and the present house was begun in 1482 when Edmund Bedingfield received a licence to erect a fortified building. It is a fine building of brick, surrounded by a moat. There is an enormous gate-house, probably the largest 15th-century brick gate-house in England. Near the hall is a small chapel built in the grounds by Pugin in 1835. This is a curious Gothic Revival building furnished with a number of genuine medieval fittings. In a side aisle of the nearby parish church is the Bedingfield Chapel, containing two lavish terracotta monuments of the early 16th century.

John Ruskin

JOHN RUSKIN, THE PRE-RAPHAELITE PROPHET

'No other man that I met', wrote Carlyle, 'has in him the divine rage against iniquity, falsehood and baseness that Ruskin has, and every man ought to have.' John Ruskin was recognised early as an intellectual prodigy by his adoring parents, and his birthplace in Brunswick Square, London, is marked with a plaque. His passionate defence of Turner appeared in the first volume of *Modern Painters,* which he published, aged 24. Ruskin developed great skill in drawing while making illustrations for his books *The Stones of Venice* and *The Seven Lamps of Architecture.* He became the first Slade Professor of Fine Art, and his drawings can be seen at the Victoria and Albert Museum, the Ashmolean Museum, Oxford and the South London Art Gallery. As the early prophet of the Socialist movement, he swept a London street to show how it should be kept, and his advanced views on care of the aged, child education and taxation, appear in the 39 volumes of his collected works.

JOHN RUSKIN *from the water-colour by Sir Hubert von Herkomer.* (*National Portrait Gallery*)

BRANTWOOD, *Ruskin's house at Coniston in Cumbria, with his boat 'Jumping Jenny'. Ruskin bought the house, without seeing it, for £1500. It is now a museum and residential study centre.*

RUSKIN'S SEAL, *with his coat of arms and motto 'Today, today, today'. He sensed that man's spirit was being swamped by machine-age evils, 'the refusal of pleasure and knowledge for the sake of money'.*

RUSKIN'S CROSS *in Coniston churchyard commemorates the champion of the Pre-Raphaelites and the man who revolutionised our ideas of Italian painting. Sculpted from hard green stone by H. T. Miles.*

UNIVERSITY MUSEUM, *Oxford. Ruskin hoped this building would realise his principles of Gothic design.*

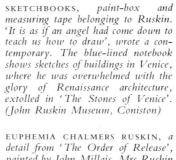

SKETCHBOOKS, *paint-box and measuring tape belonging to Ruskin. 'It is as if an angel had come down to teach us how to draw', wrote a contemporary. The blue-lined notebook shows sketches of buildings in Venice, where he was overwhelmed with the glory of Renaissance architecture, extolled in 'The Stones of Venice'. (John Ruskin Museum, Coniston)*

EUPHEMIA CHALMERS RUSKIN, *a detail from 'The Order of Release', painted by John Millais. Mrs Ruskin acted as the model, and her love affair with Millais led to the annulment of the Ruskins' marriage in July 1854. (Tate Gallery)*

COLUMN HEAD *in the University Museum, carved by Irish stone-cutters.*

WROUGHT IRON *at the Museum.*

HANDBELLS, *one of the simple forms of musical expression with which Ruskin experimented in an effort to discover an instrument which could be learnt quickly, played easily—and enjoyed—by children. (John Ruskin Museum, Coniston)*

SLATE THRONE *in the garden of Brantwood, where Ruskin in his last years would sit for hours watching a waterfall.*

NERAL SPECIMENS *at the John skin Museum, Coniston, from the ection he made. He presented the wardes Ruby' to the Natural story Museum, London, where it isplayed in the Mineral Gallery.*

ASHMOLEAN MUSEUM

The oldest public museum in Britain. Its first buildings were opened in 1683, and the present ones, designed by Charles Cockerell, in 1845. The Department of Antiquities covers the great civilisations of the Mediterranean basin, and is particularly rich in Egyptian relics. The Chinese collection in the Department of Eastern Art is especially fine, and the Department of Western Art houses one of the best collections in England. It includes outstanding works of the Italian, French and English schools, and the collection of prints and drawings is world-famous.

UCCELLO: THE HUNT *Of all 15th-century Italian painters, Uccello was the most learned in perspective and foreshortening. But it was not an arid discipline: he shows a masterly sense of design, a superb feeling for colour, and a reasonable use of space. In 'The Hunt', painted about 1469, six years before he died, rider and hounds converge on a central point—the deer herd—a spot far in a forest divided equally by four trees. Everything—tree trunks, the paths of the hounds, the hunters' staves—leads to that point.*

RICCIO: PAN *Andrea Briosco, known as 'Riccio' (curly-head) was the leading member of a school of sculptors famous in Padua in the early 16th century for their work in bronze. This is one of his most beautiful works. The subject is typical, for the main source of his inspiration was the pastoral aspect of ancient mythology: nymphs, satyrs, shepherds, goats. From those elements he created sculptures which are often profoundly moving and which, through his treatment of them, attain the status of great works of art.*

Oxford *Oxon.* 546Fc

The town of Oxford is at least 300 years older than the university. According to legend, the history of Oxford dates back to *c.* 726, but the first written reference to the town was in 912. By 1066 Oxford had clearly become a place of commercial and strategic importance, and a castle to control the developing area was built by the Normans in 1071. Of the original castle, the motte and St George's tower still survive. In 1258 the 'Mad Parliament' of Henry III took place at Oxford: Parliament openly rebelled against the king, confirmed Magna Carta, and vested the government of England in 24 councillors led by Simon de Montfort. The first school centre was University College, founded in 1249. Other colleges soon followed: Balliol (1263), Merton (1264), St Edmund Hall (*c.* 1270), Exeter (1314), Oriel (1326), Queen's (1340); by which date Oxford University was fully established as a rival to Paris, Salamanca and other Continental universities.

The Saxon tower of the church of St Michael-at-the-Northgate was once part of the northern fortifications of the city; the church adjoins the site of the prison where the martyred Bishops Cranmer, Latimer and Ridley were held. The Martyrs' Memorial in St Giles was erected in 1841 to commemorate their deaths: a cross in Broad Street marks the spot where they were burnt at the stake. The central point of the city is Carfax—probably a derivation from the Latin *quadrifurcus* (four-forked). From Carfax Tower there is an excellent panoramic view of the city.

Charles I held a Parliament at Oxford in 1644, and Charles II in 1665 and 1681.

The city was raised to county borough status in 1889. In the 1960's a ten-year programme of restoration and cleaning was initiated.

ASHMOLEAN MUSEUM Named after Elias Ashmole, antiquary and astrologer, the Ashmolean is housed in the same building as the Taylor Institution. This building was constructed in 1841 by C. R. Cockerell, RA, and paid for with money bequeathed to Oxford University by architect Sir Robert Taylor (*d.* 1835). The museum contains magnificent paintings by great masters of all periods. There are drawings by Michelangelo and Raphael, Dutch still-life and modern French paintings.

Also to be found here are a notable Oriental collection, and fine examples of 16th- and 17th-century silver, bronzes, sculptures, tapestries and miniatures. There are snuff-boxes and watches, the Hill Collection of musical instruments and an

CLAUDE: ASCANIUS SHOOTING THE STAG OF SYLVIA *Claude Gellée, usually known from the district of his birth as Claude Lorrain, painted this picture in 1682, the year of his death. He was 82. Claude spent most of his life in Rome and his pastoral landscapes have an intensely poetic quality. Light was his principal concern and his works follow the classical formula of a succession of layers going back in parallel planes to the luminous distance. The transition from foreground to background in this painting is effected by a distant bridge over which a herdsman drives his cattle. The scene in the foreground is taken from Virgil and shows Ascanius, the son of Aeneas, shooting the stag of Sylvia. But the figures add little of significance to the picture: it is the quality of the evening light which is all-important.*

THE ALFRED JEWEL *Alfred the Great, who died in 899, is generally agreed to have owned this jewel, for it bears the Anglo-Saxon inscription, 'Alfred had me made'. The jewel is gold decorated with cloisonné enamel, the technique of enamelling preferred for gold in the Dark Ages and early Middle Ages. It was found in Newton Park near the Island of Athelney, Somerset, in 1693. Its original purpose and the identity of the enamelled figure on it have been much discussed. The animal-headed socket to which the jewel is fixed shows that it once had a slender stem attached. The jewel might be the head of a pointer for following the lines of a manuscript and the figure might represent Sight.*

extensive collection of coins. The Pomfret and Arundel marbles and many European antiquities, including items from Egypt, Crete and the Aegean, can be seen.

BODLEIAN LIBRARY One of the largest libraries in the world with more than 4,300,000 volumes. It originally housed the manuscripts donated to the university by Duke Humfrey, the youngest son of Henry IV. Most of the library contents were dispersed during the Dissolution under Henry VIII: but Sir Thomas Bodley (1545–1613), a diplomat in the service of Queen Elizabeth I, restored the library in 1598–1602 and provided for extensions, including the top floor of the Schools Quadrangle (1613–c. 1620). The two lower floors, originally used for teaching, were gradually absorbed by the Bodleian, 1789–1882. The Radcliffe Camera, a circular building, built under the terms of the will of Dr John Radcliffe (1650–1714) as a private library, is now also a part of the Bodleian. In 1940 the New Bodleian building was completed at a cost of £1,000,000, much of which was contributed by the Rockefeller Foundation. The three buildings are now connected by tunnels and a book-conveyor links the reading rooms and bookstacks. Only the Divinity School is open.

BOTANIC GARDEN This is the oldest botanic garden in Britain, founded in 1621 by Henry Danvers, 1st Earl of Danby.

CATHEDRAL A magnificent Norman cathedral, with later additions which include the 13th-century central spire. The church was formerly that of an Augustinian priory, and was built during the 12th century to house the body of St Frideswide, a Saxon lady who died in 735. Her reconstructed shrine is in the presbytery. Cardinal Wolsey, who founded Cardinal College (later refounded as Christ Church), demolished the western end when building the college. Happily, he was not able to rebuild all the present cathedral, and the splendid 15th-century lierne vault with octagonal pendants was spared. There are brasses, and a 17th-century organ-case and pulpit.

The cathedral was restored in the 1870's by Sir Gilbert Scott, who replaced the east window by a more 'suitable' rose-window, an arcade and two smaller windows. Among the monuments of the 17th to 19th centuries is work by Jasper Latham, Sir Henry Cheere, William Tyler and E. H. Baily.

CHRIST CHURCH Founded in 1525 by Cardinal Wolsey, the college has a notable gateway surmounted by a great octagonal tower designed by Christopher Wren (built 1682), containing 'Great Tom', a 7 ton bell. (See p. 385.)

381

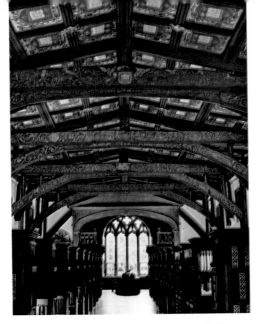

DUKE HUMFREY'S LIBRARY

Duke Humfrey, youngest brother of Henry V, donated nearly 300 manuscripts to Oxford University and the library built to house them was completed in 1488. But during the Reformation it was virtually stripped of its books, and in 1598 Sir Thomas Bodley decided to spend the rest of his life refitting and restoring it. The ceiling bears the Arms of both the university and Bodley. (Bodleian Library, Oxford)

KING ALFRED'S TRANSLATION OF ST GREGORY'S *Pastoral Care*

King Alfred's patronage of literature and learning extended to personal translation into Anglo-Saxon of a number of Latin texts. Most of them survive only as later copies, but this manuscript, of Pope Gregory the Great's 'Pastoral Care', is contemporary. It was written between 890 and 897 and sent to Werfrith, Bishop of Worcester. The book was intended for the guidance of bishops and the text illustrated begins 'This book is for Worcester' and, on the next page, continues 'When I remembered how the knowledge of Latin had formerly decayed throughout England and yet many could read English writing, I began, among various and manifold troubles of this kingdom, to translate into English the book which is called in Latin 'Pastoralis' and in English 'Shepherd's Care' . . . and I will send a copy to every bishopric in my kingdom.' (Bodleian Library, Oxford)

CHRIST CHURCH PICTURE GALLERY The large collection from which the exhibits are selected includes drawings by Leonardo da Vinci, Raphael, Michelangelo, Holbein, Titian, Rubens, Van Dyck and Rembrandt. Portraits by Lely, Reynolds, Gainsborough, Millais and others, of distinguished former members of the college, are on show in the dining-hall of the college, which is sometimes open to the public.

CHURCH OF ST MARY THE VIRGIN Oxford's famous university church, mainly of the 15th century but with a 13th-century north tower and bold 14th-century spire. The baroque south porch by Nicholas Stone was added c. 1637; it has barley-sugar columns and a standing figure of the Virgin in the ornate pediment; there are 18th-century iron gates in front. Inside, there is much of interest, including 15th-century choir stalls with tracery decoration, a canopied pulpit, and monuments and brasses.

CHURCH OF ST MICHAEL The pre-Norman tower dates from the early 11th century. The crude two-light windows have baluster pillars. The remainder of the church is 13th century and later, and there are several monuments and some medieval glass, including a Lily Window.

CHURCH OF ST PETER-IN-THE-EAST Originally Norman, with an impressive vaulted crypt below the chancel and a good Norman south doorway with beak ornament. The church has 15th-century glass, and brasses and monuments. It is now the library of St Edmund Hall. (By appointment.)

DIVINITY SCHOOL This 15th-century Perpendicular Gothic building is the oldest lecture-room in the university, designed for the teaching of theology, the most important subject at Oxford in the Middle Ages. The foundations were laid in 1420, and the building was completed in 1490. It has hardly been altered since then, except for a Gothic doorway inserted in the north side in 1669. The fan-vaulting of the roof carries 455 bosses, many bearing the Arms of benefactors.

HOLYWELL MUSIC ROOM The oldest music room in Europe, belonging to the university's Faculty of Music. Except for a brief period in 1900–1, it has been in continuous use since 1748.

MAGDALEN COLLEGE Building of this college, founded in 1458 by William of Waynflete, began in the 1470's around the 13th-century St John's Hospital. The wall along Long Wall Street including the tower at St Cross dates from 1467–73. The chapel was completed in 1474–5; it is T-shaped in plan with good proportions and graceful arches. The hall and cloister quadrangle were built in 1475. Founder's Tower, which dates from 1485–8, has profusely carved bay windows and fine vaulting beneath. The great bell-tower beside the road was built in 1492–1509. New Building (1733), facing the deer park, is a fine Georgian addition with a graceful pediment. Near by is Addison's Walk, named after a Magdalen man of Queen Anne's time who founded the *Spectator* magazine; the walk runs through the college grounds beside the R. Cherwell. (See p. 384.)

MERTON COLLEGE A college founded in 1264 by Walter de Merton, Bishop of Rochester. From this early period a number of buildings survive, but these lacked any close co-ordination in their planning. The hall was built before 1277 but was heavily restored in the 19th century. The bell-tower of the chapel (begun c. 1290) was not completed until 1450. During this time Mob Quad and afterwards the library were erected. Building has continued through the centuries; the new Warden's lodging was completed in 1963. Among the famous students of the college was William

MUSEUM OF THE HISTORY OF SCIENCE

ARMILLARY SPHERE *This Italian sphere was made between 1672 and 1684 and demonstrates the planetary system of Heracleides of Pontus who lived in the 4th century BC. According to the system, Venus and Mercury revolve round the Sun, while the Moon, Sun, Mars, Jupiter and Saturn revolve round the Earth. Jupiter is shown with only four satellites and Saturn with only three.*

COMPOUND MICROSCOPE *This microscope was probably made by John Marshall (1663–1725), a famous optical instrument maker whose shop was at one time in Ludgate, London. The stand is of gilt-brass and iron, the tubes of pasteboard, covered with tooled leather and vellum, and the base is of ebony and walnut and weighted with lead. The microscope's accessories include six objectives of various powers, a stage with a glass plate and a brass trough 'to put on the Fish that the Circulation of the Blood may be seen', another stage to carry opaque objects, and forceps and tweezers. Marshall appears to have first produced his 'great Double-Constructed Microscope' in 1693.*

Harvey, who first demonstrated the circulation of the blood in the 17th century. (See p. 385.)

MERTON COLLEGE LIBRARY Open to the public, and older than the Bodleian, it was built in 1373–8 by William Humberville. It is sited on the south-west corner of Mob Quad, and housed on the first floor to avoid damp. It contains an astrolabe said to have belonged to Chaucer, who wrote a treatise about the instrument. One book is still kept on its chain, a custom once common to prevent their removal.

MUSEUM OF THE HISTORY OF SCIENCE The finest collection of early astronomical, mathematical and optical instruments in the world is held here. The old Ashmolean building in which it is housed is one of the best examples of 17th-century architecture in Oxford, and was the original home of the Ashmolean Museum, the oldest public museum in England. The building was formally opened in 1683 to house the collection of the antiquary and astrologer, Elias Ashmole, one of the original Fellows of the Royal Society. Ashmole's collection consisted of rare geological, zoological, botanical and ethnological specimens from all over the world, together with a number of 'curiosities' typical of collections of the period.

One of the most distinguished parts of the present display is the series of Islamic and European astrolabes, once important instruments for astronomical calculation. Like many of the exhibits, these are interesting not only scientifically, but as works of art; so too are a number of the sun-dials on display and three fine orreries—machines for representing by wheel-work the motions of the heavenly bodies. There is an almost complete series of early microscopes and other optical instruments, together with photographic apparatus. Also on display are clocks and watches; air-pumps, frictional electrical machines, early X-ray apparatus, and other instruments of physics.

Of special interest for the history of science in Oxford is the penicillin material in the basement gallery, and H. G. Moseley's X-ray spectrometer—the first used in the spectroscopic analysis of elements. With this, Moseley discovered in 1914 the significance of atomic numbers, a fundamental contribution to the development of modern physics.

A more recent relic is a blackboard used by Einstein in one of a series of lectures which he gave at Oxford in 1931.

The museum also houses a comprehensive library of manuscripts, printed books and prints for students' use.

NEW COLLEGE The foundation stone of this college, the first complete complex of college buildings planned as a unit, was laid in 1380. The founder was William of Wykeham, Bishop of Winchester in 1367–1404, and most of his work survives, although much of it has been remodelled inside and substantial additions made. Wykeham's fine Gothic buildings, erected around the first quadrangle, were largely completed by 1387. The gate-house, containing the Warden's lodging, was built in 1380. In the first quadrangle opposite the gate is the library. To the right is the living accommodation for scholars and fellows, and to the left the main community buildings—the chapel and

OXFORD UNIVERSITY

The university, the oldest in Britain, probably dates from 1167 when Henry II, during a quarrel with Becket, ordered English students in Paris to return to England. His intention was to ensure that 'there may never be wanting a succession of persons duly qualified for the service of God in Church and State'.

GRINLING GIBBONS CARVING *This is part of the magnificent wooden reredos carved for the chapel of Trinity College by Grinling Gibbons about 1694. The original chapel, built in 1406, had fallen into disrepair by the 17th century, and under Dr Ralph Bathurst, who was president of the college from 1664 until 1704, a new chapel was built. The architect may have been Dean Aldrich, who was much influenced by Sir Christopher Wren. Besides the reredos there are lavishly carved stalls and screen. The chapel, begun in 1691, was completed three years later. (Trinity College)*

MAGDALEN COLLEGE TOWER *This is probably the best known piece of architecture in Oxford, since it is the sight which greets travellers by road from London as they cross Magdalen Bridge to enter the city. The college was founded in 1458 by William of Waynflete, Bishop of Winchester. Henry VI granted him St John's Hospital, a 13th-century building, and this formed the college nucleus. New building began in the 1470's with the chapel and hall, but the magnificent Gothic tower was not built until the end of the 15th century.*

MERTON COLLEGE *Mob Quad, Oxford's oldest quadrangle (above), completed in c. 1378, contains not only the oldest college library in England, but also the magnificent chapel (left) which was built in 1270–1451. Many of the chapel windows retain their original 13th-century stained glass, and the tracery of the east window is particularly fine.*

NEW COLLEGE *The first stone of the college founded by William of Wykeham was laid in 1380. The quadrangle, completed in 1387, was one of the first to be built in Oxford and was designed to contain all the buildings necessary for collegiate life; on the north side are the chapel and hall, and on the east the founder's library.*

TOM TOWER, CHRIST CHURCH *Each evening the bell that once tolled the curfew for members of this college is still rung. At five minutes past nine Great Tom, cast in 1680, weighing over 7 tons, and hanging high in Wren's octagonal tower, chimes 101 over the quadrangle begun in 1525 by Cardinal Wolsey when he founded the college.*

RADCLIFFE CAMERA

John Radcliffe, a well-known physician of William III's time, in his will left £40,000 for the erection of a library at Oxford. So it was decided to build the library between the Church of St Mary the Virgin and the Divinity Schools, but it was more than 20 years before the site was finally cleared. James Gibbs, the Scottish designer of St Martin-in-the-Fields, London, who had studied in Rome, was chosen as architect, and in 1737–48 he erected the great, circular, domed Radcliffe Camera or Library. His inspiration was probably derived from an earlier plan for a circular library at Trinity College, Cambridge, that was drawn up by Sir Christopher Wren. The Cambridge library was never built, but Gibbs's building was opened in 1749 with a ceremony at which Dr William King, the Vice-Chancellor of the University, gave a fiery pro-Jacobite speech—a flagrant act of disloyalty to the House of Hanover, the rulers of England since 1714 when George I came to the throne.

GRAND STAIRCASE IN THE
RADCLIFFE CAMERA

This graceful staircase was designed by James Gibbs, who also designed the library itself. The plasterers charged a total of £280 for their work on eight stucco ceilings in the building, including the grand staircase coves, entablatures and domed ceiling, all of which were made according to drawings by Gibbs. Gibbs also designed the staircase rail, which is made of Swedish iron, and in his estimate of the cost of the building, submitted to the trustees in 1746, he allowed £168 10s. for the ironwork.

hall (with kitchen beyond). The bell-tower and cloister attached to the chapel date from 1400. The land which Wykeham acquired for his college included a stretch of the medieval city wall which the college, by an ancient agreement with the city, is still obliged to keep in a good state of repair. The wall now survives as a picturesque boundary to one of the most attractive gardens in Oxford. (See p. 385.)

PITT RIVERS MUSEUM General Pitt Rivers gave his ethnographical collection to the university in 1883. The collection, which covers the whole world and includes archaeology as well as ethnography and European folk life material, is internationally famous. It is arranged by subjects rather than tribally or geographically.

RADCLIFFE CAMERA A magnificent circular building erected in 1737–48 by James Gibbs. It rises from a powerful base which is strongly rusticated (has stone blocks firmly outlined to give an appearance of strength and solidity). The building above has pairs of tall Corinthian columns which support a parapet topped by urns. Capping all is the dome and lantern, the buttresses of which are not, as expected, in line with the columns but are deliberately placed between them. Originally a private library, it now provides reading rooms for the Bodleian Library. The Camera is not open to the public.

ROTUNDA In 1962 a rotunda, the first to be built in Oxford since the 18th century, was opened as a museum entirely devoted to dolls' houses and their contents—the only one of its kind in the world. The period covered is c. 1700–1885—though recently an Edwardian house (complete with billiard room and conservatory) has been added. The museum does not admit children under 16, and is only open on Sunday afternoons in summer.

SHELDONIAN THEATRE This building was erected as a university theatre and to house the University Press by Sir Christopher Wren in 1664–9. It is based on a Roman theatre and is roughly semi-circular. Wren was faced with the problem of roofing a space some 70 ft by 80 ft, in wood. This he achieved with a complicated arrangement of beams and trusses supporting a flat ceiling. These are visible in the roof space which was used as a bookstore by the Press when the building was complete; the basement housed the printing presses. To save money, only the south front (the straight front) has Classical pilasters and columns; over the doorway there are the Arms of Archbishop Sheldon who gave the theatre to the university. Among those who assisted Wren was William Byrd, well known for the curious layers of knights he carved in Swinbrook church. Byrd, whose work included vigorously carved keystones on the curved side of the building, was paid £307 in 1666 for stone carving. Wren's original cupola was replaced by one designed by Edward Blore in 1838. On the south side of the theatre is a wall and railing with carved heads.

TRINITY COLLEGE Founded in 1555; portions of the old Durham College (established 1380), which formerly occupied this site, are incorporated in the present buildings. Features are the Kettell Hall, a row of gabled buildings; the Garden Quadrangle designed by Wren in 1668; and the chapel built by Bathurst in 1691. (See p. 384.)

UNIVERSITY MUSEUM In 1854 a competition was held to choose a design for a University Museum, and that of the Dublin firm of Deane, Son and Woodward was successful; work began the following year. Sir Henry Acland, later Regius Professor of Medicine, was a supporter of the scheme, and his friend John Ruskin, an ardent

SHELDONIAN THEATRE
Sir Christopher Wren was Professor of Astronomy at Oxford when Sir Gilbert Sheldon, Archbishop of Canterbury, requested him to design a theatre for the public ceremonies of the university. Sheldon provided all the money for the building, completed in 1664–9 and named after him. It is semicircular-ended: the flat ceiling was painted by Robert Streater with an allegory of 'Truth descending on the Arts and Sciences', and with a network of ropes to suggest the canvas awning of a Roman theatre open to the sky.

advocate of the Gothic revival, concerned himself in it from the start. On Ruskin's advice, the columns, windows and doorways were decorated with plant and animal motifs carved by the finest craftsmen of the day. Because money ran out before the decoration was completed, much of the exterior remains plain, but the interior carving was completed from private benefactions in 1905–14.

The museum contains the zoological, entomological, mineralogical and geological collections of the university, the earliest of which date from the late 17th century. The Pitt Rivers Museum, which is entered through the University Museum, is concerned mainly with ethnology,

and contains large collections that demonstrate the origins and geographical distribution of the material cultures of the world. To one side of the museum is the original chemical laboratory which, in best Gothic revival tradition, was built as a replica of the Abbot's kitchen at Glastonbury.

Ozleworth *Glos.* 546Cc
CHURCH OF ST NICHOLAS The main feature of this church is the hexagonal Norman tower, which is thought to have Saxon origins, standing between the nave and sanctuary. There is a pretty south door ornamented with carved foliage. Restoration was carried out in the 19th century.

P Q

Packwood House *Warks.* 546Df
A timber-framed Tudor house, built *c.* 1550, with additions made some 100 years later by John Fetherston. The house contains collections of needlework and tapestry, but is renowned chiefly for its yew tree garden (begun in 1650), fashioned to represent the Sermon on the Mount.

Padworth *Berks.* 546Fb
CHURCH OF ST JOHN THE BAPTIST An interesting church with a Norman nave and an apsed chancel. There are good north and south doors, an impressive chancel arch, and the remains of a medieval wall-painting of St Nicholas. One monument is dated 1711; another, by J. Wilton, 1776, has a mourning woman with an urn. A 19th-century stained glass window is by C. E. Kempe, 1891.

Paignton *Devon* 539Hc
OLDWAY Built *c.* 1900 in neo-Classical style by Paris Singer to designs inspired by Versailles.

Painscastle *Powys* 545Je
In many great castles the original earthworks were swept away by the medieval masons, although they were to return to favour as a defence against catapults and gun-fire in later days. Painscastle gives a vivid impression of the appearance and layout of the traditional motte and bailey castle as shown on the Bayeaux Tapestry. Both the motte, or castle mound, and the bailey, which was big enough to contain a large garrison, are defended by deep double banks and ditches.

Painswick *Glos.* 546Cc
COURT HOUSE Charles I used a room in this house as a courtroom and stayed here before the siege of Gloucester in August 1643. (By appointment.)

Paisley *Strathclyde* 561He
ABBEY The abbey was founded in 1163, and much of the present church dates from the 14th and 15th centuries, though the fall of the central tower destroyed the choir. Restoration was begun in the late 19th century. There is a monument with an effigy of a woman said to be Marjorie Bruce, Robert Bruce's daughter. (See p. 388.)
MUSEUM, ART GALLERIES AND COATS OBSERVATORY Exhibits include textiles, with fine examples of Paisley shawls, archaeological finds, British and French paintings, pottery and an extensive natural history collection.

Pakenham Windmill *Suffolk* 548Cf
An old mill that was used to grind corn until struck by lightning in 1971. (By appointment.)

Papplewick *Notts.* 552Ed
CHURCH OF ST JAMES Though the west tower is of the 14th century, the remainder of the building is Gothic of the late 18th century. The gallery is noteworthy. Also worth noting are incised tomb slabs dating from the 13th century.

Papworth St Agnes *Cambs.* 547Jf
MANOR HOUSE One of the most interesting houses in the county, part medieval, part Elizabethan, with a combination of red brick and stonework. A straight gable at one end, a great chimney with star-shaped shafts, a six-light medieval window on an upper floor, and some good stucco work give the house great character. There are also some good ceilings inside. It was built in 1585 for Sir William Mallory, a descendant of Sir Thomas Malory who wrote *Morte d'Arthur*. Most of the south front was rebuilt in 1660.

Parc Cwm *W. Glam.*   *544Fc*
This interesting Neolithic long barrow—or strictly cairn—standing near the centre of the Gower peninsula, has been the cause of some controversy. It has a horned forecourt leading to a gallery with two pairs of transeptal chambers, very like many of those in the Cotswolds. But the mound is not long, being a fairly rounded oval, more like those of the western Atlantic type. Other examples of both types are known in Gower and it may be, as some think, that Parc Cwm is a hybrid form.

Parc-y-Meirch *Clwyd*   *551Ge*
DINORBEN This remarkable hill-fort stands not far from the sea, on a hill skirting the west side of the Vale of Clwyd. In places, the natural steep scarp-slopes of the hill need no defences. But they are not continuous, and the gentler slopes between are protected by enormous ramparts. The inner rampart came first and, for a time, was defence enough. But later in its history, the second outer rampart was added. In this, the entrance was inturned with stone-built guard-chambers on each side.

This fort originated in the Iron Age, and additions may have been made before the Romans arrived. After that invasion, the fort was abandoned for a time, to be restored and re-occupied in the Dark Ages.

Parc-y-Meirw *Dyfed*   *544Ce*
In the hilly country inland lies this Bronze Age standing stone row. It is not an outstanding example of the type, but is a rarity in this part of Britain. Quite close to it stands yet another of the normal type of burial chamber, of uprights and capstone, known as Coetan Arthur.

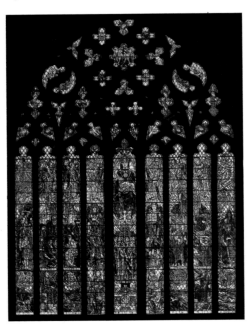

EAST WINDOW, PAISLEY ABBEY

The east window of Paisley Abbey, which was founded in 1163, is one of the largest and finest works by Douglas Strachan (1875–1950), the Scottish master of stained glass. From the west end of the abbey the window appears like a great tapestry stained with rich splashes of colour, but a closer inspection reveals the groups of figures and the carefully worked out design, which reaches its climax in the figure of Christ the King in the centre.

Parham *W. Sussex*   *542Ad*
Sir Thomas Palmer (1540–1626), who sailed with Drake to Cadiz, began this Elizabethan mansion in 1577. The great hall has unusually tall mullioned windows and a plaster ceiling. The house contains Elizabethan, Jacobean and Georgian portraits. The grounds include fine walled gardens.
CHURCH OF ST PETER A small church in the grounds of the 16th-century house. Basically Perpendicular, it was restored in the early 19th century, when the interior was redecorated in Gothic style. There are box-pews and pretty ceilings. An unusual possession is the 14th-century lead font with lettering and heraldry.

Partrishow (Patricio) *Powys*   *545Jd*
CHURCH A small remote church, mainly 15th-century, with a wonderful rood screen, which retains its gallery with delightful open-work tracery decoration.

Patrington *Humberside*   *559Ha*
CHURCH OF ST PATRICK A truly magnificent cruciform church, mainly of the 14th century, with a central tower and spire, among the best in England. There is a good Easter sepulchre, a restored medieval screen, and all around are many delightful carved details.

Patrixbourne *Kent*   *542Ff*
CHURCH OF ST MARY This is a small church, with a south tower and spire; there is a Norman door under the tower which forms its porch, with carved ornament, and a tympanum with a carved figure of Christ. The mass clocks near by are of particular interest; so too is the squint on the southern side of the chancel. There are 18 panels of delicate 17th-century Swiss glass.

Pavenham *Beds.*   *547Hf*
CHURCH OF ST PETER Most of the church is 13th–14th century, with good examples of 14th-century canopied work remaining. There is a large amount of Jacobean woodwork that was given to the church in 1848, including carved panelling, gallery and pulpit.

Paviland *W. Glam.*   *544Eb*
GOAT'S HOLE CAVE This cave now opens into a cleft in the sea-cliffs of the Bristol Channel, and visitors must watch tide conditions when visiting it. When first occupied, the cliff was fronted by a coastal plain, which made access easy. It was first discovered by Dean Buckland, early in the 19th century; he made some small excavations, and found the first British Palaeolithic burial, a human skeleton associated with the bones of extinct animals. However, Dean Buckland's belief in Archbishop Ussher's Mosaic chronology, by which the Creation was estimated to have taken place only about 6000 years ago, would not let him accept this evidence of the antiquity of man. Further excavation was carried out in the early part of this century, and flint and bone implements, objects of ivory and other substances, all belonging to various cultural periods of the latter part of the Pleistocene Age, were discovered. Above these ancient traces of human occupation, other finds showed that even as late as Roman times, men had taken refuge in this cave.

Pembridge *Heref. & Worcs.*   *546Af*
CHURCH OF ST MARY Originally a Norman building, the present church (nave with clerestory, aisles, transepts and chancel) is mainly of the 14th century, when the effigies and monuments were made; the pulpit, reader's desk and lectern are all early 17th century. The octagonally-based and detached belfry with its massive timbers was

PEMBROKE CASTLE

On a splendid natural site, almost surrounded by the Pembroke R., this castle became a key fortress in the settlement of Wales in the late 11th century. The magnificent round keep and inner bailey date from about 1200. The 13th-century curtain walls are light, the steep banks to the river themselves forming a defence. In 1648 the castle was attacked by Cromwell, and much of the outer enclosure was destroyed by cannon.

built in the latter part of the 14th century and is an outstanding feature.

Pembridge Castle *Heref. & Worcs.*   *546Ad*
A well-preserved 13th-century Welsh border castle with a moat. The oldest part, a round tower in the north-west corner, dates back to 1135. In the courtyard is a tiny 16th-century chapel with screen and furnishings brought in from elsewhere. St John Kemble, the Hereford martyr, who lived in the castle with his uncle, was hanged in 1678 for celebrating mass in the chapel.

Pembroke *Dyfed*   *544Cc*
CASTLE Pembroke became important from the late 11th century onwards, first as a key point in the English settlement of Wales, and secondly as a 'staging post' on the journey to Ireland. In 1138, the Earldom of Pembrokeshire was raised to become a County Palatine, giving the holder of the title supreme responsibility and power.

The great castle, founded here in 1097 on a promontory in the Pembroke R. where steep banks afforded a strong defence, was a reflection of this power. The great circular vaulted keep dates from *c.* 1200 and is 75 ft high with 17 ft thick walls. The fine gate-house survives. In the adjoining tower Henry VII was born in 1457.

There is a spectacular cave, once the main store-room, beneath the Northern Hall in the Inner Ward, and two rooms in the Gatehouse have been adapted to house a small local museum and shop.

Pendennis Castle *Cornwall*   *538Ca*
Like its counterpart, St Mawes Castle across the Carrick Roads from Falmouth, Pendennis Castle was a link in Henry VIII's coastal defence system. It was finished in 1546, three years after the completion of the fort at St Mawes. Similar to the other military fortifications, the castle consists of a central circular keep with semicircular bastions, enclosed by a curtain wall of further semicircular gun positions. The castle was enlarged at the end of the 16th century, but it suffered badly during the Civil War. While St Mawes had to capitulate after only one day's siege, Pendennis, in a better posi-

tion, was able to hold out against the Cromwellian troops for five months, until supplies were exhausted. Pendennis was the last stronghold in England to surrender to Cromwell.

Penhurst *E. Sussex*   *542Dd*
The medieval church, Elizabethan manor house and farm buildings together form a rare Sussex manorial group. The church, dedicated to St Michael the Archangel, is small and of almost untouched Perpendicular style; the west tower has a pyramid roof, the nave a king-post roof and the chancel a wagon roof.

Penkill Castle *Strathclyde*   *561Gb*
The modernised 15th-century keep contains mural paintings by William Bell Scott (1811–90). The castle was a favourite haunt of the group of young painters known as the Pre-Raphaelite Brotherhood. Dante Gabriel Rossetti wrote many of his poems here, and his sister, Christina, and Holman Hunt were also frequent visitors to the castle.

Penkridge *Staffs.*   *552Bb*
CHURCH OF ST MICHAEL AND ALL ANGELS A fine, former collegiate church, with work from the 13th century onwards. It has stalls, misericords and a number of 16th- and 17th-century monuments.

PENKILL CASTLE

This 15th-century Scottish castle served as the medieval inspiration and meeting place for the 19th-century pre-Raphaelites.

PENRHYN CASTLE

Hopper's fortress, the most gigantic example of the Norman Revival in Britain, was begun in 1827, and finished about 1840. The main feature of the interior is the great hall, three storeys high; it is arched and vaulted in a profusion of Norman decoration, and its north windows contain stained glass (dating from 1837) by Thomas Willement, representing the signs of the Zodiac.

Penmon Priory *Anglesey, Gwynedd*   550Fe
The foundation of the Priory Church of St Seriol probably goes back to the 6th century, but the earliest features—the font, and the cross—date from *c.* 1000. The cruciform church has a nave of 1140, and this was followed some 20 years later by the square tower and transept. The large chancel dates from the early 13th century, although it has been partly rebuilt. The church contains the best-preserved Romanesque detail in North Wales: of particular interest are the crossing arches and wall arcades, the tympanum over the south door, and the font.

South of the church there is the prior's house (now a private house) and beyond this a fine three-storied building dating from the early 13th century, which contains the cellar, refectory and dormitory. The building is roofless, but has been consolidated.

On the opposite side of the road, to the south-east, is a charming square dove-cote with a stone roof which is crowned by an open hexagonal lantern through which the birds entered; this is post-Reformation and dates from *c.* 1600. There is an ancient cell and holy well some 80 yds north of the church.

Penn *Bucks.*   547Hc
HOLY TRINITY CHURCH An 11th-century church containing one of the few Norman lead fonts in the country. There is a recently discovered medieval Doom painting above the chancel arch, and the roof of the nave, erected in 1380, is one of the finest in the country. The village is the ancestral home of William Penn, founder of Pennsylvania, and there are family monuments in the church. The ancient clock has a single hand.

Penrhyn Castle *Gwynedd*   550Ee
The medieval house on this site, from which there are magnificent views of mountains and sea, was modernised by Samuel Wyatt for Lord Penrhyn *c.* 1782; this resulted in a mixture of typical 18th-century domestic architecture and Gothic. Lord Penrhyn died in 1818 and his nephew inherited the

house; he employed Thomas Hopper to enlarge it and Hopper produced a massive Norman-style fortress in Mona marble.

At the southern end of the castle there is an immense square keep, 115 ft high and about 60 ft wide, which was probably based on the keep of Hedingham Castle.

The castle contains a collection of 1000 dolls from all parts of the world. Collections of locomotives and rolling stock are also on view.

Penrice Castle *W. Glam.*   544Fc
The ruins of a 12th-century Norman castle, with an 18th-century octagonal pigeon house close by.

Penrith *Cumbria*   557Jf
CHURCH OF ST ANDREW A medieval building rebuilt in *c.* 1720, but retaining the earlier west tower, which is probably of Norman origin. There are fragments of 15th-century glass, and 17th- and 18th-century fittings—font, pulpit, brass chandeliers.

Penshaw Monument *Tyne & Wear*   558Cg
A Doric temple, built in 1844 in honour of the 1st Earl of Durham (1792–1840), who in 1838 was Governor-General of the British Provinces in North America (now Canada).

Penshurst *Kent*   542Ce
Beside the great sandstone mass of Penshurst Place, this village has a handsome red-brick rectory which is typically Queen Anne. The lych-gate, with a house built over it, is the most picturesque corner of the village, increased to make a minute open-ended quadrangle in 1850, a most sensitive piece of Victorian development.

Penshurst Place *Kent*   542Ce
The birthplace of Sir Philip Sidney (1554–86), soldier, poet and statesman. The medieval manor house was greatly enlarged in Tudor times. It contains a great hall, built in 1340, which is 62 ft by 9 ft with a roof of chestnut timbers rising some 60 ft above the ground. The hall has a central octagonal fireplace. The house has a collection of armour, furniture of all periods from the 15th century, and portraits of the Sidney family to whom the house was granted by Edward VI in 1552. The terraced formal gardens, begun in 1560, have often been described, notably by Ben Jonson. In the Stable Wing there is a toy museum. Adjoining the North Front is the park, where specimens of rare sheep graze among the trees.

Pentre Ifan *Dyfed*   544De
This is the finest example of the local burial chambers. Not only do the great uprights carry their capstone, estimated to weigh some 17 tons, but the upright slabs which formed the forecourt of the mound, now partly restored, still stand to show that it was semicircular in plan; the stones seem to be more carefully graded than usual.

Penzance *Cornwall*   538Aa
PENLEE HOUSE MUSEUM The museum specialises in local history, showing bygones of West Penwith, including some Bronze and Stone Age relics.

Pen-y-Corddyn *Clwyd*   551Ge
This Iron Age hill-fort stands on a hill close to the sea, and has an intermittent rampart linking the stretches of steep natural scarp where no rampart was needed. The fort was built perhaps a century or more before the Roman invasion; the original defences were never remodelled, and the site was abandoned when the Romans penetrated this northern Welsh hill-country.

the old church are a 15th-century font and a 17th-century pulpit.

Pepperbox Hill *Wilts.* 540Fe
On top of the hill stands Eyre's Folly, a six-sided brick tower with slate roof, built by Giles Eyre of Brickworth House in 1606.

Pershore *Heref. & Worcs.* 546Ce
ABBEY The original abbey church, of which parts have survived to serve as the parish church, was established by 689.

Only the eastern arm—with the presbytery—the south transept and the lantern tower remain. The nave and the Lady Chapel were destroyed after the Dissolution, and the north transept collapsed in the 17th century. The presbytery itself was rebuilt after a fire in 1223, but the vaulting is early 14th century. The lantern tower (*c.* 1330) rises on massive arches.

Perth *Tayside* 566Ca
Originally called St Johnstoun, Perth grew in importance as a key crossing of the Tay and became the capital of Scotland in the 11th century. In 1437, James I, Scotland's poet king, was brutally murdered in the Dominican friary, and in 1482 Perth lost its capital status to Edinburgh.
ST JOHN'S KIRK Consecrated in 1242, but the present building dates mainly from the 15th century. Here, on May 11, 1559, John Knox preached his famous 'vehement against idolatry' sermon, which led to a riot. The mob destroyed the images and altars in the church and went on to ruin the town's four friaries. Widespread desecration of Roman Catholic monasteries and abbey churches in Scotland followed.

Peterborough *Cambs.* 547Jg
In AD 655, the King of Mercia founded a monastery on the site of the present cathedral. Henry VIII gave Peterborough city status in 1541: it was not until 1874 that it became incorporated as a municipal borough. The old town hall was built in 1671.
CATHEDRAL Peterborough is one of the most complete and impressive Romanesque buildings

PENSHURST PLACE

BARONS HALL *Penshurst Place has one of the finest surviving 14th-century halls in England, with a timbered roof of chestnut—not oak, as was most usual. The house was built for a prosperous London wool merchant, Sir John De Pulteney, in 1340.*

Peover Hall *Cheshire* 552Be
CHURCH OF ST LAURENCE The church that formerly stood on this site was rebuilt in 1811. But St Laurence's retains two earlier chapels with fine 15th- and 17th-century monuments with effigies of the Mainwaring family of the Hall. Also from

PERSHORE ABBEY

St Eadburga, the daughter of a 10th-century English king, is the most important saint venerated at Pershore Abbey. Offered the choice of necklaces and bracelets or a Bible and chalice by her father, to test her faith, the young Eadburga, who later became a nun, chose the Bible and chalice. The abbey, already an established institution by 972 when it became a Benedictine house, was deprived of large parts of its estates which were used by Edward the Confessor to help endow Westminster Abbey. At the Dissolution part of the abbey was knocked down, leaving a lopsided fragment of the original building which has been used as a parish church ever since. The vaulting of the presbytery is architecturally outstanding, with bosses deeply carved with naturalistic foliage.

PETERBOROUGH CATHEDRAL

Henry VIII gave Peterborough cathedral status in 1541; it had been one of the great Benedictine abbey churches, but the abbey was dissolved in 1539. The site was first consecrated in 655, when the King of Mercia founded a Benedictine monastery there. This was sacked by the Danes in 870, and a second monastery was destroyed by fire in 1116. The present building was started by the Abbot Jean de Seez two years later. Apart from its west front, Peterborough is an outstanding example of the Norman-Romanesque style. The Benedictines, conservative in their architecture, carried on building in this style up to the last decade of the 12th century—more than 20 years after England's first truly Gothic buildings had made their appearance.

WEST FRONT *Peterborough's crowning achievement, the unique west front, was created when a dramatic screen wall was placed in front of the old Romanesque façade. Originally it had been planned to finish off the nave with Romanesque twin towers, but the design was abandoned before these were completed. The Gothic front is dominated by three huge, deeply recessed arches, 81 ft high. For some unknown reason, the centre arch is much narrower than the other two, but the two corner towers prevent this narrowness from producing a cramped effect. The porch in the centre, in the late Gothic style, was added about 1370, probably to tie together the lofty supports of the arch and prevent them from spreading outwards.*

NAVE *Much of the original Norman fabric of Peterborough is preserved inside the cathedral, and the nave, completed under the Abbot Andrew between 1194 and 1197, is among the supreme surviving examples of the Romanesque style. The Peterborough monks owned the quarries producing the creamy-white Barnack stone from which it is built. The high wooden roof is richly decorated with paintings dating back to 1220, which have been carefully restored.*

TURNER *The Lake, Petworth: Sunset, Fighting Bucks*

When Ruskin called J. M. W. Turner's work 'the loveliest ever yet done by man in imagery of the physical world', he was implying the dominance of a quality in Turner's art which appeals today with increasing force —his concern with the vastness of nature and its physical properties of light and colour. After his father's death in 1829, at the invitation of his patron and friend Lord Egremont Turner had a studio at Petworth and did a large number of dazzling interior scenes there as well as landscapes in oils. This view of the lake, with a cricket match in progress and a herd of deer, was done about 1829–30. (Petworth House)

in England. The church belonged to a Benedictine monastery, founded in the 7th century. Destroyed by the Danes in the 9th century, it was refounded in the 10th, a new church being built *c.* 965. This in turn was burnt in 1116 and the present church belongs to the subsequent rebuilding.

Of the domestic buildings of the monastery, a few parts survive, particularly of the abbot's and prior's lodgings and various gateways. The cloister walks no longer exist. The abbey was dissolved in 1539 and refounded as a cathedral in 1541.

CITY MUSEUM AND ART GALLERY Located in a large Regency house, built as a private dwelling in 1816, the museum contains a unique collection of carved bonework and straw marquetry by prisoners from the Napoleonic Wars held in Norman Cross Barracks. The archaeological collection concentrates on the Romano-British and Anglo-Saxon periods, and the natural history and geology sections include fossil reptiles from the local clay. There is a small permanent picture collection.

Peterhead *Grampian* 567Hf
ARBUTHNOT MUSEUM The local history of Peterhead is illustrated by items in the museum. The marine section includes a collection of fishing boats showing development up to the present time, and exhibits relating to whaling and the Arctic. Other local industries represented include granite quarrying and dressing, and herring curing, which has died out. A collection of coins is also displayed.

Petersfield *Hants.* 541Je
The most handsome houses in this flourishing market town are Georgian. In the square at its centre stands an equestrian statue of William III, originally gilded.

Petersham *Greater London* 542Bg
The Georgian village still exists—a small church, and four massive town-style houses by a double-bend in the main road, where it skirts Richmond Park. The most handsome houses date from *c.* 1720. Sudbrooke Park, contemporary and even finer, designed by James Gibbs, is now the golf clubhouse.
CHURCH OF ST PETER A 13th-century church, largely rebuilt in the 18th century. There were additions in the 19th century, but Georgian fittings —font, pulpit, gallery, box-pews—remain.

Petworth *W. Sussex* 542Ad
Recorded in the Domesday Book, Petworth, a small, town at the gateway of the Duke of Somerset's great house, has many Tudor and 17th-century houses. The gateway itself is spectacular, taller than most buildings in the town. An intricate knot of narrow streets develops round the tiny market-place, where the plain arcaded 18th-century town hall stands in contrast with an exuberant bank of 1901. At New Grove House (1620), Grinling Gibbons stayed while engaged on carvings for Petworth House.
PETWORTH HOUSE J. M. W. Turner (1775–1851), the landscape artist, visited this great house to paint, and several of his pictures are here. It was raised by Charles Seymour, 6th Duke of Somerset, who, after his marriage to the Percy heiress, rebuilt the former Percy mansion between 1688 and 1696, retaining only the 13th-century chapel; the house was partly altered in the 19th century. The state rooms contain paintings by Holbein, Rembrandt, Hals, Van Dyck, Gainsborough and Reynolds. The Carved Room was decorated by Grinling Gibbons. (The park is open to the public but the gardens are not.)
SOMERSET LODGE A small 17th-century stone house, with mullioned windows and oak staircase.

Pevensey *E. Sussex* 542Dd
William the Conqueror landed here in 1066 to march to Hastings. Pevensey has the remains of a Roman fort that was converted into a medieval castle. The town was once a flourishing port.
CHURCH OF ST NICHOLAS The church was built at the beginning of the 13th century. The chancel is *c.* 1200 and the nave *c.* 1216. Extensive restoration took place in the 19th century.
COURT HOUSE Once a combination of gaol and courtroom, it is now a small museum containing treasures of the ancient borough and Cinque Port.
MINT HOUSE This stands on the site of a Norman mint. It dates from *c.* 1432 but had extensive alterations in the 16th century.

Pevensey Castle *E. Sussex* 542Dd
This Roman fort of the Saxon Shore stands guard on a harbour which is now silted up. It is not rectangular like most of its contemporaries, but oval in plan and is well provided with substantial external bastions. The military value of this coastal

PEVENSEY CASTLE

The sea once lapped against the south and east sides of this castle. In William I's reign the Normans converted the remains of the original Roman sea fort into a fortress; it was an important part of their coastal defences and despite several sieges was never taken by assault. In 1264–5, while held by a favourite of Henry III, it was besieged by the forces of Simon de Montfort under the command of his son. Subsequently the castle fell into disrepair, for the sea receded and Pevensey ceased to be a castle commanding the coastline. It was temporarily fortified during the brief threat of the Spanish invasion in 1587 and 1588.

site was recognised after the Norman Conquest, and the castle was further strengthened by Robert, Count of Mortain. A keep was built in the south-east corner, and a smaller inner bailey was fortified within the Roman walls. These were used as defences for the outer bailey, and still stand for much of their length. Subsequent alterations were limited to consolidating the inner bailey in the 13th century by substituting a stone curtain wall for the original palisade. During the 15th century the castle fell into disrepair and decay, a decline hastened by the sea gradually receding. Pevensey Castle was a Home Guard command post during the Second World War.

Picardy Stone *Grampian* 566Ff
A Pictish symbol stone; it stands in a small enclosure close to a by-road 2 miles north-west of Insch.

Piccotts End *Herts.* 547Hc
A 15th-century hall-house with wall-paintings of the period. Probably once a pilgrim's hospice.

Pickering *N. Yorks.* 558Ed
CHURCH OF SS PETER AND PAUL A Norman church with much later rebuilding. The west tower is Early English, its spire added later. There is a fragment of Saxon carving, and much 15th-century mural painting, restored in the 19th century, with saints and scenes from the life of Christ. There are effigies of 14th-century knights.

Pickering Castle *N. Yorks.* 558Ed
A Norman motte and bailey castle that replaced

an earlier one. Additions were made in late 12th and early 13th centuries, after which the castle comprised an oval inner ward, with domestic buildings and chapel, surrounded by curtain walls with towers. Only the chapel, postern gate, dungeon and three towers of the curtain walls now remain.

Picton Castle *Dyfed* 544Dd
GRAHAM SUTHERLAND GALLERY The gallery is in the grounds of the 12th-century castle, home of the Philipps family. It contains many works of the late Graham Sutherland, some of which were made especially for the gallery. The collection was a gift by Sutherland and his wife as a token of the artist's inspiration received from the surrounding countryside which he first visited in 1934. The works displayed include oil paintings, water-colours, lithographs and etchings, and works in mixed media.

Pitcaple Castle *Grampian* 566Ff
A 15th-century castle with many historical associations. James IV, Charles II, and Mary, Queen of Scots were entertained here, and the Marquis of Montrose came as a prisoner on his way to execution in Edinburgh. The castle, which has been the home of the Lumsdens and Leslies for 500 years, has 1830 additions by William Burn the noted Edinburgh architect. (By appointment.)

Pitchford *Shropshire* 552Ab
CHURCH OF ST MICHAEL AND ALL ANGELS St Michael's has Norman remains and lancet windows of a later date. The double-decker reading desk and pulpit are of the early 17th century. There is a fine oaken effigy of a cross-legged knight (John de Pitchford, d. 1284) and a series of 16th-century incised alabaster monumental slabs with likenesses of four pairs of husbands and wives of the Ottley family.

Pitchford Hall *Shropshire* 552Ab
A 16th-century black and white mansion in a setting of trees and water, with superb gables and chimneys. It was the home of the Ottley family for many generations: Sir Francis Ottley (1601–49) was nominated Sheriff of Shropshire by the Royalists in the Civil War. (By appointment.)

Pitmedden *Grampian* 567Gf
The garden has been reconstructed as originally laid out in 1675 by Sir Alexander Seton. It contains pavilions, sun-dials and fountains.

Pittington *Durham* 558Cg
CHURCH OF ST LAWRENCE There is an impressive Norman north arcade, with twisted columns and zigzag ornament of *c.* 1175, with Saxon windows above, and a west tower. There was 19th-century restoration and rebuilding. Inside are 12th-century wall-paintings, and the effigy of a cross-legged knight, *c.* 1280. There is a diminutive 13th-century monument to twin boys.

Pixley *Heref. & Worcs.* 546Be
CHURCH OF ST ANDREW A small 11th-century church, surmounted by a Victorian bell-turret, with no division between nave and chancel. The rood screen is possibly of the 14th century.

Plas Teg *Clwyd* 551Jd
This fine early 17th-century mansion is square in plan with square towers at each corner surmounted by decorative lead roofs. It has a good Jacobean stair. (By appointment.)

Plas-yn-Rhiw *Gwynedd* 550Dc
A homestead of 10th-century origin, with Tudor and Georgian additions, recently restored. It has a sub-tropical garden. (By appointment.)

Plymouth *Devon* 538Fc

Sir Francis Drake returned to Plymouth's natural harbour in September 1580 after circumnavigating the world. In 1620, the Pilgrim Fathers departed from it to settle in the New World. As a precaution against Roundhead trouble, Charles II built the great citadel which dominates city and harbour; its ramparts are 20 ft thick in places. The Elizabethan zone of Plymouth is known as the Barbican: the Mayflower Steps here commemorate the departure of the Pilgrim Fathers.

CITY MUSEUM AND ART GALLERY The Reynolds family portraits, Joshua Reynolds's diaries and the Cottonian Collection of pre-1800 paintings, drawings and printed books are among the displays in this museum. Other paintings include Old Masters, contemporary works and the Clarendon Collection of portraits. The collection of silver includes the Drake Cup and the Eddystone Salt. Pottery and porcelain are represented, with emphasis on Cookworthy's Plymouth and Bristol hardpaste. There are also departments of archaeology and natural history.

EDDYSTONE LIGHTHOUSE (RE-ERECTED) On Plymouth Hoe is one of the world's most important 18th-century lighthouses. Some 14 miles south of Plymouth the Eddystone reef was the setting of the first true rock station, the earliest being wooden, built in 1698, followed in 1708 by a wood and stone building which survived until burnt in 1755. Four years later John Smeaton's tower showed its light, and this tower, rebuilt on the Hoe after the present lighthouse replaced it in 1882, was the first scientifically designed and jointed masonry structure to be built, serving as a model until the era of reinforced concrete.

ELIZABETHAN HOUSE A 16th-century house, restored in 1931 and with fine furniture of the 16th and early 17th centuries.

PORCELAIN SWEETMEAT DISH

Made at Cookworthy's factory in Plymouth about 1770, this dish resembles three shells resting on coral. No other example with original matching spoons is known to exist. (City Museum and Art Gallery, Plymouth)

Plympton *Devon* 538Fc
CHURCH OF ST MARY THE VIRGIN A large church dating from the early 14th and 15th centuries, with a prominent west tower.

Pocklington *Humberside* 558Eb
BURNBY HALL GARDENS Gardens with lily ponds.

Polesden Lacy *Surrey* 542Af
The writer of the plays *The School for Scandal* and *The Rivals*, Richard Brinsley Sheridan, lived in a house on this site, and his wife laid out part of the gardens, beautifully set amid downland woods. The present Edwardian house was adapted in 1906 from a Regency original built in 1824 to designs by Thomas Cubitt. It contains a collection of pictures, tapestries and furniture.

Polstead *Suffolk* 548Ce
CHURCH OF ST MARY Built *c.* 1150, this Norman church has a 14th-century west tower and the oldest stone spire in Suffolk. The brickwork may be some of the earliest in England, and there is a 15th-century brass of a priest in full vestment.

Pont Cysyllte *Clwyd* 551Hd
This huge iron aqueduct, designed by Thomas Telford and completed in 1805, carries the Ellesmere Canal over the R. Dee. There is a towpath along the aqueduct for pedestrians.

Pontefract *W. Yorks.* 558Da
CASTLE Though now a ruin, this fortress has a long and bloody history as a stronghold and a dungeon. During the Wars of the Roses, it was held first by John of Gaunt and then by Henry IV; Richard II was murdered here and, later, it served as a prison for Frenchmen captured at Agincourt.

KING'S OWN YORKSHIRE LIGHT INFANTRY MUSEUM Devoted to regimental relics, medals, uniforms and pictures relating to the King's Own Yorkshire Light Infantry.

Ponteland *Northld.* 558Ch
CHURCH OF ST MARY St Mary's has a Norman west tower, and a 13th-century chancel and north transept, with lancet windows. Inside are several fragments of 14th-century heraldic glass.

Pontypridd *Mid Glam.* 545Hc
PONTYPRIDD BRIDGE The colliery town takes its name from this 140 ft single-arch bridge over the R. Taff. It was built by a local mason, William Edwards, in 1756, after two unsuccessful attempts. In order to save weight he pierced each of the spandrels with three cylindrical arched openings; the height of the arch is 36 ft.

DOMENICO POGGINI *An Acrobat*

Domenico Poggini (1520–90) was a Florentine artist who worked mainly as a goldsmith for the Grand Duke of Tuscany, but he also worked in marble and bronze. The brilliant quality of his bronzes is shown by this statuette and must owe much to his training as a goldsmith. (City Museum and Art Gallery, Plymouth)

SIR FRANCIS DRAKE,
THE GREAT CIRCUMNAVIGATOR

Drake, the Terror of the Spanish Main, was born at Crowndale, near Tavistock in Devon. His first command was a down-at-heel coastal vessel bequeathed him by the master to whom he was apprenticed. His early experiences in the West Indies gave Drake a hatred of Spain, but he gained revenge, and wealth, in 1572–3 by heading an expedition which snatched the King of Spain's treasure from the backs of mules plodding across the Isthmus of Panama. After sailing round the globe, Drake singed the King of Spain's beard by destroying 33 ships in Cadiz harbour in 1587. When the Armada sailed against England, a year later, he drummed them up the Channel to disaster. This indomitable sea captain became fatally ill on a last expedition to the Caribbean in 1596, and just before the end climbed into his armour 'To meet death like a gentleman'.

PORTRAIT of Drake painted in 1591 by an unidentified artist (National Maritime Museum, Greenwich). That year Drake diverted the waters of the R. Meve from Dartmoor to give Plymouth England's first municipal water supply.

ASTROLABE, traditionally belonging to Drake. Of the five ships which left Plymouth in 1577, only the Golden Hind under Drake's command, successfully navigated the Magellan Straits. (National Maritime Museum, Greenwich)

LODE-STONE, a natural magnet said to belong to Drake, and used to adjust compasses. (National Maritime Museum, Greenwich)

DRAKE'S MEDALLION, cut in silver and based on the world map made by the great geographer, Mercator. (National Maritime Museum, Greenwich). Drake's course, marked by dotted line, was taken because his ship was groaning with plunder, and he dared not sail it round Cape Horn.

BANNER QUARTERING *painted on silk damask; one of nine Drake used to dress his 'weather beaten bark', the Golden Hind, when the queen rode down to Deptford on April 4, 1581 to dine aboard and confer on him a knighthood after his voyage round the world. These banners are among the oldest in England. (Buckland Abbey)*

THE DRAKE CUP, *a New Year's gift from Queen Elizabeth I in 1582. The queen had told the Spanish Ambassador, who had complained about the 'master thief of the unknown world', 'The gentleman careth not if I disown him', but she had invested in Drake's expedition to break Spain's monopoly in the Pacific and happily received 400 per cent profit on her outlay. This piece is considered among the hundred best specimens of silver gilt in the country. (City Museum and Art Gallery, Plymouth)*

CYPRESS CHEST *in Berkeley Castle. It formed part of the furnishings of Drake's cabin aboard the Golden Hind, the ship which was to take him round the world. The ship was magnificently equipped, even the kitchen utensils being of solid silver, plundered from Spain. It was typical of Drake's rakish gaiety that an orchestra of four was engaged for the voyage which began in 1577 and took two years and ten months to complete.*

PORTCHESTER CASTLE

*There have been fortifications on this site to provide a
defence against invaders from the sea since Roman
times. The present castle was built in the 12th century
inside the perimeter of a Roman fort. The small
Church of St Mary, within the circle of the Roman
walls, formed part of an Augustinian priory founded
by Henry I in 1133, but the inconvenience of having
Augustinian canons in the midst of the garrison*
*probably led to their removal to Southwick about
1144–53. Two hundred years later, at the beginning
of the Hundred Years War, the threat from the
Continent revived and additions were made to the
castle. By the end of the 14th century, under Richard
II, Portchester had become a small but comfortable
royal palace. It remained in the hands of the monarch
until 1632.*

Poole *Dorset*   540Ec
GUILDHALL MUSEUM Ceramics of the 18th
century, glassware, collections of local interest and
changing exhibitions on a variety of local themes.
MARITIME MUSEUM (PARADISE STREET) Contains
exhibitions illustrating Poole's maritime history
during the medieval and post-medieval periods.
SCAPLEN'S COURT MUSEUM This medieval
merchant's house, dating from the 14th century,
has been converted into a museum. On display are
items relating to local history, archaeology and
industrial archaeology, arms and armour. Of
particular interest is the unique 33 ft long dug-out
canoe built by Iron Age fishermen. It was
discovered in the mud of Poole Harbour in 1964.

Portchester *Hants.*   541Hd
CHURCH OF ST MARY Sited in one corner of the
Roman castle, the church was originally monastic,
as part of an Augustinian priory founded in 1133
by Henry I. It is a Norman building, once cruciform and with a central tower. The west front has
a doorway, arcading and window above. The
carved font is Norman. A monument of *c.* 1618
is by Nicholas Stone.

Portchester Castle *Hants.*   541Hd
A fine example of the later type of Saxon Shore
fort, built within the last two decades of the 3rd
century AD and occupied (on the evidence of coins
found there) until *c.* AD 370. Its angular corners,
with boldly projecting bastions and brick bond-
ing-courses in the walls, are characteristic of this
type of Roman fort. It was modified by its use as an
outer curtain wall for a Norman castle, which was
built in the north-west angle.
   At the end of the 14th century Richard II began
converting Portchester into a small palace and
much of this building remains (in ruins) including
the hall, kitchen and great chamber. In the outer
bailey stands the 12th-century church of St Mary,
which survived as a garrison chapel and parish
church.

Port Erin *Isle of Man*   556Cc
MARINE BIOLOGICAL STATION A department of
Liverpool University, for research into marine

biology and fisheries. Fish and marine invertebrates are shown in the public aquarium.

Port Glasgow *Strathclyde*   561Gf
NEWARK CASTLE Begun in 1597 by Patrick Maxwell, the castle has a fine courtyard, hall and
stepped gables. It was enlarged in the 17th century.

Portland Bill *Dorset*   540Db
LIGHTHOUSE The present fine lighthouse, erected
in 1906, is typical of the period, and replaced at
least two other pairs of lights built since the early
18th century to warn sailors of this dangerous
promontory. A tower of 1869 is now used as a bird
observatory and field centre.

Portmeirion *Gwynedd*   550Ed
In 1925 the architect Sir Clough Williams-Ellis
began what has developed into a combination of
outdoor architectural museum and coastal holiday
village. His first idea was to present a 'live' exhibition of architecture and landscaping inspired by
Mediterranean fishing ports, and Portmeirion is
an integrated assembly of various buildings and
monuments dating from 1610 onwards—a barbican gate-house, campanile, lighthouse and
cloisters, for example. Sculpture, murals and
ironwork are displayed among landscaped gardens
—sub-tropical and other flowering plantations
occupying 65 acres of the Portmeirion peninsula. A splendid collection of rhododendrons can
be seen in the Gwyllt Gardens, with thousands of
hydrangeas, and among the many varieties of trees
are palms, cypresses, eucalyptus and magnolias,
and various ferns and lilies.

Portsmouth *Hants.*   541Hc
Docks, arsenal and storehouse appropriate for a
major naval base were established at Portsmouth
by Henry VIII; it remains the chief Royal Navy
seaport and, in the dockyard is Nelson's flagship
Victory and the Victory Museum. A survivor of the
Second World War air-raids is the house in Commercial Road where Charles Dickens was born in
1812, now a Dickens Museum.
CATHEDRAL This is the former parish church of St
Thomas of Canterbury, which became a cathedral
in 1927, and dates from the late 12th century; the

tower and other parts were rebuilt at the end of the 17th century. Further enlargements have been made since the 1930s.

DICKENS BIRTHPLACE MUSEUM The house in which Charles Dickens was born in 1812. It is now restored and furnished in the style of that period. One room is devoted to displays of material pertaining to Dickens and his work.

MARY ROSE EXHIBITION In an ancient boathouse in Portsmouth Dockyard are displayed thousands of articles recovered from the wreck of Henry VIII's proud warship, raised from the Solent in 1982. They illustrate every side of a 16th-century sailor's life, from carpentry and sailmaking tools to navigational equipment, weapons, surgeon's instruments, board games, and clothing. Near the exhibition is the Ship Hall, where the salvaged part of the *Mary Rose's* hull is on view.

ROUND TOWER This was constructed in 1418 to protect the entrance to Portsmouth Harbour. It is now the terminal point of a fine walk along the seaward side of the town's defences.

ROYAL NAVAL MUSEUM The museum, founded as the *Victory* Museum by the Society for Nautical Research as a complement to HMS *Victory* herself, stands opposite Nelson's famous flagship in the oldest part of Portsmouth Dockyard. It contains relics of Lord Nelson, of his officers and men and displays reflecting 18th-century naval life. There is also a superb collection of ship models and figureheads, and a 42 ft by 12 ft panorama of the Battle of Trafalgar by W. L. Wyllie.

SOUTHSEA CASTLE Henry VIII founded and built the castle in 1544 as one of his chain of coastal forts for protection against French raids. It is now a museum with a collection illustrating the naval and military history of Portsmouth. On show is the 272 ft long Overlord Tapestry, woven to commemorate the 1944 D-Day landings.

Port Sunlight *Merseyside* 551Jf
LADY LEVER ART GALLERY Founded by Lord Leverhulme and opened in 1922. Paintings, principally of the English School; water-colours and engravings; miniatures, antique Renaissance and British sculpture; Chinese pottery and porcelain; cloisonné enamel; carved stones and crystals, and Wedgwood wares. There is also one of the best collections of English furniture outside London.

Potter Heigham *Norfolk* 554Ec
CHURCH OF ST NICHOLAS This thatched church, with a 14th-century round tower with octagonal top, is mainly Perpendicular, but in the chancel is an indication of a Norman window. The rood beam still exists, and a screen features painted saints. There are 14th-century wall paintings.

Potterne *Wilts.* 540Ef
CHURCH OF ST MARY A cruciform church with a central tower, mainly of the 13th century; the later additions do not spoil the essentially Early English character. The high standard of the 13th-century work was probably due to the fact that the Bishops of Salisbury had a manor house at Potterne. There are two fonts, one Saxon with a Latin inscription, the other Perpendicular; and the wooden pulpit is also in the Perpendicular style. There is a monument by E. H. Baily, of 1821.
PORCH HOUSE A small, timbered house, dating from the 15th century.

Poulton-le-Fylde *Lancs.* 557Hb
CHURCH OF ST CHAD All but St Chad's late Perpendicular tower was rebuilt 1751–3. The galleried interior has wall monuments, heraldic panels, and the remains of the 17th-century Hesketh family pew. The chancel was added in 1868.

Powderham Castle *Devon* 539Hd
Built *c.* 1390, but much restored in the 18th and 19th centuries after damage in the Civil War. It contains some fine furniture, and portraits of the Courtenay family, Earls of Devon.

Powerstock *Dorset* 540Cc
CHURCH OF ST MARY The impressive 12th-century chancel arch, with four rows of ornament, remains from the original Norman church. The 15th-century south doorway is flanked by carved figures in canopied niches.

Powis Castle Gardens *Powys* 551Hb
The medieval castle overlooks the Severn Valley. At the end of the 17th century the long terraced gardens below were laid out in the Dutch formal manner, and remain much the same over 250 years later. On the terraces, stone balustrades and lead statuary and vases form the background to colourful trees and shrubs. Yew pyramids, planted when the terraces were laid, are clipped in fanciful topiary-work. The terraces and the sheltered ground below them provide sites for such plants as winter's bark (*Drimys*), Brazilian feijoa and Chilean flame plants (*Embothrium*). In the park are fine specimen trees. (See pp. 402 and 476.)

WEDGWOOD VASE

This lilac jasperware vase is by Josiah Wedgwood, the greatest of English potters, and has white reliefs, by John Flaxman, of Apollo and the nine Muses. Flaxman, a well-known sculptor, first worked with Wedgwood in 1775, and was later closely associated with the Wedgwood factory—an enterprise which is still in existence. (Lady Lever Art Gallery, Port Sunlight)

Presely Hills *Dyfed* 544Dd
From the Preseli Hills about 80 five-ton 'bluestones' were dragged and shipped the 240 miles to Stonehenge, where they were erected to form the inner horseshoe and middle ring enclosed by the circle of large sarsen stones. To the east of the 'quarry', on the summit of the eastern-most knoll of these hills, is the 11 acre Iron Age hill-fort known as Foel Drygarn.

Preston *Lancs.* 557Ja
HARRIS MUSEUM AND ART GALLERY Extensive collections embrace the fine and decorative arts, archaeology, ceramics and natural and social history. There are good 19th-century paintings.

Preston-on-Stour *Warks.* 546De
CHURCH The west tower, 15th century, is all that remains of the old church; the rest was rebuilt in 1752. There is a monument by Thomas Scheemakers, designed by 'Athenian' Stuart, and mid-18th-century stained glass.

HORATIO LORD NELSON, ENGLAND'S FAVOURITE ADMIRAL

NELSON *by Lemuel Francis Abbott.* (*National Maritime Museum, Greenwich*)

When England's most fêted and beloved admiral first joined the navy at the age of 12, his uncle wrote 'What has poor Horatio done, who is so weak, that he should be sent to rough it out at sea?' Two years later the boy was showing early signs of his unorthodox daring by clubbing polar bears with the butt-end of a musket, as shown in a picture at the National Maritime Museum, Greenwich.

Nelson first won fame as a Commodore in 1797. Acting without orders, he turned his ship out of the line of battle off Cape St Vincent, and with a cry of 'Westminster Abbey or glorious victory' he threw his ship across the bows of the enemy, preventing the premature union of two portions of the Spanish fleet. In June of the same year Nelson was struck during a 'land' engagement and had to have his right arm amputated. While waiting for the stump to heal he sat for the portrait here shown.

ORDERS OF CHIVALRY *which Nelson wore at every opportunity; replicas were stitched on all his uniforms.* (*National Maritime Museum*)

In 1798 he was given a fleet of ships commanded by officers who were to become known as 'The Band of Brothers', some of whose portraits can be seen in Greenwich. They annihilated the French fleet at the mouth of the Nile, leaving Napoleon, the conqueror of all Europe, bottled up in Egypt. The grateful underwriters of Lloyds presented Nelson with a silver dinner service, pieces of which remain at Greenwich, at the Portsmouth Royal Naval Museum and at the Nelson Room at Lloyds in the City of London.

NELSON'S GREAT CABIN on HMS *Victory as he left it on the morning of October 21, 1805 to go on deck for the last time. A chart of Trafalgar lies on the table, recalling the battle that broke* Napoleon's sea-power, saved England from invasion and cost Nelson his life. In the bitter contest, Victory and Royal Sovereign, leaders of the two British columns, suffered the greatest damage.

THE VICTORY, *Nelson's flagship at Trafalgar, carrying 850 men and 100 guns. The ship, on view to the public, is now in dry dock at Portsmouth, and is still used as the Commander-in-Chief's flagship.*

TWO LEFT HAND GLOVES, *and shield for his good eye. (National Maritime Museum, Greenwich)*

ADMIRAL POPHAM'S TELEGRAPHIC CODE, *used by Nelson at Trafalgar for his famous message to the fleet, 'England expects that every man will do his duty'. Nelson originally wished to put 'England confides', but there were no suitable flags. (National Maritime Museum, Greenwich)*

NELSON FIRST MET LADY HAMILTON when her husband, Sir William, was British Minister at Naples. She was beautiful—and notorious. Later, Nelson kept this pastel of her in his cabin in the Victory. He called it his 'guardian angel' and had it stowed in safety below decks before Trafalgar (National Maritime Museum, Greenwich). On the eve of the battle he wrote a last letter to Emma, which was found on his desk after his death. 'My dearest beloved Emma the dear friend of my bosom the signal has been made that the enemy's combined fleet are coming out of port . . .' (National Maritime Museum, Greenwich)

NELSON'S DEATH-BED on board the Victory, painted by Arthur William Devis. Nelson was hit by a sniper's bullet on the quarter-deck early in the action, but only died when victory was secured. His friend, Captain Hardy, standing above him, acceded to his last request to 'Kiss me, Hardy!' (National Maritime Museum, Greenwich)

NELSON'S COLUMN, towering 145 ft above Trafalgar Square, supports a statue of England's 'little Admiral' idealised and carved 17 ft high by E. H. Baily.

NELSON'S SARCOPHAGUS beneath the cupola in St Paul's Cathedral. It was originally made in the 16th century for Cardinal Wolsey by Benedetto da Rovezzano. After Nelson's death many monuments throughout England were erected in evidence of the deep affection and respect his memory inspired.

HORATIO VISC NELSON

POWIS CASTLE GARDENS

These are some of the few formal gardens surviving in Britain; they were passed by in the 18th-century vogue for natural landscaping. The long garden terraces, designed in the Dutch manner, were added to the ancient castle overlooking the Severn Valley about 1690, and were later decorated with lead statuary.

Prestonpans *Lothian* 562Cf
HAMILTON HOUSE Built in 1628, the house was restored in 1937. (By appointment.)

Prestwold Hall *Leics.* 552Ec
A Victorian house, notable for its painted marble interior and furniture. Its rose garden contains 2000 trees. (By appointment.)

Priddy Circles *Som.* 540Cf
A Bronze Age complex of four circles, each about 200 yds across. They are set in a straight line almost a mile long, the circle at the north end being divided from the next by a gap wider than the average. Henge monuments normally have the ditch within the bank but these, like Stonehenge, have the ditches on the outside. There are many fine round barrows close to the site of the circles, doubtless the burials of the people who used these sacred sites.

Princes Risborough *Bucks.* 547Gc
MANOR HOUSE A 17th-century red-brick mansion (near the church), noted for its Jacobean oak staircase and 18th-century wainscoting.

Prinknash Abbey *Glos.* 546Cd
The 14th- and 16th-century house was originally a residence of monks from Gloucester Abbey. It was a private home from 1539 to 1928, but then became a Benedictine priory.

Prior Park *Avon* 540Df
A Georgian mansion, now a boys' school. In the grounds are lakes and a Palladian-style bridge.

Probus *Cornwall* 538Cb
CHURCH OF ST PROBUS The impressive west tower here is the tallest in the county. Inside is a brass with figures, *c.* 1514, and a monument, a seated mourning woman of *c.* 1766.

Puddletown *Dorset* 540Dc
CHURCH OF ST MARY A pleasant church, chiefly of 15th-century work, with a good interior. The panelled nave roof is 15th century; the gallery, box-pews and canopied pulpit are of the 17th century. The Norman font is carved with interlaced decoration. In the south chapel are many monuments and brasses of the 15th and 16th centuries, and in the west window there is stained glass by Sir Ninian Comper.

Pumpsaint *Dyfed* 544Fe
ROMAN GOLD MINES About 8 miles south-east of Lampeter, on the hill-side on the east bank of the R. Cothi, are the remains of extensive Roman and later gold mines. At first open-cast trenches were used, up to 300 ft long and 50 ft deep, but later tunnels were dug to follow the seams. In 1935, when attempts were made to re-open the mine, a fragment of Roman water-wheel was recovered from an ancient level at a depth of 160 ft.

Purse Caundle Manor *Dorset* 540Dd
A charming 15th-century manor house with 16th-century additions. Of the five original medieval rooms, the finest are the Great Hall, with its minstrel's gallery and Tudor fireplace, and the Solar or Great Chamber which has a beautiful wagon roof. Several audible phantoms have been reported, among them the sound of chanted plainsong.

Purton *Wilts.* 546Db
CHURCH OF ST MARY An interesting church whose striking feature is that it has two towers: the central one with a spire, and the west with pinnacles. Inside, many details indicate the Norman origins of the building, which was altered during the 14th–15th centuries. There are mural paintings, including a 14th-century Death of the Virgin, and several fragments of medieval stained glass.

Pythouse *Wilts.* 540Ee
A Georgian mansion in the Palladian style.

Quainton *Bucks.* 547Gd
CHURCH OF THE HOLY CROSS AND ST MARY
A Decorated and Perpendicular church, rather
heavily restored *c.* 1877, in a pleasant setting between late 17th-century almshouses and a Georgian rectory. The importance of Quainton lies in
its 17th- and 18th-century monuments: there is
work by William Stanton (*c.* 1672), Thomas
Stayner (1689) and Giacomo Leoni (after 1735).
There are several fine brasses in the chancel.

The big monument to the Dormer family of
c. 1730 is a puzzle-work; unsigned, it has been
unconvincingly attributed to Louis Roubiliac (like
the monument at Gayhurst). It shows Mr Justice
Dormer and his wife grieving over the body of
their dead son. It stands in the base of the tower.

Quarley Hill *Hants.* 540Fe
An unfinished Iron Age hill-fort which reached
the final stages of fortification before it was
abandoned. It has a single bank-and-ditch defence,
as well as a small counterscarp bank. Excavation
made clear that, at the north-east entrance, work
had proceeded so far that the post-holes for the
timber gateway-structure had been dug, but never
equipped with uprights. There was also evidence
that these defences replaced a simple timber stockade of the Iron Age.

Quatt *Shropshire* 546Bg
CHURCH OF ST ANDREW The exterior is of 1763,
with a red-brick tower, but the interior is
medieval, of varying periods, and includes a
Norman font. Portions of the Perpendicular rood
screen remain. The pulpit and desk are dated 1629,
and among the 17th-century monuments to the
Wolryche family is one of 1614 with a baby lying
beside its mother.

Quebec House *Kent* 542Cf
General James Wolfe, who was killed while commanding the British force which took Quebec in
1759, spent much of his childhood here. The brick
house, dating from the early 16th century, was
largely rebuilt in the 17th century and contains
relics of the General.

Queensferry *Lothian* 562Bf
PLEWLANDS HOUSE A fine stone house, built in
1643 and restored in 1953. (Not open.)

Quenington *Glos.* 546Dc
CHURCH OF ST SWITHIN The two Norman doorways of this small church have elaborately carved
tympana. That on the south door depicts the
Coronation of the Virgin; on the north, probably
the Harrowing of Hell.

R

Raby Castle *Durham* 558Bf
A 14th-century fortress, with a great hall (136 ft
long) in which some 700 knights could be mus-
tered; at the western end is a minstrels' gallery in
stone. The castle was altered in 1765 and again in
the mid-19th century. It contains English, Dutch
and Flemish paintings, tapestries and porcelain.

Radbourne *Derbys.* 552Dc
CHURCH OF ST ANDREW This small church, with a
tower at the north-west, is mainly of the 13th and
14th centuries. The benches came from Dale
Abbey. As well as 15th-century monuments and
slabs, there is a large architectural monument, of
1684, by Grinling Gibbons.

Radcliffe *Greater Manchester* 552Bg
LOCAL HISTORY MUSEUM AND ART GALLERY
Temporary displays of items of local history are
on show, with frequently changing art exhibitions.

Raglan Castle *Gwent* 546Ac
The ownership of the land here can be traced back
to the 11th century, but the existing castle was built
mainly in the 15th century. Begun by Sir William
ap Thomas, who died in 1445, it was completed by
his son Sir William Herbert, created Earl of Pembroke in 1468. He was executed as a prominent
Yorkist supporter in the following year. Ultimately, the property passed to Charles Somerset,
created Earl of Worcester in 1514. The Somerset
family's tenure ended with the Civil War siege of
1646, during which the castle was severely
damaged and part of the keep deliberately
destroyed. Large parts of the 15th-century
building survive. This comprises a walled enclosure divided into two courts by a great hall set
across the middle. Each court has its own gateway,
and these entrances are each dominated from the
outside by the keep, which lies just clear of the
south wall of the main enclosure and is surrounded
by a moat.

Ragley Hall *Warks.* 546Df
A country mansion begun in 1680; a portico and
interiors designed by James Wyatt were added in
1780. The decorated great hall, by James Gibbs, has
moulded 18th-century plasterwork. There are
collections of paintings, china, furniture and
books. It is set in a 500 acre park with extensive
gardens and a lake; Capability Brown landscaped
the grounds *c.* 1750.

THE RED SALOON AT RAGLEY HALL

*Ragley Hall was designed by Robert Hooke in 1680,
but the house took many years to complete. James Gibbs
(1682–1754) and James Wyatt (1746–1813) were
both responsible for the decoration of some of the rooms.
The Red Saloon is by Wyatt. The walls of the Saloon
are papered in damask, and the ceiling was designed by
Angelica Kauffmann (1741–1804); over the fireplace
is Cornelius Schut's 'The Holy Family'.*

Rainham *Kent* *548Ab*
CHURCH OF SS HELEN AND GILES A late Norman church with nave, north and south aisles, chancel and west tower, dating from *c.* 1170. Some 13th- and 14th-century fragments of wall-paintings remain. (By appointment.)
RAINHAM HALL A small red-brick house built in Wren style by John Harle, a merchant, *c.* 1730. It has wrought-iron gates and panelling of the period. (By appointment.)

Rainsborough Camp *Northants.* *546Fe*
This oval fort of nearly 6 acres is surrounded by a bank, ditch and counterscarp bank. In the 5th century BC, the Iron Age inhabitants built a stone-faced rampart; shortly afterwards these defences were burnt and slighted, presumably by enemy tribesmen.

Ramsbury *Wilts.* *546Eb*
CHURCH OF THE HOLY CROSS A mainly Early English and Decorated church, with a massively buttressed tower built on Anglo-Saxon foundations. It contains fragments of 9th-century crosses and the ornate tomb, with reclining effigy, of Sir William Jones, Attorney-General to Charles II.

Ramsey *Cambs.* *547Jg*
ABBEY A Benedictine abbey founded here in 969 was dissolved in 1539. The eastern portion of the present building, now a school, dates from *c.* 1250. The other portions were added in 1804 and 1839. The south front can be seen from Abbey Road. The ruined gate-house, one of the most highly decorated specimens in England, is open to the public. Bodsey House, a mile and a half north, was moated; it has parts of a large 14th-century chapel and a superb 17th-century chimney-stack. (By appointment.)

CHURCH OF ST THOMAS BECKET A noble Norman church, a reminder of the abbey which was once here. There is a medieval oak lectern, and a fragment of mural painting.

Ranworth *Norfolk* *554Db*
CHURCH OF ST HELEN The church, which has a battlemented west tower and nave, and a two-storied north porch, possesses the county's finest screen, which is painted with saints and has its rood loft complete.

Ratcliffe-on-Soar *Notts.* *552Ec*
CHURCH OF THE HOLY TRINITY The 13th-century west tower has a 14th-century spire. There is a sequence of four 16th-century alabaster effigies of members of the Sacheverell family.

Ravensburgh Castle *Herts.* *547Hd*
This is perhaps the best of the Iron Age hill-forts in this area, strung along the edge of the chalk Downs, close to the prehistoric Icknield Way. Though to some extent tree-covered, the steep slopes of the hill-side and the defensive bank, ditch and counterscarp bank, together with intermittent additional works, are easily distinguishable.

Ravenstone *Bucks.* *547Ge*
CHURCH OF ALL SAINTS A generally Early English and Perpendicular church, which contains one of Buckinghamshire's three puzzling monuments (the other two are at Gayhurst and Quainton): a fine tomb to the 1st Earl of Nottingham (*d.* 1682), showing a black and white four-poster bed, on it the Earl reclining in white, on a black slab, all in marble. The mystery is the identity of the sculptor: it has been ascribed to Cibber, Catterns and William Stanton. The church also possesses some pleasing woodwork, including a fine pulpit.

Rawtenstall Museum See Rossendale.

CHURCH OF ST HELEN, RANWORTH

PAINTED PANEL OF ST PAUL *This, the finest surviving rood screen in Norfolk, carries the portraits of 26 saints. It was painted by artists who were working in the county in the 1470's, and spans the church with parclose screens enclosing the side altars.*

RANWORTH ANTIPHONER *This manuscript, illuminated by the monks of Langley in 1400, was lost for 300 years before being found in a private art collection. It is on view in the church from April to September: at other times it is kept in the Norwich Castle Museum.*

Reach *Cambs.* 548Af
A hamlet said to have once had seven churches. It
was a Roman port, and marks the Fen end of the
Devil's Dyke. The old vicarage is a charming
timber-framed and plastered house, probably *c.*
1500. Reach Lode is a waterway that was probably made by the Romans to connect with the
Cam at Upware, and thence to the sea.

Reading *Berks.* 547Gb
Reading lies at the extremities of the Berkshire
Downs and the Chiltern Hills, where, because of
the Kennet tributary, the Thames becomes a major
river; like many other key geographical towns, it
was a target for Danish raids (871 and 1006). With
the Normans it rose in importance. Henry I founded the Cluniac abbey in 1121, and was buried
there in 1136. Thomas Becket consecrated the
abbey church in the presence of Henry II. Hugh
Faringdon, the last abbot, was hanged before his
own gateway in 1539 and the abbey dissolved.
Henry VIII granted the first charter in 1542. Early
in the 17th century the cloth trade declined and
the Civil War further reduced the trade. By 1700,
the population had fallen to 7000. Prosperity
came with the opening of the Kennet and Avon
Canal in 1810, and the railway in 1840.
MUSEUM AND ART GALLERY Contains a comprehensive collection of Roman antiquities from
neighbouring Silchester. Items of natural history
and prehistoric and medieval metalwork are
displayed. There are also art exhibitions, which are
changed monthly.
MUSEUM OF ENGLISH RURAL LIFE Established in
1951 by Reading University as a centre of
information and research on all aspects of country
living, the museum contains farm implements,
tools and domestic equipment. Collections of particular interest include farm wagons, ploughs,
portraits of farm livestock, bee-keeping equipment (Bee Research Association Collection).
Records include manuscripts, photographs,
prints, drawings and a specialist library.
   A permanent exhibition is on view to the
public; the study collections and records are
available for reference on application to the
Keeper.
MUSEUM OF GREEK ARCHAEOLOGY The greater
part of the collection consists of Greek pottery,
though there is also a smaller collection of Egyptian antiquities. The museum is in Reading University. (By appointment.)

Reculver *Kent* 542Fg
Reculver (Regulbium) was the earliest Roman
fort of the series built to defend the Saxon Shore.
Though still complete at the beginning of the 18th
century, erosion by the sea has eaten steadily into
the northern part so that not more than about half
the curtain wall remains. Recent excavation has
shown that it was first occupied in the early years of
the 3rd century AD, and guarded the northern
entrance to the Wantsum Channel, now represented by the drained flats on the east side. In the
centre of the enclosure stands a remnant of an early
Saxon church.
CHURCH OF ST MARY Practically all that remains of
this church, founded perhaps in the 7th century, on
a Roman site, is the twin-towered west front.
These towers are now preserved as aids to navigation. The remainder was demolished by parishioners in 1808 for fear of the encroaching sea.

Redbourn *Herts.* 547Hd
CHURCH OF ST MARY The tower, nave and north
arcade are Norman, the chancel and south aisle

14th century, and the Lady chapel and clerestory
15th century. The church contains a 15th-century
rood screen and has unusual brick battlements.

Redgrave *Suffolk* 548Dg
CHURCH OF ST MARY A Decorated and Perpendicular church, with a font and 19th-century stained
glass in the east window. There are first-rate
monuments by Nicholas Stone, 1616, and Thomas
Green of Camberwell, *c.* 1710.

LORD CHIEF JUSTICE HOLT'S
MONUMENT
*Despite the growing 18th-century fashion for figures
dressed in Classical robes, Thomas Green of Camberwell carved this marble monument in the traditional
style. From 1689 until his death in 1709, Lord Justice
Holt was Lord Chief Justice of the King's Bench,
where he did much to discourage prosecutions for
witchcraft. (Church of St Mary, Redgrave)*

Reepham *Norfolk* 554Cc
CHURCHES OF ST MARY AND ST MICHAEL Of the
three churches with adjacent churchyards, two are
left; the third was burnt in 1543 and only part of
the tower survives. The parish church is St Mary's,
of the 13th-14th centuries. There is a square
Norman font, a brass of 1391 and the tomb of Sir
Roger de Kerdiston, who died *c.* 1337. His effigy
lies on cobbles, signifying the hard road the true
Christian must follow. Whitwell's parish church is
St Michael's, with its Perpendicular west tower
and fine Jacobean pulpit. The vestry is linked with
St Mary's Church.

Reigate *Surrey* 542Bf
CHURCH OF ST MARY MAGDALENE St Mary's has a
large monument by an almost unknown sculptor,
Joseph Rose the Elder. It dates from *c.* 1730, and
has a large architectural background, in front of
which reclines a man holding a celestial crown; on
either side of him are life-size figures of Truth and
Justice with their emblems.
   Housed above the vicar's vestry is the Cranston
Library which was founded in 1701 and was one
of the first lending libraries in the country. It can
be viewed on application to the vicar.

Rendcomb *Glos.* 546Dc
CHURCH OF ST PETER A late Perpendicular church, it was built at the beginning of the 16th century with a west tower. There are contemporary roofs and a 16th-century screen across the whole church; some glass in the Renaissance manner, and good 19th-century glass in the east window. The Norman font has carvings of 11 Apostles: the space for Judas was left blank.

Repton *Derbys.* 552Dc
CHURCH OF ST WYSTAN An interesting church, with a Saxon chancel and a remarkable Saxon crypt. The remainder of the church is mainly of the 13th and 14th centuries, with west tower and spire, a 15th-century clerestory and porch.
REPTON SCHOOL MUSEUM Housed in a 12th-century Augustinian priory, the museum illustrates the history of both Repton village and the school. (By appointment.)

Reynoldston *W. Glam.* 544Fc
ARTHUR'S STONE The peninsula of Gower, stretching several miles to the west of Swansea, has many fine monuments, of which this burial chamber is outstanding. It is in form a megalithic chamber of the Early Bronze Age, composed of uprights holding a capstone, and the mound has long since been lost. Its remarkable feature is the size of the capstone—a huge rock estimated to weigh no less than 25 tons.

Rhuddlan Castle *Clwyd* 551Ge
From here Edward I organised his administration of Wales, details of which were incorporated in the Statute of Rhuddlan (1284). Edward built the castle in 1277–82. It has concentric curtain walls, and twin gate-houses enclosing a square; a moat, fed by the sea, surrounded the building. In 1646, during the Civil War, the castle was besieged by Roundheads, and has been a ruin since 1648.

Ribbesford *Heref. & Worcs.* 546Bf
CHURCH OF ST LEONARD An interesting church with Norman remains, including a carved tympanum. The south piers of the nave are of wood; the glass in the west window was designed by Sir Edward Burne-Jones.

Ribchester *Lancs.* 557Jb
The Roman fort of Bremetennacum, on the north bank of the R. Ribble, where it guarded the crossing of the road from Ilkley to the Fylde with the main highway from Manchester to Carlisle. Parts of it were excavated last century and can be seen; in a small museum are finds relating to life in a garrison in a wild part of the country.
MUSEUM OF ROMAN ANTIQUITIES The majority of the items on display have been found in Roman Ribchester, and include Romano-British coarse-ware and Samian pottery, coins, altar stones, brooches, lamps and a tombstone; there is also a replica of a bronze parade helmet and a model of the Ribchester Roman fort. In the museum grounds there is an excavated granary.

ROMAN COINS

An aureus, most valuable coin of Gratian's reign (367–383 AD), found on the site of the Roman fort at Ribchester. (Museum of Roman Antiquities, Ribchester)

Richards Castle *Heref. & Worcs.* 546Af
CHURCH OF ST BARTHOLOMEW A church with a Norman nave, but also much later work. The detached bell-tower was added *c.* 1300. Some medieval stained glass remains, and 17th-century box-pews.

Richards Castle *Shropshire* 546Af
CHURCH OF ALL SAINTS A late Victorian church of 1891–2, by R. Norman Shaw, the architect who designed New Scotland Yard. It stands on a hill, and a notable feature is the massive tower at the south-west. Shaw drew inspiration from a variety of Gothic periods for the style of the windows and other features.

THE ROMAN FORT OF RUTUPIAE
AT RICHBOROUGH

One of the most remarkable monuments of the Roman occupation of Britain, the fort at Richborough was built at the end of the 3rd century. It was at the end of Watling Street—the road to London and North Wales—and also guarded the Wantsum Channel which separated the Isle of Thanet from the mainland. Richborough was a port and landing place of the Roman legions. Part of the north wall of the castellum remains and this is 460 ft long and 22 ft high. There is also a cruciform platform, 144 ft by 104 ft, which may once have been the base for a lighthouse. A series of defensive ditches surrounding the fortifications came to light during excavations carried out in 1926.

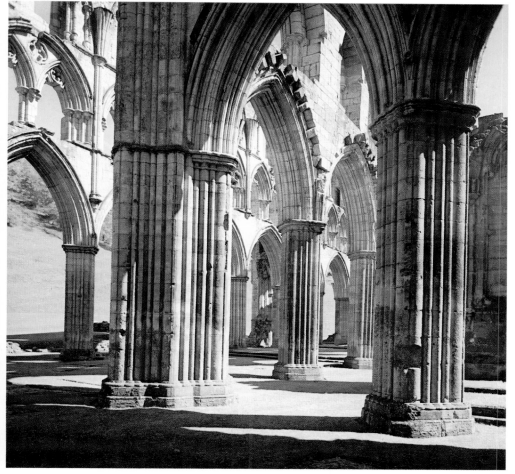

RIEVAULX ABBEY

Rievaulx Abbey's position, enclosed among the Yorkshire hills, is one of its most memorable features. Another is the austerity, for which the Cistercians were famous, of its early architecture. This can still be seen in the nave and transepts of the great church, the earliest large Cistercian church building in England.

But the chief glory of the abbey is now the choir of the church, part of substantial enlargements to the 12th-century building which were carried out in the 13th century. The choir, an unusually fine example of the architecture of northern England, was built in the period 1225 to 1230.

RIPON CATHEDRAL

An outstanding exception to the rule that cathedrals dating back to Saxon times have hardly a vestige of the original building apart from the foundations. Ripon's crypt is said to have been built about 672 for St Wilfrid, Bishop of York. The Gothic nave of master-builder Christopher Scune, built in 1502–22, is in subtle harmony with the sedate west front in the Early English style. The towers originally had spires, but the last of these was removed in 1664, some years after the central spire had fallen.

Richborough *Kent* 543Gf

Here stands Rutupiae, the key Roman fort of the Saxon shore defences. Built probably in the last decade of the 3rd century, at what is believed to have been the Romans' landing place in AD 43, it is of the developed 'late' type, with square angles and elaborate external bastions. In its later days it was garrisoned by a detachment of the 2nd Legion, who had been brought from Caerleon in South Wales. Rutupiae guarded the south-east entrance to the Wantsum channel and all the many port activities spread out along the shores of that channel.

In the museum is a collection of Roman pottery which is generally acknowledged to be one of the best found on any site; over 50,000 coins were also found here, some of which are displayed. Also on view are bronze ornaments, weapons, lamps and amphorae. (See p. 406.)

Richmond upon Thames 547Jb
Greater London
Richmond Green is a spacious turfed square, like Kew, but without the church and without through traffic. Maids of Honour Row, on the south-west side, was built *c.* 1724, and the Princess of Wales's maids of honour lived there.

Richmond *N. Yorks.* 558Ce
Dominated by the hill-top ruins of an 11th-century castle, the town has alleyways known as 'wynds', one of the largest market squares in Britain and a theatre dating from 1788.
CASTLE This castle was probably built in the years following 1071 and was held for most of the Middle Ages either by the Crown or by the holder of the Honor of Richmond. It commands a fine natural site overlooking the valley of the R. Swale. Richmond is one of the few surviving castles with 11th-century walls. (Most of the existing military structures date from the 12th century.) It was built as a large enclosure bounded by stone walls. In the south corner are the remains of the original hall, the centre of the domestic apartments—a rare survival. The castle was originally entered from the town through a gate-tower, but in the second half of the 12th century this was walled up and the tower used as a base for the 100 ft stone keep.
GEORGIAN THEATRE A small theatre, built by Samuel Butler in 1788. There were no stage presentations from 1848 until 1943, when a production was staged as part of the 850th anniversary of the Borough of Richmond. In 1960–3 the theatre was restored and re-opened.
GREEN HOWARDS MUSEUM The history of the Regiment from 1688 is illustrated by uniforms, medals, silver and trophies, campaign relics, documents, and contemporary pictures and prints.

Rievaulx *N. Yorks.* 558Dd
RIEVAULX TERRACE Adjoining the ruins of the 12th-century Rievaulx Abbey, the terrace is half a mile long and a vantage point for panoramic views. There are two 18th-century temples.

Rievaulx Abbey *N. Yorks.* 558Dd
Rievaulx was founded in 1131. Its monks belonged to the Cistercian order, and the founding mission came from Clairvaux in France, one of the foremost Cistercian abbeys, ruled by St Bernard. Within a few years it established its own colony. The main buildings were completed in the 12th century and in the 13th century substantial enlargements were made; in the latter part of the 12th century there were said to be 140 monks and over 500 lay-brothers. But by the Dissolution (1539) there were only 22 monks and the lay-brothers had probably vanished during the 14th century. Rievaulx is enclosed among the Yorkshire hills. The early architecture has all the austerity for which the Cistercians were famous, and this may still be seen in the nave and transepts of the great church, the earliest large Cistercian church building in England. (See p. 407.)

Ripley Castle *N. Yorks.* 558Cc
Both James I and Oliver Cromwell stayed in this crenellated house, the home of the Ingilby family since 1350. There is a 15th-century gate-house and a 16th-century tower. In 1780 alterations were made, in the Gothic and Classical styles. The house contains fine furniture, panelling and ceilings, paintings, armour and a secret hiding place. There is a walled garden in the grounds.

Ripon *N. Yorks.* 558Cc
CATHEDRAL The present Diocese of Ripon was only founded in 1836. In spite of such modernity, the cathedral building contains parts which place it amongst the oldest Christian buildings in the British Isles. A monastery was refounded on this site by the great Bishop Wilfrid of York in 669. From this foundation one small fragment remains—a crypt beneath the central tower of the present church. This formed a relic chamber which probably stood under the high altar of Wilfrid's church. It has a superb Early English west front and is one of those few survivals which take one straight back to the earliest days of Christianity in northern England, and provides a physical link with one of the most resounding personalities in the early history of the northern Church.

Among other interesting features in the cathedral are the 15th-century choir stalls, with their magnificent canopies, bench-ends and misericords, and the carvings of beasts and biblical scenes.
WAKEMAN'S HOUSE A 14th-century building housing the museum of local history.

Rivenhall *Essex* 548Cd
CHURCH OF ST MARY AND ALL SAINTS This stands on the site of a Roman villa and has some of the best 12th-century glass in the country. which was brought from France in 1839. In 1972 two Saxon windows dated 980 were discovered in the church.

Roche *Cornwall* 538Dc
CHURCH OF ST GONANDUS In spite of rebuilding in the 19th century, this church still possesses evidence of its Norman origins, such as a fine Transitional Norman font with a circular bowl ornamented with foliage and entwined snakes, and having at each corner a shaft topped by an angel's head (as does the font at Bodmin). Near by are the ruins of a 15th-century hermit's chapel.

Roche Abbey *S. Yorks.* 552Ef
Ruins of a Cistercian abbey founded in 1147, beautifully sited in a valley of the R. Ryton. The Gothic transepts are the chief remains of the abbey church.

Rochester *Kent* 542Dg
Since before Roman times there has been a settlement here, at the ford across the R. Medway. The walled Roman town grew up beside the bridge which carried Watling Street (the Dover Road) across the river; much of the Roman wall foundations survive within the present city. The town grew in importance when it was made a bishopric by St Augustine in 604, and the present cathedral was begun in 1077 on the site of his church. Rochester, like adjoining Chatham, is closely associated with the life and works of Charles Dickens, who made his home at Gad's Hill on the north-west outskirts of the city. There Dickens wrote *Our Mutual Friend* and *Edwin Drood*.

The Norman castle dominates the town, cathedral and R. Medway, with a keep that is one of the finest and best preserved in England. It was begun *c.* 1120. In the High Street are the guildhall and Corn Exchange, both gifts to Rochester from Sir Cloudesley Shovel in 1687 and 1706; there is

splendid brickwork and plasterwork in the Guildhall, and a colossal clock on the Corn Exchange overhanging the street; south of the cathedral stands Minor Canon Row, a terrace built in 1736, less pretentious than Shovel's buildings, and to the east of The Vines Inn is Restoration House, an interesting Elizabethan house, refaced in the 17th century with all sorts of decoration in cut brickwork.

CASTLE Set on a high chalk cliff above the river, the castle was mentioned in the Domesday Survey (1086). It was besieged by Simon de Montfort but after 1610 the castle was dismantled and now only the keep and curtain walls remain. The massive square keep, internally arcaded, is the tallest in England, standing 120 ft high and 70 ft square; Archbishop de Corbeuil completed it in 1126.

CATHEDRAL Founded by King Ethelbert of Kent in 604 and rebuilt in the 11th–12th centuries, largely by Bishop Gundulf who established an order of Benedictine monks here. Of Perpendicular design, the cathedral is one-third Norman, and two-thirds Early English.

KING'S SCHOOL A fine Tudor building dating from the reign of Henry VIII.

RESTORATION HOUSE Built in 1587, the house was given its name when Charles II stayed here on May 28, 1660, on his way to London to take possession of his throne.

Rockbourne *Hants.* 540Fd
One of the best villages in a remote and completely rural part of Hampshire. There is a pretty street and, by the church, a rambling manor house, its earliest part dating from the 13th century.

Rockingham *Northants.* 547Gg
CHURCH OF ST LEONARD Restored during the 19th century, the church contains monuments dating from the 16th to the 19th century. There is a large work commemorating the 1st Earl of Rockingham (*d.* 1724) by Peter Scheemakers and his collaborator, Laurent Delvaux, a fine 1669 font and a Jacobean pulpit.

MONUMENT TO LORD HENNIKER

This marble monument to the 1st Lord Henniker, who died in 1806, was carved by John Bacon the Younger *(1777–1859), son of the famous sculptor John Bacon. (Rochester Cathedral)*

CHARLES DICKENS, THE LITERARY
LION OF THE VICTORIAN ERA

'When I go back to the slow agony of my youth, I wonder how much of the histories I invented hangs like a mist of fancy over well-remembered facts', wrote Charles Dickens, whose birthplace in Commercial Road, Portsmouth, is preserved as a small museum. His father (the prototype for Mr Micawber) was imprisoned for debt and Charles was taken from school and put to work in a blacking factory. He taught himself shorthand, became a reporter to the House of Commons, and when his first comic sketch was published in *The Monthly Magazine,* wept with joy and pride. Dickens was 24 when the astonishing success of his monthly instalments of *The Posthumous Papers of the Pickwick Club* started him on a literary career. The essential humanity of his characters made his novels classics.

DICKENS'S DREAM *Part of an unfinished picture by R. W. Buss, it includes some of the many characters he created from seemingly futile and dull personalities, warming them with his genius into giants of wisdom and delight. (Dickens House)*

THE PICKWICK PAPERS *appeared in 19 monthly parts in 1836–7 ; it was paper-backed and sold at a shilling. The binders' order of 400 copies for the first issue rose to 40,000 for the 15th issue. This edition bound from the original parts. (Dickens House, 48 Doughty Street, London)*

THE GEORGE AND VULTURE, *a well-preserved inn in Lombard Street in the City where Dickens had Mr Pickwick stay. It was this middle-aged, bespectacled innocent whom Dickens, as a young reporter under the pseudonym of Boz, was employed to write about in a monthly magazine 'The Posthumous Papers of the Pickwick Club'. In a few issues he had perceived in this old man a romantic adventurer who would 'dance and jump, defy tyrants, experiment with life, even act the knight errant'. The British public recognised Pickwick with delight and Dickens rose from obscurity to immense fame and popularity in one year.*

NANCY'S STEPS, *now in the US with the remainder of London Bridge, was where the 'good bad' girl of 'Oliver Twist' kept the rendezvous which led to her murder. During the murder scene which Dickens re-enacted so powerfully in his famous public readings, numbers of ladies regularly fainted and had to be carried from the hall.*

AVES AT COOLING *in Kent which*
, in 'Great Expectations', says
nged to his family. This marshland
1 has strong connections with
kens, and features frequently in his
ks. Here Pip first met the convict
gwitch, who had escaped from the
ilks'—the nearby prison ships.

THE FORGE AND COTTAGE *at Chalk in Kent, which were used by Dickens in 'Great Expectations' as the home of Pip, when the boy lived with blacksmith Joe Gargery and his wife. When writing this novel in 1860, Dickens was plagued with none of his usual doubts and misgivings.*

STUDY OF FORT HOUSE *in Broadstairs which Dickens rented in 1850. The study is on the first floor, 'about the size of a warm bath', and possessing a large window commanding a magnificent sea view. At this house he spent holidays with his wife and ten children until his marriage fell apart in 1858. The novelist's hysterical letters giving details of his matrimonial problems, which he insisted on having published in the daily press, shocked an adoring public, who regarded him as a pillar of security and Victorian morality. The house was nicknamed 'Bleak House' by Charles Dickens, and this inspired the title for the novel which was planned in the house. 'David Copperfield' was actually written in the study. Relics and manuscripts by Dickens are on view.*

DICKENS'S WATCH, *a relic at the Rochester Museum. The novelist's headlong race against time ended with his premature death from overwork at the age of 58. He had asked to be buried privately and therefore the time of his funeral at Westminster Abbey was kept a close secret and only 13 people attended. It was not so much the furious pace of his writing that killed Dickens as the strain of giving a series of dramatic public readings from his works.*

JILL PEN AND INKSTAND *at ckens House, Bloomsbury, where author wrote 'Oliver Twist'.*

ISS CHALET *Dickens had five large rrors hung on the walls of the upper m, where he did much of his later iting. The chalet was given to him the actor Charles Fechter and uilt, plank by plank, among the ar trees in the garden of Gad's Hill ice. (Rochester Museum, Kent)*

Rockingham Castle *Northants.* *547Gg*
Built for William the Conqueror, the castle was used as a royal fortress until Queen Elizabeth I granted it to Edward Watson, whose descendants have lived here ever since. Here in 1095 William II (Rufus) was excommunicated by Archbishop Anselm. Charles Dickens was a frequent visitor. The present house and gardens are mainly Elizabethan, but the Norman gateway with crenellated round towers survives. The house contains fine furniture and a collection of paintings.

Roker *Tyne & Wear* *558Dg*
CHURCH OF ST ANDREW A massive church designed by E. S. Prior, built in 1906–7 with a solid-looking Gothic-inspired tower above the chancel. St Andrew's has Arts and Crafts Movement fittings: Morris & Co. wove the carpets, altar frontals and Burne-Jones tapestry behind the altar; the altar cross and lectern are by Ernest Gimson; and there are tablets by Eric Gill.

Rolleston *Staffs.* *552Dc*
CHURCH OF ST MARY The church is of mainly 14th-century work, and contains several fine monuments with effigies of the 16th and 17th centuries.

Rollright Stones *Oxon.* *546Ed*
A circle of some 100 ft diameter is demarcated by 11 standing stones and, close by, there is a single standing stone, the King Stone, which probably had its place in the Bronze Age design.

A little to the east is the stone group known as the Whispering Knights. These form a rectangular chamber with a capstone and are the remnants of the megalithic structures formerly covered by a long barrow, all other traces of which have disappeared. This is of the Neolithic period.

Romaldkirk *Durham* *558Bf*
CHURCH OF ST ROMALD Late 12th-century church with 13th- to 15th-century additions; the low tower is Perpendicular, with a vaulted roof inside. An effigy of a knight, 1304, remains, and there is a Norman font and an 18th-century pulpit.

Romsey *Hants.* *541Gd*
An ancient market town north of the New Forest. Near the abbey is King John's House, a hunting lodge built *c.* 1230; it has fine Norman dog-tooth carving.
ABBEY CHURCH OF SS MARY AND ETHELFLEDA The nunnery was founded in 907. The present cruciform church dates from later in the 10th century; it was enlarged by the Normans, and again during the 13th century. Among its treasures is a Saxon sculpture depicting the Crucifixion, and on an outside wall of the south transept is another Saxon carving of Christ Crucified. Among the monuments is an effigy of a 13th-century woman, and there is an early 16th-century painted reredos. The body of Earl Mountbatten of Burma was interred in the south transept in September 1979.

Roslin *Lothian* *562Ce*
ROSSLYN CASTLE The 3rd Earl of Orkney built this castle, now in ruins, during the 14th century, and here the Scots defeated Edward I of England in his war with King Robert de Bruce.
ROSSLYN CHAPEL The 15th-century chapel of a proposed collegiate church founded by William, Earl of Rosslyn and Orkney. It is noted for its superabundance of ornament, and the famous 'Prentice Pillar. This is purported to have been finished by an apprentice during his master's absence. The latter on his return was so enraged by this youthful skill that he hit the boy with a mallet and killed him.

Rossendale *Lancs.* *552Bg*
ROSSENDALE MUSEUM Situated in the former mansion of a Victorian mill-owner, the museum displays collections of natural history, ceramics and paintings. There is also a comprehensive collection of items of local history, including the craft of clog-making, and musical scores and instruments of the little-known music group who were called the 'Deighn Layrocks' (the Larks of Dean), and flourished from the middle of the 18th century.

Ross-on-Wye *Heref. & Worcs.* *546Bd*
Though its origins are Roman, modern Ross owes much to John Kyrle, known as the Man of Ross, born in 1637 and a natural town developer. He laid out the Prospect Gardens, raised a causeway to Wilton Bridge, created the first public water supply, and reconstructed the topmost 47 ft of the unsafe church spire. The Market House was built *c.* 1670, a red sandstone structure, on arches. The Blake Memorial Gardens were laid down by Thomas Blake, first M.P. for the Forest of Dean. The almshouses in Church Street are more than 300 years old.
CHURCH OF ST MARY THE VIRGIN Large church dating from the 12th century, with 13th- and 14th-century and later additions. There are many monuments dating from the 16th century, with recumbent, kneeling or standing effigies; one of the latter shows a 17th-century soldier, Colonel Rudhall, in Roman armour.

Rotherfield *E. Sussex* *542Ce*
CHURCH OF ST DENYS A large 13th-century church, with later additions and a west tower and shingled spire. The north porch of St Denys's has two storeys, vaulted inside, and the nave has a wagon-roof. The 13th-century wall-paintings include a Doom, and St Michael weighing souls; there are remains of Perpendicular screens. The font cover is dated 1533 and the pulpit is from the 17th century. In the east window is fine stained glass by William Morris and Sir Edward Burne-Jones.

Rotherfield Greys *Oxon.* *547Gb*
CHURCH This dates from *c.* 1100. The original entrance was on the north wall, and the Norman archway can be seen from outside. The church was enlarged *c.* 1260, when Greys Court was built by Walter de Grey, Archbishop of York. Restoration took place, and the nave was lengthened, in the 19th century. The church contains the magnificent canopied monument to Francis Knollys and his wife, erected by their son William in 1605. William's children kneel around the base; he is on the canopy with his second wife.

Rotherham *S. Yorks.* *552Ef*
CHURCH OF ALL SAINTS One of Yorkshire's grand parish churches, in an industrial town. The grimy exterior is in the Perpendicular style, with a central tower and tall spire. The interior, also mainly Perpendicular, has fan-vaulting under the tower, panelled nave and chancel ceilings, a south chapel screen, and tracery on stalls and bench ends. There is a 17th-century pulpit, and a monument of 1806 by John Flaxman. The church was restored in 1873–5 by Sir Gilbert Scott, who also designed some of the stained glass.
MUNICIPAL MUSEUM AND ART GALLERY The museum is housed in a small mansion built *c.* 1780, probably by John Carr of York for the Walker family (who founded the Rotherham iron trade), and which has been partly restored to 18th-century decorative style. The largest publicly-owned collection in Britain of Rockingham china can be

THE 'PRENTICE PILLAR, ROSSLYN CHAPEL

According to legend, the apprentice who carved this pillar was killed by his jealous master. The chapel was founded in 1446 by Sir William St Clair, dissolved in 1511, and left in disrepair until restored in 1842.

seen here, including one of the two famous 'Rhinoceros' vases. There are other examples of South Yorkshire pottery, collections of gemstones and English glass, Roman antiquities from the forts at Templeborough, a period kitchen and displays of church silver and natural history.

Rothesay *Island of Bute, Strathclyde* 560Fe
ROTHESAY CASTLE The ruins of a 13th-century moated castle of the royal Stewarts. The castle is still a royal possession and the Scottish Dukedom of Rothesay is held by the eldest son of the monarch. Four round towers are linked by a curtain wall enclosing a circular courtyard and keep—such a plan, with a keep surrounded by an outer shell, is rare in Scotland. The gate-house and apartments were added by James IV and James V (of Scotland).

Rothwell *Lincs.* 553Hf
CHURCH OF ST MARY MAGDALENE A church interesting for its Saxon west tower and the Norman work inside—nave arcades with sturdy round columns and arches with zigzag ornament.

Roughtinglinn *Northld.* 562Fd
A small promontory fort, cut off from the main hill by ramparts. The internal fortified area, less than 2 acres, is probably of the Iron Age. To the east of the fort is a rock-face with a remarkable display of cup-and-ring markings of the Bronze Age.

Rough Tor *Cornwall* 538Dd
On Bodmin Moor are many different types of structure believed to belong to the second half of the Bronze Age, though none has been closely dated by excavation. Within a radius of about a mile of Rough Tor are two stone circles, a ruined stone fort and groups of enclosed fields with remains of their owners' circular huts.

The circles, Fernacre and Stannon, are about 150 ft and 140 ft in diameter and are remarkable for having been constructed of many irregular stones, instead of the usual matched ones. Each still has 70–80 stones, of which more than half are standing. The ruined 'fort' or defensive site is on the higher part of the Tor.

Rousham *Oxon.*   *546Fd*
CHURCH OF SS LEONARD AND JAMES Standing by
the manor house, an Early English and later Gothic
church with a west tower. The lower part of the
chancel arch is Norman, and the rest has been
modified in a Gothic style; there is a 15th-century
parclose screen, and the monuments include one
with 16th-century figures facing each other in
prayer.

Rousham House *Oxon.*   *546Fd*
A Royalist garrison used this mansion during the
Civil War and shooting holes then made in the
doors are preserved. The castellated house was
built in 1635; it was enlarged *c.* 1730 when William
Kent decorated the rooms and laid out the gardens—his only surviving landscape design—with
temples, statues and hanging woods above the
Cherwell.

Rowlstone *Heref. & Worcs.*   *546Ad*
CHURCH OF ST PETER A 12th-century church with
later additions. There is an early Norman nave,
and the chancel arch and south doorway have
good Romanesque carvings of birds and foliage.
Two figures on the stones adjoining the capitals
of the chancel arch are upside down.

Royal Holloway College *Surrey*   *542Ag*
This gigantic building, in the style of a French
château, was made of stone and brilliant red brick,
as one of the first women's colleges, in 1879–87.
The founder's collection of pictures, mainly of the
early 19th century, is housed in the picture gallery.
(Open by appointment; and on advertised dates.)

Royal Leamington Spa *Warks.*   *546Ef*
The medicinal value of the spring water here was
discovered in the late 18th century and the town
grew rapidly. Many fine Regency houses like
those at Bath were built and in 1814 the Royal
Pump Room was opened. Queen Victoria granted
the Royal prefix to the town name in 1838.
ART GALLERY AND MUSEUM The oil paintings,
water-colours and drawings are mostly 20th
century, though there are earlier works by
Abraham Bloemart, Richard Wilson and Peter de
Wint. Among the modern painters represented are
Stanley Spencer, L. S. Lowry and Graham
Sutherland. The collection of ceramics includes
examples of medieval, Tudor, Delft, Wedgwood,
Worcester, Liverpool and Derby ware, and there is
a large collection of 18th-century drinking glasses.

Royal Tunbridge Wells *Kent*   *542Ce*
The wells near Tonbridge became known in the
early 17th century as a health-giving spa, through
the accidental discovery of its waters by Lord
North while staying at nearby Eridge Castle. The
place soon became fashionable, but at first there
were so few buildings that when Henrietta Maria,
Charles I's wife, went there, she was obliged to
camp in the countryside. However, the Pantiles,
the famous parade of galleried buildings with the
spring at one end, was begun, and after the Restoration of Charles II there were further developments; Evelyn the diarist thought it a 'sweet place'.
A church was begun in 1676 and soon enlarged.
Inside it has a gallery and a splendidly rich plaster
ceiling. The church is dedicated to the king's
father, 'King Charles the Martyr'. A story is told
that the first child baptised in its fashionable font
was that of a gipsy-woman passing through the
town. During the 18th century Tunbridge Wells
flourished and was visited by such personalities as
Dr Johnson, David Garrick, and Beau Nash.
About 1830 Calverley Park, a series of terraced
villas overlooking a private park, was built by

RUFFORD OLD HALL

*Rufford Old Hall was built of wood in early Tudor
times and added to between 1491 and 1523 by the
owner, Thomas Hesketh. The 43 ft by 23 ft interior
is richly carved. 'Speres'—short screens designed to cut
down draughts—stand at the serving end of the hall
and there is a movable screen which was used to shield
diners on the dais. This, one of the few such screens to
survive intact, dates from about 1500. It is covered
with intricate Gothic carving, including three
extraordinarily elaborate finials.*

Decimus Burton—a version of the idea John Nash
had put into effect at Regent's Park in London.
MUSEUM AND ART GALLERY Items illustrating life
in the town and surrounding district are displayed;
there are collections of Tunbridge ware, dolls,
18th- and 19th-century toys, costumes and old
prints. A group of Victorian paintings is included.
Other sections relate to local geology, prehistory
and natural history.

Ruabon *Clwyd*   *551Jd*
CHURCH OF ST MARY THE VIRGIN The many
monuments in this church include work by
Joseph Nollekens, a large reclining figure by J. M.
Rysbrack and, from the beginning of the 18th
century, three life-size figures, one standing and
two kneeling, by Robert Wynne of Ruthin.

Rubers Law *Borders*   *562Dc*
The forts here show evidence of two periods of
construction. In the Iron Age they enclosed a considerable area with a wall lying well below the
hill-top. Later, this was superseded by a smaller
work, a wall enclosing only the top of the hill. It
has been pointed out that some of the stones used
in this later work show traces of being re-used in
the post-Roman Dark Age.

Rudding Park Gardens *N. Yorks.*   *558Cb*
Gardens within a woodland park originally
designed by Humphrey Repton with displays of
rhododendrons and azaleas in spring. Views of the
Regency house designed by Wyatt.

Rudh'an Dunain *Skye, Highland*   *564Ee*
This Neolithic cairn is 65 ft in diameter and 11 ft
high. The eastern side has a concave forecourt,
from which the entrance leads into an ante-
chamber and a polygonal chamber. A short

distance to the south-east stands an Iron Age galleried dun. It consists of a thick wall cutting off the tip of a headland and still stands some 9 ft high. The wall contains galleries.

Rufford *Lancs.* 551Jg
CHURCH OF ST MARY A small Victorian church, built in Gothic style in 1869 to replace an earlier building. There are many monuments to the Hesketh family, including one of *c.* 1458 showing 11 children; other monuments include one by John Flaxman (1817) and one with an effigy by Matthew Noble, *c.* 1874.
RUFFORD OLD HALL AND FOLK MUSEUM Presented to the National Trust in 1936 by the late Lord Hesketh, the Old Hall is a medieval timber-framed manor house with plaster panels, and an ornate hammerbeam roof and screen. The great hall itself was built *c.* 1480, and the east wing in 1662—a good example of late Jacobean brick architecture. The folk museum in one wing of the house was begun in 1936 and consists of ancient agricultural implements, domestic appliances and items of craftsmanship from south-west Lancashire. Domestic life during the Industrial Revolution is depicted, and period costumes and Victoriana are on show. The Hall contains 17th-century oak furniture, court and press cupboards, the Hesketh Collection of 16th-century arms and armour, and Brussels and Mortlake tapestries.

Some Neolithic tools and Roman remains can be seen, and a display of antique porcelain, Staffordshire figures and china. There is also a doll museum and dolls, a Georgian dolls' house, a collection of children's games, and another related to the Duke of Lancaster's Own Yeomanry.

Rufus Stone *Hants.* 541Gd
A stone monument, erected in 1745 by Lord de la Warr, marks the probable spot where William II—called Rufus because of his ruddy complexion—was killed by an arrow in 1100. Rufus, 3rd son of William the Conqueror, became King of England in 1087; the English Chronicle records that he was 'loathsome to well nigh all his people'. The fatal arrow may have been shot by the Norman knight Sir Walter Tyrrell. Rufus was hastily buried at Winchester without any ceremony.

Rûg Chapel *Gwynedd* 551Hd
A private chapel, built in 1637 by William Salisbury, an eccentric who, after a spell at sea to learn the 'arte of pyracy', reformed and was known as 'Hosannau Gleision' ('Blue-stockings'). The building was known as 'Envy Chapel', supposedly because of a conflict between the builder and the rector of Corwen. Salisbury was a descendant of an earlier William who first translated the New Testament into Welsh in 1567. A certain amount of repainting took place in the 18th century, but the roof, the carved painted frieze and much of the furnishing are interesting.

Rumblingbridge *Central* 562Ag
The modern bridge spans a 120 ft chasm. Beneath it is an earlier bridge, which was built in 1713.

Rushton Hall *Northants.* 547Gg
John Tresham began the Hall *c.* 1500; extensive additions were made in 1590–1600 by Sir Thomas Tresham, who began Lyveden New Building. After the Gunpowder Plot the house passed out of the Tresham family. It is now a school for the blind. (Grounds only, during August.)

Ruthin *Clwyd* 551Hd
A market town whose steep streets witnessed Owain Glendwr's first blow for Welsh freedom in 1400; however, he failed to take the castle.

CHURCH OF ST PETER Basically a 14th-century church; parts of the building were demolished after the Dissolution, and restoration was carried out during the 18th and 19th centuries. The aisle roofs, which have carved bosses, are original 15th-century work; there are brasses and monuments, including one by Sir Richard Westmacott.
LORDSHIP COURT-HOUSE A half-timbered house built in 1401. At one time gallows were part of the house, as is shown by a gibbet which projects from the façade.
NANTCLWYD HOUSE A 14th-century mansion on Castle Street, the house has a half-timbered front and a gabled portico. (Exterior only.)

RUTHWELL CROSS

A detail depicting Mary Magdalene washing Christ's feet, this is probably the earliest and certainly the finest Northumbrian high cross. The reverse side shows Christ being worshipped by the beasts. The cross dates from the late 7th century and shows eastern Mediterranean influence. Two of its original four arms are missing.

Ruthwell *Dumfs. & Gall.* 562Ba
CHURCH In an apse specially built for it in the church stands a Saxon cross, 18 ft high. It is one of the two best preserved Runic crosses that survive from the Anglo-Saxon period—the other is at Bewcastle in Cumbria.

Rycote *Oxon.* 546Fc
CHAPEL OF ST MICHAEL Founded as a chantry by a 15th-century Lord of the Manor. The west tower is unaltered, and there is a two-decker Norreys' family pew and a pew believed to have been erected for Charles I in 1625.

Rye *E. Sussex* 542Ed

The name comes from the Anglo-Saxon word for an island, for the town stands on high ground well above the once submerged surrounding flat country. In Norman times Rye was a port and was added to the Cinque Ports in 1336. It was razed by the French in 1377 and 1448, and silting of the harbour caused poverty in the town in the 13th and 14th centuries. With the decline of nearby Winchelsea, Rye revived in the 15th and 16th centuries, but from the late 16th century further silting of the harbour led to a decrease in importance; today Rye itself is no longer a port—the harbour at the mouth of the Rother is nearly 2 miles away. Rye was notorious for smuggling, which centred on the 15th-century Mermaid Inn. Baddings Tower, a defence post, was sold in 1430 to John de Ypres to raise money, and has since been known as Ypres Tower, now a local museum. The Gun Garden near by was originally the site of a defence battery but was converted to a bowling green in 1649. Lamb House, built in 1722–4, was once the home of the author Henry James. The town hall dates from 1742.

CHURCH OF ST MARY THE VIRGIN This large church crowns the summit of the hill on which the old town stands. It is of 12th-century origin, and some of the Norman work is still visible though there are many later additions. The tower contains what is probably the oldest turret clock still working; the exterior face was added in 1760. There are Perpendicular screens, fine stained-glass windows, the Arms of Queen Anne and monuments by John Flaxman and John Bacon.

MERMAID STREET The houses in Mermaid Street are typical of the medieval town of Rye. In this street the Georgian houses incorporate building from the 13th century onwards; Hartshorn House, a half-timbered building from the 15th and 16th centuries, is particularly notable.

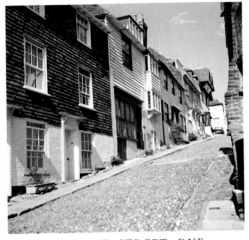

MERMAID STREET, RYE

Mermaid Street, dating from the 15th–18th centuries, suggests the prosperity which Rye once enjoyed through membership of the confederation known as the Cinque Ports. After the sea receded and its harbour silted up, the town declined in importance.

Ryhall *Leics.* 553Gb

CHURCH OF ST JOHN THE EVANGELIST Dating from the 12th century, the church has a fine tower and spire of the 13th century, wide nave and aisles, and original north arcade. There are 14th-century sedilia, and a rebuilt chancel of the 15th century. Among the memorials is a tablet of 1696 to an infant genius, and 17th- and 18th-century monuments. In the wall of the north aisle are fragments of a medieval hermitage which was dedicated to the cult of St Tibba (the patron saint of falconers) who died here *c.* 690.

S

Saffron Walden *Essex* 548Ae

An ancient town, the 'Waledana' of the Ancient Britons; remnants of their extensive earthwork fortifications remain to the west and south of the town. A Saxon burial ground has also been discovered. The keep of the Norman castle, dating from the 12th century, still survives. Near by is a series of circular excavations—the best surviving earth maze in England. Such mazes were once numerous; their origin and use are obscure, but they were probably pre-Christian and connected with fertility rites. The town takes its name from the saffron crocus, the growing of which was the most important industry from the reign of Edward III until *c.* 1790. Saffron was used as a dye and as a medicine and condiment; it is still the symbol of the town. Fine timber-framed houses of the 15th and 16th centuries and brick, or brick and flint, houses from later periods abound in the town. There are also examples of the East Anglian decorative plasterwork known as pargeting. Though now principally a market town, Saffron Walden has recently developed some light industry.

CHURCH OF ST MARY THE VIRGIN Nearly 200 ft in length, the church is probably the finest in Essex. It has a west tower with big pinnacles, and an octagonal spire added in 1841. Rebuilt in the 15th

and 16th centuries, the roofs are contemporary; the church contains the tomb of Lord Audley, a Chancellor to Henry VIII, 19th-century stained glass, and many brasses.

St Albans *Herts.* 547Jc

In Market Place most of the older houses have been altered, but No. 29, dated 1637, and No. 30, probably of the same period, give an indication of the street's character in the 17th century. In the High Street No. 17 has interesting plaster decoration work intended to imitate stonework and convey an impression of great strength. Holywell Hill, running down to the R. Ver, is mainly Georgian, but the White Hart, a timber-framed building, much restored, dates from the 15th century. St Peter's Street has some good 18th- and 19th-century houses, in particular the Grange (No. 16), a mid-Georgian country house. In Hatfield Road, the Marlborough Almshouses, built in 1736 by Sarah, Duchess of Marlborough, form an effective three-sided courtyard composition. Attractive streets with good examples of medieval and Georgian houses are George Street, Fishpool Street and Romeland Hill. At the end of Abbey Mill Lane, by the river, there is the famous Fighting Cocks Inn. This small timber-framed structure, octagonal in plan, is said to be the oldest inn in

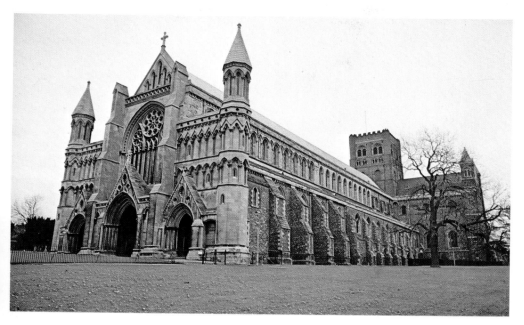

WEST FRONT *In the 12th and 13th centuries an extensive abbey, built around the shrine of St Alban, the first English martyr, existed; it was famous for its library, where Matthew Paris wrote his chronicle,* 'Historia Major'. *The present building is a fragment of the original abbey. Behind the reredos is the plinth on which St Alban's shrine once rested. A watching loft for monks appointed to guard it also survives.*

MURALS *When the Puritans' white-wash was removed from the abbey walls in 1877, a series of 13th- and 14th-century wall-paintings was discovered on the Norman nave piers.*

On their west sides the Crucifixion is depicted, with a subject such as the Annunciation (left-hand picture). On the south sides saints such as Thomas Becket are shown.

SOUTH TRANSEPT *The Normans built much of the present abbey with its lofty arcades; the pillars in the triforium here are the only bits.of the Saxon church they re-used.*

ROMAN MOSAIC FLOOR

A magnificent multicoloured mosaic floor excavated at Verulamium in 1959. It dates from the 2nd century. In the centre a lion is depicted killing a stag—a subject in keeping with the 'other-world' ideas often used as themes for Roman domestic mosaics. (St Albans)

COLOUR-COATED BEAKER

This pot with figured relief work is a good example of colour-coated ware used throughout Roman Britain. Its decoration depicts a lively scene of hounds chasing a hare, a subject popular with the Romanised Celts who were devoted to the chase. (Verulamium Museum, St Albans)

England. Opposite is the 18th-century Silk Mill.
ABBEY The history of St Alban's Abbey is obscure from the 8th century until it emerged as a Benedictine community at the end of the 10th century. The abbey church and the gate-house are all that remain of the original buildings. The core of the church, which is the second longest in England, dates from the 11th century. It is dominated by a central tower of red Roman brick, pillaged from the Verulamium site near by. The original church was greatly enlarged to the west during the 13th century, and the Lady Chapel was added to the east side in the 14th century. After the Dissolution the abbey church was taken over as a parish church, and the Lady Chapel was turned into a grammar school. In 1877 the present bishopric was created and the church restored. (See p. 417.)
CHURCH OF ST MICHAEL The church has a Saxon nave and chancel, and this 10th-century work was opened during the 12th century when aisles were added. There are 14th-century brasses, and a seated figure of Francis Bacon, who died in 1626. The Tudor pulpit is of considerable interest, and so too are the medieval Doom paintings.

CLOCK TOWER Built 1403–12, and situated in what was once the centre of medieval St Albans, this is one of the few belfries of that period to survive.
FRENCH ROW The first five houses are pre-Reformation, but a few others may date as far back as the 14th century. It is said that after King John of France was taken prisoner at Poitiers in 1356, he was for a time held in the Fleurs de Lys Inn which, despite considerable restoration, has its original timber framework.
ROMAN REMAINS The Roman *municipium* of Verulamium, one of the three towns destroyed by Boadicea during the Icenian revolt, was one of the finest towns in Britain. Rebuilt soon after its destruction, it had many excellent buildings and its full municipal status was a mark of its importance. Much of it is now covered, but the theatre—as distinct from an amphitheatre—with its stage and auditorium, is still to be seen, as are other remains. The museum close by also has material of importance. This Roman town was built partly over a former Belgic settlement, an *oppidum*, and in Prae Wood, to the west, are some remains of its defences.

St Andrews *Fife* 562Dg
At Magus Muir is the monument to Archbishop Sharp (1613–79), a pyramid of undressed rocks with an inscription in Latin describing his murder by Covenanters (Charles II's Presbyterian opponents). Near by are the Martyrs' Graves, of Covenanters routed and tortured by the Earl of Monmouth after the Battle of Bothwell Bridge, June 22, 1679. St Andrews has the oldest university in Scotland, founded in 1410. St Mary's College, founded in 1537, includes Old Parliament Hall above which the great mathematician and astronomer James Gregory (1638–75), inventor of the reflector telescope, carried out many experiments.
CATHEDRAL Founded during the 12th century, the cathedral was once large, but became ruinous after the Reformation. Beside it stands the ruined church and tower of St Regulus (or Rule), dating from the early 12th century.

St Asaph *Clwyd* 551Ge
CATHEDRAL This, the smallest of the ancient cathedrals in England and Wales, is of cruciform design with a massive central tower. The first cathedral was built on the site in 560, but the present building dates from the 13th–15th centuries, with some restoration by the 19th-century architect George Gilbert Scott. Much of the glass, too, is of 19th-century workmanship. The cathedral has a museum with interesting items of church plate on display, and a rare-books library with many 16th- and 17th-century volumes, among them the William Morgan Bible of 1588, and the William Salisbury New Testament of 1567. (By appointment.)

St Bees *Cumbria* 556Fe
CHURCH OF SS MARY AND BEGA A nunnery was founded here *c.* 650; destroyed by the Danes, it was refounded *c.* 1120. The present imposing cruciform Norman church dates from after this time, though the central tower was altered during William Butterfield's 19th-century restoration. There are some 19th-century monuments.

St Benet's Abbey *Norfolk* 554Dc
On the R. Bure, St Benet's is an early Benedictine monastery, possibly begun in AD 816. It was certainly re-established in 955, and was endowed under King Canute to become the great fortified abbey of St Benet-at-Holm. The few remaining ruins include the 15th-century west gate-house, dominated by a windmill. The outer walls (once

HUMPEN, 1691

This exquisite rare example of a humpen (tankard) is 9⅜ in. high and was probably made by Johann Keyl or Hermann Benckertt in Nürnberg. The date is shown in the enamel at the base of the scene which depicts a drunken peasant being forced into a pigsty. It was first recorded in the late 19th century, and no other is known that is comparable with it in size and quality. (Pilkington Glass Museum, St Helens)

MOULD BLOWN JUG

This jug, in amber glass with pearly blue iridescence, stands 5½ in. high. It is of the late 4th–early 5th-century period and was excavated at Karak, in Jordan. The sides show Old and New Testament motifs, the Holy Cross erected by Constantine, the Cross of Golgotha and the road to Jerusalem, and the burning bush of Abraham with Isaac and the Holy Cross. (Pilkington Glass Museum, St Helens)

enclosing 38 acres) and the church foundations are recognisable. The barn of Horning Hall Farm near by was the chapel of a hospice of the abbey.

St Briavels Castle *Glos.*   *546Ac*
Norman fortress, prison and manor court for the Forest of Dean, its Constable being Warden of the Forest of Dean. Arrowheads called 'quirrels' were manufactured at the castle in the Middle Ages—Henry III ordered 6000 in 1223. The castle is now a youth hostel.

On Whit Sunday villagers of St Briavels are given bread and cheese, a ceremony commemorating a right to gather wood.

St Buryan *Cornwall*   *538Aa*
CHURCH OF ST BERIAN A 15th-century Perpendicular church with a magnificent rood screen that stretches the whole width of the church. The screen has three sections, and the rood beam is carved with curious beasts, some with human heads.

St Clere's Hall *Essex*   *548Dd*
One of the few surviving 14th-century moated farmhouses with an aisled hall. The wings were altered in the 16th century. (By appointment.)

St David's *Dyfed*   *544Bd*
Small cathedral city. The 12th–14th-century cathedral of the patron saint of Wales is built of purple sandstone from local quarries: it is notable for its Irish oak nave roof and its 116 ft tower. The ruins of a 14th-century bishop's palace near by are preserved as an ancient monument.
BISHOP'S PALACE The impressive Cathedral Close at St David's is bisected by the R. Alun, and most of the official and residential buildings are in the western half. St David's was once the richest of the Welsh dioceses, and the palace remains reflect this wealth. Grouped around three sides of a courtyard

are the remains of three separate halls and ancillary buildings dating from the 12th–15th centuries. Most impressive is the great hall on the south, which was built by Bishop Gower between 1327 and 1345. A unique feature of his work is the arcaded parapet, which here encircles all the earlier roof: this same curious detail is to be seen at his smaller palace at Lamphey in the south of the county, and also at Swansea Castle.

St David's Head *Dyfed*   *544Bd*
PROMONTORY FORT This small Iron Age fort is one of the most beautifully sited in Wales, being at the extreme end of St David's Head, with a magnificent view of Ramsey Island and Sound to the south-west. The defences, which may not be of only one period, consist of a strong stone rampart with two outer banks. Internally there are a number of stone huts and rock shelters, while the whole area between the fort and Carn Llidi is rich in prehistoric remains.

St Donat's Castle *S. Glam.*   *545Hb*
This castle is in fine condition, due to almost continuous habitation culminating in extensive restorations by William Randolph Hearst in 1925, and finally to its present use as the United World College of the Atlantic. Basically a concentric plan, it dates from the 13th and 14th centuries, although it must have had Norman beginnings, as did the little church in the vale immediately beneath it. Hearst's restorations were thorough and skilful; he introduced masonry details and woodwork from many parts of Britain.

St Endellion *Cornwall*   *538Dd*
CHURCH OF ST ENDELIENTA A church on a hilltop, with a Norman font, and some carved bench ends. There is a tomb-chest of *c.* 1400, which might be the shrine of St Endelienta.

St Fagans Castle *S. Glam.*   *545Hb*
Only a low curtain wall remains of the original 13th-century castle; the wall now surrounds a 16th-century house, which forms part of the Welsh Folk Museum. In the house is period furniture, and domestic equipment including a dog-operated kitchen spit. Outside are a coach house with horse-drawn coaches, some craft workshops, and a range of old buildings brought from many parts of Wales, together illustrating everyday life and work in the Principality over the centuries. Exhibits include: a barn, from Flintshire, period 1550–1600, removed and re-erected; a woollen mill (1760) complete with machinery, removed from Brecknockshire; a wood-turner's shop; a cooper's shop; four farm-houses, from Denbighshire (1470), Montgomery-shire (1600), Radnorshire (1730), Gower (1630); a chapel dated 1777 from the Vale of Teifi; a cottage (1762) from Caernarvonshire, a school; and three terrace houses. Galleries in a separate museum block picture aspects of Welsh culture such as musical instruments and an Eisteddfod ceremonial sword; and show the development of soil drainage.

St Germans *Cornwall*   *538Ec*
CHURCH OF ST GERMANUS An imposing Norman monastic church on the site of a Saxon cathedral. There are two west towers: one is a 13th-century Early English octagonal tower, the other, which holds the bells, is 15th century. Major restoration work was carried out in 1888 and the east window, by Burne-Jones, was fitted into place a few years later.

St Govan's Chapel *Dyfed*   *544Cc*
The chapel and well are dramatically set above high-water mark in a cleft in precipitous cliffs, reached by a flight of steps from above. The tiny stone-vaulted chapel probably dates from the 13th century; at the side of its original stone altar is a doorway leading to a small chamber in the rock face. The well was frequented for cures as late as the mid-19th century.

St Helens *Merseyside*   *551Jf*
PILKINGTON GLASS MUSEUM The collection illustrates the evolution of glassmaking techniques from Ancient Egypt to the present day. An enamelled humpen and a mould-blown jug are typical examples. (See p. 419.)

St Helier *Jersey*   *540Ea*
JERSEY MUSEUM AND ART GALLERY Comprehensive collections illustrate Jersey life from the earliest times. These encompass archaeological finds, the ship-building and cod-fishing industries, coins, period rooms, natural history and relics of the 'Jersey Lily', Lillie Langtry. The gallery contains many paintings by local artists.

St Ives *Cambs.*   *547Jf*
Once a village called Slepe, a slippery landing place on the R. Ouse, St Ives became a manor of Ramsey Abbey in 969. A priory cell of the abbey was set up *c.* 1050 and dedicated to St Ivo, a Persian bishop whose supposed remains were miraculously found in a nearby field. The priory supplanted the village, which thus acquired the name of St Ives.

The six-arched bridge was built in 1415, but the two southern arches were reconstructed in 1716. A two-storey 15th-century miniature chapel is preserved on the bridge. Only a ruined wall remains of the priory, but the parish church dates from the 14th century. Its spire has been rebuilt several times, most recently in 1918 after it was hit by an aircraft.

The best house in St Ives is the Jacobean manor house by the bridge, with fine brick chimneys. A

ST MICHAEL'S MOUNT

This rocky Cornish island is probably Ictis, from which Mediterranean merchants obtained tin in the 1st century BC. By Edward the Confessor's time it was held by monks and, for about 100 years after, when it was owned by the island abbey of Mont St Michel off the Breton coast, it was an important centre for pilgrimages. The present buildings date from the 12th century but the Chapel of St Michael, with battlemented tower, was not begun until the 15th century. The monastery was transformed into a mansion after 1659.

great fire in 1680 destroyed 122 houses, and few built before that date have survived.

NORRIS LIBRARY AND MUSEUM Local history collection from the old county of Huntingdonshire. The museum includes an important collection of ice skates.

St Margaret's at Cliffe *Kent*   *543Ge*
CHURCH OF ST MARGARET OF ANTIOCH A fine Norman church, with a squat, battlemented west tower. There is rich decorative detail inside in the carving over the nave arches, and on the exterior in the Norman arcading along the whole length of the nave. There is also a fine west doorway. The church was restored *c.* 1869.

St Mawes Castle *Cornwall*   *538Cb*
The coastal defences which Henry VIII erected as a precaution against a French invasion after the Dissolution stretched from the eastern Kent coast right round to Cornwall in the west. Near Falmouth, where the estuary of the R. Fal is wide, two forts were built: Pendennis Castle and, on the other side of the estuary, its counterpart, St Mawes Castle. The fort at St Mawes, on Roseland peninsula, was begun in 1540 and completed three years later. As it was intended as a military defence against attacks from the sea, the landward side was neglected; it took one day for Cromwellian troops to take the castle during the Civil War. Similar in style to Henry VIII's other coastal defence forts, the castle consists of a central circular keep with three semicircular bastions for the gun positions. An unusual feature is the display of heraldic decoration and various carved inscriptions, one of which runs round the keep below the battlement.

St Michael Penkevil *Cornwall*   *538Cb*
CHURCH OF ST MICHAEL Rebuilt by G. E. Street, 1862–6. Noteworthy for the monument to Admiral Boscawen (1763) by Rysbrack, and others to the Boscawen family by Joseph Nollekens later in the same century.

St Michael's Mount *Cornwall*   *538Aa*
A monastery built on an island, like its more imposing partner off the Brittany coast, Mont St Michel. The original buildings are of the 12th century, but after the Dissolution the monastery passed through many families until the present family, St Aubyn, came into possession during the later 17th century and converted it into a mansion.

St Monans *Fife*   *562Dg*
CHURCH On a rock above the sea; dating from the 14th century, it consists of the choir, transepts and central tower with a small spire.

St Neot *Cornwall*   *538Dc*
The church stands near the Loveny R., a tributary of the R. Fowey, in a wooded valley. It is famous for its 15th- and 16th-century stained glass windows. Just outside the village is the holy well of St Neot, a Celtic monk who brought Christianity to this remote place. The parish is rich in archaeological remains, including two Iron Age camps and several Bronze-Age hut circles.

St Neots *Cambs.*   *547Jf*
An old riverside market town of Saxon origin, with a number of good houses, including the Bridge Hotel, 1685, the Cross Keys Hotel of the same period, and some old houses that belonged to merchants, flanking the Hen Brook.

St Nicholas *S. Glam.*   *545Hb*
TINKINSWOOD This slightly wedge-shaped Neolithic barrow, some 130 ft long, had a typical horned forecourt leading to the entrance. The stones of the cairn were held in position by dry-

15th-CENTURY STAINED GLASS
The oldest stained glass in the church at St Neot dates from between 1480 and 1530, the windows depicting the stories of Adam (shown above), Noah, St George and Creation being the earliest. Although restored in 1829, they are important as showing the glazing of a remote church. Almost certainly produced locally, the windows show the work of English craftsmen before their traditional style was submerged in the Renaissance. (Parish Church, St Neot)

stone walling, reinforced towards the west end by several parallel rows of upturned stones. The entrance led immediately into the chamber, which was constructed of several large slabs of stone on edge. These supported an enormous capstone, some 22 ft by 15 ft and estimated to weigh more than 40 tons. The gaps between the stones were filled by drystone walling. In addition, about half way along the length of the mound, on the north side, there was an enclosed chamber or 'pit', not approached from the side. The relationship of this barrow to the Cotswold group is very close.

St Osyth *Essex*   *548Dd*
CHURCH OF SS PETER AND PAUL The parish church is outside the walls of the abbey. Of 13th-century origin, it dates mainly from the 16th century when the nave and aisles were rebuilt in brick, with a plain hammerbeam roof. It contains some monuments with effigies, *c.* 1580.

St Osyth's Priory *Essex*   *548Dd*
The chapel and tower are of the 13th century, and the great gate-house was restored in the 15th century.

St Winnow *Cornwall*   *538Dc*
CHURCH OF ST WYNNOCUS The church is in an attractive position on the bank of the R. Fowey. It was originally a Celtic foundation. There are two windows of medieval stained glass, 16th-century bench ends and a 16th-century pulpit. The 16th-century rood screen has been restored.

SALISBURY CATHEDRAL

EXTERIOR *The glory of Salisbury Cathedral is its graceful spire, 404 ft high and the tallest in England. The cathedral is unique among English medieval cathedrals for it was planned as a single unit, and not built over several centuries as the others. Begun in 1220, the Early English Gothic building was finished 40 years later and only the spire was added afterwards — c. 1334. The impressive west front, with its rows of niches with statues of saints, is just as the 13th-century builders left it.*

CHAPTER HOUSE *This magnificent octagonal building was constructed in 1263–84. It is 58 ft in diameter and round the walls are 49 seats for the members of the Chapter. The graceful central column (shown right) was renewed in 1856 when the building was carefully restored to its original splendour.*

Salford *Greater Manchester* 552Bf
PEEL PARK MUSEUM AND ART GALLERY The art gallery has the largest public collection of paintings and drawings by L. S. Lowry in Britain, and the museum centres around 'Lark Hill Place'—a reconstruction of a small 19th-century street.

Salisbury *Wilts.* 540Fe
CATHEDRAL The Norman cathedral was at what is now Old Sarum, where its plan can still be seen in the grass, but at the start of the 13th century the See was moved to New Sarum, or Salisbury. The present cathedral is the only English one built in the Middle Ages as a single conception, and not piecemeal as were all the others. The foundations were laid in 1220, and about 40 years later work on this magnificent cathedral was finished. Its

spire was added in 1334. There are many interesting monuments, including the spectacular brass to Bishop Wyville, c. 1375, who is shown standing in a castle. The cathedral library has several illuminated manuscripts, but its greatest treasure is one of the three originals of Magna Carta, signed at Runnymede on June 15, 1215 and brought here by William, Earl of Salisbury. Apart from five years of the Second World War when it was hidden in a quarry, it has been in the cathedral since 1225. The main decorative elements inside the cathedral are the dark columns of Purbeck stone which appear throughout the building—particularly dramatically in the Lady Chapel. In the 14th century Edward III granted a licence to build a wall round the cathedral and the houses of those who served it, and much of this wall surrounding the close survives. The close is still entered through medieval gateways, and many of the houses within it date from the Middle Ages, despite the Georgian exteriors; the bishop's palace and the old deanery were certainly built in the 13th century. To the south of the cathedral lies the magnificent 13th-century chapter house and cloisters.

MOMPESSON HOUSE A fine early 18th-century town house in The Close, notable for its original plasterwork and panelling, and its elegant staircase. There is also a large collection of English Drinking glasses.

NORTH CANONRY A herbaceous garden.

SALISBURY AND SOUTH WILTSHIRE MUSEUM Nearly all the finds from Stonehenge excavations are displayed. There are collections of archaeology and local history, including the famous 'Salisbury Giant'; guild and craft relics; a wide selection of medieval pottery from Old Sarum, Clarendon and Laverstock; a Roman mosaic pavement from Downton, made c. AD 330; local costumes and bygones; and a collection of English pottery, china and glass.

THEOLOGICAL COLLEGE Built in the 17th century to designs by Wren, with extensions by William Butterfield in 1881, the college has a great staircase and interesting fire-places. (By appointment.)

Sall *Norfolk* 554Cc
CHURCH OF SS PETER AND PAUL An early 15th-century church, with a later 15th-century north transept. Among the families who contributed towards the cost of the building were the Boleyns. Both north and south porches are two-storied. The wide nave-roof and carved bosses in the chancel are decorated with angels. The seven-sacrament font was given in 1489, and is surmounted by a contemporary canopy on a pulley. The carved stalls have poppy-heads and misericords. There are many monumental brasses, including a shroud brass—unusual in that the figure is not a skeleton.

Saltash *Cornwall* 538Fc
ROYAL ALBERT BRIDGE This bridge over the R. Tamar was the last built by the engineer Isambard Kingdom Brunel, who died in the year it was completed, 1859. The difficult crossing of the Tamar, with its deep, shifting course, had for many years delayed completion of the Great Western Railway's line from Bristol to Truro, but with Brunel's achievement London, Bristol and Cornwall were at last linked. The bridge is half suspension, the other half comprising a series of flattened tubular arches; its high brick piers straddle the river.

Saltcoats *Strathclyde* 561Gd
NORTH AYRSHIRE MUSEUM The museum illustrates the history, industry—mainly shipping and coal mining—and domestic life of the old district of northern Ayrshire.

There is material here relating to the history of Saltcoats harbour, the coal shipping trade and the Steventon canal—the first industrial canal in Scotland.

Saltfleetby All Saints *Lincs.* 553Jf
CHURCH OF ALL SAINTS Once a Norman church, but there has been much later rebuilding; the Early English tower had its Perpendicular top added during the 15th century. There are two pulpits, one Elizabethan, the other 17th century.

Salt Island *Anglesey, Gwynedd* 550Df
Early in the 19th century Holyhead and Howth, north of Dublin, became the principal Irish packet ports. The engineer John Rennie was responsible for Holyhead's attractive harbour office, customs

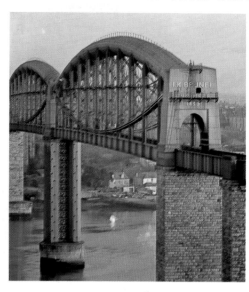

ROYAL ALBERT BRIDGE, SALTASH

Isambard Kingdom Brunel, who helped his father Sir Marc Brunel engineer the Thames tunnel from Wapping to Rotherhithe, was appointed engineer to the new Great Western Railway in 1833. It was a time of great railway expansion; after linking London with Bristol, the company wanted to penetrate into remote Cornwall—but a stumbling block was the difficult crossing of the R. Tamar which marks the boundary with Devon. Brunel accepted the challenge. The deep and shifting bottom of the river presented him with enormous problems but he persevered and by 1859 his bridge was finished. On May 14 the Prince Consort rode across in a train, and the line was open through to Truro. Today this bridge, on which Brunel's name is proclaimed in large letters, is paralleled by the road bridge of 1963.

house and imposing Doric portico reminiscent of the demolished Euston 'arch'. On Salt Island pier stands his lighthouse; though disused, this most attractive little building has survived almost intact, and is complete with original lantern and gallery. Like the light at Howth, which it closely resembles, it was lit by gas.

Saltram House *Devon* 538Fc
The original 17th-century Tudor house, set in a fine landscaped park, was acquired by the Parker family in 1712, and remained in their possession until 1957. In the 1740's it was altered, and Georgian Classical façades were added to mask the remains of the older house. Much of the interior was also redesigned then. Later the saloon and dining-room were transformed by Robert Adam. The house is noted for its fine furniture, china and a collection of pictures including 14 portraits by Sir Joshua Reynolds. (See p. 424.)

Sandal Magna *W. Yorks.* 558Ca
CHURCH OF ST HELEN A cruciform church, with a 12th-century tower that was rebuilt and enlarged in the 14th and 15th centuries; the west end was lengthened in the 19th century. Inside there is a Perpendicular screen, a Restoration font of 1662 and monuments, including two by Edward Physick (1828).

Sandford Orcas Manor *Dorset* 540Dd
Built c. 1540 in classic Tudor style on earlier 11th-century foundations, the house contains period panels, furniture, woodwork, and collections of china, stained glass and pictures.

THE SALOON AT SALTRAM HOUSE

John Parker and his wife Lady Catherine came to live in this Tudor house, with views over Plymouth Sound, in the 1740's, and they set about redesigning it in Classical style. Fine plaster ceilings date from this time, and are traditionally ascribed to Italian workmen; they show many birds, cherubs and flowers representing the 'Art of Music' in the morning-room and the 'Seasons' in the Red Velvet Drawing-room. The entrance hall ceiling has a central panel showing Mercury in Flight. The chimney-piece here is probably by Thomas Carter, and has a central relief of 'Androcles and the Lion'. In about 1768 Robert Adam designed the saloon—one of the most beautiful neo-Classical rooms in the country. The great Axminster carpet was especially woven for it in 1770. The room contains a fine collection of paintings including works by Reynolds, Rubens and Gheeraerts. One of them is after 'The Andrians' by Titian in the Prado Museum, Madrid, and its exquisite frame may have been designed by Adam as part of the room's architecture. He probably also designed the candelabra which stand at each corner of the room. Adam also repaired damage caused by fire in 1778, and the dining-room is of this date.

Sandiacre *Derbys.* 552Ed
CHURCH OF ST GILES An interesting Norman church, with later additions, on a hill. The tall 13th-century chancel is almost as long as the nave, and has good tracery in the windows and an outstanding sedilia.

Sandleford Priory *Berks.* 546Fa
Once an Augustinian priory, now St Gabriel's School, it has a 14th-century roof. The oval drawing-room was restored in the 18th century, with work by Adam and Wyatt. Capability Brown landscaped the garden. (By appointment.)

Sandling Park *Kent* 542Fe
The park is noted for its formal and woodland gardens.

Sandon *Staffs.* 552Cc
CHURCH OF ALL SAINTS A church founded in the 11th century and rebuilt in 1310. The tower and chantry chapel were added *c.* 1450. It has a Norman font, a screen, and a 17th-century pulpit; noteworthy are monuments to the family of Erdeswick, and 17th-century wall-paintings.

Sandown *Isle of Wight* 541Hc
ISLE OF WIGHT MUSEUM OF GEOLOGY More than 5000 fossils that have been found on the island are displayed. Diagrams, maps and models make the exhibits interesting to non-technical visitors as well as to geologists.

Sandringham House *Norfolk* 554Ac
A private country residence of the Queen; it was built by Edward VII when Prince of Wales in 1867–70. The palace and grounds are open to the public when the Royal Family is not in residence.

Sandwich *Kent* 543Gf
Once a thriving port (one of the Cinque Ports), Sandwich is now over 2 miles from the sea, so much has the estuary of the R. Stour silted up. The little town is a network of narrow streets, punctuated by three huge churches, two of them never properly repaired after their towers collapsed in the 17th century. The tiny oblong square in front of St Peter's Church is the centre of the town's life today. High Street, to the east, is the most handsome street, but the best houses are in the north-west corner of the town: Manwood Court, built of typical Sandwich pale yellow brick in 1574, and the King's House, also 16th century.
CHURCH OF ST CLEMENT A large and splendid church, mainly of the 14th and 15th centuries, but with a magnificent Norman central tower whose exterior has three tiers of arcading below the battlements. There is also a Norman doorway with carved decoration, and misericords.

Sarnesfield *Heref. & Worcs.* 546Ae
CHURCH OF ST MARY A pretty Norman church of the 12th century. The west tower dates from the following century and there is a 14th-century tie-beam roof in the nave. There are fragments of 14th- and 15th-century stained glass.

Savernake Forest *Wilts.* 546Db
The forest is 16 miles in circumference, and Jane Seymour's father was once its hereditary warden. It is now the domain of the Marquess of Ailesbury, and is the only English forest that does not belong to the Crown. Dating back to before the Norman Conquest, it has superb avenues of oak and beech.

Sawbridgeworth *Herts.* 548Ad
CHURCH OF GREAT ST MARY'S This large church is mainly 14th century. The east window, 1864, is by Hardman. The octagonal font is *c.* 1400, and the pulpit is dated 1632. The many brasses from the 15th to 19th centuries are matched by 14th- to 19th-century monuments by Bacon, Storey and others.

Saxlingham Nethergate *Norfolk* 548Dg
CHURCH OF ST MARY The Perpendicular church, which lies between an Elizabethan house and a parsonage by Sir John Soane, is famed for its glass.

Saxtead Green *Suffolk* 548Ef
MILL A fine example of an East Suffolk post-mill (in which the whole body of the mill revolves on its base) of *c.* 1700 or earlier. The mill proper stands on a tall round house, with a long flight of steps leading to the hooded porch. It has four main sails, a fantail, and interesting machinery. (See p. 426.)

Saxton *N. Yorks.* 558Db
CHURCH OF ALL SAINTS The chancel arch and south doorway remain from All Saints' original Norman period. Later additions include the Perpendicular west tower. Inside, there are remains of a Saxon cross and a monument to two children by J. F. Moore (1783). In the churchyard there is an unusual survival—a tomb from *c.* 1461.

Scarborough *N. Yorks.* 559Gd
Anciently called Scardeburg, ravaged by the Danes under Harald Hardrada in 1066, incorporated by Henry II between 1155 and 1163, and now a resort. The castle was built in the mid-12th century. The remains of a Roman signal-station of *c.* AD 370 can be seen in the castle grounds.
ART GALLERY The permanent collection shows modern original prints, and oil paintings and local water-colours. There are frequent temporary-loan exhibitions.
CASTLE The site of Scarborough Castle has been intermittently occupied since the Bronze Age. The headland on which it sits is a natural defensive site but the main defences now visible date from the 12th century. They were probably begun under William Le Gros, Count of Aumale, and included part of the present curtain wall. The main defensive feature of Scarborough is the keep, built in the reign of Henry II; it was completed by 1158. Scarborough was an important strategic point on the east coast of England and remained in royal hands up to the reign of James I.
Throughout the 13th century it received attention, and King John spent the then enormous sum of £2000 on it. Many of the towers on the curtain wall probably date from this period. Thereafter, like many castles, it suffered a period of neglect, but in the late 14th century funds for its repair were placed on a regular basis and it survived the remainder of the Middle Ages intact.
CHURCH OF ST MARTIN-ON-THE-HILL A 19th-century church, by G. F. Bodley. It is built in Gothic style, and contains a spectacular display of decoration by Bodley himself and many of his Pre-Raphaelite friends. There is glass and mural painting by Burne-Jones; the chancel roof is by Philip Webb and William Morris; and Rossetti, Ford Madox Brown and others worked on the walls, pulpit and stained glass.
CHURCH OF ST MARY Due to severe damage in the Civil War, St Mary's is now only a fragment of the original cruciform church; the chancel has more or less disappeared, so that what was once a central tower now stands at the east of the building. Of the remaining medieval architecture, the most interesting pieces are the arcades, the 12th- and 13th-century piers, and series of chapels off the south aisle. There are many good monuments, including one of the 18th century by Roubiliac, and one of the 19th century by Edward Physick.

SAXTEAD GREEN MILL

There has probably been a windmill on this site since 1309 and it is certain that the present mill was worked by one Amos Webber in 1796; since then it was used continuously for producing flour until 1947. It is a fine post-mill—one in which the body carrying sails and machinery rotates on an upright post—and is 46 ft tall with a sail-span of 54 ft. The body is set on top of the roundhouse containing the millstones and other machinery. The 'fantail' at the rear automatically keeps the sails square into the wind.

MUSEUM OF NATURAL HISTORY, WOOD END The museum shows material relating to the geology, fauna and flora of the region and is housed in the former seaside home of the Sitwell family, much of whose material is in the library wing.

ROMAN SIGNAL-STATION The castle stands on a headland on the north side of the town. In the narrow space between it and the cliff-edge are the preserved remains of this signal-station. The superstructure would have been a small square building surmounted by a tall tower. This station was one of five which lay along the Yorkshire coast between Saltburn and Filey. Built *c.* AD 370, they were intended to detect the approach of seafaring raiders, mainly Picts, from the north.

ROTUNDA MUSEUM The museum was originally simply a rotunda, built by the Scarborough Philosophical Society in 1829 to a plan suggested by William Smith, 'the father of English geology'. The circular form was intended to display Smith's discovery of the stratification of rocks, and the wings were not added until 1860. The collection concentrates on the archaeology and bygones of the region of North-east Yorkshire—Mesolithic finds from Star Carr, and Iron Age and Roman finds from Castle Hill. Of special interest are a Bronze Age oak trunk coffin, and pottery from the Iron Age, Roman and medieval times.

Scilly Isles   538Af
The five main islands were occupied by the Phoenicians, whose principal interest was in the tin mines of Cornwall. In the days of sail, the Isles were a notorious navigation hazard: part of a British naval squadron under Sir Cloudsley Shovel in the *Association* was wrecked here in 1707.

Scole *Norfolk*   554Ca
WHITE HART INN One of the finest old coaching inns in England. Built of red brick in 1655, and resembling a mansion rather than an inn, it is crowned with five Dutch gables in front and more at the back. It has giant angle pilasters, square chimney-stacks with arched panels and, inside, a great oaken staircase.

Scone Palace *Tayside*   566Ca
The present palace with castellated towers and battlements was built in 1803 on the site of an ancient abbey and palace dating back to the earliest days of recorded Scottish history. Here in 843 King Kenneth I brought the Stone of Destiny—possibly from Iona—on which Scottish kings were crowned. This stone, the Stone of Scone or 'coronation stone', remained here until 1296 when Edward I took it to Westminster Abbey, London, to form part of Edward the Confessor's Chair, used in English coronation ceremonies.

In the state rooms of the palace are collections of Vernis Martin vases, ivory statuettes, porcelain, French furniture and paintings.

Scotney Castle *Kent*   542De
Colourful landscape gardens surround the ruins of a moated round tower (Scotney Old Castle) built in 1379, and parts of a Tudor manor house.

Scotstarvit Tower *Fife*   562Cg
The 17th-century residence of Sir John Scot (1585–1670), lawyer and Privy Councillor.

Scrivelsby Court *Lincs.*   553He
The Lion Gate at the entrance to the park of Scrivelsby Court is the emblem of the unique office of Hereditary Champion of England, which the Dymoke family have held since the time of Richard II. The Champion's duty was to appear mounted and in full armour at the coronation and challenge to the death any man who might deny the king's right to the throne. The ceremony was last performed in 1821. Old Scrivelsby Court has been pulled down and replaced by the conversion and enlargement of the Elizabethan gate-house. (By appointment.)

Scrooby *Notts.*   552Ff
A tablet on the Manor Farm affirms that this was the home of William Brewster, a leader of the Pilgrim Fathers.

Seaham *Durham*   558Dg
CHURCH OF ST MARY The long nave of this church near the sea was perhaps built by the Saxons. The font is very old, from the early 13th century, and the chancel and west tower are also 13th century; the pulpit was made in the 16th century.

Seaton Delaval *Northld.*   558Ch
CHURCH A pleasant little Norman church (behind Seaton Delaval Hall), which has chancel and apse arches with zigzag ornament. Inside are 14th-century effigies of a knight and lady.

Seaton Delaval Hall *Northld.*   558Ch
A splendid English baroque house, regarded by many as Sir John Vanbrugh's masterpiece. It was built *c.* 1718–28. The centre block, between two arcaded wings, is the main feature of the house and has quite different architecture to its two main fronts. That on the north is noted for its great Tuscan columns and strongly emphasised jointing of its stone facing. Above rises a high, pedimented storey. All the main forms are repeated on the

SEATON DELAVAL HALL

SOUTH FRONT *Sir John Vanbrugh, the playwright who turned so successfully to architecture, began this great house about 1718 for Admiral George Delaval. It was completed about 1728, after the architect's death. The house, one of the great feats of architecture of the early 18th century, comprises a huge centre block between two arcaded and pedimented wings. At various times the house has suffered tragically by fire. In 1822 the centre block was gutted and for many years stood a gaunt ruin, but it was restored in 1959–62.*

DAVID AND GOLIATH *Although this is a 17th- or 18th-century English lead copy of a 16th-century Italian marble statue, it is one of the most intriguing pieces of sculpture in England, since it is a unique record of a lost masterpiece. In the middle of the 18th century lead copies after famous statues, classical or modern, were a fashionable way of decorating gardens. When the original was modern, it was usually in an English collection, and there is therefore a strong possibility that the original of this vigorous group is standing somewhere neglected in England. The original must have been the work of Baccio Bandinelli (1488–1560) or his pupil, the Florentine sculptor Vincenzo de'Rossi (1525–87).*

south front, but here there is a giant portico of tall, fluted Ionic columns. The house contains fine furniture, portraits and ceramics. In the grounds are extensive gardens, an orangery, obelisks and statues.

Sedbergh *Cumbria*   *557Jd*
CHURCH OF ST ANDREW Originally a Norman building, but later additions are evident, notably the Transitional arcades, and the Perpendicular windows and tower. The pulpit has a Jacobean sounding board.

Sedgefield *Durham*   *558Cf*
CHURCH OF ST EDMUND Shroud brasses dating from 1470, and 13th-century effigies, vie for attention with the 18th-century organ case and marble font at St Edmund's; but over all presides the elaborate, Gothically inspired rood screen of 1670. The choir stalls are also 17th century. The church is mainly Early English, with some later work; the west tower is Perpendicular.

Sefton *Merseyside*   *551Jf*
CHURCH OF ST HELEN The spire is 14th century and the rest mid-16th century. The interior is famous for the fine carved wooden fittings—stalls, font cover and canopied pulpit, and screens.

Also remarkable are the many brasses and monuments to the Molyneux family, including a mailed effigy of *c.* 1296.

Segontium See Caernarfon.   *550Ee*

Selborne *Hants.*   *541Je*
CHURCH OF ST MARY A Norman church with nave arcade and later additions. Much of the remainder is mid-19th century. This restoration was made by a great-nephew of Gilbert White, the naturalist, who is buried in the churchyard, and is commemorated by a stained glass window depicting St Francis.
GILBERT WHITE MUSEUM AND THE OATES MEMORIAL MUSEUM Personal possessions of the naturalist Gilbert White and exhibits related to the Antarctic explorer Captain Oates are displayed in White's former home, The Wakes, a 16th-century house in a large garden. Near by is The Hanger—a beechwood on a steep slope—where White made some of the observations he recorded in his classic work, *The Natural History and Antiquities of Selborne.*

Selby *N. Yorks.*   *558Eb*
ABBEY The abbey was founded in the 11th century for the Benedictines, and its great church survived the Dissolution of the monasteries. It is a large,

basically Norman, cruciform church, but was restored after a disastrous fire in 1906. There is a Washington family coat of arms and a 14th-century stained glass Jesse window.

Sempringham *Lincs.*   553Hc
CHURCH OF ST ANDREW Only the nave arcades and doorways remain as good examples of Norman work in this former church of the nearby Gilbertine abbey. St Andrew's was much rebuilt in the 19th century, when the chancel was added.

Sevenoaks *Kent*   542Cf
This big dormitory town for London keeps the top end of its High Street almost as it was in the 18th century (except for the traffic). Here is the church and, opposite, the Palladian Sevenoaks School, of 1727, based on a design by Lord Burlington. The Chantry, Old House and, further north, Red House, the best of all, are fine examples of gentlemen's houses of the reigns of William III and Queen Anne.

Severn Bridge *Gwent*   546Ac
A majestic suspension bridge opened in 1966. It has a main span of 3240 ft and two side spans each 1000 ft and suspended from two towers. These rise to 400 ft and take a load of 6600 tons from each cable. Unique in modern bridge design are the slender, widely spaced suspension wires, which hang in V-form to give extra rigidity to the platform.

Shaftesbury *Dorset*   540Ee
ABBEY RUINS MUSEUM The museum contains carved stones and tiles found on the excavated site of a Benedictine nunnery founded by Alfred the Great. There are models of the church and Shaftesbury before 1539.
LOCAL HISTORY MUSEUM Shaftesbury's button industry is featured in one of the collections. Books and manuscripts on local history, local archaeological finds and collections of tools and crafts and Victoriana are also included. A manual fire engine dating from 1744, complete with leather hose and buckets, is preserved.

Shalford Mill *Surrey*   542Af
An 18th-century water-mill on the R. Tilling-bourne.

Sheffield *S. Yorks.*   552Df
Symbolic of the city's industries, Vulcan, god of the forge, crowns the 193 ft tower of the town hall, opened in 1897. The Cutlers' Hall, built in 1832, contains the unique silver collection of the Cutlers' Company founded in 1624, comprising at least one piece bearing the Sheffield hall mark for each year since 1773 when the Sheffield Assay Office was opened. The first annual Cutlers' Feast was held more than 300 years ago.
ABBEYDALE INDUSTRIAL HAMLET A late 18th-century steel and scythe works, comprising a Huntsman crucible steel melting shop, forging hearths, tilt-hammers, grinding shop and work-men's cottages. The machinery is operated by four water-wheels restored to working order. The workshops are equipped, and the old warehouse block contains displays illustrating industrial development in the Sheffield area.
BEAUCHIEF ABBEY Only the west tower still stands of the 1175 foundation. Most of the present building, which contains 17th-century furnish-ings, dates from the 14th century.
CATHEDRAL CHURCH OF SS PETER AND PAUL The cathedral is the former parish church, and is basic-ally 15th century with tower and crocketed spire. Modern extensions with tower and lantern were consecrated in 1966. There are monuments from

the 16th century, including those to the 4th and 6th Earls of Shrewsbury.
CITY MUSEUM The first museum was opened in 1875; the present one, built in 1937, is a centre for information and research for North Derbyshire and South Yorkshire. It houses one of the world's largest cutlery collections, both Sheffield-made from the 14th century onwards and examples from the Stone Age to the present day from all over the world. There is also a large collection of Old Sheffield Plate. Other exhibits include Bronze Age antiquities collected from the Peak District in the 19th century by Thomas Bateman the antiquary, and Derbyshire ornamental stonework.
GRAVES ART GALLERY This houses a collection of British and European paintings, English water-colours and examples of Chinese, Indian, Islamic and African art.
MAPPIN ART GALLERY Early English and Victorian paintings are on permanent view and there are loan exhibitions of 19th- and 20th-century works.
SHEPHERD WHEEL Two water-powered cutlery grinding hulls dating back to the late 18th century, when the wheel was operated by a Mr Shepherd from whom the establishment takes its name. It is the only working example of a Sheffield cutlery master's grinding wheel to survive from this period. There was a wheel on the same site as early as 1584. (By appointment.)
BISHOPS' HOUSE The city's best surviving ex-ample of a timber-framed house. It was built about 1500, probably for minor gentry. There is nothing to support the local tradition that two bishops lived here in the 15th and 16th centuries. There are furnishings in 17th-century style, and exhibitions of Sheffield life under the Tudors and Stuarts.

Sheffield Park Garden *E. Sussex*   542Ce
Large gardens with five lakes linked by cascades, originally laid out by Capability Brown.

Shellingford *Oxon.*   546Ec
CHURCH OF ST FAITH A simple building without aisles; there is much Norman work, for example the south door and chancel arch. The windows are Decorated and Perpendicular Gothic, and some fragments of medieval glass remain. The Early English west tower has a spire, thought to have been added in 1625. There are several interesting monuments of the 17th to 19th centuries, includ-ing one by W. Tyler (1780) and one by John Flaxman (1820) of two Viscounts Ashbrook.

Shelton *Norfolk*   554Da
CHURCH OF ST MARY An almost pure Per-pendicular church with fine Tudor stained glass.

Sherborne *Dorset*   540Dd
A small country town noted for its medieval buildings, its abbey, its school and two castles. A bishopric was founded here early in the 8th century when the Winchester diocese was divided. Rebuilding of the abbey church began in the 12th century, but it was not completed until 1490. Some buildings were taken over by Sherborne School, which received a royal charter in 1550.
CHURCH OF ST MARY THE VIRGIN Founded in 705 and later a Benedictine abbey. It dates mainly from the 15th century; a Saxon doorway is still to be seen on the outside of the west wall of the north nave aisle. 'Great Tom', a tenor bell given to the abbey by Cardinal Wolsey, hangs in the tower. Inside the church there is a wealth of fan-vaulting. There are a number of fine monuments, including effigies of 13th-century abbots, but the most impressive is the large memorial by John Nost to the Earl of Bristol, *c.* 1698, with standing figures

TILT-HAMMERS: ABBEYDALE INDUSTRIAL HAMLET, SHEFFIELD

Constructed in 1785, these hammers forged scythe blades from steel made in the adjacent Huntsman
furnace. They were driven by the water wheel, 18 ft in diameter, behind the large gear wheel.

ROCKINGHAM TRAY

In 1826 Earl Fitzwilliam lent over £5000 to Thomas and John Wager Brameld, partners in the Brameld pottery at Swinton near Sheffield, and this gave a new lease of life to the factory. The Bramelds began selling porcelain as well as earthenware, and adopted the name Rockingham, and the griffin as their mark. In 1830 the Royal Dessert Service was made for William IV, but in 1842 the factory was forced to close because of financial difficulties. This small ornamental porcelain tray of about 1833 is painted in enamels with a view of Newstead Abbey, seat of Lord Byron, and is marked with the griffin. (City Museum, Sheffield)

and mourning cherubs. There is a series of interesting carved misericords of the 15th century, and stained glass of the same period.

The medieval almshouse across the Abbey Close was built in 1437. The hall is a rare example of a medieval hospital, and over the altar in the chapel there is an interesting 15th-century Flemish triptych.

OLD CASTLE To the east of the town at Castleton is the castle built by Bishop Roger in 1107–39. It is one of the earliest castles with concentric walls of the 12th century. It was acquired by Elizabeth I, who leased it to Sir Walter Raleigh in 1592, and gave it to him in 1599. Raleigh attempted to modernise the property, but gave this up in order to build another castle, then known as Sherborne Lodge.

The Old Castle suffered in the Civil War; it was badly battered by cannon in 1645, and dismantled by the Parliamentarians that same year. SHERBORNE CASTLE This is in extensive parkland adjoining the Old Castle. It was built by Sir Walter Raleigh in 1594 and has been in continuous occupation by the Digby family since 1617. It contains fine paintings, furniture, books and documents dating from the 16th to the 19th centuries. The Capability Brown gardens include a newly restored 50 acre lake.

Sherburn in Elmet *N. Yorks.*   558Db
CHURCH OF ALL SAINTS A large church with a west tower, in a commanding position on a hill. Much survives of the late Norman work—the arcades, for example—and there is also Gothic work. A rare 15th-century cross-head is carved with figures of the Crucifixion.

Sheringham Hall *Norfolk*   554Cd
Built by Humphry Repton and his son, J. A. Repton, in 1812. It is noted for its rhododendron gardens. (By appointment.)

Shifnal *Shropshire*   552Bb
CHURCH OF ST ANDREW A large church built of the local sandstone, cruciform with a central tower. Originally Norman, there are many subsequent additions: the hammerbeam roof over the nave and chancel were probably added after a fire in 1591. There are 16th- and 17th-century monuments, and several stained-glass windows of the mid-1800's. St Andrew's was restored by Sir Gilbert Scott *c.* 1876.

Shillington *Beds.*   547He
CHURCH OF ALL SAINTS The church has a wonderful hill-top site, typical of many in the Chilterns. Mainly the work of *c.* 1300, it has hardly been altered since, though the tower was rebuilt in

CHANCEL CHAIR

The Norman church at Shobdon was rebuilt at the expense of Lord Bateman in 1752–6. He entrusted the work to the care of his brother Richard, a friend of Horace Walpole, the author and antiquary. The architect is unknown but he was a friend of Walpole's, perhaps William Kent or Richard Bentley. The church was restored and decorated in the original 18th-century colours in 1971. This chair is one of a pair in the chancel and shows well the exquisite elaborate ornamental detail of the mid-18th century. (Church of St John the Evangelist, Shobdon)

the 18th century. There is a fine vaulted crypt under the chancel, partly built into the slope of the hill, and there are medieval screens and brasses.

Shipley *W. Sussex*   542Ad
CHURCH OF ST MARY There is much fine Norman carving here, and the notable monument to Sir Thomas Caryll (1616) and his wife.

Shipton Hall *Shropshire*   546Ag
An Elizabethan manor house with a stone-walled garden. There is a medieval dovecote, and a church with Saxon foundations dating from the 8th century next door to the house.

Shobdon *Heref. & Worcs.*   546Af
CHURCH OF ST JOHN THE EVANGELIST Once there was a 12th-century priory here, which was moved away. What remained of the church was rebuilt in 1752–6 (by a friend of Horace Walpole—the author and antiquary whose own house, Strawberry Hill, did much to popularise the 18th-

century Gothic style), and is now a charming example of mid-18th-century Gothic. The chancel arch consists of a trio of ogee arches, with pendants instead of columns between them. There is a three-decker pulpit with a canopied sounding-board, and a monument of 1804 by Joseph Nollekens.

Shoreham-by-Sea *W. Sussex*   542Bd
MARLIPINS MUSEUM Housed in a building dating from the 12th and 14th centuries which was probably a feudal administrative headquarters of the port of New Shoreham, the museum specialises in the history of the ancient port and borough and the life of its people. Maritime exhibits include model ships and ship paintings, and there are local topographical prints and water-colours. A turret clock dated 1690 is from the parish church.

Shorwell *Isle of Wight*   541Gc
Perhaps the most characteristic of villages on the Isle of Wight, with many thatched cottages, two Elizabethan manor houses near by, and a splendid position under the ridge of Downs that bisects the island.
CHURCH OF ST PETER A mainly 15th-century church, with traces of earlier work, in a pretty village. It contains an interesting and unusual wall-painting of St Christopher. There is a 15th-century pulpit, and many memorials to the Leigh family, including one to Sir John Leigh with kneeling figures.

Shottesbrooke *Berks.*   547Gb
CHURCH OF ST JOHN THE BAPTIST A cruciform church in the Decorated Gothic style, its central tower topped by a steeple. There are two 14th-century tombs in the north transept, one of which is probably that of Sir William Trussell, who founded the church. Brasses of the 14th and 16th centuries remain, and there are several fragments of 14th-century stained glass. The font is also 14th century.

Shotwick *Cheshire*   551Je
CHURCH OF ST MICHAEL In a village where the Dee once flowed, a remote church with embattled west tower. Though mainly 14th century, a Norman doorway remains and inside there is a good three-decker pulpit, box-pews and a canopied church-warden's seat of 1673.

Shrewsbury *Shropshire*   551Jb
ABBEY CHURCH OF THE HOLY CROSS Some Norman work is preserved in the abbey, founded in 1083 by Roger de Montgomery. The font is reputedly made from a Roman capital, and the west tower has a fine Perpendicular window. There are tombs and monuments dating from *c.*

JESSE WINDOW, ST MARY'S, SHREWSBURY

The great east window is filled with English 14th-century glass; the three panels shown above contain one of the largest representations of the Tree of Jesse, which traces the genealogy of Christ back to David and his   *father, Jesse. The glass was originally commissioned by Sir John de Charlton and his wife, Lady Hawis, for the Grey Friars; it was transferred to St Chad's after the Dissolution, and thence to St Mary's.*

ROMAN MIRROR FROM WROXETER

Found during the excavations at the site of the Roman regional capital city of Viroconium (Wroxeter), five miles south-east of Shrewsbury, this silver mirror measures $11\frac{1}{2}$ in. across. Apart from the handle it was cast in one piece, and was undoubtedly imported, the exquisite ornamentation suggesting that it came from an Italian workshop in the 2nd century or perhaps earlier. The handle is made of two loops of grooved silver wire, arranged to form a knot and soldered to the mirror back, the terminals being covered by four leaf-shaped ornaments; on each loop of wire are two six-petalled flowers. Leaves and fruits of the oak, apple and pine, with flowers, decorate the edge of the mirror back. (Rowley's House Museum, Shrewsbury)

1300 onwards, and remains of the 14th-century shrine of St Winifred. The chancel was designed by Pearson in 1887, and 19th-century stained glass can be seen.

CASTLE Built originally *c.* 1080 and besieged in 1138 by Stephen, who hanged the entire garrison. David, King of Wales, was executed in the yard by order of Edward I in 1283.

CHURCH OF ST CHAD Old St Chad's Church was mainly a 12th-century building when the tower fell down in 1788 and destroyed it. Only the Lady Chapel and fine stained glass of the Jesse window, which was transferred to St Mary's, survived. A new site overlooking the Severn was then chosen for the rebuilding. George Steuart was chosen as architect and designed the circular church built in 1790–2. This comprises a square tower linked to the circular nave by an oval anteroom containing the stairs to the gallery. In its upper stages the tower becomes first octagonal, and then circular with detached columns supporting a cupola.

CHURCH OF ST MARY The largest and most splendid of the several interesting churches in this medieval town; St Mary's is Norman, with Early English and later work. Its stained glass is especially important. There is a 14th-century Jesse window, and many windows with 15th- and 16th-century glass from Germany and the Netherlands, work by the craftsmen of Altenburg, Trier and Liège. There are several monuments, mainly of the 18th century.

CLIVE HOUSE This 18th-century Georgian house was the town house of Clive of India. It has an outstanding collection of Shropshire pottery and porcelain, and good local watercolours and portraits are on display.

ROWLEY'S HOUSE MUSEUM A 16th-century timbered house containing a fine collection of antiquities from the Roman town of Viroconium (Wroxeter), as well as prehistoric and geological exhibits.

Shugborough *Staffs.* 552Cc
Seat of the Earls of Lichfield (the Anson family) containing the 2nd Earl's collection of 18th-century French furniture. The Staffordshire County Museum is housed in the former stable and

SHUGBOROUGH

The main block of this house was built for William Anson, father of Admiral Lord Anson. The admiral was responsible for the addition of a room in Chinese taste; in about 1747 he commissioned its decoration from drawings made in Canton by one of his officers. About 1760 Lord Anson's elder brother, Thomas, an ardent antiquarian, engaged James 'Athenian' Stuart to build the wings, and a sculpture gallery at right angles to the west front (shown below); the two wings have domed bows on the east side. Together Anson and Stuart laid out the park with much ornamental architecture in Classical style, including the Tower of the Winds (shown left). In 1803, in preparation for a visit by the Prince Regent, James Wyatt extended the west front of the main block to create an elegant saloon from what had been the dining-room. J. C. F. Rossi provided the chimney-piece of the saloon and Peter Scheemakers carved the relief 'Et in Arcadio Ego'.

kitchen wing of the house. The displays include the Balston Collection of Staffordshire portrait figures (see page 440). In the park is a group of monuments based on the drawings *The Antiquities of Athens,* by James Stuart, painter and architect (1713–88), who introduced Greek-style architecture to England.

Shute Barton *Devon*   *540Bc*
A medieval castellated dwelling-house, built in 1380–90, with late 15th-century alterations. The gatehouse, with mullioned windows, is early Jacobean, but the gazebo structures on its flanks date from after 1870. The kitchen has a huge fire-place; the hall, which is above the kitchen, has a trussed roof with curved wind-braces. (Interior by appointment.)

Sibsey *Lincs.*   *553Jd*
CHURCH OF ST MARGARET A Norman church near the Fen country—the nave arcades are particularly interesting. The west tower is Early English at its base and Perpendicular above. The south porch is dated 1699.

Silbury Hill *Wilts.*   *540Fg*
The excavations of this great mound, which were completed in 1970, have determined the method by which it was built but have thrown no light upon its purpose. It was built in three stages, each

immediately following the previous one, so that it is of one period, *c.* 3000 BC, towards the end of the Neolithic period.

Silchester *Hants.*   *541Hf*
This was the cantonal town known as Calleva Atrebatum and, though no internal buildings are today visible, the essential shape and defences of the area are clearly defined. There is an amphi-theatre, seen as an oval hollow, outside but close to the east end of the walled area. Its failure to become a town-site in post-Roman times has meant that, below the modern plough-soil, the bases of all its buildings are preserved.
CALLEVA MUSEUM This was opened in 1951 as a contribution to the Festival of Britain. In 1976, the museum was comprehensively rearranged to provide pictorial and graphic displays, illustrating Silchester as it was in Roman times. The reconstruction drawings and other illustrative material show that Silchester was both a market town and a provincial administrative centre, occupied by, perhaps, 4000 people.
CHURCH OF ST MARY A medieval parish church, St Mary's has a fine early 16th-century chancel screen, a 15th-century font, a pulpit with an ornate tester dated 1639, and in the chancel medieval wall-paintings of masonry and flowers.

SILBURY HILL

The largest artificial mound in Europe, Silbury Hill is 130 ft high and covers 5½ acres. It stands near several prehistoric sites including Avebury and the West Kennet Long Barrow. Silbury is a mystery, for as yet no one has discovered what it is or why it was built. It may be a barrow—a prehistoric burial place. It was there before the Romans built their road from London to Bath, for the road goes round the hill.

Silkstone *S. Yorks.*   *552Dg*
CHURCH OF ALL SAINTS A Perpendicular, mainly 14th- and 15th-century church, with a west tower, replacing an earlier one. There are screens and a fine monument to Sir Thomas Wentworth and wife, *c.* 1675, attributed to Jasper Latham, a London mason-sculptor.

Simonburn *Northld.*   *558Ah*
CHURCH OF ST MUNGO A 13th-century church with a chancel restored by Anthony Salvin in 1863. There is a fragment of a Saxon cross.

Sissinghurst Castle *Kent*   *542De*
The great Tudor and Elizabethan mansion of Sissinghurst Castle was little better than a derelict pile when in 1930 Harold Nicolson and his wife, Victoria Sackville-West, the authoress, acquired it. Round the restored buildings they created one of the loveliest gardens in England. The design is formal, and the main axis, which is a narrow walk between high yew hedges, cuts across the length of the site, widening in the centre to a rondel. The walk leads to small enclosures reminiscent of Elizabethan gardens. Prominent among the enclosures is the White Garden, planted with all silver-leaved and white-flowered plants and divided by low hedges of clipped box. Near the large rose garden, walled on one side and with a profusion of old-fashioned roses and flowering shrubs, is the Cottage Garden. This is reached from the far end of a long walk of pleached lime trees, and in it herbaceous plants grow among paving stones. Four Irish yews guard the entrance to the south cottage, which is covered by a yellow climbing rose. The small nut grove, underplanted with primulas and polyanthuses, is enclosed by formal yew hedges. (See p. 434.)

Sissinghurst Court *Kent*   *542De*
Extensive grounds with flowering trees, a rose garden, lily ponds and fountains surround the 16th-century house. (Gardens by appointment.)

Sittingbourne *Kent*   *542Ef*
COURT HALL MUSEUM The collection, housed in a small manorial court-house of *c.* 1450, includes local archaeological specimens—Palaeolithic tools and Roman finds, and local bygones.

Sizergh Castle *Cumbria*   *557Jd*
The home of the Strickland family since 1239, the castle comprises a 14th-century tower built as a shelter against Scots raiders, and additions made in the 15th, 16th and 18th centuries. It contains fine panelling and ceilings, and the contents include pictures, furniture and Stuart and Jacobite relics.

Skara Brae *Mainland, Orkney*   *569Hg*
A Neolithic settlement of stone houses, preserved by being buried under blown sand. The houses are very closely grouped and each, internally, is roughly rectangular with rounded corners. These rooms contain furniture of stone 'planks' built into the main structure, including box-beds, dressers, wall-cupboards and tanks for live fish. Some of the small finds from the excavation are preserved on the site.

Skelton *N. Yorks*   *558Dc*
CHURCH OF CHRIST THE CONSOLER A large ornate church built 1871-2 by Lady Vyner in memory of her son who was murdered by Turkish bandits. There is some magnificent stained glass.

Skenfrith Castle *Gwent*   *546Ad*
A Welsh border castle built by the Normans overlooking the Monnow Valley. It has a round keep surrounded by 13th-century walls with towers.

Skipton *N. Yorks.*   *558Bb*
CASTLE A 12th-century Norman foundation on a rock, it was the stronghold of Robert de Clifford in 1309 and of the Clifford family for centuries. Its features include a great gateway with four towers, a banqueting hall 50 ft long, a kitchen with a huge roasting and baking hearth, a dungeon, and a 'shell room' of shells and coral. The Tudor wing was built by the Earl of Cumberland in 1536. The castle was the last stronghold of the Royalists in the North; it surrendered honourably in 1645.
CHURCH OF THE HOLY TRINITY A mainly Perpendicular church, with a simple west tower, standing by Skipton Castle. Inside are 13th-century sedilia with arches, screens of the 16th century, and a fine 17th-century font cover. There are 16th- and 17th-century monuments to the Cliffords, Earls of Cumberland.
CRAVEN MUSEUM The museum is concerned primarily with local history, natural history, and archaeology. Antiquities include remains from Elbolton cave and an Iron Age sword.

Skirza *Highland*   *569Me*
BROCH Standing on a narrow spur of cliff above the sea, the approach to the broch from the main cliff-top is protected by a wide ditch. There is a wall, very thick in proportion to the enclosed

SISSINGHURST CASTLE GARDEN

A beautiful formal garden centred around the old tower of Sissinghurst Castle, created by Sir Harold Nicolson and his wife, Victoria Sackville-West the poetess and author, in the 1930's. From a derelict site, with husband as architect and wife as planter, after much experimentation a series of gardens took shape—each a faultless example of colour and form. A main walk between yew hedges leads from the tower, and to left and right are smaller enclosures, such as the White Garden with silver-leaved and white-flowered plants, and the rose garden. Near by is the Cottage Garden shown here, with a collection of old-fashioned plants.

space, the one being 14 ft thick and the other some 22 ft across. The entrance is on the seaward side of the building and there is some evidence of minor additional structures. It is an Iron Age dwelling

Sleaford *Lincs.* 553Hd
CHURCH OF ST DENYS A grand church, dating from the 12th century; the west tower has an extremely early stone broach spire. There is remarkable window tracery and an architecturally interesting interior, with brasses and several monuments, including one by Maximilian Colt.

Sledmere House *Humberside* 558Fc
A Georgian mansion completed in 1787, with a great library (100 ft long) by Joseph Rose. On view are Chippendale, Sheraton and French furnishings, porcelain, antique statuary and fine paintings. The house stands in a landscaped park, created by Capability Brown in 1777.

Slinfold *W. Sussex* 542Ae
The L-shaped group of Georgian cottages, chequered red and blue, behind white railings, is the best part of Slinfold.

Smallhythe Place
(The Ellen Terry Memorial) *Kent* 542Ee
Dame Ellen Terry, the actress, acquired this half-timbered house, dating from 1480, in 1899. It now contains items associated with Dame Ellen, Mrs Siddons, David Garrick and many other actors and actresses.

Smarden *Kent* 542Ee
One of the most unspoilt villages in the Weald of Kent. There is a street of brick and weather-boarded cottages, leading up to the church and, to the north-west, two big half-timbered houses built by prosperous clothiers during the 17th century. One is dated 1671.

Smedmore *Dorset* 540Ec
An 18th-century manor house with a collection of antique dolls and Dutch furniture.

Smithills Hall *Greater Manchester* 552Ag
A manor house with magpie façade. The great hall and adjoining rooms date from the 14th century; the remainder dates from the Tudor and later periods. The house was recently restored and contains fine Stuart furnishings.

Snaith *Humberside* 558Ea
PRIORY CHURCH OF ST LAURENCE A big church, originally Norman but rebuilt from the 13th to 15th centuries with west tower and battlements. Inside are monuments from the 15th century onwards, including one to Viscount Downe (*d.* 1837) with a statue by Sir Francis Chantrey.

Snarford *Lincs.* 553Gf
CHURCH OF ST LAURENCE A small church begun in the 12th century, and worth visiting for three outstanding monuments: Sir Thomas St Pol (1582) with kneeling children, Sir George St Pol (1613) with recumbent effigies, and Robert, Earl of Warwick (1619) with alabaster medallion.

Snowshill Manor *Glos.* 546De
This manor house, dating from the 16th and 17th centuries, contains a collection of clocks, musical instruments, armour, scientific instruments, toys and dolls, bicycles, spinning wheels and fire-fighting equipment—over 15,000 items in all.

Somerleyton Hall *Suffolk* 548Fg
An Anglo-Italian masterpiece rebuilt in 1851. It contains tapestries, paintings and carvings by Grinling Gibbons. The 12-acre garden has a maze.

Somersby *Lincs.* 553Je
MANOR FARM Built in 1722, with four towers and a castellated north front; the design is attributed to Sir John Vanbrugh.

Sompting *W. Sussex* 542Ad
CHURCH OF ST MARY THE VIRGIN A church with a Saxon tower, unique in England because of the four-gabled spire, known as a 'Rhenish helm'. There is some Saxon sculpture in the church, which was rebuilt during the 12th century by the Knights Templar. On the south side they built a square chapel with its own small sanctuary, on the north side two small, vaulted chapels. After the expulsion of the Templars in 1306, the church passed to the Knights of St John who built a chapel on the north side connected to the tower and nave. This was rebuilt as a church room in 1971. The Knights of St John, by incorporating the old chapels into the church, gave it its present cruciform shape on different levels.

Southampton *Hants.* 541Gd
A Norman walled and fortified city-port was built here. It was used for continental trade, and pilgrims who took the route via Winchester to the Becket shrine at Canterbury passed through the port. It was also a starting point for military forces bound for France, and the French frequently attacked the town, savagely so in 1338. A splendid shopping centre has replaced the ruins resulting from the Second World War. Much of the old town, including the medieval walls, the towers, gates, and Georgian houses, still remains. The ancient ramparts are set with tablets commemorating events in Southampton's long history. Near by is the Pilgrim Fathers' Memorial, recalling their sailing on August 15, 1620.
BARGATE GUILDHALL The Bargate or Northgate was the most important gateway to medieval Southampton, where the town broker collected tolls on all merchandise entering or leaving the town. It was one of the seven main gateways, and dates from Norman times, its earliest feature being the half-round arch, *c.* 1175–1200. The guildhall, above this archway, was probably established *c.* 1400, and was originally used as the meeting place of the Guild Merchants and later of the Town Assembly. Now a local history museum, it includes among its exhibits two oak panels painted with the effigies of Sir Bevois, legendary hero of Southampton, and his giant squire Ascupart.
GOD'S HOUSE TOWER Originally part of the town's medieval fortifications, the tower is now a museum of archaeology, containing local prehistoric, Roman, Saxon and medieval finds. The oldest items displayed are a series of Old Stone Age (Palaeolithic) hand-axes from the gravel beds of the Southampton district, together with the teeth and bones of animals which inhabited the area during the Ice Age. There is a good collection of early medieval to late 17th-century pottery.
SOUTHAMPTON ART GALLERY Situated in the Civic Centre, it has a fine collection of Impressionists and Post Impressionists, and some old masters. (See p. 436.)
TUDOR HOUSE A late 15th-century building with a Georgian wing, the house displays period furniture, tapestries, glass, domestic objects, costume and accessories, local topographical prints, paintings and drawings. The garden, which is laid out in the formal style typical of the Tudor period, gives access to the remains of a Norman merchant's house dating from the 12th century, and contains a bronze cannon made for Henry VIII in 1542.
WOOL HOUSE Originally built during the 14th century as a medieval warehouse for wool prior to shipment, the Wool House is noted for its Spanish chestnut roof, which, apart from a few timber cross-ties, is of the same period as the main fabric. Carved on the beams are the names, with dates, of some of the French prisoners of war who were confined there during the 18th century. It is now the city's maritime museum.

South Creake *Norfolk* 554Bc
CHURCH OF ST MARY One of the finest village churches in East Anglia, dating mainly from the 13th and 14th centuries. The hammerbeam roof is decorated with medieval carved angels which have recently been restored. The bases of the nave pillars form seats and the larger of the two brasses is unusual in that it depicts a priest lying between his mother and father.

Southend-on-Sea *Essex* 548Cb
BEECROFT ART GALLERY European painting from the 17th century, with special emphasis on British schools from the 18th to the 20th century. A separate gallery of oil paintings, water-colours and drawings illustrates the history of Southend-on-Sea and shipping in the Thames Estuary. Temporary exhibitions of traditional and contemporary art are held every month.
PRITTLEWELL PRIORY MUSEUM The building itself incorporates the remains of a Cluniac priory founded *c.* 1110. These remains include the refectory, the half-timbered prior's chamber with its 14th-century roof, the cellars and the cloister garth. The foundations of the church, south transept and the east cloister wing are now laid out in an individual garden.

The museum collections are housed in an early 19th-century wing, and cover the archaeology, history, social life and natural history of south-eastern Essex. They are particularly strong in material on the Iron Age and Romano-British periods.

SUTHERLAND *Red Landscape*

The Englishness of English art finds in our time one of its purest exponents in Graham Sutherland. First he is English in his linear quality, which knits together with a wiry black thread the forms of his visionary landscapes, as in this 'Red Landscape'. Then he is English because landscape is the essence of his art—not landscape in the 18th-century sense, for he is not a scenic artist. He shuns perspective as it is not the look of the landscape but the feeling of it he is after. So his colour and luminosity are highly personal. His universe is one of strange forms and presences, of a hostile, sinister and mysterious Nature, of roots and thorns rather than fruits and flowers. These 'paraphrases of reality' as he has called them, are 'implications of the apparent tragedy of 20th-century civilization'. (Southampton Art Gallery)

South Harting *W. Sussex*   *541Jd*
CHURCH OF SS MARY AND GABRIEL Impressive cruciform church, containing what may be Saxon work. The present building is mainly 14th century, restored after a fire in 1576. There is a central tower and broach spire, and a 13th-century font of Purbeck marble. It also contains a 19th-century spiral staircase made by a local carpenter, a small museum, several monuments and, in the churchyard, a fine War memorial by Eric Gill.

South Mimms *Herts.*   *547Jc*
CHURCH OF ST GILES Basically 13th–15th century, with 16th-century additions; renovated *c.* 1877 by G. E. Street. There are 16th-century wood screens and stained glass, and some good tombs of the Frowyke family from the 15th and 16th centuries; also a 13th-century font.

South Molton *Devon*   *539Gf*
BOROUGH MUSEUM Housed in a building dating from 1620, the collection includes manuscripts and documents relating to local history, pewter dating from the 17th to the 19th centuries—some marked Sandringham—weights and measures from the reign of William IV, a 1725 fire engine, a 1750 cider press, 18th-century wigmaking tools, and other items of agricultural or historical interest, including stocks and man-traps.

Southport *Merseyside*   *551Jg*
ATKINSON ART GALLERY A changing collection of English 18th-, 19th- and 20th-century paintings.
BOTANIC GARDENS MUSEUM A collection of late-18th-century dolls is a principal part of the contents. The 19th-century building has one room furnished in Victorian style. There are also local water-colours and relics, and a section devoted to British birds completes the collection.

CHURCH OF ST CUTHBERT The old parish church of Southport, rebuilt in 1730. The west tower and spire date from a few years later. St Cuthbert's was enlarged in the 19th century. There is a wall monument by Nollekens, *c.* 1791, showing carved

scientific instruments, an 18th-century font, and fine early 18th-century wood-carved reredos and panels by R. Prescott (from the demolished St Peter's, Liverpool).

South Shields *Tyne & Wear*   *558Ch*
MUSEUM The museum contains the original model of the first lifeboat designed by William Wouldhave in 1789. Part of the Sir Walter Runciman Natural History Collection can also be seen, and a collection of local glass.
ROMAN FORT AND MUSEUM Headquarters, barrack blocks and guardrooms of the easternmost fort of Hadrian's Wall can still be seen. The museum contains relics from the fort including inscriptions, jewellery and the South Shields Roman sword.

Southsea *Hants.*   *541Hc*
ROYAL MARINES MUSEUM The museum, housed in the old Officers' Mess, has a display covering the history of the Royal Marines from their formation in 1664. The highlights are a medal collection which includes 10 Victoria Crosses, a display of military prints, portraits of former Royal Marine officers, a collection of military uniforms and a diorama of the action at Zeebrugge on April 23, 1918. The museum houses the offices of the Royal Marine historian, and there are many books, documents and photographs illustrating the history of the Marines.

South Stack *Anglesey, Gwynedd*   *550Df*
Set on a small island connected to the mainland by an early suspension bridge reached by a descent of some 400 steps, South Stack presents a dramatic picture whatever the weather. The present tower was built in 1809 and is little altered, and the station is still manned. One of the odd features of this site was devised in 1832: a small square revolving subsidiary light was lowered to within 60 ft of the sea when fog obscured the lighthouse.

Southwell *Notts.*   *552Fd*
MINSTER This was a collegiate church under the Archbishop of York, and there are traces of an earlier Saxon foundation. The present Norman nave was begun in 1108, and the two western towers have reconstructed pyramidal roofs; the crossing tower is squat. The chancel is Early English of the 13th century, while late in the same century the chapter house was planned. This is famous for its carved foliage decoration. The church was raised to cathedral status in 1884.

Southwick *Hants.*   *541Hd*
CHURCH OF ST JAMES A rare post-Reformation Tudor church with a magnificent 18th-century reredos decorated with cherubs and doves.

Southwold *Suffolk*   *548Ff*
A charming seaside town on a low cliff, once a centre for fishing and boat building, now a resort and holiday town. It has many open spaces, the greens being laid out to prevent further fires after a big fire in 1659. The town has flint and red-brick cottages, colour-washed houses and a white inland lighthouse. There is a museum with local exhibits in a 17th-century Dutch-style cottage.
CHURCH OF ST EDMUND, KING AND MARTYR A large, magnificent Suffolk church, with huge windows, a tall west tower, and a two-storey south porch. There is much flushwork decoration. Inside is a mutilated seven-sacrament font with 1930's cover, and a rood screen across the whole width of the church. There are also good stalls with carvings.
MUSEUM A 17th-century building, one of the earliest in the borough, houses a collection of local fossils, shells, birds, and relics, including some of the Southwold Railway.

ITALIAN SALLET

This late 15th-century helmet once hung over the tomb in Whaplode parish church (Lincs.) of Sir Anthony Irby, who died in 1610. An example of fine North Italian (probably Milanese) work, the skull is beaten out of a single piece of steel, and the whole decorated with strips of gilt copper. Originally the main surfaces would have been coloured blue. The helmet is a sallet, a popular 15th-century form of head armour. (Spalding Gentlemen's Society Museum)

Sowerby *W. Yorks.*   *552Cg*
CHURCH OF ST PETER Once a Chapel of Ease of the parish of Halifax. It has a life-size statue of Archbishop Tillotson, who was born near by, by Joseph Wilton (*c.* 1796). The original design for the statue is in the Victoria and Albert Museum.

Spalding *Lincs.*   *553Hc*
AYSCOUGHFEE HALL A 15th-century mansion restored in the 18th century, when it was the home of Maurice Johnson, who founded the Spalding Gentlemen's Society. It is now a local history museum, with a good collection of British birds.
CHURCH OF SS MARY AND NICOLAS A church of varied styles, begun *c.* 1284, with additions of the 14th and 15th centuries. There is a Perpendicular hammerbeam roof with angels, Victorian stained glass and a screen of 1875.
SPALDING GENTLEMEN'S SOCIETY MUSEUM The society began in 1710, with informal meetings of a few local gentlemen in the Abbey Yard to discuss antiquities and to read *The Tatler*. In 1712 the society was formally established. Members have included Sir Isaac Newton, Alexander Pope, William Stukeley, John Gay, Sir Hans Sloane, George Vertue and Alfred Lord Tennyson.
The society's library was created by the gift of a volume from every new member, and through gifts, bequests and purchases now contains extensive sections on archaeology, numismatics, local and natural history, heraldry and genealogy. It is one of the oldest societies in the kingdom, and the earliest provincial association for the encouragement of archaeology. (By appointment.)
YE OLDE WHITE HORSE INN Once the home of rich merchants, the Willesbys, it is perhaps the oldest dwelling in Spalding.

Spean Bridge *Highland*   *565Hd*
COMMANDO MEMORIAL Erected to the memory of the Commando forces who did their training in this area in the Second World War.

Spetchley Park *Heref. & Worcs.*   *546Ce*
Some 28 acres of garden with ornamental trees and shrubs, water fowl, and deer.

Spilsby *Lincs.*   *553Je*
CHURCH OF ST JAMES Noteworthy for its monuments to the Berties and Willoughbys, from the 14th to the 17th centuries, many with effigies.

Spofforth Castle *N. Yorks.*   *558Cb*
The ruins of the former home of the Percy family, who received a licence to erect defences in 1308. The hall has 15th-century window tracery and a moulded doorway. The kitchens were part of the undercroft.

Sprotbrough *S. Yorks.*   *552Ef*
CHURCH OF ST MARY Built between the 12th and 15th centuries, with a Decorated west tower. The furnishings include a rood screen, chancel stalls and carved bench ends. There is a brass of a knight (*d.* 1474), and other monuments.

Spynie Palace *Grampian*   *566Dg*
The ruins of a massive square fortress, built in the 15th century, and once the castle of the Bishops of Moray. The original tower is six storeys high.

Stafford *Staffs.*   *552Bc*
CHURCH OF ST CHAD A grand Norman church, with a superb chancel arch and impressive nave arcades.
MUSEUM AND ART GALLERY Items illustrating local history, social life, industry and art are on view; about 20 exhibitions are held each year.

Staindrop *Durham*   *558Be*
CHURCH OF ST MARY Seven hundred years are chronicled in the impressive series of monuments at St Mary's, beginning with 13th-century effigies to the Earls of Westmorland, and continuing to the Duchess of Cleveland's memorial of 1859. Like much else in Co. Durham, the church's origins are Saxon; the west tower is Norman, and the transepts date from the 13th century. The font and stalls are in the Perpendicular style; the stained glass was made in the 19th century.

Stalybridge *Greater Manchester*   *552Cf*
ASTLEY CHEETHAM ART GALLERY Small but important collection of medieval and Renaissance paintings as well as works by Cox, Turner, Burne-Jones and local artists. Also Greek, Roman and Egyptian antiquities and temporary exhibitions.

Stamford *Lincs.*   *553Gb*
Stamford is one of the finest medieval towns in Europe. One of the five Danish Boroughs, it was also recorded in the Domesday Book and later had 14 parish churches, together with monasteries, friaries, hospitals and medieval 'schools'. Of these, five medieval churches survive as do numerous other medieval remains. During the 16th century the town's importance waned owing to the decline of the wool trade and the silting up of the river. The 17th and 18th centuries were responsible for much of the present architectural appearance of the town, shaped by a mixture of local vernacular styles, 'pattern-book' architecture and the rich limestone belt on which Stamford sits.
ALL SAINTS' PLACE AND CHURCH The church with its fine spire dates from the 13th and 15th centuries and contains fine brasses to John and William Browne. No 3 is a particularly good 18th-century house. In the opposite corner of Red Lion Square is St John's Church, *c.* 1450, with good 15th-century screenwork and stained glass.
BARN HILL A street dating from the Middle Ages, with high-quality houses of the 17th to 19th centuries. Of note is Barn Hill House—late-17th century with the front remodelled in 1843.
BASTION Part of the medieval town wall, in West Street, which once encircled Stamford.
BROAD STREET Browne's Hospital, 1475, is one of the finest almshouses surviving in England. It was altered in 1870, but the 15th-century chapel remains with its original pews, screen and stained glass; No. 32 is a 17th-century house; Nos. 1, 2,

MONUMENT TO THE
5th EARL OF EXETER

The Earl of Exeter was a leading patron of Italian sculpture, and while on a visit to Rome he commissioned a monument to himself and his wife from Pierre Monnot (1657–1733), a French sculptor whose most important work is the tomb of Pope Innocent XI in St Peter's, Rome. The Exeter monument was shipped to England in pieces and assembled in Stamford in 1704 by the English sculptor William Palmer; it is in the Roman baroque style and apart from the effigies of the earl and his wife in Classical dress, resembles the Papal tombs of the period. (Church of St Martin, Stamford)

3, 14, 15, 19, 25 and 34 are 18th century.

BURGHLEY HOSPITAL AND ALMSHOUSES Built by Lord Burghley in the late 16th century on the site of the 12th-century Hospital of St John and St Thomas. The arch and buttress on the river front survive from the 12th century, and the main range along the river probably dates from 1616.

The almshouses were restored in 1964.

CASTLE Little remains at the foot of Castle Dyke other than three 13th-century blank arches and fragments of wall. The castle belonged to one of the barons who forced King John to sign the Magna Carta at Runnymede in 1215.

GEORGE HOTEL One of the earliest inns in Stamford, certainly in existence in 1568. The present hotel consists of a 15th-century building (the Hermitage) with original screens and a stone-vaulted cellar, and a main range built round a courtyard of the late 17th, 18th and 19th centuries. Each side of the main entrance are the *York* and *London* rooms, formerly used as waiting rooms.

HIGH STREET, ST MARTIN'S A curving street rising from the river—possibly the axial road of the Saxon 'burgh' of AD 922. St Martin's Church, *c.* 1480, is probably best known for its monuments to Lord Burghley, and the 5th Earl of Exeter, by Pierre Monnot (1657–1733).

MUSEUM, BROAD STREET Contains an interesting display of Stamfordware, the unique glazed pottery produced in the town *c.* 900–1250 and the clothes of the famous fat man, Daniel Lambert, who weighed over 52 stone.

ST GEORGE'S SQUARE Together with the adjacent part of St Mary's Street, it contains some of the town's finest Georgian architecture. The buildings are grouped intimately around the 13th–15th-century church that is long associated with the Order of the Garter. No. 17 has a medieval arch and buttress; Nos. 14–15 are 16th century with an attractive and roughly contemporary triangular window; No. 19 is perhaps Stamford's finest house, 1674, in the Artisan Mannerist style; Nos. 18, 20, 21 are fine mid-18th-century houses; in the corner, Assembly Rooms of 1727. Round the corner, in St Mary's Street, is the Theatre of 1768, recently restored; Nos. 22–26 are good Georgian houses; Stamford Hotel, 1812, is in the Greek style. In St George's Street is a medieval cottage with a circular stone chimney.

ST LEONARD'S PRIORY, PRIORY ROAD Fine Norman building with five bays of the nave and the west front intact, early and late 12th century. The Benedictine priory was founded in 1082 as a cell of Durham.

ST MARY'S HILL Dominating the hill is the magnificent 13th-century tower and the 14th-century spire of St Mary's Church, of such beauty that Sir Walter Scott is said to have doffed his hat every time he passed by. Georgian Town Hall of 1779 contains regalia dating back to Edward IV, *c.* 1460. Opposite Nos. 9A–10 is a 12th-century arch which was formerly the doorway of a Norman house. Beneath the Wine Bar at No. 13 is an early 13th-century stone-vaulted undercroft, probably the storeroom of a medieval merchant. This is the best of Stamford's many early crypts.

ST PAUL'S STREET Opposite Stamford School is the Brazenose Gateway, long associated with the Hall where rebellious students attempting a secession from Oxford tried to establish a rival university in 1333. The two east bays of Stamford School chapel are the 12th-century remains of the former parish church of St Paul. The Greyfriar's Gateway, now an entrance to the Stamford & Rutland Hospital, dates from the first half of the 14th century.

ST PETER'S STREET A street dating back to the earliest settlement of Stamford, now comprising modest 17th–19th-century buildings. The Stamford Institution, 1842, is in Greek style, and Rutland Terrace is a Regency-style terrace dating from about 1830.

Stand *Greater Manchester* 552Bg
CHURCH OF ALL SAINTS Built *c.* 1825 by Sir Charles Barry, architect of the Houses of Parliament. Like them, All Saints is in Gothic style with a tower.

Stanford Hall *Leics.* 552Ea
The home of the Cave family since 1430. The present William-and-Mary mansion was begun in 1680, and the stables finished by the Smiths of Warwick in 1730–45. It contains a collection of Stuart paintings and relics, fine furniture, and family costumes from the time of Elizabeth I onwards. Part of the stables houses a collection of vintage motor-cycles and cars, and a full-size replica of the flying machine designed in 1898 by the aviation pioneer, Percy Pilcher. There is a walled garden, and the Avon runs through the grounds.

Stanstead Abbots *Herts.* 548Aa
At the west end of the village street is an unusual red-brick house dating from 1752. It is an early example of sham-Gothic, with a circular stair turret and an embattled top. The Red Lion Inn, the Old Clockhouse and the Baesche Almshouses are all early 17th century.

CHURCH OF ST JAMES A mainly 15th-century church, with a timber south porch. The brick north chapel was added in 1577. The unspoilt interior has 18th-century furnishings, box-pews and three-decker pulpit. The monuments include early 19th-century work by John Bacon Junior and his partner Manning.

Stanton *Glos.* 546De
CHURCH OF ST MICHAEL AND ALL ANGELS A cruciform church, with remains of Norman work, it has a west tower with spire, and a Perpendicular south aisle and porch. The pulpit is 17th century; and the rood screen, reredos, gallery and some of the stained glass are by Sir Ninian Comper.

Stanton Drew *Avon* 540Cf
Here are three early Bronze Age stone circles. The central and largest is about 120 yds across and has 27 standing stones visible. From it, an avenue, with several stones still standing, runs east to join another from the north circle. The latter is smaller in diameter, and here are eight stones. The remaining circle lies to the south-west and still has 12 stones. An adjunct of this circle-complex is the 'cove', a structural remnant standing behind the Druids Arms Inn. Its precise significance is not known. The circles are known locally as 'The Devil's Wedding' from a legend that tells of a wedding party that danced on the Sabbath to the Devil's piping. Each member of the party was turned to stone, and there they stand to this day.

Stanton Harcourt *Oxon.* 546Ec
CHURCH OF ST MICHAEL An impressive cruciform church, originally Norman. The central tower is Early English below and Perpendicular above, and most of the building is of these periods; for example the chancel and screen are Early English. There are many monuments, mostly to 14th-century Harcourts; one of them shows a Lady Harcourt wearing the Order of the Garter. A fine standing figure of Lord Harcourt in peer's robes (*c.* 1832) is by R. W. Sievier.

Stanton Moor *Derbys.* 552De
In an area of some 600 yds radius there lies a concentration of monuments, all apparently of the Middle Bronze Age. Near the north end of the area stands the embanked circle known as the Nine Ladies, with which the isolated standing stone, the King Stone, close by to the south-west, should probably be associated. Away to the west is Doll Tor, a free-standing stone circle. Many of its components are still upright, though two have fallen. There are also three circular ring-cairns each with two opposed entrances and a few large stones which may once have stood upright.

There are 70 or more round cairns in the area, of various sizes. Some have been excavated and contain Bronze Age funeral urns.

Stanwell *Surrey* 542Ag
CHURCH OF ST MARY THE VIRGIN An 11th-century church with a 13th-century chancel; 14th-century south aisle; and an 18th-century wooden spire—138 ft high and leaning 6 ft out of plumb. Inside there are two medieval piscinas, and Latin graffiti on the tower pillars.

Stanwick *N. Yorks.* 558Ce
HILL-FORT Though the first defences at Stanwick may be called a hill-fort, the subsequent additional fortifications make it unique in Britain.

The first structure is the Tofts, a 17 acre area protected by a single bank and external ditch; it belongs to a period around the beginning of the 1st century AD.

About 50 years later, a 130 acre enclosure was

MONUMENT TO
LORD AND LADY KNYVETT

This marble monument to Lord and Lady Knyvett was carved about 1622 by Nicholas Stone. Stone was master-mason to Charles I during most of the period that Inigo Jones was Surveyor-General, but he also worked as a sculptor. He is particularly noted for his monument to John Donne in St Paul's Cathedral. Stone received part of his early training in sculpture in Amsterdam and introduced the use of black and white marble into England. (Church of St Mary, Stanwell)

attached on the north side, again defended by a single bank and ditch. This bank had a drystone facing and the ditch was 16 ft deep with a flat bottom.

About AD 72, an enormous addition was made on the south, nearly 600 acres being enclosed by a bank and ditch which linked with those of the second stage. This ditch was V-shaped and 15 ft deep; the bank also had drystone facing.

The history of the Roman conquest of Brigantian territory (the area occupied by the British tribe of the Brigantes—roughly from Cumberland and Durham in the north to the Mersey, Peak District and Humber in the south), gives the clue to these developments. Shortly after AD 51, civil war developed between pro- and anti-Roman factions in the Brigantes. Some 20 years later, the whole tribe revolted and another year or two were to pass before they were finally reduced to submission.

Stanydale *Mainland, Shetland* 568Ef
TEMPLE AND HOUSES Called a temple because of its semi-sepulchral features, the chief of which is a thick wall surrounding an oval area, though one end has a 'reversed' curve to its concave front, with an entrance in its middle.

Remains of stone houses surround the temple and a further group dating from Neolithic times stands near by.

Stapleford Park *Leics.* 552Fc
A mansion displaying a curious mixture of styles that resulted when the old wing, dated 1500 and decorated with sculptures depicting scenes from history, legend and the Scriptures, was embellished with Flemish gables in 1633. The house was added to *c.* 1670 and in Victorian times. It contains pictures, tapestries and notable furniture. A fine 18th-century parish church stands in the grounds, which contain a lake with herons and Canada geese, and two miniature passenger liners. (See p. 440.)
CHURCH OF ST MARY MAGDALENE A Gothic Revival church was rebuilt by George Richardson in 1783 at the Earl of Harborough's expense. The interior, restored to original state in 1968, has inward-facing seats, as in a college chapel. Monuments include a brass of *c.* 1490 and, on the north side of the chancel, a large work in marble by Michael Rysbrack, *c.* 1732.

¡VICTORIAN PORTRAIT FIGURES IN STAFFORDSHIRE POTTERY¡

QUEEN VICTORIA, ALBERT AND CHILD *Staffordshire pottery figures were popular about 1840–90, and Queen Victoria was a favourite subject for pottery groups, especially during the period when her children were being born. Later, the outbreak of the Crimean War encouraged the production of figures of the queen with her allies, and the groups became larger so that incidents from the war could be portrayed. The figures were made from fine white earthenware, painted with bold enamel colours; gilt was often used for titles and decoration.*

NAPOLEON BONAPARTE *This 2 ft high Staffordshire pottery figure of Napoleon is the tallest of the known portrait figures. The Staffordshire figures, made for a popular market, were largely ignored by museums and collectors until the 1920's when Thomas Balston started a collection. Balston specialised in figures of famous personalities, and his collection of over 400 includes portrait figures of Queen Victoria and her family, of statesmen, soldiers, and theatrical personalities. It is on display at Shugborough (see p. 431).*

Staunton Harold *Leics.*   552Dc
CHURCH One of the few churches built during Cromwell's Commonwealth; among the inscriptions inside is one over the west door recording that 'In the year 1653 When all thinges Sacred were throughout ye nation Either demolisht or profaned Sir Robert Shirley, Barronet, Founded this church, whose singular praise it is To have done the best things in ye worst times, and hoped them in the most calamitous'. The church has been little altered and its original fittings and communion plate are intact.
HALL A Georgian house (incorporating a 17th-century house), once the seat of Lord Ferrers. It is now one of the Cheshire Foundation Homes for the Physically Handicapped, instituted by Group Captain Cheshire, v.c. (By appointment.)

Stebbing *Essex*   548Bd
A village with some worthwhile houses: Church Farm of the early 16th century and Parsonage Farm, late 16th century; the Friends' Meeting House of 1674 with an 18th-century portico (now a club); and nearby moated Porter's Hall of *c.* 1600. There is also the mound of a vanished castle.
CHURCH OF ST MARY THE VIRGIN A 14th-century church, with west tower and spire. The rood screen is of stone and there is an 18th-century communion rail. The church contains a brass of *c.* 1390.

Steeple Ashton *Wilts.*   540Ef
CHURCH OF ST MARY THE VIRGIN A 15th-century church with a tall west tower, pinnacled and battlemented, which once had a tall stone spire, blown down in 1670. The chancel was rebuilt in

1853. Inside the church, there is a partly panelled roof to the nave, and the aisles and chapels are stone-vaulted, with big bosses; there are some medieval stained glass fragments, and several interesting monuments.

Steeple Aston *Oxon.*   546Fd
CHURCH OF SS PETER AND PAUL In this church is the large marble monument to Sir Francis and Lady Page, of *c.* 1730. The beautiful figures of the judge reclining behind his wife were carved by Henry Scheemakers, brother of the much more famous Peter; he was, nevertheless, an equally good sculptor.

Steetley *Derbys.*   552Ee
CHAPEL OF ALL SAINTS This small Norman chapel, only 52 ft by 15 ft, stands alone in a field and consists of a tiny nave, chancel and smaller apse, with arches between them. The chapel was derelict and roofless after the Commonwealth, but was restored by J. L. Pearson in 1880.

Stein-A-Cleit *Lewis, Western Isles*   568Cd
This enigmatic monument, some 50 ft in diameter, is possibly most comparable to the prehistoric halls of Shetland, such as Stanydale. Many of the stones were stolen before the monument became covered with peat. Traces of inner and outer faces of a massive wall can be seen, together with huge internal stone fittings. Around it is a prehistoric field enclosure, 270 by 180 ft.

Stenness *Mainland, Orkney*   569Hf
THREE STONE RINGS The Ring of Bookan is really a cairn of the Maes Howe type, but has been largely destroyed. The great surrounding ditch is

still in existence, and a mile to the north-east is the Ring of Brodgar, a henge monument. The external bank has now disappeared but the circling ditch still exists and encloses an area 340 ft across, with two entrances. Inside the ditch is a ring of standing stones; there were originally 60, but of these only 36 remain. On one stone there is a Norse Runic inscription.

A mile to the south of Brodgar is the third ring, that of Stenness. This also is a henge, of which the bank and ditch are almost obliterated. It measures some 200 ft in diameter. Originally there stood, just within the ditch, a great ring of 12 stones, of which four only remain. The tallest of these ·is nearly 17 ft high.

The group belongs to the late Neolithic–Early Bronze Age period.

Stevenage *Herts.* 547Jd
MUSEUM The collection illustrates the archaeology, history and natural history of the Stevenage area.

Stevington *Beds.* 547He
Under the churchyard's east wall is a little spring called the Holy Well, visited by pilgrims in medieval times. The Fair Maid of Kent, wife of Edward III's eldest son, the Black Prince, is said to have died here in 1386.
STEVINGTON MILL Dating from 1770, the mill was restored in 1921, bought by Bedfordshire County Council in 1951 and again restored to commemorate the Festival of Britain, 1951. It is a splendid example of one of the few remaining windmills in the county.

Stewkley *Bucks.* 547Gd
CHURCH OF ST MICHAEL AND ALL ANGELS An impressive Norman church, essentially unchanged, with nave, central space with massive tower above, and chancel, but no aisles. There is much decorative carving of zigzags and dragons. G. E. Street did some restoration in 1862.

Steyning *W. Sussex* 542Ad
CHURCH OF ST ANDREW Only the nave of this Norman church remains in its original form. The chancel, transepts and central tower were demolished about 1577 and a west tower built instead—the present chancel arch rising to nearly 40 ft was the west arch of the original tower. The font, of carved marble, was made in the 12th century. In the south aisle are the Arms of Queen Anne.

Stibbington Hall *Cambs.* 547Hg
A country mansion built of Ketton stone *c.* 1625, to an E-shaped plan. (Exterior only.)

Stilton *Cambs.* 547Jg
At the 17th-century Bell Inn at Stilton, the famous cheeses, made in Leicestershire, were loaded on to coaches for London and the North. The Bell has a long range of stone-built bays and gables, with two massive chimney-stacks and an impressive coach entrance. One gable carries the date 1642 but the inn is probably earlier.

Stirling *Central* 561Jf
CASTLE A castle has crowned the precipitous rock set at the narrowing of the Forth Valley—the Gateway to the Highlands—since the Dark Ages. Alexander I of Scotland died here in 1124 and the

STIRLING CASTLE

The strategic position of Stirling Castle in the Forth Valley has always ensured its importance. By the 12th century it was among the most important castles of the Scottish kingdom. During the Scottish wars of Edward I, Stirling Castle was recognised as a key building for the command of the country, and was the subject of a siege in 1304 when it was heroically defended against the English king by Sir William Oliphant. It was recaptured by the Scottish king Robert the Bruce after the Battle of Bannockburn in 1314. The present building is largely a royal residence built in the 15th and 16th centuries. It was the scene of the coronation of Mary, Queen of Scots in 1543. In the ensuing civil wars, it changed hands several times but ceased to be a royal palace when James VI succeeded to the English throne.

441

castle was centuries old then. It was a residence and sometimes the capital of the Scottish kings until 1603, but was several times taken by the English. In 1297 William Wallace, Scottish patriot and hero, won it back, but it was retaken and occupied in 1304 until 1314.

James III was born in the castle in 1452: he rebuilt it and added the fine Parliament Hall, 124 ft long. James V built a carved palace within the castle precincts, and Mary, Queen of Scots was crowned, at the age of nine months, in the old Chapel Royal. The castle was held by Cromwell's troops in 1651.

WALLACE MEMORIAL, STIRLING

In a niche high on this memorial tower stands Sir William Wallace, the Scottish patriot born in 1272. In 1297 he drove the English from Perth and defeated them at Stirling Bridge. Having been outlawed by Edward I in 1304, he was captured by treachery near Glasgow in 1305, brought to London, tried and executed.

CHURCH OF THE HOLY RUDE A large church of the 15th century in which James VI, later James I of England, was crowned at the age of 13 months. The church had a chequered building history. It was divided into west and east churches in the mid-17th century after a parish argument, and it was not until just before the Second World War that it became one church again.
SMITH ART GALLERY AND MUSEUM The museum, founded in 1874, contains oil paintings and watercolours, weapons and implements from Oceania, Africa, India, China, Japan, local antiquities (particularly of the Bronze Age), local rocks, minerals and fossils as well as many items relating to local domestic history—including the oldest curling stone in Scotland, dated 1511, and a 15th-century measuring jug. (Temporary displays only.)
WALLACE MEMORIAL A pinnacled tower, 220 ft high, stands on top of Abbey Craig, and from a niche near its summit a bronze statue of William Wallace, clad in chain-mail, looks out over the scene of his victory in 1297. The memorial was erected in 1867 and contains documents associated with Wallace.

Stockbridge *Hants.*   *541Ge*
The village is a single wide straight street, spanning the Test Valley between one sweep of upland and another, but there is a town hall, with a cupola, and an inn, relic of the days when coaches changed horses here.

Stockport *Greater Manchester*   *552Bf*
STOCKPORT MUSEUM The municipal museum is devoted to the history of the Stockport area from earliest times to the present. Displays in the upper galleries combine models, illustrations, room reconstructions and museum specimens to tell the story of settlement in Stockport, the development of the town, and its industrialisation.

There are relics of early man in the Stockport area, documents and items of local social and industrial history from the 13th century onwards.

The ground floor houses a reconstructed hat block-maker's workshop and related displays on the felt-hatting industry, for which Stockport is famous.

There is a resource area for the use of schools, students and local societies.
WAR MEMORIAL ART GALLERY L. S. Lowry's painting, *Crowther Street, Stockport*, and a bronze sculpture by Epstein, *Head of Yehudi Menuhin*, are the main exhibits in the gallery, which was built as a war memorial in the 1920's. The building is also used for travelling exhibitions.

Stockton *Wilts.*   *540Ee*
CHURCH OF ST JOHN THE BAPTIST Originally Norman, with later Gothic additions, the church has a west tower. An interesting feature inside is the solid wall which was built between the nave and chancel.

Stockton-on-Tees *Cleveland*   *558De*
CHURCH OF ST THOMAS There is a possibility that Sir Christopher Wren had a hand in the design of this stately church, which was completed in 1712. In addition to its fine three-decker Georgian pulpit, the interior has an 18th-century altar and communion rails, carved in oak that was taken from Captain Cook's ship, the *Endeavour*.

Stoke *Devon*   *538Ef*
CHURCH OF ST NECTAN Standing in a commanding position, looking out to the Atlantic, with a pinnacled west tower 130 ft high, St Nectan's was begun in the 14th century, and has later additions. The wagon-roofs are partly plastered and coloured—in typical Devon style—and the finely carved rood screen goes right across the church. The Norman font has carved decoration, and the bench ends were given in 1530.

Stoke-by-Nayland *Suffolk*   *548Ce*
CHURCH OF ST MARY THE VIRGIN A Perpendicular church, with a tall, ornamented west tower. There is a two-storey south porch; that on the north is 16th century, in brick. Inside is a carved Perpendicular font with figures; there are also screens, stalls, misericords and some 19th-century stained glass.

Stoke Charity *Hants.*   *541Ge*
CHURCH OF ST MARY AND ST MICHAEL Now standing alone, the church was once accompanied by the manor house. It is a small building—most of which is Norman—with a bell-turret, and some Saxon work.

It contains many monuments and brasses, a 13th-century mural painting, and a late 15th-century carved relief of the Mass of St Gregory.

Stoke d'Abernon *Surrey* 542Af
CHURCH OF ST MARY This early Saxon church with a 7th-century south wall, has the oldest thegn's doorway and brass (that of Sir John d'Abernon, 1277) in England. It also contains wall paintings, medieval glass and Tudor monuments.

Stoke Doyle *Northants.* 547Hg
CHURCH OF ST RUMBALD Built in 1722–5, St Rumbald's has a west tower with obelisks for pinnacles. Pulpit, benches and other fittings are all original. Monuments include a fine reclining effigy of Sir Edward Ward (d. 1714) by John Michael Rysbrack, and a mourning Grecian lady of a century later by Sir Francis Chantrey.

Stoke Dry *Leics.* 553Gb
CHURCH OF ST ANDREW On a hillside in remote country, this interesting little church dates from Norman times, but has much later building. Worth noting are the tombs of the Digby family, who lived in Stoke Dry from the 14th to 17th centuries, in particular the table-tomb of Kenelm and Anne Digby. The chancel screen is 15th century and the recently discovered wall paintings span the centuries from the 13th to the 18th.

Stoke Edith *Heref. & Worcs.* 546Be
CHURCH OF ST MARY THE VIRGIN The body of the church was rebuilt in 1740, but the west tower and spire of the 14th-century church remain. The present building is of stuccoed brick, with Tuscan columns. There is a three-decker pulpit, and 18th-century pews. The monuments are 18th and 19th century, except for two from the earlier building, one an alabaster effigy of a 15th-century lady.

Stoke-on-Trent *Staffs.* 552Bd
ARNOLD BENNETT MUSEUM Houses a collection of items associated with the Five Towns' most famous author, who lived here for seven years.
CITY MUSEUM AND ART GALLERY (HANLEY) The museum's main exhibits are Staffordshire, European, Near and Far Eastern and South American pottery, making up a collection that is one of the finest and largest in the world.

Stoke Park Pavilions *Northants.* 547Ge
Consists of a colonnade and two pavilions, built in 1630 by Inigo Jones. (Gardens only.)

Stoke Poges *Bucks.* 547Hb
GRAY'S MONUMENT The scene at Stoke Poges inspired Thomas Gray (1716–71) to write his 'Elegy Written in a Country Churchyard'. In 1799 this statue designed by James Wyatt was erected in the churchyard to commemorate the poet.

Stoke Prior *Heref. & Worcs.* 546Cf
CHURCH OF ST MICHAEL A good church dating from the 12th century, with a 14th-century octagonal carved font. The spire is recent. (By appointment.)

Stokesay *Shropshire* 551Ja
CHURCH OF ST JOHN THE BAPTIST Situated by Stokesay Castle, the church was begun by the Normans, had later additions, and was largely rebuilt in the 17th century after Civil War damage. Nave and tower are from that period, and the chancel roof and pulpit (which has a sounding board) are also mid-17th century.

Stokesay Castle *Shropshire* 551Ja
A fortified manor house, dating from the 12th and 13th centuries. The buildings of the castle are arranged around a walled enclosure surrounded by a moat. To the east side is the half-timbered 16th-century gate-house. Opposite this lies the bulk of the manor house, consisting of a great hall with solar, and two towers, one at either end. The north tower is the older, in spite of the later half-timbering that surmounts it; its fabric belongs to the 12th century. In the 13th century the great hall was built; it has well preserved windows with simple tracery and a fine roof.

Stone *Kent* 542Cg
CHURCH OF ST MARY Tradition has it that the building was erected by the masons of Westminster Abbey. It is the finest Gothic church in Kent west of the R. Medway, with almost all the work dating from the 13th century, and rich decoration and clustered columns. There are traces of mural paintings, a brass to John Lombard of 1408, and a 16th-century canopied monument.

Stonehenge *Wilts.* 540Fe
In Stonehenge, Britain possesses the finest Bronze Age sanctuary in Europe. The monument as we have it today (as it was when complete) was the last

STOKESAY CASTLE

One of the most attractive small fortified houses in England. It is a misnomer to call it a castle since its fortifications are minimal and it could never have resisted more than the casual marauder. In the 12th century the property was owned by the de Saye family from whom it takes its name. By 1281, however, it had passed to a Laurence de Ludlow, whose descendants
held it until 1497. In the 17th century, it came into the possession of the Craven family, and in 1865 into that of the Allcrofts who still own it. The castle is a moated, walled enclosure on whose east side is the 16th-century gate-house. Opposite is the bulk of the house, including the great hall, one of the oldest surviving buildings of its kind in the country.

stage in a long and complex history which began *c.* 2500 BC, near the end of the Neolithic period, and was completed by *c.* 1500 BC, at the end of the Early Bronze Age. The phases of building are as follows:

Phase I, *c.* 2500 BC: Ditch and bank constructed, inside which was a ring of small pits, many containing cremation burials. A few upright stones were grouped to form an entrance. (The pits are now marked by concrete.)

Phase II, *c.* 2100 BC: A double circle of bluestones, brought from the Preseli Hills in Dyfed, was erected, but never finished. The entrance was modified to suit the new orientation and 'The Avenue', leading up from the banks of the R. Avon, was constructed.

Phase IIIa, *c.* 2075 BC: The bluestones were taken down, the site levelled and the great sarsen stones we still see were brought from the Marlborough Downs, shaped and dressed, and erected as we see them today, in an outer ring with lintels and an inner horseshoe composed of five pairs of uprights with lintels. The entrance was again modified.

Phase IIIb, *c.* 1700 BC: Some of the bluestones were dressed and set along the line of the present inner bluestone horseshoe. Further holes were dug outside the great circle but these were never used and the bluestones in the centre were removed.

Phase IIIc, *c.* 1500 BC: The bluestones were now reset as we see them, in a ring between the two lines of sarsens and in an inner horseshoe. Finally, at the very centre, the largest bluestone was apparently set upright. This has now fallen and is known as the Altar Stone.

Most of the missing stones have disappeared from the Middle Ages onwards, as farmers and others once used the monument as a quarry.

The dates shown for Phases I, II and IIIc are based on radiocarbon determinations from antler fragments found in various parts of the site, and the intermediate dates are estimated from those Phases. These dates are still under investigation.

Stoney Middleton *Derbys.* 552De
An attractive old village built on narrow, hilly streets. There is an interesting octagonal church dating from 1759 whose west tower survives from a much earlier building. The 80 ft pinnacle near by is known as Lover's Leap.

Stony Littleton *Avon* 540Df
This is a chambered Neolithic long barrow still stands some 10 ft high and this has a horned forecourt. Inside the entrance, the central gallery, some 40 ft long, leads to three pairs of side-chambers and one at the farther end. The roofing is formed by corbelling and not by capstones.

Stopham *W. Sussex* 542Ad
A village at the confluence of the R. Arun and R. Rother, famed for its medieval bridge, originally built in 1309, repaired in the 16th century and again in 1865. The church contains brasses from 1428 of the Barttelot family, who from Norman times owned the lands on which the present Stopham House (18th century) stands.

Stottesdon *Shropshire* 546Bg
CHURCH OF ST MARY A church containing much Norman work, and perhaps even some Saxon. There are Decorated windows with fine tracery, and a magnificent Norman font, mid-12th century, with carvings of animals, men and foliage.

Stourhead *Wilts.* 540De
A Palladian house built in 1722 for Henry Hoare, the banker. There are landscape paintings, and also furniture designed by the younger Chippendale. Early in the 18th century a revolutionary

STONEHENGE

Set in the middle of Salisbury Plain, near Amesbury in Wiltshire, Stonehenge is the finest Bronze Age sanctuary in Europe. It may have had a religious purpose and was built in several stages starting about 2510 BC when the outer ditch and the bank were constructed. About 2100 BC the great bluestones, brought all the way from the Prescelly Hills in South Wales, were erected in a double circle. About 2075 BC this circle was dismantled; the great sarsen stones were brought from the Marlborough Downs and erected as they are today—in an outer ring with lintels, and inner horseshoe comprising five pairs of uprights with lintels. Later the bluestones were re-erected between the two lines of sarsens and in an inner horseshoe.

change in garden design took place: in English landscape gardens the irregular, curving forms of nature replaced the regular geometrical designs in the French manner of Le Nôtre. Stourhead was one of the first examples of the innovation. The gardens were laid out in 1741 by the architect Flitcroft and Henry Hoare. The meres in the bleak valley were converted into a series of lakes, and the banks decorated with architectural ornaments amid groups of ornamental trees and flowering shrubs. (See p. 446.)

Stow *Lincs.*   553Gf
CHURCH OF ST MARY A famous and magnificent Anglo-Saxon church dating from the Saxon period, with a great Norman nave. It is a Greek cross in plan, with a low central tower. Inside, there are massive 11th-century arches, and a fine Norman chancel. The carving beneath the Early English font depicts a dragon, symbolising the defeated devil. In the north transept are the remains of a wall-painting representing St Thomas Becket.

Stowe *Bucks.*   547Ge
A mansion and park produced by some of the best genius of the 18th century for the Temple and the Grenville families, later Dukes of Buckingham and Chandos. Vanbrugh, William Kent, James Gibbs and Robert Adam all worked on the house or the temples in the park. It is now a public school.

Stowlangtoft *Suffolk*   548Cf
CHURCH OF ST GEORGE A Perpendicular church with split flint decoration, famed for the superb medieval carving on the nave benches and the misericords and finials in the choir.

There are also the remains of a medieval wall-painting of St Christopher and a 14th-century font.

Stranraer Castle *Dumfs. & Gall.*   556Bg
The castle, begun in the 15th century, stands in the middle of the town. It was occupied at one time by John Graham of Claverhouse—the persecutor of the Covenanters. It was also the town gaol for a long time.

Strata Florida *Dyfed*   545Gf
The remains of a remote abbey founded by the Cistercians in 1164. The west doorway of the former church has unusual banded moulding, and there are some medieval tiles.

Stratfield Saye *Hants.*   541Hf
A largely unaltered Carolean house built *c.* 1630 by Sir William Pitt, Comptroller of the Household to James I. In 1817 it was bought by the Duke of Wellington, victor of Waterloo, out of the £600,000 voted him for the purpose by a grateful government. He had intended building a palace on the site, but wiser counsels prevailed, and with characteristic efficiency he set about modernising the old house. The plumbing and central heating he installed is in use to this day. Stratfield Saye contains many fascinating relics of the Duke and his campaigns; paintings of battles, portraits of old comrades and enemies, captured French standards and spoils of war including Napoleon's library. The Duke's famous charger, Copenhagen, is buried in the grounds.

Stratford-upon-Avon *Warks.*   546Df
Established as a market centre by Richard I in 1196, it has continued as such until modern times: its annual Mop Fair (October 12), with traditional roast pig, is a direct survival of the ancient statute fair at which farm-workers were hired. In its early days the centre was comprised of three streets running parallel to the river and three at right angles to the river, and no basic change has taken

place over the centuries. The buildings are predominantly Elizabethan and Jacobean, with picturesque 15th-century half-timbered work in Church Street; timber-framed examples of the 16th and 17th centuries in Chapel Street, High Street and Wood Street; and quite a number of 18th-century period buildings or refrontings with brick and stucco. Thus the whole town forms a natural backcloth to Shakespeare, his times and work. Interest in Shakespeare's background began shortly after his death in 1616. He had bought New Place in 1597, and to this he retired *c.* 1610. He was buried, aged 52, in the chancel of the parish church of Holy Trinity. In 1769, the actor David Garrick organised the first Shakespeare celebrations, and thus started what soon became a literary pilgrimage, to such an effect that in 1847 the Shakespeare Birthplace Trust was formed to preserve this side of Stratford's heritage.

ANNE HATHAWAY'S COTTAGE At Shottery, a mile from the town. Anne Hathaway lived here before her marriage to Shakespeare. Parts of the thatched building date back to the 15th century.

CHURCH OF THE HOLY TRINITY By the R. Avon, this is the church where Shakespeare was baptised and buried; his monument there is by Gerard Johnson. The building is cruciform and has a central spire, originally timber but rebuilt in 1763 by William Hiorn of Warwick. There is some Early English work, but the Perpendicular and Decorated periods predominate. Restoration work in 1888 and 1898 (to which William Morris objected) has been followed by a major restoration of the chancel, completed in 1976. The graves of William Shakespeare, of his wife Anne Hathaway, his daughter Susanna Hall and other members of his family can be seen in the chancel; here, too, are the remains of the font in which Shakespeare was baptised and near by are copies of the parish register showing the entries recording his baptism on April 26, 1564 and his burial, on April 25, 1616.

The late-15th-century stalls in the chancel are ornamented with charmingly carved misericords.

CLOPTON BRIDGE Built by Hugh Clopton (*d.* 1496) who became Lord Mayor of London and built New Place (1483).

GUILD CHAPEL The chapel was begun in 1269 and the nave and tower rebuilt towards the end of the 15th century. The half-timbered range adjoining the chapel was built 1416–18. The original guildhall occupies the ground floor: above is a fine hall used by the grammar school since the suppression of the guild; Shakespeare studied here as a boy.

HALL'S CROFT Home of Shakespeare's daughter Susanna and her husband Dr John Hall, it is an outstanding building with a splendid walled garden. It contains rare furniture and exhibits relating to 16th-century medicine.

HARVARD HOUSE Built by Alderman Thomas Rogers in 1596—his daughter Katherine married Robert Harvard of Southwark and their son John founded the famous American university. The house was presented to Harvard University in 1909. The adjoining Garrick Inn is of a similar date, as is the fine Old Tudor House adjacent.

MARY ARDEN'S HOUSE The Tudor farmhouse in Wilmcote village (3 miles north-west of the town) where Shakespeare's mother lived.

NEW PLACE The house to which Shakespeare retired in 1610; only the site and foundations remain. They are preserved in gardens reached through Nash's House. The adjoining Knot Garden is a replica of an Elizabethan garden.

ROYAL SHAKESPEARE THEATRE Built in 1932 to replace a theatre built in 1879 as a memorial to Shakespeare and destroyed by fire in 1926.

ROYAL SHAKESPEARE THEATRE PICTURE GALLERY
AND MUSEUM Portraits of Shakespeare and famous
Shakespearean actresses and actors are displayed
with a collection of original costumes and designs
used in Stratford productions from 1879 to the
present day.

SHAKESPEARE STATUE (GOWER MEMORIAL) The
work of Lord Gower, it was presented to the town
in 1888, and has the figures of Hamlet, Lady Macbeth, Falstaff and Prince Hal, symbolising philo-
sophy, tragedy, comedy and history.

SHAKESPEARE'S BIRTHPLACE A half-timbered
building of the early 16th century. In his lifetime it
was two separate buildings, one the family home,
the other an adjoining warehouse used by his
father John who was a glover and wool dealer.

SHRIEVE'S HOUSE Reconstructed and enlarged
after a fire in 1595: it was the home of William
Rogers, a serjeant-at-the-mace c. 1600.

TOWN HALL Of Cotswold stone, it was built in
1767, but restored after a fire in 1946.

Strelley *Notts.*   552Ed
CHURCH OF ALL SAINTS There is a 12th-century
base to the west tower, but most of the building
dates from after its endowment in 1356 by Samson
de Strelley. The chancel is the best in the county.
There are numerous monuments to 14th–16th-
century members of the Strelley family, and a
good rood screen.

Strensham *Heref. & Worcs.*   546Ce
CHURCH OF ST JOHN THE BAPTIST Standing on
high ground in a field close to the R. Avon, St
John's has a series of monuments to one family
from the 13th to the 18th century. One of them, in
marble, to Sir Francis Russell (d. 1705), is by
Edward Stanton, the mason-sculptor of Holborn
in London, whose father carved the monument to
the Earl of Coventry, c. 1700, which is at the
neighbouring Elmley Castle. On the west wall,
now set as a gallery front, is a painted rood loft
front with 23 saints.

Strethall *Essex*   548Ae
CHURCH OF ST MARY THE VIRGIN A small Saxon
church, with a 15th-century chancel and west
tower, an 11th-century chancel arch and a 15th-
century brass to a priest.

Stretham *Cambs.*   548Af
On the edge of the Fens, Stretham is notable for
its 20 ft high village cross, of c. 1400.
STRETHAM SCOOP-WHEEL ENGINE Only sur-
viving example of the type of machine used for
Fen-drainage in the early 19th century.

Strome Castle *Highland*   565Gf
For centuries a stronghold of the MacDonalds of
Glengarry and as such a constant threat to the
Mackenzies. In 1609 it was besieged by the
Mackenzie Lord of Kintail and destroyed.

Stroud *Glos.*   546Cc
SUBSCRIPTION ROOMS Built in the early 19th
century, incorporating the George Room Art
Gallery, the building is architecturally interesting
for its *porte-cochère* with Tuscan columns and
balustraded balcony above.

STRETHAM ENGINE

This scoop-wheel engine, built in 1831 by the Butterley
Company of Derbyshire, is the sole survivor of the
many similar beam engines installed in the early 19th
century to replace wind-pumps for Fen drainage. The
engine, which has been restored, has a scoop-wheel
37 ft in diameter designed to lift water 4 to 5 ft into
the dike at the rate of 124 tons a minute.

Studley Royal *N. Yorks.*   558Cc
CHURCH OF ST MARY Built between 1871 and 1878
by William Burges; the style is elaborate Gothic,
with west tower and lofty spire, polychrome
marble, alabaster and mosaic. The church is no
longer used for worship but is open in the
summer months.

Studley Royal   558Cc
and Fountains Abbey Garden *N. Yorks.*
Set in the steep-sided valley of the little R. Skell,
this is an incomparable water garden, laid out as
straight canals and geometrically-shaped pools.
There is superb statuary on the large stretches of
mown lawn; the Classical 'Temple of Piety' overlooks the Moon pond. The road from Ripon
leads through a park with 350 deer before entering the garden through handsome gates. The
water garden dates from 1716; it was made for
John Aislabie, notorious for his participation in the
South Sea Company financial scandal. The valley
at the upper end of the river was acquired by
Aislabie's son when 'natural' garden design was the
vogue. It is crowded with giant trees and, over the
lake, a great tower rises above the ruins of
Fountains Abbey. (See p. 450.)

THE PANTHEON AND LAKE AT STOURHEAD

The English landscape garden was invented early in
the 18th century, and freedom of nature with its
irregular curving forms replaced the regular geometrical
designs in the manner of the French gardener, Le
Nôtre. When he settled at Stourhead in 1741,
Henry Hoare was one of the first to create such a
garden. With the help of Henry Flitcroft the architect,
he transformed a bare valley into a magnificent

landscape. The bottom of the valley became a series of
lakes, their banks planted with trees, and dotted with
temples and grottoes, mostly in Classical style. In the
19th century a variety of ornamental trees and great
stretches of flowering shrubs were planted. Unlike
Capability Brown's landscapes where form, shape and
the green of grass and trees predominated, at Stourhead
colour and variety has been the keynote.

WILLIAM SHAKESPEARE, DRAMATIST TO THE WORLD

The Swan of Avon, as Ben Jonson named his friend, died a popular and successful dramatist. Now his reputation is such that over half a million visit his birthplace at Stratford-upon-Avon each year. Also on view at Stratford are the remains of New Place, which was the best house in the town when Shakespeare bought it in 1597, and Hall's Croft, where his daughter, Susanna, lived. Dulwich College owns the first reference to a performance of a Shakespeare play, *Henry VI, Part I*, in 1591 at the Rose Theatre, London. It was so popular it was repeated 14 times. At 30, Shakespeare had become an actor and the regular playwright of the Lord Chamberlain's players, and his name appears in the cast list of Ben Jonson's *Every Man in his Humour* in 1598 (British Museum). Shakespeare was also one of the partners responsible for building and running the Globe Theatre. This was constructed on Bankside in 1599 of material taken from London's first playhouse, which had been erected in 1576 by James Burbage and called The Theatre.

WILLIAM SHAKESPEARE, *the Droeshout frontispiece of the First Folio, or the first collected edition of Shakespeare's plays, published in 1623. It is suspected of being a fake: a medical scientist noticed the portrait had two right eyes, and there are alleged to be two left sides to the coat. (British Library)*

BAPTISM ENTRY *in Stratford Parish Register, April 26, 1564.*

STAIRS IN MARY ARDEN'S HOUSE, *Shakespeare's mother's home, at Wilmcote, near Stratford-upon-Avon.*

SCHOOLROOM *in which he studied, at the King Edward VI School. To join the school he had to be 7 years old and able to read. In those days hardly anything but Latin grammar was taught and it can be seen from his plays that Shakespeare was familiar with Virgil and Ovid.*

BAPTISMAL ENTRIES of Shakespeare's children. His marriage was not altogether happy and what little we know of his family life is through his children. Susanna was born on May 26, 1583, and the twins Hamnet and Judith on Feb. 2, 1585. (Register, Holy Trinity Church, Stratford)

ANNE HATHAWAY'S COTTAGE at Shottery, a mile from Stratford. It is thought the 18-year-old Shakespeare had to marry Anne, eight years his senior, because she was pregnant.

CLOPTON BRIDGE over the R. Avon which the 22-year-old Shakespeare must have crossed on his way to London. It is likely he walked, and the journey would have taken 4 days.

PAINTED ROOM at the Crown Tavern in Oxford, where Shakespeare is said to have stayed on his journeys between London and Stratford. The painted walls were discovered in 1937.

GRAVE OF SHAKESPEARE placed within the sanctuary of Holy Trinity Church, Stratford. It is thought he died after a prolonged celebration with his fellow dramatists.

SHAKESPEARE'S SIGNATURE appears (above the seal at the left) on this mortgage for a London house close to the Globe theatre. (British Library)

THE TEMPLE OF PIETY AT STUDLEY ROYAL GARDENS

Wild flowers and enormous trees abound in the steep valley of the R. Skell in which lies this breathtakingly beautiful garden—an abstraction of water, laid out in straight canals and geometrically shaped pools, punctuated by statuary and overlooked by the Classical Temple of Piety. John Aislabie, Chancellor of the Exchequer in Sir Robert Walpole's government, *started it all about 1727. Coming from Ripon the garden is entered beside the ornamented cascade, at Canal Gates. Part of the gardens were laid out by Aislabie's son when the fashion in gardens had changed—here is a landscape of sinuous curving lines with an irregular shaped lake above which rise the magnificent ruins of Fountains Abbey.*

Styal *Cheshire* 552Bf
Quarry Bank Cotton Mill was erected in 1784 near a half-timbered farmhouse and cottages set in fine woodlands. Shortly afterwards the village of Styal was built near by—the whole forming a rare complete industrial community.

Sudbury *Suffolk* 548Ce
Sudbury is an ancient market town and the birthplace of Gainsborough. There are attractive medieval and 18th-century houses in the streets below Market Hill. The old Moot Hall is 15th century, with an oriel window and overhanging storey; also from the 15th century are the Chantry and Salter's Hall. Gainsborough's House of *c.* 1725 has a pillared doorway, and the Bull Inn and Ballingdon Hall (across the R. Stour) are both good buildings of *c.* 1590 and 1600.
CHURCH OF ST GREGORY The principal church of the town, it is Perpendicular, with a west tower, and large windows in the chancel built by Simon de Sudbury, Archbishop of Canterbury, who was murdered in 1387. There is a towering, beautiful font canopy, and misericords.
GAINSBOROUGH'S HOUSE Birthplace of painter Thomas Gainsborough (1727–88), containing many of his pictures as well as drawings, prints and furniture of his period. Other periods are reflected in constantly changing exhibitions.

Sudeley Castle *Glos.* 546Dd
Catherine Parr, the sixth queen of Henry VIII, is buried here; in 1547, after Henry's death, she married her former lover, Lord Seymour of Sudeley, but died here in childbirth the following year. The castle was a headquarters of Charles I during the Civil War and was besieged in 1643 and again in 1644. The ruined banqueting hall dates from *c.* 1450; the chapel of the same date contains

the tomb of Catherine Parr. The castle houses much fine furniture, tapestries, needlework and china: the pictures include works by Constable, Rubens, Turner and Van Dyke. Double yew hedges, 15 ft high, are a feature of the garden.

Suie Hill See Dungarry and Suie Hill.

Sulgrave Manor *Northants.* 546Fe
Ancestral home of George Washington, 1st President of the U.S.A., Sulgrave Manor is one of the few English country houses to fly the American flag. The design of the flag is believed to have been inspired by the Washington family Arms (three horizontal stars above two horizontal bars or stripes), which can be seen carved in a stone porch at the manor. The property is first mentioned in 1086 in the Domesday Book. Some time later it belonged to a priory in Northampton, and in 1539, under the Dissolution, it was sold by Henry VIII to Lawrence Washington. The present house, in coursed stone, was built by him in 1560. Colonel John Washington, great-grandfather of George Washington, left Sulgrave Manor for Virginia in 1656. The house is a mixture of Elizabethan and Queen Anne architecture, but was carefully restored in 1920–30. It contains portraits of George Washington, and some of his possessions.

Sunderland *Tyne & Wear* 558Dg
The town's original name was Monkwearmouth; and in Saxon times it was a great centre of learning: the Venerable Bede received his early training at the monastery of St Peter. In its present form, largely expanded beyond the early boundaries, Sunderland is mainly a late 19th-century town.
CHURCH OF THE HOLY TRINITY A pleasant Classical church built in 1719; the apse was added in 1735. The interior is adorned with Corinthian columns, and the west screen (1724) bears the royal

Arms. There is also a monument, *c.* 1838, with a life-size statue by Sir Francis Chantrey, the neo-Classical portrait sculptor who left a fortune (the Chantrey Bequest) to the Royal Academy.
MUSEUM AND ART GALLERY There are archaeological and natural history sections, model ships and pottery. The gallery has a collection of works by British artists; loan exhibitions are held.

Sundridge Old Hall *Kent* 542Cf
A medieval timbered hall-house, built *c.* 1458. The great hall, several storeys high and reaching from ground level to the roof, contains the original stone hearth. The house was restored in 1923. (Open to members of the National Trust by appointment.)

Sutton-at-Hone *Kent* 542Cg
ST JOHN'S JERUSALEM Henry III often stayed at the 13th-century Commandery (headquarters) of the Order of Knights Hospitaller of St John. The Commandery chapel survives, for it was incorporated in the house, built here in the 16th century, which was later the home of Abraham Hill (1635–1721), a founder and Treasurer of the Royal Society. The house was altered in the 18th century. A weeping willow, a descendant of the tree under which Napoleon was buried at St Helena, stands in the moated garden.

Sutton Courtenay *Oxon.* 546Fc
CHURCH OF ALL SAINTS Set in a pretty village on the Thames. The broad tower is Norman, and so is the tub-shaped font with its Jacobean cover. The grave of Herbert Asquith, Prime Minister 1908–16, is in the churchyard; so, too, is that of Eric Blair, better known to the world as novelist and journalist George Orwell (1903–50).

Sutton Valence *Kent* 542Df
A village perched on a hill, which gives it its special character: the streets follow the contours, giving vast views of the Kent Weald. The many weather-boarded and brick cottages are typical of the area. At the east end of the village stand the overgrown ruins of a small Norman keep.

Sutton Waldron *Dorset* 540Ed
CHURCH OF ST BARTHOLOMEW This, reputed to be one of the prettiest churches in Dorset, was built by Archdeacon Huxtable in 1847. The brightly painted interior is by Owen Jones.

LUSTRE-WARE JUG

A lustre-ware jug made about 1820 at the Sunderland pottery, also known as the 'Garrison', which operated from about 1807 to 1865. Lustre-ware was one of many local wares produced. It had a speckled appearance and was usually decorated with transfer patterns of local commemorative interest, one of the most popular subjects being the Wearmouth Bridge as on this jug. (Sunderland Museum and Art Gallery)

SWANSEA PORCELAIN VASES

These charming vases are probably by William Billingsley (1758–1828), a celebrated early 19th-century porcelain painter. The vase on the left shows a view in Cumberland, that on the right Basingwerk Abbey; both vases have a view of Llangollen Vale on the other side. Billingsley was primarily a flower painter—he introduced a new technique for floral painting on pottery—and his landscapes are rare. After a series of unsuccessful ventures, he founded the famous Nantgarw factory, where most of the finest Welsh soft-paste porcelain was made. Billingsley later moved to Swansea where he set up a factory between 1814 and 1817. (Glynn Vivian Art Gallery, Swansea)

Swaffham *Norfolk* 554Bb
CHURCH OF SS PETER AND PAUL This 15th-century church has a steeple built *c.* 1510, clerestory, transepts, and south porch with hammerbeam roof. The nave has a superb double hammer-beam roof with angels. A 19th-century stained glass window is by Wailes, 1853.

Swaffham Bulbeck *Cambs.* 548Af
Swaffham Bulbeck has an attractive old moated farmhouse, the Burgh Hall, *c.* 1650. On the back road to Quy, half hidden among the trees, lies Anglesey Abbey, from the early 12th century—the medieval part of which was incorporated in a mansion of *c.* 1600, and later restored.

There are four notable smallish houses: the Lordship House, clunch-built, with lancet windows on one side and small mullioned windows on the other; the Merchant's House, dated 1711, a brick house with a Dutch gable; the Maltings opposite with a good shell-hood doorway dated 1697; and Abbey House of 1778, notable because the semi-basement is the vaulted undercroft of the old nunnery founded in 1190.

Swaffham Prior *Cambs.* 548Af
Swaffham Prior has many charming thatched cottages dominated by Baldwin Manor. This Henry VIII half-timbered house has an impressive over-sailing upper storey on a carved bressumer.

Swanage *Dorset* 540Ec
There are several old stone houses in the town, but most of it is modern. The town hall was erected in 1883, but the carved stone façade was designed by Wren in 1670 as the entrance to the Mercers' Hall, Cheapside, London, and re-erected in Swanage. Similarly, the Wellington Clock Tower was originally erected in Southwark, London, in 1854 in honour of the Iron Duke, but was also removed and re-erected in Swanage in 1867.

Swansea *W. Glam.* 544Fc
GLYNN VIVIAN ART GALLERY The museum contains collections of Swansea porcelain and Swansea pottery, the Deffett Francis Collection of prints and drawings, continental porcelain, a collection of glass including fine paperweights, a selection of paintings, including some by the Welsh

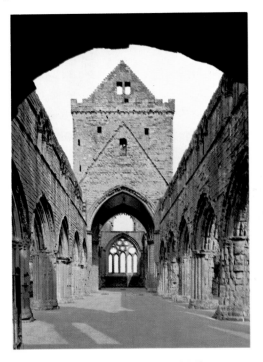

SWEETHEART ABBEY

Founded in 1273, Sweetheart Abbey is so named because of the great affection of the foundress, Devorgilla, for her husband, John Baliol of Barnard Castle. On his death Devorgilla kept his embalmed heart until her own death in 1290, when it was buried with her before the high altar of the abbey.

LOCOMOTIVE 2516

Built in 1897, locomotive number 2516 was one of 200 known as 'Dean Goods', a class of railway engines designed by William Dean, who was one of the foremost locomotive designers at the end of the 19th century. (Great Western Railway Museum, Swindon)

artists Richard Wilson, Ceri Richards, Augustus John, Kyffin Williams, and bronzes by Epstein and Barbara Hepworth.

INDUSTRIAL MUSEUM OF SWANSEA Amongst many other industrial relics is a fireless locomotive, built during the First World War, designed to be used in an explosives factory.

Sweetheart Abbey *Dumfs. & Gall.*   556Fh
Sweetheart Abbey was founded in 1273, an unusually late date for a Cistercian foundation. In plan, however, the abbey kept to the normal Cistercian rules and a range for lay-brothers was included along the west walk of the cloister. Of the convent buildings little survives, but much of the church still exists. It is a long, low building dating from the period of the foundation. The central tower still stands, and there is still some of the window tracery and the vaulting in two of the chapels.

Swinbrook *Oxon.*   546Ed
CHURCH OF ST MARY THE VIRGIN An Early English and Perpendicular church famous for its extraordinary 16th- and 17th-century monuments to the Fettiplace family. Against the chancel north wall, they resemble canopied open cupboards with shelves: on three of the six shelves reclines a man in armour. The second group of three, the effigies in similar posture but without armour, is by William Byrd of Oxford, *c.* 1686.

Swindon *Wilts.*   546Db
GREAT WESTERN RAILWAY MUSEUM GWR locomotives on display include the *City of Truro* (which on May 9, 1904, averaged 70 mph from Exeter to Bristol), *Lode Star*, Hawksworth Pannier tank engine and a replica of the *North Star* (the first passenger train to run from Paddington to Maidenhead, in 1838). Smaller items include many fine model trains, signal apparatus, valve gear, tickets, directors' passes, etc. One room is devoted to the great 19th-century engineer and bridge builder Isambard Kingdom Brunel (1806–59), who literally laid the foundations of the Great Western Railway, and probably named it as well. The building was formerly a lodging for workmen building the Great Western Railway in the mid-19th century, and later became a Wesleyan church—hence the imposingly ecclesiastical entrance. It has been a museum since 1962.

MUSEUM AND ART GALLERY The work of modern artists, including Henry Moore, Ben Nicholson, Graham Sutherland and John Nash, is contained in modern surroundings—the art gallery was built in 1964, adjoining an 1820 building which houses coins, geological collections, musical instruments, items of natural history—Wiltshire birds and British mammals—and the Manners Collection of pot-lids and ware, the largest collection of its kind on public view in this country.

Swine *Humberside*   559Gb
CHURCH OF ST MARY There was once a priory of Cistercian nuns here, and this church is the chancel of their former church, originally 12th century but enlarged in the 14th. There are misericords, a 16th-century screen and a 17th-century pulpit, while the tower and font are of the 18th century. There is a magnificent east window of 1531.

Swyncombe *Oxon.*   547Gc
CHURCH OF ST BOTOLPH A small Norman church with nave, chancel and apse, in a rather remote setting. There is a Norman font, and a rood screen with loft dating from the early 20th century.

Sycharth *Clwyd*   551Hc
This well-preserved motte and bailey—there is no castle—was one of the homes of the rebellious

Welsh leader Owen Glendower. Recent excavations have shown that he made alterations to the archaic structure, and evidence was found of its burning (during the absence of Glendower) by the 16-year-old Prince Henry in 1403.

Sydenham Damerel *Devon*   538Fc
In this picturesque village is a bridge built in 1437. It is called Horsebridge, a corruption of its original name of Hautesbrygge.

Sydenham House *Devon*   538Fd
A Jacobean mansion, whose main feature is a splendid carved staircase. Now a private house.

Sydling St Nicholas *Dorset*   540Dc
CHURCH OF ST NICHOLAS The church is mainly of the 15th century, with a west tower; the chancel was rebuilt in the mid-18th century. There are a number of minor but pretty 18th- and 19th-century wall monuments, a 12th-century font, and an 18th-century screen under the tower.

Syon House *Greater London*   547Jb
Originally a nunnery founded by Henry V in 1415. At the Dissolution in 1534, the building passed to Edward Seymour, Duke of Somerset (Protector Somerset during the life of Edward VI), brother of Jane Seymour, Henry VIII's third wife. Somerset converted the nunnery into a great castellated mansion. After his downfall in 1549 and his execution three years later on a false charge of treason, the property reverted to the Crown, and later James I gave it to the Earl of Northumberland. Repairs were made in the 17th century, possibly by Inigo Jones. In 1762, Hugh Percy (later the 1st Duke of Northumberland) commissioned Robert Adam to renovate the interior without interfering with the levels or general arrangement of rooms. The house is planned as an open square with a great courtyard. Syon contains much fine furniture and a collection of pictures. It stands in grounds landscaped by Capability Brown.

ANTE-ROOM AT SYON HOUSE

One of several ornamental tables standing beneath panels depicting military trophies that Robert Adam designed for this room, the ante-room to the dining room. Decorated in 1762–9, the room is an unusual example of Adam's style. He later became noted for paler colours and more feminine ornament. But here he used brilliant colours, stucco panels and much gilt. The room was inspired by Roman palaces Adam saw in Italy, and around the walls are green marble columns said to have been dredged from the R. Tiber.

T

Taliaris Park *Dyfed*   544Fd
This was probably built in the 17th century for the Guynne family, who lived here until *c.* 1754. There is a notable Jacobean staircase rising from the ground to the third floor. The house also has 17th- and 19th-century additions.

Talley Abbey *Dyfed*   544Fe
The ruins of a 12th-century abbey, probably founded by Rhys ap Gruffydd, Prince of South Wales.

Tamworth *Staffs.*   552Db
The great bank here once enclosed what must have been the important Saxon town of Alfred the Great's daughter Aethelflaed.

The town hall was built in 1701 by Thomas Guy (1645–1724), founder of Guy's Hospital, London, who was educated in Tamworth.
CASTLE A Norman fortress whose keep, tower and famous curtain wall of herringbone masonry were built by the Marmions, hereditary Champions of the Kings of England. The banqueting hall and other domestic offices date from the time of Henry VIII, and the Jacobean apartments are decorated with fine woodwork and a heraldic frieze.
CASTLE MUSEUM The collection of this local

history museum comprises Early English coins from the Tamworth Mint, local archaeological material, bygones, local prints and watercolours, costumes and furniture.
CHURCH OF ST EDITHA A former collegiate church dating from the Normans, but mainly of 14th- and 15th-century work. There are several monuments, and stained glass made by William Morris to the design of Ford Madox Brown.

Tantallon Castle *Lothian*   562Df
Perched high on a rocky eminence overlooking the Firth of Forth, the castle played a considerable part in the medieval battles waged between the Crowns of England and Scotland. The existing remains consist of the castle proper, an outer bailey and various defensive outworks. The main curtain wall extends along only two sides of the courtyard, for impregnable cliffs protect the other two sides. The most impressive defences face inwards towards the headland, where the 14th-century fabric included a gate-house and the East and Douglas Towers. The gate-house was later altered when it was strengthened to accommodate more artillery. The north side of the courtyard contains the remains of the chief domestic quarters.

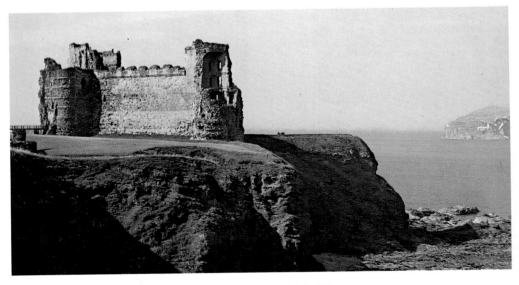

TANTALLON CASTLE

Perched on a high rock overlooking the Firth of Forth, Tantallon has had a lively and stormy history— throughout the Middle Ages it was the chief stronghold of the Douglas Earls of Angus. Although about midway between Edinburgh and the English border, the earls were frequently in open rebellion and receiving assistance from the English Crown. As a result the castle was besieged (unsuccessfully) by the royal Scots army in 1491 and 1528. However, during a third

siege by Commonwealth forces in 1651, General Monk battered the walls with his guns, capturing the castle after a 12-day bombardment. This was the last time Tantallon served in a serious defensive role. In 1699 the Douglases sold it and the whole building fell into decay. All that now remains are parts of the castle proper, an outer bailey and various defensive outworks on two sides—the steep cliffs above the sea protected the other two sides.

Tarbolton *Strathclyde*   *561Hc*
BACHELORS' CLUB A thatched house where Robert Burns and his friends formed a select social and debating society in 1780.

Tarporley *Cheshire*   *552Ae*
CHURCH OF ST HELEN A medieval church, so rebuilt as to be nearly all 19th-century work. It contains some noteworthy memorials of the 17th and 18th centuries, with effigies of the Done and Crewe families.

Tarvit, Hill of *Fife*   *562Cg*
TARVIT HOUSE A mansion, built in 1696 and rebuilt in 1906. It has a collection of furniture, tapestries, porcelain and paintings.

Tattenhoe *Bucks.*   *547Ge*
CHURCH OF ST GILES Deserted, and surrounded by the remains of a moat system, St Giles's was built in 1540 with materials from a priory. Fishponds near by are part of the moat. Inside the church are box-pews and a font made in the 18th century from 13th-century materials.

Tattershall *Lincs.*   *553Hd*
CHURCH OF THE HOLY TRINITY The church was entirely rebuilt between 1440 and *c.* 1480, and stands near the castle. Formerly a collegiate church, it has a west tower and, inside, a good 16th-century stone rood screen. There are 15th- and 16th-century brasses in the north transept; most of the original stained glass was removed in the 18th century, but the few remaining fragments can be seen in the east window.

Tattershall Castle *Lincs.*   *553Hd*
This great keep of a Norman castle is one of the most splendid and important examples of medieval brick building in the country: stone is used only for window and door frames, and a little for decoration. It was erected in the mid-15th century

at a time when brick was becoming increasingly popular as a building material. The castle itself was founded in 1231 when the owner of the manor, Robert of Tattershall, was granted a royal licence to put up a fortified building, but little remains except the keep.

Tatton Park *Cheshire*   *552Bf*
The home of the Egerton family since the late 16th century. The present house was begun in the late 18th century and was built around an earlier house dating from Charles II's time. The architect was Samuel Wyatt, who died in 1807 before building was complete. The house was finished by Wyatt's nephew, Lewis. In the house are fine furniture, pictures, china, silver and glass.

Humphry Repton laid out the park, which covers 1,000 acres with the mile long Tatton Mere winding through it. He planned to have an ornamental lake, but this proposal was turned down. However, by chance the ground has subsided at the same spot and so today there is water in the place where Repton had visualised it.

The house is superbly furnished and contains a large collection of pictures, including works by Canaletto, Van Dyck and de Heem, and china and glass. A feature of the drawing room is the silk covering on the walls. The Tenants Hall houses a fine collection of sporting trophies.

The 60-acre garden, as distinct from the parkland, contains spacious lawns, an orangery and an authentic Japanese garden with a Shinto temple that was brought from Japan and erected by Japanese workmen in 1910. Rhododendrons and azaleas provide a rich blaze of colour in the spring.

Taunton *Som.*   *540Be*
Mentioned in the Anglo-Saxon Chronicle (AD 722), and acquired by the Bishops of Winchester in Saxon times, Taunton was developed by Henry de Blois, Abbot of Glastonbury and Bishop of

Winchester, who built the castle keep. The castle had been started by Bishop William Giffard by 1129. Taunton was the centre of rebellion when Perkin Warbeck arrived with his Cornish rebels in 1497, and was again involved in strife in the Civil War. The Duke of Monmouth was proclaimed king in the market-place in 1685, and Judge Jeffreys tried 509 rebels in the great hall of the castle. In the strongrooms of the Somerset Record Office (Obridge Road) are about 2,000,000 documents dating from the mid-12th century. The castle (of 12th-century origin) was developed as a major military stronghold, with walls 13 ft thick. Its gateway dates from 1495 and the great hall is 120 ft long. Some of the municipal buildings were erected in 1522 by Richard Fox, Bishop of Winchester, and some, although built in Tudor style, are in fact from this century. The Tudor House (1578), however, is a splendid example of 16th-century domestic architecture, half-timbered and gabled. There are two sets of almshouses: one is Gray's, founded in 1635 by Robert Gray, of the Merchant Taylors of London, and has a series of all brick chimney stacks; the second is Huish's, founded in 1615 by Richard Huish, also a London merchant.

SOMERSET COUNTY MUSEUM The museum is located in Taunton Castle which dates from the 12th century, and has historic associations with the Bishops of Winchester, the Wars of the Roses, the Civil War, the Monmouth rebellion and Judge Jeffreys. Local antiquities include Glastonbury and Meare lake-village finds, Iron Age boat, Roman mosaic from Low Ham. There is a working model of a beam engine, collections of geology, fossils, natural history, and the work of local artists; local silver, ceramics, costume and dolls. The Military Gallery contains relics of the Somerset Light Infantry from 1685, and a large collection of uniforms and medals. There are also relics of the North Somerset Yeomanry.

Taversoe Tuick *Rousay, Orkney* 569Hg
One of Britain's two Neolithic cairns with a two-storied chamber (the remains of the other one is at Huntersquoy, Eday Is., Orkney). The mound is 30 ft in diameter with a 19 ft passage to the lower chamber. The upper chamber, floored by the roof of the lower, has its own entrance-passage, 11 ft long. It has two compartments and a further recess opposite the passage.

Tavistock *Devon* 538Fc
CHURCH OF ST EUSTACE A large church that reflects Tavistock's medieval prosperity as a wool town. It contains the famous Glanvill and Fitz memorials and fine 19th-century glass. The ruins of Tavistock Abbey (c. 974) may be seen near by.

Teigh *Leics.* 553Gc
CHURCH OF THE HOLY TRINITY The 14th-century west tower remains tacked on to the church, rebuilt in Gothic style by George Richardson in 1782. Inside, distinctive 18th-century features include box-pews facing each other, and a triple grouping of pulpit, reading desk and clerk's desk at the west end.

Temple Newsam House *W. Yorks.* 558Ca
This was the birthplace in 1545 of Lord Darnley, who was to become the husband of Mary, Queen of Scots, and was the home of the Ingram family from 1622. In 1922 the estate was sold by Lord Halifax to the Corporation of Leeds. The house has become a country house museum containing a collection of 17th- and 18th-century silver, furniture, ceramics, sculptures and paintings. The items include Chippendale's writing table from Hare-

THE KEEP AT TATTERSHALL CASTLE

One of the most splendid examples of medieval brick building in Britain. During the tenure of the Cromwell family the original 13th-century castle at Tattershall was greatly enlarged. The main builder was Ralph, 3rd Lord Cromwell, who held the land from 1417 to 1456. He was a powerful and ambitious politician, Treasurer of England from 1433 to 1443. The keep was built by him; it was out of date as a defensive feature even in the 15th century, and was probably planned as a grandiose and palatial set of private apartments. Many of the interior fittings have been swept away, but a set of magnificent 15th-century fire-places, complete with heraldic adornments, still survive.

TATTON PARK

This house was begun for the Egerton family by Samuel Wyatt at the end of the 18th century. It is built of local stone and is of a severely classical design with little external ornamentation. Its effect depends largely upon the excellence of its proportions and the eminence on which it was built. It overlooks a terraced garden towards a long vista of park and meres. The terraced garden is said to have been designed by Sir Joseph Paxton (1801–65). The splendid south portico is supported by four monolith columns hewn from Runcorn quarry. To the west of the south front Wyatt constructed a single-storied colonnaded wing, for which G. H. Stokes designed a second floor in 1860. Samuel Wyatt died before Tatton was completed and the work was finished by his nephew, Lewis Wyatt.

TEWKESBURY ABBEY

One of the largest abbey churches to survive the Dissolution, Tewkesbury Abbey has been used as a parish church ever since, despite its enormous size. It has one of the finest sets of medieval tombs in England. The earliest parts date from the early 12th century, the magnificent tower from about 1150. During the 14th century a new vault was added to set off the tombs surrounding the choir. These belong to successive patrons of the abbey and commemorate some of the most powerful medieval families. In the 15th century the lordship of Tewkesbury was held by the Beauchamp family, including Warwick the King-maker. Many of the family are buried in the abbey, where they endowed the beautifully vaulted Warwick Chantry (right).

wood House, *c.* 1770, and Roubiliac's marble bust of Alexander Pope, 1738. There is a fine suite of rooms, decorated *c.* 1740, culminating in a long gallery, that has retained its furnishings. The grounds were laid out by Capability Brown.

Temple Sowerby *Cumbria*   557Jf
ACORN BANK MANOR An 18th-century sandstone house, with parts dating from the 16th century. Famous for its herb garden. (Gardens only.)

Tenbury Wells *Heref.& Worcs.*
A market town with half-timbered and Georgian houses and a Tudor inn, the Royal Oak.
CHURCH OF ST MARY The tower is 12th century, with a 17th-century parapet, and the medieval chancel has a 14th-century Easter sepulchre in the north wall. There are several fine alabaster effigies.

Tenby *Dyfed*   544Dc
The old centre of this attractive holiday town lay east of the town walls, which cut off a neck of land, at the tip of which stood the castle—strongly defended on three sides by the sea. From medieval times the sheltered harbour to the north served as an important link with Bristol and Ireland. The town grew beyond its walls with the coming of the railway in 1863 and its development as a holiday resort. The parish church dates from the 13th century, and by the 15th century had developed into an impressive building. There is an excellent museum at the entrance to Castle Hill. In the summer there are boat trips to Caldy Island, where there are two ancient churches which preceded the present priory, re-established in 1929.
CHURCH OF ST MARY A large church dating from the 13th century, with later additions. The tower and 152 ft spire are between the south aisle and chapel, and there is a 15th-century chancel roof with bosses. Among the monuments with figures is a 15th-century carved skeleton; there is work by Edward Physick and John Evan Thomas.
MUSEUM The building incorporates remains of a medieval castle. All the collections on display

relate to Pembrokeshire, particularly to Tenby and cover geology, archaeology, natural history and medieval history. They include the Smith Collection of local cave-animal remains with relics of mammoths, and a fine art collection.
PLANTAGENET HOUSE An early 15th-century Tudor house. (Open to members of the National Trust by appointment.)

Tenterden *Kent*   542Ee
In the Middle Ages, Tenterden was a busy weaving centre. It is affiliated to the Cinque Ports and is now a busy market town. In the High Street there are some 18th-century houses faced with mathematical tiles—tiles hung on to an earlier wooden frame to give the impression of brickwork.

Tetbury *Glos.*   546Cc
CHURCH OF ST MARY THE VIRGIN The old Norman church was pulled down, and replaced in 1781 by one to the design of Francis Hiorne. The interior of the church is a fine 18th-century period piece, with box-pews and a pair of 18th-century candelabra which, with their 36 branches, are exceptionally large.

Teversal *Notts.*   552Ee
CHURCH OF ST KATHARINE Originally Norman, with later alterations. Remarkable Norman doorway and 17th-century furnishings—box-pews, altar rails, pulpit, squire's pew and so on. Many monuments to the local Molyneux family; one of *c.* 1741 is by Sir Henry Cheere.

Tewkesbury *Glos.*   546Ce
Tewkesbury contains many inns and old timbered houses, including the House of the Golden Key and Ancient Grudge, as well as an abbey. A row of 15th-century cottages in Church Street has recently been restored. In 1471 Edward IV defeated the Lancastrians at the Battle of Tewkesbury. About 6 miles from the town is Bredon Hill (980 ft). At the summit is a prehistoric camp known as the King and Queen Rocks. To the east of the town is the Tibble Stone, a boundary stone

probably dating from AD 600, which is referred to in Domesday Book and has been adapted as a modern signpost.

ABBEY CHURCH OF ST MARY THE VIRGIN A surprising parish church that was bought by the townsfolk at the Dissolution for about £400 and is as big as a cathedral. It was attached to a Benedictine monastery and dates from the early part of the 12th century. The tall columns of the nave form one of the chief features of the Romanesque church and make it distinctly different from most other churches of that period. The striking central tower was probably built c. 1150.

The eastern parts of the church were almost entirely rebuilt in the 14th century, and a new vault was added to the nave. The most brilliant architectural feature is the vaulting of the presbytery in which the surface is decorated with patterns similar to those used in window tracery. The impressive interior has many tombs and monuments; especially interesting is the late 14th-century Despencer chantry chapel, on top of which kneels a small effigy of Edward le Despencer beneath its own canopy. There is also some 14th-century stained glass.

Of the monks' quarters, to the south of the church, little remains.

Thame *Oxon.* *547Gc*
CHURCH OF ST MARY THE VIRGIN A magnificent cruciform church with a noble central tower and work of all Gothic periods: good windows, south porch, screens and an Early English font; also of interest are the brasses. Noteworthy among the monuments is one to Lord Williams of Thame (*d.* 1559) and his wife, in front of the altar.

Thaxted *Essex* *548Bd*
Once a Saxon village, Thaxted grew into one of the most prosperous towns in Essex during the Middle Ages through its cutlery trade. It has a large church with a tall spire, a 15th-century timber-framed guildhall and some noteworthy houses. The Recorder's House (now a restaurant) carries the Arms of Edward IV.
CHURCH OF ST JOHN THE BAPTIST The prosperity of Thaxted 500 years ago enabled the parishioners to build their spacious cruciform church with its 180 ft high spire. The pinnacled font cover, of the late 15th century, completely encases the font. There are 15th-century screens, many fragments of medieval stained glass, a richly carved timber roof and three 20th-century windows by C. E. Kempe.

Theddlethorpe *Lincs.* *553Jf*
CHURCH OF ALL SAINTS Largely a building of 1380–1400, but with some earlier work. There are Perpendicular and good Decorated windows, and fragments of medieval glass remain. There is a 15th-century rood screen and two parclose screens of c. 1535. Among the 18th-century monuments is one by Andrew Carpenter, of c. 1727.

Theobald's Park *Herts.* *547Jc*
London's Temple Bar (designed by Sir Christopher Wren in 1672) was removed from its original site in 1878, and re-erected at the end of a track to the left of the Park gates.

Therfield Heath *Herts.* *547Je*
Here there is a 125 ft Neolithic long barrow, still standing up to 8 ft high. It has a surrounding ditch and the mound was of piled turves coated with a crust of chalk. Just to the north is a group of eight Bronze Age bowl barrows. They vary greatly in diameter and are up to 12 ft high.

Thetford *Norfolk* *554Ba*
An ancient town, once important, with a known history of more than 1000 years. It was a bishop's See from 1075 to 1095. Surrounding it are many relics of Stone Age cultures, and it stands on the ancient Icknield Way. In the Middle Ages and Tudor period it had as many as 20 parish churches and several monasteries. After the Dissolution the town's importance declined.
ANCIENT HOUSE MUSEUM This 15th-century timber-framed building with an important carved ceiling houses displays illustrating the life, history and natural history of Thetford and Breckland. Finds from the Early Stone Age to the medieval period are included and there are a number of domestic objects from the 18th and 19th centuries. Ancient weights and measures are also on display.
BELL HOTEL Built in 1493, with fine timber work. Early wall-paintings and a section of the original wattle-and-daub wall tied with ropes of grass are preserved.
CAGE AND STOCKS In Cage Lane, the two-storied town gaol was erected possibly in 1581 as a lock-up with stocks and re-erected on the opposite side of the street in 1968. In Old Market Street is the gaol of 1816.
CASTLE HILL The remaining mound of a motte and bailey castle demolished in 1173. The surrounding earthworks may be from the time of the Iceni, an Ancient British tribe.
CLUNIAC PRIORY OF OUR LADY These monastic remains are near the railway station; others are the Augustinian Priory of the Holy Sepulchre in Brandon Road; the Blackfriars in the grammar school, London Road; and the Benedictine Nunnery of St George, near the Euston road.
KING'S HOUSE Used as a hunting lodge by James I; it has an 18th-century front.
THETFORD WARREN LODGE A 15th-century flint-and-stone tower, perhaps a fortified gamekeeper's house, in heathland near the Thetford to Brandon road.
THOMAS PAINE HOTEL A largely 17th-century building in which Thomas Paine, author of *Commonsense* and *Rights of Man*, was born in 1737.

Thirlestane Castle *Borders* *562Dd*
An imposing late 16th-century building incorporating a 14th-century fortress. It was altered in the late 17th century by Sir William Bruce, and contains fine plasterwork of that period and a collection of portraits by Lely, Romney and Aikmain. (By appointment.)

Thirsk *N. Yorks.* *558Dd*
CHURCH OF ST MARY THE VIRGIN This is an impressive church in the Perpendicular style; built 1420, the chancel was added in 1470. There are still fragments of medieval glass in one or two windows, and the brass and screens are also worth noting. There is 19th-century restoration by G. E. Street.

Thoresby Hall *Notts.* *552Fe*
The present large mansion, built in neo-Tudor style, is the third to be erected in Thoresby Park. The original country seat was built in 1683 for the 4th Earl of Kingston by William Talman, architect of the early work at Chatsworth. The mansion was destroyed by fire in 1745, and the only survivor was a sphinx, carved by Caius Gabriel Cibber. A few years later the house was rebuilt by John Carr of York in the Palladian manner, but in the 19th century this house was demolished. The owner, the 3rd Earl Manvers, a direct descendant of the 2nd Duke of Kingston, found Carr's house too small, and commissioned the architect Anthony Salvin to build the present mansion. (See p. 458.)

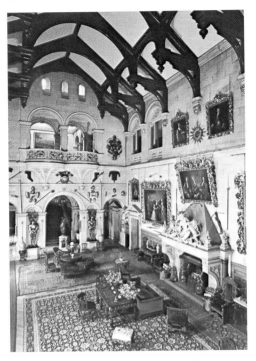

THE GREAT HALL AT THORESBY HALL

This large Victorian mansion was built by the architect Anthony Salvin to replace the smaller seat of the Earls Manvers. The outstanding features of the house, on which Salvin worked from 1864 until 1875, include the large state apartments, the three-storied great hall with its lavish hammerbeam roof, and the entrance tower, which Salvin modelled on that of Burghley House in Cambridgeshire. The mansion is surrounded by the largest park in the Dukeries, and is enclosed in Sherwood Forest.

Thorington Hall *Suffolk* 548Ce
An oak-framed, plastered and gabled house within retaining walls, built *c.* 1600, enlarged *c.* 1700, and restored in 1937. (By appointment.)

Thorney *Cambs.* 547Jh
Thorney village, only 15 ft above sea level, is the only village in Thorney Rural District, an area of 22,985 acres on the most northerly part of the Fenlands. Hereward the Wake made one of his last stands here against William the Conqueror. For a long time the village was the sole property of a single landlord, the Earls and Dukes of Bedford, who arranged the houses according to the status of employees on the estate.

At Toneham, south-west of the village, were the claypits, brick-yard and kiln used by the Duke of Bedford in building the estate houses of 19th-century Thorney.
CHURCH OF SS MARY AND BOTOLPH Remnants of the former Norman abbey church, with good late 11th-century arcades, and an impressive west front. The transepts, crossing tower and chancel have all gone, and the present east end is by Edward Blore (the architect who designed the Mall block of Buckingham Palace) in a Norman style of *c.* 1840.
THORNEY ABBEY The small island on which Thorney is built was used as a monastic settlement in the 7th century. This monastery was destroyed by the Danes in 870. The subsequent Norman abbey was dissolved in 1539 and left derelict until 1638, when part of the original was restored. Its

west front has two tall 12th-century turrets surmounted by 15th-century octagonal tops, with a deeply recessed doorway of the same period between them, over which is a 17th-century window. Above this is a stone screen, extending from turret to turret, with nine canopied niches containing medieval statues. The chancel and transept were added in 1841 in imitation of Norman style.
THORNEY ABBEY HOUSE There are two houses here. The first is of the late 16th century, and the second, *c.* 1660, was the mansion house of the Dukes of Bedford, who voluntarily contributed their vast fortunes to drain the Bedford Level of the Fens.

Around the house spread 20,000 acres of land reclaimed from swamp and mere. The house is square, built of stone, with a hipped-roof and one great central chimney-stack. Inside, there is some good panelling in the dining-room, including a great carved fire-place surround, a broad staircase, and doorcases which may have been by Peter Mills, *c.* 1660. (Not open to the public.)

Thornhill *W. Yorks.* 558Ca
CHURCH OF ST MICHAEL AND ALL ANGELS
Originally 15th century, the church was restored and rebuilt in 1879 by G. E. Street. There are fragments of Saxon crosses, and many monuments with effigies, the most spectacular being the large 17th-century edifices to the Saviles. There is good 15th-century glass.

Thornton Abbey *Humberside* 553Hg
The abbey was founded in 1139 for a community of Augustinian canons. Only parts of the chapter house and a fine gateway remain. One of the canons compiled a chronicle of Thornton Abbey from which it has been possible to date accurately the building of various parts of the monastery. The chapter house, which was begun in 1282, was paved in 1308, and must have been an impressive building. Licence to build the fine gateway was granted in 1382; it stood just inside the courtyard and had some military fortifications in the form of two round towers and an arcaded surrounding wall. It is faced partly in stone and partly in brick— an early example in England of this decorative use. The abbey is approached across a moat, spanned by a long bridge.

Thorpe Hall *Cambs.* 547Jg
A dignified mid-17th-century rectangular house, built by John Webb (a one-time pupil of Inigo Jones), during the Commonwealth period, for Chief Justice Oliver St John. It has two main floors, a high hipped-roof with dormers, and signs that suggest a Dutch influence on the later, east side. Gates with piers carrying heraldic birds frame the house perfectly. (By appointment.)

Thorpe Market *Norfolk* 554Dc
CHURCH OF ST MARGARET The church was built *c.* 1795 in the Gothic Revival style, and has open-work screens, porches on both sides, and at each corner of the building are turrets with little spires. The font is Perpendicular. One of the monuments is by Charles Regnart, 1796.

Threave Castle *Dumfs. & Gall.* 556Eg
The ruined stronghold of the Black Douglases, Lords of Galloway. It was built by Archibald the Grim, 3rd Earl Douglas, on an island in the R. Dee during the 14th century, and housed a Royalist garrison in the Civil War. The 14th-century tower-house is surrounded by walls built in the 15th century; these were more than 70 ft high and 8 ft thick. The Threave Wildfowl Refuge is on the estate and there are superb gardens.

Throwley *Kent* 542Ef
CHURCH OF ST MICHAEL AND ALL ANGELS A large church for a sparsely populated parish, with a 16th-century house adjoining. The tower between the south aisle and the chapel is battlemented; its top stage was built in the 19th century. The monastic foundation of the church explains its unexpected misericords. There are fine late 16th- and 17th-century tomb chests with kneeling effigies of painted alabaster, among the earliest in the country, with heraldry, and an 1835 monument by the neo-Classical sculptor George Rennie.

Thrumpton Hall *Notts.* 552Ec
A Jacobean house built around an Elizabethan one. The carved Carolean staircase and the saloon were added in 1667 and the stableyard wing was added in 1823–35. The house has connections with the Byron family, and contains relics of the poet as well as some fine paintings and furniture. (By appointment.)

Thurgarton *Notts.* 552Fd
PRIORY CHURCH OF ST PETER The Augustinian priory was founded *c.* 1140, and the present parish church is a tiny fragment of what must have been quite a large building with two western towers.

Tichborne *Hants.* 541He
CHURCH OF ST ANDREW The church has a Saxon chancel, an early 18th-century brick west tower, a Norman font, and fragments of medieval glass. Many monuments in the north aisle are dedicated to the local family, the Tichbornes, from the 17th to the 19th century. The box-pews are from the early 17th century.

Tickencote *Leics.* 553Gb
CHURCH OF ST PETER The huge Norman chancel arch, with its five rows of carving each in a different design, has long been famous. Much of the church was rebuilt in the late 18th century by Samuel Pepys Cockerell, but the vaulted chancel is largely original 12th-century work.

Tickhill *S. Yorks.* 552Ef
CHURCH OF ST MARY A large and impressive church, dating from the 13th century, when the base of the west tower was built. Rebuilding took place in the late 14th century, but the upper part of the tower was not completed until later, when the nave was rebuilt. There are remains of medieval glass, and monuments of the 15th–19th centuries.

Tideswell *Derbys.* 552Ce
CHURCH OF ST JOHN THE BAPTIST A cruciform church with a pinnacled west tower, almost all dating from the 14th century. It contains a Perpendicular font, some 19th-century stained glass, and many medieval monuments and brasses.

Tilty *Essex* 548Bd
CHURCH OF ST MARY THE VIRGIN This church was formerly the chapel outside the gate of the neighbouring Cistercian abbey. It has a 13th-century nave and 14th-century chancel. The five-light east window has some particularly fine tracery. The chancel also contains brasses.

Tintagel *Cornwall* 538Dd
High on the cliff-top overlooking the sea lies Tintagel, well known for its association with the Arthurian legend, for here, so the story goes, King Uther Pendragon and Ygraine, Arthur's parents, first came together. It was the site of a Celtic monastery, probably founded by St Juliot about the beginning of the 6th century. The foundations may still be seen. They were not grouped in any recognisable pattern, showing how different these early religious houses were from the later establishments, which may indicate that the first

THE GATE-HOUSE AT THORNTON ABBEY

One of the most splendid gate-houses to survive in England, probably designed for domestic use, possibly as a guest house. The upper floors contain a large hall and various small rooms including cloakrooms, and the impressive entrance façade is decorated with two rows of statuary. The Augustinian abbey appears to have been large and wealthy: at the time of the Dissolution one prior and 27 canons surrendered to the Crown. The abbey was turned into a secular college for canons for a few years during the reign of Henry VIII. The surviving walls of the fine octagonal chapter house are decorated with blank geometric tracery, and the vault sprang from a central column.

monasteries began as random gatherings of hermits, and only later became well organised.
TINTAGEL OLD POST OFFICE A small 14th-century stone house, with thick and uneven slate roof, built to the plan of a medieval manor house. It gets its name because it was a letter-receiving office for the district from 1844 until 1892.

Tintagel Castle *Cornwall* 538Dd
The castle at Tintagel was built in the 12th century, and considerable additions were made to it in the following century. By the 16th century the central portion connecting the inner ward with the lower ward and part of the great hall had been washed away by the sea. The site then became derelict until interest in the Arthurian legend revived in the 19th century. Tennyson's poems popularised the legend and the ruins were repaired in 1852. (See p. 460).

Tintern Abbey *Gwent* 546Ac
The abbey was founded in 1131. Hardly anything is visible of the original foundation, for in the 13th and 14th centuries the abbey was extensively enlarged. Most of the ruined monastic buildings are well preserved, and the church itself is an impressive ruin. It was built on an axis slightly

south of that of the first church, and the high altar was first used in 1288. The Cistercian architecture is simple: there is no triforium passage between clerestory and the main arcade, and large towers were forbidden by the rule of the Cistercian order.

Tintinhull House *Som.*   *540Cd*
An elegant small manor house built in the late 17th century. It stands in a fine formal garden.

Tiptofts Farm *Essex*   *548Be*
A moated house of *c.* 1330 with a rare surviving aisled hall. The exterior is timber-framed.

Tisbury *Wilts.*   *540Ee*
CHURCH OF ST JOHN THE BAPTIST A cruciform 12th-century church, with a central tower which, until it fell in 1762, had a spire. Inside, the font cover, pulpit and pews are 17th century; the communion rail is made from parts of a rood screen.

Titchfield *Hants.*   *541Hd*
In the main street there are Georgian brick cottages. To the north are the remains of the silvery-grey stone mansion built in Henry VIII's reign out of the buildings of the dissolved abbey. It fell into disrepair in the latter part of the 18th century.
CHURCH OF ST PETER An interesting church of partly Saxon construction. Among the monuments is one of *c.* 1615, attributed to Epiphanius Evesham, but the most striking is by Gerard Johnson to two Earls of Southampton, *c.* 1594, resplendent with effigies, shields, obelisks and heraldic beasts.

Tittleshall *Norfolk*   *554Bc*
CHURCH OF ST MARY The west tower and chancel are Decorated, the nave Perpendicular, and the octagonal font Perpendicular. But the interest of Tittleshall is in its series of monuments to the Coke (Earls of Leicester) family. Nicholas Stone, the early 17th-century sculptor, carved that to Sir Edward Coke (*d.* 1634), with a recumbent effigy. Louis Roubiliac carved the busts of the 1st Earl of Leicester, *c.* 1760, and Joseph Nollekens sculpted the large marble relief showing Mrs Coke (*d.* 1800) leaning on a broken column, whilst above an angel sitting on clouds holds out his hand to her.

Tiverton *Devon*   *539He*
A castle was built here, *c.* 1106, by the 1st Earl of Devon: only the ruins of two towers remain. The massive gatehouse on the east side is 14th century. The town acquired great prosperity in Tudor times from its wool trade, but this had declined by the beginning of the 19th century.
BLUNDELL'S (OLD SCHOOL) The original building of the famous grammar school, built in 1604 by Peter Blundell, Clothier. The north-east façade is as described in the novel *Lorna Doone* by R. D. Blackmore. (Access to the green only.)
CHURCH OF ST GEORGE An early 18th-century Georgian church, with a galleried interior.
CHURCH OF ST PETER The Greenway Chapel (1517), with its notable ship carvings, reflects Tiverton's prosperity as a wool centre. The 17th-century organ and the candelabrum are superb.

TINTAGEL CASTLE

Legend links this site—a rocky headland amid wild and romantic scenery—with King Arthur, a shadowy figure of the late 5th century who allegedly successfully led the native Celts against the invading Saxons during the breaking up of the Roman Empire. There is, however, no earlier evidence to support this link than the propagandist 12th-century writings of Geoffrey of Monmouth. The most interesting of the remains of earlier settlements on the site are those associated with the monastery which grew up around *the cell of St Juliot, a Celtic missionary who came to Tintagel about 500. This community, which was housed in a series of small, rectangular stone huts scattered across the north-east side of the headland, was governed by no formal rule but formed a loose association of individuals serving God in varying ways. Tintagel became a royal castle attached to the Earldom of Cornwall, and among its distinguished lords was Edward III's son Edward, the Black Prince, who commissioned some of the buildings.*

Tixover *Leics.* 553Gb
CHURCH A mainly Norman church with a tower, and inside an impressive tower arch (all *c.* 1140). The original medieval stone seats remain along the chancel walls. An early 17th-century marble monument to the lord of the manor has kneeling figures.

Toddington *Beds.* 547Hd
CHURCH OF ST GEORGE The church is built of Totternhoe stone and ironstone, with modern tile infilling; it is cruciform, with a central tower, and dates from the 13th to 15th centuries. The building is in keeping with the one-time prosperity of this hill-top town; inside are many monuments dating from the 14th century, including one to Lady Henrietta Wentworth, *c.* 1686, which has been attributed to both William Bushnell and William Stanton. The roof, restored after gale damage in 1976, has carved angels and bosses. The three-storied priest's house on the north side is unique.

Toddington *Glos.* 546De
CHURCH OF ST ANDREW A Gothic Revival church by G. E. Street, 1873–9. There is a tall broach spire and, inside, two marble effigies of Lord and Lady Sudeley by J. G. Lough.

Tolleshunt d'Arcy *Essex* 548Cd
CHURCH OF ST NICHOLAS A 15th-century church with an embattled west tower. The ceiling in the chancel dates from the 19th century and there is a collection of brasses in the north chapel.
HALL A house of *c.* 1500 with a fine moat and four-arched brick and stone bridge dated 1585. A wing, remodelled in the 17th century, has outstanding 16th-century panelling of linenfold divided by ranges of carving. In the grounds is a large 16th-century dove-cote. (By appointment.)

Tolleshunt Major *Essex* 548Cd
BECKINGHAM HALL An unusual Tudor brick wall surrounds a large courtyard and relatively small, partly 16th century, timber and brick house. The large turretted gate-house is the central feature of the wall, and there are other turrets at each corner of the wall. Ornamental panelling from the Hall, dated 1546, is in the Victoria and Albert Museum. (By appointment.)

Tolpuddle *Dorset* 540Dc
MARTYRS' MEMORIAL A seat commemorates the six agricultural labourers of Tolpuddle who were sentenced to transportation in 1834 for the 'crime' of demanding a wage increase.

Tomen-y-mur *Gwynedd* 550Fd
In the wild mountain country a few miles to the south-east of the Snowdon range, the Roman fort of Tomen-y-mur stood on a spur of hill some 10 miles from the sea below Harlech. The site is complicated by the presence of the motte of an early medieval castle, standing inside the outline of the early fort. However, when the fort was rebuilt in stone in the 2nd century, its area was reduced, and the wall now running through the motte is the west wall of this second fort. By the path down to the stream are the remains of an amphitheatre, bath-buildings and a parade ground. The small square mounds along this track and beyond the stream are burial-mounds of members of the garrison.

Tong *Shropshire* 552Bb
CHURCH OF ST BARTHOLOMEW A magnificent Perpendicular building dating from *c.* 1410, when the earlier church was rebuilt. The square central tower has a pinnacled and battlemented octagonal upper stage, and a short spire. The interior is dominated by superb tombs and monuments, but

MONUMENT TO THE FIRST EARL
OF SOUTHAMPTON

A fine Elizabethan monument to Thomas Wriothesley, 1st Earl of Southampton (1505–50), and his wife and son. The four obelisks are characteristic of many tombs of the period. Wriothesley, Secretary of State and Lord High Chancellor under Henry VIII, was knighted in 1540 and created Earl in 1547. At the Dissolution of the Monasteries, Henry gave him extensive lands including the Abbey of Titchfield, which he rebuilt as a sumptuous house. His grandson was a patron of Shakespeare. (St Peter's, Titchfield)

there is also a Perpendicular octagonal font, and much interesting woodwork, including screens, stall misericords and a Jacobean pulpit. There are monuments to the founders of the church, Sir Fulke and Lady Elizabeth de Pembruge, and to the Vernons of Haddon Hall, including those in the fan-vaulted Vernon Chapel (1515). (See p. 462.)

Topcliffe *N. Yorks.* 558Dc
CHURCH OF ST COLUMBA Although mainly a 19th-century rebuilding, the church still retains some of its original 14th-century work—a huge Flemish-type brass with two figures beneath a canopy containing many smaller figures of angels. There is some stained glass by Burne-Jones.

Torhouse, Stones of *Dumfs. & Gall.* 556Dg
A perfect circle of tall stones, about 60 ft in diameter, dating from the Bronze Age.

Torphichen *Lothian* 562Ae
PRECEPTORY CHURCH A hospital of the Knights of St John of Jerusalem once stood on this site. In 1756 the remains were incorporated in the present church; the tower of this church was once part of the domestic buildings of the hospital and the nave was part of the hospital chapel.

Torquay *Devon* 539Hc
The town became prosperous in the Napoleonic Wars, as a centre for officers and their families awaiting orders to move overseas; their houses are features of the old town. There are also the remains of Torre Abbey, a 12th-century foundation.
TORQUAY NATURAL HISTORY SOCIETY MUSEUM Relics of early man (Old Stone Age to Iron Age) and extinct mammals such as the mammoth and woolly rhinoceros found in Kent's Cavern near Torquay are included in the collections, which have as their themes the geology, natural history and folk culture of Devon.

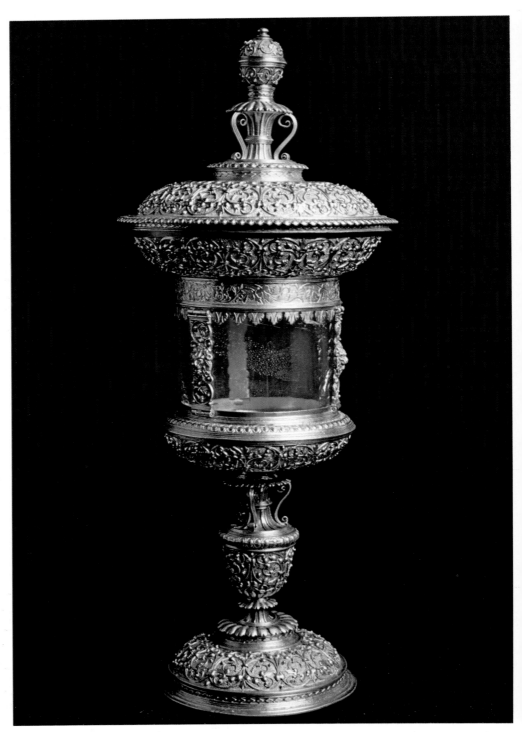

CUP AND COVER MADE OF SILVER-GILT
AND ROCK CRYSTAL

*This splendid cup is one of the many items of domestic plate to have found their way into church treasuries all over England and Wales, usually as the result of benefactions made by devout parishioners. The cup has no maker's mark at all, and it would be difficult to date it precisely from its shape alone. The bowl with its spreading cover is formed round a cylinder of rock crystal (crystallised quartz) held in place by three straps in mid-16th-century fashion, while the stem has a short pillar and brackets more characteristic of the early 17th century. Fortunately the filigree decoration of scrolling and berried foliage seems to have been used solely by a distinguished London goldsmith who used the mark 'TYL' in monogram. This mark appears on two fine standing cups with similar filigree work which were made in 1611—one is in the Victoria and Albert Museum, London and the other is at Christ's College, Cambridge —and the cup at Tong is generally thought to have been made by the same goldsmith at about the same time. It stands to a height of just over 11 in.
(Church of St Bartholomew, Tong)*

Toseland *Cambs.*   *547Jf*
TOSELAND HALL An almost perfect small Tudor manor house of three bays with a central porch, three gables, fine mullioned windows and graceful ornamented octagonal chimney-stacks.

Totnes *Devon*   *539Gc*
Totnes, on the R. Dart, existed in Norman times; by the Middle Ages it had become a walled town with four gates, two of which have survived. In Fore Street is a Tudor merchant's house adjoining the restored east gate. The guildhall houses the council chamber, used since 1624, and the court-room. The ruined castle stands by the remains of the north gate.
CHURCH OF ST MARY An impressive mainly 15th-century church, with a tall west tower. A stone screen extending across the whole church is *c.* 1460, and the pulpit is of the same period. There are arcades and good roofs.
DARTINGTON HALL On the western outskirts of Totnes. Its great hall was built in 1388–1400, and the present roof was constructed of oak from the estate in 1932. The complex of medieval buildings is now devoted to rural industries, music, the arts, a school and vocational training centre and a famous landscape garden.

Totternhoe *Beds.*   *547Hd*
Totternhoe has not only the great 500 ft high hill with a Bronze Age fort, but also the notable Cross Keys Inn, half-timbered, thatched and with a fire-place dated 1433.
CHURCH OF ST GILES Begun in the 14th century and completed in the 16th, St Giles's has a fine exterior and a pinnacled skyline. The stone came from the quarries in the village. Inside, the roof is carved with bosses and figures, and there is inter-esting brass and a font, as well as some fragments of medieval glass.

Towyn (Tywyn) *Gwynedd*   *550Eb*
NARROW-GAUGE RAILWAY MUSEUM Housed in a modern building next to Wharf Station, the museum began as an exhibition of interesting items depicting the history of the Talyllyn Rail-way, a narrow-gauge railway constructed in the 1860's to carry slates from the quarry at Bryn Eglwys. It has since been augmented from other British and foreign sources, and exhibits include name and makers' plates, signalling equipment, coach fittings, old drawings and photographs.

Tranent *Lothian*   *562Ce*
PRESTONGRANGE HISTORICAL SITE AND MINING MUSEUM Coal-mining history on a site that in-cludes a Cornish beam pumping engine and 100-year-old steam navvy. The former power house has mining artefacts on show.

Traprain Law *Lothian*   *562De*
This great hill-fort stands on an isolated hill-top north of the Lammermuir Hills. Earlier excava-tions have shown that it was occupied from the early part of the Iron Age right through into the Dark Ages.
From time to time, fresh defensive works were raised. Sometimes these obscured the earlier ones or modified them and the hill-top, as·well as its upper slopes, bears traces or parts of many of these different systems.
This fort, indeed, must have been the major settlement of the Votadini tribe. For a time this tribal area was within the sphere of direct Roman rule, but after the Roman withdrawal from the Antonine Wall to Hadrian's Wall, the Votadini were apparently a Border tribe in close alliance with Rome and in whose territory there were many detached Roman forts. It was on Traprain Law that the great hoard of looted silver from Roman Britain, now in Edinburgh, was dis-covered.

Traquair House *Borders*   *562Cd*
Mary, Queen of Scots and her second husband, Lord Darnley, stayed here in 1566. The mansion, whose origins are medieval, has remained un-altered since the 17th century. Its contents date from the 12th century onwards: tapestries, glass, embroideries, fine silver and relics of Mary, Queen of Scots and the Jacobite rebellions. There is also an 18th-century library and a priest's room with its secret staircase. In the 18th-century Brew-house attached to the main house, Traquair Ale is made, and a licence to sell the home-made brew has been granted to the owner of the house.

Trefignath *Anglesey, Gwynedd*   *550De*
A fine megalithic chambered tomb comprising three distinct chambers each built at different dates and surrounded by a cairn of stones. Though mutilated, the massive stones of the chambers still form an imposing monument, and show to what lengths Neolithic man would go to house his dead in a way he considered worthy of them.

Tremadog *Gwynedd*   *550Ed*
A small village forming part of W. A. Maddocks's scheme for reclaiming the Traeth Mawr. Built round an open square and a road junction, it included a town hall built in 1805, a hotel and shops, with terraces of cottages facing the square. At the approaches from Porthmadog is a Classical Nonconformist chapel, originally a theatre, and a Gothic church, both built between 1806 and 1810. The gate piers to the church are modelled on the Rimini gateway in Rome.

Trencrom Hill *Cornwall*   *538Ab*
A well preserved Iron Age hill-fort, with a stone wall enclosing hut circles.

Trent *Dorset*   *540Cd*
CHURCH OF ST ANDREW The church is of 13th-century origin; additions include the 14th-century south tower and spire, and a fine Perpendicular rood screen, still with its vault. Among the monuments is an effigy of a 14th-century knight. There is 16th- and 17th-century foreign stained glass. The pulpit is perhaps Dutch, of *c.* 1600, and there are some 16th-century bench ends.

Treowen *Gwent*   *546Ad*
This stone-built Tudor manor house, with Jacobean porch, has an oak open-well staircase four storeys high; there is also a four-storey spiral staircase with solid oak treads. Plasterwork, panel-ling, doors and fire-places are original. (By appointment.)

Tre'r Ceiri *Gwynedd*   *550Dd*
Here, on an isolated hill overlooking the sea, stands one of the most remarkable Iron Age hill-forts in Britain. The inner area, protected by a strong drystone wall, has a long irregular oval plan, and in this are dozens of roughly circular stone huts. Furthermore, the long north-western side has an additional stone rampart which, starting close to the south-west gate, gradually diverges in its north-easterly course. Though technically belong-ing to the Iron Age tradition, Tre'r Ceiri appears to have been occupied until the end of the Roman period.

Trerice *Cornwall*   *538Cc*
A manor house rebuilt in 1571 by John Arundell on the site of an older house. The Elizabethan plaster ceilings and fire-places can still be seen.

TRESCO

Tresco *Isles of Scilly* 538Af
TRESCO ABBEY GARDENS The terraced gardens at Tresco Abbey are unique in the British Isles for their wealth of sub-tropical plants. They were made by Augustus Smith when he became Lord Proprietor of the Isles of Scilly in 1834. Round the ruins of Tresco Abbey, Smith planted trees to act as shelterbelts; behind these lie a series of protected terraces, planted with veronicas, acacias, fuchsias, pelargoniums and cinerarias. Mesembryanthemum, a native plant of South Africa, is much used as ground cover, and in the borders native and exotic plants grow side by side. Mediterranean and sub-tropical plants provide the gardens with brilliant colour, and there are Australasian tree-ferns and Mexican cacti. In early spring the gardens at Tresco Abbey are vivid with the cultivated daffodils which Augustus Smith found growing wild among the abbey ruins.

VALHALLA MARITIME MUSEUM Housed in a mid-19th-century building of rough sea-boulders and timber from wrecked ships, the collection includes examples of wood-carving from the 17th to the 20th century, many of which are restored figure-heads or ornaments from ships wrecked off the Isles of Scilly.

TRESCO ABBEY GARDENS

These gardens with sub-tropical plants are at their full glory in earliest spring—when mainland gardens are still winter-bound. They were begun around the ruins of Tresco Abbey by Augustus Smith in 1834. He first planted trees to withstand the gales and then constructed a series of sheltered terraces. Soon veronicas, acacias, fuchsias, cinerarias, palms and many other plants were flourishing out of doors all the year through. The daffodils at Tresco are superb—some are descended from those found among the abbey ruins, probably planted by the monks.

Tretower Court *Powys* 545Jd
One of the earliest and best fortified medieval manor houses in Wales, dating mainly from the 15th century. However, the ownership of the land here can be traced back to the 11th century. The present domestic buildings were preceded by a fortress—the keep—which stands adjacent. Inside, the keep is round, but outside the stonework is polygonal in plan. The main part of Tretower Court consists of a hall, with its attendant offices, built round a courtyard; a little of the masonry probably dates from *c.* 1300. The house has a picturesque open first-floor gallery looking on to the courtyard. The hall itself, the adjoining solar and the gate-house survive more or less intact. The 17th-century mystic poet Henry Vaughan used to live at Tretower Court.

Tring *Herts.* 547Hd
ZOOLOGICAL MUSEUM Built by Lord Rothschild to house his private collection and opened to the public in 1892. The house and contents were given to the British Museum and became an outstation of the Natural History Museum in 1938. Mammals, birds and important exhibits of reptiles and fish are on view.

Trotton *W. Sussex* 541Je
CHURCH OF ST GEORGE The church is mainly 14th century, and contains a contemporary wall-painting of the Last Judgment. Beautiful large brasses compensate for the lack of a chancel arch; one, to Lady Camoys (*d.* 1310), is perhaps the oldest monument of this kind to a woman. There are also brasses to Lord Camoys (*d.* 1419) and his wife, nearly life-size figures under pinnacled and battlemented canopies.

Troutbeck *Cumbria* 557He
TOWNEND A modest farmhouse, built *c.* 1626 by a yeoman farmer. His descendants, the Browne family, lived there until 1944, and the house contains carved woodwork and their books, papers and furniture.

Trowlesworthy Warren *Devon* 538Fc
A Bronze Age moorland settlement, with six walled enclosures and circular huts. The enclosure-walls are remarkable for their massive construction.

Not far away across the moor to the south by east there is a stone row and a stone circle, both Bronze Age. Across the streams to the east, the slopes of Lee Moor have more hut circles, enclosures and other structures, evidence of extensive occupation of the western valley-slopes of Dartmoor during the Bronze Age.

Trumpington *Cambs.* 548Af
CHURCH OF SS MARY AND MICHAEL A 14th-century cruciform church with fine arches and clerestory windows. There is a famous brass of *c.* 1289, the second oldest in England, to Sir Roger de Trumpington, showing his cross-legged effigy and trumpets on his shield.

Trunch *Norfolk* 554Dc
CHURCH OF ST BOTOLPH Perpendicular church with a west tower, and another of Norfolk's hammerbeam nave roofs decorated with angels. However, Trunch is famous for its magnificent font canopy, of which type there are only three others in England. It stands on eight carved pillars, with much carving of foliage, and beneath the cover is a sort of fan-vault with a pendant. Above this are eight canopied niches, now without their statues. A large crocket finishes off the very top. St Botolph's also has a screen with painted saints of 1502, and several carved misericords to the stalls.

464

MEMORIAL WINDOW BY CHAGALL
The church of All Saints, Tudeley, contains several stained-glass windows by Marc Chagall, the famous Russian-born artist.

This window, dedicated in 1967, commemorates the 21-year-old daughter of Sir Henry and Lady d'Avigdor-Goldsmith who was drowned in 1963 while sailing. The window is built up in 12 sections. The Crucifixion is depicted at the top. Below, floating in water, is the figure of the girl whose memorial the window is, and around her are mourning figures. She is also shown climbing the ladder to Heaven, symbolising hope. The red horse and rider symbolise happiness.

Trundle, The *W. Sussex*　　　　541Jd
The Iron Age hill-fort here overlies a Neolithic enclosure, but the two do not coincide; the inner Neolithic ditch lies within the Iron Age defences, and an outer Neolithic ditch, which is not circular, but whose ends overlap in a simple spiral, partly underlies and strays beyond the Iron Age structures. These latter comprise a substantial bank with external ditch and counterscarp bank. The two entrances are diametrically opposite and there is some evidence of the remodelling of the gates.

Truro *Cornwall*　　　　538Cb
CATHEDRAL The former 16th-century parish church of St Mary stood on the site of the cathedral, which was designed by John Loughborough Pearson, who was one of the foremost Victorian architects. All the old church was demolished except the south aisle, which was incorporated in the new building. This is in the Early English style, and work on it began in 1880. There are two western towers, with another over the point where nave and chancel meet, and all are crowned by stone spires—an unusual feature for an English church. By 1903 the 250 ft high central tower was finished as a memorial to Queen Victoria. The western towers, 204 ft high, were complete by 1910, and Edward VII allowed the

south-western one to be named after him, while Queen Alexandra gave her name to that in the north-west.
COUNTY MUSEUM AND ART GALLERY Under the control of the Royal Institution of Cornwall since 1818, the gallery displays drawings by Rubens, Lely, Kneller, Hogarth, Gainsborough, Romney and Constable, and paintings by John Opie (The Cornish Wonder), Court portrait painter during George III's reign.
Life in Cornwall from the earliest times is illustrated by collections which include Bronze Age jewellery and funeral urns, items connected with tin and copper mining, ship models, vehicles, coins and tokens. The art collections include English pewter, pottery and porcelain; Japanese ivories and lacquer; and a famous collection of Cornish minerals.

Trusty's Hill *Dumfs. & Gall.*　　　　556Dg
VITRIFIED FORT A small Iron Age fort of the kind well represented in this part of Scotland. The vitrified wall encloses an almost rectangular area. The south-east entrance lies between two natural rock-exposures. There are additional ramparts with ditches lying well away from the central enclosure. Pictish symbols are carved on one of the two natural rock-faces at the entrance.

Tudeley *Kent*　　　　542Cf
CHURCH OF ALL SAINTS This small church of brick and stone is mentioned in the Domesday Book. It contains magnificent stained-glass windows by Marc Chagall, the first of which was dedicated in November 1967, when Chagall was 80.

Turin Hill *Tayside*　　　　566Eb
KEMP'S CASTLE This Iron Age hill-fort was originally a large oval enclosure with two ramparts. Later, a smaller area within the earlier enclosure was surrounded by a stone wall. This fort was abandoned later in the Iron Age and a dun about 90 ft across was built. This rested in part on the inner wall of the fort. There are apparently two other similar duns on the hill-top.

Turton Tower *Lancs.*　　　　552Bg
A 12th-century house with 16th-century alterations. It contains the Ashworth Museum in the upper storey of a large, well preserved 15th-century tower.

Turvey *Beds.*　　　　547He
CHURCH OF ALL SAINTS A Saxon church; its 14th–15th-century additions were restored and 'improved' by Sir Gilbert Scott during the 19th century. There is a 12th-century font, an early 14th-century wall-painting, and many monuments to the Mordaunt family. There are also a number of brasses, from the 15th century onwards.

Tutbury *Staffs.*　　　　552Dc
CHURCH OF ST MARY The beautiful Norman church is that of the priory founded in the 11th century. It has an impressively decorated west front with a magnificent doorway. Inside are some good arcades.

Twickenham *Greater London*　　　　547Jb
STRAWBERRY HILL Horace Walpole (1717–97) writer and Member of Parliament, fourth son of Sir Robert Walpole, settled here in 1747. He enlarged and rebuilt what had been a cottage, so that by 1776 it had become a 'little Gothic castle'. Here he set up a printing press where his works were printed. (By appointment.)

Twickenham House *Oxon*　　　　546Fc
Built in 1735 and considerably altered in 1760, this Georgian house has an unusual belvedere crowned

with a lead cupola and a ball finial. Its main internal feature is a staircase with Chinese lattice-pattern balustrade. The walled garden has a Gothic arbour and leads down to the river. (By appointment.)

Ty Mawr *Gwynedd* 550Fd
The home of Bishop William Morgan (1540–1604), who first translated the Bible into Welsh in 1588.

Tyberton *Heref. & Worcs.* 546Ae
CHURCH OF ST MARY A brick church of 1720, with a Norman doorway from an earlier building. John Wood of Bath inspired the impressive reredos in 1728. There are 17th- and 18th-century monuments to members of the Brydges family, and the Arms of George I, dated 1720. Alterations were made to the church in the 19th century.

Tydd St Mary *Lincs.* 553Jc
CHURCH OF ST MARY This is a 14th-century church, with a later west tower and spire. Inside, the 12th-century arcades provide evidence of the

former church here. The chancel windows have fine tracery work, and there is some notable carving on the 15th-century font. There are several monuments, including one by J. M. Rysbrack.

Tynemouth *Tyne & Wear* 558Ch
PRIORY CHURCH As at many other places in Northumberland, a monastery existed here in the 7th century, but raids by the Danes did great damage. The church ruins date from c. 1090–1130.

Tyttenhanger House *Herts.* 547Jc
Built c. 1660, perhaps the work of John Webb, a pupil of Inigo Jones—the architect who introduced Palladian architecture into England.
The superb staircase resembles those at Thorpe Hall near Peterborough, and Forde Abbey, Devon. The house has projecting wings, a noble entrance hall, some rich carving and much good linenfold panelling. (Not open to the public.)

Tywyn *Gwynedd* See Towyn

U V

Uffington *Oxon.* 546Ec
CHURCH OF ST MARY A large cruciform church of c. 1250. The square central tower has an octagonal top storey, the south porch is large, and three transept chapels have unusual lancet windows. The 13th-century south door has ornamental hinges, and above the north door is a large circular window.

Uffington Castle *Oxon.* 546Eb
The Iron Age hill-fort of 8 acres, has a single bank and counterscarp bank outside the ditch. The entrance lies on the north-west and the bank was apparently revetted with sarsen stones.

Uffington White Horse See White Horse.

Unstan *Mainland, Orkney* 569Hf
An almost circular Neolithic mound, known as a 'stalled cairn'. This name derives from the construction of the chamber. From the entrance a passage leads to the chamber, which is 20 ft long by 6 ft wide. It is divided into compartments (the 'stalls') and a further small cell is also present.

Up Marden *W. Sussex* 541Jd
CHURCH OF ST MICHAEL A remote 13th-century church on the South Downs, once a resting-place on the pilgrim's route from Winchester to Chichester. The interior is very simple, with brick floors, a few pews and a plain font.

Uppark *W. Sussex* 541Jd
A red-brick house in Wren style, built to designs by William Talman in 1680–1700. From the mid-18th century until 1954 it was owned by the Fetherstonhaugh family. In c. 1750 alterations

were made to the interior, and the architect was possibly James Paine the Elder. Further alterations were made c. 1770, probably by Henry Keene. Most of the interior dates from this period, and has remained untouched to this day. There are fine portraits. The grounds were landscaped by Humphry Repton for Sir Harry Fetherstonhaugh at the beginning of the 19th century, and pastures now sweep right up to the walls of the house.

Upton House *Warks.* 546Ee
A country mansion dating from the reigns of James II and William and Mary; it contains collections of Brussels tapestries, Sèvres porcelain, Chelsea figures, 18th-century furniture, and nearly 200 paintings by British, Dutch, Flemish, French, German, Italian and Spanish artists. In the grounds are fine terraced gardens. (See p. 468.)

Urchfont *Wilts.* 540Ef
CHURCH OF ST MICHAEL AND ALL ANGELS A long church, with a western pinnacled tower, built in the 14th century and added to in the 15th. The main feature of the interior is the original 13th-century chancel, which is vaulted. There is an Early English font; 19th-century stained glass; and a monument, c. 1753, by Peter Scheemakers.

Usk *Gwent* 546Ac
PRIORY CHURCH OF ST MARY The eastern part of this church has gone, but it was originally a Norman building, with central tower. Inside, the 15th-century screen extends the whole width of the building; it was restored in 1899. There is a 17th-century pulpit, and the organ comes from Llandaff Cathedral; there are also mural monuments.

THE SALOON AT UPPARK

Standing high on the South Downs this charming Wren-style house of red brick with stone dressings was built during the last two decades of the 17th century for Lord Tankerville. It was designed by William Talman, the architect of Chatsworth in Derbyshire. The building remained untouched until it came into the possession of the Fetherstonhaugh family in the middle of the 18th century. Various alterations to the interior were made in 1750–70, probably first under

James Paine the Elder, and then under Henry Keene, who was famous for the beautiful Gothic transformation of Arbury in Warwickshire. The rooms of Uppark are delightful, for by lucky chance they retain many of the original flock wallpapers, damask curtains and other textiles dating from the 18th century. The saloon especially is a fine example of an elegant early Georgian interior. Its 'fragility' anticipated Robert Adam's work by more than a decade.

UPTON HOUSE

STUBBS: THE HAYMAKERS *The passion for portraiture, so marked a feature of English taste in the 18th century, was not confined to the aristocratic landowner—it also extended to his country seat and the occupants of his stable. Of all the horse painters in this period, Stubbs was by far the greatest. But he is also a major figure in the English school, having a feeling for form and spatial organisation, and a Classicism that is more akin to French art. Stubbs had a strong spirit of scientific enquiry into the natural world, and the knowledge he gained was brought to bear on his numerous paintings of horses, and on his pictures of other animals. In addition, he often shows in his portraits—both human and animal—a fine sense for landscape. His pictures of farm labourers at work are important examples of the painting of English rural life—'The Haymakers' is one of these, dated 1783.*

SÈVRES PORCELAIN EWER *One of the few surviving pieces of Sèvres made with the rare yellow ground. It dates from 1756, the year the factory near Paris was moved to Sèvres from Vincennes, where it had been founded in 1738; its royal patronage continued until the revolution of 1789.*

Valle Crucis Abbey *Clwyd* 551Hd
A Cistercian abbey founded in 1201 by Madoc ap Gruffydd Maelor, Prince of Powys. Much of the church and the attached eastern range of the cloister still stands. The church belongs mainly to the 13th century. The square-ended presbytery is lighted by five lancet windows, forming a picturesque group when viewed from Llyn Eglwystl, the lake beside the abbey. At the west end, the façade, with its three Early English windows and later rose window above, also survives largely intact. Beneath is the richly carved west door.

The transepts still stand, and attached to the south transept lies the east range of the cloister. This was rebuilt in the 14th century and the chapter house remains, complete with its vaulting. Above was the dormitory, which was reached by a narrow staircase adjacent to the entrance to the chapter house.

Vaynol Old Hall *Gwynedd* 550Ee
This beautiful Elizabethan nucleus of the great Vaynol estate was replaced in the 18th century by the much larger Vaynol Hall. Consequently the older building did not receive the customary embellishment of the 18th and 19th centuries, and it is notable for the quality of its doors and mullioned windows, and particularly a massive oak stair which formed part of early 17th-century extensions. There is also a small private chapel of *c.*

1580, a beautiful garden and the largest barn in the county, dated 1605.

Victoria Cave *N. Yorks.* 558Ac
During the last phase of the Ice Age, this treble cave was a hyaena den only, and excavation of the lowest levels revealed only the bones of their prey. As the climate improved, Mesolithic man, perhaps *c.* 8000 BC, made his way to this part of the country, and for a time occupied the cave, where his characteristic implements have been found.

After this, the cave appears to have been deserted for many thousands of years until, during the Romano-British period, it was again occupied.

Vowchurch *Heref. & Worcs.* 546Ae
CHURCH This church has 15 dedications; it is the Church of the Blessed Virgin Mary, St John the Baptist, St Bartholomew, St Lawrence, St Ethelbert, St Blasius, St Martin, St Gregory, St Thomas, St Mary Magdalene, St Agnes, St Cecilia, St Katherine, St Margaret and St Milburga—all confirmed on one day in 1348. The nave and the chancel were built in the 14th century, and the timber bell-turret was added just after 1522. There is a Norman window in the south wall and a Norman font. The roof of the nave and other woodwork, including the screen, were renewed *c.* 1613. An unusual feature of the church is the wooden posts set beside the wall to support the roof.

Vyne, The *Hants.*   541Hf
The name probably derives from a Roman vine-growing estate on the site, but the present Tudor mansion of brick and stone was built in 1500–20 for Lord Sandys, a Chancellor to Henry VIII; the chapel and panelled long gallery date from this period. In 1654 Chaloner Chute, Speaker of the House of Commons, altered the house, adding the Classical portico designed by John Webb. John Chute redecorated several rooms and installed the Palladian staircase in the 1760's. The chapel has fine 17th-century painted glass.

Waddesdon Manor *Bucks.*   547Gd
A country mansion of French Renaissance style set in 160 acres of parkland, built for Baron Ferdinand de Rothschild in 1877–89. The contents include 18th-century French furniture, carpets, Sèvres porcelain, and paintings by Gainsborough, Reynolds, Rubens, and Dutch and Italian schools. There is an aviary of rococo design with a variety of exotic birds. (See p. 470.)

Wadebridge *Cornwall*   538Dc
BRIDGE Built *c.* 1485 on proceeds from the sale of wool, with piers sunk on wool, it is claimed to be the oldest main road bridge in Britain still in everyday use.

Wainfleet All Saints *Lincs.*   553Jd
Once a port, but now 5 miles inland; Wainfleet School was founded in 1484 by William of Waynflete, Bishop of Winchester, who also founded Magdalen College at Oxford.

Wakefield *W. Yorks.*   558Ca
ART GALLERY Contains 20th-century paintings and sculpture, with notable works by Graham Sutherland, Barbara Hepworth and Henry Moore.
BRIDGE CHAPEL One of the few chapels on a bridge still surviving in England. It is Decorated Gothic, from the mid-14th century, but it was restored in the 19th and 20th centuries, especially the west front. The bridge beneath it is also medieval.
CATHEDRAL This was formerly the parish church of All Saints, and became a cathedral at the end of the last century. Mainly Perpendicular, it has a west tower and tall spire of the 15th century. Sir Gilbert Scott restored the cathedral *c.* 1865. The eastward extension (1905) was the last major design of J. L. Pearson, and there are works by Sir Charles Nicholson and Sir Ninian Comper (the rood figures) in the present century.
CITY MUSEUM Devoted to local archaeology and history, with Elizabethan and Victorian rooms, and an inn.

Walcot Hall *Shropshire*   551Ja
An 18th-century mansion in a great park, acquired by Clive of India (1725–94) for his retirement.

Wall (Letocetum) *Staffs.*   552Cb
The remains of the Roman fort and settlement of Letocetum on Watling Street, just west of the intersection with Ryknield Street, have been

SAVONNERIE CARPET

The Savonnerie carpet factory near Paris was founded in 1627 in a former soap factory or 'savonnerie'. The workshops have produced carpets ever since despite bankruptcy, revolution and war. Many of the carpets were intended for the French royal palaces and were some of the most opulent ever made. Woven about 1680 during the reign of Louis XIV, this carpet, in baroque style so fashionable then, has Classical ornament, with acanthus scrolls and quivers of arrows all arranged symmetrically in a variety of colours. It was one of many made for the Long Gallery of the Louvre and may have been sold during the revolution of 1789, to reappear at Waddesdon a hundred years later. (Waddesdon Manor)

CLODION *Youthful Votaries of Bacchus*

Claude Michel, known as 'Clodion', was the greatest exponent of the French late 18th-century fashion for small terracotta groups and statuettes, and his skill in this racy, light-hearted medium amounts to genius. They were avidly collected a century later, and seven Clodion terracottas, collected by Baron Ferdinand and Baron Edmond de Rothschild, are at Waddesdon. The subject of this group, representing a youth with a wine pitcher, and a priestess of Bacchus leading a tiny reveller by the hand, is typical of Clodion—and so too is its freshness and vitality. (Waddesdon Manor)

excavated. The public baths clearly show an exercise hall, surrounded by a corridor with cold, warm and hot baths along its south-west side, with hypocausts and furnaces. A museum near by houses other Roman relics found in the district.

Wallingford *Oxon.*   546Fc
The town was destroyed by the Danish King Sweyn in 1006; the castle, built in 1071, is now in ruins: there are remains of the ramparts. In 1154 Henry II held a Parliament here and gave the town a charter in 1155. Life was disrupted by the plague in 1349, after which only 44 families remained. In the Civil War, fighting raged through the town, and further disaster came from a fire in 1675, in which many medieval houses suffered.

Wallington *Northld.*   562Fa
Built in 1688, altered in the 18th century and with a central hall added in the 19th century, the house is noted for its rococo plasterwork and decorative work by William Bell Scott, Ruskin and others. It contains furniture, Dutch blue and white porcelain and pictures, and stands in fine grounds.

Walmer Castle *Kent*   543Gf
One of several coastal forts erected by Henry VIII *c.* 1540, its basic structure is very similar to nearby Deal Castle which is, however, larger. Walmer is quatrefoil in plan with a central two-storied tower, and was surrounded by a sea-filled moat. Its walls are more than 12 ft thick, with embrasures for cannon. It was taken by Parliamentarians in the Civil War. Early in the 18th century it was adapted for domestic use and became the official residence

of the Lord Warden of the Cinque Ports. Several Wardens, among them William Pitt, Lord Granville and the Duke of Wellington, made it their home. The Duke of Wellington, who died here in 1852, was particularly attached to the castle and a collection of his personal effects is on show. The characteristics of the castle's former appearance are best appreciated from the fine gardens; these were laid out *c.* 1805 by Lady Hestor Stanhope, the niece of William Pitt.

Walpole St Peter *Norfolk*   554Ac
CHURCH OF ST PETER The church dates mainly from the second half of the 14th century, and has a west tower, Perpendicular windows in aisles and clerestory, two-storey south porch with coats of arms, stone-vault and carved roof bosses, a 16th-century font with an early 17th-century cover, and a 17th-century screen across the west end. Part of the painted rood screen remains, together with a pulpit of 1620, box-pews and fragments of stained glass.

Walsall *W. Midlands*   552Cb
E. M. FLINT ART GALLERY Jerome K. Jerome, the author of *Three Men in a Boat*, was born in Walsall and the gallery contains items once belonging to him. The local history section reflects the trades which made Walsall an important centre in the Industrial Revolution: the leather industry is represented by a collection of saddlers' tools and there is a collection of harness furniture—bits, spurs and stirrups. The gallery contains a group of Victorian oil paintings including some by Charles Shayer and Erskine Nicol, and there is a growing collection of modern paintings.

LOCK MUSEUM (WILLENHALL) The only lock museum in England. Willenhall has been the home of the lock and key industry since Elizabeth I's reign, and the museum contains English and continental locks dating from the 16th century to the present.
MUSEUM AND ART GALLERY The Garman-Ryan Collection donated by Lady Epstein in 1973 is now splendidly housed in a room above the Central Library. It includes paintings, drawings, prints and sculptures ranging over many periods. Sir Jacob Epstein's art is well represented, and there are fine works by Blake, Bonnard, Constable, Degas, Freud, Van Gogh, Monet, Pissarro and more than a hundred other artists. Some of the museum's local history collection is also permanently displayed, including a number of ceremonial staffs with carved heads, known as 'Bayard's Colts'.

Walsingham Priory *Norfolk*   554Bc
Walsingham Priory, founded by Richeldis de Favarches in 1061, was handed over to Augustinian canons in 1153. By the 13th century the chapel containing the Shrine of Our Lady had become a revered place of pilgrimage. Both Henry III and Edward I paid many visits, and Walsingham's prosperity probably dates from this time. The visible ruins are from this and later centuries; the most striking fragment is the east window of the 14th-century church. To the south lie the remains of the monastic buildings; the chief walls are those of the refectory, built at the end of the 13th century. Nothing remains of the original chapel, but it has been established as lying near the north aisle of the church and within the precinct wall. In 1931 an Anglican church was built adjacent to the former precinct wall of the priory. At Houghton St Giles the Roman Catholic church maintains a restored 14th-century chapel, known as the Slipper Chapel. It is said to have been one of the stations on the pilgrimage route to Walsingham. (See p. 472.)

Waltham Abbey *Essex* 548Ac
ABBEY CHURCH OF THE HOLY CROSS AND ST
LAWRENCE The remnants of the former abbey
church consist of a Norman nave, aisles, 14th-
century south chapel and 16th-century west
tower. The abbey was refounded in 1060 and built
by Harold who was buried here after the Battle of
Hastings. There is an early font and 17th-century
pulpit. The nave ceiling was painted by Sir E. J.
Poynter and the east window is by Sir Edward
Burne-Jones. (See p. 473.)

Walton-on-Thames *Surrey* 542Af
CHURCH OF ST MARY The church, dating from
Norman times, possesses a monument by the
greatest of mid-18th-century sculptors in England,
Louis Roubiliac. It is to Richard Boyle, Viscount
Shannon, who died in 1740.

Walton-on-the-Hill *Surrey* 542Bf
CHURCH OF ST PETER The church possesses a
beautiful Norman lead font. Around the bowl is an
arcade of round-headed arches, beneath each of
which is a seated figure, either reading or with a
hand raised in blessing.

Wanborough *Wilts.* 546Db
CHURCH OF ST ANDREW The church possesses a
west tower, and another, which is hexagonal and
has a spire, at the east end of the nave. Most of the
building dates from the 14th century, the monuments from the 15th century onwards.

Wandlebury *Cambs.* 548Ae
Wandlebury crowns Cambridge's nearest hill-
ridge, the Gogmagog Hills, a landmark in this flat
countryside. The earthworks enclose a circular
area of some 15 acres, which was originally rather
more, as the first defences, constructed in the first
half of the Iron Age, were the outer bank with a
14 ft deep ditch and counterscarp. This bank was

revetted with timber. After falling into disrepair, it
was refortified within a century of the Roman
conquest by the cutting of an inner V-shaped
ditch, 18 ft deep, and the erection of an inner bank,
the one now visible, entered by the south-eastern
gap. Much of the outer bank has been thrown into
the inner ditch, but traces are still visible.

Wansdyke *Wilts.* 540Ff
One of the finest linear earthworks in Britain,
surpassed only, perhaps, by the later Offa's Dyke
which traverses the Anglo-Welsh Border country.
The best remaining parts of Wansdyke are in
Wiltshire. It is a single bank with a ditch. Its
eastern end is rather obscure, but appears to be
in the extreme east of the county near the border
with Berkshire and Hampshire, not far from
Hungerford. To the west it can be traced intermittently until it is lost for a few miles in Savernake
Forest. It is then clearly visible, and at its modern
best, as far as Morgan's Hill, near Calne. From
here, south of Lacock, it is visible in part, resting on
the Roman road to Bath, where it has left
Wiltshire. It is lost near the town, but can be traced
in Somerset from Stantonbury to Dundry Hill.
Its position on the Roman road, and certain
excavations, make it clear that it belongs to the
early part of the Dark Ages.

Wansford *Cambs.* 547Hh
THE BRIDGE The fine old bridge across the R.
Nene has 12 arches: the seven northern arches date
from 1577, the next three were rebuilt in 1672–4,
and the last two added in 1795.

Wanstead *Greater London* 548Ac
CHURCH OF ST MARY THE VIRGIN An 18th-
century Classical church with a pediment, built in
1790 by Thomas Hardwick. The interior has
Corinthian columns, a pulpit with a sounding
board resting on two palm-trees, c. 1790, box-

REYNOLDS
Portrait of a Boy

*This early work, a portrait of Lieutenant
Haswell, R.N. in naval uniform, was
painted when Sir Joshua Reynolds was
only about 23 years old. He had already
completed 3 years' apprenticeship in the
studio of Thomas Hudson and was
working in London and in his native
Devon before going to study in Italy.*

*Master Haswell's parents lived at
Tiverton and the portrait reflects the
artist's close links with his home county;
some may prefer its simple style to
Reynolds' later rather more staged and
posed portraits. (Garman-Ryan
Collection)*

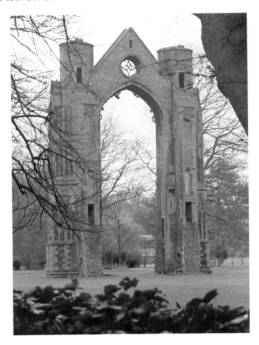

THE EAST WINDOW
WALSINGHAM PRIORY

In the Middle Ages Walsingham was one of the most famous pilgrimage centres in England. Legend tells how the pious Richeldis de Favarches in 1061 had a vision in which she was transported in spirit to Nazareth. There she was shown the house of the Holy Family and told to build a replica at Walsingham. She founded a chapel, the Shrine of Our Lady, which was served by a community of Augustinian canons from 1153. Walsingham's reputation for sanctity was revived in the 19th century, and it is now a focus of pilgrimages for both Anglican and Roman Catholic communities.

pews and wrought-iron railings. The great monument to Sir Joshua Child (*d.* 1699), with reclining and standing figures, has been attributed to John Nost.

Wantage *Oxon.*   *546Ec*
Alfred the Great, King of the West Saxons, was born here in AD 849, and a statue to him was erected in the market-place in 1877. Robert Stiles, an Amsterdam merchant who settled in Wantage, built the attractive almshouses whose entry passage is paved with the knuckle-bones of sheep.

Warboys *Cambs.*   *547Jg*
Fenland village, notorious for the trial of 'The Witches of Warboys': in 1593 an old lady, her husband and daughter were executed on charges of witchcraft based on evidence given by the five daughters of their next-door neighbour.

Warburton *Greater Manchester*   *552Af*
OLD CHURCH OF ST WERBURGH A timber church with a brick tower of 1711, and rough-hewn timber pillars, probably of the 12th century, inside. The low screen dividing nave from chancel, and the pulpit, are 17th century.

Wardour Castle *Wilts.*   *540Ee*
The old castle, built originally by Lord Lovel in 1392, was acquired by the Arundell family in 1547, and modernised in 1578 by Roger Smythson. It was damaged and abandoned in the Civil War, and

its ruins are still in the grounds, landscaped by Capability Brown, of the new 'castle', a Palladian mansion, built *c.* 1768 to designs by James Paine the Elder. At this time Paine was a leading architect in England and had just completed Worksop (Nottinghamshire) for the Duke of Norfolk. Paine's house consists of a three-storey central block with a two-storey wing on either side, containing the Church of All Saints in the west wing. The entrance front is on the north side, and the principal doorway is surprisingly insignificant beneath a tall Venetian window. The castle is now Cranborne Chase School. (See p. 474.)

Ware *Herts.*   *548Ad*
The Bull Inn in Baldock Street and Nos. 8, 10, 12, 27 and 35 are good brick and half-timbered houses from the 16th and 17th centuries. The High Street presents an effective mixture of gabled and straight-fronted houses dating from the 16th century onwards. In Bluecoat Yard stands Place House, the 15th-century timber-framed manor house which was the Bluecoat School from 1674 to 1761. Opposite is an attractive range of timber-framed cottages built in 1698 for nurses and children. The Corn Stores in Star Street include an unusual 17th-century quadrangle of storehouses with outside ladders giving access to the upper floors and open timber roofs. Facing the bridges over the R. Lea and New R. is Amwell House, an elegant red-brick dwelling of *c.* 1730, which was once the home of John Scott, the Quaker poet. The Grotto, in Scott's Road, was once in the poet's garden. Built *c.* 1770, it has a complex arrangement of intricate passages and chambers lined with shells, quartz, fragments of glass and flint.
PRIORY Built from the remains of a Franciscan friary, founded by Thomas Wake, lord of the manor in 1338; now the council offices. Part of the original work dating from this period can be seen in the cloisters; elsewhere there are a number of 17th- and 18th-century additions.

Wareham *Dorset*   *540Ec*
The town is almost ringed by pre-Roman earthworks. In the Church of St Martin is a figure of T. E. Lawrence (Lawrence of Arabia) by Eric Kennington, and the Church of St Mary has a unique six-sided lead font. The heaths surrounding Wareham figure as part of Thomas Hardy's 'Egdon Heath' in his Wessex novels.
ROYAL ARMOURED CORPS TANK MUSEUM (BOVINGTON CAMP) A collection of over 140 tanks from nine nations, armoured cars and other armoured vehicles from 1915 onwards.

Warfield *Berks.*   *547Gb*
CHURCH OF ST MICHAEL An interesting church; though restored by G. E. Street in the 1870's, it is mostly Decorated Gothic, with the north aisle partly Early English. There is fine tracery in the east window, where 14th- and 19th-century glass is combined. There are good timbered roofs, and the 15th-century screen to the north chapel retains part of the rood loft. A unique medieval sedilia bears a carving of the 'Green Man'—a pagan woodland spirit.

Warham Camp *Norfolk*   *554Bd*
Almost circular in plan, this Iron Age fort lies on the lowland coastal plain, bordered on its west side by the R. Stiffkey. Close to the stream there is a single defensive bank only, but the remainder of the 3½ acre area has two banks and ditches, the banks still standing higher than a man. Excavations have shown that it was constructed late in the Iron Age and lasted at least into early Roman times.

Warham St Mary *Norfolk* 554Bd
CHURCH OF ST MARY Norman work includes a
blocked north door, but the tower dates from the
14th century and the fittings are nearly all 18th
century—for example, the fine three-decker
pulpit. There is some early Renaissance German or
Flemish stained glass mixed with medieval
English fragments.

Warkton *Northants.* 547Gg
CHURCH OF ST EDMUND Important 18th- and
19th-century monuments to a Duke and three
Duchesses of Montagu are set in theatrical-looking
apses, with many figures, cherubs and urns. Two
monuments (1752, 1753) are by the outstanding
rococo sculptor Louis Roubiliac.

Warkworth *Northld.* 563Gb
CHURCH OF ST LAWRENCE A Norman church,
with a vaulted chancel of the 12th century and a
west tower *c.* 1200 with a later spire. There is a
monument to a knight of *c.* 1330.

Warkworth Castle *Northld.* 563Gb
For over four centuries, Warkworth Castle
remained one of the most important castles in the
north of England. Its origins are obscure but it may
have been begun in the second quarter of the 12th
century by Henry, son of David I of Scotland, who
was created Earl of Northumberland in 1139. In
1157, however, the castle and the manor were
re-granted by Henry II to an Englishman, Roger
de Stuteville, and his family fashioned the main
outlines of the castle as it exists today. The Percy
family, who acquired it in 1332, built the unusual
keep on the plan of a cross inscribed on a square
(late 14th century); and they also began a large
collegiate church whose foundations are still
visible across the outer ward. It is not clear how
much of this was actually built. Finally, some of
the fine additions made to the great hall in the
outer ward also survive, including the Lion Tower
which forms its entrance porch.

Warminster *Wilts.* 540Ef
A royal manor in Saxon times under the name of
Guermistre, when it was also an important wool
centre. The Jacobean-style town hall was built in
1830. The minster church is of the 14th century,
rebuilt and altered in the 18th and 19th centuries.
Nearby Lord Weymouth's School has its original
(1707) buildings; pupils of former days include Dr
Thomas Arnold, headmaster of Rugby School
from 1828 to 1842.

Warwick *Warks.* 546Ef
CASTLE One of the finest medieval fortresses in
Europe. The castle, perched on a crag above the
Avon, overlooks grounds laid out by Capability
Brown; it was at one time the home of the Earls
of Warwick. The 14th-century curtain wall and
massive tower defence system remain intact. The
interior was largely rebuilt in the late 17th century
and again in 1871 following a disastrous fire. The
Castle has a fine collection of arms and armour that
is distributed between the Armoury and the Great
Hall. The various State rooms, the Dining Room,
the Red, Blue, Green and Cedar rooms, contain
superb paintings and furniture. (See p. 477.)
CHURCH OF ST MARY A most interesting church,
of Norman origin, with an impressive 12th-
century crypt. Much of the building was destroyed
by fire in 1694. Rebuilt in 1698–1704, St Mary's
most noticeable feature is the commanding pseudo-
Gothic tower; nave and aisles are also in this style.
In the middle of the chancel is a monument to an
Earl of Warwick and his wife, 1369; the alabaster
effigies hold hands. The fine late Gothic Beau-

JESSE WINDOW
AT WALTHAM ABBEY

*Restored in the 1860's, the abbey contains some of
the finest 19th-century stained glass in the Jesse
window. Dated 1861, it was designed by Sir Edward
Burne-Jones who, with William Morris, Dante
Gabriel Rossetti and others, formed the Pre-Raphaelite
Brotherhood of artists and poets. The window has
three lancets with Jesse himself represented at the base
of the centre light. A vine grows from his body, each
spray enclosing a figure or incident from the Bible.
At the top is the Crucifixion, with the Nativity and
Shepherds just below.*

champ Chapel contains the tomb of the donor,
Richard Beauchamp (*d.* 1440). (See p. 475.)
COURT-HOUSE A civic building dating from *c.*
1725 which contains a fine Georgian ballroom.
DOLL MUSEUM (OKEN'S HOUSE) In an Elizabethan
house is an interesting collection of many kinds of
dolls—of wood, china, metal and wax. There are
also mechanical and musical dolls.
LORD LEYCESTER HOSPITAL The main buildings
were erected in 1383 by the United Guilds of
Warwick, who also used the Chapel of St James—
which has stood over the Westgate since 1123—as
their centre. The guilds were dispersed in 1546,
and in 1571 Robert Dudley, Earl of Leicester
(Leycester)—Elizabeth I's favourite—founded his
hospital for a Master and 12 Brethren. The Dining
Hall now contains the Regimental Museum of the
Queen's Own Hussars.

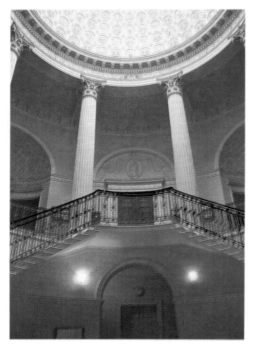

WARDOUR CASTLE
ADAM STAIRCASE

Robert Adam was one of the first British architects to feature the staircase in his designs, and to use its theatrical qualities to emphasise different floor levels. The use of space in the staircase and the fragile appearance of the wrought-iron balustrade complement the house, built in 1768 by James Paine. The first Roman staircases were merely a necessary means of getting from one floor to another, and only with the Renaissance did they become one of the main decorative features of a building—the trend first appearing in England at the Queen's House, Greenwich.

The buildings, in black and white Elizabethan style, include a great hall, guildhall (now a museum) and chaplain's dining hall (now the Queen's Own Hussars Regimental Museum).
WARWICKSHIRE MUSEUM In a market hall constructed in 1670, the museum's collections concentrate on the history, geology, natural history, archaeology and social history of Warwick and the surrounding area.

Washington *Tyne & Wear*   558Cg
OLD HALL A Jacobean stone mansion of 1610, incorporating parts of an earlier medieval house; the seat of the Washington family, 1183–1613. The house contains 17th-century furniture and many Washington relics. The arms of the Washington family—three stars and two stripes—may well have inspired the US flag, which is flown here on Thanksgiving Day and Washington's birthday.

Waterperry *Oxon.*   546Fc
CHURCH OF ST MARY THE VIRGIN In the grounds of Waterperry House, an Early English church of Saxon origin, with 14th- and 15th-century additions. The charming interior has box-pews, early 13th-century glass, and monuments including a 17th-century knight in armour facing his wife in prayer, and a mourning group by Sir Francis Chantrey, c. 1819.

Watford *Herts.*   547Hc
CHURCH OF ST MARY A large church, with west

tower and spirelet, 17th-century pulpit, and many brasses and monuments. Two of the monuments, to members of the Morrison family, are by Nicholas Stone, and have reclining effigies, allegorical figures, and big architectural surrounds.

Watson's Potteries *Suffolk*   548Cf
Bricks, tiles and earthenware have been manufactured here since pre-Roman times.

Waverley *Surrey*   541Jf
ABBEY Picturesque ruins, near the R. Wey, of the first Cistercian abbey founded in England (1128).

Waxham Hall *Norfolk*   554Ec
On the North Sea coast, Waxham Hall stands behind a long high flint wall and a 15th-century gateway. The flint and brick house, once the home of the Wodehouses, is now a farm. (Not open.)

Wayland's Smithy *Oxon.*   546Eb
This recently restored long barrow, dating from around 3600 BC, lies close to the Ridge Way, a little to the west of Uffington Castle. The visitor sees Wayland's Smithy II, a long barrow with a fine façade of upright stones and long flanking ditches. It is a typical Cotswold burial chamber in which at least eight individuals were interred. This succeeded Wayland's Smithy I, a 54 ft long barrow covering a wooden structure containing the bones of some 12 people. Wayland the Smith is a Norse god who was said to shoe horses if they were left beside the barrow with a coin.

Weaverthorpe *N. Yorks.*   558Fc
CHURCH OF ST ANDREW A good Norman church, with tower. The font is also Norman. The building was restored c. 1872 by G. E. Street.

Weldon *Northants.*   553Ga
CHURCH OF ST MARY THE VIRGIN This church tower is a rare example of an inland lighthouse. In the 18th century the Gothic spire was removed and replaced by a 15 ft high, fully glazed, octagonal lantern. In this hung a chandelier, the light from which guided travellers through Rockingham Forest. Other examples of land lights were at York, and Dunstan Pillar near Lincoln.

Wellingham *Norfolk*   554Bc
CHURCH OF ST ANDREW Contains a rood screen dated 1532, with good figure painting of saints, among them St Sebastian, and St George fighting the Dragon, in front of onlookers from a city tower.

Wellington Monument *Som.*   540Ad
An obelisk, erected in 1817–18 in honour of the 1st Duke of Wellington, victor at Waterloo in 1815.

Wellow *Avon*   540Df
CHURCH OF ST JULIAN A mainly 14th-century church, with an impressive pinnacled west tower. Mural paintings and benches with poppy-heads remain, and there is a fine roof in the nave.

Wells *Som.*   540Cf
CATHEDRAL Most of Wells Cathedral, including the west front which displays the most extensive array of medieval sculpture to survive in the British Isles, dates from the late 12th and 13th centuries, although the three towers were not built until the late 14th and 15th centuries. A new piece of sculpture by David Wynne, unveiled in 1985, depicts the seated figure of Christ with one hand upraised in blessing. It is set in a niche at the apex of the façade.
Wells is a fine example of a medieval close which has survived more or less intact, and is still surrounded by the houses of cathedral dignitaries

CHURCH OF ST MARY, WARWICK

BEAUCHAMP CHAPEL STAINED GLASS *These windows show some of the most elaborate work that a 15th-century English glass painter could produce. John Prudde, King's Glazier and fashionable artist and craftsman, used every known resource and technique to achieve the most impressive effect. Coloured jewels are inset into the borders of the robes, and the tracery angels even hold real music. Prudde obtained his royal appointment in 1440 and the windows are dated 1447.*

MONUMENT TO ROBERT DUDLEY *Dudley lies clothed in armour and the insignia of the Order of the Garter, with his second wife Lettice beside him. He was a childhood companion of Elizabeth I and scandal was caused by their attachment during the early years of her reign, culminating in the sudden death of Dudley's first wife Amy Robsart. Although the queen's infatuation cooled their friendship remained—Dudley was created Earl of Leicester in 1564 and was the predominant figure at Court until he died in 1588.*

WARWICKSHIRE MUSEUM

FLINTLOCK BLUNDERBUSS BY NICHOLAS PARIS *Blunderbusses were designed to discharge a load of shot at fairly close quarters, and had barrels which flared at the muzzle in the incorrect belief that this spread the charge more quickly. This one came from Stoneleigh Abbey, near Warwick, where it was probably carried by one of the coach-guards. The barrel and mounts are of burnished brass, and the stock is of polished walnut. It was made about 1700 by an outstanding gunsmith of this time, Nicholas Paris of Warwick.*

SHELDON TAPESTRY MAP OF WARWICKSHIRE *Some of the first English maps to show roads were a set of tapestry maps first woven by Richard and Francis Hyckes in 1588 for Ralph Sheldon; they were re-woven for his son after 1647. The counties around Warwickshire are shown with great accuracy, the designs being based on Saxton's maps of England published in 1579. Weston, the Sheldon's home where the tapestries were woven, is shown under a panel.*

To the north lies a row of lodgings built for the Vicars Choral. Adjoining the cathedral, also on the north side, is the chapter house, which is approached by a staircase and was originally used for daily meetings of the cathedral canons. To the south is the cloister and the partly ruined bishop's palace, surrounded by a moat. (See pp.478–9.)
CHURCH OF ST CUTHBERT The nave roof and west tower are striking examples of the craft of the 16th-century builders. Fragments of the original screens remain in the transepts, and there is a good 17th-century pulpit.

Wells-next-the-Sea *Norfolk* 554Bd
Wells, no longer quite next the sea, but on an estuary, is a little port with an attractive quay, extremely narrow streets and a pleasant series of Georgian houses on the green called the Buttlands. Other good buildings are Ostrich House in Burnt Street, Marsh House in Marsh Lane, and the 16th-century St Michael's Cottage in Jickling's Yard.

Welshpool *Powys* 551Hb
POWIS CASTLE Originally called the 'Red Castle', this Welsh border fortress of red limestone has been the home of the Powis family for over 500 years. The present castle was built in the 13th and 14th centuries on the site of a former stronghold; the long gallery was added in 1587 and its fine plaster ceiling made in 1592. The castle suffered considerable damage when it was taken by Roundheads in 1644, and much reconstruction, including the rebuilding of the west portals, great staircase and state rooms, was carried out in 1667. It contains fine murals by Lanscroon, paintings, furniture, tapestries and relics of Clive of India. The terraced gardens date from 1722, and have lead statues overlooking yews, ornamental trees and box hedges. (See pp. 399 and 402.)

Welwick *Humberside* 559Ha
CHURCH OF ST MARY The church was originally Norman, but was rebuilt during the 14th century. In the south aisle is the monument of a 14th-century priest. The pulpit is 17th century.

Wendens Ambo *Essex* 548Ae
CHURCH OF ST MARY THE VIRGIN The tower, with its Hertfordshire spike is Norman; the chancel dates from *c.* 1300. Inside is a 16th-century font cover, a 15th-century pulpit, fragments of wall-paintings illustrating the life of St Margaret, *c.* 1330, and a brass, *c.* 1415.

Wendover *Bucks.* 547Gc
A town of timbered houses with Civil War associations. Cromwell stayed in the Red Lion Hotel and John Hampden, the Parliamentary hero, was MP for Wendover from 1623–40.

Wenhaston *Suffolk* 548Ef
CHURCH OF ST PETER Originally Norman, but with later additions; the west tower has flushwork decoration. Inside is a large painting on wood, *c.* 1500, of the Last Judgment, 'the Doom'.

Wensley *N. Yorks.* 558Bd
CHURCH OF THE HOLY TRINITY The interest of this church is principally in the individual features. The Restoration font and cover, the early benches and the 15th-century screen are noteworthy. There are also medieval wall-paintings.

Wentworth *S. Yorks.* 552Df
CHURCH OF THE HOLY TRINITY The new church is a Gothic building, erected during the second half of the 19th century from J. L. Pearson's design. The old church is now mainly ruined, except for its chancel and north chapel, which contains several 15th–17th-century monuments with effigies.

Weobley *Heref. & Worcs.* 546Ae
CHURCH OF SS PETER AND PAUL The south doorway is in the original Norman style, but the rest of the church is mainly of the 13th and 14th centuries. Noteworthy is the north-west tower and spire with pinnacles and flying buttresses.

West Acre Priory *Norfolk* 554Bb
The remains of an Augustinian priory, founded *c.* 1100. The ruined buildings, once as extensive as those of Castle Acre, lie on both sides of the R. Nar. The 14th-century gate-house stands, and there are fragmentary remains of a church and chapter house.

West Bromwich *W. Midlands* 552Ca
OAK HOUSE A half-timbered house built *c.* 1530, with a Jacobean wing (1635). Its most interesting feature is the lantern tower, reputed to be the only one of its kind in England. The rooms are panelled and carved, and contain Jacobean furniture. John Wesley's diary records that he preached from the courtyard during his pilgrimage through West Bromwich. In front of the house there is an Elizabethan garden.

Westbury White Horse See Bratton Castle.

West Chiltington *W. Sussex* 542Ad
CHURCH OF ST MARY A pretty church in an attractive village, it has a shingled spire. St Mary's is almost entirely Norman, with the later addition of a 14th-century chapel. The north doorway is 12th century. Inside are wall-paintings of the 12th to 14th centuries, showing scenes from the Nativity and the Passion. There is an interesting very long squint (hagioscope) between the south aisle and chancel.

Westerham *Kent* 542Cf
The statue of General Wolfe, the victor of the decisive battle between the French and English at Quebec in 1759, who was born at Westerham, dominates this village built round a sloping, roughly square green. Oscar Nemon's statue on the green of a seated Winston Churchill, who lived at nearby Chartwell, was erected in 1965.
SQUERRYES COURT The Warde family has owned this William-and-Mary house for over 250 years. General James Wolfe (1727–59), a friend of the family, received his commission as lieutenant in the Marines in the garden in 1741; a cenotaph commemorates the event. The house was built in 1681 and contains a collection of Dutch paintings, family portraits, tapestries and furniture. Objects connected with General Wolfe are displayed.

West Hendred *Oxon.* 546Ec
CHURCH OF THE HOLY TRINITY A 14th- and 15th-century church, standing by a stream, with a Decorated west tower. Inside there are 17th-century furnishings (pulpit, font cover, communion rail), and many medieval tiles in the chancel and nave; also fragments of medieval stained glass.

West Humble Chapel *Surrey* 542Af
The ruins of a 12th-century chapel on what was once part of Pilgrim's Way.

West Kennet Barrow *Wilts.* 540Fg
One of the largest and finest Neolithic long barrows in Britain, a great chalk mound some 350 ft long, with a quarry ditch set well back. A kerb of sarsens surrounded the mound. A deep concave forecourt led to the entrance, held by a wall of large uprights. Inside, the gallery had two pairs of side chambers and a fifth at the end. Finally, after the last burial, the concave forecourt and the entrance were concealed by further uprights, presenting a very different false façade. (See p. 480.)

WARWICK CASTLE

GUY OF WARWICK'S SWORD *Earl Guy of Warwick's remarkable exploits are the subject of a long medieval poem, his most distinguished feat being the defeat of the Danish giant Colbran to save the English Crown for King Athelstan, who reigned from 925 to 940. The sword, supposedly Guy's, is actually early 14th century; it is a typical crosshilted weapon of its time, but over 5 ft long and designed for two hands. In Elizabeth I's time, there was an official 'Keeper of Guy of Warwick's Sword'.*

ITALIAN FIELD ARMOUR *This armour for a man and a horse dates from the late 16th century. The breast-plate and the chest protective plate of the horse, called a 'peytral', are etched with a crowned sun in splendour and the words 'Nulla quies alibi' (No rest but here). This armour was made for a very small man, or perhaps a youth. The horse's bit, reins and trappings are relatively modern. The rest for the heavy lance, when held in the couch position, is missing, but two holes for it can be seen on the breast-plate.*

PRINCE CHARLES'S TARGE *Traditionally this shield or targe is said to be one of 13 made for the Young Pretender, Prince Charles Edward Stuart. He gave them away as trophies to his supporters during the 1745 Jacobite rebellion, and this is thought to be the only one now in England. It is just under 20 in. across, and is of tooled leather stretched across a wooden frame. The silver decorations include the Medusa's head in the centre, and trophies of arms interspersed with crests in the circle around the edge of the shield.*

THE GREAT HALL *One of the exhibits in the great hall is a magnificently carved sideboard depicting the pageantry of Queen Elizabeth I's visit to neighbouring Kenilworth in 1575. The armour on view is part of one of the finest private collections in the country. It* includes a miniature suit, said to have been made for the Earl of Leicester, who died aged six, Italian jousting armour and 16th-century German horse armour. A special breed of horse, the 'Flanders Mare' had to be introduced to carry the weight of the equestrian armour.

WELLS CATHEDRAL

An attempt to remove the cathedral from Wells and to have it transferred to the priory at Bath was made in 1090. The See had been established at Wells in 909 and the canons there fought to prevent its transfer. Eventually, in 1244, they won their struggle—the bishop remained at Wells but the See gained the dual title of 'Bath and Wells'. The cathedral nave, which has elaborate foliage carving on its capitals, was built in the 12th and 13th centuries, while the east end and chapter house, with fine vaulting and window tracery, were almost entirely re-built in the early 14th century. In 1338 to 1340 the strengthening arches, which give the interior its distinctive appearance, were added where the nave and transepts meet. The cathedral contains a series of 13th-century tombs and a medieval clock dating from about 1390.

WEST FRONT *This, one of the glories of Wells, is really a screen built as background setting for nearly 400 statues. It was begun c. 1230 and is exactly twice as wide as it is high. The towers were added later, the southern c. 1384 and the northern in 1430. The tower on the north side originally housed a Chapel of the Holy Cross, and was later used as a choir vestry. The southern tower has the belfry with the heaviest ring of ten bells in the world.*

CHAPTER HOUSE *The Chapter House complex, consisting of octagonal treasury beneath, Chapter House and a staircase, was laid out between 1250 and 1260, but work was held up for lack of funds. The work was resumed in 1286, and the Chapter House itself (shown right) appears to have been completed by 1306. Round the walls of the magnificent octagonal building, with its fine vaulting and window tracery, are the seats of the prebendaries or canons.*

WELLS CATHEDRAL CLOCK *With astronomical dial over 6 ft across and mechanical figures, this clock is in the north transept of the cathedral. In the centre the earth is represented with two circles that show the phase and age of the moon. From these, rings moving outwards show the date of the lunar month, the minutes and hours. The clock chimes the quarter-hours, and as each hour strikes the figures above the dial move—four knights on horseback engage in a jousting tournament and one of them is unseated. The cathedral records mention the clock as far back as 1392; the original mechanism continued in use until 1835 when it was replaced by a modern movement.*

THE CROSSING *The magnificent central tower, which was begun in 1315 and completed in 1322, was built on Early English foundations which were not strong enough to support it. By 1338 trouble had arisen—the tower had begun to settle and tilt slightly to the west. As a result the inverted strengthening arches were constructed under the crossing between 1338 and 1340, except on the east where the stone screen already provided support.*

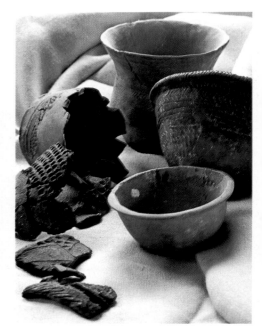

WEST KENNET BARROW

The finest example of many similar Neolithic long barrows, or burial chambers, on the Downs of North Wiltshire, the West Kennet barrow near Marlborough was excavated by Professors Stuart Piggott and R. J. C. Atkinson in 1955–6. The pottery (now in the Devizes Museum) dates from about 3000 to 1600 BC, when the barrow was used for burials by migrant peoples from the Continent who brought with them the *knowledge of farming. The pots were probably used to store grain and milk. At the top is a bell beaker dating from about 2000 BC. The two bowls, at the right and front right, are of the Peterborough type, a late Neolithic culture, and Windmill Hill type, made by farmers in Britain about 2500–1800 BC. At the left is part of a grooved-ware pot. The pieces of broken vessels date from various of these periods.*

Westley Waterless *Cambs.* 548Bf
CHURCH OF ST MARY The Early English and Decorated church once had a round tower, but this fell in the 19th century. There is a delicate early 14th-century brass to Sir John de Creke and his wife, with almost life-size figures, Sir John in armour.

West Malling *Kent* 542Df
The High Street of this small market town retains its 18th-century character. On market days stalls would have filled the lower, wider half of the street; professional people would have lived in the more prosperous houses higher up.

Westonbirt Arboretum *Glos.* 546Cc
The main arboretum is on the edge of Silk Wood Forest near Tetbury. The collection of trees and shrubs from many parts of the world was begun in 1829 by Robert Stayner Holford, squire of Westonbirt. The landscape architect, W. S. Gilpin, arranged the specimens and the arboretum has been developed and increased on a large scale ever since. Trees and shrubs are planted in groups; massed spring-flowering shrubs are displayed near huge conifers, and maple glades show autumn tints against trees with unusual barks. There are large banks of rhododendrons, magnolias and cherries. The long vistas and secluded bays, the old oaks and giant conifers are beautiful in all seasons.

Weston Park *Staffs.* 552Bb
Benjamin Disraeli was a frequent visitor to this country house, home of the Earls of Bradford for nearly 300 years, and some of his many letters may be seen. The mansion was built in 1671 and is a fine example of the Restoration style. It contains paintings by Holbein, Van Dyck, Bassano, Reynolds, Gainsborough and Lely, and Gobelins and Aubusson tapestries.

Weston-super-Mare *Avon* 540Bf
CHURCH OF ALL SAINTS Designed by G. F. Bodley between 1898 and 1902, with a later south aisle and chapel by F. C. Eden. Bodley designed the font and the pulpit.
WOODSPRING MUSEUM The museum is mainly devoted to items of local significance, including archaeological finds from Worlebury Iron Age camp and Brean Down Roman temple sites. Also on show are some old shops and a Victorian seaside holiday gallery.

Westonzoyland *Som.* 540Be
CHURCH OF ST MARY THE VIRGIN The main feature of this large church, with its tall west tower (fan-vaulted on the inside), is the magnificent nave roof, carved with angels holding shields. In addition there are fragments of stained glass, and a monument to a priest that dates from *c.* 1300. Defeated rebels from the Battle of Sedgemoor were confined here in 1685.

West Stow *Suffolk* 548Cf
WEST STOW HALL The turreted brick gate-house of what was a large house built *c.* 1520 by Sir John Crofts, Master of the Horse to Mary Tudor, daughter of Henry VIII. The gate-house is connected with the house (little of the original survives) by a colonnade of *c.* 1590. Over the gateway are Mary Tudor's Arms and in a room inside amusing Elizabethan wall-paintings showing the Four Ages of Man.

West Walton *Norfolk* 553Jb
CHURCH OF ST MARY The church, one of the best in the county, dates from *c.* 1240. The tower is completely detached and stands some 60 ft from

the church itself; it has large arches on all four sides at ground level, with arches and belfry windows above, and later parapet and pinnacles. Inside the church are wall-paintings, carved bench ends and a Perpendicular font.

Westwood Manor *Wilts.* 540Df
A 15th-century manor house, altered in 1610, with late Gothic and Jacobean windows, and Jacobean plasterwork. It contains a collection of fine furniture, and the garden includes modern topiary work.

West Wycombe *Bucks.* 547Gc
A village of fine 15th–18th-century houses along the A40.
MAUSOLEUM Sir Francis Dashwood (1708–81), founder of the notorious 'Hell Fire Club', had this curious hexagonal, roofless monument built on the hill above the village in 1763. It is decorated with imposing vases and plastered columns, and one wall once enshrined an 18th-century poet's heart. The caves in the hill are associated with the club which met at Medmenham Abbey.
WEST WYCOMBE PARK The Dashwood family came into possession of land at West Wycombe in 1698, and a three-storied brick house was erected; this was rebuilt in Palladian style *c.* 1750 by Sir Francis Dashwood. A two-storied Tuscan and Corinthian colonnade extends between the wings of the south front. The Ionic portico at the west was designed by Nicolas Revett *c.* 1770, and the Tuscan portico at the east was probably designed by John Donowell *c.* 1755. The house contains painted ceilings by Borgnis, tapestries, pictures and fine furniture.

The grounds were landscaped by Humphry Repton, and contain a swan-shaped lake and temples, one of them designed by Revett. On top of the hill in the park, next to the parish church, is the mausoleum. Caves were excavated in the hill *c.* 1750, and these are reached through a flint ruin in Gothic style.

Wetheral *Cumbria* 557Hg
CHURCH OF THE HOLY TRINITY A Gothic church, much altered and added to, but worth visiting for the large and important monument to Mrs Howard, of Corby, by Joseph Nollekens; it shows a young woman holding a baby, supported by Religion who points towards Heaven.
CORBY CASTLE A 14th-century pele forms the nucleus of the Howard mansion, built between the 16th and 19th centuries in ornamental grounds and perched high on the bank of the River Eden.
ST CONSTANTINE'S CELLS Deep in the solid rock of the river bank are three caves, said to have been occupied by St Constantine.

Wethersfield *Essex* 548Bd
CHURCH OF ST MARY MAGDALENE Mainly of the 13th and 14th centuries, the church has a 15th-century nave and clerestory. Fragments of medieval stained glass exist. Monuments with effigies date from the 15th century, tablets from the 18th century.

Weybridge *Surrey* 542Af
MUSEUM Local exhibits cover the history and archaeology of north-western Surrey, and there are displays of archaeology, social and local history and costume.

Weymouth *Dorset* 540Dc
TRINITY STREET (NO. 3) Built *c.* 1600–10, an early example of a pair of semi-detached houses (a style not common until the late 19th century).

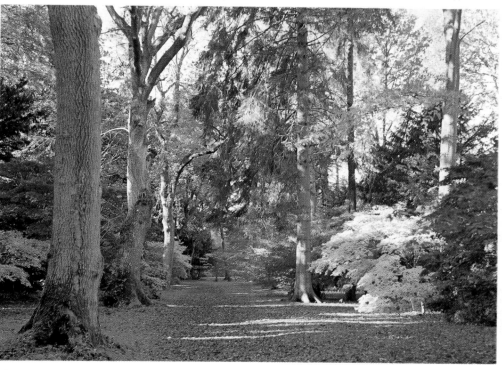

WESTONBIRT ARBORETUM

Early in the 19th century wealthy landowners began to make arboreta—collections of trees. Robert Stayner Holford, squire of Westonbirt, was one of these and in 1829 began his collection. He employed the fashionable landscape architect of the day, W. S.

Gilpin. Today, with its long vistas and secluded bays, it is a place of great beauty at all seasons. Particular attention has been paid to autumn colouring, and the maple glade when at its most brilliant in mid-October shows the tremendous success attained.

Whalley *Lancs.* 558Ab

CHURCH OF ST MARY AND ALL SAINTS Of Norman origin, St Mary's is now mainly a 13th-century building, but with Perpendicular additions. Splendid wood fittings include stalls and misericords from the nearby abbey, now ruined, screened family pews, and a magnificent organ of 1729, removed from Lancaster church at the beginning of the 19th century. There are monuments by Sir Richard Westmacott.

Whaplode *Lincs.* 553Jc

CHURCH OF ST MARY The four eastern bays of the original Norman church remain, constituting the main body of the building. The three western bays are in the Transitional style and the tower was begun in the 12th century. There are a number of monuments from the 13th century onwards, including the remarkable one of the late 16th century to the Irby family.

Wharton Court *Heref. & Worcs.* 546Af

A 17th-century stone house, with moat.

Wheatfield *Oxon.* 547Gc

CHURCH OF ST ANDREW A Gothic church converted to Classical style in the mid-18th century. It has a good interior, with an altar table said to be by Chippendale and a large marble monument.

Whissendine *Leics.* 553Gb

CHURCH OF ST ANDREW This is a large church of the 14th and 15th centuries, with a tall, pinnacled west tower. The 16th-century rood screen in the south transept came from St John's College, Cambridge, in 1869. The 15th-century roof has carved figures.

Whiston *Northants.* 547Gf

CHURCH OF ST MARY The early 16th-century church stands on a hill-side away from the road, and has a west tower with fine carvings and gargoyles. There are timber ceilings, Perpendicular windows, and benches typical of the period; also monumental sculpture by Joseph Nollekens and William Pitts.

Whitby *N. Yorks.* 558Fe

A North Yorks. fishing port and holiday resort. The Synod of Whitby, which did much to establish Christianity in Britain, met here in 664. In 1768, Captain James Cook (1728–79), circumnavigator, sailed from Whitby in the *Endeavour* for Tahiti via Cape Horn; the 17th-century house in which he lived in Grape Lane is preserved.

ABBEY Perched on a high cliff overlooking the sea, Whitby has one of the most spectacular monastic sites in England. In view of the scanty knowledge of early monastic buildings, it is of interest that excavation has revealed traces of its 7th- and 8th-century origins, including the foundations of some small scattered cells in which the inmates lived.

However, this monastery was sacked by the Danes in 867 and the present ruins belong to the monastery as it was refounded *c.* 1067. The main survival, the church, is a rebuilding of the 13th and 14th centuries. Two of the main façades (east and north) still stand to their full height.

CHURCH OF ST MARY Originally Norman, with many later alterations. There is a delightful 18th-century interior, with galleries, box-pews and a three-decker pulpit dating from 1778.

MUSEUM Contains fossils of marine dinosaurs and bone models of Napoleonic warships. Relics of Whitby Abbey include the unique 'Abbot's Book', while in the local-history section there are mementos of Captain Cook and of William Scoresby, whaling captain, scientist and priest.

Whitchurch *Shropshire* 552Ad

Midway between Deva (Chester) and Uriconium (Wroxeter), Whitchurch was known to the Roman legions as Mediolanum. Under King Alfred, its site was west of the Hundred of Hodnet, and thus became known as Westune. The Normans erected a new church which was so striking that it was praised as the White Church, from which came the name Whitchurch.

Many of the town streets have old names: Bargates, Bluegates, Watergate, Highgate, Newtown (built on the site of the old castle), Pepper Alley and Bull Ring—the town centre where the last bull was baited in 1802. Whitchurch is the birthplace of Sir Edward German (1862–1936), composer of *Tom Jones* and *Merrie England*.

CHURCH OF ST ALKMUND The present church is the fourth to be built on this site. The third collapsed in 1711 and was rebuilt in 1712–13 by William Smith of Warwick. St Alkmund's is large, with an impressive west tower, pinnacled and balustraded. The interior has tall columns and a gallery; there is a 17th-century font decorated with a Tudor rose and the Prince of Wales's feathers, and monuments from the earlier church, including one to John Talbot, 1st Earl of Shrewsbury (*d.* 1453).

Whitchurch Canonicorum *Dorset* 540Cc

CHURCH OF ST CANDIDA AND HOLY CROSS This large and interesting church contains a rare parish church feature, a 13th-century shrine of St Wite, a Saxon female saint. The building is mainly 12th and 13th century and is cruciform in design, with a Perpendicular west tower. The font is late 12th century, and there is an early 17th-century pulpit, fragments of 15th-century painted glass and a fine monument of *c.* 1611, on which lies a reclining armoured man.

Whitcombe *Dorset* 540Dc

CHURCH A Norman church with a 13th-century chancel and a 16th-century tower. It contains a Norman font, the remains of a Saxon cross, and a 15th-century wall-painting of St Christopher.

Whitehaven *Cumbria* 556Fe

A town which benefited from the Wren-style planning initiated in 1690 by Sir John Lowther and followed by Sir James Lowther (1736–1802), 1st Earl of Lonsdale, who rebuilt Whitehaven Castle.

White Horse *Uffington, Oxon.* 546Eb

First cut in Iron Age times, though later attributed to King Alfred, who was supposed to have cut it after his victory over the Danes at the battle of Ashdown. But this is certainly the oldest of the 'white horses' which dot our chalk uplands. Very similarly shaped horses are seen on some of the pre-Roman coins of the local tribes. A prehistoric trackway—the Ridge Way—runs close past the hill fort. (See Uffington Castle.)

Whithorn Priory *Dumfs. & Gall.* 556Df

The ruins of St Ninian's priory, which dates from the 12th century. The priory church was used as a parish church until the 19th century. The royal Arms of Scotland before the Union with England are carved on the 17th-century approach archway known as the Pend. A fine collection of carved stone crosses is housed in the museum. St Ninian, the first Christian missionary to Scotland, landed on the Isle of Whithorn, three miles to the south-east. There he built a chapel, the ruins of which can still be seen. To the south-west, on Port Castle Bay, is St Ninian's Cave, with sculptured stones and crosses.

CHURCH OF ST MARY, WHITBY

Whitby reached the height of its prosperity in the 17th and 18th centuries, and during this period this Norman church was renovated inside. Across the chancel arch the Cholmley pew, standing on four twisted columns with front decorated with wreaths and angels' heads, was erected in the late 17th century. The west gallery and organ were added in the 18th century, and the church was filled with box-pews.

Whitkirk *W. Yorks.* 558Cb
CHURCH OF ST MARY This Perpendicular church, with a chancel extension by G. F. Bodley, was restored in 1979. It contains a number of monuments; the most important is that to Viscount Irwin (d. 1688), designed by Edward Pierce and executed by John Nost. Also of interest is that to John Smeaton, the builder of the Eddystone lighthouse.

Whittlesey *Cambs.* 553Hb
Whittlesey has a few good buildings, for instance the manor house, of the 15th and 17th centuries; Grove House, late 17th century with a good hooded doorway; the Butter Cross, late 17th century with a tall pyramid on Tuscan columns and some mullioned windows; and the Black Bull Inn, *c.* 1650. No. 6 Gracious Street is an attractive mid-17th-century house.
CHURCH OF ST ANDREW A 13th- and 14th-century church, with a later west tower, with pinnacles. Much of the building has its original roof.

Whitton Court *Shropshire* 546Bf
A manor house built around a courtyard. It was begun in 1140 and includes a 14th-century black and white wing, and a red-brick south front added in 1621. The great hall contains the original oak panelling and a painted frieze (dated 1682).

Whitwell *Derbys.* 552Ee
CHURCH OF ST LAWRENCE The nave and west tower are Norman, the chancel and transepts 14th century. The font is Norman, and there is also a sedilia and what might be an Easter sepulchre.

Wichenford Court Dove-cote 546Bf
Heref. & Worcs.
A 17th-century half-timbered black and white dove-cote.

Wicken *Cambs.* 548Af
Wicken, notable for the unique, primeval undrained Wicken Fen, has a small but dignified Hall, *c.* 1700, near the church. The thatched Sycamores or Old House, *c.* 1650 and facing the Middle Green, was formerly a fishing and hawking box of Sir Henry Jermyn. Spinney Abbey, *c.* 1775, a mile out of the village, is a stone, twin-gabled structure which incorporates much of the Augustinian abbey of *c.* 1215. The reconstituted Fen draining-mill was presented by Lord Fairhaven.

Wickham *Berks.* 546Eb
CHURCH OF ST SWITHIN The Anglo-Saxon tower is of flint and mortar; papier-mâché elephants (shown at the Paris Exhibition of 1862) decorate the side aisle roof. The interior is 19th century, lavishly decorated (1845–9) by Benjamin Ferrey, who used carved angels to support the nave roof.

Wickham *Hants.* 541Hd
BRIDGE STREET Starts from the north-east corner of the square, and has good houses, one an unusual 17th-century building. There is also a pair of big rural-industry buildings, a Victorian brewery, and a water-mill containing timber from the American ship *Chesapeake* which was captured by HMS *Shannon* in 1813.
THE SQUARE A most handsome piece of townscape, with splendid Georgian houses of red and grey brick on three sides.

Wickhambreaux *Kent* 542Ff
The village is grouped around a grassy square with trees. The six houses, plus a water-mill, include the baroque early Georgian vicarage and the chequered post office, an Elizabethan building.

Wickhambrook *Suffolk* 548Bf
GIFFORD'S HALL A manor house of *c.* 1480, restored in 1908, timber-framed and gabled. There is a large timbered hall, great chamber with good fire-place, and much good oak woodwork throughout.

Wickhamford *Heref. & Worcs.* 546De
In 1646, Parliamentary troops led by Colonel Henry Washington defeated Royalists in the siege of Worcester. Colonel Washington was of the same family as George Washington, 1st President of the U.S.A. The family Arms (three stars and two stripes) from which developed the American flag, are on the tomb of the colonel's daughter, Penelope, in the church at Wickhamford.

Widecombe-in-the-Moor *Devon* 539Gd
A village set in a hollow on Dartmoor, which has become famous because of the traditional song 'Widecombe Fair'.
CHURCH HOUSE A 15th-century granite building near the church in the village. (By appointment.)
CHURCH OF ST PANCRAS A large 14th-century church with a tall, pinnacled west tower of granite. There is a rood screen with painted figure panels.

WILTON HOUSE *Probably no house in England has been the scene of more distinguished gatherings than took place at Wilton under the presiding genius of Mary, wife of the 2nd Earl of Pembroke. She gathered around her the nation's outstanding intellectual, social and artistic talent—including her brother, Sir Philip Sidney, and Shakespeare himself. In 1647 a disastrous fire destroyed most of the Tudor house. It was rebuilt for the 4th Earl by Inigo Jones and his assistant, John Webb, in 1648–53.*

18TH-CENTURY SETTEE *Probably designed by William Kent—the first English architect to design the furniture for a specific architectural scheme—this settee of about 1730 is in the Double Cube Room at Wilton. The carved and gilded woodwork is in Italian style, and the crouching sphinxes may have been inspired by the French designer Jean Berain. Kent himself was usually responsible only for the design of the furniture, the actual carving being executed by first-rate craftsmen.*

JENSEN DESK *Gerreit Jensen, probably of Dutch descent, worked for four English monarchs in succession, starting with Charles II and ending with Anne. The many Dutch craftsmen who followed William III to England helped to raise the standard of English work and give it an international reputation. Made of metal, tortoiseshell and wood marquetry, this desk reflects the French Court style of the late 17th century and is a predecessor of the popular 18th-century English pedestal desk.*

Wideford Hill *Mainland, Orkney*   569Hf
A Neolithic cairn of Maes Howe type. A small cell opens from each of the three walls of this chamber, the fourth being broken by the entrance from the passage.

Wiggenhall *Norfolk*   554Ab
CHURCHES OF ST GERMAN, ST MARY THE VIRGIN AND ST MARY MAGDALENE Three neighbouring parish churches which, between them, have exceptional wood fittings in the way of benches, with poppy-heads and large carved figures of saints on the bench ends, remains of painted wood screens, and early 17th-century pulpits with hour-glass stands. St Mary Magdalene dates from the 13th century in its present form and has some 15th-century stained glass. Not far away is the roofless ruin of the church of Wiggenhall St Peter.

Wightwick Manor *Staffs.*   552Bb
A half-timbered manor house, built 1887–93. It contains work by the most famous of the Pre-Raphaelite artists—wallpapers and fabrics by William Morris, a collection of water-colours by Ruskin, drawings by Burne-Jones, paintings by Millais, tiles by de Morgan, and Kempe stained glass. The gardens are mainly formal, with terraces and topiary work. They were designed by Alfred Parsons, the Victorian flower painter.

Wigtown *Dumfs. & Gall.*   556Dg
During the persecution of the Covenanters (Presbyterians) by Charles II in 1685, two women Covenanters were bound to stakes on Wigtown sands and left to drown in the rising tide; their graves are in the churchyard. A memorial to these Wigtown martyrs stands on Windyhill.

Wilderhope Manor *Shropshire*   546Ag
Built of limestone in 1586, the manor is unaltered except for plaster ceilings added in the 17th century.

Willington *Beds.*   547He
WILLINGTON DOVE-COTE One of the earliest and most magnificent dove-cotes in the country, a tall, mid-16th-century stone-built structure; it has a two-tiered tiled roof with stepped gables at each

DOUBLE CUBE ROOM *This elegant and beautifully proportioned Italianate state room on the south side of Wilton is the most important room in the house. It is 60 ft long, 30 ft wide and 30 ft high. Inigo Jones and John Webb designed it, as part of their reconstruction of the house after the fire of 1647, to house the Pembroke family's paintings by Rembrandt and Van Leyden, and family and royal portraits by Van Dyck. Over the fire-place is Van Dyck's portrait of Charles I's children. The ceiling is finely painted with the story of Perseus. About 1730 William Kent designed the suite of gilt and red velvet furniture for the room.*

PALLADIAN BRIDGE *The 9th Earl of Pembroke— the 'Architect Earl'—and Roger Morris, his clerk-of-works, built this elegant bridge in 1736–7. It spans the R. Nadder in the grounds at Wilton.*

end, and a dividing wall which carries up above the roof and is stepped like the end walls. Each part of the dove-cote is entered by a low Tudor doorway. It can hold 1500 pigeons.

The larger companion building near by is of the same material and date and has a Tudor fireplace and mullioned windows. It was once a stable.

Wilmington *E. Sussex*   *542Cd*
PRIORY AND MUSEUM A Benedictine monastery, suppressed in 1414. It now displays old agricultural implements and farm utensils, including ox-ploughs, yokes and man-traps.

Wilmington Long Man *E. Sussex*   *542Cd*
On the north side of Windover Hill, this gigantic figure of a man is carved in the chalk and outlined in bricks. It became somewhat overgrown and was renovated in the 19th century by a local man, who may have modified the original figure.

Its age is not known. It is thought to have been first cut in medieval times, but there are suggestions that it may have been as early as the mid-Saxon or even Roman period.

Wilton *Wilts.*   *540Fe*
This small town, famous for its manufacture of carpets, felt and agricultural machinery, was once politically important: here in 838 King Egbert united the Kingdoms of Kent and Wessex. Today the town is the centre of the local sheep trade.

Wilton House *Wilts.*   *540Fe*
There had been an abbey at Wilton for centuries before it was dissolved by Henry VIII, who gave the lands to Sir William Herbert. Herbert held many powerful appointments; he was created 1st Earl of Pembroke in 1551 and built a house at Wilton worthy of his standing. Tradition maintains that he consulted Hans Holbein—a porch, now detached from the house, is known as the Holbein Porch. Philip, 4th Earl of Pembroke, commissioned Isaac de Caus to construct a huge formal garden to the south of the house. In 1647 a fire destroyed much of the house and the earl asked the aged Inigo Jones to reconstruct it. Jones died in 1652 and his assistant, John Webb, completed the work; two of Webb's designs are in the Victoria

and Albert Museum. In the grounds are a Palladian bridge by Roger Morris and a casino (dancing room) by Sir William Chambers. Much alteration to the building took place in the early years of the 19th century following the designs of James Wyatt. The house contains fine furniture and plasterwork, pictures and a collection of 7000 model soldiers of the 19th century.

Wimbledon Common *Greater London*   547Jb
CAESAR'S CAMP This is of interest as being a visible hill-fort within modern Greater London. It is a roughly circular 12 acre fort defended by a single bank and ditch. The entrance was probably on the west side. Originally, the ditch was more than 12 ft deep and the 30 ft wide bank was revetted on both sides with vertical timber palisades. The height of the bank was reduced in the 19th century.

Wimborne Minster *Dorset*   540Ec
CHURCH OF ST CUTHBERGA A large church, cruciform, with a central tower, and another at the west end. There are Norman tower arches, the nave arcade is Transitional Norman and 15th century. Among the tombs is that of the Duke and Duchess of Somerset, grandparents of Henry VII, and a brass to King Ethelred, King Alfred's brother. The famous Chained Library may be visited.

Wimpole *Cambs.*   547Je
CHURCH OF ST ANDREW Near Wimpole Hall; although of 14th-century origin, St Andrew's was almost completely rebuilt by Henry Flitcroft in 1749 and Gothicised in the late 19th century. There is a superb series of monuments, from 16th-century brasses onwards: work by Peter Scheemakers, Flaxman, Bacon the Elder, Banks and the Westmacotts may be seen. (By arrangement.)

Wimpole Hall *Cambs.*   547Je
A spectacular 18th-century mansion, set in a park laid out by Humphry Repton. Once the home of Mrs Elsie Bambridge, daughter of Rudyard Kipling, it contains many finely decorated rooms and an exhibition of Kipling's life and work. Also on display is a fascinating collection of architectural and landscape drawings.

Winchcombe *Glos.*   546Dd
CHURCH OF ST PETER Built between 1456 and 1474, this Perpendicular church with 19th-century restoration, is typical of the 'wool' churches of the Cotswolds. The pinnacled west tower has a fine weather-cock, and there are gargoyles all round the church. There is a superb 16th-century altar cloth preserved in a glass case.

Winchelsea *E. Sussex*   542Ed
After the original port was devastated by storms and floods, a new town was laid out on higher ground in 1288. Of the original buildings, only three gates, the court house, the chancel of the old church and a number of vaulted cellars are left: but the original grid plan of the town can be traced without difficulty. The present houses date mainly from after 1900.
CHURCH OF ST THOMAS THE MARTYR The chancel and side chapels still remain of the original 13th-century church. There are 14th-century monuments to Admirals of the Cinque Ports, fragments of a tomb mural and good windows, *c.* 1930, by Douglas Strachan.

Winchester *Hants.*   541Ge
Winchester was a tribal centre long before the Romans came to Britain. Under the Romans Winchester became the fifth largest city in Britain. King Alfred made the town his capital. At the east end of the High Street is a statue of the king,

erected in 1901 to commemorate the thousandth anniversary of his death. In Norman times Winchester was of unrivalled eminence; as late as the 13th century it was second only to London in importance, and an important centre for pilgrims from the Continent in the Middle Ages, who paid tribute at the shrine of St Swithin and then took the route to Canterbury.

Excavations beside the cathedral in the 1960s revealed the foundations of the old Anglo-Saxon minster. The so-called New Minster, probably founded by Alfred the Great, was proved to be immediately adjacent. Parts of this church, which may have been as much as 150 ft long, and some of its domestic offices, were also uncovered.

The High Street formally ends with St Swithin's Bridge—known as the City Bridge—which was built in 1813 on the site of the original bridge built by St Swithin across the R. Itchen. To the south, along the line of the river, in a district called The Weirs, are remains of the ancient city wall, built originally by the Romans. The walls lead to Wolvesey Castle, built by Henry de Blois in 1138 and damaged by Cromwell's troops. Wren built an episcopal palace near by for Bishop Morley in 1684, and the remaining wing of this building is a residence for the Bishop of Winchester. The Plague Monument, erected in 1759 and rebuilt in 1821, commemorates the great plague that swept the city in 1666.

Outstanding post-medieval buildings are Serle's House in Southgate Street, a splendid example of the Queen Anne style; the Italianate library, built in 1838, in Jewry Street; and the new hotel immediately north of the cathedral.
CASTLE HALL At the western end of the old city are the remains of the former Norman castle which occupied this hill-top position. The great hall (1235) is Early English with Purbeck marble columns and stone window-seats, the finest and largest medieval hall in Britain after that at Westminster. Many notable Parliaments and trials were held here: in 1603, Sir Walter Raleigh heard his sentence of death, and in 1685 Judge Jeffreys held a 'Bloody Assize'. The Round Table of King Arthur hangs in the hall.
CATHEDRAL The present church was begun in 1079. At its west end it overlaps an earlier Saxon church in the immediate vicinity of the cathedral. In its present form Winchester Cathedral is, at 556 ft, the longest cathedral in Europe. The most complete remains of the early work are in the transepts, which are remarkable features of early Norman architecture. The arches have heavy plain mouldings, the capitals are undecorated, and the transepts themselves are unusual in featuring aisles that are continued across their end walls. In the 13th century the Norman church was extended to the east by the addition of the Lady Chapel. Most of the nave was subsequently remodelled, first under Bishop Edington (1345–66), but chiefly under William of Wykeham (1366–1404). The Norman masonry of the nave was carefully concealed in a casing of Perpendicular stonework. There is also a fine set of early 14th-century misericords, monuments of all periods, 19th-century stained glass, medieval wall-paintings, and the important square black Tournai Norman font, embellished with carved scenes from the life of St Nicholas.

The library of the cathedral has some notable treasures. These include a 10th-century copy of Bede's history, a 13th-century illuminated Bible and the first American Bible. (See also p. 488.)
CITY CROSS At the centre of the High Street is a four-sided, 15th-century Gothic cross, restored in

1865. It has four figures: only St John the Baptist is original, the others—William of Wykeham, King Alfred and a supposed mayor of the city—were added during the restoration. It is known locally as the Butter Cross.

CITY MUSEUM Items representing local archaeology and history include parts of Roman mosaic floors, grave finds from the 1st century AD, a Saxon ivory panel, a stone on which is cut the name of King Alfred, coins minted in the city, medieval pottery and two original drawings for the palace which Wren started to build for Charles II in Winchester. Material from Hampshire includes prehistoric pottery and tools, and a mosaic floor from the Roman villa at Sparsholt.

GUILDHALL A Gothic Revival building, dating from 1873 and containing numerous paintings from the 16th century onwards.

MIZ-MAZE The miz-maze on the top of St Catherine's hill may well be of prehistoric origin; its true purpose is now unknown, though this pattern of turf spirals is found elsewhere in Britain and abroad, and during the Middle Ages a maze or labyrinth was often marked on the floor of French cathedrals—at Amiens, for example, it was inlaid in white marble. The spirals may perhaps have been designed to guide dancers' feet in a ritual pattern, possibly connected with a fertility ceremony—although the religious use of specialised dances, to change the dancers' state of consciousness, still occurs, among the Dervishes for example.

PILGRIM'S HALL A 14th-century building with fine beamed roof.

ROYAL GREENJACKETS MUSEUM Devoted to the Oxford and Buckingham Light Infantry, the King's Royal Rifle Corps and the Rifle Brigade, now amalgamated as The Royal Greenjackets.

ROYAL HAMPSHIRE REGIMENTAL MUSEUM Items connected with the Regiment and the campaigns in which it has taken part—uniforms, badges, medals including six Victoria Crosses, silver, old Colours, photographs and records, relics of the Gallipoli landings of April 1915—are displayed in Serle's House, which dates from 1732.

ST CROSS HOSPITAL A fine complex of medieval almshouses with high chimneys. Bishop Henry of Blois, half-brother of King Stephen, founded the hospital in 1136 for the maintenance of 13 poor men—nowadays aged men. In 1445, Cardinal Beaufort added a second foundation, for men of 'noble poverty'. The inmates of the Blois foundation have a black gown and medieval cap and wear a silver cross of St John on the left breast; those of the 'noble poverty' display a mulberry-coloured gown and their regulation dress includes a silver badge incorporating a cardinal's hat and tassels as well as the Cross of St John in its design. Both are familiar sights in Winchester. A wayfarer may apply at St Cross Hospital for the dole, a sliver of bread and a drain of beer which was once served in a horn mug, but is now served in a glass.

The complex includes the Church of St Cross, the Norman church of the hospital, with a central tower; there is later work as well. Parts of the 16th-century stalls remain, and some portions of 15th-century stained glass. There are screens and medieval wall-paintings. Among the monuments is one, c. 1790, by John Francis Moore, who was noted for his use of coloured marbles at a period when white and black were fashionable. There is also a medieval wooden lectern, the only one in the county, and some exceedingly fine brasses.

TOWN CLOCK Above the main street, it was a gift to the city commemorating the Peace of Utrecht (1713). From the belfry turret of the adjacent old

WINCHESTER CATHEDRAL

The longest cathedral in Europe, begun when Winchester was the capital of England. The West Saxons had made their capital here during the 9th century and a Saxon church preceded the present building, though little evidence of it remains. The present church, begun in 1079 and now 556 ft long, overlaps the Saxon predecessor at its west end. During the Middle Ages Winchester was the richest See in England and became the ecclesiastical reward for a series of impressive men. William of Wykeham was twice Chancellor of England, under Edward III and Richard II. During his time as bishop much of the cathedral was remodelled (1366–1404) and the Norman masonry of the nave was carefully concealed in a casing of Perpendicular stonework. Cardinal Henry Beaufort (d. 1447), was a half-brother of Henry IV and played an important part in the negotiations with France in the last phases of the Hundred Years War.

VIRGIN AND CHILD

A fragment of a unique Gothic statue of stone, dating from the late 15th century. The sculptor must have been familiar with the painting and sculpture of Flanders and Holland, but there is no reason to doubt that he was English. (Winchester Cathedral)

THE WINCHESTER BIBLE

The finest ceremonial Bible produced in England in the 12th century was that written and illuminated for the cathedral priory of Winchester. It was probably begun between 1160 and 1170 and its decoration was conceived on so large a scale that although at least six artists worked on it over many years, it was never finished. The text was exceptionally accurate and a contemporary chronicler mentions that it was lent to Witham Priory at the special request of its founder, Henry II, so that the Witham monks could copy it, but this is now authoritatively regarded as doubtful. The left-hand initial shown is the 'B' beginning Psalm 1. King David slays the bear in the upper loop and the lion in the lower. The artist is known as the 'Master of the Leaping Figures'.
(Winchester Cathedral Library)

guildhall the curfew rings each night at 8 o'clock as it has done since Norman times.

WESTGATE MUSEUM The museum is situated in the original west gate of the medieval city, and its exhibits relate mostly to Winchester's civic history. There is also a Tudor painted ceiling, discovered in Winchester College about a century ago and since given to the city on 'perpetual loan'.

WINCHESTER COLLEGE One of the most famous public schools, it was founded in 1382 by William of Wykeham and served later as a model for Henry VI when he founded Eton College. The chapel has Perpendicular-style windows, and the fan tracery vaulting was designed by Hugh Herland, who was later to design the roof of Westminster Hall. Its Jesse window is a copy of the original and dates from 1822. In the centre of the cloister is Fromond's Chantry Chapel. A detached building known simply as 'School' dates from 1683; it bears on one wall an inscription in Latin meaning 'Learn, leave or be licked'. The school motto is 'Manners Makyth Man'.

Windmill Hill *Wilts.*   540Fg
This hill, encircled by three concentric causewayed ditches with internal banks, was the site of regional and possibly ritual gatherings and feasts during the Neolithic period, *c.* 3400 BC. Excavations revealed pottery and stone axes from all over Britain, showing wide contacts in this period. The summit is crowned by Bronze Age barrows.

Windsor *Berks.*   547Hb
CASTLE The castle established by William the Conqueror probably consisted, as now, of a motte, or steep mound, and two large baileys enclosed by

palisades. The stone fortifications were not built until the 12th and 13th centuries, and the defences are substantially those established by the end of Henry III's reign. Windsor was Edward III's favourite residence, and it was he who enlarged the existing royal apartments in the upper ward and established the Chapel of the Order of the Garter. Considerable additions to the castle were also made by Charles II, and an immense amount of restoration and embellishment was undertaken under George III, George IV and Queen Victoria. The exterior of the castle is largely the result of work carried out in the 19th century. The Round Tower, for example, is considerably higher than it was when originally built by Henry II, and many of the towers in the upper ward were either built or heightened during this period. (See also pp. 490-1.)

ST GEORGE'S CHAPEL, WINDSOR CASTLE This rich and complex building, begun in 1475, is the Chapel of the Dean and Canons of Windsor and of the Order of the Garter. The proportions are noble, with a beautiful vault and stalls elaborately decorated with heraldry for the Garter Knights. There is much 16th-century sculpture, but the most theatrical piece is the 19th-century monument to Princess Charlotte of Wales by M. C. Wyatt, in which the Princess is shown, chaste but bare-breasted, ascending from her shrouded corpse. Adjacent is the amazing Albert Memorial Chapel, a shrine of *c.* 1870 taste, with Baron Triquetti's monument to the Prince Consort; more important is the art nouveau memorial by Sir Alfred Gilbert to the Duke of Clarence (d. 1892), completed in 1926.

WINDSOR GUILDHALL EXHIBITION The exhibition is concerned mainly with local history, from the Palaeolithic period to the present day. It has a collection of royal portraits dating from the time of Elizabeth I (who is shown in one wearing a jewelled anchor in her hair), and a series of dioramas showing historical scenes of Windsor from the earliest times to George III's Jubilee celebrations in 1809. There is an exhibition of local natural history. Many of the exhibits, including ancient documents from the Borough Records, are changed annually and each year some special theme in Windsor's life and history is chosen. The guildhall itself was built in 1689 by Sir Thomas Fitz, a surveyor of the Cinque Ports.

Windsor Great Park *Berks.*   547Hb
The principal gardens in Windsor Great Park are the Savill Garden and Valley Gardens, both of which are open to the public—the Savill Garden all year except Christmas and the Valley Gardens daily. Begun by Sir Eric Savill in 1931, the Savill Garden contains outstanding plantings of rhododendrons, camellias, magnolias and a wide range of other trees and shrubs massed in woodland glades carpeted with drifts of daffodils. Beside the ponds and streams and in the marshy areas, primulas, hostas, irises and other moisture-loving plants thrive, the whole producing an outstanding display, particularly in spring and autumn. In a nearby formal area, roses, herbaceous borders and shrubs provide a riot of colour throughout the summer. On the north bank of Virginia Water are the Valley Gardens—350 acres of woodland containing the largest collection of rhododendron species in the world. Here, too, is the famous Punch Bowl, planted with thousands of azaleas, and the extensive Heather Garden.

Wing *Bucks.*   547Gd
CHURCH OF ALL SAINTS An exceptionally interesting Anglo-Saxon church, it has one of the four Saxon apses in England and a crypt under it. The

apse is seven-sided; the vaulted crypt has a hexagonal central chamber with a narrow passage around it. Four bays of the nave arcades are pre-Conquest; the easternmost, however, is 13th century. The west tower is 14th century, and the south aisle was rebuilt then. The lower windows were inserted in the 15th century and a clerestory added. The rood screen is 16th century, the pulpit early 17th century. All Saints is rich in monuments, and includes 15th-century brasses and two excellent tombs to the Dormer family, *c.* 1552 and *c.* 1590.

Wingfield *Suffolk*   *548Dg*
CHURCH OF ST ANDREW An ambitious church, with a clerestory to the chancel as well as to the nave, and a west tower. There are monuments to members of the de la Pole family from the 14th century, and one to Sir John de Wingfield, who rebuilt the church and founded the college.
WINGFIELD CASTLE Mainly Tudor, but with a 14th-century south front with the original central gate-house, corner turrets and door.
WINGFIELD COLLEGE Founded in 1361 and surrendered to Henry VIII at the Dissolution.

Wingham *Kent*   *542Ff*
A long village, with the best houses close to the church; there is a half-timbered group opposite it, and Queen Anne houses to the south and east.

Winkworth Arboretum *Surrey*   *542Ae*
The grounds cover 99 acres near Godalming, and contain rare trees and shrubs and a lake.

Winterborne Stoke Crossroads *Wilts.*   *540Fe*
Like the perhaps even finer barrow group on Normanton Down, every type of Bronze Age barrow, as well as a Neolithic long barrow, is present in a comparatively small area. In addition to the long barrow, there are 22 round barrows.

Winterborne Tomson *Dorset*   *540Ec*
CHURCH OF ST ANDREW A small 12th-century church with an apsidal east end, and plastered roofs. The interior is simple, and has 18th-century box-pews, pulpit and canopy; the gallery was the medieval rood loft.

Winterbourne Bassett *Wilts.*   *540Fg*
CHURCH OF ST KATHERINE A good, mainly Decorated church, with a Perpendicular west tower. There is an Early English font, and 17th-century benches, pulpit and font cover among the fittings. A 13th-century coffin-lid, or tomb-slab, is carved with figures of a man and a woman holding hands.

Winton House *Lothian*   *562Ce*
Charles I is thought to have visited this house in 1633, and the fine plaster ceilings were installed in his honour. It is said to be the 'Ravenwood Castle' of Sir Walter Scott's *The Bride of Lammermoor.* George Seton, 3rd Earl of Winton, built the mansion in Scottish Renaissance style in 1620.

Wintringham *N. Yorks.*   *558Fc*
CHURCH OF ST PETER A Norman church, with 14th-century enlargement, and a west tower and spire. Inside is a Norman font, medieval screens, 15th-century glass and 17th-century pews.

Winwick *Cheshire*   *552Af*
CHURCH OF ST OSWALD Mainly of the 14th century, with a west tower and large spire. The nave roof is panelled; the 19th-century chancel is by Pugin. There are brasses and monuments to the Gerard and Legh families; one, of *c.* 1690, may be by John Nost.

Wirksworth *Derbys.*   *552Dd*
CHURCH OF ST MARY A large cruciform church, with a central tower and spire, dating from the 13th century. Sir Gilbert Scott restored it in 1872,

THE LIBRARY IN QUEEN MARY'S DOLLS' HOUSE

This spectacular dolls' house was made and presented to Queen Mary in the 1920's as a token of national goodwill, and to provide a means of raising funds for charity. Sir Edwin Lutyens designed the building, which is a faithful replica of a 20th-century house— one-twelfth normal size—with all the intriguing details of a luxurious residence for a king and queen. In the library the books are arranged on Italian walnut bookshelves and most were written specially for the house by their famous authors. (Windsor Castle)

WINDSOR CASTLE

William the Conqueror began this stupendous royal fortress, perhaps about the time that the Tower of London was begun in 1078. The castle probably consisted, as now, of a motte and two large baileys, enclosed by palisades. The stone fortifications followed in the 12th and 13th centuries, and the defences are substantially those established by the end of Henry III's reign. Windsor has always been one of the favourite residences of the reigning monarch. Additions were made under Charles II, and much of the present fabric dates from the 19th century. The royal apartments, a series of grandiose rooms, were refurbished in the 17th and 19th centuries.

HANS HOLBEIN THE YOUNGER: SIR HENRY GUILDFORD *Holbein was the supreme portrait painter of the northern Renaissance. He first visited England in 1526 for 18 months; he returned in 1532. He probably entered the royal service soon after 1537 and did many portrait drawings as well as numerous portraits in oils for Henry VIII. It was during his first visit in 1527, that he painted 'Sir Henry Guildford'* (30½ by 26⅛ in.) *one of the king's favourites, who held various posts at Court. Here we see him with the staff of the Comptroller of the Household. Holbein combines an intensity and dispassionate clarity of observation with an austerity of linear draughtsmanship which results in a unity of the details in the costume and jewellery and the fine modelling of the sitter's features.*

THE CASTLE FROM THE AIR

Windsor encloses nearly 13 acres and is the largest castle in England. Standing on a hill of chalk near the Thames, it was originally built to guard London's approaches. Established within its present limits by William the Conqueror, its buildings have since grown continuously. St George's Chapel was founded by King Edward IV; his predecessor, Edward III, built new royal apartments in the Upper Ward, which were radically reconstructed by Charles II and again by George IV. Much of what is seen today is the creation of George IV's architect, Sir Jeffrey Wyatville, who heightened Henry II's Round Tower, remodelled others, and built several new ones during his Gothic renovations in the early years of the 19th century.

ST GEORGE'S CHAPEL CHOIR *Edward III founded the Order of the Garter, with its own chapel, at Windsor in 1348. After 1475 the building was replaced by the existing chapel, one of the most sumptuous late Gothic buildings in England. In the choir are the carved stalls of the Knights of the Garter, made about 1480, surmounted by the present occupants' banners.*

STALL-PLATE *This plaque, dating from about 1559, shows enamelling as it was practised on base metals in Elizabethan England. It is the stall-plate recording the creation of the 4th Duke of Norfolk a Knight Companion of the Order of the Garter. When a Knight Companion is created a plate showing his Arms, usually in enamel, and the date of his creation, is attached to his stall in the Chapel of the Order, St George's Chapel, and his crested helm and banner are displayed there. On his death, helm and banner are taken away but the stall-plate remains. The 4th Duke of Norfolk was involved in the Ridolfi plot to dethrone Elizabeth and put Mary, Queen of Scots in her place; for this he was attainted and executed. To be attainted meant degradation from the Order of the Garter and the stall-plate was removed from the chapel, probably in 1572; it was replaced in 1955. (St George's Chapel)* adding the clerestory. A coffin-lid of *c.* 800 is carved with New Testament scenes. There are two fonts, one Norman, the other of 1662.

Wisbech *Cambs.* 553Jb
Wisbech is one of the few Fen towns with many houses of real architectural quality. The two Brinks on the R. Nene make one of the best Georgian scenes in England, but the typical grey brick of Cambridgeshire does not complement Georgian architecture quite as well as red brick. The North Brink has inherited a character chiefly from the Dutch, who continued the reclamation work started first by the Romans and finished by the Scottish civil engineers Telford and Rennie. Wisbech, once 4 miles away from the sea, is now 11 miles inland.

The Rose and Crown Hotel has early Tudor brick barrel-vaults and an elegant 18th-century staircase with buildings at the back dated 1601. There are early 18th-century houses in Norfolk Street and the Old Market. South Brink has houses of much the same character, particularly Nos. 7–8 which belonged to Sir Philip Vavasour. Wisbech's excellent museum has the original manuscript of Charles Dickens's *Great Expectations*.
CHURCH OF SS PETER AND PAUL A large and complex church in a once prosperous town, with work of the 12th century onwards. The tower on the north side is detached from the main building. There is 19th-century stained glass and monuments, one by Joseph Nollekens; also the carved Arms of James I. The large effigy brass of Thomas de Braunstone on the chancel floor bears an inscription in Old French.
PECKOVER HOUSE Built on the North Brink *c.* 1722, is the finest house in Wisbech; the Peckover family, who also built Sibalds Home, were rich local bankers and the interior of the house reflects this wealth in the excellence of its rococo decoration work—in both wood and plaster.

Wisley Gardens *Surrey* 542Af
The Royal Horticultural Society's garden, near Ripley, Surrey. Contains a large collection of all types of garden plants and extensive trial grounds of new varieties of flowers and vegetables. Outstanding features are the rhododendrons and azaleas (May), the rock garden and alpine meadow (April) and the heather garden (September).

Withcote *Leics.* 552Fb
CHURCH This small 16th-century building served as the chapel for the adjoining Withcote Hall. It is notable for the rich contemporary stained glass.

Witherslack *Cumbria* 557Hd
CHURCH OF ST PAUL A 17th-century Gothic church, rare of its period, built *c.* 1669 by John Barwick, Dean of St Paul's. Altered in 1768 and restored in 1873, St Paul's has 17th-century woodwork and stained glass.

Withington *Glos.* 546Dd
CHURCH OF ST MICHAEL AND ALL ANGELS In a Cotswold village, an interesting church with work from Norman to Perpendicular Gothic. There is a central tower, and a good Norman south doorway. A wall monument with kneeling figures is by Edward Marshal, 1651.

Withyham *E. Sussex* 542Ce
CHURCH OF ST MICHAEL AND ALL ANGELS The 14th-century church was rebuilt 1663–72, after being struck by lightning. Its importance lies in its monuments to the Sackville family in their chapel of 1680, built to receive the monument to Thomas, a boy of 13 who died in 1677. This is by Caius

SACKVILLE MONUMENT

Caius Gabriel Cibber, who lived from 1630 to 1700, was a Dane who studied in Rome and was much influenced by Bernini's works—traces of which can be seen in this monument. Carved in marble about 1674, it shows Sir Richard Sackville, 5th Earl of Dorset (1622–77) and his wife kneeling beside their dying son. Around the base of the tomb are the figures of their children who died in early childhood.
(Church of St Michael and All Angels, Withyham)

Gabriel Cibber, and is his only known important tomb, although he carved for Hampton Court, St Paul's Cathedral, Chatsworth and other late 17th-century buildings. Other monuments of the 18th and 19th centuries are by Joseph Nollekens, John Flaxman and Sir Francis Chantrey.

Witney *Oxon.* 546Ec
Witney prospered in the past from Cotswold wool, and the Witney blankets made from it. The R. Windrush provided power and clear water for washing the wool and a number of mills stand in and around the town. In High Street is the Blanket Hall of 1721 where the merchants met to do business. The Butter Cross in the market-place dates from 1683. On Church Green, a tree-lined open space, are the church and the early 18th-century rectory at one end, and the 17th- and 18th-century houses of well-to-do clothiers down either side. On the west of the green is the old grammar school, now a comprehensive, built in 1660, the work of a local mason but already strongly influenced by the new Classicism of Inigo Jones and his followers.
CHURCH OF ST MARY THE VIRGIN A grand cruciform church, with central tower and spire, at one end of a large open green. The original Norman church was altered in the Early English and later Gothic periods; it contains a 14th-century brass with figures.

Wiveton Hall *Norfolk* 554Cd
A small manor house dated 1652, combined with a house in the same style of *c.* 1909.

Woburn Abbey *Beds.* 547He
At the Dissolution in 1539 Henry VIII granted the land and buildings at Woburn to John Russell and made him 1st Baron Russell. In 1550 Russell was made 1st Earl of Bedford by Edward VI, and later the 5th Earl was created Duke of Bedford by

William III. The Russells did not live at Woburn until the 17th century, when they built themselves a house on the monastic site. The shell grotto in the north wing, reputed to have been designed by Isaac de Caux, dates from this time. Much of this house was destroyed during the 18th century when John Sanderson and later Henry Flitcroft were employed to remodel the abbey. At the end of the 18th century Henry Holland, architect of Carlton House, London, added the east front, the Chinese dairy, and other portions of the house, including the orangery which is now the Sculpture Gallery. After the Second World War the east front was found to be riddled with dry rot, and demolished. The mansion contains magnificent collections of pictures, including works by Canaletto, Rembrandt, Van Dyck, Gainsborough, Reynolds, Velazquez and Holbein; fine French and English 18th-century furniture; and 18th-century silver. In the park, landscaped by Humphry Repton, roam 11 varieties of deer, American and European bison.

Woden Law *Borders* 562Ec
FORT AND ROMAN SIEGE WORKS The fort shows evidence, in its multivallate defences, of three structural phases, all in the Iron Age. It has, however, a still greater interest in that, outside the outermost defences, there are the banks and ditches of Roman siege works. It is not thought that these were used in an attack on the fort, but that they are the results of a training exercise by a local garrison.

Wollaton *Notts.* 552Ed
CHURCH OF ST LEONARD The church has a west tower and steeple. There is a pretty, carved wood reredos with Corinthian columns, and many monuments, from *c.* 1471 to those by the younger John Bacon and Sir Richard Westmacott.

Wollaton Hall *Notts.* 552Ed
This great mansion, now the home of the Natural History Museum of Nottingham, contains collections of exotic butterflies, British beetles and Wenlock limestone fossils. It is one of the most splendid examples of Elizabethan Renaissance architecture. The architect was Robert Smythson, who had worked for Sir John Thynne on the rebuilding of Longleat House in Wiltshire. Wollaton Hall, built 1580–8, was original for a period in which buildings planned around open courtyards were favoured. At Wollaton there was no courtyard, and the great hall was made the centre of the house. The hall rises like a great tower from the building and is ornamented with projecting round turrets at the four corners. A large tower ornamented with pinnacles is built at each of the four corners of the house itself. The facade and the sides are decorated with pilasters of the Ionic order, and the rather severe formality is broken by rich mouldings, numerous niches and huge windows.

Wolterton Hall *Norfolk* 554Cc
This fine house was designed for Horatio Walpole, 1st Lord Walpole, diplomat and statesman, and dates from 1727. It has state rooms and gardens, and is the property of the present Lord Walpole. (By appointment to interested societies only.)

Wolverhampton *W. Midlands* 552Bb
Created a county borough in 1889, the town is now famous for its engineering but was originally a medieval wool centre. After a great fire in 1590 it switched to making locks and keys in the early 17th century, and also to buckle-making—in 1770 the town had 102 master buckle-makers in steel. A feature of Wolverhampton's museums is the extensive collection of English painted enamels.

STATE SALON AT WOBURN ABBEY

Woburn has been the home of the Russell family since the 17th century. The family, created Dukes of Bedford in 1694, was given the land and original monastic buildings there by Henry VIII at the Dissolution. The 17th-century house they built was largely demolished during the 18th century when John Sanderson and later Henry Flitcroft were commissioned to rebuild it. Flitcroft had had a brilliant career. He began as a joiner and then became an architectural draughtsman for William Kent; later he joined the Office of Works as a master carpenter and eventually became Comptroller there. At Woburn he reconstructed the west front with its magnificent state rooms which were finished about 1760.

SÈVRES SOUP TUREEN

Part of a magnificent Sèvres porcelain dinner service given by Louis XV to the Duchess of Bedford in 1763, when the Duke was English Ambassador at the signing of the Treaty of Paris. Made for 16 diners, most of the 188 pieces still survive. (Woburn Abbey)

SIR EDWARD ELGAR
ENGLAND'S TRIUMPHANT COMPOSER

At the age of ten, Elgar was discovered sitting on a river bank with a pencil and a sheet of manuscript trying to write down 'what the reeds are saying'. This early display of sensitivity and talent led him to utilise to the full all the resources of his father's music shop. He gained knowledge and experience playing with the Glee Club and the Worcester Philharmonic Society and began giving music lessons. Shortly after, however, he gave up teaching to concentrate entirely on composition. The subsequent unfolding of his genius revealed him as a superb orchestral composer, and his violin and cello concertos and two symphonies give him a place among Britain's greatest musicians. His most original composition is the 'Enigma Variations' (1898), which portrays Lady Elgar, 12 of their friends and himself. His 'Pomp and Circumstance' marches are famous, but his greatest work, first performed in 1900, is 'Dream of Gerontius', of which Elgar said, 'This is the best of me'.

THE ORDER OF MERIT *(1911) and other awards bestowed on Elgar. His was the first O.M. awarded to a musician. Elgar had been knighted in 1904, and was accepted as a peer among great continental musicians while still struggling for recognition in England. (Elgar's Birthplace, Broadheath, Worcester)*

TWO PHOTOGRAPHS OF ELGAR *(c. 1902-3), who liked nothing more than to be mistaken for a general, and a part of a handwritten score.*

LADY ELGAR, *from a photograph taken in 1913. Elgar's development owed much to his wife's belief in him. (Broadheath)*

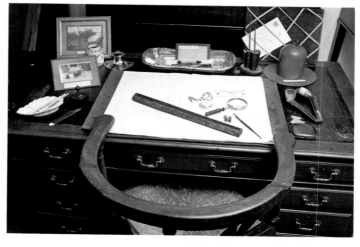

ELGAR'S DESK *and the paraphernalia he used for composition. 'Gosh, man, I've got a tune in my head' was a typical expression of the delight he felt at the prospect of musical composition. His wife acted as his secretary, ruling out the paper for most of his major scores. (Broadheath)*

ELGAR'S DIVERSE INTERESTS, *from chemistry to golf, cycling and poker-work, are here illustrated. An enthusiastic race-goer, bookmakers were awestruck with his infallible skill in picking losers. (Broadheath)*

ELGAR'S RIGHT HAND, *made of plaster and cast in Rome in 1907. He wrote 'I cannot tell how much I shall be able to work here . . .' but during that winter wrote his First Symphony, which was received with tremendous enthusiasm at its first performance by the Hallé Orchestra at Manchester in December 1908. (Broadheath)*

SECOND SYMPHONY MANUSCRIPT *written 1910–11. Elgar called it 'a frank expression of the music bubbling from the spring within me'. Also shown: his violin case, bow, metronome, rosin box and handkerchiefs. (Broadheath)*

ELGAR'S BIRTHPLACE *at Broadheath, near Worcester. He inherited an appreciation of music from his father, who was a violinist, an organist, a pianist and owner of a music shop in Worcester.*

MAESTRO'S GRAVE *Edward Elgar and his wife lie side by side in the churchyard of St Wulstan, Little Malvern; the headstone bears the crest of Lady Elgar's family. In 1970, their daughter was buried near by.*

WOODHENGE

A Neolithic ceremonial or religious site on the Wiltshire Downs, recognised from an aerial photograph taken in 1925. A circular bank—220 ft in diameter—encloses a ditch and six concentric settings of timber uprights (perhaps roof supports) now marked by rows of concrete pillars.

Wolverton Hants.   541Hf
CHURCH OF ST CATHERINE An elegant building of the early 18th century, this church suffered from Victorian insertion of mullions and tracery into the windows, and destruction of the chancel gates and the gallery. Much of the furniture and fittings, however, are original, such as the reading-desk, pews, reredos and pulpit.

Woodbridge Suffolk   548Ee
Woodbridge is a small town, concerned largely with farming. It is full of good 15th-, 16th- and 18th-century houses dominated by Thomas Seckford's Dutch-like shire hall, c. 1575, with 19th-century additions. The lower part of the structure was originally open and formed a covered market. It was sealed off in 1803. The 'abbey', another building by this Elizabethan public benefactor, is Seckford's manor house in Church Street, c. 1654; the two-storey red-brick structure, with Flemish gables, is still in excellent repair. The King's Head Inn, timber-framed in Seckford Street, the Angel Inn, also timber-framed with overhangs, in Theatre Street, and the Bell Inn in New Street are notable inns of character. There are good Georgian houses in the Thoroughfare and better ones in Cumberland Street. The post office has Jacobean plaster ceilings and fire-places from an earlier house, with a staircase dated 1634. Two unique features of the town are the old steelyards or lever weighing machines at the Bell Inn and at the Tide Mill on the quay. Rare throughout England, these are the only examples of such machines in Suffolk. CHURCH OF ST MARY A large church with flushwork decoration, a 15th-century west tower and an ornate north porch topped with double-stepped crenellations and pinnacles. There is a seven-sacrament font with a canopy and a 17th-century figured monument to a townsman and his family.

Woodchester Roman Villa Glos.   546Cc
The villa site, one of the largest in Britain, covers 26 acres and was excavated in 1796; it is generally kept covered with earth for preservation, but is occasionally opened up.

Woodcroft Castle Cambs.   547Jh
Built in 1280 and altered 200 years later, the small castle-house has an entrance gateway in the middle of the main front, with the porter's lodge on one side and the guard-room on the other; the south-west tower still stands in the remains of the moat. The room over the entrance is said to have been a chapel. Although it has no battlements or machicolations, the effect of a small, uncompromising fortress remains.

Wood Hall Hotel Suffolk   548Ee
An E-shaped house of 1579, brick-built with projecting porch and two wings. The porch has columns and pilasters, and there are mullioned windows.

Woodhenge Wilts.   540Fe
This monument lies immediately outside the Durrington Walls circle on its south-west side, its existence unsuspected until 1925. Its origins lie in the late-Neolithic period. It is marked by a circular ditch inside its bank, some 220 ft in overall diameter. The centre, when excavated, showed six concentric circles of post-holes in the chalk, with others at the entrance. They may originally have been the major uprights of a roofed building.

When the excavations were completed, short concrete pillars were inserted in the post-holes, so that the pattern is visible on the surface. Woodhenge must form part of the complex of which Durrington Walls is the largest unit.

Woodstock Oxon.   546Ed
Woodstock is dominated by Blenheim Palace. West of the main road is the cobbled market-place, and a short street of 18th-century houses leads to a

small square outside the park gates. The rear of the rectory (visible from the park) and a house on the main road have heavy, baroque details that link them with Blenheim.

OXFORDSHIRE COUNTY MUSEUM, FLETCHER'S HOUSE Opened in 1966 to display crafts and industries, building and farming methods, and life in the Oxford area through the centuries.

Wookey Hole Caves *Som.*   *540Cf*
Caves in the Mendips, worn by the R. Axe over a period of 50,000 years. During the last phase of the Ice Age, the Hyaena Den was certainly a wild-animal den for much of the time, but men also used it at various periods. Their remains included many flint and bone tools, ashes and food debris.

A few yards north is Wookey Great Cave. Here the occupation was much later, during the Iron Age and the Romano-British period. The Witch of Wookey is a massive stalagmite, said by legend to be a petrified old woman.

WOOKEY HOLE CAVES MUSEUM Little or nothing is known of the prehistoric life in the Wookey Hole Caves, but much evidence of later occupants is on display in the museum. These were the Celtic tribes from the Continent, who lived there from 250 BC until AD 450, when the Romans evacuated Britain. Earlier remains were also found, including animal and human bones, cooking articles and examples of primitive jewellery. Finds of medieval pottery and Bristol Glass give evidence of 17th-century and later visitors; undoubtedly the stalactite grottoes were a major attraction even in those days.

Woolpit *Suffolk*   *548Cf*
The last wolf in Suffolk is said to have been killed at Woolpit, whose former brick-yard supplied bricks for the construction of Royal Lodge, Windsor and Royal Pavilion, Brighton. But its chief claim to fame lies in the curious 11th-century tale of the Green Children of Woolpit, in which two children with green complexions and speaking an unknown tongue, suddenly appeared in the district. Despite misgivings, the villagers took them in, and in time, their vivid hue faded and both learnt to speak English. But neither was ever able to explain where they had come from or how they arrived at Woolpit.
CHURCH OF ST MARY A Decorated and Perpendicular church, with a 19th-century spire. There is a Venetian south porch with niches for statues and roof-bosses. Inside is a marvellous hammerbeam roof, a 16th-century brass eagle lectern, and bench ends with carved figures and animals.

Woolsthorpe Manor *Lincs.*   *553Gc*
In the quiet orchard in front of the house Sir Isaac Newton, who was born here in 1642, watched an apple fall to the ground; this is reputed to have led him to his universal law of gravitation. A descendant of the apple tree can be seen today. The house was built in the early 17th century.

Woolwich *London*   *542Cg*
MUSEUM OF ARTILLERY, THE ROTUNDA Depicts the development of artillery from Crécy onwards. There is also a collection of firearms.
ROYAL ARTILLERY REGIMENTAL MUSEUM Housed on one floor of what was the Royal Military Academy (known as 'The Shop'). The museum tells the story of the Royal Regiment of Artillery from 1716 to the present day.

Wootton Bassett *Wilts.*   *546Db*
A mainly 18th-century town, with a half-timbered restored town hall (1700) in which are stocks, a ducking-stool and an ancient fire-engine.

Wootton Rivers *Wilts.*   *540Ff*
CHURCH OF ST ANDREW Hours on the clock face are marked by the letters GLORYBETOGOD. The clock was made of old iron for George V's coronation.

Wootton Wawen *Warks.*   *546Df*
CHURCH OF ST PETER The central tower is of Saxon origin, from the early 11th century, and the church built around it has work from the Norman period to the 17th century. Inside, the octagonal font is early 14th century, and there are two screens of the 14th century. There are fragments of earlier medieval wall decoration, and some pieces of 13th-century stained glass in the east window. A variety of monuments, some with effigies, range from an alabaster knight of the early 15th century to one with 16th-century brasses.

Worcester *Heref. & Worcs.*   *546Cf*
A cathedral city, granted its first royal charter in 1189 by Richard I. Its second and more detailed charter was given in 1227 by Henry III, whom the city supported in the Barons' Wars 35 years later. James I granted Worcester yet another charter in 1621, which declared it County of the City of Worcester, separate from the county of Worcestershire. The city has suffered from its loyalty to the Crown: it was plundered and burnt in 1041 as a reprisal for the death of King Hardicanute's tax-collectors whom the townspeople regarded as agents of an invader, and in the 12th century the city caught fire during King Stephen's military action against Matilda. In 1265, Prince Edward (later Edward I) used Worcester as a base from which to attack Simon de Montfort at the Battle of Evesham, and 400 years later the first battle of the Civil War was fought at Powick Bridge, 2 miles west of the town. Prince Rupert's cavalry routed the Parliamentary horse, but next day Parliamentary forces plundered the city and desecrated the cathedral. In 1651, Charles II's army confronted Cromwell's forces at Worcester: the Royalists

WORCESTER PORCELAIN VASE

The Worcester Porcelain Company was founded early in the 18th century and grew rapidly, taking over Benjamin Lund's factory at Bristol in 1752. From 1751 the Worcester factory was run by Dr Wall, and after his death in 1776, the works were continued under William Davis until 1783, when they were purchased by Thomas Flight. This vase is from the Flight, Barr and Barr period of about 1830; it has brilliant decoration known as the 'jewellery' type. From its beginnings the factory specialised in table-wares and ornamental vases. From 1770 the distinctive vivid colours which made the works famous were used, and the development of transfer printing progressed. The material was more reliable than that of contemporary factories because of the incorporation of Cornish soapstone.
(Dyson Perrins Museum, Worcester)

WORCESTER CATHEDRAL

WORCESTER CATHEDRAL *In a superb position above the R. Severn, the cathedral is dominated by a magnificent 14th-century tower. But there have been buildings on this site since long before then. The See was founded in 680 when the large Diocese of Lichfield was divided. In the late 10th century the community of secular canons was refounded as a monastery by Bishop Oswald, later St Oswald, and this continued until the Dissolution. During the 1080's Bishop Wulfstan began rebuilding the existing Saxon church, and the oldest part of the present cathedral, the stately Romanesque crypt, dates from that time. The Romanesque church was reconstructed in the late 12th and 13th centuries. Worcester has had numerous eminent bishops. St Wulfstan was a pious and much-respected figure, and alone of the Anglo-Saxon bishops survived the Norman Conquest for any considerable time (he died in 1096). In the cathedral a number of fine monuments includes that of King John, and the chantry of Prince Arthur, eldest son of Henry VII, who died in 1502.*

CRYPT *The oldest part of the present cathedral, dating from 1084. The stately Romanesque structure was built by Bishop Wulfstan for the safeguarding and the worship of the relics of St Oswald, King of Northumbria, who was killed in battle in 642. Services are still held in the crypt.*

KING JOHN'S TOMB *This Purbeck marble effigy, once painted and jewelled, is the oldest royal effigy in England; it was probably made two years after the king's death in 1216. In 1797 the tomb was opened and the body found, wrapped in remains of a monk's cowl and an embroidered robe, with a sword and scabbard.*

were overwhelmed and the king was forced to flee.

Worcester porcelain was first manufactured by a Dr Wall in 1751, but the business was sold in 1783 to Thomas Flight of Hackney, London. One of the employees at the time was Robert Chamberlain, who left the firm to start a rival factory; this was so successful that in 1840 an amalgamation was arranged and in 1862 the Worcester Royal Porcelain Co. Ltd. was formed.

CATHEDRAL The cathedral occupies a memorable position overlooking the R. Severn. It is dominated by a fine 14th-century tower and much of the church belongs to this period. However, there have been buildings on this site for a far longer period. The See itself was founded in 680 when Theodore, Archbishop of Canterbury, separated off a part of the large Diocese of Lichfield. Its early history is obscure but in the late 10th century the community, formerly of secular canons, was re-founded as a monastery by Bishop Oswald, who was later canonised. It continued as a monastery until the Dissolution (1541). The earliest part of the present cathedral dates from the time of Bishop Wulfstan who, during the 1080's, began to rebuild the existing Saxon church. From his time survives a fine Romanesque crypt. Next in time comes one of the earliest circular chapter houses (c. 1120). In c. 1170 the west end of the nave was reconstructed in Transitional style. Finally, c. 1224, a complete replacement of the Romanesque church was undertaken, starting at the east end. A notable part of the cathedral is the 16th-century Prince Arthur's Chantry, built by Henry VII for his son who had died at Ludlow.

Among many things to see are fine misericords, one with a carved scene of a tournament, the monumental effigy of King John, and works by John Bacon the Younger, Sir Francis Chantrey, J. F. Moore, Joseph Nollekens, Louis Roubiliac, Thomas Stanton and other sculptors.

COMMANDERY The site of the former Commandery or Hospital of St Wulfstan—an almshouse for the aged and poor, from 1085 to 1540—was given to Richard Morrison in 1541. It then became a private residence and was used as the headquarters of the Royalists in the Battle of Worcester. The original 15th-century timber hall was retained, and later an Elizabethan staircase and 17th-century panelling were installed.

DYSON PERRINS MUSEUM This collection of Worcester ceramics of all periods, housed in a converted Victorian school dating from 1843, is regarded as the most comprehensive of its kind in the world. It is based on the collection of the factory of the Royal Worcester Porcelain Company, and on the private collection of the late Dyson Perrins. (See p. 497.)

GUILDHALL Built 1721–3 to a design by Thomas White of Worcester. The interesting façade is early Georgian. There are two statues flanking the entrance, one of Charles I, the other of Charles II, and above the doorway, indicating the city's strong Royalist favour, is a carved head of Oliver Cromwell, nailed by the ears as a token of undying enmity from the 'Faithful City'. Between the two central windows is a statuette of Queen Anne. Statues above an ornate cornice represent Justice, Peace, Plenty, Chastisement and Hercules. The Assembly Rooms are in Queen Anne style, and hung with paintings. The lower hall contains suits of armour used at the Battle of Worcester, two brass cannons, and a helmet (called 'Branks') for punishing scolding women.

Other notable buildings include Nash House, with Elizabethan half-timbered façade and street overhang, and King Charles's House (1577) in

similar style. Edgar Tower, the gateway to the cathedral green, dates from the reign of King John, 1199–1216. Sir Edward Elgar (1857–1934), composer and Master of the King's Musick (1924–34), was born at nearby Broadheath: his museum contains many mementoes and manuscripts. His compositions are a regular feature of the Three Choirs Festival.

Worksop *Notts.* 552Ee
PRIORY CHURCH OF OUR LADY AND ST CUTHBERT Founded in 1103, it has a fine Norman west front with twin towers and a unique transitional Norman nave. The Lady Chapel, with its lancet-Gothic windows, dates from the 13th century; the central lantern tower and choir were completed in 1974.

Just to the south of the priory is a magnificent early 14th-century gatehouse, with the old market cross in front of the entrance. Inside the gatehouse there is a 15th-century shrine, and a chapel of the same period. The gatehouse has ceiling beams, made of oak, which probably came from Sherwood Forest in 1314, when the Archbishop of York gave permission for 200 oaks to be felled for local building purposes.

Worlingham Hall *Suffolk* 548Eg
The exterior was built in 1725; the interior dates from 1799–1800. A notable feature is an octagonal hall with double staircase. (By appointment.)

Worstead *Norfolk* 554Dc
CHURCH OF ST MARY The church was begun during the late 14th century, and has a west tower over 100 ft high. The west window is Decorated, with reticulated tracery. Other features include a hammerbeam nave roof, canopied font cover and much screen-work—the rood screen, with painted saints, dates from 1512. There are also box-pews and 15th- and 16th-century brasses.

Worth *W. Sussex* 542Be
CHURCH OF ST NICHOLAS Probably the most interesting cruciform Saxon church in England, with an apse and high chancel arch. The north-east tower was built by Anthony Salvin in 1871, when the church was extensively restored. The font is from the 13th century: the woodwork includes a 16th-century pulpit and 17th-century gallery.

Wortham Manor *Devon* 538Ed
A fortified manor house, of 11th-century foundation, with carved oak porch, oak panelled parlour, newel staircase, and a most unusual feature, a double hall—one great room above the other.

Worthing *W. Sussex* 542Ad
MUSEUM AND ART GALLERY Housed in a building given to the town by its first mayor—Alderman Alfred Cortis—the museum has an archaeology collection including an Anglo-Saxon glass goblet, a late Bronze Age cauldron, and a Romano-British bronze boar, perhaps a hunter's religious offering. There is a comprehensive selection of 19th-century dolls and late 19th-century mechanical toys, including a praxinoscope theatre of 1879, in which a series of reflected images create an impression of movement. Also displayed are items of costume from 1740 to 1940, English marked pottery and porcelain from 1770 onward, and a display of scale ship models including a Viking ship of c. AD 900. The art gallery has a collection of English art, specialising in early English water-colours with works by W. Holman Hunt and William Callow, among others.

Worth Matravers *Dorset* 540Eb
CHURCH OF ST NICHOLAS A Norman church, with west tower, and a noteworthy chancel arch

and south doorway. The chancel was altered during the 13th century and has a fine modern east window. The interior was extensively restored in the 19th century.

Wothorpe Towers *Cambs.*   *547Hh*
Wothorpe ruins, *c.* 1620, are all that remain of the cruciform house originally built for Thomas Cecil, eldest son of Lord Burghley, for use as a lodge until his great house Burghley, at Stamford, was completed. It fell into ruin during the 18th century; the towers, with an octagonal top storey, are still well preserved. A gateway with a stepped gable leads to the courtyard.

Wotton *Surrey*   *542Af*
CHURCH OF ST JOHN The 13th-century church retains its 11th-century tower. The north chapel is the burial place of the family of John Evelyn, the 17th-century diarist, who lived near by, and contains many monuments. St John's was restored during the 19th century. (By appointment.)

Wotton House *Bucks.*   *547Gd*
A country mansion built 1704–14. The only historic house built to the same plan as Buckingham House, which later became Buckingham Palace. The interior was remodelled by Sir John Soane, the Regency architect, in 1820. There is magnificent wrought ironwork by Jean Tijou and Thomas Robinson, and grounds landscaped by Lancelot 'Capability' Brown.

Wraxall *Avon*   *540Cg*
CHURCH OF ALL SAINTS All that remains of the original Norman church is the south doorway; the rest of the church is mainly of the 14th and 15th centuries, with a pinnacled west tower. There is 19th-century glass by C. E. Kempe, and a coloured late 15th-century monument with recumbent effigies and shield-bearing angels.

GATES BY THE DAVIES BROTHERS

Robert and John Davies made these wrought-iron gates about 1720, repeating elements of the chancel gates inside the church, made by Hugh Davies, who was their father. The brothers are said to have worked under the French smith Tijou and their work shows traces of his influence. (Church of St Giles, Wrexham)

Wrekin, The *Salop*   *552Ab*
This great Iron Age fort crowns a hill commanding the Vale of the Upper Severn. The defences are rather complicated, but the basic structure is a bank enclosing a long oval of some 7 acres. The protection given by this bank is aided by artificial scarping of the hillside. At each end there are additional earthworks which increase the enclosed area by about half.

Wrenbury *Cheshire*   *552Ad*
CHURCH OF ST MARGARET A pleasant church, with an early 16th-century west tower, and 18th-century chancel, pulpit and west gallery. Among the 19th-century monuments are some by John Bacon the Younger and William Theed the Younger.

Wrest Park *Beds.*   *547He*
A mansion in French château style, now used by the National Institute of Agricultural Engineering. There is a fine formal garden beside the canal. (Interior not open.)

Wrexham *Clwyd*   *551Jd*
CHURCH OF ST GILES A 14th-century church, with additions of the 15th and 16th centuries and a Decorated interior. It has one of the most glorious parish church towers in the British Isles —tall, massive, pinnacled and smothered in tracery. St Giles's is rich in 18th-century monuments, among them being work by William Stanton, Louis Roubiliac and P. M. Van Gelder. The chancel gates are by Hugh Davies, father of the makers of the wrought-iron gates to the church.
EXHIBITION HALL AND WREXHAM ROOM (PUBLIC LIBRARY) Items relating to Wrexham and the surrounding area, including books and manuscripts, are displayed in the Wrexham Room. Travelling exhibitions, including art exhibitions, are shown in the Hall.

Writtle *Essex*   *548Bc*
THE GREEN Writtle, on the outskirts of Chelmsford, has a most attractive green. To the south, with the church behind them, are Aubyns, a small timbered house of *c.* 1500 (much restored) and Mundays, 17th century, with shell-hooded front door. West of the village is Moor Hall, a moated 15th-century house.

Wroxeter *Salop*   *552Ab*
In the early days of the Roman conquest, a legionary fortress was established here. It covered the entrance to the Border hills along the Severn Valley and the link with the R. Trent frontier to the north-east. When the legion was moved to Chester, its military purpose was served and, in due course, it became the cantonal town, Viroconium Cornoviorum, of the Cornovii tribe. Parts of the Roman town are still visible and there is a museum.
CHURCH OF ST ANDREW The church incorporates Roman masonry. The font is probably made from a piece of a Roman column. The Normans built the church, but there is also later work: the pulpit and box-pews are Jacobean, and there are four impressive monuments, three with effigies, from 1555 to 1708.

Wroxton *Oxon.*   *546Ee*
CHURCH A spacious Gothic church, the west tower rebuilt in the 18th century. Inside are 17th- and 18th-century monuments, including an imposing one to Lord Downe, *c.* 1631, with effigies under a canopy on black marble pillars. A monument by

John Flaxman, *c.* 1802, in memory of the politician Lord North (*d.* 1792), shows Britannia and a lion.

Wroxton Abbey *Oxon.* 546Ee
A Jacobean stone house, for centuries the home of the North family which included the 8th Lord North, Prime Minister 1770–82. It was built in 1618 by Sir William Pope, and incorporates remains of a 13th-century Augustinian priory.

Wye *Kent* 542Ef
The college, now an agricultural college adjoining the church, was founded in 1447. To the south lies the town, the houses unusually uniform and small in scale, mostly 17th century, with grotesque figures in the porches. (By appointment.)

Wymington *Beds.* 547Hf
CHURCH OF ST LAURENCE Built in 1377 by John Curteys in Decorated style and has a good ornamented tower and spire. It has square-headed side windows, turrets at the east end and the whole is spanned by a single roof. There are the remains of a Doom painting, fine old pews, fragments of colour on the capitals and arches and famous brasses of the founder of the church and his wife, a knight and his lady and a former rector. That of the knight is over 6 ft in length.

Wymondham *Norfolk* 554Cb
CHURCH OF SS MARY AND THOMAS OF CANTERBURY Roughly half of the former abbey church, now with a tower at both east and west ends. The abbey was founded in 1107, and the church was a major Norman building of which the nave arcades remain. The founder intended the nave to be parochial but, as in other cases where a church was shared, there was perpetual disagreement. At Wymondham the dispute was over the tower, so the abbey built the octagonal tower, *c.* 1400, at the present east end, whilst *c.* 1448 the parish built the west tower, and the nave was sealed off by a roof-high wall. There is a Perpendicular clerestory, and beautiful hammerbeam roofs decorated with angels and star-bosses. After the Dissolution, stone from the ruined abbey was used to rebuild the south aisle, 1544–60. There is much else to see, including the ornate modern reredos, *c.* 1935, by Sir Ninian Comper.

Wynnstay Hall *Clwyd* 551Jd
This modern building, styled as a French château, replaces the Hall destroyed by fire in 1858. In its great hall, with its ornate ceiling and a carved oak fire-place, is a rare Snetzler organ made in 1774. Since 1950, the Hall has been a school.

Y Z

Yalding *Kent* 542Df
Two tributaries join the R. Medway at Yalding, and two fine medieval stone bridges span them. The village rises gently to the north. The brick of the houses is varied in colour, especially the velvety-plum of the Old House, and the orangey Holborough House opposite. Both were built *c.* 1700, the period of the most adventurous brickwork in south-eastern England.

Yardhurst *Kent* 542Ee
A recently restored timbered house near Great Chart, built *c.* 1420. It has an oversailing upper floor and mullioned windows. (By appointment.)

Yarnton *Oxon.* 546Fd
CHURCH OF ST BARTHOLOMEW The original Norman church was enlarged in the 13th century and added to in the 17th century. It contains many interesting features: medieval glass, a 17th-century pulpit, screen, and fine monuments to the Spencer family in their chapel—also 17th century.

Yate *Avon* 546Bb
CHURCH OF ST MARY An impressive Perpendicular west tower dominates this low-built church: it is buttressed and pinnacled, and has a large stair-turret. Inside is a brass of 1590 to a man, two wives and 11 children, and several wall monuments. There is also a 14th-century font.

Yateley *Hants.* 541Jf
CHURCH OF ST PETER Of Saxon origin, but almost totally destroyed by fire in 1979. The Saxon north wall has survived, as have the 13th-century chancel and the 15th-century brick-and-timber tower. The 15th-century timber porch has a figure of St John, and there are some brasses and early tiles from the restored anchorite cell.

Yatton *Avon* 540Cf
CHURCH OF ST MARY The south porch of this impressive 14th- and 15th-century church is

highly decorated. There are transepts and the tower is central. Inside are several monuments, spanning the centuries. A Chapter House was added in 1975.

YEAVERING BELL

Snow clearly picks out the stone rampart of this hill-fort on top of Yeavering Bell—one of the Cheviot Hills—which rises to 1182 ft. The rampart encloses nearly 14 acres and has three entrances.

Yaxley *Cambs.*   *547Jg*
CHURCH OF ST PETER A cruciform church, with a
west tower crowned by pinnacles and a flying-
buttressed spire. Inside there is a 13th-century font,
a 15th-century screen and stalls, and medieval
wall-paintings.

Yeavering Bell *Northld.*   *562Fc*
A large Iron Age fort for this part of the country.
A stone rampart encircles the hill-top along its
contours and there are three entrances. The east
entrance has a protecting outer wall. Inside the
fort are the visible foundations of about 130
circular or oval houses. (See p. 501.)

Yeovil *Som.*   *540Cd*
YEOVIL DISTRICT COUNCIL MUSEUM, HENDFORD
MANOR HOUSE Housed in a converted coach-
house and stables once attached to Hendford
Manor House, the museum specialises in items of
local interest—archaeology from the Westland
and Lufton sites, prints and engravings, and local
industry. Also on view is the Henry Stiby Collection of fire-arms and an exhibition of costume.
CHURCH OF ST JOHN THE BAPTIST A large, late
14th-century town church; a fine Perpendicular
building, with west tower, large windows, and
transepts. There is a vaulted crypt under the
chancel. Among the many monuments is one by
Sir Richard Westmacott, *c.* 1855, with a life-size
half-figure. The brass lectern is *c.* 1450.

Yeovilton *Som.*   *540Ce*
FLEET AIR ARM MUSEUM Traces the history of
naval aviation from 1903 to the present day. There
are over 40 historic aircraft on display, some of
which still fly, a unique collection of aircraft and
ship models as well as exhibitions of photographs,
medals and documents. Concorde 002 is on display
in a hall connected to the museum.

Yetminster *Dorset*   *540Cd*
CHURCH OF ST ANDREW The chancel was built *c.*
1300, but the rest of the church, with a west tower,
is 15th century. Inside, the roofs still retain some of
their painted decoration. A brass with figures dates
from *c.* 1531, and there are a number of wall
monuments, mainly of the 17th and 18th centuries.
Some of the benches are 15th century.

Y Gaer Fawr *Dyfed*   *545Gd*
This is one of the largest Iron Age hill-forts in
Wales, the enclosed area being some 25 acres. Its
single massive ramparts have collapsed. The
defences did not include banks and ditches and
had simple entrances. To the north is an annex
with thinner walls.

Ynys y Pandy Slate Mill *Gwynedd*   *550Ed*
This little-known building, which forms a most
dramatic ruin against the sky, housed machinery
for cutting and dressing slate from the quarries
above Cwm-Ystradlyn, which was brought down
by tramway into the second floor. Finished slates
were loaded on to a tramway leading out of the
floor below, and eventually carried down to the
sea at Porthmadog. This building is planned
around a large water-wheel placed across the
centre, with long side-shafts driving the machinery
above.

York *N. Yorks.*   *558Eb*
The Romans came to York in AD 71, and set up a
legionary fortress, originally with a wooden
palisade, but shortly afterwards with stone walls.
The Roman occupation lasted 340 years, and the
city (raised to colony status) was visited by the
Emperors Hadrian, Severus and Constantius. A
small Christian community had assembled in the
late 2nd century and their bishop went to the
Council of Arles in AD 314. The See, overturned by
the Saxons, was restored under the influence of
Pope Gregory who created Paulinus bishop in 625.
The city then became a centre of learning with a
Saxon equivalent of a university: its head, Alcuin,
a Yorkshireman, was called by Charlemagne to
run his palace school at Aachen in 782. The city
changed its character with the coming of the Danes
who captured it in 867, and again radically when it
was destroyed by fire in 1069, enabling the
Normans to plan a new town. The Roman walled
city became five times larger, and behind new
defences a major fortress became established
between 1250 and 1300. Inside an area of 263 acres
people were crammed tightly; and York city
boundaries contained 40 churches, nine chapels,
four monasteries, four friaries, 16 hospitals, and
nine guildhalls for trade and fraternity. The city
became a major wool centre.

POSSET CUP

*York, for centuries the chief city of
northern England, possessed a fine
collection of official plate and
insignia. Many of these treasures
were lost over the years, especially
during the Civil War when the city
probably had to sell its plate to raise
money. Afterwards, city officials
rebuilt the collection, some of the
finest pieces being added in the 18th
century. This fluted silver posset cup,
one of a pair, bears the mark of the
maker—Seth Lofthouse of London
—and the year when it was made
and given, 1702. The inscription
says that it was given by the Lord
Mayor of York in 1702 to replace
a similar cup given by Leonard
Besson, who twice held the office of
mayor, in 1614 and 1626.
(Mansion House, York)*

With the decline of the wool trade and the Dissolution of the monasteries, York declined, but was revived in the 18th century when many of its medieval houses were pulled down to make way for Georgian dwellings; it further increased in prosperity in the 19th century when it became a railway centre, as it still is. Nevertheless, the medieval walls remained almost intact: the Multangular Tower dates from the beginning of the 4th century and—standing in the Museum Gardens—is a testimony to Roman stonework. Four great bars or gates commanded (as they still do) the main roads to the city: Micklegate bridged the road to the south, Bootham the road to the north, Monk the road to Scarborough, and Walmgate to Hull. These great gateways had almost every medieval device for defence, with drawbridges, portcullises, barbicans, watch towers, and guard-rooms. An existing royal charter of 1155–62 refers to an earlier one granted by Henry I.

St William's College was founded in 1461 for chantry priests; it is a fine half-timbered house with stone gateway. It was restored *c.* 1900 and is now the meeting place for the Northern Convocation. The Merchant Taylors' Hall dates from the 14th century and has been in the hands of the Craft of Tailors since at least 1415. The Merchant Adventurers built a great hall in 1357–68; it has a remarkable timber roof.

ASSEMBLY ROOMS Built 1731–2 by public subscription to designs by the Earl of Burlington, they became a great centre of fashionable society. The central hall measures 112 ft by 40 ft, the roof being supported by 52 Corinthian columns, and resembles the Egyptian Room of the Mansion House in London.

CASTLE MUSEUM One of the leading folk museums of the country and illustrating Yorkshire life during the past 400 years. The original Kirk collection contains the famous series of Victorian streets reconstructed from original shop fronts and complete with cobbles, lamp-posts, cabs, fire engines and a stage coach. A series of rooms covers the period from Jacobean to Victorian, with a barn interior to house agricultural equipment. In the Green Gallery are Georgian and Victorian fans, card cases, watches, and domestic and personal ornaments. In the Chapel Gallery are unique collections of fire insurance marks, constables' truncheons and tipstaves, and an assortment of oddities from church alms boxes to Victorian backboards. In the Music Gallery are such minstrel instruments as the serpent, bassoon and ophicleide, a virginal of 1651, a harpsichord of 1789, and a Johannes Player spinet, as well as harps and wind instruments. The Hearth Gallery has period fire-places, grates and hearth furniture.

The adjoining Debtors' Prison, built by Sir John Vanbrugh in 1705, is now an extension of the Castle Museum. The second floor is devoted to the history of the regular and volunteer forces associated with the county of Yorkshire, and there is an extensive collection of arms and armour covering four centuries. The first floor houses costumes and toys, and the felons' cells on the ground floor have been converted into craft workshops. Behind the Debtors' Prison a water-driven corn mill from Raindale has been re-erected on the banks of the R. Foss.

CHURCH OF ALL SAINTS, NORTH STREET The arcades are *c.* 1350; the roofs to the south aisle and chancel *c.* 1450. The rood, parclose screens and vestry are 20th-century additions. It has some fine medieval glass and a variety of *objets d'art.*

CHURCH OF ALL SAINTS, PAVEMENT Mainly of the 15th century, the church lost part of its east end in

'PRYKKE OF CONSCIENCE'
WINDOW

Designed in the mid-15th century, this window shows that not all old stained glass was designed to illustrate biblical scenes. Intended as a warning of what was to come, it depicts the 'Last 15 Days of the World' in 15 subject panels. The scenes, with accompanying texts, are based on the 'Prykke of Conscience' written in the Northumbrian dialect by the English mystic Richard Rolle in 1325. This panel depicts the 14th day (top) when death comes to claim all mortals, and the 11th day (bottom) when men emerge from their shelters and pray for help.
(Church of All Saints, North Street, York)

the late 18th century as a result of an early road widening scheme. The west tower, with an octagonal lantern, was rebuilt during the first half of the 19th century. There is a fine canopied pulpit of the 17th century, and a 15th-century lectern.

CITY OF YORK ART GALLERY Founded in 1879, it was re-opened in 1948 after rebuilding necessitated by bombing in 1942. In 1955 it was augmented by the Lycett Green Collection of 120 paintings by European masters of the 14th–19th centuries. The major European art movements from 1350 to 1800 are represented by works by Daddi, Guardi, Lely, Reynolds and Domenichino, among others. A selection of English paintings from 1890 to 1910 includes works by Whistler, Sickert and Wilson Steer; there is also a large collection of paintings by William Etty. Of particular interest and importance is the world-renowned Milner-White Collection of stoneware pottery which includes work by Bernard Leach, Hamada, Staite Murray and others. Topographical prints and water-colours can be seen by appointment.

CLIFFORD'S TOWER The Normans raised two fortresses on artificial mounds, one each side of the river. That on the west has disappeared without a trace except for the mound or motte known as Baile Hill. The existing tower is 13th century, erected to replace the wooden Norman keep burnt down in the Jewish riots of 1190.

GUILDHALL Built in 1456–9 by the city and the Guild of SS Christopher and George. It was largely demolished by fire-bombs in 1942. The restored guildhall opened in 1960. (See p. 502.)

JORVIK VIKING CENTRE The town that the Danes called Jorvik—today's York—is brought to life as the visitor journeys in a 'time car' along Coppergate, a reconstructed Viking street—past the shops of a jeweller, cobbler and stone carver, by a busy wharf, and even through a Viking living room. A gallery displays hundreds of everyday objects found on the site, from musical instruments, jewellery, and gamblers' dice to keys, combs, shoes, and a woollen sock.

MANSION HOUSE Built 1725–30: it houses a magnificent collection of silver, and is the home of the lord mayor. Behind it is the guildhall, built 1448, but largely destroyed by bombs in 1942 and carefully restored in 1960.

MINSTER When the mission of St Augustine came to convert England in 597, it carried instructions that the new church was to be governed from the former Roman capitals of London and York. The Archbishopric of London never materialised but that of York was successfully established by St Paulinus. The church itself was placed probably on the site of the Roman military headquarters and the present cathedral is the successor of this first tiny building. Evidence of the intermediate buildings may be seen in the crypt, in particular the surviving lower parts of some impressive late 12th-century piers and, at the lowest level, fragments of the Roman buildings underlying the whole site. The present cathedral, the largest Gothic church in England, dates from the 13th century, but building extended well into the 15th century. The last major additions, the western towers, were finished in 1472. The octagonal chapter house (built in 1260–1307) is outstanding: the huge vault span is unsupported by any central column.

NATIONAL RAILWAY MUSEUM In 1975, the exhibits from the York Railway Museum and those from the Museum of British Transport in London were combined to form the National Railway Museum. Among the engines on display is *Mallard,* which in 1938 set the still-unbroken steam record of 126 mph, and many other beloved veterans in the brilliant liveries of long-vanished companies. Rolling stock includes Queen Adelaide's coach of 1842 and Queen Victoria's saloon of 1869, complete with upholstered washroom. Nameplates, signals, posters, locomotive and station equipment, tickets, maps and timetables are also on show.

ROMAN LEGIONARY FORTRESS York, the ancient capital of the North, began its effective life as Eburacum, when the new legionary fortress of the 9th Legion was sited here on the left bank of the Ouse in AD 71. More than once it was assaulted and severely damaged, and its defences were remodelled and renewed many times. One of these attacks took place about the beginning of the 4th century and the fine Multangular Tower, which can still be inspected, was the Roman response to it. This was the external bastion at the western angle, one end of the ornate face which fronted the Ouse. Other parts of the walls are to be found and a fine collection of small remains is in the Yorkshire Museum.

ST ANTHONY'S HALL Built 1446–53 with two storeys, it became a workhouse after 1551, and later a gaol, school, armoury and meeting place for minor guilds. The Hall is now the base of the Borthwick Institute.

ST MARY'S ABBEY The 11th-century abbey is now only a ruin, but these remains are impressive, with much dating from the 13th century still visible.

TREASURER'S HOUSE A house built on the site of the official residence of the Treasurer to York Minster. Some 13th-century work survives in the vaults but the house was rebuilt in 1620.

YORKSHIRE MUSEUM A neo-Classical building designed by William Wilkins as a museum for the Yorkshire Philosophical Society and opened in 1830. The main collections include extensive archaeological material from Roman York, specimens from every geological period, and a wide range of natural-history exhibits.

Youlgreave *Derbys.* 552De
CHURCH OF ALL SAINTS An impressive church, with a Norman nave and a tall Perpendicular west tower. Restoration in 1870 was by R. Norman Shaw. The circular Norman font has a separate basin projecting from one side. The church contains stained glass by Sir Edward Burne-Jones.

Zennor *Cornwall* 538Ab
WAYSIDE MUSEUM Collections in this folk museum relate to the local trades and industries of mining, quarrying, fishing, farming, and the craft of the blacksmith. There is a fine collection of old ploughs, an original open hearth and a model of a typical Cornish tin mine, with a mill and process plant. Also on view are archaeological items of the region: stone axes, stone tools, querns and models of archaeological remains.

Zennor Quoit *Cornwall* 538Ab
This chamber tomb is of a type known as a Portal Dolmen, which is characterised by an upright stone partly or completely blocking the entrance. The Zennor tomb was probably once buried beneath a mound, but no trace of this remains.

THE GREAT EAST WINDOW
YORK MINSTER

This window, 77 ft high and 32 ft wide, is the largest single area of ancient stained glass in England. John Thornton of Coventry, who designed and made the panels between 1405 and 1408, was paid £56 for his three years' work. Of the 117 main panels, 81 illustrate the Revelation of St John: the one above shows the Dragon giving the sceptre to the Beast (Rev. xiii 2).

FAMOUS PEOPLE

Their works and whereabouts

In the crumbling ruins of an old castle, the crude medical instruments used by the *Victory's* surgeon at Trafalgar, or the ivory-handled pen which Hardy used to write his novels, there is an intangible quality—something that evokes more than a mere sense of the past. It is as if these places and things have been endowed with a living presence by the men and women they represent, whether despotic ruler or humble craftsman. This section of the book lists the places associated with the people who have influenced the quality and character of our artistic heritage.

ARCHITECTS

Architecture is said to be the youngest of the arts, since it was only comparatively late in man's nomadic existence that he sought a substitute for the cave or natural shelter. The architect, though, is more than a man who piles stone upon stone until he ends up with what is simply a more sophisticated cave. The great cathedrals of the land, the stately homes, even some of the factories, are massive if silent witnesses to the architect's passion to give a building grandeur, permanence and beauty—in other words, to make it a work of art—and at the same time make the space people live in a medium of expression.

Adam Bros.
Bury St Edmunds, Suffolk
Stamford, Lincs.

Adam, James
Hertford, Herts. Fore Street

Adam, John
Banff, Grampian

Adam, Robert
Alnwick Castle, Northld.
Bath, Avon Pulteney Bridge
Binley, W. Midlands Church of
  St Bartholomew
Brockhall, Northants.
Burton Constable, Humberside
Castle Upton, Antrim
Culzean Castle, Strathclyde
Edinburgh, Lothian General
  Register House
Fort George, Highland Regimental
  Museum of The Seaforth High-
  landers, The Queen's Own
  Cameron Highlanders and Queen's
  Own Highlanders

Gifford, Lothian Yester House
Gunton, Norfolk Church of St
  Andrew
Harewood House, W. Yorks.
Hatchlands, Surrey
Headfort House, Meath.
Hopetoun House, Lothian
Kedleston Hall, Derbys.
Kimbolton Castle, Cambs.
London Hyde Park Corner;
  Kenwood (Iveagh Bequest);
  Royal Hospital
Mellerstain, Borders
Milton Abbas, Dorset Abbey
Newby Hall, N. Yorks.
Nostell Priory, W. Yorks.
*Osterley Park House, Greater
  London*
Saltram House, Devon
Stowe, Bucks.
Syon House, Greater London

Adam, William
Aberdeen, Grampian Robert
  Gordon's College

Aberfeldy, Tayside General Wade's
  Bridge
Banff, Grampian Duff House
Haddo House, Grampian
Mellerstain, Borders
Pollokshaws, Strathclyde Pollok
  House

Ahrends, Peter
Dublin, Dublin Trinity College

Aitchison, George
London Leighton House

Allen, John
Jigginstown House, Kild.

Allen, W. Godfrey
London Church of St Bride

Allison, Sir Richard
London Science Museum

Anderson, John
Fermoy, Cork

Angus, George
Dundee, Tayside High School

Archer, Thomas
Beningbrough Hall, N. Yorks.
Birmingham, W. Midlands Cathedral
Hale Park, Hants.

Ashlin, George
Ballintober, Mayo Augustinian
  Friary
Cobh, Cork
Dublin, Dublin Church of SS
  Augustine and John
Longford, Long.
Tralee, Kerry
Tullira Castle, Gal.

Atkins, William
Killarney, Kerry Muckross
  House

Atkinson, Thomas
Brandsby, N. Yorks. Church of All
  Saints
Coxwold, N. Yorks. Church of St
  Michael

Bachup, Tobias
Dumfries, Dumfs. & Gall. Mid Steeple

Baker, Henry Aaron
Derry, Lond. Walker Monument
Kells, Meath.

Baldwin, Thomas
Bath, Avon Guildhall; Pump Room

Bardwell, William
Glenstal Castle, Lim.

Barre, W. J.
Belfast, Antrim

Barry, Sir Charles
Brighton, E. Sussex Church of St Peter
Cliveden, Bucks.
Halifax, W. Yorks. Town Hall
Harewood House, W. Yorks.
Leeds, W. Yorks. Town Hall
London Houses of Parliament;
  Lancaster House
Manchester, Greater Manchester City
  Museum
Salford, Greater Manchester Science
  Museum
Stand, Greater Manchester Church of
  All Saints

Barry, E. M.
London Royal Opera House

Bastard, John
Blandford Forum, Dorset Almshouses;
  Church of SS Peter and Paul; Old
  House; Town Hall

Bastard, William
Blandford Forum, Dorset

Batt, William
Belfast, Antrim

Baxter, John
Fochabers, Grampian

Bell, Henry
King's Lynn, Norfolk Custom House;
  Tuesday Market-place
North Runcton, Norfolk Church of
  All Saints

Bentley, John Francis
London Church of St Botolph;
  Westminster Cathedral

Bindon, Francis
Belan House, Kild.
Carnelly House, Clare
Clermont, Wicklow
Drogheda, Louth
Forenaghts (Furness) House, Kild.
Howth Castle, Dublin
Kilkenny, Kilk.
Limerick, Lim.
Newhall House, Clare
Russborough House, Wicklow

Blomfield, Sir Arthur
Alveley, Salop Church of St Mary
Bridgnorth, Salop Church of St Mary
  Magdalene
Halstead, Essex Church of St Andrew
Ludlow, Salop Church of St
  Laurence

Blore, Edward
Capesthorne, Cheshire
Castlewellan, Down
Crom Castle, Ferm.
Oxford, Oxon. Sheldonian Theatre
Thorney, Cambs. Church of SS Mary
  and Botolph

Blow, Detmar
Onibury, Salop Church of St Michael

Bodley, G. F.
Brant Broughton, Lincs. Church of St
  Helen
Cuckfield, W. Sussex Church of the
  Holy Trinity
Deene, Northants. Church of St
  Peter
Leicester, Leics. Cathedral
London Church of St John
North Stoneham, Hants. Church of St
  Nicholas
Scarborough, N. Yorks. Church of St
  Martin
Weston-super-Mare, Avon Church of
  All Saints
Whitkirk, W. Yorks. Church of St
  Mary

Bonomi, Joseph
Great Packington, Warks. Church

Boulger, James
Dublin, Dublin St Andrew's

Bowden, John
Belfast, Antrim Church of St
  George
Cavan, Cavan
Derry, Lond. Bishop Street
Dublin, Dublin Church of St Stephen

Boyle, Richard
Lismore, Waterford

Brandon, David
Hatfield, Herts. Church of St
  Etheldreda
Leicester, Leics. Cathedral

Brettingham, Matthew
Kedleston Hall, Derbys.
King's Lynn, Norfolk Church of St
  Margaret

Brettingham, R. F.
Hillsborough, Down

Brodrick, Cuthbert
Leeds, W. Yorks. Town Hall

Brooks, W.
Dudley, W. Midlands Church of St Thomas the Apostle

Brown, Capability
Claremont, Surrey
Slane, Meath Castle

Browne, Robert
Kew, Greater London Church of St Anne

Browne, Wogan
Malahide Castle, Dublin

Bruce, Sir George
Culross, Fife Palace

Bruce, Sir William
Drumlanrig Castle, Dumfs. & Gall.
Edinburgh, Lothian Palace of Holyroodhouse
Hopetoun House, Lothian
Kinross, Tayside Kinross House
Thirlstane Castle, Borders

Bryce, David
Blair Castle, Tayside

Burges, William
Cardiff Castle, S. Glam.
Castell Coch, S. Glam.
Cork, Cork
Studley Royal, N. Yorks. Church of St Mary

Burgh, Thomas
Celbridge, Kild.
Dublin, Dublin Church of St Werburgh; Steeven's Hospital; Trinity College
Naas, Kild.

Burke, John
Granard, Long.
Longford, Long.

Burlington, Lord
Boynton Hall, Humberside
Holkham Hall, Norfolk
London Chiswick House
Sevenoaks, Kent

Burn, William
Killarney, Kerry Muckross House
Pitcaple, Grampian

Burton, Decimus
Kew, Greater London Palm House, Royal Botanic Gardens
London Hyde Park Corner
Royal Tunbridge Wells, Kent

Burton, Peter
Dublin, Dublin Trinity College

Butler, William Deane
Kilkenny, Kilk.

Butterfield, William
Alvechurch, Heref. & Worcs. Church of St Lawrence
Amesbury, Wilts. Church of SS Mary and Melor
Baldersby, N. Yorks. Church of St James
Berkhamsted, Herts. Church of St Peter
Canterbury, Kent St Augustine's Abbey
Clyffe Pypard, Wilts. Church of St Peter
Heytesbury, Wilts. Church of SS Peter and Paul

Huddersfield, W. Yorks. Churches of St Thomas the Apostle and of St John
London Church of All Saints; Church of St Mary Woolnoth
St Bees, Cumbria Church of SS Mary and Bega
Salisbury, Wilts. Theological College
Trumpington, Cambs. Church of SS Mary and Michael

Byrne, Patrick
Arklow, Wicklow
Dublin, Dublin St Paul's, Arran Quay

Byrne, William
Loughrea, Gal.

Campbell, Colin
London Chiswick House
Mereworth Castle, Kent

Campion, Henry
Danny, W. Sussex

Carr, James
London Church of St James

Carr, John
Boynton, Humberside Church of St Andrew
Boynton Hall, Humberside
Bradford, W. Yorks. Bolling Hall
Burton Constable, Humberside
Cannon Hall, S. Yorks.
Castle Howard, N. Yorks.
Harewood House, W. Yorks.
Kendal, Cumbria Abbot Hall Art Gallery
Rotherham, S. Yorks. Municipal Museum and Art Gallery
Thoresby Hall, Notts.

Carter, John
Debden, Essex Church of St Mary the Virgin and All Saints

Casson, Sir Hugh
London Regent's Park

Castle, Richard
Ardbraccan House, Meath
Athlone, Westmeath
Ballinter House, Meath
Belan House, Kild.
Belvedere House, Westmeath
Carton, Kild.
Cashel, Rock of, Tipp. Cross of St Patrick
Dublin, Dublin Leinster House; Rotunda; St Stephen's Green; Trinity College; Tyrone House
Duleek, Meath
Dunlavin, Wicklow
Frenchpark House, Roscom.
Gillhall House, Down
Hazelwood House, Sligo
Ledwithstown House, Long.
Newbridge House, Dublin
Newry, Down
Powerscourt House, Wicklow
Rathbeale, Dublin
Russborough House, Wicklow
Sligo, Sligo
Strokestown House, Roscom.
Waterford, Waterford
Westport, Mayo

Cecil, William
Burghley House, Cambs.

Chambers, Sir William
Ampthill, Beds. Avenue House
Dublin, Dublin Casino Marino; Parnell Square
Kew, Greater London Pagoda, Royal Botanic Gardens
London Church of St Mary, Marylebone Road; Somerset House

507

Lucan House, Dublin
Milton Abbey, Dorset
Rathfarnham Castle, Dublin
Slane, Meath Castle
Wilton House, Wilts.

Chiswell, R.
Debden, Essex Church of St Mary the
Virgin and All Saints

Clements, Nathaniel
Beauparc, Meath
Dublin, Dublin Phoenix Park
Lodge Park, Kild.
Newbury Hall, Kild.

Coakley
Cork, Cork

Cobden, Thomas A.
Carlow, Carlow

Cockerell, C. R.
Lampeter, Dyfed St David's College
Liverpool, Merseyside St George's Hall

Cockerell, S. P.
Tickencote, Leics. Church of St Peter

Coke, Thomas
Holkham Hall, Norfolk

Cole, Sir Henry
London Victoria and Albert
Museum

Collcutt, T. E.
London Imperial Institute Tower

Comper, Sir Ninian
Chicheley, Bucks. Church of St
Laurence
Egmanton, Notts. Church of St
Mary
Eye, Suffolk Church of SS Peter and
Paul
High Melton, S. Yorks. Church of St
James
Lound, Suffolk Church of St John
the Baptist
Stanton, Glos. Church of St Michael
and All Angels

Cooley, Thomas
Armagh, Arm.
Ballymackenny, Louth
Caledon House, Tyrone
Dublin, Dublin City Hall; Four
Courts
Kells, Meath

Corbett, W. E.
Limerick, Lim.

Cottingham, Lewis
Armagh, Arm.

Cubitt, Thomas
Osborne House, Isle of Wight
Polesden Lacy, Surrey

Cundy, Thomas
Normanton, Leics. Church of St
Matthew

Dance, George, the Elder
London Church of St Botolph;
Mansion House

Davis, Whitmore
Charleville House, Wicklow

Deane, Kearns
Cork, Cork

Deane, Sir Thomas
Cork, Cork
Dublin, Dublin Church of St Anne;
Kildare Street Club; Leinster
House; Trinity College
Oxford, Oxon. University
Museum
Tuam, Gal. Protestant Cathedral

de Courcy, John
Carrickfergus, Antrim

de Lacy, Hugh
Carrickfergus, Antrim

de l'Orme, Philibert
London Somerset House

Dobson, John
Newcastle upon Tyne, Tyne & Wear

Donowell, John
West Wycombe Park, Bucks.

Drew, Sir Thomas
Belfast, Antrim

Ducart, Davis
Castletown House, Kilk.
Cork, Cork
Florence Court, Ferm.
Kilshannig House, Cork
Limerick, Lim.

Duff, Thomas
Armagh, Arm.
Belfast, Antrim St Malachy's Catholic
Church; Old Museum

Eden, F. C.
Weston-super-Mare, Avon Church of
All Saints

Edwards, William
Pontypridd, Mid. Glam. Pontypridd
Bridge

Elliot, Archibald
Glasgow, Strathclyde Royal Bank of
Scotland and Royal Exchange
Square

Elmes, Harvey Lonsdale
Liverpool, Merseyside St George's Hall

Ensor, George
Armagh, Arm.

Ensor, John
Dublin, Dublin Northland House
(Royal Irish Academy); Merrion
Square

Farrell, William
Carrick on Shannon, Leit.
Portaferry, Down.

Fetherston, John
Packwood House, Warks.

Fitz, Sir Thomas
Windsor, Berks. Windsor Guildhall
Exhibition

Fitzwalter, Theobald
Nenagh, Tipp.

Flitcroft, Henry
Ditchley Park, Oxon.
Stourhead, Wilts.
Wimpole, Cambs. Church of St
Andrew
Woburn Abbey, Beds.

Flower, William
Castle Durrow, Laois

Fogarty, J.
Limerick, Lim.

Fogerty, William
Limerick, Lim.

Fontana, Carlo
Derby, Derbys. Cathedral

Forsyth, W.
Hillsborough, Down

Fowke, Francis
Dublin, Dublin Merrion Square
London Victoria and Albert
Museum

Fowler, James
Louth, Lincs. Church of St James

Galilei, Alessandro
Celbridge, Kild. Castletown
Drumcondra, Dublin

Gandon, James
Bishopscourt House, Kild.
Coolbanagher, Laois
Daingean, Offaly
Drumcondra, Dublin
Dublin, Dublin Custom House; Four
Courts; King's Inns; O'Connell
Bridge; Old Parliament House;
Phoenix Park
Emo Court, Laois
Longford, Long.
Port Laoise, Laois
Slane, Meath Castle

Garner, Thomas
Beaudesert, Warks. Church of St
Nicholas

Gibbs, James
Bristol, Avon Church of All Saints
Cambridge, Cambs. Senate House
Derby, Derbys. Cathedral
Ditchley Park, Oxon.
Kirkleatham, Cleveland Church of St
Cuthbert
London Church of St Clement
Danes; Church of St Martin-in-
the-Fields; Church of St Mary-le-
Strand
Oxford, Oxon. Radcliffe Camera
Petersham, Greater London
Ragley Hall, Warks.
Shrewsbury, Salop Church of St Chad

Gibson, John
Charlecote, Warks. Church of St
Leonard

Godwin, Edward William
Dromore Castle, Lim.
London Bedford Park
Northampton, Northants. Town
Hall

Goldie, George
Clonmel, Tipp.
Limerick, Lim.

Goodhart-Rendel, H.
Idsworth, Hants. Church of St
Hubert

Goodwin, Francis
Bilston, W. Midlands Church of St
Leonard

Graham, James Gillespie
Elgin, Grampian Gray's Hospital

Griffiths, Sir Richard
Dublin, Dublin Merrion Square

Guy, Thomas
Tamworth, Staffs.

Hague, William
Letterkenny, Don.

Halfpenny, William
Boyle, Roscom. Boyle Barrack

Hamilton, David
Falkirk, Central Steeple
Glasgow, Strathclyde Hutcheson's
Hospital; Royal Bank of Scotland;
Stirling's Library

Hamilton, James
Belfast, Antrim

Hamilton, John
Barncluith, Strathclyde

Hamilton, Thomas
Ayr, Strathclyde Town Hall

Harding, James
Froyle, Hants. Church of the
Assumption

Hardwick, P. C.
Adare, Lim. Adare Manor;
Trinitarian Friary
Limerick, Lim.

Hardwick, Thomas
London Church of St Mary,
Marylebone Road; St John's
Wood Church
Wanstead, Greater London
Church of St Mary the Virgin

Hargrave, Abraham
Castle Hyde, Cork

Harrison, Thomas
Manchester, Greater Manchester Portico
Library

Haughy, Patrick
Strabane, Tyrone

Hawksmoor, Nicholas
Beverley, Humberside Minster
Castle Howard, N. Yorks.
Greenwich, Greater London
Church of St Alfege; Royal
Naval College
London Christ Church; Church
of St Anne; Church of St
Mary Woolnoth; West-
minster Abbey
Ockham, Surrey Church of All
Saints

Hayes, Samuel
Avondale, Wicklow
Monaghan, Mon.

Hennessey, M. S.
Limerick, Lim.

Hiorn, William
Stratford-upon-Avon, Warks. Church
of the Holy Trinity

Hiorne, Francis
Tetbury, Glos. Church of St Mary
Magdalene

Hobbs, Samuel
Cork, Cork

Holding, Matthew
Northampton, Northants. Town
Hall

Holland, Henry
Althorp, Northants.
Ampthill, Beds. Avenue
House
Berrington Hall, Heref. & Worcs.
Brighton, E. Sussex Royal Pavilion
Claremont, Surrey
Woburn Abbey, Beds.

Hopper, Thomas
Gosford Castle, Arm.
Penrhyn Castle, Gwynedd
Slane, Meath Castle

Inwood, Henry
London Church of St
Pancras

Inwood, Henry William
London Church of St
Pancras

Ivory, Thomas of Norwich
Blickling Hall, Norfolk

Ivory, Thomas of Cork
Carton, Kild.
Dublin, Dublin King's Hospital;
Municipal Buildings
Lismore, Waterford

Jackson, Thomas
Belfast, Antrim Old Museum; St
Malachy's Catholic Church

James, C. H.
Norwich, Norfolk City Hall

509

James, John
Greenwich, Greater London Church
of St Alfege

Johnston, Francis
Armagh, Arm.
Ballymakenny, Louth
Charleville Castle, Offaly
Dublin, Dublin Castle; Church of St
George; General Post Office; Old
Parliament House
Dundalk, Louth
Kells, Meath
Newry, Down
Slane, Meath Castle
Townley Hall, Louth
Tullamore, Offaly
Tullynally Castle, Westmeath

Johnston, John
Birr, Offaly Castle

Johnston, Richard
Castlecoole, Ferm.
Dublin, Dublin Green Street
Court-house

Jones, Inigo
Ampthill, Beds.
Bodrhyddan Hall, Clwyd
Castle Ashby, Northants.
Chilham Castle, Kent
Cobham, Kent Cobham Hall
Elstow, Beds.
Enfield, Greater London Forty Hall
Greenwich, Greater London
Queen's House; Royal Naval
College
Kirby Hall, Northants.
London Banqueting House, White-
hall; Church of St Benet, Paul's
Wharf; Queen's Chapel, St
James's; St Paul's Cathedral
Raynham Hall, Norfolk
Stamford, Lincs.
Stoke Park Pavilions, Northants.
Syon House, Greater London
Wilton House, Wilts.

Jones, Walter
Chasleton House, Oxon.

Joy, Robert
Belfast, Antrim Clifton House

Kay, Joseph
Hastings, E. Sussex Pelham
Crescent

Keane, Joseph
Dublin, Dublin Church of St Francis
Xavier
Longford, Long.

Keble, John
Hursley, Hants. Church of All
Saints

Keene, Henry
Dublin, Dublin Trinity College
Hartwell, Bucks. Church
Uppark, W. Sussex

Kempster, Christopher
Abingdon, Oxon. County Hall

Kent, William
Holkham Hall, Norfolk
London Chiswick House; Kensington
Palace
Milton Abbey, Dorset
Stowe, Bucks.

Kirby, J. J.
Kew, Greater London Church of St
Anne

Koralek, Paul
Dublin, Dublin Trinity College

Kyrle, John
Ross-on-Wye, Heref. & Worcs.

Lanyon, Sir Charles
Ballywalter, Down
Belfast, Antrim

Lanyon, John
Belfast, Antrim

Leeson, John
Dublin, Dublin St Nicholas of Myra

Leoni, Giacomo
Clandon Park, Surrey
Cliveden, Bucks.
Lyme Park, Cheshire

Leslie, James
Dundee, Tayside Custom House

Lethaby, W. R.
Brockhampton-by-Ross, Heref. & Worcs.
Church of All Saints

Leuventhan
Youghal, Cork

Lightoler, Thomas
Burton Constable, Humberside

Lilly, Charles
Downpatrick, Down St Patrick's
Cathedral
Portaferry, Down

Lovel, Lord
Wardour Castle, Wilts.

Lowther, Sir John
Whitehaven, Cumbria

Lutyens, Sir Edwin
Ashwell, Herts.
Barham, Kent
Lindisfarne Castle, Holy Island,
Northld.
London The Cenotaph

Lyminge, Robert
Blickling Hall, Norfolk
Hatfield House, Herts.

Lynn, W. H.
Belfast, Antrim Castle

McAllister, Alex
Belfast, Antrim

McCarthy, J. J.
Armagh, Arm.
Killarney, Kerry
Limerick, Lim.
Maynooth, Kild.
Monaghan, Mon.
Thurles, Tipp.

Mack, Robert
Dublin, Dublin Powerscourt House

Mackenzie, A. Marshall
Aberdeen, Grampian Marischal College

Mackenzie, Thomas
Fochabers, Grampian

Mackintosh, Charles Rennie
Glasgow, Strathclyde School of Art

McMullen, James
Cork, Cork

MacNamara
Letterkenny, Don.

Madden, Dominic
Tuam, Gal.

Massingberd, Sir William
Gunby Hall, Lincs.

Matthews, James
Aberdeen, Grampian Music Hall

Maufe, Sir Edward
Guildford, Surrey Cathedral

Maxwell, Patrick
Port Glasgow, Strathclyde Newark
  Castle

Meade, William
Youghal, Cork

Mendelsohn, Erich
Bexhill, E. Sussex De La Warr
  Pavilion

Micklethwaite, J. T.
Lydbury North, Salop Church of St
  Michael

Moffat, John
Dumfries, Dumfs. & Gall. Mid Steeple

Montgomery, John
Aberdeen, Grampian Mercat
  Cross

Morris, Roger
Inveraray Castle, Strathclyde
Wilton House, Wilts.

Morrison, Sir Richard
Ballyfin House, Laois.
Barons Court, Tyrone
Carton, Kild.
Cashel, Rock of, Tipp. Cross of St
  Patrick
Castle Freke, Cork
Clonmel, Tipp.
Kilruddery, Wick.
Luttrellstown Castle,
  Dublin
Lyons House, Kild.
Port Laoise, Laois
Thomastown Castle, Tipp.
Tullynally Castle,
  Westmeath

Morrison, William Vitruvius
Carlow, Carlow
Tralee, Kerry

Mottistone, Lord
London Church of all
  Hallows; Church of St Mary
  Abchurch

Mulholland, Roger
Belfast, Antrim First Presbyterian
  Unitarian Church

Mullen, Bernard
Birr, Offaly

Mulvany, J. S.
Dublin, Dublin Broadstone Railway
  Station; Dunleary

Murray, William
Caledon House, Tyrone
Dublin, Dublin St Stephen's Green

Myers
Tullynally Castle, Westmeath

Mylne, Robert
Gatehouse of Fleet, Dumfs. & Gall.
Inveraray Castle, Strathclyde

Nash, John
Attingham Hall, Salop
Blaise Hamlet, Avon Blaise Castle
  House
Brighton, E. Sussex Royal
  Pavilion
Caher, Tipp.
Caledon House, Tyrone
Helmingham, Suffolk
Killymoon Castle, Tyrone
Lissan Rectory, Tyrone
London Buckingham Palace; Church
  of All Souls; Marble Arch; Royal
  Mews; Trafalgar Square
Loughcutra Castle, Gal.
Newport, Isle of Wight
Shane's Castle, Antrim.

Newcomen, Sir Robert
Newtownstewart, Tyrone

Newdegate, Sir Roger
Arbury Hall, Warks.

Owen, W. H.
Limerick, Lim.

Ower, C. and L.
Dundee, Tayside Custom House

Paget, Paul
London Church of All Hallows

Pain Brothers
Adare, Lim. Adare
  Manor
Ash Hill Towers, Lim.
Doneraile, Cork
Dromoland Castle, Clare
Loughcutra Castle, Gal.
Midleton, Cork
Strancally Castle, Waterford

Pain, G. R.
Cork, Cork
Lismore, Waterford

Pain, James
Limerick, Lim.

Paine, James
Chatsworth, Derbys.
Chillington Hall, Staffs.
Doncaster, S. Yorks. Mansion
  House
Gibside, Tyne & Wear Chapel
Kedleston Hall, Derbys.
Nostell Priory, W. Yorks.
Uppark, W. Sussex
Wardour Castle, Wilts.

Papworth, George
Kenure Park, Dublin
Killevy, Arm.

Parke, Edward
Dublin, Dublin St Stephen's
  Green

Parke, Robert
Dublin, Dublin Old Parliament
  House

Paxton, Sir Joseph
Lismore, Waterford
London Hyde Park

Pearce, Sir Edward Lovett
Bellamont Forest, Cavan
Boyle, Roscom. Boyle
  Barrack
Cashel, Tipp. Cashel
  Palace
Celbridge, Kild. Castletown
Cuba Court, Offaly
Downpatrick, Down
Drumcondra, Dublin
Dublin, Dublin Castle;
  Henrietta Street; Old Parliament
  House
Gloster, Offaly
Newry, Down
Rathfarnham Castle, Dublin
Stillorgan, Dublin
Woodlands, Dublin

Pearson, J. L.
Appleton-le-Moors, N. Yorks. Christ
  Church
Burley on the Hill, Leics. Church of the
  Holy Cross
Crowland, Lincs. Crowland Abbey
Cullercoats, Tyne & Wear Church of St
  George
Dalton Holme, Humberside Church of
  St Mary
Iwerne Minster, Dorset Church of St
  Mary
London Church of St Augustine
Maidstone, Kent Church of All
  Saints
Shrewsbury, Salop Abbey Church
  of the Holy Cross

511

Steetley, Derbys. Chapel of All
Saints
Wakefield, W. Yorks. Cathedral
Wentworth, S. Yorks. Church of the
Holy Trinity
Truro, Cornwall Cathedral

Pennethorne, Sir James
London Public Record Office;
Somerset House

Penrose, F. C.
Escrick, N. Yorks. Church of St Helen

Pentland, George
Dysart House, Westmeath

Pentland, John
Multyfarnham, Westmeath

Peto, Harold
Garinish Island, Cork

Pierce, S. R.
Norwich, Norfolk City Hall

Playfair, William
Dollar, Central Dollar Academy
Edinburgh, Lothian Royal College
of Surgeons of Edinburgh
Floors Castle, Borders

Pollen, John Hungerford
Dublin, Dublin St Stephen's
Green

Porter, George
London Church of St Mary
Magdalene

Preston, George
Cartmel, Cumbria Priory Church
of St Mary the Virgin

Priestley, Michael
Ballymore, Don.
Lifford, Don.
Port Hall, Don.

Pugin, Augustus Welby
Adare, Lim. Adare Manor
Albury Park, Surrey
Birmingham, W. Midlands Cathedral of
St Chad
Birr, Offaly
Bishopstone, Wilts. Church of St
John the Baptist
Boston, Lincs. Church of St
Botolph
Dublin, Dublin Church of SS
Augustine and John
Eastnor Castle, Heref. & Worcs.
Enniscorthy, Wex.
Gorey, Wex.
Killarney, Kerry
London Houses of Parliament
Maynooth, Kild.
Waterford, Waterford
Wexford, Wex.
Winwick, Cheshire Church

Pugin, E. W.
Cobh, Cork
Tralee, Kerry

Rawlinson, Sir Robert
Liverpool, Merseyside St George's
Hall

Reid, Robert
Edinburgh, Lothian General Register
House

Rennie Bros.
London Hyde Park

Rennie, John
Dublin, Dublin Dunleary
London Hyde Park

Repton, Humphrey
Sheringham Hall, Norfolk

Repton, J. A.
Sheringham Hall, Norfolk

Revett, Nicolas
West Wycombe Park, Bucks.

Richardson, Sir Albert
Ampthill, Beds.
Newmarket, Suffolk

Richardson, George
Stapleford, Leics. Church of St Mary
Magdalene
Teigh, Leics. Church of the Holy
Trinity

Robb, James
Waringstown, Down

Roberts, John
Curraghmore, Waterford
Waterford, Waterford

Robertson, Daniel
Johnstown Castle, Wex.

Robertson, John
New Ross, Wex.

Robertson, William
Kilkenny, Kilk. Castle
Longford, Long.

Robinson, Sir Thomas
Claydon House, Bucks.
Glynde, E. Sussex Church of St Mary
the Virgin

Robinson, Sir William
Clonmel, Tipp.
Dublin, Dublin Royal Hospital,
Kilmainham
Kilkenny, Kilk. Castle
Kinsale, Cork

Rosse, Lord
Birr, Offaly

Rothery, William
Doneraile, Cork
Mount Ievers, Clare

Ruskin, John
Oxford, Oxon.
Wallington, Northld.

Salvin, Anthony
Alnwick Castle, Northld.
Capesthorne, Cheshire
Greystoke, Cumbria Church of St
Andrew
Hodnet Hall, Salop
Simonburn, Northld. Church of St
Mungo
Thoresby Hall, Notts.
Worth, W. Sussex Church of St
Nicholas

Sanderson, John
Dublin, Dublin Trinity College
Woburn Abbey, Beds.

Sandys, Francis
Belfast, Antrim Church of St
George
Ickworth, Suffolk

Sandys, William
Hillsborough, Down

Savage, James
London Church of St Luke

Scott, Sir George Gilbert
Aconbury, Heref. & Worcs. Church of
St John the Baptist
Alford, Lincs. Church of St Wilfrid
Aylesbury, Bucks. Church of St
Mary
Bangor, Gwynedd Cathedral
Bibury, Glos. Church of St Mary
Bradfield, Berks.
Brecon, Powys Cathedral
Bridlington, Humberside Church of St
Mary
Cambridge, Cambs. University
Library

Dunsany, Meath
Easby, N. Yorks. Church of St Agatha
Eastnor, Heref. & Worcs. Church of
St John the Baptist
Hillesden, Bucks. Church of All
Saints
Huddersfield, W. Yorks. Churches of
St Thomas the Apostle and of
St John
Leicester, Leics. Church of St
Margaret
London Albert Memorial; St Pancras
Station
Ludlow, Salop Church of St
Laurence
Northampton, Northants. Church of
the Holy Sepulchre
Oxford, Oxon. Cathedral
Rotherham, S. Yorks. Church of All
Saints
Shifnal, Salop Church of St
Andrew
Turvey, Beds. Church of All
Saints
Wakefield, W. Yorks. Cathedral
Wirksworth, Derbys. Church of St
Mary

Scott, Sir Giles Gilbert
Glasgow, Strathclyde University
of Glasgow
Liverpool, Merseyside Anglican
Cathedral
London Guildhall
St Asaph, Clwyd Cathedral

Scott, H.
London Victoria and Albert Museum;
Royal Albert Hall

Scott, Michael
Dublin, Dublin Bus Station (Busaras);
Church of St Francis Xavier

Scott, Oldrid
Kinlet, Salop Church of St John the
Baptist

Sedding, E.
Crantock, Cornwall Church of St
Carantoc

Seddon, J. P.
Hoarwithy, Heref. & Worcs. Church of
St Catherine

Semple, George
Graiguenamanagh, Kilk.

Semple, John
Abbeyleix, Laois
Dublin, Dublin St Mary's Chapel
of Ease
Tallaght, Dublin

Serlio, Sebastiano
Cambridge, Cambs. Pembroke College
Chapel

Shanahan, Michael
Belfast, Antrim Church of St George

Shaw, John
Newstead Abbey, Notts.

Shaw, Norman
Chipstead, Surrey Church of St
Margaret
London Bedford Park; Church of St
Mark
Richards Castle, Salop Church of
All Saints
Youlgreave, Derbys. Church of All
Saints

Sherrin, George
Ingatestone, Essex

Shiel, James
Killua Castle, Westmeath
Knockdrin Castle, Westmeath
Tullynally Castle, Westmeath

Simpson, Archibald
Aberdeen, Grampian Marischal
College; Music Hall
Elgin, Grampian Anderson's Institution

Slater, William
Limerick, Lim.

Sloane, Charles
Gravesend, Kent Church of St
George

Smeaton, John
Coldstream, Borders Bridge over
the Tweed

Smirke, Sir Robert
Dublin, Dublin Phoenix
Park
Eastnor Castle, Heref. & Worcs.
London British Museum;
Somerset House

Smith, Francis
Chillington Hall, Staffs.
Derby, Derbys. Cathedral
Ditchley Park, Oxon.
Lamport Hall, Northants.
Mawley Hall, Salop

Smith, James
Dalkeith Palace, Lothian
Glasgow, Strathclyde Royal Bank
of Scotland and Royal
Exchange Square

Smith, John
Aberdeen, Grampian Robert
Gordon's College

Smith, John
Dublin, Dublin Church of St
Catherine; Trinity College

Smith, William, of Warwick
Monmouth, Gwent Church of St
Mary
Whitchurch, Salop Church of St
Alkmund

Smythson, Robert
Hardwick Hall, Derbys.
Longleat House, Wilts.
Wollaton Hall, Notts.

Smythson, Roger
Wardour Castle, Wilts.

Snowdon, Lord
London Regent's Park

Soane, Sir John
Albury Park, Surrey
Aynhoe Park, Northants.
Barons Court, Tyrone
Belfast, Antrim
Chillington Hall, Staffs.
Claremont, Surrey
London Church of St John; Church
of St Peter; Dulwich College
Gallery; Royal Hospital;
Soane Museum
Wotton House, Bucks.

Southampton, Earl of
Cowdray Park, W. Sussex

Spence, Sir Basil
Coventry, W. Midlands Cathedral
Falmer, E. Sussex

Stapleton, Michael
Dublin, Dublin Belvedere House;
Ely House, Ely Place
Maynooth, Kild.

Steuart, George
Attingham Hall, Salop
Barons Court, Tyrone
Shrewsbury, Salop Church of St Chad

Stevens, Alexander
Bridge of Dun, Tayside Bridge over the
R. South Esk

Stevens, H. J.
Derby, Derbys. Church of St
Alkmund

Stokes, Henry
Lismore, Waterford

Stone, Nicholas
Oxford, Oxon. Church of St Mary
the Virgin

Stratford, Ferdinando
Newtonards, Down

Street, G. E.
Bloxham, Oxon. Church of Our
Lady
Britford, Wilts. Church of St
Peta
Clun, Salop Church of St
George
Corsham, Wilts. Church of St
Bartholomew
Cottesbrooke, Northants. Church of
All Saints
Elford, Staffs. Church of St
Peter
Haddo House, Grampian
Kempsford, Glos. Church of St Mary
the Virgin
Kildare, Kild. St Brigid's
Cathedral
Kingston, Dorset Church of St
James
Leicester, Leics. Cathedral; Church of
St Margaret
Manchester, Greater Manchester
Town Hall
Monmouth, Gwent Church of St
Mary
St Michael Penkevil, Cornwall Church
of St Michael
South Mimms, Herts. Church of St
Giles
Stewkley, Bucks. Church of St
Michael and All Angels
Thirsk, N. Yorks. Church of St
Mary
Thornhill, W. Yorks. Church of St
Michael and All Angels
Toddington, Glos. Church of St
Andrew
Warfield, Berks. Church of St
Michael
Weaverthorpe, N. Yorks. Church of St
Andrew

Stuart, James 'Athenian'
Eastnor, Heref. & Worcs. Church of St
John the Baptist
Preston-on-Stour, Warks.
Church
Shugborough, Staffs.

Sweetman, John
Dublin, Dublin Pro-Cathedral of St
Mary

Talman, William
Chatsworth, Derbys.
Dyrham Park, Avon
Little Stanmore, Greater London
Church of St Lawrence
(Whitchurch)
Thoresby Hall, Notts.
Uppark, W. Sussex

Taylor, J.
Dundee, Tayside Custom
House

Taylor, Sir Robert
Belfast, Antrim Belfast Bank Head
Office
Gorhambury, Herts.
Heveningham Hall, Suffolk
Oxford, Oxon. Ashmolean
Museum

Telford, Thomas
Bridgnorth, Salop Church of St
Mary Magdalene

Dunkeld, Tayside
Madeley, Salop Church of St
Michael

Teulon, S. S.
Ampton, Suffolk Church of St
Peter

Thomas, Sir Brumwell
Belfast, Antrim

Thompson, Alexander 'Greek'
Glasgow, Strathclyde Caledonia Road
Church; St Vincent Street Church

Thornely, Sir Arnold
Belfast, Antrim

Thornhill, Sir James
Moor Park, Herts.

Thoroton, John
Belvoir Castle, Leics.

Thorpe, John
Kirby Hall, Northants.
Montacute House, Som.
Stamford, Lincs.

Thynne, Sir John
Longleat, Wilts.
Wollaton Hall, Notts.

Tinsley, William
Clonmel, Tipp.

Tite, Sir William
London Royal Exchange

Townsend, C. H.
London Horniman Museum

Townsend, Harrison
Great Warley, Essex Church of St
Mary the Virgin

Tropenell, Thomas
Great Chalfield, Wilts. Church of All
Saints

Vallancey, General Charles
Dublin, Dublin Queen's Bridge

Vanbrugh, Sir John
Audley End, Essex
Belfast, Antrim
Blenheim Palace, Oxon.
Carshalton, Surrey
Castle Howard, N. Yorks.
Claremont, Surrey
Floors Castle, Borders
Greenwich, Greater London Royal
Naval College; Vanbrugh
Castle
Iver, Bucks. Iver Grove
Kimbolton Castle, Cambs.
Seaton Delaval Hall, Northld.
Somersby, Lincs. Manor
Farm
Stowe, Bucks.
York, N. Yorks. Debtors' Prison

Vardy, John
Milton Abbey, Dorset

Vavasar, Thomas
Ham House, Greater London

Vesey, Rt. Hon. Agmondisham
Lucan House, Dublin

Wastell, John
Canterbury, Kent Cathedral

Waterhouse, Alfred
London British Museum (Natural
History)
Manchester, Greater Manchester Town
Hall

Webb, Sir Aston
London Buckingham Palace;
Church of St Bartholomew the
Great; Victoria and Albert
Museum

Webb, John
Cobham, Kent Cobham Hall

DIVINES

In cloister and cell, men of God kept spiritual values alive through what would otherwise rightly be known as the Dark Ages; they left behind a priceless heritage in manuscript and stone. As Church clashed with State, and the old faith with the new, many died for their beliefs. Later, Nonconformism added its distinctive note of revivalism to worship in Britain.

Aidan, St
Holy Island, Northld. Lindisfarne Priory
Iona, Strathclyde

Alcock, Bishop
Cambridge, Cambs. Jesus College

Alcuin
York, N. Yorks.

Anselm, St
Bury St Edmunds, Suffolk
Chester, Cheshire
Rockingham Castle, Northants.

Augustine, St
Canterbury, Kent

Baldwin, Abbot
Bury St Edmunds, Suffolk

Barwick, John, Dean
Witherslack, Cumbria Church of St Paul

Beaufort, Cardinal
Winchester, Hants. St Cross Hospital

Becket, Thomas
Berkhamsted, Herts.
Canterbury, Kent
Reading, Berks.

Bede, Venerable
Beverley, Humberside Minster, Church of St John of Beverley

Bek, Bishop
Durham, Durham Cathedral and Castle

Beuno, St
Clynnog-Fawr, Gwynedd Church of St Beuno

Beverley, St John of
Beverley, Humberside Minster

Biscop, Benedict
Monkwearmouth, Tyne & Wear

Bolton, Theophilus
Cashel, Tipp. Cashel Palace

Bourchier, Thomas
Knole, Kent

Bourne, Hugh
Mow Cop, Cheshire–Staffs.

Browne, Jemmett, Bishop
Riverstown House, Cork

Buckland, Dean
Paviland, W. Glam. Goat's Hole Cave

Bunyan, John
Ampthill, Beds.
Bedford, Beds.
Elstow, Beds.

Canice, St, of Aghaboe
Monahincha Abbey, Tipp.

Carswell, John
Carnasserie Castle, Strathclyde

Cartach, St
Rahan Abbey, Offaly

Cedd, St, Bishop
Bradwell-on-Sea, Essex Church of St Peter's-on-the-Wall

Chad, St, Bishop of Mercia
Lichfield, Staffs. Cathedral

Ciaran, St
Clonmacnoise, Offaly

Coke, Sir Thomas
Melbourne Hall, Derbys.

Colmcille, St
Derry, Lond.
Drumcliff, Sligo
Kells, Meath

Columba, St
Iona, Strathclyde

Cosin, John
Brancepeth, Durham Church of St Brandon

Courtenay, Archbishop
Maidstone, Kent Church of All Saints

Cox, Archbishop
Castletown House, Kilk.
Kilkenny, Kilk. St Canice's Cathedral

Cranmer, Archbishop
Knole, Kent
Oxford, Oxon.

Cronan, St
Roscrea, Tipp.

de Blois, Henry, Bishop
Farnham, Surrey Castle
Hursley, Hants. Merdon Castle
Taunton, Som.
Winchester, Hants. St Cross Hospital

de Caen, Roger, Bishop
Sherborne, Dorset Old Castle

de Cardeny, Robert, Bishop
Dunkeld, Tayside Cathedral

de Clinton, Roger, Bishop
Buildwas Abbey, Salop

Constantine, St
Wetheral, Cumbria St Constantine's Cell

de Corbeuil, Archbishop
Rochester, Kent Castle

de Linton, Bernard, Abbot
Arbroath Abbey, Tayside

de Losinga, Herbert, Bishop
Norwich, Norfolk Cathedral

de Luffa, Ralph, Bishop
Chichester, W. Sussex Cathedral

Derry, Bishop of
Downhill Castle, Lond.

de Sudbury, Simon, Archbishop
Sudbury, Suffolk Church of St Gregory

de Valence, Aymer
Bampton, Oxon.

Diarmaid, St
Inchclerauɲ, Long.

Donne, John
London Lincoln's Inn; St Paul's Cathedral

Doyle, Bishop
Carlow, Carlow

Edington, Bishop
Winchester, Hants. Cathedral

Endelienta, St
St Endellion, Cornwall Church of St Endelienta

Etheldreda, St
Ely, Cambs. Cathedral

Faringdon, Hugh, Abbot
Reading, Berks.

Ferrar, Nicholas
Little Gidding, Cambs.

Finbar, St
Cork, Cork

Flambard, Ralph, Bishop
Christchurch, Dorset Priory

Fox, Richard, Bishop
Taunton, Som.

Foy, Bishop
Waterford, Waterford

Gower, Bishop
Lamphey, Dyfed Bishop's Palace
St David's, Dyfed Bishop's Palace

Gravesend, Bishop
Lincoln, Lincs. Cathedral Treasury

Grosseteste, Bishop
Lincoln, Lincs. Cathedral Treasury

Guthlac, St
Crowland, Lincs. Abbey

Hatfield, Bishop
Durham, Durham Cathedral and Castle

Hervey, Frederick Augustus, Bishop
Derry, Lond. Protestant Cathedral
Ickworth, Suffolk

Huby, Abbot
Fountains Abbey, N. Yorks.

Hugh, St
Old Clee, Humberside Church of the Holy Trinity

Hughes, Father
Llanengan, Gwynedd Church

Ivo, St
St Ives, Cambs.

John the Baptist
Winchester, Hants. Town Cross

Kevin, St
Glendalough, Wicklow

Kildare, Bishop of
Great Connell Priory, Kild.

King, Bishop
Bath, Avon

Laisren, St
Inish Murray, Sligo

Latimer, Bishop
Oxford, Oxon.

Laud, Archbishop
London Church of St Katherine Cree

Lauder, Thomas, Bishop
Dunkeld, Tayside Cathedral

Leighton, Bishop
Culross, Fife Bishop Leighton's House

Leofric of Exeter, Bishop
Exeter, Devon Cathedral Library

Le Puiset, or Pudsey, Hugh, Bishop
Durham, Durham Cathedral and Castle

Leslie, John, Bishop
Raphoe, Don.

Lloyd, Bishop
Chester, Cheshire

Loftus, Adam, Bishop
Rathfarnham Castle, Dublin

Mabon, Dean
Hougue Bie, Jersey

MacHale, John, Archbishop
Ballintober Abbey, Mayo Augustinian Friary

Magnus, St
Egilsay, Isle of Orkney

Marsh, Narcissus, Archbishop
Dublin, Dublin Cathedral of St Patrick

Mathew, Father
Cork, Cork

Milburga, St
Much Wenlock, Salop Wenlock Priory

Milles, Bishop
Waterford, Waterford

More, Sir Thomas
London Crosby Hall; Lincoln's Inn; Tower of London; Westminster Hall

Morgan, William, Bishop
Ty Mawr, Gwynedd

Morley, Bishop
Winchester, Hants.

Morton, Archbishop
London Lambeth Palace

Morton, Bishop of Ely
Hatfield House, Herts.

Mungo, St
Glasgow, Strathclyde

Neot, St
St Neot, Cornwall

Ninian, St
Whithorn Priory, Dumfs. & Gall.

Odo of Bayeux, Bishop
Dover, Kent

Odo, Dean
Clonmacnoise, Offaly Cathedral

O'Hedian, Archbishop
Cashel, Rock of, Tipp.

O'Kelly, Archbishop
Cashel, Tipp. Dominican Priory

Oswald, Bishop
Worcester, Heref. & Worcs. Cathedral

Otway, Thomas, Bishop
Kilkenny, Kilk.

Patrick, St
Armagh, Arm.
Cashel, Rock of, Tipp.
Dublin, Dublin Cathedral of St Patrick

Paulinus, St
York, N. Yorks. Minster

Percy, Thomas, Bishop
Bridgnorth, Salop

Phillips, Abbot
Kilcooly Abbey, Tipp.

Pococke, Bishop
Kilkenny, Kilk.

Rahere
London Church of St Bartholomew
the Great

Ralph, Bishop
Kildare, Kild. St Brigid's Cathedral

Ridley, Bishop
Oxford, Oxon.

Ripley, John
Leeds, W. Yorks. Abbey House
Museum

Robinson, Primate
Armagh, Arm.
Ballymakenny, Louth
Dungannon, Tyrone

Ross, Provost
Aberdeen, Grampian Provost Ross's
House

Rutherwyke, Abbot
Great Bookham, Surrey Church of St
Nicholas

St Calais William of, Bishop
Durham, Durham Cathedral and
Castle

Schmidt, Father
London Church of St Katherine Cree

Sely, John, Bishop
Kilclief, Down

Sharp, Archbishop
St Andrews, Fife

Sheldon, Archbishop
Oxford, Oxon.

Stuart, Primate
Armagh, Arm.

Sudbury, Archbishop
Canterbury, Kent Westgate
Museum

Sutton, Bishop
Lincoln, Lincs. Cathedral Treasury

Swithin, St
Winchester, Hants

Taylor, Jeremy, Bishop
Ballinderry, Antrim Middle Church

Tennyson, Rev. George
Somersby, Lincs. Somersby House

Tibba, St
Ryhall, Leics. Church of St John the
Evangelist

Trevor, Richard, Bishop
Glynde Place, E. Sussex

Turnbull, William, Bishop
Glasgow, Strathclyde

Vyvyan, Prior
Bodmin, Cornwall Church of St
Petrock

**Wayneflete, William of,
Bishop**
Oxford, Oxon. Magdalen College
Wainfleet All Saints, Lincs.

Werburgh, St
Chester, Cheshire Cathedral

Wesley, John
Epworth, Lincs. Old Rectory
Gainsborough, Lincs. Old Hall
London Wesley's House and
Chapel
West Bromwich, W. Midlands Oak
House

Wite, St
Whitchurch Canonicorum, Dorset
Church of St Candida and Holy
Cross

Wolsey, Cardinal
Great Wymondley, Herts. Delamere
House
Hampton Court, Greater London
Ipswich, Suffolk Wolsey's Gateway
Lincoln, Lincs. Cardinal's Hat
London Banqueting House,
Whitehall
Oxford, Oxon. Christ Church
College
Sherborne, Dorset Abbey Church of
St Mary

Wren, Bishop
Cambridge, Cambs. Pembroke
College Chapel

Wulfstan, Bishop
Worcester, Heref. & Worcs. Cathedral

Wycliffe, John
Bristol, Avon Westbury College

Wygun, Isabella, Prioress
Norwich, Norfolk Carrow Abbey

Wykeham, William of
Broughton Castle, Oxon.
Oxford, Oxon. New College
Winchester, Hants. Cathedral;
Winchester College

Wyville, Bishop
Salisbury, Wilts. Cathedral

York, Wilfrid of, Bishop
Ripon, N. Yorks. Cathedral

POLITICIANS AND LAWYERS

The two great contributions Britain has made to modern politics are representative government and the rule of law. Neither happened by chance or overnight: they were the work of generations of outstanding men. To visit Parliament or any law court in the land is to see these two massive principles operating through historical, often quaint, forms.

Aislabie, John
Studley Royal and Fountains Abbey Garden, N. Yorks.

Alexander, Sir William
Menstrie Castle, Central

Anderson, Sir Edmund
Broughton, Humberside Church of St Mary

Astor, Lord
Cliveden, Bucks.

Audley, Lord
Saffron Walden, Essex

Bernard, Sir Francis
Nether Winchenden House, Bucks.

Blake, Thomas
Ross on Wye, Heref. & Worcs.

Blathwayt, William
Dyrham Park, Avon

Bodley, Sir Thomas
Oxford, Oxon. Bodleian Library

Bonar Law, Andrew
Ashridge, Herts.

Boyle, Richard, Earl of Cork
Youghal, Cork

Bulwer-Lytton, Sir Edward, 1st Lord Lytton
Knebworth House, Herts.

Carlisle, Earl of
Castle Howard, N. Yorks.

Cecil, Robert, 1st Earl of Salisbury
Hatfield House, Herts.

Cecil, Sir William
Burghley House, Cambs.

Cecil, William, Earl of Salisbury
Hertford, Herts.

Chaucer, Thomas
Ewelme, Oxon. Church of St Mary the Virgin

Chauncy, Henry
Hertford, Herts. Lombard House

Choke, Lord Chief Justice
Long Ashton, Avon Church of All Saints

Churchill, Sir Winston
Blenheim Palace, Oxon.
Chartwell, Kent
Ditchley Park, Oxon.
Oldham, Greater Manchester Art Gallery
Westerham, Kent

Chute, Chaloner
Vyne, The, Hants.

Clive of India
Claremont, Surrey

Dorchester, Dorset Dorset Military Museum
Walcott Hall, Salop
Welshpool, Powys Powis Castle

Clopton, Hugh
Stratford-upon-Avon, Warks. Clopton Bridge

Cobden, Richard
Midhurst, W. Sussex

Coke, Sir John
Melbourne Hall, Derbys.

Conolly, William
Celbridge, Kild. Castletown

Cordell, Sir William
Melford Hall, Suffolk

Cortis, Alfred
Worthing, W. Sussex Museum and Art Gallery

Cromwell, Oliver
Grantham, Lincs.
Huntingdon, Cambs.
Ripley Castle, N. Yorks.

Cromwell, Richard
Hursley, Hants. Church of All Saints

Crosby, Sir John
London Crosby Hall; Church of St Helen's

Dashwood, Sir Francis
West Wycombe, Bucks. West Wycombe Park

de Albini, William
Castle Rising, Norfolk Castle

de Glanville, Ranulf
Butley, Suffolk Butley Priory Gate-house

de Rothschild, Baron Ferdinand
Waddesdon Manor, Bucks.

Digby, Kenelm
Stoke Dry, Leics. Church of St Andrew

Disraeli, Benjamin
Hughenden Manor, Bucks.
Knebworth House, Herts.
London Lincoln's Inn
Weston Park, Staffs.

Dobbs, Arthur
Castle Dobbs, Antrim

Dormer, Mr Justice
Quainton, Bucks. Church of the Holy Cross and St Mary

Eisenhower, General Dwight D.
Culzean Castle, Strathclyde

Eliot, Edward
Saint Germans, Cornwall Church of St Germanus

Eyre, Giles
Pepperbox Hill, Wilts.

Forbes, Duncan
Culloden, Highland

Fox, Sir Stephen
Fox's Hospital, Wilts.

Geffrye, Sir Robert
London Geffrye Museum

Gladstone, W. E.
Edinburgh Mercat Cross
Liverpool, Merseyside Hornby
Library
London Lincoln's Inn

Gresham, Sir Richard
Fountains Hall, N. Yorks.

Hall, Sir Benjamin
London Houses of Parliament

Hampden, John
Aylesbury, Bucks.

Harvey, Bagenal
Bargy, Wex. Castle

Hatton, Sir Christopher
Kirby Hall, Northants.

Hitler, Adolf
Dorchester, Dorset Dorset Military
Museum

Hopton, Sir Arthur
Yoxford, Suffolk Cockfield Hall

Jeffreys, Judge
Dorchester, Dorset
Exeter, Devon
Taunton, Som.
Winchester, Hants. Castle Hall

Knollys, Francis
Rotherfield Greys, Oxon. Church

Lincoln, Abraham
Hingham, Norfolk

Maitland, William
Lennoxlove, Lothian

More, Sir Thomas
London Crosby Hall; Lincoln's Inn;
Tower of London; Westminster
Hall

North, 8th Lord
Wroxton Abbey, Oxon.

O'Connell, Daniel
Derrynane Abbey, Kerry
Ennis, Clare

Onslow, Speaker
Guildford, Surrey Church of the Holy
Trinity

Owen, Robert
New Lanark, Strathclyde
Newtown, Powys Robert Owen
Memorial Museum

Ponsonby, Speaker
Bishopscourt House, Kild.

Rhodes, Cecil
Bishops Stortford, Herts.

Richardson, Edward
Rich Hill Manor House, Arm.

Roosevelt, F. D.
London Roosevelt Memorial

Sackville, Thomas
Knole, Kent

St John, Oliver
Thorpe Hall, Cambs.

Sandys, William
Mottisfont Abbey, Hants.

Scot, Sir John
Scotstarvit Tower, Fife

Trevor, John
Trevalyn Hall, Denb.

Walpole, Horatio
Shobdon, Heref. & Worcs. Church of S
John the Evangelist
Twickenham, Greater London
Strawberry Hill
Wolterton Hall, Norfolk

Washington, George
Sulgrave Manor, Northants.

Wellington, Duke of
Glasgow, Strathclyde Stirling's
Library
London Hyde Park Corner; Royal
Exchange
Stratfield Saye, Hants.
Walmer Castle, Kent

Wilkes, John
Aylesbury, Bucks.

Wolsey, Thomas
Hampton Court, Greater London
Ipswich, Suffolk Wolsey's Gateway
Oxford, Oxon. Christ Church
College

England's monarchy has endured (apart from an 11-year break after Charles I lost his head) for more than 1000 years. The institution has adapted itself remarkably to the changing needs of the nation; and in turn, individual rulers as different in style as the hasty, avaricious Henry VIII and the formidably respectable Victoria have re-shaped their kingdom in their own images.

Albert, Prince Consort
Balmoral Castle, Grampian
London, Albert Memorial; Royal Albert Hall; Victoria and Albert Museum
Madingley, Cambs. Madingley Hall
Osborne House, Isle of Wight
Portsmouth, Hants. Victory Museum
Windsor, Berks. St George's Chapel, Windsor Castle

Alexander I of Scotland
Stirling, Central Castle

Alexander II of Scotland
Balmerino Abbey, Fife
Eilean Donan Castle, Highland

Alfred
Cricklade, Wilts. Saxon burh
Oxford, Oxon.
Wantage, Oxon.
Winchester, Hants. Town Cross

Anne
London Kensington Gardens; Kensington Palace

Ap Rhys, Gruffydd
Talley Abbey, Dyfed

Arthur
Cadbury Castle, Som.
Tintagel Castle, Cornwall
Winchester, Hants. Castle Hall

Athelstan
Burnswark, Dumfs. & Gall. Hill-fort and Roman siege works
Malmesbury, Wilts. Church of St Mary

Beatrice, Princess
Brentford, Greater London British Piano Museum

Berthulf, King of Mercia
Bennington, Herts.

Black Prince, The
Canterbury, Kent Cathedral
Hellen's, Heref. & Worcs.
Tintagel Castle, Cornwall

Boadicea
Colchester, Essex
Stamford, Lincs.

Boleyn, Anne
Brighton, E. Sussex Thomas-Stanford Museum
Erwarton, Suffolk
Hever Castle, Kent
London Tower of London

Bolingbroke, Henry, Duke of Lancaster
Carreg-Cennen Castle, Dyfed
Hertford, Herts. Castle

Bruce, Marjorie
Paisley, Strathclyde Abbey

the Bruce, Robert, King of Scotland
Arbroath, Tayside
Bannockburn, Central Bore Stone
Blair Castle, Tayside
Clackmannan, Central Clackmannan Tower
Drum Castle, Grampian
Dunstaffnage, Strathclyde
Roslin, Lothian Castle

Charles Edward, Bonnie Prince Charlie
Carlisle, Cumbria Castle
Dunvegan, Isle of Skye, Highland
Lancaster, Lancs.

Charles, HRH Prince
Caernarfon, Gwynedd Castle

Charles I
Arreton, Isle of Wight Arreton Manor
Birmingham, W. Midlands Aston Hall
Blithfield, Staffs. Museum of Childhood and Costume
Carisbrooke Castle, Isle of Wight
Chester, Cheshire
Chirk Castle, Clwyd
Madingley, Cambs. Madingley Hall
London St James's Palace; Westminster Hall
Oxford, Oxon.
Painswick, Glos. Court-house
Royal Tunbridge Wells, Kent
Sudeley Castle, Glos.
Taunton, Som. Somerset County Museum
Winton House, Lothian

Charles II
Boscobel House, Salop
Chillington Hall, Staffs.
Dartmouth, Devon Borough Museum
Dunster, Som. Castle
Edinburgh, Lothian Palace of Holyroodhouse
Ipswich, Suffolk Ancient House
King's Lynn, Norfolk Custom House
London Charles II Statue, Chelsea Hospital; Monument
Moseley Old Hall, W. Midlands
Oxford, Oxon.
Plymouth, Devon
Rochester, Kent Restoration House

Charlotte, Princess of Wales
Windsor, Berks. St George's Chapel, Windsor Castle

David I of Scotland
Cambuskenneth, Central Abbey
Dryburgh Abbey, Borders
Hertford, Herts. Castle

Jedburgh, Borders Abbey
Melrose Abbey, Borders

David II of Scotland
Durham, Durham

Edmund
Bury St Edmunds, Suffolk

Edward I
Beaumaris Castle, Anglesey, Gwynedd
Caernarfon, Gwynedd Castle
Carlisle, Cumbria Castle
Criccieth, Gwynedd
Dirleton Castle, Lothian
Flint Castle, Clwyd
Hardingstone, Northants.
Harlech Castle, Gwynedd
Kidwelly Castle, Dyfed
Linlithgow Palace, Lothian
Rhuddlan Castle, Clwyd
Roslin, Lothian Chapel
St Asaph, Clwyd Cathedral
Scone Palace, Tayside
Walsingham Priory, Norfolk
Worcester, Heref. & Worcs.

Edward II
Berkeley Castle, Glos.
Caernarfon, Gwynedd Castle
Gloucester, Glos. Cathedral

Edward III
Dartmouth, Devon
London Jewel Tower
Salisbury, Wilts. Cathedral
Windsor, Berks. Castle

Edward IV
Hexham, Northld.

Edward VI
Christ's Hospital, W. Sussex
London St Thomas's Hospital
Norwich, Norfolk Priory

Edward VII
London Marlborough House
Madingley, Cambs. Madingley Hall
Sandringham House, Norfolk

Edward, Prince
Odiham, Hants. Castle
Worcester, Heref. & Worcs.

Edward the Confessor
Bury St Edmunds, Suffolk
London Royal Exchange

Edward the Elder
Cricklade, Wilts. Saxon burh

Edward the Martyr
Shaftesbury, Dorset Abbey Ruins
  Museum
Wareham, Dorset

Elizabeth I
Basing, Hants.
  Basing House Ruins
Compton Wynyates, Warks.
Dublin, Dublin Trinity College
Hatfield House, Herts.
Huntingdon, Cambs. Hinchingbrooke
Kenilworth Castle, Warks.
Knole, Kent
London Royal Exchange
Melford Hall, Suffolk
Norwich, Norfolk Market-place
Stamford, Lincs.
Warwick, Warks. Lord Leycester
  Hospital and Chapel of St James

Elizabeth II
Balmoral Castle, Grampian
Falkland, Fife Falkland Palace
London Buckingham Palace;
  Royal Mews, Buckingham Palace
Sandringham House, Norfolk

Elizabeth of Bohemia
Ashdown House, Oxon.

Ermengarde
Balmerino Abbey, Fife

Ethelbald
Crowland, Lincs. Crowland Abbey

Frederick, Prince of Wales
Kew, Greater London Royal
  Botanic Gardens

George I
London Banqueting House, Whitehall; Kensington Palace

George II
Hampton Court, Greater London
Marlow, Bucks. Marlow Place

George III
Kew, Greater London Pagoda, Royal
  Botanic Gardens
London Buckingham Palace;
  Royal Academy
Windsor, Berks. Castle

George IV
Brighton, E. Sussex Royal Pavilion
London Royal Mews, Buckingham
  Palace
Windsor, Berks. Castle

George V
Edinburgh, Lothian Palace of
  Holyroodhouse
Leeds, W. Yorks. Municipal Offices

George, Prince of Denmark
Windsor, Berks. Windsor Guildhall
  Exhibition

George, Prince of Wales
Brighton, E. Sussex Royal Pavilion

Grey, Lady Jane
London Tower of London

Harold
Waltham Abbey, Essex

Henrietta Maria
Greenwich, Greater London Queen's
  House
London Queen's Chapel, St James's
Royal Tunbridge Wells, Kent

Henry I
Cardiff, S. Glam. Castle
Reading, Berks.

Henry II
Orford Castle, Suffolk
Oxford, Oxon. University
Scarborough, N. Yorks.
Wallingford, Oxon.
Warkworth Castle, Northld.
Windsor, Berks. Castle

Henry III
Chester, Cheshire Castle
London Westminster Abbey
Montgomery, Powys Castle
Oxford, Oxon.
Sutton-at-Hone, Kent St John's
  Jerusalem
Walsingham Priory, Norfolk
Worcester, Heref. & Worcs.

Henry IV
Canterbury, Kent Cathedral

Henry V
Monmouth, Gwent
Syon House, Greater London

Henry VI
Hexham, Northld.
Muncaster Castle, Cumbria

Henry VII
London Westminster Abbey
Pembroke, Dyfed Castle
Worcester, Heref. & Worcs.
  Cathedral

Henry VIII
Arreton, Isle of Wight Arreton Manor

Berkhamsted, Herts.
Canterbury, Kent
Compton Wynyates, Warks.
Cowdray Park, W. Sussex
Durham, Durham Grammar
   School
East Barsham Manor, Norfolk
Elton Hall, Cambs.
Great Wymondley, Herts. Delamere
   House
Hampton Court, Greater London
Hatfield House, Herts.
Knole, Kent
London Banqueting House,
   Whitehall; St Bartholomew's
   Hospital; St James's Palace;
   St Thomas's Hospital
Milton Abbey, Dorset
Pembroke, Dyfed Castle
Peterborough, Cambs.
Portsmouth, Hants.
Walmer Castle, Kent
Wilton House, Wilts.

Henry, Prince
Sycharth, Clwyd

Isabella
Hertford, Herts. Castle

James I of Scotland
Linlithgow Palace, Lothian
Perth, Tayside

James II of Scotland
Dryburgh Abbey, Borders

James III of Scotland
Stirling, Central Castle

James IV of Scotland
Edinburgh, Lothian Palace of
   Holyroodhouse
Rothesay, Isle of Bute, Strathclyde
   Castle
Stirling, Central Church of the
   Holy Rude

James V of Scotland
Falkland, Fife
Rothesay, Isle of Bute, Strathclyde
   Castle
Stirling, Central Castle

**James VI of Scotland (James I of
   England)**
Althorp, Northants.
Falkland, Fife Falkland
   Palace
Hatfield House, Herts.
Hoghton Tower, Lancs.
London Apothecaries' Hall
Neidpath Castle, Borders
Pembroke, Dyfed Castle
Ripley Castle, N. Yorks.
Stirling, Central Castle
Thetford, Norfolk King's
   House
Worcester, Heref. & Worcs.

John
Dorchester, Dorset
Eye, Suffolk
Ipswich, Suffolk
Lancaster, Lancs. Castle
Liverpool, Merseyside
Scarborough, N. Yorks. Castle
Stratford-upon-Avon, Warks.
Worcester, Heref. & Worcs.
   Cathedral

John, King of France
St Albans, Herts. French Row

Katherine of Aragon
Brighton, E. Sussex Thomas-
   Stanford Museum
Buckden, Cambs. Bishop's Palace
Winchcombe, Glos. Church of
   St Peter

Kenneth I of Scotland
Scone Palace, Tayside

Knut
Bury St Edmunds, Suffolk

Laoghaire
Tara, Meath

Macbeth, King of Scotland
Dunsinane, Tayside
Iona, Strathclyde

**McMurrough, Dermot, King of
   Leinster**
Baltinglass, Wicklow

**Maelor, Madoc Ap Gruffydd,
   Prince of Powys**
Valle Crucis Abbey, Clwyd

Maeve (Queen Mab)
Knocknarea, Sligo

Malcolm III of Scotland
Edinburgh, Lothian

Margaret, Princess
Glamis, Tayside Castle

**Margaret, Princess, daughter of
   Henry VII**
Grantham, Lincs. Grantham House

Mary I
Daingean, Offaly
Elton Hall, Cambs.
Framlingham Castle, Suffolk
Lichfield, Staffs.

Mary II
Greenwich, Greater London Royal
   Naval College

Mary, Queen of Scots
Borthwick Castle, Lothian
Cadzow Castle, Strathclyde
Carlisle, Cumbria Castle
Dundrennan Abbey, Dumfs. & Gall.
Edinburgh, Lothian Palace of
   Holyroodhouse
Falkland, Fife Falkland Palace
Fotheringhay, Northants.
Hailes Castle, Lothian
Hermitage Castle, Borders
Linlithgow, Lothian Linlithgow
   Palace
Loch Leven Castle, Tayside
Lowther Castle, Cumbria
Niddry Castle, Lothian
Peterborough, Cambs. Museum and
   Maxwell Art Gallery
Stirling, Central Castle
Traquair House, Borders

Matilda
Worcester, Heref. & Worcs.

**O'Brien Donal Mor, King of
   Munster**
Canon Island, Clare
Holycross, Tipp.
Kilcooly Abbey, Tipp.

O'Conor, Cathel
Ballintober, Mayo Augustinian
   Friary
Knockmoy, Gal.

Offa, King of Mercia
Offa's Dyke
Oswestry, Salop

Parr, Catherine
Kendal, Cumbria
Sudeley Castle, Glos.

Philip II, King of Spain
Daingean, Offaly

Richard I (Lionheart)
Butley, Suffolk Butley Priory
   Gate-house
Colchester, Essex
Worcester, Heref. & Worcs.

Richard II
Blithfield, Staffs. Museum of
   Childhood and Costume
Gainsborough, Lincs. Gainsborough
   Old Hall

Hertford, Herts. Castle
Lichfield, Staffs.
Lincoln, Lincs. Stonebow and
  Guildhall
London Westminster Hall
Melrose Abbey, Borders
Oswestry, Salop
Portchester Castle, Hants.

Richard III
Grantham, Lincs.
London Crosby Hall

Rupert, Prince
Worcester, Heref. & Worcs.

Seymour, Jane
Syon House, Greater London

Stephen
Worcester, Heref. & Worcs.

Victoria
Balmoral Castle, Grampian
Brighton, E. Sussex
  Royal Pavilion
Cowes, Isle of Wight
Kew, Greater London Royal
  Botanic Gardens Museums of
  Economic Botany
Leeds, W. Yorks. Town Hall
London Albert Memorial; Royal
  Mews, Buckingham Palace;
  St James's Palace; St Thomas's
  Hospital; Victoria and Albert
  Museum

Northampton, Northants. Central
  Museum and Art Gallery
Osborne House, Isle of Wight
Windsor, Berks. Castle

William I (the Conqueror)
Battle Abbey, E. Sussex
Durham, Durham
Ely, Cambs.
Lincoln, Lincs. Castle
London Tower of London
Oxford, Oxon.
Rockingham Castle, Northants.
Windsor, Berks. Castle

William II (Rufus)
Carlisle, Cumbria Castle
London Westminster Hall
Rockingham Castle, Northants.
Rufus Stone, Hants.

William III
London Banqueting House, White-
  hall; Kensington Palace
Petersfield, Hants.
Sherborne, Dorset Castle

William IV
Brighton, E. Sussex Royal Pavilion

William, King of Scotland
Arbroath Abbey, Tayside

William the Lion
Dumfries, Dumfs. & Gall.

SCIENTISTS

Before there is any science, there must be a scientific approach; and in this sense, English science begins with Francis Bacon (1561–1626). He stressed that truth is not derived from authority, but is discovered through experiment and observation. The brilliant insights of Newton, the world-shaking theories of Darwin—even the work which led to the 'splitting' of the atom—followed, however indirectly, from this step.

Acland, Sir Henry
Wentworth
Oxford, Oxon. University
  Museum

Anderson, Elizabeth Garrett
Aldeburgh, Suffolk

Banks, Sir Joseph
Horncastle, Lincs.

Cavendish, Sir Charles
Bolsover Castle, Derbys.

Crossley, Dr John
Abingdon, Oxon. Church of St
  Helen

Curie, Mme
London Wellcome Institute of the
  History of Medicine

Darwin, Charles
Downe, Kent Down House

Gray, Dr Alexander
Elgin, Grampian Gray's Hospital

Hall, Dr John
Stratford-upon-Avon, Warks. Hall's
  Croft

Herschel, Sir William
Windsor, Berks. Windsor Guildhall
  Exhibition

Hulse, Sir Edward
Breamore, Hants. Breamore House

Hunter, John
London Apothecaries' Hall; Royal
  College of Surgeons

Hutchinson, Sir Jonathan
Haslemere, Surrey Educational
  Museum

Lyle, Sir Charles
Midhurst, W. Sussex

Lyon, Dr
Harrow, Greater London Church of
  St Mary

Milley, Dr Thomas
Lichfield, Staffs.

Newton, Sir Isaac
Grantham, Lincs. Library and Museum
Spalding, Lincs. Spalding Gentlemen's
  Society
Woolsthorpe Manor, Lincs.

Radcliffe, Dr John
Oxford, Oxon. Bodleian Library

Smith, William
Scarborough, N. Yorks.

Stukeley, Dr William
Spalding, Lincs. Spalding Gentlemen's
Society

Turner, Dr
Church Stowe, Northants. Church of
SS Peter and Paul

Van Giffen, Dr A. E.
Ballynoe Stone Circle, Down

Wall, Dr
Worcester, Heref. & Worcs.

SCULPTORS

Sculptors approach their material in two different ways: either they
are explorers, searching out the forms they want in a block of marble
or a trunk of wood, and cutting away everything that is not part of
that form; or they are builders, making a shape grow from its core as
they add wax or clay. The hidden form or the undeveloped shape were
there before the sculptor got to work; the difference between him and
other men is that he sees them.

Adams-Acton, John
Carlisle, Cumbria Cathedral

Adye, Thomas
Cuckfield, W. Sussex Church of the
Holy Trinity
Little Dunmow, Essex Church of St
Mary

Armstead, H. H.
Carlisle, Cumbria Cathedral

Bacon, John
Belton, Kesteven, Lincs. Church of
SS Peter and Paul
Berkswell, W. Midlands Church of St
John the Baptist
Bottisham, Cambs. Church of the
Holy Trinity
Hawstead, Suffolk Church of All
Saints
London Somerset House
Lymington, Hants. Church of St
Thomas the Apostle
Rye, E. Sussex Church of St
Mary
Tyrrelspass, Westmeath
Wimpole, Cambs. Church of St
Andrew

Bacon, John the Younger
Beverley, Humberside Church of St
Mary
Bradford, W. Yorks. Cathedral
Cottesbrooke, Northants. Church of All
Saints
Cuckfield, W. Sussex Church of the
Holy Trinity
Harefield, Greater London Church of
St Mary
Hawstead, Suffolk Church of All
Saints
Manchester, Greater Manchester
Cathedral
Norwich, Norfolk Church of St
George
Odell, Beds. Church of All Saints
Stanstead Abbots, Herts. Church of
St James
Warfield, Berks. Church of St
Michael
Wollaton, Notts. Church of St
Leonard
Worcester, Heref. & Worcs. Cathedral

Wrenbury, Cheshire Church of St
Margaret

Baily, E. H.
Baldock, Herts. Church of St Mary
Buckden, Cambs. Church of St Mary
Lichfield, Staffs. Cathedral
Manchester, Greater Manchester
Cathedral
Newcastle upon Tyne, Tyne & Wear
Cathedral
Oxford, Oxon. Cathedral
Potterne, Wilts. Church of St Mary

Banks, Thomas
Ashbourne, Derbys. Church of St
Oswald
Bramley, Hants. Church of St James
Carlisle, Cumbria Cathedral
Flitton, Beds. Church of St John the
Baptist
Wimpole, Cambs. Church of St
Andrew

Behnes, W.
Clifton Campville, Staffs. Church of
St Andrew
London St John's Wood Chapel

Bernini, Pietro
London Church of All Saints

Bird, Francis
London Church of St Leonard;
St Paul's Cathedral

Boehm, Sir J. E.
Bedford, Beds.
Deene, Northants. Church of St
Peter
Eastnor, Heref. & Worcs. Church of St
John the Baptist
Lewknor, Oxon. Church of St
Margaret

Bourdelle, Emile
Aberdeen, Grampian Art Gallery

Burne-Jones, Sir Edward
Mells, Som. Church of St
Andrew

Bushnell, John
Ashburnham, E. Sussex Church of St
Peter

Babraham, Cambs. Church of St Peter
Boxted, Suffolk Church of the Holy
Trinity

Bushnell, William
Toddington, Beds. Church of St
George

Byrd, William
Oxford, Oxon. Sheldonian
Theatre
Swinbrook, Oxon. Church of St
Mary the Virgin

Campbell, Thomas
Warkton, Northants. Church of St
Edmund

Carabelli, Casimiro
Ickworth, Suffolk

Carabelli, Donato
Ickworth, Suffolk

Carline, John
Hodnet, Salop Church of St Luke

Carlini, Agostino
Dublin, Dublin Custom House
London Somerset House
Milton Abbas, Dorset Abbey

Carpenter, Andrew
Amersham, Bucks. Church of St Mary
Bloxham, Oxon. Church of Our
Lady
Leeds, W. Yorks. Church of St Peter
Theddlethorpe, Lincs. Church of All
Saints

Carter, Thomas
Bramley, Hants. Church of St
James
Celbridge, Kild.

Cartwright, Thomas
Cottesbrooke, Northants. Church of
All Saints

Cass, Christopher
Great Barrington, Glos. Church of St
Mary the Virgin
London Church of St Martin-in-the-
Fields

Caracchi, Joseph
London Somerset House

Chantrey, Sir Francis
Armagh, Arm.
Ashley, Staffs. Church of St. John
the Baptist
Bamburgh, Northld. Church of St
Aidan
Bristol, Avon Church of St
Mark
Burley-on-the-Hill, Leics. Church
of the Holy Cross
Charlton, Greater London Church of
St Luke
Derby, Derbys. Cathedral
Edington, Wilts. Church of SS Mary,
Katherine and All Saints
Farnworth, Cheshire Church of St Luke
Hackness, N. Yorks. Church of St
Peter
Hodnet, Salop Church of St Luke
Ilam, Staffs.
Ingestre, Staffs. Church of St Mary
Lichfield, Staffs. Cathedral
London Royal Exchange; St John's
Wood Chapel
Longbridge Deverill, Wilts. Church of
SS Peter and Paul
Melbury Sampford, Dorset Church of
St Mary
Orton Longueville, Cambs. Church of
the Holy Trinity
Plympton, Devon Church of St
Mary the Virgin
Snaith, Humberside Church of St
Laurence

Stoke Doyle, Northants. Church of St
Rumbald
Sunderland, Tyne & Wear Church of
the Holy Trinity
Waterperry, Oxon. Church of St
Mary the Virgin
Withyham, E. Sussex Church of St
Michael and All Angels
Worcester, Heref. & Worcs. Cathedral
Wragby, W. Yorks. Church of St
Michael

Cheere, John
Aberdeen, Grampian Robert Gordon's
College

Cheere, Sir Henry
Abbots Langley, Herts. Church of St
Lawrence
Amersham, Bucks. Church of St Mary
Doneraile, Cork
Frampton, Dorset Church of St Mary
Hillesden, Bucks. Church of All Saints
Hodnet, Salop Church of St Luke
Kirkleatham, Cleveland Church of St
Cuthbert
Llandwrog, Gwynedd Church of St
Twrog
Mold, Clwyd Church of St Mary
Oxford, Oxon. Cathedral
Teversal, Notts. Church of St
Catherine

Christmas, John
Ampton, Suffolk Church of St
Peter

Cibber, Caius Gabriel
Cambridge, Cambs. Trinity College
Library
London Monument; St Paul's
Cathedral
Ravenstone, Bucks. Church of All
Saints
Thoresby Hall, Notts.
Withyham, E. Sussex Church of St
Michael and All Angels

Collins, Alan
Guildford, Surrey Cathedral

Colquhoun, James
Glasgow, Strathclyde Hutcheson's
Hospital

Colt, Maximilian
Elmswell, Suffolk Church of St
John
Hatfield, Herts. Church of St
Etheldreda
Sleaford, Lincs. Church of St Denys

Comper, Sir Ninian
Wymondham, Norfolk Church of SS
Mary and Thomas of Canterbury

Cox, Samuel
Abington, Northants.

Crutcher, Richard
Bletchingley, Surrey Church of St
Mary

Cure, William
Cranford, Greater London Church of
St Dunstan
Long Melford, Suffolk Church of the
Holy Trinity

Degas, Edgar
Aberdeen, Grampian Art Gallery

Delvaux, Laurent
Old Warden, Beds. Church of St
Leonard
Rockingham, Northants. Church of
St Leonard

Deval, John, Junior
Clyffe Pypard, Wilts. Church of St
Peter

Dick, Sir William Reid
London Roosevelt Memorial

Dunn, Thomas
Brent Eleigh, Suffolk Church

Epstein, Sir Jacob
Aberdeen, Grampian Art Gallery
Bedford, Beds. Cecil Higgins Art
Gallery
Bury, Greater Manchester Art Gallery
and Museum
Coventry, W. Midlands Cathedral
Llandaff, S. Glam. Cathedral
Oldham, Greater Manchester Art
Gallery
Stockport, Greater Manchester War
Memorial Art Gallery
Swansea, W. Glam. Glynn Vivian Art
Gallery

Evesham, Epiphanius
Cuckfield, W. Sussex Church of the
Holy Trinity
Lynsted, Kent Church of SS Peter
and Paul
Titchfield, Hants. Church of St Peter

Fisher, John
Whalley, Lancs. Church of St Mary

Flaxman, John
Barlaston, Staffs. Wedgwood
Museum Trust
Basing, Hants. Church of St Mary
Bowness, Cumbria Church of St
Martin
Bradford, W. Yorks. Cathedral
Brecon, Powys Cathedral
Campsall, S. Yorks. Church of St
Mary Magdalene
Christchurch, Dorset Priory Church
Cuckfield, W. Sussex Church of the
Holy Trinity
East Dereham, Norfolk Church of St
Nicholas
Flamstead, Herts. Church of St
Leonard
Great Brington, Northants. Church of
St Mary
Great Gaddesden, Herts. Church of
St John the Baptist
Harrow, Greater London Church of
St Mary
Hatfield Broad Oak, Essex Church of
St Mary the Virgin
Ickworth, Suffolk
Inistioge, Kilk.
Ledbury, Heref. & Worcs. Church of St
Michael and All Angels
Leeds, W. Yorks. Church of St Peter
London Christ Church
Madingley, Cambs. Church of St
Mary Magdalene
Newcastle upon Tyne, Tyne & Wear
Cathedral
Port Sunlight, Merseyside Lady Lever
Art Gallery
Rotherham, S. Yorks. Church of All
Saints
Rufford, Lancs. Church of St Mary
Rye, E. Sussex Church of St Mary
Shellingford, Oxon. Church of St Faith
Throwley, Kent Church of St
Michael and All Angels
Wimpole, Cambs. Church of St
Andrew
Withyham, E. Sussex Church of St
Michael and All Angels
Wragby, W. Yorks. Church of St
Michael
Wroxton, Oxon. Church

Foley, J. H.
Birr, Offaly
Dublin, Dublin City Hall

Frampton, Sir George
London Kensington Gardens

Franceys, S.
Broughton, Staffs. Church of St Peter

Franceys, T.
Broughton, Staffs. Church of St Peter

Frink, Elizabeth
Eastbourne, E. Sussex Towner Art
Gallery

Gatley, Alfred
Disley, Cheshire Church of St Mary
the Virgin

Gibbons, Grinling
Bottesford, Leics. Church of St Mary
Burghley House, Cambs.
Conington, Cambs. Church of St Mary
Exton, Leics. Church of SS Peter
and Paul
Felbrigg, Norfolk Church of St
Margaret
Hampton Court, Greater London
Harefield, Greater London Church of
St Mary
Little Stanmore, Greater London
Church of St Lawrence
(Whitchurch)
London Charles II Statue, Chelsea
Hospital; Church of St Mary
Abchurch; St Paul's Cathedral
Petworth House, W. Sussex
Radbourne, Derbys. Church of St
Andrew

Gibson, Benjamin
Mold, Clwyd Church of St Mary

Gibson, John
Farnworth, Cheshire Church of St Luke
Fawsley, Northants. Church of St Mary

Gibson, Solomon
Mold, Clwyd Church of St Mary

Gilbert, Sir Alfred
Bedford, Beds.
Longbridge Deverill, Wilts. Church of
SS Peter and Paul
Windsor, Berks. Windsor Castle, St
George's Chapel

Gill, Eric
Guildford, Surrey Cathedral
Hadleigh, Suffolk Church of St Mary
Lapworth, Warks. Church of St Mary
Roker, Tyne & Wear Church of St
Andrew
South Harting, W. Sussex Church

Gott, J.
Gaddesby, Leics. Church of St Luke

Gower, Lord
Stratford-upon-Avon, Warks. Shakespeare Statue (Gower Memorial)

Green, Thomas
Acton, Suffolk Church of All Saints
Dunstable, Beds. Church of St Peter
Knebworth, Herts. Church of SS
Mary and Thomas of Canterbury
Norwich, Norfolk Church of St
George
Redgrave, Suffolk Church of St
Botolph

Guelfi, G. B.
Deene, Northants. Church of St Peter

Guldo, John
Bosbury, Heref. & Worcs. Church of the
Holy Trinity
Madley, Heref. & Worcs. Church of the
Nativity of St Mary the Virgin

Harrison, Charles
Dublin, Dublin Kildare Street Club

Henning, John
London Hyde Park Corner

Henning, John Junior
London Hyde Park Corner

Henning, Samuel
London Hyde Park Corner

Hepworth, Barbara
Aberdeen, Grampian Art Gallery

527

Kingston upon Hull, Humberside Ferens
Art Gallery
Swansea, W. Glam. Glynn Vivian Art
Gallery

Hickey, John
Abingdon, Oxon. Church of St Helen

Hickey, William
Delgany Church, Wicklow

Hill, Vernon
Guildford, Surrey Cathedral

Hogan, John
Carlow, Carlow
Cloyne, Cork
New Ross, Wex.

**Hohenlohelangenburg, Prince
Victor of**
Escrick, N. Yorks. Church of St Helen

Hollemans, Jasper
Great Brington, Northants. Church of
St Mary

Hollins, Peter
Dudley, W. Midlands Church of St
Thomas the Apostle

Hollins, William
Dudley, W. Midlands Church of St
Thomas the Apostle

Horsnaile, Christopher
Ampney Crucis, Glos. Church of the
Holy Rood

Horsnaile, Christopher the Elder
Dowdeswell, Glos. Church of St
Michael

Houghton, John
Castle Lyons, Cork

Hughes, John
Loughrea, Gal.

Hunt, John
Overstone, Northants. Church of St
Nicholas

Jagger, C.
London Hyde Park Corner

John, Goscombe
Hatfield, Herts. Church of St
Etheldreda

Johnson, Gerard
Bottesford, Leics. Church of St Mary
Stratford-upon-Avon, Warks. Church
of the Holy Trinity
Titchfield, Hants. Church of St Peter

Johnson, John
Stowlangtoft, Suffolk Church of St
George

Johnson, Nicholas
Bottesford, Leics. Church of St Mary
Exton, Leics. Church of SS Peter
and Paul

Jones, Adrian
London Hyde Park Corner

Joseph, Samuel
Dudley, W. Midlands Church of St
Thomas the Apostle

Kelly, Oisin
Strabane, Tyrone

Kemp, G. M.
Edinburgh, Lothian Scott
Monument

Kempster, Christopher
London Church of St Mary
Abchurch

Kidwell, William
Finglas, Dublin
Newmarket-on-Fergus, Clare

Kirk, Joseph
Ennis, Clare

Kirk, Thomas
Caledon House, Tyrone

Landseer, Sir Edwin
London Trafalgar Square

Latham, Jasper
Oxford, Oxon. Cathedral
Silkstone, S. Yorks. Church of All
Saints

Leoni, Giacomo
Quainton, Bucks. Church of the Holy
Cross and St Mary

Lough, J. G.
Crosthwaite, Cumbria Church of St
Kentigern
Ledbury, Heref. & Worcs. Church of St
Michael and All Angels
Toddington, Glos. Church of St
Andrew

Lucas, R. C.
Chilworth, Hants. Church of St Denys
Harlington, Greater London Church of
SS Peter and Paul

McDowell, Patrick
Belfast, Antrim Castle

Manning, Samuel
Stanstead Abbots, Herts. Church of St
James
Warfield, Berks. Church of St Michael

Marochetti, Baron
Belton, Kesteven, Lincs. Church of SS
Peter and Paul
Glasgow, Strathclyde Stirling's Library
Leeds, W. Yorks. Church of St Peter

Marshall, Edward
Amersham, Bucks. Church of St Mary
Ightham, Kent Church of St Peter
Withington, Glos. Church of St
Michael and All Angels

Marshall, Joshua
Chipping Campden, Glos. Church of
St James
Connington, Cambs. Church of St Mary
Leicester, Leics. Cathedral

Middleton, John
Church Stowe, Northants. Church of
SS Peter and Paul

Mills, Peter
Thorney Abbey, Cambs.

Monnot, P.
Stamford, Lincs. Church of St Mary

Moore, Henry
Aberdeen, Grampian Art Gallery
Bedford, Beds. Cecil Higgins Art
Gallery
Dublin, Dublin St Stephen's Green
Eastbourne, E. Sussex Towner Art
Gallery
Kingston upon Hull, Humberside
Ferens Art Gallery
Northampton, Northants. Church of
St Matthew
Swindon, Wilts. Museum and Art
Gallery

Moore, J. F.
Bradford, W. Yorks. Cathedral
Cottesbrooke, Northants. Church of
All Saints
Ettingdon, Warks. Church of the Holy
Trinity
Hatfield Broad Oak, Essex Church of
St Mary the Virgin
North Stoneham, Hants. Church of St
Nicholas
Saxton, N. Yorks. Church of All Saints
Winchester, Hants. Church of St Cross
Worcester, Heref. & Worcs. Cathedral

Morris, William
Scarborough, N. Yorks. Church of
St Martin

Munnings, Sir Alfred
Mells, Som. Church of St Andrew

Nixon, S.
London St John's Wood Church

Noble, Matthew
Ashley, Staffs. Church of St John the Baptist
Flitton, Beds. Church of St John the Baptist
Hackness, N. Yorks. Church of St Peter
Holme Lacy, Heref. & Worcs. Church of St Cuthbert
Leeds, W. Yorks. Town Hall
Marquess of Anglesey's Column, Anglesey, Gwynedd
Rufford, Lancs. Church of St Mary

Nollekens, Joseph
Abingdon, Oxon. Church of St Helen
Armagh, Arm.
Cirencester, Glos. Church of St John the Baptist
Derby, Derbys. Cathedral
East Horndon, Essex Church of All Saints
Exton, Leics. Church of SS Peter and Paul
Felbrigg, Norfolk Church of St Margaret
Great Barrington, Glos. Church of St Mary the Virgin
Great Brington, Northants. Church of St Mary
Hillsborough, Down
London Somerset House
Maidstone, Kent Church of All Saints
Ruabon, Clwyd Church
St Michael Penkevil, Cornwall Church of St Michael
Shobdon, Heref. & Worcs. Church of St John the Evangelist
Southport, Merseyside Church of St Cuthbert
Tittleshall, Norfolk Church of St Mary
Wetheral, Cumbria Church of the Holy Trinity
Whiston, Northants. Church of St Mary
Whitkirk, W. Yorks. Church of St Mary
Wisbech, Cambs. Church of SS Peter and Paul
Withyham, E. Sussex Church of St Michael and All Angels
Worcester, Heref. & Worcs. Cathedral

Nost, John
Bradford-on-Avon, Wilts. Church of the Holy Trinity
Chester, Cheshire Church of St John the Baptist
Curraghmore, Waterford
Durisdeer, Dumfs. & Gall. Church
Hampton Court, Greater London
Melbourne Hall, Derbys.
Sherborne, Dorset Abbey Church of St Mary
Wanstead, Essex Church of St Mary the Virgin
Whitkirk, W. Yorks. Church of St Mary
Winwick, Cheshire Church of St Oswald

Ohly, William
New Barnet, Greater London Abbey Art Centre and Museum

O'Shea Brothers
Dublin, Dublin Trinity College

Paolozzi, Eduardo
Kingston upon Hull, Humberside Ferens Art Gallery

Parker, Richard
Bottesford, Leics. Church of St Mary

Paty, James
Chepstow, Gwent Church of St Mary

Paty, James the Younger
Monmouth, Gwent Church of St Mary

Paty, Thomas
Chepstow, Gwent Church of St Mary

Physick, Edward
London St John's Wood Chapel
Sandal Magna, W. Yorks. Church of St Helen
Scarborough, N. Yorks. Church of St Mary
Tenby, Dyfed Church of St Mary

Pickford, Joseph
Ashby de la Zouch, Leics. Church

Pierce, Edward
Chester, Cheshire Church of St John the Baptist
London St Paul's Cathedral
Whitkirk, W. Yorks. Church of St Mary

Pitts, William
Whiston, Northants. Church

Pozzo, Andrea
Thurles, Tipp.

Rawlins, Thomas
Norwich, Norfolk Church of St George

Read, Nicholas
Lechlade, Glos. Church of St Laurence

Regnart, Charles
Hadleigh, Suffolk Church of St Mary
Ledbury, Heref. & Worcs. Church of St Michael and All Angels
Thorpe Market, Norfolk Church of St Margaret

Renard Goullet, Yann
Dublin, Dublin Custom House

Rice, James
Waterford, Waterford

Rodin, Auguste
Aberdeen, Grampian Art Gallery

Rose, Joseph the Elder
Reigate, Surrey Church of St Mary Magdalene

Rossi, Henry
London Church of St Pancras

Rossi, J. C. F.
Liverpool, Merseyside Town Hall
London Church of St Pancras
Shugborough, Staffs.

Roubiliac, Louis
Armagh, Arm.
Canon Pyon, Heref. & Worcs. Church of St Lawrence
Condover, Salop Church of SS Mary and Andrew
Derby, Derbys. Cathedral
Framlingham, Suffolk Church of St Michael
Gayhurst, Bucks. Church of St Peter
Lancaster, Lancs. Church of St Mary
London Church of St Botolph, Aldersgate; Church of St Mary
Quainton, Bucks. Church of the Holy Cross and St Mary
Scarborough, N. Yorks. Church of St Mary
Tittleshall, Norfolk Church of St Mary
Walton-on-Thames, Surrey Church of St Mary
Warkton, Northants. Church of St Edmund
Worcester, Heref. & Worcs. Cathedral
Wrexham, Clwyd Church of St Giles

Royleys of Burton-upon-Trent
Breedon on the Hill, Leics. Church of SS Mary and Hardulph

Rysbrack, Michael
Armagh, Arm.
Ashby de la Zouch, Leics. Church of St Helen

Bradford-on-Avon, Wilts. Church of the Holy Trinity
Bristol, Avon Church of All Saints
Clifton Campville, Staffs. Church of St Andrew
Derby, Derbys. Cathedral
Guildford, Surrey Church of the Holy Trinity
Hardingstone, Northants. Church of St Edmund
Hatfield, Herts. Church of St Etheldreda
London, Chiswick House
Lydiard Tregoze, Wilts. Church of St Mary
Lymington, Hants. Church of St Thomas the Apostle
Mold, Clwyd Church of St Mary
Normanton, Leics. Church of St Matthew
Ockham, Surrey Church of All Saints
Ruabon, Clwyd Church
St Michael Penkevil, Cornwall Church of St Michael
Stapleford, Leics. Church of St Mary Magdalene
Stoke Doyle, Northants. Church of St Rumbald
Stratford-upon-Avon, Warks. Church of the Holy Trinity
Tydd St Mary, Lincs. Church of St Mary

Scheemakers, Henry
Bandon, Cork
Kilkenny, Kilk. St Canice's Cathedral
Steeple Aston, Oxon. Church of SS Peter and Paul

Scheemakers, Peter
Abbots Langley, Herts. Church of St Lawrence
Amersham, Bucks. Church of St Mary
Aylesbury, Bucks. Church of St Mary
Bradford, W. Yorks. Cathedral
Clifton Reynes, Bucks. Church of St Mary the Virgin
Drumcondra, Dublin
Elgin, Grampian Cathedral
Gloucester, Glos. Church of St Mary-de-Crypt
Kirkleatham, Cleveland Church of St Cuthbert
Ledsham, W. Yorks. Church of All Saints
Old Warden, Beds. Church of St Leonard
Rockingham, Northants. Church of St Leonard
Urchfont, Wilts. Church of St Michael
Wimpole, Cambs. Church of St Andrew

Scheemakers, Thomas
Bungay, Suffolk Church of the Holy Trinity
Eastnor, Heref. & Worcs. Church of St John the Baptist
Preston-on-Stour, Warks. Church

Sheehan, David
Castle Lyons, Cork

Sidnell, Michael
Bredon, Heref. & Worcs. Church of St Giles
Yatton, Avon Church of St Mary

Sievier, R. W.
Stanton Harcourt, Oxon. Church of St Michael

Smith, Nathaniel
London Somerset House

Smyth, Edward
Derry, Lond. Walker Monument
Dublin, Dublin City Hall; Custom House
Navan, Meath

Smyth, John
Derry, Lond. Walker Monument

Soldani
Glynde Place, E. Sussex

Stanton, Edward
Ampney Crucis, Glos. Church of the Holy Rood
Aylesbury, Bucks. Church of St Mary
Belton, Kesteven, Lincs. Church of SS Peter and Paul
Faringdon, Oxon. Church of All Saints
Fawsley, Northants. Church of St Mary
Knebworth, Herts. Church of SS Mary and Thomas of Canterbury
Lichfield, Staffs. Cathedral
Madingley, Cambs. Church of St Mary Magdalene
Strensham, Heref. & Worcs. Church of St John the Baptist

Stanton, Thomas
Stratford-upon-Avon, Warks. Church of the Holy Trinity
Worcester, Heref. & Worcs. Cathedral

Stanton, William
Acton Round, Salop Church
Belton, Kesteven, Lincs. Church of SS Peter and Paul
Besford, Heref. & Worcs. Church of St Peter
Blithfield, Staffs. Church of St Leonard
Croome D'Abitot, Heref. & Worcs. Church of St Mary Magdalene
Fawsley, Northants. Church of St Mary
Flamstead, Herts. Church of St Leonard
Harefield, Greater London Church of St Mary
Haslingfield, Cambs. Church of All Saints
London Church of St Paul
Macclesfield, Cheshire Church of St Michael
Quainton, Bucks. Church of the Holy Cross and St Mary
Ravenstone, Bucks. Church of All Saints
Toddington, Beds. Church of St George
Wrexham, Clwyd Church of St Giles

Stayner, Thomas
Church Stowe, Northants. Church of SS Peter and Paul
Quainton, Bucks. Church of the Holy Cross and St Mary

Steer, Wilson
Bury, Greater Manchester Art Gallery and Museum

Stone, John
Hessett, Suffolk Church of St Ethelbert

Stone, Nicholas
Acton Burnell, Salop Church of St Mary
Ampton, Suffolk Church of St Peter
Berkhamsted, Herts. Church of St Peter
Bramfield, Suffolk Church of St Mary
Charlton, Greater London Church of St Luke
Church Stowe, Northants. Church of SS Peter and Paul
Coxwold, N. Yorks. Church of St Michael
Enfield, Greater London Church of St Andrew
Great Brington, Northants. Church of St Mary
Greenwich, Greater London Chapel, Trinity Hospital

Hatfield, Herts. Church of St
Etheldreda
Hawstead, Suffolk Church of All
Saints
Kirby Hall, Northants.
London Church of St Helen's
Portchester, Hants. Church of St Mary
Portsmouth, Hants. Cathedral
Redgrave, Suffolk Church of St
Botolph
Stanwell, Surrey Church of St Mary
Tittleshall, Norfolk Church of St
Mary
Watford, Herts. Church of St Mary

Taylor, Sir Robert
Colne, Lancs. Church of St
Bartholomew

Tenerani, Pietro
Farnworth, Cheshire Church of St Luke

Theed, W.
Newcastle upon Tyne, Tyne & Wear
Cathedral

Theed, William the Younger
Manchester, Lancs. Cathedral
Wrenbury, Cheshire Church of St
Margaret

Thom, James
Ayr, Strathclyde

Thomas, John Evan
Carew Cheriton, Dyfed Church
Halifax, W. Yorks. Town Hall
Leeds, W. Yorks. Town Hall
Tenby, Dyfed Church of St Mary

Thornycroft, Hamo
Carlisle, Cumbria Cathedral

Travers, Martin
Compton Beauchamp, Oxon. Church of
St Swithin

Triquetti, Baron
Windsor, Berks. Windsor Castle,
St George's Chapel

Tyler, William
Mersham, Kent Church of St John the
Baptist
Oxford, Oxon. Cathedral
Shellingford, Oxon. Church of St
Faith

Van Gelder, P.
Warkton, Northants. Church of St
Edmund
Wrexham, Clwyd Church of St
Giles

Vierpyl, Simon
Dublin, Dublin Casino Marino

Watson, Samuel
Chatsworth, Derbys.

Watts, George Frederic
Compton, Surrey Watts Gallery

Webb, Philip
Scarborough, N. Yorks. Church of St
Martin

Weekes, Henry
Amersham, Bucks. Church of St Mary
Christchurch, Dorset Priory Church

Westmacott, Henry
Whitkirk, W. Yorks. Church of St
Mary

Westmacott, J. S.
Aughton, Lancs. Church of St Michael

Westmacott, Sir Richard
Arreton, Isle of Wight Church of St
George
Bicester, Oxon. Church of St Edburg
Blithfield, Staffs. Church of St Leonard
Cuckfield, W. Sussex Church of the
Holy Trinity
Knutsford, Cheshire Church of St John
the Baptist
London Royal Exchange
Monmouth, Gwent Church of St Mary
Ruthin, Clwyd Church of St Peter
Stratford-upon-Avon, Warks. Church
of the Holy Trinity
Whalley, Lancs. Church of St Mary
Wollaton, Notts. Church of St
Leonard
Yeovil, Avon Church of St John the
Baptist

White, Thomas
Alrewas, Staffs. Church of All
Saints

Wilton Joseph
Bicester, Oxon. Church of St Edburg
Dartrey Mausoleum, Monag.
Padworth, Berks. Church of St John
the Baptist
Sowerby, W. Yorks. Church of St Peter

Wood, Francis Derwent
London Hyde Park Corner

Wyatt, M. C.
Escrick, N. Yorks. Church of St Helen
Windsor, Berks. Windsor Castle,
St George's Chapel

Wynne, Robert
Ruabon, Clwyd Church

Zadkine, Ossip
Aberdeen, Grampian Art Gallery

STAINED GLASS MAKERS

The belief that God once walked on the earth in the flesh is the
germinating idea from which springs the glory of stained glass windows.
Listed here are the names of those who have tried to equal the
anonymous genius of the medieval stained glass makers. In churches and
cathedrals throughout Britain, Christ and the saints (and sometimes
lesser men, such as nobles or rich merchants) are portrayed in trans-
parent radiance. Until light penetrates them the colours remain dead,
and the windows are thereby themselves symbols of man and his
contact with the divine.

ackler, Joseph
udley, W. Midlands Church of St
Thomas the Apostle

urlison & Grylls
ylesbury, Bucks. Church of St
Mary

urne-Jones, Sir Edward
atfield, Herts. Church of St
Etheldreda

Ribbesford, Heref. & Worcs. Church of St
Leonard
Rotherfield, E. Sussex Church of St
Denys
St Germans, Cornwall Church of
St Germanus
Topcliffe, W. Yorks. Church of
St Columba
Waltham Holy Cross, Essex Abbey
Church of the Holy Cross

531

Youlgreave, Derbys. Church of All
Saints

Chagall, Marc
Tudeley, Kent Church of All
Saints

Childe, A. E.
Loughrea, Gal.

Clarke, Harry
·Cork, Cork
Gorey, Wex. Protestant Parish
Church
Letterkenny, Don.

Clayton & Bell
Appleton-le-Moors, N. Yorks. Christ
Church
Kenton, Devon Church of All Saints
Kings Langley, Herts. Church of All
Saints
London Church of St Augustine
Nottingham, Notts. Church of St Mary

Clayton, John
Etchingham, E. Sussex Church of SS
Mary and Nicholas

Comper, Sir Ninian
East Markham, Notts. Church of St
John the Baptist
East Meon, Hants. Church of All
· Saints
Egmanton, Notts. Church of St
Mary
Harrow, Greater London Church of
St Mary
Langham, Leics. Church of SS
Peter and Paul
Puddletown, Dorset Church of St
Mary

Easton, Hugh
London Church of St Luke

Eden, F. C.
Blisland, Cornwall Church of SS
Protus and Hyacinth
Mullion, Cornwall Church of St
Melan

Forsyth, Moira
Guildford, Surrey Cathedral

Healey, Michael
Clongowes, Kild.
Letterkenny, Don.
Loughrea, Gal.

Hone, Evie
Clongowes, Kild.
Loughrea, Gal.

Kempe, C. E.
Abingdon, Oxon. Church of St Helen
Aldwinkle, Northants. Church of St
Peter
Alfriston, E. Sussex Church of St
Andrew
Alveley, Salop Church of St
Mary
Barsham, Suffolk Church of the Holy
Trinity
Berkhamsted, Herts. Church of St
Peter
Caistor, Lincs. Church of SS Peter
and Paul
Charlcote, Warks. Church of St
Leonard
Cholsey, Oxon. Church of St Mary
Cuckfield, W. Sussex Church of the
Holy Trinity
Eastnor, Heref. & Worcs. Church of St
John the Baptist
Edlesborough, Bucks. Church of St
Mary
Froyle, Hants. Church of the
Assumption
Glynde, E. Sussex Church of St Mary
the Virgin
Kempsford, Glos. Church of St Mary
the Virgin

Ledbury, Heref. & Worcs. Church of St
Michael and All Angels
Leighton Buzzard, Beds. Church of
All Saints
Leominster, Herts. Church of SS Peter
and Paul
Monmouth, Gwent Church of St
Mary
Much Marcle, Heref. & Worcs. Church
of St Bartholomew
Norton, Cleveland Church of St Mary
Padworth, Berks. Church of St John
the Baptist
Thaxted, Essex Church of St John the
Baptist
Wightwick Manor, W. Midlands Church
Wraxall, Avon Church of All Saints

McGoldrick, Hubert
Loughrea, Gal.

Mayer & Co.
Leominster, Herts. Church of SS Peter
and Paul

Morris & Co.
Armathwaite, Cumbria Chapel of
Christ and Mary
Beaudesert, Warks. Church of St
Nicholas
Hatfield, Herts. Church of St
Etheldreda

Morris, William
Bromham, Wilts. Church of St
Nicholas
Nun Monkton, N. Yorks. Church of St
Mary
Rotherfield, E. Sussex Church of St
Denys
Rye, E. Sussex Church of St Mary
Tamworth, Staffs. Church of St
Editha

O'Brien, Catherine
Gorey, Wex. Protestant Parish
Church

Piper, John
Coventry, W. Midlands Cathedral
Liverpool, Merseyside Roman
Catholic Cathedral

Pollen, Patrick
Strabane, Tyrone

Pugin, A. W.
Kilpeck, Heref. & Worcs. Church of SS
Mary and David

Pursar, Sarah
Cork, Cork
Loughrea, Gal.

Reyntiens, Patrick
Coventry, W. Midlands Cathedral
Liverpool, Merseyside Roman
Catholic Cathedral
Odiham, Hants. Church of All Saints

Rutherford, Rosemary
Guildford, Surrey Cathedral

Scott, Sir Gilbert
Rotherham, S. Yorks. Church of
All Saints

Strachan, Douglas
Winchelsea, E. Sussex Church of St
Thomas the Apostle

Wailes, William
Bishops Cannings, Wilts. Church of
St Mary the Virgin
Bishopstone, Wilts. Church of St
John the Baptist
Swaffham, Norfolk Church of SS
Peter and Paul

Ward & Hughes
Edlesborough, Bucks. Church of
St Mary

Kings Langley, Herts. Church of All
Saints
Nottingham, Notts. Church of St Mary

Whall, Christopher
Brockhampton-by-Ross, Heref. & Worcs.
Church of All Saints

Willement, Thomas
Aylesbury, Bucks. Church of St
Mary
Charlecote, Warks. Church of St
Leonard
Leicester, Leics. Church of St
Margaret

THINKERS, MEN OF LETTERS
AND THE THEATRE

Britain's poets, playwrights and her sturdy political thinkers—Keats,
Shakespeare and Adam Smith—have enriched the world. But
England's most characteristic contribution to literature is perhaps the
novel; and her most characteristic literary figure is Dr Johnson,
massive in his commonsense—a quality that can be sensed at the
house he lived in, off Fleet Street.

Addison, Joseph
Lichfield, Staffs.
Oxford, Oxon. Magdalen College

Alexander, Sir William
Menstrie Castle, Central

Ashmole, Elias
Oxford, Oxon. Ashmolean Museum

Austen, Jane
Chawton, Hants. Jane Austen's Home
Winchester, Hants. City Museum

Bacon, Francis
Gorhambury, Herts.
London Gray's Inn
St Albans, Herts. Church of St
Michael

Baillie, Lady
Mellerstain, Borders

Barnes, William
Dorchester, Dorset Dorset County
Museum

Barrie, Sir James
Dumfries, Dumfs. & Gall.
Kirriemuir, Tayside

Beckford, William
Bristol, Avon Church of St Mark

Berkeley, George
Cloyne, Cork

Blackmore, R. D.
Tiverton, Devon Blundell's

Bodley, Sir Thomas
Oxford, Oxon. Bodleian Library

Borrow, George
Llangollen, Clwyd

Boswell, James
Edinburgh, Lothian James Court

Brontë, Anne
Haworth, W. Yorks. Brontë Parsonage
Museum

Brontë, Charlotte
Birstall, W. Yorks. Oakwell Hall
Haworth, W. Yorks. Brontë Parsonage
Museum
North Lees Hall, Derbys.

Brontë, Emily Jane
Haworth, W. Yorks. Brontë Parsonage
Museum

Browning, Robert
London Carlyle's House

Bulwer Lytton,
Sir Edward
Knebworth House, Herts.

Bunyan, John
Ampthill, Beds.
Bedford, Beds.
Elstow, Beds.

Burns, Robert
Alloway, Strathclyde Burns Cottage
Dumfries, Dumfs. & Gall.

Byron, Lord
Newstead Abbey, Notts.
Thrumpton Hall, Notts.

Camden, William
Hadrian's Wall, Cumbria–Northld.

Carlyle, Thomas
Ecclefechan, Dumfs. & Gall.
Kirkcaldy, Fife
London Carlyle's House

Carroll, Lewis (Dodgson,
Charles)
Guildford, Surrey Museum

Chaucer, Geoffrey
Berkhamsted, Herts.
Oxford, Oxon. Merton College
Library

Churchill, Sir Winston
Chartwell, Kent
Ditchley Park, Oxon.
Oldham, Greater Manchester Art Gallery

Clare, John
Peterborough, Cambs. Museum

Coleridge, Samuel Taylor
Coleridge Cottage, Som.

Conan Doyle, Sir Arthur
Grimspound, Devon

Coote, Thomas
Bellamont Forest, Cavan

Cotton, Sir Robert
London British Museum

Cowper, William
Berkhamsted, Herts.
East Dereham, Norfolk Church of St
Nicholas
Liverpool, Merseyside Hornby Library

Curwen, Henry
Amersham, Bucks. Church of St Mary

Dalton, John
Manchester, Greater Manchester Portico
Library

Davidson, John
Kirkoswald, Strathclyde Souter Johnnie's
Cottage

Defoe, Daniel
Lower Largo, Fife Robinson Crusoe
Statue

Dickens, Charles
Barnard Castle, Durham
Broadstairs, Kent Bleak House
Knebworth House, Herts.
London Carlyle's House; Church of
St Luke, Sydney Street; Cuming
Museum; Dickens House; George
Inn; Staple Inn
Portsmouth, Hants.
Rochester, Kent
Rockingham Castle, Northants.
Wisbech, Cambs.

Donne, John
London Lincoln's Inn

Drummond, William
Hawthornden, Lothian

Dryden, John
Cotterstock Hall, Northants.

Duff, William
Elgin, Grampian No. 7 High Street

Dunne, J. W.
Blair Castle, Tayside

Eliot, George
Arbury Hall, Warks.
Nuneaton, Warks. Museum and Art
Gallery

Evelyn, John
Dyrham Park, Avon

Fielding, Henry
London Church of St Benet

Flight, Thomas
Worcester, Heref. & Worcs.

Fonteyn, Dame Margot
Northampton, Northants. Central
Museum and Art Gallery

Galsworthy, John
Mapledurham House, Oxon.

Garrick, David
Hendon, Greater London Hendon Hall
Lichfield, Staffs.
Royal Tunbridge Wells, Kent
*Smallhythe Place (The Ellen Terry
Memorial), Kent*
Stratford-upon-Avon, Warks.

Gay, John
Barnstaple, Devon St Anne's Chapel
Museum

Gibbon, Edward
Buriton, Hants.

Graham, Kenneth
Mapledurham House, Oxon.

Granville-Barker, Harley
London British Theatre Museum

Gray, Thomas
Stoke Poges, Bucks. Gray's Monument

Gregory, James
St Andrews, Fife

Gresham, Sir Thomas
London Church of St Helen

Hardy, Thomas
Dorchester, Dorset Dorset County
Museum
Hardy's Cottage, Dorset
Wareham, Dorset
Waterston Manor, Dorset

Harford, John
Blaise Hamlet, Avon

Harvard, John
Stratford-upon-Avon, Warks. Harvard
House

Hawker, Robert
Morwenstow, Cornwall Church of
St Morwenna

Hazlitt, William
Maidstone, Kent Chillington Manor

Hearst, William Randolph
Gilling Castle, N. Yorks.
St Donat's Castle, S. Glam.

Hill, Abraham
Sutton-at-Hone, Kent St John's
Jerusalem

Hope, Anthony
Leatherhead, Surrey

Housman, A. E.
Much Wenlock, Salop

Hume, David
Edinburgh, Lothian James Court

Hurd, Richard
Hartlebury Castle, Heref. & Worcs.

Irving, Sir Henry
Bournemouth, Hants. Russell-Cotes
Museum and Art Gallery

James, Henry
Rye, E. Sussex

Jefferies, Richard
Coate, Wilts. Richard Jefferies
Museum

Jerome, Jerome K.
Walsall, W. Midlands E. M. Flint Art
Gallery

Johnson, Dr Samuel
Dunvegan, Isle of Skye, Highland
Edinburgh, Lothian James Court
Lichfield, Staffs.
Liverpool, Merseyside Hornby Library
London Johnson's House; Middle
Temple Hall; Staple Inn
Royal Tunbridge Wells, Kent

Jonson, Ben
Hawthornden, Lothian
Penshurst Place, Kent

Joyce, James
Dublin, Dublin Dunleary

Keats, John
London Guy's Hospital; Keats House

Kingsley, Charles
Bideford, Devon
London Church of St Luke,
Sydney Street

Kipling, Rudyard
Bateman's, E. Sussex

Knox, John
Edinburgh, Lothian John Knox's
House
Mid Calder, Lothian
Perth, Tayside

Lamb, Charles
London Middle Temple Hall

Lyte, Sir Henry
Lytes Cary, Som.

Lytton, Lytton
Knebworth, Herts. Church of SS Mary
and Thomas of Canterbury

Martyn, Edward
Tullira Castle, Gal.

Miller, Hugh
Cromarty, Highland Hugh Miller's
Cottage

Milton, John
Chalfont St Giles, Bucks. Milton's
Cottage

Moore, George
Moore Hall, Mayo

O'Casey, Sean
Dublin, Dublin Abbey Theatre

Paine, Thomas
Thetford, Norfolk Grey Gables

Pepys, Samuel
Brampton, Cambs. Pepys's House
Dyrham Park, Avon
Huntingdon, Cambs.
London Church of St Bride

Pope, Alexander
Spalding, Lincs. Spalding Gentlemen's
Society
Temple Newsam House, W. Yorks.

Potter, Beatrix
Hill Top, Cumbria

Roget, Peter Mark
Manchester, Greater Manchester Portico
Library

Ruskin, John
Kirkby Lonsdale, Cumbria Church of
St Mary the Virgin
Oxford, Oxon. University Museum

Sackville, Thomas
Knole, Kent

Sackville-West, Victoria
Sissinghurst Castle, Kent

Salisbury, William
Rug Chapel, Gwynedd

Scott, John
Ware, Herts.

Scott, Sir Walter
Abbotsford House, Borders
Burleigh Castle, Tayside
Caerlaverock Castle, Dumfs. & Gall.
Carlisle, Cumbria
Castleton, Derbys.
Craignethan Castle, Strathclyde
Dryburgh Abbey, Borders
Dunvegan, Isle of Skye, Highland
Edinburgh, Lothian Old Tolbooth
Finlarig Castle, Central
Gifford, Lothian Yester House
Inveraray Castle, Strathclyde
Isle of May, Firth of Forth
Knockderry Castle, Strathclyde
Stamford, Lincs. High Street
Winton House, Lothian

Shakespeare, William
Cawdor Castle, Highland
Clopton House, Warks.
Gawsworth Hall, Cheshire
London Crosby Hall; Gray's Inn;
Guildhall; Middle Temple Hall;
Public Record Office
Stratford-upon-Avon, Warks. Church
of the Holy Trinity; Guild Chapel;
New Place; Royal Shakespeare
Theatre Picture Gallery

Shaw, George Bernard
Ayot St Lawrence, Herts. Shaw's
Corner

Shelley, P. B.
Christchurch, Dorset Priory Church
London Kensington Gardens

Sheridan, Richard Brinsley
Polesden Lacey, Surrey

Siddons, Mrs Sarah
*Smallhythe Place (The Ellen Terry
Memorial), Kent*

Sidney, Sir Philip
Penshurst Place, Kent

Smith, Adam
Kirkcaldy, Fife Museum and Art
Gallery

Southey, Robert
Crosthwaite, Cumbria Church of
St Kentigern

Spenser, Edmund
Alton, Hants.
Doneraile, Cork
Enniscorthy, Wex.

Stevenson, R. L.
Isle of May, Firth of Forth Lighthouse

Swift, Jonathan
Celbridge, Kild.
Dublin, Dublin Cathedral of St Patrick
Kilkenny, Kilk.
Woodlands, Dublin

Tennyson, Alfred Lord
Lincoln, Lincs. Usher Art Gallery
London Carlyle's House
Somersby, Lincs. Somersby
House
Tintagel Castle, Cornwall

Terry, Dame Ellen
*Smallhythe Place (The Ellen Terry
Memorial), Kent*

Thackeray, William Makepeace
Clevedon Court, Avon
London Carlyle's House; Middle
Temple Hall

Thomas, Dylan
Laugharne, Dyfed

Trollope, Anthony
Banagher, Offaly

Ulanova, Galina
Northampton, Northants. Central
Museum and Art Gallery

Walpole, Horace
Shobdon, Heref. & Worcs. Church of St
John the Evangelist
Twickenham, Greater London
Strawberry Hill
Wolterton Hall, Norfolk

Wells, H. G.
Midhurst, W. Sussex

Wesley, Charles
Epworth, Lincs. Old Rectory

Wilkes, John
Aylesbury, Bucks.

Williams, Alfred
Coate, Wilts. Richard Jefferies
Museum

Wordsworth, Dorothy
Cockermouth, Cumbria

Wordsworth, William
Cockermouth, Cumbria
Edinburgh, Lothian White Hart Inn
Grasmere, Cumbria Dove
Cottage
Hawkshead, Cumbria

Wycliffe, John
Bristol, Avon Westbury College

Yeats, W. B.
Dublin, Dublin Abbey Theatre
Drumcliff, Sligo
Gort, Gal.
Sligo, Sligo St Stephen's Green

HOW TO USE
THE MAPS

Continuity flaps have been used in the map section to allow routes to be followed from page to page without interruption and to enable places on the flap to be seen in relation to areas to both east and west. Each map is overlapped by the maps covering the regions to the north and south. Arrows in the margin indicate the number of the pages on which the map is continued.

In production the continuity flaps have been folded over each other in groups; to use the maps divide the page and fold each flap separately.

A uniform grid has been superimposed on each map and the simple two-letter reference code is linked to the entries in the gazetteers of Britain and Ireland.

The continuity flaps provide
a link between adjacent maps. Close
the flap to see a point on it
in relation to the region to the west

Open out the continuity flap
to see a place on it in relation to
the region to the east

WHERE TO FIND THE TREASURES OF THE BRITISH ISLES

BASED ON ORDNANCE SURVEY

SYMBOLS USED ON THE MAPS

ROADS

MOTORWAY . . . .

TRUNK OR 'A' ROAD . . . . . .

'B' ROAD . . . .

OTHER TARRED . . . .

BOUNDARIES

NATIONAL . . . .

COUNTY - ENGLAND & . . . . .
WALES
REGION - SCOTLAND

SETTLEMENTS

TOWN . . . . . . READING
Dorchester . . . o

VILLAGE . . . . Silchester o

PHYSICAL FEATURES

LAKE . . . .

COASTLINE . . . .

TREASURE SITES

CASTLE/HOUSE . . . .

GARDEN . . . .

ECCLESIASTICAL
BUILDING . . . .

MUSEUM/ART GALLERY . . . .

INDUSTRIAL MONUMENT . . . .

ARCHAEOLOGICAL SITE . . . .

MONUMENT/MEMORIAL . . . .

OTHER NOTABLE
FEATURES . . . .

TOWNS/VILLAGES OF ARCHITECTURAL
INTEREST *named in black* . . . . *Acton* o

This incidence chart shows how the following 38 pages of maps, covering the whole of Britain and Ireland, have been arranged to maintain continuity and facilitate route-planning. The maps of England, Scotland, and Wales are at a scale of 10 miles to 1 inch, which gives each full map spread a coverage of an area approximately 100 miles by 120 miles. The maps of Ireland are at a scale of 12.6 miles to 1 inch and cover an even greater area on each spread.

THE MAPS OF GREAT BRITAIN HAVE BEEN DERIVED FROM ORDNANCE SURVEY MATERIAL WITH THE SANCTION OF THE CONTROLLER OF H.M. STATIONERY OFFICE (CROWN COPYRIGHT RESERVED)

THE MAPS OF THE REPUBLIC OF IRELAND AND NORTHERN IRELAND ARE BASED ON ORDNANCE SURVEY BY PERMISSION OF THE GOVERNMENT OF THE REPUBLIC OF IRELAND (PERMIT NO. 1019) AND THE CONTROLLER OF H.M. STATIONERY OFFICE

THE CONTINUITY FLAPS USED ON THESE MAPS WERE DEVISED BY THE READER'S DIGEST ASSOCIATION LIMITED, LONDON. THIS FEATURE OF THE MAPS IS PROTECTED BY BRITISH PATENT NOS. 1179103 AND 1179104

Map Labels

Scilly Isles / Land's End area (top)

St. Ives
The Carracks
Gurnard's Head
Zennor
Zennor Quoit
Chysauster
Pendeen Watch
Lanyon Quoit
Cape Cornwall
St Just
Ludgvan
Penzance
Newlyn
Mousehole
St Burian
LAND'S END
Sennen
Treen
Gwennap Head

NW Point
Lundy
Shutter Pt

Bryher
St Martin's
Samson
Tresco
St Mary's
Hugh Town
SCILLY ISLES
Annet
St Agnes

Devon / North Cornwall coast

Ilfracombe Lighthouse
Bull Pt
Berrynarbor
Morte Pt
Mortehoe
W Down
Georgeham
Arlington
Baggy Pt
Croyde
Marwood
Braunton
A361
Instow
Bishop's
Barnstaple
Appledore
Northam Tawton
Westward Ho
Northam
New Tra
Bideford
Horwood
Atherin

HARTLAND POINT
Hartland
Clovelly
Stoke
Woolfardisworthy
Buckland Brewer
Great Torrington
A388
A386
Morwenstow
Bradworthy
Stibb Cross
Merton
Petrockstow
Sharpnose Points
Kilkhampton
A39
Shebbear
Sheepwash
Highampton
BUDE
Bude
Stratton
Holsworthy
A3072
BAY Launcells
A3072
Marhamchurch
Dizzard Pt
Poundstock
Halwill
Northlew
Cambeak
St Gennys
Week St Mary
Ashwater
D E
Okehamp
Fire Beacon Pt
Boscastle
Boyton
Celtic Monastery
Forrabury Common
Tintagel Head
Tintagel
Egloskerry
Wortham Manor
Tintagel Old Post Office
Tintagel Castle
A395
Launceston
Lifton
Lewtrenchard
Lydfor
Delabole
Luneast
Chillaton
N Brentor
Brent Tor
Camelford
Lewannick
Milton Abbot
Mary T
Port Isaac
St Teath
Altarnun
North Hill
Bratton Clovelly
Bridestowe
Pentire Point
Doyden Castle
Rough Tor
Sydenham Damerel
Yelverton
Gulland Rock
St Endellion
BODMIN
Tavistock
St Minver
MOOR
A390
Gunnislake
Trevose Head
Padstow
Blisland
Pensilva
Callington
Horrab
Park Head
A30
The Hurlers
Cotehele House
Yelverton
Bere Alston
A388
St Issey
Bere Ferrers
Trev
Wadebridge
A389
Bodmin
St-Neot
Buckland Abbey
Legis To
St Mawgan
A38
Tamerton Fol
St Columb Major
Roche
Lanhydrock House
Liskeard
Bere
Royal Albert
Kelsey Head
Newquay
A392
Bugle
Lostwithiel
A390
St Germans
Saltash
PLYMO
Towan Head
Crantock
St Dennis
St Winnow
Sandplace
Antony House
Penhale Pt
Cubert
Trerice
A3058
Roche
Duloe Circle
Torpoint
Saltra
Newlyn East
St Blazey
Lanreath
Looe
Millbrook
Brixton
Perranporth
A3058
Castle Dore
Lanteglos-by-Fowey
St George's or Looe Island
Yealmp
St Agnes Head
ST AUSTELL
Fowey
Polruan
Polperro
WHITESAND BAY
Rame Head
Porthtowan
A390
Grampound
Black Head
Gribbin Head
Eddystone
Portreath
Navax Pt
Probus
Mevagissey
Rame Head
Godrevy
St Day
Truro
Chapel Pt
Gorran Haven
The Carracks
St Ives
Redruth
St Michael Penkevil
Tregony
Dodman Point
Gurnard's Head
Zennor
Zennor Quoit
Camborne
Veryan
Pendeen Watch
Chysauster
A30
Feock
Penryn
Gerrans
Cape Cornwall
Lanyon Quoit
Trencrom Hill
St Mawes Castle
St Just
Ludgvan
Leedstown
Godolphin House
St Mawes
A307
Marazion
Penryn
Pendennis Castle
Newlyn
Penzance
St Michael's Mount
Falmouth
FALMOUTH BAY
MOUNT'S BAY
Helston
Glendurgan
Mousehole
Trewavas Head
Rosemullion Head
LAND'S END
St Buryan
St Clement's Isle
Porthleven
Mawnan
Nare Pt
Sennen
Mawgan
Manacle Pt
Gwennap Head
Treen
Gunwalloe
Poldhu Pt
Mullion
St Keverne
Coverack
Mullion
Black Head
Lizard
Ruan Minor
LIZARD POINT

CORNWALL

BUCCANEERS FOR THE QUEEN

Men of Devon were renowned among the seafaring adventurers of the Elizabethan age. After the voyages of Columbus (1492) and Magellan (1520) had opened up new horizons, Spain and Portugal had the Pope's authority to divide any newly discovered lands between them. English sailors therefore had to find a north-west passage to the Orient or dispute the claims of Spain. With the support of Queen Elizabeth they took to the Spanish Seas.

Sir John Hawkins, born in Plymouth, sailed to West Africa, collected negroes and sold them in Hispaniola (San Domingo). A second trip was equally profitable (1564-5), but his third venture, in 1567, was disastrous: his convoy fell into the hands of a Spanish war fleet. Some of his men were tortured and killed; some were ransomed; others, including himself, escaped.

Sir Francis Drake, born near Tavistock, took part in Hawkins's misadventure of 1567. Intent on revenge and aware of the immense prizes to be won, he made several voyages to the West Indies. In 1577 Drake set sail for the Rio Plata, and in 1578 rounded Cape Horn. He sailed up the west coast of America, possibly getting as far north as Santa Barbara. Heading west across the Pacific, Drake began the long leg of the great circumnavigation that ended in Plymouth in 1581.

SIR FRANCIS DRAKE

Sir Walter Raleigh was born near Budleigh Salterton and educated at Oriel College, Oxford. Raleigh voyaged to North America, and returned in 1586 with a far-reaching discovery—tobacco. He attended Court for several years, but earned the queen's disfavour after a quarrel with her favourite Essex. James I was persuaded to let Raleigh undertake an expedition in search of gold, but the failure of this mission and an action against the Spanish settlement of San Tomas resulted in Raleigh being sent to the Tower—for the third time. After a summary trial, he was executed on October 29, 1618.

SHIPSHAPE AND BRISTOL FASHION

For the seamen of Bristol trade was the motive for epic voyages, and their goal was to find the north-west passage to the fabulous East.

That was the lodestar for **John Cabot,** born Giovanni Caboto in Genoa; who settled in Bristol as a merchant. In 1497, he set sail in the *Matthew* and reached Cape Breton Island, but failed to find the north-west passage. His son Sebastian joined him on some of his voyages, but by 1512 had established a reputation as a cartographer, giving service in the art to Henry VIII. In 1519 **Sebastian Cabot** was made Pilot Major to Charles V, King of Spain. Returning to England in 1547, he promoted the Company of Merchant Venturers.

The activities of the Bristol seamen, whose skill gave to the English language the expression 'shipshape and Bristol fashion', fascinated **Richard Hakluyt,** descendent of a Leominster family.

In 1582 he published *Divers Voyages touching the Discovery of America,* enabling a wide circle of potential traders to familiarise themselves with North America. Hakluyt became Prebendary of Bristol in 1586, and evolved the theory that sea power meant trading ships, not warships and guns.

TREASURE SITES

- 🗡 CASTLE/HOUSE
- ❀ GARDEN
- ⛪ ECCLESIASTICAL BUILDING
- 🏛 MUSEUM/ART GALLERY
- ⊕ INDUSTRIAL MONUMENT
- ⁂ ARCHAEOLOGICAL SITE
- ⫯ MONUMENT/MEMORIAL
- ◆ OTHER NOTABLE FEATURES

TOWNS/VILLAGES OF ARCHITECTURAL INTEREST *named in black*

SETTLEMENT OF A ROYAL SUCCESSION

During the Civil War, **Lucy Walter,** daughter of a Welsh Royalist, left England for the Hague where she became the mistress of the self-exiled **Charles II.** In 1649 she bore him a son, James. After the Restoration in 1660 Charles brought his son to England and made him **Duke of Monmouth.**

When the issue of the succession to the throne was raised, Charles supported his brother **James, Duke of**

DUKE OF MONMOUTH

York, affirmed that he had never married Lucy Walter and deprived the Duke of Monmouth of many of his posts. In 1683 a plot was hatched to assassinate Charles and the Duke of York, and though it is unlikely that Monmouth was involved he left England.

In 1685 Charles, who on his death-bed became a Roman Catholic, was succeeded by his brother James, also a Catholic. James's two daughters, Mary and Anne, were Protestants.

Knowing James's religion to be unpopular, Monmouth tried to dethrone him. With 82 followers, he landed at Lyme Regis on June 11, 1685, and issued a manifesto branding James as a Popish usurper and claiming his own legitimacy and right to the throne.

But when Monmouth marched north towards Bristol, a force of about 3000 was all he could muster. By the time he reached Taunton on June 20, where he was proclaimed king, his followers numbered 7000, but James's army barred the way to Bristol.

At Sedgemoor, north-east of Taunton, Monmouth made an ill-organised attack against the Royalists and was defeated. He was captured in the New Forest a few days later, and executed in the Tower of London on July 15, 1685.

Those who had rebelled with Monmouth were savagely punished by **Judge Jeffreys,** chief judge at the 'Bloody Assizes' in the West Country. About 80 rebels were drawn and quartered, and 292 mercilessly whipped or transported to the West Indies. One of the courtrooms was at the rear of the Antelope Hotel, Dorchester, and Jeffreys stayed at a house (now a restaurant) in High West Street.

JUDGE JEFFREYS

James's policy of 'romanising' the country led to the hope that he would soon be succeeded by his Protestant daughter Mary who had married the Protestant **William of Orange** in 1677. However, a son, James Francis Edward Stuart, was born to the king in 1688 and became a Roman Catholic heir to the throne. As James II increased his tyranny, William was secretly invited to displace him. He landed at Brixham, Devon, in November 1688. James fled to France, leaving the way open for William.

Before accepting the Crown, William demanded that the throne should subsequently go to the issue of

WILLIAM AND MARY

his wife, **Mary of Orange,** the daughter of James II, and then to her sister Anne and her issue. William and Mary were crowned in April, 1689. Mary died in 1694, William in 1702, and **Queen Anne** reigned from 1702 to 1714.

TREASURE SITES

⚔ CASTLE/HOUSE
✳ GARDEN
⛪ ECCLESIASTICAL BUILDING
🏛 MUSEUM/ART GALLERY
TOWNS/VILLAGES OF ARCHITECTURAL INTEREST *named in black*

⊕ INDUSTRIAL MONUMENT
⚒ ARCHAEOLOGICAL SITE
! MONUMENT/MEMORIAL
◆ OTHER NOTABLE FEATURES

MARGATE
Lighthouse
NORTH FORELAND
Bleak House
Broadstairs
RAMSGATE
Richborough
Sandwich
Goodwin Sands
Deal Castle
DEAL
Walmer
Castle THE DOWNS
St. Margaret's at Cliffe
Painted House
SOUTH FORELAND
Roman Lighthouse
Castle
VER

SCALE ABOUT 10 MILES TO 1 INCH (1:625,000)

CANTERBURY TALES: PRIESTS AND POETS

Thomas Becket was not the first playboy to become a prelate in the 12th century. **Rahere,** Henry I's court jester, became a prebendary of St Paul's *c.* 1115 and later built the priory hospital of St Bartholomew in Smithfield, London, parts of which still stand.

RAHERE

Becket, Archbishop of Canterbury from 1162 to 1170, had studied in France and Italy as a young man and was a close companion of the worldly prince who became **Henry II.** When Becket assumed the responsibility and austerity of his high office at Canterbury his feud with the king ended in his death: in 1170 he refused the king's command to diminish the Church's privileges and Henry's expressed anger led four knights to murder Becket in the sanctuary of the cathedral.

Henry did solemn penance, being flogged by monks at Canterbury in 1174.

THOMAS BECKET

Becket's shrine became a place of pilgrimage. Many pilgrims came by sea to Southampton, then on to Winchester, through Hampshire to the hills south of Guildford, and eastwards along the north of the Weald to Maidstone and Canterbury. Becket's shrine was broken up in 1538 during Henry VIII's Dissolution of the monasteries.

Though this put an end to the pilgrimage, an account

of it survives in the works of **Geoffrey Chaucer,** who made the journey in 1386. Chaucer, son of a London vintner, had acquired an extensive knowledge of Italy, France and Flanders before becoming a customs official in London in 1382 and making a successful career in public service. He died in 1400 and is buried in Westminster Abbey.

In his most famous work, *The Canterbury Tales,* 29 pilgrims assemble at the Tabard Inn in Southwark, London; to relieve the tedium of the journey to Canterbury each tells a story. In these tales, Chaucer drew extensively on his own experiences in England and abroad and recounted many well-known legends.

GEOFFREY CHAUCER

A worthy successor of Chaucer's, **Christopher Marlowe,** the Elizabethan playwright, was also connected with Canterbury. The son of a local shoemaker, he was educated at King's School (attached to the cathedral), and went to Corpus Christi, Cambridge.

Tamburlaine, written in 1587, was followed by *Dr Faustus, The Jew of Malta* and others. His plays influenced Shakespeare. Marlowe died after a drunken brawl in a Deptford tavern in 1593.

CHRISTOPHER MARLOWE

TREASURE SITES

- ⚔ CASTLE/HOUSE
- ✿ GARDEN
- ⛪ ECCLESIASTICAL BUILDING
- 🏛 MUSEUM/ART GALLERY
- ✸ INDUSTRIAL MONUMENT
- ✧ ARCHAEOLOGICAL SITE
- ⚑ MONUMENT/MEMORIAL
- ◆ OTHER NOTABLE FEATURES

TOWNS/VILLAGES OF ARCHITECTURAL INTEREST *named in black*

A B C D E F

Llwyngwril

Light Railway Museum
Tywyn

Aberdyfi Bar

C A R D I G A N

Borth

B A Y

Aberystwyth
Pen Dinas

Nante

Llanrhystyd

Llanon

Aberaeron

New Quay
Cilcennin

Ynys-Lochtyn *Llwyndafydd* *Llanarth*
Mydroilyn *Ystrad Aeron*
Llangrannog *Llangybi*

Cardigan I. *Aberporth* *Ffostrasol* **St David's College** *Lar*
Cemaes Head *Verwig* *Cribyn* *Llans Clydo*
Beulah *Llanwenog* *Llanybi*

St Dogmaels **Cardigan** *Llandysul* *D Y F E D*
Moylgrove **Cilgerran Castle** *Llandyther*
Dinas *A 484* *Llanyssul* *A 485*

Cerrig y Gof *Newport* *Eglwyswrw* **Newcastle** *Llandyssul* *Talley A*
Pen Brush *Dinas* *Boncath* **Emlyn** *Rhos* *Pencader* *Abergorlech*

Pentre Ifan *Crymmych* *Moelfre*

Fishguard *Pencaer* *Mynydd Prescelly* **Talley A**
Parc-y-Meirw *Llanychaer* *Brechfa*

St Nicholas *Ynysdeullyn*

Prescelly Hills *Llanfyrnach* *Cynwyl Elfed* **Taliaris**
St David's Head *Mathry* *Longhouse* *Letterston* *Puncheston* *Llanglywaen* *Llanfyr*

Promontory Fort *Llanrian* *Login* **Dryslw**
Ramsey I. **Meini Gwyr** *Llanboidy*
St David's **Bishop's Palace** *Treffgarne* *Spittal* *Llanycefn* *Meidrim* *Carmarthen*
Sulva *Llanfallteg* *Cwmtrwd* *Llanddarog*

S T   B R I D E S *Roch* *Clarbeston* *Whitland* *St Clears*
Camrose *Wiston* *Llawhaden* *A 40* **Kidwelly Castle**
B A Y *Nolton* **Picton Castle** *Narberth* *Red Roses* *Llanstephan* *Llandefarlog* *Tumble*

Haverfordwest *Mardetwy* *Templeton* *Pendine* **Laugharne**

Skomer I. *Tower Pt* *Walton West* *Kilgetty* *Llansaint* *Pontyates*
St Bride *Johnston* *Rosemarket* *Saundersfoot* *Monkstone Pt*
Marloes *Kidwelly* *Burry Port* **Kidwelly Castle**
Skokholm I. *Dale* **Milford Haven** *Neyland* **Carew Castle** *Pembroke Dock*
St Ann's Head *Angle* *Rhoscrowther* **Carew Cheriton** *Burry Holms* *Arthur's Stone*
Sheep I. **Pembroke Castle** **Plantagenet House** *Penally* **Parc Cwm**
Lamphey **Tenby** *C A R M A R T H E N   B A Y* *Bishopston*
Castlemartin **Bishop's Palace** *Caldy I.* **Penrice Castle**
Linney Head **Manorbier Castle** *Whitford Pt* *Llanrhidian Sands* *Llanmadoc* *Reynoldston*
Bosherston *Stackpole Hd* *Llanrhidian* *Rhossili* **Paviland**
St. Govan's Chapel *Porteynon* *Oxwich* **Penrice Castle**
S T   G O V A N ' S   H E A D *Worms Head* *Porteynon Pt*

B R I S T O L   C H A N N E L

Watermouth Castle
Ilfracombe *Combe Martin*
N W Point **Lighthouse** *Bull Pt* *Berrynarbor*
Lundy *Morte Pt* *Kentisbu*
Shutter Pt

GLAMORGAN'S MEN OF IRON

Present-day mining in the coal and iron valleys of the Glamorgans, which now muster nearly half the total population of Wales, dates from the early days of the Industrial Revolution.

Foremost on the scene was **Anthony Bacon,** who between 1765 and 1784 developed Cyfarthfa. He arrived by mule at Merthyr Tydfil in 1763 and two years later acquired 4000 acres of the great mineral tract at Cyfarthfa for only £100 a year rent.

Bacon retired a rich man in 1784, to give pride of place as the greatest of all the Iron Kings to **Richard Crawshay** (1741–1810) founder of a dynasty. Crawshay came from Normanton, West Yorkshire, learned his trade in London, and having won the then large sum of £1500 in a lottery used it to buy Cyfarthfa.

By 1803 the Crawshay works were turning out 70 tons of bar iron a week.

Meanwhile, **Richard Trevithick** (1771–1833) had been experimenting in Cornwall with steam locomotives. Hearing of these efforts, Samuel Homfray, another Iron King, bet Richard Crawshay £1000 that he could convey a load of iron by steam power from his works at Penydarren to the navigation canal 9 miles away—and he called on Trevithick to help him win his bet.

On February 22, 1804, Trevithick was ready for the first trial of his High Pressure Steam Tram. The course was the tramway through Thomas Town, and Trevithick's unnatural monster conveyed not only the stipulated 10 tons of iron of the bet but 70 people as well —at 5 mph.

A FAMILY ON THE BOARDS

While the Iron Kings were laying the basis for Welsh industry, one family—the Kembles—were laying the foundations of the modern theatre.

Roger Kemble (1721–1802) was one of the first actor-managers. He married Sarah Ward of Birmingham in 1753, and their first child, also called Sarah, was born

ROGER KEMBLE

in Brecon. Kemble ran a travelling company, in which all his children acted, and on one of their tours his daughter met William Siddons whom she married in 1773, when she was 18.

Appearing in a play at Cheltenham with her husband, **Sarah Siddons** attracted much attention, and was promptly engaged by David Garrick to play at Drury Lane. She failed to make much impression but on a return visit, after appearances at Manchester and Bath, she was launched on a spectacular career. She was painted by Sir Joshua Reynolds and, though she was buried in Paddington churchyard in 1831, there is a statue of her by Sir Francis Chantrey in Westminster Abbey.

John Philip Kemble (1757–1823) displayed a remarkable virtuosity in his career; during his engagement at Drury Lane (1783–1802) he played more than 120 characters from Shakespeare's dramas. He was manager of the New Covent Garden Theatre and a friend of Sir Walter Scott.

Charles Kemble (1775–1854) made many stage appearances abroad; at his best in comedy, he was said to have a greater range than any other actor except Garrick.

Stephen Kemble (1758–1822) the least successful of the family, first appeared on the stage in Dublin. Later he took over the theatre in Edinburgh, but it failed financially.

TREASURE SITES

♟	CASTLE/HOUSE	⊕	INDUSTRIAL MONUMENT
✿	GARDEN	✠	ARCHAEOLOGICAL SITE
⌂	ECCLESIASTICAL BUILDING	⌿	MONUMENT/MEMORIAL
⛉	MUSEUM/ART GALLERY	◆	OTHER NOTABLE FEATURES

TOWNS/VILLAGES OF ARCHITECTURAL INTEREST *named in black*

SCALE ABOUT 10 MILES TO 1 INCH (1,625,000)

PILGRIM'S PROGRESS, ADMIRAL'S FALL

A bronze statue at the north end of Bedford High Street commemorates a man whose career reached its peak when he was in prison—**John Bunyan,** author of *The Pilgrim's Progress*.

The son of a tinker and grandson of a brewer, he was born on the outskirts of Bedford and at 16 was conscripted in Cromwell's army and stationed at nearby Newport Pagnell. Two years later, a civilian again, he fell prey to religious remorse—black moments in which he saw his innocent pleasures of bell-ringing and dancing as heinous sins.

His sense of personal sin increased when his first child, a daughter, was born blind. Bunyan joined a Non-conformist church in 1653, and his first book, *Some Gospel Truths Opened,* appeared in 1656, the year his wife died leaving him four children. He then devoted himself more and more to studying the Bible, not the 1611 Authorised Version, but the earlier work of 1560 favoured by the Puritans.

JOHN BUNYAN

In November 1660 he was charged with 'holding a conventicle' (preaching without licence) and imprisoned in Bedford. He remained in prison for 12 years, during which time he wrote nine books, producing in 1672 a confession of his faith.

With the Declaration of Indulgence by Charles II later that year he was released and became a pastor of the Bedford church where his preaching had earlier caused trouble. When the Declaration was annulled, he was once more imprisoned, during which time he wrote the first part of *The Pilgrim's Progress from this world to that which is to come.*

By 1685 ten editions had been published and the work has since been translated into 108 languages and dialects. Three years later Bunyan died of a fever on Snow Hill, Holborn, and was buried in Bunhill Fields.

In Bedford Road at Elstow, Bunyan's Cottage is on the site of his former home; throughout the Bedford area there are places which are claimed to be the originals of such places as The Delectable Mountains in *The Pilgrim's Progress*.

THOMAS TOMPION

At Northill, a few miles from Bunyan's birthplace, **Thomas Tompion** made his name as the 'father of English watch-making'. He devised the first English watch with a balance spring and made clocks for the Royal Observatory, precision barometers and sundials. The clock he made for the Pump Room at Bath is still working over 250 years later.

At nearby Southill, **Admiral Byng** lies buried in the family mausoleum in the parish church. Byng survives as the inspiration of a French tag. An admiral in the Royal Navy in 1756, he was dispatched to prevent the French fleet from taking the island of Minorca, but was easily defeated. Recalled to face a court-martial at Portsmouth, he was found guilty of neglect of duty. He was shot on March 14, 1757.

ADMIRAL BYNG

Voltaire immortalised him by observing that in England it was necessary from time to time to shoot an admiral *pour encourager les autres*— 'to encourage the others'.

TREASURE SITES

⚔	CASTLE/HOUSE	⊕	INDUSTRIAL MONUMENT
✳	GARDEN	♣	ARCHAEOLOGICAL SITE
⛪	ECCLESIASTICAL BUILDING	♦	MONUMENT/MEMORIAL
▥	MUSEUM/ART GALLERY	◆	OTHER NOTABLE FEATURES
TOWNS/VILLAGES OF ARCHITECTURAL INTEREST *named in black*			

TREASURE SITES

⚔ CASTLE/HOUSE	⊛ INDUSTRIAL MONUMENT
✾ GARDEN	⬡ ARCHAEOLOGICAL SITE
⛪ ECCLESIASTICAL BUILDING	⚑ MONUMENT/MEMORIAL
⛫ MUSEUM/ART GALLERY	◆ OTHER NOTABLE FEATURES

TOWNS/VILLAGES OF ARCHITECTURAL INTEREST *named in black*

At the National Portrait Gallery in Trafalgar Square, London, are the portraits of some 3000 eminent Britons. Space is short and only a third of the portraits can be hung at any one time; but, given notice, gallery officials can produce any picture in the collection.

The gallery has bought or been given many collections, but none matches the extraordinary slice of history captured on canvas in what is known as the Kit-Cat Collection.

The object of the Kit-Cat Club was to bring together men of position, wit and social graces who were interested in Whig politics and literature. It included among its members eight dukes, 13 earls, two viscounts, three barons and three knights.

Charles Seymour, 6th Duke of Somerset, who lived from 1662 to 1748 and was a prominent Whig and supporter of the Hanoverian succession, probably founded the club, though **Jacob Tonson** (1656-1736), a publisher, was its first secretary and may well have been the real founder. Members met near his offices at Temple Bar at the house of Christopher Cat, pastry cook, whose mutton pies were known as kit-cats.

The original meetings at the tavern were succeeded by get-togethers at Tonson's house at Barn Elms, near Putney, or in summer months at the Flask Inn, Hampstead. The club probably broke up c. 1720-2; certainly in 1725 Sir John Vanbrugh wrote to regret that the happy meetings had stopped.

The portraits of club members were painted mainly between 1702 and 1717 by **Sir Godfrey Kneller**, Tonson's near-neighbour at Whitton, near Twickenham. Kneller painted 42 of them to a standard size of 28 in. by 36 in., so that the complete collection could be accommodated in the clubroom at Tonson's house. The pose—a three-quarter figure, showing at least one hand—has become known as a kit-cat.

Among the members whose portraits appear in the Kit-Cat Collection are:
Richard Temple (1669-1749) 1st Viscount Cobham, who built the Palladian mansion at Stowe.
John Montague (1690-1749) 2nd Duke of Montague, Fellow of the Royal Society and Fellow of the Royal College of Physicians, Grand Master of the Grand Lodge of English Freemasons, patron of the arts.
Spencer Compton (1674-1743) Earl of Wilmington, Speaker of the House of Commons, 1715-27.
John Vaughan (1639-1713) 3rd Earl of Carbery, President of the Royal Society, 1686-9, patron of the poet Dryden.
Charles Montague (1661-1715) 1st Earl of Halifax, responsible for the Act which set up the Bank of England, President of the Royal Society, 1695-8, patron of Addison, Congreve and Prior.
John Somers (1651-1716) Baron Somers, President of the Royal Society, 1699-1703, patron of historical scholarship, art connoisseur, expert in English and continental law.
William Congreve (1670-1729)

dramatist and pet of fashionable society.
Sir Richard Steele (1672-1729), an Irishman who edited the *London Gazette*, 1707-10; also connected with *The Tatler* and *The Spectator*.
Sir Samuel Garth (1661-1719) Fellow of the College of Physicians, Physician-General to the army, Physician-in-Ordinary to George I, friend of Dryden and Pope.
Edmund Dunch (1657-1719) descendant of Oliver Cromwell, Master of the Royal Household under Queen Anne and George I.
Charles Sackville (1638-1706) 6th Earl of Dorset, patron of Wycherley and Dryden, and the first protector of Nell Gwyn.
Charles Dartiquenave (1664-1737) epicure and wit, the most famous *bon vivant* of his time.
Lionel Sackville (1688-1765) 1st Duke of Dorset, considered the perfect English courtier.
Charles Mohun (1675-1712) one of Marlborough's generals, a notorious rake and duellist; twice tried for murder before he was 24, Mohun was killed in a duel with the Duke of Hamilton, who was also killed (as described in Thackeray's novel *Henry Esmond*).
Thomas Wharton (1648-1715) 1st Marquess of Wharton, rake and freethinker who 'wrote the words of Purcell's famous song 'Lilliburlero'.
Charles Lennox (1672-1723) 1st Duke of Richmond and Lennox, son of Charles II and Louise de Kérouaille (Duchess of Portsmouth), Lord of the Bedchamber to George I.

JAMES I

Newmarket's prominence as a horse-racing centre began when **James I**, 'the wisest fool in Christendom', built a hunting lodge there, called the King's House, so that he could watch the racing on Newmarket Heath.

Charles II also went racing at Newmarket. He began the custom of awarding commemorative bowls or cups, each worth about 100 guineas. (William III later initiated the custom of awarding plates.)

Charles II's devotion to racing nearly led to disaster. With his brother James, Duke of York, and a party of friends he went to Newmarket in March, 1683. At Rye House, Broxbourne, Hertfordshire, followers of the Earl of Shaftesbury plotted to seize the royal brothers as they returned to London, with the intention of proclaiming the Duke of Monmouth king. But on March 22, during a race meeting, a fire which nearly destroyed Newmarket caused the royal party to depart hastily. The plot was foiled, and though it is doubtful whether they were implicated, Lord William Russell and Algernon Sidney were charged with treason and executed.

Formal racing, similar to today's, was introduced at Newmarket by Charles II in 1667. The Jockey Club, the ruling body of flat-racing, has been established there since 1750. Important races run at Newmarket include two of the 'Classics', the 2000 and 1000 guineas, and the 'Autumn Double', the Cesarewitch and the Cambridgeshire.

CHARLES SEYMOUR

SIR GODFREY KNELLER

WILLIAM CONGREVE

LIONEL SACKVILLE

LONDON'S OLDEST THEATRES

English drama was at first inextricably bound up with religion. The first theatre licence was granted in 1574, and Shakespeare began his acting career in either the Theatre or the Curtain, both at Shoreditch, two or three years later. Some of his own plays were first presented at the Globe, a thatched-roof theatre, destroyed by fire in June, 1613.

The modern theatre owes a great deal to **James Burbage** (d. 1597) and his son Richard (1567-1619). James, a joiner, erected the Theatre in Finsbury Fields in 1576 and in 1596 acquired a house in South London, which he adapted as the Blackfriars Theatre. By 1588 **Richard Burbage** was an actor of repute who, having inherited his father's interest in the Blackfriars and Globe theatres, staged and acted in many contemporary plays. Another

DRURY LANE THEATRE

actor-manager of that time, **Edward Alleyn** (1566-1626), founded Dulwich College in 1619.

New theatres opened by licence granted by Elizabeth I were all closed by Parliament in 1642-60, but they re-opened with the Restoration, and in 1666 Nell Gwyn was starring at Drury Lane. The theatre was burnt down in 1672, rebuilt three times, partly destroyed by fire in 1809 and rebuilt again.

Covent Garden Theatre, now the Royal Opera House, which was opened in 1732, has a similar history: it has burnt down twice; and Her Majesty's Theatre in the Haymarket, originally the Italian Opera House, was totally destroyed twice, went bankrupt once, and was demolished in 1892-3 to make way for the present building.

CHARLES II

In Newmarket itself are Nell Gwyn's House and beside it Gwyn Cottage, reminders of Nell Gwyn's visits to the town with Charles II. They are amongst the few houses to survive two fires in 1683 and 1700. From selling oranges in Drury Lane **Nell Gwyn** (1651-87) became famous as a comedy actress. As Charles II's mistress she was a great favourite with the public, and it is said that her influence induced the king to found the Chelsea Hospital. She bore him two sons and is believed to have been faithful to Charles II, even rejecting suitors after his death.

LAND OF THE RED DRAGON

EDWARD II

For nearly 600 years after William the Conqueror claimed Wales and made an invasion sortie in 1081, Welshmen fought for their independence. In Wales Britons had resisted domination by Romans, Saxons and Danes; now the running battle was against domination from London.

In 1114, Henry I began to build great Norman-style castles to contain the Welsh. When **Edward I** came to the throne he demanded the people's allegiance. **Llewelyn ap Griffith** (or Gruffydd), Prince of Wales, repeatedly refused the king's summons to Westminster. He was declared deposed and Wales was invaded in 1277.

In 1282 Llewelyn, with his brother David, took Hawarden and Rhuddlan castles. English forces closed in and Llewelyn was killed after the battle near Aberedw, and shortly afterwards David was executed. In March, 1284, the Statute of Wales was enacted at Rhuddlan, in effect appropriating nearly all Wales.

A month later Edward's queen, Eleanor of Castile, gave birth to a son at Caernarfon Castle, and the king informed the Welsh chiefs that this boy would be their future prince. Edward Plantagenet, Prince of Wales and Earl of Chester, succeeded to the throne in 1307 as **Edward II**.

After many years of sporadic uprisings, **Owain Glyndwr** led the great rebellion of 1400. With aid from France, Glyndwr's forces took Carmarthen, Caerleon, Harlech, and besieged Caernarfon (1401). He continued to ravage English-held lands until he disappeared in 1415.

North Wales was again the scene of fierce fighting in 1645-9 when Cromwell's forces took castle after castle.

ORIGIN OF MAN

Today, more than 100 years after **Charles Darwin** published *On the Origin of Species,* there is still controversy about its theories. To Victorians who believed in a literal interpretation of the Genesis, Darwin's theory of evolution was heresy.

CHARLES DARWIN

Darwin's statue is set in the gardens of the museum and library at Shrewsbury, the town where he was born and educated. He went to Edinburgh and Cambridge universities. In 1831 he set out in the *Beagle* on a scientific expedition to South America and it was observations made in the Galapagos Islands that first suggested the theory of evolution to him. While secretary to the Geographical Society he published *The Zoology of the Voyage of the Beagle* in 1840.

In 1844, despite ill health, he set down his theory of the evolution of Man, but did not publish it, perhaps because he knew it would arouse controversy and opposition from theologians.

In 1858 another naturalist, Dr A. R. Wallace, sent Darwin a manuscript outlining a theory almost identical with his own. A joint paper was published (read before the Linnaen Society) on July 1, 1858, in which their theory of evolution was first given to the world, but Wallace acknowledged Darwin's prior claim to having originated the theory.

Darwin went on to write numerous works on plants and insects. He died in 1882.

TREASURE SITES

♟ CASTLE/HOUSE		✳ INDUSTRIAL MONUMENT	
✿ GARDEN		⁂ ARCHAEOLOGICAL SITE	
⛪ ECCLESIASTICAL BUILDING		⌶ MONUMENT/MEMORIAL	
🏛 MUSEUM/ART GALLERY		◆ OTHER NOTABLE FEATURES	

TOWNS/VILLAGES OF ARCHITECTURAL INTEREST *named in black*

SCALE ABOUT 10 MILES TO 1 INCH (1:625,000)

Map labels (north-west England and north Wales), including:

BLACKPOOL, LYTHAM ST ANNE'S, SOUTHPORT, FORMBY, ORMSKIRK, SKELMERSDALE, ST HELENS, MERSEYSIDE, WALLASEY, BIRKENHEAD, HOYLAKE, LIVERPOOL, BEBINGTON, Prestatyn, RHYL, Abergele, St Asaph, Denbigh, Holywell, Mold, Buckley, CHESTER, Chester Castle, Flint Castle, Ewloe Castle, Basingwerk, WREXHAM, Ruthin, Plas Teg, Llangollen, Valle Crucis Abbey, Plas Newydd, Chirk Castle, Wynnstay Hall, Pont Cysyllte, Old Oswestry, Oswestry, Sycharth, The Breiddin, SHREWSBURY, Welshpool, Powis Castle Gardens, Condover Hall, Maesmawr Hall, Montgomery, Newtown, Kerry, Walcot Hall, Clun, Stokesay Castle, POWYS, CLWYD, SHROP, Offa's Dyke

545

MIDLANDERS AT HOME AND ABROAD

Izaak Walton, Thomas Cook and the Marquess of Curzon, born within 30 miles of each other in the Midlands, distinguished themselves in very different fields.

IZAAK WALTON

Izaak Walton was born in Stafford in 1593 and later moved to London where in 1614 he had an ironmonger's business in Fleet Street. He wrote verses in his spare time but his first literary work of note was an essay on the life of John Donne.

The work for which he became famous—*The Compleat Angler, or the Contemplative Man's Recreation*—took 40 years to compile. Walton, who did not consider himself an expert fisherman, drew on the experience of amateurs all over Britain for the material in it. *The Compleat Angler* was published in 1653 and for the 5th edition in 1676 the original 13 chapters were expanded to 21, which included a treatise on fly-fishing by Charles Cotton of Beresford Hall, Staffordshire. Walton died at Winchester, and is buried in the cathedral there.

THOMAS COOK

Thomas Cook, pioneer of the travel agency business, was born at Melbourne, Derbyshire, in 1808, and in his early years was a gardener, wood turner, printer, lay reader and champion of the Baptist faith. He became a total abstainer, and in 1841 persuaded the Midland Counties Railway to let him organise a round trip to a temperance rally in Lough-

borough for 570 people from Leicester. This, costing 1s. a head, was his first publicly-advertised excursion.

'Mr Cook's Voyages' caught on, and in 1856 he conducted his first foreign tour from Harwich to the Rhine, and back via Paris. The business moved to London in 1865, organising tours to the U.S.A. in 1866 and to Palestine in 1869.

A branch office was opened in Cairo in 1873 and, with government contracts for the Egyptian and Sudan campaigns, and the organisation of Moslem pilgrims from India to Mecca and Medina, the original local service became world-wide.

Thomas Cook died at Leicester in 1892.

George Nathaniel Curzon was born at Kedleston Hall, Derbyshire, in 1859, eldest of the 11 children of the 4th Lord Scarsdale. Educated at Eton and Balliol College, Oxford, at 27 he

GEORGE NATHANIEL CURZON

became M.P. for Southport which he represented until 1898. He had travelled in the East between 1887 and 1892, and his book *Problems of the Far East* appeared in 1894.

In 1899 he became Viceroy of India. He was at first greatly popular but, after clashes with Lord Kitchener, his influence in India waned and his relations with Whitehall grew bitter.

He returned home in 1905, became Chancellor of Oxford University in 1907 and entered the House of Lords in 1908. In 1916 he was appointed Lord President of the Council, and was a brilliant Foreign Secretary (1919–24), being created Marquess in 1921.

When Bonar Law retired in 1923, Curzon expected to become Prime Minister. Stanley Baldwin was chosen instead and Curzon retired from public life in 1924.

TREASURE SITES

- ⚔ CASTLE/HOUSE
- ✿ GARDEN
- ⛪ ECCLESIASTICAL BUILDING
- 🏛 MUSEUM/ART GALLERY
- TOWNS/VILLAGES OF ARCHITECTURAL INTEREST *named in black*
- ⚙ INDUSTRIAL MONUMENT
- ⛏ ARCHAEOLOGICAL SITE
- ⬗ MONUMENT/MEMORIAL
- ◆ OTHER NOTABLE FEATURES ·

A FORTUNE IN THE SANDS

Somewhere close to the R. Nene's outfall canal in Lincolnshire, just over the Norfolk border, a treasure beyond reckoning may still lie buried centuries after it disappeared on a misty October day in 1216.

Medieval England possessed both a State Treasury and an Exchequer, but the king had his own personal treasure as well. Much of this was, for safety, kept in widely separated abbeys, but a considerable amount always went with the king on his travels.

The Court was constantly on the move, with a baggage train of heavy carts that could travel at only about 2 miles an hour. The king would often leave the train to visit one of his caches while the train went on by the shortest route.

Thus in late September, 1216, **King John** (1167–1216) having been fêted and feasted at King's Lynn, decided to go to Swineshead via Wisbech and

KING JOHN

Spalding while his baggage train moved ponderously over the Wash estuary. Several accounts of the route taken by the baggage train have been gathered over the years, and the evidence is inconclusive. What is certain is that the wagons could only cross when the tide was out, and they were partly across when the tide came

swirling in and barred retreat. The wagon loaded with the treasure was trapped in quicksands, and it slowly disappeared.

Everything John valued most was lost in a matter of minutes. He was a noted connoisseur of jewellery and gems, and with this private collection went all his regalia, his ornamented plate, dozens of gold and silver flagons and goblets, candelabra, combs, clasps, crosses, charms, bracelets, rings and ornaments, the coronation robes and regalia, and the great crown, the golden wand, the golden dove and the bejewelled Sword of Tristram, all of which had belonged to his grandmother as Empress of Germany. Nothing has been recovered from the area, now many miles inland.

At King's Lynn John had contracted dysentery. He died at Newark, having directed that his body be buried in Worcester Cathedral.

JOHN CROME

The 19th-century fashion for countryside paintings such as those done by John Constable in Essex led a group of painters to try to do the same thing for Norfolk. John Crome (1768–1821) is regarded as the founder of the Norwich School, but Robert Ladbrooke (1768–1842) who worked with him, was largely responsible for establishing the Norwich Society of Artists in 1803.

John Crome, who first exhibited at the Royal Academy in 1806, is noted for his tree paintings. A tree standing at the village of Poringland is said to be the original of the oak in his painting at the National Gallery, London, which also shows how Crome was influenced by the Dutch landscape painters—he particularly admired the work of Hobbema and Ruysdale. His son, John Bernay Crome, followed his father and also became a painter of the Norwich School.

Robert Ladbrooke exhibited landscapes at the Royal Academy between 1804 and 1815. His second son, Henry (1800–70) built a reputation for painting moonlight scenes, and his third son John (1803–79)—a pupil of Crome whose style he followed—exhibited at the Royal Academy, the British Institution and the Suffolk Street Gallery up to 1873.

John Sell Cotman (1782–1842), another painter of the Norwich School, specialised in water-colours, and interpreted landscapes as a series of flattened planes. After exhibiting in London from 1800 to 1806 he set up as a drawing master in Norwich in 1807 and from 1834 to 1842 was art master at King's College, London. He etched numerous plates of buildings and antiquities in Norfolk from 1811 to 1839. His eldest son, Miles Edmund Cotman, painted oils and water-colours of river and sea views. His other son, Joseph John Cotman, was a drawing master in Norwich in 1836 but became mentally deranged.

James Stark's most notable work is *Scenery of Rivers of Norfolk*, completed in 1834. **Joseph Stannard** exhibited with the Norwich Society between 1811 and 1816, and at the Royal Academy and British Institution between 1820 and 1829. **Henry Bright**, a water-colourist, exhibited at the Royal Academy between 1845 and 1850, and was elected a member of the Institute of Painters in Water-colours.

Cotman House is in St Martin-at-Palace Plain, Norwich, and works by all members of the Norwich Society can be seen in the art gallery section of the Norman castle in Norwich's city centre.

REBELS AND REFORMERS

THOMAS PAINE

MRS ELIZABETH FRY

GEORGE BORROW

John's treasure had been in the Wash more than 330 years when **Robert Kett** won a brief moment of fame as the first of Norfolk's reformers. Kett's birth date is not known, but the year and manner of his death are still recalled by a tree called Kett's Oak at Ryston, 3 miles from Wymondham.

Edward Seymour, 1st Duke of Somerset, had been appointed Protector of England and had introduced an agrarian policy so unpopular that peasants throughout England rose against it.

In July 1549, Kett, the son of a Wymondham tanner, led one of the most serious uprisings. The Norfolk peasants particularly resented the fact that rich landlords used common land for grazing their sheep, and from a camp at Mousehold Heath, at the gates of Norwich, Kett led 16,000 men in a blockade of the city and slaughtered 20,000 sheep. The rising was put down by the Earl of Warwick and Kett was executed in December.

Thomas Paine (1737–1809), one of the fathers of socialism, was another Norfolk rebel. He was born at Thetford, where his house still stands.

The son of a staymaker and farmer, Paine became an excise officer but at the age of 35 was dismissed for agitating for more pay. He went to America

where in 1776 he published *Common Sense*, a work on the causes of the American War of Independence which brought him a number of official appointments.

He returned to England in 1787 and between 1790 and 1792 published *The Rights of Man*. This revolutionary work advocated social services such as provision for the aged poor, maternity and funeral grants, and the limitation of armaments by treaty.

It sold well over a million copies in England alone, but aroused such feeling among the authorities that Paine prudently fled to France where he was elected a member of the Convention, the French House of Representatives. He incurred further odium in England with *The Age of Reason* (1793) and not a little trouble in France. He returned to America in 1802 and died in New York.

Mrs Elizabeth Fry (1780–1845), a Quaker and preacher, was born in Norwich. At the age of 17, in the attic of her home, she taught the poor children of Earlham. The class soon numbered 60 and gained the nickname of 'Betsy's imps'. Earlham House is now part of the University of East Anglia.

She advocated prison improve-

ment, better conditions for convicts transported to Australia, and welfare services for the vagrants of London and Brighton. In 1817 she formed an association for safeguarding the interests of women in Newgate prison. Her extensive travels on the Continent lead to prison improvements there as well.

George Borrow (1803–81) traveller, linguist and author, was born the son of a recruiting officer at Dumpling Green, just south of East Dereham. He was educated at Edinburgh High School and then worked for a short time in a Norwich solicitor's office. He travelled extensively on the Continent, in Russia and the East, and eventually published in St Petersburg a work called *Targum* which contained translations from 30 languages. He became a traveller for the Bible Society in Russia and Spain and took a special interest in gypsies. In 1843 his *The Bible in Spain*, recounting his adventures as a salesman there, was an instant success and made his reputation. There followed *Lavengro* (1851), *The Romany Rye* (1857) and *Wild Wales* (1862). In 1840 he married and settled at Oulton Broad, Suffolk, dying there in 1881. The house in which he lived in Willow Lane, Norwich, can still be seen.

LAKELAND'S ROMANTIC BROTHERHOOD

Romanticism dominated literature during the late 18th and early 19th centuries, and the landscapes of the Lake District were a source of inspiration to the romantic poets.

Foremost among the writers and poets who worked there was **William Wordsworth**, whose childhood in Cumbria he later described in his poem 'The Prelude'. Born at Cockermouth he went to school at Hawkshead.

WILLIAM WORDSWORTH

In 1798 he wrote 'Lines Written above Tintern Abbey' and in the next year settled at Dove Cottage, Grasmere, with his sister and constant companion, Dorothy (1771–1855).

Fourteen years later he was given the office of Distributor of Stamps for Westmorland and moved to Rydal Mount, Grasmere. In 1843 he succeeded Robert Southey as Poet Laureate. He is buried in St Oswald's churchyard, Grasmere.

Samuel Taylor Coleridge, the son of a vicar at Ottery St Mary, Devon, met Robert Southey in 1793

at Jesus College, Cambridge, and two years later married Sarah Fricker, whose sister became Southey's wife in the same year.

The Coleridges lived with Wordsworth for a year at Nether Stowey and Alfoxden, in Somerset. Coleridge wrote 'Kubla Khan' in 1797, after waking from an opium-induced sleep, and 'The Ancient Mariner' a year later. He spent from 1800 to 1804 at Keswick, with the Wordsworths. Coleridge was not only an outstanding poet: his *Biographia Literaria* and lectures on Shakespeare are critical masterpieces.

Robert Southey was the son of a Bristol linen draper, and though expelled from Westminster School he went in 1792 to Balliol College, Oxford. He travelled to Portugal and Spain before settling in Keswick in 1807.

ROBERT SOUTHEY

In 1813 he published his *Life of Nelson* and was appointed Poet Laureate. His next major work was the *Life of Wesley,* published in 1820. He is buried in Crosthwaite churchyard.

HUNTING COUNTRY

For 50 years **John Peel** hunted a pack of hounds from his native village of Caldbeck (Cumbria), where he was buried in 1854. His life-long friend, **John Graves,** wrote impromptu the song 'D'ye ken John Peel', noting that Peel's 'View halloo' would awaken the dead—as well as stir up the foxes. The melody is borrowed from an old air called 'Bonnie Annie'.

Robert Surtees, born in the village of Hamsterley, was a popular sporting writer who created the remarkable character of Jorrocks, the hunting hero

of *Handley Cross,* published in 1843. He defined hunting as 'war without its guilt and only five-and-twenty per cent of its danger'.

ROBERT SURTEES

TREASURE SITES

- ⚔ CASTLE/HOUSE
- ❀ GARDEN
- ⛪ ECCLESIASTICAL BUILDING
- 🏛 MUSEUM/ART GALLERY
- ⊕ INDUSTRIAL MONUMENT
- ⁂ ARCHAEOLOGICAL SITE
- �ⅰ MONUMENT/MEMORIAL
- ◆ OTHER NOTABLE FEATURES

TOWNS/VILLAGES OF ARCHITECTURAL INTEREST *named in black*

JARROW'S DARK AGE SCHOLAR

In the Saxon parish church of Jarrow, Newcastle-upon-Tyne, there is a chair used more than 1200 years ago by Bede, a monk who long after his death became known as the **Venerable Bede.**

Most of Bede's adult life was spent in Jarrow Abbey where, at a time when the ignorance of the Dark Ages held sway throughout Europe, he taught Latin, Greek and Hebrew. His major work, *Historia Ecclesiastica Gentis Anglorum*, a historical commentary on the Roman occupation of Britain and the succeeding years, interwoven with religious studies and arguments, was finished in 731.

Bede also wrote a treatise, unique in his time, called *De Natura Rerum*, in which he set out the extent of contemporary scientific knowledge. His fame spread to

VENERABLE BEDE

Europe and his works were published in both Paris and Basle, Switzerland, in the mid-16th century.

CAPTAIN COURAGEOUS

One of the great navigators of history, **James Cook** was the son of a labourer at Marton in Cleveland, North Yorkshire. Apprenticed at 12 to a haberdasher, he ran away to sea, first in the Baltic trade and then in the Royal Navy (1755).

Cook's interest in navigation began during General Woolfe's capture of Quebec when his ship took soundings in the St Lawrence R. Having surveyed the Newfoundland coast in 1762, he was made marine surveyor of Newfoundland and Labrador a year later.

JAMES COOK

His observations of a solar eclipse at Cape Ray led the Royal Society to invite him to join an expedition to observe the transit of Venus. He was commissioned lieutenant, and in 1768 sailed in *Endeavour* (370 tons), reaching Tahiti via Cape Horn in April, 1769. He then circumnavigated New Zealand in six months (discovering Cook Strait) and surveyed

the east coast of Australia before probing New Guinea and Indonesia.

In 1771, he was promoted captain and put in charge of a second expedition, led by *Resolution* (460 tons) and escorted by a smaller ship, *Adventure*. Cook sailed from Plymouth in July, 1772, to Madeira and then via the Cape of Good Hope, in search of a suspected Great Southern Continent. He crossed the Antarctic circle on January 16, 1773, wintering in the Society Islands, which he named in honour of the Royal Society.

In 1774 he probed far south, but failed to find land. He returned to Plymouth in 1775, proud that his new rules on hygiene and diet had saved his crew from fever and scurvy.

His next task was to search for the supposed North West Passage linking the north Atlantic with the north Pacific. He sailed from Britain for the Cape of Good Hope in July, 1776, discovered the Sandwich Islands in 1778, and headed for the American coast, probing northwards until baulked by a wall of ice. He charted the north and west coasts of America, and then turned for Hawaii, which he reached in 1779.

In a dispute with natives over ownership of a boat from his ships he was killed at Kealakekua Bay.

Map labels

an Signal Station
borough Castle
ARBOROUGH

Filey
Reighton
ton
Burton A166
Fleming
Bempton
FLAMBOROUGH HEAD
oynton Hall
Flamborough
Boynton A166
Burton Agnes
BRIDLINGTON
Burton Agnes Hall
es Hall

Barmston

afferton
field
Skipsea

Beeford
N Frodingham
Atwick

Brandesburton
Hornsea
even
Sigglesthorne

Long
Riston
Withernwick
ey
S Skirlaugh
Aldbrough
Wawne
Garton
Burton Constable
ham
Swine
Sproatley
Burton
Pidsea

Preston A1033
Tunstall
Roos
Hedon
Halsham
Withernsea
KINGSTON UPON HULL
A1033
Hollym
Ottringham
New Holland
Goxhill Priory
Patrington
Welwick
E Halton
Easington
Thornton Abbey
Sunk Island
Thornton
Curtis
Kilnsea

Immingham
Habrough A180
Keelby
GRIMSBY
SPURN HEAD

SCALE ABOUT 10 MILES TO 1 INCH (1:625,000)

TREASURE SITES

⚔	CASTLE/HOUSE	⊕	INDUSTRIAL MONUMENT
❀	GARDEN	⚲	ARCHAEOLOGICAL SITE
⛪	ECCLESIASTICAL BUILDING	⚑	MONUMENT/MEMORIAL
⛫	MUSEUM/ART GALLERY	◆	OTHER NOTABLE FEATURES

TOWNS/VILLAGES OF ARCHITECTURAL INTEREST *named in black*

A   B   C   D   E   F

Eilean
Annraidh

Iona

Fionnphort   Bunessan
LOCH SCRIDAIN

A849

Soa Island

Ross of Mull

Eilean a'Chalmain

Rubh'
Ardalanish

Carsaig

Malcolm's Pt

Frank Lockwood's
Island

A849

FIRTH OF LORNE

Kerrera

Croggan

Lochbuie

L. Buie

Seil

Easdale
Ferry

Luing

Cullipool

Torsa
Shuna

Scarba

Garvellachs

Lunga

Kilbride

Kilninver

L. Nell

Scamadale

Kilmelford

Balvicar

Taberonochy

Ardfern

Kintraw

Ford

A816

Kilchrenan

L. Avich

Inveraray Cas

Inver
y

A83

G

Carnasserie Castle

Craignish
Pt

Ballygowan

Kilmartin

Ardifuir

Rubh'a
Bhacain   Ardnoe Pt

Duntrune Castle

Dunadd Hill Fort

Crinan
Cairnbaan

Crarae Lodge

Minard

Furnac

Stra

G

Garbhall

R

Lochgair

Kilmichael
Glassary

Druim an Duin

An Rubha

A8?0

Kiloran
Scalasaig

A871

COLONSAY

Rubh a Geadha

Garvard

Dubh Eilean
Eilean nan Ròn

Oronsay

Rubh' an
t-Sàilein

Rubh'a'
Mhàil

Nave I

Ardnave
Pt

Ardnave

An Clachan
Sanaigmore

Bunnahabhainn

Gortantaoid

Port Askaig
Feolin
Ferry

Ballygrant

Gruinart

L
Gorm

L. Finlaggan

A846

Kilchoman

Bruichladdich

Bowmore

Bridgend

JURA

Ardlussa

Lussa R.

Rubha
nan Crann

Lagg

Ellean Mòr

Jura Forest

Small Isles
Craighouse

Rubha na
Tràille

Brosdale I.

McArthur's Head

ISLAY

L Righ
Mòr

Tayvallich

I of
Danna

Kilmory

Skervuile

Keillmore
Achahoish

Kilmichael
of Inverlussa

Ardrishaig

Otter
Ferry

SOUND OF JURA

STRATHCL

Kilberry Head

Kilberry

Pt of Knap

L CAOLISPORT

K N A P D A L E

R   REGION

Tighnabruaich

Kames

Herbert

West
Tarbert

Ardlamont
Pt

Colintraive Ferr

A886

Rothesay

I OF BUT

Rothe

Kilfinan

Auchenbreck

Kilfinan

A8003

Rubha na Faing

Rhinns of Islay

A847

Laggan
Point

Port
Charlotte

Rhinns Pt

Orsay

Portnahaven

Rubha Mór

Kilchiaran

LAGGAN
BAY

A846

Lagavulin

Ardbeg

THE OA

Lower Killeyan

Port Ellen

Texa

Mull of Oa

Rubha nan
Leacan

Ardtalla

Ardmore Pt

Eilean a'Chùirn

Achamore

Gigha I

Ardminish

Cara I

SOUND OF GIGHA

Dun Skeig

Ardpatrick Pt

Clachan

L. Ciaran

Claonaig

Skipness

Skipness Pt

Inchmarnock

West L TARBERT

SOUND OF BU

Cock of Arran

Lochranza

Pirnmill

I S L A N D

Tayinloan

Killean

Grogport

A83

KILBRANNAN   SOUND

Dougarie

Auchagallon

Machrie Moor
Stone Circles

Brodick

Brodick

Corrie

Garr

Kil

Muasdale

Glenacardoch Pt

Carradale
Dippen

Glenbarr

Saddell

Lussa
Loch

Drumadoon Pt
Blackwaterfoot

O F

A R R A N

Kilmory

Lamlash

Cla

Kilchenzie

Machrihanish

Campbeltown

Island Davarr

Brown Hd

Slidderywater Foot

Bennan
Head

Kil

A841

I N I S H O W E N
HEAD

BENBANE
HEAD

Rathlin
Island

MULL OF KINTYRE

N O R T H

BENMORE OR
FAIR HEAD

Cample Glen

Macharioch
Southend

Carskiey

Dunaverty Castle

Sheep I

Sanda I

Johnston's Pt

Ailsa
Craig

Coleraine

Garron Pt

C H A N N E L

Bennan

Ballant

Milleur Pt

Kirkcolm   A718

Leswalt

LOC
RY

HEBRIDES OR WESTERN ISLES

INNER HEBRIDES

SCOTTISH MEN OF VISION

Both Scottish and Victorian virtues found expression in men like David Livingstone, Keir Hardie and John Logie Baird. Each prized education, often hard-won, each fought determinedly for the cause he believed in, and each, except Baird, died having fallen short of the goal he glimpsed.

As a youth **David Livingstone** worked in a Glasgow cotton factory and educated himself by attending lectures at Anderson College and Glasgow University. He joined the London Missionary Society, and in 1840 he was sent to the Cape of Good Hope as a missionary.

Journeys into 'the interior', the largely unknown

DAVID LIVINGSTONE

territory to the north, led to his discovery in 1849 of Lake Ngami and the Zambezi R., and, between 1853 and 1856, to that of the Victoria Falls.

He was elected a Fellow of the Royal Society and awarded an honorary Oxford degree—but the London Missionary Society considered he had not paid enough attention to his missionary work. He resigned from its service the following year, joined the Foreign Office, and left Britain in 1858 to lead an expedition into East and Central Africa.

In 1859 he discovered Lake Shirwa and Lake Nyasa but, five years later, following distorted reports of his activities, the Foreign Office recalled him. His book on the Zambezi and its tributaries led Sir Roderick Murchison, the geologist, to invite him to search for the source of the Nile.

The expedition began in 1865; after four years of great hardships Livingstone reached Ujiji and spent two years exploring the surrounding cannibal country.

His presumed disappearance caused an American

newspaper to commission Henry Morton Stanley to locate him. The famous inquiry 'Dr Livingstone, I presume?' was uttered at Ujiji in 1871, where Stanley found Livingstone suffering from malaria.

Livingstone never found the source of the Nile. He died at a village in the Ilala country and his embalmed body was carried by mourning natives down the Zambezi. He was buried in Westminster Abbey.

Keir Hardie was at work in the coal mines near his birthplace, Legbrannock, at the age of ten. By 1880, when he was 24, his agitation for better conditions for miners had won him a place on the local pit-owners' black list.

In 1893 he founded the Independent Labour Party and in 1906 he became the first chairman of the Parliamentary Labour Party. Hardie began the Parliamentary Labour movement in Britain, but because his colleagues rejected his pacifist outlook at the start of the First World War, he died thinking himself a failure.

John Logie Baird was born at Helensburgh, the son of a minister. He studied electrical engineering at the Royal Technical College,

JOHN LOGIE BAIRD

Glasgow, and at 18 set up a small laboratory at Hastings, East Sussex. Eighteen years of extensive experiments produced an elementary television apparatus in 1924, and two years later he demonstrated T.V. in a London attic to about 50 scientists. In 1929, after he proved that transatlantic transmissions were possible, the B.B.C. took an interest in his invention and made its first T.V. transmission in 1936—though it later decided to adopt a rival system. In 1941 Baird made successful transmissions in colour. He died in 1946.

TREASURE SITES

- ⚔ CASTLE/HOUSE
- ❀ GARDEN
- 🏛 ECCLESIASTICAL BUILDING
- 🏛 MUSEUM/ART GALLERY
- ⚙ INDUSTRIAL MONUMENT
- ♣ ARCHAEOLOGICAL SITE
- ❙ MONUMENT/MEMORIAL
- ◆ OTHER NOTABLE FEATURES

TOWNS/VILLAGES OF ARCHITECTURAL INTEREST *named in black*

SCALE: ABOUT 10 MILES TO 1 INCH (1,625,000)

<!-- Map labels (left side) -->

h

g

f

e

d

c

b

a

SCALE ABOUT 10 MILES TO 1 INCH   (1:625,000)

MILES
100
90
80
70
60
50
40
30
20
10
9
8
7
6
5
4
3
2
1
0
MILES

arne Priory
nd
sfarne Castle

🏛 *Farne Islands*
Bamburgh Castle
Bamburgh

Seahouses
ker   N. Sunderland
Beadnell

Chathill
m
ingham   Newton-by-the-Sea
Charlton
Embleton
🏰**Dunstanburgh Castle**
Craster
ston   Howick

Longhoughton
rsley   Boulmer
Alnwick   Lesbury
Alnmouth

Shilbottle   Warkworth
ewton- **Warkworth Castle**
n-the- *Coquet Island*
loor
Amble
ington   cklington
Felton   Broomhill

West Chevington
rsley   Widdrington

Ulgham Ellington Cresswell
Lynemouth
Longhirst
INGTOI   Bothal   Newbiggin-by-the-Sea
Morpeth
Hepscott
ngton   Cambois
LINGTON   BLYTH

ngton
Cramlington
🏰 **Seaton Delaval Hall**
Seaton   Hartley
Masor   Seaton/
nteland   Delaval
WHITLEY BAY
Backworth
Cullercoats
TYNEMOUTH
SOUTH SHIELDS
SFORTH WALLSEND
CASTLE
PON   **JARROW**
YNE   **HEBBURN**

THE THOUGHTFUL REVOLUTIONARIES

Religion, mathematics, communications and the detective story . . . all have undergone drastic reshaping by Edinburgh men.

John Knox, founder of the Presbyterian Church, the established Church of Scotland, was born and spent most of his youth at Haddington, 16 miles east of Edinburgh. He attended

JOHN KNOX

Glasgow University, worked in Haddington as a notary between 1540 and 1543, and was then called to the ministry. In 1548, a year after he began preaching the new Protestant religion, he was captured at the fall of St Andrews Castle and imprisoned in France for a year.

Though he was made a royal chaplain in 1551, he fled to Dieppe in 1553 to avoid Mary Tudor's laws against Protestantism; he returned after five weeks there and a year later journeyed through France and Switzerland. Calvin, a leader of Protestantism, influenced his thinking.

In the same year he became pastor to the English congregation at Frankfurt, but within a year he had been charged with treason and ordered to leave. Back in Geneva in 1556, he began writing religious tracts, the most famous being *The First Blast of the Trumpet against the Monstrous Regiment of Women* (1558) which, not surprisingly, offended Elizabeth I and led to her lifelong bias against Scottish Protestantism.

In 1567 he persuaded the Scottish Parliament to approve the establishment of the Presbyterian Church. He was a minister in Edinburgh when he died in 1572.

John Napier, the mathematician, was born in the 16th-century castle of Merchiston, and became laird of the estates at Colinton and Merchiston. After St Andrews University,

Napier applied his talents to inventing machines of war (in particular, a primitive tank), and civil engineering devices, including a pump for extracting water from coal mines.

Then, as mathematics became his dominant interest, he devised logarithms, originally called artificial numbers. His thesis on them was published in 1614.

In *Rabdologia* (1615), Napier set out a method of computing by means of ivory pieces called 'numerating rods', which became known as 'Napier's Bones'. This was the earliest form of calculating machine.

Alexander Graham Bell revolutionised communications by inventing the telephone. Educated at Edinburgh and London Universities, he emigrated to Canada in 1870 and then went to the United States to work for the deaf. He became professor of vocal physiology at Boston University in 1873, and it was at Boston in 1875, the year after he became an American citizen, that he constructed his first telephone link—with Salem, 18 miles away.

At Edinburgh University **Arthur Conan Doyle** studied medicine under Dr Joseph Bell, who made an abiding impression on him. Doyle took up practice in Southsea, Hants, and there, in 1887, produced his first work of fiction, *A Study in Scarlet,* which featured Sherlock Holmes. In 1891 *The Adventures of Sherlock Holmes* appeared in the *Strand Magazine,* and brought Doyle universal acclaim.

ARTHUR CONAN DOYLE

Soon established as a highly successful author, he poured out stories about Sherlock Holmes as well as historical and adventure novels. Sir Arthur became deeply interested in spiritualism, and in 1926 published a history of the subject.

TREASURE SITES

🗡 CASTLE/HOUSE	⊕ INDUSTRIAL MONUMENT
✽ GARDEN	⚲ ARCHAEOLOGICAL SITE
⛪ ECCLESIASTICAL BUILDING	❗ MONUMENT/MEMORIAL
🏛 MUSEUM/ART GALLERY	◆ OTHER NOTABLE FEATURES
TOWNS/VILLAGES OF ARCHITECTURAL INTEREST	*named in black*

SCOTLAND
BRAVE AND ROYAL

Bonnie Prince Charlie was not the first Stuart to pursue a claim to the throne of England. His father, **James Francis Edward Stuart,** son of the deposed James II, had tried in 1715. After the Battle of Culloden Charles, like his father, sought refuge in France. In the six months before he succeeded in reaching it he was greatly assisted by **Flora Macdonald,** the 24-year-old daughter of a farmer.

FLORA MACDONALD

Flora was born in Milton, South Uist, and met the Young Pretender at Benbecula (North Uist) on his flight from Culloden. She sailed with him to Port Kilbride near Uig on the Isle of Skye. After his escape she was caught, and taken to the Tower of London for trial, but released under the Act of Indemnity (1747). She married Allan Macdonald in 1750, emigrated to North Carolina in 1774, and returned to Scotland five years later. At Kilmuir, Isle of Skye, where Flora Macdonald was buried in 1790, stands the Celtic cross inscribed with lines in her memory by Dr Samuel Johnson.

The English Crown's links with Scotland were renewed in 1852 when **Queen Victoria** leased the property known as Balmoral in the north-east Highlands. She and the Prince Consort found such personal happiness at Balmoral that the property was bought outright. **Prince Albert's** alterations and adaptations set a fashion in Scottish baronial architecture, and the queen's regular visits to Balmoral set a pattern of Royal Family holidays which continues to this day.

HIGHLAND HIGHWAYS

Following the Union of England and Scotland in 1707, **General George Wade** strengthened and enlarged the two key military bases at Fort William and Fort Augustus and introduced a network of improved roads. Ironically, they did Wade no good. In 1745, then 72, a Field Marshal, and commander-in-chief of the English armies, he was faced with putting down the second Jacobite rising, led by Prince Charles Edward Stuart, the Young Pretender.

Baffled by the speed with which Charles moved across the Highlands, Wade was replaced by the Duke of Cumberland. The rebellion came to an end with the Battle of Culloden in 1746. There are relics of the rising in the West Highland Museum at Fort William.

Wade's work was vastly extended by **Thomas Telford,** the son of a Dumfries shepherd. As a young man he worked as a mason in Edinburgh, then as a surveyor in London. The Chirk aqueduct in Shropshire, which he built between 1796 and 1801, brought him wide recognition.

THOMAS TELFORD

In 1804 he began the challenging task of linking the North Sea with the Atlantic by what became known as the Caledonian Canal. Some 23 miles of canal and 28 locks, added to the natural waters of Lochs Ness, Oich and Lochy, achieved his purpose. In the period up to 1818, Telford built 120 bridges, over 900 miles of roads and improved a score of major harbours.

TREASURE SITES

- ♟ CASTLE/HOUSE
- ❀ GARDEN
- ⛪ ECCLESIASTICAL BUILDING
- 🏛 MUSEUM/ART GALLERY
- ⊛ INDUSTRIAL MONUMENT
- ∴ ARCHAEOLOGICAL SITE
- ! MONUMENT/MEMORIAL
- ◆ OTHER NOTABLE FEATURES

TOWNS/VILLAGES OF ARCHITECTURAL INTEREST *named in black*

DRAMATIST, DUKE AND DREAMER

Fantasy, fact and something between the two centre on a few square miles of the southern Highlands.

J. M. Barrie supplied the fantasy with the work for which he is best known, *Peter Pan*. Born at Kirriemuir in 1860, Barrie began his career as a journalist,

J. M. BARRIE

first in Nottingham and then in London. An early book, *A Window in Thrums* (1889), a realistic picture of Kirriemuir, brought him fame.

But his true talent lay in drama: *Quality Street* (1901) and *The Admirable Crichton* (1902) preceded *Peter Pan* (1904). His last major work, the whimsical *Mary Rose*, was set on 'the island that wants to be visited', which is identified as at Loch Voshimid, Isle of Harris, Outer Hebrides.

Thirty-five miles from Barrie's birthplace is the magnificent ancestral home of the Murray family at Blair Atholl. **John Murray** was created Duke of Atholl in 1703. Secretary of State for Scotland from 1696 to 1698, and a Privy Councillor, he was Lord Privy Seal when, in 1705, he opposed the Union of England and Scotland so strongly that he was deprived of office.

However, he supported the government during the

rising in 1715, and captured Robert Macgregor (Rob Roy), the Highlander who followed in the wake of the Jacobite rebels but did not join the Old Pretender.

Something not fantasy and yet not scientific fact came to Blair Atholl just before the First World War in the person of **J. W. Dunne.** Dunne's advanced ideas in aeronautics had interested Sir Hiram Maxim (the Maxim gun) and H. G. Wells at a time when aeroplanes were in their infancy.

The War Office sponsored secret experiments on the Blair Atholl estate, guarded by the duke's private army, the Atholl Highlanders. Dunne's concept of a swept-back aircraft wing was too far ahead of its time for acceptance.

Dunne's most amazing experiments were set down in *An Experiment With Time* (1927). For many years he

J. W. DUNNE

recorded each morning the dreams he had had during the night. He found that a significant number came true—one 14 years later.

Dunne built this material into a thesis on the nature of time and the unconscious which gave an explanation for the 'I have been here before' feeling many people experience.

BIBLE REFERENCES

Cruden's *Biblical Concordance* is one of the first great works of reference in English. In the 1611 Authorised Version of the Bible there are 773,692 words, and Cruden's work—an index to its words and subjects—gives 225,000 references.

Alexander Cruden, who was born in Aberdeen in 1701, attended the local grammar school and Marischal College, now part of the university. Ill-health caused

him to abandon study and take up teaching. He opened a book shop in the Royal Exchange, London, in 1732, and began the compilation of his reference book, which first appeared in 1737.

Cruden suffered from attacks of insanity, but between them earned his living as a proof reader and text corrector of learned works. He died on November 1, 1770 at Camden Place, Islington, London.

TREASURE SITES

⚔ CASTLE/HOUSE	⊕ INDUSTRIAL MONUMENT
❋ GARDEN	⬥ ARCHAEOLOGICAL SITE
⛪ ECCLESIASTICAL BUILDING	! MONUMENT/MEMORIAL
⛫ MUSEUM/ART GALLERY	◆ OTHER NOTABLE FEATURES
TOWNS/VILLAGES OF ARCHITECTURAL INTEREST *named in black*	

SCALE · ABOUT 10 MILES TO 1 INCH (1:625,000)

A | B | C | D | E | F

Tully C

Inishmurray
Cliffony ● Creevykeel
Kinlough
LOUGH MELVIN
Garrison
Derry...

Benwee Head
Downpatric Head
Ardtermon Castle
Drumcliff
Grange
N16
Manorhamilton

BROAD HAVEN
Belderg
Ballycastle
Lenadoon Pt.
Easky
SLIGO BAY
Rosses Point
Hazelwood House
SLIGO
Deerpark
Parkes Castle
LEITRIM

Annagh Head
Belmullet
Binnahower
CARROWMORE LAKE
Killala
Ross Pt.
Inishcrone
Dromore West
N59
Beltra
Ballysadare
Knocknarea
Carrowmore
Dromahair
Creevelea Abbey

Bangor-Erris
KILLALA BAY
Moyne Abbey
Rosserk Abbey
BALLINA
THE OX MOUNTAINS
Collooney
N4
Markree Castle
Drumkeeran
LOUGH ALLEN

BLACKSOD BAY
NEPHIN BEG RANGE
Crossmolina
SLIGO
Tobercurry
Ballymote Castle
Ballymote
Castle Baldwin
LOUGH ARROW
Drumshanbo
 Key

Achill Head
Dooagh
Keel
Achill
Dooega
ACHILL ISLAND
Achillbeg Island
LOUGH CULLIN
Foxford
N57
Charlestown
N5
Ballaghaderreen
Ballinafad
Boyle
L. Key
Leitrim
Fe

Clare Island
CLEW BAY
Burrishoole Abbey
Rockfleet Castle
Newport Bay
Newport
Strade Abbey
Bellavary
Bohola
Kilkelly
N17
Frenchpark House
Frenchpark
Elphin
Roosky

Inishturk
Westport House
WESTPORT
N60
Castlebar
Kiltamagh
Knock
Ballyhaunis
N83
Ballinlough
N60
ROSCOMMON
Castlerea
Tulsk
N61
Strokestown House
Strokestown
Newtown
LONG

Inishbofin
Inishshark
Louisburgh
CONNAUGHT
Ballintober
Ballintober Abbey
Moore Hall
LOUGH CARRA
Claremorris
Cloonfad
Ballymoe
Ballinlough
MAYO
Ballinasloe
Roscommon Castle
Roscommon
Lanesboro
Rathcline C

SHEFFRY HILLS
Inishmaine
LOUGH MASK
Ballinrobe
Ballindine
Hollymount
N17
Dunmore
Glenamaddy
Creggs
Castlestrange
Knockcroghery
Athleague
N63
Inchcleraun
Ledw

MAAMTURK MOUNTAINS
Leenane
Clonbur
Cong
Inchagoill
Shrule
Feartagar Castle
Kilmaine
N83
Ballygar
LOUGH REE
AT

Letterfrack
Clifden
N59
Castle Kirk
Maam Cross
LOUGH CORRIB
Ross Abbey
Headford
Tuam
Knockmoy
Mount Bellew
Caltra
Clonbrock
Ahascragh

Slyne Head
Roundstone
Oughterard
N84
Annaghdown Abbey
Moycullen
Claregalway Abbey
Claregalway
Moniyea
GALWAY
Kilconnell Friary
BALLINASLOE
Clonma

St Macdara's Island
Mweenish Island
Gorumna Island
Golam Head
Inveran
Spiddal
Barna
GALWAY
N6
Oranmore
N6
Athenry
Aughrim
Clontuskert Abbey
Clonfert Cathedral
Gallen

NORTH SOUND
Kilkieran
Carna
Glinsk Castle
GALWAY BAY
Tyrone House
Kilcornan House
St Cleran's
Kilreekill
Lawrencetown Arch
Eyrecourt Castle
Eyrecourt
Clonony Castle
Banaghe

Inishmor
Aran Islands
Inishmaan
Eddy Island
BLACK HEAD
Drumacoo
Kiltiernan
Dungory Castle
Loughrea
Ballydavid
Killimor
Portumna
Derryhiveny Castle

Inisheer
SOUTH SOUND
Ballyvaghan
Corcomroe Abbey
Newtown Castle
Ballylee Castle
Kinvarra
Ardrahan
Isert Kelly
Tullira Castle
Pallas
Portumna Castle
Lorrha
Lackeen House

Doolin Pt.
Lisdoonvarna
Poulnabrone
Kilmacduagh
Gort
Lough Cutra
Lough Cutra Castle
Kiltartan Castle
Woodford
Lough Atorick
Carrigahorig
N65

Cliffs of Moher
Kilfenora
Cahercommaun
Leamaneh Castle
Lough Licken
Lough Inchiquin
Corrofin
N18
Lough Graney
Mountshannon
SLIEVE AUGHTY MOUNTAINS
Borrisokane
Shinro
Cloghjordan
ROS

Hags Head
Liscannor
Liscannor Bay
Ennistimon
Dysert O'Dea
Lough Atedaun
Feakle
Scarriff
Inis Cealtra
LOUGH DERG
Portroe
NENAGH
Toomyvara
Mon

Mal Bay
Milltown Malbay
Inagh
ENNIS
Magh Adhair
Tulla
Bodyke
Tuamgraney
Killaloe

Spanish Pt.
Mutton Island
Quilty
Kilmurry
Newhall House
Quin Abbey
Danganbrack
Kilkishen
Broadford
Silvermines
Loughm

Doonbeg
Cooraclare
Kilmihil
Killone Abbey
Carnelly House
Dromoland Castle
Newmarket on Fergus
Mount Ievers
Sixmilebridge
Birdhill
Newport
Borrisoleigh

CLARE
Canon Island
Urlanmore Castle
Bunratty Castle
Clonkeen
Ballynahow Castle

Donegal Pt.
Kilkee
Killadysert
Shannongrove House
King John's Castle
Glenstal Castle
Holycross Abb

LOOP HEAD
Kilrush
Scattery Island
KILRUSH
Labasheeda
Dromore Castle
Foynes
Carrigogunnel Castle
LIMERICK
Cappamore
THU

Carrigaholt Castle
Carrigafoyle Castle
Glin Castle
Monasternagalliaghduff
Cappagh Castle
Askeaton
Adare
Patrickswell
N24
Caherconlish
Pallasgreen
Ardmayle House

Map

TREASURE SITES

- ♟ CASTLE/HOUSE
- �֎ GARDEN
- ⛪ ECCLESIASTICAL BUILDING
- 🏛 MUSEUM/ART GALLERY
- ⊛ INDUSTRIAL MONUMENT
- ♣ ARCHAEOLOGICAL SITE
- ⚑ MONUMENT/MEMORIAL
- ◆ OTHER NOTABLE FEATURES

TOWNS/VILLAGES OF ARCHITECTURAL INTEREST *named in black*

(Map of Northern Ireland showing counties Antrim, Down, Armagh, Louth with locations including Rathlin Island, Ballycastle, Carnanmore, Fair Head Crannog, Ballintoy, Bushmills, Ballymoney, Ballymena, Larne, Carrickfergus, Belfast, Bangor, Newtownards, Strangford Lough, Downpatrick, Newry, Warrenpoint, Dundalk, Droghead, Newgrange, Mellifont Abbey, Monasterboice, etc.)

SCALE: ABOUT 12½ MILES TO 1 INCH (1:800,000)

Just as Ireland's many legends have factual origins, so the accounts of its famous saints, often confusingly romanticised by time and imagination, deal with the story of real people involved in the teachings of Christianity.

It was **St Patrick**, the Apostle of Ireland, who was responsible for bringing Christianity to the country. Thought to have been born in a Roman villa in Monmouthshire in AD 389, Patrick lived a retiring and uneventful life until he was 16. He was then captured by Irish raiders and taken back to their country as a slave. For six years he worked a lonely life as a shepherd, finding his only comfort in prayer and meditation. Finally he managed to escape to the Continent. He spent the next 21 years of his life there in study, preparing for his later work as a missionary. In 432 he returned to Ireland as a consecrated bishop and started out on a life's mission of converting the heathen. He travelled extensively, built a number of churches and firmly established Christianity. When he died on March 17, 461, at the age of 72, he had impressed Rome sufficiently for the Papacy to raise Ireland's status to an ecclesiastical province.

Someone who was still a child in Patrick's later years was **St Bridget**. Born near Dundalk in AD 452 and baptised by St Patrick, she was the daughter of a

ST BRIDGET

wealthy Leinster chieftain. Like her mother, however, she was one of her father's many slaves and worked long arduous hours on the farmland. Years later, by which time she had become a woman of considerable beauty, her father made many attempts to arrange a wealthy marriage.

But Bridget was adamant and her resolve to further the teachings of Christianity finally persuaded him to free her. With several female companions, Bridget set off for the monastery at Ardagh, there to study under Bishop Mel. Six months

later and now consecrated, Bridget and her companions returned home to found the convent of Kildare—'the place of the oak'. Stories are legion of the miracles performed by St Bridget as she travelled about the country, tending the sick, preaching the gospel and founding churches, schools and convents. She died at Kildare on February 1, 524.

The first two lines of an ancient Irish hymn dedicated to her, have a revealing eloquence about them:

'Brigit, ever excellent woman, golden sparkling flame, lead us to the eternal Kingdom, the dazzling resplendent sun.'

Fleet Street's church of St Bride is named after her

Of the many saints who travelled abroad **St Brendan** is one of the most interesting. The stories of his famous seven-year voyage in search of the Land of Promise—the earthly paradise situated somewhere in the middle of the Atlantic —are overlaid with legend, but could have had a basis in fact.

Born at Annagh in 484 on the south shore of Tralee Bay, he spent his early childhood in the care of a nun. Her religious influence prepared him for the higher studies he later pursued with Bishop Erc. Finally ordained by him as a priest, Brendan set off with great enthusiasm and energy to create two large monasteries: one at Ardfert in Tralee; the other well inland, up the R. Shannon, at Clonfert. All that remains of the latter is the famous Romanesque doorway to the church. A great seaman as well as a hillsman, Brendan covered what were then considered to be great distances, sailing not only to Scotland and the Hebrides but around the southern tip of Ireland to Wales and Brittany in his efforts to spread the influence of Christianity.

In later life he returned to his abbey at Clonfert and eventually died in 577 at the grand age of 93.

In the romantic life of his legendary voyages St Brendan's many experiences include the discovery of the Country of Perpetual Day where darkness never falls and seeing the Isle of Fleas where the insects outnumbered the grains of sand on the shoreline. He also celebrated Easter on the back of a whale, mistaking it for an island, and discovered Judas Iscariot suffering the punishment of Purgatory (except on Sundays and other religious occasions) on a tiny rock situated in the middle of the sea.

Irish history and Irish myth have long been the staple ingredients of Irish art but it was not until the latter part of the 19th century that a surge of creative writing used them to herald the famous Irish literary renaissance.

Before this period, the British occupation had almost killed continuity of tradition in the Irish way of life. Enthusiasm to restore the national language of Gaelic resulted in the formation of various literary and dramatic societies. Two of these were the Gaelic League by David Hyde in 1893 and the Irish Dramatic Movement in 1899. Two years later The Irish National Dramatic Society was formed and out of this grew the famous Abbey Theatre.

The Abbey Theatre's foundation was primarily due to the efforts of the poet **W. B. Yeats** who, with some financial assistance from England, purchased a property in Abbey Street, Dublin, and converted it to a theatre. It opened in 1904.

Yeats's other colleagues in the venture were originally **Edward Martyn** and **George Moore** but

GEORGE MOORE

being unable to go all the way with Yeats's visionary plans, first Martyn, then Moore, dropped out. They were replaced by the poet **AE** (**George Russell**, 1867–1935) and the playwright **Lady Gregory** (1852–1932).

Although the theatre originally set out to be nationalistic and draw on the wealth of Irish legends (which was Yeats's intention), its early presentations attacked many of the things the Irish held dear: mocking at marriage, ridiculing supposed miracles and pouring scorn on family relationships. For years afterwards its productions invariably provoked violent controversy at home, meanwhile earning a reputation abroad that was highly acclaimed.

After the period of civil strife ended in Ireland in 1924, dramatic emphasis shifted from the Abbey's productions to the Gate Theatre in Dublin. Founded by **Michael Mac Liammoir** and **Hilton Edwards**, the Gate presented a wider range of plays than the Abbey, embracing the work of international dramatists and subjects.

The Abbey meanwhile settled into the respectability of a national theatre, nourishing the best in Irish drama.

On the 17th July 1951, O'Casey's grim play *The Plough and the Stars* was presented at the Abbey. Its final act ends with a wild scene of insurrection and the burning of Dublin. A few hours after the curtain fell the theatre was a smoking ruin: gutted by a fire which consumed the stage props, scripts and costumes accumulated over nearly five decades. It was not until 1966 that the theatre re-opened.

W. B. YEATS

Ireland has probably reared more significant men of letters for its comparatively small size, than any other country in the English – speaking world. Of these, most seem to have been born in Dublin. The first outstanding native was **William Butler Yeats** (1865–1939). A far greater poet than dramatist (despite his activities in forming the Abbey), Yeats's early works—*The Land of Heart's Desire* (1894) and *Shadowy Waters* (1885–1906)—were symbolic, poetic dramas unrelated to contemporary life. As he developed, his writing became more intellectually obscure and an unfamiliar intensity revealed itself in his late plays, among them: *The Words upon the Window Pane* (1934) and *Purgatory* (1938).

His friend and companion, **Lady Gregory**, wrote no fewer than 27 short plays and poems. Her first two plays were written in collaboration with him: *The Pot of Broth* and *Cathleen ni Houlihan*.

This last was based upon the saga of Cuchulainn, which in turn bears a striking resemblance to the legendary labours of Hercules. She also translated a Molière play and her *Kiltartan Molière* was produced on the Irish stage.

A valuable recruit to the Abbey Theatre was **John Millington Synge** (1871–1909) whom Yeats had met in Paris. Synge, the son of a barrister, had studied at Trinity College, Dublin in 1892, and after visiting Germany and Italy decided to settle in Paris where he set himself to study Hebrew and French Drama. Ironically, it was Yeats who convinced him his real chance lay in Ireland. In 1903 Synge joined the Irish National Dramatic Society, and that same year wrote *The Shadow of the Glen*. By 1904 he was a director of the Abbey Theatre and in 1907 wrote his most famous work: *The Playboy of the Western World*. He died three years later, a reclaimed expatriate.

Another Dubliner, born in 1880, was the unschooled **Sean O'Casey**.

SEAN O'CASEY

The Abbey Theatre produced his first play, *The Shadow of a Gunman*, when he was 43 years of age. He followed this with *Juno and the Paycock*, a

drama of the Dublin slums, and its success established him as a foremost playwright. But his next play, titled *The Plough and the Stars*, is perhaps his finest. Those that followed were less successful and in 1928 the Abbey Theatre rejected *The Silver Tassie*. Living in England, O'Casey continued to write—*Within the Gates*, 1933; *Purple Dust*, 1940; *The Bishop's Bonfire*, 1955; he also produced an autobiography. He died in 1964.

In October 1856, the man many regard as the greatest wit of his time was born in Westland Row, Dublin: **Oscar Wilde**. Between 1887, when he was, for a short time, editor of the *Woman's World*, and his death in France in 1900, Wilde wrote plays— among them *Lady Windermere's Fan* and *The Importance of Being Earnest*: poems, criticisms, children's stories and the famous *De Profundis*, his final prose work cast as a letter to Lord Alfred Douglas. In this letter, written during his imprisonment for homosexuality, he claimed 'the Gods have given me almost everything', but it was society that provided the acclaim

OSCAR WILDE

he deserved and the final disaster he courted.

Two years younger than Wilde, **George Bernard Shaw** grew up in Dublin, then in 1876 moved to London. There, he wrote a number of unspectacular novels and from 1885 to 1894 was the music critic of the London *Star* and then *The World*. His first play, *Widowers' Houses*, was performed in 1892, and in 1909 the Abbey Theatre produced *The Shewing up of Blanco Posnet*, after the play had been banned in England because of Shaw's religious pronouncements. His best-known works include: *Arms and the Man* and *Candida*, 1894; *The Devil's Disciple* 1897; *Caesar and Cleopatra* 1898; *Man and Superman* 1903; *The Doctor's Dilemma* 1906; *Pygmalion* 1912; and *St Joan* 1924. In 1925 he was awarded the Nobel Prize for Literature. He died in 1950.

Among the more recent Dublin dramatists few have made a greater impact than the late **Brendan Behan**. Born in 1923, he wrote an early

BRENDAN BEHAN

autobiography, *Borstal Boy*, which vividly illustrated his experiences in prison and his activities with the IRA. He then turned to writing plays and his first work, *The Quare Fellow*, was produced in 1954. Four years later he followed this with another tragicomedy, *The Hostage*. As with *The Quare Fellow* he was largely assisted with the revision and expansion of the play by Joan Littlewood, founder of the Theatre Workshop. Unhappily Brendan Behan died at the early age of 41.

SAMUEL BECKETT

A far more complex playwright is the Anglo-Irishman **Samuel Beckett**. After a first-class academic grounding, which resulted in an exchange lectureship in Paris, he met and became associated with James Joyce and his contemporaries. Beckett's most widely acclaimed work is *Waiting for Godot*, which was produced in Paris in 1953 and later throughout the world. Beckett is now one of the world's foremost playwrights and novelists.

Although his close friend, **James Joyce**, did not write primarily for the theatre, the force of his dramatic invention influenced many of his creative counterparts. Born in Dublin in 1882, he travelled widely throughout Europe supporting himself by teaching. In 1914 he wrote a collection of short stories under the title *Dubliners*, and in the next 30 years

JAMES JOYCE

produced his greatest works, *Ulysses* and *Finnegans Wake*. He moved to Switzerland in 1940 and died in Zurich the following January.

GEORGE BERNARD SHAW

THE TREASURES OF IRELAND

A unique and little-known

land that has preserved the inheritance

of over 3000 years of civilisation

The hard facts of Ireland's history have made it dramatically different from the rest of the British Isles; accordingly Ireland is here given a separate section from England, Scotland and Wales. The story is a long, sad one of oppression by foreigners, cruel religious conflict at home and ordeal by famine; it is made bearable by the memory of a Golden Age when the Gaels, who made princes out of poets, carried the torch of Christianity through three dark centuries.

Monasteries, crosses, illuminated manuscripts and superb examples of religious metalwork still survive as reminders of that romantic period between the 6th and 9th centuries when Irish missionaries spread learning and culture across Europe. But the centuries that followed were so violent that an ancient church or monastery mentioned here must be presumed to be roofless unless otherwise stated.

Only in the middle of the 17th century was a condition of relative political stability assured, to permit the steady growth of urban civilisation. The towns, which often have a grandeur of lay-out which seems out of proportion to the size of their populations, are linked by a network of roads which again are unexpectedly large in scale.

After the famine and emigrations of the 1840's, the population fell by two million, and today is only four and a half million. One result of this is that the pace of life in Ireland seems easier than in Britain. When country houses and other occupied buildings are mentioned in this section, no implication is intended that they are all open to the public; but many people will still, in practice, prove ready to admit an interested visitor if asked courteously.

Abbeyleix *Laois* 573Gb
Laid out by the de Vesci family, with tree-lined streets and the Market House; the most interesting building is the Protestant church, with a front and spire by John Semple, altered and rebuilt by Thomas H. Wyatt in 1865.
ABBEYLEIX HOUSE Built for the 1st Viscount de Vesci in 1773–4, a square house entirely refaced in the 19th century. The interior has fine plasterwork designed by James Wyatt, and a dining-room with grisaille decoration by de Grée. (Gardens open.)

Adare *Lim.* 570Ee
ADARE CASTLE Only one wall survives of the original, nearly-square keep—surrounded by an inner bailey, a gate-house for a drawbridge and a fosse. The outer ward has a gate and two towers. The castle has two great halls by the river, the earlier and smaller being the first-floor hall, containing round-headed paired windows, dating from *c.* 1200, and the other being a 13th-century ground-floor hall. A FitzGerald stronghold.
ADARE MANOR An 18th-century mansion was joined by a new Tudor Revival manor, begun in 1832 by the 2nd Earl of Dunraven, with a long gallery and twin towers by the brothers Pain. The rest of the house was completed by P. C. Hardwick, A. W. Pugin and Lord Dunraven himself, and was finished by 1876. It has fine paintings and furniture. (Not open to the public.)
AUGUSTINIAN BLACK ABBEY Founded in 1315 by the 1st Earl of Kildare, the structure dates mostly from the 15th century. The cloister-garth of *c.* 1470, with the FitzGerald saltire carved in the north spandrels of the east arcade, is pierced with triple openings; the cloister is small and square. In 1807 the ruins were adapted as a Protestant church and much unfortunate modification took place.
FRANCISCAN FRIARY Built by Thomas, 7th Earl of Kildare, and beautifully sited in the Adare Manor demesne. The church was finished *c.* 1484 and the rest probably by 1500. Notable cloister and sedilia.
TRINITARIAN FRIARY The sole example of a Trinitarian house in Ireland, founded in 1230 and enlarged in 1272. The whole building was remodelled, with the addition of a new nave aisle, to serve as the Catholic church, by P. C. Hardwick in the mid-19th century, for the 3rd Earl of Dunraven. Near by is a dovecote.

Aghowle *Wicklow* 573Ja
The north, east and west walls survive of the early 12th-century church, whose most remarkable feature is its massive megalithic west doorway with a flat lintel and bold architrave.

Ahenny (or Kilclispeen) *Tipp.* 571Hd
Two superb 8th-century high crosses which are among the most important in the south-east. The north cross has fine abstract geometric and spiral ornaments on the shaft. The figures forming a procession on the base have not been identified.

Annaghdown Abbey *Gal.* 572Cd
The monastery traditionally founded by St Brendan of Clonfert. The cathedral, possibly a Premonstratensian church, has a Romanesque window and a Gothic north door. The ruins of an Augustinian priory of many dates and of a plain nunnery-church may also be seen. A small plain 15th-century church incorporates a late-Romanesque window with delicately carved chevron ornament.

Annaghmore *Arm.* 575Gb
A well-preserved court-cairn excavated in 1963–4, it has neat horizontal inter-filling between the upright stones.

Antrim *Antrim* 575He
The county town, site of an early monastery, whose Round Tower survives almost complete, with a cross in relief over the door and a restored conical cap. The ruins of Antrim Castle, burnt in 1922, remain; the embattled shell, by Sir Richard Morrison, incorporates an early 17th-century door. The most remarkable feature, though, is the garden, one of the rare examples of a French-style lay-out in Ireland.

Aran Islands *Gal.* 572Bc
There are three principal islands; Inishmore to the north-west, Inishmaan in the middle, and Inisheer to the south-east. On all three islands there are numerous early drystone forts and early Christian remains. The exact date of the great forts is unknown, but they are presumed to be of the Iron Age. St Enda, who is credited with the foundation of the Christian settlement, lived in the early 6th century, but it is doubtful whether the stone churches are so early; some may be as late as the 12th century.
INISHEER Among the monuments are Creggankeel, an irregular large fort; a ruined 15th-century castle, set in a circular fort; a circular graveyard called Knockgrannia, near the landing-stage; St Cavan's Church, with a nave and chancel; Kilgobnet Church, small and primitive.
INISHMAAN The principal monument is Dun Conor, one of the finest of the great forts; it is oval, with an outer bailey and restored hut-sites within. Inishmaan also has one of the few Bronze Age tombs on the islands, 'Dermot and Grania's Bed', a name commonly given to chamber-tombs.
INISHMORE Kilronan, the principal town, is in Killeany Bay on the north-east coast. The major monument is the world-famous Dun Aengus, a huge drystone semicircular fort standing on the edge of a 280 ft cliff dropping sheer into the sea. To the north-west is Dun Onaght, a large ring-fort, also restored, and at Onaght village the so-called 'Seven Churches', with the remains of only two small churches, several early cross-slabs, and some 15th-century monastic remains. Near Kilmurvy village are Temple MacDuagh and Templenaneeve, both early churches, the former with a chancel. In the centre of the island, near the highest point, is Dun Oghil, a large stone ring-fort. West of it is the 15th-century church of the Four Beautiful Saints, and their grave. South of Kilronan is Killeany (Enda's Church). Here is the tiny Temple Benen, a well-preserved oratory built of enormous stones. A mile and a half to the west is the promontory fort of Doocaher, also with a defensive line of spikes, and also restored, with clochans.

Arboe *Tyrone* 575Gd
HIGH CROSS At 18 ft 6 in., one of the tallest crosses in Ireland. Probably 9th century, it is carved with scenes from the Old and New Testaments.

Ardbraccan House *Meath* 573Je
A large stone house with wings, formerly the palace of the Bishops of Meath. The wings are by Richard Castle, and probably date from *c.* 1747. The main block is by James Wyatt. The parish church (1777) near by has a medieval bell-tower.

Ardee *Louth* 573Jf
An important strong-point on the north-west border of the medieval Pale. In the Main Street there is a castle, now a court-house, comprising a square keep of the 15th century. Hatch's Castle in Market Street is 13th century. The Protestant church includes parts of a medieval church and has a medieval font.

DUN AENGUS, INISHMORE, ARAN ISLANDS

The most spectacular of the Aran Islands' many prehistoric monuments, this dramatically sited dry-stone fort encloses nearly 11 acres. It has three rings of defence, the middle one reinforced with a line of jagged limestone uprights. The innermost rampart encloses an area about 150 ft in diameter.

Ardfert *Kerry* 570Cd
FRANCISCAN FRIARY Founded in 1253 by Thomas
FitzMaurice, 1st Lord Kerry, and now in ruins.
The rectangular building has a row of lancets on
the south side of the choir. Near by are the
remains of Ardfert House, with a garden of formal
banks and an 18th-century Gothic arch. The
splendid mid-19th-century embattled lodge gates
of the demesne are in the village.
ST BRENDAN'S CATHEDRAL This roofless early
13th-century building has a fine chancel with a
row of nine lancet windows on its south side and
three tall lancets to the east.
TEMPLE NA HOE This late 12th-century church has
lost its chancel, but the nave has angle columns
with carved capitals, a west door, a small decorated
south window and a carved chancel arch.

Ardglass *Down* 575Jc
This fishing village has seven castles or fortified
houses as reminders of its importance in the Middle
Ages. Jordan's Castle is now a museum; Ardglass
Castle was Gothicised in 1790.

Ardmayle House *Tipp.* 571Ge
Of the embattled house, a fine 17th-century wall
with mullioned windows survives.

Ardmore *Waterford* 571Gc
The foundation of St Declan still contains some of
the most striking early Christian buildings in Ireland. The Round Tower, which is one of the tallest
and most complete, has an unusual degree of taper,
a set of string-courses marking the floors at its
original conical roof. Close by stands the 12th-
century cathedral, of which the west wall is decorated with two large blind arches each containing
small arcades with figure-sculpture, above which
is another arcade of 13 arches also containing
figure-sculpture.

Ardrass *Kild.* 573Jd
ST PATRICK'S CHAPEL A small, probably late-
medieval church, noteworthy for its traditional
Irish form of stone roof.

Ardscull *Kild.* 573Hb
The great mote around which the road from
Naas to Athy pivots may have been a prehistoric
burial mound; it was certainly fortified in Cromwellian times. Near by is the rath of Mullaghmast,
where a massacre took place in 1577.

Ardtermon Castle *Sligo* 574Bc
A semi-fortified house of the early 17th century, in
the form of a long rectangle with cylindrical angle-
towers and semicircular staircase-projection at the
back. The nearly-square fortified enclosure at the
back also has a cylindrical angle-tower.

Arklow *Wicklow* 573Ka
Handsome stone Catholic church of *c.* 1840 by
Patrick Byrne, with distinguished front including
a western tower and cupola. The domed interior
has good plasterwork.

Armagh *Arm.* 575Gc
The ecclesiastical capital of Ireland, seat of two
archbishops, traditionally founded by St Patrick.
The city occupies the site of an ancient earth-fort
within which lies the Protestant cathedral. The
first church on the site was built by St Patrick, but
the aspect of the present cathedral is an entirely
19th-century restoration by Lewis Cottingham.
The cathedral dominates the city; the churchyard
is the reputed burying-place of Brian Boru, who
drove the Norsemen from Ireland in the 11th
century, and there are monuments by Roubiliac,
Chantrey, Rysbrack and Nollekens. The Book of
Armagh, a 9th-century transcription of St Patrick's
life, the New Testament and annals, is in Trinity
College Library, Dublin.

Famed as a centre of learning, Armagh was
repeatedly plundered during the Middle Ages,
and by the 16th century was little more than a
village. It now consists of the concentric circles of
the ancient settlement, side by side with the Mall,
originally the racecourse, and now flanked by
some fine Georgian houses. Much of its present
attraction is due to the influence of Primate
Richard Robinson (Lord Rokeby) who came to
the See in 1765, and remained there until his death
in 1794. Apart from the Protestant cathedral, the
principal ancient relic is the ruined church of a
Franciscan friary, founded in 1264 by Archbishop
O'Scannail. It stands in the primate's demesne.

West of the Protestant cathedral is Vicar's Hill, a
row of 18th-century houses, and near them the
library, founded by Primate Robinson in 1771 to
house his notable collection of books and the diocesan records. It was designed by Thomas Cooley,
but harmoniously extended *c.* 1820. Beside it
stands the Infirmary of 1774 by George Ensor. At
the north-west end of the Mall is the porticoed
court-house of 1809 by Francis Johnston, a native
of Armagh and a protégé of the primate. At the
other end stands the old gaol. The museum on the
north side of the Mall occupies a temple-like
school building of 1833. In Scotch Street is the
handsome town house of the Dobbin family, until
recently the Bank of Ireland, by Francis Johnston.
The Royal School on College Hill was founded
in 1608, but the present, much enlarged, building
by Cooley dates from 1774. On the hill is the
charming Observatory founded by Primate
Robinson and designed by Thomas Codley

MONUMENT TO
DEAN DRELINCOURT

*Peter Drelincourt was born in Paris in
1644, the son of Charles Drelincourt,
a Huguenot (French Protestant)
minister. He came to Ireland and
was made chaplain to the Duke of
Ormonde, Archdeacon of Leighlin,
and Rector and Dean of Armagh in
1691. He died in 1722. His widow
commissioned this recumbent monument from Michael Rysbrack, and a
school was founded under his will.
(Armagh Protestant Cathedral)*

in 1788. On another hill to the northwest is the twin-towered Catholic cathedral begun by Thomas Duff of Newry in 1840 in the Perpendicular Gothic style, and completed in 1873 by J. J. McCarthy. St Mark's Protestant church, built by Primate Stuart *c.* 1830, is approached from the Mall by an avenue of trees; near by is the wooded demesne, now partially a golf course, of the former palace, built by Primate Robinson to the design of Cooley in 1770. Beside it stands its detached chapel of 1781, with a notable Classical interior; the porticoed exterior is by Cooley and the interior by Francis Johnston.

Ash Hill Towers *Lim.*   570Ed
A Classical house with a central, pedimented, symmetrical block with a deep stable court and piers, built in 1781. The interior has Wyatt-type plasterwork. The rear façade was rebuilt in the Gothic Revival style of 1833, probably by the Pain brothers. (By appointment.)

Askeaton *Lim.*   570De
One of the chief castles of the FitzGeralds of Desmond. Mostly 15th century, it comprises two courts on an island in the R. Deel. The most interesting feature is a magnificent 15th-century great hall with florid decorated windows.
FRANCISCAN FRIARY Founded before 1400, probably by Gerald, 4th Earl of Desmond, and restored in the 15th century by the 6th Earl. The cloister buildings lie, unusually, to the south of the church which, in consequence, has an aisled north transept; the refectory, again unusually, lies to the north and south, abutting on the south walk of the cloister. The beautifully carved cloister is among the earliest and finest in Ireland.

Athassel Abbey *Tipp.*   571Ge
This Augustinian priory, founded in 1193 by the de Burgos, is one of the best of Irish monasteries. The church has an aisled nave, a tower (a 15th-century insertion) at the crossing of the transepts, with four eastward chapels and a short choir with lancets to north and south. The doorway dividing the nave from the choir is a striking feature. The dorter stands on a vaulted basement and the chapter house lies to the east of it. The refectory also stands on vaults, and there is a vaulted gate-house. Extensive precinct walls survive in large part.

Athenry *Gal.*   572Dc
A 16th-century town cross has figures of St Mary and St John. The Protestant parish church has some fragments of its medieval predecessor, and near by is the ruined north gate of the town. Extensive sections of the town walls may also be seen.
ATHENRY CASTLE This castle of the de Berminghams is irregularly shaped, with a mid-13th-century keep in good condition. There is a fine early Gothic doorway with elaborate capitals.
DOMINICAN FRIARY OF SS PETER AND PAUL Founded in 1241 by Myler de Bermingham, but most of its present features date from the 14th century. It was partly rebuilt in 1423 after a fire, and was occupied as late as 1652. Good details.

Athlone *Westmeath*   572Fd
A bridge-head on the Shannon with a much altered 13th-century castle, now used as a barracks, on the west side of the river. The Renaissance-style Catholic church was built in 1937. North-east is the demesne of Waterston, a house designed by Richard Castle, now in ruins though an octagonal spired dove-cote and a hermitage remain in the landscaped lay-out. Three miles north-east on the hill of Twyford is a cross with spirals, a hunting scene and inscription.

Athlumney House *Meath*   573Je
Adjoining the 15th-century Dowdall Castle is a fine gabled and mullioned 17th-century house.

Athy *Kild.*   573Hb
The town contains White's Castle, built in 1575. There is also a court-house of *c.* 1800 with an additional modern storey; on the outside are rather crudely carved plaques representing the Scales of Justice and the Harp of Hibernia inside wreaths.

Avondale *Wicklow*   573Kb
A square house of 1779, possibly designed by James Wyatt. It was built by Samuel Hayes, a notable amateur architect, and is famous as the birthplace and home of the Irish Nationalist hero and statesman Charles Stewart Parnell. Fine Wyatt plasterwork in the drawing-room incorporates mirrors in the decoration.

Ballinafad *Sligo*   574Cb
The Castle of the Curlews at Ballinafad, built in *c.* 1519 to control an important pass, is a small keep with four massive cylindrical angle-towers.

Ballinamantain See Kiltartan.

Ballinasloe *Gal.*   572Ed
A market town at the end of a branch of the Grand Canal, notable for the splendid mental hospital of 1838. There are also some good 18th-century houses. Near by is Garbally, originally the seat of the Trenches, Earls of Clancarty, in the grounds of which is a curious fluted obelisk. The house, by J. M. Gandy, is now a school and has a good library and art collection.

Ballincollig Castle *Cork*   570Eb
A tall medieval castle with a large bawn.

Ballinderry *Antrim*   575Hd
MIDDLE CHURCH Bishop Jeremy Taylor began this church in 1664. It is a simple rectangle with square-headed, three-light windows with oak mullions and transoms, and retains part of its original Jacobean-style fittings.

Ballinlough Castle *Westmeath*   573He
An early 18th-century house to which, *c.* 1760, a twin round-towered crenellated range was added.

Ballintober *Mayo*   572Ce
AUGUSTINIAN FRIARY Founded by Cathal O'Conor in 1216. The church was originally cruciform and had no aisle, with a tower over the crossing. There are good Romanesque and early Gothic details on the windows and capitals. The choir is vaulted, and the transepts each have vaulted eastward chapels. It continued to be used for Catholic worship throughout the 17th and 18th centuries, and in 1846 John MacHale, Archbishop of Tuam, began its restoration. In 1889 George Ashlin re-roofed the chancel, crossing and transept, and there was further sensitive restoration in 1966. The remains of a Jacobean tomb of the 1st Lord Mayo can be seen in the sacristy.

Ballintober Castle *Roscom.*   572Ee
Built *c.* 1300 by the O'Conors; a large native copy of the Anglo-Norman castle at Roscommon.

Ballycastle *Antrim*   575Gg
The town consists of a long straight street leading down to the sea from the Diamond where the Old Lammas Fair, dating from the 17th century, is held in August. Marconi transmitted his first wireless message from a cottage here in 1905.
BONAMARGY FRIARY Founded for the Franciscans *c.* 1500; it now stands in ruins, containing a mausoleum of the McDonnell family.

WILLIAM BUTLER YEATS, IRELAND'S POETIC GENIUS

The area around Sligo, in the west of Ireland, is known as Yeats Country because of its associations with the man who transmuted national legend into world poetry; a Yeats Summer School is held at Sligo every year. In his twenties, Yeats lived in London where 'he lived, breathed, ate, drank and slept poetry', striding about the streets reciting and flailing his arms. At 30, he was established as an imaginative writer with *The Celtic Twilight* (1893) and *Poems* (1895). Only a few broken walls remain of Coole Park in Galway where Yeats and Lady Gregory conceived the idea of a National Theatre. With her encouragement he developed into the colossus of the Abbey Theatre, Dublin.

'I shuddered', Yeats said, when he first saw this portrait, painted by Augustus John. 'Always particular about my clothes, never dissipated, never unshaven except during illness, I saw myself there as an unshaven, drunken bartender, and then I began to feel John had found something that he liked in me. He has found Anglo-Irish solitude, a solitude I have made for myself, an outlawed solitude.' (Tate Gallery, London)

THOOR BALLYLEE, the *roofless Norman tower built upon a small island in County Galway, which Yeats bought for £35 in 1917. He turned the place into a home, as the inscription upon it tells. The tower became the centre of Yeats's imagination, a symbol of mental solitude and questing. Publication of 'The Tower' in 1928, followed by 'The Winding Stair' in 1929, crowned his achievement as a poet. T. S. Eliot calls Yeats's work in his middle and later years 'a great and permanent example of a kind of moral as well as intellectual excellence'. The castle has been renovated and can be visited during summer months.*

MAUD GONNE, *beautiful and fiery Irish revolutionary, subject of much of Yeats's poetry, and the unrequited love of his youth. (By Sarah Purser at the Irish National Portrait Gallery)*

NOBEL MEDAL *for literature, awarded to Yeats in 1923, and a mark of his recognition as a lyric poet. It lies upon the manuscript of 'The Lake Isle of Innisfree'. (Sligo Museum, Eire)*

BRONZE *by Henry Moore in memory of Yeats, who became a Senator of the new Parliament of the Irish Free State in 1922 and founded, with Shaw, the Irish Academy of Letters. (St Stephen's Green, Dublin)*

THE POET'S HOME *in Woburn Walk, London, where Yeats lived for 24 years and, with his genius for friendship, entertained many intellectuals of his time.*

THE AUTOGRAPH TREE, *a copper beech at Lady Gregory's home, Coole Park, Galway. Lady Gregory's initials are surrounded by those of famous guests, including Yeats.*

> Cast a cold eye
> on life, on death.
> Horseman, pass by!

This epitaph, by the poet himself, is in Drumcliff churchyard, Co. Sligo.

> I will arise and go now, and go to Innisfree,
> And a small cabin build there, of clay and wattles made:
> Nine bean-rows will I have there, a hive for the honey-bee,
> And live alone in the bee-loud glade.

From 'The Lake Isle of Innisfree', Yeats's most famous poem.

PROTESTANT CHURCH An attractive 18th-century building, which was erected by the Boyd family in 1756.

Ballycopeland *Down* 575Jd
The little windmill on a hilltop outside Millisle is an 18th-century cornmill maintained in perfect working order as an ancient monument. The only other windmill in Ireland is at Tacumshane, and is not working.

Ballyfin House *Laois* 573Gb
A large, early 19th-century Classical house with Ionic portico designed by Sir Richard Morrison and his son for the Coote family. The gardens are by Lutyens. It is now a school.

Ballygalley Manor House *Antrim* 575He
A Scottish tower-house built in 1625 for James Shaw, consisting of a rectangle with a north-east tower and spiral stairs, now a hotel.

Ballygrennan Castle *Lim.* 570Ee
A large castle with a central keep and 16th-century mullioned windows, surrounded by 17th-century gabled and chimneyed buildings.

Ballylee See Gort.

Ballymakenny *Louth* 573Ke
The church was Francis Johnston's first building designed in Gothic style. It was built in 1785–93 for Primate Robinson, in the style of Thomas Cooley; it has exquisite fittings and details.

Ballymoon Castle *Carlow* 571Jf
This keep-less castle is of unique, almost square form; it dates from the early 14th century, a period from which few buildings in Ireland survive.

Ballymore *Don.* 574Df
A good 18th-century church, probably designed by Michael Priestley of Lifford. It has a heavy moulded block Venetian window to the east, and retains its interior fittings.

Ballymote Castle *Sligo* 574Bb
The keep-less castle built by Richard De Burgh *c.* 1300 has cylindrical angle-towers and D-shaped towers in the centres of the east and west walls. There was once a gateway of two such towers in the middle of the north front.

Ballynacarriga Castle *Cork* 570Db
A 16th-century castle on a rock at the edge of a lake. The arched windows of the upper room on the top floor have interesting carvings and there is a sheila-na-gig (a female fertility figure) high up in the external wall.

Ballynahinch *Down* 575Hc
A characterful town laid out in the early 17th century by the Rawdon family. The decisive battle of the United Irishmen's rising was fought here in 1798. The assembly rooms have an early 19th-century Doric timber portico. The wooded demesne of Montalto was built in the late 18th century by the first Earl of Moira and has fine plasterwork. Harris's cornmill has an early 19th-century waterwheel powered by the Ballynahinch River. The mill is still in commercial use.

Ballynahow Castle *Tipp.* 571Gf
A 16th-century castle consisting of a five-storied circular tower, well preserved, the first and third storeys being vaulted over.

Ballynatray House *Waterford* 571Gc
A large eleven-bay pedimented block of 1795–7, magnificently sited in an enormous deer park by the R. Blackwater. (Not open to the public.)

Ballynoe *Down* 575Jc
A regular circle of stones containing a horseshoe-shaped group of stones partly enclosing an oval mound, the whole about 100 ft in diameter.

Ballyragget *Kilk.* 571Hf
BUTLER CASTLE The 15th- and 16th-century Butler castle in the town retains its roof and the walled enclosure and ditch of its defences. In 1798 it served as a military barracks.

Balrothery *Dublin* 573Ke
The tower of the Protestant church resembles that at Lusk, though here there was no Round Tower to serve as the starting point; it dates from *c.* 1500.

Baltinglass *Wicklow* 573Jb
A Cistercian house, founded by Dermot McMurrough, King of Leinster, before 1167. The church and remnants of the cloister survive.

Banagher *Offaly* 572Fc
Best known for its long bridge over the Shannon, and for having once been the home of Anthony Trollope, the novelist. It has a handsome house with a porch and curved pedimented door in the Main Street. By the Shannon are early 19th-century fortifications. Three miles to the north-east is Shannon Harbour, the western end of the Grand Canal, now largely deserted with numerous abandoned warehouses and a canal hotel.

Bandon *Cork* 570Eb
On the river of the same name, the town was founded in 1608 and bought shortly afterwards by the Great Earl of Cork. One of the earliest Protestant churches, that of Kilbrogan, was founded here in 1610. This church preserves the town stocks and whipping post.

Bantry House *Cork* 570Cb
A house of many dates, from *c.* 1740 onwards, in red brick with stucco work and pilastered extensions magnificently sited in a notable garden and standing at the edge of Bantry Bay. The 14-bay south front dates from 1840, but the house is mainly interesting for the paintings and furniture assembled by Richard, 2nd Earl of Bantry. A fine stable block has an entrance arch with a Corinthian lead-domed rotunda. There are terraces and statues in the Italian style in the grounds. (Open to the public.)

Bargy Castle *Wex.* 571Kd
At the head of Tacumshin Lake, a tower-house which was the home of Bagenal Harvey, a country gentleman hanged for his participation in the rising of 1798. Now a guest house.

Barons Court *Tyrone* 574Ee
An early 18th-century house, altered by George Steuart, reworked by Sir John Soane, 1791–2, revamped by Morrison, and recently modified. The seat of the Dukes of Abercorn since the 17th century.

Barry's Court Castle *Cork* 570Fb
A large medieval castle rebuilt in 1585. There is an interesting chapel and a chimney-piece dated 1588.

Beaghmore *Tyrone* 574Fe
This Stone Age or Early Bronze Age site has recently been uncovered from beneath the peat. There are six circles of stones, with lines pointing north-east. Several cairns have also been discovered.

Beaulieu House *Louth* 573Ke
Almost the only wide-eaved, Dutch-inspired house to survive in Ireland, built in the 1660's by Sir Henry Tichborne, of rubble stone plastered

with brick dressings. The interior contains notable wooden carvings in the hall, Carolean plasterwork and a fine early Georgian staircase.

Beauparc *Meath* 573Je
A house of 1755 of cut stone with wings and convex quadrants, possibly to the design of the amateur architect Nathaniel Clements.

Bective Abbey *Meath* 573Je
The original Cistercian abbey, founded by the King of Meath in the 12th century, was much rebuilt in the 15th century, and after the Dissolution was turned into a fortified house. The triple cloister arcades are of the 15th century, and the square chapter house, with a central column, is from the 13th century.

Belan House *Kild.* 573Jb
The ruined remains of the great house of Belan, built for Lord Aldborough by Richard Castle and Francis Bindon in 1743. There is a fine stable block, a Doric rotunda and several follies.

Belcamp *Dublin* 573Kd
A handsome house of *c.* 1786 with interior plasterwork. Now a school.

Belfast *Antrim* 575Hd
Second largest city of Ireland and, since 1921, capital of Northern Ireland. It was a place of small importance until the middle of the 18th century, being overshadowed by Carrickfergus. It belonged to the Chichester family, later Earls of Donegall, who built a castle in the early 17th century on the Farset R., from which Belfast takes its name; the modern Castle Street commemorates its site. The broad High Street, continuing to the east, is the bed of the Farset R., which until the beginning of the 19th century was open between quays and flanked by the houses of a prosperous market town. A 12-arch bridge was built over the Lagan in 1682 on the site of the present Queen's Bridge, which replaced it in 1841. On the accession of the 5th Earl of Donegall in 1757, a policy of improving the town was begun. By the 1770's Belfast was showing symptoms of its future industrial development. In the 1780's, the local architect Roger Mulholland planned regular streets such as Donegall Street and Donegall Place.

Sir Charles Lanyon was responsible for some of Belfast's most distinguished buildings. He was trained as a civil engineer and his earliest surviving structure in Belfast is the Queen's Bridge, now much altered. It was Lanyon who encased Sir Robert Taylor's assembly rooms in the Barry *palazzo* style in 1845. In the same year he began the Queen's College, now Queen's University, an elegant symmetrical red-brick Tudor building with stone dressings and central tower, well set back from University Road. Many unworthy additions have since been made to it at the back and sides. The head office of the Trustee Savings Bank, which Lanyon built in 1852, is an extraordinarily successful monumental effort with a central hall lit by clerestory windows with delicate glazing. Near the university, at the east end of University Square, is the Presbyterian Assembly's College (1853–5), in a style owing something to Vanbrugh and also to Soane; for many years it housed the new Parliament of Northern Ireland. The custom house, an E-shaped building, dates from 1857; it is in the *palazzo* style, and is considered by many to be Belfast's finest building.

In Bedford Street, leading from Donegall Square to Dublin Road, the Ulster Hall of 1860 by W. J. Barre stands next to a more graceful example of his work, Bryson House. It was built in the Venetian style as a warehouse in the heyday of Ulster's linen industry. Barre's most conspicuous Belfast building is the Albert Memorial clock-tower in Queen's Square. The head office of the Ulster Bank in Waring Street, designed by James Hamilton and finished in 1860, is an exuberant work, especially the railings and lamp-standards. In the offices of the Belfast Gas Works in Ormeau Road, the staircase and entrance hall are rich with coloured tilework and pilasters.

The public houses of Victorian Belfast are a study in themselves. Kelly's Wine cellars are in the traditional style, and the Crown Bar, opposite the Forum Hotel, is of unparalleled opulence, and has recently been tastefully redecorated. Other distinguished high-Victorian buildings include Alex McAllister's Gothic Oxford Street School, although only the façade now remains.

The Ulster Brewery in Sandy Row, by Alex McAllister, has a good composition of barrels, sacks of grain and anchors in the segmental pediment. William Batt was responsible for perhaps the most notable building of high-Victorian Belfast, the National Bank of 1897, in High Street.

At the end of the 19th century, Belfast began to express its status with new public buildings. St Anne's Protestant Cathedral, on the site of the old parish church, was begun in 1898 by Sir Thomas Drew and W. H. Lynn and has been worked on ever since by a variety of people, as the changes of style show. The City Hall, begun in 1902 to the designs of Sir Brumwell Thomas, was completed in 1906. It is Edwardian baroque with a copper-covered dome visible for miles. The Presbyterian Church House and Assembly Hall in College Square East has an open-work steeple copied from St Giles's in Edinburgh. In 1902 the Sinclair Seamen's Church, built by Lanyon, was furnished with such maritime fittings as a Moby Dick corner pulpit and a binnacle as a lectern. The establishment of the local Parliament in 1921 led to the building at Stormont of a white classical Parliament House by Sir Arnold Thornely.

SIDE TABLE: CORNER DETAIL

One manifestation of Irish Palladianism (1730–60) was baroque furniture, detailed in the William Kent tradition. This grotesque animal mask, carved on the corner leg of a mahogany table, was typical of the period. (Ulster Museum, Belfast)

TREASURE FROM A LONG-AGO TRAGEDY

On October 16, 1588, the galleass Girona, *remnant of the ill-fated Spanish Armada, sank off Lacada Point, Co. Antrim; of the 1300 men on board, only four survived. The wreck lay forgotten until 1967 when it was discovered by a lone diver who gazed astonished at*

the gold and silver treasure that lay scattered among the guns. As well as coin, there were many personal jewels such as the gold-mounted cameo set with pearls and the ruby-and-gold salamander (above). The Girona *hoard is now in the Ulster Museum, Belfast.*

CASTLE Stands above the city, underneath Cave Hill. It was built in 1870 in the Scottish baronial style by Lanyon's partner W. H. Lynn, and has a tower reminiscent of Balmoral and a French Renaissance-style garden staircase of 1894. In the grounds there is a mortuary chapel containing a marble, life-size group of the Earl of Belfast on his death sofa (he died in Naples) by Patrick McDowell.

CHURCH OF ST GEORGE A building of 1816 by John Bowden of Dublin, incorporating the fine Corinthian portico of 1788 from Ballyscullion House, Co. Londonderry, built by Francis Sandys or Michael Shanahan for the Earl-Bishop of Derry.

CLIFTON HOUSE The second earliest public building in Belfast, 1774, otherwise known as the Poor House or the Charitable Institution. The composition is regular: a pedimented centre-piece, with single-storey wings pedimented at their ends in the Palladian manner; there is an octagonal tower with a stone spire. It is mostly the work of the local architect Robert Joy.

FIRST PRESBYTERIAN (UNITARIAN) CHURCH An elliptical church which was completed in 1783 by Roger Mulholland and which shows the influence of the architect Francis Hiorns of Warwick. The exterior was crudely remodelled in 1833, but the interior survives with its gallery and nearly all its fittings.

NORTHERN BANK, WARING STREET The earliest public building now surviving, though much disguised; it started life as a market-house in 1769, and was converted in 1776 to assembly rooms with the addition of an upper storey by Sir Robert Taylor. Its present form is the result of much more drastic reshaping.

OLD MUSEUM Built in 1831 by Thomas Duff of Newry and Thomas Jackson, in the Greek Revival style; it is the earliest building in Ireland to be

built as a museum, and has unusual and elegant ironwork on the stairs and balcony.

ST MALACHY'S CATHOLIC CHURCH Completed in 1848 by Thomas Jackson, partner of Thomas Duff. Externally it has to be taken a little less than seriously, with its gawky octagonal turrets surmounting the battlemented gable, but the interior is the richest in Belfast. The altar is framed by an open-work screen and tracery, the style of which is re-echoed in the pulpit. The altar paintings are by one of the Tyrolean Piccioni family.

ULSTER MUSEUM Situated in the Botanic Gardens, it contains an extensive collection of Irish archaeology, including Bronze Age Irish gold. There are geological and natural history collections and a recently opened Technology Department deals with Ulster history and industry over the past three and a half centuries. The art gallery contains modern art, British watercolours, 18th-century European paintings and Irish glass, silver and pottery. (See also p. 585.)

Bellamont Forest *Cavan*   573Hg
One of the finest Palladian houses in Ireland, Bellamont Forest was designed by Sir Edward Lovett Pearce for his uncle by marriage, Thomas Coote, c. 1729–30. It is a nearly square red-brick 'villa' with a Doric portico. The house has been very little altered, and contains some fine plaster ceilings.

Belline House *Kilk.*   571Hd
A three-storey house, it is flanked by free-standing tower-like pavilions. In the grounds there is a rustic Doric temple which was made of tree trunks c. 1790.

Belvedere House *Westmeath*   573Gd
An important example of the Irish 'villa', built in 1742 for the Earl of Belvedere by Richard Castle, with a low but complex outline. It contains a fine

staircase and rococo plasterwork of the highest quality. To the left of the house is Ireland's most important Gothic caprice, a large screen known as the Jealous Wall, built 1760. At the other end of the park is another fine piece of Gothic rustic work, an arch surmounted by an oriel window. Altogether, this is one of Ireland's most notable landscaping achievements. (Gardens open to the public.)

Benburb Castle *Tyrone*   *574Fc*
Built by Lord Wingfield *c.* 1615, it is an irregular quadrangular fort situated 200 ft above the R. Blackwater. The south-west corner is ruined. There is a rectangular tower on the north angle, and a round tower to the south-east.

Birr *Offaly*   *572Fc*
This well-planned town was laid out in the late 18th and early 19th centuries, with malls and a small square containing a column, formerly surmounted by a statue of the Duke of Cumberland. The Protestant church was designed *c.* 1810 by John Johnston. The interior, with its slender Gothic pillars, plaster vaults and a corridor of galleries, is particularly attractive. The Catholic church, with its fine tower and spire, was built in 1817 to the design of Bernard Mullen.

Also notable is an Ionic temple designed by Lord Rosse in 1828 in memory of his son; it serves as a school-house. In front stands the statue by Foley of William Parsons, 3rd Earl of Rosse, the astronomer. The Convent of the Sisters of Mercy, next door to the Catholic church, is by Augustus Welby Pugin.
BIRR CASTLE A 17th-century house built on the site of a castle. It still contains its late 17th-century yew-wood staircase, but the present aspect of the house is predominantly that of an early 19th-century 'castle', probably designed by John Johnston, of whom nothing outside Birr is known, and the 2nd Earl of Rosse, from 1808 to 1832. Its situation by the Little Brosna River and its splendid

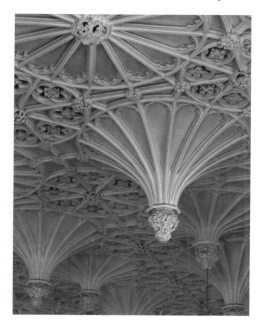

LATE GEORGIAN GOTHIC CEILING

A forest of pendants and tracery decorate this ceiling. The fan-vaults continue to the ground in the form of slender attached columns on the east wall of the church. (St Malachy's Catholic Church, Belfast)

garden, with 200-year-old box hedges over 30 ft high, magnolias and maple trees, make it one of the most ornamental estates in Ireland. The walls and barrel of the famous 'Great Telescope', built by the 3rd Earl in 1845, which was, until 1915, the largest in the world—6 ft in diameter and 54 ft long—may still be seen in the grounds. (The gardens are open to the public.)

Bishopscourt House *Kild.*   *573Jc*
A porticoed house of *c.* 1788 built for Speaker Ponsonby, who largely controlled the king's business in Ireland in the mid-18th century. It is probably the work of James Gandon, Dublin's leading neo-classical architect.

Blarney Castle *Cork*   *570Ec*
Home of the Blarney Stone, said to confer eloquence on anyone who kisses it, the castle was built in 1446 by the McCarthys of Muskerry. It consists of an enormous machicolated keep with an angle-tower containing a staircase. On one side there was formerly a considerable 18th century Gothic extension built by the Jefferyes family, who also laid out the elaborate landscape garden.

Boher *Offaly*   *573Gd*
The Catholic church here houses the relics of St Manchan in a shrine that is the largest Irish reliquary and one of the most important products of the post-Viking Irish revival. (See p. 588.)

Boom Hall *Lond.*   *574Ef*
Built *c.* 1770 for the 1st Earl of Caledon, of cut stone, it has a large cubical central hall and polygonal bay window on the east front. The house was named after the boom which the Jacobites placed across the R. Foyle to prevent supply ships reaching Derry during the 105-day siege of 1689.

Bovevagh *Lond.*   *574Ff*
In the churchyard is a house-shaped stone tomb, said to be that of a saint; a similar one is at Banagher, nearby.

Boyle *Roscom.*   *572Ef*
ABBEY Founded in 1161, it has one of the largest Cistercian churches in Ireland. The low crossing tower was an original feature, though it has since been heightened. The choir and eastward chapels are vaulted and the piers of the nave have interesting Transitional carvings.
BOYLE BARRACK A town house facing the R. Boyle, built to the designs of Sir Edward Lovett Pearce or his subordinate William Halfpenny. It is vaulted throughout and has a heavily pedimented front facing the river.

Brenanstown or Glendruid *Dublin*   *573Kc*
A fine portal dolmen with large granite capstone.

Browndod *Antrim*   *575He*
A cairn with four chambers to its gallery, on Donegore Hill. It was excavated in 1934.

Browne's Hill *Carlow*   *571Jf*
One of the largest dolmens in Europe, with a capstone estimated to weigh over 100 tons; two of the smaller supports have collapsed, and it stands in a hollow which may be original. Near by is a cut-stone Georgian house of *c.* 1763.

Brugh na Boinne *Meath*   *573Ke*
This is the most famous prehistoric cemetery in Ireland. It consists primarily of three great mounds close together in a loop of the R. Boyne: Dowth, which was pillaged in the 18th century, contains a passage-grave; Newgrange has a well-preserved cruciform chamber reached by a passage 62 ft long; Knowth has two differing chambers,

SHRINE OF ST MANCHAN

This tomb-shaped box of yew wood with metal fittings contains the bones of St Manchan. It is one of the finest surviving products of the great revival of Irish metalwork in the early 12th century. Both sides of the box have the same decoration: five bosses forming a cross and connected by short arms set with red and yellow cloisonné enamel. The borders at the base and the corners are also set with enamel. The reliquary was probably made in 1130 at the monastery of Clonmacnoise on the R. Shannon, Offaly. The row of cast bronze standing figures may have been added later in the 12th century. (Boher Catholic Church)

---

discovered in 1967 and 1968 (not open). Many of the stones in the three mounds are carved with intricate Bronze Age spiral and geometrical patterns, as are many of the massive kerbstones which surround and retain the structures. There are also outlying megaliths and secondary burials.

Buncrana Castle *Don.* 574Ef
One of Ireland's few surviving early 18th-century houses (1716), built by Henry Vaughan, with a panelled interior; it is now falling into decay. By the six-arched bridge leading up to the house is a late medieval tower-house of the Dohertys.

Bunratty Castle *Clare* 570Ef
Originally the chief seat of the O'Briens of Thomond, the castle is a late 15th-century keep with four angle-towers, the north and south of which are linked by high-level arches. The crenellations are modern and the whole castle and its interior was restored in 1956–8. Inside is a chapel with 17th-century stucco, and a collection of medieval furniture, paintings and sculptures. (Open to the public.)

Burnchurch *Kilk.* 571He
A good 15th- and 16th-century tower-house, with stepped battlements and walls honeycombed with passages and chambers.

Burncourt Castle *Tipp.* 571Gd
The many-gabled, semi-fortified house was not quite finished when in 1650 its owner, Lady Everard, set it on fire to prevent it falling into the hands of the Cromwellians. Large corbels at second-floor level supported a timber walk.

Burrishoole Friary *Mayo* 572Bf
A Dominican friary founded in 1469 on an inlet of the sea; the church with its tower and transept remains, as do some parts of the convent buildings.

Buttevant *Cork* 570Ed
A Franciscan friary founded in 1251 by David Og Barry. Most of the remains date from the 13th century, but many of the windows have been lowered and replaced in later centuries. There are eight round-headed windows on the south side of the choir, and beneath its east end is an unusual two-storied crypt. The cloister garth and the tower have gone. A mile to the south is Ballybeg, a fortified Augustinian priory founded in 1229 by Philip Barry; the belfry tower, cloister walls and dove-cote survive. The bell-rope holes in the tower are carved. Buttevant Castle, in ruins, is a good example of the early 19th-century castle style.

Cahercommaun *Clare* 570Dg
A large stone fort built on the edge of a cliff. Excavations in 1934 revealed that it was used as a dwelling in the 9th century, and traces of iron smelting were found. The fort has three concentric ramparts and contains souterrains, one of which leads outside the fort.

Caherdorgan *Kerry* 570Ad
Two ring forts, Caherdorgan South and North, each containing a group of clochans.

Cahergal *Kerry* 570Ac
A stone ring-fort, about 85 ft in diameter, with flights of steps leading to the wall-top and two ruined chambers within the wall. Inside the fort are the remains of four huts.

Cahir *Tipp.* 571Gd
The Protestant church dates from 1817 and is probably by John Nash. Beyond the castle is Cahir Park where there is a *cottage ornée* beside the R. Suir; it was probably designed by Nash, and the interior is decorated with wallpapers depicting the beauties of the Bosphorus by Dufour. Three miles north is Knockgraffon, a mote and bailey.

NEWGRANGE PASSAGE-GRAVE AT BRUGH NA BOINNE

One of the finest megalithic passage-graves in Ireland, situated in the Boyne Valley Cemetery, whose builders settled there some 4750 years ago. The chamber with three cells and the approach passage are walled with huge upright slabs and roofed with careful corbelling. The north cell (left) contains one of the finest and

most intricately carved ceiling slabs, and a pair of flat stones one above the other, hollowed out into a basin shape; cremated remains may have been put into these. A carved stone in the passage is shown on the right. The patterns appear to have been cut before the stones were put in position, and may derive from France.

CASTLE One of the chief seats of the Butlers, Barons Caher, it stands on a rocky island in the R. Suir. It is the largest castle built in Ireland during the 15th and 16th centuries, and comprises two courts, a massive keep and a great hall.

Caldragh *Ferm.*   *574Dd*
An ancient churchyard near the west end of Boa Island on Lower Lough Erne. It contains a sculptured stone with two figures back-to-back, the chests bound with diagonal straps, dating from the 5th or 6th century.

Caledon House *Tyrone*   *574Fc*
The central block of this Georgian house, dating from 1779, is by Thomas Cooley, though the second floor was raised in 1835; the colonnade and domed pavilion were built by Nash *c.* 1812. The Doric column by William Murray carries a statue of the 2nd Earl of Caledon by Thomas Kirk. (Not open to the public.)

Callan *Kilk.*   *571He*
St Mary's Church was begun *c.* 1460. It has a long aisle-less chancel, and incorporates a possibly older western tower; the arcades of the nave survive, and the chancel was used as the Protestant parish church. Also in the town are the remains of the Augustinian friary of 1462, including a fine sedilia in the chancel. The Catholic church, dating from 1836, is a good early 19th-century building.

Calliagh Birra's House See Slieve Gullion.

Canon Island *Clare*   *570Df*
The Augustinian priory was founded by Donal O'Brien, King of Munster, in the late 12th century, within an early cashel wall. The church, of the early 13th century, has a tower but no aisles or transepts, and there are two ranges of buildings dating from the 15th century.

Cappagh Castle *Lim.*   *570Ee*
A ruined 15th-century castle, originally of the Knights of Glin. It has a 70 ft high keep surrounded by a late 16th-century battlemented bawn with turrets at the eastern angles.

Cappoquin House *Waterford*   *571Gc*
A fine, cut-stone, balustraded house of *c.* 1770 by an unknown architect, overlooking the R. Blackwater.

Carbury Castle *Kild.*   *573Hd*
A picturesque Jacobean castle-like manor house, with graceful clustered chimneys. It stands beside a bailey; the mote has disappeared.

Carlingford *Louth*   *573Kf*
Like Ardglass, Carlingford is now a village, but was a town of importance in the Middle Ages. It is dominated by the massive D-shaped 13th-century castle, much altered and partly ruined. There are several medieval and 16th-century houses including Taaffe's Castle and the house called The Mint.

Carlow *Carlow*   *571Jf*
The court-house in Classical (Ionic) style is probably one of the finest in Ireland; it was built in 1830 to the design of W. V. or Richard Morrison, and occupies a commanding position at the intersection of two streets. St Patrick's College, opened in 1795, is, with Maynooth, one of the earliest centres of Catholic education surviving, and has pleasant tree-planted walks. The Catholic cathedral, a building in the Gothic manner, complete with lantern, dates from *c.* 1820; it was designed by Thomas A. Cobden, and contains a good monument to Bishop Doyle by John Hogan.

Carnanmore *Antrim*   *575Hg*
A cairn, 75 ft in diameter, containing a partly exposed passage-grave.

Carndonagh *Don.* 574Eg
Opposite the church south of the town stands a 9th-century cross carved with fine interlacing, similar to that at Fahan (Donegal), but more obviously cross-shaped and subtly carved. It is flanked by a pair of small carved stones decorated with spirals and various figures, including David with his harp.

Carnelly House *Clare* 570Ef
A square red-brick house, probably designed by Francis Bindon *c.* 1740. It has a heavily stuccoed saloon incorporating a Corinthian 'tabernacle'. (By appointment.)

Carntighernagh *Cork* 570Fc
A hill-top fort with an earlier chambered cairn.

Carrickfergus *Antrim* 575He
An old town, once an important port, on the shores of Belfast Lough. In 1778 the American captain John Paul Jones defeated the British warship *Drake* just off the shore. On a rocky peninsula projecting into the lough, this is probably the first true castle to be built in Ireland and is among the largest. It was built between 1180 and *c.* 1205 either by John de Courcy or Hugh de Lacy and is now a museum. The keep stands between the outer and inner courts at the south-west boundary of the site. The main landward entrance is guarded by four D-shaped towers of later date. The large church of St Nicholas has an elaborate monument to Sir Arthur Chichester and his family.

Carrick-on-Shannon *Leit.* 574Cb
Near the northern navigable limit of the Shannon, Carrick was given its charter by James I. There is a court-house of *c.* 1825 by William Farrell close by the remains of the gaol.

Carrick-on-Suir *Tipp.* 571Hd
The gabled and mullioned so-called manor house was built *c.* 1567 by the 10th Earl of Ormonde (Black Tom) in front of a 15th-century castle built by the Butlers, Earls of Carrick. Ormonde's building contains fine Elizabethan stucco decoration, the earliest surviving in Ireland. Beside the castle is the Tholsel, a tall square building with a clock-tower and lantern. Across the river in Carrick Beg, reached by a medieval bridge, is the Catholic parish church incorporating a tower and north wall of a 14th-century Franciscan friary. In the now disused Protestant church are two good monuments.

Carrigadrohid *Cork* 570Eb
The ruins of a gabled tower-house built in the 16th century by Dermot MacCarthy stand on a rocky island in the R. Lee, linked to either bank by medieval bridges.

Carrigafoyle Castle *Kerry* 570Ce
One of the chief strongholds of the O'Connors Kerry, an 80 ft tower-house on an inlet of the Shannon estuary. The O'Connors Kerry founded Lislaughton Abbey, on the other side of the inlet, in 1477.

Carrigaholt Castle *Clare* 570Ce
A partially restored tower-house and bawn.

Carrigaphooca Castle *Cork* 570Db
A single tower, four storeys high, on a rock by the Sullane R. It was built without fire-places or chimneys, which suggests that it was erected in the 15th century.

Carrigillihy *Cork* 570Da
An excavation in 1950 revealed a ring wall around an Early Bronze Age homestead (circular) and early Christian homestead (rectangular) on the same site; the enclosing wall is 4 ft high in places.

Carrigogunnell Castle *Lim.* 570Ee
A stronghold of the O'Briens on the summit of a rock overlooking the R. Shannon; the remains, which include a shattered keep, bawn and chapel, date mainly from the 15th century.

Carrowdore Castle *Down* 575Jd
A castellated Georgian Gothic house built in 1818 for the family of de la Cherois Crommelin. The hall has fine Gothic stucco work.

Carrowkeel *Sligo* 572Ef
A group of passage-graves in association with a nearby group of 50 mysterious circular structures which may have been the walls of vanished dwellings.

Carrowmore *Sligo* 572Eg
A large group, formerly 80 but now less than 60, of megalithic structures thickly clustered together.

Carton *Kild.* 573Jd
Formerly the seat of the Dukes of Leinster, the head of the FitzGerald family, the present house (not open to the public) replaced a Dutch-inspired winged manor house. In 1739–45 Richard Cassels raised the house one floor, totally refaced it and constructed colonnades, pavilions and terminating pedimented arches in his typical Palladian mode. However, the house was turned back to front in the early 19th century by Sir Richard Morrison, spoiling Cassels's original plan. The landscaped park possesses the balustraded bridge built after a design of Isaac Ware, and a shell house. There are two gates by Thomas Ivory. (Grounds private.)

Cashel *Tipp.* 571Ge
The Rock of Cashel rises 300 ft from the plain of Tipperary; its top is about 2 acres in area. Traditionally founded in AD 370 by Cormac, King of Munster, Cashel remained the principal stronghold of the kings of Munster until the 12th century. Visited by St Patrick *c.* 450, it soon acquired religious significance which was to outshine and outlast its political significance, and many of the early kings were also bishops. In 1101 it became entirely ecclesiastical. The remains on the rock comprise the Round Tower, Cormac's Chapel, the roofless cathedral, the archbishop's castle, the hall of the Vicars Choral and the Cross of St Patrick, all splendidly grouped together. The 11th-century Round Tower is plain but very well built and complete, at the north-east corner of the north transept of the later cathedral. The buildings were burnt in 1647 by Murrough O'Brien, Earl of Inchiquin, with much bloodshed. The cathedral continued in use, and some restoration was done as late as 1730, but in 1749 the parish church of St John was constituted as the cathedral and the old buildings on the rock were allowed to decay until the late 19th century. The hall of the Vicars Choral has been re-roofed.

In the town is the Dominican friary (13th–15th century), Quirke's Castle (15th century) and the new Protestant cathedral, begun in 1763 and completed (the west front and tower by Sir Richard Morrison) in 1788.

Near by are the ruins of Hore Abbey (Cistercian) of the 13th–15th century.

CASTLE Occupies the western half of the cathedral nave, and is in effect a tower-house, dating in its present form from Archbishop O'Hedian's time in the early 15th century. It is honeycombed with wall-passages.

CATHEDRAL Built in the 13th century, without aisles. There is a central tower; the choir is lit by five rows of lancet windows to north and south,

ROCK OF CASHEL

Dominating the town of Cashel from the north, the Rock was traditionally the seat of the kings of Munster and, until 1750, the See of the archbishopric of Munster. Amid the ruins of the 13th-century cathedral *is Cormac's Chapel, a richly decorated Romanesque church built by the last great king-bishop Cormac MacCarthy, and consecrated in 1134. The 92 ft high Round Tower is even older than Cormac's Chapel.*

being twice the length of the nave. The transepts have eastward chapels and wall-passages. The most notable tomb is that of Meiler McGrath, archbishop from 1571 to 1622.

CORMAC'S CHAPEL The largest, most elaborate and most complete of Irish-Romanesque buildings, in the angle between the choir and south transept. It was built by Cormac MacCarthy, king and bishop, and consecrated in 1134. It has a high stone-roofed nave and chancel and transeptal towers, one with a pyramidal stone roof; also an elaborate north porch and a decorated south doorway. Part of the east wall is a reconstruction of 1875. Within is a magnificent broken 12th-century sarcophagus with Scandinavian ornament.

CROSS OF ST PATRICK Stands south of the nave; it is of the 12th century, and unusual in having a rectangular frame linking the arms with the base, part of which survives.

DOMINICAN FRIARY Founded by Archbishop O'Kelly in 1243, the long rectangular church has a south transept added *c.* 1270. The south side of the choir has a row of nine lancets.

PALACE Built *c.* 1731 for Theophilus Bolton, Archbishop of Cashel, to the designs of Sir Edward Lovett Pearce, and now a hotel. The interior possesses its contemporary panelled and Corinthian-columned hall, and one of its original twin staircases.

Castle Baldwin *Sligo*   *574Cb*
A small semi-fortified house of the 17th century. It has gabled ends and was built to a simple rectangular plan with a small staircase projection giving it an L-shape.

Castlebar *Mayo*   *572Cf*
Founded in the 17th century by the Binghams (later Earls of Lucan), Castlebar is famous as the site of the battle known as Castlebar Races (1798) between the French General Humbert and General Lake, the British commander, who was soundly

defeated. The gate-piers of the old Bingham House survive. The most notable buildings in the town are the fine cut-stone 18th-century Linen Hall, with pedimented entrance, and opposite the court-house, the former Methodist church and manse, unusually combined under one roof.

Castleboro House *Wex.*   *571Ke*
The ruined remains of an immense cut-stone house with wings. Built for the Carew family, and designed by Daniel Robertson of Kilkenny *c.* 1840.

Castlecaulfield *Tyrone*   *574Fd*
Originally called Ballydonnelly, the house was built by Sir Toby Caulfeild, ancestor of the Earls of Charlemont, and finished by 1619. It was burnt during the rising against the English in 1641. Soon afterwards, Castlecaulfield was renovated and again lived in, but abandoned by 1700. The ruined house is of U-plan, and was originally three storeys high; it still has mullioned windows and some fine chimney-stacks.

Castlecomer *Kilk.*   *571Jf*
Castlecomer is an elegant town in spite of having been a coal-mining centre at the heart of the Leinster coalfield. In 1635 the Wandesford family were granted the land there, and they developed the local mines and were responsible for laying out the spacious streets of the town.

Castle Coole *Ferm.*   *574Ec*
Earlier houses were twice destroyed by fire during the 17th century. A new house was built at the beginning of the 18th century; later in the century (*c.* 1785–90) the 1st Earl of Belmore asked Richard Johnston to prepare plans for a new house but, perhaps not satisfied with the result, he called in James Wyatt who restyled Johnston's designs. The house has a central block with a four-columned portico, linked to side pavilions by tall colonnades; it contains fine decoration and furniture. (House closed 1985–6; park open.)

Castledermot *Kild.* *573Jb*
A small town in which, amongst monastic remains, may be seen a Round Tower, two 9th-century high crosses, a Romanesque west door-way and church, a Franciscan friary and the tower of a priory of the Crutched Friars.

Castle Dobbs *Antrim* *575Je*
A house built in the manner of Sir Edward Lovett Pearce in 1730 for Arthur Dobbs, Surveyor-General of Ireland and Governor of North Carolina; it incorporates later additions. (Not open.)

Castle Durrow *Laois* *573Gb*
One of the few pre-Palladian houses in Ireland, the house was probably roughly designed by William Flower, its owner. It was finished in 1732, and survives intact except for the loss of its original dormer windows, and the later addition of a bay and porch. Opposite the front door across some fields is a Roman-Doric column.

Castle Freke *Cork* *570Da*
The ruined remains of a Gothic Revival 'castle' built to designs by Sir Richard Morrison, *c.* 1830.

Castle Hyde *Cork* *570Fc*
A late 18th-century house comprising a central block with wings incorporating oval rooms; it is a design by Abraham Hargrave of Cork. The columned hall leads to a splendid cantilevered staircase which, at the top floor, gives on to a wrought-iron bridge opening on to the garden, for the house backs on to the rocky bank of the R. Blackwater. The fine entrance gates have attendant sphinxes. (Not open to the public.)

Castle Kirk *Gal.* *572Bd*
The massive ruins of a mid-13th-century O'Conor-de Burgo castle stand on a small island in a north-western inlet of Lough Corrib.

Castlelyons *Cork* *570Fc*
In the churchyard is a pedimented mausoleum, with Corinthian columns, of James Barry, Earl of Barrymore, who died in 1747. The interior contains a monument by David Sheehan, and the angels on the entablature are by John Houghton.

Castlemartin *Kild.* *573Jc*
An early 18th-century U-shaped house, notable chiefly for its wrought-iron gates and fine broken-pediment doorway. (Not open to the public.)

Castlestrange *Roscom.* *572Ed*
A ritual stone with fine La Tène ornament.

Castletown See Celbridge.

CHARLEVILLE CASTLE

In Charleville Forest, with its grotto and serpentine walks, the Earl of Charleville built this massive 'castle', complete with fine cut-stone detailing and a splendid fan-vaulted drawing-room.

Castletown Geoghegan *Westmeath* *573Gd*
Here is a conspicuous Anglo-Norman mote and bailey, and the remains of a medieval priory.

Castletown House *Kilk.* *571Hd*
The masterpiece of the Sardinian architect, Davis Ducart, a richly detailed cut-stone house with pilastered centre-piece on both fronts, and arcaded wings placed cornerwise to the main block, terminating in octagonal domed pavilions. The interior has fine plasterwork by Patrick Osborne of Waterford. The house was built for Archbishop Cox of Cashel, begun in 1767 and finished in 1771.

Castle Upton *Antrim* *575He*
Originally a Plantation castle of 1619, which was remodelled for the Clotworthy family, later Viscounts Templeton, by Robert Adam in 1788–9. It has been much altered and damaged, but the Upton Mausoleum in the nearby churchyard, of 1783, remains in good condition.

Castle Ward House *Down* *575Jc*
A strange house, built *c.* 1763–80 for the 1st Viscount Bangor by an unknown architect. Because of a disagreement over style between Lord and Lady Bangor, the south front is in Classical style with a pediment and a coat of arms above four central columns, and the north front is in Gothic style in three storeys with seven bays of pointed windows; on the battlements are urns at either end and three pinnacles in the centre. The mansion stands in fine grounds and gardens, and contains 18th-century furniture. There is also an exhibition of vehicles. (National Trust.)

Castlewellan *Down* *575Hc*
This small town consists of two squares, prettily planted with trees, laid out in the mid-18th century by the Annesley family. The market-house dates from 1764 and near by, in a park which is now a distinguished arboretum, is the 19th-century Blore-designed castle of the Annesleys. Some 2 miles south-west is the stone cashel of Drumena.

Cavan *Cavan* *573Gf*
The county town in the old territory of Breffni, it is the seat of the Catholic Bishop of Kilmore. The cathedral of the diocese, a large building of 1942, has a west front with tower and spire closely modelled on St George's, Hardwicke Place, Dublin, flanked by small domes with a large dome over the crossing. The previous Catholic cathedral in the town, a modest Gothic building, was transported to Ballyhaise, where in a simplified form it was re-erected to serve as the parish church. The pedimented court-house, with a Doric porch and the royal Arms, is by John Bowden, who also designed the Protestant parish church of 1810. Three and a half miles south-west is Kilmore, the seat of the Protestant bishop, and 5 miles to the north-west is Clough Oughter, a circular tower-castle of the 14th–15th century on a small island. On the north-west of Lough Oughter, which is less a lake than a large number of peninsulas and islands, is Drumlane, with a truncated Round Tower and the ruins of a long, plain church.

Celbridge *Kild.* *573Jd*
On the R. Liffey, dominated by large 18th-century mills, the town has, besides Castletown, an important early house, Oakley Park of 1720, possibly by Thomas Burgh, but much altered; also the Gothic Celbridge Abbey, the home of Esther van Homrigh—Vanessa in the works of Jonathan Swift. In the disused Protestant church is the magnificent monument by Thomas Carter, of *c.* 1730, with the recumbent figures of Speaker Conolly and his wife.

CASTLETOWN, CELBRIDGE

Speaker William Conolly began this, the largest 18th-century house in Ireland, in 1722. Sir Edward Lovett Pearce and Alessandro Galilei were the architects. When Conolly died in 1729 the house was still unfinished, and his widow continued in occupation until her death in 1752, without putting in the main staircase. The unfinished house then came into the hands of Tom Conolly and his wife, formerly Lady Louisa Lennox. They put in a Portland stone cantilevered staircase and employed the Francini brothers to complete the plasterwork of the staircase and hall in 1759–60.

The brothers had been responsible for the magnificent decoration in the saloon at Carton near by, where Louisa's sister Emily, Countess of Kildare was living, and where Louisa was largely brought up. Possibly only one of the Francinis was employed at Castletown, where the whole ornament is exquisite and highly Italianate, with swirls of light rococo and fanciful animals. A few of the frames contain figures (see right) and these are possibly portraits of Louisa and Tom's parents and relatives. Tom Conolly himself is portrayed in plaster, in pride of place near the foot of the staircase, and the smaller heads near to floor level represent the Four Seasons.

CASTLETOWN The largest, most influential 18th-century house in Ireland, built in 1722–32, probably by Sir Edward Lovett Pearce and Alessandro Galilei, the Florentine architect, for Speaker William Conolly. The central block reiterates the Italian Renaissance town-palace façade, whereas the curved colonnaded quadrants are in the Palladian idiom. There is a magnificent entrance hall and staircase, the latter with plasterwork by the Francini brothers of 1759–60; the first-floor long gallery by Riley is in the Pompeian manner. At the end of a vista to the north of the house is probably the most fantastic of Irish follies, built in order to provide work during the hard frost of 1740, by Conolly's widow. (Open to the public.)

Charleville Castle *Offaly* 573Gc
An extravagant and splendid 'castle' by Francis Johnston, built in 1801 for the Bury family, Earls of Charleville, now restored and reoccupied.

Charleville House *Wicklow* 573Kc
A cut-stone house built for the Monck family in 1797 by Whitmore Davis, in imitation of Lucan House. It has a raised centre-piece with engaged Ionic columns supporting a pediment.

Clara Castle *Kilk.* 571Je
The five-storied tower-house at Clara, with its small walled forecourt, is unusually complete and retains the oak timbers of the floors. There is a secret chamber in the thickness of the wall.

Claregalway Friary *Gal.* 572Dd
A Franciscan friary founded by John de Cogan in the mid-13th century. It has a slender friars' tower with stepped battlements in good preservation. The transept and east window are 15th century, and the cloister has gone. There is a de Burgo tomb, possibly of the 14th century.

Clermont *Wicklow* 573Kb
Built in 1731, almost identical to Furness, County Kildare, in red brick with wings, possibly to the designs of Francis Bindon. The interior has fine mantelpieces and elaborate plasterwork.

Clogher *Tyrone* 574Ec
The Cathedral of St Macartan was repeatedly rebuilt in the Middle Ages but now dates from the time of Bishop John Stearne, who rebuilt it at his own expense in 1745 in the Gothic style. It was remodelled in the Classical style in 1818.

Clonamery *Kilk.* 571Je
The ruined 10th- and 11th-century church has a fine massive west door with an incised cross above the lintel.

Clonbrock *Gal.* 572Ed
A large pedimented house of c. 1780. (Not open to the public.)

Clondalkin *Dublin* 573Kd
The Round Tower, which retains its conical stone top, is the best preserved near Dublin.

Clonfert Cathedral *Gal.*   *572Fc*
ST BRENDAN'S CATHEDRAL A 13th-century building attached to a 12th-century façade, the portal of which is perhaps the finest example of the Irish-Romanesque style. It is the largest of its type in Ireland and the pronounced slope of the jambs is emphasised by the 15th-century work, which does not slope, around the door.

Clongowes *Kild.*   *573Jc*
In the chapel are notable stained glass windows by Michael Healy and Evie Hone.

Clonkeen *Lim.*   *570Fe*
The small church here has a decorated Romanesque doorway.

Clonmacnoise *Offaly*   *572Fc*
The monastic 'city' was founded by St Ciaran in the 6th century, and was for long famous for its learning, a centre of manuscript-making and craftsmanship. It was repeatedly plundered by the Vikings and Irish enemies and, after 1178, by the English, whose sack of the place in 1552 proved to be a death-blow. It remained deserted, though used as a graveyard until modern times. All that remains now is the large graveyard, in a lonely site near the R. Shannon, and one outlying church. Within the enclosure are six churches, a Round Tower (and another forming part of one of the churches), three high crosses, and the largest collection in Ireland of early grave-slabs, many with inscriptions and ornaments of much beauty.
CATHEDRAL Originally a single chamber, with a late Romanesque west door and a magnificent 15th-century north door built by Dean Odo, who

died in 1461. At about the same time a vaulted three-aisled chancel was inserted into the east end. A vaulted sacristy lies to the south. The Cross of the Scriptures, alias King Flann's Cross, lies west of the cathedral and has scenes from the life of Christ, a Last Judgment, and horsemen and charioteers on the base. It dates from the 9th century. The north cross (shaft only) has a curious seated figure.
TEAMPULL CHIARAN A tiny church dedicated to St Ciaran, heavily ruined and perhaps of the early 10th century.
TEAMPULL CHONOR An 11th-century church, restored and now serving as the Protestant parish church. The south cross, of the 9th century, has vine-scroll ornament and a crucifixion.
TEAMPULL FINGHIN OR MACCARTHYS CHURCH A nave and chancel church, the nave much ruined, dating from the 12th century. It is unique in having, south of the chancel, a Round Tower as belfry, integral with the rest of the building. The tower, which is complete with its conical top of herring-bone masonry, is about half the usual size for such structures. The chancel arch adjoins it. Inside the present wall, to the west, stands the truncated O'Rourke's Tower, with a later top.

The collection of inscribed and decorated grave-slabs of the 8th–12th centuries is the largest and most varied in the country, and many are of great beauty. An ancient causeway leads eastwards from the graveyard to the Nuns' Church, rebuilt by Queen Dervorgilla and completed in 1167, in the developed Romanesque style. West of the graveyard are the shattered remains of a possibly 13th-century castle and a mote.

WEST DOORWAY AT CLONFERT CATHEDRAL

A Benedictine monastery on this site was founded about 560 by St Brendan, who is thought to have reached America in the 6th century and was nicknamed 'the Seafarer' or 'the Navigator'. The story of his voyage across the Atlantic to the 'Promised Land of the Saints' or 'St Brendan's Island' is told in one of the greatest medieval sagas of western Europe. The saga dates from about 565–73 and appeared in verse or prose in several languages, including Latin, French, Irish, Flemish, Welsh and Scottish Gaelic. St Brendan died at Clonfert in about 578. The monastery was pillaged by the Vikings in 844 and 845 during the period of their great invasions of the British Isles. It was burnt down in 1016, 1164 and again in 1179. Eventually, towards the close of the 12th century, the church was rebuilt as a small Romanesque cathedral dedicated to St Brendan, and its west façade was incorporated in a later building. In the superb, unique west doorway, the pronounced slope of the 12th-century jambs is emphasised by the 15th-century inner work which does not slope. The cathedral was wrecked in the 16th century and has suffered at the hands of later restorers; but it is notable for the Transitional east windows, the late medieval carvings on the chancel-arch and the graceful west doorway.

Clonmel *Tipp.* 571Gd
The earliest building of note is the Franciscan church in Abbey Street, which incorporates a central tower dating from the 15th century and a 13th-century choir wall. The 19th-century Protestant church by J. Welland incorporates some medieval fragments, including a fine east window with Flamboyant tracery, identical to one at St Dominic's Friary at Cashel. At one end of O'Connell Street is the Main Guard, completed in 1674 and originally the seat of the Palatinate Court of Ormond, probably to the design of Sir William Robinson. The Methodist chapel is a fine Ionic temple by William Tinsley, and the Catholic parish church of St Mary, a Classical building dating from 1837–50 (though the steeple and portico date from 1875–80), contains a particularly rich interior, including a high altar by George Goldie. The court-house, of 1800, is by Sir Richard Morrison. Along the R. Suir is an array of warehouses, evidence of the former importance of trade by water here.

Clonmines *Wex.* 571Kd
The unique fortified church of Clonmines, in appearance like a small castle, consists of a vaulted ground floor, serving as the church, with a two-storied west end.

Clonony Castle *Offaly* 572Fc
This picturesque 16th-century tower and bawn was heavily restored in the early 19th century. It is pleasantly situated near the R. Brosna.

Clontuskert Abbey *Gal.* 572Ec
A small 15th-century Augustinian house with a west doorway closely recalling that of the cathedral of Clonmacnoise, and dated 1471. The rood screen has been restored.

Clontygora *Arm.* 575Gb
An imposing horned cairn which originally had three chambers, of which the third and part of the second are destroyed; it was excavated in 1937. Near by is another cairn.

Cloyne *Cork* 571Gb
The Protestant cathedral of St Colman, for ever associated with the philosopher George Berkeley (1685–1753) is a cruciform building of the late 13th century. The nave and aisle were widened in 1856, and there is some good Classical woodwork at the west end. The monuments include one of Bishop Brinkley by Hogan, and a fragmentary font of 1611. The Round Tower stands in the village.

Cobh *Cork* 570Fb
Formerly called the Cove of Cork and, from 1849 until 1922, Queenstown, Cobh was an important naval base in the 18th century, and in the 19th a centre of the emigrant trade. The cathedral by E. W. Pugin and G. Ashlin dominates the town.

Cong *Mayo* 572Cd
The Augustinian friary, a royal foundation of the O'Conors, Kings of Connacht, dating from the early 13th century, but largely rebuilt. It retains a number of beautiful doorways showing distinct French influence, which are older than the present church. The scanty, reset remains of the cloister indicate that it had, perhaps, the first use of the dumb-bell pier which became almost universal throughout Ireland.

Coolbanagher *Laois* 573Hc
The Protestant parish church, with a west tower and spire, was built by James Gandon for the 1st Earl of Portarlington. The plaster ceiling has been replaced with an open timber one; the chancel is 19th century. The mausoleum is also by Gandon.

Coolhull Castle *Wex.* 571Kd
A late 16th-century structure remarkable for being an oblong of two storeys, rather than the usual tower-house type. The crenellations and round-headed windows are in good condition.

Coppinger's Court *Cork* 570Da
A semi-fortified house of the mid-17th century, it is shaped like a two-pronged fork, and has mullioned windows, tall gables and chimneys and elaborate machicolation for defence.

Corcomroe Abbey *Clare* 570Dg
Founded *c.*1180, this Cistercian abbey dates mostly from the early 13th century. It was originally a cruciform building without a tower; the present inadequate tower, inserted between the choir and nave, dates from the 15th century. The church has excellent masonry, delicate floral ornaments and some effigies.

Cork *Cork* 570Fb
The third city of Ireland and second of the Republic was founded in the 6th–7th century by St Finbar. The name in Irish means marsh, and the Anglo-Norman walled town occupied a pair of islands among the many between the north and south channels of the R. Lee. Nearly all these islands have now been reclaimed and constitute modern Cork, though until comparatively recently, several of the channels between them, represented by modern streets such as Patrick Street, Grand Parade and South Mall, were still open water-courses. In the 1750's the walls of the rectangular medieval city between Grand Parade and Grattan Street were removed and the city began to assume its present form. The site of the Celtic monastic settlement is some distance to the south-west; St Finbar's Cathedral, the masterpiece of William Burgess, has three spires and a lavish interior in the French Gothic style.

Among the earliest surviving buildings in Cork is South Gate Bridge of 1713, by Coltsman, and the Protestant Christ Church, a plain ashlar structure of 1720 by the same architect. The interior was remodelled and the west front built by G. R. Pain. In the church is a remarkable old effigy of a skeleton. The best-known building in the city is the Protestant church of St Anne Shandon (1722), on the high ground north of Pope's Quay; the tower is in diminishing stages, with a small cupola and a fish as a weathercock. Both tower and church have two sides in the silver Cork limestone, while the other two are in the dark red local stone. The quay-walls and bridges of Cork are also in the beautiful white limestone. The famous carillon of bells in St Anne's tower may be played by visitors. Close to St Anne's is the early 19th-century Butter Market and the L-shaped arcaded building of Skiddy's Almshouse (1718–19). The old red-brick custom house is a fine early 18th-century building with some panelled rooms still extant; it is encased in the relatively modern Crawford Municipal School of Art, whose art gallery has interesting pictures and sculpture. On the west side of North Main Street is St Peter's Protestant Church of 1783–8, in the northern porch of which is a monument with armorial bearings of Sir Matthew Down and his wife, of 1710. The church has a 17th-century font and, like Christ Church, has lost its spire. St Finbar's South, known as the South Chapel, is a remarkable Catholic city church of 1766, with its original nave and north transept with galleries.

Of mid-18th-century buildings, the Cornmarket, probably by Coltsman, retains its ground-floor arcade only, three pediments and a central clock having been added in 1843. The Mayoralty House in Prospect Row, now the Mercy Hospital, dates from 1765–73 and was designed by the Sardinian Davis Ducart, architect of the Limerick Custom House. Clarke's Bridge, by Samuel Hobbs, is of 1776.

The handsome single-arch Parliament Bridge is of 1806. Two families of architects, the brothers Pain and the Deanes, were responsible for most of the fine early 19th-century buildings in the city. Thomas Deane's first commission (in 1811, when he was 19) was the Commercial Buildings in the South Mall, adjoining the Imperial Hotel. Thomas and his brother Kearns are responsible for the early 19th-century riverside pedimented Savings Bank, on the continuation of the South Mall. Kearns Deane built the Ionic-porticoed St Mary's Dominican Church on Pope's Quay in 1832–9; the interior, with Corinthian columns and coffered ceilings, displays a 14th-century Flemish ivory figure of Our Lady of Grace from the Dominican friary in Youghal. The first building of their rivals, the Pains, was the dramatic Greek-Doric-porticoed gaol of 1818 (now part of University College). Like so many gaols of its period, it shows the influence of Piranesi and of George Dance. The front walls are slightly canted backwards from the portico and the columns are encased in a mantle, after the manner of the Temple of Segesta in Sicily.

In 1820, George Richard Pain reconstructed the interior of the Catholic church of St Mary Shandon; commonly called the North Chapel, it serves as the cathedral. St Patrick's, McCurtain Street, by George Richard Pain, is distinguished Corinthian, with a campanile. It dates from 1836, with a drastically remodelled interior of 1894. Both George Richard and James collaborated over the court-house of 1835, which has a superb Corinthian portico surmounted by sculpture; the interior was destroyed in 1891. A symptom of the battle of the styles is George Richard Pain's unusual Gothic-porticoed Father Mathew's Church (Holy Trinity Church) begun in 1832, with a spire and cupola completed by Coakly in 1880. The Ionic-porticoed Cork Steam Packet Company building in Penrose Quay is also by the brothers Pain. Sir Thomas Deane's last building was University College, built 1845–9 in the Tudor-Gothic collegiate style and modelled on an amalgam of Oxford colleges. Also in the college is the Honan Chapel, a full Hiberno-Romanesque Revival chapel of 1915 by James McMullan, with good glass by Harry Clarke and Sarah Pursar. Other distinguished 19th-century buildings are the finely detailed custom house of 1814 by Abraham Hargrave and the Corinthian-porticoed Italianate Provincial Bank on the South Mall. At Glanmire is Riverstown House, and Lota, by Davis Ducart (1765), now a convent and much altered on the exterior, with a fine mahogany staircase and some interior plasterwork.

Craggaunowen Castle *Clare*   570Ef
In the grounds of this 16th-century castle a lake-dwelling and ring-fort of early Irish settlement types have been re-created.

Creevelea Friary *Leit.*   574Cc
A Franciscan friary, founded in 1508 by Margaret O'Brien and Eoghan O'Rourke—one of the last monasteries to be founded in Ireland. Already damaged when it was suppressed in 1541, it was reoccupied for a period *c.* 1642 and later confiscated, but yet again occupied by the friars who roofed part of the church with thatch. The north side of the cloister has carvings of St Francis.

Creevykeel *Sligo*   574Cc
A magnificent 'lobster claw' cairn related to the 'Deer Park Monument'. It was excavated in 1935,

and found to contain four cremated burials.

Crom Castle *Ferm.*   574Eb
On the lake in the park is an old Plantation castle built in 1611 and destroyed by fire in 1764. The outer bawn and two flankers survive; the castle of the Earls of Erne is by Blore and dates from 1830.

Cultra Manor   575Jd
(Ulster Folk and Transport Museum) *Down*
Collections here illustrate the past and present way of life and traditions of the people of Northern Ireland, and include furnishings, costumes, tools and equipment, vehicles and a group of photographs, documents and sound recordings. The large park has cottages with their original furniture, and a small village, complete with church, school house and shops.

Curraghmore *Waterford*   571Hd
The finest forecourt in Ireland (to the designs of John Roberts, 1742–50), leads up to a much remodelled central block which contains interior decoration by James Wyatt, de Grée and Zucchi. (Not open to the public.)

To the right of the house is the charming mid-18th-century Shell House, decorated by Lady Catherine Power and containing a statue of her by John van Nost. (The Shell House is open to the public on Thursday afternoons and Bank Holidays.)

Cush *Lim.*   570Fd
A complex of earth-forts, souterrains, tumuli and ancient fields on the west slope of Slievereagh.

Cushendun *Antrim*   575Hf
A picturesque village by the sea, mostly built by Clough Williams-Ellis, the architect of Portmeirion village in Wales.

Daingean *Offaly*   573Hc
Founded as Philipstown in the 16th century by Mary Tudor of England and her husband Philip II of Spain, to be the county town of King's County (Offaly), Daingean never took root, and in 1833 lost its function to Tullamore. The small courthouse, though much disfigured, appears to be the work of James Gandon.

Dalkey Island *Dublin*   573Kc
St Begnet's Church is a small, early structure with typical lintelled west doorway and pilaster projections to both gables. The island also contains one of the Martello Towers, *c.* 1800, which are characteristic of the coast north and south of Dublin. In the Main Street of Dalkey village are two fortified houses of the 15th and 16th centuries; another stands above Bullock Harbour.

Danganbrack *Clare.*   570Ef
A fine, gabled early 17th-century tower with tall chimneys, one of the many tower-houses built by the MacNamara family in this area.

Dartrey Mausoleum   573Hg
(or Dawson's Grove) *Monaghan*
The large Tudor Revival house has been totally demolished, but in the middle of a state forest is a notable mausoleum of 1770 by James Wyatt containing a large sculptural group by Joseph Wilton.

Deerpark *Sligo*   574Cc
The 'Deer Park Monument' (Leac Con Mhic Ruis), a long cairn formerly covering a central-court grave, with three galleries opening off the 50 ft court. One gallery-portal remains standing.

Delgany *Wicklow*   573Kc
The interior of the church is chiefly notable for an enormous monument of 1789 to David La Touche, the banker, by William Hickey.

Derry (Londonderry) *Lond.*   *574Ef*
Founded by St Colmcille in 546, on a steep hill near
the mouth of the R. Foyle. The original site is now
occupied by St Columb's Catholic Church in
Longtower Street, a name which commemorates a
former Round Tower there. In 1613 the town
was granted by James I to a London livery
company (hence Londonderry), who laid it out
and surrounded it with the existing wall.
BISHOP STREET The court-house of 1813–17 is by
John Bowden and shows the same command of the
Greek-Ionic order as his church of St Stephen,
Mount Street, Dublin. The wings are surmounted
by statues of Justice and Peace sculptured in Portland stone by Edward Smyth.
DERRY'S WALLS Built in the early 17th century,
they withstood a siege in 1688–9 when the city
was attacked by the forces of James II. Derry was
relieved by a naval force after 105 days of
encirclement. Roaring Meg, a large gun of 1642
used by the defenders, still guards the walls. The
siege is also commemorated by Bishop's Gate,
and the triumphal arch designed by Henry Aaron
Baker, James Gandon's pupil, in 1788, with Classical trophies and carved masks by Edward Smyth.
PROTESTANT CATHEDRAL Built in the southern
quarter of the town in 1628–33, in an already
archaic English style, sometimes called 'Planter's
Gothic'. The west tower was crowned in 1778 by a
spire erected by Frederick Augustus Hervey, the
celebrated earl-bishop, but between 1805 and 1834
both the tower and the spire of the cathedral were
totally rebuilt.

Derryhiveny Castle *Gal.*   *572Fc*
A well-preserved tower-house, erected in 1643,
with a fortified enclosure and angle-towers; one of
Ireland's last pure castles.

Derrynane Abbey *Kerry*   *570Bb*
The ancestral home of the O'Connells, now a
museum dedicated to the memory of the Nationalist leader Daniel O'Connell.

Devenish Island *Ferm.*   *574Dc*
The Round Tower of Devenish Island, belonging
to the monastic foundation associated with St
Molaise, is one of the best and best preserved
in Ireland. It is remarkable not only for its fine
ashlar masonry but also for the decorated frieze
below the cap and the four carved heads facing the
quarters of the compass. There are also the ruins of
a small early church called St Molaise's House,
with carved bases to its antae, the 'Great Church',
and the 15th-century ruins of St Mary's Augustinian abbey.

Disertoengus *Lim.*   *570Ee*
A Round Tower 65½ ft high, with a Romanesque
doorway; near by is a ruined church—and all was
formerly enclosed by a cashel.

Doe Castle *Don.*   *574Df*
Doe Castle, surrounded by the sea and a rock-cut
ditch, was the medieval castle of the MacSweeney
Na Doe; it was restored in the 19th century.

Donabate *Dublin*   *573Kd*
On a peninsula between two inlets, an extremely
attractive Protestant parish church of 1758 with
curved gables and, at the west end, the octagonal
private gallery of the Cobbe family with a corner
fire-place and charming rococo plasterwork incorporating swans, the Cobbe family crest.

Donaghmore *Meath*   *573Je*
Just outside the town of Navan, the almost complete Round Tower of Donaghmore has a
Romanesque doorway with a crucifixion above
and human masks on either side of the architrave.

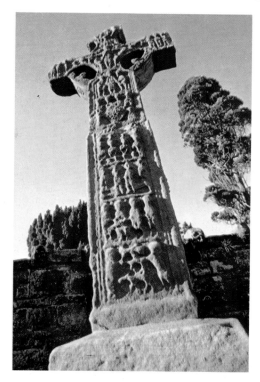

HIGH CROSS AT DONAGHMORE,
COUNTY TYRONE

*Standing in the village street, this magnificent 9th-
century high cross is one of the finest in the north
of Ireland. Although this type of sandstone weathers
badly, the intricate wreathed carving on the sides
and the scenes from the Old and New Testaments
on the back and front are clearly defined. The New
Testament panels in the photograph show the
Appearance of the Angel to the Shepherds, Christ's
Baptism, the Adoration of the Kings, the Marriage
Feast at Cana, the Anointing at Bethany and the
mocking of Christ.*

Donaghmore *Tipp.*   *571Gd*
The Romanesque church has a nave, small chancel
and the remains of a decorated doorway and
chancel-arch.

Donaghmore *Tyrone*   *574Fd*
St Patrick is said to have founded a church here,
and a 13th-century monastery on the site contained elaborate shrines. All that now remains is
a 9th-century high cross carved with Biblical
subjects, including the Fall of Adam and Eve and
the Sacrifice of Isaac.

Donegal Castle *Don.*   *574Cd*
Donegal Castle consists of a keep, built by Red
Hugh O'Donnell in 1505, to which was added one
of Ireland's finest Jacobean gabled fortified houses,
built by Sir Basil Brooke in 1610. The gigantic,
elaborate chimney-piece is particularly remarkable.

Doneraile *Cork*   *570Ed*
Originally part of the estate of Edmund Spenser,
the Elizabethan poet, it came into the possession of
the St Leger family who built Doneraile Court,
designed by William Rothery *c.* 1730 but since
altered. In the church (1816) is a fine St Leger
monument by Sir Henry Cheere; the park entrance
to Doneraile Court is a good Ionic triumphal arch,
probably by the Pain brothers. Kilcolman Castle
is where Spenser wrote parts of the *Faerie Queene.*

Donore *Meath*   *573Ke*
A 'ten-pound castle' (so-called because of a statute of 1429 subsidising the building of castles in the English Pale). It is a simple tower, built to the measurements required by the statute, having vaults over the two lower storeys and a turret incorporating a spiral stair.

Dorsey Entrenchment *Arm.*   *575Gb*
An elongated oval enclosure of the Iron Age, the largest of its type in Ireland; it must have been built to command the highway between Tara and the Navan fort.

Downhill *Lond.*   *574Ff*
The shell remains of the Earl-Bishop of Derry's irregular pilastered mansion. On the cliff the domed Mussenden Temple, fine gates, and a monument also survive. (Open to the public.)

Downpatrick *Down*   *575Jc*
This county town possesses some good late 18th-century terrace houses in English Street, Irish Street and Saul Street. The double bow-fronted judges' lodging is of *c.* 1840. Southwell School, a combined school and almshouse founded by Edward Southwell was probably designed by Sir Edward Lovett Pearce and finished by 1733. The parish church of 1560 is plain, with pedimented west tower.
ST PATRICK'S CATHEDRAL The present Protestant cathedral is a drastic remodelling, of 1798–1812, by Charles Lilly of Dublin, of what seems to have been a 13th-century choir. The carved capitals of the arcade, though much restored in plaster, embody some 13th-century work. The most attractive feature of the church is the woodwork of the pews which undulates in alternating curves and straight lines, with Gothic detailing.

Dowth See Brugh na Bóinne.

DROMANA HOUSE LODGE

Just off the road from Aglish to Cappoquin, on the Dromana House estate, is this romantic gate-house. It was built about 1840 on the lines of Brighton Pavilion in the style of the Mogul palaces of India—with an onion-shaped dome, slender spires, pointed arches and windows, and graceful filigree-like balustrades.

Drogheda *Louth*   *573Ke*
The most important of the eastern seaboard towns between Dublin and Belfast is of Norse origin, walled and fortified by the Anglo-Normans. The church of the Augustinian friary is represented by its 15th-century tower which now spans a narrow street. All that remains of the Dominican friary is the so-called Magdalene Tower of the 14th century. St Laurence's Gate, a twin-towered 13th-century structure is, in fact, a barbican which stood before the gate. On the south bank of the Boyne is the Mill Mount, the motte of the 12th-century Anglo-Norman castle, and other portions of the town walls survive here and there. St Peter's Church, rebuilt in 1753, with a later tower and spire by Francis Johnston, contains fine rococo plasterwork and several handsome monuments. In the churchyard there is a remarkable, macabre, 16th-century tomb-slab with the skeletons of Edward Golding and his wife.
The Tholsel, a cupolaed building near the north end of the bridge, is now a bank. Another notable building is the mayoralty house, a cut-stone pedimented structure on the quay by the river.
Among the fine 18th-century houses are the grammar school, originally the Singleton House; the red-brick police barracks in Trinity Street, possibly by Francis Bindon; St Peter's Catholic church, which contains the embalmed head of Blessed Oliver Plunkett, martyred in 1681. Outside the town is Ball's Grove, with a fine Classical pedimented gate.

Dromana House *Waterford*   *571Gc*
The house has been demolished; on the estate is the restored Hindu-cum-Gothic lodge.

Dromaneen Castle *Cork*   *570Ec*
A romantically sited strong-house on a rock on the south bank of the Blackwater. Access to the entrance court is by a fine Jacobean doorway.

Dromoland Castle *Clare*   *570Ef*
A splendid castle-house of 1826 by the brothers Pain; it replaced an 18th-century building of which the garden lay-out partially survives and includes a Doric rotunda and a gazebo on a hill. Now a hotel.

Dromore Castle *Lim.*   *570Ee*
The most important Gothic Revival castle in Ireland, built for the Earls of Limerick, 1867–70, by Edward William Godwin in the archaeological Gothic style based on Irish prototypes. The massing, and its situation on the rock overlooking various lakes, is unparalleled. Though the walls are enormously solid, the interior is entirely gutted.

Drumacoo See Tyrone House.

Drumcliff *Sligo*   *574Bc*
Of the monastery traditionally founded by St Colmcille, there remains a fine high cross with figure-sculptures from the Old and New Testaments, the shaft of a plain cross, and the stump of a Round Tower; the graveyard is the burial place of W. B. Yeats, the poet and dramatist.

Drumcondra *Dublin*   *573Kd*
The house, now a college, has two fronts; the south, of 1727, is by Sir Edward Lovett Pearce; the east front has an order of giant Corinthian pilasters of about the same date. On the lawn to the east is a temple, extremely Italian in character, and probably also by Pearce, or by Galilei. The church of St John the Baptist near by possesses a monument of 1740 to Marmaduke Coghill, the builder of Drumcondra House, by Peter Scheemakers. In the churchyard is buried James Gandon, the architect who designed some of Dublin's finest buildings.

Dublin *Dublin* 573Kd

A prehistoric burial site in Phoenix Park, 4000 years old, is Dublin's earliest monument. The site must have been important in Celtic times, since it had a ford and the natural harbour provided by the river mouth. Norse sea-rovers really founded the town, establishing a settlement in 841.

The Normans seized the little town in 1170 and erected a strong enclosing wall, and later a castle. The remains of this medieval city have since been largely rebuilt. After the Restoration of Charles II —and even more after the Hanoverian Settlement which was shortly accompanied by a Palladian movement headed by Sir Edward Lovett Pearce and his assistant Richard Castle—an amazing expansion began, culminating in the squares and houses of the Georgian era. Practically all the fine architecture of the city belongs to this period—an architectural heritage which remains basically intact, though momently threatened.

ABBEY THEATRE The new building by Michael Scott, opened in 1966, succeeds the historic theatre of Yeats, Synge and O'Casey, destroyed by fire in 1951.

BELVEDERE HOUSE A large five-bay house in Great Denmark Street, facing down North Great George's Street, built in 1785 by Michael Stapleton, and lavishly adorned with his richest plasterwork. It has been a Jesuit college since 1841.

BROADSTONE RAILWAY STATION (now disused). The terminus of the old Midland Great Western line to Galway and Sligo, now used as a bus garage: a massive Greco-Egyptian block by J. S. Mulvany, 1841–50, with a long colonnade.

BUS STATION (BUSARAS) An imposing L-shaped building by Michael Scott of *c.* 1952; the first modern building to be erected in central Dublin.

CASINO MARINO Designed by Sir William Chambers for Lord Charlemont in 1765–71, it is a small pleasure-house, containing finely proportioned rooms, and is a miniature masterpiece of 18th-century architecture. No money was spared in its construction, Lord Charlemont bringing Simon Vierpyl, sculptor and builder, from Rome to work on the building. There are interesting underground passages and a fine view from the parapet. It is now a scheduled National Monument.

CASTLE Originally erected in 1204–28. The Record, or Wardrobe, Tower remains, with a machicolated parapet of 1813. The arcaded red-brick buildings of Upper Castle Yard (the cross-block reconstructed 1967) and the Bedford Tower, with robust flanking gates, by Sir Edward Lovett Pearce who reconstructed the stone garden-front (recently reconditioned), contain the state apartments, including the Throne Room and St Patrick's Hall. They are still used for state functions, and possess many fine paintings, notably the ceiling of St Patrick's Hall by Vincent Waldré.

The Gothic Revival style Chapel Royal was designed by Francis Johnston and built in 1807–14. The exterior is richly decorated and the interior has fine Irish oak carving, plasterwork and stained glass. Originally a Protestant chapel for the Lords Lieutenant and Lords Deputy of Ireland who lived in the castle, the chapel was reconstructed in 1943 as the Catholic Church of the Most Holy Trinity.

CATHEDRAL OF ST PATRICK The present building dates from 1191, but it was extensively enlarged in the 13th century, and the tower added towards the end of the 14th century. It was advanced to cathedral status in 1213.

Jonathan Swift, the satirist, was Dean from 1713–45; his pulpit and tomb can be seen, as can the helmets, swords and banners of the knights of the now moribund Order of St Patrick. The cathedral is particularly rich in monuments, notably the five-storey Boyle monument.

To the east of the cathedral stands Marsh's Library, built by Archbishop Narcissus Marsh in 1707. It is the oldest public library in Ireland.

CHESTER BEATTY LIBRARY (See pp. 600–1.)

CHRIST CHURCH CATHEDRAL (PROTESTANT) A large cathedral founded in 1173 by Strongbow, the Norman Earl Richard Gilbert de Clare. The aisled six-bay nave was finished in 1234–6 and has been identified with the work of English masons of the school of Glastonbury. Soil subsidence caused the fall of the nave vaulting and south wall in 1562, and the north wall still leans about 2 ft out from the perpendicular. During the 16th and 17th centuries, the crypt was used as a tavern.

The cathedral's founder, Strongbow, is buried within. The effigy said to represent him dates from *c.* 1330.

CHURCH OF SS AUGUSTINE AND JOHN This building by Pugin and Ashlin is among the finest Victorian Gothic designs in Dublin.

CHURCH OF ST ANNE This is a well designed church of 1720 by Isaac Wills; the present Romanesque front was added in 1868 by Deane. Inside there is a finely carved wooden reredos and organ case.

CHURCH OF ST AUDOEN (PROTESTANT) This is Dublin's only surviving medieval parish church. The west door dates from 1190, and three of the bells are the oldest in Ireland, one cast in 1423.

CHURCH OF ST CATHERINE The present church was built in 1769 on a foundation dating from 1105. The architect was John Smith, and he designed a boldly-modelled Palladian elevation in mountain granite, which included pilasters, a central portico and a massive but unfinished tower.

CHURCH OF ST FRANCIS XAVIER Built in 1832 by Joseph Keane in the form of a Latin cross, with an Ionic portico. The interior of this Jesuit church has recently been redecorated under the direction of Michael Scott.

CHURCH OF ST GEORGE Francis Johnston designed this fine church in 1802; its 200 ft steeple was adapted from St Martin-in-the-Fields, London.

CHURCH OF ST MARY An early building, dating from *c.* 1700, having a tall, graceful interior remarkable for its fine west end. The handsome carved wooden case for the organ runs almost completely across the building, and embodies figure-sculpture, rare in such a church.

CHURCH OF ST MICHAN Dedicated in 1095, but largely rebuilt in 1685, it is famous for its remarkable crypt, in which corpses are mummified. The church contains a fine early 18th-century organ.

CHURCH OF ST STEPHEN On an island site, it magnificently closes the vista along Upper Mount Street from Merrion Square. It was designed by John Bowden and completed by John Welland, with elements copied from Greek originals (1824).

CHURCH OF ST WERBURGH Reputed to be one of the oldest foundations in Dublin. The present building, by Thomas Burgh (1715), was remodelled after a fire in 1759.

CITY HALL Built in 1769 by Thomas Cooley, who won an open competition for the design, it was formerly the Royal Exchange. Square in plan, it has three fronts decorated in the Corinthian order, and it is crowned by a finely lighted dome, supported by 12 columns, over the main hall. There are good sculptures by Smyth, Foley and others.

CIVIC MUSEUM Erected in 1765–71 for the Society of Artists. It has an octagonal exhibition hall, and was used as a municipal council chamber; it now houses a collection of Dublin relics.

CHESTER BEATTY LIBRARY

When Sir Alfred Chester Beatty, the American mining millionaire, died in 1968, he left his priceless collection of manuscripts, and the library he had built to house them, to the Irish nation. The collection had taken over 60 years to assemble and agents in all parts of the world were employed. The oriental section is the largest; it contains manuscripts from India, Tibet, China and also Japanese sword guards, Chinese snuff bottles and rare Chinese jade books. Middle East items include Biblical papyri, among them the oldest known New Testament manuscript dating from AD 150–250. There are a number of Korans, some in scroll form, and fine Western manuscripts.

ARMENIAN GOSPEL *Written in the 13th century for the Patriarch Constantine in Cilicia, the Armenian gospel shown here is one of four written about the same time. The photograph shows the beginning of St John's Gospel. On the left-hand page is a painting of the saint inscribed 'Saint John the Theologian'.*

THE THEBAID *This book of the poem 'The Thebaid' by the Latin poet Statius was copied in 1380–90, possibly by the Italian painter Altichiero. It has 12 miniatures, one at the beginning of each section, executed with extraordinary delicacy in grisaille (grey monotones) except for the deep blue of the sky, some green for trees, grass or water and red for blood or fire. The page reproduced is at the beginning of Book VI. Statius was born in Naples in AD 45 and proved himself to be the greatest poet in the Roman Empire. He received the golden crown for the victory in a poetical contest from the hand of the Emperor Domitian (AD 81–96). Proud of his powers of improvisation Statius (according to a description by Horace) once dictated 200 lines of poetry in an hour while standing on one leg. 'The Thebaid' is his best known work and took 12 years to write. It is an elaborate and typical story of the deadly strife of the Theban brothers, enlivened by dreams, miracles, single-combats, Homeric and Vergilian echoes and all the other familiar components of the Latin epic. Statius eventually retired to Naples in AD 94.*

CHINESE JADE BOOK *Painted for the Emperor Ch'ien Lung (1736–95), this book contains portraits and descriptions of the 16 Lohan, followers of the Buddha. The cover of the book shown here is of bronze, decorated with a repoussé dragon on an enamel ground. The whole book is painted in gold on jade.*

17TH-CENTURY COPY OF THE SHĀHNĀMAH *Written by Firdaussi, the Shāhnāmah is the national epic poem of Persia based on the collected legends of the ancient kings. In the 10th century, Mahmud ibn Sabuktagin commissioned Firdaussi to use the material, amassed from centuries of preparation, and write the poem. This is a page from a copy made for Shāh Abbas (1587–1629) by Muhammad Zaman, who had studied in Rome and acquired the art of perspective. The executioner is presenting the head of Iraj, youngest son of King Faridum, to his brothers Tur and Salm.*

CUSTOM HOUSE The masterpiece of James Gandon, with four decorated fronts; the south, facing the river, was begun in 1781 and embellished with splendid sculptures by Edward Smyth, notably the Arms of the Kingdom of Ireland on the four corners, and the series of 14 keystone-heads symbolising the rivers of Ireland. The pediment-sculpture on the south front of the friendly union of Britannia and Hibernia was designed by Carlini but executed by Smyth, who also did the statue of *Commerce* on the dome. During the fighting of 1921 the building was gutted by fire, but was soon afterwards restored. The memorial to the Dublin Brigade at the west front was carved by a Breton sculptor, Yann Renard-Goulet.

DOMINICK STREET No. 20 has the finest of Robert West's plaster. Now St Saviour's Orphanage.

DUN LAOGHAIRE Since 1821 the packet-station for Holyhead, it has a splendid artificial harbour by John Rennie, a good railway-station, and a colonnaded yacht-club by J. S. Mulvany. An obelisk commemorates the state visit of George IV in 1821, after which the town was for 100 years called Kingstown. At Sandycove the Martello tower in which James Joyce lived is now the Joyce Museum.

ELY HOUSE (ELY PLACE) By Michael Stapleton, 1770, with the most remarkable staircase in Dublin and other splendid decoration in the Adam style.

FOUR COURTS Designed by James Gandon and incorporating on the west an office block of 1777 by Thomas Cooley, was begun in 1786. It has a frontage of 450 ft to the river, dominated by a great Corinthian portico of six columns, behind which rises a massive lantern and dome. Terminal pavilions are linked to the central block by rusticated arcades. The statues on the skyline are by Edward Smyth. The four High Courts radiate from the spacious circular hall under the dome.

GENERAL POST OFFICE Designed by Francis Johnston and completed in 1818, it has an impressive Ionic portico of six fluted columns, the pediment being surmounted by statues. It was the headquarters of the Irish Volunteers during the 1916 rising, and was shelled from the R. Liffey by a British gunboat. It has since been reconstructed.

GLASNEVIN BOTANIC GARDENS Founded in 1795 by the Royal Dublin Society; they cover some 50 acres and contain many rare plants, trees and shrubs. The palm houses were built by the iron-founder Richard Turner, who later built the palm house at Kew Gardens.

GREEN STREET COURT-HOUSE Built in 1792 by Richard Johnston, it has a central recessed portico of six columns, and is mainly notorious as the scene of many famous treason trials.

HARCOURT STREET RAILWAY STATION (now disused). By George Wilkinson (1859), with colonnaded entrance at an angle to the main block.

HENRIETTA STREET Leading to the King's Inns, this is the earliest street of really large houses in Dublin. No. 9, by Sir E. L. Pearce, has a splendid Palladian interior modelled on Lord Mountrath's house in Old Burlington Street, London (by Lord Burlington). No. 10 (Blessington House), also by Pearce, has been altered externally but has good interiors.

KILDARE STREET CLUB Erected in 1860 by the partnership of Deane and Woodward, this brick Venetian *palazzo* is a most distinguished design. The whimsical carved beasts are by Charles Harrison. (Closed during 1985.)

KILMAINHAM GAOL Celebrated in Irish history, and recently reconditioned as a national monument by voluntary effort, its architect is unknown, but the entrance doorway with its powerful sculptural panel of chained serpents is noteworthy by any standards.

KING'S HOSPITAL Known also as the Blue Coat School, it is a delicate example of neo-Classical Palladianism, and was designed in 1773 by Thomas Ivory.

KING'S INNS This impressive building was one of the last commissions of James Gandon, and was designed in 1795, although it was not begun until 1802. The detailing shows Greek influence.

KINGSBRIDGE RAILWAY STATION (SEÁN HEUSTON STATION) A swaggering *palazzo* by Sancton Wood, 1845–61, flanked by cupolas.

LEINSTER HOUSE Now the Parliament House (Dail Eireann). One of the finest Dublin mansions, designed by Richard Cassels for the Earl of Kildare in 1745. It has two formal fronts, and has been claimed as the prototype for the White House, Washington. Flanking the courtyard to Kildare Street are the later fine Renaissance-style buildings of the National Library and the National Museum by Sir Thomas Deane. In the National Library are over 500,000 volumes and an extensive Department of Manuscripts. The National Museum has a fine collection of archaeological and botanical objects, Irish antiquities forming a major part.

MANSION HOUSE Though with a Victorian stucco front, it dates from 1705, and has been the residence of the Lord Mayor of Dublin since 1715.

MERRION SQUARE Laid out in 1762 by John Ensor, this is the second largest of Dublin's squares. A few of its brick houses contain the excellent stucco interiors characteristic of Georgian Dublin.

On the west side of the square is the lawn of Leinster House, flanked on the north by the National Gallery, designed by Lanyon, Fowke and Sir Richard Griffiths, and opened in 1864. It contains many outstanding examples from all European schools of painting, including the Romanesque fresco from Camp Public, the *Annunciation* of the School of Avignon, *c*. 1410, Rembrandt's *Rest on the Flight into Egypt* and Poussin's *Entombment*.

There is also a collection of 18th and 19th-century Irish paintings.

METAL BRIDGE An early single-arch cast-iron footbridge of 1816.

MOUNTJOY SQUARE This was laid out for Lord Mountjoy, and finished in 1818, but it is now sadly decayed.

MUNICIPAL BUILDINGS Adamesque, by Thomas Ivory in 1781; doubled in size in *c*. 1860.

NATIONAL GALLERY See Merrion Square.

NATIONAL MUSEUM See Leinster House.

NORTHLAND HOUSE (ROYAL IRISH ACADEMY) Built in 1770, probably by John Ensor. The plasterwork shows French arabesque influence.

O'CONNELL BRIDGE A reconstruction (1880) of Gandon's Carlisle Bridge of 1792.

OLD PARLIAMENT HOUSE Now the Bank of Ireland, it was begun in 1729 to the design of Sir Edward Lovett Pearce; the original building occupies three sides of a square, with an open colonnade round the three sides. This distinguished Ionic *piazza* was harmonised with the adjacent Trinity College by James Gandon in 1785. He extended the building eastwards and erected a magnificent Corinthian portico, joined to the earlier building by a plain quadrant screen. The House of Lords, by Pearce, survives intact with its tapestries and the silver-gilt House of Commons mace. In another room is the superb Venus ceiling from La Touche's Bank, installed in 1948. Further extensions were made westwards by Robert Parke, who balanced Gandon's work with a new west front featuring an Ionic portico. Francis Johnston remodelled the building, built the Cash Office, and harmonised the east and west quadrants.

NATIONAL GALLERY

Public subscriptions enabled this fine gallery to be opened in 1864, in a building designed by Sir Charles Lanyon. The magnificent collections comprise more than 6000 paintings and drawings, over 2000 of them on view. They include works from all the European schools, from 14th-century Florentine and Sienese paintings to the works of Irish artists of the 18th–20th centuries.

DANIEL MACLISE: THE MARRIAGE OF STRONGBOW AND AOIFE *Strongbow (Richard de Clare, Earl of Pembroke) led the Norman invasion of Ireland. In a canvas 16 ft by 10 ft, of which this is a detail, an Irish romantic gave vivid pictorial substance to his view that Irish freedom and values were lost for ever. First exhibited in 1854, the painting shows dejected Irish, and Strongbow trampling on an ancient Celtic cross.*

RUBENS: CHRIST AT THE HOUSE OF MARTHA AND MARY *The baroque style of the early 17th century introduced flamboyance and worldliness into painting. It developed early in Flanders, largely through the work of Rubens, Van Dyck and Jacob Jordaens, all of whom organised studios to undertake large series of commissions. In this work Rubens painted the figures, and Jan Breughel was responsible for the sumptuous background landscape including the birds, animals, fruit and foreground accessories.*

FRA ANGELICO: THE ATTEMPTED MARTYRDOM OF SS COSMAS AND DAMIAN *This panel is part of a series of ten small scenes which formed a base to the altar-piece 'Virgin and Child enthroned with angels and saints', painted for the Church of San Marco in Florence between 1438 and 1440. Now one of the most precious possessions of the National Gallery of Ireland, it depicts the attempt to burn the saints at the stake with* their three brothers; the flames turned away from the victims and attacked the executioners. The scene is depicted with a striking directness and clarity which are typical of Fra Angelico's serene faith in the mysteries of Christianity. The architecture in the background, the foreshortening of the foreground figures and the concept of space show how the artist had grasped the treatment of perspective, a skill born in his own lifetime.*

PIETER CLAESZ: STILL-LIFE *The Dutch middle classes maintained their homes with great pride in the 17th century, furnishing them discreetly with articles of excellent craftsmanship. It was the century of Rembrandt, Frans Hals, De Hooch and Vermeer, and paintings were in great demand—the still-life was a favourite type. Pieter Claesz (1590–1661) was a masterly exponent of the style; in this superb painting the lemon and its peel and the pewter vase show how the artist was fascinated by simple things—so that they take on an air of grandeur in his works.*

HORACE HONE: SELF-PORTRAIT *As in England, miniature painting flourished in Ireland in the 18th century. Horace Hone was his country's foremost exponent of the art. He worked in both enamel and water-colour—the technique used in this fresh and confident likeness.*

NATIONAL MUSEUM

The National Museum houses exhibits illustrating the natural history of Ireland and the history of the Irish people from earliest times. It contains one of the finest collections of prehistoric gold objects in northern Europe and an outstanding assemblage of metalwork from the Early Christian period, including richly decorated shrines of different types and personal ornaments of various kinds.

IRISH GOLD *The majority of Irish gold objects are of Bronze-Age date (2000–600 BC). The earliest are crescent-shaped ornaments called lunulae which are made of thin sheet gold. Armlets and necklets made of twisted bars are also common. From late Bronze-Age times dates a series of magnificent gold collars with elaborate mouldings and decorated terminal discs, the best preserved of which was found at Gleninsheen, Co. Clare, in 1934 (front left).*

THE ARDAGH CHALICE *Dating from the 8th century, this chalice is one of the most important examples of Early Christian metalwork. It is of silver enriched with panels of gold filigree, many-coloured glass studs and enamel. The names of the apostles are inscribed on the bowl below the encircling band of gold interlacements. On the underside of the foot are concentric zones of ornament executed in gilt bronze. It was found at Ardagh, Co. Limerick, in 1868.*

FRENCH IVORY PLAQUE: ST MARY OF EGYPT WITH ST ZOSIMUS AND THE CHRIST CHILD *This leaf of a diptych, barely $2\frac{1}{2}$ in. high, is an exceptional product of the 14th-century Paris school of ivory carving. The subject is unusual. St Mary of Egypt was a courtesan of Alexandria in the 5th century. After a pilgrimage to Jerusalem she fled into the desert beyond the Jordan, and had lived there, naked apart from her long hair, without seeing a human creature for 47 years when she was discovered by the hermit Zosimus. During this time she had miraculously contrived to live on only three loaves of bread. Zosimus gave her communion—the scene depicted here. An angel flies down with a mantle to cover her nakedness. Visiting her again shortly afterwards, Zosimus found her dead, and buried her with the help of a lion.*

PARNELL SQUARE Second oldest of the great squares, and originally known as Rutland Square. Building began in the middle of the 18th century. Charlemont House by Sir William Chambers was originally one of the best of the city mansions, now incorporating the Municipal Gallery, with good selections of pictures, stained glass and sculpture.

PHOENIX PARK The largest city park in Europe; it contains various interesting buildings such as Gandon's Military Infirmary (1787), the enormous Wellington Testimonial (1817) by Sir Robert Smirke and Lord Chesterfield's Phoenix Column of 1747. Aras an Uachtarain, originally the house of its Ranger, was built by Nathaniel Clements and probably designed by him in 1751–2. It contains notable rococo plasterwork.

POWERSCOURT HOUSE This impressive mansion was built by Robert Mack for Viscount Powerscourt in 1771–4. The interior is delicately detailed.

PRO-CATHEDRAL OF ST MARY Designed by John Sweetman, this massive Greco-Doric edifice was begun in 1816 and has a portico.

QUEEN'S BRIDGE Perhaps the most graceful of the city's bridges, with three arches and a balustrade, by General Charles Vallancey, 1764–8.

ROTUNDA This complex of buildings in Parnell Square begins with the Maternity Hospital, the earliest in these islands, designed by Richard Castle in 1751 and most notable for the exuberant plasterwork of the chapel by Barthélemy Crémillion.

ROYAL HOSPITAL, KILMAINHAM Erected in 1680–7 to provide for aged war veterans, it was designed by Sir William Robinson in Franco-Dutch Classical style, and consists of a two-storied quadrangle with a stately tower and spire. The great hall is particularly impressive, and there are exceedingly fine wood carvings and the only important florid Carolean ceiling in Ireland.

ST ANDREW'S WESTLAND ROW A fine large Catholic town church of 1832–7 by James Boulger, with a Doric portico ingeniously tied in to the street façades. It contains many monuments.

ST MARY'S CHAPEL-OF-EASE Popularly known as the 'Black Church' this remarkable and important building was erected of black Dublin limestone in 1830 by the architect John Semple.

ST NICHOLAS OF MYRA A Classical church of 1832 by J. Leeson; entrance portico and domed tower.

ST PAUL'S ARRAN QUAY A riverside Catholic church by Patrick Byrne (1835–42). Its portico and cupolaed tower go well with the Four Courts.

ST STEPHEN'S GREEN Originally a common, this, the earliest of Dublin's squares, is also the largest. The buildings bounding the perimeter present an interesting variety of 18th- and 19th-century styles. They include: No. 85 by Richard Castle (1739) with Francini plasterwork, now united with its neighbour No. 86 by Robert West (1765); also with notable plaster is Newman House of University College; the University Church (1855–60) in Byzantine style by John Hungerford Pollen; the St Stephen's Green and United Services clubs and Nos. 16–17 all on the north side; a pair of houses (Nos. 119–20) on the west side by Richard Castle; the College of Surgeons (1806–27) by Edward Parke and William Murray. Iveagh House (Dept. of Foreign Affairs) incorporates some good interiors of 1731 by Castle. In the gardens, laid out by Lord Ardilaun in 1880, are several monuments including one by Henry Moore in memory of W. B. Yeats.

STEEVEN'S HOSPITAL From a design by Thomas Burgh, it was started in 1720. It is the oldest public hospital in Ireland, and is arranged round an arcaded courtyard.

ROUBILIAC *Jonathan Swift*

In 1738 the senior students of Trinity College decided to devote their entertainment money to commissioning a bust of the distinguished Dubliner Jonathan Swift, the great satirist and Dean of St Patrick's Cathedral. They chose Louis Francois Roubiliac, the leading sculptor of his time in Britain, for the assignment. The result, dated 1745, is the most vivid portrait of Swift that survives—although Roubiliac and Swift never met. (Trinity College Library, Dublin)

TAYLOR'S HALL The last remaining guildhall in Dublin, dating from the reign of Queen Anne. The Hall, lit by circular-headed windows, has a carved wooden screen, and a marble fire-place.

TRINITY COLLEGE Founded in 1592 by Elizabeth I on the site of the Priory of All Hallows, the earliest surviving portion of the building, the Rubrics, dates from 1700. The impressive Palladian façade, built by Henry Keene and John Sanderson of London, dates from 1753. The quadrangles are bounded by many distinguished buildings—the chapel, the theatre (fine interiors), the Printing House—a miniature temple by Richard Castle—the dining-hall, basically by Richard Castle, and the fine Venetian Revival museum buildings, designed in 1853 by Deane and Woodward, with carvings by the O'Shea brothers.

The Provost's House by John Smith has a façade of Palladio derived through Burlington, and an intact interior including a splendid saloon with coffered ceiling. The great library, one of the copyright libraries, erected in 1712 to the design of Thomas Burgh, has many ancient manuscripts, including the incomparable Book of Kells, the 7th-century Book of Durrow, and the Book of Armagh. The excellent New Library, built to an international competition-winning design by Ahrends, Burton and Koralek, adjoins it to the south-east. (See also p. 606.)

TYRONE HOUSE Richard Castle built this notable Georgian mansion for Viscount Tyrone in 1740.

Duleek *Meath* 573Ke

There is a fine late 9th-century high cross in the churchyard and a sepulchral slab set in the churchyard wall. The tower and south aisle of the 15th-century Augustinian priory contain carved tombs, including the elaborate Bellew memorial.

THE BOOK OF KELLS

This famous illuminated copy of the Gospels is the greatest surviving masterpiece of early Irish art. It dates from the late 8th or early 9th centuries and takes its name from the vanished monastery of Kells, in Co. Meath. It is now believed that work on the manuscript may have begun in St Columba's island monastery of Iona, off the west coast of Scotland. When Iona was invaded by the Vikings in 802, the monks fled to Kells, taking the book with them.

The pages above are from St Matthew's Gospel, and the picture shows the arrest of Christ in the Garden of Gethsemane. On the left are the opening words of St Matthew's Gospel, Chapter 1, verse 18: 'Christi autem generatio', which, translated from the Latin is: 'Now the birth of Jesus Christ . . .' The XPI (Christ) monogram is ornamented with an intricacy and exuberance that present the eye with a feast of engaging detail. In addition to the standard motifs of Celtic art—interlaced ribbons, spirals and whorls repeated with subtle variations—the artist has included human heads, angels with spreading wings and, at the bottom of the letter P, two mice nibbling at the Eucharistic bread watched by a pair of cats—perhaps an allusion to the unpleasant fate in store for those who receive Holy Communion unworthily.
(Trinity College Library, Dublin)

The wayside pillar erected by Dame Jennet Dowdall in 1601 is richly carved with angels and saints. Duleek House is a pedimented cut-stone house, with a good door by Richard Castle or his school.

Dun Aillinne *Kild.*   573Jc
This ceremonial hill-top site, said to be an early seat of the kings of Leinster, is enclosed by a large rampart and internal ditch.

Dunamase Castle *Laois*   573Hb
The Rock of Dunamase, conspicuously situated in a gap of the West Leinster Hills, is crowned by the much-ruined fragments of a large complicated castle of numerous medieval dates, destroyed by the Cromwellians in 1650.

Dunboy *Cork*   570Ba
This was the last stronghold in South-west Ireland to be taken by the Elizabethan forces during the

Nine Years War. The ruined 'castle' of the Puxleys is notable for its spectacular Victorian transverse arches.

Dunbrody Abbey *Wex.*   571Jd
A Cistercian friary founded by Hervey de Montmorenci in *c.* 1178 but built some 30 years later. It is one of the largest abbey churches in Ireland, cruciform with an added 15th-century crossing tower; for its size the church is relatively plain.

Dundalk *Louth*   573Kf
The Protestant church of St Nicholas, though much altered, is medieval in origin, with some 15th-century windows and a 14th-century tower. The Catholic church, an imitation of King's College Chapel, Cambridge, is by Thomas Duff of Newry, and the Greek Doric Courthouse is by Edward Park and John Bowden of Dublin. Both are notable buildings.

Dundonald *Down*   *575Jd*
The fort here is an Anglo-Norman mote. In the churchyard is a fine Greco-Doric mausoleum of 1842, surmounted by a sarcophagus enclosed by six Ionic columns and a dome.

Dundrum Castle *Down*   *575Hc*
The cylindrical keep of Dundrum Castle is three storeys high, dates from 1230–40 and is surrounded by an irregularly curtained wall and a rock-cut fosse; it is among the earliest castles in Ireland. A gate-house leads to the lower ward, at the end of which stands a ruined Jacobean house.

Dungannon *Tyrone*   *574Fd*
Famous for its Volunteer Convention held in 1782, it is in origin an O'Neill stronghold. The Royal School, a Jacobean foundation, has buildings of 1786 which were erected by Primate Robinson. The Protestant church dates from 1790.

Dungarvan *Waterford*   *571Hc*
At the head of a spacious bay, it has the remains of a Norman castle now incorporated in the military barracks, and some broad quays, but is chiefly remarkable for its regular town plan and its attractive Grattan Square.

Dungiven Priory *Lond.*   *574Fe*
The church of the Augustinian priory is a simple 12th-century structure remarkable mainly for the fine 15th-century tomb, probably of an O'Cahan knight. He is in Irish costume, on an arcaded plinth containing six gallowglasses (mercenaries), the whole surmounted by a splendid Flamboyant pierced canopy.

Dungory Castle *Gal.*   *572Dc*
A 16th-century castle on a small island near the coast; it occupies the centre of an earlier earth-fort. The gabled tower adjoins one wall of an earlier hexagonal bawn. It has recently been entirely restored. (Open to the public.)

Dunlavin *Wicklow*   *573Jc*
Remarkable for its court- and market-house which stands in the middle of the square. It is a cruciform building with corner colonnades and fluted dome entirely built of masonry, probably to the design of Richard Castle in 1743.

Dunluce Castle *Antrim*   *575Gg*
On a rocky promontory jutting into the sea, Dunluce was built by Richard de Burgh *c.* 1300 and is one of the most spectacularly situated castles in Ireland. The 16th-century gate-house has Franco-Scottish corbelled turrets. In the outer court are the ruins of a Jacobean house which incorporates a great hall and kitchen. In 1639 some of the servants' quarters collapsed into the sea, taking a number of servants with them. Two earlier cylindrical towers remain.

Dunmoe Castle *Meath*   *573Je*
A 13th-century castle altered in the 16th century. The adjoining church has a sacristy with a crypt underneath.

Dunmore *Gal.*   *572De*
The remains of a 13th-century castle with a square tower and added gables; and the 15th-century Augustinian friary church, also with a square tower, founded by Walter de Bermingham.

Dunmurry *Antrim*   *575Hd*
Now virtually a suburb of Belfast, it has a handsome Unitarian church of 1779; the church is a plain rectangle with an animated rhythm of windows and doorways on its entrance front.

Dunsany *Meath*   *573Jd*
Dunsany, the medieval castle of the Plunketts, Barons Dunsany, was remodelled in the 18th century, and has a splendid staircase with 18th-century Gothic ribbing and a drawing-room with plasterwork in the Stapleton manner. The stables are by Sir Gilbert Scott. There are also two good

---

DUNDRUM CASTLE

This ruined castle, standing on a high rock, was built in the 13th century by John de Courcy on the site of an ancient fort. The castle comprises a circular keep within irregular curtain walls, with a moat cut out of the rock. In the topmost storey of the keep is a series of continuous passageways cut in the wall. Its magnificent position made the castle a much sought after prize, and for centuries it was the scene of battles and sieges until it was eventually dismantled on the orders of Cromwell in 1652.

entrance-lodges and a ruined church. The church of 1425–50, with crenellated parapets, has two western turrets and a wall dividing the nave from the chancel containing a rood. There is unusual tracery, typical of Fingall, the area north of Dublin. There is also a 16th-century high cross, a baptismal font carved with a Crucifixion and the Apostles, and a double-effigy tomb of the armoured Sir Thomas Plunkett and his wife. (Not open to the public.)

Dunsoghly Castle *Dublin*   573Kd
The massive tower of Dunsoghly is on a small hillock in a marsh on the outskirts of Dublin. The four angle-towers rise above the main level of the keep which, unusually for Ireland, still retains some of the oak timbers of its roof.

Duntryleague *Lim.*   570Fd
On a site which commands panoramic views are a ruined megalithic passage-grave, a circle of stones and a group of ruined barrows.

Durrow See Castle Durrow.

Durrow Abbey *Offaly*   573Gd
The site of St Colmcille's monastery in which was written the famous Book of Durrow, now in Trinity College, Dublin. The 9th-century high cross and other smaller stones remain. The derelict Protestant church of *c.* 1700 has a splendid baroque west doorway.

Dysart House *Westmeath*   573He
Built in 1757 by George Pentland for the Ogle family. Though relatively plain, the pedimented house has semicircular projections at both ends of the façade.

Dysert O'Dea *Clare*   570Df
The remains of a two-cell Romanesque church, badly restored. It has a Round Tower but, most conspicuously, the fine mid-12th-century high cross, with a crucified Christ above the figure of a bishop, both in high relief.

Eglantine *Down*   575Hd
A mid-19th-century house with a remarkable double ramped staircase.

Emo Court *Laois*   573Hc
A domed mansion with portico, designed by James Gandon for the 1st Earl of Portarlington, *c.* 1790, notable for Coade stone capitals and bas-relief panels. It is much altered internally.

Ennis *Clare*   570Df
The county town of Clare has a large Classical court-house of 1852 containing a statue by Joseph Kirk of Sir Michael O'Loghlen, Master of the Rolls, a column to the memory of Daniel O'Connell and some good 18th-century houses. But the principal relic of the town is a Franciscan friary, of O'Brien foundation in 1240, with features from the two following centuries; the MacMahon tomb in the friary church has a splendid relief of the Entombment dating from about 1470.

Enniscorthy *Wex.*   571Ke
There is a Norman four-towered keep, now a museum, similar to those at Carlow and Ferns. St Aidan's Cathedral is a Gothic Revival work by Augustus Welby Pugin, 1843–8.

Enniskillen *Ferm.*   574Dc
In an important site on the Erne between the Upper and Lower Loughs, it has few ancient remains save the fragmentary Maguire Castle with a Scottish turret, and the 17th-century parish church, now the cathedral, which has a handsome font of 1666.

ENNISKILLEN REGIMENTAL MUSEUM Displays of uniforms, arms, medals, colours and pictures trace the history of the Royal Inniskilling Fusiliers and the Inniskilling Dragoons.

Eyrecourt Castle *Gal.*   572Fc
Like Beaulieu, one of Ireland's few wide-eaved, Dutch-inspired houses of the late 17th century. The richly carved consoles of the cornice may still be seen. Extensive late 18th-century stables.

Fahan Mura *Don.*   574Ef
The superlative erect slab has a cross with interlaced ornament and two stylised figures on its face. The projecting lugs seem to represent arms, and may be an early stage in the evolution of the high cross form. It has a Greek inscription.

Fair Head Crannog *Antrim*   575Hg
In the little lake, Lough Na Crannagh, is a well preserved picturesque crannog, or lake-dwelling, with a drystone revetment.

Feartagar Castle *Gal.*   572De
A 16th-century de Burgo castle: a well-preserved tower-house with corner machicolation, two staircases in the walls and a vaulted first floor.

Fenagh *Leit.*   574Db
Both the churches at Fenagh have barrel-vaulted western ends, presumably to contain living quarters for the priest. The larger church has a very good east window of *c.* 1400.

Fermoy *Cork*   570Fc
Laid out in 1791 by the Scottish immigrant John Anderson, it was a notable garrison town of the 19th century. The Protestant church dates from 1802 and has a grotesque medieval stoup.

Ferns *Wex.*   571Ke
The remains of Ferns Cathedral, consisting of a 13th-century chancel, partly standing though unroofed, are far to the east of the present parish church-cathedral, which is a reduced reconstruction made in 1817 of a much larger aisled and cruciform medieval cathedral. The choir is puzzling, in being about 4 ft lower than the rest of the church, from which it is detached. Ferns Castle, the finest of the early 13th-century keeps, has cylindrical angle-towers, a type peculiar to Ireland. One of the corner towers has gone, and the principal feature is the vaulted chapel on the first floor of the south-east tower, the finest in any Irish castle.

Fertagh *Kilk.*   571Hf
A fine round tower, in good condition, though damaged by fire in 1156. In the ruined church is a double effigy, the tomb of the FitzPatricks of Upper Ossory, the sides of which are decorated with window tracery and plans of lierne vaulting.

Fethard *Tipp.*   571He
Though somewhat decayed, Fethard still has parts of its walls and four tower-houses, as well as the remains of an Augustinian friary of *c.* 1300, whose church has been re-roofed. The Protestant parish church has a medieval nave and west door, and several fine 14th-century windows.

Finglas *Dublin*   573Kd
The church contains an excellent wall monument of 1700 by William Kidwell, to Sir William Flower, the father of the 1st Lord Castle Durrow, builder of Castle Durrow, County Laois.

Florence Court *Ferm.*   574Dc
One of the most important houses in Ulster, built in the 18th century by John Cole. Very good plasterwork. (Open to the public.)

THE BOYNE MEDAL

Perhaps the first medal to be awarded for individual gallantry, and a forerunner of the Victoria Cross, the Boyne Medal was struck by command of William III after the Battle of the Boyne in 1690; it was presented to Major A. P. Rogers of the Royal Inniskilling Fusiliers, who had rescued the king as he was about to be pulled off his horse by a southern Irish supporter of James II during the battle. Probably made by Jan Luder, the medal is of 18 carat gold and was made 'repoussé': two thin gold plates were deeply embossed and then fastened together at the rim. (Royal Inniskilling Fusiliers Regimental Museum, Enniskillen)

Fore *Westmeath* 573He
The ruined 9th- to 10th-century Church of St Fechin has pilaster projections and a massive west doorway with cross-inscribed lintel; it also has an early font and a reconstructed chancel arch of *c.* 1200. There are also extensive remains of the 13th-century priory. Medieval gate-houses survive.

Forenaghts (Furness) *Kild.* 573Jc
Near the ancient Woolpack Road from Dublin to the Curragh of Kildare is Long Stone, a 17 ft high granite standing stone, in the middle of Long Stone prehistoric enclosure, surrounded by an earth ring with two entrances. West of the stone is a roofless prehistoric burial chamber, where cremated bones, pottery and flints were found.

Fota Island *Cork* 570Fb
Gardens and a fine arboretum are open to the public daily. The house, by Sir Richard Morrison, is open to the public.

Furness House *Kild.* 573Jc
Its central block is closely similar to Clermont in Wicklow, with wings, and was possibly designed by Francis Bindon in 1731. A column from Dangan in Meath has been erected in the park.

Fourknocks *Meath* 573Ke
This earthen mound was excavated in 1950 and found to contain a remarkable Neolithic to Bronze Age passage-grave with an unusually large central chamber and interesting carvings. The chamber is now covered by a concrete dome, arranged to illuminate the carved stones.

Frenchpark Church *Roscom.* 572Ef
Douglas Hyde, scholar, founder of the Gaelic League, and first President of Ireland, is buried beside the 18th-century church.

Freshford *Kilk.* 571Hf
The Protestant church, built in 1730, incorporates the west front of a church in the Romanesque style, with double recessed doorway and gable.

Gallarus Oratory *Kerry* 570Ad
A drystone chapel, a virtually unique survival of a method of building similar to that used in the Stone Age burial chamber at Newgrange and in the more sophisticated mortared stone roofs at Killaloe, Kells and Glendalough. The system makes use of corbels, with inward-sloping bowed gables and side walls that merge imperceptibly into the roof, forming a shape like an upturned boat.

Gallen Priory *Offaly* 572Fc
Little remains of the famous 5th-century monastery, but a collection of 8th- to 11th-century grave-slabs, similar to those at Clonmacnoise, is preserved in the modern priory.

Galway *Gal.* 572Cc
Originally a Norman foundation, Galway was known as the City of the Tribes. Because of its remote situation and extensive trade with the Continent, it enjoyed virtual autonomy through much of the medieval period and became to all intents and purposes a city-state, ruled by a few powerful families (the Tribes). The old Galway was built in the 16th–17th centuries and was notable for its fine architecture. Today little survives, but 16th-century Lynch's Castle (now the Munster and Leinster Bank), with its elaborate carved windows, is typical of the semi-fortified palaces of the aristocratic merchant families. Other fragments, such as the 'Spanish' Arch, survive throughout the town. In the Classical porticoed Franciscan church of 1836 are the remains of Sir Peter French's tomb, incorporating weepers in the Gothic tradition, and Renaissance ornamental detail.
CHURCH OF ST NICHOLAS The largest medieval church in Ireland, founded in 1230. It has a profusion of fine carving, much of it of the 15th and early 16th century, when Galway was at its most prosperous. The plan of the building is cruciform, and the south and north nave aisles were widened in 1500 and 1538–83 respectively, resulting in a unique three-gabled west front. The central tower was added *c.* 1500, and the south transept was extended by Nicholas Lynch in 1561 and included a private chapel approached by private stairs. The carvings include gargoyles on the south aisle and, in the interior, the 16th-century font, 15th-century water stoup and the imported 15th-century reader's desk with its cusped tracery.

ST KEVIN'S CHURCH
AT GLENDALOUGH

The valley of Glendalough contains the site of one of Ireland's holy places, for it was here St Kevin settled, and died in 618. Around him grew up a community of followers who perpetuated his fame, and this has survived to the present day. Seven churches were built in the valley; and St Kevin's Church, with its belfry—a miniature version of the nearby Round Tower—is the most perfect. The original entrance at the west end is now blocked up and the present entrance was the chancel arch. Stone crosses and other carved stones from the valley are now stored inside. The belfry is one of the earliest examples of a belfry springing from a roof or gable. St Kevin's reputed burial-place is the Church of the Virgin, in the valley.

Garinish Island *Cork* 570Cb
In 1910, John Annan Bryce began to transform Garinish Island, a desolate rocky islet, into a unique island garden. Harold Peto, the architect, horticulturist and landscape designer, laid out the garden in the Classical Italian style within a shelter-belt of trees; the formal garden gradually merges into meandering grass walks lined with naturalised trees, shrubs and flowers.

Garraunboy Castle *Lim.* 570Ee
A fine mid-15th-century keep, symmetrically sited on a rock bawn, originally with D-shaped turrets at all four corners. The interior has numerous wall-recesses and ogee-headed windows, and there is a shot-hole over the main door.

Giant's Ring *Down* 575Hd
A circular ceremonial enclosure 750 ft in diameter, with a rampart about 12 ft high, in seven sections and with a small dolmen in the centre.

Glananea House *Westmeath* 573He
A late 18th-century house, probably by Samuel Woolley, who was certainly responsible for the Glananea triumphal arch now at Rosmead, in the same county. Good Wyatt-style plasterwork.

Glanfahan *Kerry* 570Ac
An extremely dense concentration of stone forts and clochans (bee-hive huts) on the south coast of the Dingle peninsula near Slea Head, including the impressive promontory fort of Dun Beag—four defensive banks of stone and earth cutting off a spur of land which falls sheer to the Atlantic.

Glencolumbkille *Don.* 574Be
A complex site of prehistoric and early Christian remains, including a great cairn, a prehistoric chamber-tomb, ring-forts containing beehive huts, and many pillar-stones incised with crosses—all that remains of a monastery that once occupied this site.

Glendalough *Wicklow* 573Kb
Among the most renowned, and in many ways the most picturesque, of the early monastic sites, Glendalough lies at the head of a narrow valley containing two lakes. Its foundation is attributed to St Kevin, who died early in the 7th century, but the present remains are mostly of the 10th–12th centuries. Among the earliest of these are Temple-naskellig and 'St Kevin's Bed' on the south shore of the Upper Lake, accessible only by boat. The former, much reconstructed, has some early gravestones and a small enclosure. The 'Bed' is a cave. Reefert ('burial-place of the kings') Church, farther to the east, is possibly of the 10th century. Like Trinity Church, which it much resembles, it has a nave and chancel and stone brackets in place of pilasters to carry the ends of the barge boards.

East of the Lower Lake between Glendasan R. and the stream from the two lakes is the main monastic precinct, the north gateway of which, near the Royal Hotel, still survives, as does the paved causeway leading south from it. Within the present enclosure are the cathedral, the Round Tower, the 'priests' house' and St Kevin's Cross. West of it, in a separate enclosure, is St Mary's Church and south of it St Kevin's. Of these buildings, St Mary's is probably the earliest, with an added Romanesque chancel and north door. The square-headed west doorway, with inclined jambs, has a saltire cross incised below its lintel. The cathedral, dedicated to SS Peter and Paul, is a complex building consisting basically of a 10th-century nave of exceptional width (30 ft) with antae, a fine west door, and a later chancel with a reconstructed chancel arch. Three early inscribed stones are fixed to the north wall. The Round Tower is among the most perfect in Ireland, its cap being a modern reconstruction which uses the original stones.

The so-called priests' house is a small building, perhaps a shrine or mortuary chapel, probably late 12th century, and most remarkable for the lintel over its south door. Though now fragmentary, it is known to have been triangular, with a seated figure in the centre receiving homage from two others carrying bell and crozier. St Kevin's Cross is a plain granite cross 11 ft high. St Kevin's Church was originally a single-cell church with barrel-vault, roof-croft and corbelled roof above it. Rising out of the west end of the roof is a miniature Round Tower. The whole probably dates from the 9th century. Several stone fragments including the market cross are kept inside. East of St Kevin's is the much ruined St Kieran's, the smallest nave-and-chancel church recorded in Ireland.

East of this central group are two more churches: Trinity Church and St Saviour's. St Saviour's is the most elaborately decorated of the Glendalough churches and dates from the mid-12th century. It consists of a nave and chancel, with a domestic building adjoining it on the north.

Glendalough was repeatedly burnt and plundered in the 9th and 10th centuries, but from 1107 onwards was the See of a bishop, now united with the See of Dublin. In 1398 the English of Dublin sacked and destroyed it, but it remained a monastic centre until the end of the 16th century, and a place of pilgrimage until the middle of the 19th.

Glenquin Castle *Lim.* 570Dd
A tall fortified tower, carefully restored in 1840.

Glenstal Castle *Lim.* 570Fe
This massive pile includes a splendid re-creation of the medieval gate-house at Rockingham, England, and was designed by William Bardwell for the Barrington family in 1837. Now an abbey.

Glenveagh Castle *Don.* 574Df
A Scottish-style baronial castle by an unknown architect, in the centre of Ireland's only major deer forest; built for the Adair family in 1870. Park open to the public.

Glin Castle *Lim.* 570De
A Gothic castellated house of *c.* 1790–1812, which incorporates a fine double staircase and Wyatt-like plasterwork. A notable series of Gothic folly lodges surrounds the estate. (By appointment.)

Glinsk Castle *Gal.* 572Bd
Said to have been built by Ulick Burke, who died in 1708, Glinsk—a compact, three-storey, semi-fortified house—was more probably built by a predecessor around 1630. It has machicolations on the corners and a host of lofty chimneys.

Gloster *Offaly* 571Gg
The central portion is a late 17th-century house with a superimposed order of pilasters on the garden front, to which have been added two extensions with windows and pedimented niches, possibly by Sir Edward Lovett Pearce *c.* 1730. He was probably responsible also for the richly stuccoed central saloon, with its arcaded gallery and flanking corridors. In the grounds, a triumphal arch flanked by obelisks is certainly by Pearce.

Gorey *Wex.* 571Lf
The Loreto convent is by Augustus Welby Pugin, and dates from 1839–42. The Church of St Mark, in Norman style of the same date, is also by him. The Protestant parish church has fine stained glass.

Gort *Gal.* 572Db
A town well laid out by the Vereker family of Lough Cutra, but principally associated with Augusta, Lady Gregory. Her house (now demolished) at Coole Park was a meeting place for such Irish poets and authors as W. B. Yeats and Sean O'Casey in the early years of the present century. Little now remains but a cedar avenue and a huge copper beech carved with initials of many literary visitors to Coole. Some 3½ miles to the north-east is Yeats's Tower at Ballylee.
BALLYLEE CASTLE The 16th-century tower where W. B. Yeats lived during the 1920's and wrote his book of poems *The Tower*. Yeats left the tower in 1929, after which it fell into ruin. It was restored as a Yeats Museum in 1965.

Gosford Castle *Arm.* 575Gc
The first Norman Revival castle in these islands, designed by Thomas Hopper *c.* 1820. Now an hotel.

Gowran *Kilk.* 571Je
The collegiate church of Gowran, *c.* 1275, has an aisled nave and long chancel. As at Callan, the chancel now serves as the Protestant church. The 14th- and 15th-century square keep stands between the nave and the chancel. The windows and other details of the church are of high quality.

Gracehill *Antrim* 575Ge
This Moravian settlement was founded in 1746 with separate houses for the brothers and sisters, grouped around a square, plain church with baroque woodwork to the doorways. It survives almost intact. The graveyard is behind the church.

ST STEPHEN WINDOW

Harry Clarke, the son of a stained glass artist, sought to produce a more personal type of window than those produced in his father's Dublin studio. This window, dating from 1922, shows the influence of Clarke's work as a book illustrator and his interest in Aubrey Beardsley. The jewelled effect was achieved by abundant aciding. (Protestant Parish Church, Gorey)

Graiguenamanagh *Kilk.* 571Je
Almost the whole town is built inside the great Cistercian abbey founded by William the Marshall in *c.* 1207 and peopled with monks from Stanley in Wiltshire. The church is the largest Irish Cistercian example. The central tower fell in 1774 causing much damage; in 1813, the eastern parts were re-roofed to form the Catholic parish church. There was so much debris from the fall of the tower that the present floor level is 5 ft higher than the original, and architectural features are buried. There are good Transitional features, as at Kilkenny Cathedral. The seven-arched bridge over the Barrow is

by George Semple (mid-18th century). The barracks in the town has an 18th-century doorway on which the local mason who made it has worked 13th-century dog-tooth ornament. There are two high crosses, one from Ballycogan with sculptured figures, including King David.

Granard *Long.*   573Ge
A gently curving street leads up to the Catholic Church of St Mary of 1861, built by John Burke, behind which may be seen the mote of Hugh de Lacy's castle, built in 1191.

Granny Castle *Kilk.*   571Jd
A tower-house with an oriel window in good condition and one wall of its separate hall. Three round turrets and a curtain wall overlooking the river survive from the original 13th-century castle. The fortifications were later modified by the Ormonde Butlers.

Great Skellig *Kerry*   570Ab
The celebrated island of Skellig Michael, one of Europe's many rocky places associated with that saint, lies in the Atlantic 7 miles west of Bolus Head. There are nine buildings, two oratories, six dwelling huts and the church; all but the church are built of dry stone. The settlement seems to have been occupied by a community of hermits from the 9th until probably the 12th century. Access can be difficult, but the solitude, splendour and mystery of the scene is without parallel.

Greencastle *Down.*   574Fg
The De Burg keep at Greencastle, built in 1305, is a long rectangle with four angle-towers and set-back gables. It is surrounded by the fragmentary remains of a bawn, which originally possessed four corner towers.

Greyabbey *Down*   575Jd
A Cistercian abbey, founded in 1193 by John de Courcy; the church is aisle-less, with transepts and east chapels and an impressive west doorway of c. 1220. The east wall has two storeys, each of three lancets. The cloister was an elongated rectangle and the refectory, as at Askeaton, was endwise on. There are some good 17th- and early 18th-century Montgomery monuments, and a recumbent medieval tomb effigy.

Grianán of Aileach *Don.*   574Ef
A large, well preserved, though much restored drystone circular fort, probably dating from the

5th to the 12th century. It consists of three outer rings of defences surrounding the fort proper, with three internal stepped terraces and stairways. There are galleries in the thickness of the wall.

Hazelwood House *Sligo*   574Cc
Built in 1731, one of Richard Castle's earlier central block and wing houses on the shores of Lough Gill. Well detailed with William Kent-style interior decoration, the graceful building has recently been restored.

Headfort House *Meath*   573Je
A large, severe, oblong house notable for its rich Robert Adam interior dating from 1770. Now a boys' school.

Hillsborough *Down*   575Hd
Founded in the mid-17th century by Colonel Arthur Hill, who built a square fort with spear-shaped bastions and gate-house here in the 1650's. The fort has good wrought-iron gates and stone piers with urns. The present gate-house is in the 18th-century Gothic style, and dates from 1758. Much of the fort was remodelled at this time, and a charming gazebo was constructed in the middle of the north-east side by the 1st Lord Hillsborough. His son, the 1st Marquess of Downshire, virtually rebuilt the 17th-century Plantation church in 1773, with a tower and spire, at the end of an avenue framed by gate-lodges in the same style. The interior of the church is remarkable for its Gothic fittings, including box-pews, a hexagonal pulpit, throne and organ by John Snetzler and some monuments, one by Nollekens. Other notable buildings include the court-house, originally the market-house, which has a cupola, and dates from 1780, perhaps by W. Forsyth. Opposite is Hillsborough Castle, originally the Downshires' seat, designed by R. F. Brettingham in 1795, with additions by William Sandys. In front of it are elaborate gates of 1745, removed from Richhill Castle, Co. Armagh, possibly by the Thornberry brothers of Armagh.

Holycross Abbey *Tipp.*   571Ge
Founded in the 12th century by Donal Mor O'Brien and named after a relic of the True Cross; originally founded for the Tironian order, it passed to the Cistercians at the end of the century. The church has an aisled nave and choir with a vaulted presbytery and transepts, and a massive central crossing tower of the 15th century. The magnifi-

HOLYCROSS ABBEY

Once a place of pilgrimage, the abbey presents a view of the great east window of the church, with reticulated tracery, across the R. Suir. Some 4 miles south-west *of Thurles, the ruins, now being restored, include fragments of the 15th-century cloister and its ranges, and the remains of the infirmary and abbot's lodging.*

cent sedilia of the 15th century has meticulous carving. Between the two chapels of the south transept is a remarkable open-work structure, popularly called 'the monks' waking place', probably designed for the exhibition of the relic of the True Cross; it has an elaborate foliated base and twisted columns. The church, with its attractive carvings, has recently been re-roofed.

Howth Castle *Dublin* 573Kd
A medieval castle of the St Lawrence family was altered and made roughly symmetrical in 1738, possibly by Francis Bindon. He was probably responsible for the splendid pedimented front door, and the compartment ceilings and chimney-piece in the drawing-room. A part of the early 18th-century formal garden survives, with 30 ft high beech hedges. (Gardens open to the public.)

Humewood Castle *Wicklow* 573Jb
With Dromore it ranks as Ireland's most successful Gothic Revival high-Victorian essay in the castle style. Designed by William White, 1867–8, with extensive later additions including the immense circular water tower. (Not open to the public.)

Ightermurragh *Cork* 571Gb
A cruciform 17th-century house, with four gables and many fire-places, including one which records the building of the house in 1641 by Edmund Supple and his wife 'whom love binds in one'.

Illauntannig *Kerry* 570Bd
One of the largest of the Magharee Islands off the north coast of Corkaguiny. A hermitage founded by St Seanach in the 6th to 7th century, remains of the monastery, small church, three clochans and burial monuments survive in a massive drystone cashel, part of which has fallen into the sea.

Inchagoill *Gal.* 572Cd
An island in Lough Corrib, about 5 miles south of Cong, on which are the remains of an early mortar-built oratory and a 12th-century Roman-esque church. The doorway (rebuilt) is elaborately carved with human heads and other ornaments.

Inchbofin *Long.* 572Fd
A small island in the eastern arm of Lough Ree; it contains two churches and a few early gravestones. One church has a fine early Romanesque window.

Inchcleraun *Long.* 572Fe
In the north arm of Lough Ree is the island monas-tery founded by St Diarmaid. It contains a group of churches, six in all, varying in age from the 10th century to the 15th century.

Inis Cealtra *Clare* 572Eb
On an island in Lough Derg is the earliest group of monastic remains in County Clare, containing an earthen monastic enclosure, the ruins of four churches, a small building called the 'Confes-sional'—possibly a tomb shrine—a Round Tower, two high crosses and a cemetery full of early gravestones inscribed in Irish.

Inishmaine *Mayo* 572Ce
An island in Lough Mask containing an Augustin-ian Transitional church of the early 13th century, with later transepts. On the west shore of the island is a twin-crypted sweat-house (used for sweat baths), with a high-pitched stone roof.

Inishmurray *Sligo* 574Bc
This island site, 4 miles off the Sligo coast near Grange, is perhaps the most complete and per-fectly preserved early monastic enclosure in Ire-land. The monastic cashel, oval in outline, lies near the shore, in the middle of the south coast of the island, which was inhabited until very recently. It

was founded by St Laisren and raided by the Vikings in 807. Within the cashel are a small stone-roofed church with pilasters, and three clochans, of which the largest is called the Schoolhouse, and two minor rectangular buildings, the larger called the Fire Temple and the smaller St Molaise's (Laisren) Chapel. There are also several paths and causeways as well as three open-air altars or tombs, and a covered holy well outside the east wall of the cashel. St Molaise's Chapel is a very small, stone-roofed oratory with a tiny east window. Against the outside of the south wall is a long stone bench. Over the west door is a small Greek cross. The larger church, south of it—sometimes called the 'Monastery', or the 'Men's Church'—has pilasters at its east end only, and is roofless. North of it are two pillar-stones, and east of it an open-air altar. Another altar lies to the south, and to the west a stone platform on which are the five Cursing Stones; they are inscribed with crosses and other devices, and an Englishwoman is said to have used them to curse Hitler. The Fire Temple and the Schoolhouse are close together in the subdivided west part of the enclosure. The former is of medieval date, but has an early cross on its lintel. The Schoolhouse is oval, of corbelled construction without mortar.

Another church, 'of the Women', and a grave-yard with some inscribed stones, lie south-east of the cashel. Several altars, cross-slabs and pillar-stones are found in isolated sites round the shores of the island.

Inistioge *Kilk.* 571Je
A well laid-out village, with tree-lined square and a fine 18th-century bridge over the R. Nore. It was built by the Tighe family of the Woodstock estate near by.

The Protestant parish church incorporates parts of the medieval priory, and in the north tower is an effigy by Flaxman of the poetess Mary Tighe, the author of *Psyche,* who died in 1810.

Isert Kelly *Gal.* 572Dc
Standing in Castle Park is the 15th-century tower-house of the MacHubert Burke's castle; the win-dows of the second floor have arcaded embrasures, and inside is a carved chimney-piece dated 1604, with a Latin inscription.

Jerpoint Abbey *Kilk.* 571Je
The most interesting of the first generation of Cistercian houses. The silhouette of its tower with its characteristic Irish battlements, the elaboration and variety of the carvings of the cloister and other features, and its fine situation beside the Nore, combine to give it an unusual attraction. It was founded by Donal Mac Gillapatrick in 1180, but the abbey was rebuilt in the 15th century when the conspicuous crossing tower was inserted. The cylindrical piers of the nave have Transitional capitals, as have the transept chapels. The richly carved piers of the cloister arcade, re-erected in recent years, are among the finest works of Irish medieval sculpture.

Also in the abbey, and connected with the cloister carving, are examples of altar tomb-sculpture; these carved effigies of saints have a kinship with figures of angels painted in 8th- and 9th-century Irish manuscripts. Just to the north-west is Newtown Jerpoint, in which are the ruins of St Nicholas's parish church; it has an unusual groin-vaulted rood gallery and a dwelling tower dating from the 15th century.

Jigginstown House *Kild.* 573Jc
The most ambitious of Thomas Wentworth, Earl of Strafford's Irish building ventures: a huge (380

ft long) uncompleted house, dating from before 1637. It is entirely built on a vaulted brick basement faced in stone on the exterior. The upper storeys, said to have been faced with marble, are incomplete, and today one can see only the chimney-stacks and the huge window-jambs of the first floor. It is superlatively well built, and is among the earliest brickwork known in Ireland. The builder, John Allen, is reputed to have been a Dutch immigrant.

Johnstown Castle *Wex.*   *571Kd*
A magnificent group of buildings with many towers. It was designed in Gothic and Norman Revival styles by Daniel Robertson of Kilkenny in 1830–43. The castle, standing in grounds complete with a lake has an agricultural museum attached.

Kanturk Castle *Cork*   *570Ec*
In *c.* 1609 McDonagh McCarthy, Lord of Duhallow began, but never finished, this large compact semi-fortified house, resembling Burncourt in plan. Both houses are related to English examples such as Lulworth and Mount Edgecumbe.

Kells *Kilk.*   *571Je*
An Augustinian fortified priory founded at the end of the 12th century by Geoffrey de Montemarisco. The ruins have all the appearance of a many-towered walled town. They consist of two courts and cover 5 acres, making this the largest monastic enclosure in Ireland. The ruined church with a Lady Chapel—originally cruciform with a large Cistercian-type tower now half demolished—is in the north-east angle. In the north transept is a slab with a pair of high-relief portrait heads. Two miles to the south is Kilree; the early church there has pilasters and a lintelled west doorway; there is also a Round Tower 98 ft high, and a 9th-century high cross decorated with spirals, frets and figures.

Kells *Meath*   *573He*
St Colmcille founded a monastery here in the 6th century. The Book of Kells, a magnificent illuminated copy of the Gospels in Latin, was brought to the monastery of Kells in the 9th century; it is now preserved in Trinity College, Dublin. In the town are 'St Colmcille's House', a church of early stone-roof type, a Round Tower and five 9th-century high crosses, four in the churchyard and one in the middle of the town. The square bell-tower of the medieval church has a spire added by Thomas Cooley in 1783. The Catholic parish church and the court-house were designed by Francis Johnston. To the west, on the Hill of Lloyd, is the Taylour Column of 1791, in the form of a lighthouse, designed by Henry Aaron Baker.

Kenure Park *Dublin*   *573Kd*
Only George Papworth's giant Corinthian portico of 1842 remains of this once fine mid-18th-century house.

Kilbolane Castle *Cork*   *570Ed*
Two circular towers and two walls survive of the 13th-century castle built by the Cogans, and later acquired by the Earls of Desmond. The water-filled moat on the south-west side can still be seen.

Kilbrittain Castle *Cork*   *570Eb*
A picturesque remnant of a Gothic Revival castle, built around a medieval MacCarthy tower.

Kilcash Castle *Tipp.*   *571Hd*
The stronghold of Kilcash stands on the southern slopes of Slievenamon, north-west of Carrick-on-Suir. It is a typical tower-house with very large chimney-stacks and bartizans, at the side of which are the remains of a great hall. Near by is a small early church with a Romanesque south doorway.

Kilclief Castle *Down*   *575Jc*
A tower-house of the 15th century, built by John Sely, Bishop of Down, as a manorial residence after 1413. There is a high arch between its two eastern turrets. It was thatched in the 18th century.

Kilconnell Friary *Gal.*   *572Ed*
A Franciscan friary founded in *c.* 1414 by William Mor O'Kelly. It has a fine slender tower, but the north range of the cloister buildings is missing. On the eastern side of the south transept are three chapels; the middle one dates from 1512. There is evidence that galleries were inserted in the church to accommodate increased numbers of monks in the later Middle Ages. The glory of Kilconnell is in the two canopied wall-tombs in the nave's north wall. Both have arcaded bases, with tall pinnacles rising to the full height of the canopy. The west tomb, one of the finest of Irish wall-tombs, has six exquisitely carved saints on its base, including St Louis and St Denis, and an inscription to the unknown occupant.

Kilcooly Abbey *Tipp.*   *571He*
A Cistercian abbey founded *c.* 1182 by Donal Mor O'Brien, a daughter-house of Jerpoint. The church, of *c.* 1200, is fairly small and has lost its nave aisles. After almost total destruction in 1445, Abbot Phillips (*d.* 1463) undertook the rebuilding. The chancel was vaulted, the central tower added, and galleries installed because of an increase in the community; the transepts were also vaulted, and an east window, with elaborate tracery, was inserted. The church's unique feature is the use of the western piers of the crossing as niches for the seats of the abbot and his deputy. Almost 2 miles south, at Clonamicklon, are the remains of a large gabled 13th-century castle with a fortified enclosure.

Kilcornan House *Gal.*   *572Dc*
A fine Tudor Revival house with a chapel incorporating a medieval tower; now a school.

Kilcrea Friary *Cork*   *570Eb*
A Franciscan friary of neat and simple plan, founded in 1463 by Cormac McCarthy and still substantially complete. The cloister garth survives. To the north-east of the chancel is a scriptorium, well lit, for manuscript writing. Near by is Cormac McCarthy's Castle, with a tower, courtyard and turret.

Kilcullen *Kild.*   *573Jc*
The modern town is of small interest, but old Kilcullen, 2 miles to the south-west, has the base of a Round Tower, the remains of a Romanesque church, and parts of two stone crosses and a base.

Kildare *Kild.*   *573Hc*
The early remains of Kildare include a fine Round Tower 106 ft high, with a decorated Romanesque doorway. The battlemented parapet is modern. An enigmatic ruin in the churchyard is called St Brigid's Fire House.
ST BRIGID'S CATHEDRAL Probably begun 1229 by Bishop Ralph; it fell into decay during the 17th century, though a new chancel was built *c.* 1686. The church remained a ruin until the restoration by G. E. Street in 1875, which was considerably more successful than most such undertakings.

Kildreenagh *Kerry*   *570Bb*
A small oval graveyard, containing in its north-east corner a tiny oratory and in the north-west

KILCONNELL FRIARY

One of the most beautiful ruins in Ireland, Kilconnell Friary was founded about 1414 by William Mor O'Kelly for the Franciscans and built on the site of an earlier church. Little of the later cloister buildings, and the small cloister with its arcades springing from a low wall, remains. The friary was occupied by English soldiers for nine months in 1596, and in 1651 successfully withstood attack by Cromwell's troops.

corner a clochan. The rest of the enclosure is full of small gravestones. There are other monuments of this kind in the neighbourhood.

Kilfane *Kilk.*   *571Je*
The medieval church incorporates original priests' quarters on the north side. The interior has a sedilia and the effigy of an extremely impressive knight ('Long Cantwell') holding an armorial shield, of *c.* 1320.

Kilfenora *Clare*   *570Dg*
The cathedral, dedicated to St Fachtna, dates from the 12th century, and now incorporates the small, damaged Protestant church. The roofless chancel possesses good Gothic altar-tombs and two primitive medieval episcopal effigies. In the churchyard stands a magnificent 12th-century high cross. One mile east is Ballykinvarga fort, a large cashel built of great blocks of limestone with an encircling bawn of pillar stones nearly 50 ft wide (forming a *chevaux de frise*); there is also a 7 ft standing stone.

Kilkea Castle *Kild.*   *573Jb*
An 1849 reconstruction of a basically medieval castle; it has a haunted room which Gerald, the famous Wizard Earl of Kildare, is supposed to visit every seven years, riding a white horse.

Kilkenny *Kilk.*   *571Je*
In most respects the most interesting inland town in Ireland. The early monastic settlement of St Canice on top of the small hill beside the Nore, now called Irish Town, has left its traces in the Round Tower and a few stones incorporated in the Gothic cathedral. A quarter of a mile to the south on the same side of the Nore is the great Anglo-Norman castle of William the Marshall, best known as the principal seat of the Butlers, Earls, Marquesses and formerly Dukes of Ormonde. The medieval city, and the heart of the present town, was a walled rectangle lying between these points,

with the castle at its south-east corner and its northern boundary formed by the Bradoge R., which separates Irish Town from Kilkenny proper. The main street, called successively The Parade, High Street and Parliament Street, forms the backbone of the town, and its mid-point is marked by the Tholsel. Some fragments of the walls survive, especially at the north-west corner, near the Dominican 'Black Abbey'. A fine 18th-century bridge by George Smith, Green's Bridge of 1765, with five arches separated by piers enriched with pedimented recesses, survives to the east of Irish Town. In the churchyard is the bishop's palace of 1735–6, plain, except for its doorway. The interior has a fine carved and panelled staircase. In the garden is the charming pedimented robing-room, built by Bishop Pococke in 1760. To the west of the churchyard is the library, containing a notable collection of 16th- and 17th-century books; it was founded by Bishop Thomas Otway in 1679. South of this is the mid-18th-century deanery.

The church of the Dominican friary—founded in 1226, re-roofed in the late 16th century and since 1840 again in use—has a typical long preaching transept of the 14th century and a square pedimented tower, inscribed as built by James Shortall, who died in 1537. In the adjoining convent are some good 15th- and 16th-century statuettes and statues. The Franciscan friary in Smithwick's Brewery consists principally of its crossing tower of *c.* 1350; some claustral buildings have been disentangled from the Brewery. St Mary's Church (now a parish hall) has a nave, transepts and a western tower; it is now partly embedded in the raised level of the churchyard. It contains a number of notable arcaded monuments of the 17th century. The Protestant parish church of St John, on the east bank of the Nore, is an 1817 reconstruction of the Lady Chapel of the 'new' Priory and Hospital of St John; it was founded *c.* 1211. Some distance south of this, in Maudlin Street, is a small medieval tower. Kilkenny is noteworthy for the possession of more late-medieval secular buildings than any other town in Ireland. Most of these are now fragmentary, but the Rothe House, a large elaborate town-house of 1594, restored in 1965, now houses the museum and library of the Kilkenny Archaeological Society. In Rose Inn Street is Shee's Almshouse, founded in 1581. There are scanty remains of Kyteler's Inn, associated with the most famous of Irish witchcraft trials in 1324. The south-west angle-tower of the town walls survives, near the junction of Ormonde Road and New Street.

Unlike most Irish towns of its size, Kilkenny retained practical and administrative importance right through the 17th century and into the 18th. Its 18th-century buildings are thus slotted into sites in the still-living medieval city. Most conspicuous of these is the Tholsel, built in 1761, possibly by the amateur architect-builder and marble-quarrier William Colles. It has a Roman-Doric arcade of five bays over the pavement, a council room on the first floor in which are kept the city muniments, and is surmounted by a three-storey octagonal lantern with a clock and pyramidal roof, a reconstruction of c. 1948 of its timber predecessor. A few hundred yards to the north is the court-house of 1794, standing on a vaulted basement now obscured by later work. It has a pedimented Doric centre-piece, with Wyatt windows lighting the main hall and columnar features surmounting the façade. The plan of the interior is a close copy of the vanished Gandon court-house in Waterford, and the external details show mannerisms of the school of Gandon. Opposite the castle garden is a fine terrace of 18th-century houses, one of which contained the Kilkenny theatre. Elsewhere in Kilkenny are numerous 18th-century houses, some characterised by adjoining twin doorways beneath a single fanlight or relieving arch.

On the east bank of the Nore, opposite the castle, is the building (1782) of Kilkenny College, founded in 1666, where Swift and Berkeley went to school; it has a handsome front door with large, Dublin-style fanlight. South of the castle is St James's or Switsir's Asylum, an elegant set of almshouses of 1803, with a swaggering statue of the founder, James Switsir. St Ciaran's College of 1836 is by William Deane Butler, as is the Catholic Cathedral of the Assumption, a short distance south of the 'Black Abbey' fronting James's Green and built from 1843 to 1857. Near by, on the river to the south, is Mill Mount, an interesting cruciform-plan house built by Christopher Colles, the owner of the marble quarries which supplied most of the mantelpieces found in mid-18th-century Irish domestic architecture. To the south-west is Castle Blunden, possibly designed by Francis Bindon, with a later pedimented porch.

CASTLE In its present form, it is a reconstruction in the medieval manner by William Robertson of 1826. The castle was first restored in the late 17th century, but Robertson replaced practically all the remains of the 17th-century Classical work except for the Corinthian pedimented entrance gate on the west side; this may be by Sir William Robinson, and is the earliest substantial fully Classical piece of architecture in the country. Three of the massive cylindrical towers are mainly 13th-century work. Opposite are the unusual castle stables, with their court in the shape of a horse-shoe; they have been sympathetically converted for the Kilkenny Design Workshops. There is a fine collection of Butler family portraits.

ST. CANICE'S CATHEDRAL Successor to a Romanesque church, as witness the adjacent Round Tower

and a few re-used stones, it is the purest in style and one of the most attractive large Gothic churches in Ireland. It is cruciform, with an aisled nave and chapels north and south of the choir; further small chapels open eastward off the transepts, the southern one having been enlarged in the 14th century. The church was built between 1251 and 1286. The central tower fell in 1332 and was rebuilt shortly afterwards. The cathedral is remarkably rich in late medieval and 16th-century altar-tombs and similar monuments, many to the Ormonde Butlers. In the south transept is a magnificent mid-18th-century tomb of Archbishop Cox, builder of Castletown House, and his wife, by Scheemakers.

Kilkieran Crosses *Kilk.*   *571Hd*
Across the valley from Ahenny stand the three crosses of Kilkieran. The west cross, though much damaged, is richly ornamented.

Killadeas *Ferm.*   *574Dc*
The graveyard contains remarkable carved stones.

BISHOP'S STONE, KILLADEAS

Among the remarkable carved stones in the cemetery at Killadeas is this weathered monument to a bishop, dating from the 7th or 8th century. On the west side (above) the bishop is depicted full-face, while on the south side he is shown in profile with the emblems of his office—a crozier and a bell.

Killaloe *Clare*   *570Ff*
The 13th-century Protestant Cathedral of St Flannan has an earlier Romanesque doorway built into the south wall. It is one of the most complete of the aisle-less medieval cathedrals in Ireland. In the churchyard is St Flannan's Oratory, a stone-roofed Romanesque building similar to those at Kells and Glendalough. Higher up the hill, in the churchyard of the Catholic church, is the reconstructed oratory of St Molua from the island of the same name in the Shannon, which was inundated when Ardnacrusha power station was built and the dam created. The little church, which has a chancel with a vaulted stone roof, was carefully taken apart and every stone correctly replaced. Near the town is the early 19th-century Protestant bishop's palace. One mile north is Beal Boru, a massive circular earthwork.

Killamery *Kilk.*   *571He*
A fine sandstone cross; the formal carving includes a heavily weathered hunting scene.

Killarney *Kerry.*   *570Cc*
The best-known of Irish beauty-spots, it has been admired for its mountain and lake scenery and its rich vegetation since the middle of the 18th cen-

tury. Its man-made attractions are less numerous: the best of them is Muckross Abbey. The ruined Aghadoe Cathedral, just outside the town, is of some small interest. The Catholic cathedral, in the town, is perhaps the best in Ireland, and ranks among the principal works of A. W. Pugin. It was begun in 1842 and finished in 1855, the interior being completed by J. J. McCarthy, the foremost Irish church architect of the period of the Gothic Revival.

ROSS CASTLE On an isthmus in Lough Leane is a good 15th-century tower-house with some later additions and a small bawn with flanker-towers.

MUCKROSS ABBEY Founded for Franciscan friars by Donal MacCarthy Mor, probably in c. 1340, on a site said to have been settled by St Finian in the 6th century. The buildings, ruined since a visitation of Cromwell's troops in 1652, date from the 15th century. The tiny cloister is filled by an enormous yew tree.

MUCKROSS HOUSE A gabled Victorian mansion (1843) by Burn, in the heart of the Killarney lake district. The porch was added c. 1870 by William Atkins of Cork. The contents include objects of Irish historic interest—local carved period furniture, pictures, prints, maps and entomological specimens. (Open by appointment.)

Killeshin Laois 573Hb
After Clonfert and possibly Roscrea, Killeshin has probably the finest west doorway of the Irish-Romanesque style, though reset at some unknown date, with four recessed orders, and carving of unparalleled delicacy. It is probably of the early to mid-12th century. The north and west windows are round-headed with triangular gables.

Killevy Armagh 575Gb
On the eastern slopes of Slieve Gullion are two ruined churches, the earlier of which is pre-Romanesque and has a fine megalithic west doorway. The later church has sculptured heads flanking its east window. A mile to the south is a small symmetrical 'castle' of the same name, picturesquely situated, that was designed by George Papworth in 1836.

Killone Abbey Clare 570Df
The Augustinian nunnery, probably dating from c. 1225, has a small cloister-court and a church with an eastern crypt. The east wall of the church has Transitional windows with small columns. A wall-passage pierces their jambs transversely.

Killua Castle Westmeath 573He
Basically an 18th-century house covered with a Gothic mantle, possibly by James Shiel c. 1830. It is now in ruins and with its lodge, lake and follies, and its obelisk marking the alleged planting of the first potato in Ireland by Sir Walter Raleigh, is one of Ireland's most romantic demesnes.

Killyleagh Castle Down 575Jc
The 17th-century castle was almost doubled in size c. 1666, and Sir Charles Lanyon did further work on it. It retains its large walled bawn and entrance gate. (Open by appointment.)

Killymoon Castle Tyrone 574Fd
A cut-stone 'castle', built by John Nash for the Stewart family c. 1803 at a cost of £80,000. (Open by appointment.)

Kilmacduagh Gal. 572Db
The cathedral is now ruined; its western half is 10th century, its eastern half probably 15th. There is some 12th-century work and late medieval transepts to the north and south. The outstanding features are the flamboyant windows in the south chapel and the O'Shaughnessy altar-tomb. Near by stands a 112 ft Round Tower, leaning 2 ft out of the perpendicular.

Kilmalkedar Kerry 570Ad
The church is chiefly remarkable for its internal wall-colonnade of engaged columns. The west doorway has Romanesque decoration and the outer walls are sloping and show, internally, the beginning of a corbelled stone roof.

Kilmallock Lim. 570Ed
This originally walled town was founded by the FitzGerald family and was, until the 16th century, the chief seat of the White Knights. Many remnants survive, including Blossom's Gate, the only survivor of the four original medieval gates; the parish church of SS Peter and Paul, dating from the 13th–15th centuries and incorporating part of the Round Tower; the Dominican church founded in 1291 by Maurice FitzGerald, considerably enlarged in the 14th–15th century and possessing a notable 13th-century five-light window and a reticulated window of the 15th century. The last White Knight, Edmond FitzGibbon, betrayer of the Sugan Earl of Desmond, is commemorated by a monument of 1608.

Kilruddery Wick. 573Kc
A Tudor Revival mansion built by Sir Richard Morrison for the Earl of Meath c. 1820 and now partly demolished. The interior contains a fine pair of Regency drawing-rooms with splendid plasterwork and scagliola columns. The greatest interest of the place lies in the survival of one of Ireland's late 17th- and early 18th-century formal gardens. At the garden front of the house are twin canals, a further pond terminating in a lime avenue. The whole lay-out is composed of cut banks, clipped hedges, and is peopled with many statues. To the right of the main vista is a miniature amphitheatre, a circular beech hedge, fountains, and to the east of the house a huge 19th-century rock garden.

Kilshannig House Cork 570Fc
A notable house with four wings by Davis Ducart, finished in 1765. The wings, until lately partially ruined and lacking their domes, show many resemblances to Castletown House, also by Ducart. The interior contains plasterwork by the Francini brothers and a fine circular staircase. (Not open to the public.)

Kiltartan Castle Gal. 572Dc
The ruins of an extensive 13th-century castle with a strongly defended courtyard.

Kilteel Kild. 573Jc
The reconstructed remains of the Romanesque church are noteworthy for the figure-sculpture in the jambs of the chancel arch, the only instance of sculpture in this part of an Irish-Romanesque church. The subjects include Adam and Eve, Samson and Delilah, and David and Goliath.

Kiltiernan Gal. 572Dc
A monastic site with an early church, a good west door, and the remains of dry masonry; it is enclosed by a fragmentary cashel.

Kiltinan Castle Tipp. 571He
A castle of the Butlers, Barons Dunboyne, situated on a rock above a stream. Three of the angle-towers remain, two of which form a 19th-century house. It was taken by the Cromwellians in 1669.

Kinsale Cork 570Fb
A picturesque Irish seaport. The most important event in Kinsale's history was the double siege of 1601, with the Spaniards in the centre, the English under Mountjoy blockading them, and the Earls of Tyrone and Tyrconnell besieging the English.

This resulted in the massacre of the Spaniards and the flight of the earls; the James Fort on Rinnroin was then fortified by the English. In 1677 the huge Charles Fort on Rinncurran, on the opposite bank of Kinsale Harbour, was designed by Sir William Robinson, architect of the Royal Hospital, Dublin, and remained in military occupation until 1921. Most of the town dates from the 18th century and later, but the building called the Desmond Castle, or French Prison, is a 16th-century tower-house. Kinsale has one of the few medieval parish churches in Ireland still in use, St Multose; it is a substantial 13th-century cruciform building with aisles to north and south. At the north-west angle is a massive tower. The roofless south transept (Chapel of the Blessed Virgin) was built in 1550 by Geoffrey Galway, merchant of the town. The court-house of 1706 is a picturesque building with three curvilinear 'Dutch' gables, hung with slate, and a ground-floor arcade. It was restored in 1958–9 and is now a museum. The 18th-century houses of the town (though many are dilapidated and some have been destroyed) were, until recently, notable for the variety and richness of their fan-lights and ironwork, a few also being slate-hung, in the manner of south-western England. The buildings in Charles Fort include some fine robust 17th- and 18th-century pedimented gate-houses and doorways. On the hillside opposite the gate of St Multose churchyard, where there are some fine monuments, is the handsome cupolaed façade of the Catholic church of 1834.

Kirkistown Castle *Down*   *575Jd*
A tower-house with a large bawn which has twin towers at the western end; it was all built in 1622 by Roland Savage, and is still remarkably complete, having been restored in the 18th century. The Savage family were the principal Norman family occupying the Ards Peninsula.

Knappogue Castle *Clare*   *570Ef*
Built in 1467, the castle was for centuries the seat of the Clan McNamara. In the mid-19th century neo-Gothic additions were made to the medieval structure. The banqueting halls and some reception rooms have since been restored.

Knockdrin Castle *Westmeath*   *573 Hd*
A good Gothic-style castle with an arcaded central hall, built *c.* 1830 by James Shiel for the Levinge family. There is also a baronial lodge.

Knockmany *Tyrone*   *574Ed*
A large circular cairn containing a grave; three of the side stones have Bronze Age decoration. There is a similar grave at Sess Kilgreen, 7 miles away to the north-east.

Knockmoy *Gal.*   *572Dd*
A Cistercian abbey, founded in 1190 by King Cathal O'Conor as a daughter-house of Boyle Abbey. It is a transitional early Gothic building of cruciform plan, chiefly remarkable for the remains on the chancel wall of traces of painting. Their subjects include the Holy Trinity and the Martyrdom of St Sebastian. There are also *graffiti* on the plaster of the chancel walls.

Knocknarea *Sligo*   *574Bc*
On the top of the 1000 ft Knocknarea Mountain is the huge cairn known as Miosgaun Meabha, reputedly the burial-place of Queen Maeve (Queen Mab). It is 200 ft in diameter and 34 ft high, and probably covers a Stone Age grave.

Knowth See Brugh Na Bóinne.

Labbacallee *Cork*   *570Fc*
An early Bronze Age gallery grave, the largest and finest of the wedge type in Ireland.

Lackeen House *Tipp.*   *571Gg*
A 16th-century four-storey tower-house; the third storey is vaulted over. There is an extensive walled bawn. In 1735 the famous Stowe Missal, hidden for safety, was found during alterations.

Landenstown House *Kild.*   *573Jc*
An unpretentious but pleasing house, with wings joined by arches to a central block; built *c.* 1740.

Lawrencetown Arch *Gal.*   *572Fc*
Walter Lawrence built a triumphal arch to commemorate the Irish Volunteers of 1782; it spans a road through the devastated demesne, in which are other follies.

Leacanabuaile *Kerry*   *570Ac*
A 9th–10th-century stone ring-fort containing the bases of four drystone huts, some circular and some rectangular; there are two chambers in the rampart. It has been excavated and partially restored. A quarter of a mile south-east is the stone ring-fort of Cahergal, and 300 yds away another similar.

Leac-an-Scail *Kilk.*   *571Jd*
A very fine portal dolmen, with a steeply sloping capstone.

Leamaneh Castle *Clare*   *570Dg*
The O'Brien castle of Leamaneh consists of a tower of *c.* 1480 to which is joined a splendid 17th-century high-gabled house of four storeys, with rows of mullioned windows.

Ledwithstown House *Long.*   *572Fe*
An extremely interesting, but now decayed, small four-fronted square house with a pedimented front, probably built by Richard Cassels *c.* 1740. (Not open to the public.)

Legananny *Down*   *575Hc*
One of the most impressive dolmens in Ireland, standing on the southern slope of Slieve Croob.

Leigh *Tipp.*   *571He*
Of the two churches at Leigh, the smaller has antae at both ends and the remains of a steep gable; the larger incorporates a smaller, earlier church as its chancel, with much complicated rebuilding.

Leighlinbridge *Carlow*   *571Jf*
The attractively situated Protestant Cathedral of St Laserian, in Old Leighlin, is largely 13th century, with a central tower, a north chapel as wide as the choir, and a north transept. The nave has hardly any windows. The gateway of the churchyard is early 18th-century work.

LEGANANNY DOLMEN

A coffin-shaped capstone with remarkable sharp edges is poised on three graceful uprights. From an altitude of 850 ft, this ancient chamber-tomb commands an impressive view over the surrounding countryside.

THE LIMERICK CROZIER

Made by the order of the Bishop of Limerick in the early 15th century, this crozier and a mitre are still owned by his successor and are the only medieval art treasures in Ireland still in their ancient custody; both are dated 1418. The crozier, made of gilded and enamelled silver, is 6 ft 6 in. tall. It is the only medieval Irish-made crozier in the continental form of a shepherd's crook—Irish pre-Norman croziers were staff-like—and probably came from a large workshop of silversmiths. Six niches around the base of the crook contain exquisitely modelled figures representing the Trinity, the Virgin, and saints; above are six enamelled plates engraved with saints. The figures inside the crook depict the Annunciation. (Treasury, Catholic Cathedral of St John, Limerick)

Leixlip *Kild.*   *573Jd*
The medieval west tower of the later Protestant church is a very complete priests' residence, a sort of ecclesiastical tower-house. Leixlip Castle is basically medieval, altered in the early to mid-18th century by the Conolly family of Castletown. It is remarkable for its octagon Gothic-style glazing.

Letterkenny *Don.*   *574Df*
The Catholic Cathedral of St Eunan, built of Mount Charles stone by Hague and MacNamara in 1890–1901, has stained glass by Michael Healy and Harry Clarke.

Lifford *Don.*   *574Ee*
The county town of Donegal, though hardly more than a suburb of Strabane; it has a handsome court-house of 1745 by Michael Priestley.

Limavady *Lond.*   *574Ff*
A plantation town, formerly a seat of the O'Cahans, where the road crosses the R. Rose. One and a half miles to the east is Drenagh, built for the McCausland family, a chastely Classical house representing one of Sir Charles Lanyon's earliest architectural works.

Limerick *Lim.*   *570Ee*
Like so many seaboard towns, Limerick is a Viking foundation, fortified in the late 12th century by a castle, which has a better claim than most to its title King John's Castle. The city is divided into the old medieval English Town on an island in the Shannon, Irishtown on the mainland, and Newton Pery, the regular late 18th-century development.

The castle was nearly square; its north and south walls survive, the former with round towers at each end and a gateway of two D-shaped towers in the middle, and the latter with only a south-west tower standing. St Mary's Cathedral is among the most interesting of Irish medieval cathedrals. It was founded by King Donal Mor O'Brian in 1172, and its nave, most of the west front and north transept date from before 1195, when it had north and south aisles to the nave; it has now further chapels to the north and south, of later medieval dates, making it in effect five-aisled. The arches across the aisles are unique in Ireland. The 15th-century tower, with 17th-century bells, is 120 ft high and has four corner turrets embattled in the Irish fashion. The whole cathedral was extensively restored between 1857 and 1860 by William Slater of London, though various other architects were involved. The interior fittings include 15th-century choir-stalls with misericords, unique in Ireland, a Carolean tomb of Donogh O'Brian, Earl of Thomond, of 1678, and several other tombs in the chantry chapels; also the bishop's throne, designed in 1831 by James Pain. Thomond Bridge, of 1836, by the castle, is also by James Pain. In Irishtown—across the river from the court-house, presenting a plain front facing Charlotte's Quay and reserving its splendours for the relatively inaccessible river front—is the custom house. It was designed by Davis Ducart, and built between 1765 and 1769. The river front is composed of Corinthian pilasters and a channelled ashlar basement flanked by arcaded wings. In Patrick Street is the town hall of 1805, originally the Mercantile Buildings. To the left, almost next door, is a fine cut-stone Venetian door of Bruce the Banker's house, (possibly by Francis Bindon), and now ruined. Some distance to the east is the charming cut-stone St John's Square, dating from 1751, consisting of ten houses and probably also designed by Francis Bindon. Just off St John's Square is the Catholic Cathedral of St John, 1856–61, by the

English architect P. C. Hardwick, the tower and spire by M. S. Hennessy of Limerick.

The centre of modern Limerick is the cross-roads where Sarsfield Street, leading from the balustraded Sarsfield Bridge (by James Pain, dating from 1827) intersects O'Connell Street, the backbone of the grid plan of Newtown Pery, possibly laid out by Davis Ducart, which extends to the south-west as far as the Crescent. This section of the town dates from well after 1750 and owes its development to the Pery family, Earls of Limerick. Most of the houses are in fact of c. 1790 onwards. The most distinguished houses in Newtown Pery include Lord Limerick's town house and the old bishop's palace in Henry Street, the Crescent, and Pery Square of c. 1840. In the middle of the latter is the Spring-Rice Monument, by Alexander Nimmo, near by is the Church of St Alphonsus Liguori of 1858–62 by P. C. Hardwick; near it is the public library and art gallery, and St Michael's Church facing down Pery Square. In Baker Street is St Saviour's Dominican church, started by James Pain in 1817, but totally re-modelled by Maurice Hennessy, George Goldie and J. J. McCarthy from 1860 onwards. Inside is a 17th-century Flemish statue of the Virgin and Child. In Glentworth Street is a Savings Bank by W. H. Owen, in the form of a small Doric temple. Holy Trinity Church, formerly the Church of the Blind Asylum, has a recessed Ionic portico by J. Fogarty, and the Franciscan Church of the Immaculate Conception in Henry Street has an attenuated Corinthian portico by W. E. Corbett of 1876. On the Tipperary Road are the city gaol building of 1821, with a Doric grand entrance. Athlunkard Bridge on the Killaloe Road, by James Pain, dates from 1830. On the west bank of the Shannon, almost opposite the castle, is the Treaty Stone on which the Treaty of Limerick is alleged to have been signed. The modern Church of our Lady of the Rosary, on the Ennis Road, is adorned with stained glass and sculpture by modern artists.

Liscarroll Castle *Cork*   570Ed
The third largest 13th-century castle in Ireland, consisting of an enormous rectangular bawn with corner round towers and intermediate towers on the south and north.

Lismore *Waterford*   571Gc
The castle, strikingly situated high above the Blackwater on the site of a medieval episcopal building, subsequently the residence of the Boyles, Earls of Cork, was later inherited by the Dukes of Devonshire. It was extensively remodelled in 1850 by Sir Joseph Paxton and Henry Stokes. (Not open to the public.) Below, spanning the Blackwater, is the handsome inscribed mid-18th-century bridge by Thomas Ivory, the earliest of his works. The Protestant Cathedral of St Carthage was largely rebuilt in 1688 by Sir William Robinson. It has an elegant spire of 1827, probably by G. R. Pain. The mid-16th-century tomb of the McGrath family in the nave is noteworthy. A few miles to the west, in woods north of the river, are the remarkable Gothic gates and Gothic castle bridge of Bally-saggartmore; the owner spent so much money on his gates and bridge that the house was never built.

Lissan Rectory *Tyrone*   574Fe
An interesting example of John Nash's 'villa' style, built for the Rev. John Staples in 1807. (Open by appointment.)

Lodge Park *Kild.*   573Jd
The moderately-sized house is extended by four detached pavilions, giving an elongated five-part composition which is perhaps the most extreme example of this Irish Palladian style. It was probably designed by Nathaniel Clements and built 1775–7 for Hugh Henry, a rich banker.

Lohort Castle *Cork*   570Ec
A remarkably well-preserved 15th-century tower-house, reduced in 1650 by the Cromwell-

TUROE STONE, NEAR LOUGHREA

This rare Irish remnant of the Celtic Iron Age culture which originated at La Tène (Switzerland) and reached Ireland about the 3rd century BC, stands 4 ft high.

ians and restored in the 18th century. It was completely and elaborately refurbished in 1876. (Not open to the public.)

Londonderry See Derry.

Longford *Long.*   572Fe
The most distinguished building in the town is the Catholic Classical St Mel's Cathedral, started in 1840 by Joseph B. Keane, and not completed until 1893 when the portico to the design of George G. Ashlin was added; the belfry of 1860 is by John Burke. In the Diocesan College near by is a collection of local antiquities. Longford's 18th-century church has a fine tower and spire. A few miles to the north-east is Carrigglass Manor by William Robertson, of 1830, with distinguished Classical stables and an entrance arch by James Gandon.

Lorrha *Tipp.*   571Gg
The Dominican friary, built in 1269 by Walter de Burgo, has a long rectangular church with a stone screen in the centre. In the nave is a typical Jacobean armorial monument. The Augustinian church has a good Perpendicular doorway with ogee-shaped hood. There is also the elaborate base of a large cross with an animal frieze.

Lough Cutra Castle *Gal.*   572Db
The most romantically situated and the finest surviving of John Nash's extraordinary Gothic Revival castles in Ireland, begun c. 1816 and executed by the Pain Brothers. The Limerick Lodge is also by Nash.

Lough Gur *Lim.* 570Fe
One of the richest concentrations of ancient remains in Ireland, including monuments from the Neolithic to the medieval period; among them is the largest stone circle in the country, numerous forts, house sites, pillar-stones, cairns, cultivation-terraces, crannogs and a good 15th-century tower-house.

Loughmoe Castle *Tipp.* 571Gf
A 17th-century semi-fortified house added to a 15th-century tower, Loughmoe was a seat of the Purcells, whose monuments may be seen in the nearby church. There is a fine fire-place in a first-floor room, bearing armorials and initials.

Loughrea *Gal.* 572Ec
The Catholic Cathedral of St Brendan, by William Byrne of 1897–1903, though intrinsically of small merit, contains a rich collection of the best modern Irish ecclesiastical art, most notably stained glass by A. E. Childe, Sarah Purser, Hubert McGoldrick, Michael Healy and Evie Hone. The Virgin and Child in the chapel is by John Hughes, and there are embroideries designed by Jack Yeats. Part of the town gate, near the cathedral, is now a museum of ecclesiastical art; there is also a ruined church of the Carmelite friary of 1300. Four miles to the north-east is the famous Turoe Stone, covered with splendid La Tène abstract ornament.

Lucan House *Dublin* 573Jd
An important medium-sized house, free-standing; like some other Irish houses, it is joined by an underground passage to the detached service buildings. It was built *c.* 1776 by the Rt. Hon. Agmondisham Vesey, an amateur architect, partly to his own designs but with some help from Chambers and, for the very fine decoration of the principal rooms, from James Wyatt and Michael Stapleton. It has an elevated central frontispiece with Ionic engaged columns and a pediment which was copied at Charleville, Co. Wicklow. The small demesne is attractively laid out by the Liffey, and contains a fine Coade-stone monument designed by Wyatt and a Gothic rustic hermitage. The house is now the official residence of the Italian Ambassador.

Lusk *Dublin* 573Kd
The mid-19th-century church in this pretty village is built on to a 15th-century tower which consists of a square body with three circular turrets at its angles, attached to an early Christian Round Tower which is thus used as the fourth angle-tower. The whole tower was in turn copied at Balrothery, 5 miles further north, though there is no pre-existing Round Tower. There are some good medieval and later tombs in the tower.

Luttrellstown Castle *Dublin* 573Kd
Probably an early work by Sir Richard Morrison of *c.* 1800, the entrance front marred by a Victorian porch. The landscape garden—complete with lake, Doric temple, series of waterfalls and Gothic ruin—is one of the most effective in Ireland. (Not open to the public.)

Lyles Hill *Antrim* 575Hd
A large hill-top enclosure of Neolithic date, unique in Ireland and well known as having given its name to a type of pottery found in it. The extensive settlement was first spotted on aerial photographs.

Lyons House *Kild.* 573Jc
Built in 1797 for Nicholas Lawless by Sir Richard Morrison. Severely neo-Classical wings and colonnades were added *c.* 1810 by the first Lord Cloncurry. It contains notable landscape decora-

tion in the dining-room, and the demesne contains the largest artificial lake in Ireland. The pedimented arch from Brownes Hill has been re-erected here. It is now an agricultural college.

Magh Adhair *Clare* 570Ef
An inauguration place of Kings of Thomond, sited in an amphitheatre of low hills. It consists of a large mound, 20 ft high, with a flat top 100 by 80 ft, and surrounded by a fosse and an external bank.

Maghera *Lond.* 575Ge
OLD CHURCH The most interesting feature of the ruined church is the unique carved lintel of the west doorway, depicting the crucified Christ surrounded by smaller figures. It has been assigned to an early date but is probably late 11th century.

Malahide Castle *Dublin* 573Kd
Seat of the Norman family of Talbot since medieval times, enlarged by twin towers and battlements *c.* 1765, it now houses the National Portrait Gallery. There is a notable garden.

Mallow *Cork* 570Ec
Mallow was famous for its social life in the 18th and early 19th century, when it was a spa, and it still bears some signs of its former elegance.
MALLOW CASTLE Built by Sir Thomas Norreys *c.* 1600, it has a main front flanked by polygonal towers, a polygonal central porch and a polygonal projection at the back once containing the stairs and garderobes. Although the house has relatively large windows, it also has, as was usual at the time, clearly defensive features. Near by is the early 19th-century Tudor Revival manor house of the Jephson family, descendants of the Norreys. Six miles south are the ruins of Mourne Abbey, a fortified property of the Knights Templar.

Marino, Casino See Dublin.

Markree Castle *Sligo* 574Cb
An earlier house was refaced by Francis Johnston in the castle style in 1803. It has particularly fine gates and lodges, designed by John Goodwin in 1832.

Marlay Grange *Dublin* 573Kc
A seat of the La Touche family, of late 18th century date. It has good plasterwork and there are extensive stables.

Maynooth *Kild.* 573Jd
A well laid-out town, it is chiefly remarkable for being the seat of St Patrick's College, founded by the Irish Parliament in 1795 for the education of the Irish priesthood. Beside the old church at the entrance to the college are the shattered remains of the gate-tower and massive keep of the 13th-century castle. The earliest building of the college is Stoyte House, built by Michael Stapleton with additions of 1845 by A. W. Pugin, including a Gothic quadrangle culminating in J. J. McCarthy's college chapel, whose spire, the highest in Ireland, is in proportion not just to the chapel but to the whole college. The college museum has a collection of antiquities and works of art. In the sacristy is Viavicenzi's *Flight into Egypt*. On the Dublin road, to the right, is the Conolly Folly, closing the main vista to Castletown.

Mellifont Abbey *Louth* 573Je
At Mellifont, *c.* 1142, a band of Irish and French monks, at the instigation of St Malachy, founded the first monastery (Cistercian) of Classical European form in Ireland. This sounded the death knell not merely of the Celtic type of monastery, but of the whole native ecclesiastical system, and from Mellifont descend all other Cistercian monasteries in Ireland. The remains now visible on the banks of

the little R. Mattock, on a typically secluded Cistercian site, consist of the foundations of the church, the chapter house, some remnants of the claustral buildings and, most conspicuous of all, about half an octagonal lavabo which occupies part of the cloister-garth. The church was consecrated in 1157. Part of the round-headed cloister arcade has been re-erected.

Midleton *Cork* 570Fb
Founded *c.* 1670 by the Brodrick family, later Earls of Midleton, it has in the Main Street a good mid-18th-century arcaded market house, complete with clock and cupola. The Protestant church, by the Pain brothers, dates from 1825.

Mitchelstown *Cork* 570Fd
Planned on a generous scale, with wide streets and squares, Mitchelstown is particularly remarkable for the group of almshouses called Kingston College for Decayed Gentlefolk, founded by the King family in 1771. The two-storey buildings, with a chapel set in the middle, are punctuated by pedimented features by John Morrison.

Moira *Down* 575Hd
The Protestant parish church, a simple rectangle with a western tower, built in 1723, has a distinguished west front with a pedimented doorway; the octagonal spire is a replacement of 1884. The altar rails have Gothic Revival ironwork. John Wesley preached here, and W. B. Yeats's grandfather was curate in 1835.

Moiry Castle *Arm.* 575Gb
Commanding the Gap of the North, it is a campaign fort of 1600–2, consisting of a square tower eccentrically set within a rectangular bawn; the exterior corners have many musketry loopholes.

Monaghan *Mon.* 573Hg
Incorporated in 1614 by James I, the town has some interesting buildings, including a distinguished ashlar pedimented market house of 1791–2, designed and signed by the amateur architect Samuel Hayes of Avondale for the first Lord Rossmore. The Catholic Cathedral of St Macartan is a distinguished Gothic Revival work of 1861–92, designed by J. J. McCarthy. The Cross of Clogher is kept in the Diocesan College.

Monaincha Abbey *Tipp.* 571Gg
An island monastery, now in the centre of a drained marsh; it was founded by St Canice of Aghaboe, but only the 12th-century church with transeptal sacristy and part of a 12th-century cross remain. The west doorway has inclined jambs and some fine ornament, as has the chancel arch.

Monasterboice *Louth* 573Ke
The three crosses at Monasterboice are perhaps the best known of the Irish high crosses. The north cross is fairly plain, except for a simple inscription and spiral composition on the west and east faces respectively; the shaft is modern. The south cross, known as Muiredach's Cross, is dateable, for on the west face of the shaft is an inscription to Abbot Muiredach who died in 846. It is one of the finest of the earlier Irish figured crosses and the subjects include the Fall, the Murder of Abel, the Last Judgment, and SS Anthony and Paul in the desert. The summit of the cross is in the form of a shingle-roofed church. The west cross is exceptionally tall and carved with scriptural subjects. There is also a Round Tower, two early grave-slabs, two churches and a sun-dial.

Monasterevin *Kild.* 573Hc
A handsome canal-town with well-built merchants' houses and warehouses of *c.* 1800. Beside

MUIREDACH'S CROSS

During the Viking wars of the 9th and 10th centuries, in which so much Irish art was lost, carved crosses of durable stone appeared all over the country. Many survive, and this is the finest and most complete. It is 17 ft 8 in. tall and carved from a single piece of sandstone. The west face of the cross is shown and the bottom panel (below) depicts the mocking of Christ. (Monasterboice)

the canal is an austere pedimented Charter School of *c.* 1740, now a warehouse. Moore Abbey is a large 18th-century castellated house with Gothic style windows. It is now a hospital.

Monasternagalliaghduff or Old Abbey *Lim.* 570De
The ruins of this Augustinian nunnery comprise a long rectangular church with good pointed west door and, exceptionally, a walled cloister-court west of the church; other remains include gatehouses, a dove-cote and a fish-pond.

Monasternenagh *Lim.* 570Ee
A Cistercian abbey founded in 1148 by Turlough O'Brien; it is a daughter-house of Mellifont Abbey, and the remains are extremely fragmentary, but have some interesting late Romanesque and Transitional features—good leaf-carved capitals of red sandstone, a 15th-century screen and round-headed west windows.

Monea *Ferm.*   *574Dc*
In close proximity to one another at Monea are a crannog in the middle of a small lake, the early 17th-century Plantation castle, and an 18th-century or early 19th-century farmhouse, neatly representing three successive types of dwelling. The castle, which is the best Plantation castle in Ulster, is rectangular, with two Round Towers with Scottish corbelled projections.

Monkstown Castle *Cork*   *570Fb*
Built *c.* 1636 by Anastasia Archdeacon, and now empty. It is a gabled house with angle-machicolations and a good fire-place of 1636.

Moone *Kild.*   *573Jb*
An unusually slender 9th-century granite high cross, pieced together in the 19th century. The panels contain extremely stylised figures of St Paul, St Anthony, the Flight into Egypt, the Twelve Apostles and the Multiplication of the Loaves and Fishes.

Moore Hall *Mayo*   *572Ce*
The ruined shell of classical Moore Hall stands on a peninsula in Lough Carra and is evocative of the scenes in George Moore's novels and autobiographical writings. John Moore, the builder of the house, was an active participant in the French-associated Connacht rising in 1798, as President of the 'Republic of Connacht'.

Mount Congreve *Waterford*   *571Jd*
A Georgian house, seat of the Congreves, entirely refaced and remodelled in 1965; the interior, too, has been re-decorated. The gardens adjoining the R. Suir are prolific in sub-tropical flora. With an abundance in spring of rhododendrons and azaleas, the walled gardens offer herbaceous and shrub borders in mid-summer, a speciality of michaelmas daisies in September, and late-flowering shrubs as the season closes. (Gardens open by appointment.)

Mount Ievers *Clare*   *570Ef*
A remarkable example of the cubical, almost doll's-house-like verticality found in many less distinguished Irish houses. The entrance front is of ashlar stone and the garden front of brick. It was designed by William Rothery in 1736 for Henry Ievers. (Not open to the public.)

Mount Juliet *Kilk.*   *571Je*
Built *c.* 1780 for the Earl of Carrick; it has rich Adam-style ornament in the principal rooms and is surrounded by a splendid demesne. (Not open.)

Mountmellick *Laois*   *573Gc*
A town whose sober neatness is evidence of its Quaker origin; with good 18th-century houses.

Mount Sandel Fort *Lond.*   *575Gf*
One mile south of Coleraine, the earthen ring-fort stands 150 ft above the R. Bann, and was later adapted by the Anglo-Normans. It is one of the few places in Ireland that have yielded megalithic flint implements.

Mount Stewart Gardens *Down*   *575Jd*
On the narrow Ards Peninsula, the Dowager Marchioness of Londonderry began, in 1921, to transform the garden of her home, Mount Stewart. Today, a terrace leads to an Italian garden from which steps descend to the Spanish garden, so-called because the summerhouse tiles came from Spain. A paved garden in the form of a shamrock has a bed shaped like the Red Hand of Ulster, planted with red-leaved plants. The top of

a cypress hedge is shaped to represent a hunting party. From the formal gardens, paths lead to 80 acres of gently undulating ground in which, because of high humidity and lack of frost, rare sub-tropical plants thrive. The Temple of the Winds is by James Stuart. (Open to the public.)

Mount Usher Gardens *Wicklow*   *573Kb*
The gardens at Mount Usher, on either side of the R. Vartry, are between the Wicklow Mountains and the sea; they were first laid out in 1868 by the Walpole family. Although the gardens specialise in rare and tender plants, including the dazzling blue Chilean crocus, large groups of native plants grow along the sides of the river.

Moyne Friary *Mayo*   *572Cg*
A Franciscan friary on the shores of Killala Bay, begun *c.* 1460 by MacWilliam Burke and fairly complete, though burnt by Sir Richard Bingham in 1590. There is the usual slender central tower and a good cloister. The reader's desk in the projecting window of the refectory is worthy of note, as are the 16th-century *graffiti* on the plaster of the west nave wall. The west door has Renaissance detail.

Muckross Friary See Killarney.

Muckross House See Killarney.

Multyfarnham *Westmeath*   *573Ge*
A distinguished Franciscan friary which incorporates in its church the nave, tower and south transept of its 13th-century predecessor, sacked in 1601 but occupied later in the century. One and a half miles to the south-west is Wilson's Hospital, a Protestant boarding school housed in an important Palladian complex, designed by John Pentland *c.* 1760. The pedimented central block, surmounted by a cupola, has a central court with open arcading in the basement. The chapel has most of its original fittings, including a good door and a gallery. On either side, curved wings lead to pavilions in the true Palladian manner, making the arrangement reminiscent of a country house.

Naas *Kild.*   *573Jc*
The county town of Kildare, and formerly one of the royal seats of Leinster. The motte of the FitzGerald castle may still be seen. The Catholic parish church of SS Mary and David, in the Gothic style, is by Thomas Cobden of Carlow and dates from 1827. The towers and spire, of 1858, are modelled on St Andrew's Church, Ewerby, Lincolnshire.
   At Oldtown, three-quarters of a mile to the north, is the last remaining pavilion of Ireland's first Palladian house, designed for himself by Colonel Thomas Burgh, Surveyor-General of Ireland, who died in 1730.

Navan *Meath*   *573Je*
The county town of Meath has the mote of its Anglo-Norman castle, but little else of interest except the earliest known sculpture (1792) by Edward Smyth—the Crucified Christ in wood, his only religious work—in the Catholic cathedral. The cathedral was built in 1836, with galleries on three sides, but has been spoilt by later embellishments.

Navan Fort (Eamhain Macha) *Arm.*   *575Gc*
An 18-acre hill-fort enclosed by a bank 800 ft in diameter, with central mound and the remains of a ploughed-out rath. Traditionally this was the seat of the Kings of Ulster.

Nenagh *Tipp.*   *570Ff*
The cylindrical keep of Nenagh Castle, the finest of its kind in Ireland, was built *c.* 1200 by Theobald FitzWalter. The present top storey and

battlements are of *c.* 1860, but in general it is very well preserved. Fragments of its bailey and drum towers and of a rectangular gate-house survive. There is also a good 19th-century court-house.

Nendrum *Down*   *575Jd*
The remains of the monastery of St Mochaoi were virtually unknown until Bishop Reeves described them in 1845. Excavation in 1922–4 exposed the remarkably complete plan of a monastic enclosure, with three concentric cashels, numerous small buildings (some of them circular), a graveyard, a church with nave and chancel, a sun-dial and the stump of a Round Tower, all dating from before the destruction of the monastery in 974. The monastic bell was found where it had evidently been hidden in a crevice in the wall and, together with many interesting finds—writing tablets and materials of the monastic school—is now in the Ulster Museum, Belfast.

Newbridge House *Dublin*   *573Kd*
Designed by Richard Castle *c.* 1737. It has good plasterwork and a notable drawing-room picture gallery of *c.* 1745.

Newbury Hall *Kild.*   *573Hd*
Built *c.* 1765 for Viscount Harberton and probably designed by Nathaniel Clements. It is a sister-house to Colganstown, but is built of brick and has curved sweeps leading to wings with central half-octagon projections, all of brick. There is good interior decoration in the rococo manner.

Newcastle *Dublin*   *573Jc*
The parish church has a tower-house style west tower and, reset in the east wall of the roofed nave, the fine curvilinear east window from the roofless chancel. The rectory close by is a handsome small house of the mid-18th century, with traces of an ornamental canal in the garden.

Newcastle West Castle *Lim.*   *570De*
Formerly one of the chief seats of the Earls of Desmond; it has two halls, one 80 ft long, the other, known as Desmond's Hall, on a vaulted basement. They date from the late 15th century.

Newgrange See Brugh na Bóinne.

Newhall House *Clare*   *570Df*
A fine red-brick house, probably designed by Francis Bindon *c.* 1745. The entrance hall contains a cupboard masked as an elaborate organ case.

Newmarket on Fergus *Clare*   *570Ef*
In Kilnasoolagh church is a notable monument, with a recumbent figure and baroque trappings, of Sir Donough O'Brien, by William Kidwell and dating from 1717.

New Ross *Wex.*   *571Jd*
The large 13th-century ruined town church of St Mary was probably founded by William the Marshall, the effective founder of Anglo-Norman Ireland, and is among the earliest purely Gothic works in the country. As elsewhere, a much later Protestant church stands within the walls—in this case, in the nave. There are many interesting windows and tombs. The Tholsel is a distinguished cut-stone building of 1749, originally arcaded, rebuilt in 1806 by John Robertson, 'carpenter and architect' as a tablet records; it is surmounted by an octagonal and domed cupola. The early 19th-century Catholic Church of SS Mary and Michael possesses a *Pietà* by John Hogan.

Newry *Down*   *575Gc*
The town's frontier situation made it a strategic place at an early date. John de Courcy built a castle here, of which no trace remains, about 1180.

The town has a regular plan beside the canal and the river, the Main Street punctuated by two small squares; it owes much to the canal from Lough Neagh, the earliest in the British Isles, which was begun in 1729 by Sir Edward Lovett Pearce and Richard Castle. There are still some 18th-century houses, with curvilinear gables of the Dublin type, in Boat Street. Other interesting Georgian houses exist in Trevor Hill and Upper Water Street. The east gate of the White Linen Hall of 1783 has good detailing, with a key-patterned frieze and plaques of a spinning wheel and an Irish harp on either side of the arch. The Bank of Ireland occupies a town house of 1826 attributable to Francis Johnston. The court-house dates from 1843, and beside the canal are many fine warehouses with their hoists.

Newtownards *Down*   *575Jd*
The town mainly owes its origin to Sir Hugh Montgomery, who laid it out in the early 17th century, restored the priory church and built a polygonal market-house with pyramidal roof. The most distinguished building is the town hall, complete with cupola and pedimented portal, designed by Ferdinando Stratford of Bristol in 1765.

Newtown Castle *Clare*   *570Dg*
A 16th-century tower, nearly round in plan; it rises from a square base on which is the entrance door. Ingeniously placed shot-holes protect its four sides.

Newtownstewart *Tyrone*   *574Ee*
A well laid out town with a Plantation castle built in 1618 by Sir Robert Newcomen, with triple crow-stepped gables and mullioned windows.

Omagh *Tyrone*   *574Ed*
The county town, with a good Classical court-house. The Catholic church contains the 9th-century Black Bell of Drumragh.

Pallas *Gal.*   *572Ec*
A 16th-century tower-house with a bawn and gatehouse, all well preserved.

Palliser House See Rathfarnham.

Parkes Castle *Leit.*   *574Cc*
On the shores of Lough Gill, the impressive 16th-century enclosure consists of a large bawn with two flanking towers, one of which forms part of the living quarters.

Portaferry *Down*   *575Jc*
The town lies on the east side of the narrow entrance to Strangford Lough; the castle is a tower-house of the early 16th century. Portaferry House was designed by Charles Lilly in 1790 and completed by William Farrell in 1814, for the Nugent family; it has a good staircase, and Regency plaster decoration and fittings. The court-house dates from 1800.

Portarlington *Laois*   *573Hc*
An interesting town, founded by John Ruvigny, Earl of Galway, in 1667, and populated with Huguenots (French Protestants). It has two Protestant churches of which the 'English' church is now disused; the graveyard of the 'French' church contains gravestones inscribed in French, some only about 100 years old. Many of the handsome 18th-century houses facing the R. Barrow turn their backs to the street in the French fashion. In the centre of the square is the simple but beautifully proportioned market-house of *c.* 1800.

Port Hall *Don.*   *574Ee*
Built in 1746 for John Vaughan of Buncrana Castle, by Michael Priestley, the designer of Lifford Court-house, as an office, occasional dwelling and warehouse. It has been restored.

Port Laoise *Laois*   *573Hb*
Formerly, and still by many, called Maryborough, it is the county town of Laois. The Protestant church tower is topped by an obelisk spire designed by James Gandon. The court-house, by Sir Richard Morrison, adjoins the massive rusticated and pilastered façade of the old gaol.

Portumna Castle *Gal.*   *572Ec*
The huge semi-fortified house, perhaps the finest of its kind in Ireland, was built in 1618 at a cost of £10,000. It was entered via two spacious forecourts in succession, one of which has a fine Classical gateway with Tuscan columns and entablature, possibly the earliest of its type in Ireland, and now much overgrown. The castle was accidentally burnt in 1826. It still has an array of 'Jacobean' small gables, decorated with pedestals and balls, on all four fronts. There are remains of internal plasterwork. The house has massive corner towers, partly defensive, and the round-headed doorway is elaborately decorated. Portumna Abbey was furnished with a Cistercian cell, which became Dominican *c.* 1426; the church is aisle-less and has unusual tracery in its east window and in the south window of the transept. Two arcades of the small cloister have been re-erected.

Poulnabrone *Clare*   *572Cc*
A portal-grave with very large, thin flat capstone in the middle of a low circular cairn.

Powerscourt House *Wicklow*   *573Kc*
Together with its gardens and splendid estate, Powerscourt was one of the most impressive large houses in the Dublin area until the central block was accidentally destroyed by fire in 1974. It was built by Richard Castle around the core of an earlier semi-fortified house. Low arcades connect the central block to two-storey pavilions, beyond which are carved walls containing pedimented gateways and terminating in obelisks. The front is a composition of six Ionic pilasters carrying a pediment and voluted attic, and between them roundels containing busts.

The gardens (1400 acres), laid out in 1745 for the 1st Viscount Powerscourt, are among the best in the world, with terraces, wooded demesne, deer park, a 400 ft waterfall and Japanese garden. The terraces were begun in 1745, and finally completed in 1867: the top terrace is 800 ft long (oriented east–west) and from it there is a descent by steps of grass slopes to a balustraded platform which has wrought-iron work from the balcony of a German castle. The descent continues to the Triton Pool, where statues of the winged horses of Fame and Victory stand. The gateway to the garden was once a cathedral door.

Proleek *Louth*   *573Kf*
The Proleek Stone, or Giant's Load, is a massive, almost spherical capstone balanced on three points.

Quin Friary *Clare*   *570Ef*
Within the square enclosure of the great fortress built *c.* 1280, MacCon MacNamara founded in 1433 a Franciscan friary under licence from the Pope. The south curtain wall, and part of the east and west walls, were incorporated in the church, which has a tower separating the nave from the chancel, and a south transept with angle buttresses; to the north lies the cloister. The cloister arcades which support the building above have pointed arches in pairs between the buttresses; the capitals,

shafts and bases are worked with resourceful variety. The friary survived well into the 19th century, and the last friar, who died in 1820, was buried in the north-east corner of the cloister. The Church of St Finghin near by is early 13th-century, with three lancet windows in its east wall.

Rademon *Down*   *575Jc*
The Presbyterian church of 1787 is a T-shaped building in plan, with arms of equal length. There are galleries in all three arms and a pulpit in the centre of the long wall. It has good fittings.

Rahan *Offaly*   *573Gc*
St Cartach founded three small churches at Rahan; the most remarkable early feature is the chancel arch, with bulbous bases and human-headed capitals, of the larger church, which is still in use as the Protestant parish church. A very early date has been claimed for this church, but other authorities assign it to *c.* 1100. The plan of the church is unique, in having had small chambers to the north and south of the vaulted chancel, and so is the circular Romanesque east window—but this has probably been reset. The small ruined church is a 15th-century rebuilding, incorporating a fine small early west doorway.

Raphoe *Don.*   *574De*
Here is one of the last of the semi-fortified corner-towered block-shaped houses in Ireland. It was built in 1636 by the Protestant Bishop, John Leslie; the third storey, with battlements and bartizans, is probably late 18th century. The Gibbs entrance doorway must date from the early part of that century. The Cathedral of St Eunan (Protestant) incorporates some fragments of Romanesque and medieval buildings, and was rebuilt in 1700 with a 17th-century voluted porch. The tower is of 1738 and there are two pre-Romanesque doorways.

Rathbeale *Dublin*   *573Kd*
A late 17th-century house, refaced and enlarged by curved walls and wings in the Palladian manner.

POWERSCOURT HOUSE GARDENS

Eight splendid terraces lead steeply southwards from the house to the Triton Pool, and beyond are views of the Wicklow Mountains and the conical dome of the Sugar Loaf Mountain. The terraces were begun in 1745 and completed in 1867. This view is from the highest one, 800 ft long. The third terrace, the focus of the whole design, is paved with black and white stones from the nearby beach at Bray, set in a striking geometrical pattern, and flanked by 18th-century bronze statues; the wrought-iron work is from the balcony of a castle in Hamburg. Winged horses of Fame and Victory stand guard beside the Triton Pool. The gardens' gate was once the door of Bamberg Cathedral, Germany.

Rathcline Castle *Long.*   *572Fe*
A Butler house, of which a fine Classical gateway still exists.

Rathfarnham Castle *Dublin*   *573Kc*
A large rectangular Elizabethan semi-fortified house, built shortly before 1585 by Adam Loftus, Archbishop successively of Armagh and Dublin, later Chancellor of Ireland and first Provost of Trinity College. In 1767 it was bought by the 2nd Earl of Ely, who modernised it in 1770–1 with Sir William Chambers as architect. It contains fine neo-Classical decoration, and is now a Jesuit house.
PALLISER HOUSE A tall, red-brick house near Rathfarnham Castle, built for the Palliser family but most notable as the residence of George Grierson, the king's printer in Ireland. It was probably built *c.* 1730 and is by Pearce or one of his followers. It is now part of a Loreto Convent.
ST ENDAS An 18th-century house by an unknown architect. It is in neo-Classical style with a Doric portico and low curved wings. It is now a museum to the Pearse family.

Rathgall *Wicklow*   *573Jb*
Unusually for eastern Ireland, this great fort is built of dry stone, as in the west; it covers 18 acres and is 1000 ft in diameter, the central fort being 150 ft across, though much ruined.

Rathlin Island *Antrim*   *575Hg*
Ireland's largest inhabited island, Rathlin lies 8 miles north of Ballycastle. Below the lighthouse is the cave where Robert the Bruce hid in 1306 after his defeat by the English at Perth, and saw the famous spider. At Knockans are traces of an early monastic settlement of the 11th century. Boatmen take visitors to the island from Ballycastle.

Rathmacknee Castle *Wex.*   *571Kd*
A picturesque 15th-century tower-house, with stepped battlements and a well-preserved five-sided bawn with a bartizan on one corner.

Rattoo *Kerry*   *570Ce*
A Round Tower 92 ft high, with a restored roof and the remains of a small church; in the churchyard are some typical Kerry mausoleums and tombs.

Reask *Kerry*   *570Ad*
A late Celtic stone, with beautiful incised ornament—the remains of an early monastery.

Rich Hill Manor House *Arm.*   *575Gc*
An interesting mansion built by Edward Richardson, M.P., between 1655 and 1696; its Dutch gables are of a kind formerly common in Ireland. (Not open to the public.)

Riverstown House *Cork*   *570Fc*
An early 18th-century house built for Jemmett Browne, Bishop of Cloyne; it is chiefly notable for its splendid stucco decoration by the Francini brothers in 1745.

Roche Castle *Louth*   *573Jf*
Built in the late 13th century on a rock overlooking a pass in the southern Armagh hills; it consists of a large walled bailey separated from the castle by a rock-cut fosse.

Rockfleet Castle *Mayo*   *572Bf*
A typical 16th-century tower-house on the shores of Clew Bay, chiefly interesting as being the only known residence of the celebrated Grainne Mhaille, or Grace O'Malley.

Roodstown Castle *Louth*   *573Jf*
A 'ten-pound castle', so-called because of a statute of 1429 which subsidised the building of castles within the Pale, or English-controlled area. It consists of a small tower with two turrets, and has a particularly fine twin ogee-headed window.

Roscommon *Roscom.*   *572Ee*
The county town. The Dominican Friary, founded in 1253 and rebuilt in 1453, contains a late 13th-century effigy of the founder, Felim O'Conor, with 15th-century additions.
ROSCOMMON CASTLE A large keep-less castle built in 1280 by Robert de Ufford, Justiciar of Ireland, as a Crown fortress; it was later held by the O'Conors. Its courtyard has D-shaped towers, a square south gate, and a drawbridge. It was much altered, notably by Sir Nicholas Malbie, who *c.* 1580 made the many mullioned windows.

Roscrea *Tipp.*   *571Gg*
The early monastic remains of St Cronan consist of a west front and gable of the church, an elegant composition with a central gabled doorway, flanked by four similar gabled recesses within moulded pilasters, all probably of the early 12th century. Across the road is the stump of a Round Tower. There is also a figured 12th-century high cross, the shaft decorated with interlaced vine patterns, and on the west face a Crucifixion in high relief. The town castle was built on an earlier mote castle in 1280, which was granted in the following year to Edmund Butler. A tall gate-tower has stepped gables and chimneys dating

HEROIC VIRTUE

In 1734, the Francini brothers, Paul and Philip, burst on the Irish scene. Nothing is known of their origins. They introduced the use of the human figure into Irish decorative plasterwork, and their example was immediately followed by the native craftsmen, who were quick to learn the new techniques. The dining-room at Riverstown House contains eight exquisite wall plaques derived from Classical sources. There is also a superb ceiling based on a painting by Poussin entitled 'Time rescuing Truth from the assaults of Discord and Envy', now in the Louvre in Paris. The plasterwork was executed by the Francini brothers in 1745. There is apparently no theme linking the wall decoration to that of the ceiling, and this wall plaque depicts Heroic Virtue. (Riverstown House) from the 17th century, and in the courtyard is the nine-bay three-storey house of the Damer family, built in the very early 18th century.

Ross Friary *Gal.*   572Cd
The largest and best preserved friary in Ireland, founded in 1351. The church, which lies south of the cloister, has the usual slender tower between the nave and chancel, and south of the nave is a double transept, as at Kilconnell, with an eastward chapel. West of it is Jenning's Chantry. The cloister is small and square and in remarkably good condition. A further court of similar dimensions lies to the north.

Ross Carbery *Cork*   570Da
St Fachtna's Protestant Cathedral is a cruciform building with a 17th-century tower; the north transept is probably medieval, but otherwise the building is mostly of the early 19th century.

Ross Castle See Killarney.

Rosserk Friary *Mayo*   572Cg
A small, very well-preserved friary of the third order of Franciscans, founded in 1441. The church lies south of the cloister and has a central tower and southern transept, with two chapels and a sacristy cupboard. The east window has cusped tracery like St Nicholas's, Galway.

Rowallane *Down*   575Hd
South-east of Belfast, near Saintfield, this beautiful garden was created by Armytage Moore at the beginning of the century. His collection of exotic trees, shrubs and flowers from all over the world thrives in this mild climate, and many of the fine specimens were raised from seeds collected in China, Tibet and South America. (Open to the public.)

Russborough House *Wicklow*   573Jc
Built by Richard Castle and Francis Bindon for the 1st Earl of Miltown from 1740 onwards, Russborough is the longest house in Ireland. It comprises a relatively small central block, with pedimented frontispiece joined by quadrant colonnades to long low wings, beyond which plain walls pierced by baroque gateways terminate in smaller pavilions which contain the kitchen and stable courts. The interior has lavish 18th-century decoration by the Francini brothers.

St Cleran's *Gal.*   572Dc
One of the 'villas' built to designs by Sir Richard Morrison *c.* 1820.

St Doolagh's Church *Dublin*   573Kd
The chancel of St Doolagh's church dates from *c.* 1150 and has a high-pitched stone roof. The central battlemented tower is of the 15th century, while the body of the church dates from the 19th century.

St Macdara's Island *Gal.*   572Ac
On this small island off the south-west Galway coast is an early Irish oratory, measuring internally 15 ft by 11 ft. It is built of massive stones, and its pilasters continue upwards to form the portions of the roof jutting out beyond the end walls. Its original stone roof has been restored.

St Mullin's *Carlow*   571Je
Situated on the R. Barrow, little remains of the monastery of St Moling save the stump of a Round Tower, a figured high cross and the ruins of some small churches and other buildings.

Scattery Island *Clare*   570Ce
An island in the Shannon estuary where St Seanan founded a monastery in the 6th century. Six churches and the tallest Round Tower in Ireland,

120 ft high, survive, as well as two enclosed graveyards with stone slabs, and a well.

Seafield *Dublin*   573Kd
A house probably built between 1720 and 1730 for the Arthur family, on the shores of the Malahide inlet. It has a Doric portico. The superb entrance hall has two storeys of pilasters, grisaille paintings and a gallery with wrought-iron railings.

Shane's Castle *Antrim*   575Ge
Rebuilt by John Nash *c.* 1812, the whole castle was destroyed by fire in 1816. A narrow-gauge railway runs to the castle remains and a splendid Nash greenhouse.

Shanid Castle *Lim.*   570De
A castle dating from the end of the 12th century. Today only the remains of a battlemented tower stand on an impressive mote and fosse.

Shannongrove House *Lim.*   570Ee
The earliest 18th-century house in County Limerick—the front door is dated 1709 and the rear 1723. The mason was John O'Brien. The central block, with red-brick chimneys, is flanked on either side by symmetrical wings, all in Dutch-Palladian style.

Sherkin Friary *Cork*   570Ca
A Franciscan friary on Sherkin Island in Baltimore Bay. The abbey was founded in 1460–70 by the O'Driscolls, and has a typical Franciscan friary church with a cloister to the north of the nave, and a central tower and southern transept.

Skelligs See Great Skellig.

Slade *Wex.*   571Jc
The 15th- to 16th-century crenellated tower-house is well preserved and has a later oblong wing.

Slane *Meath*   573Je
The village was elegantly laid out, with four matching houses at the cross-roads.
SLANE CASTLE One of the finest Gothic Revival castles in Ireland. The building incorporates an earlier castle. The structure of the present house is largely due to James Wyatt, who was called in by W. B. Conyngham in 1785. Capability Brown, Chambers, Gandon, Francis Johnston and Thomas Hopper all designed parts of the building. (Not open to the public.)

Slieve Gullion *Arm.*   575Gb
On top of Slieve Gullion Mountain is the cairn known as 'Calliagh Birra's House'. This is a passage-grave; the chamber is polygonal.

Slieve na Calliagh *Meath*   573He
The long ridge of low hills south-east of Oldcastle is surmounted by a remarkable series of 30 passage-graves (chambered tombs in which the chamber and passage leading to it form two distinct structural units). Many of the stones have Bronze Age ornament. There is also a ring-fort, a rectangular earthwork, a pillar-stone and a stone cross.

Sligo *Sligo*   574Cc
A county town founded in 1252 by Maurice FitzGerald, who also founded the Dominican friary now known as Sligo Abbey. The Church of St John, in Perpendicular Gothic Revival style by Richard Cassels, was remodelled in 1812; the town has a tree-lined mall by the Garavogue River. Many places around Sligo, such as Lough Gill to the south-east, Drumcliff and Lissadell, are associated with the poetry of W. B. Yeats.
ABBEY The abbey contains much good 15th-century work, including a unique sculptured high altar, a good east window, a fragmentary 14th- to

15th-century rood screen, and a well-moulded cloister arcade. There are also some fine monuments, including the O'Craian tomb of 1506, with an elaborate canopy.

Springfield Castle *Lim.*   570Ed
A large, exceptionally well-preserved four-storied gabled tower-house dating from the 16th century.

Springhill House *Tyrone*   575Ge
A mile from the Plantation town of Moneymore, this 17th-century fortified manor house, with later additions, was built by the Conyngham family. The staircase is of local Irish oak, with a yew handrail. The original bell hangs in the tower. (Open to the public.)

Stackallan *Meath*   573Je
A house built for Gustavus Hamilton, Viscount Boyne, one of William III's generals. It has wide eaves and two formal fronts dated 1716. It is one of the rare survivors in Ireland of pre-Palladian style.

Staigue Fort *Kerry*   570Bb
One of the best preserved and most spectacular of the drystone ring-forts. It is situated in a hollow of the hills overlooking the Kenmare estuary. The walls are 13 ft high, terraced internally, and served by an elaborate system of stairways. There are two small chambers in the walls.

Stillorgan *Dublin*   573Kc
Of the great house and gardens of the Viscounts Allen, nothing now remains save the obelisk erected *c.* 1730 as a mausoleum designed by Sir Edward Lovett Pearce and now in the grounds of the hospice of the Order of St John of God. In the garden of a house north of the main road is a large underground brick grotto, also by Pearce.

Strabane *Tyrone*   574Ee
A town on the R. Foyle near Lifford. To the south-west, Urney Presbyterian Church dates from 1654. Gray's 18th-century printing shop, where John Dunlap, printer of the American Declaration of Independence, learnt his trade, has some 19th-century hand-printing machines.

Strade Friary *Mayo*   572Cf
Founded as a Franciscan friary by Jordan de Exeter, Strade was transferred to the Dominican order in 1252–3. There are splendid figures on the high altar, a magnificent 15th- or 16th-century tomb with superb Flamboyant tracery and weepers on the plinth, and other sculptures representing Our Lord with the Five Wounds, a layman with an ear trumpet, two bishops and St Peter.

Strancally Castle *Waterford*   571Gc
Romantically situated on the banks of the Blackwater, at the foot of the Knockmealdown Mountains, this Gothic Revival house was built to designs by the Pain brothers.

Strangford *Down*   575Jc
A small port at the narrow entrance to Strangford Lough. It has a much-altered late 16th-century fortified town-house known as Strangford Castle, and a small tower close to the shore. Strangford House was built in 1789 and has some pleasant interior detailing.

Strokestown House *Roscom.*   572Fe
The central block of the house, now refaced, was originally 17th century, but it is likely that Richard Cassels, very early in his career (*c.* 1730), added the curved quadrants and wings, which include splendid vaulted stables. (Not open to the public.)

Summer Grove *Laois*   573Gc
An attractive small house of ashlar stones hardly larger than bricks. The main front has Venetian

STAIGUE FORT

In a hollow of the hills overlooking the Kenmare estuary, this drystone ring-fort has walls 13 ft high, terraced internally and served by an elaborate system of stairways. There are two small chambers within the thickness of the walls.

windows on the first floor over the door and a semicircular window in the pediment. The entrance hall, staircase hall and drawing-room have charming rococo ornament.

Swords *Dublin*   573Kd
The village has a Round Tower 75 ft high; a 14th-century square tower, the only remains of a medieval monastery, opposite the present Protestant church; and a large castle or palace of the Archbishops of Dublin. This comprises a five-sided walled enclosure with a gateway, small tower and chapel of various dates from the 13th to the 15th century.

Synone *Tipp.*   571Ge
A circular castle of the 16th century, with machicolations and internal dome-like vaults.

Tacumshane *Wex.*   571Kd
Standing in the village is a small straw-thatched windmill (no longer working), one of only two in Ireland—the other is at Ballycopeland.

Tallaght *Dublin*   573Kc
The site of the monastery of St Maelruan, founded in the 8th century. In the 14th century Tallaght became the country residence of the Archbishops of Dublin, who built a large manorial palace there; only one small tower survives of this building, which was demolished early in the 19th century. The church to the south, by John Semple, stands detached from its medieval bell-tower.

Tara *Meath*   573Je
The hill at Tara, although little more than 500 ft high, commands a wide prospect. According to legend, the ancient kings of Tara, who ruled the northern half of the country, made their homes and were crowned here. The present names of the earthworks and monuments on the hill are traditional names only; they are probably not derived from true historical associations.

The main part of the site is about 1000 yds from north to south. Near the centre is the Fort of the Kings, an oval enclosure about 1000 ft by 800 ft. Within the fort are two adjoining earthworks, the Royal Seat, a bivallate ring-fort, and Cormac's House, a high flat mound with two banks and ditches surrounding it. On top—and serving as a monument to the local dead of the 1798 rising against the English—is the standing stone now called the Lia Fail. Within the Fort of the Kings, near its northern edge, is the Mound of Hostages, on which the original Lia Fail—the inauguration stone of the kings of Tara—is supposed to have stood; the present identity and whereabouts of this stone is not known. South of the Fort of the Kings is another smaller univallate fort, Laoghaire's Fort.

North of the Fort of the Kings, and partly encroached upon by the modern churchyard, is the trivallate earthwork called the Fort of the Synods; it has a small burial mound, the King's Chair, within its outer defences. North of the Fort of the Synods is the long narrow earthwork called the Banqueting Hall, 750 ft long and 90 ft wide. North-west of the Banqueting Hall is a group of three circular earthworks, the Sloping Trenches.

Tara was the centre of an influential pagan religious cult in the Iron Age. At that period there were timber houses on the site. The recent excavations at the Mound of the Hostages have established that it was originally a passage-grave of the late second millennium BC.

The Cross of Adamnan in the churchyard is a limestone pillar with a barely discernible carved figure. The modern statue of St Patrick, on Cormac's House, commemorates the saint's visit to the court of King Laoghaire.

Taughmon *Westmeath*   *573He*
The church here, though disused, dates from the 15th century. It has a stone barrel-vault and an added four-storey west tower, which was used as living quarters and fortified. Originally there was a first-floor room over the western part of the nave.

Thomastown *Kilk.*   *571Je*
This town was named after Thomas Fitz Anthony, the Anglo-Norman seneschal—or provincial governor—of Leinster. In his day, and throughout the Middle Ages, the town was contained within a defensive wall. Now, all that remains of the fortifications are Sweetman's Castle and Low Street.
PARISH CHURCH Of the 13th-century parish church, the north wall of the nave and the chancel arch remain. The chancel was used as a Protestant parish church until 1809. In the churchyard is the head of a high cross. In the Catholic parish church is the high altar from Jerpoint Abbey.

Thomastown Castle *Tipp.*   *571Ge*
A large, early 18th-century house with gate-house and formal garden, built by the Mathew family. It was completely refaced and extended by Sir Richard Morrison *c.* 1820. Today it is in ruins; near by is a huge walled garden.

Thurles *Tipp.*   *571Ge*
A town on the upper waters of the R. Suir. Thurles was largely the creation of the Butlers, who conquered the O'Fogartys of Eile, the former owners. The bridge is guarded by a small castle. Thurles is the seat of the Catholic Archbishop of Cashel, and the Cathedral of the Assumption by J. J. McCarthy (1865–72) has a good baroque altarpiece in the style of Andrea Pozzo. In St Patrick's College, site of the Synod of 1850, is St Caillian's Shrine of 1436. Brittas Castle, to the north, is a 19th-century reproduction of a medieval castle.

In 1980 a chalice, similar to the magnificent Ardagh chalice, and a number of gold, silver and gilt bronze objects were found in a bog near the town. The collection possibly dates from the 8th century, and is considered the most important archaeological find in Ireland this century.

Timoleague Friary *Cork*   *570Ea*
A Franciscan friary, attractively sited on a peninsula in Courtmacsherry Bay, founded either in the 13th or 14th century. Its plan is irregular as a result of the shape of the peninsula. The buildings are mostly plainly finished. Features include a wall-passage on the east and south of the choir, and the large walled courtyard to the west, a bell-tower and dormitory. The library dates from the beginning of the 16th century and the tower was

added about the same time by Edmund Courcy, Bishop of Ross. Only a small portion of the cloister remains, but the other buildings are intact.

Tintern Abbey *Wex.*   *571Kd*
A Cistercian abbey founded in 1200 by William the Marshall, it was a daughter-house of Tintern Abbey in Monmouthshire, and most of the remains date from the late 13th century. Some of the presbytery detailing is based on that at Tintern Major. The nave survives, and the central tower at the crossing may be the original, although its upper part is 15th century. At the Dissolution, the abbey and lands were granted to the Colclough family, who turned the abbey into a dwelling house, and both the Tudor and Georgian-Gothic windows date from their occupation.

Townley Hall *Louth*   *573Ke*
Designed in 1794 for Blayney Townley-Balfour by Francis Johnston, the house has a severe exterior of cut stone. There is a splendid central stone-cantilevered and domed staircase, and the principal rooms have fine joinery and plaster detail.

Tralee *Kerry*   *570Cd*
The county town of Kerry owes its origin to the Earls of Desmond, of whose castle practically nothing survives. In the 16th century, after the rebellion led by the 15th Earl, the town was granted to Sir Edward Denny, whose family held it and its borough until the mid-19th century. The most distinguished building is the Classical courthouse by William Vitruvius Morrison. Its Ionic portico is approached by a flight of steps guarded by two Crimean and Indian Mutiny memorial canons; the courts are semicircular and flank the central hall. Day Place is a street with Georgian houses. The church of the Dominican friary of the Holy Cross (founded in 1243) is by Edward Welby Pugin and George Ashlin.

Trim *Meath*   *573Jd*
The medieval town walls enclosed an extensive area; today remnants, including Sheep Gate, remain between Castle Street and Emmet Street. There are several fine 18th-century houses in the town and a column erected in 1817 to the honour of the Duke of Wellington, who spent his childhood in nearby Dangan. The gaol of 1827 has a fine gate-house. St Patrick's Church, a much-altered medieval church, has served as the Protestant cathedral of Meath since 1955. Across the R. Boyne is Talbot Castle, a fortified house of 1415, and Nangle Castle of about the same age. A little to the east rises the Yellow Steeple, the shattered remains of the splendid bell-tower of the Abbey of St Mary, founded in the 13th century; it was damaged by Cromwell's troops.

Just south-east of the town is Newtown Trim, with the ruins of the medieval Cathedral of SS Peter and Paul and its priory on the banks of the R. Boyne; it dates from 1206. Close by is the house of the Crutched Friars.
CASTLE The largest Anglo-Norman castle in Ireland, Trim covers more than 3 acres, bounded on one side by the R. Boyne. The castle was first built in 1172 by Hugh de Lacy. In its present form it dates from *c.* 1220 and the mound on which it stands is a remnant of the motte of the earlier fortress. Considerable stretches of the curtain-walls survive. The irregular bailey has towers with a D-shaped plan, sally-ports and a barbican. The keep contains a hall and chapel. (See p. 630.)

Tuam *Gal.*   *572Dd*
The town was formerly the seat of a Protestant archbishop, but now has a Protestant bishop; it is still the centre of a Catholic archbishopric. The

Catholic Cathedral of the Assumption dates from 1827–37, and was designed by Dominic Madden.
PROTESTANT CATHEDRAL A Gothic Revival building designed by Sir Thomas Deane in 1861. It incorporates the barrel-vaulted Romanesque chancel of a late 12th-century cathedral, the finely decorated chancel arch of which was the widest in Ireland. The chancel had long served as the porch of another church farther east which was used as a cathedral from the late 14th century onwards and which is now a chapter house. It contains elaborately carved Italian baroque choir stalls, dated 1740, which were presented to the diocese in 1882.

Tuamgraney *Clare* 570Ff
The Protestant church comprises a 12th-century eastern part, and a western portion of the mid-10th century with a lintelled and architraved doorway. Near the church are the ruins of a castle.

Tullabeg *Offaly* 573Gc
St Stanislaus College, a large country house now belonging to the Jesuit Fathers, has an oratory with fine stained glass by Evie Hone.

Tullamore *Offaly* 573Gc
Now the county town of Offaly, Tullamore is mainly the creation of the Burys, Earls of Tullamore, who built Charleville Castle near by. The town has some good canal architecture, including a canal hotel. There is a splendid Ionic-porticoed court-house of *c.* 1835 and an 18th-century market-house. The Protestant church is by Francis Johnston, who was also the architect of Charleville.

Tullira Castle *Gal.* 572Dc
A 17th-century tower-house, considerably added to in 1882 by George Ashlin. The interior contains a fine Gothic hall. The castle was the home of Edward Martyn (1859–1923), the dramatist and patron of the arts, who was influenced by William Morris, and was one of the initiators of the Irish stained glass revival. (Not open to the public.)

Tully *Kild.* 573Hc
JAPANESE GARDENS The flowering shrubs, miniature trees and rockeries here were arranged by a Japanese designer in 1906, and completed four years later. The gardens are symbolic of the life of a human being and features include the Cave of Birth, Peace before the Hill of Mourning, and the Gates of Eternity.

Tully Castle *Ferm.* 574Dd
A Plantation castle. The square fortified enclosure contains a T-shaped strong-house.

Tullynally Castle *Westmeath.* 573Ge
A 17th-century garrison house, Classicised in 1775 by Myers and transformed into a flamboyant Gothic castle by Francis Johnston from 1803 to 1806, with picturesque additions by James Shiel in 1825 and Sir Richard Morrison in 1842. Situated in a 1500 acre park and demesne, the castle has kitchen, museum and Duke of Wellington family relics. (Limited opening.)

Turoe Stone See Loughrea.

Tynan *Arm.* 574Fc
The four crosses of Tynan, one in the village and three on the estate of Tynan Abbey, have all been moved from their original sites. The village cross has a carved panel depicting the Fall of Adam and Eve, and was originally in the churchyard.

Tyrone House *Gal.* 572Dc
The burnt-out, ruined country house of the St George family, built in 1779 and splendidly situated on an inlet in Galway Bay. Facing it is Drumacoo church, with good 13th-century details, and the St George family mausoleum with cast-iron tracery.

Tyrrelspass *Westmeath* 573Gd
A formal landlord's village, laid out by the Rochforts, Earls of Belvedere, around a semicircular green. Several of the houses are pedimented, and the Protestant church has a fine spire and a magnificent monument by John Bacon.

TRIM CASTLE

The first castle at Trim, a fortress for the Norman invaders, was levelled by the Irish. This one dates from the end of the 12th century and the town of Trim grew up in its shelter. The square keep is 75 ft high *and has a tower abutting the centre of each face, so that there are 20 sides in all. King John visited the castle—and confiscated it. Henry V was kept a prisoner there before his accession.*

FINE SILVER AT WESTPORT HOUSE

The bog-oak bowl with its intricately wrought cover (left) and the sugar sifter (centre) were made in Ireland for Colonel John Browne, owner of the first house on the site in the early 18th century. The group of slaves (right) are on the base of a 19th-century candelabrum—one of a superb pair presented to the 2nd Marquess of Sligo, Governor of Jamaica, for his part in the abolition of slavery in Jamaica.

Ullard *Kilk.*   571Je
The ruined church has an unusual west doorway, partly reconstructed, with an inner arch at a lower level than the external one. High in the west gable above is a triangular-headed window with a small sculptured panel depicting two saints above it.

Ulster Folk and Transport Museum See Cultra Manor.

Urlanmore Castle *Clare*   570Ef
The building has a three-storied tower at one end and, at the other, a lower adjoining extension containing the remains of the first-floor hall. On the walls of the principal room in the tower are outline paintings of animals.

Ushnagh *Westmeath*   573Gd
A place of sanctity or hosting site, and thought to have been the centre of Ireland in pagan times. It contains a large number of earthworks, including the remains of an elaborate house of the 2nd century AD and a souterrain. From this 600 ft hill, 20 of the counties of Ireland can be seen.

Walpole Gardens See Mount Usher.

Waringstown *Down*   575Gd
Established in 1667 by the linen manufacturer William Waring, who built Waringstown House, a large U-shaped three-storied block with 18th-century two-storied pavilions added at the ends of the main front. (Not open to the public.) The church, of 1681, is said to have been supervised by James Robb, chief mason of the king's works in Ireland. The west tower dates from 1750 and the church was enlarged in the 19th century. The pulpit and fittings, in 17th-century style, date from 1832.

Waterford *Waterford*   571Jd
Among the most important Anglo-Norman foundations on the eastern seaboard, though owing its origin to the Vikings. It lies on the south bank of the R. Suir and consists of a long quay behind which are the narrow streets of the medieval walled town. The north-east corner of the town is marked by the massive cylindrical Reginald's Tower, probably 12th or 13th century, now a museum; other towers of the town wall survive.

The ruined Franciscan church, founded in 1240 and given to the Huguenots in 1695, has three lancets on its east wall and central tower. Fragments of other medieval buildings survive, such as the tower and belfry of the Dominican friary (Black Friars) in Arundel Square. The important medieval cathedral, which resembled Christchurch, Dublin, was demolished in 1773 to be succeeded by the present splendid building (Protestant) by John Roberts, finished in 1779; it has a western Doric portico, tower and spire, an interior with a giant Ionic order, and fine original plasterwork; the macabre monument of James Rice in the north-west chapel, and other monuments, are noteworthy. Immediately south of it is the bishop's palace by Richard Castle, dating from 1741, latterly occupied by Bishop Foy's School. Other good 18th-century houses surround the cathedral. St Olave's Church, founded by Bishop Miles in 1734, has been dismantled, and its fine fittings, including a three-decker pulpit, have been dispersed, mainly to Lismore Cathedral. John Roberts also designed the Catholic cathedral (a remarkable circumstance for the period) which dates from 1792, with double-aisled nave, a giant Corinthian order and plaster vaults. The façade is late 19th century. The cathedral has a splendid series of medieval vestments discovered during the demolition of the old Protestant cathedral in 1773 and presented by the then Protestant bishop to his Catholic counterpart. St Olave's, too, has its Catholic counterpart in St Patrick's Church of 1764, which is almost completely unaltered, with galleries carried on Doric columns. The present town hall, originally the assembly rooms, dates from 1782 and is also by John Roberts; it incorporates a 'play-house'. The decoration is simple, but there is a Waterford glass chandelier in the council chamber, installed in 1802. The present Ionic-porticoed court-house in the People's Park, by J. B. Keane and dating from 1849, is almost identical to the one in Tullamore. The Presentation Convent, by Augustus Welby Pugin, is a characteristic work begun in 1842.

Wattle Bridge *Ferm.*   574Eb
What appears to be a circle of numerous stones, 100 ft in diameter, is the kerb of a cairn removed early in the 18th century.

Westport *Mayo*   572Be
Perhaps the most elaborately planned of smaller Irish towns, laid out in 1780. The canalised river is the main feature of the plan, flanked by tree-lined quays and crossed by graceful bridges. Other streets ascend the slopes from an octagonal place containing a column. Near by is Westport House, begun by Castle, at the head of Clew Bay; it contains fine Wyatt plaster in the dining-room.

Wexford *Wex.*   *571Kd*
The county town owes its origin to the Vikings, but was captured by the Anglo-Normans. There are few remains of interest, but the Augustinian priory of SS Peter and Paul (called Selskar Abbey), comprises a square battlemented tower used as the belfry of the Protestant parish church, and a ruinous double nave. Near by, a fragment of the medieval town wall survives; there are also remains of St Mary's Church. St Peter's Catholic Church on Summer Hill is by Augustus Welby Pugin and was consecrated in 1840. Four and a half miles to the south-west is Johnstown Castle.

White Island *Ferm.*   *574Dd*
On Lough Erne, the remains of a small church with a Romanesque south doorway. Built into the wall are seven remarkable carved figures, probably of the 9th century, five of which represent sinister human beings.

Wicklow *Wicklow*   *573Kb*
A Viking foundation, now the county town, it has an 18th-century Protestant church with a square tower (1770), surmounted by a dome. The 19th-century open-work trusses, with their fan pattern, are curious. The interior retains its original Doric-columned gallery and to the left of the mid-19th-century chancel-arch is a fine mid-18th-century monument with a bust.

Woodlands *Dublin*   *573Kd*
One of the more interesting smaller houses in Ireland, Woodlands, traditionally associated with Jonathan Swift, was in fact built for his friend, the Rev. Jack Jackson, *c.* 1730, and must be by Sir Edward Lovett Pearce or one of his immediate school. The almost square plan contains a vaulted corridor leading from the front door to the centre of the house; a gazebo, or lantern, projects from the top of the pyramidal roof.

Youghal *Cork*   *571Gc*
The 13th-century collegiate Church of St Mary is among the few roofed medieval churches still in

FIGURES ON WHITE ISLAND

Some of the incredible carved stone figures built into the walls of the ruined church. Probably dating from the 9th century, five represent sinister humans. The figure on the right holds two griffins by the neck; another carries the crozier and bell of a bishop.

use. It is cruciform, with an aisled nave and a 15th-century long chancel. There is a massive fortified tower between the north transept and the nave. In the south transept is the monument of Richard Boyle, the Great Earl of Cork, to himself and members of his family, with fine effigies and remarkable wrought-iron work.

Dominating the centre of the town is the Clock Gate in South Main Street, a massive structure in limestone of four storeys above an archway with set-backs, surmounted by a domed lantern containing the clock. It was built in 1777, designed by William Meade. Near by is an altered 15th-century tower-house and, opposite, the Uniacke House (private) of 1706–15, built by a Dutch builder named Leuventhan; it has a steep central pediment with eaves-cornice and dormer. An even rarer survivor is the unique set of almshouses (possibly 1634) with pointed doorways and mullioned windows in North Main Street, where another early fragment, St John's Chapel, remains, with a small elaborate medieval window.

MONUMENT TO THE EARL OF CORK

Richard Boyle, created Earl of Cork in 1620, erected this monument to commemorate himself and his family in about 1620. He wears armour and an earl's robes. His mother reclines over the main arch above the earl. On either side of him kneel his wives—his first wife, who died in childbirth, at his feet, and his second wife at his head. Below him nine children are represented. The children appear again, this time grown up, on Lady Cork's tomb in St Patrick's Cathedral, Dublin. (Church of St Mary, Youghal)

COLLECTIONS

Specialised collections in houses, museums and galleries

The urge to collect has always been a strong characteristic of the British . . . Small boys eagerly fill stamp albums; playbills and punch ladles, seashells and swords set the scene in many of our homes, pubs and palaces.

This section of the book lists the collections, privately and publicly owned, which are notable for their special character or value. They demonstrate the diverse, cultivated and extravagant tastes of patrons and connoisseurs, the proud feeling for the past achievements of families and regiments, the scholarly and eccentric interests of learned men and dilletantes.

The collections are listed under subject headings, to assist the pursuit of specialised interests. They speak of the past as intimately as a diary and with an authority that the reflections of a historian could never possess.

ARCHAEOLOGY AND ANTHROPOLOGY

The relics of man's earliest activities displayed in British museums come from all over the world and span some 1¾ million years. They show him in his role as a hunter and warrior, as farmer, ironsmith, potter, worshipper and artist. To study these collections is to understand the relationship—often surprisingly close—between 20th-century man and his prehistoric forebears.

Aberdeen, *Grampian*
University Anthropological Museum
Abergavenny, *Gwent*
Abergavenny and District Museum
Abingdon, *Oxon.*
Borough Museum (County Hall)
Ardoch Roman Camp, *Tayside*
Ashwell, *Herts.*
Village Museum
Avebury, *Wilts.*
Alexander Keiller Museum

Aylesbury, *Bucks.*
Buckinghamshire County Museum
Barnet, *Greater London* Museum
Basing, *Hants.*
Basing House Ruins
Basingstoke, *Hants.* Willis Museum
Batley, *W. Yorks.* Bagshaw Museum
Bedford, *Beds.* Museum
Bexhill *E. Sussex* Museum
Bignor, *W. Sussex* Roman Villa
Birchington, *Kent*
Powell Cotton Museum

Birmingham, *W. Midlands*
Blakesley Hall (Yardley); City
Museum and Art Gallery; Weoley
Castle
Blackburn, *Lancs.*
Museum and Art Gallery
Boroughbridge, *N. Yorks.*
Aldborough Roman Site Museum
Bournemouth, *Dorset*
Rothesay Museum
Bradford, *W. Yorks.*
City Art Gallery and Museum
Bridgwater, *Som.*
Admiral Blake Museum
Bridlington, *Humberside*
Art Gallery and Museum
Bridport, *Dorset*
Museum and Art Gallery
Brighton, *E. Sussex*
Museum and Art Gallery
Bury, *Greater Manchester*
Art Gallery and Museum
Bury St Edmunds, *Suffolk*
Moyses Hall Museum
Caernarfon, *Gwynedd*
Segontium Museum
Cambourne, *Cornwall*
Public Library and Museum
Cambridge, *Cambs.*
Scott Polar Research Institute;
University Museum of Classical
Archaeology
Canterbury, *Kent*
Roman Pavement; Royal Museum
(Beaney Institute)
Carlisle, *Cumbria* Tullie House
Cheltenham Spa, *Glos.*
Art Gallery and Museum
Chichester, *W. Sussex*
City Museum; Guildhall
Museum
Christchurch, *Dorset*
Red House Museum and Art
Gallery
Cirencester, *Glos.*
Corinium Museum
Colchester, *Essex*
Colchester and Essex Museum
Dartford, *Kent* Borough Museum
Derby, *Derbys.*
Museum and Art Gallery
Devizes, *Wilts.*
Wiltshire Archaeological and
Natural History Society
Dorchester, *Dorset*
County Museum
Dover, *Kent*
Corporation Museum
Dublin, *Dublin* Leinster House
Dumfries, *Dumfs. & Gall.*
Observatory (Burgh Museum)
Dundalk, *Louth*
Dundee, *Tayside*
McManus Gallery
Durham, *Durham*
University Oriental Museum
Exeter, *Devon*
Royal Albert Memorial Museum
and Art Gallery
Farnham, *Surrey* Museum
Glandford, *Norfolk*
Museum of Shells
Glasgow, *Strathclyde*
Hunterian Museum
Gloucester, *Glos.*
City Museum and Art Gallery
Grantham, *Lincs.*
Library and Museum
Grays, *Essex*
Thurrock Local History Museum
Guildford, *Surrey*
Museum and Muniment Room
Harlyn, *Cornwall*
Harlyn Bay Museum
Haslemere, *Surrey*
Educational Museum

Hereford, *Heref. & Worcs.*
City Museum and Art Gallery
Hertford, *Herts.* Museum
Ilkley, *W. Yorks.*
Manor House Museum and Art
Gallery
Inverurie, *Grampian* Museum
Ipswich, *Suffolk* Museum
King's Lynn, *Norfolk*
Museum and Art Gallery
Lancaster, *Lancs.*
City Museum
Leeds, *W. Yorks.* City Museum
Leicester, *Leics.*
Jewry Wall Museum
Lerwick, *Shetland*
County Museum
Lincoln, *Lincs.*
City and County Museum
London
British Museum; Guildhall
Museum; Passmore Edwards
Museum
Luton, *Beds.*
Museum and Art Gallery
Macclesfield, *Cheshire*
West Park Museum
Maidstone, *Kent*
Chillington Manor
Melrose, *Borders* Abbey
Middlesbrough, *Cleveland*
Dorman Memorial Museum and
Municipal Art Gallery
Newark-on-Trent, *Notts.*
Museum and Art Gallery
Newbury, *Berks.*
Borough Museum
Newcastle upon Tyne, *Tyne & Wear*
Hancock Museum
Newport, *Gwent*
Museum and Art Gallery
Northampton, *Northants.*
Central Museum and Art Gallery
Nuneaton, *Warks.*
Museum and Art Gallery
Oxford, *Oxon.*
Ashmolean Museum; Museum of
the History of Science
Penzance, *Cornwall*
Natural History and Antiquarian
Museum
Peterborough, *Cambs.*
Museum and Maxwell Art Gallery
Plymouth, *Devon*
City Museum and Art Gallery
Pontefract, *W. Yorks.*
Castle Museum
Poole, *Dorset*
Old Town House; Poole
Museum
Reading, *Berks.*
Museum and Art Gallery;
Museum of Greek Archaeology
Ribchester, *Lancs.*
Museum of Roman Antiquities
Richborough Castle, *Kent*
Rossendale, *Lancs.*
Rawtenstall Museum
Rotherham, *S. Yorks.*
Municipal Museum and Art
Gallery
Rufford, *Lancs.*
Rufford Old Hall
Salisbury, *Wilts.*
Salisbury and South Wiltshire
Museum
Scarborough, *N. Yorks.* Museum
Shaftesbury, *Dorset*
Abbey Ruins Museum;
Shaftesbury and District Historical
Society's Museum of Local
History
Sheffield, *S. Yorks.* City Museum
Shrewsbury, *Salop*
Rowley's House Museum
Silchester, *Hants.* Calleva Museum

Sittingbourne, *Kent*
  Court Hall Museum
Skipton, *N. Yorks.*
  Craven Museum
Southampton, *Hants.*
  God's House Tower
Southend-on-Sea, *Essex*
  Prittlewell Priory Museum
South Shields, *Tyne & Wear*
  Roman Fort and Museum
Stevenage, *Herts.*
  Museum
Stirling, *Central*
  Smith Art Gallery and Museum
Stranraer, *Dumfs. & Gall.*
  Wigtown County Museum
Sunderland, *Tyne & Wear*
  Museum and Art Gallery
Taunton, *Som.* County
  Museum
Thetford, *Norfolk*
  Ancient House Museum

Truro, *Cornwall*
  County Museum and Art Gallery
Weston-super-Mare, *Avon*
  Municipal Museum
Weybridge, *Surrey* Museum
Winchester, *Hants.* City Museum
Windsor, *Berks.*
  Windsor Guildhall Exhibition
Wookey, *Som.*
  Wookey Hole Caves Museum
Worksop, *Notts.*
  Public Library and Museum
Worthing, *W. Sussex*
  Museum and Art Gallery
Yeovil, *Som.*
  Borough of Yeovil Museum
York, *N. Yorks.* Castle Museum;
  Jorvik Viking Centre
Zennor, *Cornwall*
  Wayside Museum

ARMOUR AND WEAPONS

Strength and pride, violence and skill: these are what weaponry
proclaims. Its purpose is deadly, and its workmanship often as delicate
as a goldsmith's or a lady embroiderer's. These are things upon which
lives and freedom have depended, and collections of them have
perhaps a greater vitality than anything else displayed to the public.

Abbotsford House, *Borders*
Abergavenny, *Gwent* Abergavenny
  and District Museum
Abingdon, *Oxon.*
  Borough Museum (County Hall)
Acton Round Hall, *Salop*
Alnwick Castle, *Northld.*
  Regimental Museum of the
  Royal Northumberland Fusiliers
Barnstaple, *Devon*
  St Anne's Chapel Museum
Birchington, *Kent*
  Powell-Cotton Museum
Birmingham, *W. Midlands*
  Museum of Science and Industry
Blackburn, *Lancs.*
  Museum and Art Gallery
Blair Castle, *Tayside*
Bodrhyddan Hall, *Clwyd*
Bournemouth, *Dorset*
  Rothesay Museum
Brecon, *Powys*
  South Wales Borderers
  Regimental Museum
Brentwood, *Essex*
  Essex Regiment Museum
Bridlington, *Humberside*
  Bayle Museum
Burnley, *Lancs.* East Lancashire
  Regimental Museum
Cambridge, *Cambs.*
  Fitzwilliam Museum
Canterbury, *Kent*
  West Gate Museum
Capesthorne, *Cheshire*
Chiddingstone Castle, *Kent*
Cotehele House, *Cornwall*
Delgatie Castle, *Grampian*
Dorchester, *Dorset*
  Dorset Military Museum

Dublin, *Dublin*
  Castle; Cathedral of St Patrick
Eastnor Castle, *Heref. & Worcs.*
East Riddlesden Hall, *W. Yorks.*
Edinburgh, *Lothian*
  Castle; Scottish United Services
  Museum
Exeter, *Devon*
Fort George, *Highland*
  Regimental Museum of The
  Seaforth Highlanders, The
  Queen's Own Cameron
  Highlanders and Queen's Own
  Highlanders
Grays, *Essex*
  Thurrock Local History Museum
Hertford, *Herts.* Museum
Inverary Castle, *Strathclyde*
Kedleston Hall, *Derbys.*
King's Lynn, *Norfolk*
  Queen Street and Saturday
  Market
Kingston upon Thames, *Greater
  London* Queen's Royal Surrey
  Regiment Museum
Kirkcaldy, *Fife* Museum
Leatherhead, *Surrey*
Leeds, *W. Yorks.*
  Abbey House Museum
Lichfield, *Staffs.* Staffordshire
  Regimental Museum
Lincoln, *Lincs.*
  Stonebow and Guildhall
Littlecote, *Wilts.*
London
  Armouries, Tower of
  London; Imperial War
  Museum; Wallace
  Collection
Lullingstone Castle, *Kent*

CLOCKS AND WATCHES

Recording time has been one of man's keenest pursuits since he began to question his place in the world, and this important activity has had care lavished on it by artists as well as clockmakers. Among the time-pieces displayed in Britain may be seen not only atomic clocks at London's Science Museum, but also the jewelled masterpieces at the Usher Art Gallery, Lincoln.

COINS, MEDALS, TRADE TOKENS

Men have always lavished care and attention on the tokens of their wealth and esteem. The coins and medals collected in Britain embody 2000 years of history. They provide a portrait gallery of monarchs and a compendium of changing styles. They are also often objects of beauty, examples of the designer's art as well as commemorations of men and events. Trade tokens, social documents on a more mundane level, are also included in these collections.

Bedford, *Beds.*
Museum
Birmingham, *W. Midlands*
Assay Office
Burford, *Oxon.*
Tolsey Museum
Cambridge, *Cambs.*
Fitzwilliam Museum
Canterbury, *Kent*
Royal Museum (Beaney Institute)
Chester, *Cheshire*
Grosvenor Museum
Colchester, *Essex*
Colchester and Essex Museum
Gainsborough, *Lincs.*
Old Hall
Glasgow, *Strathclyde*
Hunterian Museum
London
British Museum; Cuming
Museum; Wellcome Institute of
the History of Medicine

Lyme Regis, *Dorset*
Philpot Museum
Newark-on-Trent, *Notts.*
Museum and Art Gallery
Northampton, *Northants.*
Central Museum and Art Gallery
Norwich, *Norfolk*
Castle Museum;
Strangers Hall
Oxford, *Oxon.*
Ashmolean Museum
Peterhead, *Grampian*
Arbuthnot Museum
Poole, *Dorset*
Museum
St Helier, *Jersey*
Jersey Museum and Barreau
Gallery
Swindon, *Wilts.*
Museum and Art Gallery
Tamworth, *Staffs.*
Castle Museum

FOLK ART
AND LOCAL HISTORY

The roots of art are in the country, not in the town. In collections all over Britain the ordinary art of the past can be seen: things made by men whose craftsmanship came from understanding the purpose of what they made, and whose decoration has the kind of freedom that an artist might spend years trying to achieve; the exhibits provide a quiet background to the high fashions and great art of urban life.

Aberdeen, *Grampian*
Provost Skene's House
Abergavenny, *Gwent*
Abergavenny and District
Museum
Aberystwyth, *Dyfed*
University College, Aberystwyth
Alton, *Hants.* Curtis Museum
Altrincham, *Greater Manchester*
Art Gallery and Museum
Arreton, *Isle of Wight*
Arreton Manor
Ashwell, *Herts.*
Ashwell Village Museum
Banbury, *Oxon.*
Public Museum and Globe Room
Barking, *Greater London*
Valence House Museum
Batley, *W. Yorks.*
Bagshaw Museum
Bedale, *N. Yorks.*
Bedale Hall
Bedford, *Beds.*
Museum
Beverley, *Humberside*
Art Gallery and Museum
Bexhill, *E. Sussex* Museum
Bibury, *Glos.* Arlington Mill
Birmingham, *W. Midlands*
Blakesley Hall
Blackburn, *Lancs.*
Museum and Art Gallery
Blaise Hamlet, *Avon*
Blaise Castle House
Bournemouth, *Dorset*
Rothesay Museum

Bradford, *W. Yorks.*
Bolling Hall; City Art Gallery
and Museum
Bramber, *W. Sussex*
St Mary's
Bridgwater, *Som.*
Admiral Blake Museum
Bridlington, *Humberside*
Bayle Museum
Bridport, *Dorset*
Museum and Art Gallery
Burton upon Trent, *Staffs.*
Museum and Art Gallery
Buxton, *Derbys.*
Museum
Camborne, *Cornwall*
Public Library and Museum
Chichester, *W. Sussex*
City Museum
Christchurch, *Dorset*
Red House Museum and Art
Gallery
Colchester, *Essex*
Colchester and Essex Museum
Cultra Manor, *Down*
Ulster Folk Museum
Derby, *Derbys.*
Museum and Art Gallery
Dorchester, *Dorset*
Dorset County Museum
East Looe, *Cornwall*
Looe Museum
Eccles, *Greater Manchester*
Monks Hall Museum
Farnham, *Surrey*
Farnham Museum

Filkins, *Oxon.*
Filkins and Broughton Poggs
Museum
Forfar, *Tayside*
Meffan Institute Museum
Gainsborough, *Lincs.* Old Hall
Gawthorpe Hall, *Lancs.*
Glamis, *Tayside* Kirk Wynd
Glenesk, *Tayside* Folk Museum
Gloucester, *Glos.*
Bishop Hooper's Lodging;
Robert Opie Collection
Godalming, *Surrey*
Borough Museum
Great Yarmouth, *Norfolk*
Elizabethan Museum; Tolhouse
Guildford, *Surrey*
Museum and Muniment Room
Halifax, *W. Yorks.* Shibden Hall
Hall-i'-Th'-Wood, *Greater
Manchester*
Haslemere, *Surrey*
Educational Museum
Helston, *Cornwall*
Borough Museum
Hereford, *Heref. & Worcs.*
City Museum and Art Gallery
High Wycombe, *Bucks.*
Museum and Exhibition Rooms
Honiton, *Devon*
Honiton and Allhallows Public
Museum
Ilkley, *W. Yorks.*
Manor House Museum
Inverurie, *Grampian* Museum
Ipswich, *Suffolk*
Christchurch Mansion
Kendal, *Cumbria*
Borough Museum
La Hougue Bie, *Jersey*
Agricultural Museum; German
Occupation Museum
Leeds, *W. Yorks.*
Abbey House Museum
Leicester, *Leics.*
Newarke Houses Museum
Lerwick, *Shetland*
Shetland County Museum
Lewes, *E. Sussex*
Anne of Cleves House
Lichfield, *Staffs.*
Art Gallery and Museum
London
Cuming Museum; Museum of
London
Lyme Regis, *Dorset*
Philpot Museum
Macclesfield, *Cheshire*
Westpark Museum
Manchester, *Greater Manchester*
Wythenshawe Hall, Northenden
Merthyr Tydfil, *Mid Glam.*
Art Gallery and Museum
Monmouth, *Gwent* Nelson Museum
Munslow Aston, *Salop*
The White House
Northampton, *Northants.*
Abington Park Museum
North Berwick, *Lothian*
Burgh Museum
Norwich, *Norfolk*
Castle; Strangers Hall

Penzance, *Cornwall*
Natural History and Antiquarian
Museum
Peterhead, *Grampian*
Arbuthnot Museum
Poole, *Dorset* Museum
Portsmouth, *Hants.* Southsea Castle
Radcliffe, *Greater Manchester*
Local History Museum
Reading, *Berks.*
Museum of English Rural Life
Repton, *Derbys.*
Repton School Museum
Rossendale, *Lancs.*
Rawtenstall Museum
Rufford, *Lancs.*
Rufford Old Hall
St Fagans Castle, *S. Glam.*
St Helier, *Jersey* Jersey Museum
and Barreau Gallery
St Ives, *Cornwall* Library and Museum
Salisbury, *Wilts.*
Salisbury and South Wiltshire
Museum
Saltcoats, *Strathclyde*
North Ayrshire Museum
Scarborough, *N. Yorks.* Museum
Shaftesbury, *Dorset*
Abbey Ruins Museum;
Shaftesbury and District Historical
Society's Museum of Local History
Shoreham-by-Sea, *W. Sussex*
Marlipins Museum
Sittingbourne, *Kent*
Court Hall Museum
Southampton, *Hants.*
Bargate Guildhall
Southend-on-Sea, *Essex*
Prittlewell Priory Museum
South Molton, *Devon*
Borough Museum
Stafford, *Staffs.*
Museum and Art Gallery
Stevenage, *Herts.* Museum
Stockport, *Greater Manchester*
Municipal Museum
Stranraer, *Dumfs. & Gall.*
County Museum
Taunton, *Som.*
Somerset County Museum
Tenby, *Dyfed* Museum
Thetford, *Norfolk*
Ancient House Museum
Torquay, *Devon*
Natural History Society Museum
Walsall, *W. Midlands*
Museum of Leathercraft
Weston-super-Mare, *Avon*
Municipal Museum
Weybridge, *Surrey* Museum
Windsor, *Berks.*
Windsor Guildhall Exhibition
Woodstock, *Oxon.*
Oxford City and County
Museum, Fletcher's House
Wootton Bassett, *Wilts.*
Worksop, *Notts.*
Public Library and Museum
York, *N. Yorks.* Castle Museum;
Jorvik Viking Centre
Zennor, *Cornwall*
Wayside Museum

GLASS

Twists of colour and air trapped in the clear material, engraved
patterns and scenes, the diamond sparkle of expert cutting: these are
some of the pleasures of glassware, and so are the fluid shapes of this
most fragile form of art, carefully protected in collections from
Aberdeen to Wookey in Somerset.

Aberdeen, *Grampian* Art Gallery
Aberystwyth, *Dyfed*
University College, Aberystwyth

Alton, *Hants.*
Curtis Museum
Arbury Hall, *Warks.*

GOLD, SILVER AND JEWELLERY

The men who work with precious stones and metals have special skills; they can afford no mistakes, and are the aristocrats of craftsmanship, whose services have always been only for the glory of the highest— God or the aristocracy. The fine collections now on view to the public in Britain—in stately homes, museums and palaces—make the pleasure of such things available to all.

Fort George, *Highland*
Regimental Museum of The
Seaforth Highlanders, The Queen's
Own Cameron Highlanders and
Queen's Own Highlanders
Glandford, *Norfolk*
Museum of Shells
Gloucester, *Glos.*
City Museum and Art Gallery
Greenock, *Strathclyde*
McLean Museum and Art Gallery
Grimsthorpe Castle, *Lincs.*
Harewood House, *W. Yorks.*
Haslemere, *Surrey*
Educational Museum
Hereford, *Heref. & Worcs.*
Churchill Gardens Museum
Hodnet Hall, *Salop*
Ickworth, *Suffolk*
Ipswich, *Suffolk* Museum
Kedleston Hall, *Derbys.*
King's Lynn, *Norfolk*
Guildhall of the Holy Trinity;
Queen Street and Saturday Market
Leeds, *W. Yorks.* City Art Gallery
Lincoln, *Lincs.*
Cathedral; Cathedral Treasury;
Stonebow and Guildhall; Usher
Art Gallery
London
British Museum; Courtauld
Institute Galleries; Geological
Museum; Jewel House,
Tower of London; Mocatta
Museum; Royal Courts of
Justice; Victoria and Albert
Museum; Wallace Collection
Luton Hoo, *Beds.*
Manchester, *Greater Manchester*
City Art Gallery
Merthyr Tydfil, *Mid Glam.*
Art Gallery and Museum

Monmouth, *Gwent*
Nelson Museum
New Barnet, *Greater London*
Abbey Art Centre and Museum
Newstead Abbey, *Notts.*
Northampton, *Northants.*
Northamptonshire Regiment
Museum
Norwich, *Norfolk*
St Peter Hungate Museum
Nuneaton, *Warks.*
Museum and Art Gallery
Ormside, *Cumbria*
Church of St James
Oxford, *Oxon.*
Ashmolean Museum
Plymouth, *Devon*
City Museum and Art Gallery
Pontefract, *W. Yorks.*
Castle Museum
Port Sunlight, *Cheshire*
Lady Lever Art Gallery
Richmond, *N. Yorks.*
Green Howards Museum
Rotherham, *S. Yorks.* Municipal
Museum and Art Gallery
Sandford Orcas Manor, *Dorset*
Sheffield, *S. Yorks.*
South Molton, *Devon*
Borough Museum
Stranraer, *Dumfs. & Gall.*
Wigtown County Museum
Tatton Park, *Cheshire*
Temple Newsam House, *W. Yorks.*
Tewes, *Essex*
Traquair House, *Borders*
Weston Park, *Staffs.*
Winchester, *Hants.*
Royal Hampshire Regimental
Museum
Woburn Abbey, *Beds.*
York, *N. Yorks.* Mansion House

INDUSTRY, MACHINERY
AND TRANSPORT

The machine age began in Britain, and nowhere else are there finer
collections of the machines and vehicles that changed world history
than here. But there is more than historic appeal in the gleaming brass
and steel of these old machines; often they have a dramatic, almost
sculptural quality—as if their makers had had an intuition of the
changes they were about to make in the world.

Ashwell, *Herts.*
Ashwell Village Museum
Basingstoke, *Hants.*
Willis Museum
Batley, *W. Yorks.* Bagshaw
Museum
Beaulieu, *Hants.*
Beaulieu Abbey and Beaulieu
Palace House; Montagu Motor
Museum
Bedford, *Beds.* Museum
Bibury, *Glos.*
Arlington Mill
Birmingham, *W. Midlands*
Museum of Science and Industry
Bradford, *W. Yorks.*
City Art Gallery and Museum

Bradford-on-Avon, *Wilts.*
Bridgwater, *Som.*
Admiral Blake Museum
Bridlington, *Humberside*
Bayle Museum
Burford, *Oxon.* Tolsey Museum
Bury St Edmunds, *Suffolk*
Moyses Hall Museum
Caister Castle, *Norfolk*
Capesthorne, *Cheshire*
Castleward House, *Down*
Crich, *Derbys.*
Crich Tramway Museum
Cromford Old Mill, *Derbys.*
Cultra Manor, *Down*
Ulster Folk Museum
Dartford, *Kent* Borough Museum

Dartmouth, *Devon*
Borough Museum
Derby, *Derbys.*
Museum and Art Gallery
Dudley, *W. Midlands* Central
Museum
East Looe, *Cornwall*
Looe Museum
Eccles, *Greater Manchester*
Monks Hall Museum
Glamis, *Tayside*
Kirk Wynd (Angus Folk Museum)
Glasgow, *Strathclyde*
Hunterian Museum; Museum of
Transport (Eglinton Toll)
Grantham, *Lincs.*
Library and Museum
Greenock, *Strathclyde*
McLean Museum and Art Gallery
Guildford, *Surrey*
Museum and Muniment Room
Haslemere, *Surrey*
Educational Museum
High Wycombe, *Bucks.*
Museum and Exhibition Rooms
Ironbridge, *Salop*
Kingston upon Hull, *Humberside*
Kirkcaldy, *Fife*
Museum and Art Gallery
La Hougue Bie, *Jersey*
Agricultural Museum
Lacock, *Wilts.*
Lackham School of Agriculture;
Agricultural Museum
Leeds, *W. Yorks.* City Museum
Leicester, *Leics.* Belgrave Hall
London
Industrial Health and Safety
Centre; Royal Mews,
Buckingham Palace; Science
Museum
Lyme Regis, *Dorset*
Philpot Museum
Maidstone, *Kent*
Archbishop's or Old Palace
Michelham Priory, *E. Sussex*
Newcastle upon Tyne, *Tyne & Wear*
Department of Mining
Engineering, The University
Norwich, *Norfolk* Bridewell
Museum; Strangers Hall
Nostell Priory, *W. Yorks.*
Old Warden Aerodrome, *Beds.*
Shuttleworth Collection

Penrhyn Castle, *Gwynedd*
Peterhead, *Grampian*
Arbuthnot Museum
Reading, *Berks.*
Museum of English Rural Life
Rossendale, *Lancs.*
Rawtenstall Museum
St Fagans Castle, *S. Glam.*
St Ives, *Cornwall*
Zennor Folk Museum
Salford, *Greater Manchester*
Science Museum
Saltcoats, *Strathclyde*
North Ayrshire Museum
Shaftesbury, *Dorset* Shaftesbury
and District Historical
Society's Museum of Local
History
Sheffield, *S. Yorks.*
Abbeydale Industrial Hamlet;
Shepherd Wheel
Snowshill Manor, *Glos.*
Southampton, *Hants.* Wool House
South Molton, *Devon*
Borough Museum
Southwold, *Suffolk* Museum
Stafford, *Staffs.*
Museum and Art Gallery
Stanford Hall, *Leics.*
Stockport, *Greater Manchester*
Municipal Museum
Stretham, *Cambs.*
Swansea, *W. Glam.* Industrial
Museum of South Wales
Swindon, *Wilts.*
Great Western Railway Museum
Taunton, *Som.*
Somerset County Museum
Tilbury, *Essex*
Thurrock Local History Museum
Truro, *Cornwall*
County Museum and Art Gallery
Tywyn, *Gwynedd*
Narrow-Gauge Railway Museum
Walsall, *W. Midlands*
E. M. Flint Art Gallery;
Lock Museum, Willenhall;
Museum of Leathercraft
Woodstock, *Oxon.*
Oxford City and County Museum
Wootton Bassett, *Wilts.*
Yeovil, *Som.*
Borough of Yeovil Museum
York, *N. Yorks.* Railway Museum

LITERARY AND ARCHIVES

These collections take one into the private and public worlds of the
men who have helped to make English the most widely spoken
language in the world—its poets, novelists and dramatists. They live
on many levels, perhaps struggling with a sonnet and the taxman at
the same time, and their manuscripts and belongings, seen together,
convey a fascinating impression of their ideas and life: sometimes
complementary to each other, sometimes at variance. Throughout
the British Isles, carefully preserved archives and charters are fascinating
evidence of history in the making.

Abingdon, *Oxon.*
Borough Museum (County Hall)
Abbotsford House, *Borders*
Alloway, *Strathclyde* Burns Cottage

Altrincham, *Greater Manchester*
Art Gallery and Museum
Barnstaple, *Devon*
St Anne's Chapel Museum

641

Beaulieu, *Hants.*
  Montagu Motor Museum
Bedford, *Beds.*
Bembridge, *Isle of Wight*
  Ruskin Galleries
Birmingham, *W. Midlands*
  Assay Office; Museum of Science
  and Industry
Blackburn, *Lancs.*
  Museum and Art Gallery
Broughton Castle, *Oxon.*
Burford, *Oxon.*
  Tolsey Museum
Bury St Edmunds, *Suffolk*
  Moyses Hall Museum
Cambridge, *Cambs.*
  Fitzwilliam Museum; Trinity
  College Library; University
  Library
Chatsworth, *Derbys.*
Chawton, *Hants.*
  Jane Austen's Home
Coate, *Wilts.*
  Richard Jefferies Museum
Cockermouth, *Cumbria*
Dorchester, *Dorset*
  Dorset County Museum
Dublin, *Dublin* City Hall;
  Northland House (Royal Irish
  Academy); Trinity College
Dumfries, *Dumfs. & Gall.*
  Burns House
Dunvegan, *Isle of Skye, Highland*
East Looe, *Cornwall*
  Cornish Museum
Ecclefechan, *Dumfs. & Gall.*
  Carlyle's House
Edinburgh, *Lothian*
  Lady Stair's House; National
  Library of Scotland; Scottish
  United Services Museum
Elmore Court, *Glos.*
Elton Hall, *Cambs.*
Eye Manor, *Heref. & Worcs.*
Glasgow, *Strathclyde*
  Hunterian Museum
Gort, *Gal.*
Guildford, *Surrey*
  Museum and Muniment Room
Hartlebury Castle, *Heref. & Worcs.*
Hatfield House, *Herts.*
Haworth, *W. Yorks.*
  Brontë Parsonage Museum
Holkham Hall, *Norfolk*
Ingatestone, *Essex*
  Ingatestone Hall
Ixworth Abbey, *Suffolk*
Kilkenny, *Kilk.*
Kirkcaldy, *Fife*
  Museum and Art Gallery
Knebworth House, *Herts.*
Leeds, *W. Yorks.* Thoresby Society

Lincoln, *Lincs.*
  Cathedral; Cathedral Treasury;
  Stonebow and Guildhall; Usher
  Art Gallery
Liverpool, *Merseyside*
  Hornby Library
London
  British Museum; Carlyle's House;
  Cuming Museum; Dickens House;
  Guildhall; Johnson's House; Keats
  House; Lambeth Palace; Lincoln's
  Inn; Passmore Edwards Museum;
  Percival David Foundation of
  Chinese Art; Pharmaceutical
  Society's Museum; Public Record
  Office; Royal College of Music;
  Royal Geographical Society;
  Wellcome Institute of the History of
  Medicine
Lyme Regis, *Dorset*
  Philpot Museum
Maidstone, *Kent*
  Chillington Manor
Manchester, *Greater Manchester*
  Chetham's Library
Meigle, *Tayside* Museum
Mellerstain, *Borders*
Monmouth, *Gwent* Nelson Museum
Montrose, *Tayside*
Moseley Old Hall, *W. Midlands*
Newstead Abbey, *Notts.*
Norwich, *Norfolk*
  St Peter Hungate Museum
Nuneaton, *Warks.*
  Museum and Art Gallery
Oxford, *Oxon.* Bodleian Library
Ragley Hall, *Warks.*
Reigate, *Surrey*
  Church of St Mary Magdalene
Rudding Park, *N. Yorks.*
Rufford, *Lancs.*
  Rufford Old Hall
Selborne, *Hants.*
  Gilbert White Museum and the
  Oates Memorial Museum
Shaftesbury, *Dorset*
  Shaftesbury and District Historical
  Society's Museum of Local History
South Molton, *Devon*
  Borough Museum
Southsea, *Hants.*
  Royal Marines Museum
Tamworth, *Staffs.* Castle Museum
Thrumpton Hall, *Notts.*
Uxbridge, *Greater London*
  Hamson Museum
Walsall, *W. Midlands*
  E. M. Flint Art Gallery
Winchester, *Hants.*
  Cathedral; City Museum
Wisbech, *Cambs.*
Wrexham, *Clwyd* Public Library

MARITIME

Since Alfred the Great built a fleet of ships to defend Britain from
Danish attack in the 9th century, Britain's security has rested largely
on the skill and courage of her seamen. Her museums are rich in the
romance and excitement of the sea: relics of great sailors can be seen,
and great ships like the *Victory* at Portsmouth; finally the instruments
of navigation on which life at sea depends convey their own excitement, even on dry land.

Arlington Court, *Devon*
Birkenhead, *Merseyside*
  Williamson Art Gallery and
  Museum
Bournemouth, *Dorset*
  Rothesay Museum
Bridgwater, *Som.*
  Admiral Blake Museum
Bridlington, *Humberside*
  Bayle Museum

Bridport, *Dorset*
  Museum and Art Gallery
Bristol, *Avon*
  Maritime Centre
Bucklers Hard, *Hants.*
  Maritime Museum
Claverton Manor, *Avon*
  The American Museum in Britain
Colchester, *Essex*
  Colchester and Essex Museum

Dartmouth, *Devon*
 Borough Museum
Dorchester, *Dorset*
Dundee, *Tayside*
 City Art Gallery and Museum
Edinburgh, *Lothian*
 Royal Scottish Museum
Exeter, *Devon* Maritime Museum
Great Yarmouth, *Norfolk*
 Maritime Museum for East Anglia
Greenock, *Strathclyde*
 McLean Museum and Art Gallery
Greenwich, *Greater London*
 National Maritime Museum
Grimsby, *Humberside*
 Doughty Museum
Ipswich, *Suffolk*
 Christchurch Mansion
Kingston upon Hull, *Humberside*
Lerwick, *Shetland*
 Shetland County Museum
London Science Museum
Middlesbrough, *Cleveland*
 Dorman Memorial Museum and
 Municipal Art Gallery
Monmouth, *Gwent*
 Nelson Museum

Norwich, *Norfolk*
 Bridewell Museum
Peterhead, *Grampian*
 Arbuthnot Museum
Poole, *Dorset*
 Old Town House; Poole Museum
Portsmouth, *Hants.*
 Mary Rose Exhibition;
 Southsea Castle; Victory Museum
Saltcoats, *Strathclyde*
 North Ayrshire Museum
Shoreham-by-Sea, *W. Sussex*
 Marlipins Museum
Southampton, *Hants.*
 Tudor House; Wool House
Southend-on-Sea, *Essex*
 Beecroft Art Gallery
South Shields, *Tyne & Wear*
 Museum
Sunderland, *Durham*
 Museum and Art Gallery
Tresco, *Isles of Scilly*
 Valhalla Maritime Museum
Truro, *Cornwall*
 Museum and Art Gallery
Worthing, *W. Sussex*
 Museum and Art Gallery

MILITARY AND UNIFORMS

The regimental museums of the British Isles chronicle not only the changing techniques of war—red jackets to commando camouflage, sieges to ejector seats—but also its human aspect: the letters, documents and medal citations displayed all tell the private story of wartime's grief, heroism, action and fear.

Abingdon, *Oxon.*
 Borough Museum (County
 Hall)
Aldershot, *Hants.*
 Airborne Forces Museum; Queen
 Alexandra's Royal Army Nursing
 Corps Museum; Royal Army
 Dental Corps Museum; Royal
 Army Medical Corps Historical
 Museum
Alnwick Castle, *Northld.*
 Regimental Museum of the
 Royal Northumberland Fusiliers
Arborfield, *Berks.*
 Museum of the Corps of Royal
 Electrical and Mechanical
 Engineers
Blair Castle, *Tayside*
Brecon, *Powys*
 South Wales Borderers Regimental
 Museum
Bridgwater, *Som.*
 Admiral Blake Museum
Burnley, *Lancs.*
 East Lancashire Regimental
 Museum, Townley Hall
Bury, *Greater Manchester*
 Lancashire Regiment Museum
Bury St Edmunds, *Suffolk*
 Suffolk Regiment Museum
Canterbury, *Kent*
 The Buffs Regimental Museum
Cardiff, *S. Glam.*
 Welch Regiment Regimental
 Museum

Carlisle, *Cumbria*
 King's Own Royal Border
 Regiment Museum; Castle
Cefntilla Court, *Gwent*
Chatham, *Kent*
 Museum of the Corps of Royal
 Engineers
Chichester, *W. Sussex*
 City Museum; Corps of Royal
 Military Police Museum
Devizes, *Wilts.*
 Wiltshire Regimental Museum
Dorchester, *Dorset*
 Dorset Military Museum
Dublin, *Dublin*
 Cathedral of St Patrick
Dunrobin Castle, *Highland*
Eastbourne, *E. Sussex*
 The Redoubt; Tower 73
Edinburgh, *Lothian*
 Regimental Museum of the Royal
 Scots; Scottish United Services
 Museum
Exeter, *Devon*
 Devonshire Regiment Museum
Fort George, *Highland*
 Regimental Museum of The
 Seaforth Highlanders, The Queen's
 Own Cameron Highlanders
 and Queen's Own Highlanders
Gloucester, *Glos.*
 Bishop Hooper's Lodging
Greenock, *Strathclyde*
 McLean Museum and
 Art Gallery

643

Greenwich, *Greater London*
National Maritime Museum
Guildford, *Surrey*
Women's Royal Army Corps
Museum
Hereford, *Heref. & Worcs.*
City Museum and Art Gallery
Hertford, *Herts.*
Museum
Honiton, *Devon*
Honiton and Allhallows Public
Museum
Ipswich, *Suffolk* Museum
Kingston upon Thames, *Greater London*
Queen's Royal Surrey Regiment
Museum
La Hougue Bie, *Jersey*
German Occupation Museum
Lancaster, *Lancs.*
Lancaster City Museum
Leicester, *Leics.*
Newarke Houses Museum
Lichfield, *Staffs.*
Staffordshire Regimental Museum
London
Imperial War Museum;
National Army Museum;
Royal Courts of Justice
Monmouth, *Gwent*
Nelson Museum
Northampton, *Northants.*
Northamptonshire Regiment
Museum

Norwich, *Norfolk*
Royal Norfolk Regiment Museum
Old Warden Aerodrome, *Beds.*
Shuttleworth Collection
Pontefract, *W. Yorks.*
King's Own Yorkshire Light
Infantry Museum
Portsmouth, *Hants.*
Southsea Castle; Victory Museum
(Royal Naval Museum); Mary
Rose Exhibition and Ship Hall
Preston, *Lancs.*
Lancastrian Brigade Museum
Richmond, *N. Yorks.*
Green Howards Museum
Rufford, *Lancs.*
Rufford Old Hall and
Folk Museum
Southsea, *Hants.*
Royal Marines Museum
Walsall, *W. Midlands*
Museum of Leathercraft
Warwick, *Warks.*
Lord Leycester Hospital and
Chapel of St James
Wilton House, *Wilts.*
Winchester, *Hants.*
Royal Greenjackets Museum;
Royal Hampshire Regimental
Museum
Yeovilton, *Som.*
Fleet Air Arm Museum
York, *N. Yorks.*
Debtors' Prison

NATURAL HISTORY

The greatest craftsman and artist of all is Nature, the ultimate source
of inspiration. At London's Natural History Museum one can stand
beneath the great whale, dwarfed by an amazing ocean-going creature,
and only a few steps away marvel at the intricate delicacy of a hum-
mingbird's feathers or a sea shell's spiralling precision; but whatever
the size of the collection—one of the largest in the world or a small
village museum—Nature's astonishing virtuosity never fails: the
exhibits are always of the highest quality.

Abingdon, *Oxon.*
Borough Museum (County Hall)
Alton, *Hants.* Curtis Museum
Batley, *W. Yorks.*
Bagshaw Museum
Bedford, *Beds.* Museum
Bexhill, *E. Sussex* Museum
Birchington, *Kent*
Powell-Cotton Museum
Birmingham, *W. Midlands*
Cannon Hill; City Museum and
Art Gallery; Geology Depart-
mental Museum, University
Bournemouth, *Dorset*
Rothesay Museum
Bradford, *W. Yorks.*
City Art Gallery and Museum
Bridport, *Dorset*
Museum and Art Gallery
Brighton, *E. Sussex*
Museum and Art Gallery
Burton upon Trent, *Staffs.*
Museum and Art Gallery
Buxton, *Derbys.* Museum
Camborne, *Cornwall*
Public Library and Museum
Canterbury, *Kent*
Royal Museum (Beaney Institute)
Cheltenham Spa, *Glos.*
Art Gallery and Museum
Christchurch, *Dorset*
Red House Museum and Art
Gallery
Colchester, *Essex*
Colchester and Essex Museum

Colne, *Lancs.* Museum
Dartford, *Kent*
Borough Museum
Derby, *Derbys.*
Museum and Art Gallery
Dorchester, *Dorset*
Dorset County Museum
Dover, *Kent*
Corporation Museum
Downe, *Kent*
Down House
Dudley, *W. Midlands*
Central Museum
Dumfries, *Dumf. & Gall.*
Observatory (Burgh Museum)
Dundee, *Tayside*
McManus Gallery
Dunrobin Castle, *Highland*
Edinburgh, *Lothian*
Royal Scottish Museum
Erith, *Greater London* Museum
Forfar, *Tayside*
Meffan Institute Museum
Glandford, *Norfolk*
Museum of Shells
Glasgow, *Strathclyde*
Hunterian Museum
Gloucester, *Glos.*
City Museum and Art Gallery
Godalming, *Surrey*
Charterhouse School Museum
Greenock, *Strathclyde*
McLean Museum and Art Gallery
Greenwich, *Greater London*
Borough Museum

Haslemere, *Surrey*
Educational Museum
Hereford, *Heref. & Worcs.*
City Museum and Art Gallery
Hertford, *Herts.*
Museum
Hodnet Hall, *Salop*
Honiton, *Devon*
Honiton and Allhallows Public
Museum
Inverurie, *Grampian* Museum
Ipswich, *Suffolk* Museum
Kendal, *Cumbria*
Borough Museum
Kew, *Greater London*
Royal Botanic Gardens Museums
of Economic Botany
King's Lynn, *Norfolk*
Museum and Art Gallery
Kirkcaldy, *Fife*
Museum and Art Gallery
Leeds, *W. Yorks.* City Museum
Lincoln, *Lincs.*
City and County Museum
Liverpool, *Merseyside*
City Museum
London
Broomfield House Museum;
Geological Museum; Horniman
Museum; Natural History
Museum; Passmore Edwards
Museum; Queen Elizabeth's
Hunting Lodge
Ludlow, *Salop* Museum
Macclesfield, *Cheshire*
Westpark Museum
Mansfield, *Notts.*
Museum and Art Gallery
Merthyr Tydfil, *Mid Glam.*
Art Gallery and Museum
Middlesbrough, *Cleveland*
Dorman Memorial Museum and
Municipal Art Gallery
Millport, *Isle of Cumbrae, Strathclyde*
Robertson Museum and the
Aquarium
Newbury, *Berks.*
Borough Museum
Newcastle upon Tyne, *Tyne & Wear*
Hancock Museum
North Berwick, *Lothian*
Burgh Museum
Norwich, *Norfolk* Castle
Oxford, *Oxon.*
Museum of the History of Science
Peterborough, *Cambs.*
Museum and Maxwell Art Gallery
Plymouth, *Devon*
City Museum and Art Gallery

Port Erin, *Isle of Man*
Marine Biological Station
Portsmouth, *Hants.* Cumberland
House Museum and Art Gallery
Reading, *Berks.* Cole Museum;
Museum and Art Gallery
Rossendale, *Lancs.*
Rawtenstall Museum
Royal Tunbridge Wells, *Kent*
St Helier, *Jersey*
Jersey Museum and Barreau
Gallery
Salford, *Greater Manchester*
Science Museum
Sandown, *Isle of Wight*
Isle of Wight Museum of Geology
Scarborough, *N. Yorks.*
Museum of Natural History
Selborne, *Hants.*
Gilbert White Museum and Oates
Memorial Museum
Sheffield, *S. Yorks.* City Museum
Silchester, *Hants.* Calleva Museum
Skipton, *N. Yorks.* Craven Museum
Southend-on-Sea, *Essex*
Prittlewell Priory Museum
South Shields, *Tyne & Wear*
Museum
Southwold, *Suffolk* Museum
Spalding, *Lincs.*
Ayscoughfee Hall
Stalybridge, *Greater Manchester*
Astley Cheetham Art Gallery
Stevenage, *Herts.* Museum
Stirling, *Central*
Smith Art Gallery and Museum
Stockport, *Greater Manchester*
Municipal Museum
Sunderland, *Tyne & Wear*
Museum and Art Gallery
Swindon, *Wilts.*
Museum and Art Gallery
Taunton, *Som.*
Somerset County Museum
Tenby, *Dyfed* Museum
Thetford, *Norfolk*
Ancient House Museum
Torquay, *Devon*
Torquay Natural History Society
Museum
Tring, *Herts.*
Zoological Museum
Warwick, *Warks.*
Warwick County Museum
Wollaton, *Notts.*
Wollaton Hall Natural History
Museum
Worksop, *Notts.*
Public Library and Museum

POTTERY

Since prehistoric man first watched rain collect in clay hollows, and learnt to make vessels out of this special kind of earth (perhaps some of it accidentally baked in his fire), clay has fascinated him, and he has put it to innumerable uses, as varied as the Greek amphorae in the British Museum and the Staffordshire figures of Victoria and Napoleon at Stapleford Park in Leicestershire.

Aberdeen, *Grampian*
University Anthropological
Museum
Aberystwyth, *Dyfed*
University College, Aberystwyth
Abingdon, *Oxon.*
Borough Museum (County Hall)
Alton, *Hants.*
Curtis Museum
Antony House, *Cornwall*
Arbury Hall, *Warks.*
Ascott, *Bucks.*
Ashwell, *Herts.*
Ashwell Village Museum

Avebury, *Wilts.*
Avebury Manor
Aylesford, *Kent*
Barlaston, *Staffs.*
Wedgwood Museum Trust
Barnard Castle, *Durham*
Bowes Museum
Barnstaple, *Devon*
St Anne's Chapel Museum
Basing, *Hants.* Basing House Ruins
Bath, *Avon*
Holburne of Menstrie Museum;
Victoria Art Gallery
Batley, *W. Yorks.* Bagshaw Museum

Bedford, *Beds.*
  Cecil Higgins Art Gallery
Berwick upon Tweed, *Northld.*
  Museum and Art Gallery
Birkenhead, *Merseyside*
  Williamson Art Gallery and
  Museum
Birmingham, *W. Midlands*
  Aston Hall; City Museum and
  Art Gallery
Blair Castle, *Tayside*
Blenheim Palace, *Oxon.*
Bodrhyddan Hall, *Clwyd*
Bootle, *Merseyside*
  Art Gallery and Museum
Bournemouth, *Dorset*
  Rothesay Museum; Russell-Cotes
  Museum and Art Gallery
Bradford, *W. Yorks.*
  City Art Gallery and Museum
Brighton, *E. Sussex*
  Museum and Art Gallery;
  Thomas-Stanford Museum
Bristol, *Avon* Church of St Mark
Brodick Castle, *Arran, Strathclyde*
Broughton Castle, *Oxon.*
Burton Agnes Hall, *Humberside*
Buxton, *Derbys.* Museum
Cambridge, *Cambs.*
  Fitzwilliam Museum
Canterbury, *Kent*
  Royal Museum (Beaney Institute)
Capesthorne, *Cheshire*
Cefntilla Court, *Gwent*
Cheltenham Spa, *Glos.*
  Art Gallery and Museum
Chichester, *W. Sussex* City Museum
Chorley, *Lancs.* Astley Hall
Clevedon Court, *Avon*
Colchester, *Essex*
  Colchester and Essex Museum;
  Minories
Derby, *Derbys.*
  Museum and Art Gallery
Doddington Hall, *Lincs.*
Dover, *Kent* Corporation Museum
Durham, *Durham* Durham
  University Oriental Museum
Eccles, *Greater Manchester* Monks
  Hall Museum
Edinburgh, *Lothian*
  Royal Scottish Museum
Enfield, *Greater London* Forty Hall
Firle Place, *E. Sussex*
Gainsborough, *Lincs.* Old Hall
Garthewin, *Clwyd*
Glandford, *Norfolk* Museum of Shells
Glasgow, *Strathclyde*
  Burrell Collection
Gloucester, *Glos.*
  City Museum and Art Gallery
Godalming, *Surrey*
  Charterhouse School Museum
Godington Park, *Kent*
Goodwood House, *W. Sussex*
Great Yarmouth, *Norfolk*
  Elizabethan Museum
Grimsby, *Humberside* Doughty
  Museum
Guildford, *Surrey*
  Museum and Muniment Room
Harewood House, *W. Yorks.*
Hereford, *Heref. & Worcs.*
  City Museum and Art Gallery
Hill Top, *Cumbria*
Ilkley, *W. Yorks.* Manor House
  Museum and Art Gallery
Ingatestone, *Essex*
  Ingatestone Hall
Ipswich, *Suffolk*
  Christchurch Mansion
King's Lynn, *Norfolk*
  Museum and Art Gallery
Kirkcaldy, *Fife*
  Museum and Art Gallery
Leeds, *W. Yorks.* City Art Gallery

Leicester, *Leics.*
  Museum and Art Gallery
Lincoln, *Lincs.*
  Usher Art Gallery
London
  British Museum; Courtauld
  Institute Galleries; Fenton House;
  Passmore Edwards Museum;
  Percival David Foundation
  of Chinese Art; Royal Courts of
  Justice; Southall District Library;
  Victoria and Albert Museum;
  Wallace Collection;
  Wellcome Institute of the
  History of Medicine
Luton, *Beds.*
  Museum and Art Gallery
Luton Hoo, *Beds.*
Maidenhead, *Berks.*
  Henry Reitlinger Bequest
Manchester, *Greater Manchester*
  City Art Gallery; Wythenshawe
  Hall, Northenden
Melford Hall, *Suffolk*
Merthyr Tydfil, *Mid Glam.*
  Art Gallery and Museum
Monmouth, *Gwent*
  Nelson Museum
New Barnet, *Greater London*
  Abbey Art Centre and Museum
Newport, *Gwent*
  Museum and Art Gallery
Northampton, *Northants.*
  Abington Park Museum; Central
  Museum and Art Gallery
North Berwick, *Lothian*
  Burgh Museum
Norwich, *Norfolk*
  St Peter Hungate Museum
Nottingham, *Notts.*
  Castle Museum; City Museum
  and Art Gallery
Nuneaton, *Warks.*
  Museum and Art Gallery
Penrhyn Castle, *Gwynedd*
Peterborough, *Cambs.*
  Museum and Maxwell Art Gallery
Plymouth, *Devon*
  City Museum and Art Gallery
Pontefract, *W. Yorks.*
  Castle Museum
Poole, *Dorset*
  Old Town House; Poole Museum
Port Sunlight, *Merseyside*
  Lady Lever Art Gallery
Ragley Hall, *Warks.*
Reading, *Berks.*
  Museum and Art Gallery;
  Museum of Greek
  Archaeology
Rossendale, *Lancs.*
  Rawtenstall Museum
Rotherham, *S. Yorks.*
  Municipal Museum and Art
  Gallery
Royal Leamington Spa, *Warks.*
  Art Gallery and Museum
Royal Tunbridge Wells, *Kent*
Rudding Park, *N. Yorks.*
Rufford, *Lancs.*
  Rufford Old Hall and Folk
  Museum
St Ives, *Cambs.*
  Norris Library and Museum
St Osyth's Priory, *Essex*
Salisbury, *Wilts.*
  Salisbury and South Wiltshire
  Museum
Saltram House, *Devon*
Sandford Orcas Manor, *Dorset*
Scarborough, *N. Yorks.*
  Museum
Scone Palace, *Tayside*
Seaton Delaval Hall, *Northld.*
Shugborough, *Staffs.*
Sledmere House, *Humberside*

Southampton, *Hants.*
God's House Tower
Southport, *Merseyside*
Botanic Garden Museum
Stockport, *Greater Manchester*
Municipal Museum
Stoke-on-Trent, *Staffs.*
City Museum and Art Gallery
Sunderland, *Tyne & Wear*
Museum and Art Gallery
Swansea, *W. Glam.*
Glyñn Vivian Art Gallery
Tarvit House, *Fife*
Tatton Park, *Cheshire*
Taunton, *Som.*
Somerset County Museum

Temple Newsam House, *W. Yorks.*
Truro, *Cornwall*
County Museum and Art Gallery
Upton House, *Warks.*
Waddesdon Manor, *Bucks.*
Wallington House, *Northld.*
Wookey, *Som.*
Wookey Hole Caves Museum
Worcester, *Heref. & Worcs.*
Dyson Perrins Museum
Worksop, *Notts.*
Public Library and Museum
Worthing, *W. Sussex*
Museum and Art Gallery
York, *N. Yorks.*
City of York Art Gallery

SCIENTIFIC AND MEDICAL

Man's struggle for knowledge and against disease and pain has been with him as long as life itself; these collections record its triumphs, superstitions and failures, its heroes and heroines.

Aldershot, *Hants.*
Queen Alexandra's Royal Army Nursing Corps Museum; Royal Army Dental Corps Museum; Royal Army Medical Corps Historical Museum
Birmingham, *W. Midlands*
Museum of Science and Industry
Brighton, *E. Sussex*
Museum and Art Gallery
Cambridge, *Cambs.*
Scott Polar Research Institute; Whipple Museum of the History of Science
Downe, *Kent* Down House
Eccles, *Greater Manchester* Monks Hall Museum
Edinburgh, *Lothian* Royal College of Surgeons of Edinburgh

Helston, *Cornwall*
Borough Museum
London
Geological Museum; Health Exhibition Centre, Royal Society of Health; Pharmaceutical Society's Museum; Royal College of Surgeons' Museum; Royal Geographical Society; Royal Hospital; Science Museum; Wellcome Institute of the History of Medicine
Ludlow, *Salop*
Museum
Oxford, *Oxon.*
Museum of the History of Science; University Museum
Snowshill Manor, *Glos.*
York, *N. Yorks.*

TEXTILES AND CLOTHING

Perhaps the most personal of the arts, textiles have been used since the earliest days of man's civilisation to protect himself—from the elements, and from cold stone floors or bare walls—and to distinguish one man from another: priest from king, peasant from lord. Mary, Queen of Scots embroidered to pass away the time of her imprisonment, and the well brought up Victorian lady sewed as an accepted element of her social accomplishment.

Aberdeen, *Grampian*
Art Gallery
Abergavenny, *Gwent*
Abergavenny and District Museum
Abingdon, *Oxon.*
Borough Museum (County Hall)
Acrise Place, *Kent*
Antony House, *Cornwall*
Barnard Castle, *Durham*
Bowes Museum

Barnet, *Greater London*
Museum
Basingstoke, *Hants.*
Willis Museum
Bath, *Avon*
Museum of Costume
Bedford, *Beds.*
Cecil Higgins Art Gallery
Belton, *Kesteven, Lincs.*
Belton House
Belvoir Castle, *Leics.*
Berkeley Castle, *Glos.*

Birmingham, *W. Midlands*
Aston Hall; City Museum and
Art Gallery
Blackburn, *Lancs.*
Museum and Art Gallery
Blair Castle, *Tayside*
Blenheim Palace, *Oxon.*
Blickling Hall, *Norfolk*
Boughton Monchelsea Place,
Kent
Bradford, *W. Yorks.*
Bolling Hall
Bramall Hall, *Greater Manchester*
Breamore, *Hants.*
Breamore House
Brighton, *E. Sussex*
Thomas-Stanford Museum
Bucklers Hard, *Hants.*
Maritime Museum
Burghley House, *Cambs.*
Cambridge, *Cambs.*
Fitzwilliam Museum
Castle Ashby, *Northants.*
Castle Howard, *N. Yorks.*
Chasleton House, *Oxon.*
Chirk Castle, *Clwyd*
Chorley, *Lancs.*
Astley Hall
Christchurch, *Dorset*
Red House Museum and Art
Gallery
Clandon Park, *Surrey*
Colchester, *Essex*
Colchester and Essex Museum
Cotehele House, *Cornwall*
Cultra Manor, *Down*
Ulster Folk Museum
Denham Place, *Bucks.*
Doddington Hall, *Lincs.*
Dover, *Kent*
Corporation Museum
Dublin, *Dublin*
City Hall; Old Parliament House
Dunrobin Castle, *Highland*
Dunster, *Som.* Castle
Durham, *Durham* Gulbenkian
Museum of Oriental Art
Dyrham Park, *Avon*
Eastnor Castle, *Heref. & Worcs.*
Edinburgh, *Lothian*
Palace of Holyroodhouse
Elmore Court, *Glos.*
Exeter, *Devon*
Royal Albert Memorial Museum
and Art Gallery
Eye Manor, *Heref. & Worcs.*
Farnham, *Surrey*
Willmer House Museum
Forde Abbey, *Som.*
Gainsborough, *Lincs.*
Old Hall
Gawthorpe Hall, *Lancs.*
Glasgow, *Strathclyde*
Burrell Collection;
Provand's Lordship
Gloucester, *Glos.*
City Museum and Art Gallery
Glynde Place, *E. Sussex*
Guildford, *Surrey* Cathedral
Ham House, *Greater London*
Hardwick Hall, *Derbys.*
Hereford, *Heref. & Worcs.*
Churchill Gardens Museum
Hinwick House, *Northants.*
Inveraray Castle, *Strathclyde*
Ipswich, *Suffolk*
Christchurch Mansion
Kilbarchan, *Strathclyde*
Weaver's Cottage
King's Lynn, *Norfolk*
Museum and Art Gallery
Kingston Lacy, *Dorset*
Knole, *Kent*

La Hougue Bie, *Jersey*
German Occupation Museum
Leeds, *W. Yorks.*
Abbey House Museum
Leek, *Staffs.*
Art Gallery
Lerwick, *Shetland*
Shetland County Museum
Littlecote, *Wilts.*
London
Museum of London;
Victoria and Albert Museum
Loseley House, *Surrey*
Luton, *Beds.*
Museum and Art Gallery
Luton Hoo, *Beds.*
Lyme Park, *Cheshire*
Manchester, *Greater Manchester*
Gallery of English Costume;
Platt Hall, Rusholme; Whitworth
Art Gallery
Michelham Priory, *E. Sussex*
Newbury, *Berks.*
Borough Museum
Newcastle upon Tyne, *Tyne & Wear*
Laing Art Gallery
Northampton, *Northants.*
Abington Park Museum; Central
Museum and Art Gallery
North Berwick, *Lothian*
Burgh Museum
Norwich, *Norfolk*
Bridewell Museum; St Peter
Hungate Museum; Strangers Hall
Nottingham, *Notts.*
Castle Museum; City Museum
and Art Gallery
Osterley Park House, *Greater*
London
Oxford, *Oxon.*
Ashmolean Museum
Packwood House, *Warks.*
Royal Tunbridge Wells, *Kent*
Rudding Park, *N. Yorks.*
Rufford, *Lancs.*
Rufford Old Hall
Salisbury, *Wilts.* Salisbury and
South Wiltshire Museum
Sawston Hall, *Cambs.*
Shaftesbury, *Dorset*
Shaftesbury and District
Historical Society's Museum of
Local History
Somerleyton Hall, *Suffolk*
Southampton, *Hants.*
Tudor House
Stanford Hall, *Leics.*
Stapleford Park, *Leics.*
Stranraer, *Dumfs. & Gall.*
Wigtown County Museum
Stratford-upon-Avon, *Warks.*
Royal Shakespeare Theatre
Picture Gallery
Sudeley Castle, *Glos.*
Tarvit House, *Fife*
Traquair House, *Borders*
Upton House, *Warks.*
Walsall, *W. Midlands*
Museum of Leathercraft
Waterford, *Waterford* Cathedral
Welshpool, *Powys*
Powis Castle
Weybridge, *Surrey* Museum
Westerham, *Kent*
Squerryes Court
Weston Park, *Staffs.*
West Wycombe, *Bucks.*
West Wycombe Park
Worthing, *W. Sussex*
Museum and Art Gallery
Yeovil, *Som.*
Borough of Yeovil Museum
York, *N. Yorks.* Debtors' Prison

IOOO YEARS OF DESIGN

Details of architecture and decoration
re the key to recognising period style

Each period makes certain decorative elements its own. Gothic craftsmen used the pointed arch not only to vault their cathedral roofs, but to decorate their furniture. The Elizabethans covered walls, ceilings, silverware and furniture with strapwork ornament, and from the scholarship of the Georgian period evolved windows, chairs and staircases of Classical perfection. Victorian romantics harked back to the Middle Ages and to Greece and Rome to produce railway stations like cathedrals and town halls like temples. The details of architecture and decoration shown here enable the evolution of styles (described inside the continuity flaps) to be traced from Saxon times to the outbreak of the First World War, and the commentary at the top of each spread describes some of the historic events that helped to shape the appearance of things in Britain.

In this chronological style chart, subjects are grouped into horizontal bands across the pages, with continuity flaps linking the sequences from page to page. Under the flaps and across the heads of the pages background notes keep pace with the developments illustrated.

ANGLO-SAXON

EARLY SAXON KINGS	978–1042
EDWARD THE CONFESSOR	1042–1066
HAROLD II	1066

Most buildings were of wood and few have survived. The stone-built churches are more interesting for their decoration than their form.

NORMAN (ROMANESQUE)

WILLIAM THE CONQUEROR	1066–1087
WILLIAM II	1087–1100
HENRY I	1100–1135
STEPHEN	1135–1154
HENRY II	1154–1189

Characteristics of the style are round arches, barrel vaults, walls decorated with interlacing arches and arcades, highly decorated doorways, and an abundance of mouldings.

EARLY ENGLISH

RICHARD I	1189–1199
JOHN	1199–1216
HENRY III	1216–1272

Squat, bulky structures gave way to lighter, taller buildings.

DECORATED

EDWARD I	1272–1307
EDWARD II	1307–1327
EDWARD III	1327–1377

Early English innovations were improved, resulting in larger windows, tracery work, and a superabundance of decorative features covering surfaces, gables and arches.

PERPENDICULAR

RICHARD II	1377–1399
HENRY IV	1399–1413
HENRY V	1413–1422
HENRY VI	1422–1461
EDWARD IV	1461–1483
EDWARD V	1483
RICHARD III	1483–1485

A return to comparative simplicity. Buttresses were now deeper, allowing even larger windows, tracery was at its most elegant, the four-centred arch appeared, and fan-vaulting reached perfection.

TUDOR

HENRY VII	1485–1509
HENRY VIII	1509–1547
EDWARD VI	1547–1553

The slow transition from Gothic to Renaissance. Large houses were built, many of them in the new building material—brick.

ELIZABETHAN

MARY I	1553–1558
ELIZABETH I	1558–1603

The growth of a new aristocracy and the wider distribution of wealth led to a vast increase in domestic build-ing. The Renaissance brought a revival of Classical features. In the larger houses and palaces (often of a symmetrical E or H shape), galleries, grand staircases and carved chimneys appeared. Brick became the fashionable building material.

JACOBEAN

JAMES I (VI OF SCOTLAND)	1603–1625

The period from 1603 to 1625 was marked by mannered, lively ornament and profusely decorated open surfaces. The great houses showed even greater symmetry and Inigo Jones began to build in the Palladian style, derived from the work of the Italian architect Andrea Palladio.

STUART

CHARLES I	1625–1649
COMMONWEALTH	1649–1660
CHARLES II	1660–1685
JAMES II	1685–1688

The acceptance of Classical architecture was not complete until the time of Wren (1652–1723). Columns, cornices, pediments, architraved windows, and elegant proportions are characteristics of the period.

QUEEN ANNE

WILLIAM III AND MARY II	1689–1702
ANNE	1702–1714

The age of the English baroque school, which tempered pure baroque's florid ornamentation and over-emphasis of detail with the Classical.

GEORGIAN AND REGENCY

GEORGE I	1714–1727
GEORGE II	1727–1760
GEORGE III	1760–1820
GEORGE IV	1820–1830

The Georgian era brought a return to the beauty of form and proportion. For the middle classes terraced houses were built. Towards the end of the period Regency decoration emerged.

VICTORIAN

WILLIAM IV	1830–1837
VICTORIA	1837–1901

The new rich class built to impress—and architects designed in styles ranging from pseudo-Egyptian to Elizabethan, but particularly Gothic Revival and Greek Revival. Mass schemes of squalid, insanitary houses were erected for the working classes. Steel and concrete, products of the Industrial Revolution, were largely ignored by architects, but exploited by engineers.

EDWARDIAN

EDWARD VII	1901–1910

The trend in architecture from 1911 to 1914 was largely a continuation of the Victorian style. The art nouveau movement influenced decoration.

649

THE MARKS OF FASHION

The Norman Conquest removes England from Scandinavian influences and ties her politically, commercially and culturally to France and the Continent.

Norman castles overawe the people. The pointed arch, able to support stone roofs over more ambitious ground plans, is introduced. The Crusaders bring home

Arabic numerals, medicines, astrono arithmetic, the clock and a taste luxuries. Heraldry becomes importan a 'badge of rank' in feudal society as

DOORS AND WINDOWS:

arches, porches, arcades and entrances

10th-century Saxon window, Worth Church, W. Sussex. Saxon windows are narrow, with thick baluster shafts

Saxon doorway, Brixworth Church, Northamptonshire

Norman doorway, Kilpeck, Heref. & Worcs., *c.* 1140

Norman porch and staircase, Canterbury Cathedral

DETAILS OF BUILDINGS:

vaults, ceilings, roofs, buttresses, columns, capitals, gargoyles

Carved Norman capital from the crypt, Canterbury Cathedral

Norman arcaded chapel, Tower of London

Carved doorway jamb, Kilpeck Church, Heref. & Worcs.

Decorated Norman capital, Leominster Priory, Heref. & Worcs.

Norman colum chevron-incise Durham Cathe

TOWERS, BRIDGES, STAIRS:

domes, spires, parapets, balustrades

Saxon tower, Sompting Church, W. Sussex, with unusual 'German Helm' roof. Saxon towers are narrow and simple in form and detail, with small windows

CHRIST IN MAJESTY—ELY CATHEDRAL. *c.* 1100

Norman tower, Tewkesbury Abbey, Glos.

FIRE-PLACES AND CHIMNEYS:

stoves, fire-irons, kitchens

Central brick hearth with iron fire-dogs, Penshurst Place, Kent

Church authority was the most constant factor in the Middle Ages, of which this awesome figure, symmetrical and deeply carved, is typical

Wall fire-place, Rochest Castle, Kent, *c.* 1130. An advance on the centre he

FURNITURE AND DOMESTIC ARTICLES:

beds, tables, chairs, clocks, bowls, mirrors, candlesticks

St Augustine's Chair, Canterbury Cathedral. Marble, probably 13th century. Archbishops of Canterbury have been enthroned in this chair for over 700 years

13th-century carved oak chests. One is a strongbox, with wrought iron clasps; the other a storage chest, pierced with holes for ventilation

Saxon bucket with bronze bands, the top band decorated in relief; and a Saxon glass tumbler with spiral ornament

MEMORIALS, MONUMENTS AND MEMENTOES:

plaques, sculpture, tombs, ornaments

Saxon cross, 8th century. The interlaced carved motifs are also found in manuscripts of the period. Some crosses are carved with animal or human figures

Norman font, Eardisley Church, Heref. & Worcs. The carving shows soldiers with spear and sword

Details from the edges of the Bayeux Tapestry, showing the stylised treatment of strange animals and plants

Norman to in the Lady Cha Exeter Cathed It may represent Leof an early bishop of Exe The bishop's right han raised in bless

in battle. Churches have reliquaries
ade for relics brought from abroad;
lgrimages and shrines become popular.
nglish scholars returning from Paris
and Bologna found the universities of
Oxford and Cambridge. Edward I sub-
jugates Wales and builds its great border
castles. Merchant classes begin to emerge.

e tracery: rose window,
oln Cathedral, c. 1220.
v-style Gothic decoration

Multiple lancet window,
Hereford Cathedral, 1220.
Pointed, ornamented arches

West front portal, Salis-
bury Cathedral, 1234-58

Norman columns and vaulting,
Canterbury Cathedral crypt

Multiple columns,
foliated capitals

13th-century foliated
capital from Lincoln
Cathedral

Fortified gateway:
Micklegate Bar, York

Shuttered window, Little
Wenham Hall, Suffolk

Stone vault, Dur-
ham Cathedral

Fire-place with stone hood,
c. 1200. The hood gives an
improved draught

External stone castle
staircase, 13th-century

Newel staircase,
Dover Castle

ron hanging candleholder, c. 1240.
Candles were mainly for the wealthy

Carved oak chair, for the
head of the household

The Gloucester
candlestick,
made c. 1100 of
bronze or bell-
metal. The whole
surface is orna-
mented with
figures of men
and monsters.
Victoria and
Albert Museum.

Bronze sanctuary door knocker
from Durham Cathedral. Anyone
who grasped the knocker was
under the Church's protection

e Great Seal of Henry II
54-89). On it the
g is called 'Lord of
rmandy and Aquitaine'

Early medieval dog-tooth ornament

[651]

Solidity in stone.
Existing remains are from churches, cathedrals, abbeys and castles, which were built of stone. Houses and shops of less durable materials—wood, thatch and wattle—have vanished. Saxon windows are characterised by the thick baluster shaft dividing the two lights, set into rectangular blocks above and below.

The Normans brought with them from Normandy skilled masons and Caen stone. Their buildings are solid, with massive walls into whose thickness are constructed bedchambers and staircases. The semicircular arched openings of the deeply set doorways and windows are carved with chevron, billet and plant designs. By 1300, walls had become thinner, mouldings were rarely decorated, and the pointed arch was widespread—Early English Gothic style had evolved. Lancet windows and simple tracery in the window head are typical.

Columns and roofs.
The roofs of larger buildings are supported on columns or piers, with capitals, consisting of wider blocks of stone, set between support and arch. Norman capitals may be plain, or carved with beasts, devils, monsters, human figures or plaitwork. Columns are thick, and often incised in chevron (zigzag) or diamond patterns. Early medieval capitals are lighter and are often grouped above numerous shafts to form a multiple pier; and leaf decoration becomes more usual.

Roofs are generally of timber, open to the rafters, and based on collar and tie-beam construction. Some large churches from the 11th century have stone vaults in round or pointed arches with heavy, moulded ribs. As windows became larger in the early medieval period, buttresses were added to transfer the outward thrust of the roof to the ground.

Towers and steeples.
Churches are the only surviving Saxon buildings, and usually only part of such churches remains—the tower, or a window or doorway. Saxon towers are characterised by slenderness and simplicity of form and detail. Some of them have strip decoration in stone.

Norman towers are low and solid. They originally had stumpy spires—simple, four-sided structures, which were later removed or rebuilt. The tower sides are decorated by arcading, panelling and narrow window slits. Early medieval towers are often capped by a spire of broach design, in which the awkward junction between square tower and octagonal spire is bridged by side pieces extending up the spire sides.

Towns were fortified by encircling walls, with entrance gateways at intervals, and were often dominated by castles as strongpoints.

Stairs and fire-places.
Newel stairs of wood or stone were common in castles and churches of this date. They have a central post, with steps radiating spirally around it. They were suitable because they were narrow and easily built (not, as is often stated, because they were easily defensible), and took up little space in the wall thickness or the special turret in which they were constructed. There were also exterior steps, from floor to floor and, inside, ladders but no well.

Heating was provided by burning logs. One type of hearth was of brick or stone set in the middle of the floor. The logs were supported on iron fire-dogs, and the smoke escaped (when the wind was in the right direction) through a slatted opening (louvre) in the roof above. Other fire-places are of stone, with a round arch or hood above. Smoke escaped through a passage in the walls.

Rare furniture.
Furniture was scanty, and items were costly and greatly prized. The decoration was simple, carved in animal, geometric and plant forms, sometimes with pierced holes. Indigenous woods were used, chiefly oak, to make chests, benches, tables, chairs and beds.

Chests and cupboards, made in solid panels, carved and pierced, were designed to hold linen, clothes, silver, pottery and food. Most benches and tables were of trestle, collapsible type, because dining was carried out in the hall which was also used for work and leisure purposes. There were few chairs; usually only the head of a large household had one. Bedsteads were simple, mainly wooden frames with an embroidered wool wall-hanging behind.

Lighting was by candles for the wealthy, or home-made rushlights in ordinary homes.

Religious motifs.
Religion was the dominant theme of all decoration, from capitals and mouldings to silverware and pottery. One of the important surfaces to receive this vigorous, deeply cut carving was the tympanum—the solid wall panel beneath an arch. Such tympana frequently showed a religious subject, like the Day of Judgment.

In capitals, columns, fonts, doorways and window arches, motifs varied, but predominant were monsters, devils, animals and humans possessed by evil spirits, carved with great vigour and freedom of expression. In the 13th century these gave way to plain mouldings and beautifully carved leaf and plant forms. Norman mouldings were richly carved, chiefly with chevron ornament. Early medieval work is more restrained. Typical is the four-leafed dog-tooth ornament.

The Black Death kills possibly more than a third of the population in the mid-14th century. The resulting labour shortage inflates wages and accelerates the *break-up of feudalism, which tied a labourer to his lord's land. The Wars of the Roses, costly in money as well as in blood, exhaust the old warlike aristocracy* *and strengthen the position of merchant class. Standards of comfort the demand for privacy leads to Courtyard House replacing the*

The Judgment Portal, Lincoln Cathedral, 14th cent.

Decorated Gothic tracery, Exeter Cathedral, 14th cent.

South porch, Gloucester Cathedral, 1420

Perpendicular tracery, York Minster

Rose window in curvilinear tracery, Lincoln Cathedral, 1325

Bay window, Hor[...] Hall, Essex, 1510

Fan-vaulting, Exeter Cathedral, 14th century

The Becket boss, depicting the murder of Becket, from Exeter Cathedral vault

Carved capital from York Minster, c. 1310

Buttress waterspout, Thaxted Church, Essex

Nave vault, St. George's Chapel, Windsor Castle

Fortified gate-house, Herstmonceux Castle, E. Sussex, c. 1440. Defence was still important

External domestic staircase found in cities. Superseded by the internal staircase

MISERICORD AT WORCESTER CATHEDRAL

As the 15th century replaced the 14th, decoration grew less severe and natural forms became popular motifs. A new light-heartedness produced such church carvings as this misericord, and an increasingly secular attitude is revealed in the use of heraldry as a decorative device

Tower, York Minster, 1432–74

Medieval bridge, [...] sharp cutwaters. S[...] bridges were forti[...]

Abbot's kitchen, Glastonbury Abbey

Chimney-st[...] Oxburgh H[...] Norfolk

The Rokewode Mazer (drinking bowl), maplewood mounted in silver gilt, late 14th century. In front is the Pusey Horn, a Saxon relic mounted in silver gilt, early 15th century

Oak cradle, 15th century. Some cradles have curved rockers in place of a flat stand

Rushlig[...] and hold[...] Used in [...] poorer h[...]

The Ramsey Abbey Censer, silver gilt, 1325–50. It imitates contemporary stone tracery, down to the smallest details

'Architectural' tomb of Bishop Bronescombe, Exeter Cathedral

The donor, stained glass, Merton Coll. Chapel, Oxford, c. 1300

Effigy of the Black Prince (1330–76) in Canterbury Cathedral, showing the new realism in Gothic sculpture

Brass of Sir Henry Bullen in Hever Church, Kent. Sir Henry may have been the father of Anne Boleyn

...use. Caxton introduces printing. In ...s age of humanism Renaissance ...olarship flourishes. Holbein paints in ...urt. The Reformation removes educa-tion from church control; grammar schools founded by Edward VI. The Dissolution of the monasteries and the sale of monastic lands endows a new ruling class

...nenfold panelled door, ...ycockes, Essex, 1509. ...ypical Tudor panelling

Carved base of an oriel window, Hengrave Hall, Suffolk, 1538

Gateway, Trinity Coll., Cambridge

...ing buttress, ...ry VII Chapel, ...estminster Abbey.

Complex fan vault, Bath Abbey, 1501–39

Hammerbeam roof, Rufford Old Hall, Lancashire, 1463–1505

...apet, Lavenham Church, ...olk, 15th century. Lav-...am is one of the finest of East Anglian wool churches

Fortified gate-house, Oxburgh Hall, Norfolk

Carving above the gate of St John's College, Cambridge

...omestic brick fire-place, c. 1505. ...re-places followed stylistic trends ...the period, and reflected the ...eater attention paid to comfort

Baking ovens in the Tudor kitchen, Hampton Court Palace. The palace was begun by Cardinal Wolsey in 1514

...inenfold panel-...d armchair

The so-called 'Prince Arthur's cupboard', c. 1500

Elaborately decorated silver candle snuffers, 1547. Lighting was little changed from earlier times

Silver flask, 1546. Strapwork decoration

...e of the King's ...t finials at ...pton Court

The Market Cross, Chichester, W. Sussex, 15th century

[653]

The royal Arms of Henry VIII in stained glass at Cowick Priory, Devon, c. 1540

Tudor linen-fold panelling

Three periods of Gothic.

The three periods covered by these 250 years are commonly known as Decorated, Perpendicular and Tudor Gothic, and their individual features can be seen in everything from architecture to furniture and ceramics.

Decorated work is of 14th-century date. Its chief feature is the equilateral pointed arch used above doorways, windows and arcades, and also used decoratively on tombs and furniture.

In window design tracery developed rapidly. The stonework was cut into geometric and curved shapes, cusped and moulded.

From c. 1375 Perpendicular Gothic took over. In it the vertical line is predominant—noticeable in window tracery and door panels.

By 1500, Tudor style—a transition from true Gothic to Renaissance—emerged, with its flat arches, and panelling over all surfaces.

Roof complexity.

In the 14th century capitals were naturalistic, most often in plant form. Perpendicular capitals returned to plain, moulded designs. The 14th-century timber roof was of king-post and tie-beam type; but in 1394 came the hammerbeam design at Westminster Hall. Here a horizontal beam carries the vertical hammer-post. Hammerbeam roofs were constructed well into the 16th century.

The stone vault is equally well represented, especially in cathedrals. The 14th-century vaults are ribbed designs, with radiating spokes terminating in bosses. Then emerged the lierne designs, with multiple tie ribs. The fan vault marked the final phase. These elegant, traceried vaults demanded ever-increasing abutment, and the sculptured finials of flying buttresses are their beautiful counterparts.

Age of fortification.

The scope of military architecture was extended. The old idea of a strongpoint focussed on a central keep was abandoned in favour of curtain walling, with two or even three concentric rings of walls. These curtain walls were studded at regular intervals by defensive towers, and within the walls was space for a whole garrison or town with its livestock and provender. Castles, palaces, houses all had fortified entrances, and many of these gate-houses remain. Bridges have multiple pointed arches and deep buttresses; most were also fortified and had chapels.

A number of architectural features received great attention and magnificent craftsmanship. One such feature is the tower or steeple. Perpendicular Gothic towers are very beautiful, with their soaring spires, traceried windows and decorative parapets.

The chimney arrives.

Interior staircases, offering warmth and convenience, were becoming more usual, not only in churches, castles and large houses, but in smaller dwellings as well. Methods of heating, also, were slow to change, but the central hearth was disappearing, and fire-place designs were more varied, the arch following stylistic trends.

The Tudor fire-place illustrated is four-centred—that is, constructed from four geometrical centres on two different curves, a flat one in the middle and a sharply angled one at the corners. The louvre in the roof above a central hearth gave place to decorative brick or stone chimneys by the later 15th century.

Inside the abbot's kitchen at Glastonbury Abbey the medieval ovens can still be seen; outside, the kitchen displays the architectural features of the Decorated period.

Carved decoration.

There was still a minimum of furniture, even in large homes. Most furniture was made in carved oak, sometimes painted or gilded.

Carved decoration followed stylistic patterns, showing Decorated or Perpendicular cusped design, with vine and rose ornament interspersed with animal or figure decoration. Chests, carved or ornamented by ironwork in bands and scrolls, acted as receptacles for clothes and linen and were also used for seating. Food cupboards (aumbries) differed from linen and plate cupboards only in that the Gothic decoration was pierced for ventilation.

The few chairs that existed were of box pattern, carved in Perpendicular Gothic design, with panels and cusps. A drawer in the box was used for storage. Lighting methods were unaltered.

Decorated motifs.

Market crosses and impressive tombs, such as that of Bishop Bronescombe in Exeter Cathedral, present in architectural miniature the essential motifs of the Decorated period. The effigy of the Black Prince depicts the costume of the time—tight-fitting cotehardie with dagged edges, and metal plaque belt, worn low and patterned in heraldic motifs.

Misericord seat carvings illustrate the vivid interpretation in carved wood of a sometimes ironic and realistic attitude to Christian sayings. Equally, the silver flask shows the beginnings of Elizabethan strapwork so soon to dominate Tudor design, while the Hampton Court King's Beast displays the proud lion of Henry VIII as a finial.

Also typical of this time is the linen-fold oak panelling (so called because it represents folded strips of linen).

The Elizabethan Age, more settled than the preceding years of dynastic and religious conflict, sees a dazzling expansion of trade. The merchant adventurers bring exotic items from Muscovy, the East and the New World—among them coconuts, ostrich eggs and tobacco. Private wealth increases; the nobility build palaces; the rich travel and coll pictures. Under the Stuarts some England's finest glass and silverware produced. There is new interest in beau

Elizabethan window bay, Levens Hall, Cumbria. Strapwork ceiling

Carved wood door and doorcase, Levens Hall

Painted glass, Gilling Castle, N. Yorks., 1585

Entrance doorway, Hatfield, Herts., 1607-11

Oriel window c. 1610

Entrance porch, Audley End, Essex, c. 1610

Grotesque caryatid support in carved wood. Typical support for door lintels or mantelpieces

Elizabethan plaster frieze, Levens Hall, Cumbria

Plaster ceiling motif, 1599, reflecting maritime expansion

Strapwork ceiling, London, 1599

DETAIL OF BED HEAD BOARD, RUFFORD OLD HALL, LANCS.

Plaster ornamental figure c. 1600. Interiors were full of such imagery, often copied from the Low Countries

President's Gallery, Queens' Coll., Cambridge

Elizabethan half-timbering, Little Moreton Hall, Cheshire. The carved corner posts, window frames and gables are especially fine

Elizabethan dog-legged oak staircase. Built without a well

Elizabethan two-tiered chimney-piece, with figures

Jacobean carved oak newel post, Hatfield House, Hertfordshire, echoing Continental Renaissance work

Foreign lands, maritime adventure, exotic fruits and fabulous beasts begin to appear in ornament as new trade routes opened up and travellers' tales and discoveries filtered back to Europe. Often these elements appear amid a confusion of 'Classical' decoration, as builders and craftsmen used renaissance motifs on medieval structures, creating the strange but exuberant forms of Jacobean and Elizabethan work

Jacobean carved oak chest. Typical are the twisted guilloche carving, and the legs lifting the chest well off the floor

Jacobean carved oak bedstead, with curtains to keep out the draught

Turned chair, early 17th cent.

Elizabethan carved oak table. The construction is massive, with carving along the sides and stretchers to rest the feet. Bulbous legs reflect contemporary clothes

Goffering iron, for ting starched ruffs

Carved Jacobean pulpit, c. 1615.

Kneeling family effigies, from Culross, Fife. Such effigies accurately portray the costume of the age

Silver salt cellar, 1594

[654]

Carved wooden corbel, Queens' College, Cambridge

Cartouche ornamented with fantastic figures and strapwork from a map of the period its own sake, outside the service of the church. Charles I is a patron of painting and architecture; Van Dyck and Rubens paint at Court; Inigo Jones builds the Queen's House, Greenwich (1615) in the Roman manner. He visited Italy and brought back Palladio's 'Four Books of Architecture' – an influence for 200 years.

Bay window from a Jacobean drawing room, c. 1615-20

York Water Gate; London. Built as the river entrance to York House, in the Strand, c. 1626.

-based Ionic lumns, Cobham ll, Kent

Ceiling with pendant bosses, Gilling Castle, N. Yorks.

Carved Jacobean wood panel, showing Bacchic musicians

ate of Honour, onville and aius Coll., mbridge, 73-8. Built r Dr John aius, who had udied Renais-nce building Italy

Canongate Tolbooth, Edinburgh, 1591. Built of stone, like many Scottish buildings. A tolbooth was originally the place where taxes were collected

Half-timber entrance, Speke Hall, Merseyside

bean staircase, ole, Kent

Decoration of the upper stage of a chimney-piece, 1623

Elizabethan kitchen fire-place, with weight-driven spit-jack

Jacobean cast-iron fire-dog

Jacobean oak court cupboard. Carved with mythological beasts

Child's high chair, c. 1625. Carved and turned oak, inlaid with holly and bog oak

Recumbent family effigies, Swinbrook, Oxfordshire

[655]

Silver ewer, with all-over decoration, 1583

Detail from a silver salt of 1586

TIMBER AND GLASS

Houses the main theme. With the decline in ecclesiastical fortunes few churches were built, but houses of all sizes, from the mansions of the nobles to the half-timber or brick homes of the rising middle class, sprang up all over the country.

The most important exterior feature is the entrance porch, called a frontispiece. It has up to three stages, with columns to each storey and a wealth of carved stone decoration— strapwork (interlaced strap and panel designs), grotesque figures, fruit and flowers. Interior doors are beautifully panelled and carved, and have surrounding cases with columns and figures.

Windows became much larger; they are of casement type (opening on hinges), and often had coloured glass decoration. Bay and oriel windows are carved on the outside and have plasterwork ceilings inside.

Ceilings and friezes. Though a few open timber roofs were still constructed, the typical ceiling of this time is flat or coved, and made of plaster, or plaster panels between wood beams. Most examples are richly patterned all over in one of three methods: strapwork, ribbed, and pendant. The first two of these are similar, in that the whole ceiling is designed in panels of varying shapes; but one type is divided by wide decor-ated strap bands, and the other by moulded ribs. Pendant ceilings have ribs, which form downward-pointing clusters at regular intervals.

Friezes are also of plaster and richly ornamented. The plaster-work is white, and was originally painted and gilded on the enrichment—flowers and fruit, with vine and pomegranate predominating, heraldic features, human figures, animals, birds, pic-torial scenes and grotesque figures.

Craftsmen in timber and brick. Elizabethan and Jacobean craftsmen excelled in the media of timber and brick. Wooden buildings were commonly of half-timber construction—that is, the structure is timber-framed but has plasterwork panels, giving the characteristic chequerboard appear-ance. The woodwork is deeply carved in the gable bargeboards, corner posts of the doorways and on all interior features. Walls are covered by carved or inlaid panelling. This inlay is in complex floral designs.

Brick construction was expanding, for timber supplies were becoming limited, and bricks were cheap and suited to the development of Renaissance styles. Flemish bond construction (alternate headers and stretchers) was introduced, as were gauged bricks, suitable for ornament.

Stone was often used where avail-able, particularly in Scotland.

Chimney-pieces and staircases. Just as the entrance porch was the ornamental focal centre of the exterior of a house, so was the two-staged chimney-piece in individual rooms. Carved in wood, stone or marble, the lower stage includes the rectangular fire-place opening, flanked by col-umns, caryatid figures or flowers and fruits. Above is a centre-piece, either heraldic or pictorial, again flanked by columns and figures, with an elaborate cresting on top. Logs were still burnt, but coal was replacing them.

This is the age of staircase develop-ment. First came the Elizabethan dog-legged type, so-called because each short flight turns back in the opposite direction to the one below it. This evolved in Jacobean times into a proper stair and landing, set into a staircase well. Oak was the usual material. Later examples are carved with animal and human finials.

The age of oak. With larger homes, there were more rooms used for specific purposes and therefore more items of furniture, though chairs were still expensive. Oak was still the usual material; in fact, this period, and the years up to the Restoration in 1660 when walnut was introduced, is designated the 'age of oak', for it was the time when the best furniture was produced in indigenous wood.

Decoration took the same forms as in architecture: leaves and fruit, especially acanthus and vine, strap-work, grotesques and animals.

A particular feature of the time is the bulbous leg used on tables, court cupboards (a prototype of the side-board) and other large pieces of furniture, which has a clear affinity with the puffs and slashes of the contemporary costume. The bulbs were carved with acanthus decoration and glued on to the legs and posts.

Animated effigies. Sculptured tombs, memorials and effigies in churches became more animated. Medieval figures had been recumbent and depersonalised, though they were often beautiful. Elizabethan tombs were much more varied, and sculptors of note were employed.

The recumbent head of the family may be shown side by side with his wife, while the children kneel in a row or around the tomb, ranged according to size and age. As with the late medieval period, such effigies are a rich source for students of costume, portraying accurately and in detail the dress of the nobility and the middle class of their day.

Craftsmanship in silver, pottery and wood, from simple andirons to costly engraved silver tableware, displayed the same decorative motifs as everything else—above all, strap-work, and grotesque masks or figures.

Before the Civil War, Inigo Jones plans Covent Garden, the first of London's squares. During the war, fanatical Puritans attack religious images.

The most notorious, Richard ('Blue Dick') Culmer, smashes stained glass windows at Canterbury Cathedral. Roads are improved and the first regular stagecoaches

begin to run. Coffee houses open London and Oxford. The Restora (1660) brings in French and Dutch with the returning exiles. The Great

Inigo Jones doorway, Wilton House, Wilts. Classical columns with broken pediment above, 1647–52

Window at Wilton, south facade

St Paul's Cathedral, south porch. Wren, 1673–1711

Decorated doorway head, Uppark, W. Sussex, by William Talman, 1688–9

Doorway of a Wren City church, St Andrew-by-the-Wardrobe

Grinling Gibbons woodcarving in St Paul's Cathedral

Ceiling at Coleshill House, Oxon. now destroyed. By Sir Roger Pratt, 1650–2

Wrought-iron screen by the iron-smith Jean Tijou at Hampton Court, c. 1690

Part of a plaster frieze at St Michael's Mount, Cornwall, c. 1650

Ceiling centre at Balls Park, Herts., c. 1650

The dome of St Paul's Cathedral by Wren, begun in 1697. Wren had seen domes —the great Renaissance contribution to church architecture—in Paris

GRINLING GIBBONS CARVING AT PETWORTH HOUSE

The western towers of St Paul's Cathedral

Steeple, St Mary-le-Bow

Dragon weathervane, St Mary-le-B

Chimney-piece at Wilton, Wiltshire, by Inigo Jones, 1650

Staircase at Ham House, London, 1638

Staircase finial, 1637

Chimney-piece, Gibbons style, 1

Restoration Stuart four-poster bedstead, c. 1675–80, hangings all of matching velvet

A love of nature, which was simply expressed in stone and wood carving in earlier periods, now appeared in the more sophisticated and naturalistic forms of the Classical Renaissance. Wren and master craftsmen such as Gibbons and the iron-smith Jean Tijou dominated the scene.

Side-table with barley-sugar legs, flat serpentine stretchers and marquetry decoration, c. 1685

Charles II chair in walnut, c. 1675

Silver snuffer 1696

Wren pulpit at St Mildred, London, with cherubs and wreaths embellishing the sounding board

The Monument to the Great Fire of London. 1671–77

Monument to Dr Plot, a historian, 1698, at Borden, Kent. Memorials now reflect the occupations and achievements of those they commemorate

Staffordshire slipware plate, with naïve rampant lion design, 1660–80

Engraved silver tankard with flower design, hall-marked for York, 1657–8

Silver sweetmeat bo c. 1640, height 1½ in

1666) destroys much of old London and gives Wren his chance of re-planning; spires and towers prick the skyline. Pineapples appear about 1670 and be- *come a popular motif in stone and wood. The scientific revolution (Newton, Darby's blast furnace and Newcomen's steam engine) gains impetus.*

THE PALATIAL AGE

Wren's versatility. Doorways and windows were designed in correct Classical form. The orders, with columns, bases, capitals and entablatures, flanked major openings and were surmounted by pediments with sculpture and cresting. Inigo Jones's work, as at Wilton, was beautifully designed. It did not, however, possess the infinite variety which was one of Wren's chief characteristics, and which is shown by the doors and windows of his churches in the City of London. Some are plain, with columns, some ornately carved, some have brackets to support the pediment. Other architects followed Wren's lead, though their work is often coarser and less vivid. The same decorative motifs appear again and again: cherubs (heads or whole bodies), acanthus leaf and other Classical forms like the egg and dart, scrolls, and swags of fruit and flowers.

From strapwork to symmetry. The all-over strapwork patterns of the Elizabethan plaster ceilings and friezes gave place to the centrally planned design. The dominant part was a deeply recessed panel—circular, oval or octagonal—whose wide border was elaborately moulded into flowers and fruit. The rest of the design was subordinate, but in similar vein. Up to *c.* 1700 the same characteristics were to be found in all ornamented surfaces. The motifs were chiefly floral or animal, as they had been for a long time, but the treatment was new.

Grinling Gibbons, Wren's famous carver, introduced an informal method of handling carving, especially in wood. His work was extremely realistic and three-dimensional, with the work cut almost free of the background, giving a pattern of strong light and shade, and full of vitality.

Aftermath of the Fire. The Fire of London necessitated the rebuilding of 53 churches destroyed, and these, together with St Paul's Cathedral, represented much of Wren's lifework.

The great dome of St Paul's is a London landmark, but more difficult to perceive nowadays are the steeples of the remaining City churches. These show the versatility of Wren, for no two are alike.

The interesting part of each steeple is the upper part; nearly all have plain tower sides below this. Until the office rebuildings of the 1950's and 1960's the scale of the steeples was unchallenged. They are Renaissance in general features, though a few are reminiscent of Gothic spires.

The works of Hawksmoor and Archer initiated the brief span of English baroque at the end of the century.

Chimney-pieces and staircases. Chimney-pieces during the first half of the period are like the one at Wilton—though usually more modest. Still a two-storey feature, the chimney-piece extends as one unit from floor to cornice. The fire-place is rectangular, with metal basket and irons. The focal centre of the upper part is a mirror or painting, and both stages are decorated and framed by columns, figures, flowers and fruit.

The later type of design is more often in two parts: a fire-place below, and above it a separate mirror or painting.

Staircases evolved from the carved panel type of balustrade to the version with multiple balusters. The panel was in carved wood or wrought iron, with heavy carved newels and finials. By 1670–80 the barley-sugar twist motif was frequent in balusters. Wooden staircases had slenderer handrails and balusters.

The age of walnut. At the Restoration of 1660 the long 'age of oak', with its well-made but heavy designs, came to an end for fashionable homes, and the 'age of walnut' began, helped along by the influence of Continental elegance experienced by the nobility in exile. Items became more numerous.

Walnut was used mainly as a veneer, glued in thin sheets on to an oak carcase. Oyster-shell and burr patterns were obtained by using the different parts of trunk, root and branch. Marquetry was introduced—a delicate type of inlay, using coloured woods. Fittings were of brass. The twisted barley-sugar leg was in fashion, as was the elaborately carved or serpentine stretcher.

Furniture was allied to costume, notably in severe designs (Cromwellian), complicated carved frames (Charles II), and very tall chairs and beds (William and Mary).

Pulpits and candelabra. The higher quality of craftsmanship and the predominant type of ornament were reflected in the monuments, fittings, silverware and ceramics of the day. Wren pulpits were of beautiful wood, carved either by Grinling Gibbons himself, or his assistants. The metalwork of screens and sword-rests, the stonework of tombs and the sculpture of memorials showed the same high standards.

Lighting was still by candle or rushlight, but the fittings were now varied and beautiful. Silver, glass and brass were used for candlesticks and wall sconces, while brass was most usual for the giant candelabra hanging from the centre of the ceiling panels. These candelabra now had many S-shaped branches attached to a central ball. The quality of silverware, pottery and glass was improving greatly.

...ndow at Petworth ...use, W. Sussex

Baroque window, Birmingham Cathedral, by Thomas Archer, 1711–25

Doorway at Morden College, Blackheath, 1695.

...ticated doorway, ...le Ashby, Northants.

Detail of a wrought-iron gate at Trinity Coll., Cambridge, *c.* 1691

Temple Bar, by Wren, 1672; now at Theobald's Park, Herts.

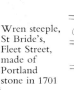

Wren steeple, St Bride's, Fleet Street, made of Portland stone in 1701

The bridge at Blenheim Palace, Oxon., by Sir John Vanbrugh, 1711. It stands in the lake created by Capability Brown

Birmingham Cathedral. Thomas Archer, 1711–25

...rought-iron scroll ...lustrade, 1695

Carved wood scroll balustrade, *c.* 1680

Enamelled brass andiron or 'fire-dog'

Staircase with barley-sugar balusters, 1700

Silver wall-sconce, 1703–4

...g-case clock with ...l marquetry, *c.* 1685

William-and-Mary winged settee with floral-patterned upholstery, walnut legs and stretchers, 1695

William-and-Mary chair, *c.* 1690

Silver case clock by Edward Webbe, 1676

...t cover with carved ...rubs, All Hallows ...he Tower

High relief chest-tomb at Elmore, Glos., 1707

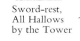

Sword-rest, All Hallows by the Tower

[657]

GEORGIAN 1714-1765

European Grand Tours become popular and the love of antiquity spreads. Foreign trade expands: custom houses and town halls are built. Duty reforms make im- | ports cheaper; mahogany is used with home-grown woods for furniture. The art of wood-turning is discovered, affecting the shape of baluster-rails and furniture | legs. Tea imports increase, potteries pand and tea-pots appear. The rich b fake ruins to romanticise their gard Seaside building begins to develop

Palladian portico at Lyme Park, Cheshire, showing the taste of the times for Classical proportions. Leoni, 1726

Guildhall, Worcs. White, 1722

ROCOCO MIRROR—HOWINGTON HALL, WARWICKSHIRE

The curves and shells of the rococo theme became dominant in decoration from 1740—lighter, freer, more elegant motifs replaced earlier florid forms with their festoons of flowers and fruit. This mirror reflects a patterned ceiling in the more formal style.

Doorcase with broken pediment Claydon House, Bucks. The sophisticated rococo style originated in France

Ornate ceiling, St Martin-in-the Fields. James Gibbs, 1722

Plasterwork, Hagley Hall, Heref. & Worcs., 1758

Classical ceiling at Houghton Ha Norfolk. Plasterwork by Artari, architect Colin Campbell, 1730

St Martin-in-the-Fields. Gibbs, 1722

St George-in-the-East, London. Hawksmoor, 1715

All Souls, Oxford. Hawksmoor, 1730

Covered bridge in the Palladian style at Wilton Park, Wilts., built 1736 for its romantic contribution to the land as much as for its utility

Heavily ornamented fire-place at Ditchley Park, Oxon. A painting framed in the overmantel is surmounted by near life-size figures. William Cheave, 1722

Wrought-iron balustrade, Stoneleigh Abbey, Warks., 1720

Chimney-stacks in the Palladian manner

Rococo chimney-piece with mirror, 1750-60

Stone and wrought-iron staircase, 1720

Trivet and place, c. 17

Brass candelabrum, 1727. Candles remain the only lighting system

Tripod table with 'pie-crust' edge, 1760

Ribband-back Chippendale chair, mahogany, 1755

Marble-topped console table, with gilt eagle pedestal, c. 1730

Chippendale sconce, gilt pinewood, c. 1755

Four-poster bedstea carved mahogany, c

Monument to Sir Nathan Wright and his son in Gayhurst parish church, Bucks., 1728

Carved oak staircase and unusually high decorated pulpit at St Martin-in-the-Fields, London

Headstone in Wisbech churchyard, Cambs., with rococo ornament and Classical cherubs, 1767. The same forms were applied to furniture, buildings and household goods

Chelsea porcelain, 'T Music Lesson', c. 176

Scarborough. Stucco is used: partly to protect brickwork from the atmosphere, partly to simulate stonework. In poorer areas cottages are built in 'pairs' and be- *come the ancestors of semi-detached homes. Religious enthusiasm creates massive congregations and high-level pulpits to address them.*

Palladian doorway, Houghton Hall, Norfolk, 1730

'Venetian' window, Holkham Hall, 1734

Window at Stoneleigh Abbey, Warks., 1720

Baroque portico, St Anne's Limehouse, 1720

Wall panels – carved, painted and gilded, 1760

Doric columns at the Circus, Bath. Wood, 1754

Coffered ceiling at Holkham Hall, Norfolk. William Kent, 1734

Florid ornamental detail, pediment ornament, St George's, Hanover Square, London, 1714

Stone parapet at Daventry Church. Hiorn, 1752

Wren tradition: St Mary-le-Strand, London. Gibbs, 1714

St George, Bloomsbury. Nicholas Hawksmoor, 1720

Rising 'Palladian' staircase, Stourhead, with Classical statues

Mahogany staircase balustrade, Bath, c. 1728 (now removed)

Engraved silver tea-kettle and stand, with burner, 1730

Silver coffee pot, with flowers in relief, 1765

Red velvet and gilded wood settee. William Kent, c. 1730

State coach, master-minded by Sir William Chambers in 1761, and an example of rococo at its most extreme. It cost £8000 to build **[659]**

Owl in Chelsea porcelain, 1752

The mausoleum, Castle Howard, N. Yorks. Nicholas Hawksmoor, 1731

SCHOLARSHIP IN DESIGN

From Classicism to rococo. Classicism prevailed in architectural detail. Porches, porticoes, doorways and windows display flanking columns, supporting central pediments. Doors are of beautiful polished wood: at first in oak or pine and two-panelled, but after the early 1740's more usually in mahogany and designed in six panels. Door furniture and panel edging is in brass or bronze.

Despite the overall influence of Italian-inspired Palladianism, two other forms of design existed. In the early years, baroque features were employed by architects like Hawksmoor or Vanbrugh. Hawksmoor's use of the baroque was monumental and uncompromising. In the mid-century years, light-hearted rococo decorative forms tended to oust severe Palladianism, replacing the correct Classicism with gayer, elegant curves.

Fine plasterwork. The ceiling continued to be the most important interior feature, whether in church or home. Plasterwork was of high quality, the best being created by Italian stuccoists. For example, the curved vault of St Martin-in-the-Fields, in London, was designed by James Gibbs and carried out by two Italians. Ceilings in most houses were flat, with a coving descending to the plaster frieze.

The Palladian school of architects, led by their patron Lord Burlington, included Colin Campbell, Giacomo Leoni and William Kent. Among the many English houses which they created, Houghton and Holkham, both in Norfolk, take pride of place. Kent, who was responsible for the Earl of Leicester's mansion at Holkham, introduced the custom of designing everything in the house—even down to the doorknobs.

Unusual new churches. London received many new churches from Sir Christopher Wren, but only as replacements for those lost in the Great Fire of 1666. In 1711 an Act of Parliament provided for the building of 50 new churches to cater for the needs of parishioners in London's expanding suburbs. Outstanding architects of the day contributed, designing fine buildings and unusual steeples different from Wren's.

James Gibbs gave us St Martin-in-the-Fields and St Mary-le-Strand, developing further the Wren tradition. Nicholas Hawksmoor built six churches—one in the City (St Mary Woolnoth), one in the West End (St George, Bloomsbury), and the remainder in the East End. Their great originality is seen especially in the steeples. All are different, but all possess a powerful monumentality, evincing Roman grandeur.

Chimney-pieces and staircases. The two-stage chimney-piece was seen until c. 1745-50. After this, rococo design began to take over. Many elegant chimney-pieces exist from the 1750's. These are more lightweight and project less from the wall. Everything about them is curved. The upper part incorporates many pieces of mirror and candle-holders; and the lower part is in carved, gilded pinewood.

The interior staircase became an important feature. Some are made entirely of wood, with barley-sugar balusters, and are set into wood-panelled stair wells. Others have stone steps with wrought-iron balustrade and mahogany handrail, set into a stucco-ornamented well. The principal entrance is often approached by an exterior stone staircase, with vase-shaped stone balusters or a wrought-iron balustrade.

Kent and Chippendale. In well-to-do homes, furnishings were becoming more comfortable, and lighting improved. Walls were panelled, stucco-decorated, or hung with silk or velvet. Until c. 1750 most of the furniture was in walnut or pine, or lacquered in imitation of Oriental designs, though mahogany imports increased after the 1720's.

William Kent and Thomas Chippendale are the paramount names in furniture in this half-century. Kent's designs set the pattern until c. 1740. His style is heavy, rich and baroque, with marble tops and gilded pedestals, often in the form of animals, birds and female figures.

The name Chippendale is synonymous with mahogany. His ribband and ladderback chairs and settees (1750's) are unmistakeable, as are the tripod stand and curved cabriole leg, with claw and ball foot.

Famous ceramic names. The quality of workmanship was rising, and there were scientific and technological advances in many crafts. This applied particularly to the ceramic industry. In the 18th century, many of the names famous in English ceramics became established—Bow, Chelsea, Derby and Worcester.

An incentive to producing new designs and techniques was the spread of the popularity for drinking tea and coffee. China tea services had long been imported from the East and later from Meissen. With the discovery of kaolin clay in Cornwall in the mid-century, porcelain manufacture began in England. Tea and coffee also influenced silver design: beautiful pots and kettles were made.

Architects did not confine themselves to buildings: Sir William Chambers even amalgamated designs for George III's gold state coach.

Pattern-books disseminate designs to builders, cabinet makers and carpenters. Because of window-tax the number of windows in old and new houses is reduced.

Town-house entrances are dignified by being raised and provided with a short flight of steps, thus creating dark, dingy basements for the servants. The first town

planning is done at Bath by the Wood family. Sir Walter Scott's romantic literature evokes nostalgia for the Middle Ages and promotes Gothic Revivalism.

Doorway by Robert Adam in St James's Sq., London, c. 1775

Corinthian capital designed for Luton Hoo, Bedfordshire, by Robert Adam

Telford's road bridge at Conwy, with the medieval castle behind. The iron suspension bridge, built in 1826, has mock towers at the ends

DETAIL OF CEILING BY ROBERT ADAM

The 18th-century custom of the European Grand Tour gave both patrons and artists a chance to study at first hand the Classical works in Italy and Greece which influenced all aspects of design. Robert Adam made the journey to Italy and Dalmatia and his ceiling designs are an 18th-century Englishman's interpretation of what he saw.

Robert Adam doorway, Adelphi, London

Orangery, Heveningham Hall, Suffolk by James Wyatt, 1790-1800

Faun and entablature from the anteroom, Syon House, London, by Robert Adam

Stucco wall decoration by Adam. Kenwood, London

Darby's bridge at Iron-bridge, Salop. The world's first iron bridge, built across the Severn in 1777-9

Early Gothic Revival St Peter's, Brighton

Hooded bay window, with balconies, in Regency Sq., Brighton

Adam staircase, 20 St. James's Sq., London

Late 18th-century steel grate

Hooded iron balcony, Cheltenham, c. 1830

Adam fire-place, Syon House, London. Adam designed his houses down to the smallest detail of the fittings

Iron balustrade by Adam, Kenwood, London

Cut glass chandelier, c. 1770. To increase the light given out by the candles, glass was used—both chandeliers and wall mirrors

Chimney glass, to go above a fire-place. Adam style

Ladderback chair, c. 1775

Shield-back armchair, c. 1775. This period was the golden age of the chair

Serpentine-fronted chest, 1775. The flowing lines are in contrast to the square furniture of earlier periods

Hanging cabinet, lyre pattern, c. 1800

Late 18th-century door furniture. Such details were often architect-designed

Veneered and inlaid knife box, c. 1770

Teapoy, c. 1820. A teapoy was a small table containing equipment for making tea

Ornamental clock designed by Adam

Classical tomb design, showing motifs used in architecture and furniture, such as the pediment and the animal foot

MacAdam's new roads and the end of foreign travel during the Napoleonic Wars, lead to increased travel at home and coaching inns. Technical develop- *ments of the Industrial Revolution and a general increase in trade breed docks, warehouses and slums. Gas-lighting starts in Pall Mall.*

...onic archway by John Nash, ...Regent's Park, 1825. Part of a giant town-planning scheme

Window at Southgate Grove, London, by John Nash, 1797

Pelham Crescent, London, by Basevi, 1820-40

...ing detail showing a Bacchic scene, by ...bert Adam. Harewood House, W. Yorks.

Ceiling decoration in the Bank of England, by Sir Robert Taylor, reminiscent of Wedgwood designs

...eek Revival: St ...ncras Church, 1822

Parapet balustrade, from Tyringham House, Buckinghamshire, by Sir John Soane, c. 1796

Bridge for Syon House, Greater London, by Robert Adam. A continuation of the Classical tradition

...erpentine scroll ...alustrade, c. 1790

Cast-iron kitchen range, c. 1800. On the right is a boiler, with a tap for hot water

Dog turn-spit, c. 1800. The dog had to keep moving, so as not to lose balance

...egency convex ...irror, c. 1810

Regency sabre-legged mahogany chair

Regency library table. Animal head and leg supports were common

Wedgwood and glass candlestick, c. 1800

...al patera, a motif found in decor-...n of all kinds, from architecture ...ottery, and especially common on ...eered furniture. Paterae are round ...val, with varied central designs

Urn motif, from a tomb. This was used by Adam and others, on buildings and furniture

Wedgwood coffee-pot 1783, Jasper-ware. Wedgwood applied Classical design to everyday household articles

[661]

THE AGE OF ELEGANCE

Adam's work and influence. The name of Robert Adam appears again and again in the field of architectural and domestic design. As he was rarely given the opportunity of designing a house from scratch, but had to re-adapt an existing one to current trends, his work is chiefly seen in detail or interior decoration.

Adam's own work belongs to the years 1760-92, but his influence was so extensive that the work of men like James Wyatt, Thomas Leverton and Henry Holland bears a close resemblance to that of Adam. Doorway and window design is delicate and restrained. Adam utilised the exquisite wrought-iron work of his day on both railings and fanlights.

John Nash is noted for his Regency terraces and houses. His most ambitious surviving works are the Regent's Park terraces, part of a planning scheme begun in 1812.

Delicate decoration. Interior decoration was at its highest level in the years 1765-90—the period of Adam and Chambers. Stucco ornament decorated the ceiling and many walls. Though still Classical, the treatment had changed and was now in delicate, low relief, rarely gilded but left white with pastel-coloured background. The overall design included circular, oval or octagonal paintings, generally figure compositions or landscapes, often painted by Angelica Kauffmann, one of the founder members of the Royal Academy of Arts and its first woman representative.

Wallpaper was gaining in popularity, and English papers were produced at Battersea. Designs were more pictorial than our all-over patterns of today. They were reproductions of paintings by artists like Canaletto, or were based on current stucco designs.

Advances in iron. While the aesthetic qualities of design slowly declined in the early 19th century, the Industrial Revolution was producing exciting new materials and methods. The advances of technique in the use of iron made Britain the foremost nation in industrial construction. This was the age of the great engineers, when Telford built bridges which were emulated all over the world.

The famous iron bridge at Iron-bridge was the first in this material —no structural masterpiece, but an experiment (still standing) in the use of iron. At Conwy, Telford built a road bridge, and blended his castellated towers with the medieval castle behind. The suspension bridges of early 19th-century engineers are among the most beautiful structures of the century.

Architecturally, churches foreshadowed the coming Gothic Revival.

Houses in terraces. The first of the terraced groups of houses were built in 1730 in Bath. Others followed in London, Edinburgh, Bristol and Cheltenham; and during the Regency, the newly fashionable seaside resorts laid out crescents, squares and sea-front terraces. In Brighton and Hove many such terraces have bow windows, extending the whole height of each house, with wrought-iron canopies and decorative balconies.

Ironwork was used increasingly for staircase balustrades, at first in straight flights but, at the turn of the century, in serpentine curves.

Adam and his colleagues continued Kent's custom of designing all the house furnishings, and the steel grates, kerbs and fire-irons of this period are some of the most beautiful ever made. Cooking was becoming easier with the introduction of the cast-iron cooking range.

Furniture evolution. The outstanding furniture designers of 1765-90 were Chippendale and Adam; in the later period, 1780-1810, Hepplewhite and Sheraton. In general, the earlier chairs have flat oval, shield, lyre, ribband, or ladderback forms; and the later ones concave oval, shield, or straight back designs. Earlier furniture is sturdy and generally carved. Later work is slenderer, especially the legs, and decorated more with inlay or painting. Regency furniture is heavier, often gilded, and with animal head and leg supports.

Though lighting was still only by candles, well-to-do homes now had hanging candelabra, wall sconces and standing girandoles, as well as simple candlesticks, in such quantity that the lighting power was considerable, though the room became odorous and hot. To increase the light, beautiful mirrors lined the walls.

Wedgwood and his successors. Porcelain was developed both technically and artistically. At the same time, Wedgwood—an artist who was also a businessman—demonstrated that the softer pottery could be made in as elegant a form as the more costly porcelain. Though Bow, Chelsea, Derby, and Worcester are household names, that of Wedgwood eclipses them. He was followed by similar men—Spode, Copeland and Minton—who made beautiful pottery available for all classes.

As in other fields, these years produced the finest of workmanship, in silver and glass, in brass and ormolu for door and furniture fittings, and in household articles of all kinds. Even an everyday article like a knife-box was veneered for display. Many of them still exist, each one a work of art, to remind us of the quality of 18th-century craftsmanship.

A widespread demand for a 'True Christian Architecture' promotes the main phase of Gothic Revivalism: Catholic emancipation and Anglican revival lead to huge church-building programmes. Railways change the face of the landscape. Prince Albert stages the Great Exhibition (1851); Paxton's Crystal Palace, derived from the greenhouse which gardening h[as] made popular, suggests a new philosoph[y] of building design. William Morr[is] forms the Arts and Crafts Movement as

Entrance porch to Bridgewater House, London, by Charles Barry, c. 1849

Oriel window, St. Pancras Station

St Giles's Church, Cheadle, Staffs., by Pugin, 1841-6

Entrance porch, Highclere Castle, Hants., by Charles Barry, 1842-4

Decorative strapwork, St Mary and St Nicholas, Wilton, Wilts., by Wyatt and Brandon, 1840-6. This stone-built church shows Italian influence

Entrance doorw[ay] Keble Coll., Ox[ford]

William Morris wallpaper, 1876. Morris's firm was famous for its fabrics and wallpapers designed by individual craftsmen

Capitals, Bristol Cathedral, by G. E. Street

Iron lamp standard, Embankment, London

Iron entrance gate, Kew Gardens, London, 1866

Cast-iron roof, Paddington Station, by Brunel and Wyatt, 1852-4. Cast-iron construction and ornament were universal at this time

Base of a column wit[h] mouse carving, Natural History Museum London, by Waterho[use]

Balcony corbel on a row of terraced houses in Grosvenor Place, London, 1867

Clock tower, Houses of Parliament, Barry and Pugin

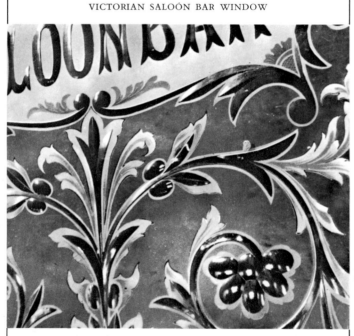

VICTORIAN SALOON BAR WINDOW

Carved base of an oriel window, P[ru]dential Assurance Building, Holbo[rn] by Alfred Waterhouse, 1878. This Gothic building is of red brick with terracotta decoration

Cast-iron and steel grate shown at the Great Exhibition, 1851

Fire irons

Balcony balustrade, Albert Hall M[an]sions, London, by Norman Shaw,

Machinery and new materials enabled the Victorians to imitate what they admired in other periods: inspired by romantic literature they made town halls look like temples and disguised cast iron as Gothic woodwork. The market for such techniques created by rising living standards is typified by the elaborate use of gilt, frosted and cut glass in their saloon bars.

Circular ottoman divided into fo[ur] seats with buttoned upholstery, c. 1840. Buttoned upholstery was popular at this period

Brass gas lamp or chandelier, used in town houses by 1840

Bamboo stand for newspapers, 1879

Iron plaque on the gates of the National Maritime Museum, Greenwich, by Philip Hardwick. One of the best examples of decorated cast-iron work

Artificial flowers protected from dust by a glass dome

'Medieval' sculptured detail, Scott Monument, Princes Street, Edinburgh, by Kemp, 1840-4. This Gothic memorial cost over £15,000

Royal lion, Victoria Tower, Houses of Parliament, by Barry and Pugin, c. 1840. Pugin designed most of the ornament

Albert Memorial, Kensington, by Sir Gilbert Scott, 1863-76

action against the machine age. Mass-production ugliness increases. Britain is now urbanised. Industry provides mass employment but creates overcrowding in towns, with back-to-back slum housing. Land values soar and mansion-flats appear. Peabody Dwellings founded in London for workmen and their families.

...way, St Mary's ...dral, Edinburgh

Lonsdale Square, Islington, 1838

Oriel window, first floor office, Paddington Station, by Brunel and Wyatt

Window, Scarisbrick Hall, Lancs., 1837

...tal, St Mary and ...icholas, Wilton, Wyatt and Brandon

Lamp, Leeds Town Hall, by Brodrick, 1855–9

Iron bracket supporting a cast-iron gallery, Coal Exchange, London, by Bunning, 1847–9. The Exchange has been demolished

Decorated capitals, Natural History Museum, London, by Waterhouse

...l, Houses of ...ment, by Pugin

Central clock tower, Leeds Town Hall, by Brodrick, 1855–60

Cast-iron and wood seat with arms carved in the form of sphinxes, Embankment, London, 1865–70. The Victorians covered all surfaces with intricate decoration

Clock tower, Cardiff Castle, by Burges

...st-iron balustrade for a ...ircase

Cast-iron fire-place, 1875. The writhing forms, moulded in iron, typify design at this period

Cast-iron slow combustion stove, 1870

...iffonier, mirror back, ...ectro-gilt, c. 1860

Balloon-back dining chair with buttoned seat, 1850

Brown glazed earthenware teapot

Doulton tankard. Factory established in Lambeth, c. 1820

...lock, Paddington ...ation, by Brunel ...d Wyatt, 1852–4

Nelson's Column Trafalgar Square, London, by William Railton, 1839. The lions by Landseer were added later, in 1866

Silver bottle stand. Victorian silverware was generally over-decorated

[663]

THE BATTLE OF STYLES

Classical and Gothic. The Gothic Revival flourished throughout the 19th century, and was at its strongest in the second half, when most buildings were in Gothic style. The spirit of the Revival was religious, exemplified by the work of Pugin, and nearly all churches were based on medieval originals. Earlier works are what the Victorians called 'English Middle Pointed' Gothic, but later all kinds of medieval work were copied.

Architects worked in both the Classical and Gothic styles. Sir Charles Barry, for example, architect of the Gothic Palace of Westminster, built many houses and public buildings in Classical style, as did also that ardent Revivalist, Sir Gilbert Scott. In civic building and terrace architecture the Classical tradition persisted, but Gothic cladding extended to railway stations, universities, town halls and hospitals.

Iron for everything. Ironwork, usually wrought iron, had been used in building for a long time, but during the 19th century its use became large-scale. After 1825, designs were less delicate and finely worked, and by 1830 iron was being used constructively as well as decoratively and became an essential building material. It was employed for columns, roofing and brackets, and structurally for tie-beams and arches.

Due to technical advances, cast iron became cheap and therefore widespread in its possible uses. By the second half of the century, it was used for everything from railings, gates and balconies to seats, bandstands, arcades and post-boxes. Though much of the work was coarse and poor in design, some excellent items were produced. Motifs were Classical and Gothic, and included animals and birds in complex ornamental schemes.

Back to the Middle Ages. There was a romantic air about many of the towers and steeples; even Classical ones on sober town halls had curving, baroque lines to the cupola. The most famous romanticised Gothic tower is the Clock Tower of the Palace of Westminster; its bell is called 'Big Ben' after Sir Benjamin Hall, Commissioner of Works. Cardiff Castle has another such turreted tower, while even a functional

building like the Natural History Museum in London has diminishing turrets in polychrome materials.

While ornament, both exterior and interior, is often crude, some is remarkably fine, though the appearance is always harder, more sharply defined and less sympathetically carved than the medieval originals. Terracotta work, as on the Prudential Assurance Building, London, was used as ornamentation on brick buildings.

Accent on bric-a-brac. From 1845 to 1885, Victorian interiors, particularly domestic ones, became darker, more over-furnished and filled with a quantity of bric-a-brac. Wallpapers and carpets were strongly patterned and coloured, and paintwork was dark. Windows were draped in layers of curtains. Chimney-pieces, tables and cabinets were shrouded in tasselled fabrics, especially red velvet, and even dressing tables coyly hid their

legs under frilled muslin with bows.

The fire-place was the focal centre of the room, providing heat from coal, which burnt in a cast-iron grate with marble and iron surround. Above the mantelpiece were shelves, cupboards and mirrors, stacked tightly with ornaments. After 1885 the pattern slowly changed towards lighter *décor*, smaller quantities of furniture and furnishing, and simpler ornamental design.

Gaslight and button chairs. By 1840 gas lighting was in general use in town houses. A metal chandelier hung from the ceiling, with three or four branches fitted with frosted globes in which the gas gently popped and purred in a flat flame. The carbon filament electric lamp was developed in 1860, but the change-over to electricity was slow. Oil lamps were in use all the century.

Most Victorian furniture design

is heavy and ornate. Mahogany was used chiefly, and the workmanship was excellent, as many pieces still in use testify. Items were large, especially dining tables, wardrobes, bed-steads and sideboards (chiffoniers). Buttoned upholstery was popular, as was horsehair covering and dark, rich colouring. Papier-mâché furniture contributed some of the most beautiful pieces of the century, as well as some of the most ugly.

Miniatures and monuments. From the quantity of knick-knacks produced, a great deal survives; and the early Victorian work at any rate is now becoming valuable in the antique market. Many of the small tables, work-boxes, porcelain groups, clocks and paperweights were beautifully made, and have a charm and attraction for us today. Silver, glass and china are of high quality, though they tend to be ornamented with

roses, violets and pictures of Windsor.

Of all the many memorials and monuments erected, probably the most controversial and typical is the Albert Memorial, which has been subjected to prejudiced comment—both for and against—ever since. Sir Gilbert Scott was inspired in his design by the Eleanor Crosses, like the reconstructed one at Charing Cross. J. H. Foley's statue of Prince Albert sits under Scott's glittering canopy.

Art nouveau flourishes against a background of Edwardian material prosperity with its town halls and monumental commercial buildings. Voysey and Mackintosh experiment with functionalism in furniture and building design, and the first garden city is founded at Letchworth (1903). Free education is introduced; schools, libraries and art galleries are built. Pho[to]graphy influences painting. The pe[trol] engine and the telephone arrive; apparent security reigns.

Gateway at the Royal Holloway College for Women, Surrey, 1886. Built to an enormous rectangular plan, in the French château style

Newnham Coll. Cambridge

Detail of an entrance porch, Cardiff City Hall, 1906. Designed by Lanchester in neo-baroque style

Oriel window, Port Sunlight, Merseyside, c. 1905

Front door, Bedford Park, London, 1880's

Doorway a[t] Queen's Ga[te] London, 18[ ] Norman Sh[aw]

Detail of a wrought-iron gate at Newnham Coll., Cambridge

ART NOUVEAU FABRIC DESIGN BY G. H. NAFFELL, 1905

Design was freed from its Victorian confinement to surfaces as artists and designers tried to invest everything with an appearance of natural growth. Sinuous plant-like forms appeared everywhere and for a short while the distinction between the 'fine' and 'applied' arts almost disappeared.

Carving from the Car[diff] City Hall, 1906. The stone crown symboli[ses] the confidence of a p[at]riotic, expansionist ag[e]

Tower of the Law Courts, Cardiff. The design is Classical, and is based on French models of a few years earlier

Tower Bridge, London, 1894, by Barry and Jones. The Gothic towers conceal a steel framework

Edwardian art nouveau staircase. A reaction against the complexity of Victorian decoration

Cooking range grate, 1910. The cast-iron chimney piece is painted

Bamboo umbrella stand. Bamboo furniture became popular in the 1870's, with the vogue for Japanese art

Washstand designed by William Burges for his house in Melbury Road, London. His Gothic designs were based on medieval furniture

Oak art nouveau table, by Charles Rennie Mackintosh, c. 1900

Electric light wall fitting, c. 1913. Oxidised copper tubing, with white glass shades

Oak chair with cane seat, c. 1900

House telephone of [a] decade before the First World War

Racing cup and cover, 1868-9, partly frosted silver, parcel gilt. At the top is St George slaying the dragon. The side shows a battle scene

Cast-iron canopy of a bandstand on the Front at Brighton

Earthenware vase, c. 1900, by William de Morgan

Silver vase on a marble stand, 1900. The swirling lines of the decoration are typical of the art nouveau period

Granite drinki[ng] fountain, comm[on] in parks, c. 189[ ]

THE LANGUAGE OF EXPERTS

*The work of the men who have
helped to create and discover our heritage
and the terms they use*

Men who share the same training and skills and are engaged in a common enterprise tend to develop their own private language. Their words are their private shorthand and the 'passwords' which help to keep away outsiders.

Many of the words in this section are like that—words such as 'gadrooning' or 'hagioscope' or 'parvise', each representing an object which is reasonably familiar to the layman, but is not generally known to him by its name.

Other words have too much vigour to be confined by their original technical meaning, and have joined the mainstream of the language. The word 'hallmark', for instance, which nowadays means any distinguishing mark of genius, began its life as the official assaying mark stamped on gold and silver at the Goldsmiths' Hall in London; the word 'sterling', once an English silver penny, much in demand on the Continent, is now used generally to suggest high quality.

But even when words have developed in this way, the experts, from archaeologists to archbishops, still use them in their original technical meanings. One key to the work of experts is simply to understand the language they use.

ARCHAEOLOGY

The last hundred years have seen archaeology reach the status of a precise science, drawing on almost every branch of learning. Today, modern technology —photography, electronics, petrology and radioactive analysis—can often discover characteristics of objects of which only the merest traces remain.

Air photography The sites of camps and ditches invisible from the ground may be seen from the air, and changes of colour in crops can provide clues to past disturbances in the sub-soil.

Artifact Any object fashioned by man.

Barrow A burial mound, strictly of earth, though often used also for a cairn, which is a similar mound of stone-rubble. Barrows are of several types. *Long barrows* are Neolithic family tombs, with stone-, timber- or turf-built chambers within the mound; they vary greatly in length. *Round barrows* are typical of the Bronze Age and are of varied shapes: *bowl barrows* resemble an upturned bowl and often have a surrounding ditch; *bell barrows* resemble a slightly flattened bell and have a surrounding ditch with external lip-mound; *disc barrows* have a small mound in a larger flat area surrounded by a ditch with an external lip-mound; *saucer barrows* are a variant of the *disc*, in which the mound is flattened into a shallow inverted saucer-shape extending to the ditch. *Pond barrows* are a rare type of burial place where a saucer-shaped hollow takes the place of the mound; in its bottom are pits for the human remains and the edge has a lip-mound.

Beaker people Two groups, of folk from south-western and eastern Europe, named after the drinking vessels they made, which were generally buried with them. They began to cross to Britain from the Low Countries *c.* 2000 BC.

Broch A Scottish type of Iron Age communal farmhouse within a tower-like stone building, having passages and chambers in its thick walls.

Bronze Age *c.* 2000–600 BC.

Cairn See *Barrow*.

Cantonal town The administrative centre of a Roman provincial local government region, such as 'East Anglia' or 'East Midlands', defined by the name of the dominant tribe. The Roman name was *civitas*.

Capstone The horizontal slab covering a stone-built chamber.

Carbon dating See *Radiocarbon dating*.

Causewayed camp 'Bank-and-ditch' protected Neolithic hilltop camp where the ditch is sub-divided by several causeways for crossing, each leading to an opening in the bank.

'Celtic' fields Small rectangular fields of Late Bronze and Early Iron Age date, commonly marked by *lynchets*. Many survived into Roman times.

Chamber Structure of stone, timber or turf, with access to the open, which contained the buried dead in a large barrow. Some of them, built of great stone slabs, are visible today, the covering mound having disappeared. These are often called *dolmens*. A *cruciform chamber* has a cross-shaped plan.

Chevaux de frise A defensive setting of stakes or similar obstacles.

Civitas See *Cantonal town*.

Clyde-Carlingford sub-type The name applied to long cairns with a distinctive pattern of internal chambers and walling, characteristic of south-west Scotland and north-east Ireland.

Cotswold sub-type The name given to long barrows with a distinctive chamber, characteristic of the Severn-Cotswold area of England.

Court cairn A pronounced variety of Clyde-Carlingford cairn, best seen in some Irish examples, in which the east end corner walls are extended to enclose a small ante-chapel outside the entrance to the mound.

Counterscarp bank A small supplementary bank on the *outer* lip of a defensive ditch with internal bank.

Cup-and-ring marks Small hemispherical hollows and incised circles, commonly found together, cut into the face of a stone slab. They appear to be a feature of the religion of the long-barrow builders.

Dolmen See *Chamber*.

Dun A Scottish type of small hill-fort.

Dyke. Ditch. See *Earthwork*.

Earthwork In prehistoric times, concentric rings of ditches (often armed with sharpened stakes) were dug around hilltop settlements as a protection. The removed earth and stones were piled up on the inside edge to heighten the defensive slope. The banks were often *revetted*.

Electrical resistivity By passing electric current through the soil between two electrodes, and comparing the resistivity between pairs of electrodes, the points at which soil may have been disturbed by prehistoric man can be recorded.

Gallery grave A barrow with an oblong chamber without a clearly separated passage to the entrance, in front of which there is generally a semi-circular space for funeral rites.

Henge A circle of wooden or stone uprights (which may have disappeared) enclosed by a circular bank *outside* a parallel ditch. Henges were ceremonial sites originating in the late Neolithic Age and are known only in the British Isles.

Hill-fort A fortified hilltop residential area (see *Earthwork*) typical of the Iron Age. Some were apparently refuges, not permanently occupied, but many—the larger ones—have been shown to have been permanently occupied by many people. Some are recognised as tribal centres, later replaced by the *cantonal town* in the valley below.

Hypocaust A hollow space under the floor of a building, which channelled heat from a furnace to heating panels of hollow tiles set in the walls. The Romans used this system for heating their houses and baths.

Inturned entrance At a point in some hill-forts the surrounding bank is turned inwards to make a passage leading to an entrance gate.

Iron Age *c.* 600 BC–AD 43.

Lynchet A small bank marking the lower edge of a field, left by primitive cross-ploughing on a hill-slope. They usually mark '*Celtic*' fields.

Maes Howe type A cairn with an internal chamber of the distinctive type best known in the great cairn at Maes Howe (see p. 347).

Megalithic Constructed of large stones; a term used generally of such chambers in long barrows.

Mesolithic *c.* 8000–3750 BC.

Mosaic Form of surface decoration used on floors and walls, composed of variously coloured *tesserae*—small cubes of materials such as marble, stone, glass or pottery.

Multivallate Having many ramparts; commonly used of hill-forts.

Neolithic *c.* 3750–2000 BC.

Palaeolithic *c.* 400,000–8000 BC.

Passage grave A large chambered tomb with a clearly defined passage leading to the chamber.

Petrology The study of rock formation and composition.

Radiocarbon dating When plants and animals die they cease to absorb the carbon needed to maintain life; the radio-active carbon they have also absorbed decays at a known rate, and by measuring their radio-activity archaeologists can date with considerable accuracy wood, charcoal, bone and other organic substances. Recent improvements in this method of dating have shown that many Neolithic and Early Bronze Age dates are rather earlier than formerly realised, and further revisions may be necessary.

Rath An enclosure, usually of a circular form, made by a strong earthen wall, and serving as a fort. (Used only in Ireland.)

Revetted Of the face of an earthen bank, having a timber or stone-built support and protection.

Ridgeways Broad upland tracks which enabled prehistoric man to travel about the country above the difficult heavily wooded valleys. The main ones converge on the great henge at Avebury.

Ring marks See *Cup-and-ring marks*.

Sarsen Local sandstone used in two of the circles at Stonehenge.

Severn-Cotswold sub-type See *Cotswold sub-type*.

Souterrain An underground chamber, store-room or passage.

Spectrographic analysis The use of a spectroscope (an instrument which breaks down light into recognisable scientific colour values) to determine the chemical and molecular structure of a substance, and thus to identify it.

Stalled cairn A long cairn with the internal chamber walls sub-divided by projecting slabs.

Trivallate Having three ramparts.

Vallum The Latin word for an earth-rampart or wall, built for defence around a camp or fort.

Vitrified fort A Scottish hill-fort with timber-laced stone walls, where the wood has caught fire and so melted or fused some stonework.

ARCHITECTURE

As well as the structural and decorative elements described below, an architect deals with certain constant factors to produce good designs:

MATERIALS. Man first built with the material closest to hand. In ancient Mesopotamia it was mud, and with only mud bricks only flat-roofed houses could be built; the Greeks, living on a limestone peninsula, used the largest slabs they could find as upright posts with slabs laid across them. From this evolved the typical Greek pillared building, and the post and lintel method of construction still used today.

The Romans discovered a local mineral which set like concrete when mixed with lime and water, enabling them to build larger structures than the Greeks and to exploit the possibilities of the arch.

When mild steel and reinforced concrete became available in the mid-19th century, architects were able to make their buildings higher and wider, the openings in them larger, and reduce the walls to waterproof skins on steel and concrete frameworks.

CONTRAST. Architects use contrast to give their buildings character. Smooth and rough surfaces imply lightness and heaviness; sculpture and mouldings produce variations of light and shadow. An arched opening can give emphasis to a plain façade, and colour can create mood—warmth and nearness, coolness and distance; dark colours suggest weight, light colours the opposite

SCALE. Reactions to a building often depend on its scale. The enormous size of an Egyptian pyramid gave the Pharaoh who built it a safe tomb, and allowed him to dominate the living even after death. Gothic churches, with their lofty spires, implied aspirations to reach Heaven itself, and seen from afar gave comfort and inspiration to the villages around them. Inside, the high vaults shrouded in darkness created a feeling of humility and reverence. Today scale can imply security in a bank, or prestige in an office building.

FORM AND PROPORTION. The Greeks discovered that the circle and the square were pleasing to the eye. By experimenting with these and other geometrical shapes they arrived at a set of ideal proportions and using them as the basis of their designs achieved buildings of unsurpassed clarity and balance. These principles were revived in the Renaissance, and in England the Georgian architects came close to matching the excellence of Greek design.

Abutment The piece of solid masonry or brickwork on a *pier* or wall that supports the arch.

Acanthus A stylised representation of a plant with thick scalloped leaves, used as a decorative feature in the carving of Corinthian capitals.

Angel beam The end of a *hammer-beam* carved to represent a human or, often, an angel.

Arcade A range of arches supporting a wall or roof. Also a covered way between two rows of arches or between a row of arches and a wall.

Architrave In Classical architecture, the beam resting on the columns.

Ashlar A wall of smooth-faced, precision-cut stones in regular courses, with fine jointing.

Bailey A fortified enclosure: the space within the outer walls of an ancient or medieval castle.

Baluster A carved column or upright post supporting a handrail.
Balustrade A series of *balusters*.
Barbican A fortified outer tower defending the entrance gate to a castle.
Barge-board A plain or carved board fixed to a gabled roof.

Bartizan An overhanging battlemented turret on a castle or church tower.
Bas-relief Carving which projects from the material from which it is formed.
Bastion A fortified projection occuring at intervals in a castle wall.
Battlements A square-toothed *parapet* used in medieval castles to protect archers.

Billet moulding Norman ornamental *moulding*.
Bolection moulding See *Moulding*.
Bond The way in which bricks or masonry-blocks are arranged in a wall to ensure strength and stability.

English bond   *Flemish bond*

Brick-nogging A timber partition with brickwork filling the spaces between the vertical timbers.
Bressumer A massive load-bearing beam used to span an opening.
Broken-pediment See *Pediment*.
Cable moulding An ornamental Norman *moulding*.
Cantilever A projecting beam secured at one end only.

Capital The carved or moulded column head on which the superstructure rests. See *Classical Orders*.
Cartouche An ornamental tablet representing a scroll of paper and usually bearing an inscription.
Caryatid A column in the form of a female figure.
Castellation *Battlements* used as a decorative feature.
Chancel The east end of a church where the altar is; the continuation of the *nave* beyond the *crossing*.
Chapter-house Assembly room for the governing body of a monastery or cathedral.
Chevron A carved zigzag *moulding* in Norman architecture usually seen around arches, doors and windows.
Classical Orders The Greeks, and later the Romans, introduced a set of architectural standards into their design for temples and public buildings. These standards or Orders regulated the proportions and relationships between the three principal parts of their buildings: the base (stylobate); the structural pillar (column); and the beams (entablature) they carried.

The first three Orders, devised by the Greeks, were the DORIC, IONIC and CORINTHIAN. The first was the simplest and most widely used; the second rather more elegant and the third, used least, the most florid.

The Romans, less restrained than the Greeks, took these three Orders and adapted them to their own taste. They then added two further Orders, the TUSCAN and COMPOSITE. The Tuscan was a clumsy version of the Greek Doric, despite an attempt at simplification. The Composite, a combination of the Greek Ionic and Corinthian, was equally less satisfying due to a coarsening of detail and extravagant decoration.

Doric

Ionic   Corinthian

Clerestory Windows near the ceiling in a high room or hall, which receive light from above the roofs of adjoining buildings.
Clunch A soft, white limestone, ideal for carving and often used for interior decorative work.
Cob Walling material of straw and unbaked-clay.
Collar-beam A timber beam connecting the mid-points of the sloping rafters of a *pitched* roof.
Colonnade A row of columns.
Composite See *Classical Orders*.
Console A large curved ornamental bracket generally occurring in Classical architecture.
Coping Brick or stone used to cap the top of a wall, to prevent weathering or for ornamental purposes.
Corbel A stone or brick projection from a wall to provide a horizontal support.

Corinthian See *Classical Orders*.

Cornice The projecting upper part of an entablature.

Cove A concave *moulding* usually seen at the junction of wall and ceiling.

Coffering Recessed panelling in ceilings, domes and vaults; used either for decoration or to reduce the weight in heavy construction work.

Crenellation See *Castellation*.

Crocket A carved decorative projection representing foliage on the edges of spires and canopies in Gothic architecture.

Crossing The central space at the intersection of the *nave* and *transept* in a church, usually directly beneath the tower.

Crow-stepped gable A gable with a series of steps in the coping.

Crypt An underground cell or burial-chamber beneath the chancel of a church, occasionally with an altar for worship.

Cupola A small spherical roof crowning a square, circular or polygonal area.

Curtain wall The length of wall between a castle's bastions; in modern use, a non-load-bearing wall.

Cusps Carved projections on the underside of a Gothic arch which separate the *foils*.

Dado The lower part of a wall when painted or decorated differently from that above.

Diapered A two-dimensional square or lozenge-shaped pattern on a wall. Brick diaper work is usually carried out with different coloured bricks.

Dormer An upper floor window projecting through the side of a *pitched roof*.

Doric see *Classical Orders*.

Dower-house A house endowed for the use of a widow.

Dressed stone Smoothly finished stonework used externally at corners, doors and windows of brick and stone buildings.

Drum-columns Cylindrical sections forming a stone column.

Embrasure See *Battlements*.

Entablature In Classical architecture, the beam-like structures above the columns: the architrave, frieze and cornice.

Entasis A slight outward swelling on columns, devised by the Greeks to counteract the optical illusion which makes vertical parallel lines appear to curve inwards. An entasis is found on most Classical columns.

Façade The front or main face of a building.

Fillet A narrow rectangular strip that separates one moulding from another.

Finial An ornamental feature, often of timber, at the top of a *gable* on the *ridge*. Also used loosely for any small pinnacle finishing off a vertical feature.

Flush-work *Knapped flint* used with *dressed stone* for decorative effect.

Fluting Shallow semicircular grooves cut into the surface of columns and *pilasters* for decoration.

Foils The inside arcs in *tracery* work between the *cusps*.

Foliate Leaf-shaped; *tracery* work with *foils* and *cusps*.

Folly A structure built solely for decorative effect, for example a Gothic-style ruin or tower.

Frieze The central division of an entablature. See *Classical Orders*. The frieze is also that part of a wall between the picture-rail and ceiling.

Gable The triangular area of wall beneath the roof at the end of a building with a pitched roof.

Gargoyle A rain-water spout on a medieval building, directing water away from the face of the wall; carved with grotesque representations of beasts' heads.

Gate-house The tower over the fortified entrance of a castle's perimeter wall.

Gauged-brickwork Bricks cut and rubbed to shape, then mortared together with fine joints in an arch.

Gazebo A summer-house or tower situated in a garden to give maximum benefit from the view.

Half-timbered Buildings with a timber framework, often of oak, with other materials—bricks, tiles or lath-and-plaster—filling the spaces between the timbers.

Hammer-beam A timber bracket that supports a trussed roof. Hammer-beams eliminate the need for a *tie-beam*.

Harl The Scottish term for roughcast, or *pebble-dash*.

Herringbone Timber blocks, brickwork or similar materials laid diagonally, to create zigzag patterns on the *façade* of a building.

Hipped-roof A *pitched* roof sloping at the ends as well as the sides.

Hood mould A *moulding* which projects from the wall over an arch, door, or window to throw off rainwater.

Hypocaust Underground chamber in a Roman house which contained a furnace and distributed warm air to the rooms above.

Ingle-nook An enclosed seat built into the wall beside a fireplace.

Ionic See *Classical Orders*.

Jamb The side of an arch, door or window.

Keep The inner tower and defensive stronghold of a Norman castle.

Keystone The central wedge-shaped stone at the top of an arch.

King-post A roof which has an upright post between the ridge and the centre of the *tie-beam*.

Knapped flint Flint stones broken in half to present a roughly squared face when used in walls.

Lancet A tall, narrow, sharply-pointed window-opening found in Early English church architecture.

Lavatorium A Latin term describing a place for washing in.

Lierne-rib The short ribs between the principal ribs in a Gothic vault.

Linen-fold Decorative carving imitating the appearance of draped or folded cloth.

Lintel A horizontal length of stone, steel, timber or reinforced-concrete carrying the weight of the wall above a window or door.

Loggia A covered veranda open on at least one side; at the front of a building.

Long-and-short work Saxon stonework with the corner stones laid alternately upright and horizontal. Often seen in *stucco* work.

Machicolation A series of openings in the floor of overhanging *parapets* in mediaeval castles, through which missiles were dropped on the enemy. See *Battlements*.

Mansard A roof with two slopes, the lower steeper than the upper.

Mausoleum An elaborate tomb, usually of monumental proportions.

Merlon One of the 'teeth' forming *battlements*.

Mezzanine An intermediate floor, usually between the ground and first floor level in a building.

Motte An artificial mound formed within castle walls, usually surmounted by the *keep*.

Moulding Ornamental carving on a wall's projections or recessions.

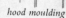

billet moulding   *hood moulding*

cove moulding   *bolection moulding*

cable moulding

Mullion A vertical bar of wood, stone or metal in a window.

Nave The main body of a church, excluding the *transept* and *chancel*.

Newel The central post of a winding staircase into which the steps are set. Also the posts at landing levels supporting the handrail.

Oculus A round window, also known as a 'bulls-eye' window.

Oratory Either a small chapel used for private prayer or a larger Roman Catholic church.

Oriel-window An upper-floor bay-window supported by *corbels*.

Pallisade A fence of stakes around a castle or defensive position.

Pantile Roofing tile with an S-shaped transverse section.

Parapet The low wall projecting above the roof level of a house. In Renaissance buildings it was usually in the form of a *balustrade*.

Pargetting Plasterwork carved with ornamental patterns. Often seen on old cottages and houses.

Pattern-book A book of designs for architectural details based on the revived principles of Classical architecture.

Pele or Peel tower A fortified tower built in the 16th century as a defence against border raids.

Pebble-dash The finish given to external walls by applying small pebbles to the surface rendering while still wet. Often called rough-cast.

Pediment The triangular space formed by the ends of pitched roofs in Classical and Renaissance buildings; a feature that often surmounts the entrance porch. A BROKEN-PEDIMENT has part of its apex omitted; a familiar feature of baroque architecture.

Classical pediment

broken pediment

Piazza A formal open space surrounded by buildings, and entered through archways.

Pier A vertical support; also the area of wall between windows.

Pilaster A flat rectangular pier or column, projecting slightly from a wall, largely used for decoration.

Pinnacle The terminating feature of a buttress or tower in Gothic architecture; usually pyramid-shaped and ornamented.

Pitched roof A sloping roof.

Plinth The projecting base of a wall or building.

Pointing After bricks have been laid, the joints between them are finished off with 'pointing'—a mixture of sand and cement. It is sometimes coloured to contrast with the remainder of the wall face.

Portcullis A heavy, gridded, defensive entrance-gate in a medieval castle, designed to be raised and lowered from inside.

Porte-cochère A large porch at the entrance of a house or mansion, big enough to receive a horse and carriage.

Portico A *colonnaded* space, with a covered roof, forming an entrance to a building.

Quatrefoil An opening carved into four leaf-shaped *foils*, occuring in Gothic architecture.

Queen-post A roof in which two uprights on a *tie-beam* help to support the rafters.

Quoins The external corner-stones of a brick or stone building.

Random-rubble Irregularly shaped stones used in wall construction.

Ravelin The part of a castle's advance defences, outside the curtain wall, whose two sides form an angle pointing towards the enemy.

Refectory The dining-hall in a monastery or convent.

Retaining wall A wall which resists the pressure from a mass of earth or water.

Revetted Faced with masonry; used of walls or banks.

Rib A projecting band on a vault or ceiling.

Ridge Top line of a pitched roof.

Roof-truss A triangular system of lightweight timbers or lengths of steel for supporting a roof.

Rose-window A circular window in Gothic architecture, traceried to resemble a rose. Sometimes called a wheel-window because the *mullions* radiate from the centre like the spokes of a wheel.

Rotunda A circular building usually with a domed roof.

Rough-cast See *Pebble-dash*.

Rustication The rough finish given to projecting stonework in a Renaissance building by chiselling. The edges or margins of the stones were left smooth.

Saddle-back roof A pitched roof on a tower.

Scagliola Plasterwork painted to represent marble. Often seen on columns. It originated in Renaissance Italy.

Shaft The main part of a column.

Shingle Thin wood tiles used as a roof-covering—often made of cedar.

Slype A covered passage, usually between the transepts and chapter-house in a church, leading to the cloisters.

Solar A quiet study or private room in a sunny or exposed place in a medieval house.

Spandrel The triangular space between the underside of a staircase and the floor. Also the triangular space between the curved parts of two adjoining arches.

Stairs An arrangement of steps made of wood, stone or metal giving access to floors above or below. These may be in straight flights between landings or constructed in a continuous curve.

Staple hall A covered market.

Stepped-gable See *Crow-stepped gable*.

Strapwork A form of ornament that imitates interlacing bands of leather.

String-course An ornamental band running horizontally across the face of a building.

Stucco Plaster used on the face of buildings to represent stonework. Also a general term describing rendered surfaces.

Swag An ornamental piece of carving resembling a garland or festoon of flowers, fruit or foliage, suspended at either end to form a loop and gathered up at the centre.

Tie-beam The horizontal beam connected to the feet of rafters to prevent them spreading out under the weight of the roof covering.

Tile-hanging The external surfacing of walls with overlapping rows of tiles on a timber framework; used in Elizabethan architecture and now becoming popular again. Slate-hanging follows the same principle.

Tracery Ornamental carving of *mullions* and *transoms* in Gothic windows.

Transept The short arms of a cross-shaped church.

Transom A horizontal bar in a window which, with the mullions, separates the panes of glass.

Tuscan See *Classical Orders*.

Tympanum The space between a *lintel* and the arch above it.

Undercroft A *vaulted* basement often found in monasteries.

Vaults Arched ceilings or roofs; vaulting is a method of roofing an area with a succession of load–bearing arches. They can be pointed or semi-circular, and usually intersect at right angles.

barrel vault

Norman vault

Early English vault

Decorated vault

Tudor fan vault

Venetian-window A triple window; the central window is arched, those on either side have flat or lintelled tops.

Voussoirs The wedge-shaped stones used to make an arch.

Waggon-roof A roof with curved braces but no *tie-beams*. When lined with boarding the interior resembles a covered waggon.

Wattle-and-daub Interlaced sticks of hazel or osier roughly plastered with a mixture of clay and chopped straw, sometimes reinforced with horse-hair as a binding agent.

Wheel-window See *Rose-window*.

ARMS AND ARMOUR

The finest products of the armourer and weaponsmith have always been esteemed as much for their beauty as for their functional qualities. Artists as eminent as Dürer and Holbein have been responsible for their design, yet the most elaborately decorated pieces are not always the most pleasing. The art of the great armourers, like that of the great potters, lay in their ability to exploit the plastic potentialities of their material, and the plain armour of the 15th century, with its elegant lines and subtle curves, can be more satisfying than the elaborate parade armour of the next century. British weaponsmiths only achieved an international reputation in the 19th century, with the work of the London and Birmingham gun makers, but fine fire-arms were made here from the late 16th century onwards, and Henry VIII's armoury at Greenwich produced armour as good as that made on the Continent.

Crossbow and Plate armour

Bolt
Crossbow rack
Crossbow
Close helmet
Visor
Gorget
Breast-plate
Lance rest
Vambrace
Haute piece
Pauldron
Rerebrace
Couter
Gauntlet
Tasset
Cuisse
Mace
Poleyn
Greave
Sabaton
German fluted armour c. 1520
Morning Star

Fire-arms

Matchlock musket
Musket with Snaphaunce lock
Musket rest
'Brown Bess' musket, c. 1750, and bayonet
Flintlock blunderbuss, c. 1760
German wheel-lock, c. 1580
Scottish all-metal flintlock pistol
Powder horn—18th C.
Colt Navy revolver
Flintlock pistol of Civil War
Webley revolver Mk. V

Staff weapons

War hammer
Battle-axe
Boar-spear
Pikes
Bill
Partizan
Halberd
Pole-axe
Vaulge
Glaive

Swords and Daggers

Viking sword—9th C.
Hand-and-a-half sword—15th C.
Broad sword, c. 1525
Rapier and left-hand dagger, mid-17th C.
Rondel dagger
Small sword
Naval cutlass, c. 1790
Falchion, 1600-20
Baselard

Cannon

Four-wheeled ship's cannon, carronade, late 18th C.
Bronze muzzle-loading cannon, calibre 88 mm, 19th C.
Chain shot
Double shot
Twelve-inch Schalch mortar, English 1726

CERAMICS

A great deal of English pottery from the 13th century onwards was derivative, but it nevertheless demonstrated peculiarly English characteristics. A peasant craft, it reflected the individual taste of the potter.

Most medieval pottery was made in monasteries; a red or buff body was covered with a green glaze. Slipware was already used in the middle ages, but earliest surviving signed examples were made at Wrotham in Kent early in the 17th century. This type of pottery was also made in Staffordshire by Ralph and Thomas Toft.

The famous Delft-ware, first made in England c. 1550, had an immediate success, and until the development of stoneware, was the most commonly used domestic ware. John Dwight of Fulham was the first potter granted a patent to produce stoneware, and in 1693 he sued the Dutch Elers brothers who worked in Staffordshire for infringement of his patent. The popularity of stoneware lasted until Staffordshire salt-glaze was invented by John Astbury in the 1730's, and the whitish finish of this ware prepared the way for the cream-coloured earthenware produced by Josiah Wedgwood, known as Queen's Ware.

During the 18th century the increasing demand for a finer and less durable ware was being satisfied by the manufacturers of fine porcelain.

Chelsea, famous for its figures and elegant tableware, was probably the first porcelain factory in the British Isles. Founded c. 1745, the factory was taken over by William Duesbury, owner of the Derby porcelain factory, who produced the porcelain known as Chelsea-Derby (1769-84).

During the same period Bow porcelain was being made in the East End of London by Thomas Frye, who took out a patent for it in 1744. Bow is best known for its figures and groups; typical colouring is dark crimson, emerald green and pale blue. The factory closed down in 1776.

The Worcester porcelain factory was founded in 1751 by a syndicate of 15 men, among whom was Dr John Wall and the brilliant chemist William Davis, who were responsible for the finest period of Worcester, from 1752-83. Worcester porcelain was resistant to heat, did not crack in hot water, and at the same time, was extremely fine with a thin, hard glaze. It is one of the few porcelains made in the 18th century that is still being made today.

During the 18th century porcelain was also produced at Caughley, Liverpool, Longton Hall, Plymouth and Bristol.

Towards the end of the century the development of Spode bone china—a compromise between hard and soft porcelain—resulted in an enormous commercial expansion. Spode predominated in the first quarter of the 19th century, until it was superseded c. 1820 by Rockingham, with its tendency to over-decoration. In 1851 the Great Exhibition popularised styles from all countries, especially Japan, and manufacturers, such as Coalport, Copeland and Minton, quickly adapted their designs to the current fashion. But towards the end of the century the formalised designs of Art Nouveau began to exert their influence, and despite popular taste 'in many Victorian servants' halls the tableware was still representative of the best of English pottery traditions, while above stairs the tables groaned under the fashionable nightmares of ceramic art'.

Ceramics The general term for objects fashioned from clay and hardened by fire, whether classed as earthenware, stoneware or porcelain. Variations of hardness and texture depending on the degree of heat used in firing are the main differences between the three types of ceramics. Soft earthenware is fired at 700°C, while the hardest white porcelain is produced by firing the clay at 1350°C.

Chelsea See *Porcelain*.

Delft The general name applied to tin-glazed earthenware in northern Europe. It originated in Asia, and was first produced in Europe in Spain and Italy where it was called MAJOLICA; in France it was called FAIENCE; and in Holland and England DELFT, from the town where it was made in Holland. There is no technical difference between these three terms, only variations in style and decoration. English Delft was first made at Lambeth in 1671.

Faience See *Delft*.

Glaze A coat of glass formed over the surface of pottery when fired; it consists of sand, flint or sandstone mixed with such fluxes as lead, potash or borax. This flux causes the glaze-mixture to melt at a lower temperature than that of clay. Its function is to make the pottery impervious to liquids, to give them a sheen, and to act as a basis or a protection for decoration. The glaze is coloured by adding metallic oxides, which are used instead of organic colours because they are not destroyed by the firing. Different colours are produced by varying either the temperature of the firing or the amount of oxygen in the kiln.

Majolica See *Delft*.

Medici See *Porcelain*.

Meissen See *Porcelain*.

Porcelain True, or 'hard-paste', porcelain is a hard, thin and translucent pottery made by fusing china-clay (*kaolin*) with china-stone (*petuntse* or 'hard-paste') at about 1350°C–1400°C. It was first developed by the Chinese and appeared in the West in the 15th century. European imitations were made of 'soft-paste' porcelain which is really a form of hard earthenware made by adding a previously fired glassy mixture to white clay. This was the first European porcelain and was produced in Italy in the 1580's; it was known as MEDICI porcelain.

It was not until 1709 that true hard-paste porcelain was produced—by J. F. Bottger at MEISSEN in Germany. Later Dresden and Sèvres became the important centres. (Meissen-ware in England is usually called Dresden.)

The earliest dated English porcelain was CHELSEA made in 1745. It was a soft-paste variety, very glassy and translucent and made in the style of Meissen-ware.

Salt-glaze Stoneware glazed with salt, thrown in the kiln at the height of firing. The process was developed in the 1730's by John Astbury of Shelton who used Devonshire clay and calcined flint in order to produce a whiter and a harder pottery, which was called 'Staffordshire salt-glaze'. Salt-glaze, which could be reproduced rapidly and in quantity, immediately became popular for domestic use. By 1750, white salt-glaze was being made in at least 50 Staffordshire potteries; much of it was undecorated and none of it bears factory marks. It led the way to the cream-coloured earthenware which became more popular in the 1770's.

Slipware One of the first earthenwares. Made by peasant potters in Kent and Staffordshire in the 17th century, it was decorated with 'slip', a clay wash of a creamy consistency.

Spode bone-china A paste midway between hard and soft porcelain. White ash from burnt ox bones is used as the stabilising ingredient because it does not impair the translucency of the porcelain and makes it easier to work. Bone-china was first marketed by Josiah Spode c. 1800.

Stoneware In 1671 John Dwight of Fulham took out a patent for this ware which fired at a very high temperature, became extremely hard and impervious to fluids. The addition of salt to the kiln at the maximum temperature produced stoneware with a pleasant rough surface. This ware was often used in bottle-making in the 19th century.

Wedgwood Josiah Wedgwood (1730–95) revolutionised the potter's craft and made it into a flourishing industry. He produced the following wares: 1759, Green glaze 'cauliflower' wares; 1765, Queen's Ware, the first cream-coloured earthenware, which was fine, light and could be pierced, moulded or decorated with transfer printing; 1760–70, unglazed stonewares including Black Basalt, hard, fine and black; and Jasperware, hard, resembling porcelain, and made in different colours.

FURNITURE

English furniture, from medieval times to the 17th century, was generally made of native oak, though other woods, elm and beech, were also used occasionally. Broadly speaking, Elizabethan, Jacobean and Cromwellian furniture was simply designed and solidly made and, since the oak was seasoned for ten to 20 years before use, lasted for centuries.

Decoration in the 14th and 15th centuries was simple, with Gothic ornament or the favourite *linenfold* pattern. In Elizabethan times it became more adventurous and was inlaid or carved with all kinds of motifs from geometric panels to festoons and swags. It was often painted and gilded, and even now there is still some colour visible on the 16th century Great Bed of Ware in the Victoria and Albert Museum.

In the 17th century the Puritan austerity of plain, unadorned furniture, produced a reaction in favour of more decorative woods and more flamboyant styles. With the Restoration, walnut came into its own and exotic woods were imported—kingwood from South America, amboyna from the West Indies, and ebony—to be used in *veneers*. Walnut was at the height of its popularity in the William and Mary period and at its best in Queen Anne's reign when it achieved an elegant simplicity of line, rarely surpassed since.

In the early Georgian period mahogany was being used, but sparingly as it was expensive. With the repeal in 1724 of the heavy duties on its import from the West Indies and Cuba, it immediately became popular with the cabinet-makers, and by 1750 had supplanted walnut in the public esteem.

Other exotic woods were imported in the late 18th century, among them satinwood, which became a minor vogue. This close-grained wood, of varying tones of yellow, with a gleam rather like satin, was often used for veneers. It was a favourite of Sheraton, who designed some of his finest pieces in it.

In the early 19th century furniture became heavier as the revived Classicism of the Regency became popular, and darker woods came into fashion, particularly rosewood. Imported from the West Indies and Ceylon, and called rosewood for its slight scent, it was dark brown with distinct, almost black, markings, and well suited to the period's style.

As the Victorian era progressed, the elegance of 18th-century line and ornament disappeared and furniture became larger, darker and more ponderous. One light-hearted production of the Victorian age was papier-mâché inlaid with mother of pearl and beautifully coloured. It was used for small objects like portable writing-desks and tables, and was highly decorative. It was in the smaller objects, rather than in their massive pieces of domestic furniture, that the Victorians were at their best.

Cabriole leg A curved leg resembling the leg of an animal. It was a distinctive feature of William-and-Mary and Queen Anne furniture, and lasted well into the 1860's. The leg often terminated in an animal claw gripping a ball, hence the term *claw and ball foot*. A characteristic of English cabriole is a scallop shell carved on the shoulder of the leg. The fashion died out with the Classical revival when curves began to be supplanted by straight lines.

Inlay One of the earliest methods of decorating furniture. The art came to England via the Germans and the Flemish. The design was chiselled out of the wood, and into this recessed ground were fitted flat pieces of different coloured woods skilfully cut to fit the pattern. In early inlay, ebony, bog-oak and holly (white in colour) were used to give a black and white effect. The designs were usually geometric patterns or formalised flowers and foliage. Later, in the late 16th and early 17th century, inlaid pictorial effects were much in favour: views of buildings, courtyards and arches.

Lacquer A form of decoration made in the East by applying layers of resin, or lac, from the *Rhus vernicifera* insect, to the wood. Each layer was dried and rubbed down to obtain an absolutely smooth surface, and sometimes as many as 35 processes were used before the surface was ready for decoration. In the 17th century lac was unobtainable in Europe, so instead the wood was usually treated with a mixture of whitening and size and then coated with several layers of varnish, made of gum-lac, seed-lac or shell-lac. The ornament was outlined in gold size and the surface rubbed down with a dog's tooth or agate pebble. As lac began to be imported, European craftsmen improved their techniques to such an extent that they were able to produce a fair imitation of the hard polish of the Oriental craftsmen, and by the late 17th century their work had reached a high standard, though in the opinion of the connoisseurs not comparable with that from China and Japan.

Linenfold A decorative pattern carved on wood, its straight flat lines looking like folded linen. The design was Flemish in origin, and was popular in England in the 15th and 16th centuries, particularly as decoration on oak chests.

Marquetry A form of surface decoration closely allied to veneer, but distinct from inlay. The design is first cut and fitted into a thin sheet of wood or veneer; then the veneer, complete with the design in one flat sheet, is applied to the surface of the furniture. Marquetry became popular in the Restoration, when designs, inspired by the work of the Dutch, took the form of flowers and birds. Towards the end of the 17th century a more intricate version became fashionable known as *Seaweed* marquetry—the pattern suggested the delicate fronds of waving seaweed. In the Classical revival of the 18th century, marquetry was popular and motifs tended to be Greek—urns, festoons of leaves and flowers, and sometimes draped figures.

A large assortment of materials was used from natural woods of different colours — black through browns and yellows, to the white of sycamore or holly; and ivory, mother of pearl, bone, tortoiseshell, copper, brass and silver.

Ormulu The word comes from the French *bronze d'orée d'or moulu* (bronze gilded with ground gold). It is essentially French and was used in France as mountings in furniture and to make small useful objects like candlesticks. The ormulu used on English furniture was probably made by French craftsmen.

Pembroke table A small table with hinged flaps which are supported by fly brackets; it came into use in the 1760's and was described as 'for a lady or gentleman to breakfast on'. Sheraton, who made designs for it, said it was called after the lady who first ordered it.

Pie-crust table A round table with a hinged top which could be folded flat against a wall, fashionable in the late 18th century. It had a carved scalloped edge rather like pastry crust on a pie. It was set on a single leg with three feet—a tripod—and often the legs were of the *cabriole* type with claw and ball feet.

Pier table Designed to be used against a wall between windows, and frequently placed for decorative effect under a mirror.

Piercing Decoration in the form of holes, originally designed to let air into 'livery' cupboards where food or clothes were stored. In the early days of oak, small holes were pierced in the form of geometric patterns; these later evolved into more elaborate cut-outs.

Woven fabric was put on the inside to keep insects out. Pierced work has been much used in every age and particularly by Chippendale for chair backs.

Splat The centre support in the back of a chair, often elegantly shaped and decorated.

Spoon-back A colloquial term used to describe a Queen Anne chair-back profiled to the curve of a spoon.

Veneer Thin sheets of wood applied to the surface of furniture for a decorative effect. Veneers first came into use after the Restoration in the late 17th century. The wood was chosen for its rarity and the beauty of its markings; at this time exotic woods like kingwood (from Brazil) ebony and amboyna were often laid on in veneers to form elaborate patterns created from the woods' natural markings. See also *Marquetry*.

GARDENS

Until Tudor times gardens tended to be utilitarian, food-producing patches. But in Henry VIII's reign Cardinal Wolsey laid out a walled garden at Hampton Court with *arbours* and *alleys* and a *knot garden*; and Sir Thomas More had a garden in Chelsea about the same time 'full of lovely flowers and blossoming fruit trees'. All that survives of Tudor gardens now are the beautiful brick walls and the occasional building—at Montacute, Somerset, for example, where the courtyard still has garden pavilions of Elizabethan date.

Greenhouses, of a rudimentary sort, were used to house plants over the winter and these became the orangeries of the late 17th and early 18th century. Many of the original orangeries still exist, at Hampton Court, Kensington Palace and Kew among other places, often designed by the great architects of the period.

It was in 1621 that the first botanical garden was founded at Oxford, known as the Oxford Physic Garden, to which travellers brought back specimens from all over the world. The gardening family of Tradescants were responsible for introducing many exotic plants to England.

But it was in the Restoration that gardens began to change again and become elaborate. Travellers, and Royalists including Charles II, exiled on the Continent, came back with new ideas, particularly from France where the great André Le Nôtre had developed the formal garden laid out with paths, woods, lakes and 'fair prospects'.

The knot garden was supplanted by the *parterre*— a great level area in front of the house where designers could introduce fountains, statues, *topiary* and summer-houses, giving the garden a new spaciousness. Walks and avenues radiated from a central point, and vistas were all-important.

At this time seeds and plants were being imported from abroad: evergreens, bulbs and flowers from Holland; seeds and plants from the Near East and America. Greenhouses began to be artificially heated, and in 1804 the Horticultural Society of London, later the Royal Horticultural Society, was founded.

In the 18th century came the landscape garden, in which Nature, assisted by man, was allowed to dominate. The two great exponents of the new style were Capability Brown and Humphry Repton: geometric patterns and mathematical precision fell out of favour, paths and streams were permitted to wind and natural contours were made much of. Garden buildings—*gazebos*, temples, and ornate summer-houses—were placed to enhance the delights of Nature. Stourhead, in Wiltshire, and Stowe, in Buckinghamshire, are two fine examples of many surviving 18th-century gardens.

With 19th-century social changes came new kinds of gardens and gardeners—suburban gardens owned by the wealthy middle class. Books on gardening began to proliferate, and in 1838 J. C. Loudon produced *The Suburban Gardener and Villa Companion;* three years later the *Gardener's Chronicle* was published for the first time. The lawn mower was invented.

The botanical gardens at Kew, which had been collecting plants for over 100 years, now had emissaries all over the world sending back rare specimens.

In the 1860's William Robinson led a reaction against the park-like style of gardening, which resulted in the more natural 'wild' garden where shrubs like rhododendrons and azaleas could grow untended year after year. Robinson advocated great expanses of lawn and borders filled with roses, flowering shrubs and herbaceous plants. In this he started a trend which is still being followed.

Alley A broad walk or path cut through trees. The *allée* was a feature of formal French gardens in the 17th century, the trees on either side of the path being clipped to retain the formal effect. They were a usual feature in great English gardens in the early 18th century. *Pleached alleys* are tree-lined walks where the boughs are interlaced and arched over the walk beneath.

Arboretum A collection of trees planted together in one area, either to act as a feature in a landscaped garden or as a grove of special botanical interest. A *pinetum* is an arboretum consisting only of conifers.

Britain is said to have the finest arboreta in Europe, with particularly good specimens of conifers. One of the oldest pineta is at Dropmore, in Buckinghamshire, where there is a unique collection of trees grown from seed as far back as 1827.

Arbour A bower or shady retreat, usually covered with climbing plants grown over trellises. Arbours or 'herbers' were a feature of gardens as far back as the Middle Ages.

Gazebo A two-storied turret set on a wall or on a high point, where a fine view could be had of the surrounding landscape; it was popular in the 18th century when to sit and gaze was fashionable.

The bottom half was often used for storing garden tools while the upper room was reserved for admiring the view through the large windows. It was in fact an 18th-century version of the earlier summer-house.

Grotto A cave-like structure, a favourite feature of 18th-century gardens, often used to house collections of shells, minerals or fossils. Grottoes were often extremely elaborate, with statues and fountains and with rivers running through them.

Ha-Ha A boundary to a park or garden in the form of a wide, sunken ditch; it prevented animals from coming in or going out and was not visible from the surrounding landscape except at close quarters. The term is said to come from 'Ha', the expression of surprise it evoked when suddenly discovered. It was a favourite device of 18th- and early 19th-century designers, especially of Capability Brown, and contrived to deceive viewers into thinking the garden extended to the horizon.

Knot garden A series of small beds laid out in a formal manner, sometimes on a terrace, and edged with dwarf hedges. In the beds, dwarf clipped shrubs or herbs like rosemary, box and thrift were planted in complicated geometric patterns, or knots. The background to the pattern might be coloured earth or gravel and the effect might rely solely on the design the green plants made when seen from above. Where the pattern was less intricate, the empty spaces in the bed might be filled with topiary-work or flowers.

Knot gardens were fashionable in Elizabethan times and extremely popular throughout the 16th and early 17th century, when the more complicated the knots, the better.

Mount A raised place or small hill, usually man-made, designed to give a view of the estate. Elizabethan gardens of any importance all had a mount up which one could clamber 'to view a fair prospect'. At the top there was usually an *arbour* or sitting-place.

Parterre The level area in front of a house below the terrace or windows. It came to England in the 17th century from France, and was part of a movement to introduce the vista to English gardens; it replaced the Elizabethan *knot garden*.

Pergola A covered walk formed by climbing plants over trellis-work, probably coming originally from Italy, where shaded walks were a necessity. Pergolas were in fashion in Renaissance England, and have more or less remained so.

Topiary The training and clipping of trees and shrubs into ornamental shapes. Topiary is an ancient art which was probably introduced to England by the Romans. It was popular in Elizabethan gardens, when hedges were cut into shapes of birds, beasts and figures. It reached the height of fantasy in the 17th century: men on galloping horses, heraldic beasts, hunting hounds, any subject that struck the fancy, might be translated into topiary-work.

The 18th century saw a reaction against the cutting of trees into cones, globes and pyramids, and the fashion died out, but there is still topiary work to be seen all over Britain in old gardens.

HALLMARKS

Gold and silver objects have been hallmarked in England for five or six hundred years. The object is to secure a uniform quality and to prevent fraud. The system is so reliable and complete that a collector can tell, with almost absolute certainty, the authenticity, maker and date of any piece of gold or silver which comes to hand, always providing he can read and interpret the hallmarks stamped upon it. Royal Plate and certain very small articles are exempt from hallmarking.

The Maker's Mark

The maker's mark is usually the first in the series that makes up the hallmark. Since 1363, it has been compulsory for the maker to stamp his mark on a piece of silver plate before sending it to the Assay Office.

At first the marks were emblems, or symbols, such as the bird appearing on the Bacon Cup (1573–4) at the British Museum. Other symbols—a hart, a hand or a cross—were chosen at a time when most of the population were illiterate, as allusions to the name of the makers.

The conjoined letters, appear-on a ewer (1597–8) at the Victoria and Albert Museum, show how the makers gradually gave up symbols and began using letters.

In the late 17th century several efforts were made to clarify makers' marks, and finally it became law in 1739 for makers to use the initial letters of their Christian and surnames. It was in response to this law that Paul de Lamerie, finest of London silversmiths, re-registered his mark. The crown indicates that he was under royal patronage. The practise of using makers' initials continues today, although the marks of firms and manufacturers have generally taken the place of the initials of individual craftsmen.

The Assay Mark

The assay mark follows the maker's mark on most British silver. English silver, in particular, accounts for nine-tenths of the desirable antique silver in existence, and the lion symbol has been used since 1544, with very few changes. The device indicates that the metal has been passed by the Assay (testing) Office as sterling silver, that is, 92·5 per cent pure silver.

From the beginning the mark was 'lion passant guardant' with its head turned outward, full face. Since 1822 it has been a 'lion passant' looking straight ahead in the direction it is going. The lion was replaced for 23 years, 1697–1720, by the seated figure of Britannia and the standard of fine silver was raised to 95·84 per cent. This mark may still be used for fine silver today.

On Sheffield and Chester plate the assay mark has always been a 'lion passant regardant'. In Ireland, a crowned harp, in Edinburgh a thistle and in Glasgow a lion rampant denote sterling silver.

Town Marks

Silver's fourth mark is the stamp of the Assay Office responsible for testing the article. Most English-made silver bears the mark of the London Assay Office. Silversmiths from all over Britain,. even in towns with Assay Offices, have always tended to

---

THE DATE LETTER

The third symbol appearing on silver is a letter of the alphabet, surrounded by a shield. This indicates the date at which an object was assayed, which is almost invariably the date it was made. Date stamps on London-made silver, indicating the date to the nearest twelve-month, have been used without repetition for over 400 years. For 20 consecutive years the 20 letters from A to U (excluding J) are used, with the same style of letter and shield. After U has been reached, the style of letter and shape of the shield are changed. The following chart gives the letter style and shield design for each alphabet since 1558.

1558–1577	1776–1795
1578–1597	1796–1815
1598–1617	1816–1835
1618–1637	1836–1855
1638–1657	1856–1875
1658–1677	1876, shield changed for rest of series 1877–1895
1678–1696 no 'u' in this series	
1696–1715	1896–1915
1716–1735	1916–1935
1736–1755	1936–1955
1756–1775	1956–1975

Other Assay Offices throughout England, Scotland and Ireland use different date marks.

Birmingham marks

The whole alphabet is used, only excluding 'J'

A	1773–1797 shields differ
a	1798–1823 'j' used
A	1824–1848 in different style
A	1849–1874 'J' used in this series
a	1875–1899
a	1900–1924
A	1925–1949 'J' used in this series instead of 'I'

Dublin marks since 1773

Whole alphabet used, with exception of 'J' and 'V'

A	1773–1796
A	1797–1820
A	1821–1845 'V' used in this series, italic 'e' alternative, and shields vary
a	1846–1870 'j' used instead of 'i', and 'v' used. Double 'f', 'g' and 'h'
A	1871–1895 'V' used in this series
A	1896–1915 ends at 'U'
A	1916–1941 'V' included in this series
A	1942–1967 this series used 'J' and 'V'

Edinburgh marks since 1780

Whole alphabet used, with exception of 'J'

A	1780–1805 'I' and 'J' used in conjunction; double 'N', double 'O' and double 'R', shields differ
a	1806–1831 'j' used
A	1832–1856
A	1857–1881
a	1882–1905 no 'v' in this series
A	1906–1930
A	1931–1955
A	1956–

Glasgow marks since 1819

Whole alphabet used

A	1819–1844
A	1845–1870
A	1871–1896
A	1897–1922
a	1923–1948
A	1949–1972 'J' and 'K' missing in this series

Sheffield and *Chester* date marks are too irregular to list in chart form, but handbooks are available giving date marks for each separate year.

send their pieces to London for hall-marking, which complicates the identification of provincial silver. In the British Isles today the only remaining Assay Offices are at London, Birmingham and Sheffield, at Edinburgh and Glasgow, and in Dublin, although many other cities have had Assay Offices in the past.

The leopard's head has been the London mark from the earliest times until the present day.

The leopard was crowned from 1478 to 1821.

The lion's head erased appears instead of the leopard's head on Britannia standard or fine silver 1697-1720, and is still valid for 95·84 per cent silver today.

A crown has been the Sheffield mark since 1773.

An anchor has represented Birmingham since 1773. The City Arms represented Chester until the Assay Office was closed in 1962.

EDINBURGH   GLASGOW   DUBLIN

Provincial Assay Offices which have closed

Newcastle Assay Office used three castles as well as the London town mark from 1702 until closed in 1883.

Exeter used a three-towered castle (plus London town mark until 1777) from 1701 until closed in 1885.

York used five lions passant on a cross (plus London town mark

until 1856). Norwich, Bristol, Salisbury, Lincoln, Coventry, Hull and Aberdeen also possessed Assay Offices.

Other Marks
A fifth mark, the sovereign's head, will be found on silver assayed between 1784 and 1890. During this period a duty was levied on gold and silver ware, and the monarch's head was stamped on the metal when the duty had been paid.

George III   William IV

George IV   Victoria

A mark commemorating the Jubilee of King George V and Queen Mary was used on silver plate from 1933 to 1935, and a coronation mark in 1952-3.

SILVER AND GOLD

English silver dates back to at least the 7th century—the Venerable Bede records that St Oswald, King of Northumbria, was served food in a silver dish—though the oldest surviving piece, the Dolgelly chalice, was made in the 13th century. The Church was chief user of gold and silver in the middle ages, and it seems that by the time of the Norman invasion both were being made in some quantity, since the Normans looted 'vessels of silver and gold . . . of which the number and decoration would be hard to relate'.

Irish metalworkers used gold as long ago as the Bronze Age, when there was an established trade of Irish gold to central Europe. The Irish goldsmiths reached the peak of their craft in early Christian times, when they produced such masterpieces as the Ardagh chalice, now in the National Museum at Dublin.

In 1150 the Goldsmiths' Guild (which also included silversmiths) was founded, and about this time silver appeared on the tables of kings and barons. Much plate was destroyed during the sacking of the monasteries and the Civil War, and it is only from the late 17th century that English silver survives in quantity.

Arabesque A style of decoration characterised by flowing lines formed from elaborately intertwined leaves and flowers. This style, named after Mohammedan decoration, was much used on silver of the 16th century and on pierced work in the 18th century.

Baroque A general term used to describe the late Renaissance style of ornament, which combined scroll-work and naturalistic detail in a strong, flamboyant manner.

Cartouche A decoration in the form of a scroll, often used by engravers like a frame around coats of arms.

Casting The technique of shaping metal by pouring it molten into a mould. Small pieces, such as handles and finials, were often cast.

Chasing A way of decorating metal in high or low relief by incising the surface with punches of different shapes without actually removing any metal. In *repoussé* or embossed chasing, parts of the design are raised into relief by hammering from the reverse side or from inside the article; the detail is then chased in by punch-work from the front. *Flat-chasing* gives decoration in very low relief and was frequently used, together with engraving, to decorate the borders of dishes, particularly in the 18th century.

Cloisonné A way of enamelling in which the various colours are poured into cells (called cloisons) separated by thin metal borders set at right angles to the metal background.

Damascening A technique of inlaying iron or steel with decoration in gold or silver.

Enamelling The decoration of the metal with coloured opaque or translucent glass. The enamel is crushed to a fine powder, then fused to the metal.

Engraving A method of decorating by cutting into the surface of the metal with a sharp tool which removes a thread of metal. Varied effects can be produced by using different tools.

Etching Decoration produced by using acid to eat into the surface of the metal. The technique was popular in Victorian times because it saved the labour of engraving.

Filigree Delicate work done with threads of silver or gold wire, finely interlaced and decorated with tiny balls of the metal. Where the balls alone are used for decoration, the work is known as *granulation*.

Finial The ornament at the top of the lid or cover of a dish. In the 18th century various shapes were popular —acorns early in the century, pineapples in the middle period and urns in the late, Classical revival period.

Flat-chasing See *Chasing*.

Flatware The term used for tableware that has no cutting edge: spoons, forks, slices, etc.

Flute A decorative groove, derived from the columns of Classical architecture. In the late 17th century, fluting was often used alternately

with *gadrooning* to form a corrugated surface.

Gadrooning A design consisting of a series of convex curves, stamped or cast, set vertically or slanting, and joined at their extremities. The pattern is typical of late 17th-century baroque ornament and was used extensively on the rims and bases of cups and on the borders of dishes.

German silver, also known as nickel silver; a tough white metal alloy consisting approximately of six parts of copper, three parts of zinc and one part of nickel.

Granulation See *Filigree*.

Guilloche A border consisting of ribbon-like bands twisting over each other in a continuous series; the spaces enclosed by the crossed lines often contain rosettes or wheel motifs.

Moulding A border formed from various combinations of parallel convex and concave forms, based on the mouldings used for decoration in architecture.

Niello Decoration made by filling *engraved* lines with a black mixture of lead, silver, copper and sulphur, and fusing it to the metal. The technique was much used in the second half of the 15th century.

Pewter An alloy of tin, and varying proportions of copper, lead, antimony or bismuth.

Pierced work Decoration cut with a saw. It has been common since early times, but particularly fine pierced work was done in the William and Mary and Queen Anne periods.

Raising The silversmith's technique of forming a hollow vessel from flat sheet metal by hammering it on a wooden block.

Repoussé See *Chasing*.

Rococo A general term used to describe the 18th-century style of ornament based on scrolls and shell forms. It is a lighter, more delicate style than the *baroque*.

Sheffield plate Plate made of copper coated with silver. Invented by Thomas Boulsover, a Sheffield cutler, in 1743, it consists of a copper ingot fused between two silver plates and rolled out to the thickness required.

Stamped work Relief decoration produced by hammering the metal from the reverse into a sunken die.

THE PARISH CHURCH

Britain's parish churches are living monuments as well as places of worship. For a thousand years of Christianity they have been the recording places of local history, and through the eloquence of their windows, carving and sculpture, the past can be felt and understood. The silverware, brasses, paintings and fabrics they contain are a vital part of our heritage—the treasures in daily use in Britain's villages and towns.

The ground plans below illustrate the typical growth of a parish church; the shaded parts of each drawing represent the additions that might have been made to the church in each period. In the exploded drawing, opposite, the most commonly mentioned parts of a church are illustrated and named.

1 Alms box (for donations)	10 Box-pew
2 Altar	11 Canopy over altar
3 Angel	12 Chancel
4 Apse	13 Chantry chapel
5 Aumbry (sacred vessels' cupboard)	14 Choir (in west gallery)
6 Aumbry lamp indicates the Sacrament	15 Choir stalls
7 Battlement	16 Church chest
8 Bell louvres	17 Clerestory
9 Boss (ornament at roof rib-junction)	

NORMAN 12th century
A simple two-cell interior with an apse at the east end sufficiently large to accommodate the altar. Access doors are opposite each other in the north and south walls, and the windows are narrow slits.

EARLY MEDIEVAL
13th–14th century
A population increase means more worshippers and the north aisle is extended. The altar space is likewise enlarged and a sedilia and piscina built in. A local family builds a chantry chapel on the south side and a porch is added for ceremonial purposes.

LATE MEDIEVAL
15th–16th century
The north and south aisles are extended, the chantry chapel screened and a new tower erected. Above the south porch a priest's room is built. A rich merchant, or guild, donates a rood and screen while another finances a north chapel.

POST-REFORMATION
17th–18th century. Bigger congregations necessitate galleried seating. The village choir sits in the west gallery. The chantry becomes the Squire's pew and the parvise a store. The north chapel is used by the village school and the chancel for quarterly communion services.

VICTORIAN RESTORATION
19th century. A fashionable architect 'restores' the church resulting in new chancel stalls, pitch-pine pews, wrought-iron altar-rails and an eagle-lectern. The altar is raised and a marble reredos set behind it. A vestry is built on the north side.

28 Communion rail
29 Crocket
30 Doom (Day of Judgment) painting
31 Dossal (back) curtain
32 Early tower
33 Easter sepulchre
34 Finial
35 Font
36 Font cover
37 Gallery
38 Gargoyle (rainwater spout)
39 Hagioscope or squint (hole in wall or pier for viewing altar during services)
40 Hatchment (Commemorative heraldry)
41 Holy water stoup
42 Houselling benches
43 Hymn board
44 Lancet window
45 Lectern

36 Ledger stone (incised commemorative slab)
37 Lych gate
38 Monumental brass
39 Mullion
40 Mural tablet
41 Nave
42 Nave altar
43 Niche with saint
44 North aisle
45 North chapel
46 Pall frontal
47 Parclose screen (separating chapel from church)
48 Parvise (room over porch)
49 Parvise stairs
50 Pier

51 Pinnacle
52 Piscina (drain for rinsing sacred vessels)
53 Poppy-head (carved ornamental feature)
54 Porch
55 Pulpit
56 Reredos
57 Returned stall (right-angled to choir stalls)
58 Riddell (side) curtain
59 Rood (cross)
60 Rood beam
61 Rood loft
62 Rood screen
63 Rood stairs

64 Royal Arms (symbol of loyalty to the crown)
65 Sedilia (seats for clergy)
66 South aisle
67 Stair-turret
68 Standard candlestick
69 Swag
70 Tabernacle (recess or canopied niche) with statue
71 Table tomb
72 Tester—sounding board
73 Tracery
74 Vestry
75 West door
76 West gallery and ringers' floor

NONCONFORMIST CHAPELS
Chapels originated from secular buildings in which Nonconformist meetings were held. Puritanism maintained the single room plan and kept it unadorned. In the late 19th century more money became available for the adoption of the fashionable Gothic revival exterior.

SYMBOLS IN CHURCHES

The old churches and cathedrals of Britain were built for a devout but illiterate population. Statues, symbols, stained glass and painting were used to make each place of worship a colourful picture-book of Bible truth and Church history. Artists and craftsmen devoted their lives to this work, and ecclesiastics, noblemen and citizens vied with each other in building more and more elaborate and beautiful shrines. In spite of destruction by over-zealous reformers, much of beauty still remains, and a knowledge of the significance of some of the old emblems increases the pleasure of visiting an ancient church.

Monograms

A monogram is two or more letters interwoven. The most ancient Christian symbol is the LABARUM, consisting of the two letters, chi and rho which begin the Greek word for Christ. This monogram is prominent in the decoration of Coventry Cathedral. A

Labarum   *Crowned MARIA*

Alpha and Omega   *IHS*   *INRI*

familiar monogram is IHS, the first three letters of the Greek word for Jesus; it was often carved on church roof beams. A favourite medieval symbol is MR for Maria Regina, Mary Queen of Heaven, also MARIA as a monogram. One of the crypt chapel roofs at Canterbury Cathedral is decorated with crowned M's. INRI is not strictly a monogram but the initial letters of 'Iesus Nazarenus Rex Iudaeorum'—Jesus of Nazareth, King of the Jews.

Alpha and Omega, first and last letters of the Greek alphabet, signify that Christ is the Beginning and End.

Numbers and Geometry

In medieval thought every number had its own mystical meaning, and numbers were easily translated into geometry. The equilateral triangle represents the Trinity; the three equal sides and angles symbolising the unity of three distinct persons. Two interwoven equilateral triangles form a six-pointed star, traditionally known as the Star of David; it is sometimes called the Creator's star, the six points representing the six days of Creation. The Triquetra is an ancient symbol whose three equal arcs express the Trinity, and whose continuous form symbolises eternity. It often appears on Celtic crosses. Baptismal fonts are often octagonal, eight being the number of Resurrection and new life.

Trinity window   *Trinity triangle*   *Octagonal font*

Triquetra   *Star of David*   *Triquetra*

The Cross

The Cross is a universal Christian symbol today, although the *labarum* monogram was used by the early Church. Monks and heralds evolved over fifty forms of the Cross. The most usual are:

The CRUCIFIX is a cross with Christ upon it. An early variety is the CHRISTUS REX (**I**), showing Christ crowned and robed. Later versions became more realistic. The ROOD (**2**)

is the great crucifix that stands or hangs in the chancel arch. The attendant figures (St Mary, St John) are reminders of Calvary.

The LATIN CROSS (**3**) (Passion Cross) has a long upright. Many churches are built on a Latin Cross ground-plan. The GREEK CROSS (**4**) has all the arms equal. The Orthodox churches of the East are built on this plan, and so are many Nonconformist chapels. Five Greek crosses incised on most altars represent the five wounds of Christ. The CALVARY CROSS (**5**) is a Latin Cross mounted on three steps, symbolising Charity, Hope and (top) Faith. The CELTIC CROSS (**6**) or Iona Cross. The circle symbolises Eternity.

Animal and Plant Symbols

In medieval times religious or spiritual meaning was attached to everything men observed in the world. Highly coloured natural history also served as a source of inspiration. The PHOENIX (**7**), the mythical bird believed to regenerate itself in the flames of its own funeral pyre was, for example, used to symbolise the Resurrection. The PELICAN (**8**), the bird that pierces its own breast to feed its young, symbolised the Sacrifice on the Cross, and the Holy Communion. Only a virgin, it was thought, could capture the UNICORN (**9**); fierce and swift, he would place his head on her lap and allow himself to be taken. This legend was taken as an allegory of the Incarnation of Christ in the Virgin Mary. The LAMB is a well-known symbol of Christ. The AGNUS DEI (**IO**) 'Lamb of God', has a halo with a cross on it to indicate the Lord, and carries a banner of Victory. The DOVE (**II**) symbolises the Holy Spirit, and is carved on font covers to show the Spirit descending at Baptism. Seven Doves represent the Seven Gifts of the Holy Spirit. The LILY symbolises Purity because of its white flowers and is specially associated with the Blessed Virgin. It is usually

shown in the conventionalised form of the FLEUR-DE-LYS (**I2**). The LILY CROSS (**I3**)—Christ is shown not on a Cross but on a Lily with three stems. This means He bears our sins in the flesh of Mary His Mother. The ROSE (**I4**) is emblematic of the two sides in the Wars of the Roses, but also symbolises Christ. The Vine and branches is based on Christ's words, 'I am the True Vine'; grapes and wheat represent the Eucharist. Palm branches symbolised victory amongst the Romans, and hence martyrs are shown carrying palms. POMEGRANATES (**I5**), symbolise the unity of the Church, as many seeds in one fruit; also new life and hence the Resurrection. It was much used as a damask pattern. The Tree of JESSE (**I6**) is used in many stained glass windows and carvings. The ancestry of Christ is shown in the form of a vine springing from Jesse, the father of King David. Kings and prophets are often added; Mary with the Holy Child is at the top, or a crucifix in some examples. The EVANGELISTS (**I7**) are symbolised by the eagle (John), winged ox (Luke), winged lion (Mark) and winged man (Matthew). The FISH (**I8**) was a secret sign used by early Christians. The initials of the Greek for 'JESUS CHRIST, SON OF GOD, SAVIOUR' make the Greek word for 'fish'.

Symbols of God and the Trinity

To represent GOD directly was considered blasphemous, so a RAY OF LIGHT (**19**) or a HAND (**20**) was drawn; CIRCLES (**21**) or FISHES (**22**) symbolised the Trinity. In medieval times, THREE CROWNED FIGURES (**23**), the FATHER (**24**) with CRUCIFIX (**25**) were used.

Symbols of the Passion

During the Middle Ages shields were used as decoration wherever possible. Emblems based on the Passion are frequently found on them and on screens, doors and bench ends, or held by angels in the roof-timbers.
(**26**) The Cross with the sheet used to lower Christ's body after His Crucifixion. (**27**) The Title (INRI). (**28**) The Crown of Thorns and Nails. (**29**) The Scourges. (**30**) The Seamless Robe, and the Dice. (**31**) The Ladder, and Sponge on Reed. (**32**) The Lantern, carried during the arrest in Gethsemane. (**33**) The Five Wounds. (**34**) The Cock that crowed after Peter's denial. (**35**) The Thirty Pieces of Silver, Judas's reward. (**36**) The Hammer and Pincers.

Saints and their Emblems

(**37**) Catherine: Princess with spiked wheel, patron of teachers. (**38**) Dunstan: Archbishop with pincers, patron of goldsmiths. (**39**) George: knight killing dragon, patron of England. (**40**) John the Baptist: bearded, carrying 'Agnus Dei'. (**41**) Clement: Pope with anchor. (**42**) Jerome: Cardinal, with lion and book. (**43**) Denis: after execution, he walked carrying his head. (**44**) Stephen: Deacon carrying stones.
A saint's emblem is often the instrument of martyrdom, as with St Clement—tied to an anchor and thrown into the sea—or based on a legend, like the pincers with which St Dunstan nipped the Devil. (**45**) a long CROSS: held by an Apostle—Philip; held by a queen—Helena. Bishops hold the crozier, archbishops a cross. (**46**) LAMB held by female saint: Agnes. (**47**) Saltire CROSS: Andrew. (**48**) SWORD held by Apostle: Paul; otherwise a common emblem for martyrs; with archbishop: Thomas à Becket. (**49**) TOWER held by princess: Barbara. (**50**) KEYS: Peter; usually paired with Paul, as the Two Pillars of the Church. (**51**) Flaying KNIFE: Bartholomew. (**52**) GRIDIRON: Lawrence. (**53**) CHALICE with a dragon in it: John the Apostle. (**54**) Three gold BALLS: Nicholas, patron of bankers and pawnbrokers: also, as Santa Claus, of children. (**55**) ARROWS: held by a king—Edmund; by a young man—Sebastian. (**56**) SPEAR: Thomas the Apostle. (**57**) PIG and T-cross: Anthony the hermit. (**58**) SCALLOP-SHELL: James the Great. (**59**) SCYTHE held by a maiden: Sidwell, a West-country saint. (**60**) INVERTED CROSS: Peter. (**61**) WINDLASS: Erasmus. Other popular emblems for saints—a woman teaching Mary to read: Anne; a giant with the Christ-child, crossing a stream: Christopher; eyes on a plate: Lucy; dragon and cross: Margaret of Antioch.

St Michael

He is shown in armour, trampling down the Devil, or with scales to weigh souls at Doomsday. 'Michael churches' are often on hill-tops and are thought to be remnants of a pre-Christian cult.
The nine medieval Orders of angels are: Seraphim, Cherubim, Thrones, Dominions, Virtues, Powers, Principalities, Archangels and Angels.

Symbolism in Church planning

Churches are orientated from rising to setting sun, a custom perhaps earlier than Christianity itself. The plan is very often a cross, and the chancel may show declination (out of line with the nave), representing the bowing of Christ's head on the Cross.
The nave (Latin *navis* a ship) symbolises the voyage to Heaven. The north door, on the 'dark' side, is the Devil's Door, opened during the exorcism at Baptism. The font is near the main door, since entry to the church is by baptism. To reach the altar it is necessary to pass under the rood; so Heaven is reached by way of the Cross.
In the churchyard the lych gate (from the Saxon word for a corpse) shelters coffin and bearers. The evergreen yew trees symbolise eternity.

Symbolism of Colours

The Church today uses colour chiefly to mark the liturgical seasons. Festivals—Christmas, Easter and Corpus Christi for example—are marked by WHITE vestments, altar-frontals and hangings; white also for the feasts of St Mary and for saints who were not martyrs. RED is the colour for Pentecost (Whit Sunday), Palm Sunday, Holy Cross Day, the Precious Blood, and martyrs. GREEN is used for the periods after Trinity and Epiphany. PURPLE is used in Advent and Lent; in many churches Lent is marked by unbleached linen to suggest penitence. BLUE is St Mary's colour. BLACK is for funerals and requiems. YELLOW was looked on as the colour of jealousy and treason; hence Judas is shown in yellow robes.

ACKNOWLEDGEMENTS

The publishers wish to thank the following people and organisations for
their permission to reproduce photographs belonging to them or of their property:

Her Majesty the Queen for gracious permission to reproduce the following
subjects: Portrait of Queen Henrietta Maria by Van Dyck. The Gold
State Coach. The Irish State Coach. The Ramillies Staircase at Marl-
borough House. Portrait of Sir Henry Guildford by Holbein. Queen
Mary's Dolls' House. And to: Aerofilms Ltd. J. Allan Cash. The Antique
Dealer and Collectors Guide. Apollo Magazine Ltd. The Architectural
Review. The Dean and Chapter of St Patrick's Cathedral, Armagh. Art-
Wood Photography. The Ashmolean Museum, Oxford. His Grace the
Duke of Atholl. The Barber Institute of Fine Arts, Birmingham. Barnaby's
Picture Library. B. T. Batsford Ltd. His Grace the Duke of Bedford.
Bedford Public Library. Captain Berkeley, Berkeley Castle. Birmingham
Museum and Art Gallery. John Bethell. The Bowes Museum, Barnard
Castle. Mrs Humphrey Brand. The Brantwood Trust. The Trustees of the
British Museum. The Trustees of the British Museum (Natural History).
The British Tourist Authority. Lord Brooke. The Trustees of Buckland
Abbey, Plymouth. The Burlington Magazine Publications Ltd. The
Burrel Collection, Glasgow Art Gallery and Museum. The Trustees of
the Burns Monument and Museum, Kilmarnock. Camera Press Ltd. The
Dean and Chapter of Canterbury Cathedral. The Royal Museum,
Canterbury. The Chester Beatty Library, Dublin. The City of London
School. The Colchester and Essex Museum. The Connoisseur. The
Council for the Care of Churches. Country Life. The Courtauld Institute
Galleries, London. The Provost and Chapter of Coventry Cathedral.
Bernard Cox. The Daily Telegraph Ltd. The Department of the Environ-
ment. Derby Museum and Art Gallery. The Devonshire Collection,
Chatsworth; the Trustees of the Chatsworth Settlement. The Trustees of
the Dickens House Museum and Library. Dorset Natural History and
Archaeological Society, Dorchester. J. E. Downward. The Rector and
Churchwardens of Dunstable Church. The Dean and Chapter of Durham.
The Trustees of the Dyson Perrins Museum, Royal Porcelain Company
Ltd, Worcester. The Trustees of Elgar's Birthplace. English Life Publica-
tions Ltd. Epton A. Eckstrand. The Marquess of Exeter. Faber and Faber
Ltd. Ferens Art Gallery, Kingston upon Hull. The Syndics of the Fitz-
william Museum, Cambridge. R. B. Fleming & Co. Ltd. John Freeman
and Sons Ltd. The Institute of Geological Sciences. Dr Georg Gerster.
Gilchrist Studios Ltd. Glasgow Art Gallery and Museum. The Glasgow
School of Art. P. M. Goodchild and Sons Ltd. The Trustees of the Good-
wood Collection. Guy Gravett. The Green Studio Ltd, Dublin. The
Gulbenkian Museum of Oriental Art, The University of Durham,
Durham. The Hamlyn Group. The Governors of Harrow School. Eric
Hartman. Lord Hastings. The Marquess of Hertford, Ragley Hall. The
Cecil Higgins Art Gallery, Bedford. The John Hilleson Agency. The
Museum of the History of Science, Oxford. The Holburne of Menstrie
Museum, Bath. George Howard. The Hunterian Museum, University of
Glasgow. Huntly House, Edinburgh. The Trustees, the Regimental
Museum, the Royal Inniskilling Fusiliers. The Bank of Ireland, Dublin.
The Irish Tourist Board. The Greater London Council as Trustees of the
Iveagh Bequest, Kenwood. Jarrold Colour Publications Ltd. The Trustees
of Dr Johnson's House. Dmitri Kasatkina. A. W. Kerr. A. F. Kersting. The
Trustees of the Lady Lever Art Gallery, Port Sunlight. The Museum of
Leathercraft. Leatherhead Urban District Council. Leeds City Art
Galleries. Lichfield City Council. The Dean and Chapter of Lincoln
Cathedral. The Treasurers and Masters of the Bench of Lincoln's Inn.
Viscount de l'Isle, Penshurst Place. The City of Liverpool Museums. The
Trustees of the London Museum. The Rector of Long Melford. Madame
Tussauds Ltd. Her Majesty's Stationery Office. Manchester City Art
Galleries. The Mansell Collection. The Countess Manvers. His Grace the
Duke of Marlborough. The Lord Methuen RA, FSA. The Rector of Middle-
ton Parish Church. Tom Molland. The Municipal Gallery of Modern Art,
Dublin. The Trustees of the National Gallery. The National Gallery of
Ireland. The National Gallery of Scotland. The National Library of
Scotland. The National Maritime Museum, Greenwich. The National
Monuments Record. The National Museum of Antiquities, Edinburgh.
The National Museum of Ireland. The National Museum of Wales. The
National Portrait Gallery. The National Trust. The National Trust,
Northern Ireland Committee. The National Trust for Scotland. The
City Engineer, Newcastle upon Tyne. Mrs F. R. Newens. His Grace the
Duke of Norfolk. The Marquess of Northampton. His Grace the Duke of
Northumberland. The City of Nottingham Museum and Art Gallery.
Norwich City Council. City of Norwich Museums. George Ovens. The
Oxford Preservation Trust. Nan Pattullo. The Earl of Pembroke. The
Percival David Foundation of Chinese Art. The Dean and Chapter of
Peterborough Cathedral. The Petworth Collection. Pictorial Colour
Slides. Picturepoint. City Art Gallery, Plymouth. The Commander-in-
Chief, Portsmouth. Pilkington Glass Museum, St Helens. The Public
Records Office, Corporation of London. Purnell and Sons Ltd. The
President and Fellows of Queen's College, Cambridge. Radio Times
Hulton Picture Library. George Rainbird Ltd. The Royal Academy of
Arts. The Director, Royal Botanic Gardens, Kew. The Royal Commission
on Historical Monuments. The Royal Scottish Museum. The Ruskin
Museum, Coniston. Lord Salisbury. The Scottish National Portrait
Gallery. The Scottish Tourist Board. Kenneth Scowen. Henk Snoek. The
Council for the Preservation of Sheffield Antiquities. Sheffield City
Museums. The Trustees of the Sligo County Museum. The Trustees of
Sir John Soane's Museum. Soho Galleries Ltd. Somerset County Museum
Governing Body. Southampton Art Gallery. S.P.A.D.E.M. George
Spearman. The Earl Spencer. The Dean and Chapter of St David's
Cathedral, Pembroke. The College Council of St John's College, Cam-
bridge. Dr J. K. St Joseph. The Dean and Chapter of St Paul's Cathedral.
The Vicar and Churchwardens of Holy Trinity Church, Stratford-upon-
Avon. The Trustees of Shakespeare's Birthplace, Stratford-upon-Avon.

Controller of Her Majesty's Stationery Office. The Sunday Times.
Sunderland Museum and Art Gallery. His Grace the Duke of Sutherland.
The Great Western Railway Museum, Swindon. The Tate Gallery.
Temple Newsam House, Leeds. Thames and Hudson Ltd. The Thomas
Coram Foundation for Children. Thomas Photos, Oxford. The Curator
of Historical Relics. Trans-Globe Film Distributors Ltd. The Board of
Trinity College, Dublin. Tudeley Parochial Church Council. The Ulster
Museum, Belfast. The Trustees of the University Museum, Oxford. The
Victoria and Albert Museum. The Walker Art Gallery, Liverpool.
Waltons Sound and Film Service. The Trustees of the Wallace Collection.
The Warburg Institute. The County of Warwick Museum. The Earl of
Warwick. Weidenfeld and Nicolson Ltd. Tom Weir. The Trustees of the
Wellcome Institute of the History of Medicine. The Duke of Wellington.
The Dean and Chapter of Wells Cathedral. Major-General Sir Harold
Wernher Bt, Luton Hoo. The Dean and Chapter of Westminster. The
Westminster Press. The Whitworth Art Gallery, University of Man-
chester. Marcus Wickham-Boynton, Burton Agnes Hall. William
Morris Gallery, Walthamstow. Directors of Warwick Castle Ltd. Jeremy
Whitaker. Simon Wingfield Digby, MP. Woodmansterne. The Dean and
Chapter of Worcester Cathedral. The York Corporation. The Dean and
Chapter of York.

The publishers also acknowledge
their indebtedness to the following books
which were used for reference or
as sources of illustrations:

Age of Wren by R. Dutton (Batsford); Ancient Art of the Americas by
B. H. S. Bushnell (Thames & Hudson); Architecture in Britain 1530–1830
by John Summerson (Penguin); The Architecture of England by D. Yarwood
(Batsford); Arms and Armour by Vesey Norman (Weidenfeld and
Nicolson); Art in Britain under the Romans by J. M. C. Toynbee (Oxford
University Press); Art Nouveau by Mario Amaya (Dutton Vista); Art
Nouveau by S. T. Schudi Madsen (World University Library); Bartholo-
mew's Gazetteer (Bartholomew); British Architects and Craftsmen by S.
Sitwell (Batsford); Buildings of England by Nikolaus Pevsner (Penguin);
Cambridge by Michael Grant (Weidenfeld and Nicolson); Castles edited
by Sir Hugh Casson (National Benzole Books); Chambers's Biographical
Dictionary (Chambers); Chambers's Encyclopaedia (Newnes); Clocks by
Simon Fleet (Weidenfeld and Nicolson); The Complete Encyclopaedia
of Antiques by L. G. G. Ramsey (Connoisseur); Concise Encyclopaedia
of Architecture by M. S. Briggs (Dent Dutton); Concise History of
Interior Decoration by George Savage (Thames & Hudson); Country
Life Book of English Furniture by E. T. Joy (Country Life); Decorative
Cast Iron Work in Great Britain by R. Lister (G. Bell); Dictionary of Art
and Artists by Peter and Linda Murray (Penguin); 18th Century Gold
Boxes of Europe by A. K. Snowman (Faber and Faber); Embroidery and
Tapestry Weaving by Mrs Archibald H. Christie (John Hogg); Encyclo-
paedia of the Arts (Thames & Hudson); English Cathedrals by Martin
Hurlimann (Thames & Hudson); English Church Monuments 1510–1840
by K. A. Esdaile (Batsford); The English Garden by E. Hymans (Thames &
Hudson); The English Home by D. Yarwood (Batsford); English Needle-
work by A. F. Kendrick (A. & C. Black Ltd); English Porcelain of the 18th
Century by J. L. Dixon (Faber and Faber); English Stained Glass by J.
Baker (Thames & Hudson); Encyclopaedia Britannica; Glass Through the
Ages by E. Barrington Haynes (Pelican); Great Gardens of Britain by P.
Coats (Weidenfeld and Nicolson); Great Houses of Britain by N. Nicolson
(Weidenfeld and Nicolson); Great Interiors by Ian Grant (Weidenfeld and
Nicolson); Guide to English Parish Churches by John Betjeman (Collins);
Guns and Rifles of the World by H. L. Blackmore (Batsford); A History of
Architecture on the Comparative Method by Banister Fletcher (University of
London, the Athlone Press); Les Instruments des Sciences dans l'Art et
l'Histoire by H. Michel (Albert de Visscher); Ireland Explored by Wolfgang
Retler (Thames & Hudson); Irish Art during the Viking Invasion 800–1020
AD by Francoise Henry (Methuen); Irish Art in the Early Christian Period to
AD 800 by Francoise Henry (Methuen); London by Nikolaus Pevsner
(Penguin); Monuments edited by Sir Hugh Casson (National Benzole
Books); Oxford by Felix Markham (Weidenfeld and Nicolson); Pagan
Celtic Britain by Anne Ross (Routledge and Columbia); The Penguin
Dictionary of Architecture by John Fleming, Hugh Honour, Nikolaus
Pevsner (Penguin); The Penguin Guide to London by F. R. Banks (Penguin);
Picture Encyclopaedia of Art (Thames & Hudson); Porcelain by H. Tait
(Faber and Faber); Regency Furniture by M. Jourdain (Country Life);
The Shell Gardens Book edited by Peter Hunt (Phoenix Rainbird); The
Shell Guide to Ireland by Lord Killanin and Michael V. Duignan (Ebury
Press and George Rainbird); The Shell Guide to Britain and Northern Ireland
edited by Geoffrey Boumphrey (Ebury Press and George Rainbird);
Tides in English Taste 1619–1800 by B. S. Allen (Oxford University
Press); 2000 Years of London by Michael Hanson (Country Life); Victorian
Comfort by J. Gloag (A. & C. Black Ltd); Webster's Biographical Dictionary
(G. and C. Merriam); Worcester Porcelain by F. Barrett (Faber and Faber);
Works in Architecture of R. and J. Adam (Alec Tiranti Ltd).

Among other people and organisations who contributed to the book
were: Victor Ball; Bord Failte, Dublin; Helena Burke; Frank Dowling;
Derek Hall; Neil Holmes; Ian Howes; Illustration Research Services;
Caroline Mackinlay; Bridget Morley; Tower of London Armouries.